JOHN FORD

THE MAN AND HIS FILMS

John Ford, ca. 1930.

JOHN F★RD

THE MAN AND HIS FILMS

TAG GALLAGHER

WITHDRAWN

UNIVERSITY OF CALIFORNIA PRESS / BERKELEY • LOS ANGELES • LONDON

Burgess
PN
1998
.A3
F5698
1986

C.2

Stills courtesy of the Robert S. Birchard Collection,
Graham Greene, Richard Koszarski, Anna Lee, Hal
Roach, the Lilly Library (Indiana University), the
library of the Academy of Motion Picture Arts and
Sciences, the Wisconsin Center for Film and The-
ater Research, Columbia Pictures, Metro-Goldwyn-
Mayer, Paramount Pictures Corporation, Republic
Pictures, RKO Pictures, 20th Century–Fox Film
Corporation, United Artists, Universal Pictures,
and Warner Brothers.

University of California Press
Berkeley and Los Angeles, California

University of California Press, Ltd.
London, England

© 1986 by The Regents of the University of California

Printed in the United States of America
1   2   3   4   5   6   7   8   9

WITHDRAWN

Library of Congress Cataloging in Publication Data

Gallagher, Tag.
  John Ford.

  Filmography: p.
  Bibliography: p.
  Includes index.
  1. Ford, John, 1894–1973. I. Title.
PN1998.A3F5698   1984   791.43'0233'0924 83-18047
ISBN 0-520-05097-5

Contents

Preface

*In the annals of American film, no name shines
more brightly than that of John Ford. Director and
filmmaker for more than half a century, he stands
preeminent in his craft—not only as a creator of
individual films of surpassing excellence, but as a
master among those who transformed the early
motion pictures into a compelling new art form that
developed in America and swept the world. As an
interpreter of the Nation's heritage, he left his personal
stamp indelibly printed on the consciousness of whole
generations both here and abroad. In his life and in
his work, John Ford represents the best in American
films and the best in America.*

—*Commendation on the presidential
Medal of Freedom given John Ford in 1973*

John Ford's career—from 1914 to 1970—spanned almost the entire history of the motion picture industry, and for most of that time he was recognized as America's finest moviemaker. His movies told good stories, had vivid characters, provoked thought, kindled down-home charms; and his own personality was apparent in them. His compositional eloquence made dialogue virtually unnecessary—scarcely for dearth of scripted richness, but because literary structure was only a single aspect of the intricate formal beauty and intelligence of his cinema.

It is this immense intelligence that critics have largely ignored. Ford's apologists laud his instincts and emotions, as though he were an artist unconsciously, unintentionally. His detractors decry his sentiment and slapstick, label him racist, militarist, and reactionary, ignoring the subtleties between extremes, the double-leveled discourses, the oeuvre's obsessive plea for tolerance.

Fault for misapprehending Ford's intelligence lies partly with Ford himself, who hid beneath masks; partly with Hollywood, whose facility is often deceptive; but chiefly with our culture's disinclination to take movies as seriously as books. To propose that John Ford was as major an artist as ever produced by America is to invite ridicule, at least today.

Perhaps I, as author of the present study, am constitutionally prejudiced in Ford's favor. I hope so. I can claim similar ethnic background, immense empathy for these movies (seen dozens of times over decades, and thus now experienced quite differently than by one viewing them for the first time), and I have wished to be useful more toward increasing appreciation and pleasure than toward revealing faults.

For assistance in obtaining prints and in research I am indebted to Joshua Bagley (United Artists), Myron Bresnick and Bea Herrmann (Audio Brandon), Kevin Brownlow, James Card, Hal Cranton (MCA-Universal), Paul Cremo, Dennis Doph (Columbia Pictures), Dan Ford, David Grossman, Joseph Judice, Kit Parker Films, Richard Koszarski, Miles Kreuger, Elaine MacDevitt (USIA), Patrick McInroy, William Murdock (U. S. Department of Defense), Bill Murphy (National Archives), Grafton Nunes, George Pratt, Adam Reilly, Patrick Sheehan and Barbara Humphries (Library of Congress), Charles Silver (Museum of Modern Art), Mort Slakoff (Viacom), Anthony Slide, John Sonneborn, John Stone, Saundra Taylor and the staff of the Lilly Library, Indiana University, and the staffs of the New York Public Library–Lincoln Center, the Free Library of Philadelphia Theater Collection, the Czechoslovak Film Archives, and the Wisconsin Center for Film and Theater Research. The American Council of Learned Societies supplied a travel grant. Olive Carey, Harry Carey, Jr., Ruth Clifford Cornelius, Cecil McLean de Prida, Gabriel Figueroa, Barbara Ford, Graham Greene, Anna Lee, George O'Brien, Leon Selditz, and John Stafford kindly shared their memories with me. I am especially grateful to the late Frank C. Baker.

Leo Braudy, John Fell, Brian Henderson, Bruce C. Kawin, William Rothman, and Michael Wood contributed invaluable editorial assistance. Gerald Mast persisted through many months of painstaking advice and encouragement; the book owes much to him. Ernest Callenbach, Mary Lamprech, and Mary Anne Stewart, at the University of California Press, have given the book a precision and beauty it would otherwise lack.

This book is dedicated to my parents and my wife, Phoebe Erb, and to William K. Everson, without whom much would be impossible.

1

Prologue: Youth and Apprenticeship

. . . man's unceasing search for something he can never find. JOHN FORD

I shall almost always be wrong, when I conceive of a man's character as being all of one piece. STENDHAL

Because John Ford shrouded himself in mystery, his life and personality remain inscrutable. His was a complex, perhaps multiple, individuality. Direct and devious, charismatic and sardonic, amusing and caustic, he generally dominated those around him, or at least retained his independence. He read voraciously, history especially, surrounding himself with books; his memory was virtually photographic, and he could get by in French, German, Gaelic, Italian, Spanish, Yiddish, Japanese, Hawaiian, and Navaho. But he posed as illiterate, hiding his erudition, as he hid his wealth under baggy clothes and his sensitivity under a tough crust. He was a man of many masks, a joiner who stayed an outsider, a man of action self-consciously reflective, a big man, Irish and Catholic. There will probably never be an adequate biography of John Ford, nor even an adequate character sketch, for there were as many of him as there were people who knew him.

Beginnings

"A cruel, hard place," a Ford character calls Ireland, and so it was for Ford's father, Sean, born in Spiddal, on the Galway coast, in 1854.[1]

Years of famine, typhus, mass evictions, and suppressed revolts had intensified the sufferings of a people already rendered destitute by a tiny plutocracy alien in race, religion, and language. Hope lay in escape, and Sean, after a visit to the harbor chapel, escaped to America in 1872, sponsored by Michael Connelly, a cousin who, after escaping enslavement by Blackfeet, deserting the Union Army, and laying track for the Union Pacific, had established himself as a bootlegger in Portland, Maine, by marrying a widow. Sean Americanized his name to John A. Feeney* and eventually succeeded to Connelly's business. His dingy restaurant-saloons down near Portland's wharves and warehouses were natural gathering places for the Irish, and John Feeney became a ward leader. He would greet new immigrants, help them settle and find jobs, register them as citizens and voters, and so built himself a political base. (A nephew, Joseph Connolly, rose to be a judge on Maine's Supreme Court.)

On July 31, 1875, Sean married Barbara "Abby" Curran, a distant cousin. Born in Kilronan, in the Aran Islands, Abby had grown up on a mainland farm, not far from her future husband, whom, however, she had not met before emigrating to Portland in 1872. She was taught neither to read nor write English (although she could write Gaelic) and her semi-illiteracy perhaps contributed to her son's ambivalence toward intellectuality.

In a season of prosperity, Feeney settled his family in Cape Elizabeth, Maine, on 190 acres of land. And here in an old farmhouse on Charles E. Jordan Road was born the future John Ford, youngest of six children surviving infancy. Although Ford went through his youth as John Augustine Feeney, and later claimed even on passports that his name was Sean Aloysius O'Feeney, and although most references, including Ford himself, cite the year as 1895, the town clerk registered him as John Martin Feeney, born February 1, 1894, and this information appears also on his tombstone and baptismal records. John was baptized March 13, 1894, at St. Dominic's, 163 Danforth Street; Edward and Julia Feeney were the sponsors. Aloysius was the name John chose at Confirmation. As a boy he was called John, Johnny, or Jack, and as he grew he acquired almost a dozen additional nicknames, while bestowing nicknames of his own on all his friends.

"We were a comfortable, lower middle class family," John Ford recalled. "We ate better than we do now."[2] "Father," said brother Frank, "was the greatest actor who ever lived. When he told a story of the elves and banshees and fairies, it was like a real experience."[3] Gaelic was often spoken in the house, midst frequent spats over pronunciation. Ford's mother, called Nana, ruled the home with an easy, quiet, but iron authority, undiminished even in her sons' manhood. She held the purse, too, and when her husband went to the races she would dole out one dollar per race—and collect the

---

*The Gaelic had various spellings: Ó Fianna, Ó Fidhne, Ó Fiannaidhe (Andrew Sinclair, *John Ford: A Biography* [New York: Dial, 1979], p.3).

Figure 1. Genealogy

EDWARD O'FIENNE m. BARBARA MORRIS   NICHOLAS CURRAN m. MARGARET O'FLAHERTY
b. Ireland   (of Killanin barony)   b. Ireland   b. Ireland

PATRICK O'FIENNE m. MARY CURRAN   FRANCIS CURRAN m. BRIDGET McLAUGHLIN
b. Ireland   b. Ireland   b. Ireland   b. Ireland

JOHN A. FEENEY = m. c. 7.3.75 = BARBARA (ABBY) CURRAN
b. 1854 S. Galway   Portland   b. 1856 Kilronan, Aran
d. 6.22.36 Portland   d. 3.26.33 Portland

—MARY AGNES (MAIME) = m. 4.9.00 Portland = John E. McLean b. c. 1876
b. 6.15.76

     —Cecelia A. McLean (or McClain) = m. Lorenzo de Prida
     —Mary McLean

—DELIA (DELLA)
b. 1878; d. 4.18.81 (measles)

—PATRICK H. = m. 10.14.12 Portland = Katherine A. Devine
b. 12.24.79   b. 1879 Portland

     —Mary Feeney
     —Francis Feeney

—FRANK T. = m. 1. = = = Della Cole
b. 8.14.81 Portland
d. 9.6.53 Los Angeles   —Phil b. 10.16.02 Portland. d. 1976 Los Angeles

     = m. 2 = = = Elsie Van Name

     —Robert b. c. 1912
     —Francis, Jr. ("Billy") b. c. 1921

     = m. 3. = = = Mary Armstrong

—BRIDGET
b. 10.4.83 Portland. d. 9.2.84 Portland (cholera)

—BARBARA (ABBY)   John E. Robinson m. Delia Malia
b. 2.4.88 d. infancy.   b. Portland   b. Portland

—EDWARD FRANCIS = m. 3.6.16 Portland = Mary T. Robinson b. 1896 Portland
b. 2.22.89
Cape Elizabeth   —Chuck
d. 1.15.69   —Sheila
     —5 others

—JOSEPHINE CECILIA
b. 12.31.91 Cape Elizabeth

—JOANNA (HANNAH)   C. E. W. Smith m. Fannie Roper
b. 12.13.92. d. infancy   b. S. Carolina   b. N. Carolina

—JOHN MARTIN = = m. 7.3.20 Los Angeles = = Mary McBride Smith
b. 2.1.94   b. 9.4.93 Laurinburg, N.C.
Cape Elizabeth   d. August, 1979
d. 8.31.73
Palm Desert, Calif.
   (cancer)   —PATRICK MICHAEL ROPER = m. 1942 = Jane Mulvaney, b. 1921 Maine
     b. 4.3.21 Hollywood

          —Timothy John. b. 2.1.44
—DANIEL   —Daniel Sargent. b. 2.12.45
b. 2.17.98
d. infancy   = m. 2 = Carroal Anderson

     —BARBARA NUGENT = m. 5.31.52 = Ken Curtis
     b. 12.16.22   div. 7.23.64
     Hollywood

winnings, if there were any. Her sons kissed her when they entered the house and when they left; more effective than any whipping was her refusal of their kiss when she was displeased. Jack was her sweetheart. He looked like her and held her in awe, and in later years, when the two were a continent apart, claimed a psychic bond. "She would send me messages. There were quite a few instances of that."[4] Probably from her, and as the youngest, he acquired the religious fervor of his childhood. Often he would rise before six and brave twenty-below weather to serve Mass. They also shared a love for movies. "As a kid I was fascinated by the nickelodeons of that period. Any time I got a nickel or a dime I would go to the movies."[5]

Feeney family fortunes tended to fluctuate with Maine's dry laws. Around 1898 they were obliged to sell the farm and, after a succession of residences, take a large third-floor apartment at 23 Sheridan Street, Portland. Sister Mary, eighteen years older than Jack, moved in with her two children when her husband died, and these, with the Myers and Mahoneys who shared the building, brought to sixteen the number of children. Dinner was open to anyone at the Feeneys. Harbor and bay could be glimpsed from the housetop, and Jack would spend hours at a nearby observatory tower, gazing out to sea. He loved the sea. "Ever since I was about four years old, I owned a boat. Some old wreck came up, and we caulked it with tar and everything, and I took that, and as I got old, I got a different boat."[6] Summers were spent sailing off Peak's Island, where Jack's father's sister had a house.

An attack of diphtheria at eight required a lengthy convalescence, and delayed Jack a year at Emerson Grammar School, but it gave him in return a sensitivity and love for books, such as he later depicted with young Huw Morgan in *How Green Was My Valley*. Nonetheless, he was an indifferent student, never opening his schoolbooks at home, and getting by through listening in class and a retentive memory; his 1906 report card graded him "fair" or "poor" in almost every subject. At age eleven or twelve his father took him to Ireland, and he went to school there for several months; instruction was in Gaelic and all the boys except Jack wore long red petticoats. Jack's father, or Gramps as he was called, took frequent trips to Ireland, whereas Nana, who had endured a terribly miserable crossing in steerage when she first came to America, was never willing to return.

Gramps was six feet two and vaguely resembled C. Aubrey Smith. "When the flag passes, take off your cap," he instructed his son at a Fourth of July parade. "But I don't have a cap on." "Then cross yourself, damnit!"

Gramps, despite his saloons, was a regimented drinker. He never drank during the day, only at dinner and breakfast. Jack was fond of relating the breakfast ceremony that would occur aboard ship when he took his father to Ireland in the 1930s. The crew would gather at the portholes to watch as Gramps ordered. "'I would like a glass of orange juice. I live part of the year in California and I want California orange juice. I want oatmeal, four eggs fried, and a double order of bacon and while you're at it put in a slice of ham.' The waiter would hesitate and wait, and he'd say, 'And bring me a drink of Irish whiskey. Bring the bottle.' He'd take a sip of the orange juice, then he'd pour himself a tumbler full of Irish whiskey, then another sip of the orange juice. He'd take that glass of Irish whiskey and down it in one gulp. Then he'd consume the whole meal. That's the only drink he'd have until supper time."[7]

Jack was reputed for drawing caricatures. "As a kid, I thought I was going to be an artist; I used to sketch and paint a great deal and I think, for a kid, I did pretty good work—at least I received a lot of compliments about it."[8] Toward girls he was shy; it took him days to get up nerve to ask for a date. He was tall and lanky, with terrible eyesight and thick glasses, but popular among his male companions. He engaged in track and baseball and made honorable mention on the state football team ("Bull Feeney, the human battering ram"—he broke his own nose and mangled his ear), despite finding himself frequently ejected from games for such antics as carrying a teammate across the scrimmage line. At Portland High he took two years of Latin, three of French, one of physics and biology; he did poorly in math— in fact he flunked algebra twice and never in his life did he achieve ease with numbers or possess any sense of chronology. But he drew honors in English and history, wrote a parody of the school song, and sold a story he had written for $25. His four-year average was eighty-four. While he never discovered himself in high school, he did have a reputation for brilliance and wit. Once a crowd gathered to watch the baseball team play bloomer girls, and Jack was spotted among the latter, in bloomers and wig.[9]

There was a feisty competitiveness among Portland's immigrant cultures—the Irish, Italians, Poles, and Jews—and a spirit of mutual tolerance united them in opposition to the Yankees. Jack picked up Yiddish from his friends and would occasionally attend synagogue for the music. The Ku Klux Klan at one point made an attempt to establish itself, but failed. There were only about a dozen black families among Portland's seventy thousand people. A large tent the Klan erected was blown down in a fierce storm, and Gramps, staring at it the next morning on his way home from church, huffed, "Well, *that* wasn't built on a rock!"[10] The blacks, Ford recalled decades later, "lived with us. They didn't live in barrios. Our next-door neighbors were black. There was no difference, no racial feeling, no prejudice. My sister Maime's closest friend was a Mrs. Johnson who was black. A wonderful woman."[11]

Jack worked mornings for two hours before school driving a fish wagon— the saloon was out of bounds—and later he worked as delivery boy and publicist for a shoe company. Evenings he would usher in the balcony of the Jefferson Theater or at Peak's Gem. Theater was a passion: he would come home and act out the whole play for his family, every part, every voice.

Jack graduated from high school on June 18, 1914. His ambitions to enter Annapolis were thwarted when he failed the entrance examination, so he looked into an athletic scholarship at the University of Maine, Orono. The curriculum was unattractive: he had had most of the subjects in high school and would have been required to major in agriculture. In addition he had to rise at 5:30 A.M. and wait tables at breakfast, and the third or fourth morning, jeered at with racial slurs, he slugged a student and got sent home. He sought the advice of his high school history teacher, William B. Jack (whom he later claimed was the most influential figure in his life after his father), and Nana unearthed from her green keepchest an exciting proposition from California. Jack headed west—just for the summer.* "I remember the last night on the train. I was coming tourist, and I had to go without dinner because I had no money in my pocket. So I arrived penniless, as the expression goes."[12] Perhaps he was conscious of repeating his father's emigration west to join an elder relative, for brother Frank had made a name for himself in Hollywood, and had stirred Jack's imagination. "I stole from my shoe factory the sole pair of seven-league boots there, and I crossed the Atlantic to join him."[13]

Francis Ford

Born August 14, 1881, and thus twelve and a half years older than Jack, Frank T. Feeney was always restless.[14] He had carved up desks at school, married suddenly at sixteen, run off to war (getting only as far as Tennessee, whence his father's political influence extracted him from a cholera camp), and then joined a circus—and disappeared. More than ten years passed, until the day Nana and Jack ran home all excited: they had found Frank—on the Greeley Theater's screen, in a Melies western! Through a New York agent, the prodigal was located and came home in cashmere and a Stutz Bearcat. After years of vaudeville, park benches, and film-mouthing (actors stood behind the screen and improvised dialogue), Frank had landed in the movies, had worked in hundreds of pictures for Centaur, Edison, Melies, and Ince, in New Jersey, Texas, and California, and now was a top star-director-writer with his own company at Universal.

---

*Various sources, among them the information in the *Motion Picture Directory* annuals from 1920 and 1921 (which Ford would have supplied himself) and also Ford's recollections of working on films shot that summer, indicate that Ford was in California in July. But other sources suggest that the days he spent at the University of Maine were in September. It has not been possible to reconcile this contradiction. It is possible—although no evidence supports it—that Ford went west in July, returned for the University of Maine in September, and then went west again. This explanation would explain why Ford at times claimed he took the train direct and at other times claimed that he worked his way west and stopped in Arizona to work as a cowboy for $13 a week. He did not go out to Frank alone but with a friend, Joe (either Joe McDonald or Joe Connolly): there is a letter to Jack from Grace Cunard, dated February 1917, in which she writes how she "promised both your mothers that I would do my best for you." (John Ford Papers, Lilly Library, Indiana University.)

Francis Ford and Anna Little, *The Outcast* (101-Bison, 1912). Typical use of a long shot with foreground figures.

Francis Ford and Grace Cunard, *Lucille Love* (Universal, 1914).

Along the way, he had changed his name to Francis Ford, inspired by the car,* to avoid stigmatizing his family.

Teamed with Grace Cunard—his red-haired, green-eyed leading lady, co-writer, and lover—the dapper, handsome Francis (five feet eleven, 160 pounds, fair skin, black hair, grey eyes[15]) was about to score his greatest mark in a virtually virgin genre: the mystery. First in a series of separate two-reelers, then in fabulously successful serials (*Lucille Love, The Broken Coin,* etc.),** detective Ford chased jewel-thief Cunard through fantastical principalities in uninhibited, peril-laden, "rattling good" melodramas ("She hates yet loves me, and everybody knows that a woman in that frame of mind is liable to do most any desperate thing."[16]).

It is not too surprising, then, that young Jack Feeney held his big brother in awe and preferred adventure in the movies to platitudes at college. So for three years Jack shadowed Frank. He could not have had a more expert teacher in every aspect of the craft; and no other major director ever got a more rigorous training. "He was a great cameraman," said John Ford in 1966. "There's nothing they're doing today—all these things that are supposed to be so new—that he hadn't done; he was really a good artist, a wonderful musician, a hell of a good actor, a good director—Johnny of all trades—and *master* of all; he just couldn't concentrate on one thing too long. But he was the only influence *I* ever had, working in pictures."[17]

Francis Ford's importance is substantial, if obscure: his most popular and personal pictures are apparently lost. Ford was greatly responsible for the westerns released beginning in 1912 under the "101 Bison" trademark (at first weekly, then twice weekly). The 101 Bisons, for their attention to minor detail, use of action to define character, exaltation of story for its own sake, epic photography, and spectacular massed battle scenes, excited the entire industry and inaugurated the great epoch of American cinema. The 101 Bisons were also the basis of the career of Ford's boss, the soon-to-be-famous Thomas Ince. But Ince, though he successfully promoted himself as a creative artist, was essentially a producer; he "invented" the production system, in which a "shooting script" details each shot and grimace prior to filming. And it was the orneriness of Francis Ford, Ince's only director besides himself until 1913, that provoked Ince to such measures. Ince, a major stockholder in his company, persistently attempted to conceal Ford's contribu-

---

*This is Frank's version, as given to Wilkinson. John Ford told Bogdanovich that Frank had replaced a drunk thespian named Francis Ford, then could not shake loose from the name; the original Ford supposedly showed up years later claiming to be "Frank Feeney" and in need of a job.

**Serials were tied to newspaper circulation wars, the weekly episodes being printed in novelized form. *The Adventures of Kathlyn,* debuting December 29, 1913, is considered the first serial (as opposed to "series"), with Kathlyn Williams starring for Selig and Max Annenberg. Hearst came next: *Dolly of the Dailies* (January 31, 1914, Mary Fuller, Edison), then *The Perils of Pauline* (Pearl White, Pathé-Eclectic, March 31, 1914). *Lucille Love* began April 14, 1914.

tions and even to pass them off as his own (as he was to do subsequently with William S. Hart); and he attempted to "steal" Grace Cunard from Ford's troupe. So Ford jumped to Universal.*

Contemporaries praised Ford's 101 Bisons for their vigorous action, picturesque style, and skill in showing action over vast distances— much the same remarks one finds in Jack Ford's early reviews. But surviving Bisons evince—in addition to specific shots later imitated by Jack—more significant similarities. *The Burning Brand*'s complicated flashback structures define the hero's psychology against varying truths of past and present, anticipating *Liberty Valance*. And the essentials of John Ford's acting style can be found in Francis's pictures: *relaxed relating*. Actors are, moreover, directed with minimal rehearsal, which gives freshness to characters and a degree of autonomy, promoting our belief that they possess lives independent of the screenplay or the director. It is difficult to imagine either Ford manipulating an actor the way Griffith did—for instance, Mae Marsh (in *Intolerance*'s courtroom) or Lillian Gish (in the closet in *Broken Blossoms***)—or "staring" at them with a brutality in cutting and framing that seems often to aim, like Hitchcock, for the maximum in sensationalism. And both Griffith and Hitchcock had a fondness for high angles and sudden close-ups that makes them seem rapacious alongside the Fords' low or level angles, gentler cutting, and more respectful distance.

Personal descriptions of Francis at the peak of his fame resemble later ones of John. Universal's *Weekly* described Francis as taciturn and active, "but running underneath this silence is a stream of humor that may be called distinctively Fordesquian."[18] Richard Willis, in *Motion Picture Magazine*, June 1915, wrote similarly: "Under the quiet, almost sarcastic manner, there is deep seriousness, and below the veil of indifference there is one of the warmest hearts imaginable."[19] Without much to say to strangers, but with ready smile and soft voice, "'Fordie' . . . speaks to the people who work with him as though he loved them. He never boasts; in fact, he is inclined to speak of his work with levity, and he gives a wrong impression to those who do not know him well."[20]

But this does not sound like John: "Good mixer without trying, good fellow without essaying to be particularly good—he is always natural and

---

*The "101 Bison" trademark went to Universal as well. The New York Motion Picture Company, Ince's employer, had agreed to merge into the new Universal combine, then pulled out. A "war" ensued, with the two staging raids on each other's facilities and Ince placing a cannon at the mouth of St. Inez canyon. But NYMPCO lost the court battle, along with the now-coveted trademark and Francis Ford, who had told Universal's Carl Laemmle that he, not Ince, deserved most of the artistic credit. Westerns, incidentally, had been issued in immense quantities (dozens per week) since 1909 and before, and were marketed in three distinct genres: Indian, Pioneer, and Civil War. In mid-1913, a year and a half before *The Birth of a Nation*, Universal announced that Civil War pictures and other westerns were stale, used-up genres and that no more would be made.

**The example is no less valid, even if Gish herself was responsible for the level of her hysteria.

always himself."[21] Indeed, in later years, the earnest John found Frank's relaxed, easygoing ways something of an irritant. Frank's superabundance of talents combined badly with streaks of impracticality. He played violin, sculpted, painted huge canvases in his garage—and would impulsively cut out sections admired by chance visitors—but lacked the stick-to-itiveness that was John's key to success. Frank's passion was variety. He enjoyed many women, through three wives and numerous affairs. And he loved makeup and disguises. Ince, writing in 1919, thought him among "the most finished of all pioneer film performers. It was nothing for him to play an Indian hero in the morning and make up as Abraham Lincoln* for the afternoon's work."[22] Often he played several roles in the same picture.

In photography, though Frank would occasionally use superimpressions to illustrate thought (as early as 1911) and generally had quietly watchful camerawork, he also (unlike John) indulged experiment for its own sake: typical, rather than exceptional, was a scene in *The Twins' Double* (1914) in which Cunard appears on screen simultaneously in three roles, in a double exposure within a triple exposure. And, again unlike John, Frank reveled in the unconventional, the shocking, macabre, and occult. The problems these caused him with producers in an era of bourgeois tastes were aggravated by carelessness with money, problems with drink, and a tendency to walk out when he could not do things his own way.

Frank flirted with success, leaving Universal to go independent, starting and failing with his own studio midst the postwar depression, returning desperately ill from the South Seas to find his wife had run off with his business manager after selling off the studio and other assets, but rebounding to form a filmmaking cooperative. That group's seven members each took turns at every job—camera, acting, directing, property—and received equal pay. They would sketch stories on postcards to suit locations, and sometimes sell for $60,000 a movie made for $2,000. "In the years we were together," said Frank Baker,** "we were just like a complete family. I don't think I ever heard a harsh word or an unkind thing said."[23]

In *Four from Nowhere*, one of thirty-some maximally cheap features Francis Ford directed in the twenties, there is a scene in which his character, awaiting revenge, sits alone in long shot in a dark-shadowed room. "Siegfried Kracauer could write a caption for it that would make it look like a collaboration between Freud and Pabst," wrote William K. Everson,[24] and perhaps the image represents one side of Francis Ford. But presently the camera cuts back, after a grim, cathartic conclusion, and one may (or

---

*Both Ford brothers were passionate Lincoln scholars. Francis also won note as a Lincoln impersonator, playing the role in at least seven pictures between 1912 and 1915.

**Frank Baker, an Australian anthropologist, sailor, and filmmaker, met the ill Francis Ford at Pangopango and accompanied him home. He became a bit player, quite obscure in Hollywood. But his tales, throughout this book, of his encounters with John Ford are illuminating, especially if taken as representative of Ford's impact on hundreds of others in his life.

Francis Ford, skeletons, and Grace Cunard, *The Broken Coin* (Universal, 1915).

may not) notice a secretary trying to hear what is going on inside. This sort of gag, unstressed, contrastive, and iconoclastic, became a *John* Ford signature. Both brothers brought charm to their pictures, and Frank's credo— keep the audience "glad they're seeing the picture"[25]—became John's.

Frank abandoned directing in 1927.* He aimed to emulate Wallace Beery and "get away from the dramatic and essay a comedy character."[26] Through more than a hundred small roles, this character evolved into a coonskin drunk, a child-of-nature who rarely spoke, but whose spittle could ring a spittoon clear across a room. Even under his brother's direction, Frank's routines were completely his own, and his "Brother Feeney" character's expressive gestures entrance his fans today as surely as any of Chaplin's or Keaton's.

"In some ways," said Frank Baker, Francis "was very much like John, but he and Jack didn't get on very well. That was a funny part of John Ford. Everything that John Ford did, I could see the reflection of Frank. Camera angles and different touches. He'd say, 'How do you like that?' And I'd say 'I've seen that before,' and he'd go as cold as anything. He had an amazing admiration for his brother, because Frank was about thirteen years older

---

*His last, *Call of the Heart* (January 1928), starred Dynamite, a dog; his other Dynamite movie, *Wolf's Trail*, has the odd distinction (Richard Koszarski tells me) of having the best cost-to-earnings ratio of *any* Universal feature (Frank made them *cheaply*)—and a speak-to-the-grave scene anticipating those in later John Fords.

Francis Ford as Lincoln, *On Secret Service* (Kay Bee, 1912).

than John, but he was completely jealous of him. He realized that this isn't me. I'm just walking in his footsteps, because I've always considered Frank the most picture-wise man I've ever known. Frank was not interested in making money, not in the least. He was an experimenter, always. Jack did the same thing, but he had this awful . . . I can say something that perhaps most people would give me the horse laugh for. I've studied John Ford for so long, and I realized that he was two completely different people. The real John Ford is so much different from the John Ford we know, the tough,

Francis Ford in his last role, as drummer, in *The Sun Shines Bright* (1952).

ruthless, sarcastic individual. The real John Ford was very kind, but he was afraid of that. And the John Ford we know is a legend, a living legend who was created by John Ford himself to protect the other John Ford, the sympathetic, sentimental, soft John Ford. I am quite assured now that John Ford was perhaps suffering tremendously from a very great inferiority complex, and sitting right at the foundation of that inferiority complex was his brother, Francis. He knew that this is where it all came from, and he took it out on Frank for the rest of his life.

"But John Ford, there was a man in my estimation. He had the touch of greatness. He was perhaps a great man, John Ford. There were many sides to him that people never saw . . ."[27]

Apprenticeship

When Jack Ford arrived in California in July 1914, Frank put him to work as "assistant, handyman, everything," at $12 a week, on the final episode of *Lucille Love*. His first (acting) credit came four months later, as Dopey in Frank's *The Mysterious Rose*.

Frank liked his action grit-real, so injuries, including at least one death, were frequent. But he paid bonuses for any injuries the camera could record; and as Jack would do too, Frank would goad his extras into surpassing themselves:

Now boys, remember you are not in a drawing room; don't bow to each other or apologize if you should happen to take a piece of skin away from the man you are fighting. This is to be the real thing—go to it. Who will roll down that bank? Who will fall off a horse? I don't believe one of you dare—huh! You will?—and you will? Good! I thought there might be one or two of you who did not want a cushion to fall on—no, I don't want any more. Listen, boys, a dollar for a bloody nose and two for a black eye.[28]

(This last line was echoed twenty-five years later in *How Green Was My Valley.*)

But Frank took care of Jack. He blew up a dynamite-wired desk where Jack was sitting by firing a cannonball through the tent. He had him jump seventy-five feet from a freight car rolling along a trestle; had him blown up in a car by mining the road; had him dodging shells on a Confederate battlefield before bouncing a powder grenade off his head (for a close shot)—it exploded just beneath his chin. "That was a close thing," Frank told him in the hospital. "Another second and audiences would have realized I was using a double."[29]

Two decades later, in *Judge Priest*, Jack had Frank playing a drunk resting on a wheelbarrow. But there was a rope tied to it, and, as a carriage drove off, Frank went suddenly careening down the street, swallowing his chaw at the first jolt. "That was for the grenade!" Jack scolded, just as if it had been the day before.[30]

Jack's roommate at the Virginia Apartments, 6629½ Hollywood Boulevard, was Edmund Richard "Hoot" Gibson, the future cowboy star from Nebraska, who was then a wrangler and occasional double for Harry Carey. In 1959 they met again:

Jack was worse Irish than me [Gibson recalled]. That time he wanted to play "My Wild Irish Rose" on the player piano and I wanted to play something else, I forget what, he picked up the piano stool and broke it on my head. And it was my piano!

It wasn't "My Wild Irish Rose" [retorted Ford], and there was no choice. He had exactly one roll for that piano—"Dardanella." He'd sit at that thing playing "Dardanella" morning, noon and night. Even now . . . anytime I have the black luck to hear "Dardanella," I notice my fists are clenched and I'm gritting my teeth. One night I had to get some sleep; I had a tough morning ahead. There he sat and his "Dardanella." Sure I knocked him off the piano stool and smashed it on his head. And then he came at me with a bottle.[31]

Ford was fond of telling how he played a bespectacled Klansman in *The Birth of a Nation*, fell off his horse, and woke up with Griffith bending over him. "Are you all right, son?" "I guess so." Griffith called for some whiskey, Jack objected that he did not drink, and Griffith replied, "It's for me."[32] Ford did not get to know Griffith until after the latter's retirement (and he was one of the few who attended Griffith's wake), but he was mightily impressed by Griffith's great epic: "I went to the premiere of *The Birth of a Nation* and at the end I actually strained my voice yelling. Before it, everything had been static. But then there were little things. Like when Henry Walthall comes home from the war and Mae Marsh has put cotton on her dress, pretending it is ermine, and while they talk he picks little pieces of cotton off the dress, shyly."[33] Taking time for "little things" became Ford's passion, too.

It is improbable, however, that the sensitivity in Jack's blue eyes was noticeable to many in the teens and twenties. Despites fights and firings he had graduated to Frank's chief assistant, and often his cameraman, by 1917. But toughness was his dominant characteristic. He had a long, powerful stride, with an arm swing, and even at age twenty he had impressed his bosses by the way he cursed and bullied the hardened cowhands who served as extras. His debut as director, he later claimed, occurred when he was obliged to substitute for his drunk brother and to entertain visiting dignitaries by having cowboys ride back and forth, take falls, and finally burn

Shooting the Ford-Cunard serial, *The Broken Coin* (1915). Francis and Grace, kneeling; Eddie Polo, on back, Jack Ford, hand in mouth. From the Robert S. Birchard Collection.

down a town. This was in 1916, and Carl Laemmle supposedly later said, "Give Jack Ford the job—he yells good." Ford's niece Cecil (or Cecile) McLean de Prida, says Laemmle's nephew Eddie was begging for a chance to direct, so Laemmle let Ford and Eddie direct one together.[34] No details of this picture are known. But Universal in these years was almost like a big family. Jack was close friends with Eddie and occasionally played little jokes even on Carl Laemmle himself.

Officially Jack graduated to director as Frank's star began to wane. With his brother's company Jack made a satiric action picture with a sentimental twist: the hero (Jack Ford) needs money to buy his mother a home in Ireland. Universal publicity gave *The Tornado* (two-reel 101 Bison, March 3, 1917) a good boost. His second movie, again with Frank's company, *The Trail of Hate*, was called "thrilling . . . teeming with life and color and action" by *Exhibitors' Trade Review*,[35] while Universal's *Weekly* ran a still from his *next* film, explaining, "When Jack has finished a picture his players are not fit for publication."[36] After the third, *The Scrapper*, in which he copied Francis by staging a fight in a whorehouse, the *Weekly* remarked (probably facetiously):

> For a long time people have said, as they heard the name "Ford" in connection with a picture: "Ford? Any relation to Francis?" Very soon, unless all indications of the present time fail, they will be saying: "Ford? Any relation to Jack?"[37]

The Fighting Brothers (1918). Hoot Gibson, Pete Morrison. From the Robert S. Birchard Collection.

Frank, in later years, used to say he was glad to get rid of Jack, was fed up with him. Jack was always getting into emotional arguments, would fight with everyone; he was a damn nuisance, a dunderhead that couldn't be relied on.[38] "As a prop man he 'stunk'; as an assistant director, he was worse, and as an actor . . . well, such a ham! When I would tell Jack to put a chair in the corner for a scene, Jack would turn and say, 'Joe, get a chair and put it in the corner'; Joe would turn around and holler, 'Dutch, get a chair and put it in the corner'; Dutch would turn around and holler, 'Jake, get a chair . . . .'"

Frank got his own chair; but, he added, anticipating the theme of *The Long Gray Line*, Jack was "durable," and he stressed the word. Jack's first film, "wasn't bad except for the acting," but the fourth one was "a little gem." "Jack was no good," he concluded, "until he was given something to do on his own where he could let himself go—and he proved himself then."[39]

The Soul Herder was the fourth film. "Delicious humor," said *Moving Picture World*, "an excellent picture in every way."[40] And we can note, even in its plot summary, many traits of the later Ford—oxymoronic humor, missing family members, the appeal of innocence, the reformed sinner. Gentle, sarcastic, communal, melodramatic, folksy, it is already an "ideal" Ford story—theatrical in a structure of myths and motifs developing in short scenes:

A terror Saturday night, tame by Sunday, Cheyenne Harry (Carey) has to have the sheriff remind him he shot up the town. In the desert he rescues a little girl from Indians. She makes him assume her dead daddy's parson's garb. After Harry rescues his girlfriend, he holds a funeral for her (dead) kidnapper, whose money he gives to prostitutes to leave town, and, since most of Buckhorn has missed three weeks of church, he escorts them at gunpoint to hear a four- (instead of a one-) hour sermon by him.

Harry Carey

The Soul Herder commenced a four-year, twenty-five-film association with Harry Carey—next to Francis Ford, Jack's most significant formative influence. In some ways it was a strange association. Ford was twenty-two, the son of a small-town immigrant, brash, intense, and ambitious; Carey was thirty-nine, the son of a White Plains special sessions judge, and a seasoned veteran. But they were both about six feet, 170 pounds, and they liked riding out to location on horseback, camping in bedrolls, and flushing out stories as they went along. Later they would let George Hively write up the stories and get screen credit.

Born January 16, 1878, Carey had given up thought of a legal career when, convalescing from pneumonia around 1906, he had authored *Montana,* a play in which he toured for some years. Henry B. Walthall then recruited him from a bar for Griffith's Biograph Company, where, always playing heavies, he became known as the "Biograph burglar"—except to

The Freeze Out (1921). Harry Carey on right. From the Robert S. Birchard Collection.

Unidentified Universal film of 1919: probably *Roped*. Harry Carey and Neva Gerber (?).

Griffith, who called him Gunboat. [41] In mid-1915 he joined Universal as one of their "Broadway Players" but gradually became identified as a western type. Once the studio's most hotly promoted star, his career was fading fast at the time of *The Soul Herder* (August 1917). According to Ford, "they needed somebody to direct a cheap picture of no consequence with Harry Carey, whose contract was running out. . . . There were numerous Western stars around that time—Mix and Hart and Buck Jones—and they had several actors at Universal whom they were grooming to be Western leading men; now we knew we were going to be through anyway in a couple of weeks, and so we decided to kid them a little—not kid the Western—but the leading men—and make Carey sort of a bum, a saddle tramp, instead of a great bold gun-fighting hero. All this was fifty percent Carey and fifty percent me." [42] Carey deliberately avoided giving his good-badman character any degree of epic stature (Hart), dandyism (Mix), or star quality (Bronco Billy), adopting instead a relaxed, receptive humility; he never seemed superior to his audience. Most Ford characters resemble this model. Good badmen appeared frequently in westerns, but Carey may have been the first to cling to the idea. Actually, his good-badman character antedates his association with Ford by some years, likewise his Cheyenne Harry persona.* He was in search of a director and, on Olive Carey's recommendation, got Carl Laemmle to assign Ford to do a picture with him.

Their next release was a war-bond comedy, *Cheyenne's Pal*, in which Harry regrets selling his horse for gambling debts, and so jumps ship and swims ashore. Then, for their next picture, *Straight Shooting*, Carey and Ford dis-

---

*The good-badman character appeared at least as early as Griffith's *The Wanderer* (Biograph: 1913); "Cheyenne Harry" appeared in *The Bad Man of Cheyenne* (Universal: December 1916) obeyed orders, turning in *five* reels instead of two: it took Laemmle's intervention to stay the confounded cutter's hand. The result was a picture Universal advertised as "The Greatest Western Ever Made."

    ***Straight Shooting* (1917).** In contrast to the agonized caricatures prevalent in later films, particularly those of today, the "professional hatchet men" portrayed by Harry Carey and Vester Pegg in 1917 seem healthy, likeable, unneurotic, and all but indistinguishable from the "goodies." Audiences today might find this "unrealistic," but, like the river serving as arbitrary barrier between *Straight Shooting's* feuding settlers,* the division between outlaw and respected citizen is fluid; Ford's people drift freely between ranch and farm, with the saloon—a perpetual halfway house—as neutral territory. The man Carey plans to kill one day becomes his father the next day; another man, a drinking buddy now, is a mortal enemy tomorrow. Life is fragile, relationships shifting, society amorphous. *Straight Shooting* records a period of transition in the land's history and the characters' lives; like most later Fords, it stresses "passage" over "permanence."

    Ford's first feature, *Straight Shooting* received critical acclaim for its graceful blend of raw action, infectious characters, compelling situations, and artful, unaffected photography. These are characteristics in which we can glimpse the mature Ford of later years. (And the Sims family bolting their food after grace will be echoed twenty-four years later in *How Green Was My Valley*.) Still, it is not easy to know how to distribute credit among Ford, Carey, and 1917. Though the western was scarcely a decade old, a decade is a century in movie history and the western had long since defined its generic conventions in marble—Universal alone had been issuing six to ten westerns a week in 1913. Agrarian, family-centered situations were among the most popular themes (which may explain something about Ford's later, populist work). And Carey, a veteran of nearly two hundred pictures, had his own notions about filmmaking. As a further difficulty, *Straight Shooting* is the sole title known to survive from Ford's Universal years (thanks to the Czechoslovak Film Archives)—one, only, of twenty-five Carey-Fords (not to mention Carey's work for other directors, including himself).

    Already remarkable for Ford in 1917 is his ability to maintain an energetic narrative while pausing constantly for tangential moments of reflec-

---

*Ranchers vs. farmers. Thunder Flint (Duke Lee) sends Sam Turner (Hoot Gibson) to evict farmer Sims; but Sam loves Sims's daughter Joan (Molly Malone). So Flint hires freelance outlaw Cheyenne Harry. But Harry comes upon Sims, Joan, and Sam mourning over the grave of brother Ted, killed by Flint's man Placer (Vester Pegg). This sight, and sudden attraction to Joan, change his life; he sends word to Flint, "I'm reforming, I'm giving up killing, I'm quitting."

    Planning to attack Sims, Flint sends Placer, Harry's drinking buddy, to bump off Harry; but wins the duel. Joan gallops to rally farmers; in the ensuing battle, Harry arrives in the nick of time with outlaw Mexicanos to defeat Flint, Sims asks Harry to take his son's place, but (in the 1917 issue) Harry sends Joan back to Sam and gazes toward the setting sun.

❧ THE ❧ NATURE DOCTOR

Dr H.C.A.VOGEL

A MANUAL OF TRADITIONAL AND COMPLEMENTARY MEDICINE

FOREWORD BY **JAN DE VRIES**

Instant
Improvement
Inc.

The Nature Doctor is not intended as medical advice. Its intent is solely informational and educational. Please consult a health professional should the need for one be indicated.

THE NATURE DOCTOR

Published by arrangement with Dr. H.C.A. Vogel
Copyright © Verlag A. Vogel, Teufen (AR) Switzerland 1952, 1991
ALL RIGHTS RESERVED

German title: *Der kleine Doktor*
New English edition prepared by Harry Selbert
Drawings by Verlag A. Vogel

No part of this book may be reproduced by any mechanical, photographic, or electronic process, or in the form of a phonographic or other recording, nor may it be stored in a retrieval system, transmitted, or otherwise copied for public or private use other than for "fair use" without the written permission of the publisher.

Library of Congress Cataloging-in-Publication Data

Vogel, H. C. A., 1902-
    [Kleine Doktor. English]
    The nature doctor : a manual of traditional and complementary medicine / H.C.A. Vogel ; foreword by Jan de Vries.
      p.   cm.
    Translation of: Der kleine Doktor.
    Includes index.
    1. Herbs—Therapeutic use   I. Title.
RM666.H33V64   1991
615'.321—dc20   91-25186
                                    CIP
ISBN 0-941683-27-3 (Hardcover)

Fourth Hardcover Printing, 1994

Printed in the United States of America

Published by Instant Improvement, Inc., 210 East 86th Street New York, New York 10028, with the permission of Keats Publishing, Inc., New Canaan, CT.

Contents

Foreword

In my mind I often relive my first meeting with Dr Vogel. It was not a lengthy meeting, yet it was to determine my future in more ways than one. During that fateful meeting I immediately realised how exceptional a person Dr Vogel was in his chosen field. It was with fascination that I listened to what this talented man had to say and I was delighted when the possibility arose for me to be trained by him.

It is now almost thirty-five years since that first meeting; in the meantime I have worked for him and worked with him, both of which I still consider a privilege. I have been able to observe him in his work with patients and have listened to him conduct lectures for thousands of people. Over the years, his tremendous knowledge has confirmed my impression of his exceptional qualities.

In those early days of our acquaintance Dr Vogel inspired in me the fervent wish to follow in his footsteps and I subsequently did everything possible to be trained to become like him, that is, to be able to help those who are suffering.

Over and over again he has surprised me by being such an excellent tutor. One only needs to read the first section of this book, one of the many Dr Vogel has written. He generously shares his ideas with the reader and in so doing passes on invaluable advice on a wide range of health problems.

I consider it a privilege to have been asked to write a foreword to this book, not only because of my admiration for Dr Vogel, but also because I have been able to turn to his books for guidance on countless occasions in order to help the thousands of people whom I have attended to at my own clinics.

In this new edition he has sought to advise the reader on new methods that are of specific relevance to today's environmental and ecological conditions.

I carefully adhere to Dr Vogel's philosophies which he has taught me over the years and I know that one of his main aims is to instruct his patients and the general public alike in the many natural ways in which suffering and pain can be relieved. As he often points the way to the simple methods available to us in nature, I have no doubt that this book will find a place in many households as a useful source of valuable information and sensible advice on treatment without side effects.

I once joined Dr Vogel on a walk through the Jura mountains, accompanied by a group of medical students. The educational value of this exercise was most impressive as he pointed out the many roots, herbs, leaves, berries and flowers along our path and explained to us their medicinal value. Dr Vogel's great knowledge and the secrets he revealed to us added greatly to the enjoyment of this walk. An even bigger revelation awaited us when we arrived at our destination. Although our guide was considerably older than any of us, Dr Vogel was the only one among us who was not totally exhausted. Surely this alone must stand as clear proof of the value of his philosophies!

Jan de Vries
Auchenkyle
Southwoods
Troon
Scotland

Preface

A Lifetime Devoted to Serving my Fellowman

It was in 1952 when I decided to publish the results of thirty years of experience in naturopathy, the treatment of disease by natural means and remedies. With the very first edition of *The Nature Doctor* (*Der Kleine Doktor*, in my native language) I hoped to stimulate a greater awareness of traditional natural medicine, to help the sick and aid the healthy to prevent illness and disease, withholding nothing that could be of benefit to my fellow man. Would I succeed?

The answer speaks volumes: since those small beginnings not only has the number of items and pages steadily grown in the course of more than fifty editions, but over 1½ million families around the globe have bought the book in one of the twelve languages in which it is published and with it have acquired a 'resident doctor' right in their own homes. That *The Nature Doctor* has proved an invaluable source of advice in days of sickness and of good health, making all my literary efforts most worthwhile, is seen in the gratifying number of letters still pouring in from appreciative readers.

So why publish another edition for the English-speaking public? I would like to reply by giving two related reasons. First, the constant changes in conditions and circumstances of our modern world call for adaptation in order to keep abreast with new developments. And second, there is my own personal involvement, my entire life being devoted to serving my fellow man, a kind of mission, if you will, urging me to enlighten, encourage and help towards a healthier body and mind.

As regards the latter, I am happy to see the worldwide fast-growing interest in natural medicine, phytotherapy (the use of plant medicines), homoeopathy, biochemical treatment, aromatherapy and other forms of alternative medicine. At the same time the modern way of life has given rise to new diseases, or an increase in the incidence of once lesser-known ailments, like viral diseases, chronic post-virus fatigue syndrome, candida albicans, stress, depressions, and AIDS, to mention but a few. Hence the need for up-to-date information, which prompted me to take on the arduous task of preparing a new edition of *The Nature Doctor*, including information on the most recent results of research, a chapter on viruses and bacteria, and details of some newly developed natural remedies.

But good health involves more than taking remedies. If we want to live healthy, happy and joyful lives, we must endeavour to re-establish the proper relationship between ourselves – the whole body and mind – and nature. There is no other way to lead a happy and satisfied life. If we violate nature, its harmony is destroyed, for we are part of nature. In the same way, all medical research is a waste of time if these holistic interrelationships are not taken into consideration.

I have always shown deep respect for nature and relied on it exclusively. Nature has been my most influential teacher and cherished university. It has been my endeavour to observe nature, to listen to it, in order to learn how to treat it and how we can use it beneficially.

I was born in October 1902 in Aesch near Basel, Switzerland. From my earliest childhood I remember that nature with its endless variety of plants and animals has always impressed and fascinated me. My thirst for knowledge, my curiosity, urged me to roam the fields, meadows and woods. My father and my grandmother in particular introduced me to the beauties of the colourful and often mysterious Creation around us. I used to wonder about things like ants, beetles, frogs and lizards until I began to understand more about them and acquire a deep sense of respect for every living creature. I esteem life as sacred. For this reason none of the body care products I have developed over the years are tested on animals, a practice that I am deeply opposed to.

My love of nature was behind my drive to explore and investigate, and led me to travel around the globe. The 1950s and 1960s were devoted to field research among native tribes in Africa, North and South America, Australia and Tasmania. I lived among them, sharing their work, their joys, their sadnesses. I was not motivated by a spirit of sheer adventure; I was keenly interested in their life-style, their diet and environment, their mind and body, and the connections and interrelations between these factors.

My fondest memories concern the Sioux Indians in South Dakota, where I spent some time. I was touched and thrilled to discover that we had a common understanding and loving respect for nature in spite of our different cultural and religious backgrounds. Nature is sacred to the American Indians and must not be destroyed. They understand that it can be used beneficially in many ways without having to violate it. Chief Black Eagle, with whom I was united in a bond of friendship, put it this way: 'I take a plant, put it in the earth, propagate it; nothing is destroyed, but I use it for myself in a natural way.'

I feel deeply indebted to the Sioux Indians for their knowledge of exceptional herbs which they shared with me. An outstanding example is *Echinacea*, the purple coneflower. I watched Indian women chew *Echinacea* leaves and apply the pulp to wounds and injuries. It was even effective in combatting the poison from venemous snakes, and particularly in cases of high temperatures and badly healing skin eruptions. Later I experimented with this plant and experienced its successful effects on my own body. I took some coneflower seed back to Europe with me, acclimatised the plant in cultivation, and developed a remedy from the flowers, leaves and roots that is now an accepted part of efficacious treatment with plant extracts.

As a nutritionist I discovered among such primitive peoples the real cause of the ever-increasing cases of 'diseases of civilisation' despite the astronomical amounts of money being spent on health and medical care. It is excess protein in the diet. Most of us eat two or three times more protein than is needed, in the form of meat, eggs, cheese and fish. Of course, protein is necessary in our diet, but too much of it triggers protein-storage diseases. Protein foods also produce excess acid, and the constant state of hyperacidity in the body is one of the causes of cancer because protein is used in cell formation and also promotes cell proliferation, as in tumours, but also as in rheumatism, gout and arthritis. I found that these diseases are virtually unknown among people who still live close to nature.

I myself have been a vegetarian for seventy years. My diet consists of nothing but natural, unadulterated, excess-alkaline food, with a high proportion of raw foods, just as is the custom among primitive peoples, who follow such a diet unconsciously. They still live in harmony with nature, the exact opposite of the modern fast-food culture. *The Nature Doctor* advises on this subject more specifically in the course of this book. Primitive peoples have no knowledge of civilisational or mental diseases. The Congo pygmies, for example, dance for joy every day, even though it rains almost daily and they hardly ever see the sun shine through the thick forest canopy.

Finding the balance between nature, body and mind has been my endeavour and philosophy, a holistic approach. I formulated my concept – which has since been proved thousands of times over – to tackle the cause of an illness or disease, and to work in harmony with nature, never against it. Ignorance and unreasonableness regarding our body's requirements contribute up to 80 per cent to our falling ill. Today's orthodox medical opinion in the main still holds to the fundamentally wrong view that it is the illness or disease itself, the symptom, that has to be treated and if possible combatted or suppressed by strong drugs. *The Nature Doctor* is designed to help us regain our basic confidence in nature, which has been pushed aside and ignored as a result of technical and scientific progress. But thousands of years of empirical medicine, proven in practice, cannot simply be brushed aside without inviting trouble.

In my long life I have collected bit by bit and expanded the traditional and empirical knowledge of European folk medicine. My activities in the interests of sick as well as healthy people began in Teufen in the Appenzellerland. This is where I established a clinic based on naturopathy, gathered medicinal plants at the foot of the Swiss Alps and first prepared extracts from fresh plants. I discovered early on that these tinctures were more effective than those made from dried plants. Driven by my love of the Creator, nature and my fellow human beings, I have communicated my knowledge freely in innumerable lectures on all continents, and since 1929 I have reported my experiences and observations as a nature practitioner and researcher in my monthly periodical called *Gesundheits-Nachrichten* (A. Vogel's Health News). Some items which first appeared in this magazine have been included in *The Nature Doctor*, others have been published in my other books, *The Liver, the Regulator of Your Health, Health Guide Through Southern Countries, Subtropics, Tropics, and Desert Zones* (a guide for holidaymakers and those living in those regions), *Nature – Your Guide to Healthy Living*, and the most recent title, *Cancer – Fate or Disease of Civilisation?*

There is not one single home remedy, piece of advice, herbal or homoeopathic remedy mentioned in *The Nature Doctor* that has not been tried and tested by myself and thousands of patients. The reader can follow the recommendations with full confidence in nature and the body's inherent defence mechanism, or immune system.

To find your way about, look at the table of contents at the beginning, and to locate a specific subject, illness or remedy, check the comprehensive subject index at the back. In many instances you will find remedies drawn from nature's bountiful medicine chest, and natural treatments that need no outsider to help in their application. Of course, there are also cases when the advice of a qualified practitioner is indicated.

I am now in my eighty-eighth year and feel the proof of my philosophy confirmed in my own life. I still enjoy working every day; I am still chairman of the board of directors of the Bioforce Company, manufacturers of natural remedies, health foods and body care products, a company I established in 1963 to cope with the great demand for natural remedies and which now operates worldwide.

I still enjoy attending meetings and conferences, and meet regularly with doctors, scientists and researchers specialising in the field of natural plant medicine (phytotherapy). On these occasions I am often amazed to find that their latest knowledge usually confirms and vindicates what I have been propagating over seven decades in my books and lectures and have experienced with innumerable patients as a nature doctor – that man is a unit of body and mind, a marvel of nature that is subject to nature's laws.

If we seek and hope to achieve a real cure, whether in the case of a single patient or of the whole human race, that is, the survival of our natural environment, we cannot expect to achieve success unless we subject ourselves in everything to nature's balanced laws. For I am firmly convinced that despite the great achievements and advancements of modern medical science we ourselves – even with the most sophisticated medical equipment – cannot do the healing. Only nature can heal and cure. We can help and support nature and its laws that make a cure possible.

And it is with this in mind that I beg the reader to consider and apply the information contained in this latest edition of *The Nature Doctor*. Good health to you!

Dr. H. C. Alfred Vogel

A Doctor in Your House

What is the purpose of having a copy of *The Nature Doctor* in your house? Well, its simple but important task is to make you aware of the many natural remedies that are readily available in your home and immediate surroundings. When a sudden emergency arises or if you suffer from some persistent ailment, simply pick up *The Nature Doctor*, locate the appropriate entry and see what help is at your disposal to alleviate the pain or overcome the problem.

Of course, I don't know whether you live in a pretty little village or a small town. I have no idea whether you have to be content with living in the built-up area of a large city or whether you have chosen to live on a farm close to nature in the quiet countryside far away from other houses, villages or towns. You may have chosen to settle in a country where distance means nothing. You may even be a forester whose home may be a solitary house among the trees, or live high up in the mountains.

Whoever you are and no matter where you live, it will be to your advantage to consult *The Nature Doctor* in your hour of need, at least until you can call your family doctor who may be able to give you further assistance. Often, however, in an emergency the immediate help offered by *The Nature Doctor* may be sufficient to overcome your problem, because the right remedy given at the right time usually has successful results.

Perhaps you think that you and your family are assured of enjoying good health and that no misfortune could ever befall you. It often happens that day after day you go about your business and various tasks without anything happening to disturb the rhythm of your life. But suddenly something goes wrong – an accident occurs, be it ever so slight, an illness strikes, a cold or a bout of flu – and the daily routine is upset. At such times you will be glad of the immediate help provided by *The Nature Doctor*.

So what do you have in your house or nearby that will give you quick and reliable help? The size of your figurative medicine chest will depend largely on where you live and what can be found in and near your home. It may be that some of the remedies you need can be found in the kitchen, the larder or the cellar. You may even have some things stored in the attic that could be most useful to you. And if you have a garden, there are many plants that can come to your assistance. Better still, if you live in the country you will find an even more abundant supply of help in the fields, woods and meadows. If, however, you live in a town, you will simply have to keep your eyes open when out walking, because you can still find many plants that will be useful in times of need.

Should you run out of the usual remedies you keep in your house, our many little plant friends can act as preventative measures as well as remedies for less serious complaints. The number of medicinal plants found hidden in the woods, sprouting in fields and meadows, growing along river banks and streams is so great that *The Nature Doctor* would be more than twice its present size if it attempted to describe all the wonderful help nature's garden has to offer.

To begin with, *The Nature Doctor* will acquaint you with some of the remedies to be found right among your everyday supplies. You will be astonished to learn that many food items can have a medicinal use, for instance flour, sugar, water, oil, salt, eggs, soft white cheese ('quark'), potatoes, carrots, cabbage, radishes, onions, garlic, horseradish and parsley – to name but a few.

Welcome *The Nature Doctor* into your home and read it carefully. It will reveal many of the remedies that have been in your home all the time without your knowing it.

At first glance, the volume and diversity of suggestions and advice may appear confusing, but a careful examination of the comprehensive index at the back of the book will help you to quickly find the information you are seeking.

The simple examples found in Part One of the book will no doubt whet your appetite and encourage you to consult the more detailed sections that follow.

Part One

Treatments to Try Out
'Can I really trust your simple natural remedies?' you may ask at
first. 'Will they encourage me to consult you whenever I am in
need?'

'Of course,' the 'Nature Doctor' replies, 'try them and see for
yourself!'

Burns and Scalds
Burns from flame or fire and scalds from boiling liquids call for
quick action. Immerse the affected part of the body immediately
in *cold water*. Where this cannot easily be done, apply a cold
compress. Cover the burn with gauze, or with a clean cloth if a
large area is affected, until medical help can be obtained. To avoid
infection, do not puncture any blisters. In cases of third-degree
burns, immediate medical attention should be sought if complications are to be prevented. *St John's wort oil* has also proved to
be an effective remedy for burns and scalds.

Cuts, Scratches and Grazes
Superficial scratches and small wounds which prove difficult to heal
can be dealt with quite simply. Use *concentrated whey (Molkosan)*,
which is one of nature's best cleansing agents. Then dust the wound
with *biological calcium powder* (for example *Urticalcin*) and, for
two nights running, apply *soft white cheese* (quark). Should these
items not be available, soak some *wheat grain* (which needs to be
minced afterwards) or *bran* in fresh milk. Then cover the wound
with the resulting mash and you will find that this also acts as a
thorough cleanser. Once again dust the wound with biological
calcium powder and after two days of treatment apply pulped
cabbage leaves, preferably using Savoy cabbage for the best results.
Cabbage leaf poultices have proved more effective than many
modern remedies. If the wound is stubborn, causing swelling or

1

discoloration, and if everything else seems to have failed, you must not lose patience but continue the treatment with cabbage leaf poultices for weeks or even months. Alleviation will be experienced even in serious cases and a complete cure is often possible.

Inflammation of the Eyes

Lengthy exposure to the reflection of the sun on water or snow can make the eyes sore. Do you know what to do when you or someone in your family are affected in this way and perhaps the eyes begin to burn during the night? The remedy is quite simple. All you need to do is take the white of an *egg*, beat it lightly, spread it on a cloth, and bandage the eyes with it. The burning sensation will subside and the patient will be able to sleep. It is more than probable that the inflammation will have diminished, if not disappeared, by the morning. If no egg is available, *soft white cheese* (quark) or even a piece of *raw meat* (veal, beef or chicken) will achieve similar results. These well-proven remedies can be used whenever you need them, including cases of snow-blindness caused by the intense reflection of sunlight from snow and ice.

Colds

A 'streaming cold' is best treated with *onions (Allium cepa)*. Dip a slice of freshly cut onion into a glass of hot water. Remove the onion after only one or two seconds, allow the water to cool and sip this throughout the day. This is also an excellent remedy for spring colds. If, in addition, you place half an onion on your bedside table, you will inhale its odour while sleeping, thus reducing the tendency to catarrh and alleviating your cold. An *onion poultice* applied to the neck during the night is equally effective. Another way to help rid yourself of a cold is by sniffing up *salt water, lemon juice*, or a natural *calcium powder* (for example Urticalcin).

Catarrh

Perhaps you are prone to frequent colds and suffer from catarrh. If you have a *pine, larch* or any other pinaceous tree in your garden, take some of the *buds* which can always be found in various stages of growth on these trees. By chewing these buds slowly and thoroughly throughout the day, replacing them with fresh ones from time to time, the catarrh will be eliminated within a few days. So, when you go skiing or out for a walk, watch out for pine trees and take the opportunity to avail yourself of this

2

simple but effective remedy. Before retiring at night, dampen a cloth with *oil* (cooking or salad oil), wrap it around the neck and cover with a *woollen scarf* to keep it warm. This will help to clear up any irritating cough.

Hoarseness

The berries of the *mountain ash*, also known as *rowan*, are a good remedy for hoarseness. There may be a tree in your garden, or in a neighbour's, or you may remember seeing one on country walks. At the same time, you can look out for the *pimpernel*. To combat hoarseness, chew either rowan berries or pimpernel root, fresh or dried. Keep chewing these for as long as possible and let the insalivated juice run down the throat. This simple treatment makes hoarseness disappear in no time at all. Of course, you do not need to use both remedies together; either one on its own will no doubt help you. When you have lost your voice, rowan berries and pimpernel root are two of the best cures available.

Chilblains and Cold Feet

Have you ever wondered what causes these two unpleasant complaints? It is unlikely that you would be troubled with them if you saw to it that your vascular system, particularly the veins, were kept free from congestion. But if you do suffer, *hot and cold foot baths* can help. Begin by immersing your feet in hot water for several minutes, then place them in cold water and keep them there for the equivalent number of seconds; in other words, if you soak your feet for two or three minutes in hot water, leave them for only two or three seconds in the cold water. This procedure may be repeated 6–8 times at a session. Finish off with cold water, rub your feet vigorously with a towel and then apply a little oil (preferably *St John's wort oil*), if you like. This treatment will soon bring the circulation back to normal.

A much older but less known method of improving the circulation is that of *walking barefoot in the snow*. If your house or apartment has a veranda which becomes covered with snow in winter, you have the ideal location for this. Incidentally, this is a similar treatment to *treading cold water*, a form of hydrotherapy connected with the Kneipp method (see page 334). To start with, practise snow-walking for ten seconds, then thirty seconds, gradually building up to 2–3 minutes. However, a word of caution is called for here. Take care not to do this to the point where you start to feel chilled. After completing the exercise, and without

3

drying your feet, go back inside to your warm bed. Do this every morning for several days in a row. If you have no balcony or veranda and have to leave your house to do your snow-walking, wear warm slippers to go outside, remove them quickly and start stamping around in the snow, preferably fresh snow. If at all possible, dry your feet vigorously with a towel before replacing your slippers to go back inside. Again, this treatment should be repeated for several days and you will be surprised to see how the chilblains disappear.

In order to prevent a return of the problem the following winter, *soak your feet* (for at least twenty minutes) regularly during the summer months in water to which *wild thyme* or *hay flowers* (*hayseed*) have been added. It is also helpful to go barefoot whenever possible so as to toughen up your feet.

You can also rub your feet with *lemon juice*. Let them dry naturally and then apply oil, *olive oil* being the best. In other areas, especially in the north, it is customary to use *paraffin* instead of lemon, although the smell is not as pleasant.

If you live near a place where cheese is made you may be able to obtain *whey*, which can be added to a foot bath. Sour whey is to be preferred to sweet for this purpose because of its more powerful action. These foot baths, although recommended for the summer period, can also be taken in winter as an alternative to the hot and cold baths or snow-walking. The water for the foot bath should be kept at blood temperature (37 °C/98.6 °F) by adding hot water whenever necessary; you can also, of course, add a decoction of herbs. The feet should be immersed for about thirty minutes and then rubbed with lemon. Finally, apply a poultice of pulped *cabbage leaves* and leave this on overnight. This treatment will not only do wonders for your chilblains, but will also be helpful when you suffer from skin eruptions.

Tired Feet and Legs
Should you be troubled with tired feet and legs, finding them even slightly swollen at the end of the day, bathe them in *potato or vegetable water*. Then wrap them immediately in a *cloth* that has been *covered with hot salt*. Do this every evening for a few days and the tiredness in your feet will disappear. If you have some *hay flowers* or other *herbs* handy, prepare an infusion and add salt, preferably sea salt, which is more effective than common salt. This salty herbal foot bath will also help you get rid of the tiredness, as well as relieving hot, burning feet. Swollen feet, especially ankles,

can be a sign of heart trouble, but *The Nature Doctor* will deal with this later (see pages 138–9).

Haemorrhages and Haemophilia

If you know someone who frequently suffers from heavy nose bleeds, or who is a 'bleeder', any advice will be welcome. What can you do if the bleeding will not stop because the normal clotting ability is impaired? This can be a serious problem unless you know that applying a piece of *fresh raw chicken* is the only natural remedy to stop the bleeding if it is caused by haemophilia. However, if it is only a temporary disturbance it can be effectively dealt with by means of a herb called *tormentil*. *The Nature Doctor* will inform you fully a little later on.

Abdominal Disorders

Girls and women frequently suffer from venous congestions in the abdomen. *Water treatment* brings great relief, and it is recommended that a long *sitz bath* (hip bath) be taken once or twice a week to combat these disorders. For expectant mothers, this kind of treatment will also make confinement easier, thus benefiting the baby. Later on, it will help prevent difficulties arising during the menopause. The body responds to such regular care, and will give you far less trouble at these critical times than it would do otherwise.

Heartburn

A number of simple remedies exist for heartburn, a symptom of indigestion experienced as a burning sensation which may rise into the chest, even causing regurgitation of acid from the stomach into the gullet and mouth. All you need do first is to grate a *potato* as finely as possible, then put this in a cheesecloth and press out the juice. Dilute with warm water, one part juice to two or three parts water. Drink this juice every morning before breakfast, before lunch and at night before retiring. For the best results, prepare fresh each time.

If you still feel some discomfort, take a teaspoon of *wood ash* mixed in a little warm water after eating. This may produce the desired result. Just pour warm water over the ashes and drink them down. If you have no wood ash, common *charcoal*, preferably from limewood, can be crushed and mixed with a little water, porridge or other *cereal*. The charcoal is easier to swallow when prepared in this way and will serve to neutralise the stomach acid.

5

If you do not find the idea of taking wood ash as described above appealing, pour hot water over them and brew in the same way you would make a pot of tea, straining through a fine sieve or cheesecloth. This liquid will also neutralise the gastric acid. *Clay* (white or yellow) dissolved in a little water is equally effective.

In the absence of any of these remedies, sipping *fresh milk* will give temporary relief. Uncooked *oatflakes*, eaten dry and well masticated, are known to serve the same purpose and should be preferred to the more harmful bicarbonate of soda. If, however, you want to normalise the secretion of the gastric juices permanently, you will have to *modify your diet*: keep off spicy food, abstain from white sugar and white flour products, and use less salt. Drinking tea made from *centaury* and *Centaurium extract* has also proved helpful.

If none of these remedies produces the desired effect, it may be that the heartburn is caused by dysfunction of the gallbladder or by intestinal worms. In these cases, the appropriate treatments would be required. Both of these complaints are dealt with in Part Two of this book.

Digestive Upsets and Cramps

Eating too much, or food that causes the pancreas to go on strike, can result in abdominal cramps. A *hot shower* will help dispel the cramps if you remain under it for 10–15 minutes until the stomach area becomes bright red. If you have no shower you can achieve the same result by applying *hot moist compresses*. Follow up by applying a *poultice of chopped raw onion* or *pulped cabbage* on the stomach. The fermentation will cease, the cramps will subside, and you will be back to your usual self. Be sure to *chew your food thoroughly*, allowing it to become well mixed with saliva. If these simple suggestions do not help you must see your doctor, for there is a possibility of a perforation of the stomach, the presence of gallstones, or perhaps an inflammation of the appendix.

Constipation

Soaked *prunes*, taken first thing in the morning and last thing at night, will often remedy the problem of constipation. Young *stinging nettles* boiled in milk have also been found helpful. After removing the nettles, drink this milk every morning on rising. This simple remedy is equally effective in cases of migraine headaches accompanied by bilious vomiting. Stinging nettles eaten raw, as a salad, are also a wonderful remedy, being good for the blood.

The simplest remedy for constipation is to drink a glass of hot water first thing in the morning. But if this does not do the trick, eat a few slices of *fig paste*, which you can make yourself in the following way. Take 100 g (3½ oz) of figs, 100 g (3½ oz) of raisins, 20 g (0.7 oz) of senna pods (preferably powdered) and 20–50 g (0.7–1.75 oz) of ground linseed. Mix all the ingredients together, grind into a paste and shape this into rolls. Cut off slices as you need them.

There is also a special *soup* for sluggish bowels which you eat in the morning with a little *crispbread* or *wholegrain bread*. To make it, cook together freshly ground whole wheat, a small chopped onion and a crushed clove of garlic. When it is ready, add some chopped parsley and a spoonful of olive oil. This simple breakfast has cured many of their constipation. For more stubborn cases, however, ground *linseed* or *psyllium seed* should be added.

In Part Two, where constipation is dealt with in greater detail, a recipe for herb soup to relieve especially stubborn cases is given (see page 224).

Sometimes just a *change in diet* will provide the answer. Avoid anything that may have a constipating effect if your bowels are already sluggish. Sudden constipation, followed by diarrhoea, could indicate a tumour in the colon and medical attention should therefore be sought.

It may be that the constipation has psychological causes or is due to a weak nervous state, exhaustion or some mental anxiety. If so, it is essential to restore the *psychological balance* to ensure sufficient *sleep* and *relaxation*. Plenty of *exercise* should be taken, particularly if the sufferer has a sedentary occupation.

Diarrhoea

If your children, especially babies, have diarrhoea, give them finely grated *apples*. As an extra help, follow up with *oatmeal porridge*. Older children can take the *oatflakes* raw. They should chew them thoroughly, insalivating well, and preferably not be given anything else to eat for a few hours. For very stubborn cases of diarrhoea there is a simple plant that helps almost without exception. This herb, called *tormentil*, has already been recommended for haemorrhages.

Put bad cases of diarrhoea on a 'tea day'. What does this mean? Depending on the gravity of the case and the child's age, nothing but herb teas are given for 6–12, or even up to 24 hours. The following herbs are recommended: *Silvery lady's mantle (Alchemilla*

7

Silverweed

alpina), *bilberry leaves, sage, Iceland moss, silverweed* (*Potentilla anserina*), and *tormentil*. Furthermore, it is advisable to take activated *charcoal* (*Biocarbosan* contains charcoal and charcoaled coffee) to absorb the toxins present in the system. *White clay* has a similar effect. Food may be directly responsible for poisons entering the intestinal tract or the toxins can originate inside through putrefaction and excessive fermentation in the bowels, causing diarrhoea. Whatever the case may be, use activated charcoal to combat such upsets.

Slimming
Do you want to lose weight? If so, beware of harmful reducing methods. For example, do not eat five or six lemons a day for the sake of a shapely waist, because this could do irreparable damage to your liver. Follow a *sensible diet*, avoiding all starchy foods. If you must have meat, choose a little veal. Eat plenty of salads, seeing to it that you have a good variety at each meal. You may include steamed vegetables such as leeks, fennel, chicory, celery or celeriac, salsify and carrots. Fruit can be eaten in the mornings and evenings.

From time to time you will find it beneficial to have a '*juice day*', drinking nothing but juice, for example carrot juice. In the autumn, you may like to have a day when you only drink freshly pressed grape juice.

However, be very careful that your slimming does not harm your health. *Sitz baths* (hip baths) with sea salt and herbs that stimulate circulation are most beneficial for people who are overweight. In the kitchen, too, use only *sea salt* (*Herbamare*) for seasoning as the trace elements it contains will stimulate the internal metabolism and will help to dispose of superfluous fat. If you take *seaweed* (*kelp*) at the same time, your slimming diet will be even more successful. More detailed advice on the subject of weight control is given in Part Two of this book (see pages 201–7).

Headaches
Recurring headaches of any sort can be relieved by applying *onion* or *horseradish poultices* to the nape of the neck, the calves of the legs or soles of the feet. In this way headaches caused by an inflammation may be alleviated or even eliminated. However, since headaches may be brought on for various reasons, it is essential to discover the cause and treat it. Any treatment that only kills the pain can be dangerous. *Petadolor* is an excellent herbal remedy for headaches.

Facial Neuralgia
Excruciating spasmodic pain in the face originates in the nerves. The best and most effective remedy for this is a *hot shower* directed against the face, or, failing that, *hot water compresses*. These should be reapplied frequently so that they are as hot as you can bear them. Stubborn cases will need a *hot herbal compress*. It is sometimes necessary to continue this treatment for up to half an hour before the pain subsides and you begin to feel better. In cases where an abcess, sinusitits or glaucoma is the cause of the pain, these simple applications will not remedy the problem.

Your Iron – a Help for Aches and Pains
It is astonishing to realise the things you can do with an ordinary domestic iron. Neuralgic and rheumatic aches and pains resulting from a chill can be alleviated by rubbing the affected parts with *St John's wort oil*. Or, if you would rather, soak a cloth in the oil and cover with this. Then cover the oiled skin or cloth with a dry cloth and gently iron over with an iron at its lowest setting, for example 'synthetic fibres'. This procedure is quite easy to do. The

heat from the iron will thin the oil, making absorption easier. The effect of this simple treatment is so good that the pain is eased almost immediately. Take care, however, not to have the iron too hot, as you do not want to burn the skin.

Urine Retention
Elderly men who suddenly find themselves unable to pass water during the night will greatly benefit from a *herbal steam bath*. Make an *infusion of camomile or any other herb*, then add this to boiling water in a largish container. Place a narrow board over the container so that the patient can sit above the rising steam. Wrap a blanket or bath towel around the patient to retain the steam. This treatment will stimulate the flow of urine, bringing great relief, and the doctor will not have to be called out in the middle of the night to perform a catheterisation, a most unpleasant procedure. Should the retention of urine be caused by the prostate, further advice can be found under the entry on 'Prostate Trouble' (see pages 173–4).

Combatting the Accumulation of Uric Acid
This is often a long drawn-out battle. If simple remedies such as *parsley tea* are not enough to ease your painful limbs and joints, take a *herbal bath* using any herbs you have available. When you check your stock of herbs in the spring, planning to gather fresh ones, use what you have left in your baths, or make an infusion of cut grass and add this to the bath. Make sure the water is around blood heat (37 °C/98.6 °F); remain completely submerged, with only your nose visible, for 10, 15 or 20 minutes, even as long as half an hour. Have someone turn on the hot water so that the temperature can slowly rise to 38 °C (100 °F), and if you can stand it, to 39 °C (102 °F), following the *Schlenz method* (see pages 433–6). While submerged, have someone brush you vigorously with a stiff brush. If you take this bath once a week, you will be rid of your aches and pains.

To reinforce the treatment place a *poultice of pulped cabbage leaves* on the aching areas and drink plenty of raw *vegetable juices*. Be sure to eat enough alkaline foods and avoid offal, such as liver, kidneys and sweetbread, as well as alcohol.

Limewood Charcoal Powder
Those who suffer from gastric acidity, problems with the stomach and intestinal mucous membranes, or the consequences of protrac-

ted jaundice, should definitely take charcoal powder, preferably from limewood. You can make it yourself by grinding pieces of limewood charcoal. Take this powder in a little milk and, although milk on its own is not always suitable for patients with liver trouble or protracted jaundice, in combination with limewood charcoal powder it is very effective.

Curing Rheumatic and Arthritic Ailments without Medication

Begin your treatment in the morning by drinking half a glass of raw *potato juice* on an empty stomach; if you like, dilute it with a little warm water. All meals should consist of natural, organically grown foods. Detailed information on 'Natural Wholefood' is found in another section of this book (see pages 463–74).

An hour before lunch eat two or three *juniper berries;* chew them thoroughly, insalivating well, and swallow. After lunch swallow 2–4 whole *mustard seeds.* To quench your thirst during the day drink the water in which *potatoes* have been boiled.

Painful areas and arthritic deformities should be treated with different *poultices;* on the first day use pulped cabbage leaves; on the second day clay and on the third day, soft white cheese (quark).

Let me also remind you of a very old but effective treatment for sciatic and rheumatic pains, the *formic acid therapy.* Once every two weeks place the painful limb, say your leg or arm, in an anthill and leave it there long enough for the ants to inject their acid. Then, wipe them off with a brush or cloth and let the formic acid do its work. This is a simple, absolutely natural injection that does not cost you a penny.

Anyone who persists in the use of these simple methods of treatment, and in eating natural foods, will not only alleviate serious cases but cure them, even where the doctor has given up hope. However, if the patient suffers from a slipped disc or other disc trouble, it will be necessary to consult a good chiropractor.

Corn (Maize) and Millet Porridge

An excellent poultice for rheumatic and some arthritic pains can be made with corn (maize) or millet porridge. If you want to increase the circulation, producing hyperaemia, these poultices are most suitable since they remain hot for quite a while.

Prepare the porridge in the usual way, but without adding anything, and apply as hot as you can bear it.

11

Itching and Burning of the Skin

This condition, wherever it may be experienced, is always exceedingly troublesome. When applied externally, *potatoes* often give relief. Peel a raw potato and cut a slice, or grate it finely, and rub on the affected part, even on the face. But this treatment alone may not be sufficient. Quite often the kidneys are to blame for the condition and you will have to observe the treatment indicated in the section on kidneys at the same time (see pages 175–83). It may also be possible that the itching is a symptom of some liver disorder. In this case it will be necessary to consider the advice given under the heading 'Liver Disorders and Nutrition,' (see pages 243–9); the recommended diet for liver patients will be particularly useful. What is more, diabetes and intestinal worms may also cause itchy skin, as can the popular remedy *arnica*, if the patient is sensitive.

Eczema and Other Skin Eruptions

When treating eczema and other skin eruptions, it is essential to make sure that the kidneys, liver and intestines are working properly. Bathing the affected area in warm *whey*, preferably sour whey (*Molkosan*), is excellent. If you can spend your holidays in the country near a dairy where you can obtain whey, you may be able to do this regularly during your stay. Using bran to bathe the eruptions is also effective. Since eczema is sometimes difficult to cure and may require a great deal of time, you should not forget that the cause may not be internal but external. Some people are allergic to certain substances and plants, for example arnica. Your skin may be allergic to terpenes, in which case you would have to keep away from plants that contain them, such as conifers, and of course floor polishes and other products made with turpentine. Even camomile can provoke eczema, and so can *Rhus toxicodendron* (poison ivy), and the primula has been known to cause urticaria. So your eczema may well have one of these external causes. As soon as the right one is identified and the necessary measures taken, the eczema will disappear.

Children may break out in a rash when they overindulge in fruit. Strawberries can cause urticaria. In every case it is good to treat and stimulate the kidneys.

Skin rashes can also have their origin in poisoning or in a vitamin deficiency. It is therefore good to avoid eating, for example, sulphurised dried fruit, and fresh fruit or vegetables that have been sprayed with chemicals. Organically grown *spinach* and young

12

stinging nettles, preferably prepared as salad and dressed with *lemon juice* or *Molkosan*, will eradicate the deficiency and cure the rash in no time at all. Drinking tea made from *wild pansy* (heartsease) will reinforce the healing process.

Boils

Whenever you notice a hot, red swelling under the skin, or if you already have one or more boils, you can help to bring them to a head in the following way. Boil some ground *linseed*, or better still, *fenugreek seed* in water. Apply the resulting hot mash and this will soften the spot and draw the pus to the surface, enabling you to discharge it. If you have neither linseed nor fenugreek available, use hot mashed *potatoes* for a similar result. The wound can then be cleansed with highly diluted *Molkosan*. Then sprinkle with *lactose* (milk sugar), or better still, biological *calcium powder (Urticalcin) and apply pulped cabbage leaves.* You will be pleased to see how quickly this simple treatment works. As an additional support for the healing process, take *yeast extract* or *dried yeast* as a dietary supplement. Finally, do not forget to have your urine tested for sugar whenever you have boils.

Whitlows (Paronychia)

A whitlow is a painful, pus-producing infection of tissues around the nails of a finger or sometimes a toe. It appears quite unexpectedly and its discomfort impels you to take immediate steps to get rid of it. Soak the affected finger or toe in *hot water* (37–38 °C/98–100 °F) two or three times a day, for an hour each time, and be sure to keep the water warm. This treatment can effect a cure relatively quickly, but if not, ask a doctor to lance the finger in order to drain off the pus and prevent stiffening. It is also useful to know that not only hot water but also soft soap can be of help. Just spread the soap on the finger, bandage it and leave on overnight.

Swelling and Bruises

Any simple swelling or bruise responds well to treatment with *cabbage leaf poultices*. If these prove to be too strong, alternate with a *clay pack*. Mix the clay with an infusion of *horsetail* or any *other herb* for a better effect. Alternating the poultices from one day to the next is beneficial because clay reduces the swelling and cabbage leaves contain healing properties and also draw out toxins. This double action ensures a rapid cure.

Ivy

Insect Stings and Bites

What a shock it is when you are stung by a bee or a wasp! Immediately, you try to pull out the sting and suck out the poison that has been injected, because you do not know how the body will react. The pain is best alleviated by means of *ivy*. Perhaps you have an ivy vine climbing up the garden wall or a tree, but if not you should easily be able to find some in a nearby forest or wood. Take a few leaves and some bark, crush them between your fingers and rub onto the sting. Of course, it would be better if you already had some *ivy tincture* in the house. This is quite easy to prepare. Gather ivy leaves and cut off some of the green bark, then pass them all through a mincer. Pour alcohol over the mash and let it stand for a week or so. When ready, press through a sieve, filter and bottle. A few drops of this tincture rubbed lightly on a sting will quickly relieve the pain. Also effective are compresses made with *salt water* to which a few drops of ivy tincture have been added. Any of these treatments will prevent extensive swelling and will neutralise the poison.

Fern (bracken) is an excellent remedy for bites from gnats and similar insects. In tropical regions fern is the next best thing to mosquito nets for protection. Stuff pillows and mattresses with fern and you will not only be protected against all kinds of unwel-

14

come insects, even bed bugs, but will also have a means of relief from rheumatism. Fortunately, education has brought about great changes in matters of hygiene and such unpleasant invaders affect us much less nowadays than in the past, except perhaps in some old farmhouses. Nevertheless, it is helpful to know that rubbing fern on an insect bite helps to avoid any unpleasant consequences.

Insect Stings in the Mouth and Throat

It is unpleasant to be stung anywhere, most of all in the mouth or throat. This can happen if you fail to notice a wasp or bee on your bread and honey or in fruit. The very moment that the insect is pressed against the palate it will sting you, and this can lead to serious problems. What can you do? Dab the sting or gargle with *whey* or *whey concentrate (Molkosan)*. If these are not available, use concentrated *salt water* instead to reduce the swelling and prevent choking. You can help yourself in this way until a doctor arrives. Gargle repeatedly with a solution of salt water – two tablespoons of salt to 100 ml (¼ pint) of water. After a while the poison will begin to disperse and will also be partially drawn out by the salt water. After gargling, a *clay pack* or *cabbage leaf poultice* applied to the neck will be of further help in reducing the poison's effect. As a good antidote, take *clay* and, if possible, biological *calcium tablets (Urticalcin)* as well.

If you add a few drops of *ivy tincture* to the salt water the effect will be better still. The preparation of ivy tincture is described in the previous entry.

In the case of hornet stings it is imperative to see your doctor immediately or go to an ear, nose and throat hospital, because there is a greater danger of choking (oedema of the glottis).

False Sea Onion (*Ornithogalum caudatum*)

This onion is related to the lilaceous plant known as starflower. Its crushed leaves when used as a poultice are an effective remedy for a number of ailments; for example, wrap around the neck to alleviate headaches and sore throats; for rheumatism apply to the painful areas. They are also efficacious in cases of blood poisoning, suppurations and serious insect stings. Where splinters or thorns are buried in the skin and difficult to extract, the crushed leaves will draw them to the surface, thus averting the need for more unpleasant treatment.

Convulsions

If your children have ever had the frightening experience of convulsions – and the problem is not uncommon – you will know that there is very little that can be done to help. Yet there is a herbal remedy that is hardly known, *chickweed*, its botanical name being *Stellaria media*. This simple weed can be found in the fields almost the whole year round, giving you ample opportunity to gather it. It is the best possible remedy for children's convulsions. An infusion of chickweed has to be taken only a few times, whether made from fresh or dried weeds, and the unpleasant symptoms of these convulsions will disappear, often never to return. At the same time, chickweed strengthens the heart and it is this that makes it especially important when treating children. Chickweed is seldom mentioned in books on herbalism because its medicinal uses are very limited. Nevertheless, it deserves full recognition since its effect in curing convulsions is absolutely astounding. What a blessing it will be if the distressed parents can find it in the garden in their hour of need!

Excessive Libido

The excessive need for, or preoccupation with, sexual activity can be quite a problem but it is possible to do something about it. Drink an infusion of *wormwood* one day and of *hops* the next, continuing to do this regularly over a period of time.

Vegetables cooked with *soda* are also helpful; this method is used in prisons and certain other institutions as a preventative measure. However, this treatment is detrimental to health if resorted to for any length of time, although the degree of harm inflicted will depend upon the individual's susceptibility.

Instead, therefore, it would be better to restrict one's diet to food that is sexually less stimulating, and include plenty of *lemon juice*. Be sure to avoid eating eggs, oysters and celery.

Take *cold showers* and *Kuhne treatments* (see pages 436–8) for a calming effect.

Conclusion of Part One

At the beginning of this section the 'Nature Doctor' asked you to try out some of his simple natural remedies. How did you get on? Have you been encouraged to consult the rest of the book in which he presents more detailed information and reveals more of nature's secrets to benefit you even further? You will not be disappointed if you do.

In the second part of *The Nature Doctor* you will find a wide range of remedies and treatments for many different ailments, as well as additional advice for some of those already discussed. Given the great number of problems that arise in life, and not wanting to hold up publication, he did not cover everything, although he touched briefly on certain subjects. The 'Nature Doctor' wants all those who gladly accept nature's ways to benefit from his extensive knowledge and practical experience gained over the years.

His advice is in harmony with nature. It will increase your skill in caring for the sick and introduce you to a great variety of remedies.

> *All that's offered, examine more,*
> *Then keep and use the best.*
> *Of friends' advice you must make sure,*
> *Man's brain oft fails the test.*
>
> *All the things that in harmony are*
> *With the laws of the One above,*
> *Do only good, won't harm or mar,*
> *Give a blessing – the way of love.*
>
> *Plants' vital forces are on tap,*
> *Natural, complete – just take.*
> *Unadulterated, pure, fresh sap,*
> *It's for one's own health's sake.*
>
> *If, in time, progress you make,*
> *Happy with the Maker's ways,*
> *And pure foods you only take,*
> *Success will bless your days.*

First published in *Neues Leben* (May 1929).

Part Two

Fever – an Alarm Bell

If only everyone realised that a fever is nature's alarm bell, and actually a defence against harmful invaders, we would allow nature to take its course and give it our full support. Instead, in our mistaken fear and ignorance, we all too often run for things like aspirin and quinine to bring down a temperature the moment it rises above normal. We should stop to ask ourselves whether we know better than the natural processes that work within us. Why do we always want to reduce a fever? Why are we not grateful for it? Why do we not listen to the advice of those who know and understand its value?

Even in ancient times it was recognised that a fever has healing powers. One physician of that time said, 'Give me the power to induce a fever and I will show you the way to cure all disease.' Although his statement may be somewhat exaggerated, nevertheless, it is intrinsically true. Exceptions, of course, are the high temperature experienced in cases of suspected tuberculosis, Graves' disease, paratyphoid fever, endocarditis, and iron deficiency anaemia. It is generally known that a low body temperature can have a serious outcome because the physician's skill will not be enough to save the patient if complications set in and his body is unable to generate more heat. We would do well, therefore, to listen to the teachings of the physicians of antiquity and regard a fever as the healing agent it is. We should be constantly aware that a fever is our ally in the fight against disease, unless it is a fever induced by drugs, that is, by allopathic medicines.

What happens, though, if the body temperature keeps on rising and the patient is faced with an untimely demise? Did we not learn in school that we are in mortal danger when our temperature reaches 40.5 °C (105 °F)? So, should we let it rise and run the risk of dying as a result?

This will not happen if we simply use our gift of observation. Indeed, we do not have to go far to find an example that will illustrate the effectiveness of fever. We all know that for a stove to work well it must be properly ventilated. If it is, we can increase the heat as much as we like without damaging the stove. But if it is not, the coals will smoulder, with serious consequences to the stove. The grate may be damaged by the intense heat if the air flow from beneath it is allowed to become blocked. However, if the stove is properly cleaned out and the air can circulate freely, you will avoid the need to replace a damaged grate.

When applied to the human body, the principle behind this illustration will help us to know what to do. In fact, we will understand that a fever is, in a manner of speaking, nothing but an accelerated burning-up process. Therefore, we must see to it that the excretory organs are kept open, just as a fire needs good air circulation. The metabolic waste products must not be allowed to accumulate in the body but must leave it, in the same way as the 'ashes' must be cleared from the grate. Good bowel function is absolutely necessary for this, as is the adequate working of the kidneys and the skin. Give due consideration to these three factors and a fever will have hardly any damaging consequences.

When a feverish condition exists, the natural therapy method requires that first of all the bowels be thoroughly cleansed. An *enema* made from an infusion of herbs can be given, or a *natural laxative* taken. If the oral laxative proves ineffective, introduce it into the rectum.

A diuretic will help to stimulate the kidneys. One of the best remedies is *goldenrod (Solidago)*, but if this is not readily available use *horsetail (shave grass)*. An infusion of *parsley, onions* or *juniper berries* may also be effective. Should none of these be available, make an infusion of *rose hips* which, although relatively mild in its effect, is still better than nothing.

Once the kidneys are working properly, elimination through the skin must also be stimulated. *Hot compresses* are always indicated for the treatment of a feverish condition. If you are uncertain as to the correct procedure, ask for a practical demonstration at a home-nursing class or obtain some written instructions. To go about it the wrong way can do more harm than good. However, a compress for the chest or buttocks should not be too difficult to handle; just take care that there are no spaces between the skin and the compress. If the patient is well wrapped, he will soon begin to perspire. If he then complains of being too hot, you can always

Goldenrod

apply *cold compresses to his calves* or put *socks soaked in vinegar* on his feet. It will not be long before the patient begins to feel more comfortable and so able to sleep. You now see how simple the natural solution is. There is really no need to give way to fear and make use of harmful pills and potions.

While nature's ways are quite simple, we tend to seek a far more complicated solution to our troubles. A prescription written in Latin, which most of us do not understand, seems to inspire more confidence than nature's easy way. We want a quick reaction, faster than natural treatment can give. Of course, we never admit that the sometimes dire consequences of such proceedings actually prove this method of treatment to be wrong. The simple and natural procedure which everyone is able to understand without any difficulty and apply in his own home, is considered to be backward and unorthodox.

Nutrition is another factor that merits our attention while a fever lasts. Normally the patient is not hungry and does not want to take anything. This is nature's way of indicating that feeding would not only be useless but actually harmful, since the digestive system is almost inactive. Encouraging a fever patient to eat will not help him at all. Often, however, in these situations we want to spoil the patient with something special. We want to show him how much we care by preparing a juicy steak, fried eggs with cheese and other attractive combinations. However, it must be pointed out that a fever patient should not receive any protein or other food that is difficult to digest, only fruit juices being indicated. Should none be available, give him a little kidney tea or some water. If you wish, these may be sweetened with cane sugar. Alternatively, just use plain water with a natural product added (Molkosan or a herbal remedy). However, the best liquids are still fruit juices, and the fever patient will enjoy these more than anything else. Squeeze some grapes or oranges; the fresh juice will provide nutritive salts and vitamins. Let him sip the cool juice slowly and he will feel truly refreshed. It is not often that a patient cannot tolerate fruit juices, but if this is the case, a good non-alcoholic wine can be given. Diluted Molkosan is equally beneficial.

Cooperating with Nature
If the fever is assisted as described above, rather than suppressed, the temperature will not continue to rise, but will decrease slowly. This is nature's way, so do not try to make it come down faster. When the temperature rises it remains high until everything that has to be eliminated has been burned up; only then will it begin to drop. This is the natural process. Anything done in haste in reality only suppresses and does not eliminate, as we might be led to believe. At best, a sort of armistice will be achieved, but never the removal of the actual cause of the problem. Everything not eliminated through perspiration, the urine and the stools remains in the body, and these toxic residues can cause a relapse at any time.

You may have a temperature and the wonderful little tablets you take to get rid of it actually relieve your very bad sore throat. However, what you have done has not eliminated the toxins and the trouble may suddenly surface somewhere else in the body and in a different way. Pericarditis or rheumatic fever, perhaps even pneumonia, may attack you. We are all too familiar with the story of how a new drug can cure a disease with amazing speed, yet bring unpleasant side effects with it. Surely even orthodox medicine must begin to conclude from experience that 'wonder' drugs do not get to the root of the disease and that nature can neither be circumvented nor overpowered with impunity. The wild animal is often wiser than civilised man when it comes to knowing what nature requires for healing and recuperation.

In future, therefore, refuse to be guided by misguided views and dulled instincts. If we follow nature's lead, it can only be for our good. If, on the contrary, we ignore its direction, we are the ones who will suffer. We should always consider fever as nature's alarm bell, and need not fear it. If we cooperate with nature instead of resisting, it will be to our mutual benefit.

Pain – an Alarm Bell

Just as fever is nature's alarm bell, so does pain act as a warning of disruption in the harmonious workings of the body. But what can you do about sudden pain? Do you feel grateful for the warning that something somewhere in the body has to be put right? Will you try and find out what is causing the pain in order to treat it correctly? Oh no, for this is too time-consuming and we are not inclined to endure pain any longer than we have to. As soon as it arises we want to expel it. Of course, there are many proprietary drugs available for killing pain, which means you would have to be crazy if you continued to suffer longer than necessary!

How short-sighted this attitude is! Consider how differently we react when it comes to repairing, say, our car or some other machine. What motor mechanic believes that the fault has been rectified if he simply plugs his ears so that he cannot hear the rattling? Will he not rather be a credit to his trade by trying to get to the bottom of the problem and repair it before a wheel comes off or some other serious trouble develops? That is what we do with a machine, but the human body, which is much more delicate, we treat superficially, even though pain – that alarm bell – may be warning us that there might be something seriously wrong. In no way should pain ever be ignored or bypassed, which is what you are doing if you simply take a painkiller.

It is interesting to note that nature is always ready to make amends for our mistakes; so if we are conscious of them and willing to learn from them we will avoid making the same ones again. How strange, therefore, that we can be so thoughtless and, for instance, fail to draw the right conclusion when an analgesic no longer gives the relief that it used to. Instead of admitting to ourselves that the analgesic effect did not mean that the cause of the pain had been cured and that we were acting contrary to nature, we foolishly take ever stronger drugs in order to suppress the pain at all costs.

The Correct Thing to Do

The conscientious doctor will most certainly do his best to find out the cause of the pain. For example, if the patient complains about pain in the region of the liver, the doctor will not simply prescribe a painkiller, but will check for symptoms of a liver disorder. He will ask whether fats disagree with the patient, what is the colour of the stool, in short, he will do all that is necessary to get to the root of the trouble. Having diagnosed the cause, he can then prescribe the appropriate remedy. At the same time, he will indicate the right kind of *diet*, including a course of *carrot juice*. *Radishes* will be permitted only in very small quantities as a remedy, since large amounts can do considerable harm to the liver. This is how the doctor will inform his patient about the best way he can help himself to improve his health.

The same doctor will proceed in a similar way if a patient complains about pain in the kidneys. He will ask whether the skin over the area feels tight, as if being contracted. He will also want to know the colour of the urine and the quantity expelled daily. If the answers lead him to suspect a kidney disorder, he will then analyse the urine in order to obtain more specific information. He may discover albumen, red and white blood corpuscles, perhaps some cylindrical or epithelial cells from the bladder, the renal pelvis or the kidneys themselves, as well as bacteria. Even if only traces of these are present in the urine, he will advise the patient to take the precautions of adopting a *low-salt diet* and wearing *warm clothing* to avoid catching colds and chills. Recommended *herbal teas* would be *horsetail, birch leaves* and *Rhizoma graminis* (couch grass root), as well as *parsley*. In addition, the doctor will advise the use of *warm compresses* to ease the painful area.

The above examples show what the doctor must do to discover the cause of pain, in order to prescribe the appropriate medication and treatment. There is no other way. Merely alleviating pain, the symptom, will be of no service to the body. People who habitually swallow analgesics little realise that their constant headaches may well be due to persistent constipation. Who would think that the toxins remaining in the bowels could be the cause of such headaches? Would it not be more appropriate to take steps to improve the bowel function instead of resorting to a constant succession of pills and powders? First for constipation, next, for a headache, and then for constipation again! And if, some twenty-five years later, cancer of the bowels is diagnosed, the patient will not be able to understand it, especially where there is no history of cancer in his family.

Heed the Warning

Some doctors fail to diagnose and treat the root cause of a patient's chronic constipation and merely prescribe a laxative. So it is not surprising that in time the patient will suffer serious consequences. It would be much better if the doctor were to consider the patient as a whole, that is, regarding his body as a unit and realising that what affects one organ will also influence others.

The same principle applies to abdominal pains experienced by many women. Often, leucorrhoea and menstrual cramps are neglected and their cause, restricted circulation, remains untreated.

Of course, there are some people who instinctively know what to do in such circumstances, whereas others have no idea whatsoever. It is the latter group who need guidance and advice.

Sitz baths (hip baths) relax the abdomen and relieve congestions. It is helpful if infusions of *herbs* such as hay flowers, camomile or juniper leaves are added to the water. The temperature of the bath should not rise above 37 °C (98.6 °F), so as not to make the blood rush to the head. Since the patient should remain in the bath for half an hour, she should maintain the required temperature by adding hot water. These hip baths will do much to relieve the cramps, and if they are continued over a period of time even the leucorrhoea may be cured. It stands to reason that every woman should give the best possible care to her abdomen, rather than letting congestions, irritations and inflammations linger and so endanger the vital organs it contains. Even the smallest upsets can, in time, develop into bigger and more serious ones. So do not neglect these early signs of trouble if you want to avoid ending up on the operating table. Rather than suffer such unpleasant consequences of neglect, it is simpler to take good care of yourself.

When it comes to the care of plants we use much more common sense than is often exercised towards our body. If a tree in your garden produces a shoot that you can see will grow in the wrong direction, you are not likely to wait until it is a branch as thick as your arm before sawing it off. Rather, you will remove it immediately – yes, 'nip it in the bud'. Because you know that 'big oaks from little acorns grow'. The same principle applies to pain. It should never be merely palliated but rather accepted for what it is, nature's early warning system. Therefore, it is essential to treat

St John's Wort

the cause of the pain before it can develop into something more serious.

Advice for Expectant and Nursing Mothers
During pregnancy and even afterwards, the mother's happiness is often marred by such troubles as phlebitis (inflammation of the veins), thrombosis and embolism.

A few words of advice on how to help and perhaps even avoid these problems will undoubtedly be welcomed by all mothers. There are certain herbs which, when combined, work wonders for the veins. In cases of phlebitis, varicose veins and thrombosis this blend is so effective that we are happy to name the herbs for the benefit of expectant and nursing mothers. They are:

−*St John's wort (Hypericum perforatum),*
−*Yarrow (Achillea millefolium),* and
−*Arnica root (Arnica montana).*

Tea made with these herbs is an excellent remedy for the aforementioned troubles. It would be even better to use the juices derived from the fresh plants, that is, the fresh herb extracts, since they are stronger.

All expectant mothers should make a note of this simple medication, because it has brought fast relief to hundreds of women – particularly nursing mothers – who suffered from varicose veins and ulcerated legs.

The therapeutic action of each of the herbs is as follows. The fresh plant extract made from St John's wort flowers and buds is an effective wound-healing remedy, as is St John's wort oil. It is an excellent remedy for severe pain in cases of injury to the nerves, concussion and injuries to the spinal cord; where the nerves are badly affected; for post-operative pains and for neuralgias, especially headaches resulting from mental strain and overexertion.

Yarrow, or millefolium, fresh plant extract is primarily indicated as a remedy for varicosis, haemorrhoids, varicose veins, venous obstructions in the abdomen and in the legs, also when there is a rush of blood to the head, frequent and excessive nosebleeding, and haemorrhaging of the bladder.

Arnica is another good remedy for the treatment of the veins, mainly in cases of stagnation of blood in veins and injuries to the soft tissue; it also relieves the symptoms of aching, heavy and tired legs and ankles. Moreover, arnica has an extraordinary effect in helping to restore the mother's organs after childbirth. Varicose veins, which are often a feature of pregnancy, can be combatted by means of this plant. It is also an excellent and reliable remedy for high blood pressure, even after a stroke, heart trouble or any similar disturbance caused by restriction of the veins. Arnica has proved its worth in the treatment of ulcerated legs, but for this purpose the extract made from the root, not the flowers, is indicated. The flowers and the tincture obtained from them are only for external use.

Pulsatilla (pasqueflower or wind flower) is another remedy for circulatory disorders. It belongs to the family that includes the buttercup and *must not* be taken as a tea because of its strong, almost poisonous effect. For this reason it should be used only in homoeopathic potency. There are no restrictions on the three herbs described above, which are quite safe.

An excellent tonic for the veins is *Aesculaforce*, a fresh herb preparation made from horse chestnut, sweet clover (also called melilot), witch hazel and arnica. The medicinal value of horse chestnut for the venous circulation has been clinically proved. Witch hazel is also prized for venous problems, and can be used internally and externally. Sweet clover strengthens the capillaries and improves the venous return, and since arnica stimulates the

Yarrow

Arnica

circulation, it is an ideal choice to complement the other fresh herbs.

For morning sickness during pregnancy there are three simple remedies. *Nux vomica 4x* usually disperses the unpleasant nausea from the first day. In some exceptional cases, if this should prove ineffective, try *Ipecacuanha 3x* or homoeopathic *Apomorphinum 4x*. For why should the mother-to-be endure the discomfort of morning sickness for weeks on end, which could mar the joyful anticipation of the coming event, when harmless homoeopathic remedies can make things so much easier?

For a trouble-free pregnancy and confinement it is further advisable to take the calcium preparation *Urticalcin*, in addition to the fresh herbs already indicated, together with a natural vitamin supplement, such as *Multi-Vitamin Capsules* or *Bio-C-Lozenges*.

Dealing with Calcium and Silica Deficiencies

It can happen that some time after the baby is born a mother develops signs of trouble with the glands and the lungs, possibly even tuberculosis. In such cases the disease has usually been latent, or the susceptibility to it was already present. Great demands are made on the body during pregnancy, which could cause an inherent weakness to manifest itself. It is generally known that the growing foetus requires large amounts of calcium in its development, so if the mother does not take care to provide her body with the necessary calcium – which she could well do – nature will not allow the unborn baby to suffer. As the foetus cannot look after itself, the calcium it is lacking will be automatically drawn from the mother's body, from her bones, teeth and tissues. Of course, this will make her own body deficient. The old saying that 'each child costs a mother a tooth', meaning that the demand for calcium is very great during pregnancy, is all too true. It is therefore important to eat plenty of *calcium-rich foods* during pregnancy, especially raw foods and, if possible, in a form that is easily absorbed. Finely grated raw carrots, cabbage salad, raw sauerkraut and other foods rich in calcium should be eaten daily. Good *calcium preparations* should also be taken, but not the more commonly sold lactic acid calcium. It is better to use preparations that contain plant calcium. Calcium obtained from nettles, for example, and other plants is much more readily assimilated.

In addition, it will be necessary to take *silica*. Plants containing silica, such as horsetail, hemp nettle (*Galeopsis*) and various others, are ideally suited for this purpose. You can either prepare infusions or use the fresh plant extracts. *Vitamin D* is also essential, for if it is lacking, calcium will not be fully assimilated and utilised by the body. Oranges, cod-liver oil, various emulsions containing cod-liver oil, and all natural products and nutriments containing vitamin D are indicated for this purpose. *Vitaforce* is a very good and balanced formula incorporating some of these substances.

Another important factor to consider is the efficiency of the kidneys and the skin. If these excretory organs are in any way obstructed, accumulations of uric acid and other metabolic waste matter will cause metabolic disorders and may prevent the assimilation of calcium.

Special attention must be given to the way you eat, that is, you should eat slowly, chewing the food thoroughly so that it becomes well mixed with saliva.

Returning to calcium for a moment, it has been observed that lack of calcium causes disturbances in the glands with internal secretions; the lymph glands can also be impaired. This can lead to flatulence, internal fermentation and putrefaction in the bowels, thus poisoning the system.

If all these factors are considered and care is taken to avoid the problems described, you will have a fairly good chance of escaping illness. It is, of course, impossible to evade every infection, but a bloodstream supplied with the necessary calcium and silica can deal with them much more easily. So, if your teeth are bad, if you are susceptible to colds, sore throats or other infectious diseases, or if you suffer from swollen glands, then you would do well to take the advice given. Why not put into practice the wisdom of the old proverb, 'Prevention is better than cure'? There is no more appropriate time to get into the habit of recognising suspicious symptoms and taking the required steps to counteract them.

Dangerous Influences during Pregnancy

Nothing gives greater happiness to a woman than giving birth to a healthy baby. No young person can fully understand the meaning of parental bliss until parenthood is realised. But how great is the distress when a sickly child is born, or worse, a deformed child, perhaps with twisted limbs, hands or feet missing, or any other of those terrible deformities which, unfortunately, can occur. How terrible must be a mother's feeling of guilt when she has to admit to herself that she might bear some or all of the blame for this calamity. Scientific research has shown that the first four to eight weeks, even the first three months of pregnancy, are the most crucial as far as harmful influences on the developing life in the womb are concerned. Some suggestions are given below on what a mother-to-be can do to best prevent abnormalities in the developing baby.

NUTRITION AND EXERCISE

Anyone who appreciates the importance of proper nutrition will readily understand that the food of the mother-to-be should be as natural and free from additives as possible. As regards quantity, she need not eat more than she was used to before she became pregnant.

A pregnant woman should make sure to inhale plenty of oxygen to guarantee the best conditions for the child's development. This is best achieved by undertaking activities outdoors in the fresh air, for example by taking walks through forests, woods and fields. On the other hand, busy roads and streets with a lot of traffic polluting the air should be avoided.

ALCOHOL, NICOTINE AND RADIATION

It should be sufficiently well known today that alcohol in the body at the moment of conception may already have frightful consequences. It is therefore utterly irresponsible to beget and bear children while indulging in alcohol. Unfortunately, this often happens after parties where heavy drinking has taken place, even though such thoughtlessness may lead to a tragedy. Every mother-to-be should understand the risk and dangers of alcohol and make it her duty to abstain from it throughout her pregnancy.

It is equally irresponsible of women to smoke during pregnancy and while nursing. Research has shown that only a few hours after smoking, nicotine is already present in the mother's milk. Who, then, can guarantee that during pregnancy the poison will not reach the placenta – and the unborn baby – just as quickly?

If at all possible, X-rays, radium therapy and any other type of radiation used in modern therapies should be avoided. Unfortunately, it is impossible to escape the radiation that contaminates the air as a result of nuclear explosion drifts, since it is not in our power to do anything about it.

CHEMICAL MEDICINES

Every pregnant woman should firmly refuse to take chemical medicines for headaches or similar complaints; nor should she take sleep-inducing drugs. Most of us will remember the shocking news about thalidomide and the tragedy it caused to possibly thousands of mothers who gave birth to deformed babies. This example alone should warn and convince any pregnant woman of the great danger of taking chemical medicines during pregnancy and while still nursing. Then it was thalidomide, tomorrow it will perhaps be a sulphonamide, and later it may be yet another product that will trigger the damage. Thus, it is better to use chemicals to clean your windows and floors and put them to other technical uses, but do not take them as medicines.

Pregnant women should take note and value their maternal duties more highly than the desire to use chemical medicines to obtain quick relief from headaches, indisposition or insomnia. On the other hand, there are plenty of harmless remedies made from plants that will help to alleviate such temporary problems. So why expose yourself to danger and reap irreversible consequences? Experience continues to confirm that natural remedies can truly aid a person without producing harmful after effects. Nevertheless, because of the unnatural conditions and unhealthy views to which we are subjected in this day and age, many people still seem to find it more expedient to rely on palliatives rather than trying to cure their ailments in a natural way. The results of their mistaken thinking should be evidence enough that the apparent detour required to adopt more natural means of healing is definitely worthwhile.

Mastitis (Inflammation of the Breast)

An inflammation which has been improperly treated, or not treated at all, frequently leaves nodules, or knots of cells, in the breast. This may possibly lead to breast cancer in later years. Gynaecologists are always on the alert when having to examine the breasts of patients, because breast cancer is very often detected. The breast being susceptible in this regard, it should be given more than the usual care and attention.

Inflammation of the breast can develop from a simple bruise. More frequently, however, an inflammation appears after delivery, during the period of lactation or at the time of weaning. It is imperative to treat an inflammation immediately, since lumps may form that lead to cysts. In cases where an abscess forms, it is best to let it come to a head and break open by itself. Of course, it may also be opened surgically. In either case scars will remain as the scar tissue will have lost its elasticity.

TREATMENT AND PRECAUTIONS

An inflammation of the breast is treated externally as well as internally. For internal treatment *Echinaforce* has proved to be extremely valuable. The use of *arnica tincture* and Echinaforce are indicated for external application. Rub them gently on the affected part, alternating between the two remedies. If the area is sensitive, the regular application of *warm compresses* with *mallow* or *sanicle* infusions will achieve faster results. For an even better healing effect, add to the infusion 5–10 drops of Echinaforce and arnica tincture.

Women who are breast-feeding and would like to reduce their milk supply may do so by rubbing the breasts with *lovage tincture* and taking an *infusion of lovage*, this herb being excellent for the purpose. In cases of miscarriage or stillbirth the milk will need to be removed with a breast pump until the remedies have decreased the flow. To prevent milk fever and inflammation of the breasts, every effort should be made to stop the production of milk by natural means. We recommend oiling the breasts regularly and, especially, rubbing the nipples with *St John's wort oil* or *Bioforce Cream* once or twice a week. This provides the additional benefit of preventing the skin from cracking.

Infertility – the Pros and Cons of Hormone Treatment

Women who would love to have children but remain childless often do everything in their power to fulfil their natural desire. This is understandable, since an unfulfilled yearning for children may lead to severe mental and emotional suffering. There are, of course, some women who have little or no desire at all for a child. Although they do not suffer by not having children, they do miss out on the joys of motherhood and the many natural pleasures which children bring to the home.

Two Solutions to Consider

The inability to have children is often connected with a hormone deficiency. In such cases there are two possibilities that can be pursued. First, the body may be stimulated in such a way that its own production of hormones is improved. On the one hand, this can be achieved through *hydrotheraphy*, by means of *sitz baths* (hip baths), alternating *hot and cold baths*, the *Kuhne treatment* and similar methods. On the other hand, stimulation of the circulatory system will boost the supply of blood to the abdomen, which in turn will step up the production of hormones and may eventually lead to pregnancy.

For stimulating the circulation remedies such as *Aesculaforce, Aesculus hippocastanum* and *Urticalcin* can be of great benefit, especially when supplemented by *wheat germ* or *wheat germ oil* (capsules). Although outdoor exercise and deep-breathing in the open air are necessary for the natural regeneration of the body, sporting activities should not be overdone. Rather, one's whole way of life should be normal and balanced. This is the natural and safe course of action to take first of all.

Some, however, immediately resort to the alternative course to overcome infertility since it may possibly assure quicker results, that of hormone treatment, especially treatment with gonadotropins. There are, however, certain risks involved. The degree of sensitivity of the female body varies greatly from one individual to the next and it is not easy for a doctor to find the right dose. Most people will be aware of the unpredictable results that an overdose of hormones can have. It is possible that a number of eggs become ready to be fertilised, resulting in twins, triplets or an even greater number of children. This would certainly be too much of a good thing, even for the woman who may have suffered previously on account of her childlessness. It is therefore preferable to try out the first solution, stimulating the hormone-producing glands in a natural way. Only if these efforts fail should one contemplate hormone treatment as a last resort.

Other Important Observations
In this context it is appropriate to take a closer look at the opposite method, the curbing of normal hormone production in the female body. Gynaecologists have observed that the inhibitory effect lasts only as long as the agent, for example the contraceptive pill, is taken. If a woman stops taking the 'pill', her body may react in such a drastic way that the end result will be multiple births. When they consider the risks of having triplets or quintuplets, some women may begin to realise the drawbacks of hormonal contraception and have second thoughts about taking the 'pill'.

Furthermore, some doctors have found that the taking of hormone preparations like contraceptive pills can increase the risk of developing cancer. This underlines the warning to women not to commit gross offences against nature, because of the unpleasant repercussions and detrimental side effects that may result.

34

Infant Care

Experience being a good teacher, no doubt many of our parents' methods in caring for their children were very good. Some of their ways, however, were quite wrong, since they were based on old customs that do not meet the demands of modern hygiene. Just think of the almost superstitious fear of water which led them to believe that bathing, especially if frequent, was bad for the health. There are still some older people who have never sat in a bath tub and, what is more, who actually boast about it! When you read that in days gone by children were carefully protected from exposure to light, air, sun and water, so that they would not catch cold, you may smile for knowing better, thinking it was a story from the ancient past. But not so; it was the custom in our parents' or grandparents' time. Again, it was also feared that children would develop crooked limbs unless they were so tightly wrapped that they were rendered practically immobile. Even today in some parts of Italy we find evidence of babies so bandaged up that they look like mummies. It is, therefore, not surprising that infant mortality was once much greater than it is today.

Baths

Frequent baths are absolutely essential for a baby, not only for hygienic reasons but also because of their importance in maintaining proper skin activity. Bathing removes congestions and stimulates the functions of internal organs and the endocrine glands. We must not forget that the baby had been in the warm, even temperature of the mother's womb for nine months, protected from the discomforts of the outside world and hidden under the mother's heart. The newborn baby is suddenly introduced into a much cooler environment to which its little body has to adapt. For this reason the baby's first baths should never be hotter than blood temperature, that is, not more than 37 °C (98·6°F). In summer the water may even be a little cooler, especially if the water has been warmed by the sun. The lively splashing and joyful shouts bear witness to the pleasures babies derive from their baths. This can also be seen in their frequent protests at being taken out of the bath when they evidently think they should be allowed to stay longer.

Any medicinal additions to a baby's bath should be chosen with the greatest care, since they can do much harm. It is impossible to stop babies from sucking their wet fingers and swallowing some of the bath water. Therefore, additions like pine essence or cubes

Camomile

containing the green iridescent colouring *Natrium fluorescentum* should be avoided. The same warning applies to acrid herbs like celandine and cranesbill which, although of great benefit for eczematous skin troubles and rashes, if used at all, should be added in only the smallest quantities. Babies have very sensitive skin and even seemingly harmless herbal additions to their bath water can cause quite unexpected reactions. The bath herbs listed below, however, are recommended for baby care. In all cases, only weak infusions should be used, since light stimulation is to be preferred for babies.

- *Horsetail* contains organic silica and exerts a beneficial influence upon the skin.
- *Lemon balm* is indicated for nervous babies who need soothing.
- *Lady's mantle* will give elasticity and tone to the tissues when they are spongy and flabby. (In cases of a tendency to hernia, this herb will help to strengthen the tissues.)
- *Camomile* is good for indigestion, stomach aches and minor metabolic disturbances.
- *Marigold* is useful when the skin is sensitive and affected by

36

rashes and impurities. (The flowers may be used as well as the leaves.)

– *Wild thyme*, also called Mother of Thyme, has proved its worth as an excellent bath herb and is especially valuable for babies who catch colds easily. Parents who themselves have weak lungs should give their babies this herbal bath from time to time.

– *Ribwort* should not be underestimated as a help in cases of a weak bladder; however, such a tendency does not become apparent in babies until they are toilet trained.

Skin Care

For cleansing the skin it is best to use a mild, super-fatted soap, 'baby soap'. Remember, the daily use of soap is not absolutely necessary. After bathing the baby a good skin oil should then be applied, but one that does not contain strong essential oils. One of the best is *St John's wort oil* with a tiny amount of mandarine, orange or lemon oil added (*Bioforce Body Oil*).

It is enough to oil the baby's whole body twice a week. The legs may be oiled every day, using St John's wort oil. Oiling is always better than powdering, as powder blocks the pores, absorbs the urine and encourages the growth of bacteria. Experience has shown that oiling is the better way and that it also prevents sores. If redness or soreness should appear, rub the skin lightly with a good woolfat cream, either genuine *lanolin* or *Bioforce Cream*, which also contains St John's wort oil.

Remedies

Household remedies and other medicines should be chosen with the greatest care. Babies react quickly to even the smallest dose and can tolerate only very light stimulants without suffering ill effects. This is especially true of teas (herbal infusions) and great care must be taken because an apparently harmless herbal tea can trigger serious upsets.

Homoeopathic remedies are ideal for the treatment of children. In fact, babies should only be given such remedies and it is lamentable that paediatricians do not prescribe them more frequently. Many allopathic drugs do more harm than good even for adults, so how much less would a young child be able to cope with their adverse effects? The amazing results achieved by homoeopathy should convince many doubters; they cannot be explained away as being 'imaginary' or 'psychological' effects, as some opponents try to do, for it can hardly be expected that babies and young children imagine these things.

It should be stressed again that infusions of herbs (teas) for small children should be very weak indeed, barely coloured. The herbs listed below have been found to be effective.

- *Fennel* (or *anise* if no fennel is available) belongs to the most common group of household remedies. Fennel, anise, caraway and dill are the so-called 'warming teas'. Whenever there is anything wrong with your baby's digestion, a weak fennel infusion will be of great benefit and will help the mother to remedy a temporary indisposition.
- *Yarrow*, given as a very weak infusion, is good for diarrhoea and loss of appetite. If this fails to stop the discharge, add a small pinch of *tormentil* and give teaspoonfuls of this weak infusion throughout the day.
- *Goldenrod* is a reliable remedy when the kidneys are out of order. The fresh plant extract from this herb, either as *Solidago* or as an ingredient in *Nephrosolid*, is one of the best and most effective medicines for the kidneys and the bladder. If you cannot obtain any goldenrod, a weak *rose hip* or *horsetail* infusion can be used instead.
- *Whey concentrate* (*Molkosan*) is a good antiseptic for minor injuries. This is a natural lactic acid product which can be used in the same way as iodine, although it is certainly less harmful than iodine.
- *Hypericum* can also be used as an antiseptic, and dabbed on externally. Dr Joseph Schier and other well-known paediatricians have recommended this simple remedy made from St John's wort even for the prevention of tetanus.

Calcium deficiency shows itself in various ways and can still be found quite frequently among small children. It prevents them from developing properly and makes them prone to catching frequent colds. If the mother wants an inexpensive, natural and good calcium preparation, she can make one up herself by doing the following. Pick some young fresh *nettles*, which can be found in most places, maybe right by the house or in the garden. Next, take some *egg shells*, which are on hand in practically every kitchen. People who live by the sea might like to use *oyster shells* instead. Crush the shells together with the fresh nettles and leave to dry in the air. Once pulverised, a light green powder will result. The child should take half a teaspoon of this 2–3 times daily. After a few months the teeth will improve and, in time, will become noticeably stronger. The bones will benefit also, and the susceptibility to colds and catarrh will diminish. If preparing this powder is too much of a bother, simply use *Urticalcin*, a ready-made calcium product containing stinging nettles.

If, in addition, the child has a deficiency of vitamin D, then you have the basic cause of rickets. Although serious cases of rickets, resulting in underdeveloped or deformed bones, are now extremely rare, less severe forms of rickets are still seen even today. It may seem strange, but children suffering from this mild form of rickets are usually very lively, react to everything quickly and their facial expression is almost too intelligent for their age. They tend to be precocious and always remind me of an apple that has grown ripe too soon. On closer examination the apple proves to be worm-eaten, and that is actually why it has ripened prematurely.

Such children who lack both calcium and vitamin D need help and can be helped. Homoeopathic or biochemical calcium triturations are excellent for this purpose, for example *Calcarea phos. 6x, Calcarea fluor. 12x* (for the teeth) and *Silica 12x*. The calcium preparation *Urticalcin* contains several calcium salts in various potencies, as triturations, as well as *Urtica* (as a vitamin D carrier), and is therefore also an efficacious remedy. *Orange juice* and *cod-liver oil* are rich in vitamin D and are highly recommended. Furthermore, *carrot juice* or the concentrate *Biocarottin*, which is made from fresh carrot juice, is another natural remedy for overcoming calcium deficiency.

Infant Nutrition

Mother's Milk
Mother's milk is the only natural and perfect food for a young baby. Nothing is more important for the infant's well-being and health in later life. This has been proved time and again by statistics on infant mortality which show that bottle-fed babies have a far greater death rate than those who have been breast-fed. In fact, the most crucial time for the baby is its first few days of life, when circumstances may decide whether it will live or die.

Even in animals we can see how nature does not tolerate any interference without serious consequences. Any farmer or country person knows how difficult it is to raise young animals, for example lambs, without their mother's milk, however strong they may seem at birth. Even the best lambs sometimes die if they are given cow's milk, or even if they are fed sheep's milk obtained from a ewe other than its own mother. Nothing is better for the newborn animal and its healthy development than its own mother's milk. A calf must have cow's milk, a lamb must have sheep's milk, and babies must have human milk. It alone is physiologically and biologically right in its composition to give the new human body what it needs for proper growth, for the development of the bone structure, nervous system and all the organs and tissues.

Breast milk, especially the very first secretion called colostrum, contains enzyme-like substances, nutritive salts and vitamins, some of which are known to us but others unknown; these cannot be found in any other food in the same quality and proportions. Moreover, breast milk is the source of immunising agents and alexins that protect the baby from diseases. Herein lies one of the greatest secrets of why very young breast-fed babies are immune to certain infections.

The argument that suckling a baby damages a mother's health and beauty can be refuted as unfounded because there is sufficient evidence to the contrary. A mother who is reasonably healthy actually benefits from breast-feeding, since during the time of nursing, under normal circumstances, the glands with internal and external secretions will function more efficiently and abundantly. The absorption of food and its vitamins is at its best at this time. The womb returns to normal much more easily in nursing mothers than in those who renounce their natural privilege and bottle-feed their offspring. Also, there is no doubt that a lasting psychological rapport and harmony are established between the mother and her breast-fed baby. In this way both mother and child profit by this natural relationship, as is always evident when we refrain from interfering with the Creator's natural laws.

For normal development and effective resistance to disease in the years to come, the foundation laid by breast-feeding is of the greatest importance to the baby. Experience and medical statistics prove that breast-fed babies recover from children's diseases much more easily and with fewer complications than bottle-fed children of a similar constitution.

Young mothers are sometimes unhappy and nervous when the flow of milk does not appear on the very first day. But it should be remembered that this would be quite unnatural as the baby should not receive any food during the first twenty-four hours of life. At the beginning, the breasts produce only the highly nutritious colostrum; the actual milk does not appear before the third, and sometimes on the fourth to the sixth, day. So, young mothers, do not despair when things do not immediately turn out in the way you may have expected. Later, if your milk supply is not enough to satisfy the baby, a few drops of *Urtica* every day, or a few tablets of calcium complex with *Urtica* (*Urticalcin*) will help the flow. Further useful information may be found in the section on cradle cap (*Crusta lactea*) on page 42.

Solid Food

Mothers often complain that their babies become constipated when they are fed brown rice gruel. It may well be that babies are more sensitive and that rice is more constipating than barley gruel, but because of its nutritional value it should not, on any account, be left out of the child's diet. The constipation can always be counteracted by natural means. Ground *linseed* is very good for the bowel action and should be added to the brown rice gruel. The amount to be used depends upon the child's reaction, but half a teaspoonful will usually be adequate. In this way the child will not be deprived of the goodness of brown rice.

Whole rye also makes a nutritious gruel. It may not be quite so creamy but it is certainly valuable, especially during teething. Rye contains not only calcium but also calcium fluoride, which is essential for the development of tooth enamel.

The best programme is to feed the baby alternatively rice, rye, barley, oat, perhaps even millet and buckwheat gruels, together with various juices, either carrot or fruit. Care must be taken, however, not to mix vegetable juices with fruit juices. In fact, it would be wise to avoid using more than one kind of fruit juice per meal, since sensitive babies may have difficulty in digesting the mixture. It would be better to mix one fruit juice with *almond cream*. This may be available already prepared from health food stores or can be made by grinding some almonds very finely and crushing them with a pestle and mortar; then mix with water in a blender. Mix the almond cream with the fruit juice in a blender and you will have the best food not only for your baby but even for older children and adults. Babies with cradle cap (see below) should definitely be put on *almond milk*, and if you want to clear up the condition, *Violaforce* and *calcium* must be added to their diet.

Infants' Complaints

Cradle Cap (Crusta Lactea)

Cradle cap in babies gives the parents a lot of trouble. Though many think that it is due to external factors, such as infections, this is not so. It is simply an abnormal oversensitivity, a so-called trophic allergy, possibly also a symptom of deficiency. If you deal with the causes the condition will soon disappear. On the other hand, the baby may have been born with the weakness of oversensitivity. Initially, treat the underlying cause: good digestion is important, so if anything goes wrong in this respect, the bowels should be normalised with the aid of *brown rice gruel, buttermilk* and other natural means.

In the case of breast-fed babies, the cause of cradle cap may be in the mother's diet. Unfortunately, few mothers pay much attention to the fact that anything they ingest, especially medicines, finds its way into their milk and is passed on to their babies. For example, a mother may be constipated and take a laxative. Then her breast-fed baby suddenly has a bout of diarrhoea. The baby is treated with all manner of things, without success, until bottle-feeding is resorted to and the diarrhoea finally stops. What a pity, though, since the infant is deprived of the best food for it – breast milk. With a little knowledge and forethought the upset would never have occurred in the first place.

While she is breast-feeding, a mother should not take any laxatives that contain aloe and other strong substances. Instead, linseed preparations, such as *Linoforce, psyllium seed* and similar remedies are harmless and can be used to regulate the bowels. Other medicines are also known to enter into the composition of milk when the mother has taken them. Among the most common of these are Luminal and many other barbiturates which are used to make up various sedatives and sleeping pills, as well as bromide, morphia and mercury preparations, quinine, salicylic acid and many remedies for rheumatism, iodide of potassium, alcohol and nicotine.

If a baby is indirectly fed such drugs we must not be surprised to see its health adversely affected. So, if your baby has cradle cap, think about the drugs you might be taking. If you have the unpleasant habit of smoking, you should certainly give it up while you are breast-feeding. Think of your child. Would you want your baby's health upset because your irresponsibility means it has to try and cope with poisonous nicotine?

Even during pregnancy nicotine has an adverse effect on the

unborn child. You can prove this to yourself by means of a simple experiment. Place a stethoscope on the mother's abdomen and count the child's heartbeats. Then let the mother smoke just one cigarette and then count the beats again. You will note that they have increased by eight per minute! Once the mother and her partner have convinced themselves of this overstimulation, they will be in no doubt that the mother should give up smoking at once.

Certain foods can affect the mother's milk in the same way as drugs. I have often seen a child's cradle cap disappear within a few days if the mother avoids eating egg white. It is, therefore, especially important to adopt a healthy diet while breast-feeding, as set out in another section of this book (see pages 39–41). Nursing mothers should remember that they are eating for both themselves *and* the baby.

Try to breast-feed your baby for as long as possible. But if, in spite of changing your own diet, the child's condition remains unaltered, then replace a meal by giving a bottle of *almond milk* or *buttermilk*. Babies suffering from cradle cap respond well to this less fatty food. *Violaforce*, the fresh plant extract made from wild pansy, can be added to buttermilk to enhance its curative effect.

If the ailing child is already weaned, instead of cow's milk give the child almond milk only. However, this requires accurate weight control. Some babies cannot assimilate vegetable protein and will lose weight. In such cases, if a protein supplement in the form of soy flour does not produce the necessary weight gain, animal protein, in this case milk, will have to be resorted to once more. Frequently, goat's milk or sheep's milk is better tolerated than cow's milk. Older children suffering from very stubborn cases of cradle cap should be given wheat germ. In all cases, nothing but natural remedies should be employed, never chemical preparations.

Sometimes the natural treatment brings very quick relief, but there are other cases that require more time and patience. As an example, one worried mother wrote to me asking for advice on how to cure her little daughter's cradle cap. She also sent a sample of the child's urine, an analysis of which revealed the existence of a liver problem. Almond milk and diluted carrot juice, to be given as a bottle-feed, were recommended, as well as a biological calcium preparation to rectify the girl's calcium deficiency. Mild stimulation of the kidneys was also necessary, for which a very weak *kidney tea* with a little *Solidago* (goldenrod) was prescribed. In addition,

Violaforce was prescribed; this is the best remedy for cradle cap and the one that especially guarantees a successful result. For external treatment it was recommended that the mother use *St John's wort oil* and then dust with *Urticalcin* powder. Bran baths are excellent for this too.

A year later the mother sent us the following brief note: 'Last year you helped us cure our little girl's cradle cap. Thank you ever so much.'

Another letter we received from a nurse reads:

'At the moment I am looking after two children. The boy, now 15 months old, had cradle cap last year. You sent me a calcium complex (Urticalcin), *Viola tricolor* and whey concentrate. Thanks to your excellent remedies the condition cleared up within a fortnight.'

In this particular case, diluted *whey concentrate (Molkosan)* was used to dab on the rash. Excellent results have also been achieved by dabbing on *Echinaforce*, a fresh plant preparation made from *Echinacea*. Water and soap are quite unsuitable for cradle cap and must be avoided. Instead, use oil, preferably St John's wort oil, to cleanse the baby's skin. It is indeed good to know that cradle cap can be successfully treated with these natural remedies, sparing the children permanent harm.

Infantile Eczema
Children's dermatitis or infantile eczema is a distressing condition, since it is not only a strain on the child, but also on the parents, due to the constant extra care and attention the child has to receive.

In 1964, at the Convention of the German Society for Child Therapy held in Munich, Dr Holt, an American paediatrician at New York University, presented the viewpoint that the 'tar therapy' was still the best method for the treatment of infantile eczema and that using tar extract of 5 per cent was also more economical than treating with steroid ointments. Also of considerable interest was Dr Holt's concession that infantile eczema is much easier to suppress than it is to cure.

With the help of the 'tar therapy' it is relatively easy to reduce the severity of the condition from degree IV to degree I, but Dr Holt admitted that this therapy is not enough to effect a complete cure. What was not mentioned was the fact that once the tar therapy is discontinued the little patient will quickly experience a worsening of the condition. Neither was there any mention that tar, with its eleven hydrocarbons, including napthalene, has been recognised as a carcinogenic – cancer-producing – substance.

RECOMMENDED TREATMENT

Unfortunately, no other paediatrician present at the convention could offer a better therapy, although several do exist, for example a *milk- and protein-free diet* and treatment with milk enzymes, that is, with *whey*. Not one of those present explained that treating infantile eczema with whey concentrate (Molkosan) can result in unexpected cures. It is indeed unfortunate that this treatment is so little known and appreciated by the medical profession, especially considering that it has been in use for many years. Centuries ago it had already been noticed that eczema began to heal when the patient was bathed in fresh, or even better, sour whey. If *Violaforce*, a fresh plant preparation made from the wild pansy, is applied at the same time, the cure is even more striking.

Since children with eczema also tend to suffer from calcium deficiency, taking *Urticalcin* will prove helpful. This calcium preparation in powder form, if applied externally, will prevent harmful bacteria from from entering through the pores of the skin. Instead of steroid ointments, use a lanolin cream such as *Bioforce Cream*. In the end, the doctor will be delighted with his little patient's progress.

Obviously, the child's diet is another important factor. Since milk proteins are to be left out completely, the inclusion of vegetable protein is vital. In this regard soy protein or almond protein, as provided in almond cream, have proved of great value. Special attention should also be paid to providing a salt-free diet. The speakers at the paediatric convention in Munich, however, made no mention of these factors whatsoever.

The subject of nutrition brought to light an interesting discovery. The doctors reported that infantile eczema was fairly prevalent among the affluent families of Nigeria, who live according to European standards, whereas among the natives who have held on to their traditional way of life it was rare or unknown. On the basis of this finding it can be concluded that the incorrect nutrition and living habits associated with our civilisation are contributory factors to the incidence of infantile eczema.

The statement, or rather claim, that infantile eczema is an allergy does not have much support. The search for an allergen or a specific antibody will probably have little success. So why not take advantage of a natural therapy that has proved to be simple and harmless in treating infantile eczema and which, in the end, does not offer just temporary relief but in many cases results in a complete cure?

Children's Diseases

Admittedly, many children's diseases can be beneficial insofar as the accompanying fever disposes of pathological material within the body that might otherwise cause more serious health problems in later life. This does not mean, however, that we should directly expose children to diseases. They will break out soon enough anyway, so the older and stronger a child is the more easily it will overcome them.

If a child's illness is correctly treated, that is to say, in a natural way and supported in the course it takes, it will be welcome as a cleansing process of the system. The fever burns up and destroys all kinds of toxins which have remained in the baby's system from the embryonic stage of development. Observant physicians agree that those who have never had any of the children's diseases accompanied by fever succumb more readily to all sorts of other diseases, even malignant ones, later on in life. This observation proves the wonderful healing power of fever.

The majority of children who do not recover easily from a children's disease owe this failure to inappropriate treatment. The worst thing that can happen to a child is the suppression of normal disease symptoms − fever and rashes − by means of chemical medicines. Remember, a fever is the internal defence reaction of the body; it burns up or destroys poisons entering from outside and those that have accumulated in the body. Rashes are often a natural way of conducting these toxins out of the system and on to the skin or through the pores. Neither the temperature itself nor its external reaction must be suppressed, because all too often the suppression results in severe damage to the heart, the nervous system or the lungs.

Chemical medicines are most harmful. Granted, it may seem convenient just to dissolve a few tablets in a glass of water, drink the solution, and see the fever obediently oblige and subside. The illness seems to fade away so harmlessly without ever reaching its climax. However, it is usually disregarded that the toxins will not have been eliminated from the body and are therefore still able to wreak damage somewhere, for example by provoking carditis, rheumatic fever, etc.

'But you can't allow the temperature to rise to a dangerous level without doing anything about it,' an overzealous nurse may object. Of course not. There is, however, a great difference between suppressing a fever and doing everything possible to encourage this internal fire. Let us always support the 'fire' and see to it that all the 'flues' are open so that it does not merely smoulder in the stove, the body, but that it really burns at full blast. All burnable wastes will then be eliminated faster, and the system will be cleansed and soon return to normal. Feverish children respond very well to the simple remedy *Ferrum phosphoricum 12x*; the tried and proven *Aconitum 4x* also helps to eliminate the toxins through the skin. If you do not yet know what course an infectious disease will take, try alternating *Aconitum 4x* and *Belladonna 4x*.

Of first importance is that the bowels are functioning properly. To achieve this, it will probably be necessary to give a small *enema*. Use an infusion of *camomile* or *horsetail*. The second important thing to watch with an infectious disease is the function of the kidneys; *horsetail tea* will be of help here, or better still, *Nephrosolid*. Thirdly, the pores of the skin must be opened to excrete toxins. To be successful, you have to follow the advice of water therapists such as Kneipp, Priessnitz and others. For effective stimulation of the skin there is nothing better than *water compresses*. Whether these should be cold or warm depends on each individual case. You can hardly go wrong with warm water compresses, but cold ones require training and skill, for you must understand when and how to use them. However, to allay any undue fear I would like to add that a body with a high temperature is not likely to chill easily and a cold pack, as a rule, will produce even greater external heat, thus reducing the internal heat.

To sum up then, we should not lose sight of the basic principle, which is never to work against nature but to direct all our efforts towards supporting the body's natural defence mechanism.

Children and adults fall victim to infectious diseases more easily if their nutrition is unhealthy and deficient. Existing deficiencies, even only slight vitamin deficiencies, encourage susceptibility to infectious diseases.

Many parents become afraid when their children have a rapidly rising temperature. But you should not forget that fevers really serve a very good purpose, because they quickly burn up the toxins in the body. Remember, too, that a child's little heart is much stronger than you might think; in fact, it can endure much more strain than that of an adult, at least in proportion to its size.

Measles

Even though in many lands this is a harmless infectious disease of childhood, in areas where it has only recently become known, for example among some American Indian tribes, the affected children often die. The causative agent is a virus, one of the submicroscopic entities that have been discovered only in more recent times. These viruses are even smaller than bacteria and cannot be seen under a normal microscope simply by colouring as can bacteria; only with the aid of modern electronic microscopes have scientists been able to study them. Even so, measles has always been considered an infectious disease because of the course the illness takes and the fact that children catch it so easily.

Most parents are familiar with the rash of pink-brownish blotches, accompanied by a high temperature. And yet, you might be uncertain as to the nature of the child's illness in its early stages, unless you check the inner cheeks in the region of the molars. In a case of measles these areas are red, and a day or two before the rash breaks out red spots with tiny white spots in the middle of them, 2–3 mm in diameter, (so-called Koplik's spots), will appear.

The disease has an incubation period of about fourteen days and it is therefore not surprising that within another ten or twelve days the next case will break out, either in your family or your neighbour's.

The first symptoms of measles can vary, but might include a head cold, nose bleeding, bronchial catarrh and conjunctivitis (with sensitivity to light, burning of the eyes and lacrimation).

Soon the child's temperature will rise to perhaps 39 °C (102 °F). It will then drop, but on the fourth day may rise again as high as 40 °C (104 °F). It usually goes down again as soon as the rash appears, but if it remains high for more than 3–4 days after its first outbreak, complications are likely to set in and more specific treatment must be given. You should immediately give the child *Lachesis 10x* to prevent the development of sepsis and apply *flannels* wrung out in a hot *infusion of herbs* (for example wild thyme) repeatedly to the affected areas. This will draw out the internal toxins through the skin. Even when the disease takes its normal course, it is advisable to apply these hot packs to bring the rash out properly. During the fever, give the child nothing but fruit juices, particularly orange and grape juice or carrot juice, the latter also being very good for the liver. If you have no juices available, give the child a mild herbal tea sweetened with honey. In addition, like all infectious diseases, a case of measles demands careful oral hygiene. For infants and smaller children, wrap a clean cloth around your finger tip, dip it in diluted whey concentrate and rub the gums, the inner cheeks and the tongue (which always become furred with measles). For older children use a soft toothbrush to disinfect the mouth.

The following remedies should be given:

- *Aconitum 4x*: 5 drops every half an hour. When perspiration has been induced and the temperature falls, it may be given less frequently.
- *Ferr. phos. 6x* (for babies use *12x*): 1 tablet every hour.
- *Belladonna 4x*: 5 drops every hour. Use when the blood rushes to the head, or with croup, conjunctivitis and ear complications.
- *Antimonium sulph. 4x* or *6x*: initially 1 tablet every 2 hours; after about three days, 2 tablets three times daily. This should be given by itself, without additional medication, when the fever has subsided. It will be sufficient to complete the cure if no complications occur.
- *Nephrosolid*: add to the fruit juice, 5 drops each time. This fresh plant preparation will help to eliminate toxins through the kidneys.
- *Cuprum acet. 4x* and *Antimonium sulph. 4x*. These should be given alternately when a hacking or whooping cough seems to be coming on.
- *Coccus cacti 4x* and especially *Thydroca* are most effective for whooping cough, if given at once when the first symptoms appear after the measles. Whooping cough can often be arrested with these remedies, without any side effects.

Children with a weak constitution who have inherited a disposition for tuberculosis and suffer from swollen glands should be treated with the following prophylactic medicines:

- *Calc phos. 4x* alternated with *6x*: 2 tablets, three times daily.
- *Urticalcin*. This is even more effective and, if given for several months, can work wonders.
- *Ars. iod. 4x*. This is indicated for thin children who grow fast. It should be taken over a period of several months in alternation with Urticalcin.
- *Kali phos. 6x*. This should be given when the lungs and bronchials are affected.
- *Sulph. 4x*. This is indicated when, in spite of packs, the rash is slow in breaking out and very mild.

When the disease has subsided the child should not be allowed outside in the cold air right away. Especially in winter, the child should be kept in bed for another week or in a warm but well-ventilated room. Such care is particularly essential for delicate children who could otherwise suffer from complications.

Mumps

This is another frequent but usually harmless childhood disease. The commonest site of trouble is in the parotid glands, but in the case of boys, the testicles and epididymis may also be affected. Serious complications can ensue when the disease is contracted by an adult male and the essential tissue of the testicles is destroyed, resulting in sterility.

An internal remedy for mumps is *Mercurius solubilis 10x*; 2–3 drops or one tablet should be taken every 2–3 hours. *Aconitum 4x* and *Belladonna 4x* should be taken in alternation every half hour (also 2–3 drops). Compresses with *whey concentrate (Molkosan)* applied to the calves are very helpful, but only when the feet are kept warm. *Hip baths (sitz baths)*, the temperature of which should be gradually increased from 36 °C to 44 °C (97 °F to 110 °F), are also excellent; after the bath the patient should be wrapped in warm blankets. If the child's bowels are not working properly, *Arabic plant essence (Arabiaforce)* is very good, but in more stubborn cases it may be necessary to give an enema. To ease the pain, apply warm compresses to the affected areas, adding a few drops of *arnica* or *calendula* (marigold) *extract* to the water. Make sure to let the child gargle with a weak solution of Molkosan. Another remedy which has proved itself over and over again is hot *St John's wort oil*. Saturate a cloth with the hot oil, or better still, mix potter's clay with St. John's wort oil, then apply to the inflamed area and cover with a very hot water bottle. This will soothe and heal. To complete the cure, give one tablet of *Silicea 12x* (silica) three times a day.

Whooping Cough

Some people still consider whooping cough to be a minor ailment, giving little thought to the distressing, hacking cough. It is, however, very important to give special attention to whooping cough, since it can cause serious complications if it is not treated properly, and may lead to permanent damage. There are a number of herbal and homoeopathic remedies for whooping cough and parents should not fail to make use of these natural treatments. Although no specific medicine exists that arrests and cures the illness completely in a given time, these remedies can reduce the intensity and duration of the attacks. First, the toxins of the pathogenic organisms have to be eliminated, as in all infectious diseases. It is also useful to do something about the patient's physical weakness so as not to encourage other infections. Whooping cough is usually followed by another illness, which is why it is important to build up the patient's general state of health as a prevention. In milder cases, the spasms will disappear after a few days.

Sometimes it will be necessary to give the child a *biological calcium preparation* and at the same time encourage the elimination of metabolic toxins through the kidneys. *Thydroca*, a fresh herb preparation containing *Drosera, Thymus, Coccus cacti, Hedera helix*, and others, is excellent for whooping cough. The homoeopathic remedies *Ipecacuanha 3x* and *Coccus cacti 3x* have also proved to be effective. As soon as the coughing attacks have stopped, the child can gradually stop taking the remedies. In their place *Santasapina* pine bud syrup can be given, as it is beneficial to continue with some medication for a little while after the cure seems to be complete.

Chest compresses are a must in cases of whooping cough. They can be either simple compresses made with a hay flower infusion or, in more severe cases, onion compresses. A horseradish poultice is stronger in its effect and a mustard poultice even more so. A correctly applied mustard poultice or a mustard bath (made using mustard powder) has saved the life of many a child who had already turned blue from a severe case of bronchiolitis (inflammation and gradual blockage of the tiniest air tubes in the lungs) and who was frantically gasping for air. But care must be taken that the skin is not exposed to the active ingredients of the mustard for too long at a time. An intense reddening of the skin is desirable, but blisters should never be allowed to form. If cases of whooping cough are treated as described above, children can be protected from serious complications.

Coeliac Disease

Since this disease causes much worry and requires great care, many parents will be relieved to learn how to go about treating it. The treatment required is similar to that used for enteritis and diarrhoea in infants and young children.

The principal remedy is *Tormentavena*; 2–5 drops are to be given 3–5 times daily, although the exact dose will depend upon

51

the age and sensitivity of the little patient. Start by giving a low dose and gradually increase it until the stool has regained its normal consistency. *Warm hip baths* or *warm abdominal packs* prepared with camomile or horsetail infusions, given frequently, will serve as a complementary treatment.

The diet should contain plenty of *brown rice gruel*, never the polished white kind. Add a little raw carrot juice or *Biocarottin*, made with concentrated raw carrot juice; just ½ or ¼ of a teaspoonful will do. While the illness persists, for children and adults, only gluten-free cereals are indicated, rice being ideal for this purpose. White flour products and white semolina are to be strictly avoided. On the other hand, potatoes boiled in their skins and mashed, skins and all, and mixed with a little raw carrot juice are quite in order. Other vegetables, with the exception of leeks, should not be given until the child is well again.

As regards fruits, finely grated raw apples mixed with mashed bananas are permissible. Bilberries, or blueberries, can also be served. When the acute stage of the disease has passed, a little grapefruit juice may be given. *Bambu Coffee Substitute* is beneficial, but only when it is taken in small quantities.

The quantity of food eaten should be kept very low. When the digestion has become somewhat normalised (noticeable in the consistency and colour of the stools) the amount of food can gradually be stepped up. Remember, however, too much food is worse than too little. Should any food item appear to upset the patient's digestion, leave it out of the diet; the choice and combination of foods depends on the individual sensitivity of the patient. Once the stool appears normal again, the remedies can gradually be dispensed with and you may slowly try introducing other foods again. If a relapse occurs, you will have to return once more to the stricter diet. Almond milk has proved to be of great help in cases of relapse.

If these suggestions are faithfully carried out and you take the child's individual sensitivity into account, patience and perseverance will lead to a complete cure. It should be remembered, however, that due to deficient digestion, which is caused by inadequate motility of the intestine, the ingested food will be only partly assimilated and particularly the absorption of minerals will be insufficient. No wonder, then, that children who suffer from coeliac disease are very prone to fractures of the bones because of their considerable calcium deficiency. However, the susceptibility to these complications can be reduced with a preparation of biological calcium such as *Urticalcin*. At the same time, this will help to curb the tendency to spasms which, in coeliac disease, are also attributable to calcium deficiency.

Poliomyelitis

Poliomyelitis is a sinister disease, yet on the whole quite brief. The polio virus is highly infectious and its virulent toxins, if concentrated, are able to attack and destroy the nerve cells, leading to paralysis. The illness itself ordinarily lasts only about 2–3 weeks. The paralysis that follows is actually the disease's aftermath. It is therefore most important to treat the disease thoroughly and with the minimum of delay. Judging by the letters I keep receiving, it is once more necessary to remind lay people as well as professionals of the fundamental rules regarding the treatment of polio.

Some time ago, a man from central Switzerland told me that his son, a strong and healthy boy, was hospitalised for tests and observation because it was thought he might have polio. Day after day passed without the doctor in charge attempting any treatment, until the first signs of paralysis appeared in the lungs. The boy was then placed in an iron lung, but he died within a few weeks, despite having been so strong and healthy. Let me add that this incident occurred many years ago and would be most unlikely to happen with the modern approach to the disease.

Famous physiotherapists, with Sister Kenny in the forefront, have proved that a life can be saved if treatment is given without delay. It is the delay that enables the virus to destroy the nerve cells. Therefore, as soon as the first symptoms become apparent it is of the utmost importance that the patient be made to *sweat*. Use a steam cabinet, a steam bath, a sauna, a tub bath of gradually increasing temperature (Schlenz bath), or quite simply hot packs; whatever you choose the important thing is to produce copious perspiration – fast. By these means much harm can be avoided and paralysis may well be averted. If Sister Kenny's treatment had been given, the boy mentioned previously might not have lost his life.

However conservative a doctor may be, he should not close his eyes to the good results obtained by new methods of treating polio. The very first symptoms should galvanise us into action. They may suggest flu, with excessive tiredness, headaches, aching limbs, vomiting, lack of appetite, etc. Whether polio is diagnosed right away or not is of little importance. These symptoms are sufficient to warrant immediate treatment, the first of which is the above-mentioned inducement of perspiration. The effect will be beneficial even if it is happily discovered later that it was the flu and not polio.

It is advisable to back up the treatment by means of natural remedies, such as *Gelsemium 6x* and *Urticalcin*, calcium always being valuable in such cases. *Nux vomica 4x* is helpful in counteracting nausea. All these remedies contribute to improvement. As for the diet, fruit juices are indicated so as not to overburden the digestive organs. What is more, never lose sight of the necessity to rid the body of toxins, not only through heavy sweating, but also through the bowels and kidneys. Since this treatment has proved to be reliable and effective in practice, it should be tried first.

Polio epidemics occur periodically and regionally, although less so today than formerly. Hot and sultry weather seems to encourage the development of the virus, for the incidence of the disease is greater in summer than in winter. In tropical countries it continues all year round. Research specialists have found that a number of people, particularly children, although immune to the disease themselves, nevertheless are carriers of the polio virus. Among primitive peoples very few cases of polio are found and this would lead to the conclusion that the advantages and disadvantages of our civilisation are responsible for our predisposition to this disease and undermine our resistance to it. Our food and life-style, living in overheated houses, and so forth, no doubt play their part in our susceptibility.

So how can we protect ourselves from this dreadful affliction? In the same way that we should protect ourselves from all infectious diseases. The main requirement is a natural way of life. Healthy exercise is also important – and we should not become 'soft'. Plenty of fresh air, light and sunshine should be our 'companions' whenever possible. Since it is now thought with reasonable certainty that the polio virus attacks by way of the nose and mouth, do not neglect to paint your children's throats with *Molkosan* when a threat of polio occurs in your locality. By doing so we can thus protect our children from infectious diseases and build up their resistance. However, should the infection have already taken place, remember the keynote to successful treatment: detoxify and eliminate – profuse sweating and elimination through the bowels and kidneys. This will help to avert the worst.

Influenza

Fortunately, not every bout of influenza is as serious as the dreadful viral influenza that killed more people in 1918–19 than the First

World War itself. Usually it is quite a harmless illness, but since so many people do not really know what to do when infectious diseases strike, the following suggestions may be helpful. The recommendations made for influenza should be followed in cases of other flu-like and infectious diseases too.

First of all, the bowels must be cleaned out by means of a natural *plant laxative*. As long as the temperature remains above normal the patient should not eat. To quench his thirst and assist elimination, give *fruit juices*, orange, grapefruit and grape juices being the most suitable. Should the liver be affected, raw *carrot juice* should be used instead of fruit juice. Under no circumstances should the fever be reduced with chemical medicines. It is a kind of defence measure, assisting the body by burning up and destroying the viral and other toxins responsible for the illness. The elimination of metabolic waste products through the kidneys is absolutely essential, and for this purpose give a kidney tea with *Solidago* (goldenrod) or *Nephrosolid*. Moreover, we can assist the fever and induce sweating by the use of *compresses*. If the patient should still find it difficult to start perspiring, let him drink hot *elder flower tea* with lemon juice.

When the normal body temperature has stabilised, first serve *raw fruit* and other *raw foods*, followed by *light meals*, keeping to a vegetarian diet, and as soon as good health has been restored, the patient can return to his usual diet, which should, however, be a natural one.

Following these suggestions, an attack of influenza can be quickly overcome and will not mean the usual long prostration. What is more, the patient will not experience the lingering tiredness and other common after effects of flu.

Virus Influenza
Although the epidemics that have hit Europe again and again for some decades no longer kill as many victims as at first, we must nevertheless regard influenza as a serious disease, especially when we consider its possible after effects. For example, it can cause pneumonia, or an acute deterioration of a chronic liver condition; it may also affect the kidneys, pancreas and abdominal organs. It is also possible for the myocardium to suffer and eczema to break out. Rheumatism can result from an improperly or incompletely treated bout of flu. All these after effects can possibly be prevented if treatment is given until the cure is complete.

Checklist for the Treatment of Influenza

At the onset of a flu virus we should carefully consider four main aspects for successful treatment.

1. In the first place we must make use of a *physical therapy* through which we can assist the body to *excrete bacterial toxins*. At the same time, we must watch the condition of the heart during sweating cures. With this in mind, we can then proceed to induce sweating through the application of compresses, wet packs or a steam bath.

In addition to the compresses, it is also beneficial to apply *cold compresses to the calves*. The patient will then be more comfortable and able to sleep.

If the illness is affecting the heart, give the heart tonic *Cardiaforce*, or *fruit juice* sweetened with *honey*. Or simply serve *herbal tea* or just water sweetened with honey. Pure *grape sugar* (condensed grape juice) also has an immediate effect in strengthening weak heart muscles.

The body should be frequently washed with an infusion of *thyme* or *juniper needles*, even if the patient may perspire only moderately.

For a severe bout of flu, the patient should take *Podophyllum 4x, Chelidonium 4x* (celandine) and *Taraxacum* (dandelion), since these remedies are good for the liver. And as already stated, the patient should drink raw carrot juice for the liver, and apply *cabbage leaf poultices* to the liver region during the night.

If it happens to be a head or nerve flu, *Avena sativa* and *Acid. phos. 4x*, in addition to a *biological calcium preparation*, are indicated; in severe cases also *Fiebrisan* and *Echinaforce*. The simultaneous application of crushed cabbage leaves on the nape of the neck has an excellent effect.

Oral hygiene must be observed in all infectious diseases, including influenza. The patient must clean his teeth regularly and remove any coating on the tongue with a toothbrush. Gargling with *Molkosan* backs up the healing process greatly.

Patients with common influenza will benefit from *Influaforce*, a homoeopathic flu remedy (see below).

All infectious diseases make the lungs work overtime in order to burn up toxins, so the sick room should be aired frequently. Provided that the patient is well covered, a pleasantly cool room is better than an overheated one.

2. Secondly, we must employ a selection of *herbal medicines*,

such as *Nephrosolid* and *Boldocynara*, for these remedies promote increased excretion through the kidneys and liver. By taking Echinaforce we can prevent irritation and inflammation. At the beginning of the illness, the flu drops Influaforce are helpful. These drops contain *Baptisia* (wild indigo), *Lachesis 10x*, Echinaforce, *Bryonia 3x* (bryony), *Aconitum 3x* and *Solidago*, and have always proved effective in minimising the virulence of the infection.

3. *Diet* is very important for a flu patient. While fever is present, neither protein nor fat should be eaten. Going on a liquid juice diet for one or two days has proved to be very beneficial. Grapefruit juice, diluted bilberry (blueberry) juice, also blackcurrant juice alternated with diluted beetroot juice will be received as a blessing by the patient. The intake of liquids should be greater than under normal circumstances.

4. After the illness has passed, we must direct our attention to the follow-up treatment, being mindful that the period of convalescence should not be short. Even though the acute symptoms have subsided, we should still apply *physiotherapy*. Also, continue taking *diuretic* or *excretory medicines* even if the fever has subsided. This will eliminate all of the accumulated toxins so that no damage elsewhere in the body is possible.

Every bout of flu should receive follow-up treatment. In fact, with any infectious disease it is advisable to continue the treatment conscientiously until the patient has fully recovered. This is the only way to prevent after effects, which can be much more unpleasant than you think. If you become impatient, just remember that you remain prone to contracting a new infection until all vestiges of the last one have been eliminated during convalescence.

The Brain

The brain is a marvellous organ and a great gift from the Creator. We would be lost without it; we could not plan, carry out or complete anything. So we have every reason to be grateful for it every day of our life. If a person voluntarily abstains from food or is made to go hungry, and as a result loses a great deal of weight, the weight loss in the spinal cord and in the brain is hardly noticeable. The fact that everything else is affected first shows the importance of the brain as the control centre of most other processes in the body.

A good illustration of the human brain is that of the walnut. The hard shell can be compared to the cranium. The two-lobed seed resembles the cerebrum, and the skin, which peels off easily in freshly picked nuts, may be likened to the meninges. At the back of the head, between the spinal cord and the brain, lies the cerebellum, which is approximately the size of an orange.

The functions of the brain, as far as they have been discovered, are amazing. Picture, if you will, the control room of a large power plant or a modern ocean liner, or the instrument panels of a jet plane. All the numerous instruments and switches elicit our amazement and admiration. These control centres are, in a manner of speaking, the brain of, for example, the ship or plane. Everything that takes place, every change in direction, every response to the changeable elements, every command, comes from that control centre, the brain. The energy needed to make everything function is supplied by generators which produce energy, or power. When the power supply is insufficient or fails completely, it can be put down to problems in the central control because it is either malfunctioning or is out of action. This can happen even though engines and equipment have been designed and built in spectacular ways.

What can we learn from the above illustration? Energy is supplied to the brain via the bloodstream. If the blood carries all the necessary nutrients, nutritive salts and vitamins so that every brain cell receives the food it needs, then everything will function properly. Not every one of the many millions of cells has its own function. The brain is divided into work groups, called centres, and more than twenty of these centres have so far been recognised.

How an entire centre can be put out of order is seen in the case of a stroke. The attack usually occurs in the inner capsule and not the outer part of the brain or the cerebral cortex. If a blood vessel on the right side of the inner capsule ruptures, the blood supply to the outer parts of the brain is disrupted and the consequences appear on the left side of the body. This inversion is due to the fact that the cerebral hemisphere controls the opposite side of the body. Whatever we sense on the right side is registered on the left side and vice versa. If the body is able to repair the damage, the paralysis will pass and the ability to speak, which was lost, will return. If the speech centre remains disturbed, while the centre governing the connecting ideas continues to function, then the person will find himself in the embarrassing situation of thinking correctly but expressing himself in a muddled way. However, this will not happen if he writes down his thoughts instead of trying to express them verbally.

What Can Damage the Brain?

If the blood pressure is either too high or too low it will adversely affect the functioning of the brain. Dizzy spells or fainting, for example, may result from too much pressure or lack of blood flow, due to low blood pressure.

Even though this single most important control centre, the brain, is well protected by the cranium, accidents and concussions can do much damage. Just think of the many falls and bumps experienced while skiing or engaging in other types of sports. On such occasions, the head – and thus the brain – often suffers severe blows or concussion without any visible sign of injury. However, if the fall is bad enough to cause a tear in the meninges, the cerebrospinal fluid will leak out and the brain, which had previously been cushioned by this fluid, will now be more like a dead weight, resulting in pressure being exerted on the various brain centres. The person will feel nauseous, the metabolic centre will be affected, and vomiting and possibly diarrhoea will occur. The patient must lie still and rest so that the tear can heal and the brain may once again enjoy the cushioning and protecting effect of the cerebrospinal fluid surrounding it.

Alcohol and drugs can influence the brain to the extent that several centres are slowed down while others accelerate. Hence the person may lose his inhibitions and temporarily act and feel differently to how he would under normal circumstances. Permanent damage, that is, softening of the brain and paralysis, may occur when vitality decreases as a result of poisoning with metals such as arsenic and mercury. These and other poisons impair and block certain processes of the brain and the central nervous system, as is known to happen in advanced cases of syphilis. The metallic toxins may remain inactive in the body for years, only to strike the victim in later life, with tragic consequences.

Meningitis is another disease which can have grave consequences, yet it is possible to prevent it by striving to keep the circulation in good condition. If, however, one falls victim to it from contact with an infected person, every effort should be made to cure the disease without delay. One of the most effective remedies for this is *Echinaforce*. If meningitis is not treated properly it can lead to partial paralysis and other permanent damage. This should be reason enough not to take it lightly but to give it the best care and attention. The patient should be kept in a darkened room and away from all noise, since he will be very sensitive to light and disturbances. Remember, meningitis is always dangerous, not only because it can bring lasting damage to the body, but also because it might lead to death.

Taking Precautions

During the productive years of youth an active person often neglects to think about the fact that the central nervous system and brain must still serve their purpose during the autumn of life. If we wish to be sprightly and in good spirits, feeling well physically and mentally during our old age, we must see to it that the engine in the control room, the brain, is given more attention than is usual in today's world.

How many of us regularly curtail the brain's wonderful source of energy and recharging by not getting enough rest and sleep! The body may be able to take one or two exceptions, but a continuous lack of sleep will undermine the health, lead to fatigue and will gradually diminish one's efficiency and productivity. Let us therefore, first and foremost, make sure to enjoy a healthy amount of sleep, going to bed early. We should also make an effort to eat wholefoods for adequate nutrition, get enough exercise for refreshing relaxation during our free time, and avoid the poisons threatening us in so many ways.

Taking these precautions will not only contribute to our overall state of health but will render an incomparable service to our brain.

The Pituitary Gland (Hypophysis)

The pituitary, 12 by 8 mm in size (like a bean), serves our body in a similar way to that of an inconspicuous general who commands a large army, or the person in the control tower who directs and manoeuvres huge jet planes entering and leaving an international airport. This gland weighs only a few grams and was at one time regarded as a vestigial organ. But when the news of its importance began to spread through the scientific world, and it was even discovered that the anterior and posterior lobes each produce completely different hormones, the amazement was great indeed. Such a small gland, yet one with so many vital functions!

The Master Gland

The pituitary gland governs the activity of the thyroid, the suprarenal gland and the sex glands. It is known as the master gland, having the leading position among the endocrine glands. Its direct link with the central nervous system in the area of very important centres at the base of the brain, the hypothalamus, has been the subject of much research, since it appears that the pituitary gland influences all the vital processes either directly or indirectly. It also appears that, together with the thymus gland, the pituitary determines growth. Since the entire development of the sex glands and sex organs is controlled by the pituitary, a hermaphrodite condition may be attributed to impaired development or disturbed functioning of this gland. A pregnancy could never run its normal course without the cooperation of the pituitary. Diabetics have to blame their ailment not only on a failure of the islets of Langerhans – located in the pancreas – to produce sufficient insulin, but also on a functional disorder in the anterior lobe of the pituitary as a contributory factor. No matter how much bile the liver produces, the process of breaking down fat will suffer if the pituitary fails to manufacture the necessary hormones. A change in the blood pressure, too much or too little elimination of water, even the start of labour pains, are all connected with the function of the posterior lobe of the pituitary and its secretion of hormones.

Until recently, science had not succeeded in fully understanding the complex hormone structure of this interesting little gland. And this is the reason why it has not yet been possible to produce its hormones synthetically. It is always a risk to prescribe medicine that has a direct effect on the pituitary, except in small homoeopathic doses. Such medicines can have a very detrimental effect on the patient if he is sensitive to drugs.

Care of the Small Wonder Gland

As a control centre of paramount importance, the pituitary should receive extra care and attention. Because of its important functions, it is well protected in an inaccessible bony hollow at the base of the skull. The only way to care for it is by looking after one's general health. Thus, it is worthwhile supplying the body with wholesome food, sufficient sleep, exercise and oxygen by deep breathing. Even though we already know a great deal about this small gland, many of its secrets have yet to be discovered.

The instrument panel of a jet plane is a complete mystery to the layperson. A radio receiver small enough to fit in a watch casing is also a marvel of technology. But what is contained in the bean-sized gland – much of which we are still not aware of – surpasses everything the human mind has created a thousand times. Appreciating the intricate design and functions of our body, we should always show deep respect for it and avoid subjecting it thoughtlessly to stresses and strains that affect our health. The biblical psalmist expressed this most aptly when he wrote: 'I shall laud you [God] because in a fear-inspiring way I am wonderfully made. Your works are wonderful, as my soul is very well aware.'

Headaches – their Causes and Treatments

Headaches should never be dispelled with analgesics. Rather, you should try and discover the cause and then treat it by natural means.

Many headaches are caused by intestinal disturbances. Putrefactive processes develop gases which enter the liver through the portal vein and, from there, find their way into the bloodstream. Headaches frequently result because the nerve and brain cells are affected by the poisons circulating in the blood. Abdominal troubles and diseases can also trigger headaches. Overwork tends to erode one's nervous energy and this condition, too, may start a headache. Other problems that may cause headaches include a ruptured disc (slipped disc) resulting from strain. This cause can be successfully treated by a chiropractor. High or low blood pressure, diseases of the blood and nephritis can all trigger headaches.

Let me point out that a headache *per se* is never an illness, only a symptom pointing to an illness that is causing it. It is for this reason that taking analgesics and chemical drugs to deaden the pain is completely inappropriate. The correct thing to do is to find and then treat the underlying cause. On the other hand, you can do something about a headache by providing the nerve cells with certain biochemical salts which will lessen and often cure the pain (see 'Four Biochemical Remedies', pages 398–402). There are also homoeopathic remedies, for example *Sanguinaria canadensis* (bloodroot), which are especially good for headaches.

Headaches can also be caused by insufficient blood supply to the brain. In this case we recommend both *Petadolor* and *Ginkgo biloba*, also known as maidenhair tree. The leaves of this tree contain active properties that can do wonders for the cerebral blood supply.

Physical therapy should not be forgotten either. Relief is often obtained from *warm showers* directed on the nape of the neck and the spine, as well as massaging with *Toxeucal Massage Oil*. If the headaches stem from an upset digestive system, warm showers directed on the stomach are the answer to alleviating the pain.

Onion, horseradish or cabbage leaf *poultices* can be applied to the back of the neck in order to combat headaches successfully.

Whatever you do, natural treatments and remedies will prove more effective than chemical drugs, which merely dull the pain. It is of fundamental importance to find the cause of the headache and to treat it accordingly.

The Tongue

Just as with any one of the other organs, the tongue is a marvellous work of Creation. The singular design, structure and arrangement of this muscular organ gives it a flexibility that no other organ in the body possesses. The tongue's shape can change from flat to broad, from thin to thick, by manipulating its muscle fibres which respond to command as does a circus horse to its trainer. Yet the most interesting feature in the structure of the tongue is its surface, which, when greatly magnified, looks rather like a lunar landscape. Every elevation and every little crater-like cavity is equipped with minute receptors of taste sensations that enable us to taste and enjoy our food and drink. The mucous glands in the taste cavities see to it that there is always a small amount of local mucus or fluid present, for chemicals taken into the mouth have to be dissolved for us to taste them.

The Sensation of Taste

Nerve cells which register the sensation of taste and transmit it to the brain are arranged in a bulb-like manner. The nerve ends may be compared to the roots, while the layers of the bulb represent the reaction controls, with built-in amplifiers. To complete the illustration, in the place of the bulb's top, there are very fine hair-like nerves that register the taste sensation.

These nerve bulbs are called taste buds, because scientists compared them to the literal buds. An adult has about 3,000 of them. But did you know that we humans probably have fewer sensations of taste when eating our food than, for example, antelopes, which have about fifteen times as many taste buds as a human? If we had as many as these animals it would be much easier for us to differentiate between healthy nourishing food and that which is harmful. Thus animals are more capable than humans in distinguishing what is good for them and what is not.

Simple experiments will tell you that there are different taste zones on the tongue. If the tip of the tongue is dipped in honey water, the sensation of sweetness is immediately apparent. A little further back on the periphery of the tongue the taste of salt is registered and even further back, also on the periphery, sourness is sensed, while zones registering bitterness are found across the posterior section. The central part of the tongue is a neutral area, as it does not register any sensation of taste.

It is noteworthy that the tongue is more accurate and reliable as a test organ than many chemical reactions. For this reason a wine merchant, or a tea, coffee or olive oil processing firm will pay more attention to their experienced 'tasters' than to the analysts in a chemical laboratory.

Imagine what life would be like without the 3,000 taste buds on our tongues. What would encourage us to eat and drink if there were no pleasure in it? If you have ever had to force yourself to eat without feeling hungry you can well understand the difference. We would also lose our incentive to prepare delicious meals for our families if there were no smile of approval and enjoyment on the faces of the happy eaters. Despite its small size, the tongue is endowed with many important functions, providing much satisfaction and pleasure.

Other Capabilities of the Tongue

Even though we know something about the anatomical structure and the functions of the tongue, we have by no means exhausted the full extent of its operations and capabilities. We know, of course, that we owe the gift of oral communication to the tongue. But that is not all. The tongue is at the same time the 'voice' of the heart, the figurative seat of the ability to feel, think and make decisions. This little organ thus may be a source of blessing or curse for ourselves and others.

From the Bible we learn that horses and ships are easier to manoeuvre and control than the tongue. Though small in size, the tongue can, metaphorically speaking, ignite a 'fire' so devastating that it destroys a forest.

How sad is its influence when spreading evil gossip and, by doing so, slandering friends and dear companions. Envy and hatred, too, make use of this nimble little instrument of the soul when sending out its poisonous arrows to do harm to successful fellowmen. As slick as oil, the tongue obeys the voice of temptation, for the chosen victim cannot escape its treacherous influence. Many a tongue cannot distinguish between 'yes' and 'no', so that its contradictions, hypocrisy and lies play a part in destroying the innocent. A disappointed person may pour out the bitterness of his heart through the tongue and infect or poison others. What dreadful words may be uttered through this inconspicuous little organ in the mouth of the mentally deranged! The confused state of mind and inner conflict of such a person often seems to surface by means of the tongue. It is hard for a healthy, normal person to understand or face such an outburst.

The Tongue Can Be a Blessing

Has the tongue been given the power to speak only in order to create unhappiness? Certainly not. The apostle Paul reminded his fellow workers to consider everything lovable and well spoken of, for the contrary use of the tongue is the root of nothing but grief and vexation. Loving, heart-warming words, words of instruction and upbuilding admonition, comfort and encouragement should pass over the lips, so that this little organ of speech may truly become a blessing. But this can only be if the heart is properly conditioned, if it has the desire to be a friend to friends, to lend a helping hand to someone in need or distress, and to overcome even hostile attitudes with goodness. In this way the tongue will become a dispenser of kindness and benevolence.

What enhances and endears springtime to us? Is it not the lovely songs of birds? Their little throats fill the air with songs of gratitude, of sheer joy and devotion. We too have been endowed with the ability to sing and can, like the birds, give vent to our joyful exuberance in harmonious song.

But the tongue must learn something else: during times of distress it must keep silent, for its indiscriminate use may cause the betrayal of a friend and brother. The tongue must know how to thwart an enemy's fatal intentions and break the power of evil. Even a foolish man will be regarded as wise if he knows when to 'hold his tongue'. This did not escape the notice of King Solomon, as recorded in the Book of Proverbs. It may be why a popular proverb says, 'Speech is silver but silence is golden.' Indeed, for many, keeping silent takes greater willpower than talking.

Is it not strange that such a little organ as the tongue serves such diverse purposes? It makes food and drink appealing to us, it warns us against indulging in spoiled or even poisonous food. In fact, if we do not force our palate to take in unnatural things, if we do not expect it to call good what is really harmful, then it will reward us with its healthy power of evaluation. It is similar with the other function for which this small organ was made, the power to express feelings. The tongue can prove to be an extremely beneficial organ, but it can also turn out to be detrimental. Whether we use it as a positive or negative outlet for our emotions depends on the state of our hearts. That is why Solomon wisely advised us, 'More than all else that is to be guarded, safeguard your heart, for out of it are the sources of life.' And out of the heart's abundance the mouth speaks.

Taking Care of the Eyes

This section is not meant to deal in detail with the complex mechanism we call the eye. Instead, all it sets out to do is give some clear and helpful hints on how to preserve and protect your eyesight, and highlight the basic principles of nature involved.

Let us begin by repeating the fact that excessive brain work causes eyestrain. The more natural and free from stress is the way we live our daily lives the better it will be for our eyes. It might be added that the poor nourishment derived from today's denatured foods also contributes to the development of eye problems.

However, many of us will admit that it is not all that easy to change these things, or we may have already made some changes and want to achieve still more. How can this be done?

The answer is quite simple. Years ago, when we were not so eager to work overtime by artificial light and went to bed early, there were fewer people with painful, weak and tired eyes. So why not try a most extraordinary remedy? Why not turn the clock back and live for four weeks without electric light? How can you do this? Well, quite simply by doing without the convenience of modern lighting. You refrain from using this miracle of modern technology; you simply do not switch on the electric light. Your painful, burning, overtired eyes, which can no longer do their work efficiently, will respond to this care and rapidly recover. But in order to be well armed against the force of habit, you must plan your day carefully so that when it gets dark, you will not be tempted to turn on the light despite all your good intentions.

Years ago, the evenings were used to relax and recuperate and to prepare oneself for the rest that was to end the day. Try to do this for four weeks. It will help you to see and experience why our Creator has given us the different lights, the bright light of the sun by day and the gentle soothing moonlight by night. Just try to work hard in the soft moonlight. You will gladly desist. Why? Because if you let its magic spell work on you like an age-old lullaby, you will soon drop off and enjoy a deep, restful sleep. Truly, if you make full use of the night for rest, you will wake cheerfully with the first gleam of daylight, without feeling drowsy, or still tired and sluggish. You will not feel morose and only partially rested, turning over on the other side to sleep on into the day. What you had intended doing by artificial light, you can do more cheerfully and with much less effort in the full light of the early morning. You will be amazed at what this compliance to nature's laws can do for you; it will renew your energies and benefit your eyesight at the same time.

The unnatural strain of artificial light, which we impose on our eyes year after year, will no longer bother us if we adapt our daily routine to the coming and going of daylight. This is the natural order of things established by God and the more we set ourselves against it, the more our eyes will tire and suffer. Indeed, if things go on much longer as they do, one day it will be hard to imagine a person without spectacles. We hardly ever stop to think about the detrimental consequences of our unnatural life-style, do we? Immersed as we are in an atmosphere of artificiality, we have lost touch with nature, we are out of tune and can no longer learn and follow its natural rhythm. How would plants fare if day and night they had to live in the light, without a chance to regenerate themselves in darkness? Their cells would tire out and suffer damage and their natural functions would be impaired. Why, then, should not man, the crown of Creation, conform to the harmony of the natural laws? Why should he not use and enjoy to the full the priceless, wondrous exhilaration of the early morning hours, rather than miss out on them, lying in bed asleep while outside the sun is shining gloriously, and do during the night what was not done in the morning hours? Why should anyone create restless nights for himself, only because they did not sleep soundly during the hours before midnight, building up strength for the next day's work? If we could only reorganise our schedule of activities our eyes would indeed benefit greatly. When light fades, let us put aside our work, and when daylight comes once more, take it up again, strengthened and refreshed. Not only our eyes, but our whole body will benefit from this natural way of life.

Spring and summer encourage us especially to give this routine a try. In winter it seems more normal to wake up with the daylight but, unfortunately, at that time of the year we are also more tempted to continue our working day far into the night. In spring, then, let us start to put our good resolution into practice. Let us give our eyes the natural daylight in the earliest hours of the morning, and in the evening, let us give them a rest rather than work under artificial light. They will then recover and become strong.

The Lacrimal Glands

Is it not a marvellous thing that the lacrimal glands, or tear ducts, serve as a safety valve to reduce the internal pressure when we are under emotional stress? How unbearable it would be, even for a little girl, if she could not cry when her doll dropped on the floor and broke, or some equally frustrating thing happened. The pain seems only half as bad when salty tears roll down the cheeks like pearls. In fact, this ingenious arrangement operates much better with women than with men.

In addition to the secretion of tears when crying, the lacrimal glands, which are located just within the upper outside part of the eye socket, embedded in a little pocket, have yet another function: the tears must keep the conjunctiva and the cornea moist in order to prevent their drying out. Furthermore, bacteria, dust and other foreign particles are washed away by the tears.

Inflammation of the tear ducts themselves is rare, but that of the nasolacrimal duct and the lacrimal sac is more frequent. If this inflammation is not given immediate attention with herbal packs of *camomile* and *eyebright*, the attacking bacteria may cause a chronic condition or even the formation of abscesses. Flushing of the eyes with *warm milk* or *mallow leaf water*, to which a few drops of *Echinaforce* has been added, is a rapid cure for simple inflammations. For those who work or live in a dusty environment it is highly recommended to cleanse the area of the eyes with the lids closed by wiping them with a cotton pad soaked in Echinaforce. Do this every evening. It prevents dirt, dust and bacteria from entering the eye itself. If the lacrimal duct is blocked you must see a doctor to have it punctured. At the same time, it is important to use Echinaforce as mentioned above and to bathe the eyes with warm milk or herbal tea. If the eyes tend to be encrusted in the morning upon awakening, it is a sign of a metabolic disorder which must be treated immediately.

It is also wise to refrain from straining the eyes when there is insufficient illumination to read by. The eyes need plenty of rest, and to be closed during the night, because they work hard during our waking hours. They are indeed very precious to us, but many people forget that and do not give them the care they deserve as the indispensable gift they are. No one will deny that the eyes are instruments that we cannot do without, physically or mentally.

Blindness constitutes an extremely heavy loss. Amongst all the other wonders of Creation, the eyes are a miracle and the lacrimal glands, despite their negligible size and apparent unimportance, are a convincing symbol of a carefully thought out design to smooth the necessary but involuntary processes of our daily existence.

Simple Remedies for Eye Problems

It is a proven fact that a *carrot juice diet* has a favourable effect on the eyes on account of the provitamin A carrots contain. Anything that stimulates the circulation and the supply of blood to the eyes helps to improve their efficiency, and this is where carrot juice is most beneficial. If raw carrots are not available, use condensed carrot juice (*Biocarottin*) instead. As supporting remedies in the treatment take *Aesculaforce* and a calcium complex (*Urticalcin*), as well as *goldenrod* for the kidneys. The requirement of silica can be met by taking *Galeopsis* (hemp nettle).

Since liver disorders, constipation and overtiredness can also be the causes of eye troubles, make sure that both the liver and the bowels are functioning properly. The liver is best restored to good working order by a *liver diet* (see page 247) and by taking *Chelidonium 4x* and *Podophyllum 4x* or *Boldocynara* liver drops. Very often constipation will disappear at the same time, but if this should not be the case, use a natural remedy for it. Above all, avoid denatured foods. Instead, eat a natural diet that is low in protein and salt. If you are feeling overworked, make sure to get to sleep at least two hours before midnight and take oat extract in the form of *Avenaforce*, and *Eleutherococcus*, a remedy made from the taiga root, since both are known for their value as general tonics for the nerves and body.

Consider each case carefully and, in accordance with the diagnosed problem, choose the right remedies and treatment.

In the case of a blocked tear duct, observe the general advice already given and for external treatment apply packs made with *clay* and a *horsetail* infusion. For conjunctivitis make up an eye bath from *eyebright* and *marigold tea*.

Infectious Suppuration of the Eyes and Mouth

Infectious eye and mouth suppuration (discharging of pus or festering) can be cured in a short time if you follow the nature treatment described in the following letter I received from a mother.

'Our little boy is much better now. The pus in his eyes and

mouth stopped within about five days after we began to use your remedies. The child looked pitiful, but now he is romping around happily again. Our treatment was as follows: before meals we gave him *Solidago* (goldenrod) and a *cod-liver oil* preparation, as well as an easily assimilated calcium preparation (*Urticalcin*). After meals he took *Hepar sulph. 4x* and *Lachesis 12x*. The eyes were bathed twice daily with diluted *Aesculaforce*. Twice a day we put an *onion poultice* on his neck. Improvement of his condition was soon noticeable. We put *St John's wort oil* on his sore lips and dusted them with Urticalcin powder. During the day we gave him *fruit juice* and *horsetail tea* to drink. Several times we prepared *white clay packs* made with horsetail tea, mixed with a few drops of St John's wort oil, and applied these to his eyes. We are indeed thankful and happy that this dangerous infection has now gone, but we continue to give the child *Solidago*, cod-liver oil preparation and the easily assimilated calcium.'

As a rule, such infections are simple enough to deal with if the body is given the right kind of help, for nature cures if we support it in its performance. It is better to take no action than to give the wrong treatment. The usual attempts to suppress the symptoms in order to destroy the germs with drugs actually undermine the body's natural powers of resistance. The same foolishness is shown by those who treat plant diseases and pests. They expect to get rid of them by spraying the plants with poisonous chemicals, but succeed only in weakening or killing the plants' own natural defence mechanism. So they are forced to increase and intensify their spray programmes. Similarly, some doctors have to prescribe more and stronger drugs because the body's natural healing powers have been weakened or even destroyed. But we must remember that man is not the healer – it is nature that really performs the cure. All we ourselves can do is support the wonderful, natural self-healing powers of the body. Let us hope that this basic truth becomes once again more widely recognised and appreciated.

The Nose

Our three respiratory organs comprise the nose, the windpipe (trachea) and the lungs. Each of these three organs has a very special and important function and only a working correlation between them assures a harmless exchange of gases.

Instead of bones, the nose has cartilage plates to give it firmness. Bones would be too brittle and the danger of them breaking too great, especially if we should fall on our nose, or a ball or some other hard object hit it. Those participating in sports such as boxing or skiing would soon have nothing but an unshapely and unsightly nose if the cartilage walls were less resilient and more vulnerable. The extent to which the beauty of the face depends on the shape of the nose becomes evident after a serious accident when the nose is crushed or badly deformed. Fortunately today, a mishap of this sort can, as a rule, be easily corrected by plastic surgery.

The Functions of the Nose

The proper functioning of the nose is very important to good health. For one thing, perhaps not everyone is aware of the fact that the nose is actually an air-conditioning organ, warming the air we inhale if it is cold outside. If the air is tropically hot, a cooling system is activated to make the climate more bearable. Furthermore, the nose regulates the intake of air that is either too dry or too humid.

What a marvellous design! Not even the smallest detail is missing in all these divine provisions and it is indeed astonishing to hear people deny the existence of an omnipotent Creator, despite the many visible testimonies of divine wisdom and creative power. God alone is capable of creating something out of nothing, for only He has control over the laws he set in motion in the first place. These laws cannot come into existence by themselves, neither is their smooth operation and application left to blind chance and whim. So let us now see to what extent a small organ like the nose may serve as proof of God's creatorship.

First of all, the nose is designed in such a way that the mucous membranes keep dust and bacteria from entering the body, provided, of course, that we breathe in and out through the nose and that it is not blocked. It is true that we can also breathe through the mouth rather than the nose, but this will make us lose the benefit of the built-in screening device, exposing us to a higher risk of catching colds and infections. Mouth-breathing poses a definite threat to the throat, the bronchial passages and the lungs.

It is interesting to note that the nostrils react to pleasant and unpleasant odours by a simple dilation or contraction of the walls, thus increasing or decreasing the flow of air. Strangely enough, the nose walls (conchae) also react to cold feet. When the feet are cold the walls contract, become cold and dry and cause the glands to stop functioning, so that dust and bacteria are no longer filtered out. It is easy to see why a cold will almost inevitably result, followed by catarrh or a runny nose. You can now understand why it is important to avoid getting cold feet and inhaling bacteria by breathing through the mouth. If the mucous membranes are functioning properly they are able to destroy all cold germs entering through the nose. It is therefore a necessary requirement for good health to cultivate the habit of breathing through the nose at all times.

Treatment for Nasal Problems

If you suffer frequently from head colds it is advisable to sniff up calcium powder (*Urticalcin*) from time to time, in the way people used to take snuff years ago. When the air is cold it is also beneficial to lubricate the nasal passages regularly with a good lanolin cream. A reliable choice for this purpose is *Bioforce Cream*; it may even prevent a head cold from developing if applied early enough. When you walk too fast or run, you do not usually breathe through the nose. Hence you should try to slow down, at least enough to allow you to continue breathing through the nose. This will also be of benefit to the heart, since there will be less of a strain placed on it.

Nasal polyps may restrict the proper intake of air through the nose. Even though these growths are benign, their presence can be a source of great discomfort. The only effective cure for them is *Teucrium marum verum* (cat thyme). But should they not yield to this treatment, surgery would be indicated.

Even more bothersome than polyps is ozaena, a disease of the mucous membranes of the nose, giving off a foul-smelling discharge or odour. Relief is obtained by sniffing up or drawing in a solution containing *sea salt*, followed by sniffing up *Urticalcin* powder. For internal treatment, *Kali iod. 4x* and *Mercurius 4x* have proved very helpful.

Rhinitis (inflammation of the mucous membranes of the nose) can also be very annoying, especially in the spring with its changeable weather pattern. As for all other kinds of inflammation and infection, *Echinaforce* taken internally is a reliable remedy for rhinitis. For a more speedy cure you could also try soaking a cotton bud in Echinaforce and painting the nostrils with it. If sores or scales should develop on the inner walls of the nose, apply Bioforce Cream for an immediate healing effect.

A 'runny nose' can be stopped with relative ease. Cut a slice of fresh *onion* and dip it briefly into a glass of hot water. It is enough to dip the slice in just once, and then drink the water in small sips. This treatment will soon cure your sniffles.

Nasal catarrh or a cold, accompanied by a pus-like sticky discharge, may be cured in its acute stage by sipping a glass of hot water to which have been added five drops of *iodine tincture*. A person allergic to iodine, especially in cases of exophthalmic goitre, may obtain the same quick result by using five drops of *camphor tincture* instead of the iodine. Again, I would like to emphasise that Echinaforce taken internally and used externally will bring sure relief.

Sinusitis can cause a great deal of pain, since the infection spreads right into the sinuses and impairs our thinking processes as well. How grateful we can be for remedies such as *Cinnabaris 4x* and *Hepar sulph. 4x* and the speedy relief they are able to give. With their help, the rapidly forming pus can be drained and the patient will be free from the unpleasant infection in a relatively short time. It is important to bring about fast relief in order to prevent it from becoming chronic, since it may reach a stage where it will stubbornly resist any treatment.

Inflammation of the Ear (Otitis)
An earache should never be taken lightly as serious illness can result from it. First of all, apply a *poultice* to the neck; even if it is only onions the effect will be beneficial. Do not use chemist's ear drops; rather, go on a *fruit diet* and avoid all highly seasoned and heavy foods for a few weeks. See your doctor for *syringing*, which may be done with infusions of ribwort, camomile, marigold or lemon balm.

If a throbbing sensation is felt deep down in the ear, or if the pain is severe on one side, particularly in the right ear, and gets worse at night, *Calcarea carbonica 6x (Calcium carbonicum Hahnemann)* will help to soothe it. The patient should receive competent treatment at this stage, because inflammation of the middle ear (*Otitis media*) can develop, and this is more serious than many people think. If the pus, instead of breaking through the eardrum and draining from the ear canal, actually perforates the thin bone wall discharging into the cranial cavity, it may spread to the mastoid air cells and reach the covering of the brain and the brain itself – resulting in a critical condition.

Improperly treated infection of the middle ear can result in meningitis. Serious problems of the ear and the middle ear are often created by incompletely treated or suppressed infectious diseases such as scarlet fever, measles, whooping cough, diphtheria, influenza and tonsillitis, because they scatter their viruses and toxins throughout the body. Hence, if a relapse is to be avoided, elimination of the toxins is of the utmost importance. Improper treatment can affect the auditory nerves and cause loss of hearing; these nerves may degenerate or atrophy altogether and lead to complete deafness.

Pulsatilla, Belladonna, sulphur and *Mercurius solubilis*, in homoeopathic potencies, are the best remedies indicated for treating inflammations of the ear. At the first sign of suppuration *Hepar sulph. 12x* is very effective, and if there is a danger of septic infection, *Lachesis 12x* can still save the situation. In cases of prolonged discharge, *Silicea 12x* taken in alternation with *Causticum* (freshly burnt lime according to Hahnemann) will help. Should there be a tendency to a relapse, recourse to an occasional dose of the constitution-building remedy *Baryum carbonicum 10x* is indicated.

Anyone prone to ear problems should take the fresh plant extract of ribwort over a longer period of time. Known by its botanical name *Plantago lanceolata*, ribwort is one of the best remedies for the ears and will also sharpen the auditory senses. *Ginkgo biloba* is excellent for the same purpose and therefore recommended for people who are hard of hearing or suffer from tinnitus (ringing or buzzing in the ear).

Middle Ear Infections

Middle ear infections are frequently not given enough attention. If a child complains of earache and has perhaps a slight runny discharge which turns to pus, we put the child in a warm bed and think our duty is done. Unfortunately, however, the correct treatment is overlooked. The reason why so many people are hard of hearing and in some cases are deaf in one ear is because an inflammation of the middle ear in childhood had been neglected. Ear infections can also affect the brain, and the eyes may suffer if the infection becomes chronic. Neighbouring organs, as well as those in different parts of the body, can also be harmed. It is therefore imperative that no time is lost in treating the ear when the first symptoms of this serious condition appear, and that treatment is continued until the patient is cured.

For a chronic middle ear infection with pus the following directions will help give the patient relief. Place an *onion poultice* behind the affected ear, but if relief is not forthcoming, change to a *mustard poultice.* If even this does not produce the desired result, you will have to resort to the *Baunscheidt method* (see page 439). It is always important that the inflammation, especially in chronic cases, is drawn away from the head by some form of stimulation therapy, so that the focus of infection is drawn from the inside to the surface. Inflammation in the ears, eyes and nose can be diverted to the neck or shoulders. Internal remedies are *Belladonna 4x*, five drops every two hours, and *Ferrum phos. 6x*, two tablets also every two hours. The patient takes one of these remedies every hour, say *Belladonna* first, an hour later *Ferr. phos.*, then back to *Belladonna* again. For as long as the ear continues to discharge and suppurate, *Hepar sulph. 4x* is effective. When there is no more pus, *Silicea 12x* is indicated to stabilise the improvement. Follow up with one drop of *St John's wort oil* and one drop of *Plantago* (ribwort juice) once daily into the ear. When the ear infection is accompanied by nasal catarrh and pharyngitis, which is most likely due to the germs spreading, use *Cinnabaris 4x* and *Plantago*. You can also put five drops of *Plantago* on cotton wool and place this in the ear, replacing it every day.

This treatment will heal even a chronic inflammation so that the hearing will return to normal. On the other hand, if the described treatment is not strictly followed, the patient's sense of hearing will be endangered. The auditory nerve together with the intricate structures of the inner ear can be permanently damaged by bacterial toxins; the infection can actually cause erosion of the ossicles of the middle ear. When this happens, no treatment will restore the hearing apparatus. So never lose time in starting an intensive natural treatment as soon as problems with the ear begin to manifest themselves. Take into account the patient's general state of health and adopt a natural diet. This will help nature to heal and regenerate.

Sinus Infections

If you know how a sinus infection can come about, you will be able to see that, using natural remedies and treatment, it is quite simple to deal with the cause of this problem. For the most part, such an infection originates in the nose, especially after a head cold, sore throat, influenza, scarlet fever etc. It can also result from pus-forming bacteria in abscesses on the gums. When this happens, secretions are blocked, the circulation becomes restricted, the normal functions can no longer be sustained and the body must find another way out. The leucocytes and lymphocytes now appear on the scene to avert serious danger. The body has several options of defence and if the normal way of dealing with infection is not open, it will find another one to ward off the greatest danger, suppuration of the antrum or sinus being just one way of preventing worse developments.

You can usually recognise this complication by a copious discharge of pus from the affected side of the nose. Acute throbbing and pulsating pains in the upper jaw or forehead, depending upon which cavities are afflicted, often accompany the discharge. In chronic cases the pain may be absent and besides the one-sided discharge only hoarseness may point to sinusitis. Merely syringing the cavities will not get rid of the causes. In addition to specific natural remedies, other measures to draw the infection away must be employed. *Onion poultices*, while perhaps not very pleasant, are simple and effective. Chop an onion finely, place it between two pieces of gauze and bind it on the neck before retiring, leaving it overnight. The two homoeopathic remedies *Hepar sulph. 4x* and *Cinnabaris 4x* will help eliminate the pus and heal the affected part. This treatment usually makes syringing superfluous. For a chronic case, and when the trouble originated with a cold, *hot compresses* and *baths* always soothe and alleviate the pain.

Sore Throats

It is a fact that a sore throat, if not correctly treated or completely cured, can have serious consequences that may do permanent injury to one's health. This particularly applies to severe sore throats such as those caused by Vincent's angina, laryngitis or tonsillitis. The toxins of an improperly treated sore throat can cause an inflammation of the middle ear, rheumatic fever and arthritis. They can also be responsible for a partial paralysis of the cardiac valves, which leaves the patient with a permanent cardiac defect. This was brought to my attention not too long ago by one of my patients, a healthy woman who had given birth to several children without any complications, until the day that a neglected sore throat (tonsillitis) put an end to her good health. The doctors shared my belief that her cardiac defect was a direct result of the presence of tonsillitis toxins in her body. To make matters worse, her stomach and intestines had been affected by the allopathic drugs she had been taking. So today, this once vigorous and healthy woman is a very sick person.

Therefore, do not overlook a bad sore throat or neglect to treat it properly, for if you do, you will lay yourself open to serious consequences and relapses.

It is also dangerous to go outdoors too soon after tonsillitis when the weather is bad. You should know that tonsillitis may take a more drastic course in a low pressure system, that is, at the beginning of a warm air current. Someone suffering from calcium deficiency or a weak lymphatic system is more prone to this type of sore throat. This emphasises the need to always have a diet rich in calcium and avail oneself of the benefits of a calcium complex, such as Urticalcin.

Careful and thorough treatment of the throat and tonsils will render bacterial toxins harmless and prevent them from spreading through the body. However, it is also important to persevere and not stop the treatment as soon as the acute symptoms have passed.

Never regard tonsillitis as a harmless complaint; it is an infection that can have serious consequences. It appears that many people still do not realise how dangerous a sore throat can be; otherwise they would be more concerned about obtaining immediate treatment for, and a complete cure of, this infection. One mother wrote to me: 'My seventeen-year-old daughter had a bad sore throat eight weeks ago and she developed an inflammation of the middle ear from it.' This is the sort of letter received all too frequently. Heart problems, pericarditis and nephritis often follow in the wake of a bad sore throat or tonsillitis. This all goes to show that the toxins are far from harmless and that this complaint should receive more attention than it is usually given.

The Treatment of Sore Throats

The first measure to be taken at the sign of a sore throat is to paint the throat two or three times a day with *concentrated whey (Molkosan)*, since this may actually arrest a case of incipient tonsillitis. Whey will destroy the germs on the surface of the tonsils and to some extent even in the crypts and channels of the throat. It will prevent the formation of toxins and help the body's own defences to advance to the infected area. In fact, this condensed, natural lactic acid product made from whey has proved far superior to the strongest chemical disinfectants and is free from the harmful properties the latter may possess.

If this remedy is not handy, the *pimpernel root (Pimpinella saxifraga)* or *imperial masterwort (Imperatoria ostruthium)* fulfils the same purpose if you keep chewing it.

Thorough oral hygiene is essential. Frequent gargling with *salt water* is good, or just suck a *slice of lemon*, unsweetened, every day, for lemon juice is equally effective. Make sure that the lemon skin has not been sprayed with pesticide. In chronic cases the use of special equipment may be necessary to clean the tonsils regularly and paint them afterwards with whey concentrate. *Dr Roeder's Apparatus*, for example, is designed to suck the pus off the tonsils.

Additionally, however, it is necessary to combat the disease from within the body by taking a calcium preparation (*Urticalcin*) and *Lachesis 12x*. For external treatment apply *cabbage leaf* and *clay poultices* in alternation. The clay for the poultice should be made into a paste using *horsetail tea*. Poultices of *grated horseradish* mixed with *soft white cheese (quark)* can also be used; these are stronger and especially effective. Pure horseradish may be too strong, so mix it with soft white cheese or finely grated carrots to reduce the strength. One-third horseradish with two-thirds cheese or carrots will still give you the full healing benefit of horseradish and do the job well. With these treatments a bad sore throat can be cured fast.

If a cough or catarrh follows the throat trouble, take syrup made from raw pine shoots (*Santasapina*) or *ribwort syrup* and *Kali iod. 4x*, besides *Imperatoria*. These harmless remedies prevent the tonsillitis toxins from invading other parts of the body. But if they are already in the blood, it is essential to stimulate the kidneys to greater activity so that the toxins can be eliminated as quickly as possible. While *Solidago* and *kidney tea* are best for this purpose, *sweating cures* support the elimination process; any method of inducing perspiration is suitable, as long as the patient can tolerate the procedure.

A follow-up cure is indispensable to eliminate the toxins completely. This can be achieved by taking *kidney drops*, such as *Nephrosolid*, and *liver drops*. *Steam baths* also help to speed up the excretion of toxins. During the treatment the patient's diet should be low in protein and salt and high in vitamins and minerals. Never shy away from the effort and bother the thorough and careful treatment of a bad sore throat may entail. It will save you the troublesome consequences that often leave a patient with permanent damage.

Hay Fever
It is certainly miserable to suffer from hay fever while those less allergic to pollen take full delight in the beauty of flowers and blossoms. To make things worse, once an attack has started it is

difficult to stop it quickly. In fact, it is generally too late to find relief. In order to check the development of hay fever, it is necessary to begin treatment early, no later than February. If you know that you are susceptible to hay fever attacks you must start treatment in the winter before the trees and flowers begin to bloom.

A treatment consisting of ten subcutaneous homoeopathic injections of *formic acid* and a *herb complex* has brought about relief, as has been confirmed by former sufferers. To ensure a permanent cure, the treatment must be repeated at the beginning of the following year. Moreover, during the entire year do not neglect to take *Urticalcin* regularly. Urticalcin powder also has a good healing effect when drawn up the nose like snuff. Furthermore, the nose should be creamed daily with *Bioforce Cream*, which prevents the mucous membranes from drying out. At the same time take *Galeopsis, Kali iod. 4x* and *Arsen. album 4x*. Also helpful are two or three teaspoons of *honey* taken daily. Make sure that the diet consists of natural wholefoods and stay away from denatured, refined foods. Animal fats are also out of the question. *Pollinosan*, a new homoeopathic medicine made from tropical plants, has already proved to be an effective treatment for hay fever and other allergies.

If you follow this advice and repeat the treatment until the hay fever has completely cleared up, you will gradually get rid of this troublesome allergy and make your life more enjoyable even when the plant world bursts out in blossoms and flowers.

Leucorrhoea and What to Do about It

Today's fashions are responsible for an increasing number of women and girls suffering from leucorrhoea, commonly called the 'whites'. In the past, when women were accustomed to wearing warm clothes in winter, very few experienced this bothersome problem. Thick woollen stockings, warm underwear, loose woollen dresses and good shoes used to provide the necessary warmth, even if there was no central heating in the house and only the living room and kitchen were heated. Today, however, we usually live in overheated rooms and dress as lightly as possible even in winter. Add to this modern way of life our inborn vanity that appeals to our desire for a figure that is slimmer than is advisable for good health, and there you have the origin of colds and their serious consequences. What is more, the hectic pace of our times encourages us to overtax our physical strength and inner resources, and if a person has a weak constitution to start with, colds and their consequences are an inevitable result.

Leucorrhoea is the result of catarrh (inflammation of the mucous membranes) and, as such, we should make every effort to cure it properly. This is of great importance because it is an uncomfortable condition and weakens the body. As with any other inflammation of the mucous membranes, we should persevere in the treatment until it has completely cleared up. Indeed, we should never neglect to treat the mucous membranes whenever there is something wrong with them. They are under constant threat from external influences and bacterial infections and a constant fight is called for. The mucous membranes are only able to withstand the attacks of invading harmful bacteria by calling the friendly ones to the rescue. The harmful bacteria must be killed, if at all possible. That is why we have mouth bacteria, for example, which are there to attack harmful invaders.

The mucous membranes of the genital organs in a healthy woman normally secrete lactic acid, which prevents the development of harmful bacteria. But if the production of lactic acid is insufficient, resistance against micro-organisms is considerably diminished, and it is easy for an inflammation to develop.

In this respect it is important to watch your diet, since inadequate nutrition may slow down and weaken the growth of lactic acid bacteria. As a result, invading bacteria soon gain a foothold and the body has to adopt a different defence strategy. It will secrete mucus and dispatch leucocytes and lymphocytes to combat the foreign invaders, all in an effort to expel them from the body. And that is the so-called 'whites', a white or yellowish discharge of mucous material from the vagina.

Knowing the origin of the trouble, we can successfully fight back if we use lactic acid. Women afflicted by this condition would do well to use *Molkosan* (whey concentrate), since its natural lactic acid content has indeed proved its worth as a disinfectant and antiseptic douche. Douching with an infusion of *camomile* and 3–4 soupspoons of *Molkosan* added to every litre (2 pints) of liquid, has given good results. The natural lactic acid in Molkosan is able to replace the lactic acid the mucous membranes are lacking. The treatment with Molkosan is therefore a biological method. Since the patient usually has a deficiency of calcium salts as well, it would also be wise to take the biological calcium preparation *Urticalcin*.

Another essential feature of the treatment of leucorrhoea is to take regular *sitz baths* prepared with herbs; the baths should last between half an hour to an hour, with the water being kept at a constant temperature of 37 °C (98.6 °F) adding hot water from time to time. Patients who follow this treatment will feel much better after a relatively short time. So take a sitz bath prepared with *thyme* or *juniper*, using *Juniperosan*, two or three times a week. These sitz baths will stimulate the circulation in the abdomen, which is an important factor in their effectiveness.

Also effective are the homoeopathic remedies *Sepia 4x–6x, Calc. carb., Pulsatilla, Ferr. phos., Kali sulph.* and *Calc. phos.*, in addition to the biological calcium preparation Urticalcin.

As leucorrhoea often affects the kidneys, although these will benefit from the sitz baths, they will need further stimulating. This can be achieved by taking a mild *kidney tea* together with *Nephrosolid*. It is understandable that leucorrhoea can have a weakening effect on the nerves. Hence we will want to build them up by regularly taking *Avenaforce* in alternation with *Ginsavena. Neuroforce* tablets are also excellent for this purpose.

On the other hand, I would advise against the use of strong antibiotic medicines. Why? Because these drugs destroy not only the harmful but also the useful and necessary bacteria, making the restoration of bacterial flora more difficult. If we want to cooperate with nature we must not first destroy its workings. Rather, we should take care and refrain from drastic medicines that destroy the beneficial organisms we want to build up, for experience shows that harmful bacteria recuperate faster than the useful ones.

The treatment of leucorrhoea, usually a very stubborn condition, requires patience, perseverance and absolute regularity in taking medication. There is no other way to achieve a permanent cure. At the same time, it is very important to avoid any detrimental habits and influences even after the cure has been achieved.

Colds

During a Change of Season

It is not unusual to hear complaints about chills and colds when seasonal changes occur. Most people accept them as unavoidable, not realising that it is really up to us to do something about them. Women seem to be more prone to catching colds, since they are usually more reluctant to exchange their elegant thin stockings for warm or, better still, thick knitted woollen ones. It would indeed be most appropriate to limit the use of elegant apparel in favour of warmer clothing, or even to put it away altogether for the duration of the winter.

The change of season is the most difficult time for the body, for it is still accustomed to the warm summer and unprepared for the sudden onset of cold weather. That is why we must protect the body with whatever clothing is appropriate for the weather. Most important of all, *keep the feet warm* and, as I have pointed out already, woollen stockings and a pair of good, warm shoes are indispensable if you wish to discourage colds. It is an accepted fact that warm feet and a cool head are necessary for good health. As long as the feet are warm we will hardly ever catch a cold, because the feet are the indicators of the general warmth of the body.

People in sedentary occupations suffer to a much greater extent from cold feet than those whose work allows them plenty of activity and movement. If you have inherited sluggish circulation, you will feel the cold even more; even overheated rooms will not seem to be warm enough for you. Of course, heating does not make up for the lack of exercise and unless the feet are covered with warm stockings and adequate shoes, they will be cold. Moreover, if you leave an overheated room inadequately clothed and go out into the cool, damp air, the body will react to this drastic drop in temperature and become chilled, with an adverse effect on the mucous membranes. And there you have the best precondition for the development of the germs that cause colds, coughs, head colds, catarrh, pneumonia and other infections. So, never seek to make up for a lack of body heat by overheating the rooms; instead, wear warm clothing, take some *exercise* and try to improve the circulation. Once we become used to the cold, we will be much less susceptible to colds.

You can see that it is not at all surprising that we need to be much more careful during the change of seasons than in the depths of winter, since we become chilled much more quickly when the body is still attuned to the warmth of sunny autumn days. Therefore, do not be tempted to sit down to your work in the morning without having taken some vigorous exercise previously. Do not despise the idea of making your own bed or tidying up your room in the morning. Even this exercise will warm you up. Again, do not just hop in the car or let the bus or train take you to your place of work. It is much better for you if you can walk or bicycle to work. If you live in an area where snow falls, enjoy the new day by shovelling snow in the fresh air. You will afterwards appreciate the warmth of your room, and it is true that brain work is much easier after brisk exercise and *deep-breathing*, which invigorates and promotes good circulation. You can also warm up in a natural way by doing early morning exercises and deep-breathing in front of an open window, and by giving yourself a good brush massage. Exhaling vigorously rids the body of waste gases and deep inhalation saturates the lungs with oxygen. This is particularly important in discouraging the conditions that favour colds.

If you do have a tendency to catch colds, make sure to eat plenty of foods rich in calcium, because the body is more susceptible when it lacks calcium; especially during the change of seasons, take a biological calcium preparation (*Urticalcin*) as well. The veins should not be overlooked either, so that the circulation remains unimpaired. Heed this advice and you will acquire more resistance to the common cold and related afflictions.

Vitamin and Calcium Deficiencies

Why is it that some people catch cold when travelling on a bus or a badly heated train, when they are probably also exposed to a draught, whereas other passengers remain totally unaffected? In answer to this question we could say that some people may have better blood circulation than others. But there may be other factors involved, because susceptibility to infection varies greatly from one person to another. The germs that can cause a cold or catarrh are often already present in the mucous membranes. All it needs is for the body to become chilled and the virus is ready to attack. The result is a cold.

Of course, we usually do not take this bothersome inflammation of the mucous membranes quite so seriously, and although we may feel uncomfortable, and often rather depressed, we are not inclined to give in and interrupt our work routine. In fact, many people, for example in Europe, have acquired an inborn immunity. No one dies of a cold anymore, do they? On the contrary, the very thought makes us smile, for who could be so weak that a mere infection of the mucous membranes could kill him? In truth, this kind of reasoning is actually quite mistaken. You may be surprised to learn that when the Eskimos succumbed to the cold virus brought to them by the Americans some years ago, many of them died, even though they were well used to cold weather. In spite of their strength, their bodies had little immunity to resist the strange and unexpected infection.

Our acquired immunity cannot completely protect us from colds either if the body lacks vitamins, for example. Calcium deficiency, a low calcium level, is another important factor. Furthermore, we have to look out for signs of exhaustion. Heavy demands on our energies are closely connected with a greater consumption of vitamins and calcium. Should circumstances require us to overtax our physical energies, we would need more vitamins and calcium to protect ourselves from catching colds than would be necessary if the body were rested.

The various ways in which we can build up our resistance to colds are dealt with below.

Foods that Build Up Resistance to Colds

Foods rich in *calcium* should be on your menu without fail. Eat carrots every day. Include kohlrabi (turnip cabbage) tops in your diet when they are in season; serve similar vegetables where kohlrabi is not grown. Celery leaves and roots (celeriac), white turnips, swedes, parsnips and the like are also good because of their high calcium content. So too are all kinds of fruits, nuts and seeds. Include plenty of figs, raisins, Brazil nuts, almonds, pecans and pine kernels in the diet. This diet will help you get through the difficult winter months with better health, until your own garden again produces fresh vegetables, herbs and berries rich in vitamins.

As long as there is no snow it is possible to harvest parsley and watercress to meet the body's needs for *vitamins A and C*. But if you live in a temperate or northern climate, it would be a good idea to sow cress seeds in flower pots or little boxes and raise them on a sunny windowsill. If you sow cress at regular intervals, you will have a constant supply of this healthy vegetable throughout the vitamin-deficient winter months. Every little help we can get will be to our advantage. The importance of foods containing vitamins A and C cannot be overstressed.

Other Remedies to Build Up Resistance

Much good may also be derived from taking natural remedies. Ideally suited for this purpose is *Urticalcin*, a natural calcium supplement of proven worth. Another natural medicine for colds is *Usnea* (larch moss or lichen), which builds up the resistance of the mucous membranes. To combat a susceptibility to catarrh and to alleviate colds, take *Santasapina* or *Drosinula Cough Syrup*.

As a prophylactic for the throat, use *Echinaforce* and *Molkosan*, since *Echinacea* extract counteracts infection and diluted whey used as a gargle disinfects the mouth and throat. If a throat infection is already under way, it is advisable to paint the throat with undiluted Molkosan. Also, massage the chest with *Po-Ho-Salve* every day.

Severe catarrh and even bronchitis may be tackled with *Imperatoria* (imperial masterwort), as it will help in every case. I often recommend to people who like to take walks through the woods and forests, even in winter, to chew *larch* (tamarack) and *pine buds or shoots*, as the sap has a preventative as well as a healing effect.

Guarding against the Consequences of Infectious Diseases

Toxins in the system, which stem from infectious disease, must be eliminated or they will lead to future ill health. A case of mumps that has been neglected or not fully cured can lead to pancreatitis (inflammation of the pancreas) in later life. An inflammation of the middle ear may be a result of suppressed scarlet fever. Improperly treated tonsillitis can give rise to heart trouble, for example inflammation of the heart muscle (myocarditis) or the endocardium (endocarditis), which in turn can lead to valvular defects or even pericarditis, although this is less frequent. The kidneys can suffer too, and rheumatic fever is often the consequence of toxic infiltrations from diseased tonsils. Many other diseases can arise when toxins remain in the body following an infection.

It is therefore most important that every effort be made to ensure the complete excretion of toxins in all cases of infectious disease. The following three main points must be observed:

1. *Elimination through the skin.* The patient should be encouraged to perspire by applying hot packs, taking hot showers etc. The Kneipp treatment might also be used.
2. *Elimination through the kidneys.* This can be encouraged by means of a simple kidney remedy, such as tea made from goldenrod or parsley, or any other natural remedy which acts to stimulate the kidneys. Onion poultices are also effective for this.
3. *Elimination through the bowels.* Fever usually tends to dry up the bowels. To stimulate movement, use simple natural remedies, for example linseed tea, psyllium seed, manna stick tea (*Cassia fistula*), soaked figs or prunes. A diet consisting solely of fruit juice is also excellent. While the infectious disease lasts, it is advisable to refrain from eating protein; nothing but fruit juices and vegetable juices is indicated.

If you pay close attention to these three points, you can avoid the complications often experienced as a result of ineptly treated infectious disease.

The Remarkable Laws of Immunity

Life's constant changeability sometimes presents us with rather unusual questions. For example, is it not strange that, in some parts of the world infectious diseases are declining whereas the death toll from metabolic disorders and other ailments associated with living in an industrialised society is showing a sharp increase? Could this, perhaps, be attributed to our having acquired increased resistance to certain infections? On the other hand, what is it exactly that makes us so vulnerable to metabolic and other disorders? While all this is somewhat puzzling, if we carefully review what experience and observation have taught us, we will find the explanation.

During the time I spent in the Amazon area, an outbreak of measles took the lives of thousands of Indians living there. Yet in Europe and North America, for instance, it is practically unheard of for a child or an adult to die as a result of this disease. Why should that be so? The virus is just as toxic and virulent as ever, but nature is always a step ahead of human wisdom. The layperson as well as the physician should become familiar with the body's inherent defence mechanisms and their capacity to face up to and adapt to new situations, and learn to respect them. Thanks to the wonderful generosity and benevolence of our Creator, these automatic mechanisms or 'laws of nature', given time, are able to produce an effective counterforce to any violent attack by invading organisms and substances. In the beginning a virus causes widespread disaster among people and takes numerous lives, but the very next generation is born with a degree of immunity and after a few more generations the illness has only negligible consequences. The history of tuberculosis provides a good example of this. Only sixty years ago tuberculosis was a major cause of death everywhere. Diphtheria and other infectious diseases, likewise, are no longer the scourge they once were.

Laws We Should All Take Note Of
By looking at the plant kingdom we can see similarities in the working of natural laws, there being the same powerful drive to adapt and produce forces for defence and immunity. As an illustration of this, let us consider our experience with DDT. Some

86

years ago, this chemical could kill all but two species of insects in Switzerland. Today, however, we know of at least forty species that have become immune to DDT. While I was staying in California I observed that it was necessary to keep on increasing the strength and toxicity of insecticides in order to obtain the desired results. The deplorable outcome of this process was that millions of birds and bees died, whilst the insects for which it was intended quickly became immune to the increased doses of poison. A few years ago, a friend of mine in Guatemala told me that an industrial firm near where he kept his beehives started using very potent insecticides, with the unintentional result that his bee population was decimated.

When the biological processes of nature are disturbed by chemicals, the interference is bound to bring about undesirable damage in its wake, yet the innocent victims are rarely given any compensation by those responsible for the losses.

In accordance with the laws of nature, we may presume that in fifty years from now the Amazon Indians will no longer die from measles, since by then they will have developed the immunity which we already have. As long as the Indians retain their traditional life-style and can avoid the detrimental effects of an ever-encroaching civilisation, they will not have to worry about many of our other so-called 'diseases of civilisation' either. The number of deaths resulting from gout, diabetes, obesity, cancer and multiple sclerosis will continue to be negligible among the Indian tribes of the Amazon.

Physicians, biologists and nutritionists who are aware of these dangers advocate a return to a natural way of life and to eating natural wholefoods as a protection against modern diseases. Like a voice crying in the wilderness, they sound the alarm again and again, appealing to us to change our life-style to a more natural one. Notable among them was the late Dr Joseph Evers, who treated thousands of people suffering from multiple sclerosis. They all hoped to find some relief from their hard lot in life. Nonetheless, it would be better to do something about preventing the illness rather than painfully trying to overcome it, because in spite of every effort made and care given, a cure is not always guaranteed. Dr Evers' book, *Gestaltwandel des Krankheitsgeschehens (Changes in the Development of Disease)*, which is published by Karl-Haug-Verlag, is so impressive that even a healthy person, after reading it, will change his life-style and diet without delay and almost subconsciously. Any reasonable person reading the book will take note of the clear and logical arguments presented by this experienced researcher. Dr Evers proves to the reader that nature has a greater share in increasing our life span than the achievements of orthodox medicine.

Why Natural Antibiotics Are Necessary

Building Up Resistance

People who have low resistance and lack antibodies, for example those who suffer from liver disorders, are rendered more susceptible to infectious diseases. Hence the need to take natural antibiotics, which will build up the body's resistance to infections. Of course, it is impossible to avoid every source of infection because we are exposed to them through the food we eat and the air we breathe. City air, especially, is highly polluted and an examination of even one cubic centimetre will reveal thousands of germs, spores and bacteria. Insects can also be responsible for transmitting diseases, flies and mosquitoes being the best-known carriers. So even with the utmost care and caution it is difficult to escape from all the adverse influences surrounding us, but we can make certain that our bodies have enough resistance and sufficient antibodies to withstand pathogenic agents, thus minimising their attacks. Certain plants, especially the medicinal herbs which contain essential oils, as well as some culinary herbs, possess antibiotic properties that ensure resistance to a wide range of germs. This will be discussed shortly, but first we will consider the effectiveness of some of the medical antibiotics, the use of which has become increasingly common in recent years.

Various Antibiotics in Practice

The discovery of such antibiotics as penicillin, streptomycin, auromycin and others which have come on the market has provided us with very potent medicines against bacterial infection. In the case of dangerous tropical diseases they have been instrumental in saving many lives. However, it is unfortunate that they are being used too frequently for the treatment of minor infections (for example a common sore throat or some other simple inflammation) which could be dealt with equally effectively by more harmless remedies.

This is where the danger lies. In the first place, the body accustoms itself to these substances and the germs develop a resistance or immunity to them until, finally, they prove useless in the fight against them when one's life is in danger. Secondly, the constant use of antibiotics, in time, harms and destroys the intestinal flora, the useful bacteria present in the intestines.

Just as certain bacteria in the intestines are necessary for the proper digestion and assimilation of food, so plants need certain bacteria to enable them to flourish as they should. For instance, it is impossible to reap a good crop of soybeans if the soil has not been inoculated with the bacteria symbiotically associated with them, or unless the beans have been grown in that particular soil before. No pine forest could grow without bacteria in the soil either. They are indispensable. A similar necessity exists in the digestive system; it, too, needs certain bacteria. That is the reason why yoghurt is highly recommended for the care of the bowels, preferably yoghurt containing bacteria of the species *Lactobacillus acidophilus*, since it encourages the normal, beneficial flora, while it hinders the harmful one, the putrefactive type, in its development. Lactic acid bacteria are good for us because they get on well with the intestinal bacteria and promote their growth. But if we take any of the various antibiotics on the market – penicillin, streptomycin, auromycin or whatever other names they may have been given – we must be prepared for their damaging effect on the intestinal flora, for it so happens that the bacteria essential to good health are also the most sensitive to drugs. No wonder, then, that the harmful bacteria proliferate and spread in the intestines after these double-edged remedies have been administered, possibly leading to chronic inflammation of the intestines. Once the beneficial bacterial flora has been damaged, the patient will have less resistance than before taking the drugs and germs can gain entrance much more easily.

If the patient then receives further doses of potent antibiotics, the body will no longer respond. In such cases even more conservative treatment may be ineffective, leaving the patient open to the gravest consequences.

Natural Antibiotics
As suggested above, persons who suffer from a liver disorder have to be cared for especially; their resistance needs to be built up with natural antibiotics. Their weakened constitution can thus be strengthened and protected. Of course, this is important not only for liver patients but also for those with weak lungs, cancer and many other crippling diseases.

Many years ago I made some interesting experiments with horseradish, watercress, gardencress and even nasturtiums. I observed that those who ate these regularly became more resistant to diseases, particularly colds and infections. At that time, I can remember how some people laughed at the idea of nasturtiums having any nutritional and remedial value, but in those days I was not able to explain why these plants have such outstanding results. This is also true of various other natural cures. Anyway, having observed the improvement in my patients' conditions, I always continued to use the treatment for their benefit, even though I could not offer any scientific explanation. To my great delight, however, I have since found in modern medical publications the confirmation that my earlier observations and conclusions were indeed correct. The research work of Professor Dr Winter, a medical scientist of Cologne, for example, has established the value of nasturtiums as a part of the diet. The thought of mixing them into a salad no longer elicits the ridicule that I had to bear years ago.

My earlier experiments had shown that the extract from the nasturtium plant was effective in killing insect pests such as aphids and others when sprayed on them. I became convinced that nasturtiums contain a very strong substance, and my assumption has since been proved by scientific research. However, there is still the question in my mind as to whether nasturtiums actually contain other substances which may have an even greater effect than their known antibiotic properties. The lethal effect on insect pests may be due to some other potent substance which science has not yet discovered. It is not only nasturtiums that yield such valuable results; the common watercress has a similar effect, as has been proved by experiments I have made over many years, especially with the cress that grows along the course of the mountain streams in the Engadine Valley in Switzerland. Eat this cress regularly and you will soon notice an improvement in your resistance to colds, catarrh and other infectious diseases.

I have made equally important observations, with even better results, in connection with another plant. Known by the names larch moss or beard moss (*Usnea barbata*), it is a lichen that grows on larch trees and its properties had not previously been analysed when I first became interested in it. During my skiing trips I would always chew some of this lichen. I noticed that deer and chamois enjoyed it too, because where there was deep snow the *Usnea* within the animals' reach had always been nibbled off. Closer investigation has now shown that *Usnea* and certain other lichens are high in carbohydrates and therefore of considerable nutritive value. The animals seem to know this and make good use of the plant as food and, incidentally, of its antibiotic properties which make them resistant to disease. There is no doubt that *Usnea* clears up catarrh. I have seen this confirmed repeatedly. On occasions, after starting out on a tour, I would feel the onset of a sore throat and runny nose. As I went along I would chew *Usnea* and by the time I arrived home again my cold would have disappeared. Such valuable experience urged me to investigate this lichen more closely, and I now use the extract in the prophylactic medicine *Usneasan*.

Observations confirm that if you have a tendency to catarrh or colds, your resistance will be considerably improved by taking this remedy regularly. So why take the risk of using manufactured antibiotics which may inflict unwanted side effects? Why not use the cultivated and wild mountain plants, whose harmless but effective medicinal properties are always present in the right composition and proportions according to the laws of nature?

Why should we subject ourselves to any dangers at all? Natural antibiotics are unlikely to have an adverse effect on the intestinal flora; neither will their regular use make germs more resistant to them. For this reason salads made from watercress, gardencress and nasturtiums are heartily recommended for healthy people as well as for the sick, and especially for cancer patients. Eat them regularly and put them in sandwiches too. Try adding some finely grated horseradish to carrot salad, or the juices can be extracted and taken in small quantities. I also recommend the seasoning salt *Trocomare* because it contains these plants. Use it as a seasoning for sandwiches and salads, and sprinkle it on hot vegetables and soups after cooking in order to avoid destroying its vitamins and minerals. When your health has been restored and you can once more think of skiing or mountaineering, do not forget to look for the lichen *Usnea*. You will find it on the bark of larch trees at an elevation of over 1,000 m (3,000 feet). Chew it while you enjoy your hiking.

Another plant which has the same potent effect is *Petasites officinalis*, the common butterbur. This plant is of special importance to cancer patients. Butterbur is a relatively rare plant, usually found near streams in mountain valleys. As it is too strong to be used in salads or as a herb, if you want to avail yourself of its medicinal value, you will have to take a *Petasites* preparation.

Improving the Value of Raw Food

Many of those people who once mocked the idea of eating 'rabbit food', raw food, are now beginning to realise that there may be something in it after all. The antibiotic properties of food are destroyed by cooking, because many substances in our food are sensitive to heat; these include not merely its vitamin and mineral content but also many other substances needed for our well-being, some of which are yet to be discovered. For the body to receive all the vital substances it needs, everyone should take a certain amount of fresh raw vegetables and fruit. As we are especially interested in the substances that help us to resist infectious diseases, if you have a garden or allotment, whatever its size, make sure to plant gardencress, watercress, nasturtiums and horseradish. Serve these plants raw in salads, chop them finely and add them to soups and stews, or mix them with cottage cheese or quark; they are also good in sandwiches. I have already mentioned that finely grated horseradish adds a refreshing flavour to carrot salad, but it can also be added to other salads. Those of you who have so far rejected carrot salad as too sweet will enjoy it with the pleasant flavour of horseradish. At the same time you will be administering natural antibiotics.

For the benefit of all who advocate health from herbs and natural foods, especially raw foods, and in defence of their convictions, let me quote the long-standing German proverb, 'You might go further and not fare so well.'

Looking After your Health – the Best Prevention against Respiratory Diseases

Various Causes

To my astonishment, when travelling abroad, I have encountered a great deal of tuberculosis even in lands which have the best climatic conditions for good health. I was amazed that even Greece, a country with an abundance of sunshine, has had to fight this disease. In Holland too, particularly in the small offshore islands, many people are affected. Doctors are probably right in blaming the damp climate of the low-lying countries, although living in such a climate does not necessarily mean that weak lungs cannot be avoided. Other factors must share the blame for such disorders, for instance a one-sided diet, especially one consisting almost exclusively of fish. Anyone who is sufficiently informed about the cause of a disease can take care to prevent it and this is clearly a wiser course to take than waiting for a disease to strike and then trying to cure it. The following observations and hints are therefore primarily intended for those who are healthy, but they will also benefit the less fortunate to improve and possibly cure their condition.

In the first place, what you eat is of the utmost importance. This has been proved by experience gained in every part of the world. It is astonishing that people living in the healthiest mountain regions, for example the Swiss Alps, where outsiders go to be cured, may actually contract TB themselves. Some time ago I met the warden of a ski chalet who had contracted pulmonary tuberculosis in spite of the fact that he had spent whole winters at a height of over 1,800 m (6,000 feet). However, the cause was obvious: his diet consisted of too much protein, too much canned food and too many unhealthy items containing refined white flour and white sugar. The bad air in the chalet also contributed to his illness. In those days skis still had to be waxed and the fumes from melted wax naturally increased the poisons already in the stale air. Moreover, in a misguided effort to save fuel, the windows were hardly ever opened. Yet fresh air is an absolute necessity for good health.

Then again, we have to build up our immunity if we are to resist respiratory diseases, for we cannot always avoid coming in contact with infection. Research specialists are probably correct in their assertion that it is unusual to find a person in Europe who, at one time or another, has not had a mild tubercular infection that could have triggered the full-blown disease if he had not had sufficient resistance or immunity. That is why our first great task is to acquire this immunity.

These observations emphasise that the best way to prevent disease is to assure good health. How can this be achieved? By putting the following suggestions into practice. First, a natural health-food diet is essential; then we need plenty of light, fresh air, sunshine, exercise and deep-breathing. The more natural your way of life and your diet, the less time spent cooped up in small rooms, and the more you use your free time to breathe and move around in the fresh air and natural light, the less you will be susceptible to disease. Whatever else you do, these rules are basic for your health and well-being.

Adequate Nutrition

It is important that your diet be made up of foods that are rich in calcium and vitamins. You should eat plenty of salads, including, for example, white and green cabbage, carrots, beets and all greens; these are the best sources of vitamins, minerals and calcium. With regard to fruits, berries, particularly organically grown strawberries, are a rich source of calcium. This important mineral is discussed in greater detail on pages 100–1.

It is equally important to eat wholefoods and organically grown foods, for example, wholegrain or wholemeal bread and plenty of dishes made from whole wheat, whole rye and brown rice. If sugar is used at all, it should be unrefined, raw brown cane sugar, never white. Honey, grape sugar, raisins, currants and other sweet dried fruits are even better than brown sugar, which retains only part of the original goodness found in the raw sugar cane juice. Natural sugar is quickly changed into glycogen. In fact, even a weak liver is able to digest fruit sugar.

Fats, too, have to be chosen with care. Do not use kidney fat and lard, other animal fat or hardened fat, or margarine made with these fats. Instead, use unrefined oils, fresh unsalted butter, almonds and nuts. Be sure to go very easy on seasonings; use table salt as little as possible. Hot spices such as pepper and nutmeg should also be avoided, if possible. It is better to season your food with savory, thyme, marjoram, basil, coriander, in other words all the popular garden or kitchen herbs. Yeast extract (*Herbaforce* and *Plantaforce*) is a wholesome flavouring since it contains the vitamins of the B complex. Gravies and sauces seasoned with yeast extract taste like meat gravy and are welcome additions to a meal.

Another important hint is to avoid eating fruit and vegetables together at the same meal. Keep them apart and you will be able to avoid fermentations in the bowels, hence stomach or intestinal gas or wind. Have fruit and wholegrain or wholemeal bread, crispbread or flake bread in the morning and evening. Together with this, have some honey, butter and, if possible, a fruit muesli with various berries or malaceous fruits (those with pips, for example apples) according to what is in season. Stone fruits, such as plums, apricots and peaches, are likely to disagree with most people unless eaten in small quantities. For lunch, eat brown rice, potatoes and cereals, with steamed vegetables and plenty of raw salads. Cut back on fried food. If you must have meat, choose veal and beef rather than pork, sausages and processed meats. Remember, too, that instead of frying, grilling is by far the better method of preparing meat for the table.

Take *Urticalcin* as a calcium supplement. Silica can be easily supplied by the hemp nettle (*Galeopsis*). To increase immunity and resistance to respiratory diseases *Usneasan* has proved invaluable. This remedy is made from lichen (*Usnea barbata*, also known as larch or beard moss) which grows on alpine coniferous trees. Its lichen acids combined with other remedial substances have proved to be very helpful. *Petasites*, made from butterbur, and *Viscum album*, from mistletoe, are also effective remedies with tonic properties. Other herbs and plants suitable for promoting resistance are mentioned in the section on natural antibiotics (see pages 89–91).

Skin Care and Other Precautions

The body's self-healing powers can be assisted greatly by proper skin care. Every day brush the skin vigorously until it turns a rosy pink colour. Afterwards apply a good oil, for example *St John's wort oil* or another skin care oil containing this ingredient. If these are unobtainable, you can use a small amount of a good grade of unrefined olive oil. It suffices to apply the oil lightly every second or every third day.

You should also take care so as to avoid cold feet. If they do get cold, take warm foot baths, massage the feet or help to warm them up by other means. Another important body function that should be given close attention is regular bowel movement. In cases of constipation, take a tablespoon of freshly ground *linseed* mornings and evenings. For really persistent constipation use *Linoforce*, a simple and reliable natural laxative. On the other hand, diarrhoea is not a good thing either, since it drains the body of energy. Two of the simplest remedies for diarrhoea are raw, dry *oat flakes* or *Tormentavena*. The latter has tormentil as its principal ingredient, with oat juice (*Avena sativa*) added for a beneficial effect on the nerves. Intestinal disturbances and fermentations can often be relieved and prevented by thorough mastication of the food we eat. So remember to eat slowly and to chew your food properly so that it becomes well mixed with saliva. This is absolutely essential for good health.

The Importance of Joy and Correct Breathing

There is no doubt that fresh mountain air has a favourable effect on our health and those who are fortunate enough to be able to spend their holidays in the mountains should take every advantage of it. Alternatively, if you are unable to visit the mountains, you may go to the seaside, where the air is not bad either, as long as it is unpolluted. The main thing is to get away from factories and busy roads.

Let me here draw your attention to the advice given in the sections 'Happiness Means Health' (see pages 624–32) and 'Breathing Means Life', (see pages 577–82). A positive mental attitude acts as a preventative to illness, signifying half the cure so to speak. For this reason it is good if the doctor keeps a careful eye on his patient's mental disposition, so that he can discuss this important factor with him. Moreover, proper breathing exercises contribute a great deal to the patient's improvement. Every nature-oriented doctor will appreciate the importance of these natural preventative measures and healing factors, knowing that health is not primarily a matter of taking medicines. He will thus be able to share in the patient's delight when the recovery is complete.

Asthma
Paroxysms of difficult breathing are one of the many signs of asthma. It is important to know that there are three different kinds of this disease, because if we want to select the correct method of treatment we must differentiate between nervous asthma, bronchial asthma and cardiac asthma. The symptoms must be carefully analysed and considered before carrying out the appropriate treatment.

Nervous Asthma (Asthma nervosum)
If your nervous system is very delicate, with a tendency to tension, and you suffer from asthma, it may well be that the cause is your weak nerves. In this case it will be clear that in order to cure this form of asthma it will first be necessary to treat the nerves.

Bronchial Asthma
Bronchial asthma is different from nervous asthma in that it is mainly triggered by certain climatic conditions. A change in environment generally brings about the desired cure. Living by the sea, where the air contains iodine, usually has a positive effect and asthma attacks will often disappear. High altitude often proves to be equally beneficial. An elevation of 900 m (2,800 feet) generally suffices, although sometimes an elevation of 1,000–1,400 m (3,600–4,500 feet) may be necessary to overcome the problem. The third alternative is the hot, dry air of the desert, which in many cases has helped to relieve asthmatic discomfort.

It is also possible that the spasms are caused by pollen in the air. This 'seasonal asthma' is similar to hay fever, which also results from sensitivity to pollen, an allergic reaction. If your domestic situation permits you to move to a different climatic zone you should do so, since a change of climate, together with the appropriate natural remedies, can lead to an eventual cure of bronchial asthma. Although a patient may be able to find suitable employment in an area where the climate would be more suitable, he may find it difficult to uproot himself from familiar surroundings and leave relatives and friends for a strange place, or his own family may be reluctant to move. It would, however, be a great pity if the patient could not receive the necessary support to move to a climate where he would find relief from his ailment.

Once a person has moved, if the attacks do not recur after a year or two, he can then consider moving back to his former home without misgivings. As a rule, once the asthma has been cured it is not likely to return if the person decides to live again in the area where it first occurred. Young asthmatics, especially, should be given this opportunity, since it can make a significant improvement to their well-being.

If, however, the bronchial asthma is a result of an old, improperly treated lung condition, it will be more difficult to obtain a successful cure. This is yet another reason why chronic conditions of the respiratory organs should be avoided at all costs. Negligence and indifference are dangerous. Such illnesses should be treated the moment they first arise and the treatment continued until a complete cure has been achieved, or else they may lead to bronchial asthma that is extremely difficult to cure.

TREATMENT WITH MEDICINES AND PHYSICAL THERAPY
Drugs used in the treatment of bronchial asthma are mainly antispasmodics. It is interesting to note that a patient who has been promised a cure does indeed feel better and remains free from attacks for quite some time after a course of simple novocaine injections. This goes to show that the patient's condition can be favourably influenced by the skilful use of psychotherapy. Incidentally, homoeopathic formic acid can be used instead of novocaine. As an alternative, give some other neurotherapeutic treatment.

Strong asthma tablets can bring about the desired relief in an emergency, but their long-term use is not recommended. These tablets contain ephedrine (extracted from an African plant) plus atropine, or an extract from thorn apples (jimson weed), as well as other potent ingredients. While the body may react favourably to these strong medicines, a complete cure is not obtained and, what is worse, the patient also runs the risk of becoming dependent on these drugs. That is why homoeopathic remedies are to be preferred. The following have proved excellent and should be selected according to the specific needs of the patient: *Arsen. alb. 6x–30x, Nux vomica 6x–20x, Zinc. valerianicum 4x, Antimon. sulph. auratum 4x* and a *Belladonna* preparation of high potency.

Among the herbal remedies, a preparation containing an extract from *Petasites officinalis* (butterbur) has proved effective. It can be taken in the form of drops, *Petadolor* tablets or, in especially stubborn cases, *Petaforce* capsules. These herbal antispasmodics are most reliable and, if administered over a long period of time, often give the most amazing positive results without any side effects at all. Our asthma drops *Asthmasan, Drosinula Cough Syrup* and *Kali iod. 4x* have also proved their worth in cases of bronchial asthma, congestion of the lungs and as antispasmodic remedies.

In addition to these remedies and positive psychological orientation, physical therapy has its place in the treatment of asthma. Of importance are *Schlenz baths*, hot and cold *foot baths* in alternation, *cold water treatment* according to Louis Kuhne, *brush massages, mustard packs* and *mud packs* on the chest. *Acupuncture* has also been reported as beneficial in cases of asthma, provided that the practitioner is highly skilled in performing this intricate form of treatment.

Cardiac Asthma

Even though cardiac asthma has the same main characteristics as bronchial asthma, no abnormalities of the bronchial passages can be detected. Cardiac asthma is the result of a weak heart. If the left half of the heart is affected, this means an accumulation of blood in the lung. Should the right half be affected, the result is poor blood circulation in the lungs, which in turn causes a decrease in the exchange of gases.

The face of a person suffering from cardiac asthma has a bluish tinge, and breathing is difficult when engaging in the slightest physical activity. As soon as the problem has been diagnosed, treatment with cardiac remedies and medicines that influence the vascular system should begin. Instead of medicines containing digitalis, which tend to accumulate in the body, it is recommended that *Convallaria* (lily of the valley) be taken, in conjunction with *sea squill*, also known as *sea onion (Scilla maritima)*. In order to strengthen the myocardium a hawthorn preparation, such as *Crataegisan*, is most beneficial. *Aesculaforce* and *Aesculus hipp.*, both medicines that stimulate the circulation, when taken with a calcium preparation such as *Urticalcin*, promote recovery. In any case, it is advisable to diagnose the cause of the disease and then proceed to treat each patient according to his medical requirements as well as applying the appropriate form of physical therapy.

Important Factors in the Treatment of Pulmonary Diseases

It is strange that orthodox medicine still does not pay enough attention to the basic healing factors in the treatment of lung patients. Much can be achieved by rest, light, air and sun, and their value has been proved beyond doubt. The words 'Lift up your eyes to the mountains whence your help comes' are inscribed over the entrance of a sanatorium in Arosa, Switzerland. They are an honest admission by orthodox medicine that it is primarily the air – mountain air in particular – which provides a cure for lung diseases.

Another factor must not be forgotten either, and that is nutritional therapy. The body must be supplied with the substances it lacks before it can attempt regeneration. First on the list are foods rich in calcium and vitamins – these are indispensable. Raw, freshly pressed carrot juice or raw, finely grated carrots, the freshly pressed juice of grapes, oranges and grapefruit, and other wholesome juices, should be taken slowly in little sips and well insalivated. If you observe this advice, the fruit acid will cause no unpleasant gastric disturbance.

Plenty of fresh raw vegetables should be served daily. Always dress salads with lemon juice, never with vinegar.

The intake of protein foods must be reduced. On the other hand, natural culinary herbs that stimulate the appetite are recommended. An easily assimilated calcium preparation is essential. I have always seen excellent results when patients have taken the calcium complex *Urticalcin* and herbs rich in silica, such as *Galeopsis*. In this connection *Usnea*, the moss or lichen found on larch trees, deserves special mention. The animals of the forest make good use of its tonic properties for the lungs and we, too, should take it to combat weakness of the respiratory organs. If you find it difficult to chew the fresh lichen, take it regularly as a tea or, for even greater effect, take the fresh plant extract, *Usneasan*. Plants like *Usnea* or *Galeopsis* are, in a sense, not medicinal but nutritional plants and bear out Hippocrates' principle that 'Food shall be medicine and medicine shall be food'. In reality, then, remedies from the plant kingdom are curative foods. Do not forget cod-liver oil or cod-liver oil emulsions; these are of great benefit and to be recommended if the patient can take them.

Furthermore, it is of great importance to influence the patient psychologically. The glandular functions must be in good order, and this depends a great deal on his state of mind.

It is also important to stimulate the skin. Give the body a daily brush massage and afterwards apply a good skin oil containing natural herbal ingredients that stimulate the function of the skin.

That good bowel movement is necessary should go without saying. Indeed, proper functioning of the bowels and the kidneys is essential for the cure of practically any disease.

Lung patients who take this simple advice to heart will benefit greatly from their rest cures and will surprise their doctors by their speedy recovery. Always remember that it is important to try and rectify deficiencies and weaknesses anywhere in the body and not just one organ. It is then understandable why recovery is faster than usual.

Calcium

Much has been said and written about the significance of calcium for our bodies. Calcium is one of the most important minerals in the human body, and the most plentiful in it. Without calcium, neither our bones, our teeth, nor the greater number of our body cells could exist. Hence the need to eat plenty of foods containing it. What is more, calcium plays an important part in our body's resistance to infectious diseases, especially diseases affecting the respiratory organs. Children who lack calcium are prone to infectious diseases, quickly develop swollen glands and are unable to ward off primary infections. When the body is deficient in calcium there is a constant struggle to fight sickness. Nature provides us with a good comparative example. Meadows that are short of lime always have a quantity of moss growing in them. If, however, you give them a lime dressing, you neutralise the acidity of the soil and the moss disappears. Parasitic plants thrive in calcium-deficient soil. From this we can draw a parallel to what goes on in the human body. Where there is a calcium deficiency all sorts of diseases, especially the infectious kinds, will thrive. Of course, this fact has been known for a long time and various calcium preparations are on the market. But all those phosphoric, carbonic and lactic acid combinations of calcium have actually failed to serve their purpose. Calcium deficiency continues to be a problem.

Many years ago I discussed this subject with a well-known chemist in Davos, Switzerland. This man had great experience in the manufacture of calcium milk and other calcium preparations and declared that he had been swamped with orders from doctors since it became common knowledge that calcium milk played an important part in the treatment of pulmonary diseases. Yet he pointed out that this remedy was of little or no use, for in order to be assimilated, the calcium would have to come from a natural source, from plants. Now this chemist, a professional man of the 'old school', told me this years ago, yet he was evidently a man who could think 'biologically', or 'organically'. And it was his sincere conviction that strengthened me in my resolve to obtain calcium in a form that the body would be able to assimilate, so that calcium deficiency could finally be overcome.

This resolve led me to produce calcium from plants, especially from the fresh green stinging nettle. I can say that I succeeded in manufacturing a calcium preparation the body can readily absorb. A well-balanced combination with other triturated biochemical calcium salts has led to the calcium complex *Urticalcin*, which has given thousands of people exactly what could be expected from a natural organic calcium preparation. However, let me point out that nobody should come to depend on any preparation, for the purpose of the advice given in this book is to make the reader aware of what he can do to help himself without them.

How to Overcome Calcium Deficiency
I would like to tell you now how to go about overcoming calcium deficiency. First of all we have in mind the children who are born with a deficiency, but there are also many adolescents and even older people who suffer from a lack of calcium and need help.

Infants and small children should be given natural foods. Do not forget to include plenty of gruel made from unpolished *brown rice*, for it contains much goodness, especially in its bran, which infants need. Naturally, there is no better food than breast milk and no healthy mother should pass up the privilege of breast-feeding her baby, if it is at all possible. She should, by the way, begin to take particular care of her health even before contemplating motherhood.

As soon as the child starts on supplementary or bottle food, natural brown rice is the best foundation for good health. From this time on, *carrot juice*, which is rich in calcium and minerals and easily digested, can also be given. Later, *almond milk* with *fruit juices* may be introduced. Be sure to obtain healthy milk, whether it is cow's or sheep's milk. Unfortunately, milk is not necessarily 100 per cent safe: in many places the cows are tubercular and judging by the way they are imprisoned continuously in stalls, it is not surprising that they become sick. Good and safe milk can only come from cows living on pasture and under natural, healthy conditions. Sheep's milk is better than cow's milk, and if you are able to obtain it from free-roaming sheep, you will have the best milk possible for your small children. It will be richer in calcium and have greater nutritional value because of the animals' healthy outdoor life. Goat's milk can also be given occasionally, but not on a regular basis. You will find more useful information in the entry on 'Infant Nutrition' (see pages 39–41).

It is important that growing children, indeed all of us, eat wholefoods and avoid white sugar and white flour products as much as possible. Food should be eaten in the same condition that nature or the Creator made it grow. In wholefoods you will find all the vitamins and minerals in the right proportions and combinations. Always bear in mind the advice to go back to natural foods and avoid those artificial refined products that human commercial greed has imposed upon us. While the manufacturer profits, the body suffers. Of course, the damage does not necessarily show up from one day to the next. The consequences of deficiencies, chemical additives and other aspects of convenience foods take time to manifest themselves, but sooner or later most people fall victim to them. Whether it is cancer, increased susceptibility to infection and disease, low resistance, a debilitation of the body, or any other known or yet unknown ailment affecting the central nervous system, they are always to be reckoned with. These frightening consequences of man's ignorance and greed are brought about by our lack of resistance, which depends on a healthy body resulting from a natural way of life and natural nutrition.

SAUERKRAUT WITH CALCIUM POWDER
If your body lacks calcium you will appreciate my special instructions on how to prepare your own home-made and excellent calcium preparation. As a matter of fact, if you live in the country this should be quite easy to do.

First of all, I realise that not everyone is familiar with sauerkraut, made from white cabbage, or knows how to prepare it. For this reason I have given the recipe later on in this book (see pages 546–7). When making your own sauerkraut, be careful to use the minimum of salt but do not hesitate to add herbs and spices such as marjoram, thyme, juniper berries and especially mustard seed, which help to preserve the sauerkraut. Sauerkraut is very high in calcium and has great medicinal value when eaten raw.

In order to increase the calcium content and actually make a calcium preparation, mix *ground eggshells* with the sauerkraut; add half a soupspoon of eggshell powder to each kilogram (2.2 lbs) of sauerkraut. You can also use washed *oyster shell powder* instead (obtainable from chemist shops or drugstores). Mix the powder with the shredded raw cabbage in the same way you would do with the herbs. The process of fermentation will then produce natural calcium lactate, which is readily assimilated. If you prepare a small wooden barrel of this 'calcium sauerkraut' every year, you will find that, by eating it regularly, in a year or two there will be no calcium deficiency in your family.

If you buy the sauerkraut in a health food store instead of making if yourself, presuming it was made with very little salt, sprinkle a teaspoonful of one of the two powders over the sauerkraut, mix it well and let it stand for another day before eating it raw. Even though this quick method of making a calcium preparation is not quite as effective as the first method, the result is still better than proprietary calcium tablets. Incidentally, you can also mix a pinch of eggshell or oyster shell powder into salad dressings if you prepare these with lemon juice. The citric acid will dissolve some of the natural calcium in the shells, making the mineral more easily assimilated.

NETTLES

Stinging nettles are another excellent source of calcium. Gather young nettles in the spring, chop them very finely or put them through a mincer, then mix into a salad. They can also be finely chopped and sprinkled over boiled and mashed potatoes or other dishes that you would normally garnish. No one will even notice that it was not one of the more common garnishes. You can also sprinkle some over soup just before serving, or spinach. It is important, however, not to cook the nettles. In these ways you can obtain your regular supply of nettles, a first-class source of calcium phosphate, vitamin D and other important minerals.

Years have passed since I gave this advice about nettles in my monthly publication *Gesundheits-Nachrichten (Health News)* and

later heard from many Bernese country women who had been
delighted with the way their children responded to nettles. They
said that the children once again had rosy cheeks and seemed to
have recovered their health and resistance – all due to this simple
remedy. So why don't you adopt this inexpensive method of
increasing your calcium intake? Why buy expensive medicines
when there is another way that is open to everyone if only we
make a little effort and give a little thought to the matter? In fact,
doing so will cause less bother than giving the constant attention
and treatment calcium-deficient children need, because there is
always something wrong with them. Calcium deficiency makes
children susceptible to catarrh, with every cold draught posing a
threat. And when an infectious disease goes round they are usually
the first to catch it. That is why prevention is better – and cheaper
– than cure!

The Lesser Known Benefits of Calcium

Everyone knows the importance of calcium as a structural component of our bones and teeth. A low calcium level indicates a calcium
deficiency that will, in time, be detrimental to the teeth and bones.
The effect of this deficiency is especially dangerous in pregnant
women, and generations ago they used to say in parts of Switzerland that every child cost his mother a tooth; in other words,
calcium deficiency was the price a mother had to pay for bearing
a child. We also know that a calcium deficiency in the blood may
bring about tetany-like conditions characterised by cramps and
spasmodic contractions.

However, calcium is not only a building material, but also one
that combines with harmful metabolic wastes, particularly acids,
which are then eliminated through the urine. One example of these
is oxalic acid, which plays a part in the formation of kidney
stones. When combined with calcium it becomes calcium oxalate, a
substance that can be disposed of easily by the kidneys.

An adequate balance of calcium in the body protects one against
scrofula and the tendency to tuberculosis. Doctors are able to tell
us a great deal about this. If the calcium level in our blood is
normal, it can protect us from the harmful effects of radioactive
strontium 90. This discovery, while still new to many of us, is
reassuring, since it is not very difficult to build up our calcium
level. Thus, the reasons for maintaining a normal level of this
vital mineral should be sufficiently clear to make us remember its
importance to our health.

Wholegrain foods, raw vegetables and dairy products are all excellent sources of calcium, and we should make daily use of them. Unfortunately, our body is unable to assimilate calcium contained in water, or in any other inorganic form. That is why we must make sure to obtain organic calcium, that is, calcium of plant origin. Since this important mineral is readily assimilated only in this form, organic calcium alone is to be preferred. But if, in spite of a proper diet, a person still suffers from a deficiency, then regularly taking a biological calcium complex such as *Urticalcin* is indicated and, of course, the need to eat foods rich in calcium is obvious. Urticalcin contains calcium obtained from nettles and is ideal for maintaining a normal calcium level in children as well as adults. Once you have tried this simple and pleasant preparation you will no longer wish to do without its benefits as a natural source of calcium. Those who are in a state of exhaustion, over-worked or whose health is low, so that no remedy seems to do them any good, will be able to improve their general condition by taking Urticalcin. The body will then soon be able to utilise other remedies too. Given that the mineral balance in the body is so important, we should heed the advice given in this section and take great care to ensure that it is achieved and adequately maintained.

Our Blood – a Mysterious Fluid

The Bible tells us that 'the soul is in the blood'. A poet of long ago also sensed the mysterious composition and working of the blood when he called it a very special fluid. He was aware of this long before his assertion was supported through the findings of various research experiments conducted in modern times. Still, it was the declarations made recently by well-known scientists that made me stop and think. They claimed that a single drop of blood reveals everything about the condition of a person's health. However, a proper diagnostic method has yet to be found which can support this assertion. Scientists must first discover this before they can properly evaluate it. The method of blood crystallisation has already taken us one step further and certainly merits our attention. No doubt other methods will be worked out and the time seems near when diseases such as cancer, tuberculosis, rheumatism, gout and many others will be detected in their early stages long before the more obvious symptoms manifest themselves.

Even though the blood has been subdivided into groups, the Rh factor has been discovered, and we know already that the texture of our blood may be either coarse or fine (similar to the skin with its coarse or fine pores), there are many singularities of the blood that remain unknown. Just think of the mysteries surrounding the content and structure of an individual's blood. It is left to the scientists to lift the veil as time goes by.

If the blood, this truly mysterious red fluid of life, had already been sufficiently researched, there would hardly be some 20,000 deaths a year due to blood transfusions in the United States alone. In the future, it is probable that surgeons, having been made aware of the great risks involved in transfusing human blood, will only make use of the much improved and effective non-blood plasma and blood replacements that are now available. Let me also mention that hepatitis, a much feared inflammation of the liver with infectious jaundice, has frequently resulted from blood transfusions. The prevention of serum hepatitis as a consequence of blood transfusions is a problem that has not yet been solved. In more recent times, AIDS too has been passed on through blood transfusions. Considering that even the medical director of an American blood bank has expressed serious concern over the risks involved in transfusions and that many surgeons, as a result of unsatisfactory experiences, prefer to work with substitutes, is there any wonder that the patient should wish to express his personal preference, talk it over with the surgeon and then make his own decision?

How could we possibly know all the secrets of blood, not having had a part in its formation? But to Him who made it, blood is no mystery. He, the caring God and Father who knows what is best, strictly prohibited the consumption of blood to the survivors of the great Flood. Eventually, this command was incorporated into the code of law of God's chosen people. Later still, the governing body of the early Christian Church in the apostle Paul's time chose not to cancel this law, but restated it as being valid and binding upon their members. The law regarding the abstinence from blood has remained valid and applicable for the entire Christian era right down to our own time. Sexual morality is another divine commandment laid down in the Bible and those who respect it are assured of greater protection from AIDS.

If we look closely at these laws, we should find that they are beneficial to our health, whether we realise this or not. The obedient observation of the divine commandments can act only for the protection and good of the individual. The person who refuses to take blood in any form into his body, whether for the sake of his obedience to God's command or for reasons of health, will receive an increasing amount of support and recognition as time goes on and research progresses, confirming the validity of his conviction.

The Lymphatic System – the White Bloodstream

Even though the lymphatic vessels are much longer than all the red blood vessels together, our knowledge of the white bloodstream is still very limited. The lymphatic vessels, which are much finer than those of the red bloodstream, are distributed throughout the entire body. In contrast with the blood, the lymph flows only in one direction and the fluid is returned to the bloodstream after its task is completed. The body can be divided schematically into four parts in the form of a cross, starting at the navel. Each of these four fields more or less corresponds to a lymphatic network, with a centre located at the right and left side of the groin area and in each of the armpit regions. Smaller centres are also located below the lower jaw, at the right and left side. Leading to these centres, the lymph glands form little nodes, which reach their maximum size in the centre itself.

Functions of the Lymphatic System

The lymphatic system is responsible for keeping the body fluids, the blood fluid and cerebrospinal fluid, in order. The total amount of fluid accounts for approximately 60 per cent of our total body weight. But the lymph has yet another important and vital function. Not unlike a police force, the lymph cells (lymphocytes) must combat and destroy all invading organisms that enter and endanger the body tissue. We are referring here to bacteria, which are more or less injurious or dangerous, depending on the type. For example, if you cut yourself, or a rusty nail penetrates the skin, millions of bacteria enter the body through the wound as if through a broken trap door. The fine, outer lymph vessels are perhaps not strong enough to resist the intruders and the bacteria continue their advance into the nodes of a centre. The centre then calls up the defences; the vessels expand and we feel a swelling in the area of the armpit or the groin, for example. The swelling can become as large as a hen's egg. If the lymphocytes, phagocytes, wandering cells, and whatever other names the defence forces may have, cannot handle their task, the lymphatics become inflamed and swollen. They become very sensitive to pressure and can be seen as red lines. This condition is called blood poisoning (septicaemia, toxaemia), even though the toxins are actually still contained in the white bloodstream of the lymphatic system. In fact, if all toxins and bacteria were passed on to the red bloodstream, no one could survive his childhood because of the many poisons that would enter the blood.

The tonsils and the appendix (see below) are also allied to the lymphatic system and have the job of cleansing the body and destroying germs. Both can be regarded as filtering systems, which explains why we should never have them removed unless it is strictly necessary. Their removal constitutes a weakening of the forces in the fight against harmful bacteria.

In the event that cancer cells escape during a biopsy or because of incomplete removal of malignant tissue in an operation, the lymph generally catches them and the centre harbours them with the intent of destroying them. If the attempt to destroy them fails, these giant cells begin to grow and multiply, and the result is the much feared lymphoadenoma, or Hodgkin's disease (see page 111), a form of cancer of the lymph nodes. That is why surgeons remove all lymph vessels and nodes during a cancer operation, especially in cases of breast cancer.

Another function of the lymph is to absorb emulsified fat and pass it on in small, tolerable quantities to the bloodstream. All so-called antibodies, which ensure immunity against infectious diseases, are formed in the lymphatic system. You can therefore understand how important it is for this system to function properly. Certain disorders of the heart, the kidneys and the blood vessels can be attributed to a partial failure of the lymphatic system.

THE TONSILS AND APPENDIX
Not everyone may know that the tonsils and the appendix possess a well-defined lymphatic network. As they also serve to filter out and destroy bacteria, they may be called sister organs. Since their importance to the body is so great, these organs should not be surgically removed as long as they do their work. Even if something is wrong with them, it would be better to see what could be done with a view to healing them and so keeping them in the body.

THE LYMPH NODES
The lymph nodes are small masses of tissue situated along the course of the lymphatic vessels. Their purpose is to filter out and kill bacteria as well as to neutralise toxins. Should one filtering station prove insufficient, another one will be called upon to help. As the bacteria advance, we notice hard red lines, rope-like and tender, leading to a swelling, for example on the inside of the

elbow. As noted earlier, the swelling may grow to the size of a hen's egg and will become sensitive to pressure. This condition is caused by an accumulation of lymph cells which have become embedded in connective tissues and muscle fibres, presenting the symptoms of blood poisoning. It is possible that in such a case the centre will not be able to cope and will call on the lymphatics in the armpit as well. If the septic injury is in the foot, the patient will feel the tight lymphatic course right along the leg and the swelling will be found in the groin.

THE SPLEEN

Although we do not yet know everything the spleen does in the body, it is nevertheless referred to as the largest lymph gland. It is located to the left of the stomach just opposite the liver, but has nothing to do with the digestive system; nor is it allied in any way or related in function to any other organ. The spleen is connected directly to the bloodstream and not to the lymph. It could therefore be located anywhere else in the body, the only explanation for its actual location on the left side being that there seems to be room for it. To this day, the spleen continues to puzzle scientists. One could go on living after its removal but the production of antibodies without the spleen would be so small that one could not survive a massive attack of micro-organisms, as might occur in a case of malaria, for example.

WANDERING CELLS

Lymphocytes and leucocytes are wandering cells; they leave the lymphatics as well as the bloodstream and, being so minute in size, pass through the capillary walls. Their movement is similar to that of starfish circulating through a coral reef. Whenever and wherever they are needed they are ready to attack, just like a special branch of the police. It is truly astonishing to note that they number in the billions, so that there are more itinerant cells in our body than there are people on earth.

How to Keep the Lymph Healthy

Despite the excellent organisation of the lymphatic system, as we have just seen, the lymph often needs help. For example, a deficiency of calcium or vitamin D creates a problem for the lymphatics. Swellings in children, notably in the region of the groin and at times on the neck or behind the lower ear, can be attributed to this deficiency. Lack of calcium and vitamin D is marked by susceptibility to colds and catarrh, sore throats and other infectious diseases, as well as loss of appetite, irritability and constant fatigue.

Plenty of exercise and fresh air are a boon for our lymphatic system. Mountain sun and sea air, if enjoyed in sensible measures, have an excellent effect on the lymph.

A proven botanical remedy especially recommended for building up the lymphatic system is the subtropical plant *Echinacea*. *Echinaforce*, the tincture from this plant, can be taken internally as well as applied externally, and brings speedy relief in cases of swollen lymph nodes and blood poisoning. For external use the freshly squeezed green leaves can be made into a pack or poultice, or a cotton swab can be soaked with the tincture and placed on the affected area. If the condition is an acute one, take ten drops of the tincture with a little water every hour. Because of its effectiveness, Echinaforce should be kept in the medicine chest of every home.

In most instances a *proper diet* can bring relief. White sugar, sweets, biscuits, pastries and other sweet snacks must be cut out. The same goes for refined food items made with white flour, refined sugar and highly processed or refined oils and fats. In their place, serve and eat more vegetables and salads. Then one is on the road to recovery. A vitamin supplement, for example *Vitaforce*, together with *Urticalcin*, has been proved to give good results. For best effect, give children this form of calcium as a prophylactic measure, long before any of the above symptoms ever appear.

Horseradish has a favourable effect on the lymph and is one of the best remedies available. Often the most stubborn disorders and ailments of the lymphatic system disappear when a teaspoon of horseradish is taken daily. It is very tasty and less pungent when mixed with cottage cheese or finely grated carrots.

Tuberculosis and Cancer
When the lymphatic system is working efficiently, it is impossible for tuberculosis or cancer to develop. As regards cancer, the proper functioning of the liver is essential too. That is why special attention should be given to both the lymph and the liver. Long before tuberculosis can be diagnosed, careful observation will disclose the presence of painful lymph nodes when pressure is applied to them. These early symptoms are often observable years beforehand and call for our special attention if trouble is to be avoided later. In order to keep the lymph in good condition, we must receive sufficient oxygen and sunlight. Dark apartments, facing away from

the sun, are veritable breeding grounds for TB bacteria and should be shunned when choosing a place to live.

Lymphoadenoma
This malignant disease of the lymph nodes, also known as Hodgkin's disease, afflicts more men than women. As early as 1832, the English doctor Thomas Hodgkin described it in detail, but to this day its origin is unknown. Since the disease begins with a high temperature, some doctors believe that it is an infectious disease. However, as yet, no virus responsible for it has been identified. Other physicians consider it a type of cancer and treat it with radiotherapy (with X-rays and cobalt rays). As a rule, the success of this kind of therapy is of short duration. In cases where only a few nodes are affected by the disease their removal is recommended, until a better method can be found to deal with it effectively. On the other hand, a complete changeover to a *natural wholefood diet* consisting of plenty of raw vegetables, soft white cheese (quark) and horseradish, as well as brown rice, has proved beneficial. Hodgkin's disease is often accompanied by anaemia. This condition can be counteracted by drinking daily one tenth of a litre (100 ml; about 3½ fl. oz) of both *carrot* and *beetroot juices* and, in addition, an infusion of nettles, flowering oat plants and alfalfa. *Petasites* preparations taken with *Galeopsis* often give good results too.

Looking After our Capillary System
Few people may know that the capillary network of the human body consists of 100 million metres (over 62,000 miles) of blood vessels. This would be two and a half times the circumference of the earth if all the tiny hair-like vessels were put together in one long line. This calculation made by scientists clearly illustrates one of the many wondrous things the Creator put in our bodies. But it is not enough to be familiar with the structure of these tiny vessels; it is equally important to know and understand their functions in the body. The exchange of metabolic waste material, the passing on of carbon dioxide to the venous blood system, and many other functions known and unknown to us, take place in the capillaries.

The body as a whole, including the capillary system, can be adversely affected and harmed by an incorrect diet and life-style. Foods that produce too much uric acid, such as meat and eggs – instead of vegetables and fruit – cause a degeneration and dilation of the capillaries to a degree that capillary photography can detect it. When magnified, dilated capillaries have the appearance of small varicose veins. Excessive alcohol consumption has the same harmful effect. Chemicals absorbed from medicines and nicotine alter and damage the capillaries and impair their function of nourishing of the cells, thus disturbing the entire metabolic process. Of what good is our marvellously equipped body if we disregard its working order and eat the wrong food, as well as follow an unnatural way of life, with insufficient exercise and deep-breathing?

Defects of the capillary system cause degeneration, slackening and aging of the muscle and nerve cells due largely to their not receiving sufficient nourishment in time. It is important to know about this when we are young, so that we can guard our health carefully. If we fail to realise it until we are old, it will be of little worth by then, and we will be like the person who wasted all his fortune in his youth. In his old age he lived in poverty while contemplating, with pain and nostalgic sorrow, the bygone luxury of his youth. We can compare youth to the seven fat years in Egypt referred to in the Bible. We should act wisely, just as Joseph did, storing up good health to be able to, figuratively speaking, live off the 'savings' during the 'lean' years of advanced age. By adopting a healthy, natural way of life, from our youth onwards, we also show the greatest care for our blood vessels.

Our All-Important Circulation

In order to illustrate the function and purpose of the blood circulation, let us for a moment consider the mail train travelling from Basel to Lugano and back, making scheduled stops to unload on the way to Lugano and picking up mail on the way back to Basel. Imagine the confusion if the train did not keep to its timetable. At each station we can see the postmaster impatiently pacing up and down the platform looking for the train to arrive and trying to calm down the people who are waiting for their mail. Such a relatively small mix-up in the commercial world could trigger undesirable delays and upset everyone.

We can draw an analogy between the mail train and the circulatory system. Let us compare the outward-bound train on its way to Lugano with the arterial network, which has the job of supplying the millions of body cells with nourishment so that they are able to perform their functions. All the necessary minerals, vitamins, enzymes, amino acids for the manufacture of protein, all the sugars and fats, and even oxygen are being transported via the arterial network on a strict schedule, every day, every hour.

Every cell is a miniature factory and needs raw materials and fuel for its processes. Only if it is supplied with all it needs, on schedule, can it be expected to perform as reliably and marvellously as it does. Shortages of the required quantities and flaws in the quality of raw materials force the cells to find a make-shift solution. It is only under the most trying conditions that the cells look for shortcuts and thereby suffer in their performance. A case in point is seen when the body begins to build giant cells, known as cancer cells. Of course, the cell itself cannot be blamed for the defect, for it fights and resists desperately to the point where failure can no longer be avoided.

We must, therefore, ensure that the 'mail trains' of our arterial system can keep their schedules by stimulating circulation through exercise and proper breathing. Furthermore, we must see to it that all the necessary raw materials are provided in the right quantities and quality. Only then can the laboratories of our cells perform their wonderful work in harmony with the divine purpose and programme assigned to them. We can then reap the full benefits of the cells' willing performance on our behalf.

Thus far we have spoken of only one function of the circulatory system, the supply. But, as in every manufacturing plant, we must also concern ourselves with the waste products the body produces. They must be promptly eliminated if congestions, in other words breakdowns, are to be avoided. The train on its way back to Basel may be compared to our venous system, which is responsible for returning all the waste products resulting from burning-up processes, for example carbon dioxide and uric acid. Some of these waste products are recycled by the liver or eliminated with the help of the kidneys. If this process of transportation becomes obstructed, problems will be inevitable, since the accumulation of waste causes tension and pressure. The train may be derailed and the mail scattered, lying undelivered on the rails. In terms of our body this means the formation of varicose veins. Advice on treating varicose veins can be found on pages 132–6.

The Marvellous Design of the Circulatory System
The Dutch scientist Dr Hoorne once said that the body is made up of blood vessels. It was he who discovered a method of making the vessels visible by injecting them with a red dye. Tsar Peter the Great, who happened to be visiting Holland at that time, was so

intrigued by the experiment that he arranged to take some of the dye home with him. Unfortunately, however, on his arrival in Russia he found that it was no longer useable. The sailors had consumed the alcohol in which it had been placed to preserve it!

Truly a wonder of creative design, every single one of the billions of cells in our body has access to the uninterrupted flow of the circulatory system. It takes the blood only about one second to move from the arterial capillaries to the venous capillaries. And it is during this second that the metabolic process takes place whereby oxygen is withdrawn from the blood and carbon dioxide from the tissue is permitted to enter. At the same time, the nutrients from the blood enter the tissue and the metabolic products from the tissue enter the bloodstream. Having fulfilled its task, the blood then flows back to the heart via the venous system.

The circulation of the blood between the heart and the lungs and back to the heart again takes about six or seven seconds. The circulation through the heart, which supplies the myocardium by way of the coronary vessels, takes place in about three or four seconds. The supply of blood to the brain takes eight seconds and to the tip of the toes, about eighteen seconds. One blood cell can make about 3,000 round trips in the course of a day. The cells are moving about incessantly, day and night. It seems that nothing in the world is more fond of travelling than our blood cells. Beginning at the heart, a cell reaches the loop of the capillaries with a swift motion. The further away it gets, the slower the motion becomes because of the thinner vessels. At last it delivers its load, as an express messenger would do, and begins immediately its return trip through the venous system. Physical stress, cold weather, excitement and fever make the blood cell speed up its pace. On the other hand, depression and psychological upsets cause it to slow down. In these situations, billions of cells receive inadequate nourishment and illness may result if the situation is not remedied by means of a positive psychological influence on the individual. This goes to show that depression and similar psychological problems may lead to physical illness if they continue for any length of time.

The Important Function of the Arteries
When I think about the enormous amount of traffic that passes incessantly over the highways leading to and from major cities such as New York or London, I must say that the expression 'arterial roads' indeed seems appropriate and justified. If for some

114

reason those traffic arteries were paralysed, life in those large cities would soon come to a standstill. The importance of the 'arterial roads' in our bodies, the arteries, will only begin to dawn on us when we study them closely. Even the most attractive human body, with shapely limbs and perfect muscular build, will begin to deteriorate and degenerate, just as the gifted and trained brain will begin to fail, when the walls of the arteries thicken and harden and thus lose their elasticity.

Even the anatomical structure of the arteries tells us a great deal about their importance. Imagine a pipe made up of various layers, the inside being a smooth, elastic tube. This tube is covered with other layers that consist of elastic, or loose but tensile, connective tissue. The tube can withstand a pressure of about 20 atmospheres (1 atmosphere equals 14.72 pounds to the square inch).

These few details give us at least some idea of how our arteries work. Like the heart, the arteries have their own blood supply. For this purpose a network of vessels, the so-called *Vasa vasorum*, is ingeniously built into their walls. Furthermore, the walls of the arteries have their own network of lymphatic vessels and nerves. The further removed the arteries are from the heart, the more branched out they become, and consequently their total cross section becomes proportionally larger; pressure decreases and the walls become thinner. A cross section of the capillaries, at the very tip of the arteries, is about 50 times smaller in diameter than that of the finest human hair.

Narrowing and Hardening of the Arteries

A narrowing or hardening of the arteries has serious, in time even incurable, consequences. The victim literally degenerates, both physically and mentally. To this day more people in the civilised, industrialised world, especially in Europe, the United States and Australia die of diseases of the arterial walls, and the number of deaths is on the increase. The length of our life is often determined solely by the condition of our arterial walls.

Hardening of the arteries (arteriosclerosis) begins with a small alteration, which looks like a flat sore or ulcer. This sore then develops into a growth of the connective tissue, followed by a deposit of calcium salts, with the result that the inside of the artery becomes gradually narrower and the blood has less space in which to circulate. The artery loses more and more of its elasticity, eventually becoming hard and brittle. The blood pressure then rises and the victim may eventually suffer a thrombosis or embolism of the brain or a cerebral haemorrhage. Dilation of the heart or haemorrhage of a blood vessel near the heart, as well as nephrosclerosis (nephritis due to a hardening of the kidney blood vessels) may also occur.

WHAT ARE THE CAUSES?
1. A diet high in fats, especially animal fats, which causes an increase of cholesterol in the blood, can contribute to the disease.

2. Nicotine is another contributory factor to a narrowing of the arteries, especially the coronary vessels.

3. A rich diet, with too much animal protein, especially too much meat, eggs and cheese, may lead to arteriosclerosis.

4. Overindulgence in alcohol is harmful to the capillaries and thus may indirectly contribute to this disease.

PREVENTION AND CURE
1. A diet consisting of *brown rice, soft white cheese* (quark) and *salads* can have almost miraculous results if adhered to consistently. By lowering the blood pressure in a natural way, it becomes unnecessary to take any radical medicines. This simple natural treatment makes it possible to rehabilitate the blood vessels right from the beginning. As I have seen from experience in Asian countries, rice bran positively influences the regeneration of the arteries.

2. Plants rich in natural *iodine*, such as seaweed, contribute largely to the prevention and cure of arteriosclerosis. The curative properties of these plants of the sea can easily be made available by including them in seasoning salts or foods; for example, they are contained in Kelpamare, Trocomare, Kelpaforce and Kelpasan.

Other medicinal herbs and spices are also beneficial, such as watercress and other kinds of cress, horseradish, garlic and leeks. A natural remedy that is to be recommended is *Rauwolfavena*, a combination of rauwolfia and oats. Further excellent remedies for the blood vessels and arteriosclerosis are *Arterioforce* capsules (containing mistletoe, garlic, hawthorn and passionflower) and *Ginkgo biloba*.

3. Plenty of *oxygen* is necessary and this means taking long walks through woods and forests, hills and mountains, or by the seaside, always deeply inhaling the fresh air. But a word of caution is necessary for those who already suffer from arteriosclerosis, such people should avoid higher altitudes because the thin air could lead to a stroke.

116

If you spend most of your time sitting in an office, the above advice and simple remedy is especially recommended. If you do not wish to be a doddery old man who shuffles along and has to be led to his office, you should give careful consideration to how you spend your time away from it. Make sure you don't spend your free time with friends in a bar instead of outdoors.

HOW TO AVOID POSSIBLE HARM
One does not have to be a fanatic in order to admit that modern, civilised man is living somewhat dangerously. Just think of all the conveniences we have gained from technology in our age of motor cars and mechanisation. They bring with them less activity outdoors and cause pollution of the air. Our indulgence in refined food products does not exactly contribute to good health either. The arteries degenerate as a result of the drawbacks of our lifestyle; symptoms of old age appear much too early, decreasing our efficiency and productivity and sometimes bringing an early end to our lives. The average increase of our life span, due to a reduction in infant mortality, does not change this picture either. It is not a question of reaching an advanced age by artificial means, by the use of drugs and special therapies, while our body is ailing and vegetating. Rather, it is much better to live to a ripe old age and still be in good health. Our life-style and what we eat should be governed by the laws of nature and not by the dictates of society, which have gone awry and, at best, contribute very little to our physical well-being.

Arteriosclerosis, Coronary Thrombosis and Heart Attacks
While I was spending some time in the Far East, I paid special attention to the occurrence of the above illnesses. It was quite evident that among the people living in the countryside of Japan, Korea and the Philippines, heart-related diseases are seldom heard of. If they do occur it is usually among the better off who have a higher standard of living. In all these Far Eastern countries the country people eat very little fat, generally not more than 50 g (a little less than 2 oz) of fat and oil a day. And let me add that these 50 g consist of mainly home-made fats with a high content of unsaturated fatty acids. Equally significant in terms of their healthy diet is their habit of eating rice to meet the need for carbohydrates. This is a custom worth copying, since rice has the quality of keeping the arteries young for a long time. Among those people whose staple diet consists of rice, I have noted that the blood

117

vessels, particularly the arteries, are in much better condition than in those who have a different diet.

And another thing. The benefits derived from a regular intake of seaweed are still a secret which may offer many answers to our questions in the future. It is the custom in Korea, Japan and many Chinese provinces to eat rice served with thin wafers of pressed seaweed. During my stay there, I adopted this habit and I must say that it made me feel very well indeed. So, if you are concerned about preventing these three illnesses, or if you are already a victim of one or more of them, you should consider the following rules, which are basic to preventative as well as curative treatment.

1. It is, above all, essential to reduce the consumption of protein and fats. If possible, avoid animal fats altogether and use natural unrefined oils such as sunflower, safflower, poppy seed or corn oil instead.
2. Make brown rice the basis of your diet.
3. Raw vegetables and soft white cheese (quark) should supplement the rice diet. Be sure to eat fresh salads every day, preferably dressed with Molkosan (whey concentrate) and unrefined oils.
4. For their curative properties, include in your diet wheat germ oil or wheat germ oil capsules, Sojaforce and Kelpasan, as well as any foods that contain seaweed. However, keep off Kelpasan if your blood pressure is high.
5. Instead of any other favourite cheese, eat only mild white soft cheese (quark) or cottage cheese. If it is difficult to give up the old habit of eating meat, eat very little of it and infrequently. The same advice holds true for eggs, which should never be eaten hard-boiled.
6. For seasoning, use salt very sparingly, It is best to change over to sea salt and Herbamare herbal seasoning salt.
7. It is of the utmost importance to provide the body with plenty of oxygen. So take long country walks at a good pace to stimulate deep breathing. If it is not possible to do this on a daily basis, at least use the weekend for that purpose. Instead of spending time in one's favourite café, bar or restaurant, sitting in front of the television or behind the wheel of a car, get out and exercise your legs in the countryside, in the woods and through the meadows.

If you try to be conscientious in living according to these seven rules, you will definitely increase your life span and help yourself to avoid many health problems in your advanced years. For example, hardening of the arteries will not incapacitate you, neither will coronary thrombosis, and you will have no need to fear a sudden end through a heart attack. It is simple to obey nature, and doing so will reward us in turn with good health and long life.

Embolism and Thrombosis

Women especially suffer from swollen veins, which often occur after surgery or just after childbirth. Generally, the blocking of venous blood vessels happens sometime between the third and the eighth day following surgery or delivery. In such cases a physician will usually give anticoagulant and vasodilator injections. However, more appropriate and helpful than this medical intervention is the following prophylactic treatment, which is to be recommended to all those who show a congenital or acquired tendency to embolism and thrombosis, and in particular to people with varicose veins.

Preventative Treatment

First of all, take proper *care of the bowels*, because intestinal disorders such as insufficient bowel movement or the retention of a faecal matter causes the blood, and hence the whole body, to become affected by metabolic toxins. Going on a juice diet for one day a week usually helps to improve regularity. The question of diet or nutrition for the rest of the week is no less important; only natural, unadulterated, unrefined foods will contribute to the eventual correction of irregular bowel movements.

Secondly, it must be remembered that regular *sweating* cures have an important place in the prevention and treatment of embolism and thrombosis. Sweating, of course, is easy for people who engage in strenuous physical activity. It can also be induced by mountain climbing, or by hiking, digging, gardening and the like, if you do not live near hills or mountains. Whatever the means, make sure to change wet or damp clothes quickly. If you happen to be one of those people who are unable to sweat even when engaging in physical activity, you have yet another way open to you. Take a sauna (up to 60 °C/140 °F) once a week. This will be of great help in reducing the tendency to embolism and thrombosis.

Thirdly, take the appropriate *medicinal herbs*. But I must point out that pregnant women should not wait until shortly before childbirth to take the herbs. They should begin to take them

119

months ahead of time in order to improve the condition of the blood and exert a positive influence on the entire vascular system. An excellent remedy is *Hamamelis*, an extract from witch hazel, a shrub known to the North American Indians as a 'miracle plant'. As early as the Middle Ages women realised that embolism and thrombosis could be prevented by taking arnica, yarrow, St John's wort and *Pulsatilla*. More than thirty years ago I began to use these herbs as a basis for a well-known fresh plant preparation, *Hyperisan*, that has since proved helpful to thousands of women in many countries around the globe. Many women have told me that serious complications at the time of delivery were prevented because they had been taking this herbal complex during their pregnancy. Much to their surprise, delivery was easy and without subsequent complications, which had not been the case for them before, when they had not been taking the preparation. A qualified midwife once wrote me an enthusiastic letter about a perfect delivery, which, according to her, could only be attributed to the fact that the mother had been taking the preparation. As a midwife of many years' experience, her observation and assessment can hardly be questioned. In addition to Hyperisan, it is recommended to take *Urticalcin*, because biological calcium is good for the vascular system. Another good supportive remedy, called *Aesculus hipp.*, a fresh plant extract from horse chestnuts, should not be overlooked either.

These are simple remedies for the vascular system, but they act in a preventative way, and this is no doubt better, simpler and less painful than leaving the problem untreated and suffering the subsequent discomfort. Once the trouble has taken root it is not always easy or possible to effect a cure, so it is more sensible to follow the advice given in good time.

Calcification and Calcium Preparations
Many people have a totally mistaken idea about calcium preparations, calcification and, in particular, calcification or hardening of the arteries. Quite often a patient tells me, 'I can't take calcium, I suffer from arteriosclerosis, and I'm sure it would be bad for me to take any more calcium; it would only be deposited in the arteries.'

But this view is entirely wrong. Biological calcium preparations such as Urticalcin have nothing to do with calcification. On the contrary, someone who is suffering from hardening of the arteries can take such a preparation without any problems, for it is easily

Horse Chestnut

assimilated. This calcium is used to repair worn out parts of the body and is never deposited in the vessels. In fact, the 'deposits' we are talking about are not really pure calcium; the term is used in the sense of arterial degeneration whereby the arterial walls gradually lose their elasticity.

First of all, fat-like substances called lipoids are deposited on the lining of the blood vessels and only later is calcium added. According to some research workers, the thickening takes place as a natural necessity so as to strengthen the walls of the arteries. It is thought that the body, as a defence measure, deposits calcium when the blood vessels have lost a degree of elasticity and stability and can no longer cope with the changed conditions of pressure. Other researchers, however, are of the opinion that it is just because of these deposits in the vessels, the so-called arteriosclerosis, that they become hardened.

Whatever the case, calcification is a sign of ageing which appears as a result of a disturbance in the general metabolism and an unhealthy diet, primarily one containing too much protein. But by no means can we hold the calcium in food or a biological preparation responsible for the pathological process of calcification. The bones of the skeleton contain reserves of calcium that would be quite sufficient to calcify all our blood vessels, yet in practice, such a contingency never arises.

As far as possible, naturopathy treats arteriosclerosis with remedies that restore some elasticity to the vessels. The blood pressure will thereby drop, for it previously had to rise because of constriction, with the lack of elasticity of the vessels compelling the heart to generate greater pressure to keep the circulation going. Of course, for arteriosclerosis we do not prescribe any medicines containing calcium. What we do indicate are *arnica* and *Crataegus*, as well as *Viscum album, garlic perles, Arterioforce* capsules and *bear's garlic tonic*. These remedies have an excellent effect. At the same time care should be taken to minimise the salt and protein intake. One of the best foods for preventing hardening of the arteries, or helping to reduce an existing condition, is *brown rice*. For this reason, anyone with arteriosclerosis should eat brown rice several times a week; it can be served morning, noon or evening and prepared in various appetising ways. The blood pressure will then fall, because a diet of fresh fruits and vegetables, together with plenty of brown rice, will gradually halt the disease and improve the condition.

If you should have to take a calcium complex such as Urticalcin for some other physical problem, remember that this preparation will not have an adverse effect on the blood vessels: on the contrary it will be beneficial. These details should reassure the patient who shies away from taking a good calcium preparation. He must by now realise that such a preparation is in no way associated with the hardening (calcification) of the arteries and positively supports rather than hinders a cure.

Older People and Calcium
Older people often raise the question of whether it is advisable to take biological calcium preparations, for example Urticalcin, or even to eat foods high in calcium, since it is known that in later years the potential danger of the hardening of the arteries and other body tissues is greater. It is an indisputable fact that during old age calcium is being withdrawn from the bones and deposited in vessels and tissues. This process causes the bones to become porous and fragile and the tissues, blood vessels and scar tissue to accumulate calcium deposits. At a quick glance, this argument would appear to favour a reduced intake of calcium. However,

experience has proved that a diet low in calcium, surprisingly enough, can even promote osteoporosis, the loss of calcium from the bones.

How can this problem be solved? Calcium is a basic mineral that compounds easily with acids. If during the latter part of life the body accumulates certain acids, for example, oxalic and other acids, which should have been eliminated with the urine, the body compounds these with calcium to form calcium salts. When reduced to an unsaturated state in this way they are rendered less harmful. If we do not permit a deficiency to develop in the mineral metabolism, and we see to it that the calcium level remains normal, we can be sure that there will be no abnormal decalcification of the bones, even during old age. For this reason, too, there will be no calcium deposits in the blood vessels and tissues. This leads us to the question: what can be done to prevent premature aging?

RECOMMENDED PREVENTATIVE MEASURES
An older person, first of all, needs plenty of *oxygen*, in other words, plenty of exercise and deep-breathing in the open air. It would be beneficial to engage in some light sport; light gardening is another good form of exercise. Long walks through a forest or wood, or walking and climbing in the soothing tranquillity of hills and dales will also provide enough refreshing exercise for the body and the lungs.

Secondly, an older person should eat foods that have a high *iron* content, which assures the proper oxygenation of the blood and normalises the metabolic processes. This can be achieved by simply enhancing our meals with plenty of raw vegetables and salads every day. Of course, this is easier to do during spring, when many kinds of cresses and the tender leaves of spinach are available. Add these to your salads without fail. Also, do not forget the young shoots of stinging nettles which provide exceptional benefits. Indeed, there are many alternatives to ensure that we can meet our daily requirements of iron and other vital substances.

Thirdly, it is essential to look after and stimulate the endocrine glands. Daily *brush massages and showers*, alternating between hot and cold water, are helpful; after using hot water, douse the body briefly with cool or cold water. But be careful not to become chilled. You should feel comfortably warm after the alternating hot–cold shower; if this is not the case, it would be wiser to refrain from using the cold water.

Another basic rule is to get plenty of *sleep* in the hours preceding midnight. Sleep does much for our health, especially during these hours. What is more, if you go to bed early sleep will come more easily, as you are less likely to be overtired. Take *kelp* to supplement the mineral content of your diet. And, as previously stated, it does not affect one adversely to eat foods rich in calcium and to take a biological calcium preparation as well. On the contrary, this will be beneficial. Finally, it is helpful, from time to time, to stimulate the kidneys in order to ensure the adequate elimination of uric materials by taking a natural herb preparation, for example *Nephrosolid*.

If you follow these rules, and eat and drink sensibly, you will reach your old age without having to become stiff and doddery. Interestingly, the preventative measures that need to be understood and followed are few and simple, but they will protect you from much greater problems.

Diets for Hypertension, Arteriosclerosis and Other Signs of Old Age

It is important to determine whether hypertension, or high blood pressure, is caused by a kidney disease or by the diminishing elasticity of the blood vessels. If the latter, it may be easily corrected through a rice diet, as this is effective in practically all diseases attributable to the aging process. Rice is a medicinal food, which provides surprisingly good results, but you must be sure to use brown unpolished rice, for this is more beneficial and valuable than the more common refined white rice. If you cannot obtain brown rice, although this is unlikely, two commercially prepared rice packages, 'Uncle Ben's' and 'Avorio' may serve as a compromise, because both of these brands still retain many of the important minerals found in brown rice.

It is not easy for everyone in countries where rice is not produced to stick to a rice diet. In many areas people are used to eating mainly potatoes and local cereals, but in the Far East rice is a staple food. In this respect people in Far Eastern countries are better off, for if they adhere faithfully to the simple brown rice diet of their forefathers, they will never have to worry about high blood pressure.

Since high blood pressure is usually associated with eating too much protein, patients would be wise to cut out from their diet all animal proteins such as meat, eggs and cheese; if they think they cannot live without these, they should at least reduce the quantities to a bare minimum. In other words, the basis of the diet should be rice, cottage cheese and salads, if high blood pressure is to drop.

The reason rice is of such importance in this diet is that it helps to restore the elasticity of the blood vessels. Soft white cheese (quark) is a good source of protein, goes well with vegetables, especially salads, and is tasty. By adding various seasonings, for example horseradish, curry and all kinds of herbs, as well as vegetable juices, you can enrich its content and taste and provide some variety. Salads, by the way, supply the body with the necessary vitamins and essential mineral salts.

A doctor in the United States has helped many people suffering from hypertension by means of a diet similar to the one suggested below. These patients would probably not have been so successful had they tried the treatment alone at home, as the temptation to lapse back into old habits may have been too strong. Through the treatment the high blood pressure was reduced, but with it went a considerable sum of money too.

As a rule, the results of this treatment begin to be seen after 3–4 months. So, if a patient can only spare four weeks to attend a clinic, he does not really have to give up when the time comes to leave, because the experience gained may be used at home and he can continue the regime. True enough, it does take a little willpower to be consistent and not revert to one's old eating habits. Of course, family members can help tremendously by showing understanding and giving encouragement. Success will not fail to come in time. In the paragraphs below we are glad to give valuable hints and directions for a recommended diet.

A Recommended Diet

BREAKFAST

Even without meat, eggs and cheese, breakfast can still be varied from day to day. We can make Bambu Coffee, have rye bread, crispbread, wholegrain or wholemeal bread, butter or a good vegetable margarine and honey or jam without additives. A dish of muesli with seasonal berries or fruits completes the breakfast menu. (Muesli, the famous Swiss breakfast food, is a mixture of rolled oats and other cereals, nuts and dried fruit.) This breakfast is tasty, nutritious and invigorating.

Instead of having fruit every morning, you may wish to introduce some variety and take your Bambu Coffee together with wholegrain or wholemeal open sandwiches. Spread the bread with butter or cottage cheese, cover it with slices of radishes in springtime, and top it with fresh seasonal herbs or tender leaves of lettuce. Finely chopped ramsons (bear's garlic) are also wholesome and, incidentally, very popular as a salad or steamed vegetable; they are especially good for people suffering from high blood pressure. When tomatoes are in season, use these in sandwiches too. At certain times of the year when horseradish and cress are available, they too will enrich our breakfast.

MIDDAY MEAL

The meal we eat at noon is an essential part of the treatment. It can indeed be curative if prepared according to the following suggestions.

Prepare rice, cottage cheese enriched with horseradish, and a salad of four or five different fresh vegetables, not forgetting to season with a little garlic in order to benefit from its healing properties. In springtime you can replace the garlic with fresh ramsons (bear's garlic). If you do not like the strong aftertaste or smell of garlic, be assured that this can usually be eliminated by eating parsley afterwards.

If you think up different ways of serving rice, it will not become tiresome. For example, it is possible to prepare tasty vegetable rice dishes, as they do in the Far East. This idea has endless possibilities, such as rice with courgettes, with tomatoes, with mushrooms, with aubergines, with chillies and with soybean sprouts. To all these dishes add creamed curds or cottage cheese with herbs, and don't forget the salad.

For the sake of variety we may want to prepare a sweet rice dish with grapes and almonds, and eat this with a fresh fruit compote. Finish off the meal with Bambu Coffee and cream.

The rice should be cooked so that the grains do not stick together. If you overcook rice it will lose its tastiness and become starchy. It is true, the Japanese usually prepare it that way deliberately, but the Chinese take care to keep the grains separate. To enhance the flavour of a rice dish sprinkle it with finely chopped parsley and a little grated cheese and brown in the oven. This will make a welcome change.

EVENING MEAL

It is advisable to take only a light meal at night and refrain from eating any hard-to-digest foods in order to ensure a good night's rest. We recommend some fruit and wholegrain or wholemeal bread, spread with butter or vegetable margarine, and a cup of Bambu Coffee. The fruit may be in a dish of muesli, or served as a fruit salad made with fresh fruit only. Fruit as a diet food has to be fresh, so that you will have to limit your choice to the varieties that are in season.

If vegetables rather than fruit are preferred, make a dish of cold buckwheat gruel (see below) and serve with any salad as an evening meal. Or in lieu of that, make some fresh vegetable soup accompanied by wholemeal sandwiches and a mixed salad.

In order to avoid flatulence, it is best to avoid eating vegetables and fruit at the same meal. If you did not know about this, it may be difficult to change your habits. But observing this rule is worthwhile, because your digestion will improve, gastric disturbances will disappear and your body's energy reserves will last longer.

WHAT TO DRINK

If we want to to have a suitable drink with our vegetable dishes, we should choose something that contains lactic acid, for example diluted Molkosan, or juices, such as beetroot and carrot juices. However, it should be remembered never to make a practice of drinking while there is food in the mouth as this prevents proper mastication and hinders the pre-digestive process.

THE ART OF SEASONING

When suffering from high blood pressure it is important to consider the type of condiments used. Since too much salt can increase the blood pressure, the diet should be very low in salt, just as is necessary in the case of kidney trouble. Instead of using salt without thinking, you must learn the art of proper seasoning. This is something that every cook should know, especially if diet meals have to be prepared. Food should never taste dull or else it will be unappetising. Instead of salt, the following spices and herbs, if used moderately, are better for your health: horseradish, parsley, marjoram, thyme, and if you like, also chillies, paprika, and curry. Garlic adds a pleasant flavour to rice dishes too.

The popular herbal salt Herbamare makes seasoning easier and is economical to use.

BUCKWHEAT

In the past buckwheat was more popular than it is today. Since this cereal, just like rice, serves as a remedy for high blood pressure, it should appear on our table for a change. It may be prepared in the same way as rice and can take its place along with cottage cheese and salads. One method of serving buckwheat is by cooking it in a vegetable broth to which has been added home-made tomato purée and finely chopped seasoning herbs. Leave to cool, then serve cold for supper, together with tomatoes and lettuce. Another variation is to mix cooked buckwheat gruel with onion, garlic and a little marjoram, let it cool and then fry like rissoles. *Bon appetit!*

Normalising the Blood Pressure through a Wholegrain Rice Diet

WHITE OR BROWN RICE?
In the United States it has been the custom for quite some time to treat high blood pressure with a rice diet. A Swiss sanatorium has employed the same diet to combat hypertension with the satisfactory result that the pressure decreased significantly, but at the same time the diet produced a bad side effect – the patients became anaemic. What could have caused this unfortunate result? Well, it was quite simply due to a lack of knowledge. No one took into consideration that white rice is not at all suitable for diet purposes; having had its goodness to a large extent removed, it gives rise to typical deficiency symptoms. Did not the outbreak of beriberi make the world aware of this fact?

A mono-diet of rice is indicated only if it is based on the whole grain; it must be *unpolished brown rice*. Only then will the patient benefit and the blood pressure drop without any accompanying deficiency symptoms. It is a good thing to observe this in everyday cooking as well, because brown rice is far more nutritional than the refined white kind, as brown rice contains 9.5 times more minerals (nutritive salts) than white rice. During the refining process, not only is the external cellulose husk removed, but so too is the tasty silvery membrane and the germ. While this process makes for a nice white rice grain, it devalues it at the same time. It is an open secret that the removed 'wastes' of the rice grains are not thrown away but are bought by the pharmaceutical companies to be included as ingredients in their tonic medicines. It is always good to look behind the scenes if you can, because you often discover some useful hints for better health.

What Can You Expect to Achieve?
It is a proven fact that a diet of wholegrain rice promotes normal blood pressure. As it regulates low as well as high pressure, it would be wrong not to give it a chance for either of these problems. Not long ago I received a letter from a friend in Germany to whom I had recommended a wholegrain rice diet for his very high blood pressure. He had followed my advice and was able to report excellent results.

He remained on the recommended diet for ten weeks and found that he had lost weight and that his blood pressure had gone down from 230 to 190. This result alone was most encouraging. He then took a two-week vacation, at the end of which his pressure had fallen even further, this time to 170. Let me add that this patient is already sixty-three years old and it is especially interesting to note that he obtained such splendid results without the aid of any medication – simply by following a diet of wholegrain rice, cottage cheese and salads. If he keeps to this diet he will experience a further reduction in blood pressure and, with it, the elasticity of the blood vessels will improve.

Even though my friend did not make use of any medicines – and still achieved a noteworthy result – it would not be wrong to supplement a diet of this kind with certain preparations which would make it even more effective. For example, *Viscum album tincture*, a mistletoe preparation, is able to lower the blood pressure. Additionally, *hawthorn (Crataegus)* and *arnica* should be taken, both remedies having a positive influence on the blood vessels. Another helpful remedy is *bear's garlic tonic*, since it is a specific for regenerating the vessels. In spring, gather bear's garlic (ramsons) and prepare it as a fresh salad, or steam it as a vegetable. For the rest of the year, take bear's garlic tonic and *garlic perles* or *Arterioforce* capsules.

If, as a result of this treatment, the arterial pressure falls, this signifies not simply a lower reading but the welcome fact that the elasticity of the blood vessels has improved – that is, a genuine rejuvenation of the vessels has taken place. If we realise the consequences of high blood pressure, we will feel it is well worth the effort to persevere with the recommended diet until satisfactory results have been obtained.

Low Blood Pressure (Hypotension)
High blood pressure as a disease has been extensively discussed and written about. All attention is focused on it in the fight to cure

it, and this is often possible by means of medication, therapies and a proper diet.

But much less is known about low blood pressure, or hypotension, and many questions are asked: 'What causes it? How does it develop? What can be done about it?' These questions are not adequately answered even in literature written by naturopaths, despite the fact that many people complain of low blood pressure.

A person with low blood pressure may be subject to dizziness or even occasional fainting spells at high altitudes of 1,500–1,800 m (4,500–6,000 feet). Every little exertion may upset the blood circulation or the normal heart activity. A change in locale is often necessary to permit the patient to live in a lower, and therefore more suitable, altitude. It must be added, though, that some patients actually feel better at a higher altitude than they do in the lowlands. In 90 per cent of all cases, the symptoms appear as a result of insufficiency of the gonads. In a woman the ovaries do not function correctly and in a man it is the male sex glands that are out of order.

What Relief Is Available?
As soon as medication that stimulates the glandular activity is given, the blood pressure returns to normal. Let me point out, however, that it is not advisable to take powerful hormone preparations, since their remedial effect is usually not permanent and can result in unpleasant side effects, or the blood pressure may be forced up too quickly. So would it not be better to stimulate the sex glands indirectly? It is possible to do this with potassium iodide preparations containing organically bound iodine from seaweed. Although all kinds of seaweed can be used, kelp is especially appropriate. No wonder *Kelpasan* tablets have for this reason gained such wide popularity. *Rauwolfia root*, which is grown in India and Sri Lanka, has also acquired a good reputation for its effectiveness and patients are also given the tincture to reduce high blood pressure. *Ginkgo biloba* drops are another splendid remedy, since the active ingredients obtained from the leaves have a beneficial effect on the circulatory system. For women, a very good homoeopathic remedy for the ovaries is *Ovarium 3x*. This excellent remedy regulates the function of the ovaries without any side effects.

Another good remedy for low blood pressure is *hyssop*, a plant that has been known and used since biblical times. Bible readers will recall God's instruction to Moses in connection with the sacrifice of the lamb at Passover. At that time the Jews were commanded to paint the door posts and lintels of their houses with the blood of a lamb, using bundles of hyssop to do so. Even today, the Samaritans use hyssop to prevent the curdling of blood of the sacrificial animal. There is a simple reason for this effect: the juice in the hyssop plant has the property of preventing blood from coagulating or clotting. In the 51st Psalm hyssop is mentioned in connection with spiritual cleansing. This singular plant does indeed possess a peculiar and mysterious power. It is most likely that its benefits in affecting blood pressure favourably and raising it are due to its influence on the gonads or sex glands.

Other Remedies and Treatments

In order to raise low blood pressure it does no harm to drink a glass of natural, unadulterated *red wine* now and again. '*Buendner meat*' (slightly salted and air-dried beef) is also indicated for this purpose. Vegetarians, however, will no doubt prefer to take *bee pollen*, which helps to increase low blood pressure due to its stimulating effect on the sex glands. The combination of *Auroforce, Kali phos. 6x* and bee pollen has been found to be effective. But here is a word of warning: bee pollen is so effective in raising the blood pressure that people who suffer from hypertension should not take any at all since doing so could provoke a stroke. I remember the case of one patient who had taken some pollen and could have had a tragic end if immediate counteracting measures had not been taken in time. You can see from this experience that even natural remedies are not always harmless if improperly employed.

Another natural remedy that increases the blood pressure is *raw carrot juice*. People with high blood pressure must therefore abstain from drinking carrot juice, but those with low pressure will benefit from it when taken in addition to the other indicated remedies. However, if carrots are eaten whole or as a salad, they will have no effect on the blood pressure; only the pure juice is curative. This applies also to *beetroot juice*.

If high altitudes make you feel dizzy and you wish to overcome the spell quickly, you might like to try *caffeine*; have a strong cup of coffee and the symptoms will quickly pass. If you live in a coastal area and have low blood pressure, *oysters* are excellent for regulating pressure and improving, at the same time, an insufficiency of the sex glands. Of course, you will have to eat them regularly.

A downward fluctuation of the blood pressure indicates a lack of vitality. It is therefore not enough simply to treat the symptoms of dizziness; a means must be sought to improve the overall condition of the person, restoring lost strength and the energy needed to keep up with the daily routine of work and life. This is much more desirable than having to force ourselves to do justice to our daily duties and chores. If the sex glands do not function properly the result is not only a loss of sexual potency, but also of vitality and energy in general. This translates itself into a lack of desire to work and a lack of creativity in physical, mental and artistic fields. A condition like this should not be left to linger on, unless one has already retired from active involvement in life and is quite happy to lead a leisurely life with no greater exertion than short daily walks.

Varicose Veins

If you reflect on the significance of the blood vessels and the blood, you can benefit from the Bible's statement that 'the soul of every sort of flesh is in the blood.' Goethe's words in *Faust*, 'blood is a unique fluid', express a similar thought. Everything in the body, its development and functions, depends on our blood and its quality, even our perceptions and feelings. If the blood is sound, our feelings and attitudes will also be healthy. We often hear about hormones, the glandular secretions present in the blood in minute concentrations, and how they influence the functions of the body and its physical activities. But this is not their only influence. They also affect our mental and emotional state and even have a bearing on our character and personality. Hormonal disturbances have been known to cause changes in character. Such thoughts make us feel very uncomfortable about taking another person's blood through a blood transfusion. Not without reason did God strictly forbid the ancient Jews to take in blood in any form.

If the blood is to fulfil its task properly, it must contain all the minerals and vitamins the body requires to maintain itself. The circulation has the important function of carrying these elements to the tissues. Thus, on the one hand, the blood itself must contain the necessary nutrients, and on the other hand, the circulation must be in good working order so that these nutrients will be taken to every cell in the body. More than that, even if the cells received everything they need they would still die if the metabolic wastes were not removed. The cells would inevitably be poisoned by their own waste matter.

If you are reasonably well acquainted with the body's functions, you will know that the arteries carry oxygenated, nutrient-laden blood to the cells, while the veins carry the depleted blood back to the heart after the tissues have received what they need. Thus, the arteries and veins are complementary to each other. Everything our Creator has made was designed so that normal function and activity can take place.

Disturbances in the venous system are much more frequent than in the arterial system, and women especially suffer from stagnation of blood in the veins. When young people complain of cold feet it is usually a sign that the circulation is malfunctioning. Lack of exercise or inadequate clothing are generally responsible for young women and girls feeling cold. And cold feet often leads to ailments of the abdominal organs and the kidneys. In this way, young girls frequently ruin their prospects of good health later in life. Their parents ignore the fundamentals of appropriate clothing and the girls themselves know little or nothing about them anyway. They are usually more interested in fashion and fads than in matters of health and what is necessary to maintain it. Their periods are frequently accompanied by cramps and all sorts of upsets, and much of this is due to stagnation of blood in the veins. Even chilblains are not warning enough for such people, because they have no idea of their cause. So chilblains are simply treated locally, where it hurts, and no thought is given to treating the veins, the origin of the trouble. In such cases alternating *hot and cold foot baths* and *long baths* would be indicated and should be complemented by taking herbal remedies.

The fashion for wearing trousers would be better for many women and girls because they would hide their knotted and swollen veins. However, if some women follow fashion blindly to the point of wearing high-heeled shoes, with the heels often pencil thin, then I am afraid to say that we lose our pity for their condition. High heels, tight clothes and underwear with tight elastic help to promote varicose veins. For this reason it would be much more prudent to dress in accordance with sensible rules for good health. Surely it would be more reasonable to find out and meet the requirements for good health, would it not?

Sclerosing
When the veins cease to function efficiently the circulation becomes impaired and varicose veins develop ('varicose' is derived from the Latin word *varix* – a dilated vein). This frequently happens during pregnancy and immediately after childbirth and should be tackled at once, for neglect at this stage will, slowly but surely, lead to

further trouble. Lack of care of the venous system can bring on thrombosis and embolism. If a good pregnancy is desired, an easy labour and a trouble-free time after birth, look after the veins!

It is understandable that one would like to get rid of varicose veins as quickly as possible. This is sometimes done by injecting a strong hypertonic saline or sugar solution into the affected vein, sclerosing it, so that it ceases to function. Each calf possesses two deep and two superficial veins, and each thigh has one of each, with smaller communicating veins. If one of these veins is put out of action, the other will have more work to do. It is obvious that this one may, in time, also become defective, for how can one vein manage to do the work of two, especially when the work was evidently too much when shared by two veins? Eventually, the second vein will also have to be sclerosed and the circulation will depend on the subsidiary veins. True, these can indeed expand a little and become stronger, but not enough to save the circulation from being impeded. Insufficient circulation will lead to further problems. Circulatory disorders, especially among the elderly, are common and often cause grave ailments, such as can be seen in senile gangrene. In many instances such afflictions can be traced back to an earlier interference with the venous system when the patient was young. Indeed, even young people can be affected. The danger of embolism and thrombosis is accentuated by meddling with the blood vessels, as many patients can confirm.

Surgery
It is, of course, also wrong to put up with varicose veins without doing anything about them. For one thing, with advancing age the condition will deteriorate and the prospects of curing it become slimmer. In very serious cases it may be impossible to avoid surgery. Such serious cases are rare among Africans, except their older women. Where a medicine man is still practising, he will cut the affected vein with a sharp piece of broken glass and then squeeze out the stagnated blood. This method, which perforce is less hygienic than an operation in a hospital, is all that is needed as far as surgical intervention is concerned. Although we in the West may not submit ourselves to this kind of treatment, nevertheless, in grave cases an operation is better and less likely to be followed by serious complications than treatment by sclerosing. It is a fact that the injected saline solution reaches not only the demarcated vessel but also adjoining cnes. As a rule, no one talks about the adverse consequences of sclerosing.

Perhaps 10 per cent of all cases of varicose veins justify surgery. The other 90 per cent of venous disorders in the legs can be treated successfully, or at least with partial success, by other means, such as those outlined below.

Natural Regeneration

It is imperative that people should be warned against any harmful, unnatural treatment of varicose veins. Why go in for dangerous methods when the veins can be regenerated by natural means? When varicose veins appear, the body is in need of a good calcium preparation, for example *Urticalcin*, as well as a preparation called *Aesculaforce*, made from horse chestnut, witch hazel, arnica and yellow melilot (sweet clover). *Hypericum perforatum* and *Millefolium*, too, are very good for this condition. The veins are regenerated in a wonderful way by means of these remedies. To alleviate a painful inflammation, take *Lachesis 10x* and *12x*. Moreover, pay attention to an appropriate *natural diet rich in calcium*. In this way, even where heredity plays a part, varicose veins can be made to recede and can sometimes be completely removed, or at least regenerated to such an extent that they will not give you any further trouble. This advice is especially important for expectant mothers because it is not only helpful to the circulation but also prevents complications during confinement. These remedies stimulate the venous system and remove obstructions so that there will be no danger of embolism or thrombosis.

Thus the veins, like other organs of the body, should be regenerated rather than removed. As has already been pointed out, the solution to varicose veins first of all requires that sensible clothing is worn, shoes with normal heels no higher than 2–3 cm or 1½ inches, and reasonably loose dresses and lingerie so that the circulation is not constricted or otherwise impaired.

A second factor worth mentioning is the detrimental effect on the veins of standing for long periods. In particular, you should strictly avoid standing for any length of time on stone or concrete floors.

Thirdly, watch what you eat. Your diet must be rich in vitamins and minerals. That is why plenty of raw vegetables and fresh fruit are important.

Rule four is to stimulate the circulation by supplying the blood with sufficient oxygen. Plenty of outdoor exercise in the fresh air will do this for you.

Then consider the general care of the legs. Put them up for a period every day and carefully empty the veins by gently stroking upwards, not massaging, as doing so may be a little too drastic. The best time to do this is in the evening before going to bed, but if you have enough time during your lunch break, you can repeat it then. Oil the legs once a week with St John's wort oil or massage oil containing this ingredient. For a change you can use a lanolin cream, such as Bioforce Cream.

At the same time, I am happy to repeat that there are some excellent natural remedies for stimulating the circulatory system. Would we have a certain number of veins, tonsils or an appendix if these organs were not vital to our well-being? Surely then, every interference and anatomical change presents a risk that is more often than not accompanied by unpleasant consequences. How strange it is that we are inclined to show more confidence in surgery than the meaningful purpose of our Creator's design! Unfortunately, the damage only becomes evident later, after the person has been considerably harmed.

Some time ago it was considered fashionable to remove the appendix, even if it was healthy, whenever the surgeon had cause to open a patient's right abdomen. Their justification for this was that it might become diseased one day and would have to be removed then anyway. Fortunately, the profession is more enlightened today and such short-sighted decisions have been abandoned so that an appendix is removed only when absolutely necessary. The same goes for the tonsils; they too can be treated and regenerated long before they are beyond repair. Really, then, there can be no excuse for neglect. We usually know our physical weaknesses. If we give immediate attention to even slight physical signals, and with persevering care and patience treat them in a natural way, the body will respond. We have the remedies; you only have to use your intelligence, understanding and willpower to apply them, and the results will be rewarding.

Anyone who suffers from varicose veins should treat them by natural means, and with perseverance. There is no immediate cure; it is impossible to blow them away from one day to the next, for it took a considerable time for the veins to become diseased in the first place. Healthy veins play such an important part in our bodies that the patient attention and care we give them to ensure their proper function will be well worth our while.

Phlebitis (Inflammation of the Veins)

Alcohol compresses are very good for phlebitis. Better still are *compresses* with tinctures from plants such as *St John's wort, yarrow* or *marigold*. These are always indicated for phlebitis. If you take *Aesculaforce* at the same time, or an infusion of St John's wort, yarrow, and *arnica*, the problem will be treated from the inside as well. The use of yet another plant, *Echinacea*, is also important for effecting a cure. The fresh herb preparation *Echinaforce* supports the body's efforts in combatting bacteria, which are always present in phlebitis. *Usneasan* and the homoeopathic medicine *Lachesis 12x* have a similar effect. By taking these remedies it will be possible to prevent blood poisoning, which sometimes accompanies phlebitis.

Changing one's eating habits will be of further benefit, bringing faster relief. A *natural diet* should be followed, preferably a vegetarian one, and plenty of fruit and vegetable juices should be included.

Leg Ulcers

Those who suffer from ulcerated legs usually are unaware that it is wrong to attempt to heal the ulcers externally without also improving the general condition of the blood. Even though a good ointment or other natural remedies may be used, it is advisable not to try to heal the ulcer too quickly. If the secretions with their metabolic toxins cannot drain away freely before the blood has been purified, the condition will give rise to increasing discomfort. This has been confirmed by many whose leg ulcers have been healed too quickly.

You must understand that, according to the principles of natural therapy, the body uses just such an ulcer, or similar afflictions, as a kind of safety valve through which it can expel material which otherwise cannot be disposed of. If this valve is closed, the toxins will remain in the body. The patient's general condition will worsen and he will feel unwell. When he begins to feel dizzy and weak it is the body's urgent plea for help to open another valve. This help is given when the patient is treated internally, with a view to restoring the efficient working of the veins.

As a rule, it will be necessary to stimulate the kidneys, since in such cases they are usually weak. If the patient takes, in addition, the special remedies for the veins as they are included in *Aesculaforce*, a complex made from horse chestnut, witch hazel, arnica and yellow melilot, as well as a course of biological calcium complex *Urticalcin*, do not be surprised if the ulcer breaks open again. Neither should you be surprised if the patient begins to feel much better. This treatment is designed to attack the problem from inside, to purify and vitalise the system by acting on the kidneys and veins. As a result, the internal condition will be improved and the ulcers will soon heal up outside without any fear of further disturbance to the patient's general well-being.

If the patient is constipated, prompt action should be taken to relieve this condition. In less stubborn cases *psyllium seed* will help, as will *soaked prunes or figs*.

If high blood pressure is noted, indicated by a feeling of dizziness, do not neglect to treat it. *Viscum album, Crataegus* and *arnica* are well-known remedies that have a regenerating effect on the blood vessels. Further advice is given in the section on hypertension (see pages 124–9). It may be that the heart requires strengthening too. All these factors have to be assessed according to each case.

It goes without saying that an appropriate diet is essential for any healing process, if it is to be successful. If by now you have come to terms with the meaning of natural therapy, it should not be necessary to re-emphasise this fact. Cleansing the body from inside requires a diet that is low in salt and protein. Meat consumption should be reduced to a bare minimum, or better still, eliminated altogether until a complete recovery has been achieved. Pork, sausages and all other processed meats, eggs, cheese, white sugar and flour, as well as canned foods, should all be avoided. In their place eat plenty of natural wholefoods, including steamed vegetables, raw salads and wholegrain products.

The above recommendations are intended to help all those who suffer from leg ulcers. If you recognise and follow these important principles of natural therapy, your recovery and future well-being will be within your reach.

Circulatory Disorders

Chilblains

Red–blue skin patches that hurt with every movement are known as chilblains. They mainly affect the hands and feet and are caused by prolonged exposure to severe cold. However, this complaint can be easily prevented if we maintain a constant effort to keep our circulation in good order.

If you have a tendency to develop chilblains or already suffer from them, you will find the simple home remedies and preventative measures outlined in the first part of this book (see pages 3–4) of great benefit. If you also take *Hypericum perforatum, Aesculaforce* and *Urticalcin* at the same time, your circulation will gradually improve and the tendency towards chilblains may disappear.

Gangrene

Gangrene is a term associated with the death of tissues due to failure of the blood supply. The condition requires immediate attention. If neglected, the skin of the legs or feet turns a bluish-red colour, becomes shiny and hard and makes the patient feel extremely uncomfortable, especially at night, when the patches begin to burn to the extent that relief can only be obtained by moving the feet from under the blankets and exposing them to the cool air.

The symptoms usually appear in older people, but have their beginnings earlier in life, possibly when the person has been repeatedly exposed to cold and rain. Gangrene can also result from untreated frostbite. This is dangerous because the tissues and vessels of the feet suffer permanent damage. Another possible cause of gangrene is the sclerosing or drying-up treatment applied to varicose veins. Prolonged standing or sitting is harmful to an older person who suffers from gangrene because the venous blood circulation slows down. Sufferers usually benefit from having an occupation which allows them to move around; with increased mobility the pain will sometimes subside altogether. Even though the disease cannot be cured completely, it is possible to alleviate it with the help of natural remedies, to the extent that the patient may go without serious complications for many years.

For an effective external treatment, add five drops of *Arnica 1x* to a little warm water and use this to make a wet pack. Take the two remedies *Echinaforce* and *Lachesis 10x* in a little water; they should be taken separately on alternate days, in the morning and at night, over an extended period. *Aesculaforce* and *Ginkgo biloba*, if taken regularly, also give satisfactory results.

The patient should not expose himself to the cold and should wrap up warmly against the weather. He should also adopt a light vegetarian diet. These measures are not difficult to follow, when he takes into account that by doing so he can find a measure of relief from his unpleasant condition and be spared much discomfort.

Haemorrhoids

Haemorrhoids, commonly known as piles, are often associated with chronic constipation. A dense network of blood vessels runs through the intestinal lining. When the stool in the rectum becomes hard and accumulates there these blood vessels become stretched. The resulting obstruction causes the walls of the vessels in the anal canal to become dilated, turning them into varicose veins in and around the rectal opening – haemorrhoids. The pressure needed to force out hard stools makes the veins in the thin membrane rupture; blood leaks out, and we have what are called bleeding haemorrhoids. At the time of evacuation, light-coloured blood will usually be noticed in the stool. If this condition is not remedied, the tissues will become inflamed and hard, resulting in the well-known piles. Hard stools can push the piles outwards so that they hang out of the anus; these can sometimes grow as large as a plum. This description alone will give an indication of the great discomfort this problem can cause. Anyone suffering from piles will therefore be most grateful for relief and a cure.

Women frequently get haemorrhoids after childbirth. Even during pregnancy the entire venous system is subjected to greater pressure than usual, often giving rise to varicose veins or enlarging those already there. In the weeks just before delivery the baby's head presses on the vessels in the pelvis and this, in turn, affects the vessels in the rectum. During delivery this pressure increases even more so that piles often appear after giving birth. Specific advice for expectant mothers is given on pages 26–9, but what can be done about this problem in general?

The Treatment of Haemorrhoids

First of all, you must take up the fight against constipation, for as long as you remain constipated any treatment will have only partial success. It must be said, however, that the cause of constipation is often more than the lack of a proper diet – one made up of wholegrain or wholemeal bread and plenty of fresh fruit and raw vegetables – and good herbal remedies such as Rasayana and Linoforce; an additional factor can be the mental and emotional stresses and tensions many of us experience as a consequence of unsolved problems in our life. An 'uptight' attitude can be an outward sign of a similar tension in the bowels, which, incidentally, are governed by the sympathetic nervous system. Once constipation has been remedied, it is relatively easy to treat the haemorrhoids successfully.

For this purpose there are some fine natural medicines available. *Aesculaforce* and *Hypericum perforatum* are good for the circulation and have aided many people in their effort to get rid of varicose veins. For this reason they are equally effective for the treatment of dilated veins in and around the anus. These remedies help to reduce the pressure in the veins and thus have a healing effect on the entire venous system.

Of great benefit also are *Millefolium*, a fresh plant extract from yarrow, *Hamamelis virginiana* and *Calcarea fluorica* (calcium fluoride). In cases of heavy bleeding, treat with *Bursa pastoris* (shepherd's purse) or *Tormentavena*. For local treatment and to ease pain, use haemorrhoid suppositories containing *cocoa butter* and *Hamamelis*. Teas made from *bloodwort* and *stinging nettles* are also beneficial. Spurge applied externally also helps to ease the pain. Although this plant is poisonous when taken internally, when crushed and applied to the anus as a poultice, it will soon help to make the pain subside.

A good way to prevent haemorrhoids is to bathe the anus with cold water every morning. The same water treatment should be given when piles have already formed.

The Heart – an Indefatigable Organ

Even before we become conscious of our existence, before birth, the heart begins to beat and continues to do so day and night throughout our life. It performs its work unflaggingly until the body is worn out and we close our eyes in death. Are we really grateful to the heart for serving us so faithfully during our lifespan of maybe 60–90 years, without even stopping for one hour, or do we take the heart for granted and neglect to look after it?

The Heart's Matchless Activity

Where could we ever find a machine that would work as efficiently as the heart? When we begin to study the structure of the myocardium we cannot help but be overwhelmed by this astounding example of divine Creation. Just look at the design of the muscle fibres. They are made up of fibrils, laid down in criss-cross layers, giving them marvellous elasticity. The cardiac wall consists of thousands of such fibres. Interwoven with this fibrous tissue we find a network of blood vessels providing nourishment and a network of nerves to register the stimuli. On reflection, we must admit that this living miracle in our body deserves more consideration than we are wont to give it. Is it not true that young people and athletes tend to treat the marvellous heart in their trust in an irresponsible and careless manner? Yet it is not only physical over-exertion that can tax and damage it. Worries and anxieties also weaken and harm the heart. The sympathetic nervous system serves to stimulate the heart and the parasympathetic slows it down. Both of these impulse conductors work in a rhythmic fashion, which means that the heart beats either slower or faster according to demand. Between every beat the heart stands still for about one-sixth of a second, the only rest it ever indulges in. But this rest in no way compensates for the amount of work we expect it to do throughout our lifetime. The heart, with all its capabilities and untiring service, is truly a miracle.

Nevertheless, it is not at all surprising to learn that about 50 per cent of all people today show some sort of abnormality in their heart function. Modern man always seems to be under stress and hurries even when there is no need, while at the same time he may be careless about attending to other responsibilities. This imbalance certainly does not make for peace of mind, as we still find it among those who enjoy their work as opposed to viewing it as a necessary evil. 'Haste makes waste', so the saying goes. Haste may indeed be harmful, but a steady pace is good for the heart.

The endocrine glands, especially the thyroid, influence the heart, a fact that can be noticed in patients with hyperthyroidism (Graves' disease). If the heart rhythm, the pulsation, is traced on paper by means of an electrocardiograph, a heart disorder can be detected. If the recording, called an electrocardiogram, shows two entwined curves, this indicates that two hearts are beating simultaneously. How can that be possible? The answer is simple if you are a pregnant woman! And if there are three curves, the happy mother-to-be can be told that she may expect twins.

Complications Deserving Attention
It is interesting to note that the heart may continue to beat even when the person is already dead. On the other hand, it is also possible for the heart to stop beating although death has not yet occurred, as in the case of suspended animation (apparent death, or asphyxia). A strong electric shock, for example, causes a spasm in the heart which may temporarily suspend its function, but death itself does not occur until later, when the oxygen supply is cut off completely and carbon dioxide accumulates because it is no longer eliminated.

Vesalius, the father of modern anatomical research, wanting to determine the cause of death of a nobleman he had treated, performed an autopsy during which he noticed, to his horror, that the heart was still beating. Witnesses who were present at the autopsy took him to court. He was found guilty of having performed a post-mortem examination on a living person and he was sentenced to death. This illustrates that life does not always coincide with the activity of the heart. So, even if death has occurred, the eyes are glassy and breathing has stopped, the heart may nevertheless continue to beat for a little while.

On the other hand, the opposite phenomenon, where the heart stops beating before the person is actually dead, has been observed in criminals who have been electrocuted. Being aware of this fact, a doctor was permitted to give a 'dead' man an injection in order to ease the spasm, because the doctor had attributed the sudden cardiac arrest to a spasm induced by the electricity. His diagnosis proved to be correct; the executed man who had appeared to be dead came back to life and had to undergo a second time the distressing procedure of the electric chair.

Many other astonishing incidents and facts connected with the functions of the heart could no doubt be cited. New surprises still come to light, some being discovered accidentally and others as a result of medical research.

Interesting Help for the Heart

The discovery of the so-called 'heart hormones' was made accidentally. A Hungarian professor was conducting experiments that involved injecting an old sheep over a long period of time with an extract derived from the heart of a young lamb. As a result of this treatment, the vitality of the old sheep increased; its heart rhythm gained in strength and it was once again able to climb around the hills as if it had been rejuvenated. When the old sheep was killed, the assumption that a rejuvenation had taken place was proved correct by the presence of new heart cells and cells which showed the nucleus to be in the process of dividing. Yet this dividing process is normally only found in young sheep during their growth period. The heart of a young animal is therefore somehow able to cause the nucleus of the heart cells to divide and form new cells. However, this process ceases to occur once the animal has reached maturity.

The cause of the observed rejuvenation, which is still unknown today, was attributed to a heart hormone, a term that seemed to be the most appropriate to designate the unknown factor. Since the substance concerned was perfectly harmless, researchers thought it might benefit humans too, and their subsequent experiments gave satisfactory results. It has since been used as an effective treatment for dilation of the heart, athlete's heart, and in cases of a tired or exhausted heart.

Nevertheless, this should not lead us to believe that if we abuse the heart and cause damage to its muscles we can always have recourse to heart hormones, which can easily correct any defects. This is not the case. Indeed, the most sensible way to ensure the proper functioning of the heart is to give it normal care and consideration. This faithful pump works wonderfully and is fully automatic if it is not constantly overtaxed. The heart hormone treatment, like any other good plant or homoeopathic medicine, is helpful in a case of real need. In such cases, there are various plant remedies available to us, for example *tincture of arnica root, Crataegus, Cactus grandiflora, Strophanthus, Spigelia*, the heart nutrient *Avenaforce*, the homoeopathic remedy *Calcarea carbonica* and homoeopathically diluted *gold*. A heart tonic made up of these ingredients will alleviate a whole range of problems. In certain cases, individuals will benefit from taking *Convallaria* and *Scilla maritima*, or a tea made from the woody partitions found inside a *walnut*, separating the two halves (see pages 153–4).

If you make sure not to overstrain your heart when you are young by engaging in very strenuous sports, you need not fear that you will have to suffer any ill consequences in later life.

Lycopus europaeus – a Remedy for Palpitations

Lycopus europaeus, commonly known as gipsywort or bugleweed, is a little known but efficacious medicinal plant. In Switzerland it is found in some parts of the Churfirst mountains at an elevation of up to 1,000 m (3,280 feet). In the valleys of the Ticino and in Pusciavo it is more abundant. European *Lycopus* is very similar in content and effect to that found in Virginia, in the United States.

Lycopus produces excellent results in the treatment of mild over-active thyroid conditions (hyperthyroidism) and the accompanying heart palpitations. Even in cases of very strong pounding and nervousness, doses of 5–10 drops have a tranquillising effect. If a hyperthyroid condition has existed for some time, *Urticalcin* is also recommended, since patients who suffer from palpitations usually lack calcium. I have often been able to achieve excellent results with people who thought they were suffering from a severe heart ailment simply by giving them *Lycopus* and calcium. It is also interesting to note that a somewhat increased basal metabolism can be normalised with these remedies if they are taken together with a homoeopathic seaweed preparation such as *Kelp 4x*. However, it is important that patients avoid the use of iodised salt. *Lycopus* and Urticalcin are also a helpful combination in cases of rapid heart beat due to over-excitability, a frequent complaint in our hectic times. Even though a calming effect can be felt almost immediately, the two natural remedies should be taken over a longer period of time for a more permanent result.

It is also important that the patient find out what is an appropriate dose of *Lycopus*, since this depends on the individual's sensitivity and response. For extremely sensitive people, five drops of *Lycopus* taken three times a day will suffice. Since the preparation is harmless the dose may be increased, if necessary to twenty or thirty drops at a time.

If a heart specialist can find nothing organically wrong, even though the patient may believe that he has a bad heart, I am confident that following the above advice will be of great benefit.

Modern Heart Poisons

Stress – Pace and Haste
The ever-increasing pace that characterises our modern way of life is one of the worst poisons for our heart. Even though, for the most part, individual productivity has not exceeded that of former times, it has become the custom to cram too many activities, especially those connected with our job, into a short space of time. Related to this, of course, is the shortened working week which has become so popular. The resulting free time is hardly ever used in a wholesome recreational or relaxing way such as pursuing a hobby, say working on an arts and crafts project, listening to good music, acquiring more knowledge through a study course or some other favourite subject or activity. Instead, we continue at the same hectic pace we use for work and seem to find enjoyment at weekends in the midst of the mad world of crowded motorways.

No wonder the result is a state of complete exhaustion instead of recuperation from the week's work. Driving at high speed creates anxiety and inner tension and affects the heart like a poison. Not only is the speed of the drive harmful, but the exhaust fumes are equally dangerous to the heart and blood vessels, particularly the fumes caused by leaded petrol. How much more sensible it would be to take a short leisurely ride to a nearby forest or the hills, get out of the car and go for a relaxing walk or hike. This kind of exercise would be invigorating for the blood vessels and, of course, the heart. The time spent in a clean environment would then permit us to return to work and our duties on Monday morning refreshed and relaxed, instead of tense and irritable as is so often the case today, when we misuse our leisure.

A similar tendency that should also be mentioned here is that of senselessly abusing our energies by allowing too little time to get to our place of work. We should always leave the house early enough so that it is not necessary to make a dash for the bus or train. Even a short run with a briefcase, bag or basket can be more taxing on the heart than most people realise. Obese people should be especially careful and remember the warning contained in the old proverb, 'Haste makes waste'. It has become a habit with many to rush around as if they have no time to lose, even though the gained time may be wasted later on in an idle telephone conversation or an insignificant chat with a neighbour. This is really most unwise, for the heart is not like a modern engine that can be accelerated from a standing start to 60 m.p.h. in seconds; the heart cannot be driven at top speed without suffering some damage.

Even young people who participate in overstrenuous sporting activities can develop dilation of the heart or other heart trouble. Sadly, modern athletic competition no longer attaches importance to purity and style of performance but requires the athlete to give his all, and it is exactly this excessive speed measured in split seconds that is dangerous. The excesses will act like poison to the heart, particularly for those athletes who are not in constant training. More often than not the damage is permanent.

The shorter working week mentioned earlier is also detrimental to the heart, since the work must be done faster if the number of working days is reduced without a proportionate reduction in the workload. The heart would only benefit from such an arrangement if the former, more sensible pace of work could be maintained. If a shorter working week depends on increased speed to produce the same results, the health of employee and employer alike will suffer.

Smoking
Smoking is harmful to the heart. We should none of us be in any doubt about this fact, especially women. The question of why women smoke if it is so dangerous to the heart, has many possible answers. One may be found in the assumption that it helps to

assert their liberated status and strengthen their self-image; or it may be the need to imitate whatever is currently popular, for no one wants to be out of step with the prevailing trends. Another reason may be the mistaken idea that smoking calms the nerves and helps to take one's mind off things. It is a fact that even fifty years ago very few women were smokers. In those days, if a woman lit a cigarette she was eyed with suspicion and dismissed as frivolous, or worse. The relatively new trend of women smoking, and thus exposing themselves to the dire consequences of this habit, may be attributed to the general change in life-style that we have undergone since then. Abundant proof exists that nicotine is harmful, as it constricts the coronary blood vessels and really has the same effect as a slow-acting poison. It is unfortunate that the tragic consequences to a smoker's sensitive vascular system do not become evident until twenty or thirty years later, so that it is all the more difficult to convince young people to stop smoking or not to start in the first place.

There is no question that nicotine is harmful to men also, but it is more so to women whose bodies are more sensitive to its effects. Also, statistics suggest that more men today smoke pipes, which are not quite as harmful as cigarettes since the toxicity is somewhat reduced due to a filtering system and a different way of preparing pipe tobacco. Nevertheless, whatever one might argue, it is more sensible and much easier to refrain from punishing the heart while there is still time.

Only One Heart!

Never forget that we have only one heart, from which we expect faithful service during our entire lifetime. It is a miracle in itself that the heart is capable of rendering this service unremittingly, and we should show our appreciation by caring for this marvellous gift. But we are failing this responsibility if we hasten its deterioration by careless overexertion and wilfully feeding it with poisons we know to be harmful. Such abuse will serve only to cut short the peaceful twilight years of our life. It is sad when proper understanding, regrets and a change of life-style come too late to save a person from an early grave.

If you are willing to make the effort to break bad habits early enough, you can bring about a restoration and strengthening of the heart with the help of natural remedies. For example, *Crataegus*, an extract from hawthorn, acts as a tonic for the heart muscles and *Auroforce* strengthens the nerves of the heart. A calming effect on

147

the heart is obtained from *Lycopus*, a harmless plant which is native to Virginia and also grown in Switzerland. If *wheat germ oil* is taken at the same time, a weak and neglected heart will soon be stronger and healthier. Nevertheless, no matter how good the natural remedy, the cure will not be lasting unless we stop subjecting the heart to harmful influences. Taking great care of this vital organ should be our first priority.

Beware of Heart Attacks

An elderly physician once told me, to my amazement, that he never came across a case of heart attack among his patients during the early years of his practice. And this was despite the fact that country people had to work much harder physically at that time because modern labour-saving machinery was not available. Why then, we might ask, do heart attacks rank as one of the most frequent causes of death today? Obviously, it cannot be linked to physical exertion from everyday labour, because modern technology has reduced the need for us to work as hard as our forefathers had to.

This question reminds me of a talk I heard during my stay in Vermont, the United States. Professor Raab, the famous research scientist who specialises in blood circulation, spoke about the 'loafer's heart' of our generation. He did not mean, however, that the 'loafer's heart' is a result of 'loafing around'; this certainly would not be true in today's increasingly busy world. Rather, it is the result of one-sided activity and a lack of exercise outdoors in the fresh air. The proper balance between exertion and relaxation has become distorted, disturbing the harmony of the rhythm of rest and activity.

We have all developed the bad habit of using the motor car for every little errand instead of walking. It is most unusual for a person who owns a car to take regular walks, not even when it is just a stone's throw to the corner shop. We have become a generation spoiled by the many inventions that make life easier: we no longer want to walk, we no longer want to use our limbs, and our muscles suffer from disuse. Many people are not aware of the danger that results from this way of life. Our circulation suffers and there may even be a deterioration of the entire vascular system as well as of the heart. Monotonous mental activity may lead to tensions, stagnation in the circulatory system, spasms, high blood pressure and many other problems. All these things are potential causes of heart attacks, especially for people in their late fifties.

Finding a Happy Medium

Many times of late I have received obituary notices concerning dear friends and acquaintances whose busy and productive lives had been suddenly cut short by heart attacks. An analysis revealed that, in every case, these people had long ago ceased to engage in any regular programme of physical activity or exercise. They would not make time for long walks or hikes in the forest or woods, or along country lanes. They had stopped participating in outings with a hiking club, which had always benefited their health in the past, and could not find time to do a little gardening. Neither did they have the time, or interest, to continue with some sport that they had enjoyed in their youth. They never stopped to think that they were actually shortening their life expectancy by twenty or thirty years, even though they may have had plenty of vitality.

This may sound contradictory, but it is a fact that the unbalanced use of one's energy, under constant stress and strain, is very taxing. Limiting our responsibilities and duties and reducing the pace of life would guarantee our heart more years of faithful service. Thus, we can conclude that a heart attack, in a sense, is often a self-inflicted blow. Every organ that is not regularly utilised or exercised degenerates and the body itself cannot exist if all activity ceases.

There is a happy medium between the over-taxed heart of a professional athlete and the under-taxed 'loafer's heart'. Anyone who does not want to end his life prematurely should certainly try to achieve this medium. It is extremely dangerous to give up physical exercise around the age of forty, because by doing so you may run the risk of having a heart attack fifteen or twenty years later and perhaps dying as a result. So, if you practise therapeutic exercises early enough and always make sure to take plenty of exercise in your daily life, you will avoid the need to go on strophanthin medication in later life.

There are times, however, when certain symptoms appear as an advance warning, making us aware of a potential problem. This happened to me several years ago when I began to have severe heart spasms. A subsequent examination showed there was nothing wrong with my heart, but I was prompted nonetheless to take a closer look at my life. In doing so I found that for some months I had been doing only brain work, with little physical activity. What made things worse, during this time my life was filled with problems and worries. It did not take much persuading to make me resume my interest in hiking and climbing in the mountains. And sure enough, within a short time I felt fully recovered.

Recommended Changes

A change of life-style would be of benefit to thousands of over-worked businesspeople, office workers, politicians and others holding sedentary positions – all executives and managers under stress – before it is too late. They should realise that it is much wiser to take some form of preventative action rather than to be concerned solely with the financial benefits, which is all their young families would be left with in the event of an untimely death that could have been prevented.

Let us not be deceived: nature has its own hard and fast rules which we cannot disobey with impunity. If an assessment or analysis of your life shows that you are in danger of having a heart attack, would it not be sensible to change your life-style and modify your daily routine? It would be wise to buy less petrol, for example, and use your legs more to make sure that your body cells receive enough oxygen. As far as diet is concerned, eat smaller quantities and stick to natural wholefoods of high nutritional value. The body will welcome such a change and show its gratitude by increasing its efficiency. Moreover, no unexpected heart failure will suddenly cut your life short. People under stress should make it a point to take the tincture made from the taiga root, *Eleutherococcus*, as well as *Ginsavita* tablets. These natural remedies, when taken regularly, with the recommended changes in life-style, will help to combat the harmful effects of stress.

Athlete's Heart

When winter arrives it brings with it the chance to partake in a whole range of snowsports, increasingly referred to as 'pleasure sports'. Some of these, however, may present a danger to the heart, because not everyone is sensible enough to choose a sport that has a beneficial effect on the health; instead, they become enslaved, body and soul, to movement and speed. Yet everything in nature is based on a wholesome rhythm of movement followed by rest. We were not created with wings, so we were not intended to dart through the air like birds. Our heart was designed to be close to the earth and we should observe its human, earthly potential.

There is a great difference between the pleasure of movement and the slavish pursuit of a competitive sport. Some light exercise after an occupation that demands a lot of sitting down is beneficial, indeed essential. But if you force yourself beyond your endurance and strength, you must not be surprised if your heart muscles become dilated because they have lost their elasticity. Yet it is still possible to do something about such a condition and, to a certain extent, regeneration can be achieved, although it is much better to take note of the old proverb, 'Prevention is better than cure.'

Athletic people usually have strength and resistance, but they must not make the mistake of thinking that their resilience and ability to spring back from overexertion has no limits. Thoughtless waste of any of our potentialities will be followed by loss of fitness. Why sacrifice to sport the energies that could serve you for many years to come? Why dash with abounding strength into overstrenuous sports and come out with chronic ill health?

Many may think that I am painting a rather pessimistic picture, but this is not so. Now and then I receive sad letters from sportsmen and women who were once famous champions; one, for example, was from an athlete who many years ago won the Swiss pentathlon and decathlon. For years now, this once energetic athlete has been suffering from loss of breath when climbing stairs, a weak heart beat, low blood pressure and ear and head noises (tinnitus). At his age he should be full of vitality.

So this is a warning not to carry any sport to extremes, yet is is a warning difficult to heed on the part of those who have already sold themselves 'body and soul' to this unrelenting taskmaster. The passion for winning in competitive sports consumes a tremendous amount of strength and energy. And who benefits from this useless drain of energy? Nobody really, and certainly not the athlete's heart, or why would it become defective so early in life?

Angina Pectoris

There are different forms of angina pectoris, the peculiar disease that produces something like heart spasms. It is caused by an insufficient supply of blood to the walls of the heart, which in turn induces oxygen starvation. The serious symptoms do not appear all at once, but increasing instances of acute heart cramps accompanied by a feeling of tightness across the chest – called cardiac insufficiency – should be a warning that immediate action must be taken.

The newest treatment with hormones has yielded comparatively good results. There are, however, various homoeopathic and herbal remedies that should not be overlooked in the treatment of this disease. Correctly employed, they are invaluable. For serious acute cases *Tabacum 6x* is helpful, and *Tabacum 12x* for chronic conditions. The cramping heart pains which induce fear, dizziness and nausea, an irregular pulse and cold sweat will be relieved by

151

Tabacum. It is noteworthy that this remedy also works well in cases of nicotine poisoning, thus proving the homoeopathic principle, like cures like. *Tabacum 6x* will greatly improve the patient's condition if he suffers from nicotine poisoning, which constricts the coronary vessels and causes the symptom-complex of angina pectoris.

Imminent collapse, with cold sweat on the forehead and a cramp that travels far down the legs, invariably requires the use of *Veratrum album 6x*. Heart hormones are very effective in cases of genuine angina pectoris as a consequence of a heart condition, in which dilation of the heart and gradual loss of tone occurs. In fact, heart hormones actually regenerate the heart. In arteriosclerotic conditions *Arnica 30x* is often extremely effective, and can be given as an injection or taken orally. Add ten drops of tincture to a glass of hot water and sip this during the day. Five to ten drops of *Crataegus* mother tincture or *Crataegisan* taken daily will strengthen the heart generally. Should asthmatic symptoms manifest themselves, *Galeopsis* mother tincture and *Cactus grandiflora 2x* will provide effective help. If the patient has a high colour, slightly bluish, and his veins are somewhat dilated, the homoeopathic remedy *Naja 12x* would be indicated. High blood pressure calls for *Viscum album*, an extract from mistletoe. *Rauwolfavena*, a preparation made from rauwolfia, has also proved its worth.

Correct breathing, with slow, sustained exhalation, can often stop an attack in its early stages, especially when the blood is then drawn away from the heart by bathing the arms. These arm baths, as recommended by Sebastian Kneipp in his water cures, have a particularly good effect when used for incipient attacks.

If congestions are also present, do not forget to take *Aesculaforce* and *Ginkgo biloba*. Moreover, a warm bath to which an infusion of *lemon balm* has been added will have a calming influence on the nervous system.

Massaging the body regularly with a good oil that stimulates the skin functions is good for relaxation of the nerves and induces a feeling of well-being.

The proper functioning of the bowels, ensuring the elimination of all waste materials, is as important with angina as it is with other diseases. If necessary, use *psyllium seed*, or a *linseed* preparation or any other natural herbal laxative to promote good bowel movement.

As regards foods, a diet rich in natural grape or fruit sugar, but low in protein and salt, is recommended for angina pectoris.

An Old Country Remedy

In general, bad heart cramps in cases of angina pectoris are relieved by radical medicines, usually amyl nitrite or Trinitrin (nitroglycerin). There is, however, an old and exceedingly simple remedy which is quite easy to come by. It relieves the spasms without any side effects or complications. The same remedy is also good for asthma attacks. This old country remedy has been in use for centuries but has now, alas, been practically forgotten even in rural areas.

Here is what you do. Take some *fermented cider*, the older the better, heat it until it reaches boiling point and quickly remove it from the heat. Then soak some towels in the hot liquid and place them, as hot as the patient can bear, on both arms, covering each arm completely. The heat plus the fruit acids of the hot cider will decongest the heart circulation, soothe the blood vessels and the nervous system and relieve the cramps. The effect of this simple natural treatment can be reinforced by placing a hot linseed, hay flower or lemon balm *compress* over the heart at the same time. Linseed is the best choice for this purpose.

Cramp-like conditions brought about by angina pectoris or other similar causes follow the course of the sympathetic nerve. They often start in the pit of the stomach near the sternum and move up to the throat, leaving a feeling almost amounting to strangulation. Such distressing conditions, if treated as described, will be relieved to the patient's greatest satisfaction.

The Woody Partitions inside the Walnut

An infusion made from the woody partitions inside the walnut is excellent in cases where the coronary vessels have become hardened, and for cardiac pains and fever. A narrowing of the coronary vessels can often be attributed to chronic nicotine poisoning. The doctor and knowledgeable friends may have encouraged the patient on more than one occasion to quit smoking because of his heart trouble, the so-called angina pectoris. Unfortunately, the nicotine addiction often triumphs over health considerations, and severe chest pains will continue to plague the smoker. Would he continue to smoke if he knew that every severe attack of angina pectoris leaves a small scar in the muscle tissue of the heart? I wonder. Still, his unreasonableness may compel him to carry on smoking and the final result will be a myocardial infarction, death of the tissues in the myocardium. Many weeks resting in bed may bring about an improvement in his condition, but it is not to be mistaken for a cure. For once again, instead of healthy pink muscle tissue, the patient will be left with yet another white scar on the heart. Even so he must consider himself fortunate, as a 'heart attack' can sometimes lead to a rupture of the heart, which would be fatal.

Needless to say, the scars themselves are far from negligible. One day, the last attack will come. A post-mortem will then reveal countless tiny scars which bear witness to the pain that accompanied each seizure and to the folly of refusing to give up smoking, preferring instead a smoker's death. If you would rather not let it come to that sad ending, stop the dangerous habit that puts your life in jeopardy – give up smoking. Moderation in alcohol and meat consumption is also indicated, and if you are able to abstain from these altogether, so much the better for your heart and general health.

The woody partitions inside the walnut contain an excellent medicinal property from which you can benefit when taken as an infusion. Remove the dividing walls of four or five nuts, soak them in water for one day, leave overnight and then boil them for a few minutes the next morning. Drink the resulting tea in the morning on an empty stomach. When taken regularly it will alleviate the feeling of constriction and pain in the chest.

This infusion is also effective in cases of high temperature accompanied by pains in the heart. Some relief is frequently noticed after the first cup, but if the pains continue, the tea should be sipped frequently until they and the fever have disappeared.

Sick without a Sickness

If you own a car you may at times hear a noise when you are driving, a noise that comes and goes. To find out what it is, you decide to take the car to a garage for a check-up, but just at that time, the noise is not there, and naturally the mechanic cannot find anything wrong with it. A few weeks later, however, your car stops in the middle of the road because the defect that had not been found and therefore not taken care of, has developed into a serious fault.

It is even harder to detect a disorder in the human body, especially if it is not a question of an actual organic disease. At times, all possible methods of examination used by the physician or naturopath do not disclose any clue of a malfunction. Intuition can be a great asset in the medical profession, but it is not enough to help those patients who feel very unwell yet the doctor is unable to put his finger on what ails them. Indeed, it often takes many years of experience to understand such patients. Many of these patients are women, whose complaints are often simply attributed to a hysterical nature or their imagination, as in psychosomatic illnesses. However, this diagnosis will only force them into deeper despair.

Hyperthyroidism

Not long ago, I was consulted by a girl who had just returned to the Engadine Valley from a trip to Italy. Her big, shiny, bulging and staring eyes showed unmistakable signs of an overactive thyroid. She explained that her doctor had practically taken her apart without finding anything wrong, although she complained of frequently feeling very ill and weak.

When staying at the seaside this 'sick person without a sickness' could sleep for twenty-four hours at a time if no one woke her up. Long sleeping periods are a typical effect of the iodine contained in sea air on those suffering from a thyroid condition. Some patients become very active, vivacious and highly strung, others feel an unnatural desire and need for sleep. It is essential for such people to be aware of what the problem is, for it will enable them to adjust to their environment and to take the appropriate remedial measures.

Some years ago I sent a patient suffering from the same symptoms to her doctor to have him check her basal metabolism. Since he felt there was nothing wrong with her thyroid, he was reluctant to check her out. But she insisted, and to his astonishment the results of the test revealed a substantial increase in her metabolism.

This condition, in almost all cases, is associated with a calcium deficiency in the blood. For this reason these patients need to eat plenty of food high in calcium. Taking a calcium-complex preparation, such as *Urticalcin*, is also highly recommended, in addition to a homoeopathic *iodine* preparation, preferably made from sea kelp, as well as *Lycopus*.

It is a source of great satisfaction to see the unpleasant symptoms disappear when the body is given the things it lacks and resumes its nature functions once more.

Neurodystonia (Autonomic Nervous Disorders)

Many disorders of the nervous system are purely psychological in nature, or they may be caused by a malfunction of the endocrine glands. Doctors call this type of problem 'neurodystonia', a descriptive term that does not really tell us much. It encompasses all disorders of the autonomic nervous system, except those of organic origin, and is therefore a rather broad and complex concept. All of the following symptoms, not attributable to organic disease, can be classified under this term: vascular spasm, sudden sweating, cramps in the vascular system and gallbladder, spastic stomach aches, intestinal and heart disorders (including organic neurosis).

Since this all-embracing term was first coined, there have been fewer people with unidentifiable illnesses. So, if the doctor cannot find an explanation for a certain complaint, he simply attributes it to 'neurodystonia'. This is convenient and benefits the doctor as well as the patient, at least from a psychological viewpoint. For to be suffering from an illness without a name is a rather uncomfortable affair. By giving it a name the doctor satisfies his patient, if only for the sake of his not being called a malingerer, one who is simply pretending to be sick.

In such cases, a skilfully handled psychotherapeutic treatment has always produced good results, especially if combined with certain tonics for the nerves such as *Neuroforce* and *Ginsavena*, as well as antispasmodics, like *Petadolor*.

Visible and Invisible Goitre

Many people, and more particularly women, often complain about a pounding of the heart without being able to explain its cause. Naturally, when climbing stairs rapidly everyone becomes aware of a faster heart beat. However, if you frequently experience a rapid heart beat without prior physical exertion or emotional upset, it would be wise to undergo a thyroid test.

A hyperactive thyroid has certain characteristics. Besides a faster pulse rate there is generally a loss of weight and an inner vibration in the chest area. Other symptoms are loss of hair, diarrhoea, and often a feeling of tension and anxiety. The basal metabolic rate is increased and the eyes take on a distinct shine. The doctor's examination will usually reveal a swelling of the thyroid gland, a goitre.

Goitre, as a result of either an overactive or underactive thyroid, is much more frequent than many people are aware, particularly in land-locked countries such as my native Switzerland, or the central plains of the United States. Many sufferers simply resign themselves to a constant state of nervousness and hypersensitivity, two of the unpleasant symptoms of this complaint.

Causes and Cures

Although iodine deficiency always plays a part in causing goitre, other minerals and trace elements are essential for successful treatment. Experience has shown that calcium is as important as iodine, so for treating and preventing goitre I recommend a diet high in calcium. White cabbage salad and sauerkraut are rich in this mineral, as are kohlrabi (turnip cabbage) – especially the leaves – turnips, carrots and beets. The latter two can be taken as juice or included raw in salads. A good calcium preparation, for example *Urticalcin*, is an excellent supplement.

On the other hand, be very careful with commercial products containing iodine. In cases of unduly sensitive people, those who suffer from hyperthyroidism, the use of iodised salt alone will sometimes cause palpitations and upsets. A person who is sensitive to mere traces of iodine should avoid such products altogether.

A calcium therapy does not cause any complications, neither does the minute amount of iodine found in some plants. For example, watercress and all the other varieties of cress contain homoeopathic amounts of iodine which even the most sensitive person can tolerate. Seaweed prescribed in homoeopathic doses, such as *Kelp 6x, 5x and 3x*, is an excellent source of iodine. When a seaweed preparation is prescribed it is best to begin with Kelp 6x, then after a few months change to Kelp 5x and continue reducing the potency until, after about two years, the patient responds well to the tablets in uncontrolled strength. The herbal seasoning salt *Herbamare* contains freshly processed cresses in addition to all the trace elements found in kelp, and is therefore a useful prophylactic.

If goitre is present and is not caused by a hyperthyroid condition, *kelp tablets* will help the patient, since they contain all the minerals found in seaweed. These tablets also help to reduce obesity without any side effects. I have also found that goitre due to hypothyroidism reacts favourably to treatment with *potassium iodide*.

Goitre not only detracts from one's appearance and is physically annoying, but it also places a burden on the mental processes because of its detrimental effect on the memory and nervous system. It is therefore advisable not to put off the treatment of goitre but to do something about it quickly. Surgery can be avoided in many cases if the proper treatment with natural remedies and therapies is administered early enough. Natural treatment will restore the normal body functions and physical strength, which is not always the case after surgical removal of a large part of the thyroid.

Post-Operative Treatment of Goitre

Where surgery is necessary, it should not be considered as a complete cure, making further treatment unnecessary. On the contrary, post-operative treatment is essential in order to eradicate the cause of the disease. Iodine remedies, especially in the case of exophthalmic goitre, are not at all indicated and should be carefully avoided. Instead, choose foods that contain traces of organic iodine, for these definitely serve to cure goitre. Once again, the two herbal seasoning salts *Herbamare* and *Trocomare*, both made with sea salt, are recommended first of all. Furthermore, effective post-operative treatment of goitre includes plant products rich in fibre and iodine. *Watercress* is high in iodine and should be eaten in salads when it is in season. It is also good for exophthalmic goitre and will not harm the patient. In addition, homoeopathic and herbal remedies can be used to good effect.

Cabbage poultices, alternating with *clay poultices*, preferably prepared with a decoction of oak bark, have been found excellent for the treatment of goitre. If the cabbage poultices prove too strong in their effect, leave them on only as long as the patient is able to stand them. In time, the period of application may be extended as the patient becomes accustomed to them. Let me add that *kelp* in combination with *Urticalcin* have given good results in post-operative treatment too.

Goitre and Iodised Salt

Many years have passed since Dr Eggenberger of Herisau first advocated the idea of iodising cooking salt and it was partly due to his initiative that iodised salt began to be used in Switzerland. The knowledge that iodine deficiency is responsible for the development of certain forms of goitre also made other countries decide to add iodine to salt. But let us examine whether this blanket arrangement makes sense.

Admittedly, iodised salt benefits those who suffer from thyroid deficiency (hypothyroidism), that is to say, tending to myxoedema, and those people can take it without it doing any harm. However, iodised salt has exactly the opposite effect on people whose thyroid is overactive, with tendency to Graves' disease (hyperthyroidism, exophthalmic goitre). Experience shows that if such people take the slightest amount of iodine they experience palpitations. So these unfortunate people think that something is wrong with their heart and run to the heart specialist to find out what is the trouble. In any case, because of the lack of a warning on the salt package, or their failure to understand the implications of iodised salt, they will have been harmed by what appeared to be a harmless salt.

This example goes to show that not everything that is meant to be good for us is necessarily good or safe for everyone. Indeed, it is incomprehensible how this salt can be offered as something that is wholesome for everyone without distinction. It should be recommended only for those whose complaint has been diagnosed as hypothyroidism, never for people with an excessive secretion of thyroid hormones, who cannot tolerate iodine.

Of course, it is an undisputed fact that a deficiency of iodine plays a part in the development of goitre, for the thyroid needs iodine for its normal function and development. But it can be found in sufficient quantity and an easily assimilated form in the food we eat, provided our diet consists of wholefoods. Such foods cause no disturbances or damage. However, if you throw away the edible skins from fruits, and vegetables, apple cores, the outer layer of cereals, such as bran, in short, anything that is part of the naturally grown whole, then you will sooner or later have a mineral deficiency. This includes, of course, a lack of iodine, which ulti-mately will encourage the development of goitre. Instead of recom-mending the use of iodised salt, it would be far better to educate people to give up eating white flour, refined sugar, canned foods and all other products of our 'civilised' way of feeding, and eat only nutritive natural wholefoods.

The introduction of iodised salt was prompted by the obser-vation that people who live by the sea hardly ever suffer from thyroid problems. The iodine of the sea, especially in sea salt, was rightly taken to be the reason for this. Even though the cause of the problem was correctly analysed, the wrong solution was adopted. A manufactured product simply does not have the same effect as a substance found in nature. Sea salt is an excellent source of iodine and everyone in 'goitre areas' should use only natural sea salt for seasoning. (The vast stretches of the mid west in the United States, for example, are commonly known as the 'goitre belt'.) Although sea salt contains iodine, nature has included it in such combinations and proportions that you need never fear any of the disturbances iodised salt brings about. Moreover, when fresh herbs are added to sea salt you get the perfect herbal seasoning salts known as *Herbamare* and *Trocomare*. A great number of people have come to appreciate these salts because of their taste and goodness.

Do you have a garden? If so, there is another way to help prevent or overcome thyroid problems. The answer lies in fertilising your garden. Feed the soil with iodine-rich bone meal and other iodine-containing fertilisers. The plants grown in such soil will be richer in iodine and thereby satisfy the body's requirements, for they are able to process the mineral iodine in such a way that our body can absorb it without any trouble and damaging effects. For the same reason iodine in sea salt can do no harm. It is a biological solution that is therefore much to be preferred to the orthodox medical way of taking iodised salt.

If you have been using iodised salt and are experiencing a faster heart beat, other disturbances of the heart, palpitations and excessive anxiety, you should definitely stop adding it to your food. This salt may be effective, though not always in the desired manner, but one thing is sure, it is by no means harmless, judging by the debates its usage has caused. Iodine is one of those medicines for which one cannot establish general rules. In the same way as one cannot say that alcohol is harmless because most people drink it, nor can one argue that nicotine is not harmful because so many people smoke. It may be true that a number of people do not succumb instantly to the bad effects of alcohol and nicotine, showing visible signs of damage right away; others, however, who happen to be more sensitive by nature do not get off so lightly and soon suffer the usual consequences of these poisons. Does this not convince you of the necessity to observe nature and abide by its rules? In accordance with your sensitivity and inherited disposition, the final effects, one way or the other, cannot be avoided. In fact, one cannot even conclude that if certain things are harmless to one person they are harmless to everyone. So, if you are a sensible person you will consider your own individual nature and reactions and let these be your guide, never making your condition worse by taking potentially hazardous substances. However difficult this may be, if you prefer to remain healthy and active rather than having to suffer unnecessarily, abstinence – the effort to cut out certain things – is no doubt the course of wisdom. After all, your health is at stake!

Iodine

Iodine is a peculiar substance that still puzzles research scientists. Taken in great quantity it is a dangerous poison; on the other hand, the body cannot exist without it. Iodine is one of the elements that the body needs only in minute quantities, a trace element; at the same time, it is of such importance that it may be compared

160

to the push button that is needed to start and stop a sophisticated piece of machinery. The human body contains approximately 0.05 g of iodine, half of which is found in the muscular system, one-tenth in the skin and a large portion in the endocrine glands, especially the thyroid. Here we find iodine attached to an amino acid, forming the hormone called thyroxine.

It is interesting to note that the so-called iodine level, that is the amount of iodine contained in the blood, is the same for all healthy people, no matter where they live, whether in the mountains, by the sea, in the polar regions or at the equator.

Where Iodine Can Be Found

Iodine is present in rocks, from which it is released when the rocks decompose during the process of weathering. It is dissolved in rain water and is carried to the oceans by the rivers. This, no doubt, is one of the reasons why the ocean is so rich in iodine, as well as other minerals which are carried to it in a similar way. While various other salts remain in the sea, iodine evaporates and is returned to the soil by means of rainfall, dew, fog and snow. Every year hundreds of tons of iodine are thus returned to replenish the soil.

In mountain valleys, however, a deficiency of iodine is often found in the population. The explanation for this may lie in the fact that the water rushes along so rapidly that it carries away large amounts of dissolved iodine instead of restoring it to the soil, as it is able to do in the flatlands.

The Effects of Iodine Deficiency

It is possible to become mentally retarded due to a deficiency of iodine. The thyroid fails to produce enough hormones, and in severe cases myxoedema can result. The deficiency may cause physical and mental lethargy. It can deaden all initiative and result in extreme lack of interest in anything, especially in work or job-related activities, while it may increase the desire to eat. The entire metabolism is affected, normal heart function is slowed down considerably, with low blood pressure following. When sexual potency is also low or lacking entirely, liveliness and emotional feelings will be missing. It is not infrequent to observe a miraculous change in a patient if he is given iodine in the form of seaweed tablets, for example, *Kelpasan*, and if he is put on a natural whole-food diet.

The formation of goitre is in almost every case connected with an iodine imbalance. This subject has been discussed in great detail in the preceding sections (see pages 156–60) and the reader is advised to refer to these for further information.

Iodine is also indirectly responsible for obesity. The thyroid and sex glands work together and if an obese person is given iodine as contained in plants, for example, *kelp tablets*, the thyroid steps up its hormone production. This, in turn, activates the entire metabolism. The gonads become more active and, as a result, the deposits of body fat decrease.

You can see that iodine is more important than one might think, because this mysterious element, even though present in minute traces, is responsible for operating the 'gears' of our body, not unlike the illustration in the proverb, 'Big oaks from little acorns grow.'

Although the effect of *watercress* is less marked than that of seaweed, nevertheless it contains a modest amount of iodine and can thus be of good service to the thyroid. Other excellent remedies are the *Topinambur* tincture *Helianthus tub.* and homoeopathic *Graphitis 6x*.

Menstrual Problems

Excessive and insufficient bleeding can both be a source of great discomfort. A heavy menstrual flow means an unnecessary loss of blood, which may even lead to a slight case of anaemia. It is important that women who suffer from this condition make sure that they do not engage in any strenuous physical activity beginning a few days prior to the period. This may be especially difficult for women who have to do physical work, because it is not easy to find someone to help and the work still has to be done.

In these circumstances, *Tormentavena* has proven to be a simple, reliable, natural remedy. It is a combination of fresh tormentil root and the juice of the green flowering oat plant. This remedy also has a tonic effect on the nerves. *Sherpherd's purse tincture (Bursa pastoris)* is also very helpful.

A very light flow of blood can cause an emotional upset. *Sea kelp* from the Pacific Ocean is very beneficial in cases of this sort because of its potassium iodide content. Generally, taking one kelp tablet in the morning and at noon suffices to normalise the flow. Do not take in the evening and continue only until the period is regular again. However, women suffering from hyperthyroidism must take kelp only in homoeopathic doses. Women who have been suffering for some time, or frequently, from the discomforts of insufficient menstrual flow should also take a preparation that stimulates blood circulation, for example *Aesculaforce*. In addition, to cure the disorder, another preparation, *Ovarium 3x*, is necessary in order to influence the ovaries and establish a regular period.

Take regular *sitz baths* (hip baths) to which an infusion of thyme or camomile has been added, to complement the treatment with the above-mentioned botanic medicines. The baths help to normalise the functions so important to women. Since the cure of menstrual malfunction goes hand in hand with the relief of emotional depression, every woman in need will be glad to follow the advice given.

Menopausal Problems

During the menopause practically every women experiences hot flushes and other distressing symptoms to a greater or lesser degree. At times a woman may be affected so severely that her nerves and emotions become totally upset, and any relief is always welcome. It is important to take even better care of the body than usual during the changes of life. Excellent benefits are obtained by *exercising* regularly out-of-doors; the importance of activities such as walking and hiking and the practice of taking deep breaths of fresh air cannot be emphasised enough and will bring about a striking improvement.

Physical therapy may also contribute to improving the condition. For example, daily *brush massages* and twice weekly *sitz baths* (hip baths) with a decoction of hay flowers or lady's mantle added to the water are recommended. Extreme emotional depression may be relieved through *Kuhne's cold water treatment* (see pages 436–8). As with menstrual problems, physical exertion as well as occupational stress should be avoided at all costs. In addition, learn to do without coffee, tea and alcoholic beverages, as it is indeed best to leave them alone altogether during the menopause.

These precautionary measures will make it easier to sleep at night and improve the patient's general health. The following remedies help to give relief and eliminate the symptoms causing discomfort: *Salvia, Ovarium 3x, Ignatia plus Sepia 6x, and Aconitum 10x.* Sounder and more restful sleep influences the mind and nerves, restoring emotional balance to people of a normally happy disposition and thus relieving constant depression and moods.

It is certainly good to know that the discomfort and upsets experienced during the menopause can be alleviated in such simple ways. For this reason, now you are acquainted with the various remedies and treatments available, use them to the full and enjoy better general health.

The Kidneys

If we were to compare our body to a modern chemical plant, the air-conditioning unit responsible for getting rid of poisonous exhaust fumes would correspond to our lungs. In the case of a prolonged breakdown of such an air-purification unit, the workers would die from poisons released into the air. The result would be just as tragic if our lungs stopped functioning. Furthermore, in order to assure the workers' well-being, it is of utmost importance to get rid of the poisonous solid waste materials too. In the body this is accomplished by the kidneys, with some help from the liver. If the kidneys were to stop operating for only two days, thus causing a retention of metabolic toxins, uraemia would set in. The accumulation of waste products, normally excreted in the urine, would cause metabolic poisoning.

This can be observed in cases of an enlarged prostate, hypertrophy of the prostate. If the enlarged prostate blocks the urethra completely – a not uncommon occurrence in older men – every effort should be made to correct the obstruction within forty-eight hours. This can be done with the help of *hot herbal steam baths* or by means of a *catheter*, a rather uncomfortable treatment. If immediate attention is not given, uraemia may develop, as already mentioned, and endanger the patient's life.

Kidney stones may bring about the same condition, that is, when they block the ureter. In such cases, prolonged *hot baths* are very beneficial. They should be accompanied by a light underwater *massage* of the kidney and bladder areas. To prevent the formation of kidney stones *madder root (Rubia tinctorum)* is still the best remedy. (For further advice on treating kidney stones, see pages 167–70).

Noteworthy Characteristics of the Kidney Structure

The structure of the kidneys is truly marvellous. All design problems have been solved with such perfection that the ancient anatomists called the kidney a *'viscus elegantissimum'*, meaning 'most elegant organ'. The kidney is really a complicated filtration plant consisting of about a million cup-shaped individual filters. Each of these filters is surrounded by a two-walled capsule and is separated by small conducting tubes which supply blood and filter out the urine simultaneously. Every day about 1.7 litres (about 3 pints) of this diluted filtrate are transported to the bladder by way of the ureter and then expelled. The remainder is reabsorbed by the bloodstream so that the entire activity takes care of about 175 litres (about 38.5 gallons) of filtrate in one day.

The human kidney is bean-shaped. The filtering units are located in the outermost layer, the cortex. The inner structures form the medulla, consisting of the collecting tubules. The size of the tubules increases towards the inside; the large vessels and the beginning of the ureter are inside the pelvis of the kidney which, by the way, has nothing to do with the basin-shaped cavity formed by the bones in the hip region.

Harmful Influences

Aside from the heart and the liver, no other organ suffers more from the consequences of our modern life-style and refined foods than the kidneys. In my practice I have been able to observe time and again the extent of the damage white sugar has done to them. Often a kidney patient has been relieved of his pains simply by abstaining from all foods containing sugar. Just to prove the point, the patient would again be given sugar on a test basis and, sure enough, the pains would return. However, this holds true only for products made with refined sugar, whereas natural sugars as contained in dried grapes (for example raisins), figs, bananas and other fruits never cause any such complications.

It is also generally known that the kidneys can be rendered a great service and protected if the intake of salt is reduced to a minimum. Bacterial poisons, likewise, have a detrimental effect on them. That is why infectious diseases such as measles, scarlet fever, diphtheria, tonsillitis and others, always have an adverse effect. Permanent damage can be prevented if proper care is taken to cure these diseases fully, and by making sure that the kidneys function properly during and after an illness. This is best done by taking the excellent plant extract of *Solidago*, as contained in *Nephrosolid*, a remedy that should be kept in every home.

Very dangerous for the kidneys are metallic poisons such as lead. This is why painters and decorators, as well as operators of hot-metal printing machines, and compositors, traditionally risked kidney problems unless precautions were taken (although these risks have since diminished as technology has advanced).

Moreover, the kidneys will function better if we protect them from getting cold. For example, when hot weather makes us feel like a cold drink, we should make it a habit to sip slowly instead of gulping it down. If you bathe in cold water or feel cold after having been caught in the rain, for example, you should immediately restore the body's proper temperature balance by taking a bath or a shower, or by applying warm water packs or any other warm water therapy. Otherwise, the cold shock to the kidneys may have adverse effects.

How to Detect Kidney Disorders

Close attention should be paid to the kidneys because kidney problems do not always manifest themselves immediately by acute pain. If the amount of water passed is less than normal over a period of time, we should have a urine analysis made. This is also indicated if the colour of the urine changes and for some time is either too dark or too light, almost colourless. If we notice the presence of blood, cloudiness, or any other residue in the urine, this is also a cause for concern. A sediment of tiny crystals indicates that the person has a tendency to develop kidney stones or gravel. Do not wait for pain or a colic before doing something about it. Seek treatment at once.

If we examine the urine sediments under a microscope, we will be amazed at the diversity of the crystalline formations nature is able to produce even in the urine. All sorts of prismatic forms and bundles of needle-like crystals can be seen. They are in fact the crystallised forms of uric acid, sulphuric acid and benzoic acid. The amino acid leucine crystal is especially interesting, forming a bundle of 'needles' more compact than a snowflake.

Such observations turn an inspection of the uric sediments into a fascinating and meaningful study. Indeed, the trained expert can draw valuable conclusions from the pictures revealed by the microscope during a urine analysis. It is even possible to find out whether the patient has adhered to a prescribed diet. For example, if numerous sulphuric crystals are present, it is evident that the patient has eaten foods containing sulphur, such as eggs, beans, peas, lentils and radishes, even though he may have been instructed not to do so. If the test shows any oxalic acid crystals, the patient has been eating spinach, rhubarb, lettuce or sauerkraut. If a large number of creatinine crystals are in evidence, the patient obviously did not abstain from eating meat.

Thus, an analysis of the urine can be most informative, often more than even some doctors may think possible. We may learn something about metabolic disorders, certain organic diseases or other functional disorders.

Having been made aware of the value of a urine test, we should not consider it extravagant to have a comprehensive examination at least once a year. On several occasions I have been able to detect diabetes through a urine test. In these cases the patients have complained for years about tiredness and thirst but no one had ever linked these symptoms with diabetes. The urine analysis, however, proved it beyond a doubt.

In view of the demands of today's ever-increasing pace of life, it is of paramount importance to care for our body at least as much as we look after our car. We all understand that it is more economical to rectify a problem with the car when it first shows up, before a major repair job becomes necessary through sheer neglect. Does our body not deserve the same consideration? Take, for example, our kidneys and think of the great demands they are subjected to; much pain and discomfort can be avoided later if prompt attention and constant care are given them.

Kidney Colic

Many people have kidney stones without being aware of the fact. The same goes for gallstones. Their presence is only noticed when the stones enter the ureter (or in the case of gallstones, the bile duct) and can move neither forward nor backward.

When a kidney stone becomes stuck in the ureter the resulting pain is so excruciating that the patient may end up in a state of delirium. It is not unusual for him to lose all control, knocking into things around him, screaming in agony and, of course, causing great concern to those around him. The pain can last for hours and there is great danger if the proper treatment is not given.

The patient must be placed in a *hot bath* and with light, careful *massage*, the stone must be made to move from the ureter into the bladder. The hot water itself will make the patient feel more comfortable. Should the heart start to give trouble or if he suffers from hyperthyroidism (exophthalmic goitre), he must also be assisted with cold compresses. The best way to do this is to apply a 'heart tube'. Place a tube in a circle around the heart area and let cold water flow through it. This will cool the heart down and bring relief. If necessary, put cold compresses on the wrists and forehead, renewing them frequently to keep them cold. With this treatment the patient should be able to remain in the hot bath for half an hour without fainting.

Internal treatment should also start at the onset of a colic. *Magnesium phos. 6x* and *Atropinum sulph. 4x* should be given. If the patient brings everything up, then the remedies must be given by means of an enema.

If, in spite of all precautions, the patient loses consciousness anyway, there is no need to panic as the spell will pass off without doing any harm, and perforation can be prevented.

Keep the bath hot by adding hot water; it should last half an hour, the patient being massaged all the while and the cold compresses being renewed. After the bath apply hot packs and give frequent herbal enemas. If blood comes instead of urine, this means that the stone has become stuck in the ureter and has damaged it. At this stage, it would be beneficial to give *Solidago* by enema in order to stimulate the kidneys, for if he has a severe attack, the patient will usually be unable to retain anything given by mouth. Continue the packs and enemas for half an hour and then follow up with another hot bath, with massage and compresses.

This treatment is to be repeated, in alternation, for half an hour each time. As soon as the stone begins to move toward the bladder the pain will move from the back to the front and then slowly diminish. The moment the stone enters the bladder the patient will be more or less free from pain. It may take several hours to accomplish this, but once achieved, the patient can then lie quietly and rest without any further danger. If he is thirsty, give him diluted *Molkosan* (concentrated whey) to sip as this reduces the internal heat and replaces the liquids lost by perspiration in the bath. It will also provide the liquid essential to eliminate any further toxins that are still in the system. Additionally, give the patient plenty of *knotgrass (Polygonum aviculare) tea* because this too helps to dissolve the stones.

However, this is not yet the end of treatment. A thorough follow-up cure, including *sitz baths* and *massage* is necessary, as the stone must not be allowed to remain in the bladder where it could give rise to irritation and bleeding.

Taking everything into account, this is still a simple method of treatment and will avert a ureter blockage with its serious consequences or even the need for an operation. It is clearly worthwhile, because the patient will recover astonishingly fast after the cure, whereas an operation can often have complications, requiring a great deal of after-care. However, should the size of the stone prevent its elimination through the natural, physical therapy outlined above, it is not too late to resort to an operation. I would add, however, that there is very rarely a need for this. In most cases it will be possible to effect a successful cure if the treatment is given with great care and thoroughness. Of course, stones can also be gradually dissolved by taking natural remedies. *Rubiaforce*, made from the madder root, is such a remedy, and one that has been tested and proven in practice. If taken over a longer period of time, Rubiaforce will dissolve even larger stones, especially if the patient also drinks a lot of goldenrod tea.

TREATMENT WITH RUBIAFORCE

Many patients whose kidney stones were dissolved by *Rubia tinctorum* (madder root) have attested to its excellent therapeutic effect. In addition to taking this remedy, however, it is most important that the patient avoids catching cold and becoming exhausted. To ensure its success, a *special diet* should be followed during and after the treatment. The patient must avoid all denatured or refined foods containing white sugar and white, bleached flour. Nor should he use salt or any sharp condiments in the food. Furthermore, the kidney patient should not eat Brussels sprouts, spinach, asparagus, rhubarb or, especially, pork, luncheon meat and other cold meats. Since vitamin A deficiency promotes the formation of gravel and stones in the kidneys, it must be counteracted by eating plenty of carrot salad and drinking carrot juice. If bleeding is noticed in the urine, no meat should be eaten, the only animal protein allowable being soft white cheese (cottage cheese or quark). For the best results the patient should stick to a diet of brown rice, vegetables and raw salads.

Physical therapy is also beneficial. For about half an hour each night a hot and moist *compress* made with hay flowers and camomile should be applied to the kidney area. Hot *sitz baths* will also help. If the stones should cause bleeding, the patient should take *Millefolium, Hamamelis virg., Echinaforce, Tormentavena and Cantharis 6x.*

While carrying out these recommendations take the *Rubiaforce* treatment. Drink less liquid when taking Rubiaforce tablets. After completing one box of tablets wait a week before starting on another, but during this interval drink as much liquid as possible in order to thoroughly flush out the kidneys and prevent the formation of new gravel or stones. At the end of the week begin to take another box of Rubiaforce tablets; drink limited amounts of a weak *kidney tea* with *Nephrosolid.* Follow up with a further week without medication but drinking plenty, as before. The treatment is completed after the third week on tablets and a further week when, again, plenty of liquids are consumed.

169

Even though the stones will have disappeared after this treatment, it would be wise to repeat it in a shortened form every three months, just to be on the safe side. However, the diet must be watched all the time. If available, a tea made from *Chanca piedra*, a plant found in the tropical jungles of Peru, will enhance the effectiveness of the Rubiaforce treatment and can be taken in conjunction with it.

The Urinary Bladder

The urinary bladder is a hollow organ made up of muscle fibres and lined with mucous membrane. Ordinarily, the bladder has the capacity to hold about 750 ml (almost a quart) of fluid. Since the fibre cells are elastic, like rubber, the bladder is able to expand greatly without suffering any damage. According to the amount of fluid collected, pressure is exerted on the walls of the bladder and, as it mounts, this triggers the feeling of needing to pass water. However, the amount of fluid present in the bladder is not the only force causing the urge for elimination. External influences such as exposure to cold produce it too. Having cold feet or stepping barefoot onto cold tiles or a cement floor cause a contraction of the bladder wall and a strong need to pass water, even if the bladder is only partially filled. A bladder infection creates the same urge, but often the patient is able to produce only a few drops of water while suffering pain and discomfort. The bladder is one of the body's most sensitive organs, and one that reacts to physical as well as emotional stimuli in an unusually strong way.

Inflammation of the Bladder (Cystitis)

Generally, inflammation of the bladder, or cystitis, is a result of a cold. 'Whatever results from a cold can only be taken away through heat' is an ancient law of natural therapy. Since it also applies to the bladder, *hot herbal packs, compresses* and prolonged *sitz baths* are very successful aids in treating cystitis. The water used to prepare a compress should be as hot as the hands can bear when wringing out the cloth. The sitz bath should have a temperature of 37–38 °C (98–99 °F) in order not to cause any congestion. This should be carefully observed, particularly if the patient has high blood pressure or a weak heart. The sitz bath should be continued for half an hour, with hot water being added from time to time to maintain a constant temperature.

Certain bacteria such as staphylococcus, streptococcus and sometimes colibacillus can often be responsible for bladder infections. In rare cases the bladder may be affected by tuberculosis, a condition more likely to occur if the patient already has a kidney tuberculosis, which permits the bacillus to enter the bladder through the kidney and manifest itself at the slightest irritation. Chronic cases of cystitis may be connected with any of the above-mentioned causes and would need special treatment.

The symptoms of cystitis are pain or burning sensations on passing urine. Due to the infection and irritation a strong urge to pass water persists. The urine generally contains some red and white blood cells, is cloudy and forms a white, often slimy sediment when left standing.

ADDITIONAL TREATMENT

The treatment with warm wet packs can be greatly supported by the use of several biological remedies. One of the best medicines with which to counteract any kind of inflammation is *Echinaforce*. Doses of 5–10 drops should be taken every hour. Also, *Nephroso-lid* has healing properties and stimulates the kidneys; *Cantharis 4x* takes away the unpleasant irritation and burning sensation experienced when passing urine and *Usneasan* contains natural antibiotic substances and fights off harmful bacteria. Meanwhile, it is advisable to stay in bed until the inflammation has completely subsided.

If at the same time the urethra (the duct through which the urine passes) is narrowed, or an enlargement of the prostate gland or bladder stones exist, the treatment must be adapted accordingly and some other remedies added. In cases where the patient is unable to control urination due to a weakness of the sphincter muscle, *Cystoforce Bladder Drops* should be taken additionally. The same drops are usually excellent for the treatment of enuresis in children too. *Galeopsis, Sabal 1x* and a tea blend made up of *marigold, yarrow and St John's wort* are also recommended.

Bed-Wetting (Enuresis)

Bed-wetting is a real problem that affects mother and child alike. Even though it may be the result of some emotional upset or nervous tension, certain remedies, physical therapy and a bland diet may greatly assist the organism and even help to overcome the emotional problems as well.

Bed-wetting in normal older children, if they do not have a cold or some other physical complaint or weakness, can generally be attributed to a psychological conflict. It can be a very unpleasant home atmosphere, or the child may have simply been spoiled by indulgent parents.

What steps should be taken to help? First, create a happy environment in the home, a pleasant relationship between parents and children. The home should be free from anxiety and the accelerated pace of modern life. It should then not be too difficult to isolate the cause of the emotional problem. Empathy and patience on the part of both mother and father will help reveal it. There may be a variety of reasons, such as fear, jealousy, ambition, over-exertion, or exciting television programmes that the parents allow the children to watch until late at night, or some other emotional upset.

Being a bed-wetter is always upsetting for the healthy, intelligent child, as well as for the handicapped one. Hence, no effort should be spared to cure the child's problem. A child whose health leaves much to be desired and who may not be so quick mentally has enough to put up with and will feel even more helpless when nothing seems to go right. Bed-wetting also means an added burden to a child suffering from cerebral palsy. So there are sufficient reasons to make use of all available natural remedies to strengthen the bladder and kidneys. In addition to these, the child must be given biological calcium and silica, but only from plants.

In order to treat the various factors involved in bed-wetting, the following remedies are recommended: *kidney tea, Cystoforce Bladder Drops, Galeopsis, Usneasan and Urticalcin*. The treatment must be supported by an appropriate *diet*, low in salt and fat. The diet should consist of brown rice and millet, together with vegetables and salads. At the same time a glass of fresh carrot juice should be taken daily. As with all types of liquid, it should be sipped slowly and well insalivated. Train the child to chew well so that the food becomes properly mixed with saliva so as to promote good digestion. No fluids should be given to the child after 4 p.m.

Considerable improvement can be brought about in time through physical therapy. A warm and moist *compress of hay flowers* placed daily on the lower abdomen stimulates the blood circulation of the urinary organs. From time to time the child should be given a *sitz bath* with a decoction of hay flowers or horsetail added to the water. But make sure that the child does not start shivering or even get cold. His whole body should be kept warm by covering the tub with large towels, protecting the parts of the body that are not under the water, or by heating the bathroom.

Also take care that the child does not get cold feet or feel chilled

Hayflower (Hayseed)

or cold. For this reason see to it that he has adequate footwear, warm socks and warm clothing to protect his body in cold weather. Moreover, make sure that he gets plenty of exercise out-of-doors, as this will stimulate the circulation and make him feel comfortable and warm. Take him on hikes or walks, possibly through a forest or wood, and encourage him to breathe deeply in the aromatic air. This will do much to build him up.

At all times the child should grow up in an atmosphere of soothing tranquillity since it will help him to relax. A happy home is the main factor that contributes to his speedy recovery; it induces a sense of balance by helping to overcome the emotions that have been a basic cause of the problem. Where there is happiness there is no room for tantrums, a defiant spirit, sullenness or depression. Engrossed as we often are in our daily routine, we tend to forget how much health, in particular the health of a child who is weak for some reason, depends on the feeling of being wanted and loved in an environment of calmness and harmony.

Prostate Trouble
It is not always possible to cure prostate problems, in fact, there are cases, especially with cancer of the prostate, where treatment

is difficult and sometimes in vain. Operating is not always the answer either, and if it can be prevented, so much the better. In cases of benign enlargement of the prostate good results have been achieved with *Prostasan*, a preparation containing *Sabal, Staphisagria, Populus, Echinacea* and *Solidago*, in conjunction with *herbal steam baths*. However, when urination has become easy again, do not take it for granted that you are now rid of your problem. Prostate conditions are seldom cured so completely that they do not recur sooner or later.

The trouble may be alleviated, but perhaps not completely cured. And do not forget, you do not get any younger either. If the enlarged prostate can be softened and brought back to its normal size, the passing of urine will once more be painless; however, it is quite likely that a degree of enlargement will remain. A slight cold, a cold beer, or anything in the nature of a temporary disturbance can cause the gland to swell somewhat, so that the trouble flares up again. Once more you may resort to steam baths and the remedies already mentioned. But to avoid disappointment you must be aware that although the treatment will probably bring you relief, it may not actually eliminate the possibility of relapses. As a matter of fact, you would fare better if you were to continue to take the remedies after the attack has subsided, reducing the quantity to half or a third of the usual dose. In this way the gland continues to be favourably influenced and the problem is kept in check, so to speak.

Prostate trouble is not unlike hardening of the arteries in that it is a condition brought on by the aging of the body and since this process is unavoidable you must remember that removing the problem once does not mean that it cannot crop up again. By using the appropriate remedies and precautions you can support nature in its own healing efforts and prevent the trouble from recurring as far as is possible.

Inflammation of the Testicles (Orchitis)

Inflammation of the testicles (orchitis) is a fairly prevalent condition yet its treatment tends to be neglected because embarrassment makes the patient reluctant to see a doctor. For this reason I would like to explain the causes and treatment of this inflammation. To begin with, never ignore this condition hoping it may correct itself. By simply trying to forget the inflammation and not caring for it properly you may invite infertility later, which can result in serious psychological problems, especially for younger men.

Orchitis is generally caused by germs that are carried in the bloodstream. They need not be of the venereal type, however; in fact, tuberculosis of another organ could be responsible for orchitis. A complication of mumps or some other infectious disease may also be the cause and the resulting inflammation can be painfully awkward for young men. Obviously, then, the correct treatment of the basic problem is called for.

For internal use, massive doses of *Echinaforce* have proved successful in cases like this. Take 10–20 drops every hour. During the night, apply a *mudpack* to the inflamed area. In order to increase its healing power and to keep the paste from drying out and breaking up, mix it with *horsetail tea* and a tablespoon of *St John's wort oil*. A helpful alternative is a poultice made from crushed *cabbage leaves*. However, if the cabbage increases the soreness, stop using it and revert to the mudpacks, which are always soothing. Finally it is important to keep the bowels open. These suggestions will work if you follow them conscientiously.

Skin Disorders

Eczema – and Other Skin Eruptions
In treating eczema it is of primary importance to discover the cause of the disease. It is usually to be found in faulty metabolism or an allergy to certain foods or other irritants. Naturally, these factors will have to be taken into consideration. In many cases a complete change of diet may be necessary. Without question, the bowels and kidneys should be stimulated so as to enable them to function adequately. Then we must find out if it is a chronic or acute skin eruption. External irritation, such as that occasioned by certain occupations, can play a part in the development of such skin diseases, but frequently it may be a hereditary condition.

For external treatment *Molkosan* (concentrated whey) has always given the best results. Molkosan is a biological lactic acid preparation which destroys harmful bacteria, stimulates the circulation and regenerates the skin by virtue of the minerals and enzymes it contains. As a rule, however, Molkosan alone is not sufficient, especially when treating psoriasis. It is then usually necessary to also powder the skin with a biological calcium preparation. For the best results use a calcium complex with *Urtica* (*Urticalcin*) in powder form. The third essential remedy is a lanolin cream, *Bioforce Cream*, which contains St John's wort oil, being ideally suited for this purpose. The complete external treatment for eczematous skin is therefore as follows:

In the morning swab the affected parts with undiluted Molkosan. If it is too strong and makes the sore places smart or burn excessively, dilute with a little boiled or distilled water. After this, powder the affected areas with Urticalcin powder. Make sure that it gets well into the cracks and scales. In the evening, dab the area once more with Molkosan, but instead of then using the powder, rub the affected parts with a little Bioforce Cream. For a change occasionally use *St John's wort oil* on its own. Repeat these applications daily.

Any skin eruption requires internal as well as external treatment; therefore the following advice is also useful for skin disorders other than eczema, particularly psoriasis. It is important to improve the condition of the blood and the lymph. First of all take a kidney remedy, either *Solidago virgaurea* (goldenrod drops) or *Nephrosolid* in daily alternation with *Violaforce* (heartsease drops). Secondly, take *Biocarottin* as a liver remedy and vitamin supplement. And thirdly, as a specific treatment, there is the '*formic acid therapy*'. This acid has to be given in form of injections, because if taken orally, it is partially transformed into carbonic acid on contact with the gastric secretions. The best results are obtained by giving hypodermic injections in the sixth and twelfth decimal potency, in alternation. During the first two weeks an injection should be given every third day, and then once every fourteen days, till the cure is complete.

Even the most difficult case will yield to this treatment, providing the proper diet is maintained and very little salt and protein is ingested. When it comes to skin disorders, salt is a poison and the metabolic toxins resulting from an excess intake of animal protein aggravate these diseases in general and psoriasis in particular. Further advice on diet is given on pages 180-1. If there is a discharge of pus from the eruption, *Hepar sulph. 4x* should be taken. If the trouble is connected with an acid condition of the body or if there is an oozing, burning, blistering rash with painful itching, then *Rhus tox. 4x* to *6x* will be the best remedy. *Arsenicum alb. 4x* to *6x* is good for both dry and oozing eruptions which burn and irritate especially by night. In cases of chronic eruptions the homoeopathic sulphur remedies *Sulphur 6x* and *Sulphur iod. 4x* to *6x* have proven their worth, particularly if the eruption is of a scrofulous nature. Finally, if the disease is the result of a tendency to rheumatism or gout, then *Calcarea carb. 4x* alternated with *Lycopodium 6x* would be indicated.

Whatever the cause, it is useful to add a calcium preparation which incorporates nettles, for example Urticalcin, to the other medication. And do not forget that Violaforce (heartsease drops) is an especially effective remedy for skin disorders.

When a Tendency to Eczema Runs in the Family

Cradle cap (*Crusta lactea*), commonly found in young infants, is often associated with a genetic predisposition to eczema and other skin disorders, passed on from one or other of the parents. Experience has shown that if cradle cap is not properly treated the child may become very susceptible to infections due to low resistance. For example, let us consider such a child suffering from whooping cough, which in turn is suppressed or wrongly treated. For this reason the bacterial toxins are not completely eliminated and it is likely that the child's heart will be affected or he will develop asthma, two conditions that are very difficult to put right.

Any kind of skin disorder, including cradle cap, must therefore receive proper treatment from the outset in order to effect a complete cure. This is the reason why I aim to direct attention in my books to combatting skin diseases by means of an appropriate treatment of the liver. The first step in this direction is a low-salt, or better still, salt-free liver diet as described in my book *The Liver, the Regulator of Your Health.*

IMPORTANT RULES FOR NUTRITION AND RELIABLE NATURAL REMEDIES

If we are careful in our choice of protein we can count on rapid success. Lactoprotein, as found in soft white cheese (quark), buttermilk and sour milk, is a good form of protein to take when skin disorders have to be treated. It is preferable to mix in finely grated horseradish, because fresh horseradish has antibiotic properties. People suffering from a skin disorder often cannot tolerate full-cream milk and should therefore abstain from it. On the other hand, they can take protein as contained in almond milk or soya milk. However, stay away from eggs, especially boiled eggs, and egg dishes, which cause strong reactions in persons suffering from eczema and similar skin disorders. The same holds true for all kinds of cheese with the exception of curds, cottage cheese, quark and most soft white cheeses made from skimmed milk, if they cause no upset.

The recommended diet consists basically of *brown rice* and foods rich in *calcium*. White cabbage salad and raw sauerkraut are among the vegetables that should be eaten regularly. Kohlrabi leaves (turnip cabbage) also have a high calcium content and should always be eaten, not thrown away.

Urticalcin, a proven biological calcium complex, makes the assimilation of calcium from food much easier and helps to prevent deficiency. Medical advisers sometimes prescribe calcium injections, which in theory may seem the correct way to supply the patient with sufficient calcium. I do not, however, recommend these, since I believe that the only healthy way of supplying the body with sufficient amounts of calcium is by eating vegetables that are rich in calcium, for example white cabbage and carrots.

When suffering from eczema it is important to keep off sweets of any kind. White sugar is harmful and may even create allergic reactions in some people. White flour, although not quite so drastic in its effect, should also be avoided. It is recommended for therapeutic reasons to confine one's diet to wholegrain or wholemeal products and wholefoods.

A kidney remedy, such as *Nephrosolid*, and *kidney tea* should be taken to stimulate the kidneys. Additionally it is recommended to drink more liquids than you are accustomed to, preferably natural fruit juices, for example bilberry or blueberry juice, blackberry juice and grapefruit juice. If you wish you may dilute these juices with mineral water, either the still kind or one with only slight natural fizziness.

Detailed recommendations on the appropriate remedies for eczematous conditions were given on pages 12–13. However, it is useful here to summarise the most important ones with a general application.

We have learned from experience that the most effective natural remedy for eczema, including cradle cap, is *Violaforce*, an extract from the wild pansy. *Urticalcin* should always be given too. This biological calcium preparation helps to heal the lesions when used as a powder. *Molkosan* and *Echinaforce* have the same effect and should definitely be incorporated in the treatment, not only externally but also internally. Eczema is generally associated with defective sebaceous glands and it is necessary to supply the skin with sufficient oil. *St John's wort oil* or *Bioforce Cream*, a lanolin cream, will accomplish this purpose very well.

OTHER NOTEWORTHY RECOMMENDATIONS

When treating skin problems, as with most other diseases, it is important that emotional upsets and difficulties be dealt with promptly and in the right way, otherwise they tend to aggravate the condition. That is why I have devoted a whole section in this book to 'Happiness Means Health'. Special attention has been given to the same question in my book about the liver, since this organ is notably sensitive to emotional influences.

Knowing how to deal with your illness is a step in the right direction, as it is clearly important to maintain mental balance in approaching any problem. One must be determined to elect for natural treatment rather than chemical therapy. By adhering strictly to a natural diet you can be sure you are on the right track. To complete the cure, it is absolutely necessary to carry out the treatment for six months to a year. The treatment need not be expensive since it is mainly a question of correcting one's dietary habits. Adverse reactions and side effects are usually minor or do not crop up at all if the treatment is undertaken correctly.

In summary, I would like to stress that in cases of eczematous skin disorders the liver needs special attention and care. The same applies to the kidneys, which must be protected from exposure to damp and cold. Furthermore, take care that the skin does not come into contact with strong detergents, floor wax and other products containing turpentine. When the kidneys and liver are functioning properly the strain is taken away from the skin and the unpleasant, often unbearable, itching will subside. At the same time the lesions will also disappear.

For those who follow my suggestions conscientiously an eventual cure is certain, but those who think that drugs and chemicals alone will suffice may go for years without finding any relief. The more stubborn the case, the more patience is needed to obtain satisfactory results.

Psoriasis

This is one of the skin diseases which is extremely difficult to heal. One successful treatment, however, is with *Formic Acid 30x* and an external application of *graphite* powder. Although orthodox doctors consider psoriasis incurable, natural therapy, especially with the help of homoeopathy, can claim a considerable number of cures. I remember the case of one girl who was almost completely covered in scaly patches, with the exception of a few small areas on her body. Anyone afflicted with this disease knows what a terrible strain it is on the nerves. Once the awful irritation starts up very few patients can bear it without scratching themselves until they bleed. It was just like that with this unfortunate girl, who was suffering from one of the worst cases I had ever seen. Often, by the morning she had scratched herself to such an extent that she was bleeding under the breast, on the legs and on the stomach. After three months of intensive treatment the girl was cured, although two follow-up treatments were later necessary to cope with a few minor relapses. Despite having been treated before, her skin was not so badly damaged that it could not be healed. For some patients who have undergone an extensive tar and sulphur treatment and have perhaps even used grey mercury ointment, achieving a cure can be much more difficult.

The chances of healing the disease are also very poor if the patient has been given radiation treatment, and I would warn patients never to resort to this particular therapy.

Skin eruptions, including psoriasis, are generally curable if the patient perseveres with the treatment until the disease is completely healed. However, if you handle skin irritants, such as terpenes, turpentine, turpentine floor wax or other strong turpentine products, the stimulus can provoke a relapse.

Psoriasis is not infectious and cannot be spread from one person to another. It is, however, possible to pass it on to one's children through the genes. For this reason such children should be given prophylactic treatment. Make sure that they have plenty of calcium and vitamins in their diet and take proper care of their skin. For further advice on treatment follow the recommendations outlined in the section on eczema.

RAW FOOD DIET FOR THE TREATMENT OF PSORIASIS

Proof of the regenerative power a raw food diet has on psoriasis is given in the following interesting letter from a patient. She writes:

'Just now I am in B., where I am on a strict raw food diet. For 23 years I have suffered from psoriasis and have had all kinds of treatments; but so far, all have been without success. After arriving here I had to fast for seven days, then I was put on fruit juices; next I was given fruits, nuts and corn bread. For several weeks now I have been eating raw salads and potatoes for lunch, and fruit morning and evening. I feel quite well and I am glad to say that the eruptions have gone. True, now and again the sun brings an occasional blemish to the surface, but it never gets big and disappears within a day or two. This does tell me, however, that

I am not yet completely cured and that I must continue the treatment. It does not really worry me, though, for I enjoy the fruit and salads. I can't quite put into words what it means to me to know that I am on the way to recovery and that I shall have the strength to work and be useful again. I only know that I shall be eternally grateful.'

The reply to her letter read as follows:

'I am truly glad and rejoice with you, knowing that with a simple raw food diet you have been able to overcome psoriasis. Now we must achieve a complete cure and you need to be patient for a little while longer. The raw food diet has stimulated the various body functions, including that of the kidneys, and has given the body sufficient vitamins and nutritive salts. This proves that psoriasis is associated with one's diet and that the function or malfunction of the organs has much to do with its development. Psoriasis is usually given external treatment only, and in various clinics this receives primary attention, which is fundamentally incorrect. In this regard orthodox doctors are, unfortunately, quite wrong in their opinion and approach. Psoriasis, one of the worst skin diseases, is not merely a visible problem, for which reason external treatment should be of secondary consideration. Of course, it is important to keep the skin clean, supply it with sufficient oil and disinfect it properly so that further complications are avoided. Nevertheless, internal treatment is far more significant, and your letter is proof of this. If you wish to improve your health still further, then let me recommend kidney tea as well as goldenrod (*Solidago*) and sufficient calcium. These remedies will be of great benefit to you.'

Nettle Rash (Urticaria)

Nettle rash, also known as urticaria, is a peculiar and very unpleasant condition. Although easily diagnosed, the actual cause is another matter. The itching variety of urticaria is accompanied by small pink eruptions on the skin. Identifying the cause of the complaint is often difficult. As a rule, it is recognised that a sensitivity to certain substances or foods is responsible for nettle rash, the kind of hypersensitivity generally referred to as an allergy. Where such a tendency exists, certain foods, such as strawberries, fish, cheese, eggs, seafood, pork and salami may be the allergens that cause such a reaction. There could also be a reaction to certain medications, even if these are biological preparations such as arnica, to cite just one.

181

What can you do if you are susceptible to attacks of urticaria? The first and obvious thing to do is to avoid every agent that could be a possible cause. Your careful observation over a fairly long period may be necessary to determine exactly what is causing the allergy. Sometimes the sensitivity may be hereditary, which unfortunately makes it all the more difficult to overcome. Still, it is possible to train the body to slowly get used to the agents that have been causing problems and eventually to eliminate the annoying symptoms. This can be accomplished by regularly taking very minute quantities of the allergens in question. Another way to successfully treat the sensitivity is by raising the calcium level, which can be achieved by taking plenty of calcium in the form of *Urticalcin*. A further remedy for nettle rash is *Violaforce*, a fresh plant extract from wild pansy. This little plant blooms in mountain pastures before haymaking time and if you suffer from urticaria, you can also make a decoction from these to wash yourself with or add to the bath water.

Simple Remedies for Neuritis

The pain of neuritis can be eased by repeatedly applying *hot water compresses*. Still better results are obtained by using *herbal poult-ices*, well heated before application. For an even more intense effect, put the herbs in a linen or cotton bag, immerse this in hot water, wring it out and apply it to the affected area.

Another alternative is to pour slightly warmed *St John's wort oil* onto a piece of woollen cloth and apply this. If you mix *potter's clay* with St John's wort oil, again, slightly warmed, and apply the resulting paste, not forgetting to place a hot water bottle on top to retain the heat, the effect will be intensified.

A very simple, old-fashioned method, though perhaps rather unpleasant, has also proved beneficial. Soak a piece of cloth or cotton wool in hot paraffin, place this on the inflamed area and cover with more cotton wool or a woollen cloth. This treatment is useful for pain in the back, arms and legs. There is nothing cheaper or simpler, even though it may be rather smelly. Take care to remove the compress as soon as the skin begins to turn red and feel warm, because paraffin can burn and blister the skin. Anyone living in a rural area where paraffin lamps are still used can easily take advantage of this method of treating neuritis.

An old doctor who served in the Austrian army once told me that they used petrol compresses for the same purpose and some-times even treated lumbago in this way with good results.

The use of *formic acid* has also proved very successful in cases of neuritis and sciatica. If a sufferer knows where there is an anthill in the woods, he should go there, expose his leg to the ants and let them 'work' on it. After a while, he can wipe off the insects with a cloth and will soon begin to feel the benefit of this inexpensive 'injection' of formic acid. Of course, the patient will achieve the same effects by applying spirit of ants, an alcoholic solution which also contains formic acid. Alternatively, if you know a homoeopathic doctor you could ask to be given injections of homoeopathic formic acid. This will be sufficient to relieve neuritic pains in most cases.

If, however, yours proves to be a very stubborn case, you can combine the various treatments described above, but you may have to persevere a little longer before experiencing relief.

It is also to your advantage to rid the body of toxins. Especially in the spring, if you live in a temperate zone, the blood can be cleansed by taking *bitter herbs*, followed by a *juice diet* that will facilitate the disposal of metabolic waste products. In order to help the body eliminate the toxins, it is important to stimulate the kidneys, bowels and skin at the same time. After the juice diet, adopt a sensible natural diet so as to avoid accumulating more poisons which may start up the neuritic pain again.

What is an Allergy?
This question is easily answered if we think of an allergy as a hypersensitivity to a certain kind, or variety, of different substances – allergens. This hypersensitivity may cause such drastic reactions that it seems as though the patient has been poisoned. For example, I am acquainted with the son of a pharmacist who becomes ill if only the smallest amount of egg is present in his food. A late friend of mine in New York would react in a similar way to wheat. Whenever he ate a piece of bread or pastry made with wheat flour he became critically ill. Professor Abderhalden once told me of one of his assistants who suffered with head swellings every time he ate white beans. Other people may have allergic reactions to daffodils, primulas, strawberries, rhubarb and even blueberries.

Merely touching certain flowers can cause skin eruptions, urticaria and other skin disorders in people who are allergic to them. Fruits can have the same effect, or they can cause a person to vomit. It is also known that some people are allergic to certain animal proteins and fats. Others I have observed become violently ill when eating seafood, such as crabs, lobster or any other shellfish.

However, that anyone should be allergic to wheat or rye I still find astonishing.

What Can Be Done about Allergies?

Many people have asked this question, but so far I have not been able to give them an answer that completely satisfies me. True, it is possible to undergo a series of tests carried out by specialists, which I understand is increasingly becoming a standard practice in the United States, for example. As a rule, however, this approach is rather expensive and requires an additional sum of money in cases where immunisation with antibodies is subsequently performed. Moreover, the effectiveness of this kind of treatment is by no means guaranteed.

The best thing is to test yourself in the following way. Every time an allergic reaction is noted write down everything that was eaten, touched or smelled. In time, a study of these notes should reveal the recurrence of a certain substance, perhaps a food item, a fruit or a flower. This may be a clue as to the cause of the allergy. Then, of course, the most obvious thing to do is to avoid the responsible agent or agents at all costs.

People who have allergies often suffer from calcium deficiency, which makes it necessary to take a good calcium preparation and eat calcium-rich foods. This will help to control if not eliminate the allergy. The homoeopathic drops *Pollinosan* have also given good results in cases of allergic colds and other allergies.

A Fast Cure for Shingles (*Herpes zoster*)

It is not easy to treat shingles and a cure often takes a long time. So it is good to know of the excellent results that can be achieved with the natural methods of treatment combined with homoeopathic medicines. For speedy relief injections of *Formisoton 6x* and *Rhus tox. 12x* are given and *Mezereum 4x* (daphne, spurge laurel) is taken orally. To stimulate the kidneys, drink goldenrod (*Solidago*) tea and an infusion of *rose hip kernels*. Locally, dab the affected area with a fresh plant extract of *Melissa off.* (lemon balm) and *Calendula* (marigold).

Attention to the diet is important. Cut down on salt and concentrated proteins such as eggs, cheese, fish and meat; they are best avoided. Fruit should only be eaten if well mixed in with flakes of wheat, millet or barley. Eat plenty of vegetables and drink carrot juice. Wholegrain cereals are also indicated, for example wheat

Marigold

grains, brown rice, barley and buckwheat. Since shingles affects the nerves, good remedies for building up the nerves are a valuable support to the treatment of this disease. Highly recommended are *Ginsavena* or *Ginsavita* tablets and *Neuroforce*, also *Kali phos. 6x*; these should be taken three times a day.

Spasms and Cramps

There is a variety of fairly severe cramps that may be caused by a nerve or brain disease such as encephalitis, or may be brought on by an infection such as tetanus. Severe cramps may also be the result of urine poisoning, as in the case of uraemia and eclampsia. Each of these conditions requires specialised treatment. However, what we want to deal with here are the simple, frequently occurring muscle spasms. Sometimes these are experienced as twitching, or clonic, cramps, brief in duration but returning in quick succession; they can also be continuous cramps, known as tonic contractions.

These simple cramps can be successfully controlled by applying *hay flower or camomile water packs* on the affected area. Alternatively, a long hot *shower* can be taken, directing the spray onto the affected area. On hot summer days, if there is no hot water available, cold water will bring relief too.

Depending upon the person's constitution, physical exertion may cause severe tonic contractions in the rectal region. These cramps can be so violent as to make the afflicted person cry out in pain. He may well believe that he is suffering from some malignant disease. In reality, however, it is nothing but a temporary cramp that can easily be relieved by taking a hot shower, as described above, for one or two minutes.

Menstrual cramps, which cause great discomfort to many women, fall into the area of cramps caused by spasms. Many different kinds of headaches may also be brought on by spasms, particularly migraine and the much-feared headache caused by the föhn, a warm dry wind blowing down into the Alpine valleys. Such a headache is worse when accompanied by a stiff neck, but the stiffness can usually be alleviated by massage.

It is a relief to know that there is no need to take hazardous medication that may even lead to addiction in order to alleviate severe pain and cramps. Instead, *Petadolor*, a preparation derived from butterbur (*Petasites officinalis*), is usually all that is necessary. This wonderful herbal remedy has proved very reliable in controlling cramps without causing harmful side effects. In addition, *arnica flower tincture*, when rubbed on the affected area, has an antispasmodic effect, and *Kali phos. 6x* builds up the autonomic nervous system.

Our 'Nasty' Sympathetic Nervous System

Our sympathetic nervous system is a greater marvel of technology than, for example, a telephone system. But if something goes wrong with it the consequences can be dreadful, which is why I call it our 'nasty' sympathetic nervous system.

Never in my life had my sympathetic nervous system troubled me as much as it did recently, during a period of much stress and worry. It was in such a state that I left St Gallen and headed for the Engadine. Shortly after I had started my journey, I felt severe spasmodic pains in the stomach area, so that I could hardly bear to continue sitting any longer. Unfortunately, I had not brought any *Petadolor* with me, which would have relieved the cramps. Usually I have a good stomach, but on this occasion it was so upset that I brought up my whole lunch. In spite of the beautiful weather, the otherwise enjoyable ride up to the Engadine was agonising. All night long I had severe pains in the stomach, which felt as if it were tied in a knot. After my arrival in the Engadine I was able to control the nausea with *Nux vomica 4x*, and *Crataegus* helped to calm my agitated heart.

Even though I did not eat a thing the next day, the cramps reached up to the breastbone and did not subside until the evening, after I had taken a prolonged hot shower.

It was this experience which helped me understand why one of my friends, who had been very worried about the sale of his business, had to undergo surgery several weeks later because of extremely painful stomach ulcers. Doctors and physiotherapists seem to be correct in assuming that practically all stomach ulcers are the result of spasms caused by worries, upsets and anxiety. This does not mean to say that the acute symptoms need be as drastic as they were in my case. Constant spasmodic cramping of the stomach muscles can, and usually will, lead to ulcers.

Prevention is Better than Cure

Since prevention is better than cure, the laudable quality of self-control should help us to overcome unexpected anxieties and problems as quickly as possible, to conquer difficulties rather than letting them conquer us. Of course, this is often a question of experience and practice, for even if we know how to react in difficult situations, old habits may prevail and prevent us from making correct decisions in a calm and collected state of mind. People with a placid nature find it much easier to remain composed when facing unpleasant and distressing events than those who are prone to making split-second decisions without giving sufficient thought to the outcome. The sympathetic nervous system, unfortunately, is not subject to control or reason, but rather to our feelings and emotions. That is why it is always important to remain composed, so that unforeseen situations may be taken in our stride. When the wise King Solomon advised us to take better care of our hearts than of anything else he made a valid and valuable point. We should heed his advice, since 'out of the heart are the sources of life', as he said. By keeping our emotions under proper control we are able to reap many benefits, not least with regard to our health. Of the utmost importance is the fact that we thus will be rendering a service to our sympathetic nervous system.

Insomnia

It is certainly annoying when you cannot get to sleep in spite of being tired. But it is even worse to lie awake for hours because the tensions of the day simply do not leave you, and are transformed into problems of insurmountable magnitude. Unpleasant daytime experiences prevent sleep and create a state of depression and the 'wheels' which are supposed to stand still during the night turn faster and faster. The restless individual tosses from side to side and finally, because he knows no other way out of his predicament, he reaches for a sleeping pill.

This, of course, is the worst thing he could do, because in no time at all, if he continues using such help, he will find he cannot do without it. He tends to forget that drugs destroy the body's ability to react and respond in a natural way and that their continued use has a destructive effect that can be far-reaching. It is far more sensible to isolate the cause of the problem that keeps you awake. Then, by resolving it, you will eventually restore your natural ability to fall asleep and rest.

If you suffer from insomnia, therefore, it will be necessary to discover and eliminate the cause of it. You may have been drinking strong coffee for years and should replace it by a cereal or fruit coffee. Should you find it difficult to give up your favourite drink, wean yourself away by mixing both kinds of coffee, gradually reducing the proportion of real coffee as your palate becomes accustomed to the new taste. In the end you will be taking a harmless drink that will permit you to rest throughout the night undisturbed.

A good drink to have before you go to bed is *lemon balm tea*, the relaxing effect of which may be increased by adding *hops*.

The homoeopathic remedy indicated for sleeplessness is *Avenaforce* (oat extract). Lemon balm, hops and *Avena sativa* taken together are sleep-inducing and a ready-made preparation containing these ingredients is *Dormeasan. Passiflora* or *Valerian* may be added to these sleeping drops for an even stronger effect. Valerian is often prescribed on its own, but as its effects are narcotic it does not provide lasting help.

Mountain guides in Switzerland know of and use another good remedy, namely *marmot oil*, and a teaspoonful of this taken daily is said to induce sleep. Since it is not too palatable it is best taken in the form of gelatin capsules, or followed by a strong herbal drink.

Of course, do not forget the habit of going to bed early, perhaps going even earlier than usual so as to be in bed well before midnight, because sleep during these hours will conserve your health and energy.

Remember, too, that retiring on a full stomach is not conducive

Valerian

to a good night's rest and is usually responsible for bad dreams. It is important when we eat, and how much and what we eat. Supper, as the last regular meal of the day, should not be taken at 8 or 9 p.m. or even later in the evening; that would be asking for trouble. If at all possible, we should have a light, easily digested meal shortly after 6 p.m. After supper, take a short walk and breathe deeply. This will aid the digestion and ensure a good night's healthy sleep.

Some Reliable and Inexpensive Remedies for Insomnia
In addition to the measures outlined above, a number of other simple approaches to inducing sleep have been found helpful by many people.

You may find it possible to put the cares of the day out of your mind when in bed by *reading* an upbuilding book or a magazine article. If one reads for long enough, it will usually lead to drowsiness and sleep.

In cases where you have overtaxed your brain, making the back of the head feel tense and painful, it is helpful to *massage* the aching area with the fingertips. This gentle massage generally relaxes the tension and induces sleep. Cold water can also help to dispel tension, and a *Kuhne treatment* is often successful in relaxing the body (see pages 436–8). *Brush massages* can also be effective, and even *fresh air* will often help.

Anything that stimulates the circulation, driving the blood back to the external areas, helps to induce sleep, since insomnia is often caused by too much blood in the brain. Our busy life today lacks balance; we often overtax our minds and do not provide enough exercise for our bodies. Consequently, our ability to relax diminishes. We cannot rid ourselves of the many problems that haunt us and thus subject our already heavily burdened mind to even more stress. Is it any wonder that we cannot fall asleep?

Another approach to inducing sleep was described in a letter I received from a former patient living in Australia. She wrote to tell me how thrilled she was with a book written by Kneipp. Her enthusiasm led her to introduce her entire family to *Kneipp's cold water cure*. Her husband, who had been suffering from insomnia for months, was cured by the brief application of cold water packs to the back of the head and neck (without drying off afterwards) just before going to bed. The treatment resulted in a deep and undisturbed sleep. One of their daughters, who could not sleep either, also tried her father's method and had been able to fall asleep without any trouble ever since. Sufficient sleep had also bucked up her spirits and benefited her general frame of mind in every way.

How gratifying it is to know that books on health have a wide circulation in every country and continent. There can be no doubt that their influence is very beneficial. The thought that my own health books, which are available in many languages all over the world, will continue to provide good advice for those who read them even long after I am gone, is enough to put my mind at rest and let me sleep peacefully.

OTHER WATER TREATMENTS

Sauna baths, once popular only in northern European countries, are now accepted in many other areas of the world. In northern Europe it is common for people to take a sauna and then roll in freshly fallen snow in winter. This exercise is said to build up the body's resistance. *Walking barefoot in the snow* as well as *snow- and water-stamping* are all favourite activities. All of these activities cause the blood to be drawn from the brain, so if practised before going to bed, they make restful sleep possible. Information on variations of these methods as practised in different countries can also be useful and enlarges the list of water treatments already known to us.

Years ago I was greatly surprised to find a sauna when I visited a colony of Finnish people in Brazil, of all places. Ask yourself, what purpose is there in having a sauna in a place where the temperature reaches 40 °C (104 °F) in the shade on hot days? The answer to this is that old habits die hard and become a necessity, which was certainly true for those Finnish people who built their sauna in a hot and humid foreign land. Perhaps it even helped them to overcome their homesickness for the old country. Moreover, in the tropics the evenings are cool and I remember that the sauna gave us a pleasant feeling of well-being. After the sauna we found a nearby jungle creek for a cool dip, which stimulated the circulation and helped to make for a restful night. Perspiring in a sauna differs from perspiring in the heat of the day in that it relaxes the mind and body and enables one to sleep soundly.

In summary, it is always useful to work out which one of the different natural treatments will be the most appropriate for overcoming your insomnia. Often all it needs is a little determination to do something about the problem and you will find what is required to give you a a full night's wholesome and restful sleep.

Epilepsy – New Views concerning its Treatment

Epilepsy, formerly known as 'falling sickness', is frequently mentioned in old writings and even in the Bible, yet although it has been around for thousands of years the therapy employed today still entails little more than a simple treatment of the symptoms. Bromine, used in various combinations, as well as Luminal, Cominal and other dangerous drugs prescribed to reduce the severity of the seizures, can hardly be called satisfactory by either the patient or the doctor.

If the patient is sensible enough to avoid alcohol, nicotine and other harmful stimulants, it may be possible to obtain more satisfactory results. Following a diet consisting of raw foods, rich in vitamins and minerals, is of definite advantage. Experience has shown that attacks are less frequent and less severe when the patient adheres to the right kind of diet.

It also appears that a new road to successful treatment has been found in positively influencing the patient's mineral metabolism. As a rule, epileptics have a low calcium level and often eliminate a lot of calcium, especially that bound to phosphorus, through the urine. For this reason a *calcium therapy*, together with an *appropriate diet*, is advisable and beneficial. In addition to eating foods high in calcium, the patient should take *Urticalcin*, a biological calcium complex, as well as other supplements as described below. Besides being very effective, this treatment has no harmful side effects. The same cannot be said for treatment with bromine because over a period of time the patient's emotional and mental health invariably begins to suffer.

Reasoning on the Evidence

Not long ago I received good news from a patient in South Africa whose epileptic seizures had formerly occurred almost daily, but had diminished to only one a month – and the monthly attacks were milder than before. The improvement had been attributed to the patient's taking *Urticalcin, Vitaforce* (a vitamin supplement) and *kelp tablets*. It is likely that the organic potassium iodide contained in these seaweed tablets was responsible for the strong influence on the endocrine glands. No doubt other minerals found in kelp had also helped to produce the desired result.

In any case, as various studies have shown, epilepsy can now be treated with less harmful medications than bromine. As suggested above, the diet should consist of mild, alkaline-based foods, supplemented by a biological calcium preparation such as Urticalcin. Vitaforce should be taken at the same time, since its vitamin D content will make it easier for the body to assimilate the calcium. The main remedy, however, is kelp in tablet form, one tablet to be taken in the morning and one in the evening. None of these are specific remedies, but nutritional supplements giving the body what it needs most. Another plant which has helped in the treatment of epilepsy is the *oak mistletoe (yellow-berried mistletoe), Loranthus europaeus*, which is native to the Balkan region.

It is unfortunate that to this day specific medicines are prescribed which treat the symptoms, the external signs, without giving due consideration to what the body may lack internally. As a result, the condition cannot be improved or cured. Hence the need to find out the cause of the deficiency and then endeavour to rectify it.

Not everyone needs the same amount of every substance. Depending on the individual's nature, his temperament and hereditary disposition, his specific deficiencies and affections, the need for a particular element may be greater than normal, requiring more vitamins, mineral salts or other substances to restore the proper balance in the system.

A report from an acquaintance in the United States, an epileptic since her youth, confirms this assumption. She wrote to me saying that she was well aware of the excellent effects of kelp for epilepsy and had been using it for more than ten years. But she also mentioned in her letter that she believed that taking a biological calcium preparation in addition to the kelp had helped her even more. Since her attacks had been severe and frequent, it was a source of great satisfaction to learn that she was able to overcome them by taking these supplements and by adhering to a diet rich in calcium.

Biologically-oriented doctors have come to the same conclusion, as a letter from one of my friends in New York indicated. He related the example of an eighty-year-old doctor who is totally nature-oriented. This well-known doctor also emphasises the excellent effect of calcium on the general state of health, especially when combined with vitamin D if the patient does not normally receive sufficient exposure to sunlight.

Although already pointed out, I would like to reiterate the importance of following a non-irritating or bland diet that is low in salt. No doubt some patients will be happy to learn that their condition can be treated by natural means, but others may find this too difficult and prefer to take a less demanding approach. Such people do not want to make changes to their life-style and prefer to lose a chance of improving or even curing their disease. What a short-sighted and unreasonable attitude! And how can help be given if it is rejected?

Tragic Hereditary Factors

When young couples decide to get married they rarely stop to think about their health and what they may pass on to their children. It is understandable that their happiness in having found each other is based on emotion rather than reason. True, they may talk about certain things before marriage, but these are usually more of a material rather than a spiritual nature. However, even though the emotions may be ruling, it is still of paramount importance to take stock of the make-up of the two individuals involved, because this factor will have strong implications for the health of their future children.

None of us is perfect and few feel so strong and healthy as not to be aware of some weakness of a physical or mental nature. If any unfavourable hereditary factor should exist, it would be better if one partner did not possess the identical genetic weakness, but instead had a positive predisposition to offset the severity of the defect in the other. For example, if the parents of both partners have poor nerves and experience great difficulty in maintaining a healthy balanced life, it often needs only minor emotional stress for their children to suffer an emotional defect for the rest of their lives. Let us take another example. If there is a history of diabetes in both families, some basic mistake in the diet of the young couple will be enough to double the inherited predisposition in one or the other of their children and insulin treatment may become necessary. For it is the case that susceptibility to tuberculosis, ulcers, cancer, arthritis, rheumatism and many other diseases may be transmitted genetically.

With this in mind, it is not unreasonable for young people, before they think of getting married, to make a point of examining their particular genetic predispositions in order to determine whether starting a family appears to be advisable, bearing in mind the possible problems concerning their children's health. If, however, they should choose to take the risk anyhow, it is even more important to consider the question of health very carefully, since much harm can be avoided through adopting a reasonable approach and by taking the appropriate action. Naturally, if the persons involved are inexperienced and have no idea whatsoever of the possible consequences, they will not be able to take any precautionary measures.

Basic Qualifications for Starting a Family
Many young people, even though properly brought up and otherwise responsible, hardly ever think about health as being a prerequisite for marriage. Their topics of conversation are often limited to the obvious: questions of where to live, how to furnish the home, holidays and excursions, leisure activities and hobbies, and perhaps the question of whether to have children and how they might bring them up.

As we all know, most employers require job applicants to complete long and detailed questionnaires. The answers help the employer to determine whether the applicant has all the necessary qualifications for the job. It would be just as informative and certainly appropriate with regard to starting a new family if the prospective marriage partners were to complete such a questionnaire. Any good physician or psychologist could easily recognise from the answers what medical risks, if any, the couple might expect to possibly affect their children.

For example, if two people who were both suffering from hypothyriodism were to marry, it is possible that some of their children might be myxoedemic and mentally retarded. The risks involved in cases of epilepsy are generally known, and epileptics are advised to forgo having children. Laws prohibiting marriage between close relatives have been made because the transmission of negative hereditary factors becomes stronger the closer the blood ties are between the two people.

Mature people, who are conscious of their responsibility towards their children, will not overlook the problems and precautions discussed above, but will give them due consideration. Only in this way may they be spared much possible suffering later on. And thanks to their reasonable and sound attitude they will have the opportunity to bring healthy children into the world.

The Treatment of Psychosomatic Illnesses and Mental Disorders

The Meaning of the Word 'Soul'

If we are to understand the meaning of the word 'soul', we shall have to turn to the Book of Books, the Bible, and ponder over a marvellous passage in the account of the Creation: 'God proceeded to form the man out of dust from the ground [one might say of the elements of the earth] and to blow into his nostrils the breath of life, and the man came to be a living soul . . .' or as another translator paraphrased it, 'a sentient creature'. Elsewhere we read: 'He poured out his soul to the very death', and yet again, 'the soul of the flesh is in the blood'.

If we pause to analyse these scriptures, we must conclude that the 'soul' (in Hebrew, *nephesh* and in Greek, *psyche*) refers to the whole person, with all his complex emotions and senses, not an immaterial entity within him or only his mind, or psyche, as defined by psychiatrists. In fact, with every pint of blood he loses, it could be said that he loses part of his soul and his sentience. If too much blood is lost, as in an accident, sentience and feeling progressively diminish, until life ceases altogether.

First God created the lifeless body, made up of billions and billions of cells; he caused the cells to live, to have in them the force of life (in Hebrew, *ruahh*). But for the life force to continue in the cells they needed oxygen, so God provided the body with the breath of life; man began to breathe because his lungs started to function. He was now alive, breathing, and began to feel and think – his existence as a living soul had begun. Thus the integrated whole of the body and mind, according to the Bible, is the living, sentient soul. Medically speaking, we must therefore treat man as a whole if any therapy is to be successful. Mental and emotional health go hand in hand with the physical, and vice versa.

The Interaction of Mind and Body

Psychological problems and disturbances lead to reactions in the physical body as well. Knowing of this interaction, it is necessary to treat the body, the physical problem, in order to relieve the psychological disorder. The reverse is also true, in that physical afflictions leave their mark on the mind of the patient to such an extent that his mental balance may be upset. Every psychotherapist will confirm that mental conditions can be responsible for physical ailments, and that organic problems can affect the mind so severely that the patient becomes mentally unbalanced. For example, a malfunction of the ovaries or the male sex glands frequently gives rise to mental disturbance, which will disappear when the physical disorder has been corrected.

Generally speaking, the field of psychosomatic medicine is still mysterious and little explored, so that it is impossible to establish doctrines and principles that are valid in every case. Nevertheless, experience and observation have clearly shown that one-sided treatment is insufficient and often fails to achieve good results, whereas the treatment of the patient as a whole, a unit, is more likely to succeed.

Natural Treatment

Electric and insulin shock treatments could be a step in the right direction. Although these treatments cannot strictly be termed natural methods, the principle behind them may be based on observations from life; for example, the shock brought on by a fright, an accident or other emotionally 'shocking' experience can jolt a person back to reason.

A change of climate, environment and latitude, long walks and hikes, breathing exercises (especially diaphragm-breathing), physical training, singing, vocal breathing exercises, etc., are all beneficial and may help to change the patient's mental outlook. Hydrotherapeutic treatments such as baths, cold or hot showers, Schlenz baths (see pages 433–6), underwater massage, walking or stamping in cold water, walking barefoot, also walking barefoot in the early morning when the dew is still on the grass, are further sources of help which can be employed according to the doctor's advice and bearing in mind the individual's needs.

In accordance with the patient's condition, doctors and nurses should try various approaches and watch and note the patient's reactions to each treatment, however small the influence of the shock effect may be. Moreover, anything contributing to a happy atmosphere should be encouraged by the nursing staff, as physical therapy and cheerfulness alone can quite often work small miracles.

From my Own Experience

Some years ago, when I still had my clinic, I had to deal with a very interesting case. A friend of mine, whose 24-year-old daughter suffered from hysterical fits that caused her to bury her head in a pillow and cry for hours at a time, asked me to treat her. I might add that her doctor's diagnosis was schizophrenia and that her sister, who was herself a doctor, could only stand helplessly by her bedside.

I took on this patient and my initial approach was to ensure the proper functioning of the ovaries by means of a *Baunscheidt treatment* to stimulate the weak menstrual flow. When this began to take effect, the patient at first became unruly, but as soon as the elimination of the leucocytes had started, a most extraordinary change occurred. The girl, now completely in her right mind, said herself that it was just as if a veil had been lifted from before her eyes. One single treatment had sufficed to bring about a complete cure and even later, after she got married, there was no relapse.

I remember another instance of such an illness, where the patient was not having any periods at all. I prescribed *mustard hip baths*, and *Ovarium 3x* for internal use. The periods were soon re-established and the emotional crisis completely disappeared.

New Approaches to these Problems

Psychological problems are not always easy to solve, but there are instances where the solution could be quite simple if only the right method of approach was first sought and then used. Every improvement in the body functions, even if it is perhaps only relief from constipation, can help or even lead to a cure. The use of physical therapy in its many forms can open up new avenues in the treatment of such patients.

As usual, diet plays an important part, for we know that pure, natural wholefoods keep a healthy person fit for daily work and help maintain general balance. Is it therefore not reasonable to expect that a proper nutritional therapy would be necessary and useful for the sick person too? Indeed, you should see to it that all denatured or refined foods are avoided. Make sure you eat only food items that still contain their full nutritional value, that is, wholefoods, and that fruit and vegetables have not been contaminated by chemical sprays and fertilisers. This careful attention to diet, in conjunction with physical therapy and a healthy psychological influence, will provide real help for both body and mind, giving the patient the chance to recover.

It is also important that circulatory disorders are taken care of, by means of natural remedies such as *Aesculaforce* or *Ginkgo biloba*, and that the patient's calcium level is raised by taking an easily assimilated calcium preparation such as *Urticalcin*.

Nursing Patients with Mental Problems

It often happens that the immediate family treat the patient with a mental problem either too gently and indulgently or else too strictly. Even qualified nurses do not always find it easy to adopt the right approach in dealing with emotional and mental illnesses.

It is true to say that strong nerves are needed to deal with such cases and the attendant's own weakness, occasional helplessness and feeling of being 'fed up' must be carefully hidden. Patients must have confidence in the one caring for them, as they are exceedingly sensitive on account of their weak nervous system and they can react very quickly. If you become annoyed because the patient has done something wrong, or if you are unhappy because his progress is slow, be careful not to irritate him for this does not encourage him to get better; rather, it will throw him back once more into mental confusion and lead to unpleasant reactions and tensions that will have both physical and mental repercussions. On the other hand, the patient is likely to abuse your kindness, so it is better not to be too gentle, soft or even indulgent; be firm but kind at all times.

Nursing staff need tremendous self-control and self-confidence, also a measure of composure and vast reserves of strength, in order to help a patient with neurasthenic or mental problems to progress. If the patient is conscious of a strong hand supporting and guiding him he will come through the wilderness of his distraught emotions and thoughts with confidence in both himself and his future. He will then cooperate with his helper and begin to think, feel and behave quite normally again.

A TYPICAL DAILY PROGRAMME

The patient should start the day early in the morning by walking barefoot on dewy grass, as recommended by Kneipp. This exercise draws the blood down to the feet and takes into the body the energy obtained from the earth. The result is a wonderful feeling of relief. If the weather does not allow this, paddling or stamping in cold water followed by physical exercises, preferably in the open air, can be done instead. In the course of the exercises, rhythmic movements, singing and vocal breathing exercises will help to disperse any mental blocks and free the inner self.

Breakfast should consist of pure, natural foods: various fruits, wholegrain muesli, wholewheat bread, butter and honey. Avoid the customary breakfast of milky coffee, white bread or rolls, and choose only natural wholefoods which contain the nutrients the body needs.

After breakfast a period of occupational therapy should follow. The purpose is to capture the patient's interest, concentration and attention by doing something practical. This distraction is an essential part of the treatment, for the patient must not be left alone and to his own thoughts, which have a tendency to become more depressing as he broods. If his attention can be diverted to everyday realities, depressing thoughts and feelings will have less chance to assert their influence on his mind. In the field of emotions an analogy can be drawn with the working of two transmission wheels: while the belt drives only one wheel, no power is transmitted to the other one. Applied to the patient, this means that we must see to it that he continually occupies himself, mentally, spiritually or physically, with the realities of life. If we succeed in this, he will gradually be lifted out of his condition marked by morbid sensitivity and imaginations, unhealthy fantasies and dreams. For those who have an artistic nature, arts and crafts projects are especially indicated as they divert and satisfy the patient without the need for constant encouragement. They also constitute a pleasant bridge between the worlds of fantasy and reality.

The midday meal should mainly consist of raw vegetables, with the addition of steamed vegetables and potatoes, brown rice or some other wholegrain dish. All highly spiced foods must be scrupulously avoided. A further period of occupational therapy should follow the meal, even if it is only washing and drying the dishes.

During the afternoon some form of physical therapy should be given, perhaps a Schlenz bath with sweat-inducing packs (see pages 433–6). Such a bath may be repeated two or three times in a week, depending on the degree of benefit derived from it. Instead of the hot bath, alternating hot and cold showers may be taken, starting with the hot, then cold, then hot again.

In cases of insufficient menstrual flow, a hip bath lasting about half an hour at 37 °C (98.6 °F), if possible with herbal extracts added, can be of great benefit.

After any one of these treatments some form of physical relaxation is called for, such as a walk in the fresh air, which will give an optimistic turn to the patient's thoughts. If some time is left before the evening meal, it should be employed with further occupational therapy.

Supper should be eaten at about 6 p.m. and be a light, easily digestible meal that will not disturb the patient's sleep. Highly recommended are muesli with fruit or a fruit salad, together with wholegrain bread, butter and honey.

As the patient's day began with the first rays of sunshine, so it should end with the fading light and he should get ready for bed as it begins to get dark. If he has trouble getting to sleep, give him *Dormeasan drops* taken in water sweetened with honey. This will help soothe the nerves.

Also, during the day the patient should be given the nerve tonic *Ginsavena*, made from oats and ginseng. In more serious cases a combination of *Rauwolfia* and *Avena sativa* is indicated (*Rauwolfavena*). The use of these natural remedies and therapies will help the patient overcome his condition. They will make it possible for him to control his morbid thoughts and depression, helping him towards mental and physical improvement. If the suggested daily programme is adapted to suit individual needs, many a patient can be helped to recover.

In all cases it follows that the diet should be planned on a natural basis and should be rich in vitamins and mineral content. If the patient's condition allows it, a juice diet or a short fast could be tried too. It is important to have his understanding and cooperation, for such diets demand the kind of effort on his part which often proves too much even for a healthy person. Never lose sight of the necessity to help him mentally by acknowledging, in a matter-of-fact way, that he is sick. He has to be cared for but at the same time the illness should not be given undue importance. The idea is to show and convince him, without pressure and almost imperceptibly, that there is a better, more favourable and simpler way out. Having gained confidence, the patient will be able and willing to follow our direction little by little. His mind will gradually begin to think correctly, coherently and, above all, logically again.

Weight Control (Underweight and Overweight)

In the past it was thought that being underweight was caused by an insufficient intake of food and that eating too much resulted in obesity. However, there are some people who eat a lot and remain extraordinarily thin, and others who eat very little and still put on weight. Everything, they say, turns to fat!

Meanwhile, research has shown that dysfunction of the endocrine glands, the glands with internal secretions, is largely responsible for both excessive corpulence and thinness. These glands are, primarily, the pituitary, the ovaries, the testicles and the thyroid. Their overactivity or imbalance usually leads to thinness, while their insufficiency (or underactivity) leads to corpulence. It has been observed that removal of the ovaries, or a disease causing ovarian insufficiency, causes a person to put on weight. Obesity following the menopause confirms the truth of this statement. Typical examples are the inhabitants of southern climates. How slim and supple the Italian or the Latin and South American girls are in the early prime of life. But as soon as the glandular secretions diminish, which is usually at a much earlier age in hot countries, they become plump. If the older generation is stout, stolid and comfortable, the reason for this can be traced to the insufficient functioning of the endocrine glands and, more than anything else, the sluggishness of the ovaries. In such cases *sitz baths* and other therapies which stimulate the ovaries (see below) would be of immense help towards reducing corpulence.

Pituitary obesity, however, is not so easy to deal with, because the pituitary is less amenable to corrective treatment than the ovaries. There are, of course, glandular preparations on the market which do act on the pituitary, but their administration is still a delicate matter. Nor do these preparations always produce positive results with the pituitary, though they often do with the ovaries.

A more effective way to reduce obesity is to take the seaweed ocean kelp. Two *Kelpasan* tablets taken twice a day are usually enough to reduce excess weight slowly but surely. Additionally, take *Helianthus tub.*, a fresh plant extract made from *Topinambur*, over a long period of time. Where the ovaries need stimulating, *Ovarium 3x*, in combination with a good diet, has given good results.

Another simple method, particularly for stimulating the ovaries, is to take various foods that contain vitamin E. The most important of these is *wheat germ*. There are some people who will not eat wheat germ for fear of getting fat, because it has also been recommended to thin people who wish to gain weight. Women need not worry about this, since wheat germ and its vitamin E content only regulate the function of the ovaries. In fact, wheat germ stimulates their function in the case of fat people and reduces their overactivity in the case of thin people; in this way it actually helps the obese to lose weight and the thin to put it on. In addition, wheat germ contains other valuable nutrients, such as vegetable protein, phosphates and natural sugar, all of which have a good effect on the body without the danger of causing an abnormal weight increase. So if you suffer from obesity, do not hesitate to eat wheat germ, for it will not increase your weight but regulate or control it.

Then there are those people who do not eat any food rich in vitamins because they are afraid they might overdose themselves. This fear is only justified where synthetic vitamins are concerned, for, indeed, they can produce an overdose. However, such a thing cannot happen with natural vitamins contained in biological remedies and organically grown food. Being an integral part of organic compounds they are never present in harmful concentrations. The body absorbs from the food only what it needs, while any surplus of certain natural vitamins is stored up or disposed of. For these reasons synthetic vitamins can never equal the natural ones. According to the Book of Books, human inability and lack of understanding bring the wisdom of the 'wise' to nothing. We may be able to analyse things, but when it comes to synthesising a biological equivalent we often fail. We simply do not know all the secrets hidden in these plants. How much more desirable it is, therefore, to turn to natural, biological sources, because the things the Creator has made for us can never be surpassed or equalled with synthetic products.

In recent times, artificial vitamin preparations have been strongly promoted by their manufacturers; before that, mineral salts ruled the scene. Fortunately, far-sighted researchers like Dr Schuessler and Dr Hahnemann found that the body requires various minerals only in minute amounts and that they can only be assimilated in triturated form, that is, ground into a fine powder.

At one time it was believed that gold could be made artificially; indeed, alchemists even tried to make an artificial man, a so-called 'homunculus', in their laboratories. Our age has become less ambitious in that it has merely attempted to produce a tablet or pill which contains all the nutrients the body requires and thus would make artificial nutrition possible, replacing our usual way of feeding. But even these efforts have been abandoned and now only elicit a smile. Before too long, synthetic vitamins will also go the same way, since they can never replace or equal those forces the Creator has put into plants, our natural food source. A return to these natural principles will prove much more profitable than all the theories the human mind has ever conceived. In this way, the natural way, the problems of obesity, thinness and metabolic disorders will be solved much more effectively.

Guidelines for Slimming without Danger

Obese people must never let themselves be persuaded to take a commercial slimming preparation. Except for seaweed, never take an ordinary preparation that contains iodine, since iodine is a dangerous element and should be used only in homoeopathic potencies and with the greatest caution. So if you do not know the contents of a slimming product, be sure to find out and reject it if it contains iodine. One should be very sceptical of any highly publicised weight-reducing remedies. Remember, the safest way to lose weight is by means of a suitable diet and a well-planned programme of physical therapy.

All chemical slimming preparations should be completely avoided. They are dangerous not only to the health but to life itself. Some people who have taken these preparations have met a tragic end. If you feel you must lose weight, take nothing but natural remedies.

When deciding how to approach a problem of obesity it is first necessary to identify its cause. It is no doubt true that excess weight is often caused by an improper diet or by eating too much. The unfortunate consequences in that case have their origin in too good an appetite. However, as discussed in the preceding section, there are some people who gain weight despite the fact that they eat very little. These people cannot reduce their weight simply by cutting down on the amount of food they consume. Advice on safe approaches to both types of problem is given below.

DISORDERS OF THE ENDOCRINE GLANDS

Those who put on weight although they eat very little suffer from impaired functioning of the endocrine glands. In my medical practice I have observed cases where the gonads as well as the pituitary gland and even the thyroid were responsible for obesity. If such functional disorders have been existing since youth, the gonads are generally underdeveloped or retarded as far as proper activity and hormone production is concerned. In such cases, fat is often deposited on the hips and waist only and never on the arms and legs, so that these limbs are not excessively big. In women the breasts show considerable fat deposits instead of being the shapely glands they normally are. Sagging breasts, due to a malfunction of the ovaries, are often an additional worry of overweight women.

This type of obesity cannot be dealt with successfully either by dieting or any other kind of slimming course. Weight loss may be possible only if the causes are treated. This means that the gonads must be stimulated and the thyroid as well as the pituitary must be given attention. When choosing medication we will certainly want to turn to seaweed, especially as contained in *Kelpasan*, for reliable results. For detailed recommendations on regulating the functioning of the endocrine glands, which includes stimulating the ovaries and pituitary gland, please refer to the section on 'Weight Control' on pages 201–3. Bee pollen will be of additional help, since it is known to have a stimulating effect; but do not take it if your blood pressure is high.

The diet should be low in protein and all white flour products should be avoided, as well as white sugar. Instead, stick to a natural wholefood diet and take plenty of juices, including beetroot, carrot and celery. Horseradish and young nettles should be eaten daily and, as a supplement to the diet, oysters, shrimps and squid have great therapeutic value.

A carrot juice diet is beneficial. Juices of grapefruit, grapes and oranges are also excellent. Experience will tell which juice suits you best, because certain acids, although harmless to people in good health, do not always agree with someone who is not quite so well. If you want to achieve good results without complications, follow the reactions of your body and take care. Also, drink only reasonable quantities of the juices, because you could do more harm than good by overdoing it. Caution is recommended even when the juices and remedies which are to help reduce weight are natural.

Extracts from animal glands may be helpful, but only if given in the appropriate doses, because they may otherwise do more harm than good. Exercise and deep-breathing, preferably in mountain or ocean air, are among some of the best remedies for stimulating the glands.

UNCONTROLLED APPETITE

Where the appetite is a contributory cause of obesity it requires attention too. People whose digestion works well or whose body metabolises food efficiently have a tendency toward a ferocious appetite. For them the most effective remedy is to follow the old and tested principle that you should stop eating when the food tastes best! A diet prescribed for this situation must follow certain rules: it must be low in carbohydrates and fats and high in raw and fresh produce, that is, raw vegetables either as salads or as juices.

It is most important to avoid all kinds of sweets and white flour products. If you like soups, forget cream soups and leave them to those who want to put on weight! Since beer is one of the worst things an obese person can drink, the need to avoid it may be a real stumbling block for some men. As regards meat, limit your intake to lean muscle-fibre cuts. What is more, it is best to remove all animal fats from your kitchen lest you be tempted to use them. One exception is fresh butter, which may be eaten in limited quantities. Season your food with the various kinds of cress, horseradish, paprika, curry and yeast extracts, as well as *Herbaforce*. These herbs and spices have a stimulating effect on the endocrine glands and the metabolic processes.

Medications claiming to melt down fat are highly dangerous and should be avoided at all cost, for one's health is more precious than a trim figure. Preparations containing seaweed and cellulose, which expand in volume, are tolerated for a short period of time, but after a while the patient gets tired of them. The best weight-reducing plan is one that utilises kelp, since it contains minerals in concentrated form and potassium iodide. Kelp not only stimulates the function of the endocrine glands, as mentioned earlier, and consequently helps to reduce weight, but it also induces a positive feeling of well-being. A word of caution, however: people suffering from exophthalmic goitre must take kelp only in homoeopathic doses.

Kelp is known to be one of the richest of all seaweeds. It will suffice, therefore, if the person takes one or two *Kelpasan* tablets in the morning and at noon, and *Helianthus tub*. A steady reduction of weight will be noticed from month to month, and the general condition of health and vitality will improve at the same time. Many patients have been helped to lose weight by taking Kelpasan and can testify to the truth of this statement.

The Stomach

As is true of any other organ in our body, the stomach is a miracle of divine Creation. The mucous lining of the stomach, like all other mucous membranes, consists of elastic rubber-like connective tissues permeated by a network of arteries, veins, lymphatic vessels and nerves. All of these minute vessels and nerve bundles taper off towards the inside into extremely fine, microscopic end loops surrounding the stomach glands. The inner lining of the stomach is not smooth, but drawn up into folds, the larger rugae, or folds, being subdivided into many smaller ones. When magnified under a microscope they look like the fins of an old-fashioned central-heating radiator. The rugate inner wall of the stomach is covered with about five million tiny secretory cells. The microscopic nozzles secrete in precise amounts the enzymes pepsin and rennin making up the gastric juice, according to the particular requirements of the kind and quantity of the food that has been eaten. A sufficient amount of hydrochloric acid has also to be secreted because pepsin is activated only when there is acid present.

Hunger and Appetite

Whenever we are hungry or fancy a particular food, this natural reaction stimulates the secretion of gastric juice. If, however, we eat without appetite, forcing ourselves to consume whatever is set before us, we will have poor digestion, which in turn can lead to other disorders. It is therefore important to ensure that we always have a healthy natural appetite. This is possible, not by working non-stop, but by taking sufficient exercise and by deep-breathing in the fresh air. So, if you work fairly near to your home, walk there instead of using transport. You can also whet your appetite by taking bitter herbs such as centaury, or artichoke tincture.

Our emotional and mental state may either stimulate or suppress the appetite through its influence on the secretion of gastric juice. So, if you easily give in to anger or annoyance, do not be surprised if this makes you go off your food. It should now be clear that happy people, who are always in a good mood, digest their food much better than those who are very serious, or worried and upset. Nor is the process of digestion helped by sitting down at the table when plagued by problems, or when the situation is aggravated by an animated discussion about them. If you are not hungry because of being too tired, it is wise to rest a little and unwind before eating. The manner in which the food is prepared and the dishes arranged on the table tends to make the meal more or less desirable.

When prepared with love, food tends to taste better. By the same token, a nicely set table which does not reflect the haste of the daily routine, but which does show care and attentiveness, most certainly promotes the desire to eat by stimulating the flow of gastric juices, encouraging good digestion and the assimilation of the food. It goes without saying that the atmosphere at the table likewise contributes to better digestion. Every meal should be a family party where not only is the good food enjoyed and appreciated but also where stimulating conversation takes place.

Skilful seasoning of food is of great importance too. This is not accomplished by simply sprinkling salt on everything, but by using different herbs, the effects of which we should endeavour to find out. Most seasoning herbs serve to stimulate the stomach lining to increase its secretions and thus aid the digestive process.

It is too bad that in modern times we have lost much of what used to be known as table manners and the pleasures of sharing a meal with family and friends. Modern man is glutted with the hurried pace of life, always on the go, confronted with an endless choice of newspapers, radio and television programmes, so that even such things as TV dinners, eaten in front of the screen, are now becoming a way of life. Is it any wonder that so many people are suffering from gastric ailments, indigestion and ulcers?

Stomach Disorders

Stomach problems, while not the number one category of illness, have been on the increase. This is especially true in the United States, where people are in such a hurry all the time that they literally gulp down their meals, often not even taking time to sit down at a table because they do not want to lose time away from their place of work. If one has acquired the habit of eating food that is too hot or swallowing it too rapidly, it should not come as a surprise when gastric problems surface. It is just as harmful to hurriedly eat ice-cream on top of a hot meal. The extremes of hot and cold can lead to gastritis. And once the lining of the stomach has become chronically inflamed, one need not be surprised if this condition develops into ulcers. How ulcers are formed and some suggestions for their treatment is discussed in a later section (see pages 210–12). Although ulcers can be cured, it is clearly preferable to treat gastritis in good time, before it reaches the ulcerous stage.

For this purpose *St John's wort oil* is excellent when taken in the morning and at night, a teaspoonful each time. And do not forget the help that can be obtained from natural remedies such as *Gastronol, Centaurium, Hamamelis* and *Solanosan.*

Whenever the stomach is upset we immediately blame it for the problem, but very often the liver is actually at fault. If fruit acids and fatty acids cannot be digested, causing discomfort, the liver is not functioning as it should. Since in such cases the stomach is not the basic cause of the problem, but only indirectly connected with it, the disorder will be corrected as soon as the liver is treated. A diet without fruit acids and fatty acids, but with plenty of brown rice, will soon achieve this. Brown rice is easily digested and does not burden the liver in any way, which is why it is so ideally suited for the necessary diet. You can also serve millet, buckwheat, whole rye or whole wheat for a change. Eat one of these wholegrain cereals together with salad; as a condiment use *Molkosan* (condensed whey) rather than vinegar, which is not really good for the stomach lining. Vinegar can upset the liver or the stomach juice, causing a burning sensation that results from excessive gastric secretion. Of course, this burning may also stem from some other adverse influence on the secretion of the mucous membranes of the stomach.

If you want to get rid of this burning sensation quickly, take a little *wood ash* in warm water. Should you not wish to take the ash like this, place it in a soft cloth, tie it up, pour boiling water over this and drink the lye you have just made. *Charcoal* is also good as a neutraliser and is available where wood is burned. But if you also find this treatment unpalatable, drink *raw potato juice* which has been diluted with a little warm water. *Dry rolled oats,* when chewed and insalivated well, are another good remedy to neutralise acid. *Centaury tea or drops (Centaurium)* are marvellous for heartburn and have a healing effect at the same time, whereas raw milk, although beneficial too, only treats the symptoms. If you follow the suggestions given here, it will be easy to stop the burning sensation that results from eating the wrong things.

Gastric Acid

Gastric acid is a peculiar wonder fluid, consisting of 0.5 per cent hydrochloric acid, which in some inexplicable way does not damage the mucous membranes or cells. The hydrochloric acid is produced from the chlorine or the saline solution circulating in the bloodstream. The healthy stomach lining is saved from digesting itself by anti-enzymes which to this day have not been fully identified. If, however, the mucous lining has suffered some damage or

Centaury

a chronic inflammation gains a hold, the protection given by the anti-enzymes is no longer fully effective and the gastric juice begins to eat away the mucous lining, with the result that gastric ulcers develop. When the strong acid reaches the ulcerous parts the so-called 'hunger pains' set in.

As soon as the patient drinks a little *milk* or chews some *dry rolled oats* the acid is neutralised and the pains temporarily subside. Even more effective is *wood ash*, taken as described in the preceding section, as this is able to neutralise the acid immediately because of its alkaline content. Ashes from birch wood or grapevines have proved to be excellent. The remedy *Gastronol* contains this ash, as well as condurango.

Hydrochloric acid acts like a disinfectant and kills the germs that cause fermentation and putrefaction. Where there is little hydrochloric acid present, fermentation accompanied by gas formation and bad breath is more likely. It is peculiar, too, that cancer of the stomach generally develops when there is a great lack of hydrochloric acid; the reason for this has not yet been satisfactorily explained. When we come to think of it, how difficult it is for man to find answers and explanations for that which we receive from the hands of our Creator!

Gastric Ulcers

It is common knowledge that more men than women suffer from peptic ulcers (gastric and duodenal ulcers). The explanation for this fact may be that women are seldom affected by anger and tension to the same degree as men. Emotional stress, anxiety and annoyance are known to be the main causes of the development of gastric ulcers. But irritation of the stomach lining, especially when the condition persists or recurs frequently, may also be responsible. It is therefore important to isolate the causes of the irritation, since only then can they be effectively avoided. On no account should you eat very hot food and, at the same time, beware of ice-cream or iced water, unless you warm it sufficiently in the mouth before swallowing. And remember that hot spices, strong alcoholic drinks and potent medications can cause unwelcome irritation.

Ulcers at the cardiac end of the stomach are rare; they are much more frequent in the region of the outlet of the stomach, the lesser curvature. As mentioned earlier, the first thing to occur is an irritation of the stomach lining. This irritation alone may cause some pain, but generally the patient ignores it and hence it goes untreated. When 'hunger pains' set in, which are so called because they characteristically appear when the stomach is empty and disappear when some food is ingested, the lining is already affected and there is a strong possibility that an ulcer is beginning to develop. The stomach wall, now no longer protected, is being eroded by the action of the gastric juice and it is this which causes the pain. Normally, the walls of the stomach are saved from self-digestion by a protective enzyme. If the mucous membrane of the stomach is already damaged, causing pain, the patient need only eat a little food and the discomfort will be relieved at once, because the gastric acid must now act on the food and is simultaneously absorbed by it.

If the pain sets in about half an hour after meals, this is an indication that the ulcer is located in the duodenum, generally 4–5 cm (about 2 inches) away from the outlet of the stomach.

A neglected ulcer, one that has not been treated, continues to grow and in time becomes a crater-like formation. Even though the wall of the stomach becomes thicker, the ulcer may eventually perforate it and allow the chyme to leak into the abdominal cavity.

210

This sets off an acute inflammation of the peritoneum (peritonitis), a very painful condition accompanied by vomiting and a racing pulse rate. The abdomen then becomes swollen and tight like a board. The patient's life will be in danger and he must be hospitalised without delay. Provided his general health is good and he is treated by a skilful surgeon, he has a good chance of pulling through.

It is possible for peptic ulcers to grow to the point where they eventually affect other organs, endangering particularly the pancreas, possibly even the liver and the transverse colon. Simple gastric ulcers are generally associated with a high acid content in the stomach, and the patient may experience belching or a sour-tasting regurgitation. If ulcers are not properly treated they may turn to cancer.

A malignant ulcer is more difficult to diagnose, since it is not normally accompanied by pain and thus not often detected until a later stage. Experience shows that malignancy is almost always connected with a lack of gastric acid, whereas a simple ulcer develops in a hyperacid condition.

THE TREATMENT OF ULCERS

Fasting has proved to be an effective treatment for stomach ulcers, provided the patient is physically strong enough.

Raw *potato juice* is recommended as a specific remedy and, taken regularly, it has a marvellous healing effect. Likewise, raw *carrot juice* and raw *cabbage juice* are excellent. Drink the juice of a small raw potato three times daily before meals and 50 ml (approximately three tablespoons) of cabbage juice, either in soup (see below) or after eating. For the best results the potato juice should be taken raw, but if the patient finds it difficult to drink these raw vegetable juices by themselves, they may be added to a minestrone or oatmeal soup. The soup should be cooked and allowed to cool a little before adding the juice. The soup makes the juice lose its strong flavour and the patient will be more likely to eat it and benefit from its goodness. These juices are indeed wonderful remedies at your disposal right in the home; all you have to do is to use them. Of course there are other useful medications, such as *Hamamelis, Solanosan* and *Gastronol*, but it is not necessary to buy something expensive from the pharmacist if the remedies are already in your garden or kitchen.

Condensed *bilberry (blueberry) juice* has given excellent results, also condensed *liquorice juice*. These juices should be taken daily

211

in doses of 20–40 g (0.7–1.4 oz). Before swallowing, they should be kept in the mouth for a minute or two to ensure proper insalivation, as this will hasten the cure.

All spicy foods and every kind of roughage should be excluded from the patient's diet, in order to prevent further irritation of the stomach lining. Provided the overall physical condition is excellent, one or two days of fasting per week will achieve good results. The diet should consist largely of milk, soft white cheese (cottage cheese or quark), cooked cereal porridge and cereal gruels. Even when the patient is completely cured and the pains have totally subsided, he will have to refrain from alcohol, nicotine, pork, cold meats, animal fats and hot spices for a long time. In fact, it would not be a bad idea to eliminate these items from the diet altogether. It would certainly be the best preventative measure possible and, considering that there are many other palatable foods which are not harmful to the body, the sacrifice involved seems small indeed.

Gastric ulcers are often the result of nervous tension, or stress. It is therefore advisable to free oneself from worries and anxieties. It is not really difficult to get rid of stomach ulcers if the simple methods outlined above are carefully followed. You are at liberty to combine the various simple remedies indicated or to conscientiously follow only one treatment until you are cured.

Poisoning of the Stomach and Intestines

Causes
It is alarming to think how easily we can be poisoned, especially today when the use of chemicals on farms and in food processing is so commonplace.

Cold meats and processed luncheon meats pose a particular risk, as do commercially prepared, precooked meals. So if you are in any doubt as to the freshness of such foods, do not eat them; they may have gone bad.

Anyone who has visited or lived in a tropical or subtropical climate knows how dangerous it is to eat fruit that has not been thoroughly cleaned. In the tropics, a cucumber salad made with unpeeled cucumbers can actually endanger your life. To be on the safe side, it is better to eat fruits that can be peeled, for example bananas and oranges.

The possibility of poisoning greatly occupied my mind when I myself fell victim to it and had to stay in bed as a result. One day I had been in search of certain herbs and while in the woods I crossed a clearing in which there were some wonderful specimens of deadly nightshade (*Atropa belladonna*). As the ground just there was very steep and slippery I involuntarily held on to the strong plants. Later, I came upon some poisonous prickly lettuce (*Lactuca scariola*), which I broke off and examined more closely. Shortly afterwards I found some wild strawberries under a luxurious growth of herbs and, forgetting I had not had the opportunity to wash my hands, I began to eat the delicious fruit. And then, to crown it all, on my way home I picked some poison ivy (*Rhus toxicodendron*) and held it in my hands. I remembered all these details later that night when I woke up with violent abdominal pains and tried to puzzle out their cause. On the whole I am not particularly sensitive to poisons, and I am sure that the poison ivy had little to do with my discomfort since it usually causes a rash in sensitive people, but I had no such symptoms. I had also eaten vegetables which we had bought from a store, since those in our own garden were late due to inclement weather and a late spring. This, too, could have contributed to the disturbance. Whatever the actual cause, the results were most disagreeable!

Successful Treatment
Intensive diaphragm-breathing eased the pain considerably, but it kept returning and woke me up again and again. At the break of day I tried to obtain some relief by going out into the open air. While there I collected some giant dock leaves which I placed on my abdomen to alleviate the pain. For a short time I did experience some relief, but later that morning the pain returned. My bowel movement was good, but I passed very little water. This surprised me until I began to realise that the body was retaining the liquids so that it might eventually help to expel the toxins. And so it was. A violent bout of diarrhoea set in, recurring several times during the morning, yet in between trips to the bathroom I did try to get on with my work. At the end of five hours, however, I had to give up.

I took sips of my medicine made up of *Lachesis 12x, Echinacea* and *clay*. Later, I decided to take *Belladonna 4x* as well, in the hope that it might do some good since I had handled deadly nightshade the day before and this could have been to blame for my condition. The remedies were indeed helpful, stimulating my system well, and at midday I was able to vomit. Strangely enough I brought up my lunch from the day before. I had not noticed such sluggish digestion before, since my system is usually quite efficient.

213

Unfortunately, by now I was much too tired to look around for a remedy to relieve the nausea, although *Nux vomica 4x* and *Ipecacuanha 4x* would have served me well. I had worked too hard during the previous week and this probably contributed to my feeling of utter weariness. But when I began to experience cramping pains in my heart I added a few drops of *heart tonic* to my medicine mixture and within five minutes my heart had calmed down. When the bowels were quite empty, discharging nothing but water, and the medicine which I kept sipping continued to work in the body, I soon began to feel better. By this time, deep-breathing caused only a slight feeling of soreness in the bowels and my otherwise healthy body had triumphed over the poison.

Special Guidelines
Many people become seriously ill from poisoning because they suffer from constipation, the bowel movement being weak or arrested, at the same time. It is therefore of the utmost importance to empty the bowels immediately to eliminate the toxins. If the bowels do not function and it is not possible to vomit either, then the body is forced to deal with the decomposing material in some other way. If it cannot render it harmless, a very serious condition might result and under certain circumstances could prove fatal, the simple reason for this being the retention of poisonous material. Hence it would be negligent not to take steps to empty the bowels when the first sign of poisoning becomes evident.

Should the patient bring up the remedies as well, then an enema to which a laxative has been added will be helpful. Do not worry about vomiting up a laxative, for the stomach will be cleansed in this way and this in itself will be of value. If the bowels are helped to function, hardened stools will dissolve, even if there has previously been constipation. Dragging, cramping pains will be a sign that things are beginning to move. The body itself may react to the situation by vomiting in order to get rid of the poison. Indeed, the body will do its part if only we give it the help it needs. Frequent diarrhoea is a symptom of poisoning, and if this natural reaction of the body should be absent, an enema is called for.

After the bowels have been cleaned out, the patient should fast for a time. If the heart is not in good condition, take a natural *heart tonic*. When you feel ready to eat again, start with light cereal gruels. In case the liver is still a bit sensitive, sip *raw carrot juice*. After two or three days *clay* mixed with water should be taken; then fast a second time for a little while, providing your heart can stand it. As soon as the feeling of hunger returns, proper meals can be enjoyed once more.

Such a case of poisoning is similar to the common children's diseases; when properly treated they promote better health. A fever and strong reactions in the stomach and bowels both help to eliminate wastes from the body, resulting in greater vitality. Even a case of poisoning can thus provide an opportunity for a thorough cleansing. The intestinal mucous membranes and the stomach lining will be cleansed, benefiting the whole body.

Never take chemical medicines which suppress the symptoms and impede the natural functions, for such a course would prove detrimental in the end. Rather, do everything you can to support the functions of the body. If you cooperate with nature you will not make any mistakes in treating illness, because nature is our best teacher. It is only we humans who tend to make mistakes.

Appendicitis

The appendix is a worm-shaped offshoot from the caecum, the blind intestine at the beginning of the ascending colon. It is this small tube which can become inflamed, the condition referred to as appendicitis, and is often removed surgically. The vermiform appendix is located exactly half way between the navel and the right iliac crest, the highest portion of the ilium and the pelvis. Imagine, for a moment, the face of a clock; if the navel were the centre, the small hand when it is on eight o'clock would then indicate the direction in which the appendix is located, exactly in the middle between the navel and the protruding hipbone.

Occasionally, an inflammation of the ovary (ovaritis) on the right side is mistaken for an attack of appendicitis. When the area of the appendix is depressed by the hand and suddenly released, the sensation of pain is radiated to the right, whereas in the case of ovaritis the pain would be local and of a dull nature. Appendicitis may also be diagnosed through the rectum. It generally makes itself known through severe, sudden pain in the right lower portion of the abdomen, appearing without warning and usually accompanied by malaise and vomiting. As a rule the tongue is coated and the patient runs a slight temperature of 37.5–38 °C (99.5–100.4 °F). If the diagnosis is difficult, the physician may also take a blood test to determine whether the number of white blood cells has increased. In cases of inflammation the usual number of 6,000–9,000 may have jumped to 15,000, and the pulse rate also climbs above 100.

Years ago the surgical removal of the vermiform appendix was considered hazardous and often ended in death. But today, with highly developed surgical techniques, it is a safe and simple matter, generally free from complications. If difficulties do arise they are usually caused by other existing circumstances rather than the operation itself. For example, the risk of thrombosis or embolism is naturally higher in people who have varicose veins or who show a tendency toward venal stagnation. However, this condition may be greatly improved or even eliminated with the help of simple natural remedies. For effective precaution, it is useful to take *Aesculaforce* before and after the operation. *Echinaforce* decreases the susceptibility to infection and also promotes and speeds up the healing process after surgery.

The danger of infection is much greater in tropical areas and if at all possible a visitor should avoid having to undergo an operation because of a sudden attack of appendicitis. An operation performed under primitive conditions could be a real problem for the traveller and his friends may later hear that 'the operation was successful but the patient died'. So, if you intend to visit the tropics and are suffering from a chronically inflamed or grumbling appendix, it may be better to have it removed before your departure, a precaution that will make the trip safer and more enjoyable.

Non-Surgical Treatment
Conservative treatment of appendicitis, that is, without operating, is primarily based on a *juice diet* and *bed rest*. Carrot, beetroot, bilberry and grape juices are particularly recommended for the cure. One part of juice should be diluted with two parts of good spring water. Sip the liquid slowly, allowing it to become well insalivated before swallowing. Add to 100 ml (4 fluid oz) of juice about 20–30 drops of *Echinaforce*. The burning sensation can be relieved by applying *cold milk packs* and nausea can be controlled with *Nux vomica 4x*, five drops to a glass of water, taken in small sips.

From the beginning it is very important to empty the bowels. For this purpose, take a harmless laxative tea or herbal laxative such as *Rasayana No. 1* or *Linoforce*. If the bowels fail to react quickly, an *enema* is called for. Either *camomile, mallow (cheese plant)* or *sanicle tea* can be used, preferably with twenty drops of Echinaforce or *Symphosan tincture* added.

Although we now know that the appendix is there for a purpose and is not just a vestigial structure of no real importance to the body, it is generally advisable to have it removed when it becomes inflamed, rather than run the risk of a perforation and resultant peritonitis. On the other hand, surgeons who routinely remove a healthy appendix merely because the abdomen has been opened for another operation are, from nature's standpoint, guilty of an incomprehensible action. Every scar carries with it the possibility of subsequent irritations and disturbances. Anyone who lives sensibly, keeps his bowels working well and makes sure that infectious diseases are completely cured, will generally be able to keep his appendix throughout life without any danger of inflammation.

It has been discovered that once the appendix has been removed the bowels become more sensitive. This alone indicates that an operation should be resorted to only when really necessary. Even then, a person should proceed with caution and seek a competent and conscientious surgeon, to be sure that the operation will be performed with the utmost care, because second operations have at times been necessary when an instrument or a piece of bandage was left inside the patient. However, such carelessness and negligence can only happen if those responsible for the blunder are not equal to the high standards of their profession.

Diarrhoea

Is Constant Diarrhoea Harmful?
Probably some 50 per cent of the population, particularly women, suffer to some degree from constipation. We hear again and again that it is bad to allow constipation to go on for any length of time, and there is no lack of good advice for its treatment. In contrast with constipation, not many people suffer from constant diarrhoea, a condition that prevents normal evacuation over long periods of time, even years, as opposed to the occasional bout of diarrhoea that passes quickly. Very little has been written about this kind of diarrhoea, even though it is more harmful than constipation.

THE FUNCTION OF THE SALIVARY GLANDS
If we are to understand this condition, we must first familiarise ourselves with the functions and processes of the salivary glands. These glands secrete a fluid called saliva which is mainly alkaline in composition and contains a variety of minerals; the body secretes these substances in accordance with the need determined by the type of food consumed. Since enzymes are important to the digestive process, these are also present in saliva. Few people may be

aware of the fact that the different glands – the salivary glands in the mouth, the mucous membrane of the stomach, the liver and the pancreas – together secrete several litres of saliva every day. Saliva begins the chemical processes of digestion, making the food ready for assimilation. When the saliva has finished its task, the colon reabsorbs its valuable substances. Once again they become part of the body fluids, and through them they eventually return to the salivary glands, ready to start all over again in the digestive process.

When diarrhoea strikes, however, the valuable salivary fluids are lost. The body is depleted of important minerals, which cannot be replaced quickly enough through food intake. As a consequence the body is weakened and the mineral metabolism becomes greatly disturbed. This does not mean to say that a temporary attack of diarrhoea lasting two or three days will occasion the loss of a great amount of valuable fluid, but if the condition continues for several months it could have serious consequences and must be treated.

Effective Treatment
To correct this condition, the patient must change his diet. Avoid all fruit, raw vegetables, sweets, cooked cabbage, and every other food that may cause fermentation and flatulence. Raw, unprocessed milk is recommended. The diet may include soft white cheese (cottage cheese, quark), any of the mild cheeses, rolled oats, crispbread, rusks, potatoes boiled in their jackets and brown rice. Not all fruits are forbidden; apples, blueberries (bilberries) and bananas have a constipating and healing effect. It is important, however, not to eat fruit and vegetables at the same meal, a precautionary measure which prevents fermentation. Make sure that everything you eat is well chewed and insalivated before swallowing. A short fast is beneficial, too, because it gives the digestive organs a rest during which time the bacterial flora can be restored and regenerated.

One of the best remedies is *tormentil tincture*, prepared from the fresh plant. It is most effective when taken in conjunction with sedative oat juice, *Avena sativa*, the combination being known as *Tormentavena*. By taking five drops in a little water every hour and preferably also refraining from eating, this excellent preparation stops even chronic cases of diarrhoea, usually within a day or two. This is a simple, completely harmless, yet most reliable botanical remedy and can be given even to infants without any danger. Temporary relief may also be obtained from *raw rolled oats* if masticated well and nothing else is added to them. *Wood ash* or *charcoal* made from lime wood have a beneficial therapeutic effect. *Clay*, white healing earth, is also recommended and is very effective.

When diarrhoea has been brought under control and can be considered arrested, it is necessary to consolidate the normal condition and complete the healing process by creating a new bacterial flora in the intestines. Two remedies are available that will help to achieve this: *Acidophilus* in powder form and the lactic acid preparation *Molkosan*. It generally takes a long time for the intestinal flora to become sufficiently established so that the intestine can once again function normally without assistance. Much care and patience are the key to beating this problem.

Chronic Constipation

The Dangers of Leaving Constipation Untreated

'Death resides in the bowels' is a warning the meaning of which we should carefully take to heart. It is an undisputed fact that constipation is the cause of many ailments. People who have been complaining about headaches for years never think that their discomfort could be caused by a transfer of accumulated metabolic toxins from the intestines to the bloodstream. Stomach, liver and kidney disorders may also stem from constipation or irregular bowel movement. Skin eruptions, spots and various eczematous conditions may be due to it. It is even possible for certain diseases or disorders to fail to respond to any kind of natural remedy until constipation, which poisons the system time and again, has been completely eradicated. Women are generally more affected by constipation than men.

If the condition is allowed to go untreated, it may have grave consequences. So never shrug it off lightly; constipation is a dangerous thing. A malignant growth leading to obstruction of the bowels (ileus) may be the result of constipation that has existed for thirty years. An artificial rectal exit (anus) is certainly not a desirable answer to the problem. We often fail to appreciate the automatic devices of our body until it is too late, that is, at the moment when these natural functions fail. They should never be taken for granted and every consideration must be given to nature's requirements. Even the most skilful surgeon can produce nothing but a makeshift solution, in comparison to the original. Only someone who has had to put up with the burden of an artificial rectal opening is able to appreciate and comprehend the marvellous working of our anal sphincter. So, never let things get to the point of neglecting proper movement of the bowels.

Some people complain about having spent a small fortune on laxatives, but all in vain. This should not be surprising when we consider the many chemical medicines sold over the counter, which, at best, offer only temporary help. It takes more to remedy the condition than just making it disappear for a few days. Just as a tree needs the right kind of fertiliser and pruning in order to grow strong, the natural functions of the human body need to be supported instead of suppressed. Instead of heeding the direction of nature, man has become too dependent on modern scientific research and reasoning.

The tribespeople in various parts of the earth would not know what to do with the best herbal laxatives, even when offered to them free. Neither the Berber tribes in the Atlas mountains, the Incas in the Cordilleras, the Vedda in the north east of Sri Lanka, nor many other aboriginal people would have any use for them. And why not? The answer is quite simple: their diet is not as opulent as ours in the developed world. Those people usually eat just enough to satisfy their hunger, whereas most of us tend to overeat.

Then there is another reason. The more primitive peoples usually have more fibre in their diet, and this provides the necessary rough-age to stimulate the intestinal muscles. We gorge ourselves on white bread, rolls, pastries, puddings and all kinds of sweets and dishes made from bleached flour and refined sugar, which all con-tribute to a slowing down of the bowel movement, causing consti-pation.

Natural Remedies
If we want to understand why these aboriginal peoples have a better digestive system than we do, we must not overlook the fact that they still live close to, and in harmony with, nature and enjoy a relaxed pace of life. We, however, who live in an 'advanced' society have come to accept a way of life where speed and bustle are the norm. We have come to feel that this is appropriate for our modern times. How wrong we are! Restlessness, anxiety, vex-ation and constant hurrying affect the sympathetic nervous system, resulting in spasmodic constipation. If we then take strong laxatives we only make the problem worse. It is much wiser to change our pace, try to find peace of mind and calmness, refuse to accept more

tasks than we can deal with and rather than pursuing every so-called pleasure keep a proper balance in our lives. We will then have enough time to get the necessary rest and relaxation. Furthermore, we will use our legs much more, walking instead of sitting around. Remember, walking helps to stimulate the bowels. Early morning exercise, massaging the stomach and brush massages, if done daily, will be of particular help to those in sedentary occupations.

We can profit from the experience of a farmer, who knows what to do when his livestock shows signs of constipation. He will take *linseed*, prepare a gruel and feed it to the animals. The linseed promotes the formation of mucous in the intestines, which in turn relieves constipation. Linseed has the same effect on humans. Another oil-bearing seed, *psyllium seed* is very effective and easy to take, even whole, because of its small size. These seeds do not have to be boiled as is the case with linseed and are more palatable than linseed gruel. If you do take linseed, it should be freshly ground each time as it goes rancid in a short time. Of course, there are ready-made linseed products on the market, for example *Linoforce*. Linseed serves as an excellent stimulation to the bowels when it is taken together with muesli and walnuts. It is interesting to note that walnuts stimulate the bowels, whereas other kinds of nuts often have the opposite effect. One reason for this is that constipation is frequently caused by malfunction of the liver. Walnuts stimulate the function of the liver and in so doing influence the bowels. Even in severe cases of constipation good results have been obtained by taking various liver remedies, for example *Rasayana No. 2, Chelidonium 4x and Biocarottin*, as well as *Podophyllum 4x–6x*, which aids the flow of bile.

There are a number of different basic causes of constipation. Nervous tension may be responsible for it, malfunction of the liver has already been mentioned, and pancreatic insufficiency can also contribute to poor bowel movement. However, diet is probably the main factor. The various causes of constipation require specific treatment.

The farmer knows that he cannot keep his animals in the stable all the time; they need exercise and a change of diet from time to time. We can take a lesson from this and make sure we get enough exercise and pay attention to our choice of food and its variation. Avoid all constipating food items and particularly chocolate and sweets. Likewise, we would do well to keep off cheese, eggs and egg dishes. Instead, eat plenty of carrots, raw sauerkraut, and bitter salads such as dandelion and chicory. Over a long period of time, it is beneficial to eat soaked prunes and walnuts for breakfast, together with a slice of wholegrain bread. Alternate this breakfast with muesli and ground linseed. During the berry season eat plenty of muesli with fresh berries added, instead of bread. As far as possible, avoid dough products made with bleached white flour and any other starchy foods. On the other hand, natural brown rice causes no complications when boiled so that the grains do not stick together. Potatoes, however, may turn out to be constipating.

By observing these guidelines, you will be able to overcome constipation, especially when you are determined to adopt proper eating habits, not gulping down your food, but masticating it well before swallowing – and always in a calm and relaxed frame of mind.

Another beneficial approach to the problem is to take a warm *hay flower sitz bath* every evening just before retiring. Relief may also be obtained from a special blood-cleansing programme, the *Rasayana Programme*. According to Indian doctors, this treatment has a stimulating effect on the entire metabolism and increases the efficiency of the kidneys, liver, bowels and pancreas. Hundreds of people have been able to get rid of chronic constipation with the help of this programme, which serves to cleanse the body fluids especially in the spring. Nevertheless, in spite of the many excellent natural remedies available today, lasting benefits can only be achieved if our many mistakes in diet and life-style are corrected. If you get to the root of the problem, make the necessary changes, and use the natural remedies and treatments suggested, you will be able to find relief from constipation.

Whether you suffer from constipation or any other functional disorder, foods that tempt the taste buds but contribute to constipation should be firmly rejected. There are plenty of delicious natural foods that are good for the digestion and the bowels, so why not choose these instead? You simply cannot eat and live just any old way and then hope to overcome the resulting discomforts by means of pills and drops. This approach will only hurt you, and eventually lead to chronic ailments. We must subject ourselves to the demands of nature and only then, with the use of good natural remedies as well as appropriate adaptations to our life-style, will we achieve the desired results. There is no other way.

Do Starchy Foods Cause Constipation?

Many people suffering from constipation claim that a diet high in carbohydrates makes their condition worse or perhaps even causes it. Looking at this argument closely, we are inclined to agree, for in such cases the pancreas does not produce enough enzymes to break down starch. Hence it is indeed true that starchy foods can lead to constipation. Potato starch is particularly binding, so that it would be advisable to restrict one's intake of potatoes or forgo them entirely until the pancreas is back to normal. Too many patients make the mistake of not finding out which foods are known to cause problems, in order to avoid them until a complete cure is achieved. They have the mistaken belief that there must be some kind of miracle cure that will do the job without any sacrifice on their part. But would it not be wiser to avoid all foods that could trigger the disorder instead of waiting until we have the problem and then depending on a remedy to overcome it? Abstinence from such foods is often the only action required to rectify the condition.

Besides potato starch, grain starch may also cause or promote constipation. However, this is only true of denatured or refined cereals. The whole grain, on the other hand, neutralises the constipating effect because of its bran content. Rice starch is the least constipating of all; it is also easily digested and therefore recommended for infants and children. Since white rice has a depleted mineral content, only unprocessed brown rice should be included in a healthy diet. Moreover, brown rice can be most palatable when well prepared.

The cooking time for rice depends on the variety used. Italian rice cooks faster than the Asian variety. If you like the grains nice and firm, which is most beneficial for the digestion, do not overcook or soak for long periods of time. A variety that does not go soft during the usual cooking time can be briefly brought to the boil the following morning and left during the morning to soak in the rest of the water. All you need to add is the seasoning of your choice. Steam a clove of garlic, finely chopped parsley and a peeled, chopped tomato in a little oil and add to the rice to enhance its flavour. Or sprinkle with grated cheese and prepare *au gratin*. Placing sliced tomatoes on top is another tasty variation. When well prepared, brown rice is so palatable that even those who have always rejected it will enjoy it. This is apart from the fact that it is very nourishing. Before long you will find the taste of white rice insipid and will become accustomed to the darker colour of natural

223

brown rice. If, however, you should still prefer a light-coloured variety, at least choose one that still contains most of its minerals, for example, the brands Avorio and Uncle Ben's.

THE RIGHT WAY TO GO ABOUT IT

Another advantage of brown rice is that it is nutritious and can sustain one over a long period of time. It is filling too, so that even a small quantity is satisfying. This is good for the pancreas, an organ that is often weakened through eating excessive quantities of food. If we stick to a natural diet, chew well, eat slowly and insalivate the food before swallowing, the pancreas is being helped to recover and efficient intestinal activity is more likely. Even small mistakes in eating habits can rob us of the vital elements so necessary for good digestion. At any rate, it is advisable to limit the intake of starchy foods and supplement the diet with vegetables and salads. Sesame seeds, eaten daily, are also helpful. And let me remind you once again, when choosing your menu, be sensible and avoid items or combinations that cause fermentation and flatulence.

So, if the pancreas should be too weak to digest starchy foods, we must take good care of it and do everything we can to restore it to its normal and full capacity. Only then will it be able to help us digest a reasonable amount of starchy food in the future.

Two Soups to Open the Bowels

There is a special soup which stimulates sluggish bowels if eaten every morning with a little crispbread or wholegrain (wholewheat) bread. The recipe is as follows. Cook freshly ground whole wheat, a small chopped onion and a crushed clove of garlic in some water. After taking the soup off the stove, add a little finely chopped parsley and a spoonful of pure olive oil.

This simple breakfast has cured many of their constipation. For more stubborn cases, psyllium seed or ground linseed should be added.

Alternatively, if you are bothered with intestinal sluggishness, have been overdosed with laxatives, if even natural plant laxatives no longer give relief, or if you simply want to normalise your bowel movement, the following recipe will be helpful.

First, make a herbal infusion. For sensitive people use cassia stick (*Cassia fistula*, also known as purging cassia) tea; for those less sensitive, use senna leaf, senna pod or some other herbal tea to stimulate the bowel movement. Brew and strain the tea, then for each person add one small raw potato, diced, with the skin. Mix in a teaspoon of bran and one of linseed. Simmer for fifteen minutes. Eat this herbal soup in the morning and also at night, if necessary. If it does not appeal to you, put it through a sieve and drink the liquid. You may eventually become used to eating it without it being strained. The effect of this soup on the bowels is astounding and it works when no other laxative does.

It is noteworthy that people who normally do not tolerate senna leaf tea respond well to this rather strong mixture if it is prepared in the way I have just described. The alkaline substances in the raw potato bind certain acids and resins which sometimes cause griping pains when senna tea is taken. I should add that horsetail (shave grass) tea is also easier to take if it is made in this way. Horsetail tea has a strong effect and it is not recommended to drink it on its own. Anyone who intends to take it regularly should remember to avoid excessive doses because of its possible side effects, which are equivalent to the symptoms of poisoning.

Dysbacteria

Much is being written and talked about the modern principles of proper nutrition. Wholegrain products, brown rice, wheat germ, natural honey, buttermilk, soft white cheese (cottage cheese, quark) and vegetable oils high in polyunsaturated fatty acids are being recommended as nutritionally sound food, and rightly so.

But it is also interesting to note that in a family of five, all eating the same healthy natural food, not every member benefits to the same degree. One member of the family may be strong, healthy and in good physical shape, whereas another may be skinny and weak, and a third member could even be anaemic and pale. Only when one of them suffers from such a marked calcium deficiency that he experiences constant cramps and spasms and can only keep free from pain by taking antispasmodics does it begin to dawn on us that nutrition involves more than simply giving the body a certain quantity of good food with a high nutritive content. Nutrition also means making sure that the body can absorb this good food, thus enabling the cells to receive all the nutrients they need.

Dysbacteria is one of the new diseases that lead to a debilitating loss of strength in thousands of people. Some degenerate totally without knowing what is the matter with them. The main causes of dysbacteria are two modern groups of medicines, first sulphonamides and second, antibiotics. To counteract their detrimental effects, it is suggested that the patient be given the liver remedy *Boldocynara*, which also stimulates production of bile. But to combat dysbacteria successfully he must take *acidophilus powder, Biocarbosan* and *Molkosan* as well.

A few days after taking these remedies, the normal appetite will return and the bowels will begin to function properly again. The patient will feel much better and notice a definite improvement in his physical condition as a result of his energy and strength return-ing. Once the intestinal bacteria have started to recover, the assimi-lation of food will improve and, in turn, the leaden tiredness caused by the illness will disappear. The body will once again be adequately nourished.

Patients with dysbacteria who are not too weak will find that going on a *juice diet* for two or three days brings excellent results. Besides other juices, beetroot juice is especially recommended. The juices should be diluted with half the quantity of spring water or slightly effervescent mineral water. If, while dieting, your stomach feels empty, eat a little crispbread.

I have often recommended a weekly 'juice day' because of its excellent effect on the general condition of health. The digestive system is able to rest, resulting in an improved absorption of food. Remember, nutrition does not depend on how much food we eat, but rather on how well the body assimilates and utilises it. These requirements can best be met when we eat unrefined, natural wholefoods.

Intestinal Parasites

In the old days, when grandmother would take a good look at her grandchildren and conclude from the symptoms she saw that they had intestinal worms, she was usually right. The children would have shadows under the eyes, be constantly picking their nose because it was itching, manifest a nervous demeanour and a lack of interest in playing and would restlessly toss and turn in bed at night instead of sleeping soundly. So what would grandmother do? She would give the children tansy or wormwood tea to drink. When tiny white threadworms appeared in the stool, she would make the children drink milk to which crushed garlic had been added. Even though the children may have hated to take this concoction, it was usually effective, but if the results were not entirely satisfactory, the garlic milk was also used as an enema. Thanks to their elders' close attention and care, the children were rid of the bothersome worms in no time, and it was a good thing

Tansy

too, because these parasites can do a lot of harm to a child's organism.

The same precautions grandmother exercised should be followed today. A child who is pale, always tired and moody could have worms and should be carefully examined. Otherwise, years may pass until someone is alerted to the problem and an examination of the stool and blood reveals their presence. What a pity, though, that these poor children meanwhile have had to suffer for years because of sheer negligence. Such lack of care can have serious consequences for the children's normal growth and development, since the worms are responsible for their discomfort and their unhappy, moody state of mind, making it difficult for them to show willingness and be obedient.

Threadworms and Roundworms
Intestinal worms should never be considered harmless or their presence accepted as a necessary evil. Although in most cases we are dealing only with threadworms and roundworms, these intestinal parasites can still be quite harmful. The tiny threadworm (*Oxyuris vermicularis*) is often the cause of much discomfort. These worms, as well as the roundworm (*Ascaris lumbricoides*), secrete

227

toxic metabolic substances which are absorbed by the body. The result is a change in the blood composition and an adverse effect on the general condition of the person afflicted. Children with calcium deficiency are especially prone to infestation with worms, which constitutes a double dose of trouble for them since their power of resistance is already low and the damage will thus be magnified.

The roundworm, which resembles an earthworm in appearance, reaches a length of 25–40 cm (10–17 inches) and has other detrimental effects besides its poisonous metabolic secretions. The eggs, which are transmitted from vegetables that have been fertilised with liquid manure, develop into small larvae which penetrate the intestinal wall and are carried into the lungs, where they settle and develop further. The patient appears to be suffering from a stubborn case of bronchitis, but the real problem is the infestation with worms. From the lungs the worms migrate through the bronchials and back into the digestive tract again, but eggs emerge in the stool only 70–75 days after the initial infection. Even so, the migration of these worms has not yet ended. When fully mature, they are found not only in the intestines, but sometimes they come down the nose and into the mouth, much to the horror of the victim. At other times they may bore their way into the bile ducts, causing jaundice. Or they may creep through the intestinal wall, which can precipitate peritonitis. Both cases are serious and dangerous. Their number may increase to many hundreds, a bunch of worms actually being able to cause an obstruction of the bowel and endanger the victim's life. I could go on enumerating the many ways in which worms can pose a danger, but what I have explained already may suffice to convince you that intestinal worms are not harmless. Their elimination must receive our attention.

Today it has become much easier to eradicate these intestinal parasites, in as far as non-poisonous plant remedies are readily available. So do not let them settle in the intestines. Papaya preparations greatly facilitate the eradication of threadworms in the colon and of roundworms which inhabit the small intestine. *Papayasan* is made from the tropical plant *Carica papaya* and is actually able to digest all kinds of worms that settle in the small intestine and the colon. Papaya is a palm-like tree with leaves similar in shape to fig leaves, but much larger. Its fruit, also called papaya, resembles a melon. When ripe it contains only a tiny amount of the vermicide enzyme papain, so it is from other parts of the plant that Papayasan is made.

Although ordinary worm medicines can sometimes have a bad effect or none at all, the Papayasan treatment is quite different. While it is an excellent anthelmintic, it is quite safe to take. Whereas other modern worm medicines kill the worms by poisoning them, leaving the body to expel what is left of them, the effect of Papayasan is based on a different principle. It does not poison the worms, but the protein-splitting enzyme papaya contains, called papain, attacks them and digests them in the intestine. It is true that the stomach, pancreas and intestinal walls produce enzymes to break down protein in the digestive tract, but the worms are immune to them. On the other hand, papain is able to literally digest the worms without harming the intestinal lining in any way. In fact, the intestinal lining is neither affected by the plant enzymes nor the body's own enzymes. It is important to maintain a low-protein diet while taking Papayasan, otherwise the proteins from meat and eggs use up the worm-dissolving enzyme for their own digestion, so that it will not be available for its intended purpose.

Sometimes it appears that worm remedies have been ineffective, because after a short time the parasites may be noticed again. However, it does not follow that the remedy was necessarily at fault; it is more than likely that reinfection has taken place. This happens during the night in a warm bed, when the tiny worms leave the body and deposit their eggs in the minute skin folds near the anus. Itching sets in and naturally the child begins to scratch, only to get the eggs under the fingernails. Since children have the habit of putting their fingers back into the mouth, the eggs are transferred back into the digestive tract. It is also possible that the microscopic eggs had been shaken from the sheets when the bed was made, dispersing them into the air, from which they were inhaled together with the dust from the room.

For this reason, the need for scrupulous cleanliness cannot be emphasised enough. During a worm treatment, the room should be dusted daily with a damp cloth. It is also imperative to change the bed linen frequently. Tight-fitting pants should be worn under the night gown or pyjamas to avoid involuntary scratching whilst asleep.

Fortunately, not everyone becomes infected when worm eggs are swallowed, because the body's natural resistance and good digestion do not permit them to develop in the first place.

Tapeworms

Tapeworms are more dangerous than the smaller nematodes. A tapeworm is extremely difficult to get rid of because of the barbed hooks on its head by which it remains firmly attached to the mucous-membrane lining of the intestines. When small segments, 7–10mm (¼–⅓ inch) wide and 10–20 cm (4–8 inches) long, are seen in the stools, this is no reason to think that the victim is now rid of the tapeworm. Rather, these are merely sexually mature parts containing eggs, which the full-grown worm casts off. Moreover, even though the tapeworm drops off segments from the end of its body, it does not become any shorter, because it continues to grow at the other end, the head, where the individual body segments begin. A tapeworm can produce hundreds of thousands of eggs which, through the excrement, eventually find their way into the cesspool. Of course, this is also true of the eggs of threadworms and roundworms. You can see why it is a hazardous thing to fertilise the vegetable garden with cesspool manure. In a heavy downpour the worm eggs may be spattered up from the ground onto the vegetables, thus providing a source of reinfection. The same danger arises when using liquid manure on a pasture where sheep and cows graze, as these animals stand every chance of becoming infected with tapeworm eggs.

There are various kinds of tapeworm. When eating meat that has not been properly cooked it is possible to become infected with the so-called bladderworms (*cysticerci*) of the cattle, pig or fish variety. The bladderworms or larvae then develop into tapeworms in the human host.

Even more dangerous than the cattle tapeworm, which can reach a length of several metres, is the dog tapeworm, of the genus *Echinococcus*. It is only about 5–6 mm (¼ inch) long but its size bears no relationship to its danger, for this little worm is capable of causing greater damage than the much longer cattle tapeworm. Although called the dog tapeworm, it has been known to infest sheep, goats, pigs and even cattle. When this happens, blisters the size of a walnut form in the lungs of cattle, and in the case of swine, these formations are found in the liver. The Swiss Information Service to Physicians reported that in 1963, for example, 508 cattle and 62 swine brought into the Zurich abattoir were infested with the *Echinococcus*. As far as domestic animals and pets are concerned, extreme precautions need to be taken, especially with dogs and cats. Adults who are otherwise meticulously clean, are often offended when reminded to be careful when handling pets. They think nothing of patting their pets while eating. But it is unwise to do this. Neither should we allow a dog or cat to lick the hand or the face, because of the danger attached to it. What is more, young animals, puppies and kittens, should be trained not to do so. To minimise the risk of infection, dog owners would be wise to abstain from feeding raw lungs or liver to their dogs. After a long journey, perhaps abroad, check your dog's faeces, since 7–8 weeks after infection small flecks with thousands of eggs may be seen. You certainly cannot be called over-fussy for taking such proper care and precautions in the interest of your health.

Since field mice can be infected from the faeces of dogs, the eggs can be transmitted to people from the cats that catch the mice. The larvae of the dog tapeworm can cause small blisters in the human liver. This is quite dangerous since worm remedies are only effective in the intestine and not in the liver.

There is another danger. The eggs can develop into minute larvae in the intestines, bore through the intestinal wall and then migrate via the bloodstream to various organs of the body, where they form blisters or cysts varying in size from that of a pinhead to a little child's head. This condition can be fatal. Do not, therefore, ignore the warning to exercise due care when handling your pets. There are no doubt many ways of playing with them and enjoying their companionship, without endangering your health.

Because international travel has now become a way of life, yet another danger presents itself. In our travels we come into contact with strangers and their animals. This is an area in which there is always a possibility of risking infection through the transmission of eggs and parasites. Being aware of this danger should make us more conscious of the need for meticulous cleanliness and hygiene.

Getting rid of a tapeworm is not as simple as one might think. I once helped a young man lose one by means of a diet and special tapeworm medication, although previous treatment with chemical medicines had done him no good whatsoever. My instructions for the diet and the remedy were as follows.

Diet: No meat, but plenty of vegetables and fruit, especially raw carrots, no bread, no potatoes, and nothing made of flour. For lunch: a stew made up of lentils, carrots, onion and garlic. Cook all the ingredients together in one pot. It may be seasoned with a little fresh horseradish. Twice a day a small dish of sauerkraut (4–5 forkfuls). In the morning, on an empty stomach, a handful of peeled pumpkin seeds and a handful of unsweetened cranberries, chewed well. Follow this up an hour later with one or two cups of tapeworm tea, without sugar. It is also helpful to sip a glass of garlic milk as well.

Recipe for tapeworm tea: Take 5 g (⅙ oz) powdered aloes, 20 g (⅔ oz) alder buckthorn (bark), 20 g (⅔ oz) senna leaves, 25 g (1 oz) valerian root, 30 g (just over 1 oz) peppermint leaves. Mix them together and use to make an infusion, one tablespoon for every cup of boiling water. Leave to brew for ten minutes, but do not boil.

Another, more radical, remedy to get rid of a tapeworm that does not seem to yield to any treatment is a teaspoonful of *Kamala powder*, taken just once. This remedy is good for adults and pets alike. Less radical but equally effective is *Papayasan* if taken over a period of time.

It is very important to avoid becoming constipated. If you tend to do so, *Rasayana No. 1* will solve the problem. And do not forget to help the body expel the tapeworm by drinking *Biocarottin*.

When examining the stools make sure that the head as well as the body of the worm has been expelled. If the head remains, the treatment will have to be repeated within two or three weeks. Should the first day of treatment produce no results, continue for another day. An *enema* with *garlic milk* given once a day can be very effective and is recommended too.

A word of caution is required at this point. The expelled tapeworm must under no circumstances be thrown on the compost heap but should be burned or buried deep in the ground.

Finally, if no treatment whatsoever is able to shift the worm, there is yet another remedy that has been successfully used in Africa, namely the *root of the pomegranate tree*. One teaspoonful of this root in powder form should be taken in a little warm water every morning and evening. Alternatively, a tea can be made by boiling the root, in which case two cups should be taken daily.

Dangers of the Tropics
Overseas travel has become commonplace since large airliners have conquered the problem of distance. It is not surprising, then, that in the more temperate regions of the earth travel agents keep issuing glossy brochures and leaflets, tempting us to travel to far-distant exotic countries. If you live in an area where glittering snow and majestic mountains predominate, it is hard to resist the call to

experience the peculiar charm of the tropics; to enjoy a walk in the balmy air under palm trees or amid banana trees, laze around in the shade of huge avocado trees, watch the crocodiles from a canoe, follow an elephant herd in a jeep driven by a watchful guide, or perhaps admire some lions roaming in absolute freedom. An added bonus would be the prospect of getting to know the customs, habits and life-style of the natives. In reality, travelling in tropical countries is often arduous and not always as pleasant as some might make us believe, even though it may be interesting. The people who encourage us to visit faraway places are usually so enthusiastic about them that it does not occur to them to alert us to the dangers the tropics can have in store for us. Not even the travel agencies see fit to do so, but as you will see from what follows below their suggested precautions and insurance are really not enough in every case.

Unseen Dangers – Parasites and Micro-organisms

For most people who visit the tropics, big game seems to be the main thing to be feared. Elephants, lions, tigers and crocodiles figure especially in our imagination and we may be fearful enough to believe that there is a wild animal lurking behind every bush. And of course we dread the snakes. However, the well-informed traveller will reassure us, knowing that wild animals are not really the great danger they are generally thought to be.

This knowledge is certainly a relief but it should not make us drop our guard. There are other threats, generally unnoticed but far more perilous than adventures with wild animals, and these stem from a variety of micro-organisms. What really makes the tropics dangerous are the things the scientist can see under a microscope and the doctor in a blood test, when examining an unfortunate traveller. A European, for example, may never have had an experience with certain micro-organisms, but what an unpleasant shock they can cause if through ignorance and carelessness he allows them to invade his body. How easy it is for a traveller to become infected and suffer the consequences of amoebic dysentery, a persistent and sometimes fatal disease. Yet one does not have to travel all that far to be in danger of contracting amoebic dysentery, as it can be caught in southern Italy, Greece and the Middle East. So if you live in a temperate zone and travel to such subtropical lands or islands, be very careful to avoid getting infected with amoebas.

In many other areas, for example in North Africa and Egypt or

233

Sri Lanka and India, travellers are exposed to the ever-present danger of hookworms. This dangerous worm is so widespread that Professor Dr Nauck, one of the foremost specialists in tropical diseases, believes that over 500 million people are infested with it. According to his estimate, every fifth person in the tropics is a carrier of this dangerous parasite.

Not only are roundworms and the tiny threadworms or pinworms extremely widespread in tropical lands and islands, but the even more dangerous whipworms are abundant in some areas, so that practically all the inhabitants are infested with one kind or another of these parasites.

REASONS FOR THE WIDESPREAD INFESTATION

If you are at all familiar with the conditions in the countries to which I refer, you will not be surprised at the widespread problem of parasites and the great number of people infested with them. The main reason is the glaring lack of sanitation and sewage systems. There are often no sewers at all; nor, in many cases, are there proper lavatories or toilets. The consequence? Human excrement lies around on the ground, even in the beautiful palm groves among all the tropical plants, and this waste matter is riddled with thousands of worm eggs. As a rule there is no safe drinking water supply either, and this of course is very dangerous. Another extremely hazardous factor is the lack of meat inspection, so that the people consume meat full of bladderworms and various other parasites. This circumstance makes it possible for the dangerous dog tapeworm to be transmitted, while filariae, another variety of parasitic worm, are spread through mosquito bites. One type of these filarial worms is known to be the cause of the dreadful disease called elephantiasis (see the following section).

Tropical Diseases

Paddling in a canoe through the dense jungle is no doubt an unforgettable experience many a nature-lover dreams about. The untouched character of nature has a special attraction, and indeed, where man has not yet created order, or disorder, the tropical environment is a unique experience. You think you are in a different world when the sun's last red-golden rays shoot through the fan-like palm branches in the evening or when the vines hanging from jungle trees appear to take on eery forms. At night, lying on a bamboo mat in a native hut under a mosquito net, never hope to find undisturbed sleep. In the solitude of the jungle unusual noises and animal sounds, often terribly frightening, reach your ears. We get the uncanny feeling of adventure, realising that what we have let ourselves in for is actually more interesting than it is pleasant. Nevertheless, we soon become accustomed to things, and what seemed strange and exotic to begin with becomes gradually more familiar. We begin to recognise plants and animals, and every day new experiences occur in the jungle. Comparatively soon we get used to snakes and wild animals and even the lack of sanitary arrangements, as well as all the discomforts connected with it.

The true dangers only begin to dawn on us when we have to lie in a hut because a cold or hot fever, vomiting and diarrhoea have laid us low, weakening us to such an extent that days later we have hardly any energy and desire to live left in us. The dangers of tropical diseases have risen drastically in recent years, especially in countries where the sanitary and health inspection is now in the hands of people who still lack sufficient training and understanding. The Congo and other African countries are typical examples. In some towns in Central Africa, where malaria had previously been eradicated, the visitor has no longer any guarantee of escaping infection. The efficiency and effectiveness of inspection and control of breeding grounds in those countries that only recently acquired independence have not been possible to maintain in areas that previously had been made safe.

It is very sad that the results of many years' efforts are being relinquished due to a change in circumstances. Malaria, typhoid fever, paratyphoid fever, elephantiasis, amoebic dysentery and dysentery are, unfortunately, once again on the increase and the danger of infection in many tropical areas can be expected to continue to grow before it falls. The white colonial powers were responsible for many wrongs, but as regards hygiene and the control of epidemics they also did a lot of good. Human weakness is often responsible for 'throwing out the baby with the bath water', particularly where childish naivety or the blindness of nationalism predominates.

It is indeed regrettable that all the good progress achieved in the course of many years of effort and work should come to nothing. It is a step backwards when tourists are exposed to greater dangers and risks of infection. So if your health is not exceptionally good and your powers of resistance are limited, or if you are very sensitive, think twice for the present before you decide to go on a safari or other holiday in tropical countries. Despite all kinds of vaccinations, you will not be immune to all tropical diseases.

For one thing, vaccines are not available for every disease; what is more, vaccination in itself can often pose a problem for the traveller, because it can weaken his general condition. And do not forget that for many serious tropical diseases prophylactics do not exist. What comfort will the most beautiful and tempting colour brochure depicting glorious beaches and colourful surroundings be if the unsuspecting tourist comes down with something serious? Moreover, the treatment of tropical diseases is not always a simple, easy or safe matter. Strong medication is required and this affects especially the liver, often inflicting great harm. I have been shocked many times when browsing through travel brochures, to see that they give no hint whether the travel agencies, tour operators and their guides have any idea at all of the dangers in the destinations advertised. One such brochure planned to take the travellers to an area in Sri Lanka, to the south of Colombo and Mount Lavinia, an area where the dreaded tropical disease elephantiasis has not yet been fully eradicated. In spite of this knowledge, the agents chose exactly that place for an overnight stay.

THE REALITY

Elephantiasis is transmitted by a mosquito. The female bites an infected person, sucks in the blood and transmits the parasite to a healthy person's bloodstream by another bite. Once the parasites, which we could call minute worms, are in the human blood, they multiply into the millions, causing fever and extreme enlargement of the lymphatics. Given time, the limbs may enlarge to the extent that they are two or three times their normal size. In fact, the disease got its peculiar name from this condition, for the legs come to resemble elephants' legs in their bulk. But it is no laughing matter: elephantiasis is a sad affliction and one that is difficult to cure successfully.

I have also heard from doctors specialising in tropical diseases that malaria has not yet been fully eradicated in all parts of Sri Lanka. It is therefore advisable to sleep under a mosquito net and to take preventative medicines. There is, however, no danger in the mountainous areas of Sri Lanka where the strikingly beautiful tea plantations are to be found. Yes, tropical countries and islands might present an especially exciting and tempting attraction and no doubt offer plenty of beauty, yet caution is definitely called for because of the unknown dangers. As I have said before, I would not recommend a tropical vacation to just anyone; weak, sickly and especially older people should not even think about visiting the tropics.

The beauties of Switzerland, in a wider sense also Europe in general and other temperate zones, have much to attract the enthusiastic traveller and holiday-maker. That is why I would like to remind the prospective traveller of the old proverb, 'You might go further and not fare so well.' Why do I recommend that you take these words to heart? Because on my many travels I have met some Europeans who had been laid low by tropical diseases and became physical wrecks as a result. So, may the foregoing words of caution serve as a warning to all those who want to travel in the tropics but have no idea of the existing dangers to their health.

Precautionary Measures

Below are listed several precautionary rules that everyone should heed when travelling in the tropics.

1. Never eat raw meat. Even meat roasted on the outside but still rare inside should be rejected. The same warning applies to raw fish of any kind. In the Far East raw fish prepared by a process of fermentation is extremely tasty and prized by many as a delicacy. Nevertheless, however tempting it may be, it can be very dangerous and should not be consumed.

2. Do not eat raw vegetables. Salads of any kind must be totally eliminated from the diet when travelling in the tropics. If the vegetables are grown in the fenced garden of a friend where you can be sure they were raised under sanitary, safe conditions, you may perhaps take a chance. Vegetables may be washed in a solution of potassium permanganate, but this does not afford 100 per cent protection either.

3. Do not eat fruit that cannot be peeled. True, it may be difficult to resist the temptation to eat strawberries or cherries in January in certain tropical regions south of the equator, but it is not worth taking the risk of exposing yourself to the great danger of possible infection with some tropical disease. Wait until you return home and pick them in your own garden.

4. Drinking water constitutes a high risk. Make sure it has been boiled before drinking it. This point applies to drinking water anywhere in the tropics, including in restaurants; it is unsafe, and so is ice, which is probably made from the same water. You must either take the trouble to boil it or try to quench your thirst by eating juicy fruit which you can peel, being careful not to transfer

any bacteria from the skin of the fruit to its fleshy part. In the jungle you can drink palm water, which is contained in the marrow of the palm tree. Even for those who normally do not drink alcohol, it would be better to quench the thirst with beer, if available, rather than run the risk of drinking contaminated water, for a little alcohol is less harmful than a dangerous tropical disease. Remember, unboiled water can be dangerous – do not take any chances.

5. Walking barefoot, although a pleasant and healthy habit in temperate zones, is hazardous in the tropics. Various parasitic larvae may stick to the skin, penetrate the sole of the foot or the skin between the toes and travel via the lymphatics and the bloodstream to various parts of the body where they can wreak havoc. If you are a nature-lover, who cannot resist the impulse to walk barefoot in these warm areas, make sure you do so only on beaches where the sand has been cleansed by the ocean tides. Even the sand dunes farther back from the beach and which are not in direct contact with sea water are a danger and must be avoided. In tropical and subtropical regions the sand farther back is often contaminated with human excrement, releasing hundreds of thousands of worms and other parasites that can be easily transferred to the foot – and their new host – while walking on the dunes.

6. In hot, humid, tropical or subtropical regions, it is advisable to take with you, and sleep under, a mosquito net at all times. A net is an excellent protection and prevention from insect bites that could result in malaria, elephantiasis, sleeping sickness, and many other tropical diseases.

Many an enthusiastic traveller may find the joys and expectations he is looking forward to dampened by so many precautionary measures and warnings. However, it is better to be sensible and take precautions, because being forewarned one can guard against any perilous circumstances to which one might otherwise fall victim. Among my closest friends I can count many who have had to pay dearly for their inexperience and ignorance of the hidden dangers awaiting the innocent traveller in the tropics, especially in recent years. Others, who have been obliged to live in the tropics for extended periods, have returned home with serious diseases or have died prematurely.

The precautionary measures mentioned in this section are not meant to spoil your expectations and joys of travelling; rather, they should serve as warnings and guidelines to help you to be adequately prepared before undertaking a trip. Preparation does not mean cumbersome equipment added to the weight of your already heavy baggage. In fact, it is only a question of some valuable advice upon which you can draw when the need arises. The old adage 'An ounce of prevention is worth a pound of cure' is of special importance to the traveller in the tropics. For further hints and suggestions on this topic see my book *Health Guide Through Southern Countries, Subtropics, Tropics, and Desert Zones.*

The Liver and Gallbladder

Causes and Symptoms of Liver Disorders

More and more people are beginning to realise that the liver is one of our most important organs and needs to be kept functioning properly. Since the liver does not send out an alarm until a disorder has made considerable progress, it is to our advantage to be especially aware of certain symptoms which can serve as early warnings. If we know and understand the various causes of liver trouble, we will be in a good position to take precautionary measures and protect this vital organ.

Almost 50 per cent of the people in Switzerland, my native country, are ill because they are overfed. The variety of things available to satisfy their palate is too great. So overindulgence is largely responsible for their disorders, whereas the opposite is true in the Far East where malnutrition is the cause of liver problems. It is astonishing to find that even in countries where rice is grown and is the staple food, only white rice is sold at the market. The only exceptions are in rural areas where the peasants prepare their own natural, or brown, rice. Generally, however, the people like only white rice and prefer to buy and cook it. The majority of the population is totally ignorant of the nutritional value of brown rice and of the many benefits it offers in its natural state as compared to denatured white rice. True, in Switzerland and elsewhere ignorance prevails as well, but at least rice is not our principal food.

If certain eating habits in Japan, Korea and China were not adhered to, the resulting deficiency of minerals would be disastrous. One habit in those countries that contributes to their good health is that they eat kelp (seaweed) as part of their daily diet. The minerals contained in ocean kelp are able to counterbalance to a great extent the deficiency caused by eating white rice. Calcium and fluoride, however, are not contained in kelp. A deficiency of these two minerals affects the teeth and this accounts for the widespread tooth decay among those people. It is only in rural or primitive areas where the people retain their teeth because of a natural wholefood diet. For instance, I have seen really beautiful teeth among the Fiji islanders.

WORMS AND LIVER DAMAGE

Unadulterated, unrefined, natural food helps to keep the liver healthy and efficient. If natural wholefood has been replaced by denatured, refined food, the cause of liver disorders may be attributed partly to this unhappy change. However, if refined food is not the reason, then a damaged liver can be the result of an infection, possibly caused by the widespread problem of parasitic worms.

In Japan, Korea, and other lands where the bad practice exists of fertilising vegetables with human excrement from a cesspit, the majority of the population are infested with worms. One of these parasites, the dangerous hookworm, can even kill its victim. Another species settles in the liver and also ruins one's life, albeit slowly.

In other areas amoebas are a constant danger, and this goes not only for the Far East but also the Near East. Amoebas can be transmitted when eating salads or other raw vegetables and fruit. They can also be passed on by people who are themselves infested with these insidious parasites. Uncleanness is only one way in which their transmission to healthy persons is possible. It is important to establish if these dangerous parasites have invaded our organism as quickly as possible, and do something about them before they are able to get to the liver via the intestines and the bile duct. Because once they have reached the liver they can destroy their host, slowly but surely. So, when travelling in the Far and Near East, never eat uncooked food or drink the water. Even fruit that can be peeled should first be thoroughly cleaned so that the parasites which stick to the fruit skins do not attach themselves to your hands while peeling it. If you fail to do this the amoebas can be transferred from the hands to the peeled parts and enter your system. You can therefore appreciate the great risk you are exposed to and it would be wise to always carry some disinfectant for cleaning the skin of fruit. I am sure you will agree that this precautionary measure is better than contracting some disease through carelessness, or even dying from the consequences. Friends I have visited in these areas often complained about a typical pain on the right side in the liver region. You cannot be too careful, for even a common attack of dysentery can permanently damage your health.

UNMISTAKABLE SYMPTOMS

It is an unmistakable symptom that the liver is somehow out of order when the patient can no longer stand the sight or smell of fatty or fried food. For instance, if you cannot tolerate fried potatoes any longer although they used to be a favourite dish, you can be sure that you are suffering from a liver disorder, which will need careful attention. Another symptom of a liver problem is an extreme sensitivity to fruit, for example, oranges or orange juice suddenly upset you, or stone fruits no longer agree with you. In this case your liver has lost its ability to digest the fruit acid. A further liver symptom may be seen in an irksome itching that can turn out to be so unbearable that you would like to scratch until you bleed. An insatiable sensation of thirst can also be considered as a symptom of liver disorder, unless, of course, it is a sign of pancreatic insufficiency or even diabetes.

On the other hand, emotional breakdown is a typical symptom of liver trouble. We feel depressed, everything seems dismal, without our really knowing why we feel that way. Nothing cheers us up anymore and we are usually morose and in a bad mood. Instead of seeking the cause of the problem within ourselves we are more of the opinion that the whole world is against us. So, when others in the family confirm that we are often quite unbearable, we can be sure that our liver is out of order.

CHANGED ENVIRONMENT

What has contributed to our having become much more sensitive than our forefathers were? Well, was not their life very different before the advent of fast-developing technology? And is it not true that two world wars have made our life more restless and less secure? Air pollution caused by various exhaust fumes is no basis for good health; neither is the threat of increasing radioactivity in the air, a relatively recent peril.

In spite of greater affluence in some parts of the world, we are burdened with greater anxieties than in the past. Although modern technology has made some heavy jobs easier and even takes care of them altogether, we seem to have less time than ever before. The paraffin lamp disappeared long ago; in those days its dim light did not allow anyone to work late into the night. Years ago people enjoyed the few hours after coming home from work, whereas today artificial light makes the day longer. Years ago people went to bed early and got up in the early morning to start a good day's work with renewed strength. Today, however, work or pleasure continues late into the night, resulting in overtiredness. Our quota of sleep is cut short and is far from invigorating, and the next morning we wake up feeling in a bad mood, remaining so all day long. Is there any wonder that our liver will be affected by such a life-style? Constant hassle and worry, anxieties and fear, the mad rush of our daily lives are all bad for it. The old, traditional customs and habits needed to remain healthy have all gone.

Indeed, we do not even make the time to sit down and eat our meals in peace anymore. But if you are not willing to take your time when eating, you will one day have to take it being ill. For it is inevitable that we will harm our health if we do not learn to relax in spite of the daily hustle and bustle around us. Instead of listening to an exciting news item on the radio or, worse, reading the newspaper while eating, we should relax and make every meal a special occasion with the family. Instead of gulping down our food in a hurry, we should enjoy it calmly, eat it slowly, insalivating well and chewing everything thoroughly. In fact, every fast eater should be condemned to eating with chopsticks, as it is the custom in the Far East. You see, this technique takes more than just practice and skill, it takes patience, because if you are fidgety and restless you will hardly be able to keep any morsel between the sticks and pass it to your mouth. I am convinced that eating with chopsticks is a wonderful method for learning how to eat in a relaxed and quiet way!

Worries, anxieties and fear engender nothing but agitation – and upset the proper secretion of digestive juices. A simple illustration will prove this point. An angry, aggressive dog will not digest its food properly. It will lie around listlessly, discontented and sullen, unwilling to eat its food when it is time to do so, actually refusing to touch anything. The dog's organism is influenced by the mood forced upon it. Newfoundlands are known to lose their appetite when they feel sad or upset. But the animal takes a much more natural approach to the problem than we do. Instead of looking for some favourite food, the dog simply fasts; it does not eat at all until the disturbance has passed and it is well again. Years ago, fasting was customary for many people, but today most of us think we would die if we did not get our meals at the usual times. Only in times of privation do such people prove that their health is actually better than they had believed it to be. If it were not so, the enormous streams of refugees from war and famine would have few survivors. No, believe me, sensible fasting will not kill but benefit us, and will benefit the liver in particular.

Even if we are knowledgeable in matters of nutrition and diet, and a day's fast presents no problem, the liver may still give problems when we are constantly under pressure because of worries, anxieties and frustration. Do not be surprised if you begin to suffer from a liver disorder when constant stress and anxieties assail you. A sensible attitude toward questions of nutrition is only helpful if our mental and emotional attitude is also right. Of course, it is not always easy in today's world to keep one's balance. There is really no better help in our daily struggle with worries of one kind and another than a calm and collected spirit. If we remain calm we will be able to shut out of our minds all distractions, retain our mental tranquillity and thus provide the best protective remedy for the liver.

Liver Disorders and Nutrition

What conclusion about the liver can we draw from what has been said above? No doubt we are more aware of the need to protect it and if some disorder should arise, we can treat it properly if we are well informed about the right kind of food to eat. For if we ignore the question of diet, we should not be surprised if deficiencies and weaknesses will not respond to treatment. Furthermore, we must be willing to continue observing the basic requirements of a sensible liver diet even after having achieved a significant improvement in our condition. It must be remembered that the liver, despite having recovered from the disorder, is usually still quite sensitive and not immediately as strong as it was previously. That is why it is advisable to be sensible. After all, it should not be all that difficult to keep up a good habit rather than give it up and have a relapse.

THE PROBLEM OF FAT

It is generally known that the liver is highly sensitive to fats when it is suffering from some disorder or disturbance. However, one cannot cut out fat altogether since the liver needs some unsaturated fatty acids in order to function properly. It is therefore important not to use any fat in which the unsaturated fatty acids have been destroyed. Heated fat should also be avoided. In fact, the basic rule for liver patients is eliminate all fried foods from your diet.

If you understand and observe this rule, you will have come to grips with a liver diet. You will then abstain from potatoes and onions fried in butter, oil or any other fat; this includes sauté potatoes and French fries or chips. If you want to help your liver recover, you will not indulge in such food however delicious it may be. Meat fried in fat will also be off your menu. As a matter of fact, any kind of dish requiring frying or baking in fat is out. Butter must no longer be used in cooking. Natural oils such as sunflower, sesame, linseed or any other cold-pressed oils may be used in limited quantities in the preparation of salads, because, strangely enough, a moderate amount of these natural, unrefined and unadulterated oils is actually good for the liver. The problem of fat is therefore one that needs careful consideration and the right solution.

This does not mean that a healthy person must be just as careful as a liver patient, but it certainly would do him no harm to heed the advice given regarding oils and fats. A little less fat would mean less strain on the system, although this fact may be disputed by those cooks who adhere to the old-fashioned opinion that we need plenty of fat to keep healthy and fit. This is untrue because the body benefits more from a modest intake of fat, since it is able to produce its own anyway. People who become obese even though they consume very little fat will confirm the truth of this statement. Just think of those who drink a lot of beer. The malt supplies the carbohydrates, which in turn produce unwanted fat deposits. We do not need much fat, although we think we might. In fact, we could reduce our fat consumption by half and still be well nourished. It would not cause a deficiency, nor would it lead to ill health. On the contrary, it would increase our chances of maintaining good health. It is an excessive intake of fat that is responsible for ill health.

THE PROTEIN PROBLEM

Once we have learned what kind and how much fat we need, we should take a closer look at the question of protein, because the liver needs a supply of good protein for maximum efficiency. Pulses, that is, peas, beans and lentils, as well as milk, are excellent sources of protein. Milk protein is the best type for the liver. Not only the sick person benefits from protein taken in the form of sour milk, yogurt, or cottage cheese and curds, but anyone who is healthy too.

If a patient suffering from a liver disorder wishes to eat some meat protein, the meat should be grilled, never fried. Avoid fatty cuts or meat that was cooked in its own fat. Very lean, muscular meat, preferably veal or beef, is the best for the patient who thinks he cannot do without it. Since pork is the most harmful of all meats, it should be eliminated from the diet. Among the divine laws given to the Israelites was one forbidding them to eat pork and, as it so happened, this abstinence proved to be in the interest of their health.

Fish protein is a food that should not be overlooked. It is important, however, that only fresh fish is used and that it is prepared with the utmost care. If fish is slightly tainted the danger of poisoning is very high, and if fish is not carefully cleaned there is the additional danger of poisoning because it may have swallowed some toxic dead matter that still remains in its entrails. Fish poisoning is especially damaging to the liver. Be particularly careful in southern regions where food goes off relatively quickly. Since fish tend to consume anything they see in front of them, they represent an immediate danger if eaten by the unsuspecting. I once watched a sick man spit into a lake somewhere in Switzerland. At once a trout surfaced and swallowed the unusual bait. Yet it could well have been the sputum of a consumptive. And it is not impossible to imagine that the fish might have been caught and served up on one's table the next day! Well, that's enough of that. The final point to remember is that should a liver patient want to enjoy some fish for a change, heed the advice given and either grill or poach it.

Eggs are also a source of protein and many people like to include them in their diet. But hard-boiled eggs, omelettes and egg salads are hard on the liver and should be avoided by anyone with a liver problem; indeed, it would be better for them to have meat rather than eggs. It is important to make sure that the eggs we consume are fresh and come from healthy chickens raised on natural feed. An egg is better for you when eaten raw, since in its liquid state an egg can be considered a valuable source of nutrients. This can also be said of soft-boiled eggs (for 2–3 minutes). Eggs are harmful, however, for anyone suffering from rheumatism or arthritis. Acting on this knowledge can only be of benefit to you.

I would like to stress the importance of making sure the eggs are safe, if you like to eat them raw, because the diseases chickens suffer from can be transmitted through their eggs. This is a problem that has received considerable publicity in recent years, particularly in the United Kingdom, and people should not forget the fact that it poses a very real danger to their health.

It is a good thing that there are other, even better sources of protein than eggs. Soybeans, for example, are an excellent supplier of vegetable protein. In certain areas of China soybean protein is the single most important protein available to the population. The lack of animal protein from milk and meat is critical in many tropical regions. Years ago the need for protein presented a particular problem for the growing population of China. Since meat was not produced in sufficient quantity to supply over 500 million people, China's population at that time, it became necessary to find a vegetable substitute. The soybean was selected because it is an excellent source of protein, able to take the place of animals as the prime supplier. In many parts of the world today the Chinese custom of germinating the soybean has been adopted and the resulting product, 'bean sprouts', has become a popular and palatable vegetable dish rich in protein.

Remember, then, that liver patients need protein too; vegetables and cereals alone are not enough. As mentioned before, milk protein, especially in the form of cottage cheese or curds, is the best protein source available in this case.

HEALTHY SEASONING

The proper seasoning of food prepared for those who suffer from a liver disorder is very important, since the liver is influenced by it for good or for bad. I must warn against certain Indian dishes because the spices are so hot that they affect the mucous membranes of the stomach. They begin to play up and may actually stop working for a few days. The palate does not necessarily like the spices either and may still feel on fire half an hour after eating the strange food. Does it not go to show that even herbal spices need to be used in the right amount? It is not good to use excessive quantities, which will only affect the liver adversely. Many Indian people have yellow mixed in with the white of the eyes, no doubt a symptom of an affected liver. Indeed, their blood sometimes contains a yellowish-red bile substance. The two main causes of this can be found in their spicy food and widespread infestation with worms. This shows that one should use spices sparingly.

Of course, if we did not season our food at all we would soon lose our appetite. It is true that bland food does not appeal to our tastebuds; instead, it can make us go off food altogether. The herbs we can sow or plant in the garden are sometimes also sold at the market. They are the basis for mild yet tasty seasoning. However, be careful with pepper, nutmeg and similar spices; better still, avoid them completely, since they are able to cause a lot of upsets. Peppers are an exception, if they are eaten only occasionally in small quantities and do not upset your digestion.

A suggested diet for the liver patient is given below. Further details about diets and care of the liver are given in the well-known book *The Liver, the Regulator of Your Health*. This book contains some excellent menus for meals, recipes and, of course, dietary instructions.

DIET FOR LIVER PATIENTS
As a good diet for the liver we suggest the following:

Morning: one glass of carrot juice; a slice of toast or crispbread with a little butter or yeast extract; a soupspoon of wheat germ, either dry or in the carrot juice.

Midday: vegetable soup; brown rice or potatoes boiled in their skins; chicory and raw carrot salad, or any other raw salad vegetable, preferably the bitter kind. Steamed vegetables may also be added. All fried and sweet dishes and desserts must be avoided.

You can vary the lunch menu as follows:
First day: brown rice; fennel root; mixed salad.
Second day: potatoes boiled in their skins, with a little cottage cheese and fresh butter; mixed salad.
Third day: vegetable soup; sandwiches made with rye or whole-wheat bread or crispbread, spread with a little butter and yeast extract, topped with onion, garlic, sliced tomatoes; mixed salad.

A little while after the meal you can have a cup of cereal coffee (*Bambu Coffee Substitute*) with milk but no sugar.

Evening: soup made with oats, barley or brown rice with a few vegetables added; mixed salad, seasoned with lemon juice or sour milk, but never with vinegar. For the sake of variety, sandwiches and different salads may be served, followed by cereal coffee with a little milk.

Always remember that fruit is taboo while the liver is out of order.

SESAME SEEDS – EXCELLENT FOR THE LIVER
Modern life with its restlessness and worries, as well as all other detrimental influences, puts a great strain on the liver, this important organ in our body. To allay our concern, it is always good to be reminded of some simple remedies, one of which is *sesame seed*. There is nothing easier than eating sesame seeds every day for the sake of your health. You will never tire of this delicacy if you

sprinkle it on your bread. I recommend this practice to all who suffer from liver problems and depend on high-quality oil and vegetable protein, but also to anyone else who wishes to protect and care for his liver and keep it sound.

In addition to eating the seeds you can also use *sesame oil*, a good source of highly unsaturated fatty acids, as well as vitamin E, which is good for the glands. It definitely benefits our health if we eat sesame seeds regularly. They contain a protein with eight essential amino acids and vitamins of the B complex which are important for cell oxygenation and thus have a favourable influence on the liver cells.

The neutral flavour of sesame seeds makes them useful for fruit salads, if sprinkled over the salad or mixed in with it, or they can be used in a similar way for vegetable salads and vegetables in general. These varied uses increase our opportunities to benefit from their goodness.

Cracked sesame seeds can also be added to wholefood muesli. And if you suffer from some kind of internal inflammation, you can still benefit from the seeds by taking them finely ground and made into an emulsion. This preparation will cause you no trouble whatsoever, however sensitive your system may be.

The sesame plant grows in subtropical soil and contains the region's abundant energy from the sun. In temperate zones you can usually buy the seeds from healthfood stores. Once you have come to appreciate their excellent effect on the bowel movement, you will never want to do without them. Unfortunately, the benefits of sesame seeds are still not as widely known as they should be. So do not only use them yourself, but recommend them to your friends, especially to those who suffer from some type of liver disorder.

Everyone in the Near East, particularly in Palestine, knows the sesame plant, uses and cherishes it. There, the seeds are sold under the quaint name 'sumsum'. Seeds have always played an important part in the nutrition of primitive or aboriginal peoples. The gathering of all kinds of seeds has always been vital in areas of the world where there is limited variety regarding food. Sometimes it is the little things that provide supplementary benefits, and this can certainly be said about sesame seeds. Let us therefore not ignore the seeds because they are so small, but enjoy them to the full.

Treating Infectious Diseases of the Liver and Gallbladder

There are a number of liver and gallbladder disorders that can come about through infection. The patient feels sick and brings up bile; he has diarrhoea and sickness and in some cases develops a slight attack of jaundice. Such symptoms call for great care.

The first thing the patient should be given to drink is *clay water*; either white or yellow clay will do, a teaspoon of clay to a small wine glass of warm water (100 ml glass, about 3½ fl. oz). Add several drops of *Lachesis 10x* or *12x* to the clay water. The effect is greater still if 10–20 drops of *Echinaforce* are also added. The patient needs to go without any food for two or three days, drinking nothing but clay water. After this time he will perhaps feel a little hungry and can then try a peeled and finely grated apple, or he can eat it whole but chew it well. To quench his thirst he can take sour whey – one teaspoon of *Molkosan* to 100ml (about 3½ fl. oz) of water – or he can drink fruit juice, such as grapefruit, raspberry, blackberry or non-alcoholic grape juice. Sip and insalivate well before swallowing. If the patient is still very sensitive he may not be able to drink anything but freshly pressed carrot juice. But let me repeat, the juice must be sipped slowly.

Solid food should be avoided at this stage, because the disturbance will be cleared up much faster if the patient fasts. Rehabilitation will only be delayed by burdening the digestive system with food. In cases where the patient vomits bile, be sure to give him liquids afterwards. *Horsetail (shave grass)* or better still, *dandelion tea* will be excellent. You can use dandelion leaves and roots to make the infusion. An extract of dandelion called *Taraxacum* will be found most effective in such cases. Avoid cereal gruels, because they always contain some fat and in the digestive process the liver will be irritated. Taking solid food can serve no useful purpose and, again, the value of fasting during the first few days cannot be overemphasised.

Once the grated apple and any of the various fruit juices can be digested and the patient feels hungry again, try giving him wholefood muesli for breakfast and supper. At midday, a little salad may be eaten, taking care that the dressing contains only a little cold-pressed, unrefined vegetable oil, or no oil to start with, just lemon juice or Molkosan. For several days after recovery fried foods of any kind should be avoided, because a certain degree of sensitivity will remain. Even slightly heated oil or animal fat will soon cause the feeling of congestion in the back of the head or in the forehead to return. A peculiar feeling of nausea may manifest itself also,

Holly

even though it may be slight. Until all germs, which may or may not be known, have been eliminated from the system, the normal diet should not be reintroduced.

No liver complaint should be treated lightly, but if the patient follows the advice given, he will soon be on the mend. *Solidago*, as usual, should be taken to stimulate the kidneys. *Horsetail* and *witch grass root tea* are alternatives. If the patient runs a temperature, and it is not unusual for it to reach 39 °C (102 °F), then *Ferrum phos. 12x, diluted holly infusion, Aconitum 4x* or any other good fever remedy is called for. A daily dose of one or two tablets of *Podophyllum 3x*, and according to the circumstances, three or four drops of *Chelidonium 4x* or the combination remedy *Boldocynara* should be taken. Condensed carrot juice, *Biocarottin*, is also beneficial.

My book *The Liver, the Regulator of Your Health* answers all questions relating to the liver and gallbladder in full detail.

Oil Cure for Gallstones
Serious thought should be given to trying the oil cure for the elimination of gallstones if the patient is willing and thinks he can take 300–500 ml (½–¾ pint) of oil in one go. Some might assume

that this treatment works by the oil entering the gallbladder and cleansing it, but this is not so. The oil merely stimulates the profuse secretion of bile. It could be said that it causes a flood of bile which carries the small and medium-sized stones with it.

The oil used for this treatment should be unrefined. Whether it is the highly unsaturated fatty acids that make it more effective than refined oil has not yet been determined, although it seems quite possible. Unrefined olive, walnut, sunflower and poppy seed oils are all suitable.

Before carrying out the cure, it would be useful to take a natural plant remedy that helps to liquify the bile, for example *Boldocynara* made from artichokes and other medicinal herbs.

For the best results, it will also be necessary to give the bowels a good clean-out beforehand. Soaked *prunes or figs*, freshly ground *linseed* or *Linoforce*, and *psyllium seed* will serve this purpose very well. But if they do not move the bowels sufficiently, give an *enema* with a warm *camomile infusion* in addition. To help even further, *hot packs* should be applied to the liver area for a few hours before and after drinking the oil. As soon as the bowels have been emptied you can take the oil. That accomplished, lie down, turn over on your right side, relax, and remain in this position for two hours. If you find it difficult to drink the oil by itself, try to take it in alternation with a cereal coffee (*Bambu Coffee Substitute*). Should even this prove to be obnoxious, you will then have to ingest the required quantity of oil spaced out, a little at a time taken over several days. This method will not be quite so effective, but at least the smaller stones may be eliminated and the remaining bigger ones may not cause any trouble for a while. However, anyone who is capable of drinking the whole quantity of oil at one time should not be surprised if all the stones are eliminated from the gallbladder. Of course, this is more likely to occur in cases which have not become chronic and where no large stones are present.

If a chronic condition suddenly flares up again, accompanied by a high temperature and an increase in the number of white blood corpuscles, there is most likely an inflammation. In that case, the patient unfortunately has no alternative but to undergo surgery to remove the gallbladder. This is not the ultimate solution, however, because after the operation condensed bile will no longer be available; it cannot accumulate as it previously had done in the gallbladder that now no longer exists. The bile entering the duodenum will always be thin and fresh and if digestive disturbances are to be avoided, a protein- and fat-restricted diet will have to be adopted thereafter. Thus, if the oil treatment can bring the desired cure, the patient will escape the need for surgery and the undesirable consequences it brings with it.

Jaundice

Jaundice is much more dangerous than is generally assumed. People who have suffered from it confirm that once they have had it, they never feel the same again. They also notice that fried foods and sweet things no longer agree with them.

A case of jaundice must not be taken lightly. There are two types of jaundice: one is caused by an obstruction or blockage of the bile duct and the other is a result of infection. Both are serious. As part of the treatment the patient must abstain from fats and fried foods for quite some time. The bowels must be thoroughly cleansed and the bile must be liquified by taking the following remedies: *Chelidonium 4x* and *Podophyllum 4x*, or *Boldocynara*, as well as *Biocarottin*, condensed carrot juice. Moreover, take plenty of fresh *carrot juice* daily, at least 100 ml (3½ fl. oz), but preferably more. *Warm water treatments* will help considerably and should always be given, either by placing a hot herbal compress over the liver or directing a shower of warm water onto the liver area. Afterwards, apply *cabbage leaf poultices*, alternating daily with *clay poultices*. At the same time the kidneys should be stimulated by drinking *kidney tea* and taking *Solidago* or *Nephrosolid*. Besides goldenrod, other suitable herbs to stimulate the kidneys are *horsetail, couch grass root, birch leaves* and the mildly acting *rose hips*. Even when the doctor pronounces the patient well, the treatment should on no account be stopped. The special diet must be continued for some time, likewise the use of poultices and warm water treatments.

When treating a case of jaundice it is always important to take care of the bowels. If regular movement is lacking, *herbal enemas* should be given to open the bowels. The bile must be removed from the blood as quickly as possible, for the longer it remains in the system and the more concentrated it is, the greater the harm that will result.

Beware of modern proprietary medicines for the treatment of jaundice. They invariably only serve to mask and suppress the symptoms and serious complications can follow their use. It is much wiser to let the illness take its normal course and assist the body with natural remedies. Even so, the healing process takes time and cannot be unduly hurried. Most cases under the supervision of an allopathic doctor will take 6–8 weeks of treatment. But if you employ the recommended natural therapy with its various measures, a cure can be achieved in two weeks in some cases. However, it must not be considered complete until the follow-up treatment has been carried out conscientiously as well. If these measures are neglected, the patient may be left with some permanent damage.

Anyone who has had jaundice should, especially in the spring, eat plenty of *dandelion salad. Artichokes, chicory*, and all bitter herbs and salad vegetables are also excellent for the liver. The various kinds of *radish* are considered medicinal and should for this reason be taken in moderate amounts, but too many can do more harm than good. And never forget to drink carrot juice, as I have already mentioned on different occasions.

If this advice is followed and the follow-up cure is faithfully adhered to, the jaundice patient will fully recuperate and suffer no unpleasant consequences.

The Pancreas

Next to the liver, the most important organ in our digestive system is the pancreas, yet it weighs only about one-twentieth of that of the liver. This small, elongated gland is located above the navel between the posterior stomach wall and the spine; below it lies the horseshoe-shaped loop of the first part of the small intestine. The left end touches the spleen and the left kidney. Small it may be, but it performs two important functions, producing an external secretion to be poured into the duodenum and an internal one to be poured into the blood.

The pancreas secretes only about one-fifth of the amount of juice produced by the much smaller salivary glands, yet its secretion is much more concentrated and important. As many as four enzymes are secreted into the small intestine immediately adjacent to the bile duct. One of these enzymes, rennin, is also produced in the stomach. It turns milk into curds, a job that is mainly done by the stomach. When the stomach fails to function effectively the pancreas has a marvellous capacity to take on part of the stomach's work load, since it can produce rennin just as efficiently as the stomach. Diastase, or amylase, changes starches into sugars, such as glycogen, dextrin and maltose. Trypsin, like pepsin, breaks down proteins into peptones and finally into the basic building blocks of protein, amino acids. The fourth enzyme, lipase, together with the bile, hydrolises fats into fatty acids and glycerol. In fact, the body cannot break down, digest and assimilate proteins, starches and fats without the enzymes secreted by the pancreas.

Neither the bile nor the pancreatic enzymes are fully efficient if the juice in the small intestine and the bacterial flora are not normal. So you can see that the digestive process involves a complicated series of relationships between many individual factors. If everyone understood this fact and fully appreciated the implications, they would no doubt make a greater effort to live more carefully and watch what they eat and drink. Excesses endanger the wonderful interplay of the digestive organs and the glandular functions.

What makes us marvel most in our quest to understand these fascinating relationships is the fact that these organs are fully automatic in their functions. We eat something and immediately the message is sent via the nerves to the cerebellum; at once another message is sent back to the intestine, the liver and the pancreas. The necessary enzymes are immediately made ready for the arrival of the food. Of course, the entire process goes on without our having to think or do anything about it. What a marvellous thing! No wonder the Bible psalmist once gratefully acknowledged that 'in an awe-inspiring way we are wonderfully made'. Anyone who fully understands this will, and can, never accept the theory of evolution. The wisdom and intelligence of a Creator's design, even in the smallest detail, is much too obvious. No sound reasoning could ever deny Creation. So let us continue our research into the wonderful secrets of the human body, for the more we understand them the stronger the proof of the Creator's power.

Embedded in the pancreas we find some peculiar cell formations, shaped rather like blackberries. They are actually small glands, but not in the least connected with the other glands. Like islands in the bigger gland, they are called the islets of Langerhans, after their discoverer, Paul Langerhans. The vital substance insulin is produced in these small glands and sent straight into the blood, not the small intestine. If these islets do not manufacture sufficient insulin, the glycogen, the sugar stored in the liver and passed on to the blood in accordance with the body's need, will not be burned up, so that the blood sugar level rises. The excess is excreted through the kidneys, which is why sugar is found in the urine. This is a symptom of the disease known as diabetes.

Proper Care of the Pancreas

Diabetics and anyone who has bad digestion need to know what to do to help the pancreas function efficiently. Since the blood carries nutrients and remedial substances to the parts of the body it can reach, the primary requirement is to stimulate the circulation. Take *hot showers* or apply *moist hot packs* for this purpose; herbal packs are especially good. As regards medicines, only few are known to act specifically on the pancreas. One such, sour whey as contained in *Molkosan*, is rich in rennin and lactic acid and gives good results. Years ago, *fermented bedstraw (Galium aparine* or cleavers) used to be prescribed with modest success. Of course, *papaya* preparations can be used to good effect, since their papain content helps to digest protein. *Lycopodium 6x* (club moss) is useful too.

You can also set aside days for *fasting* and *raw vegetable diets*, their effect being very encouraging. My book *The Liver, the Regulator of Your Health* contains instructions for diets that are good for the pancreas as well as the liver. A number of food items must be avoided completely, for example all boiled protein foods and the combination of fat, protein and sugar, either cooked or fried. Hot spices should also be avoided; use culinary herbs from the garden instead. The protein foods best tolerated are sour milk products. Prepare salads with a little cold-pressed oil and Molkosan. Of curative effect are bilberry (blueberry) juice, blackcurrant juice, weak herb teas, and occasionally a little buttermilk.

As already stated, fasting is an excellent means of resting the pancreas. Moreover, whatever the patient eats, it is important to ingest small quantities, chew everything thoroughly and insalivate well before swallowing. These are inexpensive ways and means of supporting the pancreas in the healing process. If you feel a slight pain after eating, you have probably had something that did not agree with you, did not chew your food well enough, drank too fast or ate too much. The answer to the problem is in the patient himself; he should watch himself carefully to avoid unpleasant reactions.

Regular deep-breathing exercises, with diaphragm-breathing, practised in the open air are also effective and promote the healing process at the same time. In conclusion, then, breathing exercises, together with a proper diet, warm water therapy and moist hot herbal packs, will help to rectify any condition where the pancreas is weak or upset. Many a serious, chronic ailment can be prevented if its proper function is restored. All it needs is a little understanding and perseverance with the treatment.

A Diet for Diabetics

Diabetics need to pay special attention to their diet. In contrast with most other diseases, diabetes makes the patient want to eat more. To solve the question of diet, we must therefore see to it that he eats an adequate amount of food but with the proviso that it does not consist of too many carbohydrates. This can be achieved by giving the diabetic primarily vegetables, which are rich in vitamins but low in carbohydrates.

Lacto-vegetarians obtain their protein requirements from milk products, especially sour milk, buttermilk and soft white cheese (cottage cheese or quark). If the patient is used to eating meat, he must restrict himself to only small quantities of lean, muscular cuts of meat. The following menu for one day can be taken as a model.

BREAKFAST

Take your pick from buttermilk, sour milk or cereal coffee (*Bambu Coffee Substitute*). For a change, you can sometimes have yogurt.

Make sandwiches using rye bread, flake bread, wholemeal bread or crispbread. There is also a special diet crispbread available for diabetics. Spread the bread with soft white cheese, maybe 'Gervais' fermented skimmed milk cheese or cottage cheese.

Garnish the sandwich with tomato slices or culinary herbs, such as parsley, chives or freshly grated horseradish.

If you prefer fruit for breakfast, follow my second menu:

Bambu coffee with cream, fruit muesli with rye flakes, whole rice flakes or All Bran, a well-known commercial cereal product. Use only fresh fruit in season. Bilberries (blueberries), blackcurrants and apples are particularly beneficial. Add some sesame seeds or grated almonds, but no sugar. When the berry season is over, use natural fruit juices with no additives.

MIDDAY MEAL (LUNCH)

Soya mix rissoles, creamy cottage cheese or curds with horseradish and a seasonal vegetable, either steamed or au gratin.

In addition, a large plate of salad made up of various raw vegetables is most important. Make your choice according to what is seasonally available. White cabbage, raw sauerkraut with no additives, lettuce and, above all, plenty of cress, as well as nasturtiums are all excellent. Prepare the dressing from *Molkosan* and cream; whey is very good for activating the pancreas.

For this reason diluted Molkosan is also recommended as a drink. For a change, have a cup of *Bambu Coffee Substitute* with a little cream after your meal. What you should avoid, however, are beverages containing chemical additives.

If you like meat, another typical menu is as follows:

Grilled veal or beef; steamed vegetables; and a mixed salad, as explained in my first example. Choose either diluted Molkosan or sour buttermilk to drink.

EVENING MEAL (SUPPER)
You would do well to eat only a light meal at night. For this reason, follow the suggestions given for breakfast. For a change, you might try the following:

Vegetable or sesame soup; a vegetable baked in the oven or steamed tomatoes; and a small plate of mixed salad or raw natural sauerkraut.

INTRODUCING VARIETY
You must provide for a little variety, however, so that the diet does not become monotonous and one tires of it. This can be achieved by varying the combination of the items mentioned or varying their preparation. If loving hands prepare the food, it is always possible to find new ways of presenting it. For instance, diet pasta for diabetics can be used instead of soya mixes, bran mixes or sesame dishes.

Horseradish and cress have a healing effect on the pancreas and should be used as often as possible. From time to time, mix in a little finely chopped mugwort, another herb which has a beneficial effect on the pancreas. Diabetics can also use onions to season their food. Another good seasoning is yeast extract. Spread *Herbaforce* extremely thinly on bread and cover with onion slices. This is excellent for the pancreas because it includes both yeast and onion. A word of advice for diabetics is to make a conscious effort to eat slowly, to chew everything well and insalivate properly. This will help to utilise the food more effectively and to satisfy one's hunger more quickly. Even though the diabetic has a greater craving for food, it is not advisable to eat too much, since the excess will only place a greater demand on the digestive system. For this reason it is extremely important that the patient eats only natural whole-foods that are rich in nutrients.

Multiple Sclerosis

Just hearing the name of this disease can inspire fear. It is a strange disease, progressive and insidious, and it can have tragic consequences for the rest of one's life. Multiple sclerosis, often abbreviated to MS, is not known among people in less developed parts of the world, where the diet is still 100 per cent natural and unadulterated. Hence it must be a disease of our modern civilised world, a typical disease caused by civilisation.

The Real Cause

It is understandable that we want to know the cause of an illness, and it is no different with multiple sclerosis. Unfortunately, however, the cause of this dreaded affliction has not yet been conclusively pinpointed despite continuous research. Although there is no certainty, the symptoms seem to suggest a pathogenic agent, but it has not yet been identified. It is also thought that the reason that some people are susceptible to this agent is probably a deficiency of some vital substances.

The Symptoms

The symptoms of multiple sclerosis are not always the same, so that the identity of the disease sometimes escapes diagnosis, especially in its early stages. One of the earliest symptoms is often the absence of the abdominal reflex. A fairly reliable diagnostic sign concerns the optic nerves. In this case, by using an ophthalmoscope the eye specialist will observe demyelination where the optic nerve enters at the back of the eye.

There is no doubt that multiple sclerosis is a progressive disease of the central nervous system. It rarely strikes before the age of twenty or after the age of forty. Women sometimes fall victim to it after giving birth and men after an accident or a neglected infectious disease. The first signs of illness may also be a disturbance in the sensory nerves, especially in the feet. The patient gets the feeling of walking on cotton wool and runs the risk of stumbling on uneven ground. After the attack on the sensory nerves there follows a disturbance of the nerves controlling movement, a paralysis of the limbs. A little while later, the patient begins to drag his legs, walking stiffly. In accordance with the focus of the disease, the feet and lower organs or the arms and hands, perhaps even the jaw muscles and facial muscles are involved. When the intestinal muscles or the bladder sphincter are affected or put out of action, the condition is indeed serious. As the disease progresses, the muscles of the mouth and the vocal cords can become involved, causing impairment of speech. Pain is not always present and when it is it is rarely unbearable. There may be inexplicable periods of remission, with the symptoms subsiding; or there may be a sudden worsening of the condition, a relapse. The disease may go on for decades and it is not surprising that a lot of patience and mental energy is needed, both on the part of an MS patient as well as his family and those who take care of him.

It is important to begin treatment as soon as the disease has been diagnosed, since the chances of success are then better than if it is neglected, although many orthodox medical doctors do not agree with this view, or do so only reluctantly. Years ago, a lady from eastern Switzerland came to me for treatment. Three or four doctors and a professor had diagnosed multiple sclerosis. The symptoms of paralysis were only slight to begin with. About three months later, when the lady went to see a specialist, he did not believe that she had suffered from multiple sclerosis, since she was found to be in good health. If she had had multiple sclerosis, the doctor contended, she could not be well again, because there was no cure for it and no one had so far been cured. The treatment she was given is the first of those outlined below.

Various Approaches to Treatment

TREATMENT NO. 1

This treatment is a nutritional therapy, similar to the one employed by Dr Evers. Even before Dr Evers became well known, I had based my approach on the view that the patient's diet should be kept the same as that enjoyed by the primitive people who were not affected by multiple sclerosis. That means eating plenty of raw foods and only boiling those vegetables which cannot be eaten raw. The basic diet plan includes brown rice with soft white cheese (cottage cheese or quark) and horseradish, and mixed salad. Eggs are allowed very occasionally and only when raw. Meat is left out of the diet entirely and in its place milk and soya protein are consumed. White flour products are also cut out completely. Bread is only permitted in limited quantity, and nothing but wholegrain, wholemeal and crispbread. Since canned foods cannot really be called natural or a wholefood they, too, must be avoided altogether. Fruit must be natural, organically grown fruit that is in season; it can either be eaten whole or added to muesli. Honey and fruit sugar as obtained from grapes, also chopped currants, raisins and grapes are the only sweeteners permitted.

TREATMENT NO. 2
This is a stimulation therapy according to the *Baunscheidt method* or *Chinese treatment*. First the upper half of the back is treated and about ten days later the lower part. After about twenty days the treatment is repeated; once again treat the upper half of the back first and then the lower part. The same treatment is given three times, so that a total of six applications are performed. The dietary treatment will not achieve the same results in a year that this stimulation therapy can bring about in a matter of a few months. However, it is advisable to let an experienced therapist give this treatment.

A CASE HISTORY SPEAKS FOR ITSELF
Some years ago, when I was still operating a clinic, one of my patients was serving in the armed forces. He had consulted a neurologist and was given little hope of improvement. This diagnosis shattered the man's interest in life. One of his colleagues noticed his state of mind and asked him to consult me. We accepted the patient and gave him both treatments outlined above. About three months later we discharged him and I can still see the young man's happy face when he, for the first time, was able to walk with feeling in his feet.

During the course of his illness the patient described how the feeling in the nerves was returning. He noticed that it returned in the same sequence in which he had lost it in the limbs. Shortly after going home he had to surrender his military equipment and the army doctors were most surprised to see him do this personally. They asked him about the treatment he had received and one of the younger doctors was rather disparaging when he heard of it, but another doctor present, an older man, spoke up in defence of the treatment on the basis of the obvious results. The young man was very happy when he told us about the incident later on.

TREATMENT NO. 3
There is now another method of treatment available which was unknown in those earlier days. I am glad to say that it also helps considerably towards achieving a successful result. It is a fresh

hormone treatment. As with the treatment of poliomyelitis, it is necessary to obtain the fresh testicles of a healthy young bull. Take off the skin and chop up the tender inside with a sharp knife or put it in the food processor. Then apply the mixture to the whole extension of the spine, from the nape of the neck to the coccyx, massaging it in vigorously. This massage treatment should be given once a week in two stages, in the evening and early the following morning. The portion to be used in the morning will need to be kept in a cool place during the night.

A TESTIMONIAL OF SUCCESS

On 31 March 1964 I received the first letter from a patient in Brussels who had been suffering from multiple sclerosis for sixteen years. A year later, on 30 April 1965, he wrote again, about the effect of the recommended treatment. His letter read as follows:

'I have been taking your reliable medicines for one year now and have very much improved. It is exactly a year since I started taking Petasites, Usneasan, Echinaforce, Aesculaforce, Urticalcin and Biocarottin regularly. Every week I receive a massage with fresh bullock testicles. My nurse always waits at the slaughterhouse when a bull is killed, so that she can get the testicles quite fresh. The massages are indeed excellent for me. But let me give you a few details of my progress. All symptoms caused by the illness – cold feet, problems with the bowel movement, insufficient urination, bad eyesight, half the head going numb – have completely disappeared. However, I am not yet able to walk. True, I can stand up now and my right foot is already 60 per cent active; only the left foot does not respond yet. But considering that I have been ill for seventeen years, I have made very good progress in just one year. May I add that I had not been able to hold a long conversation without getting tired out; but this is no longer a problem.

'Now I can watch television for hours without any difficulty, participate quite normally in conversations, and I read a lot.'

Letters like this one from our Belgian patient are indeed encouraging. They show that if we support nature it has the power to bring about a regeneration even in serious cases of illness. The patient in question had been ill for many years and I am sure that his progress and success would have been better still if the treatment could have been given right from the start. The remedies mentioned by the patient are good for raising the calcium level and curing circulatory disturbances, inflammation and spasms.

However, the remedies alone could not produce the fine results he experienced.

Considering the mental anguish multiple sclerosis patients are subjected to, it should not be too much work or trouble to apply the treatment described. It should be followed conscientiously even when the healthy person, who still has full use of his limbs, finds it hard to understand what it means to the sick to wait for years, perhaps decades, seemingly without any hope, until he is relieved of his affliction.

Arthritis and Gout

It is estimated that 4–7 per cent of the world's population are afflicted by the dreadful, painful scourge called arthritis. Two to three hundred thousand people in Switzerland have fallen victim to it and millions of people elsewhere in Europe and the United States can speak of their personal experience of arthritis, many of whom may have suffered from it for decades. Arthritis and gout mar the sufferer's happiness and can be sheer agony. It is the purpose of the following discussion to help as many of these people as possible.

Arthritis often has its origin in a chronic infection somewhere in the system. It may be the tonsils, a dental abscess or some other purulent inflammation which keep discharging minute quantities of toxins and poisonous waste products of the protein metabolism into the bloodstream. The effect is damaging to the joints and the internal organs such as the heart and kidneys. Apart from that, arthritis is definitely a disease of civilisation, the outcome of eating the wrong kinds of food and a wrong life-style. In many cases we may also have inherited a predisposition to it; we suffer the consequences of what our forefathers passed on to us, in the words of the Bible, 'Fathers are the ones that eat unripe grapes, but it is the teeth of the sons that get set on edge.'

A disturbance of the mineral metabolism makes it mandatory that we change from a diet that produces too much acid to one yielding an alkaline surplus. In the first place meat, especially sausages, cold meats, all kinds of processed meat and beef soups, as well as foods cooked with eggs and cheese, should be avoided wherever possible. If you feel you cannot give up meat entirely, at least confine yourself to freshly prepared unprocessed meat and keep off all preserved meats, sausages and processed meats.

Secondly, stay off all processed foods, white sugar, white flour products, canned foods, in other words everything that is no longer in its natural state or original form. The diet should consist of potatoes, cereals, unpolished brown rice, fresh vegetables and fresh fruit or naturally dried (unsulphured) fruit and vegetables containing no chemical additives or preservatives.

The simpler and more natural the diet, the greater will be its contribution to our all-round health, well-being and long life.

The most important remedy for arthritis is *potato juice*. It is not only its alkaline constituents which contribute to curing arthritis but possibly other, as yet unknown factors. Patients should take the juice of a potato daily and in severe cases the amount should be slowly increased. Grate the potato, squeeze out the juice and take it first thing in the morning before breakfast. It can also be taken in warm water or added to soup if you feel you cannot drink it neat. This is the most important remedy and should be taken every day. There should be no difficulty at all in obtaining potatoes anywhere on earth. Additional curative juices which should be taken daily are those of *white cabbage* and *kale*, as well as *carrot*. These principal medicinal juices should be taken every day without fail, even if only in small amounts, in addition to following a simple, natural diet. If you do not like the taste, mix the juice in with vegetables after they have been boiled or otherwise prepared. The best way to take the juices is, of course, undiluted. Sip them slowly so that they are insalivated before swallowing.

Externally, apply crushed *comfrey root* to the affected parts and you will find that the pain will gradually subside. Tincture of comfrey (*Symphosan*) is excellent also, and *butterbur (Petasites officinalis)* is a good supporting remedy. For further supportive medicine you can prepare an infusion made of *birch leaves, imperial masterwort (Imperatoria), restharrow (Ononis spinosa), anise (Pimpinella anisum), goldenrod (Solidago virgaurea), dandelion (Taraxacum)* and *meadowsweet (Spiraea.)* Naturally, the fresh plant extracts of these herbs are of excellent help too. Further recommendations are *Juniperus, Berberis vulgaris, Urtica* and, in addition, attenuated doses of *Colchicum.* These ingredients are all contained in our excellent remedy *Imperarthritica*, which should be taken as follows: five drops in a little warm water, or for better results, in potato juice, three times daily before meals. Add an extra drop every day until you reach twenty, or perhaps thirty drops if there is no sign of a severe reaction. Then reverse the procedure and decrease gradually to five drops, before increasing again to thirty drops. The dose must be adjusted to suit individual requirements even if it means reducing it to only two drops, if the effect on the respective parts or joints is strong. Imperarthritica can be used externally too: put a few drops on the hand and rub gently into the affected area. Finally, if an infection is the cause of the trouble it must be either healed or removed by other means.

Can Tomatoes Cause Cancer and Arthritis?

One often hears or reads in the newspaper that eating tomatoes encourages cancer, meaning that tomatoes could cause malignant growths. Even doctors often voice this opinion, which is based on various erroneous conclusions of certain researchers. Many patients, especially those whose parents or grandparents had cancer, ask me: 'What about tomatoes? Can I eat them?'

Cancer mortality has absolutely nothing to do with eating tomatoes. Research carried out by careful investigators has shown that cancer mortality is highest in those countries where the intake of protein, particularly animal protein, is excessive. A diet in which protein predominates can ultimately lead to the development of cancer and arthritis, especially when a predisposition towards these conditions, either inherited or acquired by inadequate nutrition, already exists.

Another factor is the constant irritation of cells through medicinal or mechanical, that is, physical, action. Chronic ailments and conditions, even constipation, can irritate the tissue to the extent that degenerative changes in the cellular system appear, which may sooner or later become malignant or cause arthritis, if the other two factors are present. Experience shows that cancer and arthritis may have the same basic causes, especially as far as incorrect eating habits and our modern life-style are concerned; it is only in their detail that they differ.

Many women say that after having received a blow or similar injury to the breast or other delicate part of the body, it has led to an induration of the tissues involved, which was later diagnosed as cancer. Needless to say, not every blow results in a tumour. If the person has no predisposition to malignancy, the immediate results of such an injury to the tissues will naturally disappear without leaving any ill effects.

Of course this has nothing to do with tomatoes! In fact, there are hundreds of cancer patients who have never eaten tomatoes in their life. If tomatoes were responsible for the disease, we should find the greatest incidence of cancer in the area around Naples, in Southern Italy, for instance, where people consume immense quantities of them. Yet I have come across few cases of cancer in this district and, indeed, mortality from this disease is extremely low there because great emphasis is put on fruit, vegetables and pasta, with very little protein other than fish being eaten. No doubt, the diet is a contributory factor to the low incidence of cancer in this area, despite their appetite for tomatoes.

Sufferers from arthritis or gout are often frightened by the same argument, that tomatoes encourage their development. This view has been propagated by researchers whose experiments have been confined to laboratories, without the necessary field work. It is true, however, that green or unripe tomatoes are not good for the health, since they contain toxic substances that are only rendered harmless by the process of ripening. But is it not also true that unripe apples, or any other unripe fruit for that matter, are detrimental to the health for exactly the same reason? Of course it is. However, it is wrong to argue that such toxins are contained in ripe fruit merely because they are found in the unripe ones. In reality, tomatoes that have fully ripened on the plant are wholesome and contain at least five different vitamins which are essential for the human body.

Rheumatoid Arthritis

Rheumatoid arthritis belongs to the category of rheumatic-arthritic diseases called 'Polyarthritis' in German, literally 'multiple arthritis', for it occurs in several joints at the same time. Did you know that it imposes by far the greatest financial burden on the social welfare and health institutions of most developed nations? Few people realise that each year huge sums of money are spent in an effort to help the millions who suffer from this terrible disease. Since I have had cause to treat many patients with rheumatoid arthritis, I would like to write a few words on this subject.

THE NATURE OF THE DISEASE

Academic debate about the real origin of this illness still persists. It can be caused by micro-organisms, perhaps in the wake of an infection, or by any of a number of toxins. More often than not, we find in association with arthritis some local focus of infection which discharges a constant stream of toxins or pathogenic agents into the blood. The quantity can be so small that the person may remain totally unaware of what is going on, until the body finally reacts, and becomes seriously ill. As a rule, various changes take place in the blood and scientists such as Dr von Bremer, recently also Dr Isel, have found viruses in the blood as well. Nevertheless, no definitive and conclusive explanation has so far been presented despite all the research and theorising.

I have observed that patients suffering from rheumatoid arthritis usually have a family history of gout, arthritis or some other rheumatic disease. There would thus appear to be a definite predisposition to this condition, as it is the case with many other diseases. Not everyone with a dental abscess will be afflicted with rheumatoid arthritis. One person may come down with some kidney problem, another with a heart condition, while yet another one is likely to find that a circulatory disorder develops; only a fourth one may develop rheumatoid arthritis or some other ailment. And there may also be one who will escape unscathed. You see, it very much depends on the predisposition mentioned above, and even though the individuals concerned have the same life-style and diet, the disease is triggered either by some pathogenic agent, that is, microorganism, or by toxins.

The frightening thing about rheumatoid arthritis is that, without an apparent reason, the joints in any part of the body can become afflicted. The heart may be affected too. There are times when it seems that the ailment is improving because a loosening-up of the joints and great relief is felt. Then, suddenly, for some inexplicable reason, there is a relapse and the condition deteriorates. These relapses usually occur during the cold seasons, in late autumn, winter or early spring. A warm dry summer often encourages what appears to be a real improvement.

TREATMENT GIVEN BY ORTHODOX MEDICINE
Orthodox medicine has not so far been able to find any satisfactory cure, although the pharmacies are overflowing with 'remedies' for rheumatism. For the most part, the disease has been, and still is, treated with salicylic acid preparations. At first it was thought that this was at long last a specific for a hypothetical, supposed causative agent, but these hopes were soon shattered. Why? Because the duration of the disease was hardly shortened and heart complications began to appear as frequently as they did before – and all this, by the way, was openly admitted by orthodox doctors. The salicylic acid preparations merely palliate the pain and inflammation in the joints, but not without unpleasant side effects. Gastric troubles may follow, head noises, cases of dizziness that can take on such proportions that onlookers believe the patient to be drunk. These are additional disorders brought on by medication. Aspirin and similar salicylic preparations may be better tolerated,

but they are not so effective as pure salicylic acid. Then, one day, Schottmueller introduced Pyramidon to combat rheumatic arthritis – and what happened? This drug had even worse effects on the general well-being of some patients. The formation of white blood cells (to be more exact, granulocytes – containing granules that become conspicuous when dyed) was prevented. This gave rise to agranulocytosis, from which some patients died. Sulphonamide drugs were indicated only for the primary infection, not for the already established rheumatoid arthritis.

CORTISONE

Then the great need for a cure seemed to have found its answer in the discovery of cortisone, a hormone secreted by the adrenal cortex. It was acclaimed as the wonder cure. Such enthusiasm about a new remedy is frequent, but when it does not justify the faith placed in it it is quickly forgotten. The reasoning behind the use of cortisone was a theory put forward by a Canadian scientist named Selye. He maintained that the cause of arthritis was to be found in the normal defence mechanism of the body and that cortisone prevents this mechanism from becoming active, in other words, it paralyses it. According to him, this should cure the disease.

When cortisone is administered, the pains and inflammation immediately disappear, but the patient is not really cured, because as soon as its action has been exhausted and if no further dose is given, the old symptoms return. So the duration of the illness is not at all affected by the drug. What is more, it is known from animal experiments – and autopsies on patients who died during treatment – that prolonged medication with cortisone tends to atrophy the adrenal cortex. In fact, cases have been known where the cortex had virtually wasted away completely. If the body is given a substance which it should produce itself, then the organ which normally has this function will degenerate because it has become superfluous. The same principle applies to the muscles. If they are not exercised they will grow weak and flabby, resulting in atrophy, wasting away. We have the same evidence of such a thing happening in the case of diabetes and treatment with insulin. The doctor will readily admit that insulin is a help but not a cure. Part of the pancreas, the part that actually produces insulin, begins to degenerate if too much of the medication is given. Orthodox medicine is aware of this fact and a conscientious doctor will prescribe the absolute minimum dose necessary. He does not want to discourage the pancreas from manufacturing its own insulin, or perhaps even cause the still active islets of the pancreas to degenerate as well. It is obvious that the treatment which produces results without the need for insulin is to be preferred at all times.

ACTH

The hormone product ACTH (adrenocorticotrophic hormone) has been on the market for some time now. It is a hormone produced by the pituitary gland and in some ways its effect is the same or similar to that of cortisone. In this case, however, the body is not given the adrenal hormone direct, that is, administered from outside, but the adrenal cortex is stimulated by a hormone to manufacture its own. Far from degenerating, it hypertrophies, or grows much larger in size. The effect of this medication is not as sudden as that of cortisone, for the adrenal cortex must first be activated by ACTH to produce a sufficiently high hormone level in the blood, which in turn is intended to ensure freedom from pain. When administration ceases, the harmful consequences experienced with cortisone will not occur, because ACTH preserves the function of the adrenal gland. Nevertheless, the question arises as to whether we have not merely carried the catastrophic effect of cell degeneration one step further. In this case degenerative changes take place in the pituitary gland, which normally produces ACTH for the body. Since the pituitary holds a key position in the body's hormone production (it manufactures a considerable number of different hormones), the hormone balance is disrupted and the resulting damage may be even more difficult to rectify than the arthritis itself. As far as hormone preparations are concerned, however spectacular their effects may be, one must always remember that only one side of the coin is seen at a time, and the other side may look quite different.

I once had the opportunity to discuss these points with a doctor who had lectured on this subject and he frankly admitted that he would not use these remedies for himself. Should the need arise, he would look for another, more conservative way of treating the disease. Of course, I do not deny that in some cases the use of the new medications may be justified, but let the doctor and patient alike consider very carefully what side effects they might produce and what the ultimate, rather than the immediate, effect might be. Careful analysis and observations have led me to conclude that all hormone and organ preparations should be viewed with the utmost caution before prescribing or taking them.

COMBINATION TREATMENT FOR ARTHRITIS

Very good results can be achieved in the treatment of rheumatoid arthritis by combining or applying the available therapies. First of all, the patient must change over to an absolutely natural diet, which is, of course, always indicated for cancer, arthritis or gout and all similar diseases. The conclusion about diet is supported by the fact that these diseases do not exist in less developed parts of the world, as I have seen for myself. It must be that our faulty eating habits and way of life in the West account for the problems we bring upon ourselves, or that they are at least contributory factors. Unfortunately, this opinion is not shared by many and even some doctors still do not seem to consider their patients' diet as a decisive factor for their improvement and cure. Not long ago a patient told me that her previous doctor had always taken good care of her but never once did he mention a change of diet. Rather, in his opinion diet did not play any part even in the treatment of cancer and the patient could eat anything he wished. Such an attitude and advice call into question the professional capacity of a doctor who is obviously behind the times. Surely nutritional therapy has yielded convincing proof of the importance of proper diet in treating most ailments and a doctor should not overlook the potential benefits, especially when it can contribute so much to his patient's welfare. The clear evidence should be enough to make him want to change his opinion. For my own part, I am firmly convinced that there is no illness in which a proper diet does not play a part, whether it concerns the laying of a good foundation from which to counteract the patient's sensitivity or the provision of healing factors. Diet should be given serious consideration even if it only assumes a supporting role on the way to recovery.

DIET

A diet of natural foods is of primary importance when treating rheumatoid arthritis. Follow the diet given under the heading 'Natural Food' (see pages 463–9). Only unadulterated, unrefined foods should be eaten, just as the Creator provided them in nature. In preparing them we should be guided by the same principle: food should be left in its natural state as far as possible. Cooked animal protein, such as meat, is detrimental according to my experience. For better results, adopt a predominantly vegetarian diet and include plenty of raw foods. Curds or cottage cheese, as animal-derived protein, are good for you. If you cannot abstain from meat altogether, it is permissible to eat a little beef or veal, but pork, sausages, and processed and canned meats should be completely out of bounds. Caution should be exercised as regards fats; they should be of vegetable origin, cold-pressed and unrefined. Keep off heated fats or fried food. Vegetable oils, such as cold-pressed olive, sunflower, poppy, or linseed oils, should be used in their unrefined state. Anyone suffering from rheumatoid arthritis should never have denatured white sugar on his table. For sweetening, honey and natural sweetness from grapes, sultanas, currants and raisins must take the place of refined white sugar. These dried fruits can be put through a mincer so that they can easily be added to foods for sweetening. Raw rose hip purée made without white sugar is an excellent substitute for the usual jams. Not only white sugar but also white flour and white flour products must be scrupulously avoided. On the other hand, wheat germ taken in limited quantities is an excellent addition to the diet. If vegetables are not eaten raw, care should be taken in their cooking. Never boil vegetables but simply steam them in a little water to preserve their minerals and vitamins. Raw salads are very good seasoned with whey concentrate (*Molkosan*) or with lemon juice and oil; never add salt and sugar.

If at all possible do not use table salt or sharp spices, but replace these by fresh culinary herbs and yeast extract, or use *Herbaforce*.

NATURAL REMEDIES

For internal use, *Nephrosolid* is an excellent remedy for the kidneys, as it increases the secretion and expulsion of urine. Nephrosolid contains *Solidago* (goldenrod) and other herb extracts. Another effective remedy I like to prescribe is *Imperarthritica*, also a fresh herb extract. It contains, among other important ingredients, *Petasites off.*, *Polygonum avic.*, *Betula* and *Viscum album*. To remedy circulatory disorders and venous stagnation, *Aesculaforce* is indicated. This herbal complex contains horse chestnut, melilot (sweet clover), witch hazel and arnica, all excellent for the veins. *Kelpasan* is a good mineral supplement and increases the haemoglobin content at the same time. *Echinaforce* will relieve inflammatory conditions. These remedies, in combination with *Petasites officinalis* and *Viscum album*, will make great improvement possible, the latter helping considerably to regenerate the affected tissues.

Should the breathing be restricted in any way, you will find *Usneasan* of great help. This remedy is prepared from larch moss and if used in conjunction with external applications of mucilaginous extracts such as *Wallwosan* or *Symphosan*, a fresh herb preparation containing comfrey, you will obtain a great deal of relief. Furthermore, it will be to your advantage to alternate with a massage oil such as *Toxeucal*, made from camphor and various extracts, including eucalyptus and the fresh leaves of poison ivy (*Rhus toxicodendron*). Packs made up of *clay* and *pulped cabbage leaves* are also beneficial. To obtain the best results apply them in alternation. It has been found that an application of *grated carrots* also relieves the pain.

Biological injections will overcome the pain even faster. Homoeopathic remedies are injected subcutaneously and quickly take effect. *Formic acid 12x, Lachesis 10x* and *Urtica 6x* (stinging nettles), all have proved their worth in this respect. Mistletoe preparations, especially *Plenosol* (Dr Madaus), lend additional support to the curative action of these medicines. Start with the potency 0 and increase gradually to the stronger 1.

By following the above advice, rheumatoid arthritis can be successfully treated. You should find that most doctors who practise natural therapy will be prepared to give the appropriate homoeopathic injections.

FANGO (MUD) CURES

I remember some particularly severe cases where the patients followed all the advice given above, yet a fango treatment in Italy was still necessary to effect a cure. Where professors and doctors at Swiss clinics have been hard pressed to find some satisfactory treatment for their patients, a fango cure in conjunction with the natural remedies suggested in the previous section has proved a superb biological treatment – the best there is. Patients who could hardly move around anymore became quite capable of taking up their normal work once again. Should a fango cure in Abano or Montegrotto in Italy become necessary, the financial sacrifice it may require will no doubt seem worthwhile if the patient can regain his health and former efficiency.

If you combine a fango cure with the other three treatments already mentioned, you will not only make possible a cure of the disease, but will also ensure that it is permanent. Take the biological remedies and ampoules for injection with you so you can use them to a limited extent. When taking the fango cure, be careful not to force or overdo things. After four or five treatments take a day off.

For a change, take a bath in the hot springs of a grotto. These natural sauna baths are widely available in these Italian spas. It is

271

a good idea to sweat in the bath one day, and then to have a fango treatment the following day. This programme may prove to be rather strenuous for some patients, but it will be easier than having to put up with the dreadful consequences of arthritis when it is not treated naturally. The natural way is always the best way. As to the question of diet, as the suggested regime could be a little difficult to follow in Abano or Montegrotto, it may be advisable to take some crispbread, raw cane sugar, honey and raw carrots with you, or try to obtain them locally.

FURTHER ADVICE ON HOW TO GET WELL AGAIN

If you wish to regain your health, you will have to pay special attention to what is natural and follow the advice already given. This implies that you should beware of the many patent medicines that claim to be able to cure or improve your condition quickly. For a permanent cure, more is required than just a few injections. In fact, both the doctor and the patient need a lot of patience and perseverence. The doctor must pay close attention to the patient's reaction to the various treatments if rheumatoid arthritis is to be cured. Still, the important thing is that that relief is possible. If the result achieved is to be permanent, the patient must continue to follow a diet of natural foods and to take limited amounts of the remedies from time to time. The idea is to prevent a return of the same illness. If you have the financial means you might take a fango cure in Italy once a year; doing so will help combat an existing disposition to arthritis. This treatment, together with the other advice presented, if followed, will give the patient every chance to keep fit in the future.

The Living Cell

The cell is a tiny but perfectly designed and incredible unit of every living thing on earth. Like so many other things it is a miracle of Creation. Our body is a harmoniously cooperating organisation of single cells, similar to the many individual citizens in a country. The earth's population is now five billion, a tremendous number when you think about it, but relatively small in comparison with the total of about 100 trillion (100,000,000,000,000) cells that make up the body of an adult person. And this miracle, the human cell, is on average only 0.02 mm (1/1000 inch) in diameter. If you want to get some idea of this tiny structure, take a soft-boiled egg as a comparison. On the outside is the cell membrane (the shell), then we find the cell plasma (the white) surrounding and protecting the nucleus (the yolk), the most important, highly organised and complex part of this tiny unit – the control centre.

Cell Metabolism

The cell's metabolism is yet another miracle at work, one whose workings scientists rack their brains to puzzle out. Although we do have some knowledge of the internal processes, this represents only a fraction of what actually goes on in the cell. We know, for example, that the cell takes in proteins, sugar and salt solutions together with various minerals and that it releases some substances, in a sense, waste material. But why is it that one kind of cell selects this or that substance for itself, while another kind attracts different substances? In other words, what enables the cells to make this selection? No one has yet been able to discover the answer to this question.

Sick Cells

If an engine is not lubricated for any length of time, it will overheat. If we ignore the whining and grinding noises caused by dry bearings and do not replace the oil at once, the engine is bound to suffer damage. Similarly, a cell's efficiency will diminish if it lacks the required substances, or if it does not receive sufficient quantities. The cell will become sick if such a deficiency continues for some time so that it has to draw on and eventually exhaust its reserves. In the case of vitamin deficiency we speak of 'avitaminosis'. As soon as the deficiency is recognised and the required substances are provided, the individual cell will recover and with it the complex organisation of cells, the tissue, will be restored to health and begin to function properly again. For this reason the art, or rather the capacity, of a good doctor becomes evident in his ability to diagnose these deficiencies and choose the appropriate natural remedies. The damage will then be rectified.

The Degenerated Cell

A degenerated cell could be described as a criminal in the cellular 'state' or organisation, since it operates in a way similar to criminals in society. They ignore the law, do what they want and take what they like without any concern for those around them. Of course, it takes time for a person to sink so low mentally and morally that he becomes a cold-blooded criminal.

The same applies to a cancer cell, a cell that has degenerated into a malignant one. It is just like a criminal who lives at the expense of others and without consideration ravishes and destroys whatever lies in his way. But, you may ask, what makes a healthy cell degenerate and become malignant? What complex series of errors and detrimental influences cause the degeneration? Careful observation and experience has already given us a good insight into the things that may contribute to the change, although we do not yet understand all the causes leading to the mutation that transforms a normal cell into a giant or malignant one.

KNOWN CAUSES

I am fully convinced that many causes work together and put such great stress on the healthy cells that they have to give in; the harmony of their natural life and function becomes so disrupted that they degenerate and become malignant.

1. Predisposition is often responsible for cell degeneration, that is, it may be due to the inherited genetic make-up. However, such a predisposition need not lead to cancer if one's life-style is sensible.

2. An inadequate diet, a constant companion of our modern way of living and eating, upsets the body's biological balance and so damages the entire cellular system.

a) Too much protein intake, and of a poor quality, plays a considerable part.

b) Fats have a bearing on the development of cancer. Animal fats and fats lacking in unsaturated fatty acids are especially detrimental.

c) Disturbances in the mineral metabolism caused by the consumption of refined foods have proved to be a contributory cause of cell degeneration.

d) Avitaminosis, as well as a deficiency of other vital substances, seem to be strongly implicated in the development of cancer, but research in this area is still inconclusive.

e) Metabolic disorders, for example chronic constipation and constant fermentations in the intestines as a result of dysbacteria, are also very damaging.

3. Lack of oxygen plays a decisive part in the development of cancer. Experience has shown that people who take plenty of exercise in fresh, clean air are less at risk than those who engage in mental work or have to work in closed rooms. It would therefore be advisable to walk more rather than go everywhere by car, to spend one's free time walking in the woods and meadows instead

of sitting in a pub or bar talking politics, or wasting one's time in front of the television set or in the pursuit of similar pleasures.

4. Toxic gases and radiation which pollute the air today are also carcinogenic, or cancer-producing, factors. So beware of them!

5. It has been proved beyond doubt that some chemical additives to our food are carcinogenic. Colourings, flavourings and preservatives are worse cell poisons than was previously thought, and it is for this reason that many government agencies have started to ban them. They follow the example of Germany in this respect, where the efforts of doctors, especially those engaged in research into vitamins and minerals, succeeded in persuading the Government to take such measures.

6. Certain medicines, such as those that are, unfortunately, still used all too frequently in chemotherapy, especially derivatives of tar, contribute to cell degeneration. This is of particular significance today, when people are accustomed to swallowing tablets for just about anything.

7. Poisons in the form of pesticides and herbicides are often used indiscriminately. These can stick to vegetables, for instance, and are taken into the body through carelessness or lack of forethought. The result can be extremely damaging since lead, arsenic and copper are much more toxic than is generally realised.

8. The biological balance in plants can be disturbed because of errors when using fertilisers. If such produce is eaten for any length of time, it can also upset the biological balance in the human body.

9. Tenseness and indurations disturb and slow down the metabolic processes and foster the development of cancer. It is therefore strongly recommended that regular exercise be taken for relaxation as a prophylactic therapy. Indurations, lumps and growths such as scars and warts should be carefully watched. Never scratch or irritate them.

10. One of the most serious factors in the development of cancer is stress, that is, worries and anxieties. The extent of its influence is, of course, closely linked to our mental attitude, whether we give into negative thinking rather than being positive and optimistic whenever we feel depressed. Worries and anxieties are detrimental to the liver and have been a contributory cause of cancer for thousands of people. There is nothing more harmful to the life of our cells than continuous or repeated mental stress. Indeed, it poisons the blood and lymph and undermines the very life of the cells to a greater extent than some of the other factors listed above, even when taken together.

The long list of detrimental influences on the health of our cells shows that determining the possibility of cancer is simply a question of calculation. Every one of the described factors adds a few more percentage points to the possibility of contracting the disease, and as soon as the total of 100 per cent is reached, the negative influences will pull down the scales, the cells will become damaged and the disease, which can bring such pain and sorrow, will strike.

Once a tumour has formed, surgical intervention helps to calm one's fears by removing it. However, the danger to the rest of the tissues can only be stopped if all contributory factors to the cancer are tackled. We should not be content with the surgeon's reassurance that he has been able to find and remove everything and thus feel absolutely safe. Hormone treatment and radiotherapy create added problems for the cellular system and will not save a patient who has undergone surgery from the need to completely change his dietary habits and life-style.

The patient's mental attitude towards the illness and all other vital matters must be put on a healthy basis. True, this may not always be easy for the convalescent, especially if members of his family lack the necessary understanding and do not support him. Nevertheless, he should make a serious effort since it will help to improve his condition and contribute significantly to his cure. At the same time, he will make life easier for himself and those around him. No doubt, this will be a blessing in itself.

The Spectre of Cancer

While the world's medical specialists argue about the causes of cancer, more and more victims die every year. Some researchers try to blame a virus for its development, considering the disease to be a localised one affecting certain groups of cells. Others are just as bold in defending their view that cancer is a disease affecting the whole organism.

It is possible that viruses do play some part in the disease, but the researchers who believe that cancer is a disease that affects the whole body may be closer to the truth than the others. The view that cancer is a disease brought about by civilisation finds strong support through the investigation of conditions in less developed parts of the world, where cancer is comparatively unknown. According to my observations, cancer has more than one cause, it is the culmination of a combination of many causes, in other words, it is a complex disease.

A Question Still Unanswered

Thousands of pages have been written about cancer, yet our critical questions remain practically unanswered. Histologists with their modern ultramicroscopes or electron microscopes have so far not been able to tell us why a healthy cell becomes a cancer cell. It is for this reason that the early diagnosis of cancer is so difficult. Public information and lectures often make cancer appear to be a simple and straightforward problem and, for example, women over forty are encouraged to visit the doctor for a regular check-up. The doctor keeps telling them that there is no reason to be anxious, that everything is in order – and the women lose their fear of cancer. Then, quite suddenly, and in spite of the doctor's reassurances, a woman notices a hard lump. She rushes to a specialist who asks, with a slight tone of reproach in his voice, 'Why did you not come to see me sooner?' When she answers that the family doctor has been checking her regularly for years the specialist is naturally embarrassed and worried. Indeed, cancer is a difficult problem even for a capable physician and his efforts to prolong a patient's life can often be in vain.

OTHER BAFFLING QUESTIONS

The conscientious doctor is sometimes baffled because a seemingly serious case takes an unexpected turn for the better. On the other hand, the opposite can also happen: the patient seems to be making fine progress but suddenly the picture changes and the illness takes such a rapid turn for the worse that no skill, no effort, is able to arrest it. Even the best surgeon, highly skilled in his profession, may suffer the tragedy inflicted by the merciless Angel of Death in that his best friend, sister, mother or even his own wife passes away prematurely. Or the scourge of cancer may take hold of the doctor himself and all the efforts of his colleagues, using the most up-to-date therapies, prove to be in vain.

All this is very sad and we are filled with sorrow. For how can one help the patient to escape such an end? It would be a great relief for all of us, would it not, if there were some natural remedy that could cure the disease. Sadly, though, even the most experienced specialist knows of no such remedy. True, there are some good medicines that may have brought relief for some patients, but unfortunately there is no specific remedy for cancer, one that cures it without fail. What is more, it seems that we will never find one. This, too, is a tragic prospect. Once again, patients, nurses, pharmacologists, as well as doctors, are confronted by a puzzle. Is it not true that conscientious efforts are being made to find a cure, and endless hours and huge sums of money are being spent on research? Should it all be to no avail? Is it not true that those who seek will also find?

A plant may lack sufficient, or the right kind of, soil. Its fruits may be affected by a fungal disease. Insect pests may destroy some too. The site where the plants grow may not be the best one; perhaps they need plenty of light and sunshine but they grow in a dark and shady area, or they need a little sun but receive too much. If the orchard-keeper neglects the proper care and fertilising of his trees, the specialist to whom he turns for advice will not be able to overcome these deficiencies by using a single patent remedy. I think we will all understand this illustration without any difficulty, and by applying it to the factors contributing to cancer, we should also understand the difficulties of treating this disease. A remedy may be the best there is, yet it can only help towards effecting a cure. We can take a plant remedy that stimulates the liver, for example barberries from the Himalayas or the common butterbur, which have done much good in treating the disease, but the problem of cancer will not be solved by just one remedy alone. Perhaps it may alleviate the pain, arrest the growth of a tumour, even bring about an appreciable improvement to the patient's general condition. Other improvements may be noticeable, but none of the available remedies will actually be responsible for a complete cure. The reasons for this are explained in the sections below.

Is Cancer a Localised Disease or One Affecting the Whole System?
It will first be interesting to consider some of the arguments put forward by doctors of the highest calibre about some of the basic questions concerning cancer during a recent court case in Germany. How difficult it must be for judges to reach the right decision in such cases, especially when the views of specialists contradict each other! How can judges possibly be expected to make sense of it all?

Professor Bauer from Heidelberg, a famous and respected expert in the field of cancer, maintained that cancer is a localised disease and can therefore be tackled by means of the scalpel and radiation, that is, by surgery and radiotherapy, with varying degrees of success. However, two other well-known surgeons, Dr Albrecht and Professor Zabel, expressed opposing views. In common with many others, they were of the opinion that cancer is a disease affecting the whole system and that with the surgical removal of a tumour the actual disease is only partially treated, let alone cured. The great number of deaths that occur during the first year after an operation, in spite of radiotherapy, seem to speak out strongly in favour of this second view. A further aspect may be added, for it is thought that certain materials leave the malignant tissues, enter the bloodstream and lymph and, of course, the cells. This has a detrimental, if not poisoning, effect. According to this opinion, we can conclude that it is not only migrating cancer cells but also these separate materials that can lead to metastases in the course of time. The American school of thought seems to support this opinion. However, the available literature is not clear on whether the detached and circulating materials are in fact the same as those viruses discovered first by Dr Nebel of Lausanne and later by Professor von Brehmer.

The claim that cancer is a communicable disease, under certain conditions, may no doubt be a new thought to many. As many people find this possibility alarming, the question is dealt with separately below (see pages 280–1).

THE COMPLEX NATURE OF THE CAUSES

In spite of all the new views about cancer, I am sure we are not mistaken in taking the cause to be a combination of factors, including nutrition, housing conditions, occupation, lack of oxygen and necessary exercise, as well as the mental state and attitude of the person. What is more, it can no longer be denied that an inherited predisposition contributes to cancer. The empirical fact that it is possible for therapies to be useless even if employed in the early stages of the disease, according to personal disposition and the reaction of the body, is a reason for sadness on the part of all therapists. No other illness presents more surprises to the doctor, even the specialist, than cancer. He may be successful in treating a severe case, but a seemingly mild one can suddenly take a turn for the worse against all expectations.

There is a practical lesson to be learned from this. It is absolutely necessary to take certain precautionary measures, particularly once you have reached the age of forty. You should be sure to avoid all carcinogenic influences. This means primarily tobacco, most chemical medicines, also colourings and flavourings in food and drinks. Another thing to avoid is constant or prolonged overtiredness. Mental and emotional stress and strain, worries and constant feelings of depression are equally dangerous. They should be combatted right away and every endeavour made to overcome them.

Anyone who has seen the suffering and pain of someone afflicted with cancer of the larynx or lungs will not find it too difficult to give up smoking for ever. If you suffer from rheumatism or arthritis and are sensitive to volcanic influences, you should keep away from radioactive treatments because the water of volcanic springs that are radioactive can also cause cancer.

All in all, do not be overanxious, yet still be sensible and careful. You do not want to do what is harmful while thinking you were doing yourself some good. Strong stimulations can destroy, whereas milder ones can be beneficial.

Is Cancer Communicable?

Even though it is said that in experiments it has been possible to transmit cancer from sick animals to healthy ones by infecting them with toxins from malignant tissues, there is absolutely no evidence that cancer is communicable in humans; it has also been proved that cancer can result if certain tissues are subjected to the influence of poisons over a period of time.

Nevertheless, it has been noted that when a marriage partner has died of cancer the other partner often falls victim to the insidious malady some time later. But this observation does not prove that the disease was transmitted to the partner; there is indeed another reason.

As a rule, both partners will have eaten the same food and lived in the same house and environment. Their work or occupation would often be similar, and the same is true of their philosophy of life, producing similar mental and emotional demands and stresses. In accordance with their physical predispositions, the existing bioclimatic conditions can also have the same effect on them. All these deliberations show that the cancer which killed one partner did not directly infect the other, but the same illness resulted from a combination of the same causes. Working together, these causes eventually led to cancer in the other partner as well.

Then there is the time spent in caring for the patient and the deep sympathy felt for his suffering. Both are a strain on the energy reserves, apart from the shattering experience of the loved one's eventual death, the resulting loss being difficult to bear. The feeling of loneliness after decades of companionship can be overwhelming. In fact, just as joy and happiness strengthen and help to overcome an illness, so constant sorrow and anxiety can contribute to producing an illness, turning it into infirmity that may end in death.

We must not forget that not everyone has the necessary inner strength to recover from losses and problems successfully, and this fact should be taken into account as another factor to be added to the total of all other causes.

If cancer really were communicable, it would no doubt claim many more victims than it does and would be far more dangerous than it already is.

Susceptibility to Cancer Despite a Healthy Life-Style

Vegetarians often claim that one cannot get cancer if one leads a natural life. So it is an understandable tragedy when someone with a healthy life-style and strictly vegetarian diet falls victim to cancer. But what explanation is there for the fact that vegetarians, advocates of natural remedies and treatments, even leading figures in this field, succumb to cancer? Unfortunately, this really does happen, even though they may try to keep it a secret. True enough, experience has proved that a diet too rich in protein, especially animal protein, can contribute to the development of cancer, whereas a healthy diet based on vegetables and fruit does reduce one's susceptibility to it.

ADDITIONAL PRECAUTIONS

It must be taken into consideration that vegetarians, perhaps even without realising it, can take into their system a number of carcinogenic substances. How? Mainly through pesticides and similar sprays, as well as colourings, flavourings and many other chemical food additives. Food that is natural and 100 per cent pure can only be guaranteed if you produce it yourself, and then by organic growing methods. Furthermore, it must be noted that the development of cancer is not solely dependent on diet. It is no doubt beneficial to our health, however, if we eat the right kind of food, because we are then more likely to avoid the substances that promote cancer.

However, it is easy to minimise the advantage gained from a healthy diet by ignoring other factors that are closely linked with a natural life-style. If you have to live and work inside all the time you are subject to a serious lack of oxygen, which must be remedied through plenty of exercise. It is also wrong to curtail the time allocated for rest and relaxation only because of being too conscientious and responsible. Why? Because doing so only produces a situation in which you live under constant stress, and this inevitably leads to tensions in the body, which in turn trigger mental and emotional ups and downs. Once physical tension has disturbed the mental balance the result can be cell irritation, and if this continues over the years it may also be a factor in the development of cancer. For this reason, true inner happiness and optimistic confidence are wonderful remedies, creating a different basis for life. Worries and anxieties, however, when added to overtiredness, can be even more dangerous in stimulating the development of cancer than can errors in diet.

This may well explain why some people who stick strictly to sound rules of nutrition nevertheless fall victim to cancer. No doubt you can now see that caring for our mental condition is just as important as adopting the right kind of diet. It is also true that the person who is able to maintain his mental balance finds it much easier to relax, slow down and keep calm, even though life may be stormy all around him. This ability will save much energy and help to avoid tension. If your duties are highly demanding, and you cannot reduce them, then make it a point to get plenty of oxygen, at least before going to bed; take a quiet walk and, what is even more important, do retire early. Is it not true that you get little done in the evening or night when your mind is tired? You will not be able to do as much as you want to, and you will have to make a far greater effort than you would in the morning after a good night's rest, when the problems we face seem much less overpowering and are easier to solve than the night before when vigour and efficiency levels were low.

So there are quite a few things we have to watch in our difficult and critical times if we want to protect our health. Happily, we can do justice to what we have to do if we use sound common sense and judgment and act circumspectly, even though we may have to make some sacrifices. Such precautions are all in the interest of good health.

Birthmarks and Cancer

I have noticed many times that we cannot be too careful with birthmarks. Take care not to scratch them; they are best left alone, for to try and get rid of them by means of remedies or surgery is not without danger. In fact, it can mean that cancer cells, which might be present, begin to spread. Probably the best time to do something about a mole (nevus), if you do want to remove it because it is too unsightly, is during childhood. Even then it is most important to choose a highly skilled surgeon who is fully aware of all the dangers involved in its removal.

Birthmarks may remain inactive for decades and then, quite

282

suddenly, at the age of fifty or over, they begin to play up. A Swiss immigrant in British Columbia, western Canada, told me recently about such a case. A friend of his who had a birthmark on his lower back finally had it removed. Eighteen months later he began to notice glandular swellings and other abnormalities all over his body. On further examination they were found to be metastases of a malignant kind.

Even a simple irritation of a birthmark, especially when the irritation is continuous or repeated, can pose a grave danger. Clothing can cause such an irritation or the habit of scratching the mark, perhaps even making it bleed. In time, this irritation can have serious consequences.

PRECAUTIONARY MEASURES

If you insist on having a birthmark removed surgically, go on a strict *liver diet* in preparation for the operation. The best diet is one that serves as nutritional therapy for cancer patients. Take *Petaforce* at the same time, since this remedy helps to prevent metastases. The point to remember is that you should not simply go to have the mark cut away without first preparing the body in a prophylactic sense. Nor is it advisable to have a little tissue cut out for examination (biopsy) unless the same precautionary measures have been carefully observed and the liver diet adhered to consistently for one or two months. In this case, too, it is necessary to take Petaforce as a precaution to avoid the formation of metastases. Following this advice could certainly save many a person from disaster, possibly even from death.

In lectures and medical literature doctors keep pointing out that it is important to begin treatment early whenever cancer is suspected. But what is meant by 'early'? There are many people who regularly visit their doctor, are carefully examined, and yet fail to prevent what is going on in the body which neither they nor the doctor can detect or foresee. Hence the question, 'What should you do to successfully prevent cancer?' Providing an answer to this question is not at all easy. In our modern times there are too many factors that disturb the normal cell in its biological balance, changing a normal cell into a cancerous one. Mutation, the process of a healthy cell changing into a sick or degenerated one, is still a mystery and all efforts to solve it have so far been unsuccessful.

No one can deny that the stresses of modern life are partly to blame for various diseases, whether it be vascular disorders or cancer. Neither can anyone deny that increased radioactivity contributes to cancer. Chemical sprays as well as chemical additives in food are also contributory factors, as discussed above, together with the refining of food items and the thoughtless consumption of these foods. In addition to the constant stress and strain, the increased mental tension of our times probably plays a great part in laying the foundation for the development of the disease. We know, for instance, that worries and anxieties are bad for the liver, and what is bad for the liver is also detrimental to the endocrine glands. The resulting effects also share the blame in the disease's development.

Therefore we must consider the contributory factors and then make a conscientious effort to avoid them. Of course, it goes without saying that it is essential to follow a natural rhythm, or way of life. Overdoing things, in other words extremes, should be avoided, as should everything that is not in harmony with nature; these things can only be detrimental to an already weakened constitution. Once we have come to understand that we must adopt a positive attitude and life-style in order to escape the tentacles of one of the worst illnesses of our times, a birthmark will not be the reason for putting ourselves in danger of dying from cancer.

Smokers' Cancer

The tobacco industry has all the power and money to prepare and mount an effective campaign to play down the warning sounded worldwide against smoking, especially the smoking of cigarettes. It sets out to silence all knowledge concerning the fact that smoking causes cancer. What is more, it is just possible that the tobacco industry may be successful in finding some scientists, well-known chemists and medical professors who will endeavour to prove the contrary. However, even though the American Medical Association might accept another ten million dollars from the tobacco industry – as it has happened before, to our disbelief – the damage to health is there for all to see. Much can be bought with money, but not necessarily good health.

Of course, there are other causes of cancer of the lips, tongue, larynx, bronchials and lungs, but this fact does not mean that smoking is less of a cause of cancer, or, more accurately, an irritation and causative factor. It is not the nicotine, which affects the coronary vessels, that is to blame for smokers' cancer, but the tar, or phenol to be more specific. This chemical irritant is able to make the cells degenerate, leading to cancer. It is true that not every smoker becomes a victim of cancer. The chemical cell irritation caused by the tar is not enough, as a sole cause, to trigger cancer. As stated earlier, a predisposition to the disease is necessary. Not every smoker can be sure whether he has this predisposition or not. But he can be quite certain of it if his parents suffered from cancer or arthritis.

HEALTHY HABITS

It is certainly unwise to expose oneself to the danger of cancer because of some so-called pleasure. Think of the terrible suffering cancer of the larynx or lungs can mean. If you have ever had to watch a victim of this tragic condition slowly dying in agony, no doubt you will muster the courage and consider it your urgent duty to warn others of the dangers. Honest records and statistics show that by far the greater percentage of the above-mentioned kinds of cancer occur in smokers and those who work with tar.

It is not difficult to admit that smoking does not quite agree with a young person to begin with. This is a fact. Still, the tiniest bit of inherent cowardice may cause the young person to overcome the natural aversion to smoking because he does not want to be different from his peers – he does not want to be an outsider. Nor does he fancy being teased; above all, he wants to appear grown up and so imitates the adults.

Instead of trying to overcome inhibitions and inferiority complexes by doing commendable work, some young people learn to smoke and drink, habits that are detrimental to their health. While acquiring a taste for these things they develop an internal insensitivity but this price is paid without much thought, since the end result helps to suppress their feeling of inferiority.

It is a strange thing that if something tastes bad and bitter or burns on the tongue, once one had become used to it, the palate even comes to like it. But should not exactly this reaction move us to embrace only good and healthy habits? Of course it should! And by the way, the craving to suck something can be satisfied in a completely harmless way. Simply keep some raisins in your pocket and eat them whenever you experience the desire for a cigarette. Raisins are stimulating because of the valuable grape sugar they contain. This is not only nourishing and strengthening but also much tastier than nicotine and tar products. If you are able to help someone give up the vice of smoking, you will be helping him not only to save a considerable amount of money but, what is more important, you may also save him from the cancer that might otherwise catch up with him in later years.

Deadly Dangers in the Water

My experiences in the tropics have often urged me to point out the dangers that await a traveller if he drinks unboiled water in tropical or subtropical regions. By doing so, it is possible to take in pathogenic agents and parasites that can actually put one's life in jeopardy.

Unfortunately, even in our temperate zones it has become a hazardous thing to drink water, as was evidenced in an article published as long ago as 19 April 1964, in the journal *Nationalzeitung* (No. 178), entitled 'Carcinogenic Substances in Water'. The article discussed the results of analytical tests of the water in Lake Constance and its catchment area. According to the author, the results indicated that the water analysed contained considerable amounts of carcinogenic substances. Even though the author did not sufficiently exploit the material, his presentation of the findings was enough to make us take note. We must remember that many toxins, besides the effluents from industries, can enter rivers and lakes without our realising it. For example, quite a number of poisonous sprays are used in agriculture, and deposits of leaded petrol and diesel oil accumulate on the roads. Rain and the water from melted snow take up these and many other substances, eventually washing them into the rivers and lakes. Tests have also shown that the groundwater in certain places already contains certain amounts of such pollutants, none of which are at all conducive to good health.

All these factors make carcinogenic agents accumulate in our system. Say someone is a smoker. The tar from the tobacco will give him a few per cent of carcinogenic substances; radioactivity in the air will add a few more per cent, so will sprays, especially if they contain DDT; then a few more per cent will be absorbed from chemical medicines, especially if derived from tar; a further amount will come from food additives, irradiated foods, as well as smoked meat and fish. If the carcinogenic substances from polluted water are added to these other tragic influences, it is quite possible that the total of 100 per cent cancer-producing substances will have accumulated in that person's body. This may be enough to form a tumour if an appropriate irritation in the body also takes place. Since cancer claims an increasing number of victims in our times, it is essential to identify the many causes that can lead to it.

Beware of Carcinogenic Substances

Now that it is generally known that certain substances are carcinogenic, many people are more careful about what they eat and drink. It has been found that all tar products have a carcinogenic effect. Some of these are medicines, for example headache and sleeping tablets, or analgesics, but so, too, are some artificial colourings, flavourings, preservatives and improvers that, unfortunately, are so often added to our food. Tar released in the process of smoking tobacco can also produce cancer. Sadly, people who have to live in towns and cities are unable to avoid inhaling air that is polluted with carcinogenic agents. It is also almost impossible to escape from increased radioactivity, which is present in our food, even in milk and water, and in ever-increasing quantities. How sensible and necessary it is, therefore, to keep away from any carcinogenic substances when we are able to.

To do this, however, we need to know and remember what they are at all times. We must not remain indifferent, telling ourselves this or that is not so bad after all. It is a fact that many little things add up to make one big one, and that the cumulative effect results in the disaster we are all trying to escape from!

SOME WARNING EXAMPLES

I could quote many examples to prove that there are a number of possibilities leading to cancer. Once a farmer from Emmental came to consult me about a large tumour he had. First I asked him what he himself thought might have caused the problem. Without much hesitation he told me that he had always tended to eat too much pork and smoked meat. As smoked meat is indeed carcinogenic because it contains tar, the patient was perhaps correct in his assumption. Moreover, many a gardener and farmer may not even realise that most of the sprays they use, especially those containing derivatives of tar, can cause cancer.

Years ago it was nothing short of a celebration if a person went to a fashionable coffee-house in order to enjoy some cake baked with 100 per cent natural ingredients. During the Second World War many food items were not available, or at least were in short supply. It was then that substitutes began to be introduced, and since it is often easier to use essences and the like, substitutes continued to be preferred. Using artificial products instead of natural ones has become more and more prevalent today. But few people stop to think that when they eat a cassata or any other ice-cream made with artificial colours and flavours, they are actually

287

ingesting carcinogenic substances. The chance of adding carcinogenic agents is ever-present wherever chemicals are mixed in food to improve its flavour, aroma and colour. Today there are enough dangers around that can lead to sickness that we do not even know about. Knowing this fact should deter us from exposing ourselves to damage by things we do know about and so could avoid.

It is unfortunate that so few people attach any importance to leaving nature natural. Nevertheless, we should take care and do everything in our power to eat and drink nothing but natural food and drinks that will do us no harm.

Seven Basic Rules for the Prevention of Cancer

The following seven rules will give you an idea of some of the effective precautionary measures you can take to prevent cancer as far as you possibly can. You should endeavour to follow these rules at all times.

RULE ONE

We live in restless, uneasy times, beset with many failures and disappointments. Instead of putting the emphasis on the manifold problems and difficulties confronting us, we should try our best to keep calm and maintain our equilibrium. If we let worries and anxieties dominate us, we should not be surprised if our health begins to suffer; we will become agitated and our mental and emotional life will be impaired, even come under stress. In such circumstances is there any wonder that spasms occur and mental tensions attack and damage our cellular system?

We must fight against depression in our outlook and attitude, because constant mental and emotional pressures, given time, can act like a physical cell poison. Depressive worries lead directly to tension in the body and if the condition is allowed to continue, it will contribute considerably to the development of cancer. So if we do not want to suffer undue damage through worries and the like, we must make a determined effort to shake off everything that might upset our equilibrium, our inner calm and balance. However, that does not mean we should become apathetic or lethargic, for indifference is no remedy whatsoever. On the contrary, we must endeavour to go about our work with a happy spirit and with bold determination try to find release from our worries. If we do all that lies in our power to do, then we can remain calm and take care that our spirit is filled with uplifting, optimistic things and that we enjoy nature's precious gifts with joy and gratitude. There are some people who give in to their worries and anxieties to such an extent that their depression makes them oblivious to the most beautiful scenery and glorious sunshine. It is to them that we especially recommend the precept 'Happiness means health'.

RULE TWO
We should make sure to always eat what nature offers, in as unadulterated or natural a state as possible. Proper nutrition is more important than you might think. It is a proven fact that devalued, refined foods containing artificial additives and residues of sprays, but lacking vital substances and other nutrients, help to prepare the groundwork for the development of cancer.

Our diet should always contain more alkaline foods than acid ones. A lack of minerals and unsaturated fatty acids can also contribute to the degeneration of cells. Furthermore, overeating and digestive upsets accompanied by fermentations and intestinal gases are basic causes of cancer. If you turn these remarks over in your mind, you will realise that it is up to yourself to make the necessary changes in your diet, always laying stress on a choice of wholesome, unadulterated natural food.

RULE THREE
We must not poison our body fluids and cells with chemicals. For this reason it will be clear why it is essential to avoid all medicines used in chemotherapy that are capable of disturbing the normal cell metabolism. Watch out especially for medicines based on tar. The compulsive consumption of tablets and narcotics is also responsible for upsetting the biological balance, physically as well as mentally. Smokers may delude themselves into thinking that nicotine is not really harmful and has no influence on cancer, but it is an established fact that the phenols – tar – contained in tobacco are carcinogenic. Why be foolishly deceived and suffer the tragic consequences?

RULE FOUR
No one but a person who cannot walk can imagine life without the use of his legs. The importance of our legs only begins to dawn on us when we see someone who cannot use them. And yet, time and again we commit the error of giving in to convenience; we take the car instead of walking. The way things are going it appears that before too long many people will use their feet and legs only

to operate the accelerator! But this neglect is absolutely wrong; it robs the body of an essential source of strength. Walking and hiking help us to breathe deeply, so that we regularly inhale sufficient oxygen to keep the cells healthy and elastic. Cancer cells lack oxygen, and since lack of oxygen is one of the main causes leading to cell degeneration, we must never neglect the regular intake of oxygen. Engage regularly in walking and hiking!

RULE FIVE

Take great care that the cells do not receive any unnecessary physical irritation. The liver, too, should be paid constant attention and given more care than all the other organs. If the liver does not experience any functional upsets or failure, it is impossible for cancer to develop. The liver is the most important bulwark in the fight against cancer, and no cancerous cell degeneration is possible as long as this marvellous laboratory is working properly. We should therefore always make every effort to keep it working efficiently.

RULE SIX

Since the hazardous effects certain rays have on our body cells are known today, we should beware of them. Not only do radium and X-rays constitute a double-edged sword for the cells, but the ever-increasing radiation in the atmosphere plays an important part in cell degeneration. Volcanic areas with high radiation levels can trigger cancer, depending on the individual's predisposition and susceptibility. I have seen cases where lymphogranulomas developed within a few days, especially in women who had received treatment in hot volcanic springs and with fango (mud) packs. Cosmic rays, which together with the so-called earth rays can cause tensions, are also able to trigger cancer if someone is exposed to them regularly over a period of time. We should always be aware of these dangers and avoid them where possible.

RULE SEVEN

The endocrine glands play an important part in our body and should be cared for so as to keep them functioning normally. Maintaining the right balance will prevent unnecessary problems. Interestingly, there are some people who have such a favourable predisposition, despite the unbalanced and turbulent times we live in, that they experience no problems with the functioning of their glands, particularly the sex glands. However, not everyone is so fortunate and well-balanced; there are some people who push themselves too hard, while others suffer constantly from inhibitions. Both tendencies are responsible for unnatural conditions of irritation and are harmful to the cells. Excessive irritation and tension encourage cancerous degeneration of the cells if they occur repeatedly. In this case, harmony in one's emotional life is a necessary requirement if one wants to keep healthy.

FURTHER HINTS

If you make a determined effort to observe the seven rules given above and take care to put them into practice, you need have no fear of falling victim to cancer. Following this advice will benefit the general condition, even for those who may have inherited unfavourable tendencies and susceptibilities. It is true that it is not always easy today to lead a life that is in harmony with these rules, but when you consider the pain and trouble you can save yourself and those close to you, surely the effort would be worthwhile!

Even if someone already has cancer toxins in the blood, or perhaps even a tumour, he should not give up hope. A thorough change of life-style and diet can be a purposeful and decisive step towards a cure. Good natural remedies lend added support in this direction. *Petasites* preparations, for example *Petaforce*, have often reinforced the healing process.

It is, however, a different story if the liver is already affected. In this case, not only one battle but the whole fight is lost, and there is little point in continuing to bother the patient with diets and treatments. True, for some patients it has been possible to stabilise the condition even where the liver was affected, but where all other circumstances were favourable, although it must be said that such cases are rare exceptions.

PREVENTION IS EASIER AND BETTER THAN CURE

People whose parents have succumbed to cancer, even one parent, usually inherit a certain predisposition to the illness. Anyone falling into this category would be advised to be doubly careful and go over the seven rules at least once every three months. This review will help you to make the necessary changes while there is still time for it. Mind you attend to this early enough, so that you will not fall victim to a terminal illness.

Unfortunately, only a few people heed the warning and take preventative measures when they are young. And it is for their sakes, for those who are grateful for the right directives, that I consider it worthwhile giving the above advice. If you follow the recommendations, you will live to see that prevention and caring for your body will pay rich dividends. It is better, less expensive and less painful than first succumbing to sickness and then trying to combat it by means of costly and often useless therapies. If this principle is true of any illness, it is certainly so in the case of cancer.

Remedies for Cancer

Although there is no such thing as a specific remedy for cancer, and probably never will be, nature makes some helpful plants available to us. These plants are able to aid and exert a prophylactic effect. The plants described below represent just a sample of those that can be useful. Additional information can be found in my book *Cancer – Fate or Disease of Civilisation?*

BUTTERBUR

Known by the botanical name *Petasites officinalis*, butterbur has achieved wide recognition as a remedy. In the first place, its antispasmodic effect eases tension in the cells and reduces the patient's susceptibility to pain. Secondly, it has an anticarcinogenic effect. No wonder that some doctors claim to have noticed fewer cases of metastases after operations when the patient had been given a good *Petasites* preparation before and after surgery. As butterbur is a nonpoisonous plant, it can be taken in large amounts without any danger of side effects. Some cases are known where this simple plant, in conjunction with a change of life-style on the part of the patient, has produced remarkable results.

MISTLETOE

This peculiar parasitic plant likes to live on certain trees and is also known as *Viscum album*. It, too, has proved to be a good plant remedy for cancer, because of its effect of stimulating the cell metabolism. As this is generally very weak in cancer and arthritis patients, mistletoe preparations are beneficial for both diseases. Mistletoe can be given in the form of drops or by injection.

CELANDINE AND OTHER REMEDIES

Celandine, also known by its botanical name *Chelidonium*, is a further effective help, as are preparations made from *Podophyllum*, *Boldocynara*, *Lycopodium*, *barberry* and all other plants that stimulate the liver. Cancer patients always suffer from liver insufficiency, so it is understandable why plants that stimulate the activity of the liver can help to improve the patient's condition. Since there is usually a vitamin C deficiency as well, we recommend that the patient take *Bio-C-Lozenges*, in addition to a diet rich in vitamins.

ECHINACEA

This plant has proved its reliable effect on all kinds of inflammation and is therefore a good supportive remedy. It can be used internally and externally.

COMFREY (WALLWOSAN)

Comfrey (*Symphytum officinale*) is a fine pain-reliever in cases of cancer of the stomach and intestines. For this reason it is usually prescribed for diseases of these organs.

LACTIC ACID PREPARATIONS

In more recent times research has shown that lactic acid is also beneficial in caring for cancer patients and should be considered for this purpose. *Molkosan, sauerkraut juice and vegetable juices* taken alternately will improve the patient's condition and quench his thirst, however great it may be.

Bacteria and Viruses

These two types of micro-organism have been the subject of many books and lectures. There are even university institutes wholly devoted to research into them. So what do we know – and what can we do about them?

Bacteria

Bacteria are very tiny, but are discernible under a microscope. Even though they have been thoroughly researched, they are still as dangerous as ever. Just think of the bacteria that at one time caused such dreadful diseases as the bubonic plague, cholera, typhoid fever and tuberculosis. Improved sanitation has helped to eradicate the epidemics that in medieval times decimated entire towns and villages, so we have cause to thank hygiene, including effective sewage systems and clean drinking water, for stemming the tide.

In the past, tens of thousands used to die of tuberculosis. As recently as fifty years ago consumption, as it used to be called, was still considered more dangerous than cancer because men and women were carried off in the bloom of their youth. Happily, a change of life-style, healthier housing and living conditions, more nutritional food rich in calcium and vitamins, breathing oxygen-rich air and exposure to plenty of sunlight were found to be the means to almost eradicate tuberculosis. Moreover, the patients who were released from sanatoriums as cured would have developed an immunity to the disease. The bacteria would have been encapsulated and rendered ineffective and if the patients continued to observe certain guidelines they would be unlikely to suffer a return of the disease.

The important thing in protecting oneself against bacteria is, therefore, to strengthen the body's defences – the immune system. A deficiency in vital substances or nutrients, as well as unhealthy external conditions, can weaken this wonderful defence system or even destroy it. Expressed in military terms, this would mean creating a weak position in an otherwise well-protected and defended front line. The enemy would be able to penetrate where the defences were down – and so it is with the immune system in its fight against invading bacteria.

Viruses

For a long time the existence of viruses remained unknown, perhaps for the reason that they are much smaller than bacteria and invisible even under an ordinary microscope. However, since the invention of powerful ultramicroscopes and electron microscopes it has been possible to use more sophisticated methods of investigation and make viruses visible. We have therefore been able to learn more about what they do and the dangers they pose to man and beast. In the case of bacteria, specific medicines have been developed that retard and stop their multiplication and growth, in some cases actually destroying them. But viruses are much tougher and in no way affected by, say, antibiotics. Little has so far been achieved in finding a way to combat them successfully.

MY OWN EXPERIENCE

Some twenty years ago, one of my patients displayed certain symptoms which made me suspect a virus as being the cause of her illness. The woman, a Yugoslavian, complained about unnatural tiredness, accompanied by headaches, susceptibility to colds and catarrh, loss of appetite and intestinal trouble. It seemed as if everything in her body was upset. Her symptoms reminded me of a condition I had read about in a medical publication, for which a virus was to blame. The fact that all known herbal and homoeopathic remedies had failed to bring her relief strengthened my suspicion that nothing but this specific virus could be responsible for her condition.

The syndrome observed in the patient matched the symptoms attributed to the cytomegalovirus. However, as I wanted to be absolutely certain I sent the lady to a hospital where the laboratory was headed by a virologist I knew personally. I explained to him that I suspected the cause of her problem to be the cytomegalovirus. He did not think so, however, especially as the symptoms were not so obvious to him that he could confirm my opinion there and then. Nevertheless, he agreed to do a blood test. To his great astonishment what I had suspected proved to be true.

I then asked him what he would recommend to help the patient, and he suggested building up and improving her general condition of health since there was no specific remedy to combat the virus.

TRIAL WITH NATURAL REMEDIES

I had no choice but to try out the remedies I knew and had available. To strengthen the immune system and regenerative mechanism I prescribed *Echinacea*, a plant that builds up the body's own defences. I can speak from my own experience because when I visited the tropics *Echinacea* helped me to acquire resistance to malaria, which is one of the reasons why I decided on this remedy to fight the virus. Moreover, I put her on *Lachesis 10x*, a snake poison in homoeopathic dilution, in order to tackle the viral toxins. Thirdly, I indicated *bee pollen* and *royal jelly* to support the body with special nutrients. Besides taking these remedies, the patient was asked to change her diet to one made up of raw food, raw vegetable juices, natural brown rice and lactic acid products.

THE RESULT

Three months later the patient was feeling much better. After another hospital check-up, performed by the same virologist, he confirmed that the lady's condition had improved significantly, providing the basis for an encouraging prognosis. In answer to my question as to whether or not it was possible to get rid of the virus altogether, he told me that he did not think so. Then he used an interesting comparison to illustrate what was going on in the patient's body.

THE NATURE DOCTOR

A HELPFUL ILLUSTRATION

The virus, my virologist friend explained, could be seen as a villain who has been thrown out of the house itself but has stayed on the veranda. As soon as the circumstances in the house change – or the body's overall condition deteriorates again – the villain is there ready to slip into the house to cause havoc once more. This illustration reminded me of something that once happened in our own house. A family of sables climbed from the trees into the attic, where they created an awful racket. What could I do but have some of the trees near the roof cut down, and close up every hole through which they could possibly enter. A few years later, however, a creeping plant grew up the wall unnoticed, giving the sables the chance to climb in and become a nuisance yet again. Once more we had to block everything up, but this time we got rid of them for good because we made sure there were no openings left anywhere.

Perhaps this is an odd, not quite scientific, way to illustrate the problem we have with a virus, but it helped me to understand the researcher's point of view.

We have only one option in order to fight pathogenic agents, in this case viruses, for which there is no known antidote or remedy, and that is to support the body in defending itself, by helping to mobilise its defence forces, or mechanisms. Thus, if we want to take up the fight against viruses and win it, we must do all we can to back up the body's own regenerative power. The virologist in the Swiss hospital agreed with me. This is the only correct way to treat viral diseases.

LOSS OF IMMUNITY

We are no longer absolutely in the dark when it comes to treating cancer. There are some biological means that help to normalise the body's weakened defence system without causing undesirable side effects. It is now understood that cancer, the disease, is not restricted to a tumour, that is, a localised problem; rather, it is a chronic ailment affecting the body as a whole. For this reason measures must be taken to detoxify the body. How do we do this? First, we stimulate the liver, the organ whose role it is to filter out toxins. Then there is the need to regularise the intestinal flora. Next, the body must get plenty of oxygen. Finally, the patient requires a natural wholefood diet, with plenty of raw food, brown rice and lactic acid products. In this way we can fight cancer or do much to prevent it. At no time should we consider it an inevitable blow of fate.

With viruses the situation is similar, although less simple, because they usually attack the immune system. Where the body's resistance has been damaged by the sum total of pathogenic effects and an inherited weakness in the immune system, a viral attack is able to destroy what is left of the existing regenerative forces. In such a case, not just one battle but the whole war will have been lost.

AIDS – Worse than Cancer

Acquired Immune Deficiency Syndrome, AIDS for short, is the worst disease known to us that is caused by a virus. Hundreds of thousands of people, all over the world, have been gripped by shock and fear. So far, however, the orthodox medical profession has not found a remedy. Every victim is, in a sense, condemned to death. True, there is a waiting period of 2–5 years before resistance breaks down completely. Death is then caused, not by the destructive virulence of the virus, but by a lack, or loss, of the body's defences, a failure of the regenerative mechanisms, a disease the patient might easily have overcome under normal circumstances.

WHAT PROTECTION IS THERE?

If the media are right, hundreds of thousands of people in the United States and Europe alone have already fallen victim to AIDS. What can be done to prevent it? A widely read American newspaper gave the advice (with which I agree) to lead a morally clean life, rejecting all sexual excesses and other perversions of the body, mind and emotions. This disease has spread mainly, but not exclusively, among those who practise these things, having taken on epidemic proportions. Infection is said to be possible via the mucous membranes, primarily the sex organs. I do not like to write about things like these, I would rather talk about positive aspects of therapies and treatments that are intended to take care of our health and fitness. Still, I may be able to transmit a glimmer of hope, comfort and advice to the fearful.

A GLIMMER OF HOPE

I am aware that virological institutes are working frantically to find an antidote for the ultramicroscopic villain. It is hoped, and it would be good fortune if this hope could be fulfilled, that the search will be successful and that many people will thus be spared great suffering. But what can one do before medical science discovers a specific remedy?

Protection against the virus can only come from the help we give the body by leading a healthy life and by improving and strengthening its general condition.

For this reason the intake of food rich in vital substances, vitamins and minerals, is essential. The food of modern civilisation actually weakens the body, undermines the defences and hinders the system from deploying its forces and displaying its regenerative powers in the first place.

It is important to try and reduce the virus's chances of development as much as possible by eating, pure, alkaline food with a high vitamin content. Doing so, it is likely that the body's own regenerative forces will be built up. I read a newspaper report only recently which confirmed the assumption that a diet made up of such food can bring successful results. The case in question concerned a child born with the AIDS virus whom the doctors at the Robert-Koch-Institute had given two more years, at the most, to live. At the same time they told the mother that the baby's life could possibly be extended a little longer with the help of a vitamin treatment. According to the newspaper article, she followed this advice and every day gave the child two kiwi fruits, two grated apples with lemon juice, rusks and the juice of three oranges, in other words, pure, excess alkaline food with natural vitamins. Every two months she took her child for a check-up at the paediatric clinic. After some time the doctors were able to tell the happy mother that the last examination revealed a negative result – the AIDS virus no longer showed up. The child could be considered cured. Judging by this example, can we not draw the logical conclusion that every AIDS patient should live on only pure fresh food, that is, a diet of fruit and raw food? Besides the fruits mentioned in the article, the patient should also eat avocados, papaya, and perhaps bananas – fruits that are available all the year round.

A well-known tennis player came down with AIDS, and was diagnosed as such by the doctors of St Vincent hospital. This same person was completely cured by means of a special diet high in vitamins but low in protein, a protein-free fruit diet. Today he plays tennis with the same verve and vitality as he did before.

PLANT REMEDIES TO BACK UP TREATMENT

There are a number of plants that I have come to know for their efficacy in combatting viral diseases: *garlic, horseradish, bear's garlic (ramsons), butterbur (Petasites), lichen-acid-containing Usnea, and Echinacea, the purple coneflower.* I can vouch for the good results achieved with patients with viral infections who had taken these natural remedies, in addition to adopting a sensible and healthy life-style.

It would be worthwhile if doctors were to try these plants when treating their patients. *Echinacea,* in particular, contributed to keeping myself and my friends free from malaria in the tropics, and should therefore be included in any treatment given to those suffering the dreadful viral disease AIDS. Instead of sitting around waiting for the end to come, an experiment could be made involving a complete change of life-style and the indicated plant remedies. It may be that a cure is possible.

There is no doubt the AIDS disease has scared many, above all the young, making them rethink and modify their ethical views, especially their attitudes towards sexual morality. And I appeal whole-heartedly to doctors and dieticians to try everything in their power so that something positive rather than alarming will soon be reported by the media.

Remember, nature is bound to have a way, but it must be sought. And he who seeks can expect to find a solution.

Our Teeth

The importance to our health of having good teeth is still not sufficiently appreciated. It is the same with health in general. We begin to value it only when we have lost it and are sick. Many people think it is enough to know that there are doctors available if they need them, and they do not worry any further. They similarly rely on the dentist if something goes wrong with their teeth, and for this reason they do not give any thought to the importance of keeping their teeth healthy. In a figurative sense, we could call the teeth the front line defences of our body.

Healthy Teeth and their Defence Action

Metaphorical speech being the oldest and most effective way of explaining something, I would like to compare the teeth to armour-plated turrets. The hard outer tooth enamel could be called the armour-plating because the enamel is the toughest tissue of the body, built up of very hard calcium fluoride. The enamel possesses a thick enough layer of calcium fluoride – in our illustration a strong armour-plating – to be able to do justice to all the demands made on it for the usual 60–80 or even more years of our life, provided we have inherited the proper basis for this from our parents, especially if our mother's mineral metabolism was efficient and her body had all the necessary minerals when she was carrying us.

Next to the armour-plating is the calcified tissue called dentine, which can be compared to porous limestone. The dentine is protected by the tooth enamel, the armour-plating mentioned above, and cannot be damaged or injured in any way as long as the enamel is intact.

The canals in the tooth leading to the root are the pulp canals. The larger central part is known as the pulp chamber, the spongy tissue of the tooth containing nerves and blood vessels. In our illustration these canals and chambers might represent crew quarters, from which it is seen to that all operations in the turret are properly directed.

In both the pulp canal and the pulp chamber there is also a breathing system, and a lymphatic and nervous system. The nerves could be compared to the crew manning and operating the test instruments, warning and listening devices, in short, all possible communication instruments and apparatus. Any unusual happenings, any attacks from outside, an unexpected bump, an excessive demand and the like are immediately reported to the central control, figuratively speaking, the headquarters. If a break-in or some other danger is imminent, a warning is sounded – pain sets in. The attackers in this case are bacteria. No doubt the Creator made the nerves, which transmit the feeling of pain, not to torture us but to make us aware that something is wrong in the body. We are then able to do something about the problem.

WHY WE NEED HEALTHY TEETH

We need healthy teeth to enable us to chew well, which is essential for proper digestion. Only if we make full use of our salivary glands will our food be properly assimilated and agree with us. There is a reason, then, why we have six large and many more small salivary glands, which secrete various alkaline substances that are of the utmost importance to the whole digestive process. If food particles are sufficiently insalivated, the later stages of digestion will be made much easier.

It is interesting to note that the teeth stay healthy if they are used correctly and given hard food to chew. This is exactly the opposite of what we know about other instruments, which usually wear out when used a lot. The pressure exerted when biting acts as a kind of stimulus for healthy teeth. The periodontal nerves transmit this stimulus to the blood vessels and more blood is supplied. The increased blood supply means better nutrition and guarantees constant regeneration of the tooth. Thus, anyone who eats hearty meals that force him to chew vigorously strengthens his teeth and keeps them healthy. On the other hand, if you get into the habit of eating primarily gruels, soup and soft food you miss the chance of forcing your teeth to be active and stimulated, laying the groundwork for later tooth decay. Apples are an excellent fruit to eat as they need chewing and their acidic juice also cleanses the teeth.

To keep physically healthy and fit, adopt a good and natural diet and take care that your teeth remain healthy and strong.

Dead Teeth

Unfortunately, it is possible to have dead teeth, and these could be likened to turrets without a crew. Their defences are gone and the enemies from outside are able to invade. No one is left to carry out repairs; no one is there to replace the damaged calcified tissue of the dentine or to take care of regenerating what becomes defective. Such a tooth may be repaired and closed up from outside, but if the dentist does not sterilise everything properly, bacteria may spread again inside the tooth and sooner or later cause its destruction. The only protection still left is the cementum around the root. Also surrounding the root is a network of nerves and blood vessels.

WHY CORRECT NUTRITION IS NECESSARY

Not only solid food but also wholefood is necessary to keep the teeth healthy, for the blood can only supply the nutrients and materials needed for regeneration and repair that it has available. If we do not take in enough calcium, even the best machinery ready to do the repair work cannot function because the necessary substances are lacking. A bricklayer will not be able to build a strong wall if he does not use enough lime or cement in his mortar. The same principle applies to our teeth. Deficiencies of calcium, vitamin D and fluoride, besides other vital substances, tend to prepare the way for weakness and degeneration.

Such degenerative symptoms, particularly dental caries and also degenerative effects apparent in the jawbone, are the consequences of our modern denatured food, our eating habits and life-style. People in less developed parts of the world, who have not yet been affected by modern ways but live a healthy natural life, generally possess fine teeth. There are indeed some primitive tribes, as we might describe them, who would provide a dentist with no work whatsoever. He could merely admire their beautiful teeth. For one thing, these people have inherited good teeth with the necessary armour-plating of excellent enamel.

So if you have children, see to it that they eat plenty of food rich in calcium and, in addition, give them a calcium preparation such as *Urticalcin*, the well-known nettle calcium supplement, as required. Should anything abnormal be noted, for instance oversensitivity to heat and cold, or perhaps painfulness when chewing, a visit to the dentist is called for. Any minor damage may then be quickly put right. Bacteria can easily invade once the protective cover or armour-plating, the tooth enamel, is broken, however small the crack may be. They cannot eat the enamel since it is too hard, but they enter the cracked protective surface and settle in the dentine, proliferate and ultimately destroy it. It is therefore of the utmost importance to act quickly. Do not wait until you get toothache, but visit your dentist regularly for a check-up and repair of minor damage, if necessary. Following this advice can help you to avoid the discomfort of a nerve treatment and dead teeth, which, after all, constitute a health hazard. The subject of caring for your teeth is discussed further in a later section (see pages 303–8).

THE CONSEQUENCES OF DEAD TEETH

As the expression indicates, a dead tooth is completely lifeless. Since it can no longer be regenerated, bacteria are able to form pus and abscesses. It may seem strange, however, that pain, or a toothache, is not always felt. An X-ray picture will disclose the presence of a granuloma full of bacteria at the root apex, or there may be an abscess full of pus. Still, even this unfortunate condition does not always cause pain. These abscesses or cysts scatter toxins, triggering headaches, dizziness, indisposition, rheumatic pains, neuralgias, neuritis and many other illnesses. The effect on some people is such that they never again feel quite well, and the slightest overexertion or change in the weather will make them feel indisposed. Good natural remedies and other medicines often give little relief, because the problems I have just described return again and again, making the person feel depressed. Of course, these symptoms may stem from a liver disorder. Conversely, the cysts may affect the liver if they happen to be in the teeth, tonsils or certain other parts of the body. When the dangerous abscesses are tackled by resection of the dental root, or the bad teeth are simply pulled out, the patient is suddenly freed from all his problems.

I have known patients who lived a healthy life and were never really ill, yet they were not really well either, because they did nothing about their dental abscesses. They would suffer from head-aches, slight indisposition, excessive tiredness or pains somewhere in the body, but these would temporarily disappear with treatment. The condition always changed, however, when the abscesses were finally dealt with. These patients would suddenly feel better than they had done for years.

It is especially important for those of us who live in our so-called civilised society to take much better care of our teeth than we generally do. For this, of course, we need to have a good dentist. However, there are other things we need to do in order to care properly for our teeth. These requirements are dealt with below.

Care of the Teeth

THE DISADVANTAGES OF CIVILISATION

After considering the facts, it will be agreed that from the point of view of our health, care of the teeth is more important than any beauty or body care. Of course, when I was a little boy I am afraid I heartily disagreed with the idea of cleaning my teeth every day. It seemed enough of a restriction to my freedom to have to wash daily and keep blowing my nose. Why should I be bothered with even more work? Couldn't my teeth keep themselves clean? I wondered. Indeed, I thought they could, because I had heard of primitive tribes who live a natural life, close to nature, and they had beautiful teeth without ever having to brush them or give them special care. But eventually I learned that on account of our modern diet and way of living, we have lost many of the advantages that those primitive peoples still enjoyed. My parents told me that bacteria settle between the teeth, attack and destroy them. They get into every crack, multiply and eventually cause tooth decay. The questions remained, 'How do primitive people cope with bacteria? Why do their teeth remain healthy and beautiful? Are the bacteria unable to invade, multiply and cause decay, just as they do in civilised people?'

303

THE ADVANTAGES OF PRIMITIVE PEOPLES

Of course, primitive people in unspoilt areas of the world are exposed to the same tooth-destroying bacteria that affect people in the industrialised world, but the enamel of their teeth is harder and does not allow the bacteria to penetrate and lodge in crevices; that is why their teeth remain healthy and resistant. But why are the teeth of those people so excellent? The answer is simple: their food is unadulterated, natural, not like ours that has been changed, refined, denatured, bleached and adulterated – to our detriment. Our faulty nutrition impairs healthy resistance, not only in the teeth but also in the bones, indeed the entire organism; we have become soft.

Solid, unrefined food as originally produced by nature enables those primitive peoples to use their teeth for the purpose originally intended by our Creator. They use their teeth in such a way that the function of chewing is properly exercised, and the teeth are cleaned at the same time. Wholewheat bread and bread or cakes made with whole corn require vigorous chewing, and so does all the rest of the hard food that makes up their diet. Thorough chewing guarantees a maximum health benefit from the outside, while healthy nutrients make for internal health, vigour and resistance.

A NATURAL DIET AND DENTAL HYGIENE

A healthy, unrefined diet will supply sufficient calcium, fluoride and other important elements to keep the dentine and enamel in perfect condition. Primitive people have such beautiful teeth because their crude diet supplies all the elements they need to preserve their teeth in a healthy condition, whereas we, with our denatured food, suffer from all sorts of deficiencies. Beautiful teeth do not depend on being Chinese, African or Indian or whether you are white, yellow, black or brown; they depend on a natural diet. The proof of this is found among North American blacks who have been living in that modern, industrialised society for some generations. It is only since they left their native lands and adopted the diet and customs of their new environment that their teeth have begun to show signs of deterioration. Now dentists have plenty of work among the blacks of Chicago or Virginia. Their healthy resistance has disappeared and those who turn their backs on natural foods have to care for and brush their teeth just as much as anyone else. Anyone who adopts the life-style and eating habits of our modern 'civilised' society becomes prone to disease, including, of course, bad teeth.

Should we clean our teeth? Certainly we should, for we no longer possess natural resistance to tooth decay and therefore have to assist nature mechanically to remove all food particles, plaque and undesirable bacteria from the surface and crevices of the teeth.

To ensure healthy teeth, we should adopt a natural diet. This is the first decisive step. It is essential to have a wholesome diet of natural foods and also plenty of exercise in the open air and sunshine. The teeth will then be able to do their work for an entire lifetime. As regards proper nutrition, it is important to choose wholegrain or wholemeal (wholewheat) bread that contains rye in addition to wheat, since rye is rich in fluoride which is necessary for the development of strong tooth enamel. Among some tried and tested breads are 'Walliser Roggenbrot' (100 per cent rye bread made in Switzerland), Vogel's wholegrain flake bread, Risopan crispbread and 'Waerlandbrot'. Other similar breads may also be available in your locality.

However, because our bodies have become degenerated through the introduction of modern foods, we must, as a second step, go in for special tooth care. Even if we occasionally eat some black rye or wholegrain bread, this will not make our teeth any healthier. True, there are still some people who have good teeth, even among Europeans, but if an analysis is made of their diet it will be found that it is based on wholefoods and that they follow a natural way of life. In the mountain areas of the Swiss canton Valais the people still eat a famous dark rye bread, and this is no doubt one reason why they seem to have excellent teeth. Vigorous chewing gives the jaw muscles plenty of exercise, and this kind of natural massage assures better blood circulation. There must be other countries, too, where in some areas the population lives primarily on natural food and has good teeth as a result.

When I was a young man in my late teens I too had bad teeth as the result of an unnatural diet. I then changed my eating habits and within three years my dentist assured me that my teeth showed definite signs of hardening. At the end of six years, he congratulated me on my change of diet and said that my teeth were in excellent condition, with hard and healthy dentine. Now, in my old age, I still have the same good teeth I had in my youth. So, to safeguard the teeth, all refined foods should be avoided. To start with, white sugar and flour should definitely be left out of your diet. Every school and every dentist's waiting room should display comical educational posters, acting as constant reminders of the two enemies of strong teeth, white sugar and white flour, and the cartoons on these posters should become as popular as Mickey Mouse. Such vivid warnings would make our schoolchildren constantly aware of the agents responsible for bad teeth. Who knows, maybe they would even contribute to banning the culprits from our tables!

BASIC RULES FOR CARE OF THE TEETH

A few rules for care of the teeth might be useful to everyone. First of all, the teeth should be cleaned every day with a good and simple cleansing agent. It can be a toothpaste that does not contain any strong chemicals, for example *Rosemary Toothpaste*, or it can be ashes or some other natural material. Every small sign of decay should be given immediate attention so that you will be spared the problem of dead teeth. Small defects when neglected may result in having to kill the nerve, and years ago that was often the practice.

A tooth without a nerve is a dead tooth and, in a manner of speaking, becomes a foreign body in the mouth. Such a tooth must be watched carefully, for it may precipitate the formation of granulomas, ideal nesting grounds for germs. A little thing like that can endanger a person's general health because the bacteria and metabolic toxins discharged into the bloodstream can cause various ailments, although the teeth themselves may not be painful at all. Nothing seems to be wrong with the teeth, yet the person may suffer from rheumatic fever and does not know why. Arthritis may develop, possibly leading to rheumatoid arthritis and other serious ailments, all stemming from granulomas or abscesses. Some of the other problems attributed to them include cardiac pains and troubles, palpitations when walking upstairs or uphill, kidney and liver dysfunctions, as well as other organic upsets – all without our knowing what the cause might be.

American doctors are generally credited with the discovery of these problems emanating from germ-ridden dead teeth. The sad thing was that in the case of articular rheumatism, rheumatic fever, some dentists short-sightedly extracted not only the dead teeth with their abscesses, but also all the good ones. This, of course, was wrong, although many doctors worldwide followed this method. The error was later recognised, but not before a lot of damage had been done.

An acquaintance of mine, a railway employee, was forced to have all his excellent teeth extracted because a doctor had decided that they were the cause of his heart trouble. He was unwilling to have this done, but gave in because he was afraid the insurance company would refuse to continue his policy. Unfortunately, the removal of his teeth did not cure his heart problem. A nature cure did eventually succeed in doing so, but, alas, nature treatments, however effective, could not bring back his extracted teeth.

DENTAL TREATMENT

Never deceive yourself into thinking that a small dental defect will eventually correct itself. Visit your dentist right away. Have your teeth checked regularly and have the dentist look out especially for any dead teeth.

A capable dentist, at the first sign of articular rheumatism or heart trouble, for example, will X-ray the teeth to see if an abscess may be the cause of the trouble. The effective treatment of this type of inflammation requires professional knowledge and skill. If you have waited too long, so that you need large fillings, be careful as to the material used. Some people experience unpleasant side-effects when certain amalgams are used to fill a cavity, chief among which are mercury and silver. Depending on the individual's constitution and potential resistance, these amalgams can trigger heart trouble, a dazed state or headaches, making him unable to perform mental work efficiently. These symptoms persist until the amalgam fillings are removed. Once that is done, the problems that may have been plaguing a person for years usually disappear. Some material resembling the tooth substance should be used to fill the pulp canals, wherever possible. Gold crowns have often proved their worth, too, but they are not suitable for everyone, especially those sensitive to metals. The reaction in this case may be a mild form of heart trouble. Remove the gold and the problem goes too. If such a sensitivity to metals exists, the dentist cannot use them for your fillings, particularly silver, since its effect is worse than that of gold. However, the degree of sensitivity will vary from one person to another, depending on the individual's constitution, especially the lymphatic system.

When fitting a crown, a good dentist will take great care to see that it fits well. It must come well up into the neck of the tooth, leaving no space, as this would become a breeding ground for micro-organisms. Neither should a crown be too long, as this might cause irritation and inflammation. The solution to these problems depends upon the dentist's skill. A loose crown can lead to suppurative conditions and an abscess formation which, when prematurely closed in, can cause the most dreadful pain imaginable because of the gases that are produced that have no way out. Under such painful circumstances the taking of anodyne drugs will be unavoidable. A further consequence of incorrect treatment could be the infiltration of bacterial toxins into the system, a situation that is not only bad for health but can endanger one's life. The heart may be affected; it may even stop beating momentarily. Great skill and experience in natural treatment methods would then be required to eradicate such an infiltration.

It should be quite clear from this explanation that it is foolish to take such problems lightly and to neglect seeking treatment at the earliest opportunity, even if you think you are too busy and have no time for it straight away. On the other hand, it is also important to consult an extremely experienced dentist because his knowledge will be indispensable in recognising the problem and subsequently providing the proper treatment.

Periodontal Disease (Periodontitis)
Despite any amount of skill and experience, it is extremely hard for a good dentist to treat the ever-increasing number of cases of periodontal disease with more than limited success. This disease, characterised by chronic gingivitis (gum inflammation) and the gums becoming detached from the tooth surface, presents a difficult problem for dentist and patient alike. In fact, the teeth may become loose and fall out (periodontitis).

Massaging the diseased gums with *Echinaforce*, in alternation with *rhatany tincture* or a *herbal water containing rhatany and myrrh*, is a partial solution to the problem. In addition to cleaning the teeth, the necessary daily dental hygiene and massaging of the gums, take *Urticalcin*, in order to supply the body with additional calcium, and adopt a diet rich in vitamins and minerals.

Periodontitis is definitely not an infectious disease; it is the result of a deficiency, an avitaminosis, and this, of course, can arise quite easily if we live on modern refined foods. It is quite a different story among the American Indians and Africans, for example, who have not abandoned their traditional natural diet. Gingivitis and periodontitis are unknown among them.

Improvement can often be noticed when the patient changes his diet to a natural one, eating plenty of raw foods and avoiding products made with white flour and white sugar. However, patience will be necessary, since it will take time for the benefits of a change in diet to manifest themselves. Still, even though you might have to wait several months before the problem disappears, you will be all the more grateful and happy in the end. Alternatively, if you do not see fit to change your diet to a natural one, you can, in time, expect to face bigger problems, in spite of your dentist's efforts. The disease can spread to the jaw and cause you to lose all your teeth.

Beautiful Hair – a Natural Adornment

Visitors to oriental countries cannot help but notice the many, mainly young, Buddhist monks clad in orange robes and with their heads shaved. They are to be seen everywhere. Without even thinking you will compare them to the ordinary people with their beautiful dark hair. You will be convinced that hair is indeed an adornment. We in the West like blond, brown and black hair; even auburn or red hair can be very appealing. Women with auburn hair were considered especially beautiful in ancient Greece. But when we compare the thick bluish-black hair of the Indians in the Americas and India, and other peoples, it is not easy to say whether it is because of mere admiration or a little envy that we consider their bountiful hair so desirable. The inhabitants of those lands do not yet see any need to spend money on preserving their beautiful locks. Baldness is a peculiarity predominant among white people. It must be an acquired characteristic, for baldness simply cannot have been the Creator's original purpose; it is presumably a consequence of civilisation.

The Structure of the Hair

The anatomic structure of the hair, like so many other things in the body, is a technical miracle. Although the hair has no feeling, it is not dead matter either. Perhaps it could best be compared to a plant with a bulb-shaped root. The hair root, or bulb, is embedded in the skin, about 3–5 mm deep (⅛–⅕ inch), and is connected by blood vessels from which it receives the nutrients necessary for the hair to grow. The daily rate of growth is about ¼–½ mm. A tightly knit network of lymphatics envelops the hair roots. The salty lymph is thought to act as an electrolyte in the electrical function of hair. Strong electric charges in hair cause visible sparks when combing it in the dark. The hair of very excited or ecstatic people lights up in the dark and when photographed the effect is seen as a kind of halo. Great mental disturbance and agitation is observable in the hair, when viewed under a microscope, as notches of variable depths. So it is possible, for example, to discover if someone has had a nervous breakdown the previous year.

A medical book I once read described hair as a 'barometer of the soul'. In fact, extreme shock can make one's hair turn grey in a short time. Some people who were buried under rubble when conscious and could only be freed some days later, emerged grey-haired. When I visited a hospital in Guatemala I also observed Indian children whose long black hair showed strains of white, in this case caused by vitamin deficiencies. Their bodies lost the ability to produce black pigment the moment the deficiency disease had started, and the colour of the hair remained white as long as the disease lasted. Only after recovery did the colour return to its original black.

We can see, then, that the hair not only mirrors what goes on in our mind but also our physical condition. For instance, during pregnancy some women's hair becomes very oily due to increased activity of the sebaceous glands. But once the child is born the function of the glands returns to normal. This again goes to show that the condition of the hair is closely linked with one's physical condition. The same principle applies in the case of animals. A shiny coat in dogs and horses is a sign of good health, but if it is dull or rough looking, it is high time for the vet to look for the underlying problem in the animal's system.

A healthy hair is strong, being able to support a weight of about 80 g (just under 3 oz) without snapping. A diseased hair, however, will tear when a weight of 30–40 g (about 1½ oz) is suspended from it. The healthy pigtail of a Chinese or Indian woman is able to support about 2½–3 tons before it snaps. Of course, the resistance of a single hair depends also upon its relative thickness. People who live close to nature have thicker and stronger hair than those who do not. Generally speaking, the more refined our food and life-style, the finer will be our hair.

When a hair is pulled out, the root, held fast in the dermis, is able to manufacture another hair shaft. However, eczema and other diseases affecting the scalp can make this part degenerate and die, so that the affected areas become bald. Typhoid fever is usually responsible for the loss of all hair, but the hair bulb does not actually die and the hair has been known to grow back even more luxuriantly after recovery, when the capillary vessels and lymphatics have returned to their normal function.

Hair Colour
The colour of the hair is manufactured near the hair roots, where an inner layer of cells contains pigments of various colours. That

310

is why there are so many shades of hair, from blond to red or black. Hair colour is part of an individual's genetic make-up. True, the hairdresser can use chemicals to change your natural shade to one that is completely different. Nevertheless, the original colour will return at the roots as the hair continues to grow. So, if your hair is dyed or bleached and you do not wish it to be known, you will have to see your hairdresser regularly for a touch-up. It has become the fashion to change one's hair colour according to whim, but this may not always be appreciated by the passport control at international borders, for example, unless you have the entry 'hair colour' altered accordingly. Irrespective of the modern extremes and changes, the natural variety of hair colours and characteristics is just as lovely as the charming variety of shape and colour seen in butterflies, birds, fish and other marine creatures, not forgetting the beauty of flowers.

Turning grey seems to be somehow connected with the activity of the sex glands. The hormone production of these glands diminishes with advancing age and the hair seems to go grey at the same rate. As already mentioned, however, dramatic mental and emotional shock, as well as continual stress and worries, can also be responsible for premature greying. It is often noticeable at the same time that the activity of the gonads is weakened. It could be genetic that some people turn grey in the bloom of youth. Unfortunately, however, grey hair does not usually suit the person's youthful looks. It is different with a face wrinkled as a result of rich experience and a hard life; silver-grey hair in such a person often seems a fitting crown.

Care of the Hair

Natural beauty calls for care if it is to remain, and this principle applies to our hair too. The best care we can give it is a natural way of life with plenty of exercise in the open air and a sensible diet. Remember, the hair is a reflection of our general condition of health.

Since hair contains silica, iron, copper, arsenic, manganese and sulphur, it stands to reason that plants in which these elements are found prove to be excellent for its care. Naturally blond people will find that washing their hair with *camomile* and then applying *onion hair tonic* is a superb treatment. Dark-haired people achieve better results with *birch* or *nettle* lotions. If you rinse your hair with diluted *Molkosan* (3 tablespoons to 1 litre/1¾ pints of water), it will retain its natural brilliance.

311

For care of the scalp, and to combat hair loss, massage it with *Bioforce Cream*, preferably a day before washing it. This natural cream contains lanolin, genuine St John's wort oil and the extracts of fresh plants. If fungal disease has caused a loss of hair, dab the affected areas with diluted Molkosan and, after drying, dust with *Urticalcin* powder. This treatment usually helps to get rid of the infection in a short time.

Excessively oily hair is often a problem for young people around the age of puberty. In the case of girls, this is generally due to a temporary disruption of the ovarian function. In order to help, the cause must be treated; *warm underwear* is recommended and *warm herbal sitz baths* are necessary, taken every night until relief is achieved. Some older men try to keep their hair by using expensive tonics, but these preparations often benefit the manufacturers and advertisers more than those who would like to see an end to their bald pate. Really, all is in vain, because once the hair bulbs have gone, no new hair can grow.

Most people look after their hair in one way or another, even though they may not have grasped the idea that the basic care and treatment has to be from inside the body itself. In other words, by eliminating any existing internal deficiencies, the appearance of the hair will improve. I often hear from patients who have taken silica and a biological calcium preparation who tell me, 'My hair is beautiful again.' They are elated and surprised at the same time.

External care will no doubt benefit your hair to some extent, and so will a good hair tonic. However, if you do not see to it that you put your 'internal house', your body, in order, and do not take in sufficient calcium and silica, all external treatments will be of little use. And it is really quite easy to do something about it. The usual problem is lack of calcium and silica, but if a woman's hair is too greasy, her hormone production is poor. Then it is important to treat the hormone glands, perhaps by taking a good homoeopathic preparation such as *Ovarium 3x* and regular *sitz baths* in order to assure good circulation. If the stagnation is bad, *Aesculaforce* will help rectify the trouble. Proceeding in this way, there will be an indirect beneficial influence on the hair. Moreover, if you follow this treatment you will not merely benefit your hair; the general condition of your health will improve, since many other body functions depend on the proper functioning of the glands.

HAIR AND SCALP LOTIONS AND HAIR RESTORERS

There are all kinds of hair and scalp lotions advertised and no doubt some of them may be quite good. However, there is one remedy that is always available and does not cost much; it is also the best possible hair tonic and restorer. It is the common *onion*. Onions contain sulphur and this natural sulphur is an excellent skin lotion. If you have any hair or scalp problems, take half a raw onion and rub it well into the scalp before washing your hair. This treatment is very effective and will stimulate hair growth. If you do not feel like using raw onions, use an *onion hair lotion*. For better results use a hair nutrient as well, *lanolin*, which contains vitamin F. In its natural state pure lanolin (*Adeps lanae*) is too thick and sticky, so that it has to be processed or at least mixed with oil. *Bioforce Cream* is such a simple preparation. Incidentally, lanolin (wool fat) is not obtained from sheep's meat but from sheep's wool. It is certainly biologically appropriate if we use the things nature provides for certain purposes. Since lanolin serves to keep the sheep's wool, hair and skin in good condition, it can be of service for our hair and skin too. My own successful experiences of using lanolin have proved this assumption to be true. Of course, *nettles*, in the form of an infusion or a fresh plant extract, provide us with an excellent hair tonic, especially in the case of skin eruptions on the scalp. Many people recommend *birch leaves* too, but the best tonic of all, I believe, is the onion.

So if you wish to have a healthy scalp and beautiful hair, there are plenty of remedies from which to choose. The ones I have just mentioned will no doubt give good results.

The Skin

The Functions of the Skin

Not everyone is aware of the fact that the skin is an organ just as vital as the kidneys, stomach and intestines, and even as essential as the liver. A person would die in a few hours without the function of his skin, and that is much quicker than if his stomach and intestines were to be taken out. One third of the blood in the human body is to be found in the capillary vessels in the skin. In an adult the skin covers an area of approximately 2 square metres (21 square feet), and it is therefore one of the largest organs of the body. One square centimetre (0.155 square inch) contains about three million cells and a number of tiny structures whose functions are essential to good health. We do not feel the cold as acutely as heat and therefore feel less pain when exposed to severe cold than to extreme heat. This is because every square centimetre of our skin contains two or three structures that register cold sensations and about six times as many that register heat. Depending on the area of the body, there are about 10–20 hairs to every square centimetre, also 12–15 sebaceous glands and 90–120 sweat glands, in accordance with the texture of the skin, whether it has fine or large pores. If all the fine capillaries were to be connected together, they would extend to about 1 km (⅝ mile), and the even finer nerves would be four times as long.

If we touch a piece of material with our fingertips, trying to find out whether it is pure silk or linen, twenty-five tiny structures cooperate to help us test the fabric. We could catch a finger in the door and feel nothing at all if it were not for the 200 sensation structures per square centimetre of skin that communicate the injury to the brain via the sensory nerves. Scalding, burning and a Baunscheidt (stimulation) treatment can cause the formation of large blisters filled with fluid, with the top layer of skin becoming separated from the one beneath it.

The outermost layer is called epidermis and consists of cells. The deep inner layer, the corium or dermis, is much thicker and consists of fibrous tissue. The epidermis has more than twenty cell layers that contain no blood vessels, which is why the skin does not bleed when it is rubbed off, nor produces any sensation of pain. However, when the dermis, which lies under the epidermis, is touched or brought into contact with water, there is an immediate reaction. When engaged in physical work, handling earth, sand, lye and the like, soapy water rubs off several layers of the epidermis when the hands are subsequently washed. But on the following day there will already be the same number of layers as before, because the epidermis is continually replaced from underneath. Once this function is disturbed, we get hard and horny skin or abnormal flaking, with loose scales of dry, dead skin, as is so often the case with the scalp. If you wear the same underwear for too long, the offensive smell is due mainly to millions of dead skin cells and dried sweat.

THE SEBACEOUS GLANDS

Our skin is like living leather, with a built-in automatic lubrication system in the sebaceous glands that becomes active in accordance with the skin's needs. Dry skin (lacking oil) is extremely sensitive, making one much more susceptible to colds and infections, and also to radiation damage. When washing with soap, not only is the dirt removed but sebum is dissolved at the same time. This means that the skin is deprived of the necessary oil and its protective function is diminished. For this reason it is especially important in the winter to use a good skin oil after washing with soap. Experience has shown that *St John's wort oil* is the best skin care oil known to us; it is truly excellent for the skin and especially for the capillaries and nerves embedded in it. However, since it is rather greasy it should be mixed with essential oils from plants, which provide the added bonus of enhancing the soothing effect of the St John's wort oil. We have produced such an excellent mixture with our orangy-red-coloured *Skin Oil*. It would be a good idea to keep a bottle in your bathroom on account of its importance in skin care and as a massage oil.

If there is an insufficient secretion of the sebaceous glands, causing the skin to be rough and chapped, the application of a cream containing lanolin is indicated. *Bioforce Cream* is a natural and effective remedial cream that is soon able to revitalise the skin. This tried and tested cream contains lanolin as a base, as well as arnica, sanicle and other medicinal herbs that have proved their worth in skin care. Bioforce Cream is also recommended as a protection against sunburn, with the best results being obtained if it is applied to the skin the day before exposure to the sun.

THE EFFECTS OF SUNLIGHT
Sunlight of a certain wavelength is especially intense in the mountains and by the sea, changing white tyrosine to a brown colour. This pigment, which tans the skin so beautifully, is on the one hand a protection against burns and on the other, a stimulus for the manufacture of antibodies for various infectious diseases, especially tuberculosis and diseases of the throat and chest.

As individuals it seems that we are still not well enough informed about the importance of sunlight for our well-being. Otherwise we would find out just how much or how little can benefit our health. If we were to put our children on a natural diet rich in calcium and let them spend more time in the open air and sunlight, rickets and scrofula (tuberculosis of the lymphatic glands) would be unknown. The ultraviolet rays change ergosterol, which is present in the human body, into vitamin D. And it is generally known that a deficiency in calcium and vitamin D is mainly responsible for rickets and lymphatic problems.

Beauty and well-being are highly dependent upon the general

tone and buoyancy of the body, and both are significantly increased by exposure to sunlight.

With regular exposure to sunlight, the way we look and feel will both improve, giving us a better physical appearance than we had before. It has been found that exposing the skin to sunlight increases, in a manner of speaking, the voltage of the nerve system so that the whole body will experience greater vitality. The skin is like an antenna that absorbs and emits rays. For this reason some people appear to refresh us and others sap our strength; when in the presence of the latter if feels as if all our energy were being drained, tiring us very quickly.

It is interesting to note that sunlight on the skin also heightens the efficiency of our sensory organs. We are able to hear and see better when we let the sun recharge us.

THE SWEAT GLANDS

The manifold functions of the sweat glands have only gradually come to be recognised. The body has about two million sweat glands, each one being about 5 mm (about ⅕ inch) long. Without perspiring, they evaporate 1–1.5 litres (1.7–2.6 pints) of water during the course of a day. If exudation is increased by means of a steam bath, a sauna bath or by living in the tropics, the body is able to give produce up to ten times this quantity of water.

If it were possible to combine all the sweat pores into one single tube, its diameter would be about 25–30 cm (10–12 inches). The size of such a tube makes it easy to understand why so much water is able to escape. Taste a drop of sweat and you will see that it is salty; on litmus paper its reaction is acid. In fact, sweat contains sodium salts, potassium, sulphuric acid, iron, phosphorus, lactic acid and as much urea as one kidney excretes, for which reason the skin could be called the 'third kidney'. The skin can exude arsenic and other poisons, possibly resulting in eczema and other skin eruptions. This shows the wisdom of treating skin problems internally as well as externally. Indeed, it explains why sweat treatments have cured many an illness.

The sweat glands are the units of a temperature control system that makes life in the tropics more bearable. By evaporating water through the sweat glands it is possible to lose heat of up to 500 calories. Keep the functions of the skin in good working order and you will be observing one of the most important rules for good health.

DETRIMENTAL INFLUENCES

When I visited Mesopotamia (between the Euphrates and Tigris rivers) I went to a small museum at the edge of the ruined city of ancient Babylon. There I saw vessels that had been used by women of those bygone times for the storage of oils and creams. According to ancient records, the women even used plants as a basis for the preparation of cosmetics and aromatic oils, as it is still the practice in those areas among Arab and Bedouin women. On another visit, this time to the Indians of the Amazon region, I became acquainted with a plant from which a fatty red dye is obtained. The natives use this extract to paint the body and face and it adheres to the skin for weeks, not even soap being strong enough to remove it.

Beauty culture is almost as old as the human race. The desire to look attractive and to improve one's looks is somehow inborn and it is especially women who take full advantage of the possibilities. However, although cosmetics can be beneficial to the skin and its functions they can also be detrimental, as, for example, are all creams and other preparations that block the pores and impair or stop the exudation of sweat, thus making the skin flaccid and tired looking. Frequent powdering also has the same effect. This explains why some women with tired skin certainly do not look their best without their make-up and can give you quite a shock if you see them first thing in the morning. Without make-up a forty-year-old woman who has been accustomed to applying non-biological cosmetics for many years may look like a seventy-year-old grandmother.

The skin is, and should be, the expression of one's good health, so if you want to help nature a little by caring for your skin, use nothing but biological cosmetics, especially those of natural plant origin, since they stimulate and support the skin's natural functions. Other cosmetics are little more than paint, a veritable deception.

WHEN THE FUNCTIONS OF THE SKIN ARE IMPAIRED

It is understandable that the indigenous peoples of, for example, Africa, South America and the South Sea islands enjoy a better skin function than people who have to wear thick clothing all the time; the native people in hot climates often walk around wearing very little clothing, if any, and their bodies are in constant contact with the air, sunlight and often with muddy water, thus promoting a more efficient skin function. Since in colder regions of the earth it would be impossible to do this, the people living in northern

Peppermint

Europe must have followed a healthy instinctive desire to stimulate their bodies by taking regular saunas and improving the effect even further by cooling down afterwards in cold water or by rolling in the snow, for these customs also keep the functions of the skin in good order and, in turn, benefit the whole body. For the same reason some people with a healthy instinct like to go hiking or swimming. They practise such a sport on a reasonable scale, and if they ski it is done in a sensible way, climbing up the mountain slope instead of using a ski-lift. Other people find greater pleasure and advantage in massaging the body or having it massaged regularly. They use an effective oil that stimulates the functions of the skin, keeping it healthy and in top condition.

Impaired skin functions can have extremely detrimental consequences. When you do not perspire enough you should frequently drink an infusion of *elder flowers, peppermint* and *lovage;* you can take them either in alternation or as a mixed herb tea. In addition, it is recommended to take a weekly *sauna* over an extended period.

Certain parts of the body can sweat excessively, for example the hands, feet and armpits. Is there anything one can do about this condition? Yes there is; you can stimulate the kidneys with a good *kidney tea* containing *Solidago* (goldenrod), and *Nephrosolid kidney drops.* The skin, the so-called 'third kidney', will be relieved as soon as the kidneys themselves have been activated. Additionally, in accordance with the method of the ancient Chinese, take *sage tea* or *Salvia drops* (made from fresh sage) regularly. If the perspiration, especially under the arms, has an unpleasant smell, the best external remedy is *Hamamelis Soap*, which contains witch hazel and thyme, and is an excellent means of supporting the treatment with sage drops or tea. Daily washing with Hamamelis Soap followed by the application of *Bioforce Cream* has also proved successful in cases of feet that sweat excessively.

Dry, scaly skin that is flaking off can be effectively treated by the external application of *St John's wort oil*, in alternation with *Symphytum Cream* or *Symphosan*, which contain comfrey and other herbs. At the same time, take *Violaforce*, a tincture made from heartsease (wild pansy). If the condition is caused by dry psoriasis, you will also have to dab the affected area with *Molkosan* every day. Callouses, causing skin that is as hard as a lizard's, are the result of a disease of the endocrine glands, often connected with avitaminosis (a disease caused by vitamin deficiency), and will require special treatment of the underlying cause.

Sensible Skin Care

It is important that the skin care you practise protects and benefits the skin rather than damages it. The reason why I raise this point is the great number of cosmetics on the market and the persuasive advertising used to sell them. Unfortunately, only very few of this host of products really are kind to the skin. You see, the term 'skin care' only applies correctly to products that protect the skin, are good for it, keep it healthy, indeed, even heal and rejuvenate it. Only skin that functions properly can remain healthy and reflect freshness, perhaps even youthfulness. This requires, first and foremost, good circulation, for this alone guarantees adequate nourishment of the skin.

The second factor to consider is the importance of stimulating the skin's ability to breathe, or at least ensuring that this is not impaired. Cosmetics that block the pores prevent the skin from breathing properly. Such products include powder, certain other cosmetics and many creams containing fat, filling materials and stabilisers which the skin is unable to absorb. If the skin is not treated in the right way, it will begin to look withered and will age prematurely.

In addition to physical treatment to stimulate the circulation and regenerate the skin, there are some first-class plants that can be used for this purpose. *St John's wort* (*Hypericum*) is most frequently indicated and widely used. Its oil-soluble ingredients promote good circulation in the skin because even the finest capillaries will be activated. Plants that contain mucilage, for example, comfrey and some mosses, rejuvenate the skin and, in time, can even soften wrinkles, since the skin tissue will recover its youthful tone. It is therefore most beneficial in the care of your face if you soak some cotton wool with *Symphosan* and dab your face with it after washing, or regularly apply *Symphytum Cream*. Should you suffer from eczema and dry skin, wash the affected areas with an infusion of heartsease (wild pansy) every day.

Badly functioning sebaceous glands tend to dry the skin and require the use of a cream made from plant oils, lanolin and vitamin F. Whatever cream you decide on, it should supply the skin with the substances it lacks. Creams with a vaseline base are not truly satisfactory because vaseline is difficult to saponify and the skin cannot absorb it. *Bioforce Cream*, on the other hand, is excellent for dry, even cracked and chapped skin. I would advise that any rich skin cream be applied sparingly; remember, too, that the skin absorbs oil or fat more quickly in cold weather than in warm weather.

Non-greasy creams based on something other than plant mucilage generally contain ingredients that block the pores. The skin suffers and loses its smoothness if the treatment continues for some time. Oiling the skin, especially after a bath and washing with soap, is to be recommended, since soap removes the natural oil produced by the sebaceous glands. A good oil that stimulates the skin is indispensable in winter and whenever engaging in water sports.

It is imperative that the perfumes added to skin oils and creams be only from natural essential oils. Perfumes derived from chemicals can harm the skin. Also remember that the skin derives no benefit whatsoever from being covered with thick layers of all kinds of cosmetics. Healthy skin only needs a little help when greater demands are put on it through exposure to the sun, water, cold and wind. The wisdom expressed in the saying 'You can have too much of a good thing' applies to the care of your skin and cosmetics too.

SKIN BLEMISHES
No one likes to have skin blemishes, yet it is not uncommon for young people to have a problem with spots, especially at the age of puberty. A spotty face can even create an inferiority complex if

all lotions and creams fail to help. This is another reason why the problem of impure skin should be tackled at the roots. The recommendation to be careful about what one eats and adopt an appropriate diet is not always received with appreciation, but it is necessary, since the trouble is basically the result of ingesting the wrong food.

If you suffer from spots it is of the utmost importance to reduce your intake of fats by half or three-quarters. What is more, take great care to avoid heated fats and oils, animal fats being especially detrimental. Cakes, biscuits, pastries, and all other sweets should be left out of the diet altogether or at least drastically reduced. Eggs, particularly boiled eggs, omelettes and other egg dishes are like poison for impure skin. Only fresh, soft white cheeses such as cottage cheese or quark are digestible, but no other kind of cheese. Raw vegetables, natural brown rice, potatoes boiled in their skins, cottage cheese and horseradish are nutritive and remedial and contain plenty of essential vitamins and minerals. Hot spices tend to make things worse. Some external remedies that have proved very effective are *Echinaforce* and *Molkosan;* one day apply Echinaforce to the affected area, the next day use Molkosan, and continue in daily alternation. Apply a little *Bioforce Cream* to any patches of dry skin. For internal treatment take *Violaforce*, a tincture made from heartsease (wild pansy), and also Echinaforce.

Avoid squeezing spots and blackheads, unless you apply Molkosan to disinfect them right away. Otherwise you will only spread the bacteria, which usually settle in the inflamed skin pores. In other words, if you want to prevent the condition from getting worse you have to be very careful. Also, do not handle or work with turpentine, floor wax, paints and modern detergents; if you have to use them, make sure to wear rubber gloves for protection. *Symphosan* helps to improve and regenerate skin that has large pores and looks withered. Its content of plant mucilage is responsible for this action. And another thing, it is not always advisable to wash with soap. Cleansing the skin with oil and then wiping it with alcohol is often more beneficial for impure skin. Finally, I cannot emphasise strongly enough how important it is to improve your general health by adopting a natural way of life. Your skin will then derive great benefits too.

SHOULD OILS BE USED FOR SKIN CARE?
It is true that nature itself sees to it that our skin receives the oil it needs, and for this purpose we have been given the marvellous

sebaceous glands, which work automatically. I have noticed that people in less developed parts of the world tend to have much oilier skin than we have and they never have to worry about dry skin. Unfortunately, the sebaceous glands of people living in industrialised societies work less efficiently and there is a very good reason for this. The fact that we go against, rather than cooperate with, nature – through our unnatural way of life, our food, clothing and general living conditions, and doing our work shut inside closed rooms that are often overheated in cold weather – discourages the proper functioning of the skin and the sebaceous glands.

To remedy this situation we must give our skin all the help it needs in the form of a good oil. It is advisable to always lubricate the body well before going for a swim, whether in a cool freshwater lake or river or in the sea. Doing this will help the body to retain its warmth and you will not shiver or feel chilled even if the water is cold. I am writing this from personal experience, although I must admit that I have a good basal metabolic rate and circulation, so I do not chill easily. The oil treatment is especially recommended for sensitive people, even more so for the prevention of chills after stepping out of the water.

On the other hand, it is not necessary and does not benefit the skin in any way to smear so much oil on the body so that it looks all greasy. Oil should be used sparingly and massaged well into the skin. Avoid oils that are scented with synthetic perfumes, which make the bathers smell even from a distance. Pure *olive oil* mixed with a little *lemon oil* is a good and inexpensive skin lotion for bathing. If you want to buy a ready-made oil, look for a skin oil that is based on *St John's wort oil*, because this is a most excellent skin-food on account of the lipoids it contains. It is important, when shopping, to ask for a skin oil that is made from natural, red St John's wort oil; reject any oil that is artificially coloured.

Care of the skin requires not only the use of oil but involves common sense when exposing the body to the sun, light and air. An efficient skin function is the basis for proper glandular function and for general well-being.

WRINKLES AND SKIN WITH LARGE PORES
As a rule, smooth skin is a sign of youthfulness and good health and it is not surprising that women in particular make a great effort to maintain this desirable condition for as long as they possibly can. But it is not simply a matter of giving nature a helping hand by applying plenty of powder, make-up and creams. In fact,

the liberal use of such products may achieve just the opposite of what is desired. The real answer lies in taking care in one's youth, living in a natural way and not worrying too much or constantly giving in to anxieties, for we know that stressful problems are wearisome and undermine the body's reserves and well-being. They do indeed age us prematurely and foster the formation of wrinkles. Of course, constant tiredness on account of overwork or pursuing pleasures night after night can also harm one's health and impair one's youthful looks. It is understandable why so many people want to cover up these flaws in their faces by using all kinds of cosmetics.

What is less understandable is why some girls plaster their young and radiant faces with make-up. Make-up is supposed to hide what is ugly, but what could be more beautiful than glowing health, smooth and youthful skin, red cheeks and lips as nature coloured them.

The skin cannot breathe naturally if the pores are blocked with cosmetics. In consequence it degenerates; the pores become larger. It is just as unsightly when the skin begins to slacken early, developing more wrinkles than would be expected as a result of the normal ageing process.

NATURAL BEAUTY CARE

Much time is often wasted in efforts to improve one's looks cosmetically. Yet how much easier it would be to keep the body healthy and, in particular, to take good care of the sex glands right from the start. Their efficiency contributes to maintaining youthfulness longer. For this, sunlight, deep-breathing and exercise are important. Anyone who spends most of his time in heated rooms, rarely moves around in the open air, never goes for walks or hikes or practises some other sport in moderation, should not be surprised if he becomes like a hothouse plant and grows old before his time. Remember, exercise in the open air, perhaps gardening or walking, has much to do with keeping young and fit. Regular showers, alternating between hot and cold water, are also beneficial since they promote good circulation. Recommended, too, are good plant remedies for effective external application, such as *Symphosan* tincture or *Symphytum Cream*, and *Violaforce*. These two remedies, applied in alternation, help to reduce the size of the pores and rejuvenate the skin.

For a reliable skin care programme rub in Symphosan, a tried and tested comfrey preparation, every morning after washing.

Afterwards, as a protection against strong sunlight or biting wind, apply *Bioforce Cream*, which contains lanolin, but it is not necessary to do this daily. Then, before going to bed, soak a cotton pad with *Violaforce* and dab over the whole face. In order to help the sebaceous glands, use a natural skin oil, or the lanolin cream already mentioned, two or three times a week. This treatment may be sufficient for everyday use, provided you are not too exposed to cold and sunshine. It is quite a simple treatment and you will derive great benefit if you take care of your skin like this for a few months. It will look much younger and the pores may even return to normal.

Impetigo

Young people often suffer from pustules all over the face and on the back. The condition may be attributable to a disturbance in the internal hormone secretions and especially associated with the sex glands. At the same time, an external bacterial infection – mainly staphylococci or streptococci – may also be diagnosed. This unpleasant condition usually provokes inhibitions and the sufferer tries to get rid of the disfiguring infection as quickly as possible. So he keeps squeezing the pustules and spots, only to spread the infection with his fingernails. The bacteria keep on spreading, the affected areas and spots growing larger and more inflamed. In time, the lesions secrete a fluid which, when dry, develops into yellowish crusty sores, of a rather unsightly appearance. In the past mercury ointments were used to combat this condition, but in modern times penicillin or sulphonamide creams have become more popular, both of them giving better results than those with a mercury or tar base.

Biological Treatment

This unpleasant condition can also be treated with biological remedies, an excellent one being *Molkosan*. Used externally, this natural, concentrated, whey product, containing 15 per cent lactic acid, will give good results. Soak a cotton pad with it and dab the affected areas. Repeat the application after about five minutes, this time using *Echinaforce* instead. Molkosan kills the bacteria and Echinaforce prevents infection. When a pustule comes to a head and you feel like squeezing it open, do so only with sterilised cotton wool. Immediately afterwards, apply Molkosan and Echinaforce as indicated above. Do not use soap for washing, but cleanse the skin with 45 per cent *alcohol* to which a few drops of *arnica tincture* have been added. When you suffer from pustules your skin is rarely dry, but if it should be, apply *Bioforce Cream* once a week.

Internal treatment is also necessary and you should adopt an appropriate diet. My book *The Liver, the Regulator of Your Health* contains guidelines for such a diet. In addition, you should take Echinaforce regularly. And if you want to reduce the formation of pus, take *Hepar sulph. 10x.* On the other hand, if you want to stimulate it in order to promote faster cleansing, take the same remedy in the fourth potency (4x). In order to activate the glands, it is also advisable to take at least one *Kelpasan* tablet daily.

Reliable Remedies for Fungal Infections (Mycosis)

No matter where mycosis occurs, it is difficult to eradicate. However, as with all skin conditions, *whey* has proved to be of excellent value even for mycotic diseases, that is, fungal skin diseases. But since not everyone is able to go to a dairy in the country and obtain fresh whey, many patients like to use the concentrated whey as available in *Molkosan.*

A patient told me once that she had suffered from this troublesome problem for years despite all her efforts to get rid of it. The fungus had settled under her breasts and on her arms, causing frequent soreness, and for more than twelve years she had used all kinds of remedies without success. Then she learned about Molkosan and an African plant remedy, *Spilanthes*, which complements and reinforces the healing effect of Molkosan. After applying these two remedies in alternation for about two weeks, she was pleased to note great improvement. The skin had been rehabilitated and was clear once again.

It goes without saying that such a splendid result makes one glad, if only because of the great patience the sufferer must have had in order to endure the unpleasant problem and its bothersome effects in spite of years of treatment. Think of the discouragement and disappointment first of all, then the great relief when the stubborn fungus disappeared in a relatively short space of time, restoring the skin to normal.

Diseases of the Nails

It is one of nature's wonders that the body is able to use silica and other minerals to provide the toes and fingers with tough horny plates. By diseases of the nails I do not mean deformities of the nails and diseases of the nail roots caused by the use of nail polish and manicures etc. The nails and hair are usually an indication of the person's general condition of health. As a rule, those who suffer from metabolic disorders have neither strong nails nor healthy-looking hair. The nails and hair become brittle and lose their natural structure when there is a deficiency of minerals and trace elements. In such cases, the only worthwhile thing to do is to treat the basic cause of the problem.

Athlete's foot and nail mycosis are stubborn infections. It is easy to acquire the fungus from infected scales of skin dropped on the floor of changing rooms in public swimming baths, or through contact with persons who suffer from the infection. If you want to treat these infections successfully you will have to cut the nails to the quick, perhaps even using a nail file. Apply *Bioforce Cream* during the day and, before you go to bed, tie some absorbent cotton soaked in *Molkosan* round the affected areas, leaving it on all night. The following night *Spilanthes* should be used instead of Molkosan. Continue using these two remedies in alternation for quite some time. I remember one doctor from Berlin telling me once quite excitedly that in his many years of medical practice he had never known an effective remedy for athlete's foot and nail mycosis until, by chance, he came across Molkosan whey concentrate when he was standing in for another doctor elsewhere. The good results in combatting these infections may be due to the effect of concentrated lactic acid together with lactic enzymes and nutritive salts.

A simple inflammation of the cuticle can be treated successfully with *Bioforce Cream, Molkosan* and *Echinaforce*. For the treatment of more serious cases of inflammation, for example onychia, use *horseradish tincture* instead of Molkosan. Finally, eating food that is rich in calcium and silica is an excellent way to strengthen the nails, as is the supplementary intake of *Urticalcin* and *Galeopsis*.

The Feet – our Faithful Servants

Only when we look upon our feet as faithful servants will we show enough appreciation to pay them proper attention and give them the good care they deserve. Do you realise what an important function the feet have to fulfil through an entire lifetime? They carry the body, irrespective of its weight, and take us wherever we wish to go. Yet looking at the changing fashion in footwear, especially as indulged in by the ladies, we begin to see the discrepancy existing between the unfair treatment of our feet and the constant care they need and deserve. We must not close our eyes to this fact.

When I was young I often heard adults use the term 'flat-footed Indian' when they were describing someone who had really bad flat feet. Later on in life I had the opportunity to visit the Indians personally and, to my enlightenment, I saw for myself that such a description of their feet was completely out of place. True, there are Indians called Blackfeet, but I never saw one Indian with flat feet, a sad and frequent occurrence among many other people. People in less developed societies, as long as they stick to their traditional habits and walk barefoot most of the time, have strong and healthy feet that make others living in a more industrialised society truly envious.

Is it not true that our poor feet spend much time imprisoned in often unsuitable shoes? No wonder they are often just as degenerated as our teeth! It is indeed important that we give appropriate care and attention to our feet in return for their lifelong faithful service.

The Structure of the Feet and the Need for Proper Care

The bones of the feet are of a very simple design, but the structure and arrangement of the muscles is a technical masterpiece. The muscles are designed for walking on uneven ground, that is, natural ground. If they are not exercised they degenerate and the shape of the foot will change. The foot will lose its efficiency and especially the long muscles, the long flexors of the toes, will become slack. Changes in the natural structure of the feet will lead to deformities such as flat feet, splay feet, club feet, and whatever other names they are known by.

It was for a good reason that Priessnitz, Sebastian Kneipp, Rickli and other nature cure teachers recommended again and again that we walk barefoot as much as possible, particularly in the summer. It is good to walk on dew-wet grass early in the morning. This is refreshing and strengthens the foot muscles, while walking on uneven natural ground provides the feet with an invigorating massage. These recommendations are explained in greater detail on pages 332–4. However, there are many other ways in which we can care for our feet. These are the subject of the following sections.

Care of the Feet

What long and faithful service is rendered by our feet! We take it for granted that they will support the whole weight of our body and take us wherever we want to go every day of our life. Nevertheless, as a rule we neglect the daily foot bath that they so urgently need and deserve. For the feet perform not only a mechanical but also an eliminative function, although this may generally be ignored. Everyone knows about perspiration of the feet and although it can become offensive and unpleasant when excessive, so that we would like to get rid of it, it does have a purpose. Suppressing this perspiration can have extremely serious consequences. Granted, it is most disconcerting when others become aware of the strong odour, and cases have even been known where smelly feet led to a divorce. Excessive sweating of the feet should really be looked upon as being the action of a safety valve of the body; when it reaches the point where it becomes embarrassing the sufferer should do something about stimulating the kidneys and the skin by natural means. For if you try to suppress foot sweat, the toxins will remain in the system and cause havoc, leading to various ailments. The types of problem that might arise from such action, together with some suggested alternatives for dealing with excessive foot sweat, are discussed on pages 330–31.

Above all, it is most important to look after our feet and wash them daily. Since the feet are excretory organs and the sweat rids the body of toxins, it is even more important to wash your feet every day than it is to wash your face. This cleansing is very important to one's general well-being. Although there are incidents mentioned in the Bible where 'washing of the feet' had a symbolic meaning (for example humility), we should never overlook the intrinsic therapeutic value either. The washing of feet in the Middle East is almost a ritual because most people wear sandals and recognise the hygienic and health reasons for doing so. We should do it for the same reasons. To convince yourself, try washing your feet every day for one month and you will notice how your general feeling of well-being improves.

At the end of the day, if you feel tired and perhaps have a headache, try a *herbal foot bath* and see how it will soothe you. Add to the bath wild thyme, juniper needles or any other aromatic herbs and your feet will feel refreshed and invigorated. To increase the effect, after the foot bath apply a good oil that stimulates skin function; *St John's wort oil* or *olive oil* can be used for this. Even if done only once a week, this oil treatment is most beneficial. Another soothing foot oil is *Juniperosan*.

Daily care of the feet takes only a few minutes but it pays dividends in good health and saves medical bills. Try to do it on a regular basis. Further guidelines for proper foot care are given immediately below.

USEFUL ADVICE FOR PROPER FOOT CARE

The importance to our health and well-being of caring for the feet will be clear from the preceding sections. Other interesting points will also be explored in the following pages. However, this section sets out to provide some useful guidelines on caring for the feet in general, as discussed above, as well as dealing with specific problems that may be experienced.

1. To start with, go and buy yourself shoes that are sensible and fit the foot rather than the fashion.
2. In the second place, take note of the following three points:
    (a) Wash your feet daily; afterwards knead and massage the muscles, then rub the feet with a little foot oil, such as *Juniperosan*.
    (b) If you suffer from rheumatism, arthritis or an ailment that causes water to accumulate in the feet, it is useful to add a tablespoon of *herbal sea salt* to a foot bath. This bath should last 15–30 minutes, at a constant temperature of 37°C (98.6°F).
    (c) Sore feet should be bathed in an infusion of *mallow* or *sanicle*.
3. Never try to suppress foot perspiration by means of strong substances. The result could be damaging to internal organs. The correct approach is to stimulate the kidneys for better elimination of wastes. Bathe the feet in an infusion of *sage* and afterwards rub them with a little *Juniperosan*. This amounts to a pleasant foot care regime and can get rid of foot perspiration in a natural way, given time.
4. For eczema and athlete's foot a foot bath with an infusion of *wild pansy (heartsease)* or *cranesbill* is recommended. After the bath dab *Molkosan* on the affected areas and as soon as it has dried, apply *Bioforce Cream*.
5. Blue areas, which are caused by dilated capillaries, should be treated like varicose veins. Take *Aesculaforce* orally and apply it externally as well.
6. For cold feet take *foot baths*, alternating between hot and cold water. Prepare the warm bath with an infusion of thyme, immerse your feet for three minutes, then place them in cold water for three seconds. Repeat this sequence for a total of about twenty minutes.

Make sure the temperature of the warm water remains constant by adding fresh hot water whenever necessary.
7. A burning sensation in the feet, as often experienced by older people, should be treated in the same way as item 6. The burning is caused by strictured vessels, and remedies that act to dilate them again must also be taken internally.

If you have ever had any trouble with your feet you will keenly appreciate that healthy ones are a real blessing. It is always recommended that they be given preventative care, for our general condition of well-being often depends on the state of the feet. Also remember that cold feet are bad for the kidneys and, in the case of women, the pelvic organs.

Dealing with Excessive Foot Sweat
Is it a good thing to get rid of foot sweat? Or is perspiration a natural process through which the body disposes of toxins tnat it could not otherwise eliminate? This second assumption seems to be correct, or else so many unpleasant consequences could not have resulted when sufferers tried to suppress perspiration of the feet.

Just recently I received a letter from a woman in Zurich telling me that while her husband was doing military service his foot sweat was suppressed and as a result he developed a skin disease. Foot sweat is often suppressed by people in military service, but this is no cure; rather, it can be detrimental in as far as the effects will be either a skin disorder or some other problem. For example, I have never found a person suffering from any form of lung trouble to be plagued by excessively sweaty feet. Specialists in lung diseases with whom I have discussed this phenomenon have confirmed my observation. Hence the logical conclusion that the direct and deliberate suppression of foot perspiration or some other excretory body function, can mark the beginning of lung problems or may be connected with them. If you want to get rid of the troubles incurred there will be no other way but once again to induce the feet to sweat. You may wonder how this can be done. Well, the suggestion below is simple enough, but carrying it out successfully is quite another matter.

A doctor in Berlin once helped himself by sprinkling carbide powder on the insoles of his shoes. The moisture exuding from the feet generates heat through its contact with the carbide, which serves to draw out yet more moisture. In this way foot sweat is induced artificially. It was reported that the doctor used this method to cure several cases, including patients with lung diseases that had previously failed to respond to any other treatment.

The thing to remember is that it is fundamentally wrong to try to suppress foot sweat. If the odour becomes too unpleasant, bathe the feet frequently; wash them with a herbal infusion and afterwards oil them with a good, aromatic skin oil, for example *Juniperosan*, that is easily absorbed. Also, change your socks and stockings frequently. These measures will do no harm and can only be beneficial. Remember, the natural functions of the body should never be suppressed because through them the system is able to work properly.

High Heels or None at All?

The question of heels does not arise in areas of the world where people walk barefoot. In temperate and cold regions, however, the question is a valid one. It is interesting, however, that when travelling through South America you will see many more high-heeled shoes worn by women than is common among modern women in more northern regions. In fact, I had the impression that South America might have been the birthplace of high-heeled shoes. On one occasion I was watching an Indian girl from the slums of Lima. As soon as she was out of sight of her shack she quickly took off her shabby footwear, hid it under a bush and put on a pair of fashionable high-heeled shoes. She then proceeded to swagger along the street like a queen!

In rural areas where there are only dirt roads, high heels are, of course, most uncomfortable. The natural uneven ground, meadows and fields call for sensible shoes or going barefoot. So if someone leaves a lonely farmstead and goes to live in the city, the temptation to follow modern fashion trends is often too great; high-heeled shoes are worn, even though they may make walking rather awkward and difficult, indeed even painful. And if a woman is so used to wearing high heels that she cannot do without them, her feet will no longer be normal and healthy. Her tendons will have become so deformed that it will be difficult and painful for her even to stand on her bare feet.

FOOD FOR THOUGHT

I am often surprised to see young girls strutting along in high-heeled shoes, or else in slipper-like shoes with thin soles and no heels at all. Both extremes are harmful and inappropriate; both

331

force the body into an unnatural position, causing it to tire more quickly and suffer damage. The blood can become congested, leading to varicose veins.

There is a natural reason why walking barefoot does not cause any problems. You simply would not walk for long along a hard and even road surface, but over meadows, fields and forest ground, all of which are uneven surfaces that support the arch of the foot, for movement acts like a massage. Judging from the standpoint of zone therapy, you will happily realise that the whole body benefits as a result. It is for this reason that walking barefoot in warm weather when you are on holiday or when working in the garden is an effective and invigorating natural treatment.

In contrast, when you have to walk on surfaced pavements and roads, a heel of 2–2½cm (about 1 inch) is just right. This height will provide the position for the foot that tends to tire the legs and body the least. Additionally, an arch support may be the answer for feet that ache or tire easily. There is usually no need for special insoles because there are carefully made shoes with a built-in support on the market.

If you stop to think that the feet have to carry your whole body weight day after day, you will agree that they most certainly deserve comfortable, well-constructed shoes in addition to daily attention. All this is surely part of a proper health programme.

Walking Barefoot

Walking barefoot is increasingly becoming a thing of the past. In fact, nowadays many people associate it with poverty or eccentricity – they look down on it. Just try it and dare to go for a long walk without your shoes and watch how many glances of surprise, pity and even contempt you will attract. What does this indicate? That the onlookers have all but forgotten or never learned the benefits of walking barefoot. They know nothing of the peculiar, mysterious power it can convey, or else they would not react the way they do.

Of course, there are many whose feet are untrained and would not be capable of walking barefoot over stones. But if you go for an early morning walk on dewy grass you will soon notice that going barefoot makes you feel really good, generating new strength when you have been feeling tired and worn out. It is like recharging one's batteries, so to speak, recharging your run-down nerves with energy. It seems as if Mother Earth is giving off energy that improves the glandular functions. That is why I consider it rather strange that, although overtired and worn-out, we do not take full advantage of this simple regenerative treatment, which is able to stimulate our endocrine glands to increase their activity.

Whenever we are in the garden, woods and forest, fields and meadows, we should make full use of the opportunity to take off our shoes and socks or stockings and walk barefoot, especially in the summer when the ground is warm. Take care, however, to walk only on natural ground, for the more unspoilt the ground the greater will be the benefit derived from its magnetic field. Never believe that walking barefoot on asphalt, concrete or any other artificial surface will do the same good. No, it is better to wear your shoes on this kind of surface, because you will not stand to gain anything by it, rather the opposite. Also, do not cool down your body even further by going barefoot when it is cold or wet. In certain mountain or rural areas the children can often be seen going without shoes throughout the entire summer, even when it is cold and raining. Their parents follow the custom of putting away their children's shoes and socks at the beginning of spring, only bringing them out again when the winter has set in. But even during the summer months a rainy spell can cool the atmosphere so much that bare feet will no longer benefit the health. It should be clear that it would be much better to be reasonable and sensible as regards the wearing of shoes in inclement weather.

On the other hand, if walking barefoot is done sensibly, it cannot be recommended highly enough as a remedy for all those who are worn-out and overworked, and who suffer from glandular insufficiency and other problems. If you feel tense because of stress and overwork, why not try it and see how you will obtain soothing relief.

The ancient Greeks were not as weak as the people of our modern age, yet they seem to have understood the revitalising benefits coming from the ground, or else they would not have passed on to us the old legend of Gaea, the energising Mother Earth. The legend tells of the giant Antaeus, son of Gaea, who was invincible as long as he touched his mother, the earth. When wrestling with him his adversary was able to defeat him only because he noticed that Antaeus regained new strength every time he touched the ground, but that his strength diminished as soon as he was lifted in the air. Granted, this is only a legend, but the story must have been based on certain observations of natural phenomena, for it is a fact that the earth holds wonderful regenerative powers capable of imparting energy to our bodies. A simple test is all that is needed to prove this assertion. Even though it has not yet been possible to discover and prove scientifically the actual cause of this elemental force, our experience of it cannot easily be refuted.

WALKING AND EXERCISING ON DEWY GRASS IN THE MORNING
Not everyone may find it easy to get up early in the morning and walk, run or do their exercises on the still dewy grass. Perhaps you live in a town with narrow streets and would find it inconvenient to go outside and seek out a green meadow before breakfast in order to do a little morning exercise. Still, it would be a most refreshing activity for all the many town dwellers who are normally locked up in their rooms and offices, before actually having to surrender to the hustle and bustle of a busy day.

How much to be envied are those who still live close to nature, who in the early morning carry out their natural exercise by making hay or doing general farm and garden work. Even though they may not realise it, these people are conditioning their bodies all the while. To them it is nothing but their work, part of their daily routine. It would be a first-class restorative to take a holiday on a farm and get up early and join these people in their early morning chores so as to regenerate our bodies which have been wearied and worn out during the working year. Think, too, of the opportunity you would have of learning from nature, helping you to adopt a more optimistic view of life.

Early morning exercises require deep-breathing, and this will help to drive out the remaining traces of weariness from our bodies, enabling us to start the day's work refreshed, even more so if we are able to walk on dewy grass. Sebastian Kneipp was one who called attention to the effects of dew, and it is beneficial to our health if we make use of nature's gifts. Civilisation has robbed us of much of our freedom by forcing us to live in cramped houses and towns, but nature teaches us little things that can make up for this loss to some extent. Observing these lessons can help us to maintain a reasonable physical balance while having to accept the hustle and bustle of everyday life.

Periostitis
'Just a minor cut on the foot, a little torn skin. Such a thing is bound to happen when working in the garden or fields. I'll let the wound bleed freely and will be able to forget all about it.' So I thought when I injured my left foot some time ago. Over the

years such injuries had often happened and no further trouble had resulted. I naturally thought that it would be the same this time.

Within two days, however, the foot became inflamed and the first signs of blood poisoning could be detected. Two clay poultices made the symptoms disappear; but instead of continuing the treatment as I should have done, I did nothing further, being too busy to look after myself. From time to time, especially at night, I noticed a dull pain which seemed to go deeper and deeper. After about ten days it became so bad one night that I could hardly bear it. Because of neglecting to treat the infection, inflammation of the membrane covering the bone (periostitis) had evidently set in. Clay poultices no longer helped, or to be more specific, I could no longer tolerate the poultices. Soaking the foot in a herbal bath did nothing towards relieving the pain either.

After two terrible nights I decided to apply the *Baunscheidt (revulsion) treatment* (see pages 438–9) and after about two hours the pain had completely disappeared. The inflammation had been drawn to the surface and the cause of the pain eliminated. How much more simple is such a treatment than the allopathic method involving pain-killing drugs and surgery. Had I undergone allopathic treatment it would have meant weeks or even months in bed. Only someone who has experienced relief from pain through natural and reliable means can appreciate how wonderful it is to draw from nature's storehouse the wide variety of remedies and treatments available to us.

Strained Ligaments and Sinews, Sprained Ankles

There is a way to alleviate the pain and restore to normal any sprains and strained ligaments in the quickest possible time. This is what you must do.

Beat until stiff the whites of 3–5 eggs. Add a strong substance that will increase the rate of the blood and lymph circulation to a maximum. If you live in a southern region, use *eucalyptus* or *camphor leaves* but before adding them to the egg whites put them through a mincer two or three times until they are transformed into a paste. Dried leaves should be ground to a powder, or crushed in a mortar. Or maybe you have some eucalyptus or camphor leaves already in powder form. If you have camphor powder available, use 20–30g (about 1 oz). At any rate, add the leaf powder or camphor powder to the stiff egg whites, mixing the ingredients thoroughly. If neither camphor nor eucalyptus powder is on hand, use finely chopped *pine buds or needles* (from any coniferous tree) for the paste and mix with the egg whites. Spread the mixture on the painful area, then dress with wide strips of cloth and bind loosely with an elastic bandage. As the egg whites harden the paste will provide a firm and strong dressing. If necessary, renew the dressing after two days. After that, massage the affected part with *comfrey tincture* (*Wallwosan*), followed by the application of *raw cabbage poultices. Pulped raw potatoes, curds* or similar ingredients can also be used for the poultices.

This treatment will relieve the pain after only a short time, perhaps within a few days, and it is therefore better than suffering pain and not being able to walk for 4–6 weeks or even 2–3 months.

Massaging the injured part with light movements directed towards the heart will speed up the healing process.

Finally, warmth is necessary in the case of all bruises and internal injuries of ligaments and muscles. So see to it that the affected parts of the body are kept warm at all times.

Back Problems

After some great physical strain or effort, particularly at the end of a day of heavy housework or gardening, people often complain about their aching back. Yet the cause of the pain is not necessarily connected with general tiredness caused by the work. Many other causes can be responsible for backache and if it keeps returning it is advisable to look for the true source of the problem.

If the pain is relatively high up, causing a feeling of contraction, the person may actually be suffering from kidney trouble. Should the pain be felt a little lower down it may be the symptom of prostate (in the case of men) or bladder trouble. Backache can also stem from a degeneration of the bones, for example in a case of 'arthritis deformans'. A change in the position of the uterus can also trigger backache, and even muscular rheumatism may be interpreted as backache, as can sciatica when it starts higher up.

Backache being a nuisance, the sufferer seeks to get rid of it quickly. For this purpose use a good warming ointment. Apply *Symphosan* for a change. It is also beneficial to place some moist, hot *hay flowers* or *camomile*, tied in a cloth, on the painful area. Should this treatment not alleviate the pain and improve the condition, it is advisable to consult a doctor in order to identify the real cause of the pain, which can then be treated accordingly.

Hernias (Ruptures)

The peritoneum is so well designed that it does not easily become ruptured, even if it is subjected to exceptional strain once in a while. The healthy body is equipped with such good reserves of strength that one really wonders how it is possible for the abdominal wall to rupture in so many different ways. Observations show that some people inherit a tendency to ruptures, while with others a post-operative scar serves to weaken the abdomen. Once a weakness exists, it only needs a degree of pressure or a violent bout of coughing for a hernia to result. Thus, a hernia is not only caused by lifting heavy weights.

When the peritoneum is torn, the intestine can protrude through the front wall of the abdominal cavity. If the intestine is not pushed back in at once, flatulence can make it impossible for it to be returned to its normal position. The result is a so-called strangulated hernia, which requires immediate surgery. However, if the hernia is not strangulated, it is possible that a well-fitting truss can retain it in place, thus giving some relief.

Preventative Measures

It is always useful to know what you can do to prevent certain problems from arising and this also applies to preventative measures after surgery. For example, it is advisable to massage the abdomen regularly with *Symphosan*. This will help to strengthen the stomach muscles and prevent unwanted deposits of fat. At the same time, if every week you take two *sitz baths* in an infusion of *oak bark*, the effect of the regular massage will be enhanced. Keep-fit exercises also strengthen the abdominal muscles and the entire front wall. But be careful not to overdo the exercises. Be sensible, too, when practising a sport, whether it be rowing, skiing or whatever. A sensible approach guarantees good exercise that will strengthen, but not strain, the abdominal muscles and wall. Incidentally, if you practise some physical exercise regularly and sensibly, you will be much less prone to hernias in the first place than if you only sit around and do mental work.

For internal treatment, herbs that contain silica, such as *horsetail* and, especially, *Galeopsis*, are excellent. And to not forget to take *Urticalcin*, a biological calcium preparation.

A Selection of Medicinal Herbs

Only some of the more important herbs are considered in the following pages, since a detailed description of the extensive domain of the plant world would demand far greater attention than could ever be given in this limited space.

How a Good Herbal Remedy Is Developed

Establishing the Therapeutic Effects

To establish the effects of a natural plant medicine one must first of all be capable of observing accurately and interpreting correctly. In every age there have been people endowed with intuitive insight which enabled them, by personal experience and observation of others, to determine what plants are most suitable for curing a given condition or illness.

The effect of various substances on the human organism can be observed with greater accuracy after two or three days of fasting. Needless to say, one would only experiment with plants and substances known to be nonpoisonous. After taking one plant or another, it is possible to judge the relative merits – how it affects the bowels, the kidney, the stomach or the appetite, or whether it stimulates the functions of the body in some other way. If the body is in good condition, certain important effects can be easily perceived. In homoeopathy this is the so-called 'proving' of remedies on healthy people.

A doctor or other health practitioner can observe the effects of a remedy on the patient himself. If the patient reports that a particular remedy has other effects on him than those already known, the doctor will naturally take note of such observations. If other patients experience the same effect, then the doctor will realise that the medicine has a novel, so far unknown, reaction. A new remedy, or a new application of one, will have been discovered!

Sage

Combining Remedies

The purpose of combining remedies is to enhance the effect of one through the addition of another.

If a calcium deficiency is to be treated, it will be necessary to make sure that there is not a deficiency of silica at the same time. If there is, the patient must take both minerals. Supposing he also suffers from night sweats and at the same time wants to get rid of a bad cough; for the first, *sage (Salvia)* would be needed and for the second, extract of *pine buds* or *lance-leaf plantain (also known as ribwort, or Plantago lanceolata)* would be the indicated remedy.

It will be clear, therefore, that in order to cure different illnesses, the doctor can choose a suitable combination of remedies, but he must be careful that the individual remedies are compatible. There are some that vitalise the body, while others have a relaxing effect. As a rule, a knowledge of pharmacology is required to be able to choose and combine remedies correctly. Still, even in former times, when physicians were not so well trained and informed as they are today, they hit upon remedies by accurate observation and careful analysis of their findings. They were successful in discovering effective combinations, with one remedy increasing the effect of another, so that the action of the combined ingredients was greatly improved. However, if the combined remedies do not complement one another, not being compatible, the total effect can be reduced rather than enhanced.

The importance and effectiveness of combining different substances is illustrated in the case of vitamins. For example, an easily assimilated calcium preparation is not necessarily absorbed into the system if there is a deficiency of vitamin D, or if the two are not taken together. The body cannot absorb the calcium if there is a lack of vitamin D and, conversely, the vitamin D will not benefit the body if there is a lack of calcium. One complements the other.

In the body we find a similar interdependence of functions. Hydrochloric acid and the digestive enzyme pepsin work in close association with each other in the stomach. Pepsin can break down the food proteins only if the gastric environment is kept acid through the presence of hydrochloric acid in the right concentration; otherwise pepsin is completely ineffective. There are many associations like these, and if we are to produce medicines that fulfil their intended purpose, we must find out more about them.

To combine just any kind of herb or extract with another, hoping that eventually one may be lucky and suddenly invent something outstanding, is clearly the wrong thing to do. There are certain herbs and other natural remedies which, when combined, tend to harm rather than benefit the system. To ascertain the overall effects and be able to combine them correctly requires the gift and powers of accurate observation and a certain amount of intuition, a flair that comes from experience and training. Moreover, it is not always possible to judge the material components alone, for there are many substances and factors which have yet to be discovered but nevertheless play a part in the total effect. For this reason it is necessary to reckon with unknown as well as known factors.

Consider, for example, certain combinations of remedies that were used in the Middle Ages and are still as effective today as they were then. This is undoubtedly because of their rich content of vitamins and enzymes. Even though such factors were unknown when these remedies were originated, the skilled observers became aware of their effects and a new remedy was found and from then on employed in curing sickness. Practical experience in such circumstances is just as valuable, if not more so, than scientific knowledge of the exact chemical composition.

Unknown Factors
Very often an alkaloid or some other chemical substance in a plant is believed to produce a certain effect. If the alkaloid is extracted and administered, the symptomatic effects may be the same or similar, but the lasting effect will probably be different. The chemist is unable to explain this, because his analytical procedures are not sufficiently refined for him to be able to pinpoint those substances which are commonly termed 'unknown factors' and which are responsible for the overall effect produced by the plant. It is therefore essential that all natural remedies be taken as an organic whole, in the same form as nature produces them. Those who merely consider the so-called 'active substance' in a herbal preparation demonstrate a superficial understanding of the subject.

For example, if we extract arnicin from the arnica plant, it will never have the same effect on the heart and blood vessels as the extract that has been made from the whole arnica root. The same principle applies to carrot juice. By using just the isolated carotene as a provitamin, it is impossible to obtain the same medicinal effect as it would by drinking the pure and natural juice. Pure lactic acid as found in sauerkraut also differs in its action from the whole sauerkraut, because the acid is associated with other substances in the fermented cabbage and these possess their own curative properties. Some of these intrinsic properties are still unknown.

These few examples show that the things nature provides in their unadulterated and complete state represent the best source of our remedies. Nature is and will remain the most reliable pharmacy. Anyone gifted with an awareness of what nature has to offer will not be disappointed in his search, whether he be a medical researcher or just eager to learn. Nature will be his willing teacher and will unlock the secrets of its marvellous healing powers.

How Herbal Remedies Can Be Used
Every plant contains various minerals, vitamins, ferments, enzymes, oils, resins and mucilage. All these components in their natural proportions have a specific effect on the body.

Tea (Infusion)
In many places it is still customary to make a herbal tea or infusion in order to treat health problems. In fact, this is the oldest form of preparing herbal remedies. Unfortunately, however, an infusion only utilises the water-soluble properties of a plant.

341

Tincture

The preparation of a tincture using alcohol as a base, as opposed to water in the case of an infusion, is more advisable, since in addition to the water-soluble substances, those soluble in alcohol, such as resins, oils and other specific active ingredients (for example arnicin and petasin), will be extracted. What is more, an alcoholic tincture keeps well and can also be diluted, that is, to obtain homoeopathic potencies. The body is able to assimilate substances contained in an alcoholic solution better than those dissolved in water. In times gone by, only dried plants were used in the preparation of tinctures but today fresh plant extracts are preferred, since they contain a higher concentration of the active ingredients.

The Spagyric Process

Many years ago Dr Zimpel developed the spagyric process in which plants are fermented by means of yeast fermentation. The carbohydrates ferment and are changed into alcohol. During this process certain medicinal properties are released and are also changed. New enzymes develop and these enhance the overall effect in the case of some plants, whereas in others, for example plants containing mucilage, the effect is diminished. This fermentation process, like any other method, has its advantages and disadvantages. In more recent times, Dr Strahtmeier has again started to use the fermentation process, with good results.

Lactic Fermentation

Lactic fermentation has been used for centuries in China, Korea and Japan. In those countries it is employed to prepare medicinal herbs and to change vegetables into hearty condiments and what are known as *kimchi*, spicy pickled dishes similar to sauerkraut. Although the lactic fermentation of various vegetables has the great advantage of activating a plant's beneficial properties, this method of preparing food has not yet found the popularity it deserves. The remedial effects of plants used in the treatment and prevention of diabetes, arthritis, rheumatism and cancer could be even more beneficial if they were prepared in this way. That is why *Molkosan* and vegetable juices should not be regarded merely as food, but also as remedies. It appears that the importance of preparations containing lactic acid will increase as radiation levels increase in our modern environment.

Powder and Tablets

The whole, dried plant can also be made into a powder, which in turn can be used to produce tablets. The advantage of a powder and tablets is the fact that they retain all the plant's substances, including the ashes. On the negative side, sensitive ingredients are lost in the drying process, although the minerals, oils and resins remain fully effective. Remedies taken in powder and tablet form are ideal for use as laxatives and to stop diarrhoea, as well as to aid the digestion and eliminate worms. Papaya preparations are a good example in this respect.

Fresh Plant Trituration

In this method of preparing plant remedies, freshly cut or harvested plants are triturated with lactose, grape sugar or some other basic medium. Experience has shown this method to be one of the most effective. Unfortunately, as the process is slow and intricate, it is rarely used. Trituration has proved its worth in the manufacture of *Urticalcin*, since it allows the natural calcium to be prepared in such a way that the body can easily absorb it.

Oil Extracts (Preparations Made with Oil)

Oil is used in the preparation of *St John's wort oil* and other body oils, since it dissolves resins and other oil-soluble substances, which the skin will absorb for the benefit of the whole body. For example, the red dye of St John's wort is oil-soluble and much more effective in the form of an oil than as a tincture.

Crushed Fresh Plants for Poultices

Applying fresh crushed plants to an affected area is also a reliable form of treatment and has become more popular in recent times. Many people have either heard of or experienced cures effected by applying cabbage leaf poultices. If followed correctly, this method does a lot of good, avoiding the need for expensive medication. Besides cabbage leaves, many other medicinal plants and herbs can be used for poultices, so that their active ingredients will be absorbed via the skin. *Rumex alpinus* (giant dock) is an excellent medicinal plant. When crushed and applied to the back of the neck overnight, it will alleviate headaches and nervous tension. In the tropics, crushed greater plantain (*Plantago major*) is used for the treatment of ulcers and boils with good results. Crushed *Echinacea* leaves are marvellous for inflammations, and crushed comfrey leaves relieve arthritic pain.

343

The above examples show that medicinal plants can be used in a variety of ways to obtain reliable results. Plants are indeed the link between inorganic minerals and the human and animal body. Since the body is only able to absorb and assimilate minerals in the finest form possible, it is of great benefit that plants were designed to do the preliminary work of processing the minerals. They absorb these inorganic substances from the ground, processing them in such a way that our body is able to assimilate them.

Alpine Plants and Lowland Plants – Which Are of Greater Value?

Observations and Practical Experience
The above question does not have a simple answer. There are many aspects that have to be taken into consideration. For instance, I first noticed that strawberries grown in my garden in Teufen (about 900 m/3,000 feet above sea level) had less sugar content that the same variety grown in the Engadine (about 1,500 m/5,000 feet above sea level). I wondered if this could be attributed to the humus in the soil of the Engadine moors or to the intensive sunlight there. Interestingly, I also noticed that the sugar content of the lowland strawberries increased if the summer was a warm and dry one. I had to conclude from this observation that warmth and sunlight are mainly responsible for sweetness. Feeding also plays an important part; our strawberries are given a sufficient quantity of organic lime, which would account for their being sweeter than if the soil was not fed at all. So then, various factors must be weighed up before we can come to the right conclusion. By the way, carrots also do better in the Engadine than in Teufen, being sweeter and better flavoured. For this we must not only thank the strong, warm sunshine but also the higher elevation of the Engadine, its excellent climatic condition, and the richness of the soil.

Not every high elevation has the same merits. The southern Alps enjoy many more hours of sunshine than the northern range. For this reason plants do much better in the more southern areas than in the northern regions. In some of the latter areas they have only stunted growth before dying. Naturally, medicinal plants are also affected by these regional and climatic differences. For example, *Solidago* that has been grown in the higher Engadine has a better and stronger effect on the kidneys than that grown in the lower region of Teufen and, interestingly, that grown in Teufen is still better than any grown in the districts below an altitude of 500 m (1,500 feet).

344

Scientific Experiments

Some time ago, Professor Flueck delivered an interesting lecture to members of the Swiss Association of Apothecaries dealing with exactly these observations and the many factors that combine to produce active substances in plants. The lecture was based on the results of experiments in which various medicinal herbs had been grown at different altitudes but in identical soils. The experiments enabled Professor Flueck to prove beyond doubt that the therapeutic value of the plants does not depend solely upon the altitude at which they grow. In order to accurately identify the other factors involved, the experiments were fully controlled; the same plant was grown at different altitudes but in the same kind of soil in every case.

Better growth and content of active substances was achieved with the plants grown in sheltered mountain valleys, exposed to sunshine but protected from the winds, than with those grown at higher altitudes with equal exposure to the sun but unprotected from the winds. For this reason certain plants were found to do better at middle elevations than at higher altitudes. Others produce a higher content of medicinal properties if grown in the shade, or at least semi-shade, but these are usually exceptions to the rule.

So if an alpine herb proves to be more effective than others, having a higher content of active substances, it cannot always be attributed to altitude alone. Rather, it depends upon the kind of plant, its hours of exposure to sunshine, the temperature of the atmosphere and the degree of protection from severe winds. It is therefore not at all surprising that plants growing in mountain valleys protected from the winds tend to contain more active ingredients than those growing at lower altitudes.

However, Professor Flueck's experiments led to the astonishing observation that plants grown in the middle altitudes had a higher content of nutrients than those grown at high elevations. In view of my own experience, having been successful in growing mountain plants, his findings made me wonder. However, further investigation gave me the solution to the mystery: it was the species, or variety, of plant rather than the elevation at which it grew that really mattered.

Alpine Plants

The alpine plant is usually richer in its constituents and medicinal value than its lowland relative. I have proved this for myself through analysis. For example, the lowland yarrow contains less

345

essential oil and is less aromatic than the highland yarrow from the Engadine, the Lower Engadine to be exact. Mind you, it may be true that the soil and the abundant sunshine and warm atmosphere, also the greater intensity of ultraviolet rays, exert an influence on the quality of the plant.

The conclusions drawn from Professor Flueck's experiments were arrived at with little, if any, consideration of the influence of ultraviolet radiation and this would lead one to believe that these rays are not so important in plant life, at least as far as their principal active elements are concerned. However, there are other constituents to be reckoned with, even though they are not generally considered 'active substances'. These elements, especially the trace elements, seem to depend upon ultraviolet light to a far greater extent than the more common principal substances, although little is known about the relationship between trace elements, ultraviolet radiation and mountain climate, as Professor Flueck admitted. To obtain scientifically acceptable evidence in this matter would involve costly experiments. In any case, what really matters are the results of our practical experience with herbs and herb extracts. For instance, we know it to be true that St John's wort grown at alpine altitudes is richer in active substances and more efficacious than the same plant grown in the lowlands or at an intermediate elevation. The tincture obtained from the former is a much darker shade of red than that prepared from the lowland plant. Hence we must conclude that the medicinal dye content is greater. The plant itself looks different from the ordinary lowland *Hypericum perforatum*; it is shorter and more compact. And since it is indigenous to the alpine regions it is distinguished by the name *Hypericum alpinum*. You will see, then, that it is the alpine plant which is richer in medicinal value and content; the variety of plant is the clue to the mystery's solution.

What is true about St John's wort also applies to goldenrod. The alpine variety is small and bushy and instead of one flower stem, like the lowland kind, it has 12–15 arising from its small rootstock. The alpine variety of *Solidago* is more aromatic and stronger, contains more essential oil, and its diuretic effect is far stronger than that of its lowland cousin.

Other Noteworthy Influences
It is quite obvious that experiments made with some lowland plants, *Belladonna* for instance, are less conclusive as regards the influence of mountain climate and than those made with plants

that are actually native to higher elevations. The condition of the soil has to be considered too, because the bacterial flora of lowland soil has usually been damaged by artificial fertilisers and cannot offer the same favourable basis for growth as the naturally fertilised ground of mountain valleys, the humus of which is brought down to the valleys every spring by the avalanche snow from where the ecology has not been interfered with. This kind of soil is ideal for promoting exceptionally good growth of plants, their medicinal content being the best possible because the mountain valleys provide the perfect biological conditions for these plants. Additionally, the sheltered valleys offer another advantage in as far as the plants are less exposed to strong winds than on mountain heights. That is why they thrive in these alpine valleys, and are especially aromatic and effective as raw materials for fresh plant preparations.

Scientific research is no doubt of great interest to the therapist and can tell him a lot. But when it comes to assessing the medicinal value of a herbal preparation, there is no substitute for practical experience with actual patients. A pure remedy, made from the whole plant, contains a complex of active elements, some of which are known and others unknown. For this reason, it is the practical treatment of a patient that really matters in determining whether a preparation is effective or not. This is why the medical researcher needs the cooperation of the herbal therapist in order to develop the best remedies from nature's bountiful storehouse for the benefit of the sick. After all, is this not the real purpose of all medical research? At least, that is what it should be!

Angelica (*Angelica archangelica*)

When the black death, the plague, raged in the Middle Ages, terrified people scoured the woods and marshes for medicinal herbs. They dug up angelica by the running streams and in damp clearings, for they felt certain that this plant would help them. Next to a plant called butterbur (in German, 'plague root'), angelica was considered the most important remedy for combatting the plague. Contemporary descriptions of those dreadful times contain the most remarkable stories of the reliable help these remedies must have given. The old chronicles report that anyone who kept a piece of angelica root in his mouth all through the day would be preserved from the plague. Be that as it may, the strong aromatic taste of this root is due to an essential oil and the valerian, malic and angelic acids it contains.

Angelica

The fresh plant extract has a marvellous effect on the digestion, helping to overcome loss of appetite, irritation of the stomach lining and also stomach cramps. For these complaints, take ten drops in a little water three times a day, half an hour before meals. Moreover, it is excellent for bronchial and deep-seated catarrh if a few drops are taken with a little honey once an hour.

The seeds of angelica are also used. For example, a liqueur can be made from them. And here is the recipe for the genuine angelica liqueur known as '*Vespétro*':

Angelica seeds (or chopped angelica root, if you are unable to obtain the seeds) 60g (2 oz)
Fennel seeds 8g (¼ oz)
Anise seeds 8g (¼ oz)
Coriander seeds 6g (⅕ oz)

Grind all the seeds together in a mill or crush in a mortar, put in a bottle and add 200 g (8 fl. oz) of pure alcohol. After eight days strain the mixture through muslin or cotton wool and mix it with a solution of 1–1.5 litres (2½ pints) of water to which 500 g (1lb) sugar (preferably grape sugar) has been added. And there you have it!

There is no better or more pleasant remedy for digestive upsets or flatulence. Let us imagine a monastery in the Middle Ages. There the monks would enjoy a glass of this golden drink before appearing for duty in the morning. Late in the evening a guest arriving with an upset or chilled stomach would be given a glass of 'Vespétro', and just a small sip would have a quicker and better effect than any of today's chemical liquids or tablets.

Bear's Garlic/Ramsons (Allium ursinum)

This outstanding medicinal plant has been wrongfully neglected for a long time and in quite a few books on herbalism it has not even been mentioned. Even in some of the best books only garlic is listed. *Allium ursinum*, with its distinct pungent smell, is generally called bear's garlic or ramsons. Its leaves resemble those of the lily of the valley and, as both plants grow in the shade of the woods, one is often mistaken for the other. Bear's garlic thrives in damp but healthy ground and is sometimes found so plentifully along the sides of streams and brooks that it could actually be cut with a scythe.

The considerable sulphur content of bear's garlic acts on the skin, the bones and the bronchial tubes, especially when there is an abundant secretion of phlegm.

Intestinal flatulence, with a burning sensation in the abdomen and an irritation of the bladder, accompanied by a strong urge to urinate, will be alleviated by means of bear's garlic. So, too, will chronic intestinal catarrh, when the mucous lining of the stomach and intestines has become very sensitive. Best of all, however, is the effect that bear's garlic has on hardening of the arteries. In this respect it can considerably lengthen the lives of older people. Bear's garlic juice or bear's garlic tonic can help prevent a stroke, and if a person has already suffered a stroke, this simple plant can restore him to health better than some of the most expensive proprietary medicines. Elderly people who have high blood pressure and are in danger of a stroke can ward it off with four plant remedies: *bear's garlic (Allium ursinum), mistletoe (Viscum album), hawthorn (Crataegus oxyacantha)* and *Arnica (Arnica montana)*. So why risk falling victim to paralysis when simple natural remedies exist that will prevent a stroke and at the same time strengthen the heart and the vascular system, giving new life to the body?

To benefit fully from bear's garlic it may be eaten fresh and uncooked as a salad or mixed with other vegetables. Steamed with a little oil, it is similar to spinach and, although not as beneficial as when eaten raw, it is still better than ordinary vegetables.

Butterbur

Taken as a wine or tonic, or an extract in the form of drops, it has also proved invaluable. If you do not wish to go to the bother of gathering the leaves yourself to use as a vegetable, you can take advantage of the fresh plant extract, in which all the goodness of the plant is preserved.

Butterbur (*petasites officinalis [hybridus]*)
During the past few years butterbur, or *Petasites*, has proved itself as a valuable remedy, one that has achieved quite astonishing results. Since it is a strong remedy, the mother tincture is not usually tolerated by the average patient and it has to be potentised to 1x or 2x, or even higher. If the patient, for example one suffering from a tumour or cancerous growth, notices a very strong reaction, he will have to take the remedy in a weaker potency. Let me add that this reaction is a sign of having made the right choice, that the remedy is appropriate. All that is left to do is to ascertain the potency that is tolerated by the patient. To find the individual tolerance, it will be necessary to ignore the usual directions; instead, add one drop of *Petasites* to a glass of water (200 ml/7 fl. oz) and take frequent sips during the day. After 8–10 days the body will have become used to that particular strength and the dose can be increased, using one drop to 100 ml (3.5 fl. oz) of water. Continue taking this dilution for eight days, then add one

350

drop to 50 ml. In time, the body will tolerate *Petasites* in even stronger doses.

This remedy attacks tumours, growths and all other pathological cell changes very forcibly. In cases of diseases of the respiratory tract, for example the lungs, *Petasites* should be given highly diluted. Recently, I spoke to a professor of medicine in Germany with whom I had left samples of the tincture for experimental purposes, and he confirmed that *Petasites* is a 'strong' medicine. He said that doses of only one drop gave rise to severe reactions in sensitive patients. It must be added that *Petasites* is quite harmless and nonpoisonous, so that strong reactions need not be any cause for alarm. Doctors who complain that our natural remedies are not potent enough to produce a satisfactory therapeutic reaction should try some of them to find out for themselves that fresh plant extracts can be as spectacular in their effects as many chemotherapeutic drugs, with the added advantage of their being harmless and nontoxic. This fact proves that nature holds many hidden powers which could be utilised for the benefit of the sick.

Not long ago I received a letter describing the treatment of an animal with *Petasites*. A terrier had developed a growth on one of her nipples, but this remedy soon reduced it in size.

Petasites is one of the best, if not *the* best, natural remedies, often giving better results than one hopes and expects in cases of tumours, especially those of suspected cancer or actual cancer. If it is taken together with *Viscum album*, the reliable fresh plant extract from mistletoe, or in the form of a combination remedy made up of these two remedies, it is possible to experience satisfactory results even in cases where chemotherapy has no more to offer.

So when the doctor says that he has done everything possible, and that there is no hope left for an improvement in a patient's condition, remember *Petasites* and *Viscum album*. These two remedies, together with an appropriate diet containing plenty of fruit juices and vegetable juices, can often achieve an improvement in the patient's general well-being. At any rate, this treatment can definitely reduce sensitivity to pain and make life easier.

Latest Research Findings

The medicinal use of *Petasites* goes back to the Middle Ages, or even earlier. The more we study the plant the more impressed we become with its good effects on a whole range of complaints, and the therapeutic spectrum of its active substances.

Petasites has a wide range of applications as an analgesic (a pain-relieving drug) and excellent results have been reported in connection with its use for headaches, migraines, menstrual cramps, toothache, painful wounds and many other aches and pains. It is at its most effective when taken in tablet form as *Petadolor*. This remedy provides temporary or complete relief from pain, and has also been known to cure the underlying problem.

Considering the fact that many people swallow chemical analgesics almost without thinking and become dependent upon them, it is understandable that doctors and patients alike appreciate the availability of a nontoxic and nonaddictive pain-killer.

A real-life experience proves that *Petadolor* is absolutely harmless. A patient from the Swiss canton of Graubuenden who felt tired of life swallowed some eighty Petadolor tablets hoping to put an end to his suffering. However, afterwards he must have had second thoughts because he contacted his family doctor. The doctor telephoned me, as the manufacturer of Petadolor, in order to find out about the remedy's ingredients and toxicity. I reassured him that the remedy is completely nontoxic and gave him the name and address of a pharmacologist who had conducted many experiments with it. The phamacologist subsequently confirmed that Petadolor is harmless. In fact, the doctor did not even have to pump out the patient's stomach, even though an overdose had been taken. Later on, he telephoned again, reporting that the patient felt none the worse except that he had passed a large amount of water and in a short time had lost a lot of weight. But despite his experience he felt very well indeed and no longer intended to commit suicide. Incidentally, the doctor went on to suggest that the remedy might be used for the treatment of dropsy and obesity.

Petadolor is not as fast-acting as many chemical medicines, but its harmlessness no doubt offsets this small disadvantage. In approximately 50 per cent of patients who take it the pain-killing effect is relatively fast, but in 30 per cent it is slower, taking about an hour to counteract menstrual cramps and migraine. In approximately 10 per cent of patients, especially cancer patients, it begins to work only after about three days, but then the effect is stronger than that of morphine. About 10 per cent of all patients respond very little or not at all to the remedy. It may be, however, that in time a greater concentration of the active substances will bring relief to these people too.

Since Petadolor is able to ease cramps and spasms, it helps to calm and tone the nerves. Faster results are obtained when Petadolor tablets are dissolved on the tongue, because in this way the active elements are dissolved by the saliva and absorbed via the mucous membrane.

Curing an Addiction to Chemical Analgesics

In recent years there has been a frightening increase in the number of people becoming addicted to pain-killing drugs. It is therefore welcome news indeed that *Petadolor*, if taken regularly, can cure the habit comparatively easily. Thousands of people can now obtain great relief through this simple herbal remedy. Taking one tablet every hour can break the addition within a few weeks. Petadolor can even relieve in a relatively short time severe cases of migraine headaches that are accompanied by the typical vomiting of bile. Some patients had suffered from such attacks for years before taking Petadolor. However, it must be said that the normal dose of two tablets three times a day is not sufficient for this purpose. In severe cases the tablets should be taken every hour, or even every half hour, and allowed to dissolve on the tongue.

Welcome Help for Painful Menstruation

It is a relief for women and girls to know that *Petadolor* can help most cases of dysmenorrhoea, the pains and cramps associated with difficult menstruation. I have received testimonials from women who have been helped by this simple natural remedy, where stronger chemical medicines had previously failed. Hence Petadolor should be kept in every medicine chest and travel bag, every hotel and factory reception desk and the staff room or sick bay of every store. In one Basel store Petadolor was given to about forty saleswomen for headaches and menstrual pains, and they all expressed their appreciation for this natural remedy that has no side effects whatsoever.

An Effective Remedy for Asthma

Of all the available plant remedies for asthma the various butterbur preparations stand out as being the most effective. These are *Petastites officinalis extract, Petadolor tablets* and, for exceptionally stubborn conditions, *Petaforce capsules*. All these preparations are made from 100 per cent plant extract and are reliable antispasmodics. A senior consultant at a Kneipp sanatorium once related the case of an asthma attack that would have killed the patient if it had not been for the doctor's help. The strongest chemical medicine, which the doctor had reluctantly administered before, was not as effective as the *Petasites* preparations he then gave the patient. Moreover, it is gratifying to know that *Petasites* not only provides effective short-term relief but in time will bring about a cure.

The effect is not always the same with every patient, since there are various kinds of asthma (see pages 96–8). To back up the treatment, it is often necessary to prescribe a biological calcium preparation, for example *Urticalcin*. One asthmatic told us that such a treatment with *Asthmasan* had practically rid him of his problem, even though he used to suffer from almost unsupportable attacks every time there was an atmospheric depression, or föhn, in the air.

Treating Cancer with Petaforce

Petasites in a high concentration has been given to cancer patients for some years now and the good results achieved have induced researchers to continue their tests. It is not impossible that desperate cancer patients who face an uncertain future will eventually be helped by means of *Petasites*, and this possibility gives us reassurance and hope. Much store has been placed on certain potential cancer remedies that have been publicised widely in the press, causing a sensation, but almost as suddenly as they appeared so they disappeared. However, observations relating to the use of *Petasites* extracts have consistently shown for decades that the plant has a certain influence on the general development of cancer. Of course, only time will tell how far this plant can help to solve the problem of cancer.

Encouraging results have already been recorded. For example, the senior consultant of one large hospital told me that he gave *Petasites* extract to all patients after surgery, with the result that no metastases occurred (the cancer did not spread) and the patients' condition remained stable. Another example concerns a sixty-year-old patient who was taken to hospital suffering from a ramified malignant growth in an advanced state. The doctors held out no hope and informed the lady's son that they did not expect her to live much longer. Nevertheless, the patient was put on *Petasites* extract and, to the great astonishment of the doctors, she was discharged from hospital a few weeks later.

Cases like this last one give grounds for the hope that *Petasites* contains active substances that can be of great help in the treatment of cancer, and no doctor should ignore its potential. Experience has shown that *Petasites* definitely alleviates the unbearable pain suffered by cancer patients in the advanced stage of the illness, when even morphine injectons begin to fail. Every cancer patient should be given *Petaforce*, a *Petasites*-based preparation, in addition to the doctor's usual therapy. Our own results justify the assertion that Petaforce can be of great benefit to cancer patients: it reduces the danger of metastasis, considerably improves the patient's condition and prospects of a cure, and makes the existing pain more endurable. Moreover, Petaforce is a harmless, nontoxic plant remedy without any side effects, for which reason doctors and patients should not hesitate to make full use of its medicinal properties.

Notable doctors continue to use Petaforce and to obtain promising results from their experiments. It is hoped that, together with a special regime, it will eventually play an essential part in solving the difficult problem of cancer. There is another specific observation to back up this hope. As a rule, a turn for the better is noticed on the third day of treatment with Petaforce; the patient's condition improves and pain becomes less severe. Satisfactory results have even been obtained in cases of cancer of the liver, which usually leaves little hope for the patient.

Comfrey (*Symphytum officinale*)

Comfrey grows, for the most part unnoticed, near farmyards, in ditches and by river banks. Because of its excellent medicinal effects it should be lifted from its obscurity and used more widely. Even in ancient times it was employed to heal wounds and broken bones, especially fractures of the leg. It is for good reason, then, that people gave it common names such as 'knitback', 'bruisewort' and 'healing herb'. Considering its good services in cases of fractures alone, it deserves more attention than it usually receives. Comfrey, especially when taken in a homoeopathic form, promotes the healing process and speeds up the formation of new bone cells, which is probably due to the fact that it contains 0.8–1.0 per cent allantoin. This substance is known to encourage granulation and the formation of epithelial cells. Comfrey also contains choline and other, still unknown, elements.

Symphytum growing in the wild has a strong effect on the central nervous system and should be taken only in small amounts. There are about twenty varieties of comfrey, some of which are cultivated for fodder. One is *Symphytum asperum* or *asperrimum*, which is mainly grown in the Caucasus area, while *Symphytum peregrinum* is a Ukrainian variety. *Symphytum orientale* can be found in an

Comfrey

area covering Armenia and running all the way to the north of
Iran. These three varieties are valuable because of their leaves.
While animals avoid the leaves of common comfrey, or *Symphytum
officinale*, they enjoy these three kinds; pigs especially like them.
The leaves of these three varieties of *Symphytum*, as well as of
Siberian comfrey, are said to contain vitamin B_{12}. The curative
mucilage is present in the leaves, but in larger amounts in the roots.
In the United States the leaves are even used in salads.

Comfrey is a fine remedy for an injured periosteum (the connective tissue covering the bones), for festering wounds, wounds which
refuse to heal, and leg ulcers. There is hardly a better remedy to
be found for the external treatment of gout, in which case the raw
root should be grated and applied to the affected part as a poultice.
If fresh roots are not available, use the tincture (*Wallwosan*)
instead. The tincture also provides effective relief from neuralgic
pains, for instance troublesome facial neuralgia. In both cases,
Symphytum 3x is a good supportive remedy if taken internally.

Wallwosan should be rubbed very lightly into the affected parts,
because gouty conditions, injuries to the periosteum and periostitis
react unfavourably to forcible massage. After applying the tincture
it is beneficial to follow up the treatment with *packs of clay,
cabbage, giant dock (sorrel)*, or *goldenrod*.

Wallwosan should be taken internally not only in cases of fractures, gout and neuralgic pain, but also for all sorts of injuries, as well as before and after an operation. Once the bandages, stitches or clips have been removed, the fresh scars can be treated with Wallwosan. Apply the tincture lightly and the healing process will be speeded up.

Additionally, healing can be accelerated and unpleasant post-operative conditions avoided by drinking *vegetable water*, chiefly that from *boiled potatoes* and *leeks*. The *raw juices* of the *cabbage* family are excellent and have a curative effect. The idea is to make use of all these available means in order to derive their combined benefit. It is to your advantage to let comfrey help you, and to increase its effect by using all other available remedies as well.

Symphosan – a Tried and Tested Remedy

Symphosan consists of a mucilaginous tincture prepared from the fresh, raw *Symphytum officinale*, a hairy boraginaceous plant, and various other fresh plant tinctures.

Years of experience have shown that Symphosan, when taken orally, is excellent for treating inflammations of the stomach and intestinal linings. However, even more important is its external use. Applied as an ointment, it will alleviate gout and pains in the joints which manifest themselves when degenerative changes in them begin to occur and a grating noise can be noticed when flexing the joints.

It is important to adopt a strict natural diet as well, for the cure must come, in the first place, from within the body. Gratifying results can be achieved with this treatment if the patient is willing to follow it faithfully. There is no reason for arthritis sufferers to lose hope if they use Symphosan and plan a well-regulated diet. In this way, the degenerative progress of arthritis or gout can be arrested, as has been proved in long-standing cases where all other therapies had failed.

Inflammation of the nerves (neuritis) may also be treated success-fully with Symphosan. In fact, wherever there are painful parts in the body, or wherever there is any sensitivity to pressure which manifests itself in the peripheral nerves, Symphosan can be rec-ommended as a simple, natural and efficacious remedy.

It is extraordinary what a regenerating influence Symphosan has on the skin. Wrinkles, crow's feet and other signs of premature aging will be regenerated by its continuous use. As far as age allows, it is possible to have a firm, youthfully fresh skin. Sympho-san is therefore a valuable cosmetic and should not be missing

357

from the dressing table. It does more than improve the appearance, it promotes good health, and true beauty is identified with health. If Symphosan is used for cosmetic purposes, it should be alternated with a good skin oil.

Abrasions, cuts and injuries which take a long time to heal will respond favourably to Symphosan and heal more quickly. It relieves pain and is anti-inflammatory, and also helpful for haematomas, that is, blood blisters and swellings filled with effused blood.

Use Symphosan externally and take *Aesculaforce* orally for good results in cases of phlebitis. Leg ulcers respond to a local application of Symphosan. First, dab the affected part, but if it stings too much, just dab the surrounding area until the pain subsides, for this too has an alleviating effect.

SYMPHOSAN'S SEVEN INGREDIENTS
To obtain a therapeutically balanced preparation, the fresh plant extract of *Hypericum perforatum (St John's wort)* is added to the pure product of *Symphytum officinale (comfrey)*. St John's wort is well known and proven as a remedy for the blood and for wounds, and as such, helps to intensify the effect of Symphytum.

Hamamelis (witch hazel) is, in the experience of the North American Indians, one of the important wound-healing remedies. It has gained a deserved place in modern medicine too.

Sanicle is another tried and proven country remedy, especially indicated for badly healing wounds, cuts and grazes. It has been used by people in the country for centuries. Unfortunately, it is quite rare in many areas.

Solidago virgaurea, also known as *goldenrod* and *woundwort*, has also been used to treat wounds since time immemorial. It is anti-inflammatory and speeds up the healing process. Its content of essential oils, tannins and saponins may be responsible for these valuable effects.

Arnica, which may be found anywhere in Switzerland up to a height of about 2800 m (8,500 feet), has been recognised as an aid to healing wounds for thousands of years and is acclaimed as such in the oldest herbal records. Contusions with extravasation of the blood into the adjoining tissues are also cured by means of an extract from the root. Arnica will encourage proper capillary circulation, which makes it an important ingredient that enhances the effectiveness of the other plant remedies.

Besides these six ingredients making up Symphosan, there is yet one more. It is *houseleek (Sempervivum tectorum)*, a plant that

Ginkgo biloba

used to be found growing on the roofs of old houses in Switzerland, especially on thatched ones. It may not have been a good thing for the roofs, but the householders certainly knew how to take advantage of the fresh plant to treat inflamed eyes, burns, scalds, ulcers or sores and wounds, for which it is a cooling and healing medicine.

All these outstanding herbs are combined to make Symphosan a truly remarkable remedy that should be kept in every medicine chest and rucksack.

Maidenhair Tree (*Ginkgo biloba*)

I first came across the tree called *Ginkgo biloba* some years ago, while on a visit to the Far East. There were some very fine specimens near Nagasaki, Japan – the city destroyed by an atom bomb. The trees had fortunately survived. Now *Ginkgo biloba* is also grown in Europe's temperate zone, its leaves containing the same active substances as those grown in Asia. In fact, I planted a maidenhair tree, as it is also called, in my garden ten years ago, and it is doing well.

As a result of our modern life-style and environmental disruptions, vascular diseases have increased considerably; in this context it seemed appropriate for me to take a closer look at the *Ginkgo*

359

biloba tree. My contact with Dr Wilmar Schwabe and his research team enabled me to gain a thorough knowledge of the medicinal effects of this extremely valuable plant, and it is noteworthy that preparations made from it have caused no side effects whatsoever. In cases where the brain does not receive sufficient blood, the tincture made from the leaves has proved to be efficacious. Also, a deficient supply of oxygen to the brain can be remedied quite rapidly, which is very important after a stroke. Blood viscosity, that is, its consistency and rate of flow, will improve in a short time. This makes it possible to eliminate the symptoms of a defective circulation, such as headaches, buzzing in the ears, problems with hearing and sight, depression, and a state of fear and panic.

Some people over the age of seventy have registered a notable improvement in health after only 4–6 weeks when they have taken a double dose of the tincture three times a day (the normal dose is 15–20 drops three times a day). Relief is even more certain when a low-protein diet, but one that is rich in vital substances, vitamins and minerals is also followed. Although scientists believe that ginkgo flavone compounds are responsible for this plant's diverse effects, other yet undiscovered substances in the plant must also be given some credit for these benefits.

It is possible to normalise high blood pressure after just a few weeks of taking *Ginkgo biloba*, probably because the blood's viscosity will be favourably affected. We do not know of any other plant remedy that is as beneficial for the brain, central nervous system and vascular system. Moreover, it is interesting to note that the tincture produces a welcome secondary effect, the stimulation of the kidneys and pancreas. Improved blood circulation and supply of oxygen ensure that the cells of the central nervous system are better nourished, hence more efficient. Furthermore, the circulation in the skin, therefore the functioning of the finest capillaries, will be promoted. When *Hypericum* is taken at the same time, ten drops on an empty stomach every morning before breakfast, this will influence the circulation even more. Anyone over the age of fifty would do well to take *Ginkgo* drops for a few months, since various body functions can thus be improved. For when there is better blood circulation, the entire body will benefit from a general cleansing process. The use of this remedy in daily alternation with *Vinca minor* has also given very good results.

Vascular constriction caused by nicotine can also be favourably influenced – but one has to stop smoking. Circulatory disturbances in the arms and legs, even diabetic vascular damage, will diminish.

In cases of varicose veins, the regular taking of *Ginkgo* drops will counteract the formation of blood clots (thrombosis). Everyone who is reasonably sensible and natural in his approach to nutrition and life-style will be able to achieve a veritable regeneration and rejuvenation when taking a course of these drops.

I have received many encouraging letters from patients who have found *Ginkgo biloba* to be an excellent remedy for a variety of complaints. In February 1986, one lady wrote:

'I have been taking this remedy since October 1985. For years I kept getting a pain behind my left eye and when out walking I would involuntarily swerve to the left, often bumping into people. I even feared I had a brain tumour, but neither the eye specialist nor X-rays discovered anything like that. Tests of the throat, nose, ears and sinus were all negative. One doctor said that vascular and circulatory problems were to blame and prescribed *Ginkgo biloba*, "the best remedy there is," he added. And that reminded me of your article in *Gesundheits-Nachrichten (Health News)*, where you recommended *Ginkgo biloba* for the same complaints.'

A nursery-school teacher recently told me that her eyesight had deteriorated so that she could no longer read even when wearing her glasses. Several months earlier she had started taking *Ginkgo biloba* regularly, about thirty drops every morning and night. When she tried her old pair of glasses again she was amazed that her sight had actually improved. I asked myself why this might be so and came to the conclusion that *Ginkgo biloba* had had a regenerative effect on her eyes because it promotes good blood circulation even to the capillaries, thus also improving the supply of oxygen. In fact, I would be glad to hear from anyone whose eyesight had improved after taking *Ginkgo biloba* for some time. Incidentally, it stimulates other sensory functions too, for example the hearing.

Another patient said: 'I began to notice an improvement in my circulation after taking 15–20 drops daily for about a month. The feeling of heaviness in my left foot and leg has almost gone and the migraine headaches are now less frequent.'

A further effect is highlighted in the following letter:

'A little while ago I began to drink *Ginkgo* tea and I must say that its effect is outstanding. Blood supply to the head has improved. Every night my nostrils seemed to be blocked, but now this is better. What is even more important, I'm not as forgetful as I used to be, and if I do forget something I find it easier to recall what it was. Another thing, before I began to take *Ginkgo biloba* my right arm tended to go numb while I was asleep and I had to shake and massage it several times to get the circulation going again. Now I no longer suffer from this.'

I might add here that *Ginkgo biloba* tincture, made from the fresh leaves is stronger and more convenient to use than the tea prepared from an infusion of dried leaves.

A lady in Bremen, Germany, had a similar experience to the one recounted above:

'I have been suffering from insufficient blood supply to the brain since my youth. It has caused me a great deal of anxiety, even an inferiority complex and lots of tears. As soon as I learned about *Ginkgo biloba* I went to get it from our local pharmacy, which stocks your remedies. That was three weeks ago, and I already notice that I can think better and more clearly and my memory, indeed my general health, has improved. I feel happy again.'

Ginkgo biloba is also indicated in cases of concussion. As soon as the patient feels better and has recovered, the remedy should be taken to stimulate blood supply to the brain. Pain and complications in the legs caused by menstrual problems can be eased if *Ginkgo biloba* is taken in alternation with *Vinca minor*. It is recommended to take the first remedy early in the morning one day and the second one the next day, and so forth. Doing so will improve the circulation right down to the finest capillaries.

Horsetail/Shave Grass (*Equisetum arvense*)
Horsetail, or shave grass, is to be found as a rampant weed growing chiefly in damp clay and sandy soil, on railroad tracks, untilled ground, on meadows and alongside paths in the fields. In former times this silica-containing plant was used to clean tinware in some areas of Europe. There are more than twenty varieties in Switzerland, although only *Equisetum arvense* is used for medicinal purposes. Some varieties are even poisonous, for example *Equisetum heleocharis* which contains a toxic alkaloid called equisetin. This variety is larger than the common horsetail and, like *Equisetum palustre*, a marsh plant, it should never be used as a medicinal herb. In the remote past shave grass grew considerably taller, attaining the height of a tree, as has been proved by fossilised specimens dug up from the earth.

Today we must content ourselves with the small, rather delicate plant. It has a finely wrought structure and it stands like a tender young fir, pliant yet tough. A flood can knock it to the ground and drag it from its roots, but the little horsetail takes root anew and stands erect. What gives it this toughness and resilience? If we

Horsetail

analyse its ash constituents, we will find that it contains 60–65 per cent silica and 15 per cent calcium, with the balance of 20 per cent being made up of other minerals.

From this analysis it is evident that silica, as the predominant element, is mainly responsible for its curative effect. *Horsetail tea* has a diuretic effect, stimulating the kidneys; it also helps to cure haemoptysis (the spitting or coughing up of blood), whether it comes from the lungs or the stomach. There is only one other remedy that can compete with horsetail in alleviating this condition and that is tormentil extract. Silica is of great importance in the regeneration of the tissue, as is calcium. Diseases of the respiratory tract (the lungs, bronchial tubes and pleura) and the glandular system likewise depend upon silica for help. Hence an infusion of horsetail or an extract from the fresh plant will be most beneficial. There is only one other plant so far known that contains more silica than horsetail and that is the hemp nettle (*Galeopsis dubia*), with 72 per cent. These silica-containing plants are also very good for the skin and shave grass baths are frequently recommended for the treatment of various skin diseases.

Lady's Mantle (*Alchemilla vulgaris*)

Was this plant given its name because its leaves are shaped like a cloak, or because it can ward off women's illnesses in particular, and so protect them from harm? Perhaps both attributes have influenced the choice of this name. At any rate, let us look at this herb more closely. To do so we must leave the flat lowlands and climb up into the hills, not too high, though, for lady's mantle grows at about 550–640 m (1,800–2,100 feet). Its true home, however, is the alpine meadows of Switzerland, where in close proximity we also find silvery lady's mantle (*Alchemilla alpina*), a plant which looks a little more attractive but is less demanding as regards nutrient intake since it grows in poor stony soil. The less conspicuous common lady's mantle (*Alchemilla vulgaris*) favours rich soil and it can be seen growing alongside the proud monks-hood (*Aconitum napellus*) in hollow places where the earth contains the humus and nitrogen in which these two plants delight. You can also come across it near alpine dairies, where it proliferates together with the giant dock (*Rumus alpinus*). It grows very large in these places because of the rich soil.

The healing potential of lady's mantle is of particular benefit to women and has also proved its worth in cases where the connective tissues lack sufficient strength, causing a tendency to hernia. It should be pointed out, however, that such constitutional problems require that an infusion made from the plant should be taken regularly for at least a year.

The freshly pulped leaves of lady's mantle help wounds to heal quickly when applied externally. If you sustain a scratch or a cut while walking or hiking in the mountains, there are plenty of effective remedies all around. A few flowers of St John's wort rubbed between the fingers and placed on the cut (or crushed arnica root), with pulped lady's mantle bound on top, will make an inexpensive curative dressing. A word of caution is needed here: pick the plants only where they are clean and never from the wayside or near an alpine dairy.

Formerly, good ointments used to be made from the fresh leaves of lady's mantle and also its root. These ointments and creams were used to dress wounds and treat mild ruptures. A tea made with lady's mantle will also stop children's diarrhoea without any side effects.

Lily of the Valley (*Convallaria majalis*)
This woodland plant with elegant sword-shaped leaves and delicate
white flower bells not only brings joy to our hearts in the spring
when we come across it on our walks, but also strengthens and
stimulates this organ, albeit that few people are aware of it. As
long ago as the Middle Ages, lily of the valley was held in high
esteem as a heart medicine. Later, however, when the more potent
digitalis, or foxglove, was discovered, lily of the valley fell into
disuse. An English doctor, by the name of Withering, found digitalis in the tea mixture of an old woman herbalist who used it to
cure dropsy. This happened in the year 1785 and digitalis has been
used ever since.

However, in recent times, we are beginning to realise that we
have wrongfully neglected lily of the valley and that the plant that
produces the most dramatic effect is not necessarily the best one.
After many years of using digitalis as a heart medicine we have
come to know some of its side effects. For example, we know now
that digitalis is cumulative, which means that it remains in the
heart muscle for quite some time and so prolonged treatment may
seriously damage the heart. Lily of the valley, however, does not
pose the same danger, since within four hours the glycoside, the
active substance, is broken down by the body, although its medicinal effect continues for much longer.

Convallaria – the Latin name for lily of the valley – is best used
in the form of a standardised fresh plant extract, together with
Scilla maritima (sea onion or squill). It strengthens the heart
muscles and extends its favourable effect to the blood vessels. If
the patient is given the same dose as would be given with digitalis,
its action will be more gentle and produce no side effects such
as are engendered by accumulation. Digitalis sometimes proves
ineffective in cases of a weak heart resulting from influenza, pneumonia or other lung and infectious diseases, whereas lily of the
valley invariably does the job more effectively. This plant can, and
should, be used as a pre-operative heart tonic and it will also have
a salutary effect if used after an operation. Those who engage in
competitive sports, where a strain is often placed on the heart, will
find *Convallaria* a real help. I have also had excellent results when
using it to treat heart complications which occurred during or after
kidney diseases and have found it most reliable in the treatment
of arteriosclerotic conditions, high blood pressure and symptoms
characteristic of degenerative and premature aging processes.

There is no doubt that lily of the valley is a remedy to be used

Mistletoe

for all kinds of heart trouble. In addition, the unpleasant heart symptoms accompanying hyperthyroidism will be alleviated by taking it, in which case digitalis would not be indicated at all. *Convascillan* is an excellent heart remedy combining lily of the valley with sea onion or squill. The latter plant is described on pages 380–81.

Mistletoe (*Viscum album*)

Each December, as the festive season approaches, shop windows and market places are decorated with the famous mistletoe branches with yellow-green stems and white berries. How many people realise, however, that this plant contains within it such wonderful curative powers? Mistletoe, known also by the Latin name of *Viscum album*, is not only used in the observance of an ancient custom, but is also important in the treatment of prematurely aged arteries. The fresh extract of mistletoe is one of the best remedies for the loss of elasticity in the arteries, a hardening of the arteries accompanied by high blood pressure. Combined with bear's garlic and hawthorn it will safely arrest, perhaps even cure, the progress of this tragic accompaniment of old age. These herbs, together with garlic and passionflower, are contained in *Arterioforce* capsules. Also, when combined with the Indian drug *Rauwolfia serpentina*, mistletoe becomes a high-blood pressure medicine beyond compare. Centuries of experience with mistletoe and the latest results of research on *Rauwolfia* have enabled us to produce the outstanding combination remedy called *Rauwolfavena*.

However, for the treatment to be effective it is important that the levels of salt and protein in the diet be drastically reduced. The importance of mistletoe as a remedy can be illustrated by the quantity used in Germany alone, where 170–190 tons are processed every year.

Mistletoe extract is, of course, used to treat more complaints than just high blood pressure. It is indicated for headaches that are accompanied by dizziness, for spells of vertigo where there is a tendency to fall backwards, for people suffering from agoraphobia and a wavering gait and for those who experience attacks of 'pins and needles' in the limbs and who suffer from constant cold feet. *Viscum album*, used in conjunction with the indicated heart remedies, is beneficial for sudden attacks of palpitations coupled with vascular spasms, difficult breathing and nightly attacks of asthma. For treatment take 5–10 drops, 3–5 times daily.

Moreover, in the search of an effective herbal remedy for cancer, mistletoe and butterbur have given good results so far. For this reason, no one suffering from malignant growths should forget to take mistletoe. The fresh plant extract, as well as homoeopathic injections, have proved invaluable in this respect.

Finally, it is a matter of record that people who have suffered for years from pains in the joints because of chronic arthritis or arthrosis have been cured by homoeopathic mistletoe injections.

Mugwort (*Artemisia vulgaris*)

Pliny, writing in ancient Rome, as well as Gmelin in modern times, noted that *Artemisia* derived its name from the ancient practice of lining the shoes with the leaves to prevent tiredness. It is also said that Roman soldiers put mugwort in their sandals in order to ease their march into Helvetia.

People who have spent their holidays in the canton of Tessin, Switzerland, must be familiar with mugwort, for it is one of the toughest and most widespread weeds in that district. It is easily recognised because it reaches a height of almost 2 m (5–6 feet). Anyone not well acquainted with the various members of the *Artemisia* family might mistake mugwort for wormwood, as it resembles the latter in taste and smell.

The claim that mugwort relieves tired legs can be proved quite simply. After a long walk, bathe your feet in an infusion of mugwort and discover for yourself its soothing effect.

Apart from an essential oil and bitter substances, the herb also contains inulin, a substance similar to a carbohydrate but one that is tolerated by diabetics, unlike ordinary starch and carbohydrates. This makes it possible for the body to receive natural sugar-like substances without the need to engage the pancreas (the islets of Langerhans) in their digestion. Diabetics should take advantage of mugwort. The finely chopped leaves can be used in salads as an additional flavouring. In former days mugwort was also well known as an ingredient for stuffing geese and ducks. In fact, this is still the custom in some areas.

In cases of chronic diarrhoea, stomach or intestinal catarrh, and the widespread problem of intestinal worms, mugwort is an ideal remedy. Moreover, the fresh plant extract is one of the few effective medicines for the treatment of hystero-epilepsy, a form of falling sickness which appears to be connected with ovarian dysfunction. Mugwort is also an ingredient in *Dr Zimpel's epilepsy medicine*, which is closely based on the formulae developed by Paracelsus.

Mugwort is a diuretic and also encourages the menstrual flow when it has for some reason become retarded. Five drops of the fresh plant extract in a glass of water, sipped throughout the day, will suffice for this purpose.

Nettles (*Urtica dioica, Urtica urens*)

In the spring, when the snow has melted and the warm wind thaws the ground, life once again begins to stir in Mother Nature's womb. On sunny slopes, steep paths and even on disused refuse heaps, the green, finely serrated leaves of the nettle appear. Hardly anyone notices it, but it quietly grows while using its juices to produce a medicine that can bring health to many, and even save lives. If only people knew about the benefits of this plant and used it. Many a sufferer of tuberculosis would not have died had he but gone out of his way to gather nettles and avail himself of their goodness. How many children might have had their waxen looks changed and their red cheeks restored, if only their parents had realised what wonderful medicinal value the despised nettle has to offer! Much hard-earned money would not clink unnecessarily into the pharmacist's till, if young nettles were used as a restorative every spring.

No other plant can equal the nettle as a remedy for anaemia,

Nettle

chlorosis, rickets, scrofula, respiratory diseases and, especially, lymphatic problems.

It is most appropriate that nature has given this plant the protection of stinging exterior. Without it, we would probably never have the opportunity to benefit from its healing power. Animals, with their instinctive knowledge of what is good for them, would not leave us even one leaf.

The stinging nettle is rich in calcium, phosphorus, iron and other important minerals. It also belongs to the small category of plants that contain vitamin D. We already know that this vitamin is important in the development of the bones as well as for the assimilation of calcium. That is why eating raw nettles, either pulped or in the form of nettle juice, has a quick and reliable effect on rickets.

Many years ago I gave a lecture in Winterthur and mentioned that the stinging nettle was a wonderful help to those suffering from tuberculosis or weak lungs. A year later, I again delivered a lecture in that same hall. This time, a man from the audience stood up and announced in front of everybody that he had heard me describe the marvellous healing powers of the stinging nettle the previous year. His wife was then at home ill with tuberculosis of the lungs. Since her doctors could hold out no real hope of a cure, he began giving his wife food that was rich in calcium. Every day he gave her the juice of raw nettles, or added finely chopped nettles to her soup. Now, a year later, to the astonishment of her doctors, this man's wife had regained her health. I myself was just as surprised as the 300 members of my audience. I do admit that the daily nettle hunt and the trouble of putting them through the mincer to extract the juice is quite an effort. However, it is worth-while considering that it can help a sick person to regain health.

Young nettles can be finely chopped and sprinkled on soup as a garnish or added to salads. Since the juice is not very tasty it is better to mix it in with whichever soup you prefer – vegetable, potato or oatmeal. A tablespoon per day for an adult and a half to one teaspoon for a child has sufficient medicinal properties to take effect. For an infant, 5–10 drops of the extract each day, added to different dishes of mashed foods should suffice. If you want to profit from at least part of this healthy remedy and at the same time enjoy a pleasant vegetable dish, you can also steam young nettles in oil with a little onion. This will give you an excellent spinach-like dish that goes well with mashed or sauté potatoes, besides being tasty. So make it a point to search out the places where you can gather nettles; only pick the young shoots and you will be able to have nettles on your menu for months.

Perhaps some of my readers feel that they have no time to look for and prepare these wild plants and would prefer to buy the juice ready-made. Of course they can do this; but no prepared medicine – even an extract from fresh plants – can have as good an effect as the extracted juice from a plant freshly gathered or the fresh plant used by itself.

The calcium complex *Urticalcin* contains *Urtica*, which is the Latin name for nettles. As the name implies, Urticalcin is a com-pound containing various kinds or combinations of calcium, with the addition of fresh nettles. The way in which homoeopathy makes use of nettles will be explained in the section on 'Homoeo-pathic remedies' (see page 397).

Oats (*Avena sativa*)

It is common knowledge that horses derive their strength largely from eating oats. They are nourishing for people too. Whenever we have an upset stomach we most likely take oatmeal gruel or porridge, for this will usually correct the trouble. As a food oats

Oat

are good for man and beast, but that is not all: oats are also a wonderful remedy. Even in its earliest stages, when the oat plant is just a tall grass, it has remarkable healing powers. Few people realise that when the ears are just beginning to form, when it is juicy and breaking into flower, this green grass is at its richest in avenin, which is unsurpassed as a nutrient for the cells of the nervous system.

You can prepare a perfect nerve food at home simply by putting the flowering oats through a mincer, or by chopping them up in some other way. Cover the green mash with warm water and let it stand for about two minutes. Then strain and sweeten with honey, unrefined sugar, grape sugar or grape concentrate. The green oats can also be put through the mincer together with raisins or currants, then covered with warm water and strained as before. In this way they will be sweetened during preparation.

When the green oat plant is about 40–50 cm (15–20 inches) high it is usable for this oat drink, and is most potent during the flowering period. As long as the grains are juicy the oats can be used for this tonic.

The resulting oat drink is a wonderful tonic which, if taken

371

regularly over a period of time, will calm and regenerate the nervous system, giving it new energy. Its use is also recommended for diabetics.

Even after the oats have been harvested the straw can be used to make an infusion, although it is not as potent as the juice from the green oats. Still, it will be found quite effective in cases of catarrh, coughs and febrile conditions. A decoction of oat straw added to the bath water is especially good for children whose skin function needs stimulating.

There are still other uses for oats, for even the grains make an excellent tea. If you cannot find gleanings in the field, use the oat grain together with the husk, as fed to horses. Sweeten the tea as you would the oat drink described above. It has a tonic effect, and if taken when the mucous membranes of the stomach or intestines are inflamed, it is a superb soothing remedy.

Homoeopathy employs the freshly pressed juice from the green oats for its outstanding nerve remedy *Avena sativa*, which is the Latin name for the oat plant. This remedy is particularly useful for children and sensitive people. The same extract, together with the extract of Korean ginseng, is used to make the reliable nerve tonic for adults called *Ginsavena*.

Papaya (*Carica papaya*)
Every time I see papaya fruits on display in a shop I remember the time I spent in Lagunas, on the Marañon river. It was there that I acquired the habit of looking for a papaya plant after every meal. I would break off a leaf and eat some of it to aid the digestion and as a prophylactic, even if it was only a piece the size of a large coin. It may even be possible that my regular chewing of papaya leaves may have seen to it that the many kinds of parasites did not really bother me on my repeated travels in the tropics, even though I may have swallowed them with my food. True, I was always very careful, but even so, dangerous amoebas, hookworms, oxyurias, ascarids, whipworms and many other parasites, are rampant in the tropics and multiply rapidly, laying millions of eggs. There are some that draw blood from the intestinal linings; others cause inflammation, even abscesses and ulcers. They penetrate the liver and as a direct or indirect consequence thousands of victims die, often literally wasting away.

Papaya

A Superb Remedy

It is interesting to note that wherever there are dangers to our health nature provides a local means of resistance or remedy. Papaya thrives in hot and humid tropical regions. I came across some marvellous specimens in Lagunas, where the trees grew to about 3–4 m (about 10–13 feet), the trunk to a diameter of about 20–25 cm (8–10 inches), bearing 20–25 fruits, which hang on the trunk between the axils of the large leaves. The ripe yellow fruits hang more towards the bottom of the tree; further up they are still green and unripe. They look like melons, are hollow inside and full of small, black, moist, round seeds. The active substance of papaya is to be found mainly in the unripe fruits and in the skin of the ripe ones, but this skin is usually peeled off and thrown away. The fruit pulp is yellow or pinkish, with an unusual taste, which it may take a while to become accustomed to.

As I suggested above, the fruit aids the digestion, so make it a habit to eat a slice after meals if you are visiting the tropics. The strong taste is less noticeable when papaya is mixed in a fruit salad together with pineapple, bananas and mangoes. It also helps to add a little lemon juice. Incidentally, papaya and pineapple mixed together in a blender make a tasty and refreshing drink.

Although a certain German pharmaceutical company mentions the use of only ripe papaya in their product, the real medicinal

373

effect is not obtained from ripe fruits. The curative properties, especially papain, are found in the unripe fruit, the seeds and leaves. Papain can be obtained by scratching the skin of unripe fruits. Immediately, a white juice oozes from the incision, similar to latex in a rubber tree. Left to dry, this milky juice becomes a yellowish rubbery substance – raw papain. This is an excellent remedy, employed to deal with two specific problems. First of all, it kills – or rather, digests – all intestinal parasites that usually settle in the large and small intestines. So if you eat a piece of papaya leaf after every meal, as I used to do, you will not be plagued by troublesome worms. You can also chew and swallow a teaspoonful of the black seeds for the same purpose. This simple preventative measure, if taken regularly, will keep you free from infections too. The second type of problem for which papaya has proved an effective remedy is described below.

Help for the Pancreas
Papaya stimulates the pancreas and helps to digest protein. If you happen to indulge in too much protein, eat some papaya and you will find that the feeling of fullness and listlessness disappears in a matter of minutes. No wonder, then, that *Papayasan*, which is made from papaya leaves and the juice of unripe fruits, is such a helpful natural product. In fact, Papayasan has proved to be an excellent remedy for a range of pancreatic problems, including fatty stools caused by insufficiency of the pancreas, even typical pancreatitis. Papayasan should preferably be taken in conjunction with *Kelpasan* because of the latter's potassium iodide content. Diabetics will benefit from Papayasan too, since it is a great aid in digesting fat and protein. Anyone who suffers from diabetes should take two Papayasan tablets after every meal and will be delighted at the effect of this natural remedy.

If you intend to travel to a subtropical or tropical region, even if only for a short visit or vacation, do not forget to take some Papayasan with you. Remember, two tablets after every meal can save you from a lot of trouble. It is much better to pay a little attention to your body and care for your health than fall victim to amoebic dysentery or some stubborn worm infection and the bothersome consequences.

Pimpernel Root (*Pimpinella saxifraga*)
In the Middle Ages, women must have often sat talking and exchanged advice on all sorts of subjects. The medical practitioner

often lived miles away from a hamlet or fortified castle and there were no telephones to summon him or her. Sometimes it might have happened that some young noblewoman was unable to give her new-born baby sufficient milk and, often within the walls of the castle itself, some wise old woman would be found to give advice. Later, a young girl would be hustled through the gates and over the drawbridge with orders to find some pimpernel roots somewhere outside. Having been well washed, these roots would be placed in the noblewoman's bosom and within 6–8 hours there would be so much milk that the pimpernel roots would have to be quickly removed and thrown away.

Thus, old stories and records tell us of the wonderful effect produced by the little pimpernel. Today we have other remedies that may be easier to come by and apply (for example *Ricinus communis 3x*) but wherever the pimpernel may be found, it should prove to be as great a help as it was in days of old. Nursing mothers might try to discover whether its effect is as good as the old records say it is.

Today, the pimpernel's main attribute is the wonderful effect it has on the vocal cords in cases of catarrh and sore throats. Pimpernel roots, chewed throughout the day, will have a much better effect than all the expensive patent medicines with their fancy packaging and labels that promise miracles. There is only one drawback, pimpernel roots are far from palatable, even though they are not so bad that one would want to reject them altogether. In the wintertime, when catarrh is so prevalent, one can come to appreciate the pimpernel's great benefits.

If hoarseness is allied to the catarrh, chew pimpernel roots with rowan berries; both remedies can usually be bought in a dry state at a pharmacy or herbalist. For extremely bad cases, *fresh pine bud syrup (Santasapina Cough Syrup)* is another excellent remedy.

Formerly, pimpernel root was recommended in cases of calculus and skin eruptions. That our forefathers prized pimpernel as one of the means of protecting themselves against contagious diseases can be seen from the old saying:

> *To be healthy and fit, eat garlic and pimpernel,*
> *You can then hope to live to an old age as well!*

Purple Coneflower (*Echinacea*)

Purple Coneflower (*Echinacea purpurea* and *angustifolia*)

My Introduction to Echinacea

It was in the 1950s when I met Black Eagle, the chief of the Sioux Indians. Besides his tribal tongue, he spoke very good English, so we were able to talk about our mutual appreciation and love of plants, their curative powers and practical uses for various ailments and emergencies. I found even his philosophy of life to be very similar to my own. He too looked at nature as a creation of the great Artist of the Universe.

We both shared the same views regarding man's responsibility towards nature, which involved not only thinking of what we can get out of it but rather doing all we can to protect and preserve it. Because of the many things we had in common, a close bond of friendship developed between us and one day he embraced me affectionately and professed his feelings of brotherly love towards me. It was a most interesting experience, not least because of the different tribal customs he introduced me to. Being over ninety years old at the time, he was able to relate many experiences he had had with the white man. More than once I had to interrupt, expressing my deepest sympathy and sadness at all the injury and suffering the people of my own skin colour had inflicted upon him and his people.

Black Eagle's ideas about illness and disease were of great interest to me, and in this respect we discussed the importance of medicinal herbs as well as nutrition, or proper diet. He believed that the white man's customs and habits had overtaxed the regenerative powers our Creator, or nature, had implanted in us and that he often had only himself to blame for the resulting diseases.

A Sacred Plant

It was from Black Eagle that I learned about the curative effects of various plants growing in South Dakota, the home of his tribe. One plant in particular enjoyed his special appreciation. Considered as sacred, this medicinal herb had been a life-saver on many occasions. His ancestors, he said, used it to cure cases of blood poisoning.

Even snake poison could be made ineffective with it. When someone was bitten by a poisonous snake, he told me, another person would suck the bite until blood began to flow. Of course, the attendant would spit the poison out. Next, the leaves and roots of the plant were chewed up, preferably by the unfortunate victim himself. The juice was swallowed but the masticated plant was applied to the bite and bandaged. This treatment was repeated at least twice, and then repeated again on the second and third day. By the fourth day, the effect of the poison would have disappeared and the victim would be out of danger.

These Indians used to do the same thing to treat injuries. Again, the masticated plant would be placed on the affected part, and a serious situation would never arise provided this plant was on hand and was applied immediately. Certain arrow poisons could be neutralised by the same method. And if one wanted to prevent susceptibility to colds and catarrh in bad and blustery weather, he only had to chew the leaves or roots of the plant. The ingested juice would build up resistance to everything we now call infectious diseases.

The Two Varieties of Echinacea

Then Black Eagle showed me this highly prized plant, or plants to be more exact. I discovered that it was the coneflower, *Echinacea*

377

angustifolia and *Echinacea purpurea*. One of the two varieties, *Echinacea angustifolia*, has a tap root, and I still remember how deep I had to dig to get it out. The other variety has a rootstock and does not penetrate quite so deep into the earth.

The chief explained that both plants were equal in their effect. But having heard so many marvellous things about what this plant could do I began to think it was almost too good to be true. Still, I took some seeds back home with me and began to grow *Echinacea* in the Swiss lowlands as well as at an elevation of 1,600 m (4,500 feet); that was in Teufen and in Brail (in the Engadine), where I used to have a house with a large garden. At first, the plants were quite sensitive to the cold in the mountains, but I persevered for ten years until they became acclimatised and began to produce flowers.

Blood Poisoning Cured

One day I was cutting grass on a steep meadow when I hit my foot with the scythe. It was careless of me, but I did not immediately disinfect the cut, only bandaged it with a handkerchief and carried on with my work. Because of this negligence, it was not surprising when blood poisoning set in. Well now, I thought, this is a chance to put our herb to the test and see whether the Indians were right. I proceeded exactly the way Black Eagle had taught me. Already a long blue line was visible on the leg and higher up, in the groin, there was a swollen lymph node. So I covered the whole leg with a dressing of crushed *Echinacea* leaves. Furthermore, I chewed some and swallowed the juice. In fact, I ate the whole plant. Now came the surprise, for within quite a short time the inflammation and infection were gone. This experience convinced me that everything I had been told about *Echinacea* was true.

Protection against Malaria

Some time after the above experience, I travelled to the Amazon region and visited a jungle where malaria was rampant. I was accompanied on this study tour by a colleague who had been working with me in Peru, a man who was well acclimatised to South America.

I took the risk of travelling without malaria drugs, but I did take *Echinacea* tincture daily, about forty drops every morning and evening. During the first few days we put up a mosquito net, but in the native huts the mosquitoes were able to slip through the chinks in the bamboo floor. We even killed some blood-filled insects under the net.

My colleague had no confidence in *Echinacea* and declined to take any. Like myself, he must have been bitten hundreds of times. The area we visited around the Upper Marañon was notorious and feared for malaria. Although I was bitten all over, I was astonished that I did not once come down with a fever attack, whereas my colleague returned home with a bad case of the disease. Unfortunately, he had not taken any remedy. He believed that his sixteen years in Peru had made him immune to malaria. However, the area where he had been living, at our farm in Tarapoto, was malaria-free, unlike the Amazon region we visited on this occasion.

Thirty years later, a medical check-up brought to light that I had once had a malaria infection, which could only have been during this visit to the Marañon. As I had never suffered so much as a bout of fever or any other symptom of the disease, I came to the obvious conclusion that *Echinacea* may well help to prevent malaria.

Reinforcing the Immune System
Researchers have been taking a keen interest in *Echinacea*, with the aim of isolating its medicinal properties. First they tried, without success, to find the substances that prevent the growth and development of pathogenic organisms, since it was thought that this is what happens.

It was much later, however, when they discovered that the effect of *Echinacea* is not attributable to some antibiotic property, but to its ability to reinforce the body's own defence mechanism. Medical science began to realise then that here was a very remarkable plant indeed. After all, the immune system is one of the most important things in our body. Without its proper functioning, without a good defence mechanism, we could not survive. We are constantly subjected to the attacks of millions of germs. However, these agents can multiply and cause damage in the human body only if they find the breeding ground necessary for their survival and if the defence system is weak.

The immune system is weakened by our modern, unnatural way of life. It is therefore understandable that a herbal remedy such as *Echinacea* is gaining in stature.

SCIENTIFIC EVIDENCE

Scientific research has confirmed that *Echinacea* improves and builds up immunity, even though it has not been possible, to date, to isolate a specific substance that is responsible for its remedial effect. I myself am convinced that no such active substances will ever be discovered because it is not some specific chemical that can be credited with the medicinal effect, but the complex of vital substances contained in the plant as a whole. It is the same with all other medicinal herbs; it is the entirety of substance – all the active and supporting substances in the plant – that achieves the desirable results. This is especially true in the case of a herb whose properties stimulate the immune system, since it acts not just on a single organ but on the body as a unit.

I have been able to prove for myself that *Echinacea* activates the immune system, and that it is therefore a great aid to the body's resistance to micro-organisms. Time and again I have seen those with a weak lymphatic system and who suffer constant attacks of colds and catarrh, particularly children, overcome this susceptibility when put on regular medication with *Echinacea* preparations such as *Echinaforce*. Many parents have told me that their children have become more resistant to infectious diseases; the same is true of sensitive adults. Because of my practical experience, I maintain that *Echinacea* builds up the body's own defences, above all, the efficiency of the phagocytes.

Scientists have discovered that *Echinacea* is able to render the hyaluronidase (an enzyme) produced by bacteria ineffective, preventing their proliferation. This helps us to understand why *Echinacea* neutralises snake poison, which also contains hyaluronidase.

Without doubt, *Echinaforce* can be used with confidence for every case of infection or infectious disease. It supports the body in every part where its defence mechanism needs to be improved, increasing overall resistance.

Sea Onion or Squill (*Scilla, Urginea maritima*)

Along the shores of the Mediterranean, more specifically the blue waters of Greece by the Peloponnesian peninsula, an extraordinary plant is found. It shoots up out of the dry ground on a stem more than a metre (3 feet) high and is crowned with a dense spike of small white flowers. The stem has no leaves and if you dig down for its root, you will come upon a large bulb which, on average, is about 15 cm (6 inches) in diameter and over 1 kg (2 pounds) in weight. This is the genuine sea onion or squill that flourishes in

380

the dry ground and the fragrant sea air and is known to the botanists as *Scilla maritima*. The plant contains an essential oil, scillitin, or scillin, besides other important substances, and was used as an internal as well as external remedy even by the ancient inhabitants of the Mediterranean region. They praised its medicinal effects in the treatment of various heart troubles, oedematic congestion, and breathing difficulties. They also used it to aid those who suffered from extreme cold in the hands and feet, whose urine was pale and watery, whose pulse was light or rapid, or whose upper air passages were affected with catarrh. It was found especially helpful in treating the kind of heart trouble that is accompanied by difficulty in dispersing water and expelling phlegm caused by catarrh, and by itching of the skin. More recent observations, based on the experience of those ancient herbalists, have confirmed the efficacy of fresh squill extract in curing the range of symptoms just described.

This natural plant remedy can be of great help in treating these problems. Large doses are unnecessary. In fact, to achieve good results no more than five drops of 3x potency (1/1000 dilution of the mother tincture) need be taken at one time.

A combination of lily of the valley and sea onion produces a very good remedy, *Convascillan*. Where once it was necessary to give strophanthin – a virtual whip for the heart – it is now possible to provide help with this gentle and reliable *Convallaria* complex, which supports rather than drives the heart. The effect of Convascillan is also long-lasting, another point in its favour.

Wild Fruits and Berries

Barberry (*Berberis vulgaris*)
Roaming through the valleys of the Swiss cantons of Valais and
Graubuenden, bright with the autumn sun and a riot of colours,
the happy wanderer will find not only hedgerow after hedgerow
of wild rose hips, but also many bushes replete with sprays of
barberries. Of course, barberries grow in other areas too, but
wherever they are, most people go past the wild fruits without
realising that they have wonderful healing powers. The clusters of
these red oblong berries are a delight to the eye and, together with
autumn flowers and leaves, make a beautiful bouquet. Still, few
people are aware that these berries can be eaten and are, in fact,
one of the best nerve tonics available. No other wild berries are
as rich in vitamin C and many people suffering from 'nerves' could,
on their walks in the country, benefit enormously by picking some
and chewing them slowly before swallowing them. A general check-
up of the population would no doubt prove that many people
nowadays need such a tonic.

A raw barberry conserve, made from well-ripened berries, is rich
in vitamin C (ascorbic acid) and other vitamins. However, if copper
vessels or utensils are used to cook and strain the conserve, the
copper acts as a catalytic agent and destroys most of the vitamin
C.

Since the vitamin content is mostly lost in cooking, the barberries
should be processed raw in order to obtain a nutritious and
remedial conserve that keeps well. Thorough tests have shown that
the best way to produce barberry conserve is as follows. Put the
freshly picked and fully ripe barberries through the mincer. Then
squeeze the pulp through a sieve. The pips and skins will remain
in the sieve and you will have the clean purée and juice. Add 100 g
(3 oz) of raw cane sugar to 500 g (1lb) of barberry purée and stir
well. When the sugar has dissolved, add 200 g (7 oz) of honey and
finally 200–250 g (7–8 oz) of thick grape sugar syrup. Stir the

382

Hawthorn

mixture until well blended. If the mixture is too thin, add a little more raw cane sugar. Then, pour into glass jars as you would with jam.

On a commercial scale, this conserve is made by condensing grape sugar under a vacuum and then slowly adding the raw purée. Experimental research has established the excellence of this natural remedy in the treatment of bad nerves. It also has a wonderful effect on the kidneys and on any scorbutic tendency, such as bleeding gums.

Hawthorn (*Crataegus oxyacantha*)
The splendid remedy, *Crataegisan*, is made from the dark red berries, haws, to be found hanging in small bunches from the thorny hawthorn shrubs by the wayside or in the meadows every autumn. When I was a child, my friends and I called them 'mealy berries'. We children did not know anything about them, except that they were good to eat (their pulpy inside is not unlike cooked sweet potato) and of course we ate them because there was probably nothing else at that particular moment. Certainly we did not need those berries when we were young, for *Crataegus* is a heart remedy, and is particularly valuable in cases of weak heart muscles.

When arteriosclerosis, high blood pressure and, especially, a hardened and constricted coronary artery are diagnosed, there is

Juniper

no doubt that *Crataegus* is the best, the most harmless and the most reliable remedy that can be taken. *Arnica*, mixed in the right proportion with *Crataegus*, makes up a compound remedy that has benefited many elderly people, even to the extent of lengthening their lives.

Crataegisan is a successful remedy for angina pectoris, when heart cramps occur. These cramps are usually accompanied by stabbing pains in the region of the heart resulting in difficult breathing and a weak, irregular pulse. In this case, where immediate relief is necessary, take 5–10 drops every half hour. When the pains subside and the cramps have eased, 15–20 drops taken three times a day will suffice.

For cardiac dilatation, the main treatment should consist of *heart hormones* and *Crataegus* taken at the same time.

Juniper Berries (*Fructus juniperi*)
People who like sauerkraut will be familiar with juniper berries because they are often added for flavouring. But then what do we do? We pick them out and leave them on the side of the plate. Occasionally they are mentioned in a cookery book as a spice, and it may also be remembered by some that grandfather often used to chew them first thing in the morning. Besides that, juniper

berries have been more or less forgotten. Old herbals say that the eagle lives to an old age because it feeds on juniper berries. They contain a delicate essential oil and much sugar, yet they do not taste sweet because their bitter constituents override the sweet ones.

Sufferers from gout and rheumatism find that juniper berries are an excellent remedy because they help to increase the elimination of uric acid by way of the urine. Be careful how you use them, however; too much may irritate the kidneys, and this is easily done if you take the juice or extract. If someone suffers from nephritis or similar kidney conditions, he should take juniper only in homoeopathic doses, *Juniperus communis 1x* or *2x*.

For cases of asthma, and particularly the excessive mucous catarrh that may result from the disease, juniper extract is most beneficial and its use should be alternated with that of barberries and rowan berries.

Oedematous conditions (excessive accumulation of fluid in the body) and acute inflammation of the bladder (cystitis) will respond to juniper in the form of an infusion, essence or extract.

Eat juniper berries every morning before breakfast, one berry the first day, two the second day, and so forth until you reach twenty and then go back, reducing the amount day by day to just one. This is very good for stimulating the appetite and strengthening the stomach and will benefit the glands.

Moreover, if you tie some juniper needles in a muslin bag, and place this under the hot tap when you run a bath, you will have a good remedy for rheumatism and gout.

Rose Hips (*Rosa canina*)

Not only are the modest but beautiful flowers of the wild rose, so unjustly called *Rosa canina* or 'dog rose', a pleasure to behold, but the fruit too is delightful as it splashes its bright red across the autumn landscape. Where the hips have not been harvested they look, in winter, like little red gnomes with white caps of snow, and many a hungry bird has enjoyed these nutritious berries when everything else has been buried under the ice.

As a food, rose hips are excellent for many reasons. The fully ripe hips contain natural fruit sugar and taste as sweet as any jam. They are nourishing because of their many mineral salts, such as calcium, silica, magnesium and phosphorus. Incidentally, phosphorus is good for the brain and no doubt our little feathered friends have to use theirs, dashing about in the winter weather,

Rose Hip

and who knows whether the phosphorus in rose hips is responsible for their feathers being always so bright and shiny. On the other hand, silica may contribute to the beauty of their feather coats. Our little friends must owe their peace and contentedness, in spite of their lively acrobatics, to the vitamin C in rose hips, since this vitamin has a calming effect on the nerves.

Now you know why rose hip products are also valuable for us humans. Nature always shows us the way, while science can only try to give us an explanation of the reasons.

Rose hips are one of the best sources of vitamin C. Rose hip pulp is not only a tasty, slightly tart conserve but a medicine, a nerve food, conforming to the old principle, 'Let food be your medicine and medicine your food.' It is important, however, to remember that rose hips should not be boiled as heat destroys much of their remedial properties. Eat a slice of bread thickly spread with raw pulp every day and you will be taking your daily requirement of vitamin C. If a conserve is made from the pulp and sweetened with grape sugar or other fruit sugars as described below, you will have the added advantage of getting the best kinds of sugar, ones that are easy to assimilate, and you will be providing yourself with food of a high calorific value.

Rose Hip Conserve
Gather the ripe berries of the wild rose, the hips, and spread them out to mellow in a dry shady place. Make sure they are not piled up on top of each other in the box or basket, otherwise they will go mouldy, rather than overripe. When they are nice and soft, put them through a mincer to obtain a thick red purée. Use a wooden spoon to rub the mash through a sieve in order to separate the little seeds. A red paste will come through the sieve and can be scraped off with a knife or spoon. This paste, rich in vitamin C, should now be mixed with half the quantity of honey or grape sugar (the consistency of honey). That is all there is to it! Although uncooked, the mixture will keep well, preferably in the refrigerator. It is wholesome and delicious. A teaspoonful a day will provide the daily requirement of vitamin C and can help a hard-working person more than any of the commercially manufactured vitamin C tablets.

Rose Hip Tea
Having made the conserve, you will have the seeds, skin and some pulp left over. These can be dried and used for making tea, especially in winter. Rose hip tea is most beneficial. It has a delicate flavour and can be served with lemon or milk, according to taste. It is rich in silica and, perhaps for this reason, is an excellent kidney remedy. Seriously ill people who cannot take any other herbal infusion are quite safe with rose hip tea.

Rowan Berries (*Fructus sorbi*)
In the autumn, the rowan tree (European mountain ash) produces beautiful red berries. If you spread these berries out in a shady place and dry them, you will have a reliable remedy for hoarseness. Just chew them and the problem will quickly disappear. Also, some people in rural areas still make jam from the ripe berries.

Sea Buckthorn (*Hippophae rhamnoides*)
There is hardly another shrub with edible berries that is so widely distributed as sea buckthorn. It can be found growing from the north of Portugal to the Pyrenees, across the Alps, then south in the Balkans, over in Turkey, and to the east in central Russia, Mongolia, Korea and Japan. If all the berries could be gathered and processed, they would be more than enough to cater for the vitamin C requirement of all humankind.

Once our bodies have become deficient in vitamin C, we are

much more liable to succumb to infectious diseases. That is why we should see to it that the deficiency is rectified, especially in springtime. Although barberrry and rose hip purées no doubt play an important part in correcting vitamin C deficiencies, sea buckthorn berries are no less valuable in terms of their extremely high content of vitamin C. During the time of year when a wide selection of fresh vegetables are difficult to obtain, or very expensive, and fruits have lost part of their vitamin content because of long storage, the need for vitamins is even greater and many people like to tide themselves over the vitamin-poor period by eating *Bio-Buckthorn-Conserve.*

Vitamin C has to be taken daily since the body can store only minute quantities. It is found in the endocrine glands, the suprarenal and pituitary glands, and there is no doubt that it is essential to the normal functioning of these important glands.

As a rule, cancer patients show a definite lack of this vitamin. It is therefore recommended that people with a predisposition to cancer and those who are victims already, increase their intake of foods that are rich in vitamin C.

To ensure good health, the daily intake of vitamin C should not be less than 50 mg, and it is better if it can be obtained from such natural sources as sea buckthorn, raspberries, lemon juice and rose hip and barberry purée.

Sea buckthorn has even more to offer us than its high vitamin content. Its berries also contain other vitamins, for example, water-soluble vitamin B, fat-soluble provitamin A and even vitamin E. These natural, biological vitamins are vital for keeping the body healthy, fit and efficient. Various acids, such as malic and tartaric acids, have also been identified in these berries. The sea buckthorn berry seeds can also be used to produce an oil of which the dietary value is unquestionable.

If you suffer from constant infections and bleeding of the gums and mucous membranes, you would do well to take sea buckthorn products as a dietary supplement. Sea buckthorn berries being rich in many vitamins and trace elements, it is obvious that the products based on them are recommended for children and adults alike as food supplements and a tonic.

In Switzerland, sea buckthorn grows abundantly in the upper Inn valley and in Ticino, especially in the Maggia valley. When ripe, the orange-coloured berries nestling between olive-green leaves are quite conspicuous, and in the wintertime birds can be seen enjoying them to the full. We use sea buckthorn extract as one of the ingredients in our vitamin preparation called *Bio-C-Lozenges*.

A Brief Guide to Selected Homoeopathic Remedies

The subject of homoeopathic remedies is so vast that the examples given below represent only a small selection of what would otherwise fill several volumes.

Aconitum napellus (Aconite, Monkshood)

The erect and splendid aconite, with its hood-like, blue-purple flowers, can be as poisonous as it is medicinal. This beautiful plant is known by many names, for example monkshood, friar's cap, wolfbane and mousebane, and is native to the Swiss Alps. There you will find it on the alpine meadows, where the ground is rich, in damp hollows between low shrubs and in thinning woods right up to the highest elevation where the conifers grow.

Every part of the plant is highly poisonous. The whole plant, including the subsidiary tuber, which is developed from the root for the following year's growth, is used to make a tincture for homoeopathic purposes. If this tincture was to be taken pure, it would result in certain death caused by cardiac paralysis and damage to the spinal cord. But diluted a thousand or one hundred thousand times, aconite becomes one of the best and most reliable homoeopathic medicines.

Aconitum is the best first aid in cases of inflammations that tend to become febrile. In infectious diseases, especially when the skin is hot and dry, *Aconitum* in the third and fourth decimal potency (3x or 4x) has a rapid and highly beneficial effect. It diverts the toxins from the blood and the tissues to the skin and encourages perspiration. A rush of blood to the head (hot flushes), such as many women experience during the change of life, is best dealt with by *Aconitum 10x*; for even better results this should be taken together with *Ovarium 3x*. It is helpful to take *Aconitum 4x* in alternation with *Belladonna 4x* at the onset of an acute illness when fever, a feeling of unrest, hot flushes, palpitations, uneasiness and a state of anxiety are present. When perspiration breaks out and the patient has calmed down, the treatment with *Aconitum* can be stopped and only *Belladonna 4x* or some other indicated remedy need be taken.

Homoeopathic *Aconitum* and *Belladonna* should be in everyone's medicine chest, for they are more frequently used than any other remedy for first aid. However, we do not recommend *Aconitum* tincture as it is dangerous, even though some doctors prescribe it for neuralgia caused by a cold, for gout and for rheumatism. There are other, safer remedies available that are just as effective. *Aconitum* is a mydriatic, that is, it dilates the pupil if it is put in the eye. *Belladonna* has the same property due to its atropine content. To achieve the best results, *Aconitum* should be given in the fourth decimal potency (4x), for stronger persons perhaps in the third (3x); five drops in a glass of water taken at hourly intervals will be enough.

Atropa belladonna (Belladonna, Deadly Nightshade)

This attractive plant with its thick stems or branches and leaves is somewhat similar to the tobacco plant. However, its axillary flowers, dull brown to dark purple in colour, indicate that it is neither the tobacco plant nor the ground-cherry (Chinese lantern), but belladonna, the medicinal as well as deadly nightshade.

The ripe, shiny black berries often entice children to pick and eat them – with fatal results. Many a child has had to pay with his young life because of being tempted. On the other hand, in considering this plant we cannot overlook its many benefits, even though we are aware of its poisonous properties. As is true of people, plants can have good and bad characteristics, and this is the case with belladonna. It is known to have killed people, but it is also famed as a life-saver.

Belladonna is partly responsible for the rediscovery of the homoeopathic principle of similarity. Dr Hahnemann once found himself completely at a loss as to what remedy to prescribe for a sick woman, until an unconscious child was carried in to him. The child's face was suffused by a bluish-red colour and Hahnemann realised immediately what had happened when the father showed him the pretty black berries he had snatched from the child's hands – belladonna poisoning! By chance, the physician noticed that there was an extraordinary similarity in the appearance of the women and the child; both had a bluish-red flush on the face. The causes were different but the results were the same. The doctor suddenly realised what he must do, the significance of which has only become fully recognised and appreciated in our time: 'Similia similibus curantur', the ancient Hippocratic teaching and principle of similarity.

As soon as Hahnemann had given the child something to make it vomit, he went out with the father, broke off a branch of the belladonna with flowers and fruit, and squeezed the whole thing into some water. By diluting it to about 4x he prepared the yellowish-green liquid into a medicine, which he then gave to the sick woman. Noting her reaction, the doctor followed this up with a second dose, and a few more, until the woman was finally out of danger. Thus, the child's belladonna poisoning saved the woman's life and at the same time brought about a deeper understanding and knowledge of another law of nature.

Belladonna can always be given with success where a condition is the result of poisoning, whether from an internal or external cause, and where it manifests itself in the nervous system and the brain, for example through headaches, a rush of blood to the head accompanied by a racing pulse, delirium and where every movement of the body, even a simple movement of the eyes, aggravates the condition. *Belladonna 4x* is indicated when an illness reaches a sudden crisis; when the patient is sensitive to light and his pupils are dilated; when the mucous membranes are dry, hot and inflamed – and when any one of these symptoms is accompanied by a high temperature. For the intellectually alert, the vivacious person, young people who have to concentrate mentally and draw heavily on their brains, or for those who lead an intellectual life, *Belladonna 4x* is a wonder medicine.

Belladonna 4x is a quick and reliable help in cases of infectious diseases such as measles, scarlet fever, whooping cough, conjunctivitis, whitlows and even pneumonia, especially in its early stages.

It is important to keep *Belladonna* in your medicine chest; if used at once when needed, many a serious problem can be avoided. The remedy works if there is a threat of meningitis. If grandfather exhibits a suspiciously red face, the same remedy will avert an imminent apoplectic fit. Auntie may be troubled by sudden neuralgic pains, a brother or sister may come home from work with stomach, intestinal, liver, bladder or biliary cramps, or the cramps may be somewhere else in the abdomen – they will all find relief from five drops of *Belladonna* taken in a small glass of water. This first aid rarely fails. Cramps that develop suddenly, beginning in the anus, are relieved within a few minutes by *Belladonna*. It has even been effective in cases of bed-wetting.

With respect to dosage, the potency used generally is 4x. Typical *Belladonna* cases should not receive potencies below 6x.

Coccus cacti (Cochineal)

This is a marvellous remedy for whooping cough and when combined with *Drosera* (sundew) its effect is astonishingly fast. *Coccus cacti* (cochineal) is one of the ingredients in *Thydroca*, the reliable whooping cough drops. If these drops are used at once, possibly prior to the onset of the characteristic symptoms, as a prophylactic, the whoop may be aborted.

It is strange that *Drosera* is a carnivorous plant and *Coccus cacti* itself has little to do with plants. To obtain the raw material for this whooping cough remedy one must travel far: to Algeria, the Canary Islands, or to Central America where cactus plants abound in desert areas and stony wastelands. The search goes on to locate a genus of cactus called *Opuntia coccinellifera* and on it one will find a small insect about 3 mm long, which feeds on the juicy flesh of its host. The insect has a broad shell and leaves behind a red stain when it is squashed on a piece of white paper. Do not be shocked to learn that this is the female cochineal insect, the raw material for the wonderful homoeopathic whooping cough remedy called *Coccus cacti*.

In addition to its beneficial effect on whooping cough, students and supporters of Dr Rademacher have found that *Coccus cacti* has an excellent effect on the kidneys. Observations made at a Vienna clinic confirm that all kinds of spasmodic blockages, respiratory blockages and pneumo-tubercular coughs also benefit from it. In the great Homoeopathic Repertory by the well-known American authority Kent, *Coccus cacti* is recommended for diseases of the central nervous system.

Physicians in earlier times used this remedy in material doses, that is, the mother tincture, for severe kidney disorders, but homoeopathy generally employs the medium potencies 4x–6x.

Guaiacum officinale (Guaiac, Resin of *Lignum vitae*)

In Paracelsus' time, merchants brought home a sort of wood that was said to contain a medicinal resin. This wood was extraordinary because it sank in water, obviously being heavier than water, and this made it different from any other wood known at the time. It was found in the West Indies and South America and, when heated, a resin flowed from it that became a remedy for consumption.

Today, *Guaiacum 1x* is one of the best medicines for pharyngitis. Five drops on a little sugar, taken every one or two hours, will almost certainly stop the symptoms in a short time. In fact, after two or three doses the patient will notice that the soreness has already begun to ease. *Guaiacum* acts as a specific in such cases, and bad-smelling sputum or perspiration is usually a sure indication for its use, at a medium potency, three times a day. Stabbing, tearing pains in the joints, with gouty deposits in them, have also been relieved by means of this remedy. *Guaiacum* is therefore an important ingredient in several ointments and embrocations. Used together with *Lachesis, Guaiacum* will bring quick relief for those who suffer from tonsillitis.

Kalium iodatum (Potassium Iodide)

This is one of the remedies that is greatly misused by orthodox medicine, insofar as it is given in large material doses. Professor Bier has promoted the success of potassium iodide and has proved that it is one of the best expectorants for catarrh and will even arrest the development of catarrh if used in the strengths 4x and even 6x.

Those who are predisposed to rheumatism and chesty colds will find *Kali iodatum 4x* an excellent and speedy means of help, even for bronchial and pulmonary catarrh. Even chronic cases respond favourably to the remedy. *Kali iodatum* is indicated for post-pneumonia treatment, in cases where phlegm is still present and seems to sit deep in the chest, threatening to develop into consumption. The best results are obtained when it is alternated with *raw pine bud syrup* or *Imperatoria (imperial masterwort)*.

As a final observation, the main effect of kelp can no doubt be ascribed to its content of *Kalium iodatum*.

Lachesis

Do not be shocked, dear readers, when I tell you that this remedy is made from snake poison, taken from a viper (*Lachesis muta*, or bushmaster) whose bite, if unattended, leads to certain death. However, when homoeopathically potentised, in this case diluted a billion times, *Lachesis* is a valuable medicine.

We owe the discovery of this remarkable remedy to Dr Constantin Hering. It has no doubt saved many more lives than have ever been lost through the bite of the bushmaster. Blood poisoning, septicaemia, chronic ulcers, boils, carbuncles, smallpox, scarlet fever, severe cases of measles and other diseases just as serious, can be safely and reliably treated with *Lachesis*. Whenever a disorder is accompanied by a bluish appearance of the skin, you can be sure that *Lachesis 12x* will help.

Lachesis 12x is a superb remedy for problems occurring in the left side of the pelvis, especially women's complaints.

After a serious illness, when all sorts of toxins are circulating in the bloodstream and the body is fighting to eliminate them, *Lachesis* can be of great service.

Where typhoid fever is concerned, *Lachesis* is one of the most useful and reliable medicines. After a stroke, especially in cases where the left side is paralysed, *Lachesis* as well as *Arnica* are often given with good results.

In cases of pulmonary abscesses, gangrene of the lung or very bad tonsillitis and other serious throat diseases, this remedy can help where all others seem to have failed. I have often seen tonsillitis completely disappear after an injection of *Lachesis 10x*, without any ill effects.

This remedy should be kept in every home, for whenever a serious illness threatens to induce blood poisoning, there is no better medicine available. The safest potencies to use are 10x or 12x.

Daphne mezereum (Daphne, Spurge Laurel)

The last muddy streaks of snow are still lying on the upland meadows and under the rhododendrons when the bright red blossoms of the daphne already catch our eye. The homoeopathic remedy *Mezereum* is prepared from the bark of this attractive but poisonous plant.

It is a wonderful remedy for shingles, facial erysipelas and vesicular eruptions, those itching little blisters on a red background that become worse when scratched.

For deep-seated varicose ulcers this remedy is second to none.

Mezereum is indicated for dry mucous membranes accompanied by dry and irritating cough and a feeling of constriction across the chest, which occurs especially during the night, as well as intense thirst with burning pains in the throat and a raw nasal discharge. Even in acute cases the remedy must not be given in potencies below 3x.

Sepia officinalis (Sepia)

Let me describe the merits of this wonderful homoeopathic remedy, one that is not recognised by the orthodox section of the medical profession, and you will no doubt become quite enthusiastic about it. First, however, do not turn your nose up when I tell you that *Sepia* is obtained from cuttlefish 'ink'. If you have ever visited the Mediterranean or other southern seas you must have come across those curious creatures with their tentacles and know that they eject a dark brown ink-like fluid. In former times painters used this ink from the cuttlefish but today the chemical industry produces a dye known as sepia.

Did you know that *Sepia* is one of the best medicines for women's problems? Frail women who tire easily after only a short walk or who perspire excessively, causing them to smell unpleasant and feel listless, have their best friend in *Sepia*, a remedy that benefits the whole body. In the United States they call it the washer-woman's medicine. It helps the overworked, the tired, the sad, and those who complain of backaches.

Chronic skin eruptions that itch and burn, little blisters around the joints, the desire to sleep during the daytime and insomnia during the night, vertigo, a poor memory and similar conditions can all be alleviated and cured if *Sepia* is taken for a certain period of time.

The potency required depends upon the sensitivity of the person; robust people can use a lower potency (4x), while those with a more delicate constitution may require higher potencies (6x–12x) for the best results.

Tarentula cubensis

It is hardly believable that the poison of the hairy Cuban tarantula should possess such remarkable curative powers when homoeopathically diluted, but it does. Boils, felons (whitlows), or any other infection of the fingers or under the nails are cured by *Tarentula cubensis* as if by a miracle. In most cases the affected parts are characterised by a bluish colour and cause severe, burning pains, particularly during the night. For small abscesses on the hands and feet, as well as whitlows, there is no better medicine. *Tarentula* is without a par among homoeopathic medicines in the treatment of furunculosis (the recurrent appearance of furuncles and boils). To produce immediate results, use the injection method.

As a word of caution, *Tarentula cubensis* should only be used in high potencies (8x–12x). It is also important not to confuse *Tarentula cubensis* with *Tarentula hispanica* (Spanish tarantula).

Urtica dioica, Urtica urens (Stinging Nettle)

The fresh plant extract from the stinging nettle (see pages 368–70) is known in homoeopathy as *Urtica mother tincture*. In addition to glycosides, tannic acids and formic acid, it also contains a good quantity of silica (40 per cent of the ash constituents), the same proportion of calcium, as well as phosphorus, iron, sodium and a little sulphur.

Urtica is a most reliable remedy for arthritic ailments, inflamed joints of a gouty nature, diminished urine with increased sedimentation and bladder irritation.

In such cases, exudation through the skin becomes acrid and is accompanied by an unpleasant odour. This is the result of an insufficient kidney function and may in time lead to a skin eruption that itches and burns, especially at night. For these symptoms, take ten drops of *Urtica* mother tincture in a glass of water, sipping it during the day. In addition to *Urtica*, the kidneys can be further assisted with *Solidago* or *Nephrosolid*. Take sips of both remedies, alternating one with the other.

Four Biochemical Remedies

Calcarea fluorica (Calcium Fluoride)

If your teeth hurt when you eat, if they feel a bit loose, or if the enamel becomes brittle and chips off easily so that bacteria can enter through the crevices, causing tooth decay, then it is high time for you to remember *Calcarea fluorica*, a biochemical remedy to counteract mineral deficiency. At the same time, *silica* (see page 401) should also be taken because it is equally important for the construction of the teeth and bones.

Incidentally, it is not surprising that the mountain peasants of the Swiss canton of Valais possess such beautiful teeth, because the famous whole rye bread they consume is a rich source of calcium fluoride.

This mineral is important for the connective tissues and for this reason should be taken before and after operations so that granulation, such as scar formation, can take place more quickly and without interruption. It has also been suggested that a deficiency of calcium fluoride in the system must play some part in the tendency to hernias.

Always remember that nature will be able to rectify problems as long as the necessary raw materials are present. This principle should be observed in our diet and if it is, the body will respond, but if our diet is deficient, we must see to it that the necessary materials are supplied.

Recently, interesting observations have been made concerning the effect of this mineral on hard swellings of the tendons and ligaments, dilations of the tendon sheaths (known as 'ganglia') and even glandular tumours and hard cyst formation. It is gratifying to know that, besides other treatments, such a simple natural medicine as *Calcarea fluorica* will benefit these conditions. It would, of course, be unreasonable to expect too much from any given remedy, because we must remember that disease is hardly ever attributable to the deficiency of a single cell salt. Others, too, may be lacking and need to be replaced.

It has been found that cataracts of the eyes are usually associated with a deficiency of *Calcarea fluorica*, and their treatment should include taking this mineral in alternation with *Kali chloricum* (potassium chlorate). Sclerotic deposits on the eardrum, which may give rise to deafness and 'head noises', as well as painful whitlows and itching, and eczematous diseases of the skin are also relieved by taking this remedy for a period of time. *Calcarea fluorica* should be taken together with *Millefolium* (yarrow) or *Aesculaforce* to improve the elasticity of the walls of the veins in all cases of haemorrhoids (piles), varicose veins and phlebitis (inflammation of the veins).

Babies with teething problems will respond to *Calcarea fluorica*, taken in alternation with *Calcarea phosphorica* (calcium phosphate). I should also mention that mothers can more quickly regain their figure after the birth of their babies and prevent a pendulous abdomen, which is caused by a relaxation of the abdominal muscles and ligaments, if they take *Calcarea fluorica* or the calcium complex *Urticalcin* regularly during pregnancy.

Calcarea fluorica is generally given in the potency 12x, but for some rare cases it may be 6x. The normal dose is two tablets (0.125 g each), three times daily.

Natrum muriaticum (Cooking or Table Salt, Sodium Chloride)

The type of person most likely to benefit from *Natrum muriaticum* can be described as follows: puffy face, with watery-looking skin; thin, in spite of having a good appetite; feels the cold acutely especially along the spine and back, as well as in the hands and feet; easily exhausted by mental and physical work; cannot stand the heat of the sun; inclined to headaches and migraines; easily agitated and upset. If one tries to comfort such people they become bad tempered or angry. Their bowels function badly and the stool is dry, hard and crumbly. In the case of women these symptoms are accentuated during and after their periods, which are always irregular. A typical aversion to bread can often be noted. There either seems to be a great yearning for salt or a definite aversion to it. Those who have a number of these characteristics will find *Natrum muriaticum* an excellent and quite harmless remedy.

It has an immediate effect on infants and small children when there are disturbances of the bowels or liver, and it is a splendid worm remedy if taken regularly for a long time.

Patients with Graves' disease (exophthalmic goitre) will find speedy relief by taking *Natrum muriaticum*. In cases of vasomotor disorders, palpitations with a feeling of faintness, and an irregular pulse (such as every third stroke out of rhythm) the medication has a very good effect. Skin eruptions with light-coloured watery secretions, eczema, acne and skin blemishes, especially when accompanied by dry mucous membranes, also respond to treatment with *Natrum muriaticum*.

In cases of constipation, the potency 3x is indicated. All other disorders will benefit from a medium potency, such as 6x, or better still, a higher one, from 12x to 30x. Highly strung persons always respond better to higher potencies.

Natrum sulphuricum (Glauber's Salt, Sodium Sulphate)

The German chemist J. R. Glauber discovered this salt in 1658 and it still bears his name today. Although it is water-soluble, it is absorbed with difficulty by the intestines and, if its curative powers are to be utilised, it has to be taken in biochemical trituration and attenuated to the sixth decimal potency. Only then is *Natrum sulphuricum* fully absorbed, benefiting the body without any side effects.

One of its important merits is that it increases the secretion of bile into the duodenum, thus aiding the digestion generally and that of fats in particular. Its action also extends to the blood. In cases of haemophilia, a disease characterised by loss or impairment of the clotting ability of blood, so that even a minor cut or injury can put the patient at risk of bleeding to death if the right action is not taken, *Natrum sulphuricum* will improve the condition. Naturally, it must be taken over a long period of time; moreover, its effectiveness is enhanced when *Millefolium* (yarrow) is taken at the same time.

Diabetics will find *Natrum sulphuricum* a great help if taken in conjunction with the fresh plant extract of *tormentil*. Other indications include liver problems, especially after recovery from jaundice, an inflamed bile duct or an inflammation of the small intestine.

For 'early-morning diarrhoea' with flatulence, it is a specific, but should be alternated with doses of *clay water* (healing earth). Metabolic disturbances, having their origin in a liver dysfunction, are remarkably improved by *Natrum sulphuricum 6x*, two tablets taken three times daily – a simple remedy that gives fast relief! Also in cases of obesity, mild cases of dropsy, certain kinds of asthma, chronic malaria, and the well-known spring rashes from which many adolescents suffer, *Natrum sulphuricum 6x* brings prompt relief.

Nursing mothers should not take this remedy because it reduces the flow of milk. On the other hand, at the time of weaning it has been found to be of great help. People who are always pale or whose eyes are slightly yellowish instead of white and tend to feel depressed and moody should take this remedy from time to time.

Terra Silicea purificata (Silica)

This fine remedy is valued in biochemistry as much as it is in homoeopathy, and I will try to describe its most important uses as briefly as possible.

Silicea is used for suppuration of every kind, but only when it has established itself properly or is already dispersing. In the early stage *Hepar sulph. 4x* should be given to encourage the elimination of pus. The healing process should then be left for *Silicea 12x* to accomplish. In northern lands, silica is used by the peasants for every sort of suppuration, especially for boils. For inflammation of the bones, necrosis of the bones, tonsillar abscesses, dental fistulas, indeed for any sort of fistula, silica is a slow but sure remedy.

Silica is the right remedy to use for felons (whitlows), problems with the hair roots and the disrupted growth of hair and nails.

Give silica to lymphatic-scrofulous children with swollen glands; there is no better remedy than this for improving the child's whole constitution. As a rule these children are thin, or else puffy with a swollen stomach, and have a poor appetite and little stamina, as well as an uncertain state of mind.

Those who suffer from lung problems and scrofula should take silica together with a homoeopathic calcium preparation. Silica is very good for the skin and the connective tissues, and is successful in the treatment of excessive hand and foot perspiration that has an unpleasant odour and causes the skin between the fingers and toes to become sore. Problems arising from suppressed foot sweat can also be dealt with satisfactorily by silica, but it is probable that the sweat will be re-established after having been wrongly suppressed in the first place. This is something to be welcomed. In fact, never do anything drastic to suppress foot sweat, unless you also stimulate the function of the skin and kidneys so that elimination is increased through these two escape routes. In that case, the foot sweat will eventually disappear without any harmful consequences.

People who always feel cold and shivery, even when they are active, might try taking silica. After several weeks it will improve the basal metabolism, and their vitality and joy of living will gradually return.

Hard lumps in the breast, perhaps even malignant ones, will benefit from the continued use of silica. Wounds that refuse to heal will improve if it is sprinkled over their surfaces. This external method of treatment has proved its value for leg ulcers (*Silicea* for external use, *Hypericum perforatum* and *Aesculaforce* to be taken internally). Apart from its medicinal value, if silica is taken over a long period of time, it will improve the condition of the hair and promote a clear complexion.

Silicea is sometimes prescribed in the 6x potency, but usually it is 12x. Some physicians use 30x with good results. Take two tablets two or three times daily.

If you wish to use *Silicea* as a powder, simply crush the tablets.

Modern man and woman,
Living under constant stress,
Must go back to Nature
And relearn how to live
In harmony with its peace and tranquillity.

Seasonings

Culinary Herbs Are Medicines

Culinary herbs could be such a rich blessing if only we were
sensible enough to plant and cultivate them in our own garden.
Moreover, if we realised that these herbs not only make our food
tastier but also have real medicinal value, we would not hesitate
to avail ourselves of their curative properties by adding them daily
to our food. Seasoning that is good for health means using herbs,
but it is sad to say that the importance of fresh herbs for our well-
being is still too little appreciated. All of us should know each herb
and its value as a flavouring and as a medicine, however small or
ordinary it may be. To help you acquire this invaluable knowledge,
let us consider some of these herbs more closely.

Parsley

Parsley is, of course, well known but often only used to garnish a
dish. But did you know that it is a good remedy for the kidneys?
Bearing this in mind, why not add it, finely chopped, to soups,
sauces and dressings, to cottage cheese, and sprinkle it on salads,
potatoes and other dishes? It will enhance the taste of your meals
and provide you with vitamins A and C, as well as traces of vitamin
B_{12}, which is important for the formation of red blood corpuscles.

Celery, Celeriac

Celery (leaf-stalks) and celeriac (the turnip-like root) are good
vegetables for people suffering from rheumatism and gout, and for
those who want to do something about preventing these two diseases. If you use the roots, stalks and leaves to season your food
on a regular basis, it is most unlikely that you will ever suffer from
renal gravel or stones. Celery is also a notable remedy for dropsy.

Thyme

Marjoram

This herb originally came from North Africa, where it is still valued as a mild but reliable nerve tonic. Marjoram increases the amount of water eliminated by the body and is therefore used to ease bladder trouble. It also stimulates the bowel movement, helping to regulate it.

Thyme

Thyme is very popular because of its fine aroma and flavour. What is more, it has an antiseptic property and is able to regenerate mouth bacteria.

Rosemary

Isabella, Queen of Hungary, had much to do with rosemary's reputation as a rejuvenating tonic. This simple but beautiful shrub with its little leaves and flowers is known everywhere as a sweet herb and a remedy and is used in herbal medicine because of its beneficial effect on the vasomotor nerves and the heart nerves. This aromatic herb should be used much more widely for culinary purposes, to enable us to benefit from its goodness. In fact, famous

Rosemary

chefs have been adding rosemary to sauces and gravies, roast meat and saltwater fish for a long time. Vegetarians, too, should not forget to use plenty of this herb.

If you add rosemary to old wine you will get a good heart tonic, which will benefit anyone suffering from low blood pressure or who is always pale and weak, as well as older persons. A glass of rosemary wine is a good pick-me-up for convalescents recovering from a bout of flu or similar infectious disease; it will speed up their recovery.

Savory

In the Middle Ages, savory, or bean herb (*Satureja hortensis* in Latin), grew in every monastery garden and still today it is prized as a kitchen herb. It was used for seasoning and as a remedy, and Abbess Hildegard of Bingen, Germany, a reputable medieval herbalist and recognised as such even in modern times, recommended savory as a valuable herb.

The common name 'bean herb' tells us something about its culinary use; indeed, some cooks maintain that there is no better flavouring for beans. Moreover, if you season vegetables with savory, you will not suffer wind as an after effect. Many good cooks also flavour meat dishes and chicken with aromatic savory.

Anyone suffering from low blood pressure would do well to use savory in addition to hyssop in the preparation of food. This herb was also highly valued in the Middle Ages because it was thought to stimulate the gonads.

Lemon Balm

Lemon balm is often grown in kitchen gardens, its pleasant aroma not only attracting humans but also bees which feed on its nectar. It makes a fine tea, and if your nerves are frayed and need calming, a cup at bedtime, sweetened with honey for an even better effect, will help you sleep since it is mildly soporific. Many women like to drink the tea because it is good for menstrual problems and cramps. In days gone by, balm tea was recommended for tobacco poisoning. And in the seventeenth century the Carmelite monks in Paris prepared an excellent 'balm spirit' that soon became famous. The ingredients were lemon balm, betony leaves, lemon peel, a little coriander, cloves and cinnamon.

Although you may know lemon balm mainly for its use as a tea, it can also be added to food for flavouring. It may also be true that few people know of another application of balm; the fresh leaves can be crushed and gently rubbed on bee or wasp stings. This has a soothing and healing effect, similar to that obtained by applying crushed ivy leaves.

Basil

This plant has been cultivated since ancient times. It is probably native to India, where it was known as *Arjaka* in ancient Sanskrit. The aromatic herb is a good source of food for bees, but is also valued as a kitchen herb and a remedy. In ancient Egypt basil served as a medicine for snakebites, scorpion stings and eye troubles. The crushed leaves were also applied to painful parts in cases of rheumatism. Basil's remedial effects are due to its content of rhymol, eugenol and camphor. Pliny recommended basil tea as a remedy for nerves, headaches and fainting spells. The Greeks used basil not only to prepare aromatic baths to strengthen the nerves, but also for flavouring must (the juice pressed from grapes before it has fermented), wine and liqueurs. Basil is used in northern Germany to season the famous Hamburg eel soup and in the preparation of gherkins (pickled cucumbers). In Italy, particularly in the south, it is found in practically every garden because it is used widely for seasoning – and food to which is has been added is always very tasty.

Lovage
Lovage can reach a height of over 2 m (6 feet) and is used in the same way as celery and celeriac (see page 404). It is probably native to Asia, where it is used to make highly flavoured sauces. The plant is known for its diuretic effect, which is no doubt due to an essential oil. Lovage stimulates the appetite and makes a good soothing remedy for flatulence and digestive problems in the intestines.

Chervil
This herb, called *Anthriscus cerefolium* in Latin, is much appreciated as a medicinal plant in Bern canton, Switzerland. The smell of chervil is strong, somewhat sweet, aromatic and slightly reminiscent of anise. Chervil's effects are digestive, dispersing, blood-thinning and diuretic. You can prepare an excellent herbal tea in the spring by adding it to dandelion and yarrow. This combination is particularly indicated for the treatment of scrofula, dropsy and a tendency to eczema.

Caraway, Anise, Coriander, Fennel and Dill
The seeds of these five plants have a warming effect and are good for the stomach and intestines, especially in cases of chills and inflammations, as well as other upsets.

An infusion of fennel and anise is also appreciated for its good effect when small children suffer from stomach and bowel problems of any kind. Nursing mothers will find dill helpful in stimulating lactation.

Leek and Other Varieties of Allium
A number of the *Allium* varieties – there are about 250 in all – serve as vegetables, spice plants and remedies. They contain garlic oil, its chief component being allyl sulphide, which is responsible for their characteristic smell. All varieties of *Allium*, for example leeks, are good for the blood vessels, keeping them elastic and preventing premature aging. If you eat plenty of chives, garlic, and, in the spring, bear's garlic (ramsons) – all of which are from the *Allium* family – intestinal worms will be eliminated.

Chives
Of all varieties of *Allium*, chives (*Allium schoenoprasum*) are probably used the most widely. Chives are found all over Europe, East Asia, the Orient, and from the Caucasus right up to Siberia.

Add finely chopped chives to salads, gruels, cottage cheese, potatoes and vegetables for flavouring and to enrich the nutritional content. If you have no garden, you can grow chives in a pot on a window sill or balcony. During the winter months, move it to another light area of the kitchen.

Bear's Garlic (Ramsons)

Bear's garlic also belongs to the *Allium* family and is called *Allium ursinum*. Use it for seasoning or as a steamed vegetable. Mix finely chopped bear's garlic with other salads or serve it on its own.

As a hot dish, steam it together with spinach in a little oil, but even without the spinach bear's garlic is very tasty. As a spring treatment, bear's garlic is the best remedy for cleansing the blood, gallbladder and liver of wastes that have accumulated during the winter months. For those suffering from arteriosclerosis (hardening of the arteries) with high blood pressure, bear's garlic is a remedy and food at the same time. They should eat it regularly every day, finely chopped and added to salads.

Garlic (*Allium sativum*)

Today, tourists visiting the great pyramids of Egypt, seated unsteadily on the back of a camel or in a sleek automobile, are probably unaware that the overseers of the pharaohs were not only responsible for the construction of these great architectural masterpieces but they faced the additional problem of feeding a great army of workmen. Herodotus, the Greek historian, wrote that during the time of the building of the Cheops pyramid 1,600 silver talents (about 3.5 million pounds sterling) worth of garlic, onions and radishes were purchased to keep up the workers' strength. The Egyptians considered garlic and onions as sacred plants, to which they attributed all manner of magical powers able to ward off evil spirits and the effects of their wicked deeds. The Greeks and Romans also used garlic as a medicine and for seasoning. From the Bible we learn about the prominence the Jews gave to it, and their constant use of garlic for thousands of years is perhaps partly responsible for the endurance and tenacity of this people. The Semitic people seem to suffer much less than others from hardening of the arteries and poor functioning of the lymphatic glands. The Turks and Russians make much use of garlic to season their food and their older people are less likely to suffer from high blood pressure because they eat it regularly.

Many people, however, do not like the pungent smell of garlic.

Wormwood

Yet there is a simple remedy to dispel it quickly; just eat some fresh raw parsley at the same time. You can make a tasty sandwich by slicing a garlic clove onto a slice of buttered bread and adding a little *Herbaforce*.

Like all foods that have a penetrating smell and a strong taste, garlic should be taken in small amounts only, otherwise it could be harmful, especially to the kidneys. Garlic as well as onions contain a sulphurous essential oil that is probably responsible for its effectiveness as a vermifuge, an agent that causes the expulsion of intestinal worms. Garlic milk is excellent for this purpose, as described below. Crushed garlic can also be added to a wormwood infusion instead of milk, to be drunk or used as an enema in the same way as garlic milk.

Half a clove of garlic, placed between the gums and cheek, will often soothe a headache. Earache and headaches often respond to a garlic or onion poultice applied to the back of the neck.

Garlic Milk
This is an effective remedy for eliminating intestinal worms, as well as for sciatic pains. If taken over a prolonged period of time it will also cure sweaty feet.

A garage mechanic who had suffered from sciatica for a considerable time, and for whom the doctor could not offer any help, was advised to drink garlic milk daily. He took the advice and within a few days the pain was greatly relieved. At the end of a fortnight it had disappeared completely.

Garlic milk may be prepared cooked or uncooked. In the raw state, uncooked, it is more potent. Cooking lessens the smell some-what and the effect is still quite satisfactory.

To make garlic milk use a garlic press, obtainable from hardware stores, to crush the garlic. Add the pulp to uncooked milk (two raw cloves to 100 ml/3.5 fl. oz) and drink it. If you prefer, you can boil the garlic in the milk.

For the maximum effect one should drink 200 ml (half a pint) of this mixture daily. The same mixture can also be used for enemas.

Of course, not everyone reacts in the same way and not every remedy produces the same results in every person, but in the case of a bad sciatica attack, it is well worth giving this simple remedy a try. According to the individual, one of three different therapies should produce results: formic acid treatment, adjustment by a chiropractor, or garlic milk.

Onion (*Allium cepa*)

Although onions are healthy and can be used for seasoning in many ways, they do not agree with everyone, especially people whose digestion is not too good and who tend to suffer from intestinal fermentation and flatulence. Such problems can be exacerbated when onions are eaten.

Raw onions have a mild diuretic effect. They are rich in vitamin C, and if eaten regularly and in small quantities they are good for the nerves. In cases of congestion, a headache, earache, toothache and inflammation of the eyes, especially after a chill or cold, an onion compress on the back of the neck can relieve the pain and often disperse it entirely. For this purpose, wrap the finely chopped onion in gauze.

When a person is feverish, with a congested, burning head, an onion compress applied to the soles of the feet will be very helpful, and if the heart is affected, a compress on the calves of the legs will give quick relief, or at least act as an auxiliary to another remedial treatment. For gout and diabetes, as well as for hardening of the arteries, onions as a food are a vital part of the treatment.

A sulphurous essential oil is responsible for the onion's good effect on the skin and scalp, especially in cases of dandruff and loss of hair.

In homoeopathy *Allium cepa* is the best remedy for a running cold. It is often enough just to leave half an onion on the bedside table so that the odour can be inhaled through the night. Every morning and evening cut the dried part away. If this does not effect a cure, it will still bring great relief and help towards a speedy recovery.

For colic and wind in the umbilical region, and for infants and small children who have bladder cramps along with reddish, smarting urine, *Allium cepa* is a harmless and reliable remedy. If you do not have extract of *Allium cepa* in your medicine chest, cut a thin slice of onion, dip it into a glass of warm water for a few seconds then remove it and take a sip of the water every hour. You will be astonished at the prompt relief this will bring.

Shallot (*Allium ascalonicum*)
In addition to the common onion, the small, flavoursome shallot, also called scallion, is widely used for flavouring. Its botanical name is derived from the name of the ancient Philistine town Ascalon on the Mediterranean coast, which has been rebuilt in modern times.

The shallot is native to Palestine, where the crusaders came across it and brought it back to Europe. With regard to its use in cooking and as a remedy, it can be used in a similar way to the common onion and the leek.

Cress
Some of the cress varieties used for food are garden cress (*Lepidium sativum*), watercress (*Nasturtium officinale*), nasturtium (*Tropaeolum majus*) and alpine cress (*Hutchinsia alpina*). In all, about 90 different varieties are known in the temperate zones of the earth. Some are used for flavouring, and most of them have a medicinal effect, although varying in strength.

According to recent research, cress (like horseradish) contains a kind of penicillin and is a great help in improving mouth and intestinal bacteria. Having a modest content of iodine, cress is a dietary remedy for thyroid problems. It is recommended as a remedy for scrofula, and when taken regularly it will reduce an inherent tendency to skin eruptions. At the same time cress is good for kidney problems; in particular, it helps to prevent the formation of kidney stones.

Horseradish

Cress on its own makes a wholesome salad, but it should also be added to other salads. In fact, it is very important that we avail ourselves of its medicinal values by eating it regularly. If you are in the habit of preparing vegetable juices daily for the sake of their vitamins, always add a little cress. The popular seasoning salt *Trocomare* contains various cresses among its ingredients which largely account for its fine aroma and taste.

Horseradish (*Armoracia rusticana*)

Since horseradish is one of the healthiest seasonings there is, it should be used much more in the kitchen. It is rich in vitamin C and is the best known dietary remedy for scurvy, only raw sauerkraut being equally effective. Horseradish has a regenerative effect in cases of dysbacteria and helps to overcome functional disorders of the pancreas. It is a good seasoning agent for diabetics, being curative at the same time. If you use it as a seasoning in the spring, in small amounts but regularly, it will help in the fight against 'spring fever'.

It has recently been discovered that horseradish contains a considerable amount of antibiotic substances, including a kind of penicillin, which explains why horseradish syrup (see below) is so effective in cases of throat diseases. Also because of its antibiotic properties horseradish tincture is of great benefit when treating

413

wounds that are not healing well or are forming proud flesh. Even when other remedies have proved ineffective, horseradish tincture will not only bring relief surprisingly quickly, but will actually cause the wound to heal.

For home use, tincture of horseradish may be prepared in the following manner. Grate some fresh horseradish, mix it well with pure alcohol and let it stand for an hour or so. Then filter it through some gauze or muslin. The resulting tincture can be used on wounds, cuts and grazes as an antiseptic. Although it may sting somewhat, it will be most effective and the pain and soreness will quickly disappear.

Grated horseradish can be used in place of onions when these, applied as a poultice, have not succeeded in stopping, for example, a bad headache. Simply apply the grated horseradish to the back of the neck.

Horseradish being one of the spice plants that have a reliable medicinal effect, it should be grown in your garden, if you have one. It will then always be available. Add horseradish to carrot salad and the latter will be less sweet and more palatable; many men, especially, prefer it in this way. The flavour of cottage or curd cheese is also improved by horseradish, and the same is true of salad dressings.

Always mix a little grated horseradish into your salads. In addition to making the salad taste better, horseradish will reduce any tendency to colds and chills.

For older people, horseradish, as well as garlic, is a most excellent medicine. Both regenerate the blood vessels, especially the arteries, and reduce the blood pressure. If you are over the age of forty, you should give these two remedies serious consideration. They serve an important purpose, act in a regenerative way, and are stimulating.

However, you must be careful not to use too much horseradish, since it is very strong. The Chinese make a horseradish relish that, if eaten without your knowing what it is, will take you by surprise as the pungent flavour goes up your nose, indeed, it seems, even to your brain, causing temporary discomfort. The sensation is severe and definite, as with any other strong stimulation, but do not forget that the effect is also one of cleansing.

Horseradish Syrup
If the symptom of catarrh refuses to disappear, try horseradish syrup. This remedy is also indicated for the treatment of weak lungs

and other bronchial and respiratory problems, since horseradish contains an antibiotic substance similar to penicillin.

Prepare the syrup by adding honey to the grated horseradish. Mix well and press through muslin. The residue should be cooked with a little water and raw (unrefined) cane sugar, pressed out again, and then added to the syrup. This provides a strong medicinal mixture.

Black or Spanish Radish (*Raphanus sativus*)
The black or Spanish radish is the best possible liver medicine you can have right in your home. But you should not eat too much of it, or else it will be harmful. Taken frequently in small quantities, it can help liver patients to prevent bilious colic and many kinds of digestive problems.

Radish Syrup
Finely grated radish, sprinkled with raw cane sugar in order to make a syrup, provides a good medicine for chronic bronchial catarrh. To save on the amount of sugar used, first press the grated radish through muslin and then add sufficient sugar to form a thick syrup. Made in this way it should keep for weeks and you can take some every day. This is also an inexpensive and reliable help in the treatment of persistent whooping cough. For those who do not want to take the time to make the syrup, or who are unable to obtain black radishes, radish syrup prepared in much the same way can be bought.

In cases of gallbladder trouble, ten drops of raw radish essence (*Raphanus-Perkolat*) in a tablespoon of water, taken three times a day, are sufficient to give relief. You may use this radish essence for whooping cough and bronchial catarrh in conjunction with the syrup. Add ten drops to a glass of water, sweeten with honey and sip throughout the day.

Salt as a Medicine
Salt is a remedy for many ailments, but not in the form in which it is usually ingested. Bathing in sea water is recommended for glandular disturbances, which so often result in obesity. The thyroid also benefits from sea-bathing, and anyone who suffers from goitre or similar thyroid problems (hypothyroidism and hyperthyroidism) will obtain good results from it too. If you live in a landlocked area and do not have access to the sea, you can use dry or moist salt packs at home to draw away water from the

tissues. For this reason, anyone suffering from oedema, swellings of a dropsical nature, will find salt packs an answer to his problem.

Gargling with salt water is an excellent substitute for the more expensive antiseptics and herbal mouthwashes sold over-the-counter – the effect is just as good.

In cases of catarrh or inflammation of the mucosa, tepid salt water should be sniffed up the nostrils, which should then be rinsed with clear water. This simple treatment, when practised regularly, will reduce any susceptibility to respiratory ailments, that is, catarrh and sore throats. Naturally, if you do live by the sea, it would be better to use sea water, provided that it is uncontaminated. Use cooking salt instead, if that is all you have available.

Salt has a good effect when used externally and it is also beneficial when taken orally. However, for internal use common cooking salt, iodised or fluorinated salt should not be used if at all possible, only sea salt or herbal salt, which are much better. The trace elements found in sea salt and herbal salt benefit the endocrine glands and normalise both hypofunction and hyperfunction. Obesity is often the result of insufficient glandular function, and in such cases ordinary salt will aggravate the condition by increasing the body weight still more. On the other hand, a herbal salt containing seaweed has the opposite effect. In fact, if *Herbamare* seasoning salt is used regularly, quite a few pounds of excess weight will be lost in a natural way.

Salt is an excellent preservative, even for fresh plant extracts, and does not reduce their therapeutic value. *Trocomare* herbal seasoning salt contains eight different fresh herbs with an antibacterial effect. If you are susceptible to, or are exposed to, infectious diseases, Trocomare will prove invaluable as a prophylactic and will also have a favourable influence on any existing problems.

Salt is widely used in homoeopathy too (see page 399), where it is known by the name *Natrum muriaticum*.

Various Diets and Treatments

Serious Vitamin Deficiency in the Spring

In the past, the consequences of vitamin deficiencies through the winter months and into the spring used to be much more drastic than they are today. The problem was little understood and therefore left without any real solution. People in remote areas often suffered greatly during these months because of an acute lack of food rich in vitamins. Many old people would die in the winter or spring because their strength was at an all-time low for this very reason.

Even today at this time of the year there is a general susceptibility to colds, bronchial catarrh and infectious conditions of the mucous membranes; these are always a result of a deficiency of vitamin A and other substances. By taking food rich in vitamin A you can, as a rule, avoid inflammation of the eyes, eyelids and cornea, and the nuisance known as 'night-blindness'. A lack of vitamin A in the body is responsible for the stubborn failure of wounds to heal properly.

It is good to know that the varieties of pepper, as well as tomatoes, contain plenty of vitamin A; unfortunately, however, in winter they are not always widely available or are relatively expensive. It is therefore more than welcome that carrots are usually on the market – and somewhat cheaper. Their vitamin A content is, of course, well known. So make it a point to eat fresh carrot salad every day, or to drink fresh carrot juice. Commercially prepared carrot juice with lactic acid is also recommended, and is appreciated by those who have little time to prepare the juice themselves. Health food stores stock concentrated carrot juice, such as *Biocarottin*. This is a good supplement to overcome vitamin deficiency. A word of caution is needed, however, for people who suffer from high blood pressure; try to eat more salads rather than depending on juices alone, since the regular intake of carrot juice can raise the blood pressure.

Further Observations

In a series of experiments some animals were given food that did not contain vitamin A, resulting in the development of gravel and stones in the kidneys. To eliminate the stones, they were then given food rich in vitamin A. The experiments were indeed successful and the elimination was confirmed by means of X-ray pictures. This is a clear warning to us never to go without food that is rich in vitamin A.

Other symptoms of vitamin A deficiency are bleeding gums, which are more frequently seen in the spring, and blue-red spots in the skin, which occur when blood seeps into the tissues as a result of leaking blood vessels caused by the deficiency. These undesirable blue-red spots show up mainly in the legs, where they can eventually turn into ulcers. Vitamin A deficiency can also lead to a loss of appetite and the limbs feeling as heavy as lead. In some cases frequent nose bleeds are experienced or existing piles begin to bleed slightly; these symptoms are often accompanied by cardiac insufficiency.

Scurvy used to make itself known with similar symptoms, posing great problems to ships' crews for a long time, until the importance of vitamin C was discovered. Sauerkraut then came to the rescue. The great seafarer James Cook used it successfully to keep his crews free from scurvy, and others later followed his example. Instead of sauerkraut you can eat white cabbage salad, flavoured with a little lemon juice; the effect is the same.

Way back in the Middle Ages a physician by the name of Carier discovered that an extract made from pine and fir buds or shoots was a good remedy for scurvy. Later research proved that the buds or shoots of coniferous trees have the highest content of vitamin C. You have here the reason why pine bud syrup, when prepared with the raw juice, as in *Santasapina Cough Syrup*, has a twofold effect: in cases of catarrh it soothes the mucous membranes and it also improves the general health of the patient because of the pine buds' vitamin C content.

Nearly all wild fruits are rich in vitamin C and contain valuable fruit sugar. Barberries, rose hips and sea buckthorn berries are marketed in the form of tasty conserves that keep well. Your vitamin C requirements in the winter and spring months will therefore be met if you take these purées. An especially effective addition to them are combinations such as *Bio-Sanddorsan;* this contains sea buckthorn as well as rose hip purée, both of which valuable for your health and also very tasty. Children like to eat Bio-

Sanddorsan as a sandwich spread. It is an advantage when something that is necessary can also be made palatable, especially as far as sweet-toothed children are concerned, because then they will happily take in the thing that benefits their health. I once overheard a child say, with sad face, that things that were tasty were bad for you, but things that were supposed to be good for you had a nasty taste. I have never forgotten this remark and since then have tried hard to produce health foods that taste good at the same time. This is possible by using well-thought-out combinations, such as the one I achieved in *Bio-Sanddorsan*. Another easy way to avail oneself of vitamins is by taking *Bio-C-Lozenges*, made from fruit extracts such as acerola cherries, sea buckthorn, rose hips, passion-fruit, lemons and blackcurrants.

It is not only wild fruits and berries that are good for us in the spring, there are also a number of wild vegetables that sprout in the milder regions where there is no snow, or where it has melted. To name but a few, we can find dandelion shoots, watercress, nettle shoots, bear's garlic (ramsons) – and many others that can be used for salads. These plants often seem more like weeds and we might pass them by without a glance. It would be much better if we were to make use of them and their appreciable content of natural vitamins.

Internal Cleansing in the Spring

As soon as the warm rays of the sun hit the windows in the spring conscientious housewives are usually gripped by a peculiar restlessness that urges them to declare war on every trace of dust, dirt and disorder in the home. Similarly, such a challenge to spring-clean confronts each and everyone of us and we get the overpowering feeling that our bodies need cleansing, in order to rid them of all accumulated wastes. Then a certain 'spring fever' or fatigue seems to gradually reduce, or slow down, our enthusiasm. Even though we may have had enough exercise during the winter to keep our bodies in trim through movement and deep-breathing, we still feel that somehow our reserves of energy are at a low ebb. Of course that is quite true since the food that was stored in the autumn will have been losing more and more of its vitamins and other vital substances. Another problem are the many days without any sunshine, so that our body is even less able to utilise the vitamins properly. Heavy winter clothing, especially thick water-proof coats, hinders the normal breathing and perspiration of the skin and in this way contributes to impaired body functions.

What You Can Do

There are a number of things you can do to combat 'spring fever' successfully. First of all, practise more physical and breathing exercises. Even vigorous walking or hiking will help you to exhale a substantial amount of accumulated wastes. It may make you sweat a little, and that is good because it stimulates the skin and helps it to exude toxins. Only be careful not to catch a cold; as soon as you arrive home, change your damp underwear.

You can do even better than that by sweating properly in a steam bath, either taking a sweat bath at home or a sauna. This will make the skin eliminate toxins faster than anything else. But beware of overdoing it; be reasonable and watch your heart. This treatment can be made easier and safer if you take a natural heart tonic.

At any rate, you can see that there are some wonderful possibilities for assisting the body to eliminate wastes and toxins by excreting them through the skin as much as possible. So do not forget to treat your body to this kind of beneficial 'spring-cleaning'.

FOOD RICH IN VITAMINS AND MINERALS

The fact that 'spring fever' is partly a result of a deficiency in vitamins and important minerals should impel us to include in our diet plenty of early spring and wild salad greens and fresh vegetables. Then there are certain flowers and leaves that make superb herbal teas. For example, the bright yellow flowers of coltsfoot are a means of eliminating any phlegm and catarrh that may still linger on after the winter has passed. An infusion of various new leaf shoots is a rich source of minerals; as soon as the raspberry plants, blackberry branches and blackthorn and hawthorn bushes put forth tender new shoots, busy yourself with gathering them to prepare a wonderful spring tea from these fresh leaves. Do the same with young strawberry leaves and the tender shoots of the birch tree. Not only does such an infusion supply you with certain nutritive salts, but it also stimulates the kidneys to function more efficiently – an important aspect of any spring-cleaning treatment.

When the stinging nettles have grown large enough, gather some young shoots every day and add them, finely chopped, to your salads. They are delicious when lightly steamed as a vegetable, tasting something like spinach – which, incidentally, can also be used – or make them into a salad if you prefer. A little finely chopped bear's garlic (ramsons) will enrich any salad and a number of people enjoy bear's garlic leaves lightly steamed as a vegetable.

Coltsfoot

Remember, however, bear's garlic has a piquant flavour and it is better to use it fresh according to the principle 'You can have too much of a good thing.' Of course, this guideline applies to all strong flavourings and seasonings. Another spring vegetable is the radish, of which there are several varieties. Use them wisely in accordance with the same principle, for a little is good for the liver, but too much can harm it.

Many people in the country know of another wild salad herb that stimulates the liver – young dandelion leaves. When these are fresh and tender they should be eaten as a salad every day. If we want to avail ourselves of their benefits even during the warmer season of the year, when the plants are already fully grown, bearing flowers and seeds, there is still a way to enjoy dandelion salad. Here is how. On a mild spring day, when the soil is sufficiently moist, lay out a dandelion bed by making deep grooves into which you plant a row of dandelion roots. Lay the roots in such a way that they appear to be like a long rope in the groove. Cover them with garden peat and soil. When the shoots push through the earth, cut them immediately. This method will give you tender dandelion shoots right into the autumn months. Their effect on the liver is marvellous. During our cleansing treatment in the spring we must do all we can to stimulate the liver. Only by doing so can we be sure of success in fortifying one of the body's most important organs.

Many people are of the opinion that a 'spring cure' has fulfilled its purpose when the bowels are thoroughly cleansed. And, it is true, the intestines do have to be paid due attention. Nevertheless, strong laxatives will not benefit them as much as they deserve. Any treatment should not only cleanse or purify, but also build up and heal.

A WELL-BALANCED PROGRAMME TO IMPROVE THE METABOLISM

In order to improve the body's metabolism it is necessary to stimulate the bowels as well as the liver, gallbladder and kidneys. The normal activity of these organs can be achieved by a treatment that helps to cleanse the blood and which has been put together according to an Oriental 'cure' or formula. Known as the Rasayana Programme, it cleanses and purifies the blood, normalises the metabolism and helps the organs to function properly. This programme is outlined in detail in the next section.

It is important to point out that no drastic or extreme measures should be taken in any such treatment. Years ago, some people in the country would use arum, a strong plant, to cleanse the lungs in the spring, but their view was based on the principle 'the more the better'. However, this is not true, nor is it sensible, for much harm can come from it. Rather, be reasonable in following a spring-cleansing programme. Consider your general health and take sufficient time to allow your body to gradually adjust to the change. If you are sensible in carrying out the treatment, and follow it through successfully, the result will be better health and increased efficiency and vigour. The care and effort required will certainly be worthwhile.

Programmes to Purify the Blood

In the past it used to be the custom in the country to carry out a programme of cleansing the blood every spring. People would gather fresh leaves from blackberry and raspberry bushes, strawberry plants and ribwort (ribgrass), coltsfoot flowers and, where possible, cowslip. They would pour boiling water over these young green shoots and flowers and drink the infusion in the morning and evening. Honey was added to sweeten it.

English Cowslip

This 'spring tea' is still recognised for its pleasant effect on our well-being. Those who take it regularly are convinced that it purifies the system, purging it of the winter's metabolic wastes and infusing the new energies of spring. Some medical practitioners may turn up their noses, discarding the idea of blood-cleansing as being erroneous and unscientific, but there is no doubt that such herbal cleansing stimulates the body's mechanisms and in this way achieves an overall cleansing effect.

According to the views held in ancient India, the blood and the circulatory system can and should be purified from time to time. *Rasa* is the ancient Indian word for the blood or body fluids, and *Rasayana Kalpa* is the name used for a blood-cleansing programme following the model and method of the ancient Indians.

In fact, the programme consists of four remedies, one each to stimulate the intestines, liver, kidneys and stomach:

1. *Rasayana No. 1* is a herb tablet that stimulates and cleanses the intestines.
2. *Rasayana No. 2,* is also a herb tablet; it contains curcuma root (Indian saffron) and serves to stimulate the liver.
3. A special *kidney tea* stimulates the kidneys and the excretion of wastes through the urine.
4. *Arabiaforce,* an Arabian plant essence, improves, regulates and

423

balances the function of the stomach lining and the mucous membranes of the intestines. This remedy is made according to an old herbal recipe that was brought to Europe by Paracelsus. The herbal ingredients come from the Near and Far East.

These four remedies taken together serve to 'spring-clean' the body and are of special benefit to all those who suffer from constipation and sluggish metabolism.

For even better results and to consolidate them, take the above-mentioned 'spring tea' after completing the Rasayana Programme. Your body will respond to this good care, and will enjoy greater vitality and energy.

Kelp and 'Spring Fever' or Fatigue
Since kelp is a seaweed some may wonder what this plant from the cool ocean has to do with the feeling of laziness or listlessness experienced by many people at the onset of spring. Well, many things in life are astonishing, not least the fact that this ocean plant can help to replenish the body's deficiency of minerals and vitamins that causes this unwelcome and bothersome feeling.

Kelp, a species of seaweed from the Pacific Ocean, is rich in minerals and for this reason has been successfully used to reduce obesity and treat thyroid problems, as well as to combat 'spring fever'. Its successful application for both purposes has been confirmed by an increasing number of people. Kelp is always at our service with its rich content of important trace elements and it is therefore the simplest, and possibly the best and least expensive, remedy to combat 'spring fever'. The easiest way to go about it is to take one *Kelpasan* tablet after each meal. If you suffer from Graves' disease (exophthalmic goitre) or hyperthyroidism, it is important to take kelp only in homoeopathic potency (1x–6x) because the effect of the remedy depends on the appropriate dilution being used.

Water and its Therapeutic Effects
Several years have passed since I visited the headwaters of the Amazon river, but I still remember watching the natives bathe in the dirty waters of a tributary of the Marañon. In other tropical areas I often saw the same thing happen, natives enjoying themselves in the muddy water, in some cases the water being absolutely black, while other streams appeared more yellow or red. The Indians and, especially, their children would romp about in these dirty

rivers without any fear of becoming sick as a result. At any rate, they always seemed very happy and seemed to enjoy their dip. In spite of the obviously good effect a swim seemed to have on them, I never mustered enough courage to go in the water myself.

However, one day I felt exceptionally tired and worn out and decided to derive some benefit from the refreshing water. After all, the temperature was 40 °C (105 °F) in the shade and took a lot out of me after a while, especially as it was combined with extremely high humidity. I had to keep reminding myself of the need to breathe deeply in order to cope a little better with the unbearable atmosphere. All I wanted was a refreshing bath to bolster my spirits. Even so, I still did not have the courage to jump in the river, but it occurred to me that I could ask a native woman to go and fetch me some water in a large earthenware jug. I stood on a bamboo footbridge between two huts and as she brought the water I poured it over my head, letting it run down all over me. The Indian woman was kind enough to keep bringing one jug of water after another, and it was not long before I felt quite refreshed, even though the water was not as cool or as clean as I would have wished it to be.

The Mystery Solved

Much later I took a bath in a mud pond in the north of Scandinavia. When I stepped out of the muddy water I felt completely refreshed and began to think about the effect a little more closely. It suddenly crossed my mind that we apply clay-water compresses because they are better than simple water packs. And then there are mud baths and fango mud packs; these too are judged to be more effective than simple water packs. Then it dawned on me that the muddy, that is, dirty, water was not that bad after all; I realised that it can still have a therapeutic effect in spite of its uninviting appearance, provided, of course, that the muddiness is nothing but natural dirt accounted for by clay or some other kind of earth.

On a later visit to the southwest of the United States I came across a river that looked red, quite appropriately called Red River. The puzzling question was 'How do this and similar rivers get their strange colour?' The answer is quite simple: there is either red or yellow clay dissolved in the water, thus colouring the water accordingly, or they contain marshy soil and are black as a result.

I can well imagine that Sebastian Kneipp would have been over-joyed if he could have seen such coloured river water. His natural instinct and intuition would have encouraged him to immediately investigate the medical effects of these waters. In fact, some time later an analytical chemist proved to me, by means of an apparatus which measured the electric tension in the water, that water carries energy that is transmitted to the human body. We filled a bath tub and then used the apparatus to measure the electric field in it. After the bath had been used we measured this once more and found that the electric field had decreased, thus proving that the energy had been transmitted to the person in the water.

The Origin of Water's Therapeutic Effects

Not every kind of water has the same electric field, nor does it have the same therapeutic effect. The result depends upon the 'ballast' substances contained in the water, such as clay or black mud, which are responsible for the electric charge. Minerals dissolved in the water can also add medicinal properties. These substances are usually picked up by the water as it flows from its source deep in the earth and on its way passes over mineral deposits. It is these substances that account for the remedial effects of water when used for bathing and drinking. Any colouring matter, which we at first consider to be impurities or dirt, will have been added to the spring water as it flowed over deposits of clay and minerals. Thus the therapeutic value, as well as the content of minerals and its energy or power, is produced in a natural way, and that is of importance to us.

When I was visiting the South Sea islands I had similar opportunities to see the natives bathe in dirty, muddy waters. But please do not misunderstand my meaning, for I am not referring here to dirt resulting from the unhygienic environment I also saw there – human excrement or pollutants, or bacteriological dirt from other sources that can be channelled into the water. I am not talking about this kind of real pollution, but rather the natural process of earth and minerals being absorbed by the water, changing its clear colour. Naturally, coloured water is not necessarily unsuitable for bathing, although one has to be extra careful in the tropics because of the abundance of parasites that pollute the streams. Just think of the dangerous schistosomes, liver flukes and micro-organisms galore, which transmit all kinds of dangerous diseases.

You have to be even more careful with drinking water. There are some wonderful mineral waters available, but some water also contains poisonous minerals, some of which I came across in North, Central and South America. It can happen that a stream may come from a mineral spring in which is dissolved arsenic, copper or other heavy minerals that make the water poisonous and dangerous to drink. For this reason it is not possible to drink water from just any spring or source as one is able to do, for example, in Switzerland. It is often possible to recognise such dangerous springs by the discoloration of the rocks and stones, which turn yellow, greenish or other colours. Sometimes crystals can be found in the riverbed which taste sharp and burn the tongue.

The same rule applies to water for internal or external use as applies to plants: many plants are curative whereas others are harmful or can only be taken in a diluted form. It is true that nature has much to offer that is beneficial, but we must also keep our eyes open and make sure that we use only the things that are truly good for our health. There is no point in being careless and ignorant and so causing ourselves harm. Remember, always make sure to use only the things that are helpful and safe.

It is common knowledge that not all mineral waters have the same effect and it would be foolish to ignore the fact that the mineral content of a certain water may be beneficial in the case of one particular illness but may not be so for some other physical disorder. Similarly, not everyone is helped by the same thing. For example, strong people are more resistant, whereas those who are sensitive and weak always have to remember that although a mild stimulation can be good, anything stronger may be harmful. Hence, be careful. Volcanic areas with strongly radioactive springs can do much harm to sensitive people, and may even have a paralysing effect and endanger their glandular functions. If you become aware of an adverse reaction when staying in such places or taking the waters, it will be better to avoid them. On the other hand, do not forget that people of a stronger disposition and nature may benefit from a stay in volcanic areas. What may harm a weak person can possibly cure a stronger one. The simple rule is 'Know your own limitations and weaknesses.'

The Therapeutic Value of the Sea

People who do not live by the sea dream of the beach and surf, especially when they sit down to plan their holidays. They long to see the play of the waves, how they break on the immovable rocks, roll and foam and then fizzle out on the golden sands. The waves approach the beach, powerful and inexorable, run up on it and disappear, yet in spite of their awesome power they instil a feeling

427

of being soothed. We never tire of watching them; we are just happy and content to admire their endless movement.

Sea Air

In the morning and evening we feel the urge to stretch our legs and go for a walk along the beach. Some holiday-makers may still be tucked up in bed when we are already up and about, enjoying every minute of the exhilarating experience. The bracing sea air is tangy, salty, high in iodine, and its effect on us is instant. Old and lingering catarrh is loosened. Whatever else is left over from the colds and chills of the previous winter is on its way out because we breathe deeply on our regular walks along the beach.

Let me tell you, sea air is indeed a remedy for our respiratory organs and the endocrine glands; it cleanses and stimulates them marvellously. It has been said before that the thyroid in particular is stimulated by sea air and also by sea water and seaweeds, especially on account of their iodine content. However, if you suffer from Graves' disease (exophthalmic goitre) or hyperthyroidism, you must be careful to limit your exposure to these stimulants; in other words, if the sea air or bathing in the sea increases your pulse rate or causes a faster heartbeat, you should spend only short periods on the beach every day. Given time, the body will become accustomed to the impact of the marine atmosphere and you may gradually increase your exposure to a few hours daily. The more the disturbing symptoms diminish, the longer you can permit yourself the pleasure of spending time on the beach. So if you take care to do what is sensible and reasonable and not extreme, the therapeutic effect and cure will be much faster.

Sea-Bathing

Bathing in the sea has different effects on people. Salt water has an osmotic effect in as much as it draws water from the body. As a result, those people who always have some excess fluid in the legs will feel considerably better after bathing in the sea. Sea water will do the same for them as sea salt packs would do. If you tend to obesity, sea-bathing will usually help you to lose weight, even though you may not eat less. Excess weight and fat can be reduced because the sea stimulates the thyroid and gonads, thus benefiting the entire metabolism. All this is good for the figure and slimness may thus be within reach for some people. Sea air and sea-bathing are beneficial in cases of circulatory disorders, and diabetics will find sea-bathing good for them when they swim a lot and walk along the beach and over sand dunes. When stress and tension threaten your health do something about it quickly: take a holiday by the sea – there is no better remedy. However, while you are away from your work and duties, put them completely out of your mind and do not let the telephone interrupt your treatment. So, no telephone in your hotel room! 'Switching off' is absolutely essential during your holiday if you are to benefit fully from the 'cure' the sea can give you.

And there is one other rule you must observe: go to bed early during your stay by the sea. That means that you must cut out any kind of night life and remember instead that the early morning hours are the best. In fact, after an early and restful night it is easier to wake up, then go for a walk along the beach, feeling fully refreshed and fit. Remember, early to bed and early to rise, makes a man (and woman) healthy and gloriously hungry for breakfast! What better ingredients could you have for this meal than a delicious fruit muesli, wholegrain or wholewheat (wholemeal) bread with honey, and fruit-cereal coffee (*Bambu Coffee Substitute*)!

If you are able to organise your days by the sea properly, you can expect to benefit as much from them as you would from a holiday in the mountains. If we provide the body with all its needs, we will reap the desired health benefits irrespective of where we spend our holidays. However, just lazing around in the sun and heat is of no benefit anywhere. Instead, move around and exercise in the unpolluted air, breathe deeply and get plenty of rest during the night. If you eat healthy natural food at the same time, you will return to your duties after the holiday feeling rested, refreshed and optimistic.

Alternating Hot and Cold Water Therapies

Alternating hot and cold water applications are excellent for poor circulation and a fine aid to removing any congestion.

Apply hot water or herbal packs for about three minutes, then replace by a cold water pack, but leave this on for no longer than half a minute. Repeat the hot pack, followed by the cold, and continue in the same way for 20–30 minutes. The same principle applies to water-treading. Tread your feet in hot water for three minutes, then half a minute in cold water, and so forth. If you take alternating hot and cold baths, you must stay in the cold water only the same number of seconds as you were in the hot for minutes. This rule also applies to alternating hot and cold foot and arm baths. These applications should never make you feel chilled, but always warm and comfortable.

Steam Baths at Home

Steam baths are useful for dispersing congestions, making the urine flow again when retention occurs (older men often suffer from this difficulty) and relieving cystitis (inflammation of the bladder) and similar conditions of the bladder, as well as prostate problems.

These baths are easy enough to prepare at home. First make a steaming hot infusion of hay flowers (using the stalks, leaves, blossoms, seed and the hay itself), camomile, wild thyme or similar aromatic herbs. When this is ready, pour it into a large vessel, place a narrow plank or board over it, on which you can sit. Keep the steam and heat from escaping by covering yourself from head to toe with towels or sheets.

If you find sitting on the board to be uncomfortable, you might use some sort of wicker chair instead. If you do not have one, it may be possible to cut a hole out of the seat of an ordinary chair so that the steam can rise from underneath. In any event, you must keep your body warm and well wrapped in towels.

Keep adding more hot herbal infusion or hot water so that the steam continues to rise. It will be even more efficient it you can keep the infusion on a hot plate.

Such a steam bath is very effective, inexpensive to construct, and serves an excellent purpose.

Sitz Baths and their Medicinal Value

Sitz baths (in which only the hips and buttocks are immersed, hence their other name, hip baths) are part and parcel of good health care and, at the same time, complement effective beauty care. If you take regular hip baths, the circulation will be stimulated, which, in turn, will benefit the abdominal organs and health in general. Such regular care and attention is especially good for the ovaries, since they are easily affected by cold and congestions. Sitz baths increase the blood circulation and eliminate congestions, stagnation, irritations and any initial stages of inflammation of the ovaries and Fallopian tubes. Deformations and infertility can thus often be prevented.

Of what use are the best natural remedies if they do not reach the affected parts of the body because of congestion or circulatory disorders? We all know that life and healing forces are contained in the blood and that it is therefore important for the blood to

Balm

reach the ailing parts of the body. The best remedies for this purpose are water therapies, and for women, hip baths, or sitz baths, are the most indicated. Did you know that external symptoms such as oily skin, blackheads, dandruff, skin eruptions and itchy skin can be the result of poor functioning of the abdominal organs? One basic requirement of a thorough health and body care programme for modern women is the treatment and care of these organs.

A woman's mental and emotional balance and attitude are highly dependent on the good working order of the abdominal organs, especially the ovaries. Keep-fit exercises, walking and regular sitz baths help to provide the proper circulation a woman needs. Taking into account that her general well-being has much to do with the conscientious care of her health, surely any woman will want to see to it that this care is just another important part of her daily routine.

The addition of herbs in the form of infusions is highly recommended. For those who are nervous and tense, add lemon balm to the bath water; those who tend to feel tired and easily chilled will find thyme a good help; dry and flaking skin benefits from an infusion of wild pansy (heartsease); while comfrey is good for rough skin with large pores. Another way to treat rough skin is to apply Symphosan (comfrey tincture) after every bath. If the skin is sensitive or sore, it is advisable to add an infusion of mallow (cheese plant) or sanicle. Oily skin responds well to herbal sea salt.

Hay flowers (hayseed) and juniper needles can also be added to a hip bath. Or if you can obtain some eucalyptus leaves, they too are a good addition. Some of the aromatic herbs are stimulating while others have sedative properties. You will have to make your choice according to the intended effect. Even oat straw can be a beneficial addition, although it is often considered useless as a medicine. Whatever the case, a hip bath is more efficacious when a herbal infusion is added than if just water is used. It would be a pity to take so much time and trouble preparing a sitz bath if full use of the herbs as remedies were not made at the same time.

One or two hip baths should be taken every week. In cases of illness and necessity they can be taken more frequently. The time spent in the bath may vary from twenty to thirty minutes, and the water must be kept at a constant temperature of 37°C (98.6°F), which is accomplished by pouring off some of the water and replacing it with hot water. It is recommended that a hip bath be taken in the evening before going to bed, because you should not step out into the cold air afterwards or sit around in the house to cool off. A warm room is essential for such a bath, as a cold room absorbs too much body heat. Additionally, it is advisable to wrap up well with warm towels for extra warmth. A reduction in body temperature or even beginning to feel chilly is detrimental when taking a bath.

The best vessel to use for a sitz bath is, of course, one specially designed for that purpose; it will enable you to run off cooling water and add hot water, in order to maintain the required temperature. Lacking that, an ordinary bathtub will do, but you will have to keep a bucket of very hot water by the side of it. Use this hot water to top up the bath after removing some of the cooling water; to do this you will need a jar and another bucket for disposal. If all you have is a bathtub, you can take such a 'half bath' with the water reaching no higher than the navel. If you have an ordinary bathtub and a small hip bath, you can simply put a plank across the tub and stand the hip bath on it. You will need another plank or board as a foot rest. A hand shower attachment will make it quite easy to add more hot water, while the cooling water can be left to run out into the unplugged bathtub underneath. The advantage of this arrangement is obvious; at the end of your bath the water can be emptied straight into the tub.

Regular sitz baths are beneficial to your health, will preserve your youthfulness and, of course, have a great influence on your mental and emotional disposition and attitude.

The Schlenz Method (Baths of Increasing Temperature)

I once met the old high school teacher Rudolf Schlenz in Innsbruck and shortly afterwards discussed the Schlenz method with his son, Dr J. Schlenz. My conversations with these two men conveyed to me some of the spirit of the late Maria Schlenz, who had developed this type of hot water therapy.

Mrs Schlenz was neither a medical doctor nor a naturopath, but a simple housewife and mother. She had, however, an appreciation for nature and a gift for observation. In caring for her children she realised that they were too delicate to benefit from Kneipp's cold water treatment, so she thought of giving them hot water treatments instead. Some doctors had given baths of increasing temperature (*Überwärmungsbäder* in German) with good results even before she began to use them and continued to do so after the introduction of her method, but orthodox medicine in her native country paid no attention to her experience.

Later on, I made the acquaintance of Dr Devrient in Berlin, who was so enthusiastic about the Schlenz method that he published a book explaining these baths, as well as sauna baths, as used in practice. He made reference to the practical experiences with these baths recorded by his colleagues Dr Wilhelm Winsch and Dr Walenski. Whenever Dr Devrient stood in for another colleague, Dr Keller-Hoerschelmann, he came into contact with Swiss folk medicine. He himself was an ardent advocate of natural therapy methods and holistic medicine. It was obvious, then, that he also approved of hydrotherapy and, of course, the Schlenz method. Professor Lampert employed the same method with great success; in fact, it is known that he cured over a hundred cases of typhoid fever during World War II, without losing a single one of his patients.

Some time later I learned about the regenerative and curative effects of hot water treatments as used in Japan. The temperature of their baths surpasses that of blood temperature, and it is interesting to note that rheumatism and cancer are seldom heard of where these hot water baths are taken regularly. Some researchers even claim that swollen tissue can be rehabilitated if the water is kept 2–3 degrees Celsius above normal body temperature (39–40°C/102–104°F). And when the temperature is raised 4–5 degrees higher, that is, up to 41–42°C (105.8–107.6°F), tumours are changed and in time dissolved, according to these researchers.

It is possible that these claims are somewhat exaggerated; nevertheless, experience has shown that 'baths of increasing temperature' make a positive contribution in the treatment of tumours, especially when the effect is heightened by the use of appropriate herbs. Many a malignant ailment can be prevented by their use, and the prevention of frightening diseases such as cancer has become a great necessity in our time. *The Nature Doctor* has already given some good advice regarding the prevention of cancer (see pages 288–92) and here we add the further recommendation that you take a prolonged bath or Schlenz bath once a week. Its prophylactic effect can help to maintain your health. However, you should not simply be satisfied with knowing these things without acting upon the knowledge. That would be of little use to you. You should rouse yourself and apply the recommended treatment on a regular basis.

Schlenz Baths at Home
Before you decide to try out a Schlenz bath in your home, you should first get to know the exact method as used in a recognised Schlenz bath centre, to enable you to become familiar with all the relevant details. The bathtub used for Schlenz baths is generally longer than an ordinary one and should preferably be made of wood. But in modern homes this is rarely the case, so that a conventional enamelled or plastic bathtub will have to do. It is also necessary to remember that the head will have to be immersed, too, so that you will have to bend your legs a little in a shorter tub.

Since the head is submerged as well as the rest of the body the warmth will be equally distributed over the entire body and congestions towards the head will be avoided. A Schlenz bath will therefore give no trouble at all, even though you may not be able to stand an ordinary hot bath. Keep the mouth and nose just out of the water so that you can breathe. On the other hand, as this position is uncomfortable and difficult to maintain for any length of time, attach a belt at the top end of the bathtub, or a strong cloth, for use as a support for the head. Rest the head on this support under the water, leaving only the mouth and nose above it. To begin with, keep the water temperature at 36–37°C (97–98°F), that is, blood temperature; but be careful not to let the temperature drop. For this reason, it is important to have some

Elder

hot water ready to add as necessary, letting the temperature rise to at least 38°C (100.4°F). Before taking the bath, drink one or two cups of hot herbal tea – lemon balm, peppermint, elder or goldenrod. Add a few drops of *Crataegisan* if your heart is a little weak.

Increasing the body temperature by several degrees induces a kind of artificial fever, which is able to burn up a lot of wastes, just as with a natural fever. In this regard, we cannot help remembering a statement made by Parmenides, the father of metaphysics: 'Give me the power to induce fever and I shall cure every illness.'

Indeed, more healing can be done through increasing the body temperature than is generally thought possible. By raising the temperature to 40 or 41°C (104–105.8°F), disease-causing agents that are sensitive to heat will be destroyed. Regular Schlenz baths will have an effect on sensitive tumour cells or tissue, since they do not tolerate heat very well. Those who suffer from metabolic and circulatory disorders will benefit from a weekly Schlenz bath, as will anyone who has problems with the skin function and lymphatic glands, or who suffers from skin eruptions and eczema. In the case of all these disorders and ailments, regular Schlenz baths can lead to a complete cure.

When you first start, a Schlenz bath should last only half an hour. In time, you can increase the duration to two hours. In cases of obesity it is advisable to add sea salt, brine or a good bath salt to the bath water, in addition to the herbs. An attendant should use a tough brush to vigorously brush down the patient's entire body once or twice during the bath. This has the same effect as an underwater massage and stimulates the capillaries. It removes congestions, and any unpleasant feeling of constriction will disappear.

When the time for the bath is up, sit upright, apply a little *Po-Ho-Oil* under your nose and inhale slowly, deeply and vigorously; then stand up, wrap yourself in a warm bath towel and go straight into a warmed bed without drying yourself. You will continue to perspire while you are there. Maria Schlenz, by the way, used hand-knitted wool blankets to keep the heat in. Your head and wet hair should be wrapped up warmly so that no part of the body can cool down.

A Schlenz bath taken at home has the advantage that you can go straight to bed and sleep. As soon as the body has stopped perspiring, wash it down with lukewarm water and apply *St John's wort oil* or some other body oil that contains this oil. Afterwards you will feel relaxed and pleasantly tired and will go soundly to sleep.

A few Schlenz baths can dispense with the need for costly hydrotherapy treatment at a spa. Then there is the added advantage of being able to prepare Schlenz baths right in your own home. If you wait until evening for the bath, you can still do some urgent work during the day, and you will feel fresh and energetic the following morning, after a good night's sleep.

In cases where the initial symptoms of poliomyelitis are present, the fresh hormone treatment recommended by *The Nature Doctor* (see page 53–4) should be followed up by a Schlenz bath. This can help you to prevent paralysis. Schlenz baths are of equal benefit to those who suffer from multiple sclerosis. They help to prevent the sad complications of this illness, which can make life almost unbearable. In view of the many benefits a course of treatment with Schlenz baths can give, this method deserves to be much better known and utilised than it actually is.

Kuhne's Cold Water Treatment
Louis Kuhne had an astute mind and understanding of natural healing and was able to use water most effectively for what is called 'stimulation' or 'irritation' therapy. He perfected his method to such an extent that his handbook came to be translated into

many languages, circulating in all parts of the earth. Unfortunately, he had no direct successor and no society or clinic took up his ideas with a view to spreading the Kuhne method, as was the case with the cures developed by Priessnitz, Sebastian Kneipp and other hydrotherapists.

Cold Water Friction Treatment

Especially valuable and important is a cold water massage Kuhne developed. A simplified form of this treatment can be undertaken in your own home. First, take a large container and fill it three-quarters full with cold water. Then put a board over the container to cover half of it. Sit on the board, having taken off the clothes covering the lower part of the body. Take a brush with a long handle, wrap a cloth around the brush, dip it in the cold water and rub round about the genitals. The cold reaction must only affect one part of the body and for this reason your hand should not be put in the cold water but remain dry all the time. Because of the cold reaction it is essential to maintain a constant body temperature by wrapping yourself in warm cloths or towels during the treatment, as is done during a steam bath.

The Kuhne treatment is best done at night, for it ensures more restful sleep because it draws the blood from the head to the abdomen, with the effect that it is much easier to switch off from distracting thoughts. If you find it difficult to go to sleep, you should try this method. Five minutes are often enough to draw the blood away from the head to the centre of the body, resulting in hyperaemia, increased blood flow. In accordance with the body's reaction and the purpose intended, the treatment has to be carried on for 10–15 minutes. However, always remember that you must not allow yourself to become chilled; the body should remain nice and warm for the effect to be beneficial. If you think that you could catch a cold because you keep dipping the brush in cold water and going over the same area again and again, you are actually mistaken. This part of the body has an abundance of blood vessels and is therefore less sensitive to the cold. When massaging, do avoid the region of the bladder because it is more sensitive. If your body does not respond to the cold water friction by making you feel warm, and you are quite sure that it does not, it would appear that the Kuhne method is not for you.

However, if your body responds well to cold water applications, the Kuhne method will give you the desired results. These cold water friction or massage treatments relieve headaches, congestions in the head, leaden fatigue, stomach upsets, loss of appetite and many other complaints. Frigidity as well as an exceptionally strong sexual drive can be treated successfully, so that in time it is possible to experience normal function of the sex organs. After a few weeks, cases of depression and melancholy can be improved and they may even be cured if the treatment is continued over an extended period.

Following the instructions given, you can practise these cold water massages at home and as long as the necessary care is taken, you will do no harm whatsoever. On the contrary, you will have reason to be astonished at the excellent results.

Revulsion by Means of Stimulation (Irritation) Therapies

It is the Chinese who seem to have a great deal of experience in the field of stimulation (irritation) therapy. On my visits to the Far East I was able to witness their mastery of this kind of therapy. I even watched them treat and cure gangrene by means of it. There was an old monk in a Buddhist monastery who gave this kind of treatment. One European patient told me in confidence about the excellent result in his own case.

Of course, the modern treatment is much milder than the old-fashioned methods. In the old days a white-hot iron was passed quickly over the affected area in order to induce stimulation or revulsion. Nowadays pungent roots containing mainly mustard oil, are used instead. First, hot compresses are applied to the area to be cured, then the grated roots are rubbed in, bandaged with cotton to keep warm and left to act for 4–5 hours. The active substances contained in the root pulp induce powerful stimulation, making the blood circulate vigorously in the area. The body responds by sending a great detachment of leucocytes and lymphocytes to the spot, so that an artificially induced inflammation breaks out. The purpose is to rally all available forces in the body. Congested blood vessels, tiny thromboses, toxins and metabolic wastes are dislodged and excreted. If the treatment is done properly, it is possible to cure old and even chronic disorders.

Some years ago I had the opportunity to give such a treatment with complete success. One day an old man from the Jura mountains came to see me about his leg, which the doctors were intending to amputate. The stimulating treatment I gave him opened up an ulcer on his leg that had been a long-standing problem. You should have seen the quantity of blood and pus that burst forth! And then the pain subsided all at once. Needless to say, after this thorough cleansing action the wound began to heal and the old watchmaker's leg was soon as good as new.

The Baunscheidt Method

The Baunscheidt method is similar to the Chinese treatment just described. However, Baunscheidt did not take it from the Chinese but developed his treatment based on his own experience and conclusions. This method achieves a simulation or irritation of the skin by means of an apparatus known in German as *Lebenswecker* (life reviver). After pricking the skin, *Baunscheidt oil* is rubbed in, the area is covered with cotton wool and the ingredients are left to work overnight. The following day the treatment is continued with the application of a lanolin cream (*Bioforce Cream*).

This therapy has given good results in the treatment of chronic ailments, even multiple sclerosis. The application is made on the left and right side along the patient's spine. However, it is not advisable to undertake a Baunscheidt revulsion treatment on the off-chance that it might work, but without being really familiar with it. If you want to use this method it is absolutely essential that you know the correct way of applying it. The same rule applies to any stimulation therapy and it is better to let a physiotherapist or biologically oriented doctor with the necessary experience give the treatment. The needles have to be used with great care and only on the muscles; never touch the glands or periosteum, which must not be irritated.

Stimulation therapies can be used successfully in cases where medicines fail to give results because the circulation in the affected parts is insufficient and the remedies do not reach them. The stimulation provided by these therapies is then an alternative and welcome means of assistance.

The Medicinal Value of Clay

From time immemorial clay has been used to cure many ailments. Yet this old remedy has often been rejected by those who could have benefited from it. Nevertheless, clay has never been totally forgotten and today it is once more finding favour. Among other things, it is particularly recommended as a treatment for tumours where external application is possible.

Also, there is an interesting account in the Bible of how Christ used clay to cure a blind man (John 9:11). Even though it may have been a symbolic act, we should not lose sight of the fact that

439

earth or clay was used and that the Teacher of Nazareth surely knew of the healing elements of nature and respected them.

People who live closer to nature in less developed parts of the world treat many illnesses with clay, and veterinary surgeons make use of it too. Beauty specialists recommend it for face packs and athletes use it for strains and sprains. Clay applications have proved their worth for centuries. A combination of clay and herbs is especially recommended. Instead of using simple herb poultices, the herbal properties are combined with those of clay. Usually the clay is mixed into a paste, to which the hot herbal infusion is added to form a poultice. The poultice is then applied to the affected part of the body and the double action of the clay and herbs results in a more potent effect.

If you want to get the best out of a treatment with clay, you must be certain that you understand how it works. There are those who use clay where linseed or fenugreek seed should be applied, and this is quite wrong. For instance, clay should not be placed on a boil to collect the pus and draw it to a head. Hot linseed or fenugreek compresses will do this job far better, for the action of clay disperses, it never draws together or gathers.

Directions for the Use of Clay
According to the time of the year, clay poultices may be used either hot or cold. Those who are sensitive to the cold may prefer a hot poultice; a bag of hot herbs can be placed on top of the clay to help retain its heat. With a cold clay pack you can reduce the feeling of cold by a hot herb bag used in the same way.

For a small clay poultice, a tablespoon of clay, mixed with a herbal infusion to make a thin paste, will suffice. Spread the paste evenly, about 3–5 mm (⅛–⅕ inch) thick, onto a piece of gauze or linen and place on the affected part. In cases of inflammation, especially inflammation of a nerve (neuritis), *St John's wort oil* mixed with clay can work wonders and has the added advantage of keeping the poultice soft and easy to remove. Otherwise its removal can be unpleasant for those with sensitive skin as clay becomes hard and brittle as it dries. It is recommended that the poultice be applied at night and left on until the morning.

There are certain instances, usually in cases of chronic ailments, where it is advantageous to apply *clay and cabbage poultices* alternately. Since we know that clay disperses and cabbage draws together, the alternating actions will produce effects similar to those of a counter-irritation. This is often desirable in chronic rheumatic and arthritic conditions.

Taken internally, clay has a remarkable effect on diarrhoea and inflammation of the intestinal mucosa. Whatever medication is taken for these problems, it should be added to clay water.

Everyone could profit physically from an intestinal cleansing twice a year and the best clay to use for this purpose is the white, sand-free kind, although yellow clay is suitable too. Such a course of treatment should last a week at a time.

What Herbs to Use

For applying to tumours an infusion made from *horsetail* (shave grass) or *oak bark* produces good results when mixed with clay. Inflammation of the nerves is best treated with a mixture of *lemon balm* and clay; and for rheumatic problems, an infusion of *eucalyptus leaves,* needle-like *juniper leaves,* or *wild thyme* with clay is recommended. Never boil aromatic herbs and leaves; merely pour boiling water over them and allow them to steep in the hot liquid (infusion). Non-aromatic herbs can be boiled a little. When ready, strain and mix the liquid with clay to make a paste. If you infuse the herbs in a small cloth bag, this will be useful for laying on top of the clay-herb poultice when it is in position. As previously explained, this will help to retain the heat.

Herb Poultices

Herbs that favourably influence the function of organs when taken as teas, tinctures and extracts will also benefit us if we apply them as poultices, as practical experience will prove. Kidney herbs such as *Solidago (goldenrod), birch leaves* and *horsetail,* can be crushed or minced and applied raw to the region over the kidneys. This external application will enhance the effect of the same remedies taken internally.

The application of fresh plants will benefit the circulatory and lymphatic systems and ease stagnation in the vascular system. In fact, fresh plant therapy is easy. For example, *crushed sorrel, giant dock* and *rhubarb leaf* poultices applied to congestions, bruises, swellings and the like, have an excellent effect. They will dissipate the trouble much better than expensive commercial plasters and ointments. Various leaves found in the garden and fields are suitable, but care must be taken not to employ the leaves of poisonous plants. The leaves of *Rhus toxicodendron* (poison ivy) can cause a severe rash. *Belladonna* and other poisonous plants must not be used either. In fact, poisonous plants, it must be remembered, are safe only in the hands of a professional phytotherapist. Other leaf poultices, for example ones made with *cabbage leaves*, can be applied without having to fear any complications. They are helpful in treating numerous ailments, and if there should be a strong reaction, simply reduce the time the poultices are allowed to remain on the affected area.

These poultices are easily prepared and always beneficial.

Cabbage Leaf and Other Herb Poultices

The curative properties of *cabbage leaves* are becoming more widely known now, even though the use of crushed medicinal plants on diseased parts of the body is by no means a new idea. Dr Blanc has written a booklet on the subject and many people have benefited from this inexpensive treatment. Many years ago I started to apply crushed *St John's wort* leaves and flowers in the case of inflammations of the nerves, with wonderful results. Whenever I used to get blisters from walking barefoot in the mountains in search of herbs, I always found some *goldenrod*, bruised it and put it, raw and fresh, on the sore spot, covered it with a leaf of lady's mantle and bandaged everything with a handkerchief. This enabled me to carry on walking and go about my business. The blisters did not bother me anymore and soon began to heal. In the case of kidney trouble it is a good thing to crush or mince fresh *birch leaves and goldenrod* and apply the raw pulp over the kidney area. Wrap them round with warm towels and place a hot water bottle on top for added warmth.

Cabbage leaf poultices or packs are excellent for the treatment of tumours. In the case of cancerous growths, their effect is very good when alternated with clay poultices. It sometimes happens that the condition or pain becomes aggravated at first, but after a while improvement usually follows. Cabbage pulp can cause a strong reaction; it can increase the secretion of urine, cause blisters, or simply dry out on the skin. Tests on myself and the testimonies of patients have always proved the effectiveness of these poultices.

Cabbage leaves are usually available in your kitchen, so why not try a pack when you suffer bruising, notice a growth or experience some internal inflammation? Apply the crushed leaves, in addition to taking the necessary oral medicine. Many chronic ailments can be successfully treated with *cabbage* and *clay packs* applied in alternation; one day apply the pulped leaves, next day the clay packs. In this way it is often possible to avoid the surgeon's knife.

Good results are also achieved with *onions* and *raw horseradish*. Some skin diseases clear up when a paste made up of *bran* and an infusion of *marigold* or *horsetail* is applied. Or you can soak some *wheat*, put it through a mincer, then mix it with marigold or horsetail to make a soothing and curative paste.

THE EFFECTIVENESS OF CABBAGE POULTICES – TESTIMONIALS

In many cases the orthodox doctor goes to no end of trouble to help a patient, but unfortunately, without success. Then, when a simple natural remedy like cabbage leaves produces a cure, we are astonished at how natural active forces, without depending upon laboriously collected human knowledge, can bring about almost miraculous results.

The case of a 62-year-old patient, who suffered considerably, serves as a good example. An infection, aggravated by eating sprayed cherries, resulted in the development of a fungus the size of a small coin on the lady's tongue. The doctor removed it with cautery (silver nitrate) and found it necessary to prescribe, in addition, eight days of radium treatment. After three weeks the patient left the hospital with a paralysed tongue.

Five weeks later, a large swelling appeared on her neck. It seemed that another operation would be necessary to remove it. Discouraged by the prospect of more surgery, the patient kept postponing it. Eight weeks later the pain had become almost unbearable but now an operation was considered out of the question. Instead, she received forty-three radiation treatments. Afterwards, the patient felt weak and thought death was inevitable.

At this point the doctors had given up all hope of curing her. The wound would not heal and constantly exuded pus. After nine weeks the patient asked to return home from the hospital and her family and relatives continued treating her with much care and devotion. Every ten minutes the dressing on the wound had to be changed and a special ointment applied. But despite all this kind attention the pain could not be relieved.

An acquaintance of hers who had read of cabbage poultices in my monthly magazine *Health News (Gesundheits-Nachrichten)* recommended this treatment and – lo and behold – within four days of trying it, the pus was discharging freely and the terrible pain receded. In spite of suffering from chronic constipation and headaches resulting from it, the patient felt much better and was delighted to be on the mend after a year and a half of illness. It is hard to believe that cabbage can achieve such success, but if this patient had not taken advantage of the treatment her condition would probably have greatly deteriorated instead of improving as it did.

The marvellous effect of cabbage leaves is truly remarkable and no doctor or medical practitioner who has the well-being of his patients at heart should ignore this lowly plant.

Here is another example, taken at random from the many testimonials I have received. A worried mother wrote asking for advice on how to deal with her child's swollen neck glands. Having followed the prescribed treatment, this is what she wrote:

'The trouble was soon put right by the remedies and cabbage poultices. Cabbage, in general, seems to be a marvellous thing. It seemed our thirteen-year-old son, who is 175 cm [5'9"] tall and whose voice has already broken, would not be able to get rid of a cold before having to go back to school the following Monday. He then complained of a really bad headache and yesterday afternoon, of a pain in and above his right eye. I was afraid of sinus trouble, so I put a cabbage poultice on his head just above the eyes and left it on for two hours. Monday came and off he went to school, returning in the evening still cheerful. The pain had completely gone.'

It is quite peculiar that the humble cabbage should have such outstanding healing powers and can give unexpected relief without any harmful side effects. What explanation is there? Well, cabbage not only supplies curative elements to the tissues but also eliminates toxins and other harmful substances from these same affected areas. This kind of remedy fills an important place, especially where nothing else seems to be effective.

The Potato as a Remedy
Raw, grated potatoes, mixed with a little milk, are an ideal remedy for the following conditions: slow-healing wounds or cuts, wounds that form proud flesh, infections or inflammations that secrete putrid matter, swellings, bruises, articular rheumatism and inflammation of muscles and of the periosteum.

Potatoes boiled in their skins, mashed when they are still hot and mixed with a little raw milk, can be applied as a poultice, like a clay pack. If you have a poor reaction to cold applications, use warm poultices. Those who benefit from cold packs, on the other hand, should use raw potatoes, grated or pulped.

A remarkable effect can be obtained by alternating three applications on three consecutive days. On the first day, apply a *potato poultice*; on the second day, a *cabbage poultice*; and on the third day, a *clay poultice* made with a *horsetail infusion* and a little *St John's wort oil*. If you continue to apply these poultices for some time, even a severe swelling will yield.

Old potatoes should have their sprouts carefully removed because they contain a poisonous substance called solanin. These sprouts should neither be fed to animals nor used as food or as a remedy. If you prepare juice from fresh potatoes, or from old ones after removing the sprouts very carefully, do not be afraid that the juice could harm you. On the contrary, raw potato juice is well known as a remedy and has helped to cure many a gastric problem.

Raw potato juice is especially good for inflammation of the gastric lining (gastritis). For stomach ulcers drink the juice diluted with warm water first thing in the morning, before breakfast. The juice of one small potato will do. If you find it difficult to drink potato juice because of its not too pleasant taste, add it to a warm oat gruel or soup that has already been cooked. Potato juice, *Gastronol* and a mild, fibre-free diet will cure the most stubborn gastric ulcers, if attention is given to proper mastication and thorough insalivation of the food one eats.

Potato juice is highly alkaline and is a very effective antidote for uric acid conditions such as rheumatism and arthritis. Just remember that care must be taken to remove any solanin-containing sprouts before preparing it.

Papain – its Origin and Uses

In the lush woodlands of Florida there are found not only thousands of cabbage palms and many other tropical plants, but also a great number of wild papayas. The Indians living there have always enjoyed the juicy fruit because it is delicious and healthy. They also made use of the plant in cooking. Since time immemorial those primitive tribes have known that papaya leaves, stems and fruit contain a substance that breaks down protein. So, whenever the hunters happened to kill an old animal the cook would wrap the tough meat in papaya leaves and leave it overnight. On the following day it would be tender enough to be roasted over a fire. The substance which tenderises meat, called papain, causes a kind of predigestion process, one might say.

The handsome papaya plant resembles a small palm and has big leaves similar to those of a fig tree. It grows mostly in the Western hemisphere and is found in Central America, Guatemala and San Salvador, the islands of the Caribbean, in Brazil, even in the jungle, as well as in Florida. If you could visit the sites in the Brazilian jungle where trees are cut for timber or the area is cleared for other purposes, you would be able to make a very interesting observation that almost borders on the miraculous. In the dense forests there are no papayas to be seen anywhere, but shortly after the trees have been felled, papaya plants begin to sprout here and there. I met some Swiss settlers in the area who told me of their surprise at finding papayas growing where not one single plant could be seen in an area of 100–200 square kilometres (about 40–80 square miles) before it was cleared.

Where do these plants suddenly spring from? The answer escaped me for quite a while, but I found it in the end, and it is actually very simple. You see, birds like papaya too and when they find the fruit growing in clearings they swoop down and pick at them, seeds and all. Off they fly again and on the way their droppings, together with the undigested seeds, fall back onto the jungle floor where they remain dormant for ten, twenty, or perhaps even a hundred years or more, the reason being that the dense forest shuts out all sunlight from the earth, and without light they cannot sprout. However, as soon as a clearing is cut in the jungle the sunlight warms the earth, the seeds begin to germinate and within a year, because their growth is very fast indeed, you have a plant the height of a man.

The Indians enjoy eating plenty of papaya where they grow, and the white settlers have noticed this habit and copied it. Eating papaya after a meal makes for better digestion. Food rich in protein will cause no problems if you eat papaya, since papain breaks down protein. Being a good observer, you will soon discover that all those who eat papaya remain free from intestinal worms. In fact, all worms disappear when papaya is taken over a period of time. The seeds are especially effective as a remedy and it is recommended to chew some of them every time you eat the fruit. What is the reason for this desirable effect? Research has shown that papain simply digests the parasites made of protein; it not only helps to digest cheese, meat, eggs, and other protein foods in the digestive tract, but also any intestinal worms that may have settled there. It dissolves their protein organisms and destroys them in a simple and harmless way. Papaya could not be better described than as a simple food and an excellent vermicide. Even amoebas are destroyed by the papain in papaya seed as long as they are still in the intestines and have not settled elsewhere.

Because the ripe papaya fruit is perishable it cannot be trans-

ported over long distances. However, it was discovered that the unripe fruit, the stems and the leaves contain more papain than the ripe fruit – and this solved the problem of shipping. Obviously unripe fruits can be transported far more easily. Furthermore, the use of the milky juice which contains the most papain suggested itself. Preparations made with this juice aid the digestion and are useful remedies for the elimination of worms – a widespread problem in many areas of the world.

Papayasan contains papain in combination with the ingredients of the whole plant. It can therefore act in the same way as the whole plant provided by nature and taking it is the equivalent of eating the unripe fruit with its rich papain content.

Every doctor, nature practitioner and pharmacist, as well as every caring mother, will no doubt be glad to know that there is at last a worm medicine that is absolutely safe. According to the third edition of Professor Eichholz's *Pharmakologie (Pharmacology)*, even experts regard the usual worm medicines as risky and far from harmless, for he writes: 'The toxicity of all anthelmintic medicines should prompt the prescriber to consider whether it is preferable to tolerate the presence of parasites, rather than to take the risk of poisoning the patient.' If this is of concern to pharmacologists and pharmacists, how much more should it make the patient think. However, with a papaya preparation no one need fear, for it is beneficial to the digestion, assisting in the assimilation of proteins, and is absolutely harmless – even for pregnant women and people with weak constitutions.

In the short time Papayasan has been available it has helped many hundreds of people, and in the future it will aid thousands more who want to be free from the harm and danger of intestinal worms without any risk of side effects.

Worms are by no means to be taken lightly, whether it is *Oxyuris vermicularis*, the little threadworm that causes an itching irritation in the anus and can be found by the thousands in the large intestine; the ascaris or roundworm inhabiting the small intestine; the *Trichocephalus dispar* (whipworm), or any other intestinal parasite. They are all extremely harmful and can lead to severe disturbance in the composition of the blood, and cause conditions such as eosinophilia, anaemia, chlorosis and liver disorders. The chief factors responsible for these and other serious conditions are no doubt the metabolic toxins secreted by the worms.

The botanical enzymes of Papayasan break down protein and hence dissolve the cuticle of roundworms, threadworms and whip-

worms, and with the help of intestinal ferments will completely digest them.

The Therapeutic Effects of Milk

Milk has always been regarded as a remedy, not only as a food. Everyone knows that milk is an excellent source of minerals. It contains magnesium, manganese and many other minerals, including calcium in a form that can be easily assimilated. These minerals are found in a concentrated form in sour whey, the watery liquid that separates from the curd when milk is made into cheese. At the same time, they are improved and enriched through the process of lactic fermentation. The concentrated lactic acid with the milk enzymes, such as contained in *Molkosan*, has antiseptic properties, making Molkosan a good remedy for sore throats, catarrh and even laryngitis.The numerous applications of this valuable remedy are described in greater detail below.

Just as sour whey is a remedy, so is milk on its own and curds or soft skimmed milk cheese. They are each good for certain illnesses. For example, an inflammation of the gallbladder can be quite painful, but a compress of cold, unboiled milk will relieve the pain immediately. The actual inflammation will often subside after a short while and pass faster than with any other medication. Heartburn caused by indigestion, an overacid stomach, is easily neutralised by drinking unboiled milk, and this natural remedy is to be preferred to aluminium silicates. Milk, given in the form of injections, has also been effective in revulsion or stimulation therapies. Soft skimmed milk cheese (quark) has been used in poultices for grazes, bruises and benign swellings for longer than anyone can remember. The application never fails to give good results.

Molkosan (Whey Concentrate)

Although curd packs and several other milk applications are well enough known, whey, the serum of the milk, is the form most frequently used in caring for the sick. Both sweet and sour whey contains most of the milk's mineral nutrients, while cheese, which separates from the whey, is valued chiefly on account of its high protein and fat content. Enzymes, especially rennet used in the manufacture of cheese, doubtlessly play an important part in the therapeutic effects of whey. Milk itself is a wholefood, which implies that it contains all the necessary elements to sustain life. Among these elements are protein, fat, sugar, minerals and trace

elements. So whey, the by-product of cheese manufacture, still has considerable nutritional value, actually much more than it was once thought to have. It is, therefore, of little wonder that in former times royalty and the famous from France and other countries made special journeys to Switzerland to take the world-renowned Swiss Whey Cures. Usually the visitors were afflicted with meta-bolic problems such as obesity, circulatory congestions, intestinal complaints, pancreatic insufficiency and flatulence. Whey cures also rectified conditions of dysbacteria, a complaint that is even more widespread today. Artificial preservatives and food additives, pesticide sprays etc., all contribute to the harm done to the body, which will have to put up a fight against them and their conse-quences.

Molkosan has helped a great deal in this struggle. If you want to assist the digestion, add a teaspoon or tablespoon of Molkosan to a glass of mineral water and drink this at mealtimes. Of course, you do not have to take mineral water, ordinary water will do just as well.

Molkosan regulates the secretion of gastric acid; it reduces an excess of acid and increases its quantity when there is a lack of it. Molkosan also benefits diabetics because the lactic ferments stimu-late the pancreas. Thus, it is without a doubt one of the best drinks these patients could wish for.

Regular use of Molkosan will lower the blood sugar level and, at the same time, reduce the quantity of sugar in the urine. Of course, an appropriate natural diet must be observed too. A little patience is necessary, but after several weeks a positive change for the better will be noticed.

Having an efficient pancreas is important to obese people, as this gland influences the fat metabolism. Regular use of Molkosan will slowly reduce excess weight, especially if *kelp tablets* are taken at the same time. This does not mean, however, that people who are underweight will have to avoid taking whey concentrate, for it regulates the metabolism rather than having a specific catabolic effect. So both underweight and overweight persons will benefit. In short, Molkosan makes for better assimilation of food.

Molkosan can be applied externally with the same success as when it is used internally. It has proved to be more valuable in the treatment of pimples, eczema and cradle cap than many more expensive preparations. For the most part, eczema can be treated by dabbing on undiluted whey concentrate. In cases of skin impurities and blemishes fine results are achieved if Molkosan is both taken internally and applied externally. Where athlete's foot and nail mould have not yet yielded to any other remedy, Molkosan will give quick and reliable relief. Just soak some absorbent cotton in it, bind this on the affected part and leave it on overnight. Dr Devrient of Berlin has confirmed that no other remedy for mycotic diseases is quicker and more reliable than Molkosan whey concentrate. When used to clean minor wounds, scratches and cuts, it is a first-class antiseptic.

For incipient tonsillitis or during the course of this disease, painting the throat with whey concentrate is most helpful. In fact, if it is done in the early stages, it may well prevent the disease altogether, especially when *Lachesis 10x* is taken at the same time.

Many years ago, I drew attention to my experience in the treatment of internal and external carcinomas with whey concentrate. Frequently, the mere swabbing of external cancerous growths and skin cancer has proved very effective. I vividly remember one special case of a cancerous tumour on the calf of the leg. When the surgeon had removed it he told the nurse in attendance that he felt doubtful about the wound ever healing. Still, we swabbed it with Molkosan and, to the surgeon's astonishment, it did heal very well and fast. Other successful cures have been achieved by giving whey concentrate orally and externally and I am happy to say that Dr Kuhl, having made his own experiments, now acknowledges the importance of lactic acid in the treatment of cancer.

Of course, I do not wish to say that such lactic acid preparations are a panacea, a cure-all, but they have certainly brought the treatment of cancer a step further along the road. Because Molkosan has a fairly high percentage of natural lactic acid, it is of immense value in a cancer diet. As a drink, diluted with mineral water, it is both prophylactic and curative in its effect. Dr Kuhl also recommends *raw sauerkraut* for this purpose, because of its lactic acid content.

It is, indeed, a great pleasure to see how the experiences and observations we began to report on in our magazine and books many years ago are now being confirmed as facts.

Once you are familiar with the many good effects of whey concentrate you will appreciate it and stop wondering why, in the past, even high-ranking personages did not consider it beneath their dignity to take 'whey cures' for the benefit of their health.

The Curative Effects of Wheat Germ Oil

In my discussion on wheat and wholegrain bread (see pages 516–9) I highlight the merits of wholegrain products and how the various cereals grown in different parts of the earth are a useful source of food that does not perish easily. It was only a few decades ago when researchers discovered that wheat germ is, in fact, an excellent remedy; this equally applies, of course, to wheat germ oil. Since more and more people are rejecting the use of chemical medicines, physicians, naturopaths and physiotherapists are ever more compelled to turn their attention to remedies that are made from basic materials as nature provides them. Many competent and skilled researchers have been studying the oils contained in cereal germs, and have found that the remedial effects of wheat germ oil are remarkable.

Wheat Germ Oil and its Two Important Elements

Wheat germ oil is high in polyunsaturated fatty acids and these play an important part in the development and maintenance of healthy body cells, as well as in the protein metabolism. They also contribute to the therapeutic solution of the problem of cancer. Polyunsaturated fatty acids, also known as essential fatty acids, promote internal oil oxygenation and, generally speaking, benefit the entire metabolism.

In the second place, wheat germ oil is important because of its valuable vitamin E content, which has also been called the fertility vitamin. Expectant and nursing mothers should take wheat germ oil regularly. Experience has shown that vitamin E is useful in helping to overcome a tendency to premature birth and miscarriage, since a deficiency in this vitamin is often found to be the cause. An extended course of wheat germ oil can help to prevent these unfortunate occurrences.

Furthermore, wheat germ oil can serve as a real help for menopausal problems and scanty, irregular or painful periods, if it is taken for some time. Weak sexual impulses, even impotence, can also be improved or cured if wheat germ oil is taken regularly. Yet this oil is not a stimulant drug, as is the case with preparations made from the African yohimbe tree bark; rather, it strengthens and normalises the functions of the organs in an absolutely natural way. It simply supplies the body with enough vitamin E to keep it functioning normally. For sexual weakness we recommend *A. Vogel's Wheat Germ Oil* or *capsules*; to increase the effect, take *Kelpasan* at the same time.

Heart Trouble and Circulatory Disorders

Wheat germ oil has proved such a good tonic for the heart that its use for this purpose deserves a special mention. The oil is always beneficial for circulatory disturbances in the heart, myocardial insufficiency or disorders, as well as stricture of the coronary vessels and other degenerative heart conditions.

Many people suffer from peripheral circulatory disorders and their consequences, others from circulatory disturbances in the brain, causing a weak memory, fainting spells, vertigo and related complaints. For all these conditions wheat germ oil is a superb remedy, especially when taken in conjunction with *Aesculaforce* and *Ginkgo biloba*, both of which are proven fresh plant preparations. We are certainly glad to have these preparations and wheat germ oil as a welcome natural remedy for many conditions.

Normalising Body Weight – Obesity and Leanness

Wheat germ oil improves the activity of the sex glands and is therefore an excellent help in the fight against obesity. If the treatment is supplemented by the intake of *Kelpasan*, a seaweed preparation, the thyroid and other endocrine glands will also be stimulated. The body weight will be regulated and the general condition of health improved without having to follow a strict diet. Furthermore, it is most gratifying to know that skinny people can normalise their weight with the help of wheat germ oil.

Incidentally, it is marvellous that sufferers from liver and gallbladder disorders can take wheat germ oil very well. My book *The Liver, the Regulator of Your Health* describes a practical liver diet which will benefit such people, especially if it is supplemented by wheat germ oil.

Hypertrophy of the Prostate

For this condition, an enlarged prostate, wheat germ oil has proved most effective, with even better results being achieved when it is taken together with *Sabal serrulata*, which is obtained from a palm that grows in Florida. Experience has shown that this plant remedy causes the enlargement to recede. If wheat germ oil is taken at the same time, its stimulating effect will give the success which *Sabal* alone could not produce. There are, of course, other good remedies for this complaint, and physical therapies are often necessary for a complete cure, but in the initial stages *Sabal* or *Prostasan* together with wheat germ oil capsules will suffice.

Dosage and Duration of Treatment

The normal dosage for adults is one tablespoon of wheat germ oil in the morning, at noon and in the evening. For children it is sufficient to give one teaspoonful three times daily. Wheat germ oil has a strengthening effect and is especially recommended when children and adolescents suffer from tiredness as a result of studying. As a tonic or prophylactic, adults should take one teaspoonful daily. Alternatively, you can take wheat germ oil in soup or in your breakfast muesli.

The duration of the treatment depends entirely upon the individual's needs. Generally speaking, if a vitamin or mineral deficiency is to be rectified, it is necessary to take the medication for several months. When the deficiency has been overcome, it is recommended to continue the treatment by taking half the dosage only, then a quarter, and then slowly phasing it out altogether.

After recovery, if you replace the former deficient diet by one made up of wholefoods, you will be able to manage without having to take any more concentrated vitamin products. However, if you continue to follow the denatured diet of the majority of people today, one including white flour and refined sugar, you will need to supplement it with vitamin preparations. Only in this way will it be possible to avoid a relapse. For this purpose, wheat germ oil is strongly indicated.

A. Vogel's wheat germ oil is a 100 per cent Swiss product and has the advantage of being cold-pressed in modern oil presses. That is why its content of the two main components – vitamin E and polyunsaturated fatty acids – is so high. According to absolutely reliable and objective analysis, it meets with the highest demands of both doctors and consumers.

Vitaforce

Besides the carefully manufactured wheat germ oil, there is also available a fortifying and body-building tonic called *Vitaforce*. This product is especially appreciated by those who have a sensitive liver and wish to use a good food supplement. It is a natural product, whose carefully balanced combination of ingredients is the result of exhaustive research, containing mainly sea buckthorn juice, orange juice, wheat germ and malt extracts, honey, bee pollen and the effective ingredients of a tropical fruit called durian (*Durio zibethinus*). The combination is a concentrated food supplement ideal for fortifying and maintaining the muscle tone and the functions of the sex glands. The effective ingredients of Vitaforce make it an excellent tonic for all those who work hard, and particularly those who use up more energy than most, such as athletes. The tonic compensates for the high loss of energy.

Honey – its Specific Therapeutic Effect

It is interesting to study how that little wonder, the bee, makes its honey. We marvel, too, at the bee's body and how this small and delicate structure is able to manufacture a substance that would need such cumbersome machinery if done by humans. Then we marvel at the diligent industry of the bee as we watch its flight over the flowering countryside – but these aspects are not what I wish to speak about right now. Our interest, at the moment, lies in the remedial value of honey, which has earned a high mark for itself in natural medicine.

In the ancient world honey was well known and appreciated for its healing properties but as time went on that knowledge fell into oblivion. The rediscovery and scientific explanation of the value of honey, however, has enabled it once more to assume its rightful place among natural remedies.

A doctor wrote in a medical journal about having successfully used honey in the treatment of diphtheria. A 25 per cent addition of honey to another remedy was found to act as an antiseptic and prevented the diphtheria bacilli from propagating.

This experiment is without doubt proof of the fact that honey deserves attention as a folk medicine of long-standing. It is certainly no coincidence that years ago honey was prescribed as a remedy for exactly this disease. In those days, unlike today, there were no effective treatments for diphtheria, and honey, together with other remedies, no doubt was beneficial to the patients and may have helped to save many lives.

As regards natural remedies in general, I am sure that scientific research would find many an old piece of folk wisdom to be true. The Bible's recommendation, 'My son, eat honey, for it is good', is clearly well founded. Honey is indeed good for us because it has healing properties.

Dr Müller asserts that potential carriers of the diphtheria bacillus can render themselves much less dangerous to other people by the systematic consumption of honey. 'Carriers' are those who harbour the micro-organism of a disease but are not necessarily affected by it themselves, although they constitute a potential source of infection for others. Any remedy that eliminates this danger is most welcome.

The effectiveness of honey places it on the list of tried and proven remedial foods and our confidence in it is fully justified, even though there may be some people who cannot take it and have to forgo its goodness.

The Medicinal Value of Honey

There is no doubt that honey and its medicinal value were known as far back as biblical times, as it is mentioned in a number of ancient records. Honey is the best form of carbohydrate and is easily absorbed by the body. What is more, experience has shown that honey increases the medicinal effect of natural remedies that are good for the respiratory organs. If you want to take advantage of this fact, simply add the indicated number of drops of a given remedy to a teaspoon of honey or to warm water sweetened with honey. Sipping this honey water together with the remedies will enhance their effect; for example, in cases of catarrh or disorders of the bronchial tubes or lungs, the prescribed medicines will have a much faster and stronger effect if taken with honey. It is for this reason that the pine bud syrup *Santasapina* contains honey.

Honey Salve – a Healer

Mix a teaspoon of honey with 20–30 drops of *Echinaforce* tincture and you will have a splendid healing salve for grazes, minor wounds and cuts, boils, and even scabs and crusts.

For wounds that are refusing to heal properly, mix some honey with 10 per cent *horseradish*; the horseradish can be finely grated, or use the fresh juice or tincture. Apply this reliable natural remedy to the affected part, and you will be surprised at the good result. This mixture is an excellent remedy for whitlows, nail mould and similar stubborn conditions that suppurate and take a long time to heal.

Treating Arthritis and Gout with Honey Packs

If you suffer from arthritis or gout you will find the external application of honey a great relief. Add one teaspoon of *comfrey tincture* or *Symphosan* to four tablespoons of honey, mix thoroughly in a cup, then heat the mixture in a double saucepan (bain-marie). Fold a cloth three or four times, soak it in the hot honey mixture and apply to the parts where the pain is worst – the hands, elbows, knees and feet. This treatment is best given in the evening, so that you can leave the pack on overnight. In order to retain the heat for longer, place on top of the pack a bag of cherry stones that have been heated on the stove; a bag of hot hay flowers or camomile will serve the same purpose. Then wrap a warm cloth around everything.

Some patients have been helped by this treatment to the extent that they were once again able to walk or move their hands without feeling any pain. It is worthwhile repeating these honey packs for several weeks until you find relief. If you do not have any herbs at your disposal, honey packs can be made without them. The effect will still be very beneficial, even though it might take longer.

The Wonder Jelly for Queen Bees – Royal Jelly

An Unsolved Mystery

Not everyone knows that a worker bee's busy life is over after twenty-eight working days. Or did you know that the egg cells that normally produce worker bees can, when fed with a special substance develop into queens? There is something mysterious about this wonder of nature. For one thing, the queens are considerably bigger than the other bees, and, what is more, they live sixty times longer. A very special nutritive fluid is collected by the workers for those cells which ultimately produce queens. Although this phenomenon has been the subject of extensive scientific investigation, the understanding of its exact nature still eludes the researchers and only some of the jelly's constituents have been isolated. The ancients perhaps knew more about it than we do, as we frequently find references to 'ambrosia', 'nectar' and other wonder foods in their writings and it is not unreasonable to assume that they were referring to what is now called 'royal jelly'.

Unfortunately, no reference as to how this ambrosia was obtained is to be found, so our assumption must remain speculative. There is no doubt, however, that royal jelly possesses biological qualities of the highest order, for it enables the queen to lay as many as 2,000 eggs daily, and this with a single fertilisation. This is, indeed, a marvellous biological achievement, which stands unrivalled in nature.

Royal Jelly Makes the Headlines

Scientific and popular periodicals have devoted much space to the subject of royal jelly. True, this promotion no doubt has something to do with cleverly disguised advertising, since every manufacturer believes his product to be the best on the market. On the other hand, these efforts demonstrate that today's world needs a biologically safe natural tonic, as opposed to a chemical or synthetic one. No one really knows how the bees manufacture the natural compound. All we can say is that the Creator gave them the necessary instinct to make this complex substance from the raw materials they have available in nature. What they produce proves the truth of the concept that 'Food should be medicine and medicines should be food.'

Some years ago the newspapers reported that the Pope had recovered from a severe illness after his personal physician, Dr Galeazzi, had prescribed royal jelly as a tonic for him. It also was reported that Dr Paul Niehans, an eminent endocrinologist and specialist in live-cell therapy, was of the opinion that royal jelly vitalises the glandular system in a similar way to an injection of fresh endocrine cells. These observations are a strong enough indication that it is indeed appropriate to pay much more attention to royal jelly in the future.

As long ago as in April 1956, at the Second International Biogenetic Congress held in Baden-Baden, Germany, under the chairmanship of Dr Galeazzi, many of the papers presented dealt with the research findings in connection with royal jelly.

Then there were the articles written by Professor Belvefer of Paris, who had been conducting research on royal jelly for decades. It is amazing to read his references to the findings made by a number of researchers, for example the fact that the queen bee is able to lay 300,000–450,000 eggs a year as a result of her feeding on this remarkable nutritive complex. This feat cannot be matched by any other creature on earth.

Further reports explained that royal jelly not only vitalises and rejuvenates through its effect on the endocrine glands, but also successfully combats whooping cough and asthma, especially in children. It has been found that children with a weak constitution soon pick up and have better appetites when given royal jelly. Benefits can also be obtained in cases of bronchitis, migraine, stomach and gallbladder troubles, digestive disorders, bad nerves and the peculiar kind of fatigue resulting from weak functioning of the endocrine glands. These and many other health problems can be improved considerably, if not cured, by taking royal jelly regularly. Moreover, it is maintained that people with a predisposition to cancer will benefit from a regular intake of royal jelly. It is also good for the skin when taken orally and when used for massage. For the latter, dilute some royal jelly with honey and water and massage the solution into the skin.

A Question of Cost

Many people have questioned the cost of royal jelly, since there is no uniformity of price. In the United States it can cost five, six or even ten times as much as it does in Europe, but the price tags on European products can also vary considerably. It is unfortunate that such products are not always honestly priced and, as a consequence, a good natural remedy can become discredited.

Our own *Gelée Royale* is marketed in 10 g (0.353 oz) jars and this quantity gives about a month's treatment. It is also available in the form of ampoules, called *Apiforce*.

Pollen

Every time sensational articles about pollen appeared in newspapers and magazines, the questions would be asked. 'What actually is pollen? Is it a product of the food industry or of nature?'

According to the biblical account of the Creation, pollen existed long before man. The earth had to be thoughtfully prepared for man's existence. For this reason, the plant world had to be made first, then came the animals and finally, man. So pollen existed even before the bees started flying from flower to flower. Pollen contains the male gametes of plants, which are essential to their propagation. Perhaps the wind carried these reproductive cells; otherwise the plants could not have been fertilised or pollinated before the arrival of insects. Today, bees are especially responsible for pollination, together with the wind. We have probably watched these busy insects in their constant activity many times. When bees visit individual flowers with their untiring zeal in gathering nectar, they collect something else at the same time. Their little legs touch the pollen, which in turn sticks to them in tiny grains, making the bees look as if they were wearing tiny yellow pants.

Since beekeepers are usually good observers, it occurred to them to make an experiment of collecting this pollen and feeding it to the bees during inclement weather. The result was that after 8–10 generations the bees that had been given this pollen food had grown bigger, stronger and healthier. They even built larger honeycomb cells. Their tongues had grown longer in relation to their overall size, and this was also an advantage, for these bees were able to obtain the nectar from flowers that ordinary bees were unable to reach.

So the beekeepers were prompted to look at pollen more closely. Experiments were made with mice, giving them a supplement of pollen. This resulted in several benefits. It was noticed that the mice became less susceptible to disease, their fertility increased visibly, their coats became shiny and healthy, and they remained free from skin diseases. The rodents' vitality increased noticeably, and they lived longer. These findings led to a further examination of pollen. An analysis showed pollen to be rich in vitamins and to contain nearly all the minerals and trace elements vital to man and beast.

Tiredness and Low Blood Pressure

Experiments have shown that pollen has a strong action on the human sex glands and, through them, on all the endocrine glands. People who always feel tired and weary are able to get rid of this tiredness by taking a teaspoon of pollen in the morning with their breakfast.

Pollen is excellent for low blood pressure, especially when taken together with seaweed, that is, *kelp*. If one drinks carrot juice in addition, which can be in the condensed form of *Biocarottin*, the unpleasant symptoms of low blood pressure, for example fainting and weakness, will usually be rectified after a short time. People who suffer from low blood pressure are often subject to sexual weakness, too, and therefore a deficiency in the sex glands. As a rule, taking pollen in combination with seaweed preparations can remedy this condition.

High Blood Pressure, Exophthalmic Goitre, Metabolic Disorders

If the blood pressure is too high, it is not advisable to take pollen. A necessary precaution would be, first of all, to bring down the pressure by eating a natural diet of whole rice, soft white cheese (cottage cheese or quark) and salads. This diet is described in detail on pages 128–9. Only when the blood pressure has been normalised can a person start taking pollen.

Those who have exophthalmic goitre, that is to say, a hyperfunction of the thyroid, should take pollen only after the functional disorder has been eliminated.

On the other hand, metabolic disorders such as constipation and diarrhoea can benefit from treatment with pollen.

Mental Strain

Those who do taxing mental work find bee pollen to be an extremely simple and natural energy food. With its help they are able to stand up to the intensity of their work for longer and feel less tired. In today's hustle and bustle of everyday life pollen is a welcome food supplement, providing the help needed when great demands are made on one's mental capacity.

Not all the active substances of pollen have yet been discovered, but those that have been isolated, as experience has shown, are cause enough to recommend this natural product to everyone who lives a modern life.

Bee pollen, being very rich in vitamins and containing almost all known minerals and trace elements, has become a popular energy booster. Since nature provides us with this wonderful tonic food, we should prefer it to artificial or chemical products every time.

The Curative Properties of Chicken and Chicken Fat

The following story confirms the efficacy of an old natural remedy. A French-Swiss woman tried to lift a heavy pot of boiling water from the fire and, in doing so, slipped. She sustained scalds and second- and third-degree burns over a considerable area of her body, including the neck and chest. According to the doctor, her life was in danger. Fortunately, her husband remembered his mother's treatment for burns and scalds. She always used raw chicken fat. So, as fast as he could, he got some fresh chicken fat and proceeded to spread it liberally over the parts of the body that had been scalded. Before long, the burning pain was relieved and his wife calmed down, being able to sleep that same night. Within a few days the pain had completely gone and new skin was beginning to form over the scalded areas.

As I have already mentioned, fresh chicken fat is an old natural remedy and, next to *St John's wort oil*, one of the best treatments there is for severe burns and scalds.

And here is another experience with chicken fat which is just as interesting. In a lonely farmstead a young man hurt himself badly while felling a tree. The axe went right into his knee and cracked the knee cap. He dragged himself to the house with difficulty. There was no doctor for miles around and, of course, there was no such thing as a telephone. His father could not think what to do. Meanwhile, the boy's leg had become very swollen and discoloured. The lymph glands in the groin became swollen and painful. Blood poisoning had already set in. His mother then remembered that her grandmother had always used chicken fat in cases of blood poisoning. So she killed several chickens and spread the raw fat on the whole leg as thickly as possible.

The doctor, whom the family finally succeeded in contacting, could only come the following morning. As an experienced travelling country doctor, he did not consider the chicken fat treatment strange and appeared well satisfied with the young man's condition. He took the patient with him to the hospital for surgical treatment and in a short time the leg was completely healed. The mother was convinced that she had saved her boy's life by rubbing on the fat as soon as the blood poisoning became evident.

Some doctors may smile or scoff when reading about such simple natural remedies. However, they should not forget that these remedies have been known and used for hundreds of years and have outlasted many a modern chemical drug. These natural treatments are always near at hand and invariably provide help when other remedies fail. They will continue to do so long after many of the present-day products of the pharmaceutical industry have been discarded and forgotten.

Chicken as a Styptic

No less interesting is the story I heard from a Berlin doctor who was attached to the famous hospital 'Charité'. A person suffering from haemophilia had to have a minor operation and the doctors were worried about stopping the bleeding. A peasant who was a patient in the hospital happened to hear of their anxiety and when one of the doctors was making his rounds, he told him in his blunt rustic way that he knew of something that would stop the bleeding and was better than all the strong-smelling ointments in the hospital.

The doctor, who had formerly been a country practitioner for many years and had often obtained valuable information from his patients, did not ignore such words but asked, 'Well, what would you say was good for stopping bleeding?'

'Chicken would help, Doc, but it must be put on absolutely fresh and warm,' replied the peasant, and the conversation ended there.

However, the doctor did obtain a chicken before the operation, although perhaps more out of curiosity as to what would happen if he actually used it. After collodion treatment and everything else had failed to stop the bleeding, as a last resort, he cut a piece from the chicken and laid it while still warm on the patient's small incision, which was still bleeding. As if by magic, before the unbelieving eyes of the other doctors, the bleeding stopped.

Red Slug Syrup (*Arion rufus*)

When suffering from a serious condition, and everything else has been tried without success, red slug syrup, however unattractive it may sound, should be given a chance. Extraordinary results have been achieved with this syrup in the treatment of diseases where bacteria or bacilli play a part, for example ulcers, gastric ulcers and pulmonary infections.

Its preparation is quite simple. Place a layer of the large red forest slugs (*Arion rufus*) in a jar, cover with a layer of sugar, then add further layers of slugs and sugar until the jar is full. The minimum quantity of sugar should be about the same weight as the slugs, although you can use a little more.

After a short time the sugar begins to dissolve the slugs. On the second day, strain everything through a sieve. Then add a third part of alcohol, that is, one-third of the whole weight of the mixture. The remedy is then ready. (The residue in the strainer is of no further use and can be disposed of.) A tablespoon, or in serious cases a liqueur glass of the syrup, should be taken every morning before breakfast. The curative effect of this syrup is so extraordinary that even doctors who have experimented with it are simply amazed.

Although the preparation and perhaps even the mere idea of slug syrup may seem repugnant, such feelings can be disregarded when grave necessity arises. Farmers, who are less fussy about such things, are often pleased to avail themselves of this remedy. One young farmer who had stomach ulcers and was spitting blood had found no relief from chemical and natural remedies. He consented to take the slug syrup, this repulsive-sounding remedy, with the result that he recovered and today is once more able to look after the family farm.

Another report tells of a man who was suffering from some form of lung disease. The doctors had despaired of curing him. He too tried the slug syrup and is now quite well again. Many other successful examples prove that it is better to take a remedy, the thought of which may be repugnant, than to accept defeat in matters of health and perhaps even die as a result of neglect.

Of course, if you do not know what the syrup is made of you will not worry, for it does not have an unpleasant taste at all.

I would like to make one final observation. Cases of chronic bronchial catarrh can also be treated successfully with slug syrup, even if it has not responded to other medicines. Remember, however, when you buy the ready-made syrup, to make sure it is actually made from slugs.

Questions of Nutrition

Natural Wholefood

It is certainly difficult for a housewife to feed her family along scientific lines, for even an expert in the field of nutrition would find it a problem. In fact, what should you eat so that the body obtains all the nutrients, minerals, vitamins and trace elements for it to be adequately nourished? Who can dare to say that he knows what our individual requirements really are? Is it not true to say that every year, every decade, new discoveries are made in the field of nutrition? In fifty or a hundred years from now, if we could look back at the things we now think of as necessities for our bodies, we would probably be surprised at our ignorance of the elements which make up a healthy diet.

How much simpler it would be if man could accept the idea that a wise Creator has provided everything that is necessary including our food, in nature. If we look upon our food as something prepared for us by Him, for our well-being, then we will know we have at our disposal all the known and unknown nutritive elements we need. Being in their right proportions, they will contribute all that our bodies require. Primitive peoples are more sensible than we are in this respect. They take their food just as it grows and prepare it very simply, thus preserving its nutritive value. Does that not give our ailing society cause to think on these things?

New drugs are being discovered every day, yet we do not see a decline in the overall incidence of disease. On the contrary, certain diseases are becoming more prevalent, especially those that are connected with the metabolism of the cells and the central nervous system. Among the most notable are cancer and multiple sclerosis. Yet those two diseases are practically unknown among the natives of various so-called 'uncivilised' areas of the world. It is noteworthy, then, that degenerative changes in the cells, as they occur in cancer and multiple sclerosis, are chiefly restricted to the people who live in 'civilised societies'. Moreover, it is only in the industrial world that many infectious diseases are rampant, where refined food has weakened the people. Interestingly, more primitive people living near industrialised communities are not affected by many of their neighbours' diseases, even though the causative agents could attack them just as well. I am referring especially to multiple sclerosis, although here is as yet no conclusive evidence that it is caused by micro-organisms. But similar diseases cannot gain a foothold among such people either, simply because they live more naturally and therefore have sufficient resistance to germs and other causes of disease.

Nothing but wholefood offers real sustenance and protection and this is shown by the example we have in whole rice. Everything offered by nature consists of an integral whole and if only a fraction of it is removed, whatever it maybe, we are deprived of something that would otherwise provide us with complete nutrition. The Creator meant cereal to be a complete formula and to benefit fully from it we should prepare our food from the whole grain.

Whole Rice (Brown Rice)

Let us look at a rice grain. The inner kernel, the endosperm, consists mainly of starch, as is the case with all other grains, for example wheat and barley. From this we get white flour. Starch is a carbohydrate, and supplies energy, without which we cannot live. That is why it would be unwise to throw away the starch and use only the bran, for example, because the proportion in which starch is associated with the others substances contained in the grain is intimately related to the needs of our bodies. The proportion matches the correct formula. To meddle with it would be equivalent to altering the proportions of the ingredients of a perfect recipe, the one our wise Creator provided for our benefit and that of other animals.

Besides the starch, the grain contains bran. This, in turn, is made up of layers of gluten, various minerals and trace elements. Research has shown that only the most minute amounts of these trace elements are required, yet if they are missing altogether, the various functions of the system begin to suffer. These known and unknown trace elements are found in the outer layers of the grain, the bran.

Another vital part of the grain is the germ. Fats, proteins, phosphates and valuable vitamins are found in it. Of particular importance is the vitamin E in the germ, because it regulates the functions of the sex glands.

There is yet something else in the grain, cellulose, and some may argue that we can do without this outer preservative layer that envelops each grain as if with a fine cellophane film. True, it is indigestible and cannot be assimilated, but its action is nevertheless a necessary one for the intestinal tract. It cleanses its lining, which is studded with villi, tiny microscopic processes that assist assimilation. These hair-like processes are apt to become clogged up if the food ingested consists of too much material lacking in roughage. It is here that the cellulose-containing bran or fibre, comes in. Its particles scrape along the intestinal walls, cleaning away the filmy adhesions and at the same time stimulating peristalsis, the wave-like contractions of the intestines that press their contents onward and so prevent constipation. In fact, if everyone ate natural whole-foods, containing starch, minerals, nutrients and roughage in the right proportions, no one would suffer from poor digestion or constipation.

The importance of the bran and germ of the rice grain was drastically demonstrated when people in the Orient began to copy those in the West by refining their staple food, their rice. A disease known as beriberi became rife among them and after all the known medicines had been thrown into the combat against the disease without success, a colonial doctor, Dr Eijkman, as well as other researchers, discovered that rice bran alone was able to cure the scourge. This definitely established the fact that beriberi was a deficiency disease, an avitaminosis, not an infectious disease as had been thought previously.

Fortunately, our Western diet is much more varied than that of the Oriental nations and such pronounced deficiencies rarely occur. If our diet lacks one substance or another, the deficiency can usually be compensated for, at least partly, by the substances contained in other foods we eat. However, it is only a partial compensation and we still often suffer from an imbalance in our food intake, as will be discussed in a later section. Many people in the Orient suffered the sad consequences of beriberi, but as soon as they began to take food supplements or returned to their former way of preparing whole rice, their health was restored.

This experience provides a strong argument in favour of changing over to whole cereals, including whole wheat and whole rye. It is incomprehensible how students who have seen films or experiments showing what happens to pigeons when they are fed on refined rice can continue to eat the very food that is responsible for such devastating results. They seem blind and thoughtless in the face of the evidence. Why spend time and effort in tireless research if the findings continue to be ignored by the consumer? Is it not strange that the consumer often prefers to take the consequences and become sick, rather than make a change in his diet?

Remember that natural rice, also known as unpolished, whole or brown rice, contains nine and a half times more minerals than the polished, refined kind. It is these minerals that are of vital importance to us. Observations have shown that whole rice contains substances that keep the blood vessels elastic for much longer and it is for this reason that Asians seldom suffer from hardening of the arteries and high blood pressure.

Whole or brown rice should be prepared in the same way as refined rice, only do not pour away the rice water. The rice should be soaked in as much water as it is able to absorb and cooked in as little water as it requires to soften without the grains sticking together. Then the nutritional elements will not be wasted or lost. Brown rice can be served in a number of ways, and many Chinese and Middle Eastern recipes are excellent for this purpose.

What about the Wheat Grain?
What I said about the rice grain also applies to the wheat kernel. Its valuable constituents are to be found, not in the inner part, but in the outer one, the bran. Like rice, the wheat grain should be used in its entirety, ground coarsely as wholewheat flour or flakes. Groats, coarse meal, are especially suitable for soups, rissole mixes, bread and biscuits. If you have no rough-grinding mill to make you own wholewheat flour, soak the wheat overnight and then put the soft, swollen kernels through the mincer.

This flaky wheat can be added to your muesli. Of course, you can use *Vogel's Wheat Bran and Germ* instead. According to taste, sweeten the muesli with raisins or sultanas, putting these through the mincer together with the soaked wheat. The raisins will give you natural sugar. You see how easy it is to prepare a delicious muesli! Add some honey, perhaps some finely ground almonds or almond purée and a variety of fruit according to what is in season. Berries are an ideal addition. If you tend to suffer from constipation, mix some soaked linseed into the muesli to encourage the bowel function.

A high-energy food can be obtained by keeping the wheat moist and warm so it can germinate. According to the temperature, the wheat takes about two or three days before it begins to sprout; then use the sprouted wheat in the same way you would the ungerminated kernels. Germinated wheat is good for the blood and is a tonic for the whole body. Let the sprouts grow 2–5 mm (up to about ¼ inch) long, but remember to put the grains in a warm place so that they are encouraged to germinate. Do not add more water than the grains can soak up. On the other hand, instead of soaking the wheat in water, you could spread it on a wet cloth; the sprouts will then be greenish in colour. These green sprouts are necessary for people suffering from anaemia, who need chlorophyll.

Bread and cakes can also be made with germinated wheat, or rye, barley, or any other cereal. Bread and muesli prepared in this way are far more nourishing than anything made from flour that has been stored, and that you may have to store even longer before use. The oxygen in the air is harmless as long as the grain remains whole, but as soon as it is milled into flour it begins to destroy many important nutrients, especially the highly active ferments. If used fresh, and if possible germinated, the goodness of the whole grain is available to us. A more detailed account of the uses and benefits of germinated wheat is given on pages 520–21.

So, if you eat wheat raw, either in muesli or using any other method of preparation, you will have at your disposal an energy food that contains all the important vitamins and minerals of the grain in their complete and unchanged form.

It is amazing to see the effect of such a wholefood on sick people. They derive infinitely greater benefits from it than from the most expensive remedies. Natural food is without doubt the best medicine for every nature-oriented person.

Vegetables and Herbs

If you want healthy vegetables they must be grown organically. They depend upon the soil in which they are grown and for the soil to be healthy it must be worked and looked after properly. If you live in the country, take advantage of the various edible plants growing wild in the woods and fields. You will find wild spinach and many other wild vegetables, all tasty and nutritious. Do not neglect to gather and eat them. *Bear's garlic (ramsons)*, for example, is a prized vegetable, one of the best blood-purifying plants there is, and it should be gathered and eaten in the spring. It regenerates the blood vessels, and lowers and normalises blood pressure. The blood pressure problems that often accompany old age, brought on by the loss of elasticity of the arteries, can be effectively counteracted with brown rice, bear's garlic and mistletoe tea, if taken on a regular basis. Young *nettles*, finely chopped and mixed in with salads or steamed like spinach, are also very good for the blood.

Dandelion salad, which is rich in vitamins, cleanses, stimulates and assists the liver to do its job. Every spring this delicious salad should be on the table. If you have a garden you can grow your own dandelions. Dig up some roots and plant them in a trench, fill in with compost, forest soil or peat and then dress the top with a layer of pine needles, if available. The roots will soon begin to sprout and the shoots will show their tender green tips. Then remove the pine-needle dressing or peat, cut the shoots as far as the roots, put the cover back on again and leave to sprout anew. This method will give you fresh dandelion leaves for an extended period, in fact, until well into the summer – and if you are blessed with 'green fingers' you will be able to obtain a continuous supply throughout the growing season.

Watercress is often found growing wild too. As it is rich in iodine, it will benefit your thyroid and all the other endocrine glands, the hormone glands. The iodine in watercress is present in the right amount and combination with other substances. If you have thyroid problems, such as palpitations, oversensitivity to every little influence, or enlargement of the gland itself, you should definitely eat watercress on a regular basis. You will find it a marvellous remedy if you lack vitality and are always listless and tired, symptoms that are usually caused by the poor function of the endocrine glands.

It is also good to add a little *yarrow*, finely chopped, to your salads, but do not overdo it. You can mix it in with your salad dressing, giving it a delicate, slightly bitter flavour. This is most effective for treating the venous system. It would not be a bad idea to mix in a few leaves or flowers of *St John's wort* as well. As we have said before, natural food is remedial at the same time.

In cases of circulatory disturbances, if the veins are responsible, yarrow and St John's wort can be used with good results. Piles benefit too. All these medicinal plants are easily collected from meadows free from chemical fertilisers, unpolluted waysides and even near the garden fence. Even if you are not troubled by any ailments, these plants should be used as a means of preventing disease, thus avoiding the subsequent need to cure one.

Anyone who suffers constantly from respiratory problems, catarrh and sore throats, should take a little *ribwort*, chop it up

Ribwort

finely and mix it in a salad dressing. When finely chopped, the herb is absorbed in the dressing but still enhances the medicinal value of the salad.

All these herbs are rich in minerals and vitamins. They are beneficial to our health even though used in small quantities.

If you have a garden, the cultivation of culinary herbs such as savory, tarragon, thyme, marjoram, lovage and many others will be found most rewarding. Their effect on the system is second to none.

Further information on these and other herbs can be found in the sections on 'Medicinal Herbs' (pages 338–81) and 'Seasonings' (404–16).

Fertilising and Conditioning the Soil

If you work your own garden, any manure you use should be organic. Compost, bone meal, hoof and horn meal and forest soil can all be used for soil improvement. According to your soil's particular need, if it is loamy or peaty, it may require stone meal. All these natural materials are appropriate for organic fertilising. Strong chemical or artificial fertilisers should be avoided at all costs. The keeping quality and the flavour of produce grown in organic soil are vastly superior to that of produce grown in soil treated with inorganic fertilisers.

If you have liquid manure and dung at your disposal, do not spread it directly on the soil but incorporate it into compost to improve its quality. The compost heap will mature more quickly if layers of dung are alternated with yarrow or pine needles in its construction. In the first year you can add animal dung and liquid manure to the compost. But in the second year, no new material should be added to the heap; it should merely be turned over to let the air get to it. At the end of the second year you will have valuable compost that is of great importance to the plants. Vegetables that require nitrogen will do better if the compost has bone meal added to it, while legumes like peas and string beans, as well as roots and vegetables that are rich in potassium, grow better with wood ash compost, since wood ash is rich in minerals, including potassium.

If we are to benefit from the minerals in the plants we grow we should avoid boiling them, as the minerals pass into the water. It is better to steam the vegetables or, if cooked in water, use the bare minimum so that hardly any is left when the cooking has been completed.

GREEN MANURE

For years now I have no longer simply dug or turned over the garden or a field and spread the manure over the soil, in other words, applied a top-dressing. Rather, I cover the manured soil with grass, carrot tops or other vegetable waste, so that the organic manure, such as compost, cannot be dried out by the sun. I plant seedlings with a dipper, then spread freshly cut grass around them, about 1 cm (about ½ inch) thick. This top-dressing, or cover, is renewed after about three months when the soil is still moist, the bacteria have multiplied and the plants have grown much faster than when treated the usual way. This method has also given good results with berry bushes and shrubs. However, you must take care that the grass or weeds used are still young; do not use them when they contain ripe seeds.

This green manure will make hoeing unnecessary. And since any germinating seeds under the green cover will suffocate and die, weeds will not be able to grow.

CALCIFIED SEAWEED

If you would like to enrich your soil with valuable trace elements from the sea, spread it with calcified seaweed (seaweed lime) from time to time. The soil will then receive potassium bound to iodine.

It has been observed that plants given calcified seaweed are much healthier and less susceptible to mould and similar diseases.

Raw Vegetables and Vegetable Juices

Raw vegetables possess greater therapeutic value than cooked ones. Deficient digestion and assimilation require raw juices. Cabbage juice (green or white cabbage), for example, will improve and often cure such conditions as arthritis, stomach ulcers and metabolic disturbances. Raw potato juice is another superb remedy for stomach ulcers and is most effective when taken in combination with cabbage juice. If you cannot take raw vegetable juices neat or diluted with warm water, you might like to try adding them to soup (vegetable, oatmeal or barley) immediately before serving. Most people find this idea more appealing, apart from the fact that juices usually enhance the flavour. While not everyone is keen on soup, in this case it is a useful means of taking the vegetable juices. You can also add a little raw juice to cooked vegetables or a gruel. Boiled cabbage frequently causes indigestion or flatulence, while raw cabbage, taken finely grated or as juice, will create no such consequences. White cabbage can be made into sauerkraut, another perfect medicinal food, which should be eaten raw, if possible, in order to retain its full value. The cabbage family is rich in calcium and anyone suffering from calcium deficiency should eat plenty of cabbage, including sauerkraut, as a simple and inexpensive source of this mineral.

Although juices are good for us, they should not be enjoyed to the exclusion of anything else; our digestive tract also requires cellulose, roughage, if it is to remain in proper working order. Juices are potent and should not be taken in excessive quantities over long periods of time. After a course of juices, go back to eating the whole vegetables. Raw vegetables demand good teeth and should be thoroughly masticated and properly insalivated to promote the digestive process. The fibres must be broken down if they are to release their nutrients. If your teeth are bad, grate the vegetables or put them through a mincer or blender. The reason why many people do not tolerate raw vegetables is not that they are indigestible, but that they have not been properly masticated and insalivated. Fruit juices and vegetable juices should be well mixed with saliva and not just swallowed. Acid fruit juices need to be neutralised by the alkaline saliva before they reach the stomach. Vegetable juices are more easily tolerated than fruit juices, and even liver patients or people who have a sensitive liver or suffer from kidney trouble have little difficulty in digesting them. Particularly recommended are juices that have gone through a process of lactic fermentation; they also keep better. For further advice on raw fruit and vegetable juices, please read the sections on pages 495–9.

A Good Natural Diet
A good natural diet consists partly of cooked and partly of raw foods. For very serious diseases such as cancer a raw food diet works wonders and is often the only measure that will get to the root of these pathological problems.

The patient who has lost the ability to digest and assimilate his food should begin the diet with juices, then start taking small amounts of finely grated raw vegetables and fruit. Gradually, the quantity is increased until he is able to eat the foods in their natural raw state.

If there is no need to change over to a diet made up entirely of raw food, it would still be beneficial to incorporate small quantities in your daily menus.

Vegetables and fruits should not be served at the same meal, but taken separately, as breaking this rule will mean you are likely to be bothered with flatulence. This important rule is explained in greater detail on pages 493–5.

On the other hand, in spite of contrary opinions, cereals, organically grown and stone ground if possible, are good companions to both fruit and vegetable dishes.

Milk
When milk is uncontaminated and pure, it is a valuable food, providing protein and fat. However, since there are many sick cows and the main causes of sickness are tuberculosis and brucellosis, milk – especially unboiled, raw milk – cannot be recommended without reservation. In cases of cancer, arthritis and many other serious illnesses, it is better to avoid milk altogether. Then there is the question of whether one should drink it fresh or sour. Some say one thing, some another. There is obviously more nourishment in fresh, untreated milk direct from the cow. Sour milk has lost the lactose which, through fermentation, has been transformed into lactic acid, but it is nevertheless easier to digest and more beneficial to the intestinal flora, which it regenerates. From this it will be seen that both kinds of milk have their advan-

tages, whether fresh or sour, or as yogurt, even though the substances contained in them may vary.

More advice on how we can gain the many benefits of milk is given in a later section (see pages 536–40).

Eggs

Eggs should come from healthy, naturally fed, free-running (free range) poultry, if at all possible. When eaten raw, they are more wholesome than any other way. However, since it is quite possible that eggs contain hazardous bacteria, great care should be taken in choosing one's supplier. Sick chickens usually carry these bacteria and can transmit them through their eggs. Duck eggs are known as carriers of the paratyphoid bacillus, although the birds themselves may appear to be quite healthy. For this reason, be especially careful with duck eggs.

Nevertheless, eggs are rich in lecithin, which is a valuable nerve food. Raw egg stimulates the flow of bile. Healthy eggs can be beaten raw into soup before serving, or mixed with honey or some other natural sugar and eaten in this way. Eggs are also rich in protein, especially the yolk, although most people make the mistake of assuming that the protein is found chiefly in the egg white.

Eggs do, however, have the disadvantage of causing the formation of uric acid. This gives rise to the release of sulphuric acid, which can be noticed on the breath after one has eaten boiled eggs. For this reason, people with arthritis, rheumatism or cancer should abstain from eggs in all forms. Yet again this example goes to show that it is always necessary to consider whether any food can be eaten without detriment, or whether it should be avoided altogether. Fruit and vegetables, however, are always recommended, provided one's digestive system tolerates them and the bowels do not react adversely, producing flatulence.

Avoiding Fruit Sprayed with Pesticides

When you buy fruit, make sure that it has not been sprayed with pesticides. Traces of lead, arsenic and other chemicals pose health hazards and will make the fruit inedible. Eating sprayed fruit need not necessarily bring on an acute case of poisoning, but chemical pesticides may have a cumulative effect and continuous doses, however small, can, sooner or later, lead to the development of pathological conditions (see also pages 557–60).

In any case, fruit purchased at the market should always be properly cleaned and it is a good idea to peel it if spray spots can be seen. Many orchards are sprayed with chemicals to which has been added a substance with a special adhesive property so that the rain cannot wash the spray off the fruit. It is true, however, that by peeling the fruit you will lose valuable elements that are found in and under the skin, so it would be much better still to be discriminating when buying your fruit and to look for organically grown produce. If you have fruit trees of your own, make sure that no hazardous sprays are used.

Spices and Seasonings

It is best to avoid nutmeg, pepper and other hot spices and use safe and wholesome seasonings and herbs instead. Yeast extract, especially pure culture yeast extract, can be recommended since it is natural. Pure culture yeast extract contains the vitamin B complex and is about the best seasoning you can use. It is good as a sandwich spread or dissolved in warm water and added to soups and stews as a liquid seasoning. But it should never be boiled, in order to preserve its ingredients.

By now it should be self-evident to every reader that, as our daily bread nothing but crispbread, coarse-grained wholewheat (wholemeal) bread, in other words, bread made from *flour of the whole grain*, should be on our table.

The body will react favourably to natural foods prepared with skill and left in their natural state. Various ailments will disappear without the need for medication of any sort if we feed our bodies in the proper manner. Only natural food, wholefood, contains the elements we need to keep our bodies healthy and in a balanced condition, as it provides all the necessary known and unknown nutritive factors. One does not have to be a dietician to realise that the 'divine formula' embodied in every fruit of the earth cannot possibly be improved upon by man if it is to remain health-promoting. We benefit fully from the food provided only if we eat it in its natural form. If we reflect on the unhealthy state of mankind in the civilised world, we must conclude that man apparently throught himself wiser than the Creator by changing, refining and otherwise adulterating the food that was offered to him in the most perfect condition possible. So then, back to natural wholefood!

Helpful Diets for the Sick

A Low-Protein Diet

A low-protein diet is of paramount importance in treating all metabolic and digestive disturbances, high blood pressure, arthritis, rheumatism and gout, and should be adopted for some time. Protein is found chiefly in meat, eggs, cheese, milk and milk products, peas, beans and lentils, so vegetarians should reduce the intake of milk products and pulses (legumes). People who have previously enjoyed a mixed diet ought to refrain from eating pork, sausages and cold meats and restrict the diet to veal, beef, lamb and mutton.

Eggs and cheese and dishes prepared from them should also be avoided. But if you must eat eggs, have a limited amount and eat them raw. They can be beaten and added to cooked soup. Since eggs produce a great amount of uric acid, sufferers from arthritis are better off without them. Women troubled by insufficiency of the ovaries may eat raw eggs in moderate quantities.

Those who like cheese should restrict their intake and then only eat the mild types, along with vegetables, for their midday meal. Soft white cheese (curds, cottage cheese or quark) is much better than hard cheese, because it has none of the drawbacks of other high-protein foods and assists the function of the liver – a fact of which all liver patients should take note.

Avoid eating high-protein foods in the evening because they are usually the cause of restless sleep. Heavy food is more appropriate for the midday meal, as it generally requires longer periods for digestion than breakfast or tea would allow. If a heavy meal is eaten at night, the digestive system will not be able to cope so easily with the demand placed on it.

Avoid Fried and All Denatured, Refined Food

Fried foods have no place at all in a liver diet, or where a person has a sensitive liver. Of all fats, only fresh butter or a good vegetable margarine is permissible, or a little unrefined oil. Although vegetable oil may be better tolerated when used for frying, it is to be avoided in more serious cases of illness.

To complement a proper diet and support any treatment you may be taking for the good of your health, you would do well to cut out all white flour and refined sugar products, also all canned food and any other refined and denatured food items.

Suggestions for a Health Diet
In planning a healthy diet, the following suggestions should provide some useful guidance.

BREAKFAST

For breakfast to be nourishing and wholesome, the ideal foundation is muesli with apples or other seasonal fruit. Add nuts and wholegrain flakes to enrich it further. A highly nutritive addition is whole wheat, first soaked and then put through the mincer. Raisins or sultanas can be mixed with the wheat before it is minced; these are excellent for the blood. A level tablespoon of ground linseed may also be added if constipation is a problem. Use honey or grape sugar to sweeten.

Crispbread, wholewheat or whole grain bread (for example *Vogel's Whole Grain Flake Bread*) with a little butter, honey or rose hip conserve can follow the muesli. If you like, sprinkle some wheat germ on the bread or over the muesli.

For a drink, make a cup of rose hip tea sweetened with honey or grape sugar. If desired, top the tea with a little cream or even less milk. Cream is better than milk because it contains fat but little protein, although liver patients will find milk or almond milk more tolerable. For a change, you might try some cereal coffee.

These suggestions give you an idea of how to plan your breakfast according to the season and the availability of fruit, as well as your own preferences.

An occasional fruit juice breakfast is beneficial, and grape, orange or grapefruit juice can be recommended. Grapefruit juice is especially good because it stimulates the kidneys, the liver and the entire glandular system.

In cases of impaired liver function take 100–200 ml (about 4–8 fl. oz) of pure, raw carrot juice and a slice of buttered crispbread sprinkled with wheat germ, rather than sweet fruit dishes such as fruit salad with citrus fruits. Muesli with apples is permissible too. If this does not satisfy you, sandwiches as described under 'Supper' can supplement your breakfast.

MIDDAY MEAL

Depending upon the time of year, a great variety of salads may be served. The dressing may be prepared with lemon or *Molkosan* (whey concentrate), which is a great aid to digestion, but never use vinegar. Another tasty dressing can be made with sour cream or yoghurt, and herbs such as savory, marjoram and thyme may be added to give a zesty flavour. Every kind of cabbage is good, but it is best eaten raw as a salad, because cooked cabbage can easily cause flatulence. Cabbage salad (coleslaw) is not only well tolerated, but is also very tasty, healthy and nutritive.

Then you might have vegetables which, when steamed, should not cause fermentation and flatulence.

A third category, food containing starch, or carbohydrates, should also be on the menu. From a dietetic point of view, whole rice is the best choice. It has a good effect on the blood pressure, helping to normalise it and to regenerate the veins. For variation, substitute potatoes, either boiled in their skins or baked. Of course, they can also be served in other ways, but they can harm the liver when fried so this method should be avoided.

Whole wheat also provides an ideal dish and should be prepared in the same way as rice. Instead of a risotto you would then get a 'wheatotto', so to speak. Other good carbohydrate foods containing nutritive salts are millet and buckwheat.

If you like soup, choose a vegetable soup, but only mildly seasoned. Meat soups are not particularly healthy for they promote the formation of uric acid in the system. Vegetable soups, on the other hand, are very beneficial for those who suffer from arthritis. Before you sit down to eat the soup, add some fresh herbs and raw vegetable juices. And if you do not like raw vegetables prepared as a salad, they too can be added to soup, finely chopped or grated. Finely chopped nettles, bear's garlic (ramsons) and other herbs will improve both the nutritive value and the taste of the soup.

For those who like meat, beef or veal may be added to whatever dish they have chosen, but this should be considered as just a small addition to the main meal, for it is best to restrict oneself to a minimum of the protein-containing foods.

A sweet course or dessert has no place in a health diet because it encourages fermentation, that is, flatulence. If you cannot overcome your desire for fruit or some other naturally sweet food after a meal, postpone indulging in your fancy until at least 4 p.m. It is better, however, not to make a habit of such snacks between meals because it is always better to eat a little rather than a lot. A small amount of nutritious food goes a long way towards good health. Eating slowly and thorough insalivation will enable you to obtain the maximum value from whatever you eat; it prevents the pancreas from being overburdened and the formation of intestinal gases.

For your midday meal, instead of soup, you may substitute vegetable juices or natural unsweetened yoghurt. Sugar does not go well with the lactic acid in yoghurt, as it causes fermentation. If you wish to increase your weight, by all means take soup, but if you tend to be overweight and wish to reduce your weight, you would do better to go without it.

EVENING MEAL (SUPPER)

I prefer to call the evening meal 'supper' rather than 'dinner' because it should be a light meal rather than a heavy main one. Nor should it be eaten too late at night. A light meal will be well digested before it is time to go to bed. Supper may be the same as breakfast, but it does not have to consist of sweet food and fruit, although a fruit salad makes a pleasant change, especially if served with any of the whole cereal flakes or corn flakes. A good and inexpensive mixture is one made with ordinary oat flakes, currants or raisins and chopped nuts.

Be careful to use nuts sparingly at the end of the day. True, they are nourishing, but are intended for moderate consumption. Pine kernels make a pleasant change from walnuts and are tasty and nutritive. Crispbread and wholegrain (wholewheat) bread with a little butter or a good vegetable margarine go well with fruit salad, but if you have a problem with your liver, consider using honey or raw rose hip purée instead of fat.

As a change from fruit, a meal of sandwiches and salad can be very enjoyable. If you wish to drink something with it, have some cereal and fruit coffee (*Bambu Coffee Substitute*) with a little cream or milk. Liver patients should have a glass of carrot juice instead. For variety's sake you might have a good vegetable soup.

Sandwiches: You can use your imagination to create quite a variety of sandwiches. Serve wholegrain (wholewheat) bread or crispbread, lightly spread with butter, then perhaps just a touch of vegetable extract such as *Herbaforce* or a yeast extract. A variety of fillings can be used, such as curds or cottage cheese mixed with chives or some other culinary herb. If you like garlic, chop some finely or mince it and spread it on the buttered bread. Garlic, chives and watercress go very well together in a tomato sandwich and so does finely chopped onion in place of the garlic. Grated carrot and a little horseradish is also a tasty combination. There is almost no end to the variety of sandwiches that can be prepared according to your taste and preferences. Herbs mixed with soft cheese and a little cream can be spread on bread or eaten with potatoes boiled in their skins. In the spring, radishes are a welcome addition to the sandwich menu, but they should be used sparingly because they are quite strong and too many can overstimulate or even irritate the liver. The resulting upset would be contrary to the objective of a health diet. Small cucumbers, thinly sliced, are delicious in a sandwich, and even white cabbage, also finely sliced, tastes surprisingly good.

So there are many variations possible; all you need is a little imagination and natural good taste. If you like, fresh tomatoes can be put on the table as well. A juicy tomato is always refreshing and will enrich the meal with its vitamins. Arthritis patients, however, should take great care to eat only the fully ripe ones.

General Advice

A health diet should be planned in such a way that it does not cause unnecessary disturbances in the system. Special attention should be given to the requirements of the individual organs that are weak. The liver and the pancreas cannot tolerate unhealthy fats or excessively sweet things; the kidneys react to too much salt and spices. As regards salt, the latest research has shown that sea salt is vastly superior to mined stone salt because in its unrefined state it contains many of the substances and trace elements that are found in healthy blood. Moreover, if the sea salt is enriched with herbs you have an excellent seasoning. We have such a tasty and wholesome preparation in *Herbamare*. For those who are prone to catarrh and similar infections or inflammations, there is also *Trocomare*. This herbal seasoning salt is also indicated as a prophylactic for infectious diseases. It is a dietary salt made up of natural sea salt and enriched with eight different fresh plants whose antibacterial effects are similar to those of penicillin, but without the danger of the body becoming resistant to them or the intestinal flora being damaged. As with herbal seasonings, *Trocomare* should never be boiled, but should be added after the food has been cooked so as not to destroy any of the active ingredients. Remember, *Trocomare* provides valuable remedial properties as well as flavouring.

Of course, sea salt should not be used indiscriminately either, only in small quantities. Those who suffer from diseases that require an absolutely salt-free diet, for example, nephritis and cardiac oedema, should not even use sea salt. Seasoning has to be done sensibly and always restricted to a minimum. This does not mean that food should be bland. Far from it. If vegetables are steamed instead of boiled, they will retain all their own rich flavour and by making use of the many kitchen herbs that are at our disposal the palate will have no reason to find fault with any dish.

That salads should not be salted almost goes without saying. And as a dressing, use lemon juice or *Molkosan* whey concentrate, not vinegar.

By adhering to a correct diet we can do much to help achieve success with whatever natural remedy or treatment we may be taking. There is little point in swallowing medicines or taking water treatments if, at the same time, we pay no attention to the food we are eating. Actually, our diet should be the first thing to come under scrutiny since it is useless to take remedies to cure, for example, the accumulation of uric acid, if at the same time we encourage its formation by eating eggs and other concentrated protein foods. It is senseless to take kidney and blood-purifying teas and steam baths to eliminate metabolic wastes from the system if we continue on the diet that is responsible for our problem in the first place.

Manure is for the plant what food is for the human body. The gardener or farmer will only be wasting precious time if he uses the wrong kind of manure when caring for his plants. It is the same with our nutrition. If we eat the wrong kind of food we will not achieve our goal of keeping fit and healthy. What we have become used to eating for no better reason than its pleasant taste or convenience, must in the future be considered from the standpoint of what it will do for us. Only then can we expect to benefit to the fullest degree from the food we eat. Moreover, it is only with persistence that health can be restored, for did it not require equal persistence in eating the wrong things that made us fall victim to disease? We should all remember that good health does not depend upon our physician alone; a lot depends upon ourselves. It often takes years to become sick, so it would be foolish to think that good health could be regained in a matter of days. Yet with perseverance many patients have overcome their ailments and recovered their health.

Fasting

One of the best remedies to maintain general well-being is fasting. If we do not feel well because we have eaten too much, or if our stomach is upset because we have eaten unsuitable food, perhaps making us vomit and causing diarrhoea, then fasting is a most natural remedy. Under similar circumstances our domestic animals have more sense than we do; they simply refuse all food. When unwell, dogs and cats usually eat grass or some cellulose, so as to bring it up again with the mucus. They follow this up by being off their food for at least a day. Animals instinctively know they must not eat until they feel well again. This natural treatment of upsets is even more closely followed by animals living in the wild. They, too, know of no better remedy than fasting if they are ill. They just lie down in the shade, rest and fast until they feel well again. It would also be good for us if we gave the body a chance to purify itself.

When a person fasts the body has an opportunity to rid itself of accumulated harmful metabolic wastes. From time to time it is a good idea to plan ahead to have a fruit juice day and follow this up with one or two days of taking only clean pure water. However, before you begin the fast, make sure the bowels are empty. Mucilage-producing substances such as linseed or psyllium seed, or a herbal laxative, perhaps manna, will help move the bowels. If your liver is in good order you can then begin the fruit juice diet with orange, grapefruit or grape juice, according to what is in season. During the berry season, add berry juice to the list. Any wastes in the body will be eliminated and your organs will begin to function more efficiently.

Should you feel sick during the fast, you will be well advised to speed up the elimination by encouraging the skin function. Friction baths, vigorous washing and towelling or brushing down will stimulate the circulation, while deep-breathing exercises will likewise help to get rid of the feeling of sickness. Short walks in the woods and along country lanes, breathing in the aromatic air, will soon restore a feeling of health and well-being.

If you feel very hungry, chew a few raisins slowly and thoroughly. The Bedouins wandering in the desert often live on nothing but a few dates a day, because they obtain the full benefit from this frugal meal by chewing it thoroughly and so predigesting it properly. In the same way we can help ourselves during our special period of fasting. Spit out the skins of the raisins and just enjoy the grape sugar.

You must observe an important rule when fasting; never begin a fast while feeling disturbed, annoyed or worried about something. A happy frame of mind is a natural medicine that stimulates the endocrine glands and keeps them at the peak of their efficiency. This is one reason why our modern way of life with its constant hustle and bustle, and its problems, worries and upsets, can damage our health so much.

How long should a dietary fast last? The answer to this will be determined by the needs of the individual. Two or three days may be sufficient; however, having kept it up for three days, it is perhaps a pity to stop. The first three days are like climbing a high mountain with all its initial difficulties. Having scaled the hardest part, the worst is over and, to one's surprise, the going becomes easy and enjoyable. So it is after the first three days of fasting. The body will have adapted to the change and can easily stand another five days. An eight-day fast, taking only fruit juice, will give your body a complete 'spring clean'. If you suffer from arthritis, a condition that cannot easily be shifted, you will find it beneficial to continue the fast even longer. Remarkable men like John the Baptist, and a still more distinguished person, Jesus Christ himself, fasted. Of course they did it not for the purpose of cleansing their bodies, but to achieve the utmost mental concentration. As documented in the Scriptures, Christ fasted for forty days. It is an established fact that when great demands are made on the mind, fasting will help to make one's thoughts crystal clear, one's understanding precise and accurate.

If fasting has improved your well-being, do not encourage a friend or neighbour who suffers from Graves' disease (exophthalmic goitre) or tuberculosis to undertake the same treatment. Such a course would definitely be harmful because you cannot cure these two diseases by fasting. Be very careful, therefore, about recommending a fast to others. A long and complete fast might also prove dangerous to people with certain types of heart trouble, even though the fruit juice diet would make it less strenuous since the body is being nourished to the necessary extent while the work of cleansing is going on. If a liver disorder is suspected, take vegetable juices or Vogel's vegetable juice mixture, rather than fruit juices, because the fruit acids do not usually agree with the patient. Carrot juice is particularly good in such cases. You see, then, that each case should be considered individually with respect to what one can or cannot do.

When you are fasting and taking natural medication at the same time, take only a third or even a quarter of the normal dose of your remedies. While on a fast, your system works more efficiently and will respond to medicines much more promptly than usual.

During the fast it is necessary to maintain the normal rhythm of movement and take adequate rest. All extremes are harmful, so avoid them. For instance, do not spend your days on the couch or in bed in the mistaken belief that you must conserve your energy while not eating. On the other hand, do not engage in arduous sports or walks; it would do you no good. The balance of movement and rest during your fast will revive you, restoring vitality and giving you a new foundation for health and well-being. However, I want to stress that it is important to lead up to your fast days slowly and also to return to your normal diet in the same way.

Fattening-Up Diets

Although it should be sufficiently well known that fattening-up diets are anything but sensible, and contrary to the findings of modern nutritional research, they are still occasionally recommended. Lymphatic children with swollen glands and shadows on their lungs are overfed during their stay in Swiss mountain resorts to such an extent that they return home quite plump. It is not surprising that when they are back home in the lowlands and complain of excessive tiredness, show signs of some liver trouble, or even succumb to jaundice. The weight increase achieved by stuffing butter, milk and rich foods into them is no longer the accepted procedure of the nature-oriented, progressive doctor, since it has been found that there are other factors of even greater importance.

The fattening-up diet produces something like an optical illusion. Fat, heavy-bodied children somehow create the impression of being in the best of health, but that this is not always true is borne out by past experience and common knowledge. Excessive feeding usually affects the liver because the diet contains too much fat. This, in turn, leads to other metabolic disturbances which eventually have to be corrected. So forget fattening-up diets. They are not sensible. The resistance to infection is nearly always lowered after such an extreme feeding programme and, all in all, nothing good is ever gained by it.

How Much Food Do We Need?

I have often been asked how much an adult should eat. Should we adopt the system of calories as a measure of our need or is there another way of knowing how much food will prevent us from becoming undernourished?

Like most systems, reckoning in terms of calories is not the perfect system, and should therefore be considered as a purely theoretical guide. An exact method of calculation is not possible because an individual's need for food depends upon so many different and constantly varying circumstances, so that the adoption of a strict and definitive system can do more harm than good. True, a person's body weight or build plays an important part in determining how much food one should eat. Theoretically speaking, a stout and tall person should require more food than a slim one. It is possible, however, that the slim person has a more vigorous nature and burns up more energy than the fat, placid, calm person and in this case our theory already ceases to be valid. A happy, jolly type needs less food than a discontented, unhappy person, because cheerfulness promotes better glandular function and consequently better digestion and improved assimilation. The happy person gets more out of his food. There is much truth in the old saying that one does not live on what one eats but on what one digests.

A person who works in the garden with a spade and a fork has a different food requirement to someone who sits in an office all day. Climate must be considered too, according to whether one lives, for example, in Sweden, Switzerland, Africa or California. It has a bearing on one's need of food as far as quantity and kind is concerned.

I myself never rely on systems that will probably change anyway, like so many other things in life. The only reliable guide is that furnished by the body itself, its automatic mechanisms the Creator endowed it with. Its demands will automatically vary or change with the prevailing circumstances. I fared well by listening to my body's voice when I lived in a cold northern region, in the temperate region of my native Switzerland, and in the tropical regions with their steppes and deserts.

The basic rule to remember is that if you take care to eat only natural foods, wherever you are, you cannot go far wrong. Avoid refined products and imbalances in your diet. If you let nature guide you it will help you to follow your inner urges and interpret them correctly. In this way you will be able to feel more than just hungry; you will develop those finer instincts that nowadays only the more primitive peoples have retained.

Vitamins

Natural Food for the Nerves – Vitamin C

Every year, come autumn and winter in my garden in the Engadine, the little clusters of scarlet barberries between the leafless thorny branches of the berberis shrubs just beg to be harvested. A little earlier it would have been the ripe redcurrants, shining in the autumn sun. So when I am there, I pick some of these berries most days and enjoy their acidic flavour which is due to ascorbic acid, or vitamin C. These berries are, in fact, a natural food for the nerves. Before long, even the slopes facing south become covered in thick snow, and the birds will be daily guests on the shrubs, feasting on the beautiful red, oblong berries in order to obtain their requirements of sugar, minerals and vitamins. The red fruits of the *Rosa canina* (wild rose), the rose hips, will still be peeping through the snow. When these hips are ripe they are deliciously sweet. Because of their vitamin C content they, too, are a wonderful food for the nerves. No wonder that rose hip purée and barberry purée are a perfect source of vitamins during the bleak winter months. They should be on every table because they fill an important gap in our nutrition, since practically all other foods lose some of their vitamin content during their months of storage. Wild fruits, in the form of fruit purée or conserve, prevent vitamin C deficiency while being tasty and pleasant food. But not only barberries and rose hips are rich in vitamin C, even richer are the berries of sea buckthorn, which grows abundantly in the lower Inn valley, the Tessin and the Maggia valley in my native Switzerland. Their orangy-red colour, bright amongst the olive-green leaves, can be spotted on slopes and along brooks and rivers – a delight to the eyes of every nature lover.

THE MERITS OF FOOD RICH IN VITAMIN C

In order to show someone how important it is to prevent vitamin C deficiency, we would do well to refer to Captain Cook's famous experience. Realising the disastrous effect of a lack of vitamin C in the diet, and to guarantee the success of his expeditions, he carried on board whole barrels of sauerkraut. His farsightedness spared him and his crew from falling victim to scurvy. Every 100 g (about 3½ oz) of sauerkraut contains approximately 20 mg of vitamin C, about the same proportion as in raw potatoes, but the latter, of course, are less palatable when uncooked.

The symptoms and consequences of vitamin C deficiency are muscular weakness, bleeding under the skin, bleeding of the gums and loosening of the teeth, which can even fall out. Resistance to infectious diseases is greatly reduced and susceptibility to catarrh, sore throats and tonsillitis, pneumonia and pleurisy is considerably increased. The capillaries are weakened and damaged, severely affecting the circulation.

DAILY REQUIREMENT OF VITAMIN C

Although there is no unanimous opinion as regards the daily requirement of vitamin C, for adults it seems to be between 75–100 mg, or about one-tenth of a gram (0.0035 oz), and for children about half this amount. The following list will give you some idea of how to cover your daily requirement. The quantity of each food item for this purpose is given in grams (1 g = 0.035 oz; 1 oz = 28 g); for example, you would have to eat 12 g of sea buckthorn berries to obtain the amount of vitamin C needed for one day.

- 12 g sea buckthorn berries or raw sea buckthorn purée
- 20 g ripe rose hips or raw rose hip purée
- 70 g blackcurrants
- 120 g green cabbage salad
- 170 g strawberries
- 180 g spinach salad
- 200 g white cabbage salad or natural sauerkraut without additives
- 300 g dandelion salad
- 500 g potatoes boiled in their skins

The amount of vitamin C contained in each item is only approximate. The actual figure varies according to where the plants grow and the season, but the fresh fruit or vegetable has the highest content when just picked, as a certain amount is lost in storage. It goes without saying that you will only need part of the amount given for each food item containing vitamin C because you will eat more than one category of such foods in the course of the day. If sugar is added to the raw, freshly prepared fruit purée, a larger amount of fruit will be needed to cover your requirement.

To set your mind at rest I would like to point out that the natural vitamin C in our food does not harm the system, even though we might take in more than the indicated daily quantity. However, this cannot be said about the synthetic vitamins. These artificial products should only be taken in accordance with the prescription and are never equal to the vitamins contained in plants or fruit. *Bio-C-Lozenges*, on the other hand, are made from fruit extracts with a high natural vitamin C content and help to prevent vitamin C deficiency. So if you believe the principle that food should be a remedy at the same time, you will not take synthetic vitamins but see to it that your daily requirement comes from carefully chosen and prepared food.

Vitamin A
At one time there was not much one could do about conjunctivitis and dehydration of the cornea caused by vitamin A deficiency.

While it was more common in infants and small children, adults were sometimes affected too. Vitamin A deficiency also predisposes one to pulmonary ailments, pneumonia, inflammation of the middle ear, suppurations and abscesses. So where do we find this important vitamin? In butter, cod-liver oil, dandelion leaves, stinging nettles, parsley, savoy cabbage and carrots. Fruits which contain the most vitamin A are apricots, dates and rose hips.

Vitamin A deficiency in children and adults can quickly be rectified by taking *Vitaforce*, rose hip conserve and date sugar. Children and patients whose assimilation is poor should take the condensed juice of organically grown raw spring carrots (*Biocarottin*), which has the additional advantage of being a liver remedy.

Natural food serves our purpose much better than anything else. To illustrate, 1 g of mother's milk contains 2–5 international units (IU) of vitamin A; the same amount of blackcurrant juice, 3–5 IU, and rose hip conserve, 60–100 IU.

CARROTS, CAROTENE AND BIOCAROTTIN

Carrots are so rich in important minerals and vitamins that they can rightly be called a remedial food. You should eat them every day in one form or another, especially during the low-vitamin winter months and early spring. They should preferably be eaten raw, because when uncooked they retain all their goodness.

Children like to nibble carrots as if they were sticks of rock or candy. So when mother puts them on the table cut up into four pieces, maybe grandmother would not be so pleased with her meal, but this is perfect for the children since their teeth are given a little extra work to do. I remember the time when carrot salad used to mean a dish of cooked carrots, sliced and dressed. However, since the importance of their vitamins has become common knowledge, boiled or cooked carrots are hardly ever served as a salad, instead, grated raw carrots have taken their place. With a little grated horseradish added they taste exceptionally refreshing.

WHY CARROTS ARE SO GOOD

One kilogram (2.2 lb) of carrots contains approximately 2.5 g potassium, about 300 mg calcium, 6 mg iron and 0.6 mg copper. If you consider the importance to our blood of iron and copper in organic form, that is, from plants, you will have every reason to give your children plenty of carrots or *Biocarottin*. Moreover, it is good to know that there are about 300 mg of phosphorus in every kilogram of carrots, and we all appreciate the significance of phosphorus for the brain, particularly our memory. Carrots are also good for the glands because of their content of iodine. Furthermore, they are a source of magnesium and cobalt, as well as carotene (provitamin A) at the rate of 70 mg per kilogram of carrots.

Carotene is extremely important in our effort to keep the cellular system healthy and the digestive organs functioning efficiently. It promotes healthy growth and the development of strong, resistant teeth. In fact, vitamin A, that is, carotene, together with calcium and vitamin D, contributes considerably to good teeth.

Did you know, too, that carotene, if taken plentifully, is able to prevent the formation of kidney stones? This has been proved by careful observations. And another thing, a lack of carotene is one of the factors that contribute to a greater susceptibility to infections, especially coughs and sneezes.

Taking plenty of carotene helps to achieve a faster and more complete recovery in cases of pneumonia, various heart troubles, eczema and psoriasis. Women should also take greater amounts of it during pregnancy. It is generally known that it is good for the eyes, helping to improve the eyesight and, if taken in sufficient quantities, it can be the means of overcoming night-blindness – a tremendous benefit to pilots and night-drivers. Carotene has another welcome benefit in that it reduces the tendency to form cataracts. In addition, experiments and observations are said to have shown that carotene improves the function of the sex glands because it exerts a certain influence on the production of sex hormones; thus it can be of assistance in overcoming sexual weakness and impotence. This effect may be attributable to the high vitamin E content in carrots, for there are about 25 mg of it in every kilogram (2.2 lbs). Finally, just let me mention some other vitamins in carrots: one kilogram contains 0.5 mg vitamins B_1, B_2 and B_6, as well as the important vitamin K, and about 50 mg vitamin C, the valuable nerve food.

CARROTS IN WINTER

In the winter our diet should include carrots every day, either in the form of a good fresh salad or a glass of freshly prepared raw juice.

An abundant crop of carrots provides the basis for a beneficial use of the surplus. Let me add that we grow our carrots organically. When harvested, we produce juice and condense it under vacuum at a low temperature. The result is our concentrated juice product known as *Biocarottin*. Among its other valuable applications, if Biocarottin is taken together with *Papayasan* it is possible to keep one's intestines free from worms. Biocarottin has also proved its worth as a supplement in a liver diet, since the goodness of carrots is even more readily available in the concentrated juice. So why take chemical medicines, which are unnatural and foreign to our system, when nature has given us so many good raw materials that are of real benefit to our health?

Vitamin B Complex

Vitamin B_1, or thiamine, is considered to be the anti-beriberi vitamin. *Beri* is a Hindustani word referring to a sheep's fetlock; in Sinhalese, *beri* means weakness. The weakness or loss of energy experienced by those whose main diet is white rice leads to a partial paralysis of the limbs, making the patients drag their feet similar to the way sheep do. For this reason the disease, which is caused by a dietary deficiency of vitamin B_1, came to be known as beriberi, a reduplication of the word *beri*.

The anti-beriberi vitamin is contained in the aleurone layer of cereals; a good quantity is also present in yeast. The substance consists of various chemical compounds which, although not related to one another, have the same quality of being water-soluble.

The vitamin B complex is essential to enable the cells of the nervous system to take up oxygen. The primary and best remedy available in biological medicine for the treatment of painful inflammation of the nerves, as well as for strengthening the entire nervous system, is a steady supply of vitamin B. It is also a reliable help for those who suffer from poor stomach and bowel action and the lack of appetite connected with these disorders. If taken in greater amounts, vitamin B will often relieve disturbances during pregnancy. In cases of circulatory disorders and heart trouble and prescribed natural remedies will act faster and better if vitamin B is taken at the same time. In the past, explorers on arctic and Himalayan expeditions took along supplies of yeast extract for the sake of its concentrated nutrients and, not least, its sufficient amounts of vitamin B.

Today we have a fine supplement in *Herbaforce* because of its content of cultured yeast extract and fresh plant extracts. It is very tasty and most suitable as a sandwich spread, for snacks and food for journeys. It enhances salad dressings and is a splendid flavouring for soups, stews and other dishes.

VITAMIN B$_{12}$ AND THE BLOOD

A doctor friend of mine told me once that he was of the opinion that a certain patient's anaemic condition had its basic cause in his vegetarian diet. This patient, who was otherwise quite healthy, was unable to overcome his condition, and the doctor was adamant that the man should add meat to his diet because it is rich in the haematinic vitamin B$_{12}$. But when the doctor found out that I have been a vegetarian since I was seventeen, and have a constant haemoglobin count of 100–105 and otherwise excellent blood, he was extremely astonished and had to change his opinion. Mind you, a healthy vegetarian diet must include plenty of green vegetables and all the green culinary herbs, such as all kinds of cress and parsley, because these contain sufficient levels of vitamin B$_{12}$. All these green herbs, in particular parsley, stimulate the kidneys and urination and should therefore be used regularly, and not just as an occasional garnish on prepared dishes. In fact, your health will benefit greatly if you chop up some kitchen herbs daily, mixing them in your salads and cottage cheese and sprinkling them over vegetable and potato dishes. You can ensure a regular intake of these green herbs by always using the herbal seasoning salt *Herbamare*, which is made from fresh green herbs. If you use natural products regularly in your kitchen you will reduce the risk of succumbing to vitamin deficiency.

Vitamin E – the Fertility Vitamin

The Roman gladiators had no idea about hormones and vitamin E, but they knew from experience that they became more energetic and efficient when they ate bulls' testicles the day before their contests. No doubt it needed clear thinking and some degree of biological understanding to come to this conclusion. Not infrequently it was mere chance, an acute observation or clear and logical thinking that led to discoveries that serve us today in our quest to rectify errors in nutrition that plague us in the form of deficiency diseases and avitaminoses.

DEFINITE MERITS OF VITAMIN E

It was many decades ago (in 1922) when the American scientist Herbert McLean Evans discovered vitamin E. Since then it has been proved that there is no better natural remedy for sterility and infertility. Many a woman could have saved herself great heartache if she had known about vitamin E. Not only does this vitamin prevent miscarriage, but it also promotes the healthy, normal development of the foetus, ensuring a normal pregnancy without complications.

However, vitamin E is not only important for women; men too depend upon an adequate supply of it for the normal functioning of the sex glands. In turn, vitality, pleasure in work and stamina are dependent upon the efficiency of these glands.

Vitamin E influences the development and function of the smooth and striped muscles, being able to prevent muscle degeneration. This is of great importance for the cardiac muscles. In fact, vitamin E, together with natural heart remedies such as *Crataegisan* and *Auroforce*, has proved most effective as a tonic for weak heart muscles. It can be added that a vitamin E deficiency is very bad for the nerves too.

In cases of vitamin E deficiency swelling of the intercellular substance in the connective tissue and impaired firmness of the vascular walls have been discovered. Stagnation in the capillaries and bad circulation are connected with this condition, and all of these things lead to metabolic disturbances and increased oxygen consumption.

If these disturbances are diagnosed in the years of development and growth, an increased intake of vitamin E can help. Menopausal problems also respond well to average doses of vitamin E, as do rheumatic ailments. All in all, vitamin E is important in keeping the body functions healthy.

Cows can succumb to brucellosis (undulant fever, Bang's disease), an epidemic infectious disease causing miscarriage, if they lack vitamin E. It can be cured by giving the animals feed that is rich in vitamin E, such as bran that contains wheat germ. Brucellosis can be transmitted to humans, for example by drinking contaminated and unpasteurised milk and by eating infected butter or cottage cheese.

The correct daily dosage of vitamin E has not yet been established. It is assumed that the daily requirement is 15–25 mg. One litre (1.76 pints) of wheat germ oil contains 1 g of vitamin E, so that we would have to take 15 cc (about ½ fl. oz) every day to meet our requirement.

SOURCES OF VITAMIN E

Vitamin E is rarely found in meat, except in those parts that are unsuitable for human consumption, for example bulls' testicles, the spleen, placenta, pancreas and pituitary gland. It is, however, found in fish and egg yolk, and in small amounts in milk as well as butter.

It is more abundant in vegetable products, primarily in cereal germ, oil fruits and cotton seed, also in corn (maize), peanuts and all varieties of cress – watercress, garden cress, nasturtium and American cress. For this reason the formulae of *Herbamare* and *Trocomare* include these cresses. Vitamin E is also present in spinach, lettuce and alfalfa (lucerne), as well as in most leafy salad greens. That explains why vegetarians probably meet their daily vitamin E requirement more effectively than meat-eaters. If you suffer from a deficiency, make use of the above-mentioned sources. For quick results take wheat germ oil, and if you do not like its taste, use wheat germ oil capsules, which are quite easy to swallow. The gelatine capsule dissolves in the intestine and there is no danger of the taste repeating on you.

Overcoming Protein Deficiency

Lactovegetarians will not find it easy to prevent protein deficiency if they travel in countries where there is little dairy farming. In fact, a vegetarian may have difficulty even in our temperate regions in obtaining his eighteen amino acids every day in the food available to him, yet they are essential building blocks for the protein in his body.

Millet was the staple diet of our forefathers; together with milk and meat it provided the necessary protein. Later, potatoes were added as a valuable source of protein, and in more recent times, soya beans. Soya has proved to be an excellent vegetable protein, and was responsible for saving millions of Chinese from starvation when overpopulation made the production of sufficient animal protein impossible.

Because they are so good for us, we should give much more attention to soya products. The beans contain first-class protein, as well as minerals and other vital substances. Millet proved its worth in the past when it served to satisfy our forefathers, giving them strength and energy. For this reason alone it, too, deserves to be on our table now. Over forty years ago, millet began to go out of vogue and was only used for chicken feed. More recently, however, as a result of the serious efforts being made to enrich our diet with valuable plant products, millet has begun to be revived as a food and it would be to our advantage if we used it regularly in alternation with potatoes and soya.

On travels through tropical regions in the developing countries of Africa and Asia, a frequent sight are many adults and even more children with pot-bellies and skinny limbs. This condition is generally a symptom of protein deficiency. Although it is true that pure calories, that is, carbohydrates, are often plentiful in the form of tropical fruits, and the body is able to produce its own fat, in hot countries it is very difficult to obtain sufficient protein. Because of the great heat, cattle yield less milk. It is therefore not surprising that in those areas all kinds of seeds are considered important for food. In folk museums we can also find that seeds, kernels and nuts stand out as a special feature in the nutrition of ancient peoples.

Seafood – Saltwater Fish and Shellfish
As suggested in the previous section, non-meat-eaters may find it difficult to get the necessary protein in tropical countries. Milk and milk products are usually scarce or unobtainable because the climate is too hot for productive dairy farming. Soya is not grown everywhere and nuts are often unknown. So what can be used to provide protein? Small island populations could not survive if it were not for seafood. Shellfish are a welcome and valuable source of protein in these areas.

Of what benefit is seafood for those of us who already obtain enough protein from other sources? The addition of seafood is then not really essential. Still, we are accustomed to eating many things that are not absolutely necessary; for example, we could live without citrus and tropical fruits, yet we are glad and grateful for the added variety. Seafood contains good quality protein, is easily digestible and many prefer it to animal protein. Important, too, is the fact that seafood contains traces of iodine.

The great progress in civil aviation has made foreign travel easy and has brought us into close contact with people from other parts of the world, who visit us and are pleased when they can get their own food and fruit in our shops. Conversely, many of us venture out and travel to faraway places, where we become familiar with other customs and habits. The result is that we now have many food items in our shops that were rare or even unknown until relatively recently.

Eating Vegetables and Fruit at the Same Meal
I keep receiving letters and reports that confirm the fact that digestive problems often arise when fruit and vegetables are eaten at the same meal. Let me quote the following account as an example.

'There has been much talk lately about modern diets, with many lectures being given on the subject. My daughter and I went to an interesting one given by Dr Bircher. The speaker made the point that, before every meal, fruit and raw vegetables or a salad should be eaten. So my whole family started a regime of eating an apple before our meals. The result? My goitre scar from an operation eleven years ago was dreadfully painful for three or four days and a small swelling developed. Then the pain diminished, although it did not disappear entirely. I should also tell you that on the evening of the lecture, I hurried a little and for the first time in my life I was conscious of my heart beating rather rapidly and ever since I have felt sick almost every day. We have now stopped eating an apple before our meals, for it seemed to give us flatulence as well.'

All things considered, what does this account emphasise? It is good to serve a dish of raw food before the main meal, but be careful to stick to one variety of food. Before a vegetable meal eat raw vegetables, never fruit, and before a meal composed of sweet dishes, you may eat fruit. Dr Bircher-Benner's theory may apply to healthy people whose organs function properly, but if there is a tendency to dysfunction of one or more organs, especially the liver and pancreas, the consumption of fruit and vegetables as part of the same meal can encourage further disturbances.

A urinalysis disclosed that the writer of the above letter had trouble with her liver and pancreas, and it was no doubt for this reason that she suffered from flatulence when she ate fruit and vegetables at the same meal. Where the liver and pancreas are working efficiently, the digestive juices are able to break down fruit and Dr Bircher-Benner's theory would be correct. It would then do no harm to eat fruit before a vegetable meal. However, if the organic mechanism is impaired, the enzymes will clearly be unable to digest the fruit acids, resulting in a reaction between the fruit acids and the alkaline vegetable components. The unpleasant consequences are excessive fermentation and flatulence.

We are naturally grateful to Dr Bircher-Benner for his great achievement in the field of modern nutrition, but we regret that he did not see the importance of keeping the two classes of food, fruit and vegetables, separate. For one thing, even taste-wise they do not necessarily go together. Take strawberries and cabbage or radish salad, for instance; the very thought of having to eat these salads after strawberries is far from tempting. Our sense of taste alone tells us not to mix these foods.

In a personal interview, Dr Bircher-Benner told me once that he could find no scientific reason for separating fruit and vegetables. Nevertheless, many of his patients complained about disturbances, especially fermentation or flatulence, in connection with his diet. Of course, if someone follows the Bircher method and experiences no disturbance at all, there is no reason why he should not continue. On the other hand, if upsets do occur, it would be unwise to stick to a regime that causes trouble. Rather, it is better to follow the lead of nature which, after all, is more important than all our theories. The rule about not eating vegetables and fruit at the same meal applies to the combination of food items in general; in particular, it is important to avoid fried food and sweet things when the liver and pancreas are affected, because they cannot cope well with these.

Fruit and Vegetable Juices – their Effects on You

Perhaps you do not know which juice will agree with you. Or the choice may be difficult if you want to recommend juices to relatives and friends. The following hints will provide you with the information you need.

Carrot Juice

The essential oils contained in carrots have an effect on the mucous membranes and stimulate the blood circulation in the stomach and intestinal tissues. Because of its balancing action carrot juice is good for constipation and diarrhoea. With small children it usually stops the dreaded attacks of diarrhoea and vomiting in no time at all, and also eliminates intestinal worms. Other complaints, such as headaches, eczema and skin blemishes (for example acne), may be connected with bad digestion and can be rectified with the help of this juice. Many women prize carrot juice as an ideal natural remedy that acts from within the body, keeping them slim and ensuring a good complexion. Carrot juice is refreshing and soothing if taken during convalescence after an operation or a serious illness, coughs and colds, and infectious diseases accompanied by fever. We owe it to the rich content of carotene (provitamin A) that this juice improves the eyesight and stimulates the production of rhodopsin (visual purple), the lack of which causes night-blindness.

Beetroot Juice

This juice contains betaine, which stimulates the function of the liver cells and protects the liver and bile ducts in cases of disturbance. Every 100 g of beetroot juice contains 5 mg of iron, in addition to a number of trace elements, which, it is believed, encourage the absorption of the iron in the blood. A healthy body needs plenty of iron, especially in the first two years of life, during puberty, in pregnancy, when breast-feeding and during the menopause. Beetroot juice is highly recommended for these crucial periods of life. If your child is pale, do not forget to give him or her a small glass of beetroot juice before meals every day, morning and evening. In the case of infants (six months to two years) one teaspoonful will suffice.

Celery Juice

Celery juice is distinctly alkaline and eliminative. It is therefore recommended for all disturbances caused by the accumulation of wastes and toxins, for example rheumatic and arthritic ailments. Celery juice regulates the water balance and puts new life into elderly people.

Tomato Juice

Tomato juice is recommended as a protection against premature aging, as well as the symptoms of overtiredness and unpleasant body odour. It is refreshing and cleanses the body.

Potato Juice

Unlike the other juices, which are good for health but also delicious taken before meals to stimulate the appetite, potato juice is strictly remedial, and is particularly indicated for the treatment of stomach ulcers.

Vegetable juices enhanced by lacto-fermentation have a stimulating and balancing effect on our vital intestinal flora.

Raw Juices, Medicinal Juices

SCIENTIFIC RESEARCH

While living on 57th Street in New York for a short time during 1950, I used to go for a drink of freshly squeezed orange juice at a certain 'health bar'. Whenever I went there I was amazed to see people drinking cabbage juice from enormous glasses. I had, of course, known the benefits of raw cabbage juice for certain disorders for along time, but I also knew that it was a rather unpalatable drink.

Later I came across an article in the Toronto *Magazine Digest*, which extolled the virtues of cabbage juice in the treatment of gastric ulcers. Here, then, was confirmation of a treatment we in Switzerland had known for quite a while, based on our own experience with cabbage juice. Dr Garnett, the author of the report, referred to experiments with 'vitamin U' (U standing for Ulcer) which, according to him, is responsible for the curative effect of this juice. What he may not have known, however, is that raw potato juice is even more effective, and it is quite likely that he would have found 'vitamin U' in it as well. Another researcher, however, may advance Ragnar Berg's explanation proposed many years ago. According to him, the alkaline properties of raw juice neutralise the free acids in the system and so rehabilitate the mineral metabolism, making possible the successful treatment of gastric ulcers.

THE EVIDENCE OF EXPERIENCE

It is not essential to know exactly how a cure takes place. The mere knowledge that juices can cure is infinitely more valuable than any scientific explanation advanced in this connection. Science, after all, only confirms the discoveries made decades ago. Many years ago, as a young man, I lectured on this subject and drew attention to the value of raw juices. Today it is easier to convince people because science has, in the meantime, confirmed our assertions of the past that raw juices and raw vegetables are wonderful remedies. It is, and will remain, a fact that the raw juices of potato and cabbage will heal gastric and duodenal ulcers.

Even more interesting is the observation I made in connection with raw potato, cabbage (green and white) and carrot juice in the treatment of gout, rheumatism and allied conditions. If these juices are taken in conjunction with a strictly natural diet, these diseases will eventually respond to the treatment.

A SPECIAL DIET

Before *breakfast*, on an empty stomach, take half a glass of raw potato juice diluted with a little warm water. The breakfast itself should consist of whole wheat that has been soaked in water for a day or two. It can be made more palatable with the addition of a good vegetable stock or fresh butter. If the bowels need special attention, add psyllium seed or freshly ground linseed to the wheat. Crispbread with butter and wheat germ will complete your breakfast. If the liver is not functioning properly, drink a glass of raw carrot juice. Chew all the food well and insalivate it thoroughly.

Midday Meal: Eat a good, hearty vegetable soup with a cup of raw cabbage juice, which is added after the soup has been taken off the heat. Then have a dish of natural brown rice, steamed vegetables and a salad. Never use vinegar to make your salad dressing; use lemon juice, or sour milk or whey concentrate (*Molkosan*) if you cannot tolerate lemon. For variety, in place of the brown rice you can use whole wheat, buckwheat or millet. If you feel nervous and tired out, beat a raw egg and mix it in with your food every other day. On no account should the eggs be cooked because this would destroy most of their vitamins and, in addition, produce too much uric acid. Only when eggs are eaten raw do they have a place in a therapeutic diet, if it is at all advisable to include them. Thus, raw eggs can be used, as indicated, in a diet for stomach ulcers, but those who suffer from rheumatism should avoid eggs altogether.

Evening meal: This can be along similar lines to the breakfast. The wholewheat dish can be varied by taking oat flake porridge or, even better, raw, soaked oat grains, put through the mincer.

Keep off fruit on this special diet, only use vegetable juices.

CHANCES OF A CURE

With this diet it is possible to cure a stomach ulcer within a month. Gout and rheumatic complaints will improve within two or three months and then slowly disappear. Afterwards, continue with the diet but have only fruit every second day. Avoid sausages, cold meats, pork, canned foods, white sugar and white flour and everything made from these. In fact, you would do well to forget these items altogether. You may start eating meat again after six months, but only veal or beef.

If you follow the suggested diet consistently, you will find that even the most stubborn case of gout will eventually disappear. Of course, you can back up the healing process by means of natural remedies. *Wallwosan* or *Symphosan*, applied externally, will give relief; take *Petasites* internally, also *Nephrosolid* to stimulate the kidneys. For gastric ulcers *Gastronol* is recommended, to be taken after meals. But never lose sight of the fact that the cure depends fundamentally on the raw juices.

Since these juices, with the exception of carrot juice, are somewhat unpalatable on their own, try mixing them in thick minestrone soup. The vegetable flavours will neutralise the strong taste of the raw juice. As pointed out already, add the juice only after the soup has been taken off the heat, so as not to lose the medicinal value. If this should make the soup lukewarm, gently warm the juice in a double boiler before adding it to the soup. You will have to eat this soup with the raw juices twice a day and between meals take an additional 200 ml of juice (about 8 fl. oz). In grave cases, 400–500 ml (just under a pint) of raw juice daily is absolutely essential.

Proponents of nature cures and nutritional therapy were advocating the use of raw juices long before scientific research began to confirm their value. Patients should remember the proven effects and be willing to persevere with the treatment until the hoped-for results are obtained.

It is amazing that it was in the United States where these drastic methods of treatment were developed and practised, for it is there, more than anywhere else, that poor nutrition has led to such modern diseases of civilisation.

Patients elsewhere should show the same perseverance in adhering to a raw juice diet that may be relatively unpalatable but will eventually lead to rehabilitation. Mere taste is a small price to pay for health restored!

Which Juices Are Compatible?
Some people assume that it is permissible to combine fruit and vegetable juices, such as orange with carrot juice. This, of course, is no better than eating fruit and vegetables at the same time, which, as already discussed, is apt to cause fermentation and flatulence, especially in sensitive people. Generally speaking, one juice can be mixed with another of the same kind, so that the best way is to take, for example, carrot and beetroot juices at one time, and orange and another fruit juice some other time. This way your digestion will not suffer. As a rule, it is better to drink only one juice, not a mixture. What is more, sipping is much better than gulping it down, because little sips, properly insalivated, will avoid flatulence or any other digestive disturbance. The curative effect will be greater too. Insalivating well helps to warm ice-cold juice in the mouth and so avoid chilling the stomach. A bite of crispbread or rusk with each sip of fruit juice will help to neutralise the acidity somewhat and protect the stomach lining.

If, in spite of all their goodness, you simply cannot tolerate fruit juices, mix them with muesli, while vegetable juices are best incorporated in soups and stews, after these have been cooked.

Difficulties in Adjusting to a Raw Food Diet

High blood pressure, thick blood, venous ailments and similar conditions, demand a change in the viscosity of the blood and this can be accomplished by following a protein-reduced diet. Meat, cheese, eggs and other protein foods have to be cut down to a minimum in such cases. However, it is not always easy to change over to a fruit diet. Elderly people in particular are likely to be troubled because gastric acid does not always mix well with the acids found in fruit. When changing over to a fruit diet it is of prime importance to eat very slowly, insalivate the fruit and fruit juices thoroughly and eat some crispbread, wholewheat rusks, oatmeal biscuits, toast or any other flakes or wholegrain crackers or biscuits, as the starch contained in them will help to neutralise the acids, rendering them more acceptable to the stomach.

Those who change to a raw food diet must take into account that the digestive organs will not immediately adapt themselves to the change from a mixed or one-sided protein diet. A little time and patience are needed before a really successful changeover is achieved, and the body must be given all the help it needs. Let me use a motor car as an illustration. A driver knows that he cannot change from a high octane to a low octane petrol without first making adjustments to the carburettor. Similarly, the digestive organs must be adjusted to the new diet. Many people fail in making this dietary change simply because this point has not been given the necessary attention.

When Raw Food Causes Problems

It is known that crude oil can produce more power than a refined product, but it requires that an appropriate carburettor be fitted. There is a similarity with a diet of raw food. Some people have health problems, weak digestive organs, and are not able to tolerate raw food in its solid form. Their condition may only allow them to take it in the form of juices.

Since raw fruits and raw vegetables contain the highest amount of vital substances, every meal should include at least some raw food, so that we can obtain sufficient quantities of vitamins and enzymes. A weekly raw food day will benefit us if we are able to take and digest them well. Bearing this prerequisite in mind, it will be beneficial to go on a raw food diet for a while, especially when the weather is amenable during the change from winter to spring. The diet will give the body a chance to be properly cleansed.

However, if you find that nuts and salads are eliminated without being digested, a raw food diet is not for you. In particular, children with digestive problems or who suffer from coeliac disease should not be given any food they cannot digest. It would be closing one's eyes to the facts if a diet were continued although the patient was slowly dying of a complete loss of energy – a kind of foolishness I remember seeing once in the case of a girl who would not listen to reason.

It is true that some primitive peoples live almost entirely on raw foods and remain fit and strong. We in the industrialised world, however, should not draw the wrong conclusions from this. Figuratively speaking, civilisation has inflicted many wounds on us, and many of us have acquired extremely weak digestive organs, making it almost impossible, or at least very difficult, to digest raw foods. If this applies to you, you will have to make the food more digestible by cooking it. Only a modest addition of raw food in the form of purée or juice will be permissible. Facing the facts is the answer to keeping your body from being put under unnecessary stress. When the system has recovered sufficiently and the digestive juices are once again able to break down the raw vegetable cells and assimilate the nutrients, you can begin to enjoy some raw foods, but with great care. Even then, you should never forget that proper chewing and thorough insalivation are called for. Never eat in a hurry. So if you want to benefit fully from raw foods, you will have to take more time eating them than you do with cooked food.

THE DANGER OF INTESTINAL WORMS
The danger of ingesting intestinal parasites together with raw salads is not unknown. But if you are able to grow vegetables organically in your own garden, that risk should be eliminated. With bought vegetables, however, you are never quite sure whether they were fertilised with liquid manure and thus infected with worm eggs. Hence the warning to wash salad greens thoroughly in salt water, rinsing them afterwards, to make sure that you have at least some protection. The effects of intestinal worms are most unpleasant and you would be wise to take care to avoid infection. Mind you, some people have had intestinal parasites for years, possibly decades, without realising it. They have no idea why they are always on edge, often unwell and anaemic. Nor do they know the cause of the black rings around the eyes. People who recognise these symptoms should consider the possibility that they may have intestinal worms. As mentioned above, one precautionary measure

501

is to be careful when preparing raw food; another good suggestion is to take a course of *Papayasan*, the plant remedy that effectively eliminates worms.

TYPHOID FEVER, DYSENTERY AND OTHER INFECTIOUS DISEASES

Imported vegetables can pose dangers if they are not 100 per cent clean and so are perhaps infected with typhoid bacilli or carriers of dysentery or some other infectious disease. If you live in a hot country or in the tropics, never eat any raw food or fruit that you cannot peel or disinfect. The same advice goes for anyone who travels to such countries. It as advisable to be scrupulous in this respect, for the damage is quickly done. When peeling fruit, do not forget to disinfect the skin first, since anything adhering to it can stick to your fingers and, in turn, infect the peeled fruit before you eat it. Constant caution is indispensable, even though it may make life a little more complicated.

Conclusions

If, after all the above considerations, you conclude that the value of raw food does not really compensate for the many disadvantages and dangers, you are wrong. I have only made you aware of the disadvantages to show what could minimise the value so that you can exercise the necessary care and draw the full benefit from it. These reflections should stimulate anyone able to do so to take up organic gardening in order to obtain produce that poses no danger. So, if you have a garden or plot of land, there is nothing to prevent you from doing this. It is also gratifying to know that organic cultivation methods are winning more and more advocates.

Berries

If it were generally known how rich in vitamins berries are, they would figure far more in our everyday diet. Most of them contain a considerable amount of vitamin C. The importance of this vitamin is fully realised by those who have had bleeding gums, loose teeth, a tendency to chills and colds and a predisposition to haemorrhaging. All these forms of bleeding become immediately apparent when vitamin C is lacking.

Blackcurrants are rich in vitamin C, although not everyone likes their distinctive taste. But if you ate 50 g (2 oz) of these daily, you would provide your body with its full requirements of vitamin C for a whole day. Rose hip, sea buckthorn berries, raspberries, redcurrants, cranberries and nearly all other berries are excellent sources of vitamin C.

Vitamin A is supplied by various other berries. For example 100 g (about 4 oz) of fresh bilberries (blueberries) contain as much as 1.6 mg of pure vitamin A, and 100 g of blackberries, 0.8 mg. It is clear, then, that during the berry season you need not be solely dependent upon carrot juice and watercress as sources of this vitamin. Various berries will help to meet your daily requirement. This fact should be remembered by all those who suffer from the consequences of vitamin A deficiency, usually showing up in skin diseases, pathological changes in the hair, teeth and nails, softening of the cornea, obesity from glandular dysfunction, night-blindness (nyctalopia) and other conditions (see pages 486–8).

Although much has been done, said and written about vitamins, the last word on the subject has yet to be spoken. We are today catching a glimpse of the intricate interplay between vitamins, enzymes and hormones. Vitamin B_{12} is an indispensable component of the yellow respiratory enzyme; vitamin A, the opponent of the thyroid hormones and so on. Hyperthyroidism can thus be checked by eating plenty of food containing vitamin A, such as the berries mentioned above.

It is generally known that berries are also valuable because of their high mineral content. All berries, with the exception of cranberries, are predominantly alkaline. But in spite of their acidity, cranberries are still valuable, mainly for those who eat a large amount of raw food.

Experience has shown that berries are good for the liver and pancreas. In cases of disturbances in these organs, bilberries (blueberries) will do much to restore their proper functions. Although stone fruit, pears and other fruit can upset people with these disorders, berry juices will have a beneficial effect.

The one fruit that has to be watched is the strawberry. Many people are allergic to strawberries and they can also affect the kidneys, although much depends upon the fertilisers used in their cultivation. If the right organic manure or compost is used, that is, a natural compost, bone meal and natural lime, then reactions such as nettle rash (urticaria) may be avoided. If you are allergic to cultivated strawberries, try wild ones, because there is a difference. On the other hand, you may forget strawberries altogether and stick to the other kinds of berries that do not cause allergic reactions and are just as good.

People of a lymphatic constitution, who frequently have reason to complain of swollen glands, should make the fullest use possible of all available berries. They are excellent for the glands, and may also help to reduce susceptibility to infectious diseases of the respiratory organs.

Mothers-to-be will similarly benefit from berries. When there are sufficient vitamins and minerals in the blood, most of the ailments associated with pregnancy can be avoided. Since vitamin C prevents morning sickness, it is recommended to eat food rich in this vitamin during pregnancy.

Allergic problems and the weariness often felt in the spring, the so-called 'spring fever', will be alleviated or even overcome by eating plenty of berries. Of course, we are referring to berries in their fresh, raw state. Eat as many as possible before preserving or bottling the surplus. You must remember, however, not to use white sugar for preserving, since it is a calcium robber and can cause problems. Rely on the fruit's own sugar instead, which, after all, is the most valuable sugar of all and berries are very rich in it. Since extra sugar is needed to make jam, use unrefined brown cane sugar with at least 10–20 per cent grape concentrate added, to give it still greater nutritional value.

The Curative Value of Berries
The outstanding curative properties of berries come into their own when they are eaten raw. When we let them ripen fully in our garden, their own fruit sugar suffices so that we do not need to add cane sugar or honey. Their vitamin content, their vital substances and natural colouring are an inestimable source of nourishment that is also remedial. When the liver or pancreas is sluggish, bilberries (blueberries) are not only acceptable but can actually bring about a cure.

Wild berries are also good for people who suffer from arthritis, rheumatism, cancer and multiple sclerosis. Those who are allergic to cultivated strawberries can usually take wild ones without experiencing any trouble. Since the endocrine glands, besides the liver, benefit greatly from the curative and vital substances of berries, they are, in a manner of speaking, a food for rejuvenation. This should not really surprise us, because by eating them regularly we can reduce excess weight, along with exerting a favourable influence on the ovaries, the thyroid gland and the hypophysis – in short, on all the endocrine glands. Wild fruits have the advantage of having been grown organically, so that we can be fully confident of their undiminished medicinal value.

The Properties of Sour Berries

Anyone who avoids eating sour berries for fear of ingesting too much acid is mistaken, because not everything that tastes sour is also chemically sour. Even in very sour-tasting berries the alkaline substances predominate. The only berry with an excess of acid is the cranberry. All the others can help to neutralise excess acidity, even in the overacid bodies of people suffering from rheumatism and arthritis.

Berry Juices

We have established that most berries are rich in vitamin C, so when they are in season they can supply us with what our bodies need, and that their alkaline minerals are also most beneficial. So as long as berries are there to be picked we should preferably eat them whole rather than only drinking the juice. We can do the latter once the season is over, enabling us to benefit from the curative properties of berries until the next crop. For those suffering from liver disorders bilberry juice is known to be excellent. Drinking blackberry and blackcurrant juice can be to our advantage. We know that the berries' colouring substances share in their curative effect. For instance, they cleanse and regenerate the intestinal flora. So it is for our good if we do not let the berry season pass us by and during the rest of the year make good use of natural pure fruit juices for the sake of our health.

Be Careful with Stone Fruit

People who have problems with the liver and pancreas must take care not to eat stone fruit, such as plums and peaches, in any great quantity, for if they do, they will probably pay for it with increased discomfort and pain. It is also important to remember that stone fruit should never be eaten on an empty stomach. What is more, be absolutely sure to eat slowly and insalivate the fruit thoroughly before swallowing. If you eat some crispbread, rusks or wholewheat bread along with the fruit, the gastric reaction to the acids, especially hydrocyanic acid, will be diminished. Healthy constitutions used to raw foods can probably digest stone fruit very well and eat it at any time, but sick or delicate people should not take the risk. It is better to abstain from eating stone fruit than to eat it and suffer the consequences, only because other people might be able to enjoy it. If you should happen to eat some and upset the gastric and intestinal mucous membranes, you can obtain relief by taking a tablespoon of clay in water, morning and evening for a few days. Should excessive gastric acidity develop, take a teaspoon of wood ash before each meal and the disturbance will quickly disappear.

Rules for Eating Stone Fruit

Stone fruit is known to be more digestible when dried than if eaten fresh. But whether fresh or dried, it is essential that we observe a few basic rules in order to enjoy these tasty fruits without having any problems.

Stone fruit cannot be stored in the cellar, nor would it ripen there. It should always be picked when fully ripe, and should also be ripe when bought. Partially ripe stone fruit causes problems, and also tastes unpleasant. Thus, anyone who buys unripe stone fruit will subsequently be disappointed and feel cheated. You will never see unripe apricots, for example, miraculously ripen. You can wait as long as you like, but they will not become juicy and sweet; rather, to your great dismay, they will shrivel up pitifully. Cherries should be ripe and what is more important, unsprayed, otherwise they will be harmful. When we eat fully ripe and unsprayed cherries together with some wholewheat (wholemeal) bread, chewing everything well, they will not cause fermentation and will exert a good influence on the liver. Another thing, we should never drink water while eating cherries, or immediately afterwards. This rule applies to all stone fruit. Remember, too, that this kind of fruit is not to be simply swallowed before being properly chewed, as is usually done. Stone fruit, if well insalivated will not give any trouble, as long as it is ripe and unsprayed. In the case of dried fruit (see below), it is also important to ensure that it is unsulphurised.

It is true that nowadays it may not be easy to follow through this advice if you cannot obtain your fruit from the right sources. Our own gardens, which we tend ourselves, will provide us with all we need, as will also the produce of farmers who look after their trees in an absolutely natural way, who pick and sell nothing but fully ripe fruit.

Jam-Making and Dried Fruit

An abundant crop of stone fruit is an inducement to use the surplus for making tasty jams. But you must be careful that the fruit's value and taste are not unduly spoiled by boiling it for too long. Well-made apricot jam is delicious. Cherry jam is also always popular, not only that made from the sweet but also from the sour cherry, which is customarily used more for jams than for eating fresh. Those who have no time to make their own will find the natural and carefully prepared *Vogel jams* worthwhile trying.

It is peculiar that stone fruit when dried does not cause any problems; rather, this process brings out its real goodness. However, when buying dried fruit we must make sure that it is natural, unsprayed and unsulphurised, for only then will we enjoy its full benefits. Dried apricots are a wonderful, thirst-quenching food to take with us when out walking, but again they must be absolutely natural and pure.

Health Benefits

Since natural food is indispensable for good health we can count on its benefits. Even if the vitamin content of cherries is relatively low, it is still important, because it is easily absorbed by the body. Cherries contain 0.05 mg per 100 g (2 oz) of vitamin B_1. This anti-beriberi substance, also known as thiamine, is good for vascular problems, circulation disorders and heart trouble, as well as for low blood pressure. This makes even small quantities of these vitamins welcome. Another of the B complex vitamins, known as nicotinamide, which is used in the treatment of pellagra, is also present in cherries at 0.01 mg per 100 g. If a person's gums often bleed or are inflamed, or the teeth are loose, natural food rich in vitamin C is needed. In this case we should eat unsprayed, fully ripe cherries. Sour cherries contain more vitamin C than the sweet kind, but they have 1 per cent less sugar. In spite of their sour taste, these cherries are alkaline-forming. They contain less sodium than sweet cherries, but in comparison they have more potassium and sulphur, and are very rich in malic and citric acids.

Formerly, a specially prepared syrup made from cherries together with the stones, which contain hydrocyanic acid, served as a diuretic for dropsy and as a refreshing drink. The fruits and their stones were crushed together, the pulp was squeezed out, and sixty-five parts of sugar were added to thirty-five parts of juice. Cherry stones were also once used for people who suffered from kidney stones, six to be taken daily. Even cherry stalks, especially those of red and sour cherries, were used for medicinal purposes; a tea was made from them to treat infections of the respiratory tract and to increase the flow of urine.

In former times, dried cherries were a remedy for chlorosis and anaemia. And even today, prunes, soaked and eaten before going to bed and before breakfast, are still used for sluggish bowels.

507

Continuing this simple treatment over a period of time will help even in stubborn cases of constipation.

Fully ripe and uncontaminated apricots and peaches are a wholesome addition to our food. They are relatively rich in vitamin C, contain some vitamins B_3 and B_2, a substantial amount of carotene and also pantothenic acid, which helps to prevent the hair turning grey.

SLOES – A STONE FRUIT

Not everyone knows that the blackthorn or sloe is a shrub that also bears stone fruit, sloes, although they are not edible. Nevertheless, to complete our list of the various stone fruits that have healing properties, we must not omit to mention it. As far back as antiquity this shrub was widely used. The flowers were picked and the essence made from them was used to cleanse the blood, as a laxative, as a remedy for the stomach, for coughs and for the lungs. A syrup made from its fruits, especially in combination with tormentil, was good for chronic diarrhoea. It is also beneficial for the mucous membranes of the stomach and intestines. Even anaemic persons will find sloe syrup to be a good and natural remedy. So the fruits of blackthorn serve exclusively for curative purposes, while we enjoy the other stone fruits as wholesome and healing food.

Fruit Sprayed with Pesticides

As more instances of poisoning from eating fruit sprayed with pesticides come to our attention, we would do well to consider the different aspects of this dangerous practice.

Some people do not react immediately to poisons such as lead, arsenic and copper sulphate used in sprays, being less sensitive. Others are more sensitive and immediately show signs of poisoning upon eating sprayed fruit. Be it as it may, when buying fruit one should make sure it has not been sprayed. It is common to find blemishes or an occasional brown spot on fruit that has not been treated with insecticides, but the fruit is still edible and its goodness is not impaired, since these blemishes are harmless plant fungi.

If you are uncertain as to whether a fruit has been sprayed, caution commands that you peel it, which unfortunately also removes the phosphates and other valuable materials which lie immediately under the skin. It is better to do without these minerals, however valuable, than to risk poisoning. If the fruit trees are sprayed in winter, when they are bare, the fruit cannot suffer

508

since there is none; the only damage that can then be done is to the ground and the micro-organisms in it. The poison adhering to the bark will not find its way into the fruit later on.

It is hoped that the practice of spraying poisons, chemical pesticides, will eventually stop as there is the possibility of using harmless biological pesticides that will help increase the yield of crops without the risk of harming the consumer. However, such harmless products can only be discovered if an effort is made to find them, as is the case with natural remedies as opposed to chemical ones.

Experiments carried out with herbal sprays, containing extracts of horsetail (shave grass), yarrow and nasturtium have given very satisfactory results and trials are continuing. We also recommend spraying with tobacco extract because it is organic and much less hazardous than chemical sprays.

Rhubarb

I am often asked whether rhubarb is harmful as a food. There are some good things to be said about it, for instance that it is rich in vitamins, acids and various essential minerals. On the negative side, however, it must be said that rhubarb can be hard on the kidneys, especially when there is a tendency to kidney stones. One should always be very careful with rhubarb, as well as asparagus and Brussels sprouts, as all three of these are excessively acid-forming. Although they are beneficial if taken in small quantities, they can have an injurious effect on the kidneys if eaten in large amounts. Particular care should thus be exercised by anyone suffering from kidney stones or gravel, rheumatism and arthritis. For them it would be better to limit their intake of these foods or avoid them altogether.

Furthermore, it is important to choose the right kind of manure for rhubarb. If artificial fertiliser or unfermented liquid manure is used, the rhubarb can actually become poisonous. It is indeed lamentable that what is good for the farmer often turns out to be bad for the consumer. Still, we have to draw attention to these things. And then: 'let the buyer beware!'

Sugar

It is necessary to clarify certain questions connected with the various kinds of sugar, since many people are not sure of the difference between unrefined cane sugar and refined white sugar. In fact, it has been said that brown sugar (unrefined cane sugar) is treated with sulphur and is therefore no less detrimental to health than refined white sugar, which has been bleached and dyed for the purpose of preservation.

However, white sugar is dyed solely to enhance its whiteness, not to make it keep longer. This is done following the same principle as is applied in the manufacture of washing powder, to which is added 'blueing agents' to make the linen appear whiter than it actually is. Without this addition it would soon begin to look greyish. Sugar keeps indefinitely on its own and needs no preservative. If stored correctly, it will last a hundred years and still be sweet. It is 'blued' for eye-appeal and for no other reason.

Refined sugar, like refined flour, is a product of our civilisation, an unnatural 'food' and a contributory factor to ill health. We should keep away from anything that is detrimental to our health and reduces the nutritional value of our food. It is therefore obvious that denatured, refined foods are to be rejected. Unrefined cane sugar, on the other hand, contains various minerals, which are alkaline-forming and, at least, make some contribution to our health. Moreover, the allegation that it is treated with sulphur is untrue.

The best sugar is, and always will be, that found in nature, that is, in fruits, either fresh or dried. Raisins, sultanas, dates and figs are ideal sources of natural sugar. Since it does not need to be digested, it is the best and quickest source of energy. In fact, it is completely wrong to believe that protein foods are the only energy source. And why? Just think of a bull and its tremendous power, yet it does not eat any kind of protein food at all. Or think of a cow and the enormous quantity of fat it produces – all from the grass it eats!

If you wish to sweeten your morning dish of muesli, you do not need either sugar or honey. Currants or raisins will amply sweeten your breakfast dish; just put them through the mincer and add them to the rest. Honey and grape sugar are excellent, nutritious sweeteners. Condensed sugar cane juice, pear or peach syrup and similar forms of sugar, which have not been refined, can also be used with confidence.

The commercially prepared so-called grape sugar, glucose or dextrose, made from corn (maize) starch, does not belong in the category of natural sugars. The chemical formula of synthetic grape sugar happens to be the same as that of natural sugar made from grapes. The two have nothing else in common. In fact, the 'grape sugar' or dextrose that is sold over-the-counter in powder or tablet form is a misnomer. To be sure, it supplies calories, it gives energy, but it lacks the nutritive and curative properties of the genuine grape juice. After all, we are not so interested in the chemical formula of sugar, but in its effect on our health.

So what do we mean by 'grape sugar', as referred to in this book? We refer to the genuine sugar made from grapes, the condensed pure grape juice made from vine-ripened grapes. The manufactured grape sugar is artificial, but the genuine article can be described as nutritive grape sugar or grape concentrate. This syrup can also be made from raisins, sultanas and currants. It is by far the best sweetener available, in many ways equal to honey and in other respects even superior to it because some people cannot take honey, whereas practically everyone can tolerate real grape sugar.

Infants and children, patients with a feverish condition, and seriously ill adults suffering from metabolic disorders should use only grape sugar, rather than white sugar, to sweeten their drinks. It oxidises in the system without any waste and does not impose any additional burden on the body. Unlike white sugar, grape sugar is not a calcium robber. It should be part of the diet of every convalescent and those with weak hearts or frayed nerves because of its soothing quality. Sleeping drops, lemon balm herb tea or heart tonic sweetened with grape sugar in a little water and taken at night encourage restful sleep. Grape sugar has only one drawback: it is relatively expensive. But this is not at all astonishing in view of the cost of grapes nowadays.

Since reports continue to circulate that seek to discredit natural foods and justify the use of denatured, refined products, it is high time that we clarify the question of sugar once and for all, so that the consumer can be sure of what is genuine and wholesome, and what is misleading and false.

The goodness of fruit sugar is not in any doubt, but when you buy dried fruit take care to select only the produce that is not sulphurised, bleached or denatured in any other way. Nothing but natural, pure fruit guarantees the benefits we intend to derive from it in the first place.

The Value of Natural Unrefined Sugar

I shall never forget the Indian children we met in Central America. They would approach us slowly, smiling timidly, while chewing on a piece of sugar cane. This seemed to satisfy their sweet tooth and helped them to overcome their shyness. Practically all children like sugar, the peculiar carbohydrate that gives our taste buds the pleasant sensation of sweetness. The young Indians enjoy raw sugar cane and also the raw fresh juice that is then condensed over a fire, making what they call *pilosillo*. Most astonishing to me was the fact that although they ate a great deal of the sweet brown syrup their teeth were strong and beautiful. In fact, if they had no knife handy, I often saw them using their teeth like one.

JUSTIFIED WARNINGS

More than ever before, we read and hear about the dangers of eating too much sugar. Are these warnings justified? Why are we nowadays told that sugar and sweets are harmful, especially to our teeth and bones? Is the appalling condition of our children's teeth really the result of their eating too much sugar and sweet things? Again, is the assertion true that even unrefined cane sugar is not the healthy natural product it is made out to be?

Being good observers and knowing how to use practical experience, we can draw the following conclusions. We must look for the problem's solution in what our sweets consist of, what goes into their making. The Indian children probably indulge as much in sugar and sweet products as do our young ones, yet 90 per cent of our children have bad teeth in spite of good oral hygiene, using a toothbrush and toothpaste, while the Indians lack these modern implements and have good teeth. However, the sweet things the young Indians enjoy are not refined products, but still contain all their natural substances, a combination of minerals such as calcium, fluoride, magnesium, manganese, iron, silica and phosphorus. And that is the crux of the matter, because what our children eat is refined sugar without the minerals, which is bound to disturb the whole mineral metabolism and result in a mineral and vitamin deficiency. This serious state of affairs is made even worse by our eating other denatured products, for example white flour and white rice. The resulting deficiencies then lead to bad teeth and other damage to our health.

Alternatives to Refined Sugar

People who move to our regions from far away lands and exchange their natural foods for a diet of our refined foods will soon begin to experience dental problems. It is a fact that sweets and refined sugar can cause much more damage to our health than is commonly assumed. Yet there are other good sweeteners around, for example honey, grape sugar syrup made from grapes and dried fruits such as raisins, sultanas, currants, figs and dates. All these fruits contain easily assimilated natural sugar, but with an abundance of minerals.

So, when you prepare a dish of breakfast muesli, a gruel or porridge, think of including raisins; put them through the mincer and then add them to your dish as a sweetener. You may ask, 'Can I use crude sugar?' Sugar made from sugar beet is unsuitable for the table; it would not be a good sweetener for fruit muesli because it often makes it taste like soap. There is another drawback to unrefined beet sugar; it is treated with lime, a process that reduces its mineral content. Unrefined cane sugar, as we know it, is not equal to the *pilosillo* mentioned earlier. *Pilosillo* is simply condensed and crystallised sugar cane juice, whereas the kind we buy in Europe has already been through one refining process, again generally using lime, and is therefore no longer 100 per cent pure. However, it does contain some of the molasses and a total of about 2 per cent minerals, so that it is still more valuable than the white, completely refined, sugar.

Another very good natural sweetener or sugar is maple sugar, which the Indians of North America make from condensed maple syrup. This is very tasty and well worth trying. A further alternative is date sugar, which is discussed below.

If you want to remain healthy, watch what kind of sugar you eat. Parents should heed the advice given regarding sugar and sweets, because it is intended for the sake of their children's well-being. If you observe these guidelines your health will benefit because of eating natural food, and you will save a great deal of money on dentist's bills!

THE GOODNESS OF DATES

The visitor to Mesopotamia and the Persian Gulf is greeted by millions of date palms. Growing in unspoilt, mineral-rich soil, they bring forth thousands of tons of a wonderful fruit sugar year by year, the great benefits of which, however, rarely extend beyond these geographical borders. It is a joy to admire the Arab children's beautiful teeth, but the sight also fills the visitor with sadness. Why? On the one hand we are glad for the Arab children, but on the other hand we are sad because the teeth of our own children and youths, according to the reports of school dentists, are in a very poor state indeed.

When I visited the ruins and vicinity of ancient Babylon, an Arab boy climbed up a date palm, happily and with enviable ease, picked some ripe dates and threw them down to me. It gave him great satisfaction to see that his generosity was gratefully acknowledged, his beaming smile showing a row of healthy white teeth. His firm and strong muscles and his lithe body, which gives those sons of the desert the agility of a wild cat, impressed me greatly. Although these children of nature can be presumptuous and brash, they do leave an unforgettable impression.

While our children spoil their teeth with all sorts of sweets made from refined sugar, the children of those desert tribes have nothing but dates to satisfy their sweet tooth. It is not without good reason that dates are called the 'meat' of the desert Arabs. Their children eat a large amount of date sugar but still have healthy teeth, just like those of the Indian children who satisfy their desire for sweet things by eating green sugar cane or *pilosillo*, the condensed sugar cane juice.

What a pity that we are not similarly inclined and satisfied with simple natural things! If we could avoid the use of refined sugar, which contributes to tooth decay and many other degenerative conditions, our children's teeth would be much better. What is more, refined sugar is now about three times dearer than it was just a few years ago. So there are many reasons why we should try to eliminate it from our diet as much as possible, substituting fruit sugar instead.

Date sugar and grape sugar, made from raisins and currants, are so valuable that everyone who is interested in his or her family's health should make the effort to sweeten all fruit dishes with it. This would provide the entire family with valuable carbohydrates and the vital minerals and vitamins needed to prevent sickness.

In view of my observations I am sure I was right to give consideration to the problem of sugar while sitting in the shade of some Mesopotamian date palms. There and then I made up my mind to experiment with the valuable natural sugar of dates and come up with a product that pleases the taste buds and is also a healthy food. Indeed, every food item, and especially sweets, should be such that they cannot spoil our children's teeth in the future. We want their teeth to be just as healthy as those of the Arab children who obtain their sugar from Mesopotamia's date palms.

The Value of Canned and Bottled Fruit

Some time ago I received a letter with the following query: 'The other day I read in a book on diet reform that preserved fruits and those bottled hot have no nutritional value. I have been wondering about this, because during the past year I have bottled a quantity of fruit, thinking it would have greater food value than fruit commercially canned.'

I would like to answer this enquiry in print because it will be of interest to everyone. It is quite true that in preserving fruits and vegetables by the heat process many of the vitamins are destroyed. However, the statement about preserved fruits having no nutritional value is absolutely untrue. The actual nutrients, such as carbohydrates, sugar, starch and minerals, remain unchanged and for this reason preserved fruits and vegetables do have considerable food value, assuming that a natural process is used to preserve them.

It is quite a different story with commercially canned fruits and vegetables. The bleaching, blanching and chemical additives definitely affect the nutritional value. If I speak out against canned foods, it is because it so often happens that, just for the sake of convenience, factory-preserved foods are used when the meal could, with a little extra effort, consist of at least some fresh fruit or vegetables. Canned foods are served all too often in hospitals and sanatoriums. If sick people are to get well, they must have health-giving nourishment, which can be obtained at its maximum value only from fresh vegetables and fresh fruit. For this reason one should eat fresh foods as much as possible – fresh berries, fruit and vegetables – when they are in season. Eat your vegetables raw in salads and fruit in muesli or fruit salad. Any surplus that cannot be used this way should be preserved and bottled immediately, so that provision is made for the winter.

You can guarantee healthy nutrition if you always supplement a dish of preserved vegetables or fruit with some fresh produce. Not everything you eat need have a high vitamin content; it suffices when part of the meal meets this criterion. The important thing is to make sure that you do not leave out anything essential when planning your menu. Let us suppose that, for lunch in winter, you have yogurt, which contains vitamins, and some fresh carrot or beet salad. In addition you may have some of your preserved vegetables, as well as potatoes or natural brown rice. The body will then obtain its vitamins from the fresh vegetables, and other nutrients from the preserved or bottled food. All in all, you will be adequately and correctly fed.

Preserve and bottle all surplus from your garden produce, but do not make the mistake of depriving the children of fresh fruits and berries just because you want to keep them. I remember as a child having to watch the blackcurrants and raspberries I longed

515

to eat being made into jam. Parents, in their eagerness to preserve them, forget about the value of fresh fruit.

Our Daily Bread

Bread has always played an important part in our nutrition. It is still on our table today and every day as a staple food. The age-old request 'Give us this day our daily bread' illustrates to what extent we depend upon it. We may have an abundance of other foods, but bread remains the foundation of our diet. How much we disliked having it rationed during the war years. Things have changed since then, although the need for good and wholesome bread is as great as ever.

Nutritious Bread

It has always pleased me when, here and there on my travels, I have been served with bread as it was once made in my own country – from the whole grain. I found that the North American Indian women prepared their bread from grain that they had ground themselves with a stone mill. Arabs, Bedouins and other African people still keep up the custom of making their bread from wholegrain cereals. Some use wheat, some rye, others barley and each of these breads tastes good and provides the body with all the goodness of the whole grain, because whole cereals contain most of the elements needed to build up the organism and maintain it in a healthy condition. They abound in minerals, enzymes, vitamins and other essential factors.

The Greek mountain peasants also use good wholewheat bread as the foundation of their diet. Wherever you find good bread, the health and resistance of the people consuming it is better than among those living on white bread. Where white bread and rolls are the common fare, I have always found more bad health. True, white bread may not be the only reason for this, but it does share the blame for lack of good health.

One cannot imagine Ruth, a woman of biblical fame, having gleaned the valuable ears of grain from Boaz' field, only to turn it into refined flour. The Book of Books reports that in ancient times the whole grain, barley or wheat, was ground in a stone mill, then honey was added to it and it was made into cakes.

The Correct Baking Process

We know from the history of ancient Rome that their legionaries were issued a certain quantity of wheat every day. Wheat grain can be stored almost indefinitely without losing any of its value, but this is not the case with flour. As soon as the external sheath has been broken and the grain has been milled, the oxygen in the air begins to take effect, and the longer the flour is kept, the more it will lose of its value. The enzymes are probably the first to suffer from such exposure. These are active elements in the grain, for example diastase, which comes to life during the process of germination and changes the starch of the grain into maltose, then dextrose.

An interesting observation will illustrate this. Make some dough from freshly ground flour and knead it well with your hands. You will notice that the hands become quite red as hyperaemia is produced. It is the active enzymes that are responsible for this phenomenon and these are found especially in the bran and the germ. If you make dough from the same flour after it has been stored for 5–6 weeks, this reaction will no longer occur to the same extent, if at all, because the enzymes will have decreased in effectiveness or died off during the long period of storage. That is why it is better to use a stone mill for grinding – as our forefathers did and certain primitive peoples still do – then prepare and bake the bread immediately. Thus the full value of the enzymes is preserved and the bread will be more nourishing, for it contains the healthy substances of the wholegrain cereal.

Wholewheat or any other wholemeal bread should be prepared in the way just described, and we should make it a point to make or buy bread which is prepared and baked according to this natural method. When we consider the great demands placed on our system today, it is only sensible that we should prefer bread that retains its full nutritional value and reject the less valuable.

The Milling Process

The manner in which bread cereals are ground is quite important. Some time ago I visited an old miller, who showed me an old-fashioned stone mill, now unused, beside the beautiful new machinery that replaced it. Without any prompting on my part, the miller began to tell me that his old mill had produced excellent flour, while the other two modern machines seemed to take all the goodness out of it. At first I thought this was rather exaggerated, but in the light of subsequent observations I was forced to agree with him.

The ancient Romans, who knew something about metallurgy, were certainly in a position to make metal rollers or discs, if they had not been convinced that the use of stone was more appropriate for milling grain. Every metal mill, if it creates too much friction heat, does something detrimental to the flour which, ultimately, is reflected in its taste and quality.

Today it is known that copper destroys most of the vitamin C content of food that is brought into contact with this metal. Similar effects take place with other metals too. Thus it is possible that an iron or steel mill could affect the taste or composition, or both, of the flour, even though this has not yet been proved conclusively.

The Question of Bread – a Solution

All these deliberations urged me to find a solution to the bread question that would comply with all the requirements I have mentioned. Many years ago I carried out a series of experiments with the help of a master baker. I decided to use not only wheat, but also rye, because of its high fluoride content. As a rule, the bread we eat is mainly made from wheat, but rye is particularly important for the teeth and bones. In areas where much rye bread is eaten, good teeth and excellent bone structure stand out as a characteristic among the people. There is no doubt that rye bread and rye cripsbread lay a healthy foundation for this.

On the other hand, wherever white bread is now consumed, deficiencies have developed to such an extent that dental caries and other problems affecting the teeth and bone structure are very much in evidence, sometimes as early as in the first generation after the changeover.

On account of this definite link between white bread consumption and poor dental health, I decided to bring out a natural bread, called 'Risopan'. It is, in content, comparable to the bread eaten by primitive peoples, being made of whole rye, wheat, barley, rice bran and rice germ for the sake of their richness in vital minerals. Unfortunately, for the most part, we are used to eating refined white rice instead of the whole brown rice and it is advantageous to compensate for the deficiency somewhat by means of bread that contains all its nutritive substances. 'Risopan' is prepared in accordance with the principles I have just outlined. The grain is ground in a stone mill and the flour is immediately made into a dough and baked. It keeps very well and is most suitable for taking on long journeys. The new Vogel wholegrain flake bread is also made in a similar way to 'Risopan'.

It would be a good thing if other wholegrain or wholewheat bread were always made according to the same natural method. If you eat such bread year in and year out, it is reasonable to assume that your body will benefit greatly from it. Remember that nature is not guided by our palates, moods and appetites, but works according to its eternal laws. If we ignore or reject nature's dictates, we will have to suffer the eventual consequences, or at least our children will. So make sure to serve nothing but good and wholesome bread. It alone is the foundation of natural and healthy nutrition.

Whole Wheat and Other Cereals

However intensively one may campaign against the use of white flour and other refined foods, there is still far too little attention given to the fact that cereal deprived of its germ and bran is no longer a health food. Vitamins, minerals, highly valuable oils and other substances are no longer present in refined flour. As a result, it is not the least bit surprising that the general standard of nutrition is decreasing despite the abundance of other varieties of food. Even though many may not want to see that the health and physical strength of the people are drastically reduced when white flour, white sugar and other refined products are the common fare, the facts cannot be denied. Modern nutritionists and researchers tell us clearly that minerals and vitamins are essential to good health, yet what do we do? Most of us simply ignore such clearcut statements based on scientific research.

Our grandparents could certainly tell us a thing or two about the more natural way of life. Their diet, simple though it was, did not produce the deficiencies of today, because it consisted of wholefoods, lacking none of the vital elements. In the country bread was baked in the home and this good, old-fashioned cereal bread formed the basis of their daily diet. We really should abandon the lamentable custom of refining and canning food, a custom of our civilisation that has been nothing but detrimental to our health, and return to the simple, natural ways of our forebears.

You, the individual, can do something about this for yourself. Eat whole wheat, which is no doubt one of the best foods available, containing just the right amount and combination of elements, and should be used in its entirety. You will find it very tasty and wholesome. Soak the grains, then steam them with a little butter or oil and onions, and season with one of the many culinary herbs. If you prefer not to use onions, they may be omitted. The dish can also be prepared 'au gratin' in the oven, or you can add soaked wheat kernels to soups, stews, casseroles, etc. Wheat prepared in

519

the same way as a risotto makes a delicious 'wheatotto'. Why not use whole wheat in every form possible? If you like, you can even sweeten it with almonds, raisins or currants.

Whole rye and barley can be used in the same way, although they are not quite as palatable as wheat. Seasoned with fine culinary herbs, the soaked grains can be put through the mincer and made into rissoles. There are many possible methods of preparation and the resourceful cook will never be at a loss to find and make many cereal dishes that are tasty and healthy. A dish made with whole wheat is an energy food for growing children and ravenous youths, as well as for those who do heavy work. Add vegetables and fresh salad and you have a combination of foods that provides the basis for first-class nutrition. Since it is amazing what strange combinations of food are sometimes dreamed up, I would like to stress that you should never eat a salad or vegetables together with a sweet wholegrain dish; it is better to combine sweet things with stewed fruit or grated raw apple muesli and cream. For a good effect, grate some fresh fruit and mix it in with the *compote*. A cup of rose hip tea also goes well with a sweet wholegrain dish.

Germinated Cereals – an Inexpensive Tonic

It is quite common to spend good money on expensive tonics, so you will be pleased to learn that there is something much cheaper within your reach. I am referring to germinated cereals, whether it be wheat, rye or barley. These cereals offer us what many an over-the-counter potion promises but does not provide.

So how can we obtain germinated wheat? Well, all that is necessary to make grains sprout is moisture and warmth. Place a wet cloth on a plate, sprinkle it with grains and put it in a cupboard or similar warm place. Be sure to keep the cloth damp or germination will be retarded or even stopped altogether. When the sprouts have grown to a length of about 2–5 mm (up to about ¼ inch), put the grains through a mincer and use as a foundation for muesli. Or eat the mince just as it is, but remember to chew it thoroughly and insalivate well.

As soon as germination takes place, the enzyme diastase becomes active and transforms the polysaccharide starch into disaccharide sugar, or malt, which is easier to digest than starch. This process, by the way, is used to turn barley into malt. If you chew the germinated grain you will notice its sweet taste. This fresh 'malt' is rich in enzymes, especially diastase, and this is what makes it such a wonderful tonic food. It can be eaten together with linseed as is done in Sweden, where the dish is called *kruska*. It aids the digestion of other starchy foods and is recommended for those who have poor assimilation and have trouble gaining weight. It is a simple, inexpensive and excellent tonic food and is also good for the blood. If, at the same time, you eat plenty of raw carrots or drink fresh carrot juice, perhaps going on a grape diet as well, you will be able to build up your strength without having to pay a fortune. Together with plenty of grapes or fresh grape juice, this diet is recommended for people with heart trouble. Anyone suffering from constipation should avoid the skin and pips of the grapes. The advice also holds true for those who tend to suffer from fermentation and flatulence, since not eating the skin and pips prevents these intestinal problems.

Good results with germinated wheat encouraged Dr Bircher-Benner to recommend it to his patients too.

Wheat Germ

Wheat germ – those tiny yellow flakes – is far too little valued and used. If people only realised how wonderfully nourishing and curative these flakes are they would serve them every day in one way or the other, including in their breakfast muesli. Girls and young women in particular would eat more wheat germ if they appreciated what marvellous properties it has to offer.

Wheat germ contains a first-class protein and much oil. More important, however, are the phosphates in it, and we should all know the vital role phosphates and their combinations play in keeping our nervous system healthy. Still more important than phosphates is the high content of vitamin E in wheat germ. Let me briefly remind you of what vitamin E means to us.

It is not for nothing that vitamin E is also called the fertility vitamin, since it plays a considerable part in the development and function of the reproductive organs. But the ovaries and testicles are more than just reproductive organs, they actually discharge their secretions into the bloodstream and therefore belong to the category of organs known as the endocrine glands. Vitamin E is of great importance for the correct functioning of these glands and thus for the entire metabolism.

Provided there is no physical disability, vitamin E often acts as an aid to conception when a woman eats foods rich in this vitamin. Due to its high content of vitamin E, wheat germ is the single most indicated item for this therapy. Every 100 g (4 oz) of wheat germ contain as much as 30 mg of pure vitamin E.

Wheat germ is one of the best remedies that can be recommended to help overcome a tendency to premature birth. In fact, if pregnant women were to eat sufficient wheat germ or take wheat germ oil capsules, the painful experience of miscarriage could often be prevented.

Brucellosis (undulant fever, Bang's disease) has been successfully treated with vitamin E preparations and there is no better specific remedy than wheat germ and wheat germ oil for this purpose. For years, farmers have observed that feeding their cattle with good bran, which contains wheat germ, reduces the incidence of brucellosis and abortion. The results of experiments in which cattle suffering from brucellosis were fed with wheat germ have confirmed that sufficient quantities of vitamin E in time enable the body to build up resistance to the germs which cause this disease.

Girls and women who become obese because of ovarian insufficiency should take *herbal sitz baths* and eat plenty of wheat germ, as this will stimulate the ovaries, increase the metabolic rate of the body and so dispose of undesirable fat. In addition, they should take the seaweed preparation *Kelpasan* for even faster results.

Lack of vigour and stamina, tiredness because of overwork and neurasthenic conditions call for foods rich in vitamin E, which have a better effect than all expensive medicines if taken over a period of time. Anyone suffering from impotence should not give up hope, but take a long-term course of wheat germ or wheat germ oil capsules and, at the same time, *Kuhne treatments* (see pages 436–8), which will certainly help, if not cure the problem completely. In addition to wheat germ, other sources of vitamin E are *lettuce, watercress* and *soybeans.* So make sure to eat enough of these natural products if you suffer from any of the above-mentioned conditions. Moreover, it is interesting to note that experiments on vitamin E have shown that no side effects have resulted if too much of the vitamin is taken.

Thus there are many reasons why we should ensure that our families eat wheat germ regularly. Among other things, it will ensure that our children's most important glands will develop properly. Wheat germ has a delicious taste, not only when sprinkled over muesli and in soups, but also on bread and honey – a much healthier snack than sugary buns from the baker's.

Wheat germ as a concentrated food is an absolute necessity in our modern world, where so much low-value, denatured food is eaten, causing an increasing prevalence of deficiency diseases. People living in areas relatively untouched by modern development and those of us who live on natural wholefoods, generally speaking may not need to take concentrated food such as wheat germ on a regular basis. If you make it a habit to eat whole grains and other wholefoods, you will obtain the essential substances in the right proportion. In wheat germ they are in a concentrated form.

Wheat Germ and Bran

If we slice a wheat grain lengthways we will find that the white inside is mainly made up of starch. White flour comes from this part. The yellowish germ is located at one end of the kernel. Years ago the wheat germ was not fully used because no one knew about its great value as a source of vitamin E. The outer protective cover over the starchy part is the bran, consisting of a tough sheath which, being pure cellulose, is indigestible. This roughage should not be eaten if one suffers from gastritis and stomach ulcers, for it is so tough and sharp-edged that it would actually irritate and inflame an already damaged stomach lining. In the case of ulcers it may even trigger pain and light bleeding.

A number of valuable minerals are found in the layers between the starch and the outer cellulose sheath. These layers contain vitamins of the B complex, gluten and amino acids essential for the building up of body protein. It is exactly these valuable and important parts of the wheat kernel that are usually fed to cattle, the bran together with its roughage or cellulose and germ. It is quite an achievement that modern milling machines are able to separate the valuable layers without including the indigestible cellulose, so that we can actually obtain the important elements of the grain and include them in our diet. This product is sold as 'wheat germ and bran.'

Buckwheat (*Fagopyrum esculentum*)

If you travelled down to Pusciavo during the war you could have seen in the districts adjoining the Italian border many fields sown with buckwheat, a crop which is almost unknown to this day in other areas. Our fellow citizens in the south were smarter than we in the north when it came to looking after themselves. There was a government requisition order on wheat flour, but buckwheat, a wild cereal, was exempt. So the farmers started to grow buckwheat, which was known to be highly nutritious and wholesome.

Buckwheat is satisfied even with poor and sandy soil and has a short growing period. In fact, the crop matures within three months and for this reason it is cultivated in northern climates where the seasons are short, as in Siberia. The plant attains a height of half a metre (1½–2 feet) and has reddish white flowers which provide a good supply of nectar for the bees. American buckwheat honey is known far and wide.

The French name for buckwheat, *blé sarrasin*, seems to indicate that buckwheat must have been brought to France from the south by the Saracens, whereas the Russian name, *gretsikha, grikki* suggests that the Greeks probably introduced this valuable food into their neighbouring lands. In many parts of Russia it is a national dish and the people prepare a most delicious oven-baked buckwheat.

Whole buckwheat can be cooked in the same manner as rice, and buckwheat groats are excellent in soup and for rissoles. The flour makes what is called a 'short' pastry and is good for mixing with wheat flour. The resulting pastry is better than that made with wheat flour and a high proportion of butter.

German biologists have discovered that buckwheat reduces high blood pressure, a finding that has since been confirmed by American scientists. An extract of buckwheat is thus claimed to combat high blood pressure and arteriosclerosis (hardening of the arteries). Unpolished brown rice has the same attributes as buckwheat in this respect. It would be to the advantage of older people if they were to change their menus slightly, to include more natural brown rice and buckwheat, but fewer eggs, cheese and pulses (legumes), for these two cereals have a rejuvenating effect on the blood vessels, especially the arteries. The intake of protein and salt should also be reduced to a minimum as one advances in age or if one suffers from high blood pressure.

Buckwheat Dishes

Whole buckwheat: Precook some buckwheat in a little water or vegetable stock. Make a sauce from two teaspoons of wholegrain (wholemeal) flour, finely chopped herbs and unseasoned tomato purée and mix with the buckwheat. Add some stewed onion and a little oil, and cook until the grains are soft but still whole.

Cold buckwheat: Prepare some buckwheat as above, pour it into a mould and leave to cool. When cold, remove from the mould and garnish with parsley and tomatoes. Serve with a green salad.

Fried buckwheat: Prepare a buckwheat gruel, then add some finely chopped onions, garlic and a little marjoram. Form into small shapes and fry in oil on both sides until golden brown.

What You Should Know about Potatoes

What else is there to know about potatoes other than that they are tasty? That is about the extent of most people's knowledge about the peculiar solanaceous plant we call potato and botanists call *Solanum tuberosum*. Because potatoes belong to the same family as the deadly nightshade, our forefathers had some rather unfortunate experiences with them when they were first brought to Europe. No one knew this strange plant native to Peru's highlands.

If ever you get the chance to visit the mountainous areas of that country you will be surprised to see how many varieties of potato actually grow there, many not even known to us. In the Altiplano, from Cuzco as far as Puno on Lake Titicaca especially, the Indians cultivate some beautiful vegetables.

It was as late as the sixteenth century when Spanish sailors and Sir Francis Drake first brought potatoes to Europe, with the intention of cultivating them as a food on the European continent. They gave them to their friends but did not explain anything about the new plant. Why not? Well, it often happens, does it not, that someone knows something but does not tell it to another person simply because he thinks that he will be aware of it already. That is exactly what happened with the potato. No one who planted the tubers seemed to realise that the unknown plant was a member of the deadly nightshade family and had poisonous properties. Neither could anyone imagine that it was the tubers themselves that served for food and not the round green berries growing on the plant. In fact, no one took any notice of the actual potatoes. Of course, the result of eating the berries brought only trouble, because anyone who tried the new vegetable from overseas soon suffered from diarrhoea and vomiting.

The story goes that, very upset and disappointed, some of those participating in one of the potato meals went and uprooted the plants, tops and all, and flung them onto a bonfire. Involuntarily, they had also pulled out the potatoes attached to the roots. Meanwhile, these roasted nicely in the fire and one or two rolled out of the embers. In anger, someone stamped on them, but they smelled so appetising that the person picked one up. A little hesitant, he tried it and to his surprise it tasted as delicious as it smelled. So that was it! What they were to eat were not the green berries on the plant but the tubers that grew under the ground! The mystery was solved and Europe had gained a new food, one that is not only a source of protein, starch and vitamin C, but also a remedy.

Potatoes as a Remedy

Raw potato juice has proved its worth in the treatment of arthritis and it is also a fine remedy for stomach ulcers. Patients are advised to drink the juice of a medium-sized potato (about one-third of a glass) before breakfast on an empty stomach. The ulcers usually disappear within 3–6 weeks. If a little fresh *carrot juice* is added to the potato juice the taste will be improved, making it easier to take. If the patient is unable to prepare his own juice because of lack of time, he can take the lacto-fermented juice sold in health food stores.

Raw potato juice, together with *centaury*, is a splendid help in neutralising excess acid in the stomach, which is generally the cause of heartburn. The simplest way to do this is to add fresh centaury drops to the potato juice. It has not yet been discovered whether the remedial effect is attributable to the solanin content (about 0.002 per cent) or to the alkaline mineral salts.

An interesting letter informed us recently that *Solanosan*, together with *Petasites*, helped a stomach and liver patient to find relief from pain, providing restful sleep, an improved appetite and weight gain. Solanosan complex is made from the potato plant, which can have a poisonous effect, but the remedy is in homoeopathic potency and therefore efficacious in treating the indicated illnesses. Large amounts of Solanin, however, can cause poisoning and even endanger one's life.

BEWARE!

The green potato leaves contain approximately 0.06 per cent solanin, the flowers 0.6 per cent and the fruits, which look like green berries, about 1 per cent. The white eyes or sprouts on the potatoes themselves are very dangerous, the green ones even worse. As soon as they begin to appear, in winter or spring, cut them out carefully. They are especially bad for the eyes. When the tubers grow a little above the soil and turn green, make sure to cut the green part off since it is poisonous. These rules are simple and can be followed without any difficulty. However, this need for care does not mean that a plant which is considered dangerous cannot also be most useful, even contain food and remedial properties – as the potato clearly proves.

Oils and Fats

Their Role in Degenerative Diseases

In the search for contributory causes of gout, arthritis, cancer, multiple sclerosis, liver trouble and other serious diseases, investigators always discover something new after years of research. Almost all experts agree that hereditary factors play an important part in the predisposition to certain diseases. Mental and physical strain, overwork, constant hurry, irritations, fears and worries cannot be ignored as contributory causes, or they may even trigger the diseases. Poisons finding their way into the system through drugs and unnatural foodstuffs, preservatives and additives, must be recognised as detrimental to health. Modern refined and nutrient-deficient foodstuffs also share considerably in the blame and invariably undermine our health. We are thinking especially of canned foods that are prepared in such a way that they retain none of their original nutritional value. Then there is a particular substance that has so far received little attention, but the absence of which may lead to degenerative diseases. I am referring to the polyunsaturated fatty acids that are contained in natural oils and fats but are destroyed by heating, refining, hardening and other factory processes. A lack of these acids gives rise to disturbances in the metabolism of the cells, and it is obvious that this must have a bearing upon other pathological processes as well. A few years ago, little was known about the unsaturated fatty acids and few, if any, references were made to the importance of natural oils and fats in a balanced diet. Only recently has it become possible to see what part these substances play in degenerative diseases or their prevention.

The Nature and Properties of Oils and Fats

Oils and fats do not have a highly complicated chemical formula: on the contrary, they consist of the common elements carbon, hydrogen and oxygen. All fats and oils used for food contain one or more of the three types of fatty acids, the saturated, the unsaturated and the polyunsaturated. If we consume an excess of saturated fatty acids, as found in refined fats and oils, too much energy is required to digest them and for this reason we feel tired and sleepy after a meal.

The saturated fatty acids are chemical compounds that are exceedingly poor in oxygen and their consumption would require us to exercise and breathe deeply – something we feel no inclination to do after eating such foods. These heavy fats, are mainly of animal origin and have a high melting point, while the unsaturated oils occur chiefly in seeds and have a low melting point. Vegetable oils are richer in unsaturated, even highly unsaturated fatty acids. For this reason natural, unrefined oils are better for you than others. Oils with a low melting point are hardened or hydrogenised because transporting and stocking them in bottles is more difficult and costly. So the oil industries prefer the method of hardening because firm slabs of fat can be more easily packed and transported than liquids.

However, the hardening process has a detrimental influence on the quality of the product since metallic compounds can remain in the fats, even if only in homoeopathic dilution. Furthermore, the unsaturated fatty acids are transformed in the process into high-melting stearic acids, which do not have the same health value. If you want to remain healthy, avoid the hardened fats, even though they may be easy to use and store.

Why, then, do the unsaturated fatty acids have the above-mentioned advantages, whereas the hardened fats have lost them? The answer is quite a simple one. They are not saturated and therefore able to become saturated. That is, the unsaturated fatty acids are still able to combine with other elements. Figuratively speaking, they are still single, unmarried, and therefore ready and willing to enter a relationship. They will combine with the minerals, proteins and oxygen in the body and in this way encourage normal cell metabolism and oxidation. If these functions are interfered with over a period of years, even decades, the cells degenerate and disease will inevitably manifest itself. Cell growth may become abnormal and malignant, cancerous. The phospholipoids may degenerate and this can lead to thrombosis. Where there is a lack of polyunsaturated fatty acids and in their place an excess of saturated ones, the cholesterol in the blood will combine with the fats and deposit itself on the walls of the blood vessels, giving rise to hardening of the arteries (arteriosclerosis), high blood pressure and the danger of apoplexy or a stroke.

Considering all these factors, it will be seen how vital it is to change over to unrefined fats and oils, such as those made from sunflower and safflower seed, olives, poppy seed and linseed. Also, fresh tree seed products, or nuts, are suitable for meeting our vital requirement of unsaturated and polyunsaturated fatty acids. A first-class source of highly unsaturated fatty acids are sesame seeds, which contain up to 43 per cent of these oils, in addition to interesting combinations of minerals and proteins, making these seeds a valuable food item indeed. Sesame seeds and products made from them serve millions of people in the Near East as a daily health food. So it would be quite appropriate to include them in our diet. It would help to rectify a deficiency in our unnatural diet that has been permitted for much too long.

Evaluating Fats and Oils Today

When an Arab friend and I walked through the olive groves in Upper Galilee, taking pictures of gnarled trees that might have been several hundred years old, I began to realise why olive oil was considered so important even as long ago as in biblical times. The South Sea islander looks at his coconut palms with the same reverence, seeing that they provide him with clothing and food. To the Russian peasant in the Caucasus his sunflowers are equally valuable, providing him with necessary oil. When he eats the seeds, spitting out the husks, he knows that this food will give him strength and tenacity. The Egyptian peasant feels the same way when he harvests sesame in fields irrigated by water from the Nile.

A TOPICAL QUESTION

Which of all the oils and fats provided by nature is the best for our consumption? This question is a difficult one to answer. To start with, the criteria for judging or evaluating an oil or fat must be clear in our mind.

Today, oils and fats are primarily rated according to their content of unsaturated fatty acids. It has been found that these are necessary to guarantee the normal growth of many body cells and also to keep them healthy. Furthermore, we know that premature aging of the vascular walls, above all, the arteries, can be caused by a lack of unsaturated fatty acids. Even a cancerous degeneration of the cells has been attributed to this deficiency. Unsaturated fatty acids are therefore a vital factor, and we cannot remain healthy without them.

But it has not yet been proved that an oil or fat should be judged only by the amount of unsaturated fatty acids in it. It almost goes without saying that when a vital substance is discovered, it is at first highly overrated, such as once was the case with vitamins and the great fuss that was made over them. While this fanfare was going on, it was all but forgotten that minerals, the nutritive salts, are just as vital as vitamins. For example, olive oil has only a modest content of unsaturated fatty acids and therefore tends to be unjustly downgraded. In contrast are the interesting findings of one scientist, who observed that the composition of the fat molecules of olive oil compare the closest to those found in mother's milk. Hence it could be assumed that olive oil is probably the most acceptable kind for human consumption, because the body will find it the easiest to process for assimilation. Whether this researcher's view is right or wrong, his findings make us sit up, listen and think. It should also prevent us in the future from being too quick and one-sided in judging a natural product. The benefits of a single constituent, in this case the value of unsaturated fatty acids, should never lead us to ignore the others – which may prove equally important in the end.

REASONABLE EVALUATION CRITERIA

The Creator made all natural products with a rich and varied content. All are extremely valuable in their original composition. But man has often overlooked this wisdom and learned little or nothing from it. In this connection I remember one of Professor Kollath's expressions: 'Let nature be natural.'

However, it has been quite a while since nature's produce was left simple and natural; instead it has been violated by refining, denaturing, devaluing, colouring and flavouring, often with chemical additives. While enumerating these violations, we cannot help thinking of Kurt Lenzer who speaks in his writings about 'poison in the food'.

REFINING AND SOLIDIFYING

Oils and fats have not escaped being tampered with either. By being refined and solidified, and by having emulsifiers added, they have received a bad name, and rightly so. Not only polyunsaturated fatty acids, but the whole structure of natural products with all their known and still undiscovered qualities, has been thrown off balance. Every oil or fat, left as nature made it, would provide us with what we need to meet our nutritional requirements. It is only when we interfere by introducing chemical and technical methods in the manufacturing process that damage is done and loss of value ensues. More often than not these interferences cause health problems. Of course, oils have been refined, and their taste improved, for many years, but simpler methods were used in the past. Oil was refined by means of wood ashes, because their alkaline substances removed some of the excess acid in the oil, thereby improving its taste. A further advantage of the old methods was that large quantities of oil were not stored, but a fresh supply was pressed from time to time. Oil-bearing fruits keep longer than the oil once extracted.

It is especially harmful when fats are hardened by electrolysis, as metal salts are used in the process. Although this method destroys much of the goodness in the natural product, this is not the only bad result. The traces of metal salts remaining in the oil can cause further damage to health by acting like poisons in homoeopathic potencies. Scientific research, as well as information disseminated by groups promoting a more natural way of life, have accomplished a great deal of good by encouraging greater awareness of these problems in recent years.

FIRST THE SMALL, NOW THE LARGE MANUFACTURERS BECOME
MORE NATURE-ORIENTED

Forty years go there were not even a dozen health food stores in Switzerland selling natural, unadulterated foods and only very few manufacturers produced such items. It was around that time that Mr Klaesi founded the company 'Nuxo-Werk'; besides this company I knew of only Messrs Phag in Gland who made an effort to market unhardened natural fats.

Subsequent research and an ongoing campaign of enlightenment have resulted in even larger manufacturers producing unhardened, naturally pure oils and fats, and it is most gratifying to see that substantial progress has been made in the field of fats. In all these necessary innovations, health food stores must continue with their pioneering work, so that in the future they will become even more popular as specialists. However, providing healthy natural and pure food cannot be left just to the health food stores; everyone has a right to be able to obtain such food from his local shops. It is the duty of large companies and manufacturers to rectify the neglect so far shown in this respect, because commercial interests have taken precedence over those of health for too long. However, since oil and fat manufacturers are clearly beginning to see the light, it can be assumed that other food industries will soon wake up too. As far as the chemical industry is concerned, it should stay where it belongs and not get mixed up with the food business! The growing tendency of people to suffer from liver disorders and cancer should suffice as a warning signal to encourage us to remove at least some of the causes that are closely connected with nutrition.

A sensible solution to the fat problem is at the same time an important solution in the fight against the diseases I have mentioned. This is a clearly proven fact. With the exception of fresh butter, the sale of animal fats has rightly fallen to a minimum; this can no doubt be attributed to the consumer wisely beginning to take his health into consideration. As far back as 3,500 years ago, Moses demanded that all animal fat be burned sacrificially. Without doubt this law would have benefited the health of the entire nation. I find it gratifying that the tendency these days is to make vegetable oils and fats in their natural form available to many more people, permitting them to meet their dietary requirements with wholesome products. Nevertheless, our total fat consumption is still too high, and too much fat is bad for us. Although the increase in serious diseases is certainly regrettable, we do want to discover the various causes and possibly combat anything that contributes to their development. It is a fact that fats contribute to this problem. Thus there is need for a change in this respect, a change that can only be to our benefit.

The Importance of Oil Seeds and Fruits

It surprised me to find that among many primitive peoples, seeds or fruits from which oil is produced appear to play an important part in their diet. Not only do they use the oil, but also the whole fruit, which is crushed or cut up and added to another dish. People who live close to nature, untouched by civilisation and its corrupting habits and customs, usually have good health, which most definitely has something to do with their natural diet. Science is slowly being forced to admit that natural wholefoods, among which we can certainly count the oil-bearing seeds or fruits, are of great value and importance to our health.

The Whole Seed

Throughout my many decades of practical experience I have always noticed that it is far more beneficial to utilise food in its entirety, as a wholefood, if at all possible. We should use not just the oil extracted from the seeds, but we should also consume the residual matter, the oil cake, adding it to our food. If the liver is sensitive and cannot tolerate certain oils, especially those that have been refined, it will usually accept the unrefined ones. It is even more beneficial for the liver if the whole oil seed or fruit is eaten. This observation has been confirmed in many cases and will no doubt become a universally accepted fact in the near future following its endorsement by scientific research. It is obvious that, as far as modern nutrition is concerned, new ways should be found and followed in the interests of everybody's health.

Meanwhile, we can at least take advantage of our present knowledge and make a dish of oil seeds and honey. In doing so we will prevent oxidation and the deterioration of the nutritional value of the oil seeds. Creamed into a spread, poppy seeds, freshly ground sunflower seeds or any other oil seed and honey, is about the healthiest and most strengthening food that exists. Furthermore, it is a splendid food and remedy for those who suffer from liver problems.

Linseed

First, let us consider linseed, the seed of the flax. People who are used to eating linseed regularly have no problems with their livers. Indeed, recent experiments have confirmed that linseed is important for good liver function.

Before eating linseed, grind it with a small mill or mincer. If you buy it already ground, make sure that it is fresh because after four or five days ground linseed begins to go rancid. The reason for this change is the effect of oxygen on the ground seeds and, after just a few days, although their goodness is barely reduced, the unpleasant taste is most off-putting. Thus, it is better to buy the seeds to grind yourself and use them right away. Take care to select good linseed, rich in active substances and highly unsaturated fatty acids. A small mill or a blender can be used to grind; set on the lowest speed for the best results. There are various ways of using linseed, for example, mixed with honey or curd cheese and herbs, all nourishing and delicious. These seeds can be called a strengthening food, a tonic, and once you have become used to their taste you will not want to do without them.

Sunflower Seeds

It is regrettable that these oil-bearing seeds receive so little attention as food for human consumption. They are delicious when mixed with raisins, for example. In fact, sunflower seeds are much more valuable than sunflower oil because the seeds contain a first-rate protein, besides highly unsaturated fatty acids. Unfortunately, the sunflower oil we buy is usually refined and although it is still relatively valuable, it cannot be said that it has the value of unrefined oil with its full content of highly unsaturated fatty acids. So if you use whole sunflower seeds you will have a food that is beneficial because of its oil and other elements.

Poppy Seeds

What has been said about sunflower seeds applies equally to poppy seeds. As part of the diet these seeds are worthy of far more consideration than they have hitherto received. One should not be content with making a poppy seed cake once in a while, or on certain holidays during the year as they do in Hungary. Instead of putting them in cakes, poppy seeds should be eaten regularly. They do not contain opiates as some people think, as the opium is obtained from the seed capsule and not from the seeds themselves. It sometimes happens that fruits or nuts do have a slight trace of a harmful substance, for example the hydrocyanic acid contained in plums. However, this is no cause for worry. The substance is an integral part of the fruit and, as such, does not act in the same way as the pure, extracted acid would. It is only found in infinitesimal quantities, in what one could say was a homoeopathic potency, and far from being harmful, it can actually do some good.

Sesame Seeds

These small oil-containing seeds of the subtropical sesame plant are comparatively little known worldwide, although in parts of Europe and North America they are commonly used. They contain an abundance of minerals and high quality protein. As these are partly combined with highly unsaturated fatty acids, they are directly transported to the cells and assimilated. The same fatty acids also supply the body with oxygen necessary for the combustion of calorific foods and so contribute to more efficient metabolism and to proper elimination. Sesame seeds will be found useful in preventing constipation and in combatting suppurations, cradle cap and eczema, and even tumours. They strengthen the nerves, stimulate the heart muscle and, because of their vitamin E content, can be taken with confidence during pregnancy. Patients afflicted with liver and gallbladder problems will welcome not only the seeds, but the raw oil as well, because both can be easily tolerated.

Because sesame is beneficial to health in so many ways, it is good to make use of the seeds themselves and also the different sesame products on the market, which children especially like to eat as snacks, only at the same time they actually provide the extra nourishment needed during their growing years – unlike sweets. Sesame seeds can be considered a perfect wholefood.

Almonds

Few people know about the high quality of almonds as a food, and they are hardly ever used by anyone who lives in the country. Almonds were quite expensive during the Second World War and so they went out of vogue. It is quite understandable that their excellent nutritional value has also been forgotten. However, almonds are cheaper today and it is well worthwhile reconsidering their food value. No doubt they will then receive more credit than they do at present.

About a quarter of the total weight of an almond consists of a high-quality protein and approximately 60 per cent is a fine oil, the almond oil. This oil can be recommended to liver patients who may not be able to tolerate any other fat. Almonds are also rich in minerals, especially potassium and calcium. They also contain valuable magnesium and, last but not least, nerve-nourishing phosphates.

It is necessary to masticate almonds thoroughly if the body is to digest them and obtain the full benefit. A particularly practical way to eat almonds is in the form of a purée. This is easily digested and assimilated and can be recommended to anyone who has problems with the liver and pancreas. Pour the almond purée into a blender to make almond milk, a nourishing drink that is rich in vitamins and easily digested.

Almond purée is a suitable food for babies, and almond milk should be substituted for ordinary cow's milk in cases of cradle cap. Only very rarely does almond protein not agree with a baby and more than 90 per cent of them tolerate it much better than the protein found in cow's milk. Many grateful mothers are aware of the fact that it was this milk that helped their babies to overcome cradle cap, as well as gastric and intestinal disturbances. Almond milk, if given regularly, will eventually rectify even the most stubborn disturbances. It is especially beneficial in the spring, when cow's milk does not always agree with some babies because the animals feed on fresh grass. Couple almond purée with a good *biological calcium preparation* and *Violaforce* in homoeopathic form, and cradle cap will soon disappear in most cases.

Because of their outstanding value and properties, almonds should find an esteemed place in every modern kitchen.

Walnuts

The walnut harvest is an unforgettable experience for all those who have had the privilege of growing up in the country. It was always a red-letter day for me when, armed with a stick, I was allowed to climb the high walnut trees and beat down the nuts, which, though ripe, were not quite ready to fall out of their green outer shells. Even the bravest climber had fearful moments sometimes, when some outer branch would not release its precious load, and it was neither safe nor easy to persevere until the last nut dropped to the ground.

Searching for walnuts in the leaves under the trees, piling them together, then prising the nuts out of their shells, although not the cleanest thing for the hands, was great fun. Such work was not for the ladies with their delicate fingers and polished nails, because for more than two weeks afterwards the yellowish-brown stains would still be impregnated in the hands.

Many of us will be familiar with the good fresh taste of newly harvested walnuts. Eaten with wholewheat bread and sweet apple cider or freshly pressed grape juice, they are both delicious and nutritious. But did you know that walnuts are especially good for those suffering from metabolic disturbances and constipation? When drugstore laxatives do not produce the desired results, walnuts may solve the problem. Walnuts are recommended for people with liver disorders and although most liver patients cannot tolerate fat they will find that moderate quantities of walnuts will agree with them quite well.

So, do not wait for the festive season to eat walnuts. They should be eaten all the year round. Make a point of including them with fruit dishes and snacks.

Milk and Dairy Farming
While milk is a valuable food for growing children, is must be free from impurities and pathogenic matter, which it may contain if the animals are housed under poor hygienic conditions. The quality and biological value of milk also depend upon the animals' feed. Some farmers use excessive quantities of concentrated feed or artificial fertilisers for their fields. Milk produced by their cows is not 100 per cent safe and the consumer would be advised to boil it. Since in some countries there is still the danger of brucellosis, in this case, too, it would also be advisable to boil milk. However, if you are fortunate enough to live, or spend your holidays, in the mountains where the cows roam freely, no such safety measures will be needed and you can drink the milk without any hesitation or risk. Good pure milk and wholewheat bread, and of course

vegetables and fruit and other natural, wholesome foods, are essential to good growth and health.

Milk – a Recommended Protein Food

If we meet our requirement of protein with meat, including processed and cold meats, the body will respond by producing more metabolic wastes, but this will not happen if we concentrate on milk as a source of protein. Most people can take and assimilate milk protein quite easily, which is why milk products are excellent protein foods; for example, the soft white cheese known as 'quark' in German-speaking lands, or curds and cottage cheese in other areas, are excellent foods. Quark is ideal for making cheesecake, a tasty and wholesome sweet addition to our menu. Many Swiss families enjoy sweet quark, that is, quark mixed with almonds, berries or other fruits. Other healthy dishes are potatoes boiled in their skins, or jacket potatoes, and quark with horseradish. If you cannot obtain this type of soft cheese, cottage cheese or curds are equally good. They can be enriched with vegetable juices and are very popular for stuffing fresh tomatoes.

Another milk product is hard cheese, which satisfies the hunger of the labourer very well. From the point of view of health, however, soft white cheese is better. It is recommended that hard cheese be eaten together with salad and raw vegetables, so that it can be chewed and digested better, causing less disturbance to the stomach. They say that cheese is like gold if you eat it in the morning, like silver at noon, and like lead in the evening. In other words, you should watch what time of day you bite into a piece of hard cheese.

Milk – a Nourishing Drink

Although milk is a popular food in Switzerland, it should be used much more for drinking. Many other countries have a much better arrangement, for everywhere you go in the United Kingdom or the United States, for example, milk is available in small cartons, so that workers, schoolchildren, travellers, in short, anyone who wants a cool, nourishing and strengthening drink of milk can obtain one without difficulty. I have even seen some railway stations where milk automats have been installed. It is definitely better and cheaper to enjoy a cool, fresh drink of milk in the heat of summer rather than alcoholic beverages or sweet soft drinks with artificial additives.

Milk is a natural product with many benefits. It is only regrettable that not every dairy farmer is well enough equipped to produce and supply uncontaminated milk, but efforts are being made to improve the quality.

Unfortunately, deliberate interference in nature can reduce the value of the best quality milk, especially when the cows are inoculated. It is necessary, therefore, to raise this subject and draw the dairy farmers' attention to the problem.

The Consequences of Inoculation

When cows have been inoculated against tuberculosis, on no account should their milk be drunk raw for at least four or five days. It would be best to discard such milk altogether, at least for human consumption. Unpleasant consequences from drinking this milk may be experienced, such as liver and digestive disorders, headaches and feverishness; those who live on a natural diet are especially affected. The strange thing is that the feverishness does not cause a loss of appetite and the affected person continues to eat normally. The problems can be counteracted with *Echinaforce, Usnea* and *Urticalcin*. It is advisable to stimulate elimination through the kidneys and liver, thus enabling the toxins to be disposed of. Be careful then, if you do not want to harm your health. The best thing you can do is not to drink this contaminated milk.

Dairy farmers who deliver milk from sick animals should think twice and consider the health of their fellowmen as more important than the small financial return they might gain. But it is unfortunately true that monetary advantages often take precedence over a farmer's sense of responsibility.

Other Factors that Impair the Quality of Milk

Poorly kept cowsheds can result in tubercular cows. Only good housing conditions for the animals will avoid their contracting disease.

The incidence of tuberculosis is reduced considerably if the animals receive sufficient exercise in the fresh air, because even the best fodder is not enough to keep them healthy if they are cooped up inside all day. They should be allowed to enjoy the benefits of light and exercise in the fresh air, for this is an absolute necessity for their health and well-being.

The danger of tuberculosis is often minimised, and although it is true that it is only when the udder is affected that the disease is directly transmitted to the milk, who would dare to assert that tuberculosis of the lungs, or of any other organ for that matter, would not reduce the quality of the milk. Only healthy animals can produce milk that is safe and wholesome. The milk of a diseased cow must be affected in some way, even though the animal might not be tubercular. This is not difficult to understand because it is the same with humans. If a mother is sick, suffering from mineral and vitamin deficiencies, she will be unable to pass on these vital elements to her baby because she lacks them herself. Only a healthy mother can transmit healthy nutrients.

What do we learn from these considerations? That certain basic principles must be put into practice. We have to go full circle if we want to eradicate any mistakes. We have to provide healthy conditions before we can successfully combat today's nutritional problems. First, we must see to it that the soil is healthy and provides healthy food for the animals. Then we must make sure that their housing is adequate if we want them to produce safe milk. By observing these requirements we can be more certain of better health for the consumer.

American Dairy Farming

It would be a salutary thing to compare Swiss dairy farming and its various deficiencies with American dairy farming. The Swiss farmer, and, no doubt, those from many other countries, can learn much from the organisation, installations and hygienic conditions and rules found in the average American dairy farm. There are many American ideas that could be applied elsewhere for the benefit of producer and consumer alike. Admittedly, the American dairy farmer has larger herds and more extensive facilities, but with a little good will, some improvements could be made. If milk is to be wholesome, it must be equal to the requirements demanded of healthy food.

Dairy Farming and the National Economy

There are vegetarians who assert that they can get by quite well without dairy products. True, this is perhaps possible in the lowlands where practically all the land can be used for farming and vegetable growing. A typical example of turning pasture land into arable land is provided by China, where the huge increase in population required the conversion of much of their pasture land to allow the cultivation of more grains and vegetables, which yield more protein, minerals and vitamins. The Chinese example, however, would be impossible to apply to mountainous regions where fruits and vegetables will not grow. With very few exceptions, dairy farming is usually the only activity that can be success-fully undertaken for the production of food. In my own country, Switzerland, the best milk comes from the mountainous regions and is instrumental in stabilising the national economy through the production of various kinds of cheese and other dairy products.

WHEN FINANCIAL CONSIDERATIONS ARE OVEREMPHASISED

The subject of dairy farming leads me to comment on a strange policy among some dairy farmers. There are some farmers who muzzle calves to prevent them from eating hay or aftermath. By feeding them only on milk their flesh will remain white, the idea being, of course, that white meat fetches a better price. This view of things, aided and abetted by the consumer, is extremely short-sighted, because red meat is of better nutritional value. However since the white meat is more tender, it is also more expensive.

The same principle applies to white bread, white rolls and other white flour products, showing once more the power of advertising and how demands are created to spoil the palate so that artificially prepared foods with all their additives seem to taste better. The knowledge that they are greatly inferior to products made from whole cereals is simply ignored. If one continues to eat white bread, lack of fibre will soon weaken the peristalsis of the intestines and lead to constipation, which, in turn, encourages a host of other troubles that will ultimately be dealt with by injections and all sorts of harmful drugs and medicines. One mistake after another is made and, sooner or later, the price for choosing one's food according to the dictates of the palate will have to be paid for by chronic ill health and physical suffering.

How much wiser it would be to adapt oneself to the more healthy foods, which give a true sensation of taste, instead of the cultivated taste for the artificial. It is not only the individual who would be the ultimate beneficiary from eating natural health foods, but the economy of the land would be boosted as well.

Yogurt

Yogurt reminds me of the old Bulgarians, whose longevity and health have commonly been attributed to their eating plenty of this healthy dairy product.

What is yogurt? One usually receives the answer that it is a kind of curdled milk. In a certain sense this is correct, the difference being that ordinary sour milk contains approximately 6 g of lactic acid per litre while yogurt contains only about 2 g.

Lactic fermentation does play an important part in the preparation of yogurt, but its particular properties and flavour are due to the Maya bacillus, which works in symbiotic association with the ordinary oriental lactic acid bacillus.

Is yogurt better for you than ordinary sweet milk? Sweet milk coagulates in the stomach into curd. The same process is used in making cheese, when rennet from the stomach of calves is added to warm milk, which then turns into curd. The process of turning milk into curds imposes quite a bit of work on the stomach, which it accomplishes only insufficiently, or not at all, if there is a disturbance in the secretion of the gastric fluids or if the stomach lacks tone. Some people find it difficult to digest sweet milk if the stomach is not performing well. On the other hand, most people can tolerate yogurt or sour milk, the reason being that yogurt enters the stomach in a predigested form, that is, a fine curd. Proof of this can be seen when a child vomits after having drunk some milk and the milk returns in big white lumps, whereas yogurt or sour milk is brought up as a flaky fluid.

Yogurt benefits the intestines most of all. It will cleanse the intestinal mucous membranes and encourage the development of healthy intestinal flora. The yogurt bacillus will eliminate the pathological kind. All this promotes better digestion and assimilation of food.

Yogurt should be eaten as the first course of a salad meal, that is, first the yogurt, then salad and finally, vegetables. It is often eaten with fruit but this is less beneficial because it can lead to undesirable fermentation. Anyone inclined to flatulence should particularly avoid taking sugar or fruit with yogurt.

Intestinal putrefaction, which manifests itself by offensive smelling stools, can be gradually overcome by eating yogurt. I would emphasise the qualification 'gradually', for there are some people who think that an occasional bowl of yogurt will rid them of all their digestive disorders. This, of course, is not so; it will take time. It is a good idea to keep a stock of yogurt at home; in fact, you may find that it pays to make it yourself. Yogurt has an even greater health value if *Lactobacillus acidophilus* is also used in its preparation.

Lactobacillus acidophilus
Milk is an ideal culture medium for all kinds of bacteria. If you leave unpasteurised fresh milk in a normally warm room in summer it will turn sour. The curdling is caused by lactic acid bacteria

whose spores were either present in the milk or invaded it while it was in the kitchen. We do not recommend using milk that cannot turn sour because of chemical additives that make it stringy and go off if left outside the refrigerator.

There are various species of lactic bacteria, each one playing an important part in the preparation of special cheeses. Yogurt is made by inoculating the milk with lactic acid bacteria. Some of these bacteria should not be ingested constantly because they affect the intestinal flora. Thus yogurt is good for you if you eat it occasionally; if, however, you take it regularly all year round, its influence on the intestinal flora is one-sided and therefore detrimental. Some researchers claim that yogurt, if eaten every day over a long period of time, will cause the essential coliform bacteria in the intestines to degenerate. For this reason it is not recommended to eat yogurt continuously.

Acidophil bacteria help to build up new intestinal flora in cases of dysbacteria and the connected destruction of useful bacteria. American researchers also claim that acidophil bacteria are important in the formation of vitamin B_{12} in the intestines due to intestinal biosynthesis.

We know that vitamin B_{12} is important in the formation of red blood corpuscles, so we can conclude that the *acidophilus* is a tremendous help in cases of anaemia, as well as in the fight against pernicious anemia, in a supportive role. The intestinal flora is impaired when there is too much or too little gastric acid. Flatulence and poor digestion may occur. Acidophil bacteria have done much to relieve this condition as well as easing other problems too. For example, they are helpful in treating enteritis and similar inflammations of the intestines, and some causes of constipation. In view of these beneficial effects, it is recommended to take *acidophilus* two or three times a year for about a month on a regular basis. Any problems with the intestinal flora will then be rectified.

Coffee

The Effect of Coffee

Coffee, as a product of the coffee tree, has such a general acceptance all over the world that millions of tons of beans are consumed annually. Because of its composition, it is not surprising that many people concerned with their health are talking about it in conferences and in the press and other media.

Coffee can damage our health, for it has been shown to have an injurious effect on the nerves of those people who are already 'living on their nerves'; it peps them up. Although I disapprove of the regular use of this nerve poison, I drink coffee to stay awake and alert on occasions when I am forced to drive long distances at night. Still, I know it does not do my nerves any good. True, I cannot justify drinking coffee except that on such occasions it is better than falling asleep over the steering wheel and causing an accident. If one is not a regular coffee drinker and only takes it occasionally as a stimulant, that is, a medicine, its immediate effect is amazing. If, however, you have been drinking coffee regularly, perhaps three or more cups of a strong brew every day, you will be used to it and the effect will be weaker or not apparent at all. Caffeine dilates the blood vessels and coffee, used as medicine, is therefore indicated as a chemical vasodilator.

Coffee the Arabian Way
Generally speaking, coffee has the dilatory and stimulating effect described above; however, I learned an interesting fact with regard to coffee as the Arabs drink it. It surprised me that it can be prepared in a way that is much less harmful than the coffee made in the European or American home. In fact, I was quite astonished to see that the usual stimulating and insomniac effect was barely noticeable when I had coffee in Arab lands.

The Arabs serve it as the Turks do, in little cups together with the grounds. As a rule, they do not keep it roasted and ground but prepare it when the guests arrive. They roast the beans and grind them shortly before use, bring the ground coffee rapidly to the boil, let it bubble briefly, and pour a little cold water over the froth to settle. Then it is served very strong and thick with plenty of sugar.

In comparison with regular coffee, which I normally take with milk or cream and without sugar, the Arabic coffee did not cause me any trouble and seemed less stimulating. The unfavourable side effects of the coffee somehow appear to be eliminated by the Arabian method of preparation. After many observations and experiments I found that the grounds contain certain materials that, to a certain extent, neutralise the soluble substances in coffee, including caffeine, weakening its stimulating properties.

If you like the pleasant taste and aroma of coffee, why not try the Arabian method and take only a small cup, together with the grounds. However, you should only indulge if your nervous system is in good working order; sensitive or nervous people should leave coffee alone.

Bambu Cereal and Fruit Coffee Substitute
Since most coffee drinkers should give up drinking coffee completely for the sake of their health, the question arises as to how they can achieve this. Efforts to find a satisfactory substitute for coffee have been continuing for a long time, with the result that there are several good cereal and fruit mixtures on the market today, including our own *Bambu Coffee Substitute*.

These substitute coffees are healthy and have none of the undesirable effects of the coffee bean. Even the milk in fruit coffee suffers none of the drawbacks it encounters in ordinary coffee. Milk taken in 'bean' coffee coagulates or curdles in the stomach, with each mouthful becoming a little ball of curd in the acid medium of the stomach. However, if ingested in cereal and fruit coffee, milk curdles in fine flakes, making it much more digestible.

Bambu coffee also mixes well with raw milk for a cold drink in summer. Its bitter constituents, which come from acorns, and other minerals, are all of importance to the body in general and the liver in particular, which may well apply to bitter elements in other foods too. However, the principal benefit of this coffee is its coagulating effect on milk, as described above. Of course, if you are fit and healthy, none of these considerations will mean much to you, but if your health is not so good, or you are nervous, sensitive and highly-strung because of a life-style that is contrary to nature, it is a different question. In that case, you should definitely choose only mild food and drink.

THE BENEFITS OF CEREAL AND FRUIT COFFEE
It is not unreasonable to suggest that a modern health diet should be accompanied by a good coffee substitute, one that is pleasant to the taste and has none of the side effects of regular coffee – important factors when choosing any food product. A confirmed coffee drinker might think that it would be impossible to get used to a substitute, no matter how badly regular coffee affected his health. Fortunately, it is possible to train our palate and even use a trick to help us change its likes and dislikes. Those who feel that making such a changeover might be difficult should at first try drinking their coffee with only a slight addition of the cereal and fruit mixture, then gradually increase the quantity of the substitute and decrease that of the regular coffee until eventually they are

drinking only the cereal and fruit coffee. A coffee addict who suffers from insomnia because of drinking too much will gradually effect a change in taste and then really enjoy his cereal and fruit drink. The health benefits will be obvious, especially for those who are accustomed to drinking their coffee with milk. By drinking a good cereal and fruit coffee substitute rather than regular bean coffee, the heart and nerves will benefit tremendously.

These substitute coffees are usually available at health food stores and delicatessens and, interestingly, the modern substitute is often similar in taste to regular coffee. Moreover, the availability of instant cereal and fruit coffee, such as *Bambu Coffee Substitute*, makes its preparation an easy matter: simply put a teaspoon of Bambu in a cup, pour hot water or milk over it, and serve a fine and aromatic beverage to your family and friends.

Sauerkraut (Fermented White Cabbage)

We gratefully accept all the information science can supply us regarding effective substances found in natural foods and medicines. However, more important than long-winded dissertations on the subject is the practical application of such knowledge – at least to the patient. Anyone who has seen people suffering from scurvy, in camps and institutions and on ships, will appreciate why foods containing anti-scorbutic elements are so necessary for them. Their diet may be adequate in all other respects, but if certain vitamins are missing, their food alone cannot overcome the deficiency.

Apart from lemon, sauerkraut is the best anti-scorbutic remedy and it was sauerkraut that enabled the daring explorer James Cook to sail the farthest seas for years without any of his sailors falling victim to scurvy. Of course, in those days, such things as anti-scorbutic vitamins were unknown, but through trial and error men like Cook, who observed and understood the ways of nature, eventually discovered the remedy for the insidious disease. Captain Cook always made sure that there were sufficient barrels of fermented cabbage on his ships. The supplement of sauerkraut with the sailors' meals provided them with food and medicine at the same time, so that the devastating effects of scurvy were avoided and Cook could carry on with his explorations and discoveries.

If your gums bleed easily or become soft and spongy around the teeth, if you constantly have small ulcers or sores on your gums and oral mucosa, if your skin bleeds easily, if you notice swellings near the joints, or if you suffer from a general feeling of weakness and weariness, then you must add raw sauerkraut to your daily diet and make your salad dressing with lemon juice. The old Central European saying that 'sauerkraut every day keeps the doctor away' is undoubtedly true, for raw sauerkraut is a wonderful remedy and should have a place of honour in every home. If you have no opportunity to make it yourself, go and buy some at a health food or delicatessen. In addition to vitamin C, its content of natural lactic acid and other effective enzymes makes sauerkraut a remedial food.

Sauerkraut water or juice is an excellent remedy for many gastric and intestinal disorders and ailments, but beware of the highly salty, factory-made sauerkraut, which cannot be considered good for health. Remember, too, that only when it is raw does sauerkraut have the above-mentioned anti-scorbutic elements, supplementary substances and healing properties.

Making Sauerkraut at Home

If you want to make your own sauerkraut, you might like to try the following recipe for *sauerkraut with onion*.

Shred a head of white cabbage, not too fine, not too coarse. Spread a layer about 2 cm thick (a little less than 1 inch) on the bottom of a container, preferably one made of wood or glazed earthenware. Scatter some juniper berries and mustard and coriander seeds over the cabbage and add a small pinch of salt. You can leave out the salt, but then add more mustard seeds to compensate. On top of this, place a layer of sliced onions about 1 cm (about ½ inch) thick. Add another layer of cabbage and seasoning, then onions; continue until the container is full. Press the cabbage and onions down firmly and cover the vegetables, using a lid or plate that will fit inside the neck of the container. Place a heavy stone on the lid to weigh it down, and allow the cabbage to ferment. If you want to speed up the fermentation process, dilute some yogurt ferment or whey concentrate with water and pour over the cabbage.

Of course, sauerkraut can be made without the onions. It is important, however, that the preparation is done in a warm room and that the cabbage it left to stand for two or three weeks in a room not under 20 °C (68 °F). After that, place the container somewhere cool so that there is no butyric acid fermentation, which could ruin the contents. If you prepare sauerkraut without salt, you must make sure that you exclude all air from the container and that everything is scrupulously clean so that it will keep well.

Formerly 1–2 per cent salt was used, in other words, 100–200 g for every 10 kg of cabbage (4–8 oz for every 20 lb). Nowadays, 0.5 per cent salt or less is considered enough, since it has been found that too much salt reduces the lactic acid fermentation, resulting in an inferior product.

The Art of Cooking Depends upon Proper Seasoning

If you have been able to travel extensively, your judgement in many things will be better than that of the person who has been used to looking at everything from the limited experience of his immediate environment and local events. Through travelling, we become acquainted with the art of many cooks and come to appreciate those who know how to prepare healthy and nourishing food and not only tasty dishes that merely appeal to the palate. In this respect, three entirely different types of cooking have impressed me no end: the French, Arabic and Chinese cuisines. Each of the three follows the principle that the art of cooking is based on the correct use of spices, seasonings and flavourings. Food that is naturally bland needs careful preparation and seasoning if it is to be made palatable so that we will want to eat it again. Simply adding plenty of salt will not achieve the desired result and cannot produce the flavour that the food lacks in the first place. Cooking is an art that some people develop naturally, but others have to learn it. What helps to make our food healthy and tasty are the herbal or vegetable seasonings that are added to it, certainly not just the use of salt.

The Characteristics of Chinese, Arabic and French Cuisines

Chinese cooks prefer not to boil vegetables until they are soft; instead, they leave them about 20 per cent raw. In this condition they may taste somewhat bitter and so must be properly seasoned to make them more palatable. But the Chinese cooks know their job and prepare their food in such a way that you will enjoy it, even though you may have to chew more than with food prepared the European way. They also use a wider variety of spices and condiments, for example, curry and soy sauces, various kinds of peppers and all sorts of spicy pods that resemble red and black chillies. Moreover, they almost always include a little seaweed, which, although not much of a taste in itself, adds something to Chinese dishes that is unique.

Centuries of tradition lie behind Chinese cuisine and its habitual use of seaweed, and this ingredient is appreciated for the sake of its minerals and trace elements that are so necessary to our health. This goodness is present in very small quantities, or not at all, in other plants, and the ancient Chinese must have used seaweed instinctively as they would not have known about these substances. However, they must have been good observers and noticed that nature offers us many things that may not be visible to the eye, nor tangible, but are nevertheless of vital importance to us. This precious gift of observation has no doubt contributed to the way in which Chinese cuisine has developed. Even though much else has been forgotten that once was an intrinsic part of their culture, the Chinese people still benefit from this tradition, as they have for thousands of years.

The distinctive nature of Arabic cuisine also depends upon its use of various seasonings and condiments. Arab cooks, however, indulge in one habit of which many Europeans are not so fond: they mix spicy things with sweet ones, and bitter with mild aromas or flavours, creating peculiar contrasts of taste that may indeed tickle the palate of some but, as a rule, put us off. It often takes a while for outsiders to get used to these contrasts, but the Arab is not bothered in the least by eating peppers together with oranges or other fruit, whereas it would take me a long time to enjoy the combination of these contrasting tastes. On the other hand, it must also be said that the Arabs do not just salt their food but season it. And this is to their credit.

French cuisine is famous, not least because its secrets are found in the kitchen garden where a great variety of herbs abound and beg to be used. Escoffier, the modest Frenchman of small stature, came to be known as the King of Cooks because he mastered the use of culinary herbs in our European gardens and markets in a way that no one else has been able to match. No wonder his skill and art enabled him to produce the tastiest and most stimulating sauces, gravies and dressings that inspired the enthusiasm of even kings and princes!

Practical Experience Put to Good Use
When travelling abroad, any useful experiences and observations in connection with food should be recorded and utilised, if necessary adapting them to suit our own circumstances. I have tried to put this suggestion into practice by experimenting at home with new blends of herbs and spices according to specific rules and principles. The combination of fresh herbs, fresh vegetables and sea salt, as

in *Trocomare*, and partly also in *Herbamare*, is an example of my efforts.

Years ago, herbs were dried and powdered before use, but today we know and appreciate that fresh herbs are much more active and effective for seasoning. A fresh herbal seasoning is therefore more savoury and full-tasting. Herbamare and Trocomare seasoning salts are available in convenient shakers and offer you the goodness contained in the fresh vegetables and herbs from which they are made. The plants are organically grown, gathered from the garden and used immediately in the manufacturing process, while still fresh. A wonderfully green mush is made first, to which pure sun-dried sea salt is added. The salt dissolves and absorbs the juices, while the mush is dehydrated without heating. When ready, the seasoning is packed into the shakers. Modern nature-oriented families appreciate having these seasonings on their tables every day.

Another product for daily use is the seasoning sauce *Swiss Alpamare*, also called *Kelpamare*. This product is made from the juices of fresh vegetables and herbs and is also manufactured by means of a special fermentation process. For this purpose suitable herbs are fermented in accordance with old Chinese and Japanese methods, using edible fungi (mushrooms), which develop in an absolutely natural organic way. When fermentation comes to an end we have a seasoning sauce similar to the soy sauce found in Japan and China.

Instead of having to extract the salt using hydrochloric acid, which destroys a number of vital elements, the natural method makes for quite a different product that is far superior in taste and content to the products made according to our old-fashioned methods. Furthermore, Swiss Alpamare (Kelpamare) also contains seaweed, which is added during the manufacturing process and therefore integrally mixed and blended with the herb extracts.

The sandwich spread *Herbaforce* has the same herbal base and, in addition, is enriched with yeast extracts containing vitamin B. *Plantaforce* vegetable concentrate makes a delicious vegetable bouillon or drink. A teaspoonful of this added to a cup of hot water is enough to provide our guests with a nourishing and strengthening drink. We will also be glad to enjoy a cup of hot vegetable broth when we come home hungry and thirsty but it is not yet time to sit down to a wholesome meal. This drink is prepared in a jiffy and is invigorating as well. Plantaforce thus saves time, and time saves energy.

This brief discussion of how we can put our experience and observations to good use will no doubt help everyone to prepare tasty meals that benefit our health at the same time. Neither special knowledge nor ability is necessary, and this is most welcome for all those who have little time and a busy schedule. On the other hand, even if you have enough time to prepare your meals with care, the seasonings and flavourings we have just considered can bring you nothing but natural goodness and will enhance the goodness of your food.

Cooking Salt

How Much Salt Do We Need?

It is appropriate to consider this question, since many people hold mistaken views about salt. We were taught in school that a person requires 7 kg (about 14 lb) of salt a year in order to stay alive. It is true that man and beast cannot do without it, although it is also acknowledged that certain diseases demand a low-salt or even a salt-free diet. This apparent contradiction resolves itself when we realise that our salt requirement need not necessarily be obtained from the crystalline kind of salt known as common or table salt, but can equally well come from our food. Cases in point are the inhabitants of the Asiatic steppes and the Indians living at the headwaters of the Amazon River. They have never heard of salt, nor do they have a word for it, but as they could not survive without it, it is obvious that they must cover their requirement by means of their food.

Adequate Salt Intake

How can we solve the problem of obtaining enough salt without overloading the body with too much common or table salt? We can take advantage of the vegetables that contain plenty of it, for example leeks and onions. All plants contain salt, for when we talk about salt we mean sodium chloride, which is found in plants. Nevertheless, the fact that fresh, raw vegetables are a source of salt is frequently overlooked and many believe they must use ordinary salt to avoid deficiencies. But doing this puts a strain on the kidneys. Many well-known physicians, such as Gerson, Riedlin, Hermannsdorfer and the noted surgeon Professor Sauerbruch, have discovered that in cases of tuberculosis of the bones, too much salt has a markedly bad effect, whereas a low-salt diet or abstinence

550

from salt improves the general condition and stimulates the healing ability of the body.

Those who suffer from kidney ailments know that little or no salt is one of the important rules of their treatment if they are to recover rapidly. So, even for those in excellent health, it would be sensible to reduce our salt consumption as much as possible so as to avoid overburdening the kidneys. We should definitely give more consideration to these facts, since many other diseases and ailments also require a low-salt or salt-free diet in order to protect the kidneys or effect a cure.

Yeast and Yeast Extract

Earlier this century, the British began to experiment with yeast and yeast extract as a concentrated food for various expeditions. From the point of view of weight and size, they turned out to be most suitable for this purpose. An individual can keep going longer on a pound of yeast extract than on a pound of any other concentrated food. In the beginning, the value of yeast was known only by the results that were obtained from its practical use, as little was known of its vitamin content. If today yeast and yeast extract are looked upon as the most valuable concentrated foods at our disposal, scientific research and experiments have amply justified this opinion.

Yeast contains various vitamins of the B complex, especially vitamin B_1 (thiamine), and is very important to the cells, helping to take up oxygen supplied by breathing (vitamin B_2). The vitamin B_1 content of yeast is also most beneficial to the nervous system and the process of burning up carbohydrates.

Professor Abderhalden has discussed yeast and yeast extract in his publications, even calling them a kind of vegetable insulin. Yeast and yeast extract have a stimulating effect on the pancreas if it is not functioning properly and the internal secretion is upset, that is, if the islets of Langerhans are weak and do not secrete sufficient amounts of insulin. Diabetics should therefore use yeast extract for seasoning and as a sandwich spread, with a topping of sliced onions, in order to benefit from the sulphur they contain.

Yeast extract and yeast itself should only be taken in small but frequent quantities.

I would like to stress that 'live' yeast has certain disadvantages for those whose intestinal flora is disturbed. When the yeast cells, a kind of fungi, reach the intestines they usually cause fermentation and flatulence, although this is not a problem when the intestinal flora is normal. If you are sensitive, take yeast extract, which is also much more convenient to use as a spread and in stews, soups and the like. Simply dilute the extract in warm water.

It is well known that yeast taken regularly in small quantities has a medicinal effect upon furunculosis (boils) and wounds that refuse to heal. It is worthwhile mentioning that small quantities may cure the condition, while large amounts can actually provoke the problem, thus confirming the homoeopathic principle that any substance that leads to pathological conditions when taken in excess, will act as a curative agent if administered in attenuated or potentised form.

Yeast and yeast extract relieve disturbances of one's general state of health. Yeast extract is also good for neuralgic pains, trigeminal neuralgia and similar aches caused by inflammation of the nerves. Owing to its high vitamin B content, it has also been found to be of special benefit during pregnancy.

Those who suffer from stomach and intestinal problems and those with circulatory disturbances have a splendid food supplement in yeast extract. In fact, yeast fulfils the requirements the ancient medical researchers looked for in food: that food should be remedy and a remedy should be food.

At one time barm or beer yeast was used to produce yeast extract, but its bitter taste, which cannot be completely eliminated without altering its health value, led to this method being replaced by a precultured and special control method, usually using molasses as a base. So, if possible, obtain the cultured extract.

Herbaforce and *Plantaforce* are yeast extracts enriched with juices from organically grown herbs and vegetables. Their taste and flavour are superb. Herbaforce is especially suitable for use as a sandwich spread.

Miscellaneous Topics

Impoverished Earth, Rich Sea

How many rivers annually rush into the seas, their mighty waters carrying tons of minerals, lost to the earth forever. True were the words of ancient Solomon, who clearly recognised the water cycle: 'Every river flows into the sea, but the sea is not yet full. The water returns to where the rivers began, and starts all over again.' Untiring is the journey and untiring also, therefore, is the disappearance of minerals. In spite of the water cycle, they are not returned to the earth. The water that evaporates and returns in the form of rain or snow is like distilled water, lacking minerals. When we consider not only the rivers that have their sources in the Alps, but also the far mightier ones, the Amazon, Rio Grande, Mississippi, Ganges, and Nile – all the powerful rivers of our planet – we can begin to appreciate how much the earth must have lost in the form of minerals over the millenniums. Rain and snow continue to dissolve potassium, calcium, magnesium, manganese, iodine, boron and many other mineral substances found in the earth. They are washed into the rivers and thus carried into the seas and oceans. As a result, our earth becomes poorer in minerals and the seas correspondingly richer.

Efforts to Retrieve the Loss

Such reflections have caused some far-sighted people in various countries of the earth to reclaim at least something from the sea. We only have to think of the different kinds of seaweed that grow in it, their rich mineral content being most beneficial. In the first place, seaweed should be used to fertilise the soil, in order to return to the soil some of the substances that it lacks. In California seaweed has been used for quite some time as a fertiliser, for cattle feed and as a food supplement, sometimes even for medicines. Since the 1930s sea-foam and seaweed have been used for fertilising

553

in Holland. And for centuries farmers in France have been spreading a calcium-rich seaweed onto their fields.

The success of these farmers caught the attention of scientific circles and Professor Boucher reported amazing things about the effectiveness of a reddish-coloured seaweed powder, known as 'Calmagol', that has been used as a fertiliser on the isles of Glénan, south of Brittany. It was found that the plants not only grew better, but were healthier because of the addition of seaweed meal. Subsequent experiments with vegetables, fruit and berries provided good results. Mildew, fungi, scab and even pests such as greenfly were said to have disappeared when the plants were dusted with seaweed meal. It was therefore not only good for the improvement of the soil, but had the additional benefit of serving as a plant remedy, so to speak. While kelp is rich in iodine, the iodine content of the seaweed preparation 'Lithothamne Calmagol' is low, although the latter is rich in easily dissolved calcium.

Professor Boucher claims that one region in France escaped an outbreak of foot-and-mouth disease because the farmers treated their land with seaweed meal. Since these reports come from a reliable source, one can rightly expect them to be true. It can therefore be assumed that seaweed is good not only for fertilising and improving the soil, but also for regenerating exhausted, sick soil. It would be worthwhile if more farmers and gardeners made their contribution to improving the soil by adopting the use of seaweed.

No Life Without Iodine

I once read a fairy story about a prince who was never happy, and nothing seemed able to relieve his melancholy. Finally, the king prepared a feast to which he invited princes from all over the world. The guests enjoyed themselves, dancing and applauding the amusing performances of the entertainers and jesters, as it was the custom at court in those days. Although most of the people present gave way to laughter and merriment, our prince remained indifferent and sad. When the king promised a large reward to anyone who could make his son happy, a goatherd from high up in the Alps came forward. He had noticed how frisky and playful the chamois became whenever they licked at a certain area of the rock where salt deposits were located. So he had scraped some off and brought it along, thinking that it might bring good luck to the prince and himself. He gave some to the prince, who made a face as he put it in his mouth, but then slowly began to liven up and join in the fun. His disposition was improved and he felt happy once again. Were this story true, five millionths of a gram of iodine could have performed the same miracle.

Correct Dosage

Scientists have calculated the daily iodine requirement of the entire Swiss nation to be only 25 g (less than 1 oz). Perhaps this small estimate is correct. At any rate, only minute amounts of this mineral are necessary to meet our needs. On the other hand, if it were lacking, an abundance of the best nutrients and vitamins could not prevent the stupefaction and death of the Swiss people. It is a fact that a deficiency of iodine especially affects the thyroid gland and triggers strange symptoms. For example, a goitre can form, or myxoedema can result, leading to mental stupefaction. Conversely, an iodine disorder can cause exophthalmic goitre. This problem is recognised by the symptoms of hypersensitivity accompanied by frequent heart palpitations and nervous internal fluttering, which uses up nervous energy through overstimulation of the sympathetic nerves. The intestinal glands, the liver and pancreas, indeed most organs, will thereby be overstimulated. Even the perspiratory glands will be affected, and excessive perspiration can break out and weaken the body. Depression, characterised by mental imbalance and emotional ups and downs, is often the unpleasant consequence. This condition only deteriorates and becomes insupportable if massive doses of iodine are given.

We can see, therefore, that the intake of the miracle substance iodine has to be measured carefully, for both deficiency and excess mean trouble. Thus, to avoid harm, it is imperative to give iodine only in high potencies of homoeopathic dilution.

Some years ago, since the Swiss and the inhabitants of other land-locked countries often displayed signs of iodine deficiency, Dr Eggenberger from Herisau, a noted goitre specialist, supported the idea of adding iodine to common salt. This was meant to help those people in Switzerland who tended toward goitre, but it caused those with a tendency to Graves' disease having to put up with an increased heart beat and other unpleasant side effects.

Sea salt and sea water both contain iodine, and for many people these can have the effect of a specific medicine. But those who have a predisposition towards Graves' disease will find it better to take the small amounts of iodine found in plants, which will give them no trouble.

Iceland Moss

Plants Containing Iodine

In Switzerland very few plants contain iodine. Iceland moss, lung moss, reindeer moss, larch moss (*Usnea*) and carrageen (also called Irish moss) are some of the plants that do contain vitamin A and a reasonable amount of iodine, as has been proved by the pharmacologist Professor Gessner. In Switzerland there are thirty-eight different varieties of these mosses, which are described in botanic terms as lichens. Professor Gessner reports that these additionally contain antibiotic substances with a strong tuberculo-static effect. Some of these lichens are used in *Usneasan drops* and *Usneasan Cough Lozenges*. Genuine eelgrass (*Zostera marina*) and thrift (*Armeria maritima*), which can be found on the shores of the North and Baltic Seas, contain iodine, fluoride and bromide, three essential trace elements. Small amounts of iodine are also found in watercress.

All seaweeds contain iodine, the amount varying according to the kind and where it grows. The species known as bladder wrack (*Fucus vesiculosus*) grows to a size of 5 cm (2 inches) wide and 1 metre (3 feet) long. Its iodine content varies between 0.03 and 0.1 per cent, and it is used to treat obesity, struma and scrofula. However, it is unsafe for some people to take large amounts of this seaweed, especially those with a sensitive thyroid.

Kelp is the longest seaweed, reaching up to 700 metres (over

2,100 feet) in length. It is probably the longest known plant in existence. Kelp has the advantage over other seaweeds of having a fairly predictable iodine content, so that it is relatively easy to gauge the correct dosage.

By regularly taking very small quantities of seaweed or food items made with it, it is possible to eliminate an iodine deficiency without running the risk of taking too much. For this reason it is beneficial to include small amounts of seaweed in our food, above all in soups and vegetables. Doing this, especially in land-locked countries, would gradually overcome any deficiency of iodine and other trace elements.

These logical considerations caused me to add seaweed, kelp to be more specific, to a number of my food products, for example *Herbamare* and *Trocomare*, the two popular herbal salts, as well as *Herbaforce*, the practical and tasty sandwich spread. The seasoning sauce *Swiss Alpamare (Kelpamare)*, and the vegetable soup concentrate *Plantaforce* are also enriched with it. In this way it is possible to make use of varied and different food items in order to counterbalance an existing deficiency. The more the population increases and the prevalence of diseases of civilisation grows, the greater becomes the necessity to recognise and make use of the sea, with its rich mineral content, as a source of food.

Poisons that Are Difficult to Eliminate

The virulence of poisons should be judged not merely on the basis of their specific effects, but on their long-term influence. Poisons that trigger typical symptoms such as vomiting and diarrhoea but are easily expelled from the body or neutralised may be unpleasant and considered dangerous by the person so affected; however, poisons that produce none of these symptoms but remain in the body, causing degenerative or insidious conditions, are really much worse. In fact, they may have a considerable role to play in the development of cancer, and it is unfortunate that physicians and the health authorities in general find it difficult to recognise them.

We have not forgotten the disastrous results when a large number of women took the thalidomide drug, in good faith, during the 1960s. It seems that only after hundreds, or even thousands, of people have suffered from taking such drugs, the real danger is discovered. Experience has shown that no one knows the long-term effects of any strong chemical medicine. No chemist, experienced physician or pharmacologist can predict the effects with any degree of certainty. Granted, laboratory and animal experiments do give a limited idea of the general effects in each case and this may help in the specific or symptomatic treatment of a certain disease. However, how is the drug to be judged and what is to be done when suddenly deformity, sterility, and neural and genetic damage is observed, as was the case with thalidomide? If legal proceedings are taken, will it not be difficult even for a very alert and observant doctor to prove his point? What is more, he will have to think very carefully about whether he dare take on a mighty chemical or pharmaceutical company and sue them successfully.

To illustrate this point further, I know of one representative of the chemical industry, involved in the manufacture of pesticides and insecticides, who challenged the opponents of the industry to produce evidence of fatalities resulting from the application of such chemicals. No one would deny that arsenic is a dangerous poison, nor that opium is a hazardous drug. But it would not be easy to provide conclusive evidence that, say, the death of a woman who had eaten arsenic to improve her complexion and looks had been caused by her doing so. Even if it were possible to discover such a case, another expert would almost certainly stand up and prove a different cause of death. The same holds true of opium addicts.

The More the Better?

Preservatives, pesticides and herbicides can be highly dangerous, but if the proper care is taken there will be no acute symptoms of poisoning. Normally, if the directions for use are observed, there will be no evidence of chemical damage. However, what happens when farmers follow the opinion of those who say 'the more the better'? What are the consequences when they use too much poison and spray too late, or when the poison cloud also covers the plants growing under the trees or the neighbour's cultivated garden or field?

I have seen the results of tests conducted in Switzerland and elsewhere that even the experts considered disturbing. I once visited an American institute that operates with government support where the professor in charge acquainted me with the results of experiments conducted with animals, and the things I saw and learned were more frightening than impressive. No one should simply close his eyes to the lasting effects of chlorinated hydrocarbons such as DDT, Duldrin and Aldrin, and it is irresponsible if the damage caused by them is hushed up. I do admit that these chemicals have saved the lives of a number of people, especially in tropical regions. On the other hand, one must face the fact that one cannot shoot sparrows with cannon balls. Honestly, I would not like to eat vegetables and fruit every day knowing that they contained measurable traces of these poisons, which actually remain in the body. For this reason they steadily accumulate in the system until a certain degree of concentration is reached that puts the person's health and life in jeopardy.

Eichholz, a well-known and outspoken professor from Heidelberg, Germany, has stated that in large cities hardly an autopsy takes place where the fatty tissue does not show traces of DDT. People who lose weight during a severe illness are in danger when poisons begin to settle in the fatty tissue, because the body will draw on its own tissues and the toxic matter will enter the bloodstream and trigger reactions that not even the physician is able to explain.

Vegetable Feed for Babies

It is certainly a sign of progress that babies are today given vegetable juices to supplement their usual gruels and milk food. I am sure that this is one reason why vitamin deficiencies are much rarer now than years ago. Infant mortality has also decreased considerably, and it is quite possible that better nutrition has contributed to the improvement.

But what happens when the loving mother has prepared the juice with such care but the carrots, for example, contain poison? How puzzled she must be when her baby does not put on any weight or, worse, loses weight, despite her constant attention. The baby's stool becomes thinner and thinner, but the doctor is unable to diagnose the cause, having eliminated the possibility of its being coeliac disease. Not long ago, on a visit abroad, I was shown the results obtained from tests on carrots grown in Germany, Switzerland and Italy; they all contained considerable amounts of poisonous chlorinated hydrocarbons. The implications of this are quite frightening. The offspring of animals that had been given these carrots to eat did not live beyond the age of babyhood.

Now the thing is, if a mother presented her dead baby in court to prove that the poisoned carrots were responsible for her baby's death, she would be hard pressed to find even one scientist willing to back up and prove her case. The short-sighted farmer is unable to realise the consequences of the excessive use of pesticides, or their application at the wrong time, so the question of poisonous sprays and the people's general health is more acute and urgent than ever. It is the responsibility of our governments to do something about this danger, to subject the poison-spraying to government inspection and to see to it that the problem is judged without prejudice; after all, our governments have the power to introduce appropriate legislation and give the necessary direction whenever damaging practices come to the fore.

The Call for Safe Pesticides

The call for pesticides that do not harm our own health or that of our children is more urgent than ever before. If it is really impossible to fight pests without some kind of poison, then we should at least employ plant poisons that are easily eliminated, neutralised and made ineffective. When I was in South America I came to know of certain roots that were used as an insecticide. They had hardly been discovered when the industry replaced them by synthetic chemicals. Systematic research, I am sure, would no doubt find ways of using tobacco extract, products made from derris (of the *Artemisia* family), and various tropical plants. Such products could be used without disturbing the biological balance in nature or harming our health. It is possible that plant pesticides may be considerably more expensive than chemical products, but it is only right that people's health should come before financial considerations.

ORGANIC FARMING

The call for organic farming will have to be given more and more attention, and it is good to see the results so far. No longer is organic farming palmed off as eccentric or a dream. Organically grown vegetables, for example carrots, are absolutely essential for children. If you have your own garden, however small, you can be truly happy because you will be able to cultivate it organically and ensure the growth of pure vegetables. Our condensed carrot juice is made from organically grown carrots. However, if you are unable to grow your own vegetables, they are now available at most health food stores, an increasing number of supermarkets and from farmers who have changed over to organic methods.

Poisonous chemical sprays are detrimental and a health hazard not only when used on the land, but also on fruit trees. This practice still demands careful investigation and we should always remember that the consequences can be disastrous when financial profits are put before health and safety in the production of food.

DOES ANYONE REMEMBER THE BEES?

Having become used to disregarding the health of human consumers, who worries about the welfare of the bees? Hardly anyone gives a thought to the fact that millions of bees and other useful insects are killed every year by poisonous sprays. Perhaps we will realise one day the extent of the damage that has been done. We should never forget that insects have other functions besides pollinating our fruit trees. To give one example, the ichneumon wasp is able to keep millions of the larch roller (tortricid moth) larvae, or caterpillars, in check before they can destroy all the beautiful greenery of the larch trees. On occasions, when insufficient DDT is available, the trees are cleaned up and saved from these pests by these small wasps, which finish them off.

DEVASTATION IN THE JUNGLE

I became aware of the ruthless manner in which some enterprises are conducted through some friends in Guatemala. For years, our contact in that country, a Canadian married to an Indian woman, has produced honey for us. One day, quite unexpectedly, a powerful cotton company established itself in his neighbourhood and began to clear vast forest areas and plant cotton. Without any real necessity, only because of habit, the owners had their cotton plantation dusted, not manually of course, but on the generous lines the Americans are accustomed to, by plane. The finely distributed poison was intended to prevent supposed pests from settling on the cotton plants. It did not worry the commercial giant that various other insects, including bees, were killed as a consequence of their dusting. In fact, our contact lost 300 colonies of bees! Moreover, he was forced by these circumstances to pick up what was left and move to another area. The beekeeper, a simple, uninfluential man, has decided not to sue for compensation; he could not risk losing the case and facing bankruptcy as a result.

Today, totally untouched places in nature are few and far between, and their number continues to decrease, so that we wonder where it will all end. I remember talking to a zoologist I met in Guayaquil, Equador, as he was preparing to travel to the Galápagos Islands to study the iguanas, large lizards, living there. He poured out a tale of woe about the devastation being inflicted and how, soon, he would hardly know where to go anymore to study certain animals in their natural habitat. Wanton destruction and killing and the advance of civilisation were changing the environment so drastically that these animals were being robbed of their habitat and chance of survival. Something or someone has to pay when short-sighted, one-sided measures are taken and the biological balance of nature is disturbed.

Look Out – Metallic Salts Are Hazardous

More than twenty years ago, Dr E. Eckmann gave a lecture in which he pointed out that metallic salts, especially of heavy metals, become deposited in the lymphatic system. Other scientists have proved that these salts can form a barrier in the kidneys and that they also become lodged in the spine, causing problems even decades after originally settling there, as is the case with arsenic.

Plant poisons can also do us harm, but it is usually much easier to expel them, whereas metallic poisons remain in the body and do extensive damage, as a rule, years later. It is not quite clear yet how far metallic poisons contribute to the onset of paralysis, muscular dystrophy, lymphogranuloma and all kinds of conditions connected with the spinal column and cord.

How Do Metallic Salts Get into the Body?

You may wonder about the answer to this question. Well, there are various medicines that contain metals, for example Salvarsan. If this is taken, the patient will be ingesting mercury and arsenic, since both of these are ingredients of Salvarsan. There are also certain medicines for the blood that contain iron and copper.

Secondly, metallic salts are used in some old-fashioned preserving processes and, of course, in pesticides; these contain copper, lead, arsenic and so forth. In the case of pesticides the danger arises even as they are being sprayed or dusted, because they can thus be inhaled. They then settle on vegetables and fruits, posing an added danger, since it is difficult to remove the traces even by washing the produce.

It is still not fully known which of the new and frightening diseases are connected with the insidious effect of toxic metallic salts. Some of these diseases cause partial or total paralysis, confronting the doctor with an unsolvable problem and subjecting the patient to painful infirmity. Most likely this is due to poisoning through metallic salts, in addition to the influence of radiation. It is for this reason that we cannot be too careful in our efforts to ensure that we do not take into the body dangerous poisons in the form of metallic salts that undermine our health and future.

Chemical Sprays Are a Health Hazard
Only recently I heard from a mother whose child came down with an extremely dangerous form of poisoning after eating sprayed grapes.

Another report came from a woman in her sixties who loves the grapes from the Ticino canton in Switzerland. Although she should have known better, she would eat the grapes that obviously still had traces of pesticide on them and then, without fail, would suffer from digestive upsets accompanied by strong fermentation in the bowels. At first she thought that the problem was caused by eating too much raw sauerkraut, but as soon as the grape season came to an end so did her intestinal trouble, even though she continued to enjoy eating sauerkraut regularly. Moreover, she only consumed sauerkraut obtained from a reliable source, which was prepared in a natural way and not detrimental to health. These facts pointed directly to the sprayed grapes from Ticino as the cause of her upset.

I received another account from a woman who had observed similar reactions in the case of an old friend in her eighties. This old lady had been bedridden for twelve years following a stroke, paralysed from the spine to her chest. For eight weeks her organs failed to function, but then her digestion returned to normal. Still, the patient could not eat berries or stone fruit brought by her visitors, because half an hour after eating such fruit she began to feel a tightness and dragging pain in the bowels and experience flatulence, followed by diarrhoea. This condition lasted for about one or two days and the patient, understandably, felt miserable all the while. So she avoided all fruit which she felt might have been sprayed or fertilised with chemicals. The point was that she experienced no problems whatsoever if she ate cherries, strawberries, plums, grapes, currants, raspberries or blackberries that had been organically grown and not treated with chemicals. But whenever she did experience some disturbance, the cause was always the same – chemical sprays and fertilisers.

The lady who reported these findings had read an article in our magazine *Gesundheits-Nachrichten* (*Health News*) dealing with 'sprayed grapes' and was now sure of her observation and conclusion. She was glad to have discerned correctly the cause of her friend's problems, even though she had been laughed at by some, who were of the opinion that the patient had simply been imagining these things.

Although the above causes of poisoning can be avoided if proper care is exercised, there are still other, undiscovered, sources that can be even more disastrous because their potential danger is not discernible.

AN EXAMPLE OF POISONING THROUGH CHEMICAL SPRAYS

I recently visited the family of a farmer whom I knew through friends. It was a chance visit, and the farmer's wife, who had heard of me and had also read some of my publications, took advantage of the opportunity to talk to me about her little daughter's condition. She described the girl's symptoms, and how she usually lay in her bed quite listless and apathetic, and it occurred to me immediately that this was probably some form of poisoning. The little girl had been treated with penicillin in hospital, yet her condition had deteriorated. It so happened that I knew the senior consultant of the hospital personally and would say that he is an excellent physician, but unfortunately he was looking for the pathological cause in the wrong places.

I asked the unhappy mother about the circumstances she could still remember from before her little daughter fell ill and whether she could think of any influences that might have been responsible. Sure enough, what she remembered confirmed my suspicions because she told me that her husband had been spraying the trees round about that time; in fact, the girl had walked straight into the poison cloud. From that moment onward, her mother said, the trouble started. I was in no doubt at all that the circumstances and symptoms proved what the cause really was.

Now all I wanted to know was whether the doctors had been told of the incident, and she said that they had. Yet only one doctor at the hospital considered pesticide poisoning to be the cause of the girl's condition, whereas his colleagues flatly rejected this opinion. It was perfectly clear to me, however, why penicillin could not even relieve the symptoms, because it would have given at least temporary improvement if bacteria, instead of chemical poisons, had been the cause of the illness. Having made the correct diagnosis, I had no problem in choosing the appropriate treatment and remedies, and I suspect, no, I am convinced, that the natural treatment and necessary natural remedies helped the little girl to recover.

EARLY WARNING

I have always been against the spraying or dusting of crops with poison. But if anyone is of the opinion that he cannot do without it, he should at least ensure that it is done in the winter. Moreover, it is important that farmers take their responsibilities seriously and protect their workers and, especially, children from any possible harm. The consequences are not always immediately recognisable, because the chemicals may contain slow-acting poisons, such as copper, lead, arsenic and tar. The modern products, chlorinated hydrocarbon compounds and phosphoric acid esters in their various forms, are even more dangerous, since these poisons do not merely stick to the outside skin of fruit but actually penetrate the leaves and circulate in the sap. It is too late to sound a warning when a farmer or farmworker comes down with lung cancer ten or fifteen years after exposure to poison. Telling him that he should have worn a face mask when spraying his trees will be of no help or comfort to him then.

Never think that the body becomes used to the poisons so that in time they will do no harm. This, unfortunately, is untrue. A quarry worker does not become used to stone dust either and it will be of no use to inform him of the danger he is exposed to when he has already fallen victim to the incurable condition of silicosis. It is certain that this disease will end his life prematurely. It does no good to become careless or complacent as regards obvious dangers, or to lose one's fear of occupational hazards and neglect to take the necessary precautions.

ANOTHER CASE OF PESTICIDE POISONING

Pesticides can cause other disturbances when, for example, sprayed fruit is eaten. The headmistress of a girls' boarding school telephoned me during one cherry season because all but one of the girls were suffering with diarrhoea; some were even feeling so unwell that they had to stay in bed.

My first question concerned the menu, as I wanted to know what the girls had eaten the day before. The answer pointed straight to the cause of the problem, the girls having eaten cherries fresh from the trees at 4 o'clock in the afternoon. The one girl who had not been affected was also the only one who had not eaten any cherries because she did not fancy any. It will be quite obvious how this circumstance led us directly to the cause of the trouble.

I asked the headmistress to let me have some cherries for testing and recommended her to check with the farmer about spraying. And indeed, the investigation brought to light that the farmer had sprayed his trees shortly before the cherries were ripe for harvesting; in fact, they still had spots of dried pesticide on them.

How much simpler it would be if people of responsibility were to continue the search for harmless, nonpoisonous pesticides. If sought with patience and perseverance, no doubt such substances could be discovered among the great number of plants available to us. What a boon and blessing this would be, circumventing all kinds of damage and upsets.

Copper Cookware

Disadvantages and Possible Danger
Copper vessels were used much more in days gone by than they are today. Copper pots and pans were the pride of every prosperous home. But since the knowledge of vitamins has become widespread, the use of copper cookware has gone out of fashion. It was found that copper is a catalyst and, as such, destroys vitamin C. If rose hips, barberry purée or other vitamin-rich foods are cooked in copper pans, only a small amount of this vitamin remains intact. The same foods, if cooked in an enamel or stainless steel pot, will retain a much higher content of valuable vitamins. As far as health is concerned, copper pots and pans have no place in the kitchen. What is more, copper oxidises easily and forms harmful verdigris.

I have observed many cases of problems with the mucous membranes of the stomach and intestines resulting from eating food that has been prepared using copper utensils. The liver may also be affected since everything that passes the portal vein from the digestive organs comes into contact with the liver, the poisons having to be broken down. It is nothing unusual that jaundice results when large amounts of such metal oxides and metallic salts are regularly taken into the system. Changes in the blood are also possible and certain forms of anaemia may be connected with them. Kidney damage is another possible result of poisoning with metal oxides. And it has been noticed that copper, just like aluminium, can trigger a mild disturbance of the central nervous system.

The Question of Health
All these factors are important enough to make us look at our pots and pans and check whether some should be discarded in the interest of good health. Certainly all copper pans should be removed from your kitchen and no longer used for cooking. Homoeopathy prescribes *Cuprum* (copper) in potencies of up to 20x. So, if such high dilutions produce a medicinal effect, surely

it is most appropriate to consider the potential danger of your cookware.

Copper has an interesting effect on microscopic organisms. Put some copper shavings in a cloth bag, place this in some water and watch what happens to the microscopic protozoans, algae, fungi and bacteria living in it. They all die. Without losing much of its weight, copper can produce such a powerful catalytic effect that it kills these microscopic organisms.

Silver-plated or nickel-plated copper can cause upsets when they are used for toys, because once the plating has been abraded, the oxidised metal can harm the child playing with such a toy.

All these considerations should make us want to keep away from copper. If you wish to cook and live in a way that is conducive to good health, you must take care to choose safe cookware. Why add to the already existing detrimental influences in our modern life? As it is, our food loses much of its natural value because of chemical additives, preservatives and the refining processes, apart from other influences such as chemical sprays and fertilisers used in its production. You are merely following a course of wisdom if, in your kitchen, you take care not to add to all this pollution but keep the standard as high as possible so that your health will benefit.

Are Synthetic Fibres Detrimental to Health?

Professor Jaeger devoted much time to the question of fibres, or materials, some fifty years ago. The main point of the arguments current at that time was whether silk, wool or cotton were to be preferred. Dr Lahmann of Dresden, at the 'White Hart', joined in the controversial debates on underwear and fibres. Those who had the money wore silk, which was considered the healthiest fibre of all. Depending on its quality, wool may cause itching and not everyone can wear it next to the skin. In particular, women in the change of life and after are usually very sensitive and cannot stand wool; it may be that even cotton causes itching and they have to resort to buying expensive pure silk lingerie, which produces no reaction and feels pleasant to the skin.

The Arabs and Bedouins living in the desert prefer to wear wide, flowing woollen clothes and coats as a protection against the heat of the day and the cold of the night. Cotton had many opponents at first, but in time it came to be accepted and established itself as a good, inexpensive material, especially as a substitute for linen, which was much more expensive. Eventually, cotton began to replace linen more and more.

All these fibres are produced by nature, yet each one has its own characteristics and qualities. Wool and silk are better insulators than cotton and linen, making them more suitable for winter weather and cold days. Interestingly, however, silk is also pleasant to wear in the heat of summer because it has a cool feel.

Synthetic Materials

For several decades now there have been new materials and products on the market, based on fibres that are made synthetically by machines. The principle of manufacture is similar to the one used by the silk worm in making its fibre or thread. Indeed, every time man intends to produce a substitute for a natural material he has to learn from the marvels of nature. A liquid pressed through fine nozzles hardens into a tough thread when exposed to the air. The thread is then spun and woven like silk. The resulting artificial fibre, called nylon, perlon or other names, is of great importance to industry. However, is wearing such synthetic materials healthy and can it be recommended? The answer to this question is of great interest to the many patients whose letters have so often made this enquiry.

We can only base our answer on experience and observed facts; for example, these artificial fibres had hardly been on the market any time at all when many women began to complain of aches and pains after wearing stockings made from them. Synthetic lingerie produced the same unpleasant reactions, such as pain similar to that experienced with rheumatism. Yet it is strange that not all people are affected in the same way when wearing synthetic materials.

It seems that artificial fibres are able to influence or partially destroy the body's electric field. Adults and children who notice such disturbances should wear only natural fibres. It is careless when symptoms of pain are ignored only because it is easier and more convenient to look after synthetic fibres than it is to treat natural ones. Wearing artificial fibres can even trigger spasms. Those who suffer from rheumatism and nervous problems should not wear artificial fibres, nor should people who have circulatory problems, since these may be aggravated. It is, however, impossible to give a general rule and each person must find out for himself which fibre suits him the best, because personal experience is of greater value than a whole series of well-meaning suggestions and advice.

Every material develops or possesses energy of the electromagnetic kind, which can be easily observed in the evening when undressing. Some pieces of clothing and underwear may crackle and spark, depending on the kind of fibre worn. Science does not understand everything involved in this area, and research is still in its infancy. For this reason we ourselves, in the interests of our own well-being, must watch our physical reactions to certain fibres, draw the right conclusions and then act accordingly.

Animals and Insects as Carriers of Disease

Some years ago, on my arrival in La Paz having travelled from Cuzco, the Swiss consul warned me to be careful of the Indians on the Altiplano, saying they were riddled with parasites. However well meant the advice was it actually came too late, since I had been living among the carefree native Indians for quite a while and had seen for myself that many individuals had lice.

From the reports of German doctors who had accompanied the troops on the German campaign in Russia I knew that lice can transmit typhus. Of course, not all lice are infected with this disease but they are an awful nuisance anyway. I have often had to give medical advice to patients who returned from foreign countries complaining about intense itching, especially in the hairy parts of the body. Mind you, I could not be so blunt as to tell them outright that the itching was caused by lice.

Parasites, Tropical Leeches and Mosquitoes

In tropical countries there are many tiny parasites, such as mites, that penetrate the skin and cause cold or hot fevers. I myself once caught such an infection in the tropical jungle and only DDT was able to save my life. These tiny parasites are not visible to the naked eye. They stick to plants and when touched with bare arms or other parts of the body they attach themselves to the skin and enter through the pores. The resulting infection is referred to as 'cold death' because the body temperature progressively decreases until life ceases if no help is forthcoming in good time.

When you are roaming through the jungle, leeches may fall from the trees, drop onto you and attach themselves to your skin. These tropical bloodsuckers, however, are not harmless like their cousins in temperate zones, because they can cause blood poisoning. The mosquitoes in those areas are also dangerous and able to transmit malaria. This disease is rampant near the headwaters of the Amazon and no traveller there should dare to sleep without a mosquito net. Even so, these carriers of disease are equipped with a peculiar instinct that enables them to find every chink in a hut and tear in a net and so torment their victims. When I was visiting that area I often discovered some mosquitoes under my net in the morning and, on squashing them, would find them to be full of blood. It could have frightened me, but perhaps I am immune to malaria or the modest quantities of quinine I took to be on the safe side were enough to protect me. In Sri Lanka I came across another type of mosquito dreaded by everyone because it transmits the fateful disease called filariasis, or elephantiasis.

Rats, Mice, Domestic Animals and Flies

Some time ago I visited San Francisco, where I met a scientist with whom I discussed a number of problems. Among other things he told me that in the dock area rats are often caught that are infected with cholera. In such a way it is possible for international ports to be endangered by foreign ships even though no sick person is on board, the reason being that rats and mice are disease-carriers. If more efforts were made to eradicate not only mice and rats but also flies and mosquitoes, I am sure that foot-and-mouth disease would spread much less. It is a documented fact that in the tropics, the jungle and the prairies more people die from diseases transmitted by insects than are killed by tigers, leopards, snakes or any other wild animal.

On the other hand, our own domestic animals are not necessarily safe either and can also transmit disease. For instance, it is possible to contract brucellosis by drinking infected raw milk. This animal disease, which is characterised by a recurrent or undulating fever is by no means pleasant and is difficult to cure, unless powerful doses of vitamin E are given. Most people know that cats and dogs can easily transmit worms to humans if no care is taken and close contact with the animals maintained. For one thing, never let these pets lick your hands when they try to show their joy and enthusiasm. Then there are some forms of eczema that can be transmitted to humans by cows, mainly the calves. Beware of these conditions too, since it is often very hard to cure them. Dab the eruption at once with diluted *Molkosan* (whey concentrate). It usually helps to kill the causative agents.

Even if pets and animals are dear to you and you love them, remember the reasons why it is necessary to keep them at a proper distance. Moreover, do not think of flies and mosquitoes as being harmless and entitled to fly around your home. Make a determined effort to rid the home of these and other insects and you will be much less likely to suffer from infectious diseases.

Climatic Influences

Today, many unnatural influences undermine our health and we often lack enough strength and energy to put up with the vicissitudes of the climate. To be exact, many of us are much more sensitive than were earlier generations. This should not surprise us if we look at our modern circumstances, yet it is more difficult to understand why the influence of climate can be so strange and inexplicable in its effect. Perhaps the laws governing climate and weather may still elude us despite scientific and meteorological progress.

On a visit to Sri Lanka I had the opportunity to make an extraordinary discovery in connection with the climate and its miraculous effect on us. The case in question concerned a nurse who had suffered from severe asthma attacks in her native Australia. The hot and humid climate of Colombo should, on all counts, have aggravated her condition but, instead, it had such a favourable influence that her asthma disappeared altogether. This change in her condition was in complete contrast to the usual experience with the disease, since dry, warm climates, particularly mountain and desert climates, generally have the best curative effect, or at least help to alleviate it. However, when this nurse visits her brother in the dry and cooler air in the higher altitude of the island, her health problem returns immediately. Once back on the hot and humid coastland, the trouble is as if blown away. For this reason the nurse has been living in the low-lying area for some years without as much as a twinge of her asthmatic problem.

No Rule without Exception

The above case shows that rules formulated on the basis of experience and observation do have exceptions and that some people respond well to something to which they should not. Most people suffer and experience intense disturbances when the seasonal winds blow, for instance the föhn, khamsin and monsoon, but there are some who feel well in this kind of weather. The sea air may not agree with some individuals, while they may feel good in the mountains, perhaps when engaging in winter sports.

Whatever good advice the doctor can give you, it would be

appropriate to get to know yourself a little better, to find out what your body needs in order to feel fit and well. You cannot always go by what others think or tell you. It is useful to watch yourself and see what benefits your well-being so that you can be guided by the favourable effects and so be able to choose the best place for your holidays or work. I can tell you from experience that some people suffer from liver trouble in Europe but the moment they change their habitat and move to the United States they are completely rid of their disturbances. Then I know patients who simply did not feel well while living in Basle, but after moving to the Appenzellerland where the föhn is often blowing, they had no complaints whatsoever. The opposite is also true, for many people feel unwell in areas with much föhn, but when they go to the Jura where it is unknown, or stay by Lake Geneva, even with a northeasterly wind, they remain fit and well.

Unfortunately, there are not many books that deal with bioclimatic influences on general well-being and the various illnesses. The only such manual so far published that I am aware of is one by the American physician Dr Manfred Curry.

The Sun Means Life and Death
If we put a hot-house or indoor plant outside in the blazing summer sun, it will probably die. Remembering that the sun throws out powerful radiation can save us from experiencing such a disappointment. The sun's rays consist of different wavelengths, a bundle of rays that can be likened to a cable made up of many wires, each one with its own frequency. We should not forget that the ray complex of the sun puts a great strain on plants, animals and humans. The effect can be illustrated by considering the sun's energy in terms of electric voltage. For example, if a power point has been set for 380 volts and we plug in an appliance that is adjusted for 220 volts, the difference in voltage will create heat and can burn out the appliance. Similarly, a destructive effect can result in unhealthy plants because, figuratively speaking, the higher voltage will damage the weak plant. Instead of charging or invigorating the plant, the sun's energy will destroy it. Plants that are damaged, maggoty or infected with insect pests will live longer if they are not exposed to intense sunlight, better still if they are kept out of the sun altogether.

The Sun's Effects on Humans

Animals seem to know about the sun's effects instinctively, because you will never see a sick animal lying in the sun. They carefully avoid sunlight and rest in the shade. We, too, should know and understand that we cannot expose ourselves to the sun if we are not well; in fact, doing so could lead to death. When a friend or acquaintance dies suddenly we invariably wonder about the actual cause of death. Recently a lady with whom I was acquainted had a stroke and died. Now I know that she had suffered from high blood pressure, yet just prior to her stroke she had been working outside in the blazing sun without a head covering; this, of course, would have raised her temperature considerably. The same kind of thing is repeated in hundreds of cases every year.

Patients who suffer from, or once had, tuberculosis should also avoid sunbathing. It should always be remembered that sunlight may even have a stronger effect in the winter when it is reflected from the snow. Intense sunlight may cause a focal reaction; increased circulation or hyperaemia can trigger bleeding and have serious consequences, even causing death. Inflamed parts of the body, infections and latent infections in the lymphatic system should never be exposed to strong sunlight because they could be caused to erupt or become acute, leading to serious reactions that place the patient's life in danger.

APPROPRIATE PRECAUTIONS

Even if you are healthy you should not expose yourself to the sun's rays indiscriminately if you want to avoid trouble. You will have to be patient and adjust your body gradually, staying in direct sunlight for only short periods at a time. And another thing: it is much better for you to move around in the sun rather than lie in it passively. Sunbathing in half-shade is far healthier and can even be recommended for the sick.

In low-lying areas the sun has little power in the winter months and more and more people prefer to spend their holidays in the mountains. High up in the mountains amidst the snow and ice it is quite common to see girls and young women in their bathing suits. They hope to get an even better tan in winter through the reflection of the snow than they would in summer. Watching this effort could really be a great comfort to the dark-skinned populations of the earth, especially those among them who strive to look as light-coloured as possible and escape the contempt they think white people might have for them because they are dark!

Both healthy and sick people should take the same precautions in winter and in summer. If you have never had the opportunity to see for yourself the amount of care taken by desert dwellers in order to find protection from direct sunlight, you would be surprised to find them walking around in voluminous woollen gowns and thick head coverings in spite of the heat. As a rule, it is quite cold during the night in desert areas and a warm head covering is no luxury, but the fact that the natives do not go without it in the daytime either shows that it is pleasant, comfortable and a protection. There are still some natives who wear little or no clothes at all, but remember that this is less dangerous for dark-coloured skin than it is for white, since dark skin absorbs part of the rays.

Anyone who knows how to appreciate nature's gifts recognises the sun's value as a source of energy. At the same time, however, no one should forget to exercise caution and show respect for its power. Every year we hear of cases with tragic consequences and these remind us of the absolute necessity to familiarise ourselves with both the good and bad effects of sunbathing. As with any other therapy, we should be guided by our personal condition and decide on the most beneficial length of exposure. Take the example of water treatments where we have to take into consideration the individual's predisposition in order to know whether hot or cold would be better. Similarly, it would be foolish to decide on taking some physical treatment if we know that medication would give better results, or vice versa. Five minutes in the sun may do us real good, whereas an hour's exposure may be disastrous, even more so for those who are sick already.

People in today's industrialised society should never forget that they cannot expose themselves to the sun's energy indiscriminately. We have not been used to walking around in nature since infancy without much clothing, exposed to all kinds of weather without fear or trouble. Instead, for generations we have been trained to protect our bodies from inclement weather by sitting and working in heated rooms and wearing thick clothing. We are not toughened-up, but reared more like hot-house plants, and this is a great disadvantage when we want to let the full impact of solar rays work on our bodies without any protective measures. So, do not do it, or you will have to reckon with the consequential damage to your health.

Intense Heat and its Dangers

I am always reminded of visiting a hospitable desert Bedouin in his tent whenever someone complains about a hot summer's day in my native Switzerland, where cold and rainfall are well known but not real drought. In the shade of his black goat's-hair tent the temperature must have been around 40 °C (104 °F) and the air outside was shimmering in the heat. In spite of this the bearded man, whose deeply lined face betrayed his advanced age, served me hot tea. I was astonished and wanted to know the reason. His answer was quick. It was completely wrong, he said, to drink cold water in the intense heat; it would only increase the thirst instead of quenching it. And so would sweet drinks, he added. It would be asking for trouble and not healthy either. At the time of our conversation I was still doubtful about his conclusion, but eventually it was confirmed by my own personal experience. It is really true that a hot drink or juicy fruit are better than anything else to quench one's thirst in the heat. What is more, they may prevent you from catching a cold, but there is no guarantee for that if you gulp down ice-cold beverages.

It is also important to breathe through the nose when it is very hot, not only when you are in the cold. The nose is equipped with a built-in air-conditioning system, or temperature control, which warms up the incoming air in the winter and cools it down in the summer.

Additional Advice

People who live in the desert keep themselves fit in spite of the continuous heat and we would do well to learn from them and imitate their habits and customs. Since not only hot beverages are important but also the way they dress, we might try comparing their ideas to ours; in so doing we will be surprised to find that the desert people do not at all agree with our custom of wearing light clothing when it is very hot. On the contrary, in the desert they wrap themselves in loose woollen robes that are more like cloaks and keep their heads covered. Watching these people you can see that they feel comfortable and seem to suffer much less in the intense sunlight than we do when wearing tight clothes or swimwear. The loose robes protect the Bedouins wonderfully and we obtain the impression that they do not perspire. We give much too little thought to the fact that the sun's intense rays are extremely damaging to anyone who has not sufficiently adapted to them. There is the danger of sunstroke, and sunburn can set off

575

permanent or prolonged damage to the peripheral nerve and vascular systems.

The Bedouins do not feel the need to lie around motionless in the hot sun for hours on end; they do their work and moving around early in the morning or in the evening. We can also take a look at animals and their habits to see whether such exposure is beneficial. In fact, no animal, domestic or wild stays in the direct sunlight when it is hot, preferring instead to seek a shady spot or half-shade.

What do all these observations teach us? They suggest that we, too, should use common sense. The sun's rays have a stronger effect in the mountains than in the lowlands or by the sea, and if you are used to living at a high elevation you will be able to stand the sunlight there better than in low-lying areas. The converse is true of people who are used to living in lower areas. They would do well to avoid the sun's rays in the mountains but become less tired when exposed to the sun in their habitual lowland climate.

Let me tell you an experience from Sri Lanka that confirms my point. Together with our friends who lived by the sea we went to visit some other friends in the beautiful hills. How amused the hill dwellers were when they saw the lowland folk quickly make for the shady places because the mountain sun was too much for them. Not so with us Swiss; we felt much better than we would by the sea, where our lowland friends were at home and on their best form. The conclusion we must draw is that we should never go beyond what does us good. Brief spells of indirect sunlight are more beneficial and healing than the more common sunbathing. Moving around in the half-shade is a healthy exercise. People who suffer from high blood pressure and heart trouble should never expose themselves to intense heat or strong sunlight. Doing so could lead to sudden death.

When it is extremely hot you must be careful to avoid cooling down suddenly. Bathing in very cold water, for example in a mountain lake or a river with glacier water, can pose a great risk. Although I have mentioned the matter of drinking before, I would like to reiterate in this context that it is bad for us to drink water that is too cold. So, if you are on a mountain tour and nothing but cold water from a spring is at hand, add a little thirst-quenching *Molkosan* but no sugar and sip the water slowly while insalivating well. In this way you will avoid the chilling effect your body would otherwise experience and your thirst will be quenched much better than if you had taken a sweet soft drink. It is thus worthwhile putting a small bottle of Molkosan in your rucksack when going on a hike in the summer.

Breathing Means Life

The peculiar connections between our psychological and physical life are reflected in the sentence 'Breathing means life'. Again and again we find this concept discussed in journals and lecture halls and it may be of benefit from a scientific as well as a practical point of view if we examine and analyse what lies behind it.

It is a fact that mental stress can have a potent effect on our general health. I have experienced that myself. If one's profession requires one to be in the public eye, hostile people will engender malice and slander and make life difficult. Not everyone has a 'thick skin' and is able to shake off any and every kind of attack without feeling hurt, letting storm and the sound of ruin blow over him without upsetting his inner balance. You may think that you know your own strength and believe that your mental health is greater than it really is, but some problems can upset you so much that, in spite of having a healthy body, your organs begin to weaken, and may even give in and stop functioning. Anger, worry, disgust, disappointment and frustration are bad companions for health as they gnaw at our nerves and, eventually, the liver and pancreas become affected. This is what happened to me. My stomach began to play up in spite of my maintaining the best possible diet. Flatulence followed. Breathing became difficult and heart problems appeared. And, to top it all, appendicitis set in. A colleague examined me, confirming the diagnosis and expressing concern and fear. He advised me to have an operation.

Instead, I fasted, drank only carrot juice, and took hot water treatments. I felt slight relief, but the condition did not really improve.

What was I able to do to regain my resistance and get rid of the disturbances?

Breathing Exercises

Thinking things over, I hit on the idea of exercising the abdominal organs by rhythmic breathing. At first I practised this by drawing in the abdomen when I inhaled, and pressing it out when I exhaled. On further consideration, however, I decided to reverse the order of things and draw in the abdomen when I exhaled and press it out when I inhaled. This resulted in considerable relief after a little while. The gases escaped and I felt better.

It is true to say that the exercises made me a little tired to begin with and gave me light pains that reminded me of aching muscles, but soon I noticed a peculiar warmth surge through the body. The pain in the heart region disappeared. I increased the breathing exercises daily, doing them once, twice, three times, four times a day, very briefly at first, then for five, ten, fifteen minutes. I exhaled slowly and steadily while pulling in the abdomen at the same time, then inhaled and slowly pressed out the abdomen. If this is done vigorously, the chest really fills up well and, in time, can hold twice as much air as before.

First thing in the morning I would do my breathing exercises, repeating them at noon during my lunch hour and again at night before going to bed. I began to sleep better, as the intensive breathing exercises gave me a feeling of pleasant tiredness and relaxation. Sleep became more restful and worries, sorrows and anxieties were no longer able to wake me up in the middle of the night. What a marvellous thing it is that breathing exercises have such a profound effect, even being able to influence our mind!

From a physical point of view, my abdominal muscles seemed to be the first to benefit. They became stronger, my diaphragm developed and my digestion improved. I no longer felt any trace of pain and the inflammation which had plagued me for weeks disappeared.

No doubt the natural remedies I took also helped, but without the breathing exercises it would have been difficult to achieve such success.

Some time after this experiment I saw a chiropractor, who was a friend of mine. The X-rays he took showed a normal spine, no arthritis, in fact, no signs of degeneration. Happily he assured me that my diaphragm muscles were exceptionally well developed, better than average, which I attributed to the breathing exercises. Slowly, I began to realise that the exercises had contributed to relieving the mental pressures that had bothered me. It only took five, ten or fifteen minutes each time, but eventually I began to feel more cheerful. It was now easier for me to bear the problems that had weighed so heavily on my mind. Light and sunshine entered my life once more. Indeed, in my case, 'breathing meant life'!

Breathing through the Nose
Many years ago I had an experience when, quite by chance, I applied the same breathing method. My lungs were damaged in a

car accident and the resulting problem could have posed great difficulties for me.

I decided to go to the mountains for the sake of pure air, adopted a natural diet and was making satisfactory progress. The 'finishing touches', however, were provided by regular deep-breathing exercises. I concentrated on thorough exhalation, followed by equally thorough inhalation. I began these exercises in front of an open window in fairly cold weather. In time, my condition became so good that I was able to do the breathing exercises in a temperature of −10 °C (14 °F), in front of the open balcony door, with the curtains drawn and without clothes, for fifteen minutes. In spite of the cold, the strenuous exercise made me perspire.

At the same time I combined the breathing exercises with a relaxation exercise. While standing on a carpet, I tightened and loosened my muscles again and again, tightening when I inhaled and loosening when I exhaled. I then took a short rest before starting the exercise again. The air seemed to flow through my body like a warm, pleasant stream. If I had been breathing through my mouth, I would have undoubtedly caught a chill, with the possibility of pneumonia developing. Thus I became aware of the importance of breathing through the nose and could appreciate why this is recommended in all health books.

We possess a heating element in our nose which warms the air as we breathe it in; thus air below freezing point will be warmed up to natural body temperature as it passes through the nostrils. Our lungs would suffer if we breathed in cold air all the time and it could not be warmed before entering. That is why it is important in cold climates to breathe through the nose and when it is really cold to wrap a woollen scarf over the mouth and nose to protect the membranes. In extremely cold weather no one likes to breathe through the mouth anyway, but if you did, you could become so ill that you would have to stay in bed and not be able to enjoy yourself in the mountain snow. If you persist in this lack of care, you might eventually suffer to such an extent that you stop breathing altogether and then, of course, will never again benefit from your vacations in the mountains!

It is different in the tropics, where the nose acts as a thermostat in the hot and humid air, cooling down the hot air that passes through it to approximately blood heat.

This air-conditioning system in our nose is a marvellous thing. It maintains the air temperature at a level that is appropriate for our needs.

Correct breathing exercises, always breathing through the nose, will help to relieve certain types of headaches. If, in spite of having had a good night's rest, you are still tired in the morning, or if you wake up with cartarrh in the throat, then you must pay particular attention to breathing through the nose. You can tie a handkerchief around your mouth, or put a piece of adhesive tape over it at night, until such a time as breathing through the nose comes easily and naturally. Once you establish the habit of breathing with your mouth closed you will no longer catch cold even in an unheated bedroom and will wake up refreshed for the day ahead. Also, if you snore, you will soon overcome this tendency through nasal breathing.

There is no doubt that correct breathing has a salutary effect on the brain, since the air passes beneath the bony roof of the post-nasal cavity over which the important brain cells lie. Every anatomical detail of the human body serves a specific purpose. For example, why is the nasal space divided into three corridors through which air must pass before it can enter the nasopharyngal canal and the bronchial tubes? In flowing past the blood-vessel-lined interior of the nose the air is warmed and prepared for the lungs. In addition, the anterior nostrils are considerably smaller than the posterior nares and this causes a partial vacuum in the nasal interior, which sucks the warm air from accessory nasal cavities and mixes it with cold air coming in with each breath. With what extraordinary ingenuity the construction of the nose has been designed! Even the smallest detail has a purpose.

This finely tuned detail of anatomical construction becomes more obvious to us when we consider the ear. If the smallest detail in its structure is changed, the acoustic requirements, the reception of sound waves and the transmission to the auditory nerves, will be disturbed and our hearing impaired. Any deformation produces damage and problems. Of course, the same thing applies to our nose.

The Influence of Correct Breathing on Illness

Correct breathing is not only good for the head, abdomen and the whole body, but it influences and stimulates the activity of the sympathetic and parasympathetic nervous systems. These interesting anatomical mechanisms, which could be described as being able to function without a brain, are responsible for the involuntary or subconscious functions of the body. All depend upon correct breathing. In fact, if deep-breathing is practised, you will notice that the sympathetic nervous system works more efficiently, also influencing the activity of the heart.

Even conditions such as angina pectoris may be improved and perhaps even rectified with the help of deep-breathing, if other curative measures are employed at the same time.

If the bronchial tubes have not degenerated beyond repair, deep-breathing can sometimes even cure asthma. If not a cure, then at least a significant improvement is possible.

While constipation requires the regular intake of natural food for improvement, it is put right with correct breathing. If you breathe in and out correctly and sufficiently you will notice that the bowels begin to function better. Five, ten or fifteen minutes, each morning, afternoon and evening should be devoted to deep-breathing exercises. It may take a week, two weeks or even four weeks before the bowels will begin to function more efficiently, but regular movement will not fail to come.

A slim figure can be obtained or retained by correct breathing. A 'spare tyre' will disappear more quickly if, at the same time, attention is given to the diet. Even if one is careless with the diet, correct breathing alone will ensure a 50 per cent success rate in achieving a good figure.

Anyone suffering from enlarged adenoids may do so because of faulty breathing, since it can lead to the formation of these growths of lymphoid tissue. On the other hand, correct breathing, day and night, will prevent them and even make existing ones recede.

Some people lose their sense of smell. For them we recommend a diet of natural foods, for a time perhaps even raw food, and correct breathing exercises. This combination can slowly bring back the sense of smell. Indeed, no illness or disease exists that will not benefit from correct breathing techniques.

If women would but breathe properly, most of their abdominal complaints, tumours and growths could be prevented. Confinements would be much easier because nervous congestions would disappear. Tight clothing, belts and tight-fitting elastic girdles should be avoided if abdominal breathing is to be unrestricted. It is preferable to exercise the abdominal muscles to maintain their elasticity, rather than to control their shape by girdles that restrict and only serve to weaken the muscles. As soon as such an artificial contrivance is removed, the muscles which have been kept in place by pressure alone will again bulge out and the whole purpose of maintaining a pleasing appearance will be defeated.

If children were to be taught correct breathing at school, their lungs, chests and diaphragms would develop properly and respiratory problems of the chest and lungs, as well as obesity, would remain practically unknown. At the same time, they need to be given calcium-rich foods. All these things make for healthy growth of the internal organs and prevent the lungs from weakening.

Singing teachers take great care in helping their students to achieve success by training them in proper breathing techniques. This is why professional singers never lose sight of the importance of correct breathing.

How much time should we spend on breathing exercises? To begin with, one minute may be sufficient. Gradually the time should be increased, to two minutes, then five minutes and so forth, until the correct way of breathing becomes habitual and automatic under any circumstances. As already stated, the exercises should gradually be extended to fifteen minutes. Regularity in practising the exercises is of the utmost importance because it helps the body to become accustomed to a new rhythm; in this way we will find that deep-breathing is better than any other form of exercise. This is a 'medicine' that is within the reach of everyone and costs nothing but a little effort, concentration and perseverance.

We recognise with gratitude the help obtained from natural remedies and food, from rest and proper exercise. But are we aware that it is only through correct breathing that we will crown the other therapeutic successes, adding the finishing touches to them? Once this is so we will then prove the principle that 'breathing means life' to be true.

Fresh Air
The benefits of fresh air are far too little known and appreciated. One so often enters a bedroom, living room, study or work room and finds the air so heavy that it is almost impossible to breathe. These rooms should be aired frequently. A sickroom, in particular, requires a regular change of air because the exhaled gases and germs are harmful to both the sick person and those who care for him. Fresh air must be let in regularly. However, the question might arise as to whether it is wise to air rooms at a time when fuel is scarce or expensive? Heating engineers will answer that our concern is not at all warranted. The fire in a stove will not burn efficiently if it is deprived of oxygen. That is why we will benefit the fire if the room is ventilated frequently, though quickly, letting

oxygen-rich air in. The room will heat up more quickly because fresh air becomes warm faster than stale air lacking oxygen.

In the case of a sick person, never deprive him of fresh air, even though he may have a fever. If he is properly covered he will not become chilled, and do not be surprised if I tell you that a fever patient cannot catch cold easily under normal circumstances. He is in fact overheated and a quick cold breath of air will do him no harm, so that you will have nothing to fear on this account. See that the sick person is well tucked up in bed, then open all the windows for a few moments. Nothing untoward can happen when this is done; on the contrary, the fresh air will help the patient on his way to recovery.

Oxygen as a Healing Factor

Cancer specialists will tell you that cancer cells are cells that lack oxygen. Doctors specialising in rheumatism, arthritis, diabetes and similar diseases have also pointed to oxygen deficiency in their patients. We must therefore conclude that modern man may have money and all sorts of conveniences but he lacks oxygen. In fact, many diabetics would not enter a coma if they were made to increase their oxygen intake early enough.

Let me illustrate this by an experience I have already mentioned elsewhere in my publications. A doctor once spent his vacations in the mountains together with a diabetic friend. When he realised that his friend's condition was threatening to send him into a coma he resorted to a ruse to save his life. Having no insulin on hand, the doctor could see the patient getting weaker and more listless and knew that the only way he could help was to oblige the man to walk faster, or better still, run, in order to get rid of the acetone in the lungs and make him inhale more oxygen. To force his friend to do this, the doctor had to try and make him angry and did this by whispering something in his ear! As expected, the sick man turned on his doctor friend furiously and then ran off as fast as his legs could carry him. The excitement and movement provided the man with the oxygen he needed to prevent him going into a coma. Later, when he found out that his friend had made him angry only in order to save his life, he was most grateful and both men rejoiced over the successful outcome.

A Simple Remedy

Monotonous work can be so tiring that our limbs feel heavy, while an interesting activity can involve our whole being to such an extent that we forget to breathe properly. The deficiency, however, can be rectified in a simple way if we take an evening walk in the fresh air in order to unwind. For the best results go uphill because this will necessitate deeper breathing. Our feeling of tiredness will soon vanish, faster in fact than if we decided to lie down and rest in a room with little oxygen.

The healing processes will proceed much faster in the case of illnesses that enable the patient to move around, if he increases his intake of oxygen by walking briskly in the fresh air, possibly through an aromatic forest or woodland, on a regular basis. Anyone putting this 'prescription' conscientiously into practice will enjoy positive results. As a rule, even depression can be overcome by taking a brisk walk in the fresh air for as little as an hour. Mind you, a slow walk will not have the same effect or benefit as would a strenuous march requiring vigorous breathing, which results in oxygen rushing to the brain cells and normalising their function.

Patients who are unable to go for walks should have their sick-room aired regularly in order to allow oxygen-laden fresh air to replace the stale air and so accelerate their recuperation. Lack of oxygen will retard their progress.

Those who practise winter sports will benefit more healthwise if they climb uphill with their skis for an hour rather than using the ski-lift. The lazy or convenient way does not benefit them as much as they would like it to. Modern means of transport have a similar effect, hindering us from using our legs. We appreciate our legs when we use them vigorously, letting them benefit our health. Walking briskly makes us breathe more thoroughly and this, in turn, supplies the body with plenty of oxygen. Our daily activities and work deprive the body of oxygen, yet it needs this vital element to keep it fit and healthy and to recuperate from illnesses. How good it would be if we resolved not to fill up with more petrol but, instead, with more oxygen! Better health would surely follow.

The Effects of Smoking
When a young person first starts smoking, how unpleasant he or she usually finds it. To be honest, it is far from enjoyable. On the contrary, the young person must fight all the way through nausea, disgust, nervous shock, dizziness and a general feeling of natural aversion in order to overcome the ill effects the learner smoker is subject to.

As with all harmful practices, the person trying to enjoy smoking insists that the pleasure outweighs the risks involved and that it can't be all that bad anyway. He may even point to his grandfather who, although an inveterate smoker, lived to be eighty years or more. It is true that a person with a strong constitution may be able to stand poisons without any apparent damage to his health. However, if there are people who can take drugs and grow old in spite of doing so, that does not mean that everyone has the same strong powers of resistance. On the contrary, millions of people have died prematurely because of tobacco or nicotine, narcotics, alcohol and other drugs.

Focusing on smoking, however, what are the dangers inherent in nicotine? It is the arterial system in general and the coronary arteries in particular that are affected by nicotine. If the addict has constitutionally weak blood vessels to start with, the danger of smoking will be all the greater for him. The vessels lose their elasticity, become progressively narrower and thus restrict the flow of blood to the heart, the walls of which are poorly nourished and begin to deteriorate.

If we could see through the chest and look at the heart we would be shocked to notice the change in its appearance under the influence of chronic nicotine poisoning. The delicate, toned muscles become relaxed and their beautiful red colour gradually changes to a dirty brown. If a person's heart muscles constantly suffer from lack of adequate nourishment, they will begin to look like those of a very old person. Pathological anatomy speaks of 'brown atrophy' in describing such cases, because the worn-out brownish pigments are deposited in individual cells of the heart muscles. In addition, a number of small white streaks are noticeable. These indicate that minute particles of the muscle itself have been destroyed and are now replaced by connective, or scar, tissue. Once the tissues of the heart muscles have been ruined, they cannot be replaced, not even by the best possible natural remedies. All one can do is to strengthen whatever undamaged tissue is left so that it can now do the work that had previously been done by the scarred tissue.

So, if one values life, the heart muscle ought to be well cared for. This brings to mind some words of ancient wisdom: 'More than all else that is to be guarded, safeguard your heart, for out of it come the sources of life.' Even though these words have a deep symbolic meaning, they indicate nevertheless that our heart is an organ that demands our whole attention, for if the heart fails what else remains but death? When the liver or the kidneys fail the patient is able to stay alive for a little while, but when the heart suddenly stops beating the person will drop as if struck by lightening and death follows instantly. Anyone who has witnessed a case of heart failure is extraordinarily affected by the tragedy – the sudden transformation from life to death. The pathologist will probably say that the heart muscles had been starved of blood for many years and were therefore terribly changed. The information that nicotine had been responsible for the fatal damage is then, unfortunately, no longer of any use. It is too late. Fortunately, it need not come to this, because the mere fact that the effects of nicotine poisoning become apparent long before the possible fatal consequences should make the addict decide to give up the habit before it is too late. Or would it not be better to give up smoking long before disturbances arise?

The blood pressure and the pulse rate also react adversely to nicotine, as has been proved in extensive tests undertaken by the Americans Mathers, Patterson and Levy, who investigated the link between circulatory disturbances and smoking. It was found that the average rise in blood pressure after inhaling one cigarette was 15 mm, while the pulse rate increased by fifteen beats per minute, and in cases of special sensitivity to nicotine, by twenty-five beats. The results of the tests varied according to the nicotine content of the respective cigarette brands and the individual smoker's sensitivity.

Tobacco smoke can also damage plants, as a simple experiment will prove. Put some cress seeds in two small dishes and when they begin to sprout, place a clear glass cover or jar over them. When the plants are about 2½ cm (1 inch) high, under one of the glass covers blow cigarette or cigar smoke; repeat two days later. Within a week the smoked plants will be dead, completely shrivelled up, while the ones in the unpolluted dish will be perfectly healthy.

Any gardener will tell you that tobacco extract kills insect life and that he uses it to destroy aphids. This particular use of tobacco can be recommended, but you must watch that the plants are sprayed when the fruits have not yet developed or are very small, so that the rain can wash away the extract.

How Dangerous is Tobacco Tar?

There is a general idea that tobacco is only dangerous because of its nicotine content. This view is incorrect. There is yet another evil inherent in tobacco and that is the phenols and tarry substances that are released in the process of smoking. The latter are, to a great extent, responsible for the development of cancer. Smoker's cancer of the tongue or throat results directly from tar contamination rather than nicotine. Experiments with rabbits have shown that tobacco tar can cause malignant ulcers. The ears of some rabbits were brushed with tobacco tar every two or three days, and within a few weeks or months most of the animals developed cancerous ulcers. If these experiments are repeated using ordinary tar, the same form of cancer develops, thus proving that it is not the nicotine but the tar in tobacco which is responsible for cancer. Thus, it is wrong to draw the conclusion that low-nicotine or nicotine-free tobacco is safe to smoke.

Smoking – a Vice of Modern Times

If someone maintains that our ancestors were tobacco smokers too, he is actually quite mistaken. The widespread habit of smoking is not very old. True, we know that the North American Indians used to smoke and so did the people who lived where tobacco was grown, on the various Pacific islands, but tobacco was brought to other countries only through maritime traffic. Our ancestors in the West did not know the tobacco plant, and it is amazing how fast it spread over the globe and got a hold on people, making them think that they could not live without smoking. Somehow the idea developed that you are not 'with it' or lack credibility if you do not indulge in smoking. It is not surprising that Dr A. H. Roffo, a university professor, wrote: 'I consider tobacco a narcotic such as cocaine, morphine, opium and other drugs. In my opinion, tobacco is much more dangerous, for the number of people who are addicted to cocaine, morphine, etc., is ridiculously small in comparison to the ever-growing number of tobacco users. Besides, cocaine and morphine addicts, more often than not, are sick people, while tobacco, for the most part, attracts healthy young people.' Although narcotics are much more dangerous than tobacco, the latter is a far greater menace to our health because it has become so widespread. Since the 1970s the proportion of women smoking has grown steadily, but the female body is even more sensitive to such poisons, posing great risks and producing disastrous consequences during pregnancy and lactation.

Stress – a Disease of Modern Times

Leisure, a cosy home atmosphere, tranquillity and contemplation, as well as a period of relaxation at the end of a working day, are things that will soon only be known from reading descriptions of

the past. Even at mealtimes modern man is in the grip of restlessness connected with his busy schedule. Mind you, the body cannot
stand this pace of life for ever and the natural outcome is seen in
the constant increase of gastric disturbances. We should not be in
a hurry when we sit down to eat; in fact, we should rest for a few
minutes beforehand and then enjoy our meal with a calm mind
and a healthy appetite. Most gastric problems will disappear if we
make an effort to be relaxed at mealtimes, eat slowly and chew
the food thoroughly. It will then be better assimilated and cause
fewer disturbances in the intestines. Also, when chewing
thoroughly you will be less tempted to eat too much, giving you
a chance to combat excess weight more effectively. It is an unde-
niable fact that in the Western world more people become sick
and die as a result of overeating than because of going hungry. We
would do well, therefore, to reduce our intake of food and so
benefit our health.

A Miscalculation
If you have been so infected by a hurried pace of life that it becomes
a habit and you cannot even slow down when you should rest and
relax, the end result of rushing about will not be what you expect.
It will not save time and enable you to relax for longer. If the
spare time is not devoted to relaxation but sacrificed to other
business activity or intense efforts, do not be surprised to find your
interest in work declining.

Our ancestors used to start the day at 4 a.m. in the summer and,
as the poet Johann Peter Hebel wrote: 'The work you do at four
in early morning light, will not affect your health and rest at nine
at night.' A working day was not an eight-hour period in which
certain work had to be done; but rather, the day was long enough
to make work a pleasure and the evening hours a time for 'recharging one's batteries'. Because people today want to get more out of
life and enjoy it in a different way, all these former pleasures have
gone. However, the calculation has misfired. The outcome has not
provided a beneficial basis for relaxation. On the contrary, a
shorter working week has demanded greater effort from us, often
taxing the energy reserves beyond capacity.

An overtired person derives less benefit from a longer period of
inactivity than those who work steadily, without hurrying and
feeling under pressure, because they prefer to spread their workload over a longer period of time.

The shorter working week has given us more free time and if

this time were used to relax and unwind, there would hardly be anything wrong with it. However, since the hurried pace has also invaded the most popular forms of entertainment and pleasures, sooner or later there will have to come a collapse somewhere. So far, the willingness to work has been greatly impaired, and the long weekend has led to people turning their backs on work, showing open dislike for it. The German poet Goethe observed that rest from work can be detrimental to the work ethic, saying, 'Everything in life we can endure, except too many free days, to be sure.' Many people find it much easier to stop work than to start it again. This is understandable, because work that does not give pleasure is like a punishment. On the other hand, if you use your free time in a leisurely manner, slowing down the pace, you will be able to return to your place of work with renewed vigour; the week will pass enjoyably because fresh strength will make your tasks and duties easier and so lead to happiness. A steady, persistent and joyful pace of work, and shorter rest periods, are better for our life, for our physical and mental health, than the unnatural change of pace that modern life has forced upon us.

Housing Problems and Sickness

Years ago, rich people who were able to build large houses and mansions had a peculiar custom that helps us to understand why it is necessary to let the humidity and chemical processes going on in the new building settle down for some time before taking up residence there. For the sake of their own health, they allowed poor people to live in the new building rent-free during the first year. Even if the house was built of natural and quarried stone, this precaution was considered necessary in the interests of health. Of course, it was the health of the rich that benefited; the poor derived only financial benefit.

Concrete Structures and their Dangers

What about modern concrete structures? Do they not represent a far greater hazard to health than buildings made of stone? If so, there are still some strong people around who, apparently, are not affected by living in concrete buildings. At least they are not aware of any disadvantages healthwise. Not everyone is so favourably endowed, however, and some people notice twinges of rheumatism and neuralgia after only a few weeks – a more accentuated stiffness of the limbs, or a stiff neck. The gouty nodes one may already have become more painful, perhaps even depression may set in, even if not experienced previously. If you notice these or other disturbances shortly after moving into a concrete building, you should experiment by spending a holiday with friends who live in a brick, wooden or stone building. If the symptoms disappear while you are there, it would be reasonable, in the interests of health and if you are able, to move from the concrete structure, despite its modern conveniences, to a healthier dwelling place.

A humid home with little sun can damage your health just as much as a concrete building. We often calculate incorrectly, economising on the wrong things, for what good does it do us to pay less rent if we have to pay more than what we save on doctor's fees and medicines! Pain and psychological suffering can also be avoided if, when deciding where to live, we consider not only the cost but also the possible effect on our health. Living in a healthy home is of greater value than having modern conveniences and should take priority. Unfortunately, neither the authorities nor the individual are sufficiently interested in solving the question of housing from the standpoint of health. How people's health would benefit from this knowledge if those in positions of responsibility could be moved to transfer a few million from the military budget to that of health. Such a humane action would definitely be worthwhile, especially if some of the money were to be used to improve the housing conditions in the poorer sections of our towns and cities, where there is little sun and where insect pests, even rats and mice, can still contribute to the transmission of infectious diseases. It would be most appropriate if every country had an effective programme for healthy housing as one of its main targets.

Taking Health into Consideration when Building a House
Thousands of years ago the Chinese princes would order their builders to test the ground of a new building site before work commenced to see that it corresponded to the requirements for healthy living. We do not know exactly how they went about it, but we can see from old records that the order was carried out each time. In order to provide the healthiest possible conditions, it is important to consider whether a house is to be built on rock or gravel, on clay or marshy ground, whether the foundation is laid in wet earth with a high groundwater level or whether the ground is dry. One might have no other choice but to accept the plot of land that does not have the best conditions, in which case it is up to the builders to minimise the existing deficiencies and

590

disadvantages by means of technical devices, perhaps by drainage and insulation or lagging.

You may have never given any thought to the importance of checking a building site from the standpoint of whether it provides a basis for healthy living. Watching animals in their habitat can help you appreciate this point. You will notice how careful they are in choosing a spot where they want to spend the night, and where they intend to build their burrows, nests or whatever. You will never see wild deer choose wet and marshy ground to sleep on. No fox or marmot will built its den in wet marshland. Even dogs and cats are often quite choosy when it comes to selecting a place to sleep if given the opportunity. A dog will not stretch out on a concrete floor, even though it may provide a cool spot on a hot day.

Exhaustive scientific research and subsequent discoveries have brought to light many aspects of bioclimatics, electromagnetic waves, electric fields and other things that sensitive persons have always experienced reactions to but had no plausible explanation for. Our ancestors based their approach on experience and observation, taking into account many of these things even though they probably knew nothing of their exact nature. We still do not have all the explanations, but modern technology and science have come up with many a revelation that years ago had been perceived instinctively or intuitively, or simply on the basis of supposition.

Where to Build or Buy Your House

If you want to move house, you should check the location you have chosen from the standpoint of bioclimatology; of course you will also wish to see whether the area is suitable, that is, whether you actually like it and it suits you. For this reason it would be useful if you could live in the selected area for a while before finally deciding to build or buy a property there. In accordance with our constitution and sensitivity, various circumstances can be significant, for example atmospheric humidity, elevation, and whether the area is known for the föhn or any other influential winds. You should also take into account whether you feel the cold or the heat, your preference as regards food and exercise or movement, or whatever type you are. In view of the different idiosyncracies and natures we have inherited and from which we cannot escape, it is by no means of little importance where and under what conditions we live. The various members of a family often differ in their needs and preferences, in which case it would be advisable to be guided by the more sensitive ones, choosing your site to suit them.

BASIC RULES

Of primary importance is a dry building site. The foundation must be sound, and it is essential to provide adequate insulation. The choice of building materials has a bearing on health, wood being the healthiest of all, especially in a dry climate. In second place is brick, fired clay; next follows natural stone as a third choice. Concrete, especially the reinforced kind, must be considered as the unhealthiest building material there is, so one should keep one's distance if at all possible.

The Electric Field

Every person and every material has a certain connection with electricity. When undressing at bedtime you may have noticed that some items of clothing crackle, or you may even see them momentarily light up in the dark. The electric charge causing this varies with different people; some have more than others. Not only every human but also every animal, and even dead matter, is electrically charged. The electric charge can be restored or increased. Since we use up energy through life's processes and functions, it is necessary to replace it constantly. We do this by eating food, taking tonics and food supplements, as well as by breathing deeply. The electric field and charge are also influenced by where we live and in what conditions. It is even possible for those factors to upset the natural balance.

Once the balance of the electric field is upset, all kinds of disturbances may manifest themselves; for example, we can be overcome by an unnatural heavy fatigue, or persistent headaches, sometimes leading to troublesome migraine and depression. A lack of vigour and initiative often comes in its wake. Worry and nervousness may set in, bothering the sufferer so much that he does not know what to do with his fidgety limbs. He may fall victim to an unpleasant nervous condition, coupled with inner discontentment.

Since modern technology enables us to measure this electromagnetic field, we know that concrete, and reinforced concrete in particular, is able to rob much energy from those people who have to live in concrete buildings, the amount depending upon their individual sensitivity. For this reason, if you have the choice, select instead natural stone, brick or, better still, wood as the main building materials if you plan to build your own house.

The place we live in is very important to our health in these modern times. For many, though not all of us, where we live depends largely upon our own personal decision, whereas we may not be in a position to influence other important health factors. For instance, we are more or less left to accept the levels of air and water pollution and the frightening increase of radioactivity in the atmosphere without being able to do anything about it. Since we have to eat contaminated food and inhale polluted air, the accruing influences progressively weaken our bodies, to our detriment. Taking care that the house or apartment we live in is as healthy as possible is therefore a sensible and well-founded decision.

Questions of Health and the Protection of Nature

In the not too distant past, the Swiss were generally trained to keep their land clean and tidy. They were brought up with this attitude from earliest childhood at home, and when they started school, strict order and tidiness continued to be taught; in fact, teachers took great care that on outings and excursions the children never left litter lying around.

However, this order was soon disrupted when other habits and influences found their way in. I remember a beautiful wooded area in the Rhine valley, a delightful place where one could always relax. But one day, I found that the scene had changed and the picturesque landscape was littered with paper and wastes. Many a person resented this untidiness, but during the following year their anger could turn to gladness because a litter bin was installed – a quiet hint to put the rubbish where it belonged. This preventative education allayed our fears for the future and impressed upon observers that the Swiss were not inclined to let the beauties of nature be spoiled by thoughtless people who threw their rubbish just anywhere.

Nevertheless, in spite of local efforts, the new habit spread faster than the protective defence could educate. There is an awful attitude and saying that poisons the minds of children, youths and adults alike: "That's the way it's done today. Someone else can clean up after us!' Just take the following experience. While waiting for their train, two fresh-looking girls from the Engadine littered the whole platform with peanut shells. An observer's remark of 'Well, now!' caused nothing but the weakest indication of embarrassment on their part and the thoughtless excuse: 'Everybody does this nowadays; the cleaner will sweep it all up anyway.'

If this is the attitude of modern youths, it is no wonder that we encounter a lack of concern and love for untouched nature even in the most beautiful areas. Today, it is quite common to see rubbish in gorges and streams. A campsite, picnic area or wayside frequently tells us that visitors have enjoyed themselves without giving as much as a single thought to the fact that other people want to enjoy the beauty unspoiled. How can they do so if they have to sit down in the midst of empty cans, bottles, paper and all kinds of rubbish? Neither meadows nor forests, not even rhododendrons and the white snow escape this antisocial behaviour! It is amazing how quickly good habits become forgotten when bad influences take over. How superficial the sense of beauty really is when it can close its eyes to ugly disorder!

Whenever I travelled abroad to faraway places and had to watch how thoughtless and ignorant some people were in treating their surroundings, I felt pride in knowing that tidiness prevailed in my native land. Such actions upset and often repulsed me, and I would never have thought it possible for things to change so much in my own country. I vividly remember an incident in Central America where I saw a stream full of rubbish and dead animals. The same contaminated water flowed downstream and was used to irrigate gardens, for people to bathe and wash their clothes in; it was even used in their kitchens. Maybe the natives were tougher there, but they nevertheless suffered from infections on an epidemic scale, as I saw for myself. The blatant lack of hygiene among people living in such conditions, has led to rampant infestation with worms, so that in certain areas all the inhabitants can be infected with intestinal worms and amoebas. The authorities care little or not at all about taking the necessary precautions, even though such unhygienic conditions are responsible for damage to health, and can even contribute to a slow death.

Water Pollution in Europe

Are the waterways and lakes in Europe any better than elsewhere in the world? I have it first-hand from the experts that people in Europe are exposed to ever greater dangers. I once saw a good film on the preparation of the Upper Rhine for commercial navigation that provided eloquent examples of the appalling condition of our rivers and lakes. It was clear that the exploitation of this river for economic advantages was not worth all the accompanying disadvantages. But it is not enough to inform the people; governments should also be quick to take remedial action in order to stop the pollution and killing of our lakes and rivers. The entire fish population is put in jeopardy and may die if the water continues to be poisoned. Soon it will be impossible for the aquatic animals and birds that live on these fish to survive. Most of us know that in many areas bathing is no longer permitted because of contaminated water.

Those who are aware of the existing problems can help by joining in the protests, which are gaining strength all the time. All of us can contribute personally by doing everything in our power to care seriously about tidiness and order with a view to preserving the beauty of the land, things that used to be automatic and taken for granted years ago.

Air Defence in Another Sense
There is also another thing which needs to be protected in the interest of health. It is our right to breathe good, unpolluted air, is it not? Clean air is necessary for life, and the sanitary measures taken everywhere should definitely embrace this important requirement. Appropriate laws should be made and enforced. For is it not still possible for anyone to pollute the air without anything being done about it? We all know that air is just as important as water. So if industry is not allowed to poison the water, it goes without saying that the many factory chimneys should not be permitted to belch out their fumes into the atmosphere without any consideration for the well-being of the human race.

Think of those people who have built their homes and picked the spot carefully so as to enjoy it, only to find that in time the increasing traffic brings an endless stream of cars and lorries passing right outside their front doors, forcing them to inhale stinking exhaust fumes instead of clean and healthy air. Since the motorways have already been built, it is imperative that remedial measures be sought and taken in order to protect the health of people who now live near them but did not choose to do so. If every motor car had to be fitted with an exhaust emission control device, the costs of installation would certainly not ruin us economically, but would improve our environment.

Each and every one of us should remember that the air is free and belongs to all, being a valuable gift we cannot do without. Yet how many people blow foul-smelling cigarette or cigar smoke into the air, completely oblivious to the fact that the atmosphere also belongs to their fellow human beings, who all have a right to inhale pure air. To all those people we could put the same question an American friend of mine once asked a smoker, saying with a tone of surprise: 'I didn't know that you couldn't stand clean air.' The poisons in our body change our natural sensitivity, yet great apathy has taken over regarding the things that merit special protection and care. Instead of being given greater protection, the air is expected to absorb all kinds of poisonous gases!

Nansen once said with regret that everybody is on the move and everything is possible when it comes to making war and destroying life, but when life and health demand protection, no one and nothing is forthcoming to help!

Television and Health

Living with Technology

During the last eighty years or so, the inventions made have been truly amazing. According to biblical chronology, thousands of years have passed since the days of Adam and Eve, yet during all those millenniums, until the turn of the last century, the achievements of technology amounted to nothing like the progress that has been made in my lifetime.

The modern developments have opened up a vast field of knowledge and the great number of inventions are certainly useful to us if we apply them in the right way and learn to strike a happy medium. However, many of us find this very hard to do. Already we feel lost without a motor car, because our business has to be done quickly. We have become so used to rushing around and the convenience of driving that, in time, we almost forget how to walk. That is a great pity. It is all very well to move quickly when there is a need, but it should not extend to our whole life. We should retain the pleasure of walking in our leisure time. Similarly, the modern business world is unthinkable without the telephone – it being a major disaster when the telephone is out of order, even for a short time. However, if the telephone worries us at all hours of the day and night, the otherwise useful invention turns into a nuisance which we could describe equally well as a 'worriphone'. No wonder we look forward to our holidays without the constant ringing to disturb the peace. The blare of the radio can be another undesirable disturbance when it intrudes relentlessly from a neighbour's apartment without any consideration for our peace. In such circumstances even this useful invention becomes annoying.

The Pros and Cons of Television

Let us now consider the television, an invention that most of us could not imagine being without. This is no exaggeration, for no sooner has it cast its spell than people rush out to buy a set, whether it is necessary or not and whether they have the means or not. Those who can ill afford a television set are often the ones most interested in acquiring this costly form of entertainment come what may.

Let us now examine this desire to be entertained by what we watch on the screen from the point of view of our health. No doubt it is a marvellous invention that can transmit much valuable knowledge and broadcast many important world events. Could one ever forget observing the animals in Kruger National Park? We are amazed at the giant lizards on the Galápagos islands, those surviving animals that give us an idea why legends tell of dragons. Although we may be sitting comfortably in our armchair, television transfers us to those distant shores, making us believe we are actually there, so engrossed do we become in the life of some strange creature. And what about the presentation of a heart operation in a well-equipped modern operating theatre – a gripping experience for anyone who is interested in the human body. Such educational programmes can fill many a gap in our knowledge and give us pleasure and enjoyment. At the same time, moderation is called for if we do not want to run the risk of losing time and control and suffering as a consequence.

DANGERS TO HEALTH

I learned about the danger of television to our health some years ago when staying with friends in the United States, where I noticed that their children sat in front of the screen for hours at a time. The parents usually had great difficulty in persuading them to come to the table to eat or to go to bed. The consequences of this unnatural enthrallment were not in the least welcome; in fact, they were disturbing and difficult to combat and overcome. The children were in an overwrought state, with a poor appetite; their scholastic achievements had dropped; they were absent-minded, lacked concentration and were much more subject to infectious diseases. Indeed, even at such a young age their health had already been undermined.

Scientists have pointed out that watching television puts a great strain on the eyes and that the oscillations harm the nervous system, especially in the case of children. I do not want to go into details here about the additional mental and emotional harm inflicted by programmes that are inappropriate for children, since that has been done elsewhere. Every person is impressionable to a greater or lesser degree, but children in particular are easily influenced because they have not yet acquired a firm position and are therefore receptive, and vulnerable, to everything that rushes into their minds. As it is, our modern times with their frequent changes and innovations in every field, their dangerous radical changes with respect to moral codes and values, do more harm than one can bear. Whether we want to or not, we transmit unrest and bad impressions to our children, who are entitled to protection from these things. So why should we let television programmes put additional stress on them and divert them from their wholesome course through life? Parents should be constantly aware of these factors and take great care.

IT IS EDUCATION'S TURN TO SPEAK

Years ago people were highly selective in the choice of intellectual nourishment for their children's minds. Today, however, we have become spoiled with the great variety of things on offer, unfortunately not all for our good. The demand, even need, for constant saturation with ready-made entertainment suggests that we no longer appreciate what it means to relax in tranquillity and peace. Having reached this point ourselves, we cannot expect to retain an educational hold on our children, for they are good observers and covetous copiers of enjoyment, wanting the same things they see their parents indulge in. A child begins to be demanding when he notices that his parents exercise no self-control. The parents may want to be strict in determining what programmes their children can watch and for how long, yet they are frequently powerless in the face of their children's disobedience. All these reflections have to do with education, and if we adults let ourselves be influenced by advertising and other pressures we should not expect that our children will want to be any different.

Yet, today, obedience is more necessary than ever before if a child's desires are to be curbed and not become too demanding. A child who has learned to be obedient and comply with his parents' wishes will only have to train himself in the practice of moderation, whereas badly brought up children who always get their own way succumb hopelessly to the gripping power of television. This is much more dangerous than many parents may think, because a growing child who is allowed to absorb anything he likes, without restrictions, is left to the mercy of bad influences. So, if parents do not set a good example in all they do and say, they can hardly expect self-control from their children. Where self-discipline is lacking it would be much better not to have a television at all.

The Need to Relax
If there is one thing the busy person finds difficult to achieve, it is the ability to relax correctly. Whether we are conscious of it or not, our modern technological age transmits its restless rhythm to everyone. Whatever we do has to be done quickly because we have so many other things waiting. The modern procedure of concentrating on one job enables a person to become skilled and adept in his field, but at the same time it is apt to kill one's interest in the whole thing to be made or done – the overall picture. The individual does not, or will not, see how his part fits in with the rest, so that the immediate consequence of his attitude is an unsatisfactory condition of joyless existence. Where interest in work and verve are missing, the job itself will not prevent boredom from encroaching into our lives, and we feel that our free time must be arranged so that it is more eventful, rather than used to provide wholesome relaxation.

It is different, however, with the person who enjoys his work. The time will fly, instead of drag by and he will derive pleasure from what he is doing. However, because of his good disposition such a person may be asked to fill in here and there and, in time, he will become overloaded. So beware!

Shorter Working Hours – No Solution
Working shorter hours tends to cause more stress because less time is available, and more concentration and haste has to be packed in. The change to a five-day week implemented some years ago has, in the main, failed its original purpose. The working week lost another day so that more effort had to be crammed into five days, resulting in greater fatigue which, together with the increased tension, is difficult to shake off and the additional day of rest cannot be enjoyed fully.

In addition to work there are usually too many other obligations, not to mention the diverse opportunities to engage in new and exciting activities, crowding out the intended relaxation. Years ago, people came home from work and were happy to sit on a bench in front of the house and relax until it grew dark. Nothing exciting happened to disturb the peace and pleasure hours of leisure. No noise and no radio programmes subjected the body to further tension and no television shows demanded the undivided attention of the viewer. In the place of these canned programmes there was often heard rising from the valley a beautiful song that refreshed the singer and the listeners alike. These aspects of life led to wholesome relaxation which we search for today but seldom find in spite of all the money spent. Often, sound sleep escapes those who did not retire early enough, not wanting to miss out on some nocturnal pleasure. For them the hours of the night become more arduous than even their work during the day, but sleep is an indispensable and natural requirement.

While some people are never able to relax, there are others who cannot do enough to make money. Some workers, for example in the catering industry, do not enjoy their days off as a time of rest and relaxation, but to make more money they accept casual work as well. Such demands on the body may be possible for a little while but they will sap the person's energy reserves in the long run. We must recognise that the rhythm of life consists of periods of tension and relaxation, the latter being necessary to recharge life's batteries. Another modern tendency is to seek the necessary relaxation in sport, but unfortunately this often degenerates into competition and the body is overtaxed once again.

A Programme to Unwind
As well as having a work schedule, I recommend that you also have one for relaxation. If you are a housewife, you can plan your time quite well after your husband has gone to work and the children to school. When your housework is finished in the morning, take a break for five or ten minutes. You will be surprised to discover the benefits resulting from such a short rest period. The same relaxation can be observed at midday, and if it becomes habitual, you will build up a store of energy, enabling you to deal with daily problems more easily. Whether you stay at home or go out to work, you will have more opportunity to relax if you do not feel obliged to scrutinise every little item in the daily newspaper whenever you have a break. There is better nourishment available for the brain – things that edify – and it is this you should turn to in order to supply the mind and spirit with food that fortifies. The right kind of upbuilding material will also serve to relax the body, proving the truth of the saying 'Man does not live by bread alone.'

There are many people who believe that it is beneficial to have a lie in after a hectic week's work. But unless you are ill, spending the whole morning in bed only makes you feel worse. It is much better to go to bed early the night before, get up in the morning soon after you awake and take a long walk through the woods or forest, or along a bubbling stream. Doing this will do wonders for your nerves. Once in the aromatic air you will automatically breathe more deeply and soon feel wonderfully refreshed. Doing some gardening is also a great way to relax after engaging in strenuous mental or office work. Then there is the possibility of berry-picking and gathering medicinal herbs, a meaningful distraction that helps you to revive.

So you will see that in spite of all the modern hustle and bustle and the air and environmental pollution, there are still a number of opportunities to unwind in a natural way. As a rule, these opportunities are inexpensive. All you have to be is content with them and they will benefit you in every way.

Tiredness – a Natural Symptom

In a medical book I read recently it said that man is not a machine and has to rest after making a strenuous effort. If the author, a medical doctor, had a proper understanding of technology he would have known that even machines cannot go on running forever, but need rest periods just as much as we do. It is not without reason that engineers speak of fatigue and stress in the case of machines. In fact, many railway and aeroplane accidents happen as a result of metal or mechanical fatigue. The molecules lose their strength and resilience when the metals remain in constant use, creating a greater risk of them breaking. So when a lifeless machine or engine is subject to symptoms of fatigue, how much more so is the living human body!

It is possible that a person cannot eat or sleep because he is just too tired. His condition is then one of exhaustion. But what can be called mere tiredness, and where is the border between tiredness and exhaustion? Normal activity is good for the mind and body, but laziness and idleness are harmful. An engine that runs at a reasonable pace has a longer life than if it is hardly ever used; mechanical parts that are left idle become rusty, oxidise and seize up due to hardened lubricants; in other words, they suffer damage. An engine runs best at a certain number of revolutions per minute and an adequate temperature, and it becomes damaged if it is overheated. This is the reason for installing gauges that tell you the best temperatures for running the engine so that its life can be extended. We humans also possess a reliable gauge that indicates whether our 'body engine' is running properly or whether we are overtaxing it. This motor is, as we all know, the heart. When running at high speed, it should not be left to a colleague or the 'motorist' to decide the maximum rate, or speed; let the heart itself tell you. As soon as it beats considerably faster than usual, this should be taken as a warning that you must slow down. It is true that we can let our 'heart motor' run at a higher speed for a short time, but when the exertion continues over an extended period, our energy reserves become drained, fatigue sets in and our health is adversely affected.

The normal strain of work stimulates the circulation and, with it, the entire metabolism, so that the body is kept resilient and healthy. Of course, a normal and healthy metabolism also produces wastes, resulting in a feeling of tiredness when these waste products reach a certain concentration. This symptom of tiredness should always be met with rest and relaxation, even by young people who are usually able to work 8–10 hours a day with ease. A healthy, properly nourished body experiences the sensation of pleasant tiredness in the evening, and 7–9 hours of sleep, the exact amount depending on our individual needs, will be quite enough to restore a feeling of refreshed well-being. We will then be able to carry out our duties quite happily the following day if our body has had sufficient rest during the night.

The Need for Common Sense
It is mainly young people and athletes who find it difficult to be sensible and not go beyond what is physically good for their health. There are times when they do not seem to understand the importance of warming up in order to help the muscles and internal organs to acquire sufficient elasticity. Sports physicians, gynaecologists and other specialists are well aware of this since they have to deal with the consequences of carelessness. We should not overtax ourselves to the point of exhaustion in our work, and how much less should this be done in sports activities! Those who go beyond what is reasonable when they are supposed to relax and restore their energies show a lack of knowledge and understanding. In some cases they are driven by ambition that, strictly speaking, creates an attitude which has nothing to do with sportsmanship.

It is impossible to establish general rules that would constitute an exact standard or yardstick regarding the energy we can safely spend, because each person has to take into account his constitution, his physical and mental reserves and, last but not least, his age. It really depends upon our individual capabilities and need for rest and sleep, which can vary enormously from one person to another. For this reason, what follows are only guidelines, intended to point you in the right direction regarding how much you can do.

How to Judge your Capabilities

Let us take an example. A twenty-year-old has at his disposal 100 per cent energy, of which he may spend 80 per cent on work and sporting activities without damaging his reserves. He will not be so tired at the end of the day that he would speak of exhaustion. When calculating one's potential it is necessary, according to age, to deduct the years of one's life from the 100 per cent starting point. This means that a forty-year-old can risk spending 60 per cent of his energy potential, while a sixty-year-old will have to be satisfied with spending a mere 40 per cent. It would obviously not be good for him if circumstances forced him to spend as much energy as he could if he were only twenty years old. The result would be that instead of feeling normal tiredness in the evening, he would be completely exhausted. He would not find proper rest in sleep and would wake up still tired. This condition of exhaustion reduces vitality and shortens life expectancy, which means that the individual would have more years to look forward to if his use of energy were to be more sensible and moderate.

The Beneficial Rhythm of Life

In modern times the normal rhythm of life that once was a hall-mark of country life has been turned upside down. You can only expect to wake up feeling bright and breezy in the morning if you refuse to follow the spirit of our times and, instead, go to bed early, well before midnight, in order to do justice to the body's need for rest. Those who fall victim to the modern trend of indulging in nocturnal pleasures will not dream of leaving them to retire early. Radio, television, the cinema and so forth keep them prisoner and demand an even greater amount of their energy and strength than would have been lost in the course of their daily occupation and consequent normal tiredness. These additional nightly demands at the expense of sleep upset the balance that is maintained by a normal pace of life. Even young people who extend the day into the night in order to get more out of life will, in time, suffer from a form of fatigue that manifests itself in irritability, feeling uptight and, in the end, insomnia.

How wise it would be to interrupt this deteriorating condition in good time before it takes over one's being, leading to the need for strong sleeping pills that can become addictive! People who feel overtired should decide to spend their holidays in the country, where they can go on easy excursions and for walks in the forest or woods and the hills or mountains, rather than choosing a travel programme that would involve great strain and effort. They need to breathe deeply in the fresh air, enabling them to feel naturally tired in the evening and so enjoy restful sleep once again. Anyone who thinks that he can get rid of overtiredness by sitting in an armchair all day is mistaken, because he needs more than rest: he needs sufficient exercise and deep-breathing. This will eliminate the tiredness and metabolic wastes from the body. Townsfolk would benefit more from their holidays if, instead of lying around, they helped the farmers make hay and went for short walks, besides eating and drinking well.

If you do not want to become overtired, you should observe and become familiar with the rhythm of exercise and rest. Plan to have sufficient time to get ready if you work away from home, so that you will arrive at your place of work without having had to rush. Moreover, it will be of special benefit if you choose, not the shortest way to work, but the most pleasant – perhaps passing through a park or some gardens. Remember, this can be a protection from exhaust fumes at the same time. Following this advice, anyone can derive physical benefits from his daily walk to and from work and this cannot be appreciated enough in view of the limited opportunities to move about in our jobs. If the distance is too great or walking to work presents other problems, why not train yourself to get up a little earlier in order to go for a brisk walk before setting out to work? It would also be to your advantage if you repeated this in the evening. A balanced combination of exercise and rest maintains our efficiency and well-being and helps us to avoid getting overtired. So why should anything prevent you from putting this advice into practice conscientiously and with perseverance?

No one can prevent the process of aging, nor waning vitality, which can take place at different rates for different people. There is little point in being too grieved about it; just remember that you have gained experience, wisdom and skills in those past years, things that can help you to replace the decreasing energy to the extent that the achievements of an experienced man are able to surpass those of a youth still full of vitality. Even in the area of technology it is not so much the existing knowledge and power but their skilful use that raises its potential to the maximum heights.

Beware of exerting yourself to the limit, leading to complete exhaustion, because every violation of biological laws will find its revenge and you may have to pay a bitter price.

What Is Exhaustion?

The human cell is a marvel made by the Intelligence that has shown endless ingenuity in technical design, forever presenting scientific researchers with surprises.

Although each kind of cell is different in structure from the others, they all have basic similarities. The cell's most important part is the nucleus, just like the yolk of an egg. The nucleus is, as a rule, surrounded by a nutrient reserve, similar to the egg white that envelops the yolk. The cover holding everything together in the cell is the cell membrane. The cell itself is a small state within a state and enjoys a certain independence. There are even cells that circulate or wander for the purpose of being on hand wherever their help may be needed. That is why they are called 'wandering cells'. We can say that every cell has it own internal regulations, and absorbs and releases certain substances. This process is called metabolism. The cell uses the absorbed nutrients and changes them into energy, or it converts them into a new substance that serves the body, especially in its growth.

The breakdown and conversion of nutrients produces wastes, in the same way as wastes are formed in the process of combustion or oxidation. We are talking about the so-called 'metabolic waste products'. Exercise, breathing and rest are responsible for the elimination of wastes from the body, and if these processes are restricted, hindering their removal, then congestions and deposits occur that lead to rheumatism, gout and arthritis. Besides the nutrient reserves, the body has other reserves that can be so substantial that they influence the body weight. Active cells retain their elasticity, and work and exercise that requires plenty of movement maintain the health of individual cells, therefore benefiting the whole body.

The Use of Energy

In accordance with effort and demand, cells use up nutrient materials during the day, which are replenished during the night. This is the normal rhythm of life. In the evening, when the cells have exhausted their supplies, we become tired. If we use up more energy than normal, the cells draw on their reserves. If the energy consumption is excessive over a period of time, we have to spend more than can be replaced during the night. The inevitable result of this mismanagement is a deficiency that gets progressively greater. The normal reserves diminish and are finally used up; the cells are now completely exhausted. We suffer from a kind of fatigue that is like a sickness, in time leading to a condition of painful tiredness. People who are constantly on the move, always doing something, can easily reach this state, and if nothing is done about it, or if it is stepped up by increasing the overexertion, this senseless condition can trigger a sudden reaction and suddenly snap, like a short circuit. This explains the cases of sudden death that may puzzle even the doctor.

Activity and work produce a natural tiredness which should not be resisted but given in to. We do this by taking a break or going to bed to obtain the necessary rest.

This natural rhythm refreshes, letting the preceding exercise of the muscles serve to strengthen the body. However, if the strain and effort are not followed by the necessary rest, the consequence will be exhaustion, causing the opposite to happen, because constant overexertion damages the cellular system and thus the whole body. It is important to avoid exhaustion in our daily life as well as in sport and exercise. Those who ignore this advice will often have to reckon with permanent damage that may be far greater then they imagine or would like to be true.

Natural Sleep

How Much Sleep Do We Need?
The question of how much sleep a person really needs has occupied the minds of many clever people who, try as they might, have never arrived at a satisfactory answer. Some say that seven or eight hours sleep are necessary if one wants to be rested and ready for work, while others seem to think that they can manage quite well with four or five hours. Regarding those who sleep fewer hours, it is questionable whether the nerve cells will have sufficient time to become regenerated and whether, in time, some deficiency will become apparent. An unusual failing of strength, shorter attention spans and becoming easily tired are definite indications that one is not getting enough sleep, no matter what kind of theories anyone has on the subject.

When should we sleep and for how many hours? There are many different answers to these two questions and it is better if we ask, not other fellow humans, but nature itself – the most appropriate teacher. Nature sets before us a splendid example in the lively, ever-active world of birds. What can we learn from our feathered friends? When and for how long do those cheerful little singers sleep? Well, we all know the answer, don't we? They begin their songs at the break of dawn when the average person is wasting the sunny hours of an early spring morning lying asleep in bed. They are already about their business and do not return to rest until the last traces of twilight have gone. For the birds this seems to be a natural and proper way of life and, indeed, primitive man adopted it.

Our eyes were given to us by our Creator to enjoy and explore the light and what each day unfolds. They are a miracle and we should look after them well. The daylight opens them in the morning, and when night falls it is natural to close them in rest. For what other reason were we given alternate light and darkness? Modern man, however, came along and invented artificial light for himself, allowing him to prolong the day indefinitely. First he used kindling and candles, then paraffin and gas, until the invention of the electric light bulb made it even more simple to switch on the artificial light and continue working at any time of the night. No longer can we say, as once was said: 'Come, let's make an end to the day and go to bed, for we have endured its cares for long enough.' Now we can think of other ways, besides sleep, for banishing the cares of the day – by doing more work or by dissipating our night hours in pleasures to help us forget our troubles. Thus, although artificial light seems useful and practical to us, we have forgotten that we have changed the natural rhythm of life to suit our own transient mood, personal need, or perhaps just to comply with a certain set of circumstances.

Instead of waking with the first rays of sunshine so as to use every moment of natural light, we sleep through the most beautiful hours of the day and, of course, it it impossible to get our work done before the departing light invites us to sleep once more. In the summer, could we but follow the natural rhythm of life, like the animals in the wild, we would have longer working hours; we would then have a wonderful opportunity for resting and becoming regenerated in the winter. We do not have to hibernate, but by enjoying sweet sleep before midnight, we should be well enough rested to rise with the dawn and work during the daylight hours, giving in to the body's natural demand for sleep at night. Perhaps you have never wondered why daylight appears and then disappears. We should do our business during the hours natural light is available, because this is nature's way and rhythm. Natural sleep lasts from sunset to sunrise.

What would our civilisation say to such a way of living? Obviously a resounding 'No!'. How could habits and customs be changed so drastically? From a social and economic viewpoint it would, at this time, seem impossible to adapt to this once natural pattern, although it would be healthier for us.

Try this way of life as an experiment either during your holidays or when you are convalescing from an illness. Instead of going out in the evenings on some social occasion that may last far into the night, take the opportunity to enjoy some natural sleep several hours before midnight. If, during our holidays, we accustom ourselves to this way of life, perhaps when we return home we may succeed in cancelling our social obligations on two or three weekday nights in order to enjoy the regenerative power of natural sleep. Our business and social life will actually benefit, for our energies and strength will be renewed. If, on the other hand, we behave like most people on holiday and stay up all hours of the night indulging in social life to the full, then we should not be surprised if our body and mind are still tired once it is over.

As I have said before, sleeping far into the day does not compensate for those hours lost before midnight. An old rule of country folk says: 'One hour of sleep before midnight equals two hours after.' This is no delusion but a fact confirmed scientifically, and one that anyone can prove to himself over a two-week period, by going to bed when the sun goes down and getting up when it rises. He will find his nerves have become regenerated and his general health and vitality greatly improved. A clinical experiment carried out for one week produced interesting results. One person went to bed every night at midnight and slept for twelve hours until midday, while another slept from seven or eight o'clock in the evening until four or five o'clock in the morning. Even though the second person slept three or four hours less than the first one, it was found that he was more refreshed, more rested and in better physical shape. This was obvious proof that hours spent in rest before midnight are far more beneficial than the hours after midnight, since they recharge the system with energy more effectively.

Natural sleep is a simple and easy way to help the body stay strong and healthy. All that is needed is a little willingness, a little determination and perseverance.

Sleep and Salutary Conditions

You may never have thought about it, but did you know that it matters where we sleep, whether in a healthy environment and bed or not? It strikes you first when travelling and your customary routine and sleeping place are not possible. The first time I slept in an Indian hut in the jungle I looked around in vain for a mat or some other soft surface to lie on. In the end I had to sleep on the bare bamboo floor like the Indians themselves, but at least I had my jacket, which I rolled up and used as a pillow. The only luxury I found was a mosquito net to keep out the malaria-carrying insects. If it had not been for the screeching sounds of monkeys and parrots or the cries of wild animals that kept rousing me, I would have slept comparatively well, because lying on a hard base is actually healthy. But when one is not accustomed to sleeping on a hard surface the old bones do rather object! Nonetheless, I did sleep better in that hut than the time I used a farmer's bed that was too soft and gave me the feeling of being smothered under a mountain of downy feathers.

A HEALTHY BED

It used to be the custom in country homes to cover the mattress with a quilt for greater warmth and softness. But it is hard to understand how it was possible for the habit of sleeping on a soft foundation to creep in, especially in areas where the people are usually tougher. Soft beds that sag when you lie down are not healthy. And if there is a bolster and thick pillow as well, do not be surprised to find that the spine will adopt a distorted position. If the sleeping person could be X-rayed from the side, this would be seen quite clearly. That is why old beds in country homes, where great-grandmother had had difficulty in sleeping, are far from ideal for healthy sleep today.

A good bed must have a certain degree of firmness, because if it is too soft the blood vessels, in particular the veins, become congested and this impairs the circulation. Many people do not sleep properly on foam rubber, and those who suffer from rheumatism may find metal springs unfavourable to their condition.

Blankets should be light and porous. A duvet filled with down provides beautiful warmth but a heavy old eiderdown is uncomfortable. Woollen blankets are popular in many places, but in really bad weather anyone who feels the cold will probably need an additional duvet. On the other hand, those who become warm easily will find a light duvet is better in the summer, as opposed to a woollen blanket that keeps in the heat and is heavier. Our choice, then, depends upon our individual disposition and the time of year.

In Guatemala, where two woollen blankets did not keep us warm enough during the cold nights, they gave us newspapers to use as insulation material between the blankets. True, it made us feel warmer but the constant rustling of the paper disturbed our sleep. Blankets made of pure wool, especially camel and angora, are excellent; for instance, they provide good insulation and create an electromagnetic field. Less favourable are synthetic fibres since many people, including those who suffer from rheumatism and arthritis, are susceptible to their unpleasant effect.

Bed linen, too, has its place in providing the basis for healthy sleep and should be changed frequently. While in use, we should hang it out to air in the sun from time to time. Well-aired sheets will help to stimulate the skin pores so that they will function more efficiently. In fact, it is no idle imagination to feel a sense of pleasure and well-being between fresh sheets, but a clear sign that the frequent changing of bed linen makes for healthier sleeping.

OTHER REQUIREMENTS

In the past it was considered important to sleep with the windows open. Today central heating is the accepted norm in many homes and it is therefore essential to open all windows before going to bed, letting in fresh, cool, oxygen-rich air. Unfortunately, this may have other drawbacks because in modern industrial towns there are many pollutants present in the air. Should you be fortunate enough to live in a relatively unpolluted area, keep a small window open for ventilation if your bedroom is heated. Draughts can be prevented by closing the curtains. It is important to realise that stale air in the bedroom disturbs the normal exchange of gases and sleep will not provide the rest it should. No wonder so many people still feel tired in the morning!

It is one thing to take care and change the bed linen frequently, but it is equally important to keep the body clean by daily washing. Never go to bed when the body is hot and sweaty; first take a shower or at least wash yourself down and remove all sweat and dirt. Sweating is healthy because it brings out toxins, but it also demands thorough washing. Dried up sweat clogs the pores and the toxins stick to the skin. Therefore, a clean body is part and parcel of salutary sleep.

Poor blood circulation can be helped with a hot water bottle or bed warmer if you cannot warm up naturally. Better still, take a foot bath, or alternate hot and cold baths, to warm your feet. A warm shower or bath is recommended when the body has cooled down considerably and just does not get warm. If you do have poor circulation, never go to bed with cold feet because they can keep you awake for hours. In that case it is better to make the effort and have a warm bath.

Sleeping drugs are the worst thing anyone can take because they do not cure insomnia, unless you use natural remedies. A person who does not subject himself to the laws of nature as regards sleep and rest can become a slave of chemical drugs when constantly resorting to sleeping pills.

Salutary sleep means learning to go to bed early. Soft harmonious music, not loud noise, may send you to sleep, and uplifting reading has a calming effect, in contrast to some exciting television entertainment. Quietly meditating on the deeper meaning of life can free us from the sickening happenings of our times and help us find the necessary rest.

So then, salutary sleep is based on many small necessities and requirements. Give due consideration to them before you consult your doctor about insomnia, because the answer to your problem is generally to be found simply by observing them.

Sleep, the Remedy We Cannot Do Without
The best medicines, money and possessions cannot take the place of sleep. When travelling it may overcome us on a train or plane, to the homeless it may come as a relief in open fields, and at night it gathers the more fortunate ones among us into its soothing arms on soft pillows. It is always necessary when it comes, and we should not drive it away; otherwise it may one day take revenge by avoiding us.

Do we really know what sleep means to our senses? Do we show understanding for its necessity? Have we ever stopped to think how it recharges our batteries by letting us rest and relax? While we are asleep we forget everything. When a day has been full of heavy burdens we can bring it to an end by means of merciful sleep. For the nerves, brain, muscles and blood vessels it is an important break. While we sleep, millions of our body cells can rest and renew themselves. In its wonderful effects sleep remains a mystery, a phenomenon of nature, in spite of all that has been written about it.

Since it is said that every cell is subject to a rhythm of tension and repose, it is astonishing to hear that millions of heart cells, from before our birth to the last moment of our life, never stop working. It is strange that not all cells have been given the same potential. While some require the regular rhythm of rest, others are capable of working throughout life with untiring pliability, without ever resting. What miracle makes this possible is known only to the One who put the building blocks of life together and imparted the life force to them in the first place.

AN EXTRAORDINARY THING — THE NEED FOR SLEEP

One thing we know for sure from experience: we must not let the body go short of sleep since there is simply no substitute for it. Experience and observation also tell us that bedtime has something to do with the coming and going of daylight. We are aware of the fact that sleep before midnight is more refreshing and relaxing than sleep afterwards. If we postpone our bedtime to the hours after midnight we will not derive the strengthening benefits from sleep that we would by going to bed earlier, because the hours before midnight provide double the benefits. Not everyone needs the same amount of sleep. Individual requirements generally lie between six and ten hours.

If we want to derive the most from sleep as a source of energy we must definitely make sure that we allow ourselves the time we individually need. Anyone who cuts sleep short so that he can work more will soon notice that he has calculated wrongly. During the day his energy will decline and his efficiency will diminish. If we need a great deal of sleep in order to feel fresh during the day we should not compare ourselves with those who get by with less. We must by all means obtain the amount we personally need. May we therefore never forget the mysterious renewing power of sleep. It is essential for good health.

What Do Dreams Tell Us about Ourselves?

If you watch a dog asleep on the floor after an exciting chase, you can often see his legs twitching and hear him making strange noises. The dog is dreaming and the chase or something similar is still going on in his subconscious mind.

After telling a child a story about the wolf who wants to devour it, or some other exciting story, do not be surprised if the child

612

wakes up screaming from a nightmare and runs to his mother or father because he is frightened. Modern teachers avoid exciting childrens' minds unnecessarily, but what about some of the television programmes children watch that are really inappropriate for them and can lead to real addiction?

Life Goes On While We Are Asleep

Strong impressions, agitation, fear and panic usually disturb the sleep pattern. The reflexes of the subconscious mind prevent quiet relaxation during sleep. After all, not every part of the body is asleep, many functions such as the circulation and, with it, the activity of the heart and the lungs, never stop to rest. If they stopped working our life would stop too. Digestion and everything linked with our metabolism continues working during the hours of sleep. Part of the brain rests, consciousness in particular being switched off, but other parts continue their function at a reduced rate.

We should not eat much in the evening and should avoid heavy or indigestible food completely; neither should our last meal of the day be taken late if we wish to prevent the subconscious mind, with its reactions and reflexes, giving us excitable and restless dreams that rob us of valuable energy for no good reason at all. It is of equal importance to try and forget the day's happenings, perhaps by listening to some soothing music before going to bed. Another means of unwinding is to read something pleasant or take a leisurely walk where we can take in calming impressions from nature around us. The result will be a relaxed state of mind leading to undisturbed repose. I am in no doubt that exciting radio broadcasts and television programmes that last until the early hours of the morning are the worst enemies of restful sleep.

On the other hand, not all dreams are troublesome; indeed, some dreams are quite pleasant and may let you experience some beautiful things you may never have had the chance to see in real life. As a result, you will wake up happy and contented after your 'trip' to far-distant lands. A feeling of joyful surprise may fill your being as you visit the jungles and other sights of nature, without having to spend the time and money that would have been necessary had it all been reality.

Diagnosing Illness

Dreams can, in a limited way, betray our condition of health and help us discern what illness may lie dormant in us. Dreams of being chased while the facing wind holds one back from escaping can indicate blood congestions that require attention. Oppressive dreams may be the result of lying uncomfortably so that the limbs go to sleep, or indicate that the bedroom is too hot or badly ventilated. These dreams often wake you up and you are then able to solve the problem.

The Interpretation of Dreams

The general interpretation of dreams as practised by private individuals or by psychologists usually goes too far. It is interesting, however, that you may find an answer to some problem you have been looking for in vain while awake, the reason being that the rested brain is able to draw more logical conclusions. Some researchers and inventors have even found the solutions they were seeking while asleep and dreaming. The solutions were proved to be correct on subsequent examination of all the details involved.

According to God's inspired writings in the Bible, the Creator revealed his purposes on several occasions in the form of prophetic dreams way back in antiquity. On the other hand, dreams can also be inspired by magic, metaphysical powers that are neither in harmony nor accord with the Almighty. Dreams have always had an important place in ancient cultures, as can be clearly seen from Daniel's reports about King Nebuchadnezzar of ancient Babylon, as recorded in the Bible. However, the memorable dream in question, telling of a mighty tree, came in fact from God Almighty, and the King's magicians and interpreters of dreams were unable to understand its meaning. No one but Daniel himself, with God's help, succeeded in presenting the correct information to the frightened ruler. A similar thing happened to the Egyptian pharaoh in the time of Joseph. In that case, too, no one but Joseph knew the divine dream's interpretation.

PRECAUTIONARY MEASURES

Based on this difference between divine and magical dreams, we must bear in mind that God has not used dreams to transmit the progressive steps of his purpose since the conclusion of his inspired Word. The fulfilment of his written prophecies is sufficient to reveal his purposes. Knowing this will protect us from falling victim to metaphysical influences. Once you understand their real origin you will reject them in the interests of your own well-being, guarding yourself against their evil intent. The disastrous influence of metaphysical powers to which some people open their minds can be clearly seen in India and other Far Eastern lands, where dreams and visions have been known to plague and mislead the population.

As regards modern interpretations of dreams, it would be better to treat the subject with healthy scepticism and sobriety. In spite of scientific research, dreams are still a borderline area of unexplained processes and it is most advisable to observe a healthy, natural way of life that will keep your sleep as free as possible from vivid dreams.

The Symptoms of Old Age

Medical textbooks dealing with the signs of old age mention all kinds of conditions that have as their cause the progressive deterioration of the body. Ossification of the cartilages increases, elasticity of the ligaments decreases, and the whole body becomes stiff, the entire bone structure bent. The joints are less flexible and moving them becomes more difficult, often painful. Walking becomes less safe and the person feels as if the joints lack lubrication, easily said after hearing them creak and crack! The memory deteriorates and the increased hardening of the blood vessels leads to high blood pressure. Strenuous physical effort and exposure to strong sunlight can no longer be tolerated but cause giddiness and the danger of a stroke.

This description is enough to make you lose a little of the joy of life if you are past sixty. But does it have to be like this? Is this fate immutable? Have a look at those who are much older and you will meet many eighty-year-olds who are full of vitality and energy, sometimes more so than other people who are only fifty. This reminds me of my grandmother's sister who, at the age of ninety-six, was still able to read the newspaper without glasses. Her memory and mental alertness were so sharp that I had great admiration for her when I was a young man.

A Sensible Way of Life

On examining the life-style of such people we can generally find the following basic characteristics. Their life is simple and they are moderate in their ways. They work, but do not go without time spent in rest and relaxation. They do not go short on sleep and know how to retire, in the proper sense of the word, when night falls; indeed, they are able to shut out the impressions of the day and forget whatever worries there might be. In fact, such people have the ability to overcome the ups and downs of life with a calm and cheerful spirit and without worrying themselves sick. Any problems are tackled with determination and are soon solved.

Admittedly, this way of life cannot prevent old age but it does keep one young and flexible inside. Such people are content with the experience and maturity age has given them, knowing that these qualities compensate for their former youthful agility and energy. This attitude helps them to use their energy reserves moderately even at a highly advanced age, rather than squandering them in senseless pursuits. It is no doubt an art not to let the many worries and annoyances irritate and upset us too much and, instead, think more about the good and beautiful things, showing grateful appreciation for them. But this art can be learned and it is worthwhile doing so, since it helps to make the twilight of one's life more pleasant and happy.

Some old people take a constitutional walk every day, inhaling a good supply of oxygen in the fresh air, even though it is almost impossible nowadays to find a quiet country road free of all traffic. Everywhere you go there are cars, leaving only narrow meadow paths and remote trails in the forests where they have not yet been able to advance. So, if older people escape from the motor exhausts and flee to nature's solitude, the exercise, healthy air and available oxygen will be a boon to them. In addition, older people should eat natural food and in moderate quantities, with only a little fat. Their protein intake should also be limited, which avoids the formation of too much cholesterol.

Experience teaches us that the normal signs of old age can be put off by years, even decades, if the right and natural measures are taken in time. But this is only possible if we do not let the speed of our times infect us; rather, we should remember Goethe's advice and take things slower and calmer as we get older. The transition from a fast pace of life to a quieter one may not be easy; on the contrary, many people complain as different physical problems crop up and they find it increasingly difficult to cope. They confirm Solomon's observation that the years of old age are far from welcome. For this reason the wise man of biblical fame admonished the young: 'Remember, now, your Grand Creator in the days of your young manhood, before the calamitous days proceed to come, or the years have arrived when you will say: "I have no delight in them".' All those who maintain the right attitude towards the Creator throughout life will not moan about the difficulties of old age, because their heart will remain young.

Gratitude – a Remedy

I was made aware of the importance of gratitude in our life some years ago when a good friend who was an instructor at a missionary school in the State of New York asked me whether I had expressed thanks for the air I had inhaled that day. In a way, this unexpected question startled me, because I had never before thought of expressing gratitude for this indispensable gift, but had for years taken for granted its being there to receive daily. Of course, I am sure that I am not alone in having been thoughtless in this respect. At the same time, I realised that I had reason to be grateful for many other precious gifts. Moreover, I became conscious of the fact that everyday life with its hectic demands and its various joys, but also its many obstacles, often crowded out the invaluable precious things we receive from the Giver of all good and perfect gifts at no cost to us whatsoever. Once we have begun to realise that, in spite of many difficulties, we have reason to be grateful for all the indispensable things that we cannot produce ourselves, then the awakening gratitude will permeate our being with a warm feeling, and this inner warmth is a gift of which we can always avail ourselves without cost.

Many years later I was living among the carefree inhabitants of a small South Sea island. I was curious about the cause of their happiness and found that they subscribed to gratitude without thinking. They never forgot to express gratitude for all the many little and greater joys the Creator gave them day by day. Without tiring they felt grateful for the sunshine, the warmth, the blue sea with its abundance of food, the coconut trees, various other fruit trees and many other things. Gratitude not only transmits warmth, it also produces contentment, which in turn awakens happiness. It stimulates the endocrine glands, promotes good circulation, and thus influences the metabolism for better health, with all the important body functions being activated. The German poet Schiller once described joy as an animating spark, believing that joy in fact makes the world tick. With two world wars behind us, and all the subsequent wars, we realise that the spring in the world clock can be equally well wound by destructive powers. However, since these powers are never able to rob us entirely of the divine gifts of light, sunshine, air and others, we have reason enough to express our joy about them daily.

Maintaining a Positive Attitude

One of the worst enemies that could be unleashed on the primitive peoples of the world was greed. It made them lose contentment and their inner balance, and it is therefore not without reason that many dangerous conflicts resulted. The same consequences may be triggered in children. Take an unspoilt child who is happy and content when playing with fir cones, pebbles and bits of wood. If the child is suddenly given purpose-made toys they arouse a feeling of desire and craving in him that cannot easily be allayed but demands satisfaction. In time, the desire inevitably increases. In the end, even an abundance of such toys will no longer be enough, because contentment will have been rejected and his greed will have become insatiable. Of course, this process is not confined to one child, it can take hold of whole nations, permeating them with discontent. It is this evil process which the 'civilised' world introduced to the developing countries, resulting, inevitably, in conflict and unrest.

Fortunately, there are still some people left who resist being infected by discontent but know how to remain cheerful in spite of difficulties. I remember a very sick farmer's wife who suffered from multiple sclerosis and had been paralysed for fourteen years. When she achieved a slight improvement with great effort and was able again to use her arms and eat without help from other people, she was so happy and grateful for the fact that she could cope so well with her still deplorable condition. Whenever I had to face some unpleasant jolt such as cannot be avoided on our bumpy earth my mind always returned to this lady and her quiet contentment.

Especially when we are tired we tend to look at the present, future and past with a negative spirit, but this does not contribute to a contented attitude by any means, nor will it provide the basis for restful relaxation and refreshing sleep. Therefore, we would do better to think of all the positive things that have happened to us and are still going on every day; in other words, we should count our blessings. This attitude will allow a pleasant sense of gratitude to enter our heart and will help to restore the mind and body to a state of well-being. We must admit that every person has sufficient grounds to feel upset, to worry and feel unhappy. However, if you place these negative factors on one side of the scales, then the same quantity of active, positive factors should be placed on the other side in order to balance them. So when you feel depressed and beset by problems, think about all the valuable things you have, the good you have been able to do in your life, your successes, the many gifts nature offers you day by day. All these encouraging memories and experiences are able to fill your heart with gratitude so that life's burdens, all your complaints, appear small indeed.

Even sick people and those who are seriously ill can relieve their frame of mind and, in so doing, ease their suffering by adopting a positive attitude. Why should your disturbed condition of health dominate the whole spectrum of your life and emotions?

Should a sick person not be happy because at least some of his organs still function well? Could he not think up ways of how he may contribute to a quicker recovery by taking the proper measures? An illness that is properly treated and cured can, in fact, help to eliminate wastes from the body and thus improve one's general well-being. However, if a morose attitude is taken and the pain is dulled by means of chemical drugs instead of proper treatment leading to cleansing and a cure, you should not be surprised to see your hopes of success vanish. Gratitude and contentment during an illness are the best basis for recovery. Often, when you think you have good reason to give free rein to sadness and despair, why not remind yourself of the dangerous times of war or the millions of refugees who lost, and continue to lose, their homes and possessions. These thoughts would awaken gratitude in you for what blessings you have and make all your little sorrows disappear. For is it not wonderful to have a roof over your head that protects you from the rain and cold, and to live in a reasonably orderly environment and land? Gratitude and appreciation for all the many things we take for granted, that embellish our daily life, can cheer us up and dispel any feelings of depression. Try it out and you will see that it works.

The Therapeutic Power of Music

If harsh, clashing sounds such as those made by machines get on our nerves and can damage our health, it is easy to believe that harmonious music would do just the opposite for us. Science has studied the effects on humans of various kinds of sound, and the consensus is that the right sort of music definitely has a beneficial effect on our state of health.

The lullaby a mother or grandmother sings at a child's bedside is a good example of how a soft melody can have a calming effect. On the other hand, is it not true that the loud blare of pop music coming from a neighbour's open window, when one is trying to relax and rest, has just the opposite effect? How often have

Mozart's delightful melodies boosted our morale? How many troubled and wrinkled brows have been smoothed by listening to the works of the great composers? The power of a Beethoven symphony has quietened many an agitated heart. Even the twittering of birds is often able to disperse worry and anxiety to such an extent that those who see no solution to their troubles return home from a walk in the woods comforted and strengthened, hardly realising from what source the power came. A child might fall and immediately begin to scream to attract attention and assuage his pain. If, just then, a robin or blackbird in the garden hedge starts to sing, the child invariably stops wailing. At first he is interested to know where the voice is coming from, then is comforted by the cheerful little minstrel; soon the pain is forgotten and the little face is all smiles again.

It is not surprising that intelligent doctors assert that music has a soothing influence on their patients when under stress and in pain. It relaxes cramped muscles, improves the function of the glands and influences good digestion, which is directly dependent on glandular secretions.

The Choice of Music

It goes without saying that not every sort of music has the same effect. Some lovers of light music might think it strange that classical music has the best effect on some sick people. It may also seem odd that musicians often do not react to music in the same way as those who do not make music a part of their daily lives. Perhaps this can be attributed to a sort of professional diffidence.

Music for the invalid must be chosen just as carefully as medicine, even with regard to 'dosage', so that its therapy can work properly. We should bear in mind the homoeopathic principle that strong stimulants are destructive but weak ones vitalise.

It is interesting to note that there is a resemblance between all biological laws and principles. Just as a stimulating and invigorating medicine is given in the morning and a sedative at night, in the same way, lively music will be found suitable for the mornings and soothing, soft music for the evenings, helping to relax the patient and induce sleep. It is understandable that the choice of music and the volume must be right if the patient is to benefit.

Great care should be taken that someone suffering from Graves' disease (exophthalmic goitre) and others with an increased heart beat are only exposed to soft harmonious music, which will be of greater benefit to them than fast, exciting sounds. On the other hand, a slow heart that can do with perking up will benefit from a little more movement and rhythm, so as to catch a little of the enlivening spirit.

As with all biological methods of treatment, it is necessary to apply intuition, understanding and feeling. Those who lack such sensitivity and do not have the ability to develop it, should at least be considerate and spare the patient at home or in the neighbourhood from the worst of the blaring noises that go under the name of 'music' today. It is sad to see the abuse that has been inflicted on us since radio has been invented.

In summary, try the influence of some healing music with your family, friends and acquaintances, at the same time not forgetting to show consideration for your neighbours and especially those who are ill.

The Therapeutic Power of Peace and Quiet

Have you ever stopped to think about the great healing power that dwells in tranquillity, in undisturbed peacefulness? Have you ever got to know it and sought refuge in it from all the noise around us? Did you know that there are, in fact, some people who are afraid of quiet and solitude? They are not used to seeking rest and relaxation in peacefulness. They need noise, the unsettling rushing and chasing around, the feverish restlessness that does not give them even time to think. They flee from tranquillity, the healing power that could do so much for them if they only would trust in it. But they do not know it and it passes them by. So they drown in the noisy hustle and bustle of our times, letting the wondrous relaxing power of peace escape them, though with mixed feelings and suspicion. How strange that it is often the very people who are in urgent need of peace and quiet as a remedy that often shirk it!

Where to Find Peace

It is increasingly difficult to find peace in certain areas and lands, or only in such remote and inaccessible places that might frighten even those who love it. But in those areas where it still displays its beauty and serenity it should be taken advantage of as the wonderful recuperative remedy or tonic it really is. If you have not yet come to know peace, do not ignorantly shut it out or reject it. A good opportunity to become familiar with it is in the wintertime.

Imagine, for a moment, that you are walking home alone one wonderfully clear starry night. The delicate hoarfrost on the shrubs and hedges glistens in the cool moonlight. The snow under your feet sparkles and in the stillness around you the crunching of your shoes sounds almost deafening. Without thinking, you stop to take in the peacefulness and the glistening beauty. You feel as if you are in another world. No sound disturbs the enchanting silence and stillness. Have you ever before realised the beauty of the birch trees in their white winter coats? It is as if you are seeing everything for the first time.

How many gifts of nature have you passed by without even looking? But look at your garden, how everything shines and sparkles. As you contemplate it, the beauty and splendour grows on you, the silence and peace take a hold of you. Involuntarily, you cast your eyes up to the sky, the Milky Way with its millions and millions of solar systems – what a tremendous, silent, quiet wonder! In fact, have you ever wondered how long the twinkling stars have already been in their places? For millions, or billions, of years they have been shining in silent peacefulness. What are you in comparison? Your life has gone on under their light for twenty, thirty, forty or fifty years, yet you have never before seen them so beautifully still, so remote but so majestic. Slowly you begin to meditate on the meaning of life, wondering whether you actually fulfil its purpose, or even whether you know and understand what that purpose is. Perhaps hitherto you have merely let the noisy current of the modern world propel you along.

Somehow you may feel weak, possibly even ill, and you ask yourself whether the noise, the hustle and bustle, the restlessness of our world have contributed to your condition. Does sickness make sense at all? Is it part of the purpose of life? There is something in you that just cannot accept the idea of sickness being inevitable. Was there not a man in antiquity who also could not accept it, doubting that sickness served a sensible purpose?

Slowly you walk to your study, still turning these thoughts over in your mind and, without prompting, you reach for a book on the shelf, the book that tells you about Job and his painful disease. Your room is quiet too. Nothing disturbs your meditation, and your reading tells you that the man Job was able to prove his devotion and integrity to God despite his suffering.

You put the book back on the shelf and now turn your eye to the pictures of your parents and grandparents that look at you from their places on the wall. They have been hanging there for years but never before have you noticed their calm, benign expressions. Of course, you know that their times were quieter times, even though the people in their day had to work hard to be successful. But there you have it, an easier life is not always a successful one. You cannot help pondering over all this. You may have come to know just the tail end of their days, before humanity was plunged into wars and many disastrous cravings, putting an end to peace and quiet.

You eye the radio in the corner as if it were an enemy. Why, is it not a source of noise? Does it not force foreign thoughts on to you, robbing you of your peace? And what about television? From the moment you let it in through the front door, it is in the home like an intruder, like some evil thing intent on stealing your time and tranquillity, while parading before your eyes all the disastrous happenings in the world. How fortunate are those of us who never let it in and have never become used to it! However, it is up to you to keep your room quiet and peaceful if you want to!

THE AWAKENING OF GRATITUDE
You are tired and decide to go to your bedroom. There is your bed in front of you. It is cold outside but you have a roof over your head and own many other things that millions do not have at all. You remember the pictures you have seen, pictures of refugees with nothing but the clothes on their backs. You still have it quite good. So why be sad? How many people go on living without a bed, or even a room, of their own. Poor people, herded together somewhere in the world, feeling cold and afraid, hungry people with no way out of their predicament – these thoughts cause you to reflect on what you have and can be grateful for. It is wrong to take everything for granted. Indeed, even the air you breathe suddenly appears to be worthy of gratitude and so does the peace and quiet around you. You feel it surging through you with a warming kind of joy and you go to bed feeling content.

You are still alone, your family has not come in yet, and they cannot know what has gone on in your heart and mind. You pull up your blanket, still deep in thought, comfortable in the calmness surrounding you. You fall into a sleep that has not been so good and restful for a long time – and all because of those moments of peace and quiet, solitude and gratitude you had enjoyed before closing your eyes. The healing powers at our disposal would make our stressful times much more endurable if only we could recognise and use them.

Happiness Means Health

Promoting health through happiness is an interesting pursuit. The poet Conrad Ferdinand Meyer thought deeply about this subject and concluded that a heavy heart is not cured by unrestrained hilarity but responds very quickly to even a little happiness. Was he really right? Can life's problems be sorted out by just a little happiness, even though our everyday demands, worries and sufferings continuously erode our energies?

Imagine a beautiful peach tree espaliered against the wall of your house. Each spring it blossoms anew and a few months later it brings forth delicious fruit. Why should we think it could be otherwise? Yet suddenly the unexpected happens. The peach tree flowers as usual, but just as the flowers open they fall to the ground. The bark of the tree dries up and the tree dies. What has happened? The tree was the pride of the household; its healthy growth, its beautiful blossoms and delicious fruit were the talk of the neighbourhood. How could this tree die so quickly and unexpectedly? What malicious enemy could have attacked it? You ask yourself all these questions but you can only find the answers by digging up the tree. It is then that you discover the cause: field mice have eaten the roots and so killed the beautiful tree.

What a joy it would have been to see the tree recover and again send forth its blossoms. Sometimes it is only by losing things, either material or spiritual, that we become aware of their value. Young people would not be so casual about their health if they could but know that they might soon lose it. How bewildered we are by the loss of health and until we know the cause there is not much we can do about it. Good health should be treasured and never abused, for good health leads to happiness.

Negligence, ignorance, inexperience, ineptitude, often force of circumstances, as well as a lack of knowledge on how to sustain health and prolong life, are all, metaphorically speaking, rodents that are gnawing away at our life and bringing us eventually to ruin. So does the little word 'happiness' imply that having it will bring back health and save our lives from an untimely end?

If you inherited good health and vigour you should always cherish and appreciate these valuable gifts. Inherent advantages should be enjoyed and used to make others happy too. An old proverb puts it this way: 'The happiness we give to others will return to make our own hearts rejoice.'

Life is like good garden soil. It brings forth nothing if we do not sow, till, water and care for it. Without good seed even the best soil will not produce a thing. If we do not put anything into life, we cannot hope to get anything out of it. Again, the poet's words come to mind: 'Know that the noble mind puts goodness into life, but does not seek it there'! All the things that raise our spirit and give us strength are like valuable and beautiful plants in our lives. The useless things that hang about us, imperfect beings that we are, are as weeds, which should be pulled out and destroyed.

Undoubtedly one of the best and most useful plants or attributes we possess is happiness. This not only brings peace to our spirit but also healing to our body.

Happiness as a Remedy

Happiness can indeed be spoken of as a remedy. Mysterious functions take place in our bodies, which are responsible for equally mysterious and inexplicable effects. No less puzzling is the interaction between the mind and the nervous system. In what a wonderful and simple way the central nervous system executes the orders of the mind! Millions of muscle fibres work like obedient little horses, harnessed and driven by millions of reins and guided by our will, the driver. To this wonder-system of divine design we owe the movement and rhythm of life.

How differently the sympathetic nervous system works! Unguided by the cerebrum and uninfluenced by the will, it performs those functions that could not possibly be maintained and attended to by our conscious minds. The circulation and digestion, as well as all the organs involved in these processes, are regulated by the autonomous nerves on which our physical and mental well-being depends. Although the will has no power over them they can nevertheless be influenced by our imaginative faculties, by our feelings and emotions. Joy will get hold of the hidden switches of the sympathetic nerves, and release cramps and flood away congestions in the liver, the kidneys and the pancreas. Even the heart cannot escape the positive influence of joy and happiness.

By helping those around us to see and appreciate the beautiful things in life, to achieve happiness, we are administering to them the best biological medicine possible. Showing them the meaning of life and the opportunities to do good to their fellow human being will bring joy and happiness into their life.

If you know a diabetic patient, you can be of great service if you teach him to enjoy the good and beautiful things in life. Point out the beauty of the spring buds and blossoms; encourage him to rejoice in the golden splendour of the ripe wheat fields of the summer, to take pleasure in the autumnal symphony of colours and to admire the ornate beauty of wintry ice and snow crystals. To experience this happiness will touch his heart, improve his breathing and instil him with a vitality that will carry him through the woods and over the hills with opened eyes and a thankful heart. The pancreas will begin to function better; the secretion of digestive enzymes and consequently the digestion, will improve. A lower intake of food will be of advantage to him in his condition, since better digestion means better utilisation of the food eaten. The inner secretions will be stimulated, the islets of Langerhans will increase their production of insulin and the sugar in the blood will be oxidised. Aided by physical measures such as hot abdominal packs and good natural wholefoods, especially by plenty of raw vegetables in the diet, all eaten slowly and well insalivated, his health will visibly improve. If joy and happiness are added to the diet, before long he may be fortunate enough to have regained his health.

You can help people who suffer from liver disorders, too, by telling them of this happiness cure. They will have reason to be grateful to you. If your own liver, the most important gland in your body, is not working as it should, let happiness set about casting out trouble and anxiety. It can wage a successful war against these saboteurs and will effectively counteract the damage done by them. Take and use this help which, though sometimes buried deep within you, is always ready to come to your assistance. Be filled with the rhythm of the pulsating life of happiness; be glad, even if the gladness at first is somewhat artificial and forced. Breathe deeply and at the same time concentrate upon something of beauty and value. Eventually you will find that happiness will pervade your whole being and so master your body and all its functions.

Happiness is like warmth. Even the coldest heart must melt if this warmth is allowed to penetrate for long enough. If whatever you do can somehow help your neighbour, the resulting happiness you receive will permeate your entire being. Whether you are a farmer, salesperson, housewife, office worker, doctor, lawyer, butcher, candlestick maker, or whatever, your fellow human being needs your skill and by rendering a service to him it should bring happiness to you. Do not go about your work sullenly, thereby spoiling the blessing of it. If you are a teacher or a doctor and perhaps you feel that what you do does not receive proper recognition, at least take comfort and happiness from the fact that you are in a position to help those who need and want to be helped. Those who work only for the sake of making money, or are forced to because of circumstances, gain very little, if any, satisfaction from their work. If there is no pleasure to be found in what you are doing or in your achievements, then you are cheating yourself, to be sure. If your eight- or nine-hour working day is pervaded by ill-will and discontent, and you sleep for another eight hours, it is fairly certain that you will not have many happy, cheerful and thankful feelings during whatever time remains. Such a life is one of slavery and drudgery. Your work would be so much easier and enjoyable and it would make fewer demands on you if only it could be permeated with happiness. In the evening you would be much less tired, your dinner would taste better and your morale would be higher. The hours of leisure spent with your family and friends would be filled with pleasure and peace of mind. Even though others contaminate the atmosphere with hate and discontent, your happiness would be strong enough to triumph over such discord.

Envy and jealousy are powerful enemies that corrupt the mind. They can destroy and gnaw away at the plant of happiness in the garden of your heart and lay hold of your innermost being.

There once was an Indian prince who marvelled at one of his fellow believers, a poor man, who could rejoice without envy at the beauty and gracefulness of the prince's wife. The prince, puzzled, questioned him and the poor man explained happily: 'Why should I not rejoice in beauty, especially if it does not occasion me any worry or responsibility? You have the burden of overseeing all your wealth and of providing for all your wife's needs while I, on the other hand, can rejoice in just looking at her, without any worry or dismay.'

Those who can enjoy looking at the good fortune of others without feeling envious have passed their first big test, which will ensure them happiness and peace throughout their lives. Possessions always mean responsibility but there are many things we can relish without such cares. Our walks can be taken not only for the healthy exercise they give but also for the joy of seeing the beauty of the flowers, the distant mountains, the fine woods and rich fields. We need not consider the fact that the cool, blue lake and the rushing stream do not belong to us. We can rejoice in the graceful gambols of someone else's young animals without fearing that, by some mischance, we might lose them. We can enjoy all these things so much better than their owner, because ownership is a heavy burden that demands work and care. Many who strive for it with envy or jealousy in their hearts perhaps could not enjoy such a burden successfully. So, if you wish to enjoy beauty to the full, do not let envy and jealousy encroach upon your joy in appreciating the possessions of others.

If, one day, you find yourself robbed of happiness, just exert yourself by doing something to please others and you will find that it will return. A kind, friendly word, an understanding smile and a comforting look or remark are the things that can do much good in giving pleasure to others. If you have the capacity to comfort someone in his sorrows, you will undoubtedly find comfort for yourself, for it is well known that one derives more pleasure from giving than from receiving.

Is not every day a gift from heaven? Why spoil it with grumbling and discontent? How much more sensible it would be to fill the day with useful thoughts and deeds, for each day comes but once and by nightfall it is gone forever. Even though troubles may arise, happiness and thankfulness can offset them and thus the day never needs to be lost and wasted.

If you are alone, you can rejoice in the quiet and collect your thoughts. If you are among friends, then rejoice in their company and make good use of the occasion to profit by such companionship. Build one another up by conversation that gives moral improvement and mutual benefit, like the echo of a beautiful symphony. Empty chatter produces spiritual emptiness that craves for distraction. Boisterous laughter does not generate joy but is like darnel, a weed whose ears are empty.

When you go to bed – when the sun sets if at all possible – the last thing you should do before going to sleep is to thank your Maker for the day he has given you. Rejoice in the good you have been able to do and if you have received a kindness, then remember it with quiet happiness and breathe deeply, for joy comes from the depths of the spirit and is carried on the breath of life. When borne aloft to higher spheres by this feeling of joy, you will realise how small and insignificant your everyday troubles really are. You will gently slip into the land of unconsciousness, like an aeroplane crossing from day into night. The higher the flight path the safer the flight because there is less danger of coming into contact with the obstacles on earth, the air currents and gusts. It is the same with us; the higher we reach in the spiritual realm of joy and peace, the more peaceful our inner lives will be, and thus our sleep. Our dreams, if they appear at all, will be quiet and no longer based on our former restlessness.

To change our way of life so that we can find this deep, satisfying joy in the midst of our everyday life, must of course take a little time and practice. Our nature is not used to controlling our mind and spirit as it is to ordering our muscles and sinews.

When the new day dawns, do not hurry agitatedly into the unknown, wondering what new worries it will bring. Try to remember that it has been given to you completely new, to do with it what you will. After all, should we really take it for granted that light and sunshine return day after day for our benefit? So thank your Maker for these important gifts of everyday life, as thankfulness always fills the heart with joy and this happy frame of mind will never nourish the hard-hearted attitude that there is no divine Power interested in our welfare. On the contrary, it will prompt you to express thanks to your Maker for the wonderful gift of light and warmth. Full of joy, your first step in the new day will be a happy one. Whatever problems that arise to worry you can be dealt with more easily; in fact, you will look at them in a different light, giving you a better chance of success, whereas sadness and discontent will rob your time and drain your strength, or they may even lead you into further trouble. Those who begin their day in a happy frame of mind are more likely to end it in the same way.

If you are not in a happy mood when you wake up, think of something joyful. Open your windows, breathe deeply for about five minutes and the lingering tiredness will soon leave you. This exercise will put a different, happier face on things, even though you got out of bed on the wrong side. Moreover, if you do something for the body at the same time, you are well on the way to acquiring a positive mood. According to your nature, this may be washing yourself down with hot or warm water or taking a shower. Additionally, it would be useful to do some exercises, resulting in a pleasant feeling of warmth and a good start to the day. You will enjoy breakfast more than usual if you clean your teeth properly beforehand and gargle to cleanse and refresh your throat thoroughly.

Take pleasure in your food and make sure that it is both tasty and natural. Do not be a slave to time with one eye always on the clock. Eat peacefully and slowly, chewing your food well. In this way you will extract all the nourishment possible and your internal organs will benefit from the work your teeth and salivary glands have done for them. Those who enjoy and value what nature's garden so generously gives us should remember to be grateful and not take the well-laden table for granted. There are so many things in which we can rejoice that there is really no time left for discontent.

If, however, some sorrow strikes you down, face things bravely with determination to overcome it. Eventually you will reach the place where the warm sun of peace and happiness will once again soothe or even heal your pain completely. Always look ahead with optimism.

Should the enemy of all living things rob you of one of your loved ones, try not to be overwhelmed by inconsolable grief. Prophetic words have been written, which promise us a time when there will be no more sorrow, when pain and death will no longer exist. These are not empty illusions. The God of Life will put a stop to evil and destruction and the resurrection of the dead will become a reality. This faith in a happier future brings a warm glow of comfort and hope to our hearts. Nothing can strengthen our morale as much as the thought of the restoration of all things to a state of perfection. What a comfort it is to know that our pain- and fear-ridden world will one day be freed of all destructive forces! No one who wilfully wielded evil power will be allowed to return from death to spread sorrow and anguish once more. Those who mourn their dead, a result of inherited imperfection, should not stubbornly reject joyful hope and faith in the resurrection. True, the superficiality of our lives and the cares of day-to-day living are apt to obscure our understanding of such matters. We think that things have always been and always will be the same. We cannot envisage a time when blood will no longer be spilled, when swords will be turned into ploughshares, spears into pruning knives and man will no longer learn the art of war. This must now seem a quite unbelievable blessing for our war-weary and war-mongering world. However, the God of Life, the God of Peace, will make good his promises. Each one will have his own vineyard and sit beneath his own fig tree, at peace with the world and without fear for the future. These are sacred words of hope and comfort spoken under inspiration by the prophets of old and can be considered as good as fulfilled. The kingdom for which we learned to pray as children is no Utopia, no matter how much the worldly wise may scoff at the idea. Those who believe these words must eventually be filled with hope and positive happiness, even though they may have many trials and tribulations to overcome.

'Yes,' some sigh, 'if only we could understand and believe.' Because many love the dissipations that have become common and seemingly necessary to their superficial lives, they cannot achieve real happiness in life and the joy of worthwhile things. For them the future is gloomy and will remain so, to the extent that they seek a way out with drugs. While they think it is pleasurable, there is no health and joy in this escape.

Our pleasures should be salutary so that they can impart health. Some people become slaves to a passion and regard it as their real and only pleasure in life, yet it is quite possible that indulging in it is doing them great harm. This applies very much to the passion for sports. From a healthy pleasure in movement and rhythm, sports have now become so exaggerated and competitive that they can damage and sometimes even destroy your health. Anything that can harm you is not a true pleasure, which should always make for good health.

If you take pleasure in the beauties of nature you will find that other passions cannot make too many demands on you, especially those that blind you to all true happiness. Concentrate on and enjoy the bounteous riches of creation, which are limitless and offered to you for your delight. Only the normal biological rhythm of a healthy way of life can ensure for you the happiness that strengthens and regenerates. For example, you will not be able to enjoy the fresh, clean mountain air, nor the scent of the meadows and the larch or fir trees if you have ruined your sense of smell by smoking.

Happiness is a soothing balm for a sick heart and the best remedy for a wounded spirit. Even when you lose all that you thought was worth living for, or when the friends you thought you could depend upon desert you, you will still find that happiness is inexhaustible, once you know where and how to find it. A ray of sunlight coming through the window can make you happy. It can transform the unnoticed spider's web into a silver diadem. Light, air and sun are possessions that we place too little value on, yet they enrich our lives by scattering many joys in our path. All we have to do is open our eyes to these things. Even when the sun's light is withdrawn, the inner light which we should have stored in our hearts should continue to illuminate our lives.

Unfortunately, it does not seem to be a characteristic of our times to seek out and enjoy the little things in life. So much unhappiness has embittered people's hearts, too many hopes have been raised and shattered, and peace – that great giver of happiness

– has too often been destroyed. It is very difficult for an overtired nervous system to be relaxed and at ease so that strength and peace-bringing happiness can enter and do its good work. It is never easy to rid oneself of unhappy memories and impressions, but if you wish to regain your health through happiness, then you must do your utmost to forget. Happiness can then take root and a healthy, joyful spirit will provide the best conditions for making and keeping your body healthy.

Recommendations for Breakfast

If you want to do justice to the physical and mental demands of today's world, you must do all you can to obtain and eat natural wholefoods containing plenty of nutrients and vitamins. Many people think that it is enough to watch their intake of calories, as this is generally recommended. However, that this consideration is not the only important one can be seen in the resulting deficiencies and various other disturbances, as well as tiredness, not to speak of sudden symptoms of illness. It is necessary to change to natural, organic wholefoods in order to stem the tide of environmental pollution, and the stress of our modern unhealthy life-style.

You can begin by making the right start with your breakfast. In Continental Europe coffee or tea, white bread, white rolls, butter, jam or marmalade, perhaps some cheese spread, is usually considered sufficient to keep one going until midday, whether in hotels or at home. The idea is that a more substantial lunch will supply the necessary balance. In the United Kingdom and the United States, however, it is often customary to have a quick 'bite' in the lunch hour in order to interrupt the work schedule as little as possible. For this reason people tend to eat a substantial breakfast including plenty of protein (just think of the English breakfast), because the meal has to last until the evening when, on returning home from work, the main meal of the day is served.

Years ago it was the custom in rural Switzerland to eat either specially prepared sauté potatoes, polental, (a dish made of cornmeal) or porridge. This kind of breakfast was more nutritious, even though it can still be described as one-sided, not balanced. Then, in Switzerland, the idea of the now widely known 'muesli' arose, based on the nutritious rolled oats, *mues* (meaning dish). Muesli is a mixture of uncooked cereal flakes with grated nuts or almonds, dried fruit, and grated raw apples or berries. Dr Bircher-Benner became one of the early advocates of muesli and his recommendations were so convincing that the expression 'Bircher Muesli' established itself, especially in Switzerland.

A Special Wholefood Muesli

The experience I gained on my travels encouraged me to formulate a special muesli that contains all the nutrients we need, as well as many vitamins and all trace elements. No wonder it deserves the name 'Vollwertmuesli' (Full Value Muesli) and is on sale in every health food store in Switzerland. It contains six cereals – whole grain rye, wheat, oats, barley, brown rice and millet – all made into flakes. Another ingredient is sprouted soybeans (the sprouting takes away the bitterness and makes soya more digestible), to provide a valuable source of protein. Chestnut flakes are added for flavouring and nutritional value. It is sweetened with granulated dried grapes (organically grown); the valuable grape sugar, like honey, is directly absorbed into the blood. The granulation is achieved using pure lactose and this is a boon for the digestion and intestines. Dried, organically grown fruits enhance the taste of the muesli besides giving it valuable fruit sugars. Ground almonds are another ingredient. A further addition to this nutritious muesli is rather exceptional: it is the tropical fruit known as durian which only grows in rain forests. The natives eat this fruit for its nutritional value, giving them the strength to achieve exceptional tasks. In my own case, by eating durian I was able to keep up my energy and endurance all day long in spite of high humidity and heat. If it were not rich in vitamins and other nutrients it would hardly be so effective. Most of my friends like *Vogel's Breakfast Muesli* so much that they would not be without it in the morning and some even have it for supper as well.

According to the season, I recommend enriching the muesli with berries, fruit and a little milk or cream; you will then have a nutritious breakfast that will keep you going even if you have to do strenuous work. Additionally, I would recommend as a drink a cup of rose hip tea sweetened with honey, or *Bambu Coffee Substitute* with milk or cream, if you prefer it. A piece of wholegrain bread with butter and honey is also appreciated by some. Those who feel more hungry in the morning may appreciate Vogel Bread, if it is available where you live.

A breakfast based on such a nutritive muesli provides the body with enough energy to cope even with hard work without the need to draw on its reserves. Vogel's Breakfast Muesli is also an ideal food for growing children, as well as for young people who have to study or work hard.

Recommendations for Lunch (Midday Meal)

The consequences of unhealthy nutrition are usually felt more keenly when we are older, although nowadays more and more young people suffer from 'diseases of civilisation'. Listeners at my well-attended lectures in Europe keep asking me to what I owe my remarkable vitality and vigour, in spite of my advanced age and heavy work load. I have already explained what I eat for breakfast and, for the benefit of my questioners, I will here outline my nutritious lunch at midday.

Salad, vegetables and starch for lunch supply minerals, which we should never overlook, in addition to vitamins. The salads are made up of what the garden offers fresh, so that the variety depends upon what is in season. The salad dressing is usually made with soft white cheese (cottage cheese or quark), sunflower oil and *Molkosan* (whey concentrate), and possibly horseradish and seasoning herbs. The vegetables, too, depend upon what is seasonally available in the garden.

I recommend wholefood items such as *A. Vogel's Soya Dinners* in place of meat, especially for those who wish to eat a vegetarian diet or need to reduce or eliminate their intake of animal protein for health reasons. These soya dishes are meat-free, being made from carefully selected vegetable products. As they are available in a variety of different flavours they will definitely enrich your lunch table.

The range of easily prepared ready-to-serve dishes has been increased by the new range of *Soya Mixes*. These too contain no meat, and are therefore valuable food supplements for those who are on a meat-free diet. It is possible in this way to supply the body with purely vegetable protein by means of a delicious and pleasant lunchtime meal.

The Soya Mixes are especially indicated for vegetarian diets. Vegetable fats rich in unsaturated fatty acids help to reduce and stabilise the cholesterol level in the blood. The mixes are enriched with important trace elements and their fibre content has a positive effect on the movement of the bowels.

In these restless times, every person interested in health should never forget that proper nutrition is a key factor in protecting one's health and that it is possible to prepare tasty dishes that please the palate while being absolutely natural.

It is important, however, that a person makes sure to eat food that contains protein, starch and vital substances (vitamins and minerals) at least once a day.

Suitable protein foods other than meat are dishes containing soya, or cottage cheese (quark) or other soft cheeses.

Starchy foods are mainly potatoes, brown rice or wholegrain cereals, including millet and buckwheat.

Foods that contain vital substances (vitamins and minerals) are vegetables and salads.

Recommendations for Supper (Evening Meal)

As a light meal is better for you in the evening, the menu should possibly be the same as in the morning. You will sleep better after it than if you eat a lot of food that is hard to digest.

What is more, high-value wholefoods satisfy even in smaller quantities and keep you going to the next meal without feeling hungry, so that you can actually eat less. Every meal should be a happy family occasion and it will be just that if everyone appreciates the companionship as well as the food on the table. If you partake of it with gratitude you will forget the haste and bustle of the day and automatically chew it more thoroughly. The body will then be able to obtain the full benefit of the goodness in the food, all the nutrients and remedial properties.

The laws governing healthy nutrition are the same for man and beast and similar for plants. A healthy diet is especially important for older people and so is moderation in eating. So, if you want to learn the art of how to stay healthy as you grow older, remember that the right mental attitude and diet are of paramount importance.

Important Basic Rules for the Healthy and the Sick

The rules I outline below will help the healthy in a preventative sense, and the sick will find them beneficial when followed in addition to their therapeutic treatment. In fact, a patient who takes these rules into account will have greater success with his medical treatment.

1. Since overfeeding with protein is one of the principal causes of the 'diseases of civilisation', you should conscientiously observe the optimum intake of protein, that is, not more than 40 g (1.4 oz) daily. This is about half or a third of what people usually eat in the course of the day.

2. Your choice of foods should be restricted to natural foods, so avoid eating refined or devalued, denatured products. At the same time, see that you select organically grown cereals, fruit and vegetables.

3. The evening meal (supper) makes healthy sleep difficult if it consists of heavy protein foods. You will find it quite easy to become used to 'Full Value Muesli', enriched with fresh fruit according to the season. Some *Risopan* crispbread with a little butter and a cup of *Bambu Coffee Substitute* or rose hip tea will be enough to complete the meal.

4. I recommend a weekly fast day when you only drink vegetable juice, made from organically grown vegetables. Drink half a litre (just under a pint) of juice and about 1½ litres (about 2½ pints) of a mild kidney tea in the course of the day.

5. Eating correctly will aid the digestion. Always insalivate your food well. Anyone who does not wish to take the time to chew his food thoroughly will one day be forced to take time to stay at home sick.

6. Natural remedies should be taken regularly. In cases of a strong reaction take a smaller dose than indicated, until the disturbances disappear.

7. There are already enough poisons in our environment to upset your body, so take care to avoid as many of them as you can; nicotine, drugs and alcohol all weaken the body.

8. The order for every day is: 'Fill up with oxygen not petrol.' By this I mean that you should make a point of getting enough exercise in the fresh air every day.

9. Do not forget that the usual mad rush and demanding stress of our times not only overtax our nerves, but can also cause painful tension and circulatory disturbances. Therefore, do not let yourself be affected by more than what cannot be helped. A useful antidote is internal peace and calmness. They protect us, save energy and are an aid to beneficial relaxation.

10. Worries, anxiety and discontent harm the liver. So try to be generous and forbearing as regards human weaknesses. Those who can bear such loads preserve the peace that builds up, whereas strife and conflict destroy the things that are valuable.

11. The peace of the twilight hours provide relaxation and time for quiet meditation. When the day has had its fill of necessary duties and obligations, we should not let television programmes unnecessarily whip up our emotions still further. Uplifting spiritual food is soothing. Listening for a little while to soft music can also

help us to relax. Years ago the day was usually rounded off by singing songs of praise and gratitude, but the problems of our modern times have fundamentally changed all that.

12. Sleep is the best and least expensive remedy for good health and relaxation and should not be cut short for the sake of night-time pleasures. The hours before midnight count double and help one to go to sleep quickly. Before going to bed, a short walk in the fresh air can be relaxing, so that even the most tiresome day can end in wholesome rest.

Fasting – a Means to Combat the Damage Caused by Civilisation

People advanced in years tell us that life before World War I was more natural and hence more healthy than it is today. If the statistics of those days are correct, in the industrialised countries one person in thirty died of cancer or a heart attack, whereas today it is already one in four. The reason for this difference is mainly to be found in a change of nutrition as the simple demands people had in the past have given way to greater demands today. This applies especially to the increased consumption of protein foods and low-value carbohydrates, in particular, products made with refined sugar and refined white flour.

Comparing these nutritional trends with the modest require-ments of more primitive peoples who had not yet become familiar with the diet of our advanced industrial society, I discovered that for this reason those people had as a rule, been spared the dangers and sorrows caused by our 'diseases of civilisation'. They knew neither rheumatism nor arthritis, hardening of the arteries accompanied by high blood pressure, or cancer. The symptoms of these insidious diseases appeared only when the traditional and natural diet gave way more and more to one made up of food produced by our commercialised society. As long as people living in their natural, untouched environment were used to eating only a little protein every day – about half or even a third of the quantity consumed in more advanced societies – they were able to maintain their biological balance and good health.

This observation made a strong impression on me in every case I studied and as long ago as the 1920s I published my findings of those days in a booklet that is now out of print. In 1935 I followed this up with the publication of my first book on nutrition, entitled *Nahrung als Heifaktor (Food as a Healing Factor)*. It was clear to me that refined, denatured foods had to lead to deficiencies and could give rise to serious diseases. So why not overcome the problem by means of natural wholefoods that have not been robbed of their goodness?

Eating food as it is presented to us by nature, without anything removed, helps to avoid physical problems and can also contribute to a cure, if some harm has been done already.

At first the World Health Organization (WHO) held the opinion that a relatively high daily intake of protein was necessary. This advice was generally followed, but since the view was in fact incorrect, what was done has led to ill health. On the basis of experience the WHO later changed its opinion, recommending a daily protein intake of only 0.7 g per kilogram of body weight. In more recent times even this recommendation has been further reduced to only 0.5 g. For a 100 kg (15½ stone) man this would mean a consumption of 50 g (about 2 oz) of protein per day. Taking an average weight of 60–70 kg (9½ stones), the daily intake should be approximately 30–35 g (just over 1 oz).

More and more attention has been given to nutrition and efforts are being made to overcome or rectify existing damage to health. In an effort to renew the body fluids, some hit on the idea of fasting. A little time before that, the Austrian farmer and nature healer J. Schroth recommended a diet of solid foods without liquids. However, when it was observed that this diet had dangerous side effects, the 'cure' was given up and small quantities of liquids were taken during the period of fasting. Eventually the use of purifying teas was started, without adding sugar but sweetening them with a little honey. Pure spring water was then employed, as well as mineral water low in carbonic acid or, better, without it. The body reacted wonderfully to this cleansing cure of drinking 1–2 litres (2–4 pints) of pure spring water.

The idea of these fasting cures was to refrain from eating proteins and starchy foods over a period of time, with the benefit that the bowels could rest and the kidneys and liver had the opportunity to cleanse the body, getting rid especially of metabolic waste toxins. By observing the rule of reduced protein consumption, the diseases resulting from an increased intake would decline considerably too, and success in treating existing ones would undoubtedly be greater than when the various recommended medicines, treatments and therapies were taken.

It is with reservation that I mention the fasting treatment with tea, spring or mineral water, because it is, in a sense, a starvation diet and the person is forced to live on his body's own protein. Interestingly, the pH value of the blood changes, becoming more acidic. Anyone who wishes to undertake such a fast for any length of time should have the necessary reserves and attitude or else it could be detrimental.

Fasting with fruit or vegetable juices, on the other hand, places less of a strain on the system, avoids the starvation effect and can more easily achieve the desired cleansing of the body fluids. In South Africa I observed good results achieved by a diet based on freshly pressed grape juice. However, the grapes must be unsprayed in order to avoid taking in blue vitriol and residues of other chemicals. If the juice is contaminated the poisons will enter the system and thwart the purpose of drinking it. You need absolutely pure, organically grown and treated juice if you intend to bind and eliminate toxins that have accumulated in the body.

Since the juices must be made from biologically pure fruit and vegetables, there is yet another important factor to be considered. The soil where they are grown must on no account by subjected to chemical fertilisers because they harm the otherwise good foundation, resulting in a decrease in useful micro-organisms; the bacterial flora suffers and the entire condition of the soil becomes imbalanced. Soil that has been saturated with chemicals, with nitrates, phosphates and nitrogen compounds is definitely 'sick'. But how can soil that is itself 'sick' produce healthy fruit and vegetables? Obviously its produce is by no means 100 per cent. Moreover, chlorinated hydrocarbons, such as DDT, Aldrin and other dangerous chemicals, are bad for the soil.

The many detrimental influences attributable to environmental pollution must also be considered responsible for the deaths caused by cancer and vascular diseases. Then there are the mental pressures resulting from increased stress and constant hurrying, as well as other circumstances. Even though juice diets can work wonders because they cleanse and renew the body fluids, you must take care that the unfavourable influences of our times do not cause additional harm to your health. Be cautious, therefore: never go beyond what the generally weakened condition is able to cope with. If you suffer from heart trouble, you cannot embark upon such a ruthless diet without being cautious. I knew the doctor in charge of a well-known clinic in South Africa. He was a clever man but also quite fanatical as regards encouraging his patients to fast. Having failed to take into consideration the weak heart of one of them, the eventual death of the patient in question was really the fault of the doctor. A patient has to be strong enough before starting a juice diet. The doctor in attendance should act with great caution since a patient with heart trouble may not always be able to take the strain of such a diet.

Protecting the Body Cells

It is true that our cells are wonderfully made, with each one in the system being autonomous, independent. When healthy the cell possesses a marvellous metabolism as well as the remarkable ability of internal regeneration. What occurs inside the cell could be compared to the work of a computer, one that has come from the Creator's hand. It is also true to say that we understand very little about the workings of the cell. Still, the cell's ability to repair or regenerate damage is always ready in its defence. This readiness on the part of millions, indeed billions, of cells is most important to the whole cellular system. In fact, a cell can fight off unfavourable influences for years and, supported by the lymph and enzymes, it is able to absorb the best nutrients from the blood.

If, however, in the course of time it no longer receives the things it urgently needs, it will gradually give up. The cell is then like a business person who is in the red because of unfortunate circumstances and can no longer escape bankruptcy. However, with a cell the situation is far more tragic, because its condition is then what we know as cancer. The cell is forced to give up its normal functions. Since it can no longer hold off the influence of poisoning, it becomes antisocial and begins to act, we might say, like a person who has lost his reason. It becomes a sick giant cell. Juice diets have often proved effective in such cases, but, again, they should not be undertaken without careful thought.

An important rule demands that any treatment should only be given after first considering the patient's physical condition. I remember an occasion when I ignored this rule and went on a carrot juice diet without actually needing it. After two weeks my body suffered a peculiar reaction: I turned yellow, as if I had jaundice. At the time I happened to visit an eminent haematologist from Innsbruck, who was amazed at the excessive amount of carotene in my skin. An analysis brought to light that the haemoglobin count had been increased by 100 per cent. The effect was like a strange fire in the body, as if I had a high temperature, yet the examination showed no fever at all. I stopped the diet and two weeks later the disturbance had subsided.

This experience led me to be more careful and future experiments did not play such tricks on me. For my own purpose, I found a blend of about 30 per cent carrot juice, 60 per cent beetroot juice and about 10 per cent cabbage juice to be most satisfactory. In cases of dysbacteria sauerkraut juice, which contains lactic acid, is excellent; dilute it with half the quantity of spring water or non-carbonated mineral water. Lactic acid is a fine healing factor for the intestines. Juices that are fermented with lactic acid are more easily tolerated than freshly pressed ones, and it is possible to take at least one-third more of the lactic-fermented juices than of those prepared from fresh produce at home. You have to go by the experience gleaned from experiments and then be guided by what your body finds the most effective.

Scheduling Occasional Juice Days
A beneficial way to get used to a juice diet is to go on a one-day fast each week. If this juice day is successful and does not make you feel ill, then you can extend it to two days a week, later on even three days. As time goes by and your body becomes used to juice days, you may be able to go on such a diet for two weeks. But do not forget that you need to get plenty of oxygen during this time.

Grape juice diets are beneficial even in serious cases of cancer, since the juice is able to renew the body fluids to a great extent. For those who respond well to grapefruit, a juice diet using this fruit will be most beneficial, but not everyone tolerates grapefruit, for which reason it is important not to be fanatical as regards any form of treatment.

Whenever you go on a juice diet, a trustworthy, biologically oriented doctor should supervise its progress and the patient himself should carefully monitor his condition and reaction. The doctor must keep a check on the heart, blood pressure and other physical aspects so that the diet will produce the desired effects. In the fight against the diseases of our industrialised society, especially cancer, I have seen the best results when the patient is given the following mixture of lactic-acid-fermented juices: 60 per cent beet, 30 per cent carrot and 10 per cent sauerkraut.

Emptying the Bowels – Indispensable for Juice Diets
Never go on a fast without first eliminating all faecal matter. This applies with greater force to those who already suffer from constipation. If you ignore this advice you may have to reckon with unpleasant, possibly even disastrous, consequences. The peristalsis of the intestines is stimulated by the ingested food and if this stimulation is lacking, as is the case during a fast, the encrusted

materials will keep sticking to the villi of the intestines. Of course, this is extremely harmful to the body; it can even poison the system and cause serious consequences. This can be avoided, however, if the right measures are taken. The patient is therefore advised to consider these words carefully if he wants to escape the detrimental effects of such negligence. Do not forget to undergo a thorough cleansing of the bowels before going on a diet, even if it is only intended to be a short one, lasting a few days.

There are some good botanic laxatives you could use to stimulate the intestines. Some people like *Linoforce*, a tried and tested linseed preparation; others prefer to take *Rasayana No. 1 or No. 2*, or the mucilaginous *psyllium seed*. All these remedies are purgative but do not exclude the need for an enema before beginning the diet. For this purpose it is usually not enough to use an ordinary enema syringe, but a douche should be able to clean out the colon very well. Clinics and sanatoriums use a special douche for irrigation. For the duration of the diet it is advisable to give an enema every morning. This has been found to be very beneficial, because impurities are still eliminated often four or five days after beginning the diet. This faecal matter will have been encrusted in the villi but is softened, dissolved and finally eliminated by means of the treatment.

It depends on the health reserves and the condition of the heart whether a longer period of fasting is advisable. Some people extend the diet up to three weeks, if not longer. Let me add that with this long fast it is still necessary to give an enema every morning. In order to prevent the mucous membranes from drying out, use a decoction of *mallow*, instead of just water, or you can add to the water a little mother tincture of *Symphytum officinalis*, which is made from comfrey. If you happen to have some comfrey in the garden prepare a decoction from it and use this for the enema.

There is also another good suggestion. Add the mucilage prepared from *quince seed* to the water for the enema; or a mucilaginous infusion made from mosses such as *carragheen* (Irish moss). The addition of *Usnea* is recommended too, especially because of its excellent disinfectant action for the colon at the same time. Disinfecting can also be done with the addition of 10–20 drops of *Echinaforce*; this has a good effect on the intestinal bacteria. A tablespoon of Molkosan is beneficial to the intestinal bacteria since the lactic acid promotes their growth and health. When on a fast it is indispensable to follow the advice just given in order to protect the colon.

Mallow

At the end of the diet it is important to make a slow transition to your normal eating pattern. Begin with a soup made with oat-flakes or barley. Rice gruel is also to be recommended. However, meat, egg and cheese dishes should be left off the menu during the first week after the diet. Instead, it is preferable to take light vegetable dishes, brown rice, mashed potatoes, corn and millet. Also, have salads and soft white cheese (cottage cheese, quark) mixed with a little garlic and parsley.

It is important to pay proper attention to the transition from your normal food to the fasting diet and from the diet back to normal food again. This is essential to give the body enough time to adapt gradually to the new situation.

Health Benefits from Taking Vegetable Juices with a Specific Purpose

Are vegetable juices really indicated as a curative therapy for various diseases? What is their benefit to our health? These questions are a waste of time to those who do not think that nutrition plays an important part in keeping healthy. At the same time, observation tells us that the diseases resulting from life in our industrial society are on the increase. These illnesses have been termed 'diseases of civilisation' because they are caused by the diet or nutritional habits of people in the more affluent countries. In particular, the daily consumption of protein is generally too high, leading to a condition of overfeeding. Thus, if we are able to achieve a proper dietary balance by a purposeful intake of vegetable juices our health will definitely benefit. In fact, a day a week on a diet of vegetable juices will be beneficial to anyone. If we can see the reason why, it will be easy to keep one day a week reserved for this purpose.

A total of 500–700 ml (18–25 fl. oz) of vegetable juice during one day may be sufficient, but according to the physique of a person, up to 1 litre (1.76 pints) a day can be taken. It would be wise to take the juice in sips during the course of the day, making sure to insalivate it and not just gulp it down. The body will then obtain the full benefit of the vital substances, the minerals as well as the vitamins. At the same time, it will have a rest from the usual intake of carbohydrates, fats and protein. It is especially successful when you reduce the daily intake of protein to 35–40 g (1½ oz). This may be only half or a third of the quantity you are probably used to having every day.

Since 1935 I have been prescribing vegetable juices with notable results. The juices I have used are beetroot, carrot, cabbage and sauerkraut, either pure or mixed. Whatever the disease concerned, these juices have helped to solve the dietetic difficulties. However, since not everyone finds it easy to get the quantities right when mixing the juices, I thought it well worth using my experience and produce a ready mixed combination of juices, known as *A. Vogel's mixed vegetable juice* containing 60 per cent beetroot, 30 per cent carrot and 10 per cent sauerkraut, all three being fermented with dextrorotatory lactic acid. Only organically grown vegetables are used in the normal, biological manufacturing process.

This excellent mixed vegetable juice has an additional benefit in its content of provitamin A, which is important for the eyes. For this reason it is a dietetic help for night-blindness, xerophthalmia and other eye problems. It is suggested that you begin by diluting the pure juice with still mineral water until you are used to the hearty taste of A. Vogel's mixed vegetable juice. This is advisable because excesses should be avoided when on a diet. I have also been successful in helping many people with gastric ulcers by prescribing raw potato juice. It is best to press the juice fresh and drink it right away.

A vegetable juice diet achieves a reduction of protein, fat and sugar consumption without harming one's health. It is therefore an alternative method in the treatment of diseases brought about by modern civilisation. These findings, after years of practice, have prompted me to recommend juice diets for the benefit of all those suffering from these diseases.

In order to step up the elimination of wastes through the urine, it is of paramount importance to drink 1–1½ litres (2–4 pints) of weak *rose hip, goldenrod or kidney tea* daily throughout the duration of a juice diet or fast.

The Excellent Effect of Juice Diets on Various Diseases

The general advice for a prescribed juice diet is especially applicable in cases of rheumatism and arthritis, and following it carefully can only bring good results. For this purpose, go on a vegetable juice diet for two or three days every week and you will ensure that the body obtains plenty of alkaline substances in an easily assimilated form. No strain is put on the body through having to deal with breaking down fats, carbohydrates and proteins while taking only juices. The juices are highly alkaline, able to bind the acid elements and eliminate them through the kidneys and urine. In this way it is possible, figuratively speaking, to balance the acid/alkaline composition, since acid elements, which are partly responsible for causing pain, crystallise and are gradually eliminated. This apparently unimportant process alone is able to effect a considerable improvement in the patient's condition after only a few months. The elimination can be stimulated and the results accelerated if the patient takes *Solidago, Nephrosolid* and other good kidney remedies at the same time.

The use of a good *oil* that stimulates the skin functions is further recommended, as well as the external application of *Symphosan* following a warm shower in the morning or an invigorating herbal bath. If you follow this advice, your skin will benefit and the treatment can have greater success.

If so far you have not bothered much about proper nutrition, you should definitely make an effort to eat only natural wholefoods, avoiding white flour and white flour products. With respect to cereals eat only wholegrain products. The right way of eating your food is important too, because it benefits the digestion. For one thing, forget the usual hurry. Before sitting down to eat, relax and let your insides calm down. Eating slowly and chewing the food thoroughly, with good insalivation, will then be easy. This advice is worth remembering in order to achieve good results.

Then you should give attention to another important requirement, sufficient exercise in the open air. It provides fresh air and the necessary oxygen, essential for those of us who are healthy and even more so for the sick who want to get better. This is another step in the direction of recovery. Painful myogelosis, hardening of tissue, is not uncommon nowadays. Massage by a skilled practitioner can help to remove the problem. If you follow the advice given, the treatment can be taken at home with the same success as in an expensive clinic or sanatorium. So then, remember the various possibilities at your disposal to reach the goal of recovery.

The same treatment applies to those who suffer from various vascular problems and especially when a heart attack is in the offing or has already occurred. If you are in this position you should by no means think that everything is lost and there is no reason left to change your habits. It would be much more intelligent to strengthen your determination to improve and accept whatever help is available. Vascular diseases are often a symptom of a potassium and magnesium deficiency in the body, so it is appropriate to change one's diet to a protein-reduced and vitamin- and mineral-rich one.

A. Vogel's *mixed vegetable juice* made from carrot, beetroot and sauerkraut juice is a superb means of preventing such deficiencies, since these three vegetables are known to be rich in potassium and magnesium. Its alkalinity is three times as high as its acidity. People prone to heart attacks should have at least two juice days a week, one at the beginning and the other in the middle of the week. The body will soon benefit from doing this because of the reduced intake of fat and protein, and also because of the added provision of minerals and vitamins contained in the juices.

However, heart patients still need plenty of oxygen, which they can obtain by inhaling good air when walking or hiking or by doing some moderate work in the garden. Be careful, though, to avoid direct sunshine; cover the head with a light hat. Any existing congestions should be treated by reflex zone massage and moderate but regular exercise therapy. The heart muscles and nerves can be strengthened if the hawthorn fresh plant preparation *Crataegisan* is taken at the same time. Conscientious efforts to follow the advice given will enable the patient to prevent the disaster of having a heart attack.

An apopleptic must be careful, too, in order to counteract the degeneration of the blood vessels successfully. In this case, there is the danger of a stroke caused by high blood pressure. Such a person should also take the aforementioned advice seriously and follow it as a preventative measure. It is not enough for him to rely on mistletoe preparations or rauwolfia extract alone. The right diet is absolutely essential, because it was poor nutrition that undermined his health over the years and decades. If he does not want to succumb to the consequences of increasing high blood pressure, he must avoid everything that caused the problem in the first place. This means reducing the intake of protein to the normal and reasonable optimum quantity of about 40 g a day, or 0.5 g per kilogram of body weight, in accordance with the quantity established by the WHO (see page 638). The reduced quantity of protein and starch should be replaced by vegetables and salads. Soft white cheese (cottage cheese, quark) or soya protein are best suited to cover the protein requirement. As regards starch, apoplectics should take advantage of the goodness brown rice has to offer. A natural brown rice diet comprises three rice days a week, and this is most appropriate since brown rice has a regenerative effect on the blood vessels, as has been proved in the case of many patients. So do not overlook the great benefit of brown rice.

The question of fats and oils must also be solved in a sensible way. When one's health is endangered it is no doubt advisable to do without fats and oils in cooking in order to avoid the temptation to use heated fats and fry food in fat or oil. The use of fat will then be restricted to cold pressed oils for salads, which is all you need.

Pay careful attention to seasoning. Cooking salt should be avoided; use moderate amounts of the herbal seasoning salts *Trocomare* and *Herbamare*. Healthy and wholesome substitutes for salt and other seasonings are small amounts of garlic, horseradish and parsley. Do not use vinegar to dress your salad but wholesome *Molkosan*, which aids the digestion. While on a diet or treatment it goes without saying that you should really cut out all alcohol and nicotine. If you follow this general advice conscientiously you will notice an improvement in the blood pressure after only a few weeks, and after some time your doctor will be happy to confirm that the pressure has returned to normal. Such a result based on natural treatment is to be highly appreciated, but the method of reducing blood pressure by means of strong medication always presents a risk that has led to disaster for some patients. As with heart attack patients, it will be of great benefit if an apoplectic goes on a juice day at the beginning and in the middle of each week.

Those who suffer from a disturbed lymphatic system tend to be bothered by catarrh. They keep having trouble with their respiratory organs and are prone to anaemia. In view of this they would do well to go on a vegetable juice diet two days a week. At the same time, their general condition should be built up by taking *Urticalcin* every day. This preparation increases the calcium level and is therefore of importance to the patient with lymphatic trouble. Refined sugar and products made with it must be avoided at all costs, even in the case of children, who are usually sweet-toothed. It would be a mistake to give in to their craving during the treatment because it would be detrimental, reducing the up-building and regenerative benefits of the cure.

Besides the wholesome effect of carotene, A. Vogel's mixed vegetable juice contains vitamin B_{12}, which is important for the blood. In order to overcome their susceptibility as quickly as possible, those suffering from lymphatic problems should become used to taking about twenty drops of *Echinaforce* regularly every morning and evening. This remedy helps the body to improve its own powers of regeneration and build up natural resistance against infections, which is most beneficial to the patient.

Diabetics and those who suffer from obesity can also derive benefits from juice days. In addition, diabetics should acquire the habit of taking a glass of A. Vogel's mixed vegetable juice with every midday and evening meal.

As far as obesity is concerned, it can be of the normal kind or hypophysial, although the latter is very rare. A. Vogel's mixed vegetable juice diet is of great benefit in the case of normal obesity. It is recommended to take nothing but juice, together with rice crispbread, such as Risopan, for two or three days every week. At the same time, support the stimulation of the endocrine glands with a seaweed preparation, preferably on an empty stomach in the morning. Good results have been gained with *Kelpasan*, taking 1–2 tablets every morning before breakfast. This, incidentally, helps to combat early-morning tiredness too.

A fast day, eating only apples and grapefruit, besides the vegetable juice days, is also beneficial and helps to reduce weight. At any rate, grapefruit is well suited to reducing excess weight. For this reason always add half a grapefruit or the juice to your muesli in the morning and evening. If you are prone to obesity, make it a point to eat half a grapefruit with your breakfast every morning. Furthermore, reduce your intake of protein to 40 g (1½ oz) and also limit that of carbohydrates considerably; try to meet your daily requirements by eating wholegrain products. On the other hand, you may eat salads to your heart's content without any restriction as to quantity, since they do not share in building up the body weight. However, keep away from white sugar products and sweets; your craving for something sweet can be satisfied with dates and figs in moderate quantity. Brown rice dishes are to be preferred to those made with flour and potatoes.

The Influence of a Vegetable Juice Diet on Cancer and Leukaemia
Why are cancer and leukaemia, as a rule, unknown among more primitive peoples? As long as these people live on food that is rich in vitamins, minerals and high in alkalinity, without any items produced according to our 'civilised' ideas, they are able to maintain their biological balance. Another factor is the ease of obtaining plenty of exercise in the fresh, unpolluted air, and with it, deep-breathing, which provides the lungs with more than enough oxygen. The same factors are important in our own case, if we are to arrange our life in such a way that prevents problems. Should there be cases of cancer and leukaemia in our family we must be especially careful.

Whenever the problem runs in the family, it is definitely indicated to change one's eating habits, that is, to replace the foods of civilisation with full-value natural wholefoods. We can only endeavour to regain and maintain the biological balance in our body if we follow a strict diet that is high in alkalinity and vital substances, vitamins and minerals. If cancer is suspected, or someone suffers from leukaemia, or is recovering from a cancer operation, a low-protein diet is urgently recommended. In preparation for the actual therapy, which requires a very strict diet, not more than 20 g (0.7 oz) of protein daily are permissible. In such a case, an extended vegetable juice diet makes a virtually protein-free diet possible. However, it is most important for the therapist or doctor to check the patient's heart carefully before putting him on the diet, because the heart must be strong and healthy in order to stand the recommended protein-free juice diet.

Whether the diet is based on fruit or vegetable juices, in every case the body will be forced to obtain the necessary amino acids from somewhere. According to experience, it draws them rrom the cancerous cells rather than the healthy ones. For this reason it is possible that cancerous tissue shrinks and is absorbed after a protein-free diet extending over three or maybe even four weeks. This is possible where the juice, rich in vital substances and highly alkaline, attacks the cancerous tissues with such force that these cells are unable to withstand the violent action. Even in serious, sometimes hopeless, cases surprising changes for the better have been reported. It is additionally beneficial to take plant preparations that tend to prevent cancer, such as *butterbur (Petasites), mistletoe, garlic, horseradish* or another plant containing *germanium. Symphytum*, the wild comfrey plant, is also helpful in this connection.

It is not always advisable to extend a juice diet over a period of three or four weeks only because the patient wants to see quick results. It is much better to go on a juice diet for one week and then follow it up with a low-protein natural diet, and then another juice week. If you do decide on an extended juice diet, you should only tackle it under the supervision of a qualified therapist or practitioner. A good choice would be a doctor who specialises in holistic medicine and nature cure methods.

Before embarking on a juice cure, the colon must be thoroughly cleansed. Use *psyllium seed* or a *linseed* preparation such as *Linoforce* for this purpose. It is sometimes advisable to support the cleansing process by taking *wheat bran*. The diet will be more successful if the prescribed quantity of juice is sipped during the day, rather than taken in large amounts each time. Should you feel heartburn at the beginning of the diet, neutralise the acid right away by means of *wood ash*, best of all birch wood ash; take a teaspoon of ash in a glass of water.

Years ago it was the practice in the United States and in South Africa to go on grape juice diets for the treatment of cancer. I remember hearing of excellent results that were achieved to the astonishment of everyone. Unfortunately, it is today no longer advisable to go on such a diet because it has become universal to spray the grapes with pesticides. Naturally, this procedure is responsible for contaminating the grape juice with an excess of copper and chemicals. However, unsprayed grapes still produce a fine juice that can be used for grape juice diets.

The danger of poisoning is minimised in the case of vegetable juices, since the vegetables for juice diets must be organically grown anyway. *A. Vogel's mixed vegetable juice* made from beets, carrots and sauerkraut, all fermented with lactic acid, is especially recommended in the fight against 'diseases of civilisation'. The results have been outstanding even in cases of cancer and leukemia, although it is not at all easy to be successful in treating these two dreadful diseases. Constant vigilance and careful observation of the condition in each individual case are indispensable.

A. Vogel's Rheumatism Cure

Simple treatments are often more effective in curing troublesome diseases than those that require a lot of bother and are costly. So why does not everyone readily acknowledge their worth and take them? The reason is that they require certain sacrifices to be made. The treatment recommended for cases of rheumatism, arthritis and gout is only successful if followed for at least six months or, better still, for a whole year, and involves cutting out completely any food with excess acidity, replacing it with foods that are high in alkalinity. In other words, the patient must go without meat, fish, eggs and cheese.

You can see why this idea does not appeal to everyone and is often considered too difficult to follow. On the other hand, is it really a pleasure to suffer constant pain which may also become twice as bad when the weather changes and the humidity in the air increases? Of course, no one really relishes this idea. True, it may be that the transition period of changing from one set of dietary habits to another requires effort and determination, but the palate is able to become accustomed to such a change, even though it may be reluctant at the start. A little good will goes a long way and it is not, in fact, so difficult to adapt oneself to a special diet; all it means is that the taste buds must be re-educated. Moreover, dietary food, if prepared properly, can be made so tasty that you will want to continue with it after the treatment has ended. What is more, if an improvement in one's condition is noticed within a few weeks the patient will not regret having taken the plunge and changed his diet. Feeling that the aches and pains are actually beginning to recede is a most welcome relief and makes the personal sacrifice well worthwhile.

In the morning, on waking up, the first thing to do is to follow a routine of invigorating personal hygiene. As a rule, a warm shower is recommended; slowly get used to it by gradually increasing the temperature of the water. Then use *Symphosan* to rub down the whole body. The principal ingredient of this herbal preparation is comfrey and it stimulates the skin functions, helping it to become more supple and soft.

After completing this general hygiene and body care have breakfast consisting of 3–5 tablespoons of high-value muesli (*A. Vogel's Breakfast Muesli*). Mix in the juice of half a lemon. According to need, you can also choose half a grapefruit or the juice of 2–3 mandarin oranges or clementines, if available. Next, add half a tablespoon of pure honey, three tablespoons of coffee cream or half a tablespoon of almond purée. Then add two or three grated apples, depending on their size. Instead of apples you could mash and add some berries when in season. These ingredients make a juicy, refreshing muesli. In addition to this dish, have one or two slices of wholegrain (wholewheat) bread with butter or a good vegetable margarine. A cup of rose hip tea is excellent as a mild stimulant for the kidneys. If you need to activate the kidneys a little more take a *kidney tea* and add ten drops of *Nephrosolid* or *Solidago*. For a change, you may prefer to have a cup of *Bambu Coffee Substitute* with a little coffee cream.

Lunch should be prepared without any frying, for the benefit of the liver. For every meal it is enough to have a 100 per cent natural food containing starch, such as brown rice, potatoes, millet, buckwheat or corn. Soya can be considered a source of starch as well as protein. The choice of our starchy food determines what is to accompany the meal. Whichever you choose should first be steamed, then browned without fat in an earthenware pot in the oven. Most vegetables are suitable for this method, for example leeks, fennel, courgettes, aubergines, cabbage stems and kohlrabi (turnip cabbage). Tomatoes grown in your own garden and ripened on the plant should be eaten raw in salads. For a change, however, you can cut them into three and prepare them *au gratin* in the oven. Fresh green beans and peas supplement the protein foods. The beans are very tasty when prepared with the appropriate herbs.

Salads constitute food with healing properties. According to the season, use cress, tender dandelion shoots or lamb's lettuce. White cabbage makes an especially refreshing salad (coleslaw) but should be served without bacon or ham. Equally valuable is raw sauerkraut. Carrot salad is also very popular, and beetroot salad is usually preferred when made with cooked beetroot. Beetroot salad is a good substitute for raw salad. Many people like chicory salad made with the white variety. The Brussels variety can be made into an appetising dish too.

The salad dressing is also important; it should be stimulating and tasty. Soft white cheese (quark or cottage cheese) is a good base, but yogurt (natural, without any fruit), *Molkosan* or lemon juice can be used to give slight acidity, with the addition of a little cream or cold-pressed oil. Season with crushed garlic or grated horseradish and culinary herbs, but everything in moderation so that the dressing is pleasantly seasoned. Such a dressing is valuable because it whets the appetite and so aids the digestion. If you want to put on weight have an additional supplement of cottage cheese or quark every day, seasoned with herbs, garlic or horseradish. Or you may prefer curd cheese.

To drink, choose a good mineral water, a still or slightly carbonated type; add some Molkosan for the sake of the digestion. Instead of wine, try A. Vogel's mixed vegetable juice, 100–200 ml (4–8 fl. oz) with each meal.

The total food intake per meal should be moderate. In fact, when eating wholefoods it is possible to eat 40–50 per cent less and yet be better nourished than before. The evening meal should be similar to breakfast because a lighter meal is easier to digest and guarantees restful sleep.

If you want to speed up the results of the treatment go on a vegetable juice diet for one or two days a week. Take one litre (about 2 pints) of juice during the day, sipping it regularly every hour. You may take a slice of Risopan crispbread with it, since this bread has the highest mineral content.

If the treatment is followed properly it will regulate the functions of the bowels and kidneys. But if you suffer from constipation, especially the chronic kind, do not neglect to take *Psyllium* or *Linoforce* daily at the beginning. After a while you will no longer need to take it because the bowels will respond to the diet and begin to function efficiently, even more so when the food is eaten slowly, chewed well and insalivated.

These rules have been tried and tested. Now and then during the treatment have your urine tested so that you can see what is being eliminated from the body. The urine test is, in a manner of speaking, a test of the treatment's success. Improvement and cure depend upon the alkaline/acid balance being restored.

Are Nitrates Poisonous?

We could also ask whether phosphorus, fluorine and chlorine are poisons, for they are all important to the growth of plants and neither human nor animal life would be possible without them. It was not idle talk when Moleschot said, 'No thought without phosphorus.' Phosphorus is necessary for the brain and the bones. Like fluorine, chlorine and iodine, it is an element, but only when it is combined with other elements, for example potassium, calcium, sodium or magnesium, are nutritive salts formed.

Nitrates are just as necessary as the other substances; in fact, they are actually a harmless source of nitrogen. Plant life would be impossible without any one of these salts or substances, including nitrates. What does matter, however, is the quantity of these substances contained in a plant. If the level is too high, they are detrimental to health and therefore dangerous. For example, it is possible to achieve an excess of acidity in plants that normally are high in alkalinity when artificial fertilisers containing too many phosphates are spread. All minerals existing in nature and necessary to life are detrimental, even poisonous, if they are so highly concentrated and used in order to produce greater yields in an unnatural way (massive fertilising). This cannot possibly happen when the land is worked organically; there will be no overdose of phosphates, fluorides or nitrates. Organically grown vegetables indicate a more balanced content of nutritive salts than those grown with artificial fertilisers. The nutritive salt content varies from plant to plant; for example there are, more nitrates in beets than in carrots or other tubers.

For people who eat too much protein, large quantities of nitrates can be harmful because the nitrates are changed into nitrides in the body, forming dangerous nitrosamines (carcinogenic substances). But even these compounds are rendered harmless when sufficient amounts of vitamin C are taken. Even though beetroot absorbs a relatively high amount of nitrates in a natural way, beetroot juice is one of the best plant remedies for providing cancer cells (which are known to lack oxygen) with plenty of oxygen, thus opening up the way to regeneration and a cure. At the same time, it is essential to adopt a low-protein diet, forcing the body to derive its amino acids (component molecules of protein) from pathological cell tissues such as growths, myomas, even malignant tumours. The vitamin D and betacyan, the nitrogen-containing colouring of beetroot, actively help to regenerate the deteriorated cancer cells. Nitrates are therefore not harmful even in cancer therapy, as long as they are used as outlined above. In this regard we agree with Paracelsus who said that 'Everything is poison; it all depends on how much you take.' It also depends on the circumstances connected with ingesting it.

The 'Nature Doctor' Takes His Leave
Much advice has been given in this book and I hope that it will help many of you. There is so much we can do for ourselves by natural means. With the proper intelligent attitude perhaps we can live with the things that cannot be remedied by leading as healthy a life as possible, by permitting our spirit to rise above our physical suffering.

More could certainly be said about our mental attitude towards life and health but this would take us into another book. The important thing to remember is that we should live our lives according to nature's rules. The more we feel and think in a healthy way, the less will those damaging influences, which are so difficult to disperse, make their way into our bodies.

If we admit the value of the good, which is always at hand for ourselves and those around us, we will achieve something for our health and spiritual balance in these insecure and restless times. How we react to life depends upon our innermost selves. The hurrying stream of time tries to blot out the healthy habits established in the past and thus lead us along strange paths that make it so easy to go astray. But once you have peered into the rich treasure chest of *The Nature Doctor* you will never be deceived again. You will know that there is an answer in nature.

So, open this book when you need advice on matters of health. It will save you many disappointments and you will avoid useless and perhaps harmful treatments. In any event, the advice given here can never do any harm, unless you go your own way contrary to the suggestions. I would encourage you, however, to follow the advice carefully and you will find the balanced middle way, neither being fanatically extremist nor indifferent.

On the other hand, let me say that there is one little 'herb' I do not know either, the one referred to in an old proverb:

There's many a herb to cure,
Not one, however, for death, to be sure.

I am fully aware that my medical advice is but a help for dealing with the times in which we live.

A Special Note
The quantities or doses of natural remedies indicated in this book are based upon the author's experience acquired in many years of practice. The adequate quantities prescribed can vary according to the sensitivity of the patient. More robust persons may take larger amounts to achieve the desired result, whereas children and more sensitive patients may achieve the full effect with half the quantity or even less. Since botanic remedies and homoeopathic medicines are given in order to rectify and cure the cause of an illness, not merely the symptoms, it is more important to take the remedies regularly and for some time than to watch the exact quantity.

Index

Index

The Index will help you locate the subjects of interest at a glance. The page numbers in bold print refer to more explicit information on the listed subjects. This makes the answers to your questions about certain diseases and health problems much easier.

INDEX

INDEX

INDEX

INDEX

INDEX

Ignatia, 163
Immunity, building up resistance, 86, 88, 93
Immunity laws, 86–88
Imperarthritica, 263, 270
Imperatoria ostruthium, see Imperial masterwort
Imperial masterwort (Imperatoria ostruthium), 77, 78, 263, 394
Impetigo, 324
Indurations, 275
Infant care, 35–39
Infantile eczema, 44–46
Infant nutrition, 39, 41, 101–102
Infectious diseases, 30, 47, 51, 54–57, 85, 88, 89, 92, 100, 175, 216, 236, 258, 324, 365, 390, 392, 464, 488, 502, 504
Infertility, 521
Inflammations, 261, 408
Influaforce, 56, 57
Influenza, 54–57, 74, 75, 365
Injections, homoeopathic, 367
Injuries, 27
Insect bites, stings, 14–15, 407
Insect pests, 90
Insomnia, 187–189, 611
Insulin, 61, 254, 267
Intestines, bowels, 24–25, 85, 89, 213–215, 217, 228, 240, 399, 408, 422, 465, 481, 547, 581, 641
  care of, 12, 119, 642
  cleansing, 252, 441, 641–643
Intestinal bacteria (flora), 89, 91, 219, 225–226, 254, 472, 479, 505, 541, 542, 551, 642
Intestinal catarrh (enteritis), 368, 542
  disorders, 8, 62, 399, 406, 547
  gases, fermentation, 408, 541, 551
  mucous membranes (inflammation), 10, 372, 441, 505, 541, 642
  parasites, 12, 226–233, 372, 399, 410, 446, 489, 495, 501
  poisoning, 212–215
  putrefaction, 541
  ulcer (duodenal), 497
  worms, 12
Iodine, iodised salt, 42, 130, 155, **158–162**, 203, 412, 468, 554–557
  deficiency, 157, **161**
Ipecac, Ipecacuanha (Cephaelis ipecacuanha) poison, 29, 51, 214

Iron, 397, 487, 496
Islets of Langerhans, 254, 368, 551
Itching of the skin, 12, 241
Ivy (Heder helix), ivy tincture, **14**

Jam-making, 506
Jaundice (hepatitis), 11, 106, 228, **252–253**, 483
Joint(s)
  diseases of, see Arthritis
  inflammation of (arthritis), 397
  painful, 357, 367, 394
Juice(s), **495–499**
  day, 8, 226, 641
  diets, 471, 641
  fasting, 119, 183, 226, 645, **649**
Juniper (Juniperus communis)
  berries (Fructus juniperi), 11, **384**
  needles, leaves, 20, 25, 56, 81, 263, 328 432, 441
Juniperosan, 81, 328, 329, 331
Juniperus communis, see Juniper

Kale, see savoy cabbage
Kali chloricum (potassium chlorate), 399
Kali iodatum (potassium iodide), 72, 79, 98, 394
Kali phosphoricum (potassium phosphate), 49, 131, 185, 487
Kamala powder (Glandulae Rottlerae), 232
Kelp (seaweed), 9, 124, 130, 145, 155, 157, 161, 192, 205, 394, **424**, 449, 459, 557
Kelpamare/Swiss Alpamare, 116, 549, **557**
Kelpasan, 116, 118, 130, 161, 205, 270, 325, 374, **424**, 451, 522
Kidneys, 12, 20, 24, 38, 51, 54, 55, 81, 85, 113, 124, **164–169**, 179, 363, 385, 393, 405, 410, 420, 442, 472, 479, 509
  care of, 12
  elimination of toxins, 54, 56, 420, 645
  inflammation (nephritis), 385
  stones, 104, 488, 509
  (stone) colic, 167–168
  tea, 55, 78, 81, 172, 178, 252
Kneipp, treatments advocated by, 3, 47, 85, 152, 190
Kohlrabi (turnip cabbage), 84, 157, 178
Kuhne, treatment according to, 16, 33, 98, 163, 190, **436–438**, 522

667

Sunflower seeds, 533
  oil, 251, 528, 533
Suppuration, 15, 401, 487
Suprarenal gland, 60
  adrenal cortex, 267
Sweat, 314, 316, 390, 394, 396, 555
  glands, 53, 55, 78, 85, 119, 420
Sweet clover (Melilotus off.), 27, 135
Swellings, lumps, 7, 13, 350, 434, 439, 441, 443, 448
  on fingers, see Whitlows
Sympathetic nervous system, 140, 142, 186
Symphosan, 216, 263, 270, 319, 320, 323, 357–359, 432, 455, 651
Symphytum off., see Comfrey
Syphilis, 59
Syringing ear, 73

Tabacum, 151
Tapeworms, 230
Tapeworm tea, 232
Tarentula cubensis, 396
Taraxacum off., see Dandelion
Taste, sense of, 63
TB, see Tuberculosis
Teeth, 29, 39, 100, 104, 306–309, 398, 512
  bad teeth (decay), 398, 512, 514, 518
  care of the, 303–308
Television, 596–598
Temperature below normal (hypothermia), 19
Tenseness, 275, 288, 392–393, see Silica
Testicles, 201
  inflammation of the (orchitis), 174–175
Teucrium marum (cat thyme), 72
Threadworm, pinworm (Oxyuris vermicularis), 227, 234, 447, 448
Throat
  inflammation of the, 76–78, 88
  sore, 15, 72, 375, 395, 448, 468
Thrombosis, 26, 119, 134, 216
Thydroca, 49, 51, 393
Thyme, wild, Mother of thyme (Thymus vulgaris), 4, 56, 81, 94, 127, 163, 319, 329, 405, 431, 441
Thymus gland, 61
Thymus serpyllum, see Thyme
Thyroid, 60, 142, 201, 412, 415, 428, 452, 468, 503, 504, 555
Tincture (how made), 342

Tiredness, getting tired, 53, 459, 592, 601–605
Tobacco, see Smoking
Tobacco tar, 586
Tomatoes, 264, 478
Tomato juice, 496
Tongue, 49, 56, 63–65
Tonics, 451, 456, 520
Tonsillitis, 74, 76–78, 85, 165, 365, 394, 395, 450
Tonsils, 76, 108
Tooth
  decay, cavities, 398, 512, 514, 518
Toothache (headache), 410, 411
Tormentavena, 51, 95, 141, 162, 169, 218
Tormentil (Tormentilla erecta), 5, 7, 38, 95, 141, 162, 218, 363, 400, 508
Tormentilla erecta, see Tormentil
Toxins, 22, 53, 107, 262, 265, 306, 557–562
Trace elements, 459, 463, 464, 496
Treatments, courses of cures, diets, 417–444
Trocomare, 91, 116, 158, 413, 416, 479, 492, 549, 557, 647
Tropical diseases, 88, 232–239
Tropics, visits to the, dangers in the, 232–239
Tuberculosis, 19, 49, 86, 89, 92, 104, 110, 171, 175, 293, 370, 550
Tumours, 276, 278, 442, 435, 450, 587
Turpentine, 12
Typhoid fever, 235, 293, 395, 502, 569

Ulcers
  chronic, 395, 462, 523
Uraemia, 164
Uric acid, 10, 113, 445, 475
  (combatting)
Urinary bladder, 170
Urine (urinalysis), 24, 104, 166, 170, 171, 213, 405, 412
  retention of, 10, 430
Urticalcin, 2, 15, 29, 39, 41, 45, 53, 54, 69, 72, 78, 80, 81, 83, 84, 95, 99, 101, 105, 110, 120, 122, 135, 138, 139, 144, 155, 157, 172, 175, 192, 198, 261, 302, 326, 337, 370, 538, 648
Urtica urens/dioica, see Nettles
Usnea barbata, see Larch moss
Usneasan, 91, 95, 137, 171, 172, 261, 270

Vaccinium myrtillus, see Bilberries

INDEX

INDEX

Dr. Alfred Vogel—
"The Nature Doctor" in Person

For most of this century Dr. Alfred Vogel has been learning the secrets of natural healing and the curative powers of herbs, and for almost as long has shared that knowledge with patients at the clinic he ran for many years and with countless readers of his many books. Born in 1902 near Basel, Switzerland, he eagerly absorbed herbal lore from his grandparents and parents, eventually becoming familiar with the whole body of European empirical folk medicine. In later years he traveled to the remotest parts of the world, and absorbed the curative lore of tribal peoples in Africa, Asia, Australia and the Americas. His stay with the Sioux Indians in South Dakota was among the most informative and inspiring of his many tribal encounters, and gave him some literally lifesaving information as well as deepening his sense of union with nature.

At his clinic in Teufen, treatment was based on naturopathic principles, using medicinal plants gathered at the foot of the Alps, and his great interest in all methods of natural healing led him to the study and use of homeopathic treatments as well. In his worldwide lectures and the newsletter he has published for more than sixty years, Dr. Vogel has brought his experience and wisdom to many thousands, but it is his books, beginning as far back as 1925, that have carried that wisdom, and a legion of practical instructions for the full range of health problems, to countless readers in many countries. His most famous work is *Der kleine Doktor,* published in English as *The Nature Doctor,* and translated into eleven languages. It has now been completely revised and substantially enlarged for this edition.

Dr. Vogel's decades of research and discovery have brought him professional recognition in many countries as well as the gratitude of those he has helped: he was granted an honorary doctorate in medical botany by the University of California at Los Angeles in 1952, and in 1982 was awarded the coveted Priessnitz Medal at the annual Congress of German Nature Cure Practitioners.

Though nearly ninety, Dr. Vogel still puts in a five-hour work day and attends many professional meetings and conferences, often discovering that the latest research "discovers" what he has been practicing for seven decades—and what folk medicine has known for centuries. "Only nature can heal and cure," Dr. Vogel is fond of observing, adding the corollary that "we can help and support nature and its laws that make a cure possible." This has been the basis of his lifelong work.

In 1963, Dr. Vogel founded Bioforce, now one of the major manufacturers of herbal extracts, homeopathic medicines, specialty health foods and biological body care products. The enterprise was started in the small farming community of Roggwil, but now has extensive production facilities in Switzerland and distributors and offices in many parts of the world.

tion. At one point, he even pauses to watch the ranchers listening to a record—in a silent movie! Impressively deft are the seemingly crude reaction shots—Vester Pegg quivering in fright before the duel's final moment, or Molly Malone* gazing out her door after Harry, or the kinetic representation of terror as a static crowd suddenly flees the frame in all directions at the news of the coming duel. Filming through doorways was a standard practice in 1917, given the construction of sets, and so was the blocking of characters in triangles, but Ford (who was still doing both half a century later) makes it emotionally meaningful, as he does everything else—in this case, another instance of "passage." The famous scene of Molly fingering her dead brother's dish was probably inspired by Mae Marsh and her baby's shoe in *Intolerance* (October 1916), but Ford intercuts Molly at her pantry with Harry on the riverbank, where leaves, breeze, and flickering light mirror moods Antonioni-ishly. The exciting finale, as Molly gathers horsemen to ride to the rescue, derives directly from the gathering of the klans in *The Birth of a Nation*. Yet via Francis Ford, *Straight Shooting* owes more to the "Ince tradition" of simple lyricism than to Griffith's exalted epic. In place of Griffith's dramatic shaping, all events in *Straight Shooting* have equal value, and thus ignite a more active symbolism into land, light, water, and foliage, a plate, a donkey by a stream, a horse's tail, a glass of whiskey, a bartender's bald head.

According to contemporary accounts, the picture originally ended with tainted Harry sending Molly back to still-pure Sam, refusing her hand and a respectable life in favor of something "just over yonder" that keeps calling to him, and he is "left facing the setting sun alone."[43] The present "happy" ending—in which Harry accepts Molly—appears to have been clumsily edited into the reissue of 1925, an era less tolerant of tragedy than the heroic teens. And the earlier ending is truer to Carey—who often walked away in last scenes, an outsider—and to the Fordian hero (e.g., *The Searchers*—wherein John Wayne imitates Carey's signal arm gesture).

★

"Harry Carey tutored me in the early days,"[44] said Ford; "I was scared to death, but . . . Harry helped me immeasurably."[45] Carey's was a rare sort of screen personality, uncommonly charismatic, and this spirit, relaxed and communal, vivifies not only the *acting* style in Ford's work, it also epitomizes that unattainable ideal society that Ford would so often and

*Molly Malone, leading lady of Ford's first "stock company," was nineteen and had played western heroines for two years before being cast in *The Soul Herder*. She loved outdoors and hated cities and teamed with Carey and Ford in nine films in as many months, then in a tenth three years later. Sweet Molly Malone had a song named after her, but her career petered out in the twenties, and she died in 1952.

so wistfully invoke. Ford, in fact, lived much of the time on a ranch Carey purchased in 1917, just after Carey married actress Olive Fuller Golden.*

The "ranch," down a road going to "Happy Valley," near Newhall, California, covered barely three acres. The house had three tiny rooms and no electricity; the bathhouse stood fifty feet away; the "convenience" was the bush. There were a cow, some chickens, a couple of pigs, and the guys who made the films: Jim Corey, Pardner Jones, Hoot Gibson occasionally, Teddy Brooks. They slept outside in bedrolls. Jack had a spot in the alfalfa patch; always a hard riser, he had to be awakened by Harry's dogs. Olive, the only woman, did all the cooking. It was "a very good time," she recalls. Gilhooley McConigal, a propman with Ford for decades, had a car they called an EMF, Every-Morning-Fixit, because it would never start. Harry's $150 wage went mostly to alimony payments for two ex-wives, and they were all broke. Jack moaned he always had to pay for the butter. He was "adorable," Olive says. "He had a beautiful walk, not too argumentative, a good listener."[46] Her main function was to keep them all sober.

Always basically the same, Ford was cocky, full of questions, but secretive himself, fearless, at times aggravatingly persistent. His wit, caustic, even mean, was made bearable by a terrific sense of humor. He was always wrapped up in his work, never wanting to relax, drink, and raise hell, always going full steam.[47] He virtually never had a girl—Olive remembers only a single brief affair with a certain Janet, "the first girl he ever slept with."[48] "He was movies, that was it, that was all his life until he met Mary."[49]

Probably from Carey, if not already from Francis, Ford saw the importance of characters *relating* on the screen—and this is arguably Ford's key quality. But Carey in turn gave credit for his ability to relate to Griffith: "He taught us to listen, so it would show on the screen, and he taught us to read the dialogue—despite the fact that our films were silent. I am still reading my dialogue the same way."[50] It was a lesson Ford would one day pass on to John Wayne. "Duke," Ford told him, "take a look over at Harry Carey and watch him work. Stand like he does, if you can, and play your roles so that people can look upon you as a friend." ("That's what I've always done," Wayne later said.)[51] Also from Carey, Wayne got his broken speech patterns: e.g., "Take your . . . [*pause*] . . . stuff and run down to the . . . [*pause*] . . . creek." At the end of *The Searchers* (1956), Wayne strikes a signal Carey pose in homage (placing his hand on his elbow) and, as Carey so often did, walks away (in fact, walks away from Ollie Carey's house). To understand this, one might recall

---

*At Universal since 1913, Olive met Harry in 1915 during *A Knight of the Range*. She, but not he, remembered an earlier meeting. In Griffith's 1913 *Sorrowful Shore*, Harry had swum out to rescue her, terrifying with big bushy eyebrows and liquor on his breath. He had not said a word to her, just put her down on the beach and walked off. Their marriage in Kingman, Arizona, in 1917, turned out to be illegal—one ex-wife was suing for divorce as late as 1919—so they were married in California again in 1921.

that the role that made Wayne a star—a role Ford had saved for him for years and fought to allow him to play—was, in *Stagecoach*, that of a good badman.*

The actors most at home in Ford's movie-worlds are, in fact, all similar to Carey: Will Rogers, J. Farrell MacDonald, Francis Ford, Ben Johnson, to name a few. Carey's son Dobe thinks Harry gave Ford the model for this basic type. Ford saw the charismatic, relaxed hero in Carey, then made him improve on that, making him "more of a Harry Carey than he really was."[52] This technique of locating an actor's eccentric traits and amplifying them into a screen personage was one Ford followed all his life.

In May 1918, Carey's salary jumped from $150 a week to $1,250, then to $2,250 in 1919. (Jack's salary went from $75 to $150 to $300, which so annoyed him that he would later claim it had dropped from $50 to $35.) During a publicity tour, Carey stated, "I wish to Jack Londonize the Western cowboy—that is, present him as he really is in life . . . a sturdy, manly fellow, totally unlike the one we see in comedies. He has his distinctive characteristics and they are amusing enough without exaggeration."[53]

But the realistic cowboy was not what audiences wanted; tastes were

*Ford also used Carey's black, triple-creased hat on future characters, notably for Henry Fonda in *My Darling Clementine*.

Desperate Trails (1921). Harry Carey, George Stone, Irene Rich. From the Robert S. Birchard Collection.

The Outcasts of Poker Flat (1919). Cullen Landis, Gloria Hope. A lost film.

switching to the flashy, dandified, fantasy types. Carey mellowed, too, into a boy-scout figure. But in the heroic teens, although sometimes the sacrificial good thief *The Soul Herder* suggests, he more often had the raw-edged meanness of Wayne in *The Searchers*, but without the namby-pamby censorship of the 1950s. Harry wreaked trails of vengeance through bars and whorehouses. *Exhibitors' Trade Review*, in November 1918, groaned that the filth and rats in prison were entirely *too* realistic: "The only wonder of it is that anyone should attempt to heroize such a type [as Carey's rough character]. There may be such men in the west, but it is best on the screen to show them up as horrible examples of what a man may be."

Carey worked for a number of studios after leaving Universal, but his career declined steadily. In 1928 a flood wiped out his ranch. Broke, he and Ollie hit the vaudeville circuit. His career resurged in 1931 when Irving Thalberg cast him in *Trader Horn*; but when Edwina Booth sued Metro for a disease she claimed she got while filming in Africa, and Carey refused Metro's request to testify against her, the studios reportedly blacklisted him, and Carey returned to B westerns on poverty row.

Building Status

In 1920, at a Hollywood Hotel St. Patrick's Day dance, Rex Ingram introduced Jack to Mary McBride Smith. She was twenty-seven, a trained nurse from New Jersey and a former Army Medical Corps lieutenant. Her father was a New York Stock Exchange member; uncle Rupert Blue was U.S. Surgeon General, uncle Victor Blue an admiral and Chief of Naval Operations. She was Scotch-Irish Presbyterian. Jack's shanty-Catholic parents had a harder time accepting Mary than her upper-crust family did accepting him. Her Carolina ancestors stretched back to Thomas More, Washington, and Lee; Sherman had burned the family plantation—an incident Ford wrote into *Rio Grande*. "He went down with me to visit my folks," said Mary, "and to my horror told my family what a nice kindly old gentleman Sherman was, and I had to sit there and take it!"[54] Jack was a practicing Catholic and a member of the Knights of Columbus, but as Mary was divorced—she had wed a soldier leaving for the war—marriage in the Church was not possible. Accordingly, they were married July 3 at the Los Angeles courthouse. Irving Thalberg and William K. Howard were ushers; Allan Dwan gave them a keg of whiskey. They all went to Tijuana for the Fourth, in Jack's blue Stutz Speedster. (In 1941, after Mary's first husband's death, they were married before a priest, in Washington, D.C., and they

John and Mary Ford, with Patrick and Barbara, ca. 1926.

pronounced their vows again on their fiftieth anniversary.) Their first home was a rented two-bedroom stucco at 2243 Beechwood Drive. In October, for $14,000, they bought a house at 6860 Odin Street, on a hill overlooking the site of the future Hollywood Bowl, where they stayed thirty-four years. Patrick was born nine months to the day after their wedding, and Barbara on December 16, 1922. Maude Stevenson ("Steve" or "Steves") began a long tenure as governess. "He said he only married me because I didn't want to get in pictures," said Mary. "I never went on the [movie] stage the whole years I was married. Never went near. That was one of the agreements we had. He said, 'If I were a lawyer, you wouldn't sit in my office. If I were a judge, you wouldn't hear my cases.' He said, 'That's where all the trouble starts.' He'd bring scripts home, but he'd never ask me to read them. It was very funny, his work was a closed organization as far as the family was concerned." She reconciled herself. "I'd had my feelings hurt when I was first married, so I said, 'That's that!' "[55]

By 1921 Ford had been at Universal four and a half years and had made thirty-nine pictures, twenty-eight of them features. The qualities critics singled out are notable in his later work as well: "Mingling of pathos and humor . . . wealth of human touches . . . clever details . . . experimental photography . . . optic symphony . . . thrills, excitement, action, realism." But life at Universal seemed to be going downhill. Harry Carey had been dropped; the Stern brothers, in control, were always shouting at everyone; Ford's salary was still low. So in 1921 Ford signed a long-term contract with William Fox at $600 a week. Fox, like Universal, was a minor company catering to blue-collar and rural audiences. Perhaps typical (but delightful) is **Just Pals** (1920), the first of fifty Foxes Ford would make, and a simple story in which a village bum (Buck Jones) and a boy hobo thwart a robbery. The small-town detail, folksy characterizations, and elfin charm resemble less such actual Griffith as *True Heart Susie* than they do King Vidor's Griffithian *Jack Knife Man* and *Love Never Dies;* Fordian swift pacing and plentiful action replace Griffith's formally wrought presentations and lordly distance. Parallel editing in climaxes, developed by Griffith, had become endemic by 1920 (even in a modest C-budget western like Francis Ford's *The Stampede,* 1921); nonetheless Ford's finale excitingly fuses five plot lines, typically counterpointing chases, fights, and robberies with the humor of a sheriff displaying his badge to avoid a church collection. Typically Fordian too are the lynch mobs, hypocritical social strata, pompous churchgoers, busybodies, and the unobtrusive blacks (unnecessary in a story set in Wyoming, yet ignored by whites and drama). Humor is already gruff and sentimental, fighting a necessary part of friendship.

But unlike Universal, Fox's management, in the persons of Fox and Winfield Sheehan, was dynamic, and the company would shortly become a titan in the industry. As a bonus, Ford was given a trip to Europe. Mary, probably because of seven-month-old Pat, did not go along. But she did see

Unidentified person, Douglas Fairbanks, Mary Pickford, John Ford, ca. 1928.

him off from New York, and he wrote her as the boat sailed, November 19, 1921:

On Board S.S. *Balls-tic*

Dear old fruit: I am going to keep a sort of diarhea for you about happenings on board (with the provision of course that I am able). We are just leaving. I hope you are not on the wharf yet with that throng of handkerchief waving maniacs. . . .

5:30 P.M.

Darling: I am sorry to say I am slightly drunk. Yes sir!! Bummed! I also have hiccoughs. Mary, how I wish you were with me! Gosh. We would have had such a delightful trip. It's really wonderful on this boat. I have spent the entire afternoon in the "BAR" drinking Bass's Ale and feel quite wonderful. (Except for the hiccoughs.) . . .

Sunday

. . . Just as the priest lifted the host, the clouds and fog lifted & three miles away we could see the shores of our beloved fatherland, "The Emerald Isle" as green and fresh as dew on the down. Even the priest stopped, gazed and then with a gulp of joy in his throat went on with the Mass. Of course all the tads has tears running down their cheeks and when the prayer of thanksgiving came, it sounded like a hymn of heaven, so joyous these old folk were. . . .[56]

Jack hurried to Ireland from Liverpool; it had been his chief reason for making the trip. The Sinn Fein nationalists were engaged in a bloody revolution against England. Jack's father had of course contributed generously and Jack himself wanted to get involved. He wrote Mary about it in January, after his return to New York:

At Galway I got a jaunting car and rode to Spiddle and had a deuce of a time finding Dad's folks. There are so many Feeneys out there that to find our part of the family was a problem. At last I found them. Spiddle is all shot to pieces. Most of the houses have been burned down by the Black and Tans and all of the young men had been hiding in the hills. As it was during the truce that I was there I was unmolested BUT as Cousin Martin Feeney (Dad's nephew) had been hiding in the Connemara Mountains with the Thornton boys, I naturally was followed about and watched by the B & T fraternity. Tell Dad that the Thornton house is entirely burned down & old Mrs. Thornton was living with Uncle Ned's widow while her sons were away.

I went to London (which I didn't like), Paris, Marseilles, Nice, Monaco (Monte Carlo) & Italy. I had quite a wonderful trip but as I say, I missed "my family.". . . As I will be here a couple or three weeks more [shooting a picture], I will try and hick up and stand it, but it is sure tough. I hate this place. No New York for me. . . .[57]

Cousin Martin in fact had a price on his head. Years later he told Dan Ford how Jack had sought him in the hills and given him food and money, and how the British had "roughed up [Jack] pretty well" before putting him on a boat to England with the warning of imprisonment if he ever came back to Ireland.[58]

Jack Ford returned home with a much strengthened sense of identity and commitment; he channeled funds to the IRA the rest of his life. He also returned to a rather chagrined wife and a pile of debts. He was soon making good money. His salary in 1921 had amounted to $13,618, but in 1922 it came to $27,891, and in 1923 to $44,910. Moreover, at Universal he had been allowed to make only two non-westerns, whereas in his first two years at Fox, his subjects included the London theater, New York's Jewish ghetto, rural New England, Maine fishing towns, and Mississippi riverboats. And along with new prestige and bigtime money came a new name: with *Cameo Kirby* (1923), Jack Ford died as a screen name and John Ford was born.

Three Jumps Ahead (1923). Tom Mix. A lost film.

Hearts of Oak (1924). Theodore von Eltz, Hobart Bosworth, Pauline Starke. A lost film.

Ford soon found grist for his ambition. Isolated in the Sierra Nevada while filming *The Iron Horse* (1924), the story of the transcontinental railway, he commanded, it is said, 5,000 extras; construction of two whole towns; 100 cooks to feed the crew; 2,000 rail layers; a cavalry regiment; 800 Indians; 1,300 buffalo; 2,000 horses; 10,000 cattle; 50,000 properties; the original "Jupiter" and "116" locomotives that had met at Promontory Point May 10, 1869; Wild Bill Hickcock's derringer; and . . . the original stagecoach used by Horace Greeley![59] A planned four-week schedule stretched into ten as blizzard followed blizzard, shooting became impossible, and magical community grew in the troupe. "All sorts of things happened," Ford recalled, "births, deaths, marriages, and all in the icy cold. There was only one single day of sun."[60] "We nearly froze to death. We lived in a circus tent, had to dig our own latrines, build up a whole town around us. Saloons opened up; the saloon-girls moved in."[61]

"The Ford outfit was the roughest goddamdest outfit you ever saw, from the director on downward," said assistant Lefty Hough. "Ford and his brother, Eddie O'Fearna, were fighting all the time. This goes back to the days in Maine when Eddie and the others ran a saloon and they used to kick Ford out of there and wouldn't let him drink. Ford never got over this. I had to break up the fights. When we were doing some of the stuff on the tracks, they got in an argument and O'Fearna went after the old man with a pickhandle."[62]

There had never been a scenario—only a short synopsis—and Ford kept making it all up as the weeks went on. Back in Los Angeles the studio, frantic for footage, pleaded, cajoled, threatened, blasphemed, then ordered retreat. Ford tore up the wires, or held them in the air and had Pardner Jones shoot a bullet through the sender's name. Production boss Sol Wurtzel, come up to inspect, fell prey to a three-day crap game. Finally William Fox, who, on the strength of Paramount's successful *Covered Wagon* (1923) and faith in Ford, was backing the project, looked at what had been shot and said, "Let them finish it."

John Ford's career was on the line. He avoided premieres like poison—his nerves could not control his stomach—and feigned casual aloofness toward his work. Thus he played bored while those who had attended the Los Angeles opening aired their verdicts. But when Francis Ford meekly offered some suggestions, Jack jumped wildly to his feet: "Who the *hell* asked *you!*" he shouted, and stormed off, slamming doors behind him. He avoided strong language at home, but Frank awakened pathological sensitivity. (Hence it was partly to humiliate Frank that Ford cast him always as a loony or drunk, never as a Lincoln. "I want to see him *lashed*," Jack would chortle—and did, in *The Black Watch*.[63]

If *The Iron Horse* dawdles today, it is partly because we are deprived of its marvelous score; Ford rhymed rail layers' movements to songs his Uncle Mike had taught him, accelerating the tempo as the rail layers raced. And it is partly because the edition generally available is the European cut, rather than Ford's far more dynamic version.* *The Iron Horse* uses its thousands sparingly; Ford never allows them to detract from his simple human story.** To add comedy, he added three soldiers (Francis Powers, J. Farrell MacDonald, James Welch) who stole the show in the twenties. Only during boy Davy's black-lit expressionistic poses over his father's dead body does *The Iron Horse*'s B-western feel turn artful. It is an epic chiefly by suggestion. As the father heads west from Springfield, a bystander remarks, "Poor dreamer! He's chasing a rainbow." "Yes," replies a Mr. Lincoln, "and someday men like [him] will be laying tracks along that rainbow."

The Iron Horse was among the decade's top grossers; against costs of $280,000, it returned over $2 million. It made Ford internationally famous and put a Fox film on Broadway for the first time. As Bill Fox escorted John and Abby Feeney to that Broadway premiere, he told them that if he had had a son, he hoped he would have been like Jack.[64] (Fox's precepts were also Ford's at this time: action, folksiness, uplifting sentiments, spiced with humor.)

But two years later an attempt to repeat *The Iron Horse*'s success flopped. Although *3 Bad Men* (1926) is a far better picture by any standard and, in fact, was better liked by contemporaries who saw it, box-office tastes had veered sharply away from westerns. *3 Bad Men* had to be severely cut after previewing, and Ford, having made forty-three westerns in nine years, was not to make another for thirteen years—until *Stagecoach*.

3 Bad Men mythicizes its genre. Villain Layne Hunter (Lou Tellegen), with fancy dress and a Liberty-Valance-like whip to spur his depraved minions, pertains to western fantasy. As does the wrath of Bull Stanley (Tom Santschi), punching down doors, heaving varmints from balconies, or, flanked by torchmen, descending a staircase, his dead sister outstretched in his arms. Iconically, the parson begs mercy by a flaming cross with black smoke swirling. And the three bad men make their entrance mythically silhouetted against the horizon, preceded by their reward posters (like Harry Carey in *Straight Shooting*, or the Cleggs in *Wagon Master*). Below them, a wagon train stretches across a prairie[†]—an early instance of Ford envisioning life as a parade. And at the end, their ghosts, pledged even in death to watch over Lee (Olive Borden), join hands and ride into the sunset, their memory perpetu-

---

*Two negatives were customarily shot simultaneously, one for domestic prints, one for foreign. Ford's version (the domestic), according to John Stone, has many more tracks and pans during hunts and battles, closer shots of horse-falls, more emphatic cutting. Track-laying is more rhythmic, building in one long single sequence (rather than split into two) to climax in the meeting of the tracks. Most titles differ, are more rhymed to the beat, and sometimes change motivation. Into both versions mismatched close-ups of Madge Bellamy were interpolated against Ford's will. The Lincoln scene was Fox's suggestion.

**Headin' west, Davy sees his father killed by (fake) Indians. He grows up (into George O'Brien) to scout for the railway constructors, and reencounters his childhood sweetheart engaged to his father's murderer.

†Dakota land rush, 1876: three outlaws befriend orphaned Lee, encourage romance with Dan (George O'Brien), and give their lives to thwart Hunter stealing her gold map (but then the plot—or cuts?—forgets the map). Tellegen partnered Bernhardt in the famous 1912 *Queen Elizabeth*

The Fighting Heart (1925). Billie Dove. A lost film.

ated (like Colonel Thursday's in *Fort Apache*) by Lee's baby's triple name. Epic themes enunciated in a prologue—immigrants on sailing ships, Dakota gold rush, ploughing oxen—are forgotten, midst informalities, plot, and comic interludes, until after the land rush. Then a broken wagon's slogan is updated ("BUSTED—BY GOD") and the wife declares, "This soil is richer than Gold." Throughout, the quaint chivalry of the good badmen punctuates Fordian themes of friendship and life's preciousness. Similar hero trios recur often in Ford (cf. *3 Godfathers*), always associated with the myth of the three kings and redemption through self-sacrifice.

Spectacle, by 1926, was no more novel than today. But who will ever forget that pan of hundreds and hundreds of Conestoga wagons waiting along a line miles long? Said Ford:

> Several of the people in the company had been in the actual rush. The incident of snatching the baby from under the wheels of a wagon actually happened. And the newspaperman who rode along with his press—printing the news all through the event —that really happened. We did a hell of a land rush—hundreds of wagons going at full tilt; it was really fast.[65]

and married Geraldine Farrar. Santschi appeared in *In the Sultan's Power*, the first story film shot entirely in California. Existent prints of *3 Bad Men* preserve none of the photographic quality whose vistas of Jackson Hole and the Mojave thrilled contemporaries.

Like *Straight Shooting* and *The Iron Horse, 3 Bad Men* chronicles a micro-society, motley and fluid in class, and essentially in passage. Against the *chaos* of this milieu is counterpointed the *order* of individuals' initial typing (by race, nationality, class). Counterpointed also are quotidian and mythic dimensions of events. The Fordian hero, a sacrifical celibate, intervenes to preserve social harmony.

Such weighty and germinal narrative structures may, however, seem in the long run not so impressive as the inventiveness of ***The Shamrock Handicap*** (1926),* Ford's twenties *Quiet Man*, an Irish comedy. Here is much of his fifties compositional style, painterly, spacious and balanced, deep in field. Here a large cast and wealth of inventive incident create breezy pacing (where earlier Foxes meander). Stratifications of class (Irish, black, Wasp, Jew, doctor, etc.) function not solely as themes but as motifs to be juggled playfully. Typically for Ford, downbeat material receives comic treatment, and humor has a wacky quality uniquely his: a doctor tells laid-up Neil he's done what he could, then walks out with a golf bag on his shoulder; jockeys bring flowers "got cheap at the undertakers"; Finch shrugs off adversity by biting a banana. Contemporaries cheered the Kildare marketplace, which comes alive midst ruins, dusty roads, barefoot boys in maxi-skirts and jackets, children carrying geese and sheep, donkey carts, jigging couples, and a "corker" of a steeplechase.

Less successful was (and is) ***Kentucky Pride*** (1925):** narrated by a horse, the plot plods dully, but abruptly explodes into the sort of finale that became a Ford trademark in *The Quiet Man*. In seven brief vignettes:

1. Beaumont gazes greedily at his winning tickets.
2. Confederacy and Virginia's Future are reunited.
3. Donovan stands boasting with both in winner's circle.
4. Greve Carter says, "It's hard to tell you, but I've lost everything" — betting against Confederacy — and the ex-Mrs. Beaumont leaves him, word for word repeating the earlier scene when she left Beaumont.
5. Cameramen have comic difficulties taking pictures.
6. Little Mike, Jr. (the jockey) and Virginia are revealed kissing when fat Mrs. Donovan moves from in front of them.
7. Virginia's Future, who began the film admonishing, "Pride of race is everything," now concludes: "When I saw my baby flying ahead, all the aching disappointment, the bitterness of my own life [in failing to run true],

---

*Ireland: The O'Haras sell their horses for taxes, and Sheila (Janet Gaynor) bids adieu to Neil (Leslie Fenton), whom Finch takes to America to jockey. But the O'Haras mortgage everything, go to America with handyman Con (J. Farrell MacDonald) and a pet goose, enter Dark Rosaleen in the stakes, and win.

**Virginia's Future trips at the finish line, and her desperate owner Beaumont (Henry B. Walthall) disappears. Saved by groom Donovan (J. Farrell MacDonald), she foals and is sold. Donovan, now a cop, finds Beaumont selling bourbon trackside, reunites him to his daughter, rescues the mare from a junk dealer after an epic fight, and rides her in tails and tophat proudly down Main St., to see her daughter Confederacy win, 20-1.

The Shamrock Handicap (1926). Janet Gaynor, Leslie Fenton.

seemed to melt away. . . . Suddenly I knew that I had not failed, that I too had carried on. . . . My darling baby . . . had paid my debts in full."

This is the first extant appearance of the "Tradition & Duty" theme that—prominent in early Universals also—will be found important in nearly all Ford's subsequent films. And in this incipient vignette style lie seeds of Ford's greatness. Through broad playing and multitudes of tics, somewhat in the manner of the British stage or commedia dell'arte, it characterizes instantly and narrates economically. Each shot becomes a vaudevillelike "turn." Cutting isolates a character within his own "atmosphere," yet juxtaposes him between contrasting shots of others and *their* atmosphere. By rapid passage through a variety of "turns" (shots or scenes), as above, an entertaining, kaleidoscopic suite of emotions is obtained.

Always fascinated by character, Ford had drawn caricatures in school, had acted them out at home, and incessantly robbed real life to fuel his movies. His description, some forty-five years later, of a dinner at William Fox's home in 1924, has precisely the same taste for personality as his pictures:

A butler came over to Grampy [i.e., Ford's father] with a bottle of Jameson Irish Whiskey, and he lit up like the bulb on a Christmas tree when he saw it. He took his water glass, dumped the water into a potted plant, held it up for the butler, and didn't let him stop pouring until the glass was filled right up to the brim. Then he gulped the whole glass

Figure 2. Early Ford Films
Many mysteries would be clarified, were fewer early Ford films lost.

Year	Films	Survived	Westerns	With Carey	Reels			Fox	Universal
					2	3	5+		
1917	9	1	9	6	4	1	4	—	9
1918	7	0	7	7			7	—	7
1919	15	0	15	9	6		9	—	15
1920	4	1	1	0			4	1	3
1921	7	0	6	3		1	6	2	5
1922	2+	0	0	—	1?		2	2+	—
1923	5	2	3	—			5	5	—
1924	2	1	1	—			2	2	—
1925	4	2	0	—			4	4	—
1926	3	3	1	—			3	3	—
1927	1	0	0	—			1	1	—
TOTAL	59+	10	43	25				20+	39

down in a shot. He didn't bat an eye. I remember Mr. Fox staring at him in disbelief.[66]

Congeniality such as this is the outstanding characteristic of Ford's early movies. But he was valued for efficiency rather than artistic ambition. Surviving Foxes evince thrills, beauty, and invention, but little depth. Characterization abounds, but without development or complexity. Overloaded with titles, the Foxes seem more like illustrated stories than movies, their editing generally logical rather than expressive.

Oddly, *Straight Shooting*, back in 1917, did not share these failings; it alone suggests genius—along with bundles of ideas merely reworked in the subsequent ten years. And this reminds us that Ford's first three years passed as junior partner in collaboration with Harry Carey—whom, as with brother Frank, Ford ever after regarded with love and antagonism.[67]

Ford's "years of apprenticeship" would shortly come to an end. Meanwhile, he continued, as much as possible, to work with a familiar crew and company of actors (at least in bit parts), as had been the custom for many filmmakers in the teens. As assistants he employed, for forty years, his brother Edward O'Fearna* and his brother-in-law Wingate Smith. Meanwhile he was building status. In 1927 he was elected president of the Motion Picture Directors Association and sailed with Mary on a fêted voyage to Germany. The next year, his *Four Sons* would rack up spectacular earnings, and it, along with his *Mother Machree* and Murnau's *Sunrise*, would give Fox three simultaneous hits on Broadway. And meanwhile . . . .

*When Nana entered the theater lobby for *The Iron Horse*'s premiere, there were huge posters of everyone connected with the picture. She inspected them all, then queried Fox:

Upstream (1927). Earle Fox as Hamlet. A lost film.

Building a Legend

Ford was building his legend. George O'Brien,* who became a star in *The Iron Horse*, was a nobody when he auditioned for that film. But Ford's opening line, as always, was "Call me Jack," and immediately he established affection—cajoling O'Brien into exchanging a dimestore necktie for Ford's knit import—before inventing a test for O'Brien. Dozens had tested already for the part, and more weeks went by. But Ford called O'Brien back to watch him leap on a horse from the back, over and over, then snatch a glove off the ground while galloping past, over and over—until the cinch broke. O'Brien bounced painfully to the ground, but picked up the glove. Pleased, Ford got comfortable and had O'Brien wrestle for him

---

"Where's my Eddie?" And forever after Winfield Sheehan referred to him as "My Eddie." But Edward used the name O'Fearna to differentiate himself—and misled hosts of movie writers into thinking O'Fearna a Gaelic version of Feeney. Eddie directed a single film at Universal in 1920 and was erudite in history, but sometimes a dud on the set, where it was said his chief function was to echo Jack's "Quiet!" He would send people home before their roles were finished, or, more amiably, keep them on for months after they were through (according to Frank Baker). But John thought him indispensable. (Patrick, the eldest brother, stayed in Maine as a fishing captain.) Fox also gave Nana an immensely expensive black sable coat; characteristically, she returned it to the store and gave away the money.

*O'Brien, born San Francisco, 1900, son of the police chief, got into films with Tom Mix's help, played leads in six other Fords after this first big part, then in cameos as late as 1964. His career highpoint was *Sunrise*; after 1931 he starred in numerous B westerns.

with Fred Kohler. O'Brien wasn't getting paid for any of this, but he thought Ford had a great sense of humor. He, like John Wayne, always figured Ford as a coach. "Go in and do this for me," Ford would say, and whatever it was, they'd do it.[68]

John Wayne met Ford in 1926. His name then was Michael Morrison, and he was working summers as a prop boy at Fox to pay his costs at the University of Southern California. But Ford, learning he was a football player, kicked him face-first into the mud, and laughed. Morrison, in reply, challenged Ford to a scrimmage and took the opportunity to kick him in the chest. Everyone gasped. But Ford liked this: testing people's goat was his way of making friends, and Morrison was a hard sort to arouse. Later, during *Four Sons*, Morrison raked leaves into a shot Ford had sweated over all day, and Ford marched him around the set roaring like a lion, pinned an Iron Cross on him, ordered, "Assume your [football] position," and gave him a kick. But Morrison admired Ford. "[Ford] was the first person who ever made me want to be a person—who gave me a vision of a fully-rounded human being."[69] Ford took a liking, too, to Morrison's thick-hided classmate Wardell Bond. He gave them bit parts, then recommended Morrison as a new face for Raoul Walsh's epic western *The Big Trail* (1930). Walsh thought a name change was in order, Ford suggested some historical figure, Morrison said he liked General Anthony Wayne. The "John" perhaps imitated Ford. Decades later Wayne observed that many people had directed his films but that John Ford had directed his life. "I really admired him. I wanted to be like him."[70]

Part of Ford's legend came from the disciplined efficiency of his sets: since he would never tell an actor anything, they were scared at the penalties a moment's inattentiveness might bring, and hence riveted their attention totally on Ford. Fear—and fascination—were cunningly reinforced by selection of a "whipping boy," whom Ford would castigate mercilessly for days on end. Often the whipping boy was a buddy, like Bond or Wayne; but anyone expecting star privileges earned special gall: Ford would ask them for their pictures and maintain a steady current of ridicule. He could be cruel, with his cold face and sarcastic tongue: "When does your contract come up for renewal?!" he'd crack into his megaphone so everybody would hear. Big men like Victor McLaglen or Wayne would break down and cry like children, and Ford would jibe deeper, always on the megaphone: "D'ya know, McLaglen, that Fox are paying you $1,200 a week to do things that I can get any child off the street to do better?!" And he got away with it. A cult grew up around him. But if you fell from grace, if you said the wrong thing or turned down an assignment, you'd get "put on ice." For two, five, ten years you didn't exist, until one day he'd pat you on the back and ask you where you'd been all this time, why you hadn't called him.[71]

But his sets, says Dobe Carey, were not tense—rather quiet, full of reverence, like church, in part because he always had music going. This was supplied by Danny Borzage (director Frank Borzage's brother). For forty years, beginning with *The Iron Horse*, when sets were struck at production's end, Danny's accordion would play "Bringing in the Sheaves." Every mid-afternoon, there was a break for tea (Earl Grey)—and anyone who talked about movies had to pay a twenty-five-cent fine. Toward women he was generally considerate; using foul language in front of women was one way to get kicked off the picture; drink was another. Ford seldom touched a drop while making a movie. Instead he chewed handkerchiefs, big linen ones, handmade in Ireland. His wife would stick a dozen in his pocket every morning; by day's end their four corners would be chawed to shreds. Off set, he would "bleed" people, as Frank Baker put it: "He'd get you talking and talking and suddenly you'd find half of what you said in the picture he's making."[72]

He never looked at the script or consulted his script girl, Meta Sterne; he kept everything in his head, and no one but he knew what he was doing. His concentration and memory became part of the legend. He argued once with Baker about which direction a figure on a soldier's medal was supposed to face; Ford was sure the reproduction was in error. Twenty years later, sitting with Baker and paging through a book, he suddenly stopped: "There! See! I was right!" "What're you talking about?" "The medal . . . don't you remember . . . ? *Four Sons.*"

Squabbles became silently cherished traditions. Baker was playing his first bit part for Ford in *Hearts of Oak* (1924): "I thought I was wonderful. He said, 'Is that the best you can do?' And I got on my high horse right away. He said, 'A five-year-old child could show more intelligence than you did. You're the worst actor I've ever seen in my life.' I'm starting to boil. He's got me where he wants me. I said, 'Now may I reciprocate? You are the worst director that I have ever worked for.' The only other director that I'd ever worked for was his brother! Then he said, 'That is impertinent!' I said, 'I'm an older man than you, and I think your use of pertinence is altogether wrong.' 'All right,' he said, 'As long as you work for me, you're not going to get screen credit.' I didn't know what the hell screen credit was. He said, 'Your name will not be on the screen as playing a role in this picture.' I said, 'I'm very pleased to hear that. I have some friends in different parts of the world, and I'd hate to have them see my name on a John Ford production.' He said, 'You'll never ever get screen credit from me,' and I never did. And I worked on forty pictures for John Ford."[73]

Ford enjoyed playing rough. One frigid night he marooned Baker on a desert island; "You weren't cold, were you?" he asked. The Archduke Leopold of Austria, playing a bit in *Four Sons*, was kind of haughty, so Ford told Baker to knock him into a shell hole during a battle scene, "and hurt him when you do it." The hole had been filled deep with mud and Ford was there to laugh when they pulled Leopold out.* Once, at home, Jack was

---

*The impoverished archduke did not make a go of it in Hollywood, and Ford paid his way home to Austria.

drunk and pesty; Baker ran him upstairs and told him to go to bed. "He made a pass, I flopped him down the stairs right in front of Mary, who'd walked in that moment. As we stood talking, Jack came crawling up on his hands and knees, suddenly knocked me down the stairs, then ran into his room cackling." Next day, rubbing his chin, Ford caught Baker watching. "Yeh," he said, "you punch like a bloody mule."

There was a fellow called Vince Barnett who played elaborate tricks. Ford was shooting at a railroad station for *Strong Boy* (1929) when Barnett, identifying himself as the "Western Controller of Traffic," threw the film crew out. Ford spent four days back at the studio building a station set before he learned Victor McLaglen was behind the gag. He said nothing, but some weeks later the company went down on the track, where the railway ran a short distance into Mexico. Officials boarded the train, McLaglen had forgotten his I.D., Ford would not testify for him. What is more, Abdullah, McLaglen's Arab masseur, whom he had illegally imported, was found hidden in the toilet and confessed McLaglen's crime. So McLaglen was taken off the train, sobbing plaintively, locked up on bread and water, permitted no calls. "Next time you hire Vince Barnett," said Ford, "you'll think twice, won't you?"[74]

In 1934, temperatures and tempers soared as they shot *The Lost Patrol* on the Yuma Desert. One night in the commissary, Baker, his back to Ford, read a headline about a murder, "He was stabbed," and from behind came Ford's cold Maine voice: "He was shot." "He was stabbed," reiterated Baker, and back and forth it went, getting tenser as the two rose to their feet, their backs rubbing against each other. Suddenly Baker screamed, "Don't you dare call me a liar, you shanty Irish sonovabitch," and socked Ford across the table. So, Baker figured he was through on this film. He went to his tent and stretched out. Presently a voice, Ford's, came from the neighboring tent. "Are you there, Frank Baker?" "I'm here." "I want to talk to you." "You know where I am." Ford walked in, carrying a bottle and two glasses. "Will you take a drink with me?" "I'll take a drink with you, but in the commissary bar!" "You proud Australian bastard. Come on." And Ford spoke to the barman so everyone could hear: "I want you to give this stiff-necked Australian bastard a drink on me."[75]

One day during the Depression, Ford was approached outside his office by an old decrepit Southerner, an actor from the Universal days. It was pitiable. His wife was desperately in need of an operation, the hospital wouldn't admit her without a $200 deposit, and they didn't have a dime. As the old man nervously told his story the crowded room grew deathly still. Ford, staring as though terrified, kept backing away. Then, all of a sudden, he hurled himself at the actor, knocking him across the room and onto the floor. "How *dare* you come here like this?" he shouted. "Who do you think you are to talk to me this way?" And he stomped into his office.

The room seethed in indignation; the old man crawled shakingly to his feet. Frank Baker left furious. But, outside, he hid behind a bush as he saw Ford's business manager, Fred Totman, come out the door, hand the actor a $1,000 check, and have Ford's chauffeur drive him home. There, an ambulance was waiting, and a specialist was flown from San Francisco to perform the operation. Sometime later, Ford purchased a house for the couple and pensioned them for life.

"I've been trying to figure Jack since the day he was born and never could," exclaimed Francis Ford when he heard this story from Baker. "This is the key. Any moment, if that old actor had kept talking, people would have realized what a softy Jack is. He couldn't have stood through that sad story without breaking down. He's built this whole legend of toughness around himself to protect his softness."[76]

Baker acted as Ford's swallow during the Depression, sending weekly checks to twenty-two families, forwarded from various points around the country, so that Ford, who could not bear thanks, would not be connected with them.[77]

Dropping Out

Life with John Ford required forbearance—Irvin Cobb dubbed Mary "the lion tamer." When Ford was filming, the picture was never out of his mind for a minute—and one quickly learned not to disturb John Ford when he was deep in thought. After a picture he would lock himself in his room, dress in a sheet, and go on a three- or four-day binge. Objections were of no avail. "Fuck you!" he would scream defiantly, "I'm going to get drunk!"[78] Then he would repent and sign solemn pledges with his parish priest: he would never drink again.

"When we had a fight," said Mary, "it was a fight, but not very many, because Jack would go upstairs, and he'd do the worst thing a man could do. He just wouldn't speak to me for two weeks. He wouldn't answer my questions. He'd put cotton in his ears, and he just wouldn't hear me. It was the most aggravating thing."[79] Once she threatened to leave: John ran out, started the car, and held down the horn for her to come.

Drinking had been one of the things uniting Jack and Mary. During Prohibition days they made their own gin and kept it hidden in a panel over the mantel that slid back. Every Sunday cowboys and navy officers would come over to Odin Street to drink.* But as time drifted on, Jack became a lone drinker. His friends had disapproved of his marrying Mary. They thought,

---

*Among them, Tom Mix was Mary's favorite: he was always doing wildly extravagant things for her. And he sent her a Mother's Day card every year. ("You're not the type," he explained to his own wife.) No one ever made more money for a movie company than did Mix for Fox, but that Ford and Mix made only two pictures together, both in 1923, suggests Ford's discomfort with the tinsel aesthetics of Mix's personal production unit. And Mix for his part bowed out of the Ford-dominated *3 Bad Men*. Surviving fragments of their *North of Hudson Bay* hold little interest, save for a rapidly edited canoe-in-rapids chase (during which Ford, in furs, subbed for a baddy).

she said, that he was "stepping outside the fold. His gang. Ollie [Carey] wasn't nice to me at all [at first]."[80] As Jack began calling himself Sean Aloysius O'Feeney, Mary changed her middle name from McBride to McBryde and, spending fortunes on clothes, fortified her niche in Society. Religion was another thing that failed to unite them. And between Mary's socializing and drinking and Jack's filmmaking and drinking, the children were raised largely by Steve. Pat was pushed through school by Jack, at times with a razor strap, but Barbara—who never finished high school—was coddled by Mary without the slightest discipline. Whenever there was trouble at school, Mary would put her in another school—five or six schools: it was always the school's fault, never Barbara's.

Jack had become famous and wealthy—his earnings came to $279,000 in 1929 and 1930—but success made him unhappy. He loathed the panoply of position so dear to Mary—"When I became admiral she was very proud," he quipped years later, "She realized that she had achieved her mission in life"[81]—yet her aristocratic disdain for Hollywood goaded his disgruntlement with the synthetic aspect of his career. Truth to tell, he was never content unless making a movie. But he yearned for excitement; he wanted to be "one of the boys."

"Whataya doing tonight?" he asked George O'Brien the day they finished *Seas Beneath*, "Why don't you come with me to the Philippines?" "When you going?" "Tonight. Just give me $200 for the ticket."

It was the best offer O'Brien had heard all day, so that night he was standing beside Ford on the Oslo freighter *Tai Yang*. A bachelor, he was touched when a car drove up and Mary and the kids stepped out. "Gee, that's wonderful!" he thought; "Family comes down, Mary has a tear in her eye—'Don't cry, Mary!'"

"You'd cry too," she replied, "if you were me. You've got my ticket."[82]

Jack, henceforth signing himself Daddy, wrote Mary at sea in early January 1931:

> We've had ten days of typhoons, hurricanes, gales, etc. The weather has been terrible. The ship was under water all the time. Mountainous waves broke over the bridge. This is the first time it's been steady enough to even write a letter. We'll probably be 10 days late. In spite of that I've had a good time. . . . O'Brien's behavior has been exemplary. I am proud of him. Never once has he been disorderly or uncouth and at all times he is a credit to the industry. . . . This trip has done me a lot of good. I've never felt better and certainly never looked better in my life. Even O'Brien looks at me admiringly. (However it will do him no good.) . . .[83]

In the Philippines, after a twenty-seven day voyage, they spent mornings on polo, swimming, tennis, and boxing, and evenings being royally fêted. On a "stinky steamer" they sailed south around the archipelago: Cebu, Illoweila, Dumagita, Jolo, Zamboanga, Mindanao. On impulse, they decided to go home, but went to Hong Kong instead, up the Yangtse to Shanghai and

George O'Brien, Lawrence Peyton (?), John Ford, ca. 1931. From the Robert S. Birchard Collection.

Peking, then to Japan, ribbing each other constantly. Three weeks surfing in Hawaii preceded their docking, artifact-laden, in San Francisco on April 11, 1931. Jack thought he should go see Mary; it had been almost four months. "Don't you think I should do that, George?" "Yes, I think you should do that, Jack."

In the years ahead, echoes often reached O'Brien of Fordian accounts of O'Brien's doings during their trip. Most frequent were tall tales of O'Brien's South Sea "orgies." According to another tale, George, eager to meet a Moro sultan with twenty-three wives, had spent days practicing court ritual; but when he walked down the palace aisle, bowing low to the ground, and lifted his eyes, there on the throne sat Jack Ford.[84] Yet despite their comradery, Ford, O'Brien confessed years later, "was the most private man I ever met. I guess I never really understood him."[85]

Mary begrudged her missed cruise, and Jack went back to being unhappy. He staged a dispute near the end of *Arrowsmith*,* walked off the picture, and holed up day after day drinking darkly mid his books.[86] Then

*Ford disagreed with the crowds assistant Bruce Humberstone had used to populate a lobby, wanting it empty, for a proper mood. Goldwyn backed Humberstone.

he sailed to the Philippines again on October 31, with Mary on *her* trip.* A few halcyon weeks in Hawaii, as Jack simmered his irritation with Mary's trunkloads of luggage—the very thing he had wanted to avoid—preluded a greater binge, a morbid slobbering in the dark, and ended after two weeks in hospitalization.[87]

Steve brought the children to Honolulu, they all sailed to Manila, and for awhile Jack showed Mary a good time. But the itch would not go away, and on January 22, 1932, he set out on a "man's trip," with Fox representative Larry de Prida, through Macassar, Bali (four days), Surabaya, Semarang (Java), Batavia (Jakarta), and Singapore.** His ability to share Mary's sort of fun was limited; he thrived midst dirty casualness, variety, and adventure. Mary, unwilling or unable to join in, had to resign herself to a certain aloneness.[88] In mid-February the four Fords sailed to Hong Kong, Shanghai, Kobe, Yokohama, and Honolulu, and reached San Francisco March 8.

Jack tried to make up for his shortcomings. In December, they sailed round the Panama Canal to New York and spent a month on Peak's Island. That spring, 1933, he bought her a creamy beige Rolls Royce, with a mink coat on the back seat, and a note: "This ought to shut you up for twenty years."[89] Mary wanted a chauffeur's uniform in matching colors, but that she had to pay for herself.

Ford's own car, naturally, was a filthy, littered Ford roadster. He seldom rode in the Rolls, as Mary would not permit him to smoke in it. And his personal "style" once made him miss a meeting at MGM, when a gate guard, refusing to believe he was a director, denied him admittance. In fact, when he slouched in, during the Depression, to the Rolls Royce showroom, wearing his usual scuffy sneakers, dirty baggy trousers, and grimy shirt, and began slamming doors, kicking tires, and bouncing on leather seats, they were just coming to throw the tramp out when he banged the woodwork, declared the car look solid, and announced he would take it. A certified check for $22,000 arrived ten minutes later.[90] Ford used a similar incident in *Tobacco Road.* He never carried cash; Totman kept him on a small allowance, and Ford borrowed constantly from friends.

Ford's proudest possession—the one thing he *did* lavish money on—was a two-masted 106-foot ketch he purchased in June 1934 for $30,000 (and spent another $36,235 on in repairs over the next eight years). Originally called *The Faith*, it had been built by A. D. Story in Essex, Massachusetts, in 1926, from a John G. Hanna design. Ford rechristened it *Araner*, after his

---

*Typically, Ford told an interviewer, Axel Madsen, that the Philippines were the only part of the Pacific he never got to.

**In Singapore de Prida met and married Ford's niece, Cecil McLean (with whom Ford had grown up and who appeared in several of Frank's films); she had traveled with John and Mary as far as Hawaii, as a Max Factor representative. She and her husband were interned by the Japanese in the Philippines during the war. While her husband was hospitalized, Cecil gave birth to their daughter. They were freed in February 1945. Cecil McLean de Prida has been the source of much information for all Ford biographers.

mother's birthplace. It was capable of about eight knots, flew Ford's buddies' Emerald Bay Yacht Club ensign and the house flag—orange, green, and white—and became a moviestar in *The Hurricane* and *Donovan's Reef.* Here John retreated to prepare pictures, rest after them, and every other chance he got. It had two fireplaces, two bathrooms, red carpets, a four-poster marriage bed, a dressing room for Mary, and a teakwood deckhouse Ford adopted as his hideaway and whose roof he raised so John Wayne would stop bumping his head. Here the Fords spent half their lives, cruising winters to Baja and Mexico or to Hawaii, where their children were going to high school. As the image of America in Ford's pictures grew increasingly bitter and alien, *Araner* more and more became his refuge.

2 First Period (1927-1935): The Age of Introspection

Wer den Dichter will verstehen,
muss in Dichters Lande gehen.   GOETHE

(Whoever wishes to understand a poet
must go into the poet's land.)

John Ford, by 1927, was becoming an artist. Henceforth—and progressively more so as the decades pass—understanding his pictures is the key to (and more important than) understanding the man.

His was a complex personality, and, indeed, he adored paradox. In himself, in the world, in existence itself, he searched out contradictions dear and dreadful to beggar his comprehension. Like any well-raised Irish Catholic, he strove compulsively to be a saint and to understand. Such understanding entails reconciling irreconcilables, a task easy for a simple soul, impossible for a schizoid. But to amplify irreconcilability while still suggesting a higher harmony, this is the task of the wise man, this was John Ford, and his movies, his art, are nothing less than an attempt to formulate, in aesthetic terms, this Blakean vision.

Naturally, neither his life nor profession made steady progress. There were periods of retreat, of reformulation; there were peaks and valleys. At times, particularly in the later years, the "vision" fragments, disintegrates, leaving only contradiction. It is no easy thing to find a "language," a style, a cinema capable of expressing feelings, experiences, consciousnesses that one can nowise articulate until that cinema exists. So pure must that language be, that it is identical with what it is trying to communicate; if not, we will have only description, not consciousness.

Ford's art, though, is not his autobiography; it is more a parallel existence. If his work seems to fall into general "periods," as does Beethoven's music, the rationale for the division lies more in each period's differing approaches toward certain recurrent styles and themes than in Ford's private or professional life. Certain subdivisions appear in these periods; unsettled, "transitional" stretches of experiment and strife alternate with plateau periods. The best (and poorest) movies tend to be found in plateau periods, while those from transitional periods tend to be unevenly inspired. Although the *best* work of a later period is sometimes superior to the best of an earlier period, many earlier movies are immeasurably superior to later ones.

The first period tends to be relaxed, airy, concerned with being and with contemporary social life. The second period tends to be more manipulative, closed and formal, concerned more with mood and the past. The third period is brighter and more vital, formal but open, concerned with pilgrimage and subsistence. The fourth period, following a "season in hell," is eschatological, existentially and aesthetically.

EVOLUTION OF FORM AND THEME (1927–1931)

*The camera exists in order to create a new art—to show
things on the screen that cannot be seen anywhere else,
on stage or in life; aside from that, I have no use for it;
I'm not interested in doing photography.*   MAX OPHULS

Mother Machree (4/7ths lost)	1.22.28	Fox	Effects and music
Four Sons	2.13.28	"	"
Hangman's House	5.13.28	"	Silent
Napoleon's Barber (lost: a short)	11.24.28	"	All-talking
Riley the Cop	11.25.28	"	Effects and music
Strong Boy (extant only in Australia—maybe)	3.3.29	"	"
The Black Watch	5.8.29	"	All-talking
Salute	9.1.29	"	"
Men Without Women (sound version lost)	1.31.30	"	"
Born Reckless	5.11.30	"	"
Up the River	10.12.30	"	"
Seas Beneath	1.30.31	"	"
The Brat	8.23.31	"	"

In ten years John Ford had gained distinction as an efficient taskman and had made many "nice" movies. Yet suddenly in 1927 he began to make pictures on an altogether more ambitious level of artistry, the true characteristics of his mature work began to emerge, and, with smashing commercial successes, his position at Fox became preeminent. The first segment of this

Figure 3. Ford's Mature Career

1st Period		2nd Period		3rd Period		4th Period	
1927	1935	1935	1947	1948	1961	1962	1965
· · · · · · · ·├————┤		· · · ·├————┼· · ·		├————┤ · · · · · · ·		├—————————┤	
1931		1939–1941		1956			

Dots indicate transitional phases; lines indicate plateau phases.

period is, nonetheless, transitional, whereas the second (1931–35) comprises a series of masterworks.

In brief, Ford's artistic leap resulted from marriage of his vignette style (see page 35) with Murnau's atmosphere-enriching expressionism. This marriage of "turn" with composition greatly intensified rapport between character and milieu, and soon blossomed into a theme that dominates Ford's work: milieu, through tradition, duty, and ritual, determines individual character. Similar themes occur in many Hollywood expressionists, and in much of the era's literature as well. What is distinctive in Ford is his juxtaposition of disparate moods, styles, and characters—suggesting a variety of possibilities, which, in turn, imply an off-setting modicum of freedom; and soon the Fordian hero emerges to moderate further the worst ravages of determinism. Ford aimed, moreover, for empathetic understanding from his audiences; satire was not an end in itself, nor the sort of identification and sensationalism one finds in, say, Hitchcock. (And it is not too much to claim that most misunderstanding of Ford results from identifying a character with oneself or with Ford.) Ford's richness thus is due to dialectical tensions at almost every level: between audience and film, between themes, emotions, compositional ideas. Not surprisingly, the "typical Ford shot" is a geometric depth in which people stare at each other across space.

Besides Ford's natural evolution, three momentous events combined to propel his sudden artistic leap: the expansion of the Fox enterprises; the advents of Murnau and *Sunrise;* and the coming of sound.

Fox

In 1925 William Fox, while retaining absolute control in his own hands, began to transform Fox Film Corporation and Fox Theatres Corporation from a New York–based enterprise with holdings in less than twenty theaters producing programs for blue-collar consumption into a $300 million giant with over a thousand theaters producing high-quality specials in the most modern studio in Hollywood. Under production boss Winfield Sheehan (but with Fox's omniscient supervision), product image was upgraded and stars created by pictures such as *What Price Glory?* (November 1926: Victor McLaglen and Dolores del Rio) and *7th Heaven* (May 1927:

Janet Gaynor and Charles Farrell)—two of the top grossers of the decade. Ford, with the success of such high-budgeted specials as *Four Sons* (possibly Fox's top grosser) and *Mother Machree*, found himself at the top of the heap of Fox directors, flanked, in company promotion, by the likes of Walsh, Hawks, Borzage, Murnau, and Blystone. Even the critics raved over his "weepies." (Besides, it was estimated that 87 percent of film audiences were women.[1])

Murnau

To gild his company's new image, Fox imported Friedrich Wilhelm Murnau from Germany, where *The Last Laugh* had made him the reigning cinema artist. And to gain the prestige a masterpiece would give, Fox gave the filmmaker carte blanche. Indeed, *Sunrise* was more prestigious than popular (and in 1958 *Cahiers du Cinéma* voted it "the most beautiful film in the world"), but, with Murnau at the Fox studios from August 1926 to March 1927, *Sunrise* had an immense and immediate stylistic effect on nearly everyone on the lot (Borzage's *7th Heaven*, for example) and thus on much of American cinema over the next two decades. Ford, after seeing a rough cut in February, told the press "that he believed [*Sunrise*] to be the

Desperate Trails (1921). Harry Carey. From the Robert S. Birchard Collection.

Desperate Trails (1921). Ed Coxen,
Barbara LaMarr. From the Robert S.
Birchard Collection.

Desperate Trails (1921). Harry Carey.
kneeling. From the Robert S.
Birchard Collection.

greatest picture that has been produced [and doubted] whether a greater
picture will be made in the next ten years."[2] He then rushed off to Germany, where Karl Freund headed Fox interests, "to shoot exteriors" (none
of which appear in the finished film) for *Four Sons,* an almost self-effacing
imitation of Murnau's style. In Berlin, he visited Murnau and was greatly
impressed by the director's sketches, designs, and production methods.

Ford was enchanted by the intense stylization of Murnau's painterly invention, in which a character's conscious rapport with his physical world
seemed suddenly palpable. Ford's movies had been relatively unstylized.
But henceforth lighting creates dramatic mood through emphatically contrasting blacks and whites, macabre shadows, shimmering shafts of light,
chiaroscuro, and other abstractions. Scenery, too, sometimes distorted
from everyday norm, becomes dramatically active — not just a passive container. Actors, their gestures formerly natural, now often calculate the specific mood-effect of each movement. And compositions, camera movements,
and montage, previously pretty, logical, and rudimentary, now aspire to
expressive force. The camera becomes a narrating persona, activating a
compelling distance between frame and image. "Cinema", writes Erich
Rohmer of Murnau, "organizes space as music organizes time, taking that
total possession of space that music takes of time. . . . [Cinema] organizes
emotion's disorder. [So that, inserted into cinematic space, a gesture of]
man's internal tumult affirms his profound affinity with the rhythms of the
universe."[3] These ways of articulating ideas, impressions, and emotions became what, for convenience, we label Ford's "expressionism."

The term may be confusing, as it implies kinship to the brutal Expressionist (big *E*) movement that arose paroxysmally out of German anxiety
following World War I. The advent of the German artfilm had indeed been

heralded by *The Cabinet of Dr. Caligari* in 1919, but this single movie's few Expressionist roots were immediately abandoned by its successors. Nonetheless "expressionism" (small *e*) has survived to designate all in cinema that is not realist; expressionism is concerned with the subjective or poetic aspect of things, and is virtually equivalent to "style." "Subjectivity" implies meaning (or, more properly, sensibility, for artistic meaning is inseparable from emotion)—meaning imposed by form. "Reality," on the other hand, is by definition meaningless and emotionless; thus filmic realism is, in theory, styleless. For the pure realist, distrustful of man's coloring dialectic with objective reality, cinema is not an artistic experience but a means of recording reality without human interference. In practice this ideal is unachievable; the very act of framing imposes form, while disparities between human sight and cinematography produce poetic effects of intensification, particularly on sunlit air and sea. Although all so-called realist filmmakers are to some degree expressionist, the two terms are used (with confusing vagueness) to indicate antinomal tendencies.

Subjectivity may infuse a film's world through either (1) prefilmic interpretation of what is to be photographed (by story, dialogue, acting, lighting, scenery, etc.) or (2) filmic interpretation by how it is photographed (framing, camera movement and focus, cutting, etc.). Music may be either prefilmic or filmic. Composition (visual, aural, temporal) is the product of prefilmic and filmic elements, is equivalent to what we mean by "cinema," and is the artist's imposition of the judgments of his sensitivity on reality. There is no "innocent eye"; only art and lies.

Films that emphasize prefilmic qualities are usually called expressionist. Their subjectivity reflects their characters, camerawork occurs within prefilmic space and seems dictated by the action; and it is in his design of the action that the film artist may be found. *The Cabinet of Dr. Caligari* is a good example, as is most filmed theater and most sensationalist cinema.

Films that deemphasize prefilmic qualities have traditionally (and arbitrarily) been called realist. Their subjectivity reflects their director, camerawork occurs outside prefilmic space and seems imposed on the action; and it is in his arbitrage that the film artist may be found. In Rossellini's *Viaggio in Italia*, for example (although this is scarcely an essentially realist movie), when Ingrid Bergman looks out to sea, we may feel that Rossellini feels a surge of (qualified) romantic effusion, but we really do not know what Ingrid feels. Our vagueness, contradictory and ambivalent, results from certain aspects of the film—the acting— being intentionally left "not-made": Ingrid's feelings are not interpreted for us, not subjected to formalization so that they become readable.

Most major directors (including Rossellini) combine emphases of various elements, both prefilmic and filmic. These "realist-expressionists" (or "expressionist-realists," as the case may be) conjure up a genuine dialectic between their own subjectivity and that of their characters with their world.

Murnau's *Tabu* (1931) is an excellent example. *Tabu's* sets are not at all stylized as in *Sunrise* or *The Last Laugh,* and what Murnau photographs he leaves quite alone. With one exception: the acting of the three principals is intensely formalized, infused with each character's subjectivity. Filmic qualities, on the other hand, are extremely pronounced. Cutting and angles are as arbitrary as in Eisenstein, with the arbiter (Murnau) coherently exterior to the film's storyworld. Character point-of-view shots are ostentatiously avoided, with a handful of notable exceptions; cutting tends to be discordant, even jarring; and even the shadows that fall on the sleeping lovers seem, insofar as they formulate our understanding of the scene, imposed.

A camera angle should *intensify,* asserted Murnau,[4] and what Rohmer meant by calling Murnau a "cinema of presence"[5] is powerfully evident when *Tabu's* characters appear in isolated close shots. Their fluent bodies radiate their private sensibility, their feelings are palpable without the slightest vagueness, and the space they habitate is utterly infused by their subjectivity. When Murnau cuts away, we may feel their gaze infusing subsequent shots with their subjectivity; but a cut to another character is instead a conflict of private worlds. Such moments of space-dominating isolation are few, however. Characters are generally contained by a "raw," uninfused reality (their village, the sea), and thus isolated in quite a different way. Murnau surrounds art (the characters) with the real world, rather than with a poetic world, and the characters are thus isolated ontologically. They cannot impose their will on reality, but the reality their imagination creates imposes itself on them. Yet this internal dialectic of the film between man and the physical world that contains him would be as nonexistent as it is in most films that have close shots and long shots (and how many films do not?), were it not for Murnau's throwing it into relief by his external presence all through, cutting and imposing angles and articulating his own dialectic with his characters and their world. It is, moreover, the fact that we are conscious of Murnau's gaze that accounts for our feeling we behold reality.

Contrasts between subjective and objective reality, theater and documentary, character and directorial presence become vital aspects of John Ford's cinema. But such contrasts are not equally apparent in all the dark, moody movies of twenties Germany, nor in the national cinemas influenced by the Germans. We can note, in fact, two opposing strains of expressionism, one stemming from Murnau (*realist*-expressionist: Ford, Sternberg), the second from the other major German filmmaker, Fritz Lang (*expressionist*-realist: Eisenstein, Hitchcock), and we can cursorily contrast the two strains and their imitating directors. Of course, each director mixes prefilmic and filmic elements in quite different proportions, and one might be tempted to question the placement in their respective columns of the montage-heavy Eisenstein and the decor-and-acting-heavy Sternberg. Yet there is generally a greater dialectical tension between prefilmic and filmic elements in the Murnau group, and thus a stronger tendency to meditate on consciousness and reality, whereas the Lang group tends to pursue relatively monolithic goals and to aim for sensation rather than for reflection.

Murnau–Ford–Sternberg	*Lang–Eisenstein–Hitchcock*
characterization	symbol
passion (character's consciousness of dilemma)	action (character's working out a dilemma)
gesture (motion)	shape (stasis)
angular stage (deep)	geometric picture (flat)
style for realism (realist-illusion)	reality stylized (antirealist)
people acting freely within determining milieu: organic	people as agents of determining forces: mechanical
Lumière	Méliès (French company)

So frequently does each of these six directors exhibit tendencies opposite those ascribed him (Ford's *Informer* particularly fits into the Lang column), that such pigeonholing may seem tendentious. And, in fact, Murnau is hailed as much for the "expressionism" of *The Last Laugh* as for the "realism" of *Tabu*. Nonetheless there *is* a close intermeshing of style and theme within each strain. Lang, Eisenstein, and Hitchcock are commonly praised as cerebral, calculating filmmakers, Murnau, Ford, and Sternberg as sensual, instinctual filmmakers. The former, the "stern moralists," locate their dramas intellectually— in psychology, subjectivity, or (as in early Eisenstein) in doctrinaire analysis of virtually characterless historical events; their techniques are rigorously calculated to convey the subjectivity of their subjects and to arouse the viewer; their moral viewpoint seldom admits much ambiguity—corruption may be endemic, but right and wrong are seldom in doubt. Murnau, Ford, and Sternberg, the "photographers," are as equally interested in milieu as in character, and their emphasis on determinism and passion hopelessly tangles moral issues; their techniques are calculated to involve the viewer in dialectical problems that admit of no facile solutions: they, not Eisenstein, are the true dialectical artists, aiming for a coherent cognitive experience of vastness and contradiction.

Anticipations of expressionism can be found in individual scenes of early Ford movies (and of course in many pictures of the teens). Oft-repeated citings of dark images in the 1919–21 years, descriptions of *Hoodman Blind* (1923) that suggest Murnau's *Nosferatu* (1922), and criticism of excessive amounts of characterization detail confirm, far more than isolated instances in extant movies, a predilection in Ford for what he was to find in Murnau. Yet there is an essential difference between pre- and post-Murnau Ford. Ford's cinema became totally stylized. Whereas previously his movies illustrated stories, they now tell stories, *are* stories: articulating emotions and moods and states of the soul and tactile impressions of being alive. Ford found cinema could be completely poeticized; he discovered movies might be art.

Sound

Ironically, although Ford was to retain a silent-film style (i.e., visual articulation) throughout his career, such a style only really becomes manifest in his work with the coming of sound.

Fox was a good studio for sound, having pioneered a sound-on-film process simultaneously with Warner Brothers' development of the Vitaphone disc system. The turn-around year for sound was 1928; some eighty-five features were issued that year with synch-score or some talk, in contrast to five or six in 1927. Ford directed Fox's first dramatic talkie, a lost three-reeler called *Napoleon's Barber*, and shot their first song sung on screen in *Mother Machree*.

Some critics have theorized that sound made movies more theatrical and less cinematic. The opposite was true for Ford. Sound freed his characters from enslavement to intertitles, allowing them to communicate directly to the audience. And it allowed the filmmaker to dictate precisely the music and sound effects he wished. He thus had more control over an audience's total experience during their time in the dark, and that experience became immeasurably more intense. Ford wrote at the time about exploring "sound as well as sight images,"[6] and it is clear that he thought of sound not merely for convenience but for poetic effect. Perhaps had Ford been able to use sound in early 1926 he would have used it in natural ways, but now, influenced by Murnau, he employed it expressionistically to contribute to mood.

Thus both sound and Murnau prompted Ford toward creating cinema that would itself be an experience rather than a mere means to an end (i.e., to illustrating stories or to treating a script). Suddenly his work evinces consciousness of the dynamically expressive potentials of movement within the frame and of cutting, which, when wedded to predetermined music, Ford develops into his particular sort of "music-drama" cinema. Combined with vaudevillian cameos, Ford's cinema can, without too much exaggeration, at times be likened to a trailer for a musical.

Evolution of Expressionism and Sound . . .

We can follow in four films certain developments of sound and of Murnau's influence, and see them come to fruition, along with John Ford, in *The Black Watch* and *Salute*. Millions wept over **Four Sons** (1928), while Fox cheered the "Biggest Success in Last Ten Years" and I. A. R. Wylie, struck by the "restraint" with which her story had been filmed, praised the "simple, half-completed gestures and the commendable absence of tears."[7] *Photoplay* voted it best film of the year. The plot concerns a Bavarian mother who loses three sons in World War I, then goes to America to join the fourth, but has to sneak through immigration when she forgets the alphabet the U.S. requires she know.

Strangely, the extravagantly mobile camera, which Ford aped from *Sunrise* and other German movies and which tracks ceaselessly with characters, in front or behind, the longer the better, was not singled out for mention by reviewers. Rather they were fascinated that he kept actors still for long moments. Indeed, however atypical the mobile camera for Ford, ponderous pacing was, at this date, even more so. Each muscle movement is parsed with elaborate detail, as in Murnau's *Last Laugh;* framings are high, as in Murnau; the script derives from a stream-of-consciousness treatment by Herman Bing, a Murnau assistant; and even the sets of the Bavarian village and New York are reused from *Sunrise*—as in many other Fox films of the day (not surprisingly, considering the city street alone cost $200,000 to construct).

So alien to Ford are these aspects of *Four Sons's* style, and so singular this instance of blatant imitation, that one wonders whether his declared fondness for it does not stem solely from the technical tour de force of his homage to Murnau. Fordian melodrama often inspires tears without appreciable effort, but Margaret Mann's studied eloquence, so lauded in 1928, seems now surprisingly unempathetic for a Ford mother.

It was remarked (and imitated) at the time that Ford had reversed the usual rule and photographed intimate moments in long shot rather than close-up, thus achieving greater intimacy.* When, for example, the mother

---

*Good filmmakers, of course, had always used long shots for intimacy, notably Griffith in *Intolerance* (1916).

Mother Machree (1928).

learns two sons are dead, she sits in still dejection, the room dark except for a single stream of light. Extending the poetry, pigeons fly from a belfry, and in the river water the clock tower is reflected upside down; the postman throws a coin into the water, and it makes rings. *Four Sons* is filled with such sustained meditation, sometimes dynamically, but too often overly studied.

In contrast, Murnau's influence is well digested in **Mother Machree** (1928) and the score (with sound effects), unlike the insipid thing plastered onto *Four Sons,* is wholly sympathetic to nuances of action.* Oddly, the movie got put *back* into production after sound (and Murnau) came along, having originally been shot in September 1926. Instructively, pre-Murnau Ford—pretty and picturesque, just like *The Shamrock Handicap*—contrasts with post-Murnau expressionism: light and perspective. Angled shots of a tenement staircase express hardship's struggles (as in *The Crowd*). Scenes are center-lit, with darkened top and bottom (much like thirties Fords). During a night storm, a mother and child shiver anxiously in their hut, viewed from a theatrically expanded perspective—i.e., the distance from the camera to

---

*An Irish fishing village, 1899: Ellen McHugh's husband is lost in a storm. Later, in difficulty in America, three Irish sideshow folk find her work as a "half-woman" on the midway. Forced to surrender her son to a school principal, she becomes housekeeper for a wealthy Fifth Avenue family. Years later, the son falls in love with their daughter, and rediscovers his mother.

Alas, only reels 1, 2, and 5 of the original seven are extant, and the only available copy of Ford's best (?) silent resides in the Library of Congress.

them is more than twice the length of the hut itself. All is total darkness, except for a rotating beam of light that shines intermittently through the windows from a lighthouse. The mother's later hysteria is the most expressionistic acting in Ford, coupled to unusually trenchant cutting and framing. Most importantly, for the first time in extant Ford work, tensions are created in the spaces *between* characters, and their motions in relation to one another are fluidly choreographed. Generally expeditious on set, Ford all his career virtually exhausted himself over such choreography. It remains today virtually unimitated (except in actual musical numbers) by any other filmmaker, and is thus perhaps the signal peculiarity of Ford's *mise en scène*.

The Murnau influence, no longer imitative, pervades *Hangman's House* (1928), a darkly moody studio-Ireland created from colorful mist, expressive acting, cutting, and decor; but pacing is swift, camera movements few, and framings, though not yet at slanted angles, have recognizably Fordian balance and tension.* Expressionism blends with Ford's nineteenth-century romanticism. Glenmalure Castle's echoing halls and stony gargoyles reflect its owner, who looms menacingly over his daughter's Gothic-chapel marriage and her wedding-gown encounter with Hogan just after, and who dies midst fireplace visions of scaffolds, decapitated heads, and crying widows spinning vertiginously toward him. As in *Four Men and a Prayer* (1938) and *The Long Gray Line* (1955), death is signaled by a dropped hand. Use of such *signifying gesture* is another expressionist trait that became a Ford hallmark.

Misty forest love scenes and a festive-village steeplechase provide some contrast to the gloom. And toward the end of the castle holocaust, the camera tilts down to the castle's reflection in a lake: already Ford puts emphasis on memory and legend.

Hogan's motivation for returning from Algeria remains tacit until the final scene, near a grass-thatched seacoast cottage; now he emerges as a romantic self-sacrificer, a Fordian hero in the Carey tradition. Having bidden farewell to the girl and her lover ("I'm going back to the brown desert, but I'm taking a green place with me in my heart"), he is left alone on the shore. Ford cuts closer, and swiftly Hogan's smile fades and a lump forms in his throat; we realize it is not just Ireland he loves. Hogan is the first Ford character to possess incipient qualities of alienated consciousness. Such a development was perhaps inevitable in Ford, given expressionism's obsession with psychological moods (German Expressionism having originated in articulation of *Angst*).

*Ireland: Dying, a hanging judge compels his daughter (June Collyer) to forsake Dermott and wed scoundrel D'Arcy (Earle Foxe), who kills her horse and steals her estate. Fighting Hogan (Victor McLaglen), an exiled patriot whose sister he killed, D'Arcy is consumed in the burning castle.

John Wayne debuts as a spectator so excited he busts fence pickets unawares; he appears earlier, in silhouette in the judge's fireplace, as a man being hanged.

Hangman's House was announced in May 1927, filmed in seven weeks starting in January, but not released until May. Though Fox was heavily promoting Victor McLaglen* and Ford, it let the picture die, providing neither Movietone score nor mention in publicity. But Wilfred Beaton, editor of the trade review *Film Spectator* and an incipient auteurist, praised it as "the finest program picture ever turned out by a studio, [its] merit due [not to any] sure-fire hokum," like *Mother Machree* and *Four Sons*, but to Ford's direction: "There could have been no more of him in [it] than if he had played the leading part." Beaton called it

> an Irish poem . . . spread [up] on the screen. . . . The photography almost outdoes for sheer beauty the amazing shots in *Street Angel* and *Sunrise*. . . . As [Ford's] humans move through the gorgeous settings we keep our eyes on them and are concerned with what they are doing, but all the time the beauty of the scenes and the wistful quality of the atmosphere play upon our senses as an alluring and soothing obligato.

And Beaton noted how Ford, to achieve such (expressionist) context for his characters, is "one of the few directors competent enough to avoid sticking in close-ups at each opportunity."[8]

Rediscovered after half a century of oblivion, *Hangman's House* justifies Beaton's claims; as does **Riley the Cop** (1928):**

> [*Riley the Cop*] is composed of the darnedest lot of rot ever assembled in one picture, but so deftly is it handled, so intelligently directed, that it is the funniest thing that has been brought to the screen this year. . . . When Jack Ford made his other pictures, he had stories, and all he had to do was to tell them. When he tackled *Riley* he had nothing except a cameraman. At least I imagine that there was no script. Every excruciatingly funny bit in the picture gives you the impression that it was shot the moment someone thought of it. . . . The beauty of the job from a craftsman's standpoint is that there is not a single broad stroke in the whole thing, not a caricature, not an extravagant costume or make-up. It's just funny because it is downright brilliant. . . . Farrell MacDonald[†] [Riley] gives the finest performance of his career . . . but it's a director's picture and my hat is off to Jack Ford.[9]

*McLaglen, born 1885, South Africa, son of an Anglican bishop, ran away at sixteen; as prizefighter became British Empire champ; served as deputy provost in Bagdad during World War I; made twenty films in England before coming to America in 1924 and leaping to stardom in *What Price Glory?* (1926). He played romantic leads (e.g., *Dishonored*, 1931), not assuming slapstick until later.

**When Davy leaves to visit his girl vacationing in Germany, lovable Officer Riley is sent in pursuit of a missing $5,000. He takes Davy from a Munich jail to a beergarden, has to be hauled by Davy onto a plane to Paris and, drunk again and pursued by a beermaid, has to be handcuffed onto a taxi. On ship Davy finds his girl; a cable exonerates.

†John Farrell MacDonald (1875–1952) graced twenty-four Fords. Born in Waterbury, Conn., schooled in Toronto, he held a B.A. and LL.B. from Yale and an LL.D. from Stewarton University, had worked as a civil engineer, a mining engineer, on geologic surveys and newspapers, till joining the Comstock Minstrels and touring light opera. He composed music and once sang

Indeed, the very aspect that hampered development of deep, complex characters in Ford perfectly suited comedy: the vignette technique, with its successions of representative "types" and their "turns," yielded surface variety. And Ford's invention of such variety is almost profligate. Most gags in *Riley* are visual. The broader ones, such as the running joke about Riley's big feet, counterpoint the more abundant "invisible" humor. While principal action occurs centerframe in a Paris nightclub, a foreframe dandy sniffs a rose all the while, which goes unnoticed through the long scene, till Riley unaffectedly takes, sniffs, and returns it without comment. Although *Riley's* topic, tone, and treatment derive somewhat from a Francis Ford series about a comic cop, this Fordian comedy benefits, thanks to Murnau, from a heightened visual style. Players and milieu seem more physical, the camera more contemplative, editing something more than mere pacing. (There are even multiply exposed half-naked chorus girls and spinning trumpeters to show Riley is drunk—imitative of Lubitsch's 1926 *So This Is Paris* and the city scenes of *Sunrise*.) With a buoyant Movietone score, *Riley* is the one Ford silent that does not give the impression it is illustrating the titles and would rather be a talkie. This is a *movie*.

. . . and Evolution of Character and Theme

Expressionism had originated as a means to externalize psychology. And Murnau found that, just as detail and atmosphere could intensify "thereness" and give "soul" to water and trees, so too they could deepen the personality and realism of characters. That his characters, like virtually all twenties expressionist ones, were fairly simple souls, and that his "cinema of presence" stayed on their exterior, suited interwar popularist doctrine, which tended to view exteriority as determinant of man's ethnic (and even personal) identity, and which lauded representation of common-man group consciousness ("social realism") as art's highest representation. Two-dimensionality was less important than elucidation of determining social mechanisms.

These attitudes influenced a generation of moviemakers, for all of whom drama lay in the relation between society and the alienated (separated) individual. For "Jansenists," like Eisenstein, Lang, Hitchcock, and Vidor, bad political, social, or economic systems have been imposed on basically innocent humanity and cause individuals to become alienated—divorced from the community—which is bad. In Eisenstein, such systems encourage people's worst traits and punish their good ones, but in the long run virtuous

---

baritone in Lillian Russell's *Princess Nicotine;* he loved football and golf, and exhibited eighteen paintings in Los Angeles in 1924. His film career started with Selig and Biograph (Griffith), then, after stage work, continued with Imp, Pathé, Universal (where he joined the Oz Company, had his own production unit as director, and probably knew Francis Ford), Tiffany, and, in 1915, Biograph (as feature play director).

ideas will win out. In Lang and Hitchcock, alienation leads people into greater misery and lunacy, away from community, where alone there is hope for security and happiness. In Vidor, alienation incites a search for individual answers to universal questions, but what is learned is that answers can only be realized within the family fold. Of course, there are many exceptions to these broad thematic tendencies; Ford's *Informer*, for example, belongs to the "Jansenist" school. But generally, for "Franciscans" like Ford, Murnau, and Sternberg, hope (and fault) lies in the individual rather than in the community. Alienation refers not to the malicious pettiness of everyday life but rather to a critical dialectic of consciousness whereby the individual may rise above his culture; group consciousness and conventional wisdom enslave society to neurosis, intolerance, and war. The alienating dialectic may take the form of love, power, or wisdom. In Murnau, love sets individuals apart, but in *Tabu* their culture destroys the lovers, and without malice. In Sternberg, love makes people saints, power makes them monsters; his Dietrich characters (somewhat like the Ford hero) perceive more truly the nature of things—for better or worse.

Symptomatically, Lang and Eisenstein heroes—Siegfried, Freder, Jr., Nefsky—and even Hitchcock ones (although Vidor rejects heroism entirely) tend to be paragons of simplicity personifying common-man purity, whereas their villains and victims tend to be complex. Only the most symbolic villains are simple in Ford, Murnau, and Sternberg; their heroes tend to be paragons of anguished complexity—*Tabu*'s lovers, Shanghai Lily, X-27, Blonde Venus. In Ford, Cheyenne Harry (*Straight Shooting*) undergoes such traumas of alienation on his way toward moral responsibility that he turns completely against everything he formerly stood for and ends by exiling himself even from the love that initially ignited his alienation.

But between *Straight Shooting* (1917) and *Arrowsmith* (1931), as far as surviving films allow one to judge, Ford's characters are simpler sorts. Not until *Hangman's House* (1928) do we know of someone evincing incipient alienation. But Hogan's anguish, like that of subsequent principals in *The Black Watch, Salute, Men Without Women*, and *Seas Beneath*, is not critical self-awareness, but only fear that failure in duty will result in ostracism from the group.

Truth to tell, Ford characters, after the youthful fluidity of the Harry Carey years, rarely change. As their subjectivity affects their space, so their space affects them. It is because the worlds they inhabit are so drenched with their own sensibility that changes become violently difficult for them. Ironically, change is everywhere around them. But this is all the more reason to resist change, even if imagination and culture did not already imprison them in static definitions. How can we define our beliefs, duties, morals, goals, loves, even our selves, if everything is in constant flux? Culture—communal subjectivity—provides surety midst chaos.

In full maturity, the Ford movie abounds with tensions between individuals, cultures, change, and subsistence. But in this 1927–31 transitional phase, it is social mechanisms, intensified in presence and detail, that interest Ford: any progress in characterization is coincidental, for the individual's morality merely represents class consciousness (King emerges out of, and returns into, the chorus; Paul Randall yearns to fit in; *Up the River's* cons sneak *back* into prison for a ball game). *The Black Watch* and *Salute* exemplify the Ford formula at this date.

Ford's first talking feature, **The Black Watch** (1929), is virtually a neo-Wagnerian music-drama, exploiting aural-visual storybook pageantry in order to intensify milieu—the social structures (ethnic customs, values, rituals, myths) by which an individual is formed and of which he becomes a perpetuating instrument, and which, by their insularity, breed intolerance, greatest of evils.

The underlying plot structure is simple: a Scottish regiment's war rally is juxtaposed with a Pashtu liberation movement's war rally; then the suicidal bravery of the Scots during World War I is juxtaposed with the suicidal bravery of the Pashtus. Both groups die for duty, a duty necessary for their societies. In the triumph of this duty, some spectators may find satisfying celebrations of accepted social values; others may find a lament that such familiar duty is unquestioned by those who die, and that the very structures that maintain society also destroy its heroes. Duty leads people astray.

Midst ritual in the Black Watch officers' mess—parading regalia, the colonel's World War I entry speech ("Your forefathers rest their honor in your keeping"), a toast (to "Bonnie Laddie"), Davey's song ("Annie Laurie")—it is disturbing that Captain Donald King is summoned away. Notably, he is signaled out of the chorus. We have glimpsed him before, in brief cut-aways, but as one of the regiment rather than a man apart. As King, Victor McLaglen has the stature and simplicity to support this character, for whom self-identity is indistinguishable from chivalric pledge; only within the closed society of his regiment, with its rites and mystiques, will he be the story's hero. But he is told to skip out on his brethren, to "slink away" from the war, to transfer to the Khyber Rifles, then to desert and to seduce a white-goddess stirring up an Afghan hill tribe! To his protests of horror comes the reminder: "Your father was a soldier and he obeyed orders."

So now he stands reluctant in the foyer, taking an eternity to put on his greatcoat, unfold his cap, and light his pipe, until the savored song ends. It is typical of Ford to prolong such an incident, realizing in its sentimentality the psychic milieu out of which King's —and the regiment's—motivation will flow. Now King stands apart, the regiment visible in the room behind him; but protracted parallel editing marks his split, King walking into fog while his "pals," hands entwined, sway to "Auld lang syne," then again, at the train station, where King from the crowd watches their departure.

The regiment marches in, piping "Bonnie Laddie" (a seventy-second take); a sergeant's wife lectures, "Poul doun yer kilt. Dounna ferget yeh're a member of the kirk, an' hide yer shame!"; a woman mounts a box and sings

"Loch Lomond"; like most, she holds heather (the sort of detail only Ford would find); a little girl begs, "Tat' mi wi yeh, pay-tr!" The Colonel thrusts a bitter "Cheerio" at King, whose feelings the singing crowd echoes:

> You'll take the high road, and I'll take the low road . . . For me and my
>   true love will never meet again . . .

To this polyphonic orchestration of incident and sound (ritual demonstrative of cultural bonds), Ford adds spatial representation (demonstrative of cultural depth and power). A shot through the gate displays five distinct layers of field: background, train, policemen, triangle of sailors, gate. Typically, having established a composition quickly, Ford sets it into choreographic motion. One movement balances another: the train rightward, the crowd upward, more entering from below (to reinforce the motion). Bagpipes cede to a hymnal "Annie Laurie," train bells chime, a woman cries, "O Angus! Angus!" and some elderly parents make their way in halting contrapuntal motion out the gate.

Wonderfully uneconomic, at seven and a half minutes, the sequence is an ultimate Fordian mixture of pathos, comedy, and romantic spectacle, its hokum redeemed as it takes on the profound aura of documentary truth about a sentimental era.

The contrasting warrior society in Peshawa receives equally modal, if briefer, treatment: golden sunlight to contrast Scottish fog, Moslem songs, mysticism, rituals, and beliefs that bind. Yasmani is bathed in translucent veils, shimmering jewelry, and shifting chiaroscuros; Myrna Loy's awkward, stilted performance is not inconsistent with goddesshood. Steeped in storyland dew, she dwells "beyond British rule—in the Cave of the Echoes": outside, mist, howling wind, tinkling bells, squawking blackbirds; inside, midst gusts of smoke, ragged prisoners are chained to a mammoth wrench beneath a cracking bullwhip (among them, King's "chum"—Francis Ford). In the cave below, huge, chiaroscuroed, long-echoing, a hundred tribesmen howl curses on unbelievers. King, to prove himself, wrestles a Pashtu above a flaming cauldron, while Yasmani gazes excitedly from a rocky precipice (cf. *7 Women*, when Anne Bancroft distastefully watches two Mongols fight over her). A boiling fire billows smoky flame, prisoners crouch in tiny cages hung from the cavern ceiling, and Yasmani, in white transparent robe, bestows a herd of virgins for her followers' "desire." Fantastic? Yes. But Scotland was almost equally exotic, equally emotional.

Yet, is their juxtaposition contrast or metaphor? Perhaps both. The Pashtu are anonymous and almost "campy" beside the Scots' sincerity; and they seem pure fantasy, while the "opera" in Scotland had at least theatrical realism. But exaggeration in degree is only the metaphor's poetic license, the better to hold a mirror to our own (Western) society—and there is certainly no exaggeration in the similar results obtained by the two societies.

The truth—the war in Europe—is revealed to King in Yasmani's crystal ball. High-angle forward tracking shot: the regiment marching through woods into battle, pipes playing; the men have trouble keeping up with the Colonel, who trots along brusquely ahead, smoking his pipe and carrying a walking stick, oblivious to enemy fire. Dissolve, low-angle: men leap logs. Dissolve: a piper, MacDarvish, falls wounded. Dissolve: another falls in fog, and a hymn, piano and male chorus, appears briefly. Dissolve: another falls, and we hear the little girl, "Tat' mi wi yeh, pay-tr." Dissolve: the men line up, along a tree-bordered road, vertical on the screen. Dissolve: the Colonel, wounded against a tree, rebuffs solicitations, "Carry on!" Dissolve: over a hundred mass along the road; the pipes play "Bonnie Laddie" and their sound blots out the battle for the remainder of the sequence. The men charge across the screen, and, as they do so, Ford dissolves (typically) into the receding angle of the road for a closer shot. Dissolve: they rush by the Colonel. A bomb explodes, bathing the screen white, and a "white" dissolve into the fog shows Malcolm (King's brother) falling. Dissolve: his face lies in the mud, eyes still, wide, staring open; men pass over him. King's face appears in superimpression, watching, calling; and we return to Pashtustan.

The sequence is among Ford's best: swift, muscular, lucid spectacle in picture and sound. How can men watch friends die and then rush eagerly themselves toward certain death? But King's men have mounted machine guns atop a colossal staircase, and the tribesmen, with swords, shields, and Islamic banners, charge up to the guns' mouths and die. Yasmani expires in King's arms, as Ford pans laterally along the British line, staring at the faces of the killing colonial soldiers.

Duplicity, betrayal of love, mass suicide, all in the name of Duty. King, drawn to Yasmani (who loves him), had moaned, "Dirtiest job I ever tackled"; but it was necessary, because this "native Joan of Arc" threatened to "turn these wild tribesmen loose to ravage a peaceful country." He had not reflected, earlier, on the wisdom of opposing "Joan of Arc," and he did not get a chance, later, to reflect on the "ravage" in Europe before his command perpetrated its own ravage on the Pashtus. The irony of citing right and wrong to justify slaughter is caricatured in Mohammed Khan (Mitchell Lewis), who, like many Ford "fool" characters,* reveals social values by exaggerating and theatricalizing them in comic skits. The big bearded Pakistani's skit is thrice repeated: he swats a beggar, slits a prisoner's throat, slaps another off a precipice, and each time intones, "For all the violence I have displayed toward my fellow men, Allah, forgive me!" But Khan's caricature is not of Moslem society: his initial skit is prefaced by his introduction by a British general, who describes him as holding "the highest rank possible in His Majesty's Service, a gallant soldier, and a gentleman!" Thus Khan's colonial chauvinism parodies King's own native chauvinism.

Slow fade to the regiment in another dining hall, framed by a bunkered doorway where two sentries stand in battle dress: only half as many men at

---

*Such as Mose Harper (*The Searchers*), many Francis Ford characters, and the feisty cavalry sergeants sometimes played by McLaglen himself—in his later career as a comedian.

table; the Colonel speaks, the pipers march round, the hands toast, the drummer twirls his sticks. Then King appears, in a stunning high-angle reverse shot, his back to us, overlooking the table. "I'm reporting for *duty,* sir."

Davey's arm is in a sling, a blanket hangs over his chair, but the Black Watch is never unable to sing; individuals may die, but the parade goes on. He starts weakly "Auld lang syne"; others join for the chorus, those on the right rising, to heighten rhythms toward climax. The left side rises, hands interlock, and all sway. Outside, three common soldiers stand cold in overcoats, caps, mittens, and foggy breath; they also sing with joined hands; we recognize the two sergeants. Within and without, everyone starts simultaneously to wish a "Happy New Year," and the most operatic of all Ford movies fades out Renoiresquely to the buzz of muffled conversation. The soundtrack continues over the black screen for a few seconds. It is the sound of the group.

In order to elucidate the social mechanisms that lead to war, *Salute** (1929) assumes, as did *The Black Watch,* a formidable myopia by which it is true to the subjectivity of its microsociety, if not to that society's objective situation in the greater world. Nothing could be more typical of expressionist-realism, and *Salute*'s comedy of manners documents establishment gentility in twenties America. Our impression that Paul Randall is heir to wealth beyond care is supported by the ancestral portraits, ancestral colored servants, and ancestral estates overlooking Chesapeake Bay, but nowhere does the film suggest there is anything extraordinary in this (unless it is the intensity of open-air atmosphere, or the way wind and sun flicker tree leaves). Rather than overtly criticize Paul's myopia, his lack of consciousness that life could hold problems greater than his schoolboy sense of dynastic duty, Ford represents Paul's class consciousness as an onerous actuality:

Grandfather: (indicating the ancestral portrait gallery) These are the men of our family—all Navy men.

Paul: I'll try to be worthy of these men, grandfather. Well, most of all, I want to be worthy of you.

At Annapolis, Paul finds in ceremonies, uniforms, exercises, hazing, and music ("Anchors Aweigh" at every occasion) equivalents of Black Watch regalia. But Duty and Tradition prove enticingly pretty, too, in the person of Nancy Wayne. Little surpasses, for lovely ingenuousness, Paul on her windowsill being taught "*Anchors Aweigh*"; their gentle voices blend sweetly, and explain in one magic moment all the wars ever fought. For wars

*Setting out for Annapolis, raised by his admiral grandfather, Paul does not notice girlfriend Marion flirting with his big brother John, who, raised by the *general* grandfather, is a West Point football star. At Annapolis, Paul meets Nancy Wayne; but too light for football and accused of ratting on upperclassmen, he nearly quits. At the Spring Weekend ball, Marion ignores Paul, and brother John devours Nancy. But next fall, Paul beats John in the army-navy game, and realizes Nancy loves him.

are not caused, says Ford, by "bad" people, but by "innocent" ones, for whom war becomes an extension of every fine impulse. Witness this incredibly "cute" dialogue, whose attitudes seem to our heroes all the more legitimate in virtue of their being enunciated midst the bright air of a campus walk* (filmed by Ford in a single frontal tracking shot):

Nancy: What's amatter? Bad news? Trouble?

Paul: No, I'm alright. Nothing wrong. Nothing at all.

N: Oh. I see. It's a lovely morning, isn't it?

P: Is it?

N: Yes, it is. Come on, let's walk and see. Now, tell me, what is the trouble?

P: No trouble, I told you, Nancy. No trouble at all.

N: I suppose that's why you're absent from formation without pass, looking as though you'd spent the night sleeping in a gutter.

P: I didn't sleep. I just walked, walked all night.

N: No trouble?

P: Oh, well, I might as well tell you. I quit the Academy.

N: Oh!

P: Hmm. You're disgusted with me, aren't you?

N: Well, no, but I'm disappointed. Why, you see, I'm a naval officer's daughter, Paul. Dad's a . . . invalid at home from the North Sea Patrol and the Navy means a lot to me. Well, it should to you too, Paul, with your grandfather.

P: Oh, granddad will understand. He'll know I'm doing the right thing.

N: Well of course he will, but he'll be disappointed too. Why, he's part of the tradition of the fleet. And he expected you to carry on that tradition. And now it dies with him.

P: Oh, I've tried, Nancy, I've thought of that and I've tried, but, well, I just can't seem to live up to it. It's too big for me.

N: I see. Do you suppose everyone will understand that? This girl, Marion?

P: Marion?!

N: Girls are funny, Paul.

P: Do you think Marion would be disappointed if I quit?

N: Terribly disappointed. 'Course she'll never let you know how disappointed she really is, if she cares for you. She'll just go on fighting the whole world for you, shielding it from everyone as much as she can, even from yourself. 'Course, sometimes she'll wish she didn't have to fight, she could just sit back secure and be proud of you.

P: You think Marion would want me to stick it out?

*Fox Movietone News first shot sound outdoors in 1927, and Walsh's *In Old Arizona*, a talking outdoor western, had been released nine months before *Salute*. Still, the sequence, filmed on location, is noteworthy for 1929.

As Paul, William Janney is bland, likeable, and (unlike the rest of the cast) anxious in diction. An early instance of many a guileless young brave in Ford, his abashed sensitivity does not essentially distinguish him among the naval officer caste (more aristocratic and Southern than Ford's army). As Nancy Wayne, Helen Chandler* makes a difficult (because so admirable) character credible and intriguing. Ford had a miraculous knack for milking fascination from ingenues in trite situations, their subtle turns of intonation and gesture due probably to deliberate underrehearsal and the resulting cloying mixture of uncertainty and sincerity.** It is the surreal quality of the performances, the patent artifice of James Kevin McGuinness's dialogue,† and Joseph August's realistic photography that lift much of *Salute* into realms of fond whimsy and poetic prosaism.

Ford will increasingly indict indoctrinated, ingenuous dutifulness, such as Nancy and Paul's, as cause of most social evils. In *Salute*, "evil" is latent, at worst, and even attractive (although too aristocratic to attract recruits), and no connection is made between cultural values and war, when beauty pays its dues to duty. Did postwar audiences require explicit reminders? Perhaps. But it is not primarily important to question how much Ford finds Nancy and Paul admirable, how much lamentable, how much objects of praise or satire. What *is* important is that *Salute* holds up a mirror to its age, and shows clearly enough the social dynamics that produce myopic naval officers.

When satire does appear, Ford does not, like Mel Brooks or Stanley Kubrick, announce it with flashing neon lights. Yet, short of thinking Ford a mindless racist jingoist even more ingenuous than Paul, how else, than as satire, can one interpret the scene immediately following Nancy's pep talk?: Stepin Fetchit (as Smoke Screen [?!], an old Randall servant) shows up at Annapolis, and proclaims to Paul, "I's yer Mammy!" Surely among the more redolent symbols in twenties movies, Smoke Screen has snuck away from the Randall household in the admiral's dress uniform (sword, tails, mammoth hat) to take care of Paul. For it appears that this navy world of manly tradition is a matriarchy, and despite a paragon of navy wifehood like Nancy (especially in comparison to Minne Wead in *The Wings of Eagles*, 1957), Paul, and the navy, still need a Mammy. Fetchit, in keeping with the theatrical traditions of the "original Negro,"†† is acting as a mirror, satirically reflecting establishment values—like many Ford "fool" characters.

---

*Janney debuted in Mary Pickford's *Coquette* and had a small role in *Dawn Patrol* the following year. Chandler (1909–68) retired her unusual personality in 1935; cf. *Dracula*, *Outward Bound*, *Christopher Strong*.

**Claire Luce (*Up the River*), Karen Morley (*Flesh*), Rochelle Hudson (*Doctor Bull*), Anne Shirley (*Steamboat Round the Bend*), and Grace Kelly (*Mogambo*) easily surpass their screenwork elsewhere. *Riley the Cop* has another lovely open-air (park) scene between ingenuous young lovers; this sort of purity is lacking after World War II, when Ford's youths are naive, but awkward.

†McGuinness (1893–), Catholic publicist, drinking buddy ("Shaun" dubbed him "Seamus"), later a production chief at MGM. Credits include *Rio Grande*, *Tarzan and His Mate*, *China Seas*.

††Stepin Fetchit (né Lincoln Theodore Monroe Andrew Perry, 1892– , his stage name a

Satire of big brother John is more ambivalent, with some suggestion in his "American credo" lecture to Paul that, in flirting with Nancy, John had wished to arouse therapeutic anger in the callow youth:

John (to Paul):   If you want anything, you've got to grab it. After you grab it, hold onto it. No one in this world is going to give you anything, not even your own brother. So make up your mind to what you want, and then go and take it.

But George O'Brien cannot portray so vainglorious a character without slightly alienating us—and Ford's purpose is to reflect, not to nauseate— so, whatever the soundness of his advice, there is no reason for not supposing John the paragon of grabbiness he seems. Thus the staging—an expressionistically lit depth-of-field confrontation—seems less a "moment of truth" for Paul than a "study in contrast" for us. A second confrontation, after Paul beats John in the game, is similarly ambiguous:

John: I had a spill coming to me, Paul. I've been a big shot here too long. In fact, it was good to learn I could be spilled, 'cause, Paul, when I get that ole commission and go out to the army, I'll only be a punk shavetail. Some grizzled ole sergeant probably knows more about soldiering than I'll ever know, 'have to take me in hand and play nurse to me. Huh? I'm not sore, Paul, I'm thankful to you. I'm proud of you.

Paul: Gee, John, you're sure regular!

---

racehorse's, but also suggesting "step and fetch it") entered Fox films from vaudeville (*In Old Kentucky*, 1927) and became the studio's house darkie and the only really successful black moviestar of the era. He flaunted his wealth among blacks—a pink Rolls Royce with his name in neon lights—who adored his success while regretting his roles (the only sort available to blacks), but he hid his intelligence from whites, touting himself in trade ads as "a convincing, unexaggerated original or modern negro . . . that will meet the approval of the Board of Censorship and the patrons of North and South." His stereotype was not all his humor (and he is funny aside from it), but was an exaggeration by which to satirize Uncle Tomism. His skits and dialogues were of his own invention. "He played for two audiences," wrote Thomas Cripps, "giving to one a reassuring vision of Southern nostalgia, and to the other a covert, unstated metaphor for insurrection." John Wayne (who, with Ward Bond, had a substantial part as an upperclassman hazing Paul) was Fetchit's personal dresser on *Salute*. In later years, however, Fetchit found it almost impossible to find work; he hoped to film Satchel Paige's life, but was desperate for *any* work, and wrote Ford often. To Ford's suggestion that he be cast in *My Darling Clementine* in 1946, Darryl Zanuck replied: "No one has laughed longer and louder at Stepin Fetchit than I have, but to put him on the screen at this time would I am afraid raise terrible objections from the colored people. Walter White, when he addressed us on the problem of colored people, singled out Stepin Fetchit, as I recall, as an example of the humiliation of the colored race. Stepin Fetchit always portrays the lazy, stupid half-wit, and this is the thing that the colored people are furious about." (Memo, February 5; in the John Ford Papers, Lilly Library, Indiana University). It was an act of fierce independence for Ford to cast Fetchit in *The Sun Shines Bright* six years later—and he paid for it with that film's commercial failure. But Ford believed in Fetchit who, for his own part, was still defending himself as a liberator who paved the road that others tread. See: Joseph McBride, "Stepin Fetchit Talks Back," *Film Quarterly*, Summer 1971, pp. 20–26; Thomas Cripps, *Slow Fade to Black* (New York: Oxford University Press, 1977), p. 286.

What is "regular" about John is his hubris, a hubris perhaps ultimately equivalent in myopia to the naiveté that infests Paul.

Tradition and Duty, growing out of ethnic origins and with generally gloomy consequences, will be a major theme in virtually every subsequent Ford movie. Sensibly, in most of his early talkies (as in most of his post-1945 pictures), he sets his theme within highly structured societies in which social mechanisms motivating duty manifest themselves clearly. Even when Duty is not indicted, as in *The Black Watch* and *Salute*, it nonetheless precipitates noble tragedy. In *Men Without Women*, a disgraced officer redeems himself by staying behind in a sunken submarine so that others can escape. In a third navy movie, *Seas Beneath*, the conflicting duties of Americans and Germans, treated with remarkable equanimity, lead to sacrifices in love, liberty, or life for all the principals.

Despite *Salute*—Fox's biggest grosser of 1929—Ford was obliged, as with *The Black Watch*, to share credit on his next three pictures with dialogue directors.* Perhaps he was inflicted with an uncredited one on *Salute*, also. Some technical problems were inevitable: since rerecording had not yet been developed, *actual* army-navy-game footage *with* crowd noise alternates awkwardly with *staged* field action *minus* crowd noise. Yet how could Ford have been responsible both for the technically difficult but graceful outdoor dialogue scenes (often with traveling camera) and also for the technically simple but woodenly staged indoor ones (with mikes ill-disguised as lampcords)?

Interference had been disastrous for *The Black Watch*. It had been planned as a part-talkie, with only a couple of dialogue scenes, but Ford's train-station farewell, with its astonishingly virtuosic sound, had so bowled over Fox executives that production was shut down in order to replan the project as a full-talkie. Even so, Ford was not allowed to direct dialogue, which was entrusted instead to Lumsden Hare (a British stage actor who also plays King's colonel). Thus King and the Field Marshall speak with pompous slowness, stand stiff, project two nuances per minute: here where drama ought to peak—as King is ordered to desert—narrative halts. Hare also added love scenes ("I wanted to vomit when I saw them," said Ford, still bitter thirty-five years later) and seems to have taken over whenever there was extended talk. Perhaps it was as much to evade Hare as to try out his expressionist sound theories that Ford's portions (85 percent?) avoid dialogue in favor of operalike spectacle. And, of course, Ford's endless digressions never disrupt suspense. King, for example, arrives at the Field Marshall's midst a long foggy skit with tweedy streetsingers ("'Ome Sweet 'Ome"), then traverses one of filmdom's first offices of clapping typewriters.

Up the River does not suffer from whatever William Collier, Jr., contributed. Andrew Bennison may have added to *Born Reckless*'s woodenness, but *Men Without Women* is unassessable, the only extant copy lacking a soundtrack.

It was, in any case, a period of experimentation for Ford. For his first talkie, he used a single microphone (as he would always do!), and enjoyed underlaying foreground conversations with background talk, or the decrescendo effect of people walking away from the mike, or having characters perform with their backs to the camera. Insofar as they enhance *presence*, such techniques concur with Ford's expressionism. Foreign accents also provide fun, pipes and drums play at every opportunity, there is more singing than in most musicals, and as many sounds as possible are deliberately included.*

In *Men Without Women* (1930), Ford used a real submarine, dove his camera in a glass box, and took "impossible" dolly shots down bars and streets, with men carrying microphones on fish poles overhead. In *Up the River*, to accentuate Claire Luce's charisma and helplessness, he abandoned for once his eye-or-lower camera angle to frame her from above in three-quarter profile. The final shoot-out in **Born Reckless** (1930), mimicking a Ford western, complete with beloved bartender, is realized within a single long take—as are many action scenes in *Seas Beneath*. Such pyrotechnics are exceptions, rather than the rule; but in *The Brat*, the camera is unusually fluid throughout—Ford even mounts it on a garden swing.

Experiment—and comic invention—outside the plotline were Ford's invariable approaches to unsympathetic or inferior material. *Salute's* platitudinous plot is redeemed by sheer quantity of invention, and building up tangential incidents in *Born Reckless* nearly diverts us from its pointless story.

The Brat (1931), a trivial Maud Fulton drawingroom comedy of manners, becomes thoroughly enchanting because of rapid pacing and a light, pointed touch. Piquant Sally O'Neil's fascination is heightened by her huge intense eyes, Yankee-Cockney accent, and friendly youthfulness wedded to sophisticated theatrical manners. Rather than try to lessen the "typing" of the "stock" roles (which would only have further dehumanized them—one might as well discard the whole play!), Ford has his actors play them for all their worth— with constant confirmatory "business," often in Ford's "wacky" manner: Mac-Millan's self-proclaimed genius is mocked by his confusion when handed an olive away from table, and his affectation by his habit of writing in a Russian shirt at a monk's desk. When June Collyer dismisses "Cyril," we see a Viking helmet and spear turn round to reveal a Brooklyn goon in pants who, seeing her cubist portrait of him, begins punching his head. Also added by Ford is a night-court prologue, whose half-dozen docket cases are a sideshow of freaks, while in a back room some cops (Ward Bond among them) "destroy" (Prohibition) champagne, wishing for beer and pretzels.

*Various drums, bagpipes, accordion, piano, honking and backfiring car, train bells and whistles, locomotive steam, squeaking brakes, tomtoms, wrench-wheel, whip lashes, tiny tinkling bells, squawking birds, bubbling oil, gunfire, machine guns, bombs, horses, howling wind, swords and shields, disembodied voices, a soda dispenser, a phonograph, dog barks, clapping typewriters.

In *Up the River* (1930), Ford again accentuates types to mock-epic propoɪ-tions, drawing out caricature to suit the personalities of three fresh new actors—befuddled Warren Hymer, anxious Humphrey Bogart, and roguish Spencer Tracy—then sets them to trading lines in a spontaneous, quasi-vaudevillian style. *Up the River* had been planned as a grim prison drama, was nearly canceled when MGM released one first (*The Big House*), and then was rewritten delightedly by Ford and William Collier into a comedy.* Tracy, for example, arrives for prison by limousine, and poses for photos while the band plays "Stars and Stripes Forever." Commented Mordaunt Hall in *The New York Times*:

> Whatever may be one's opinions of depicting levity in a penitentiary, this screen offering often proved to be violently funny for the thousands who filled the seats of the [Roxy].[10]

In fact, the bizarreness of the project was especially fortuitous for Ford. Throughout this period, some sequences in *The Black Watch* aside, Ford impresses far more in comedy than in drama. And *Up the River* has lots of his wacky humor: dowagers touring prison, a pixilated mother (Edythe Chapman), a show, the unstressed presence of the ball team's mascot—a zebra—another instance of Ford's "invisible humor." But, in *Up the River* this humor counterpoints tragedy: marching files of prisoners, cellblocks, Claire Luce's depression, lovers' shame, the horror of a youth whose arrest killed his mother. And the result of this counterpointing was to throw both drama and comedy into relief and to create numerous "magic moments" that moved audiences. In a way, it was proof of expressionism—the movie once again creating its own reality.

Ford's comedies had always used vignette techniques, presenting char-acters initially as stock types in poses and situations supporting their basic definitions. The vignetting made them memorable, and made them fun to contrast. Each such character study constituted a world; their juxtaposition accentuated the bizarre qualities of each. Ford's expressionist techniques, meanwhile, came to be employed in drama for purpose of, essentially, "typ-ing" atmosphere, milieu, and psychic vibrations of entire sequences. Basi-

---

*St. Louis (Tracy) deserts Dan (Hymer) during a prison escape, then shows up looking opulent in K.C., where Dan, street-singing for a gospel group, slugs him, and, as the band plays, both are hauled back to Bensonatta Penitentiary. There, Judy (Claire Luce), who plans to marry parolee Steve (Bogart), hears ex-boyfriend Frosby is blackmailing Steve to help cheat their wealthy New England neighbors. So St. Louis and Dan break out during a variety show, hop a freight, set things right for Steve—and return to prison for the big ball game with Upstate.

Up the River was Tracy's first film. Ford had seen him on Broadway in *The Last Mile*, talked baseball with him afterwards until 4 A.M. at the Lambs Club, and persuaded Fox to sign him despite an earlier rejection. Tracy, as ever, is quietly impressive, but even more quietly so than in later career, and, compared to the older, more affected actor, fresher and more natural at thirty. Bogart was also signed on Ford's advice (it was his second film), but Fox soon dropped both actors.

The Seas Beneath (1931).

On set, *The Seas Beneath* (1931). William Collier, Sr., in chair; John Ford with elbow on knee. From the Robert S. Birchard Collection.

cally methods of "weighting," expressionist techniques can have only limited (though vital) applications to comedy. But by applying comedy to expressionism, kaleidoscopic results were obtained. Not only would Ford contrast emotional *moods*, juxtaposing tragic and happy moments, but also *style* (slapstick with impressionism, expressionism with naturalness, theatricality with realism), and also *cinematic elements* (shapes, motions, light and dark, color, sound, music, cutting, camera movement) as autonomous "lines" of polyphonic formal inventiveness. This triple level of contrast is the

route that all Ford's best movies follow. Like his penchant for choreograph-
ing movement, it is a signal quality.

There are few incidents anticipating such contrast prior to *Up the River*,
and they tend to be unartful, or else to lack the pointing of comedy.*
Whether or not serendipitously discovered in *Up the River*, these poly-
modal techniques were applied quite deliberately by Ford to his next picture, *Seas Beneath* (1931), and for the first time to a dramatic subject, rendering it, despite dreadful acting** and splendid photography, an instruc-
tive failure for its three distinctly incompatible modes of "realism":

1. Documentary Realism. The camera stares watchfully at immense varieties of natural lighting (Joseph August, again) and at water. The gaze
from hundreds of yards' distance is steady as sailors board a lifeboat, row
away, and the trawler sinks—nearly a minute, but seeming much longer.
Another long take accentuates bizarre humor, as a girl wistfully watches her
lover's departure on a funnily contrived submarine. A half-hour battle sequence almost follows real time, with little "action" but with weighty concentration on waiting, communication, and events between gunshots.

2. Comedic Vignettes. Despite a fat, braggart, McLaglen-like bo's'n, all
the characters are low-keyed and humdrum, with George O'Brien average to
the point of banality; thus both corn and naiveté have flavors of authenticity.

3. Operatic Mannerism. The Latin music accompanying siren Lolita's
every appearance is matched by the white lace draping her and the exotica
of her gesture and language (like Myrna Loy in *The Black Watch*). Though
overdone, such atmosphere aims at least for inner realism.

DEPRESSION (1931–1935)

Arrowsmith	12.1.31	Goldwyn–United Artists
Air Mail	11.3.32	Universal
Flesh	12.9.32	Metro-Goldwyn-Mayer
Pilgrimage	7.12.33	Fox
Doctor Bull	9.22.33	Fox
The Lost Patrol	2.16.34	RKO
The World Moves On	6.27.34	Fox
Judge Priest	10.5.34	Fox
The Whole Town's Talking	2.22.35	Columbia

*The bizarrely mismatched prologues to *Men Without Women* (boisterous bar scenes) and
The Brat (police cars screaming down Broadway midst black expressionist night and alternating high /low-angles) seem contradictions of all that follows them, rather than contrasts.

**Canary Island, 1918: Commanding a Q-boat—a German-hunting schooner with hidden
cannon, reservist crew, and trailing U.S. sub—Capt. Bob (George O'Brien) romances Anna
Marie, who, unknown to him, is German U-172's commander's sister. Ens. Cabot, drugged by
Lolita, later dies sinking a German trawler; Anna, rescued by Bob, fails to warn off U-172,
which is sunk. She, her brother, and fiancé go off to prison, leaving Bob hoping she'll return at

John Ford in the Dutch East Indies, 1932.

In contrast to the uneven experiments of this period's first half, its second half contains a series of mature and major masterpieces. No longer tentative, "polyphony" in mood, style, and element, whether subdued in moody tragedy or ebullient within depressed comedy, is fully adequate to thematic material. Contemporary America, in eight of nine films, is insular, static, misanthropic, and oppressive, every individual victim to determinist forces. Cultural values alone no longer provide surety. The Duty that formerly propelled bold heroes to get things done now seems full of contradictions; heroes find themselves ridiculous and destructive, and turn introspective. Their alienation symbolizes the common woe, serves to mature and reintegrate them, but only gradually becomes a positive force for altering social rot. Arrowsmith and Hannah Jessop are the first Fordian characters to attain critical consciousness and, with Jones (*Whole Town*), DeLaage (*Hurricane*), and some postwar instances, are the only ones who achieve *change*—but with what violence! Only with Hannah, then more fully with Will Rogers, in *Doctor Bull* and *Judge Priest*, does the Fordian hero appear,

war's end. (Marion Lessing (Anna) turns the ambivalence of her parting into total confusion; Ford was obliged to use her.)

There is even more atmosphere in the German edition's reedited music track: Wagner, Wagner, Wagner. Their sub sinks to the "Liebestod." But it contains a scene, missing from the U.S. edition, in which the Germans bury Cabot at sea—to "Taps." (Ford was unhappy with Fox's editing.)

as one capable of containing the contradictions that in earlier heroes threatened sanity and demanded resolution. The hero, of whom Abraham Lincoln will be typical, has a priestly quality: both of and above the people, he is a mediator, a lonely soul, continent but tragic. He alone brings light to an otherwise intolerably bleak existence: *Tabu's* was a world lacking a hero. He is a Christ figure in the Augustinian scheme, a hero in the Hegelian—one whose knowledge of right and wrong transcends ordinary human limits and who single-handedly elevates his community out of its sloughs of intolerance and onto a higher moral plane. Outside normal human history, he is generally celibate.

These thematic developments were implicit in earlier pictures. Still, one can see here a commentary on the social catastrophe of the Depression years. But while there are attacks on business and government, Ford defines the horror not by 33 percent unemployment (12 million out of work) but by the moral meanness corrupting social bonds at every level—including, especially, the common man.

Although Ford wrote off $76,000 of stock losses between 1930 and 1932 (a lot of it in Fox subsidiaries), his earnings in those years came to $268,000 and exceeded $1.4 million between 1933 and 1941. His personal depression was not financial but moral, externalized in two wandering voyages to the South Seas and, in contrast to his ten steady years at Fox, in wandering visits to Goldwyn, Universal, MGM, RKO, and Columbia. A new contract negotiated by a newly acquired agent, Harry Wurtzel (brother of Fox production chief Sol Wurtzel), kept Ford under salary as a Fox contract director, but permitted him to work elsewhere as well. The advantages of this nonexclusive clause were less artistic than financial. Ford's Foxes are better and more personal than his movies at other studios, but production was long stagnant at Fox, following William Fox's ouster and the bankruptcy into which the new owners milked the company.

Arrowsmith (1931). Ford's first picture* away from Fox was a prestigious and ambitious undertaking for Ford, and it scored a box-office and critical triumph (with four Oscar nominations).

---

*Dr. Martin Arrowsmith (Ronald Colman) declines research under Prof. Gottlieb at famed McGurk Institute, choosing to practice medicine with Leora (Helen Hayes) in yokel-ful Wheatsylvania, S.D., where his cure for Blackleg wins him his own invitation to McGurk. There, a crazed burst of research is deflated, first by supercilious director Tubbs announcing it as "A Cure for All Disease," then by similar findings published in France. A year later Martin accompanies eccentric doctor-soldier Sondelius to the plague-ridden West Indies, where indignation greets Gottlieb's insistence on testing Martin's serum by treating only half the islanders, until a black doctor offers his people. Leora is left behind, Martin contemplates adultery with Joyce (Myrna Loy), Sondelius dies, then Leora, alone. "To hell with science!" screams Martin, releasing serum to everyone. In New York, a hero, he confesses his failure as scientist to Gottlieb, but Gottlieb has gone insane. Martin rejects Tubbs, refuses Joyce's hand, and rushes madly after a departing colleague to be a "true" scientist.

There is more than a fleeting similarity between Sinclair Lewis and John Ford in this period. Lewis wanted to expose the barrenness of American life, its hypocrisies, its insipidities, its myopia, and this, together with such gestures as refusing the Pulitzer Prize because of its advocacy of novels that would represent "the wholesome atmosphere of American life and the highest standard of American manners and manhood," gave Lewis a reputation as an angry, engaged writer. Where Ford differed was not so much in his low estimation of America, as in satiric sense. For him the dumbest bumpkin had a soul, and ugly personalities might have some charm. Lewis's satire concentrates on a character's defects, Ford's on his likeable qualities (e.g., Arrowsmith's purposefulness, Leora's agreeableness). Ford's less condescending satire increases empathy while simultaneously increasing distance. When you are amused with someone you like, you may also view him with some objectivity, and his defects, if clearer, seem less alienating. It may be argued that Ford's approach is better suited for films than Lewis's, since a more palatable movie may (ultimately) be more seditious.

Arrowsmith had appeared in 1925 and won Lewis the Pulitzer the following year. In 1930, again for *Arrowsmith*, he became the first American to be awarded the Nobel Prize for Literature. It was apparently assumed that the public was familiar with the book when the movie was made, for the adaptation by Ford and Sidney Howard (himself a Pulitzer winner in drama), attempting and failing to telescope the novel into a dramatic structure, has a shorthand quality to it, which today may leave an unprepared viewer somewhat mystified. And the confusion begins with the opening legend: "The story of a man who dedicated his life to science and his heart to the love of one woman"—which, while hinting at the antinomies, is not quite true.

Lewis's Arrowsmith is a stuffed shirt, lacking the bedside manner, unable to get along with the laity, hopelessly misplaced outside the laboratory. The movie sought a more sympathetic character, and with Ronald Colman playing the part, Arrowsmith becomes more empathetic, less satiric, and frailer. Howard-Ford even invented a scene in which Arrowsmith pulls a young boy's tooth with a painless trick, thus demonstrating character traits quite contrary to the novel's Arrowsmith. Two qualities, however, do set Colman-Arrowsmith apart. One, ironically, is Colman's suavity and assurance, which, when combined with his neglect of Leora for the glory-road,

---

Commentators claim McGurk refers to the Rockefeller Institute, and that Gottlieb and Arrowsmith are loosely based on Drs. F. G. Novy and Paul de Kruif. In the novel, Martin marries Joyce, who tries to train him into a society figure, until he leaves her to join Terry in a rustic Vermont lab. But when the movie was reissued under the more rigorous Production Code of 1934, nearly all Joyce's scenes were omitted; even the thought of adultery—Martin and Joyce going to bed in separate rooms—was unpalatable. Thus, glimpsing Joyce only once or twice in the background in St. Hubert, we are puzzled in the reissue when she pops up proposing in New York. Martin's lines over his dead wife ("I loved you Lee, didn't you know that? Didn't you know I couldn't love anyone else?") are deleted—the silence makes the scene more moving—and also his rush into her closet where he strokes and kisses her clothes.

makes him subtly pompous and silly; his theatrical manner suits a character so abstracted from reality. The second distancing quality is a peculiarly cinematic device: speed, his impatient drive. Thus, for example, a scene not in the book: on their date, Martin and Leora decide to get married, and she puts a coin in the jukebox, wanting to hear soft music. Instead she gets the "Lone Ranger" portion of the William Tell Overture, a prophecy of the galloping vigor of the man to whom she is tying herself. (The "tying" quality is expressed in another interpolated scene, when the county clerk gives the marriage certificate to Leora, insisting, "The lady gets it.")

Lewis's Leora was a much admired character at the time, although today so self-effacing a woman would not inspire plaudits. Ford beefs her up a bit, and the casting of Helen Hayes doubtless had that intention; but Hayes's screen-presence is not quite charismatic enough to permit her to compete with Colman and give the requisite force to Leora's side of the drama. She is still wholly Martin's and although in the book he is never forcibly accused of neglect, in the movie's telescoped sequencing implications become more explicit: the miscarriage Martin discovers she has suffered when he returns home having proved his Blackleg serum anticipates the dead woman he will discover when he returns having proved his plague serum. Thus the film becomes virtually the story of their *non*relationship. Martin's quest for glory kills Leora.

The implied antinomy between science and humanity is echoed in the use of the serum. While Lewis is at pains to indicate the need for scientific knowledge, as opposed to traditional "cures," mostly worthless yet widely accepted and whose value has never been ascertained, the movie, in the severest defect of its shorthand method, declines to make a case for the scientific method— i.e., for having a "control group" from which medication given to another group is withheld. We are left, like John Qualen's quaint Swedish farmer, feeling that it was a trifle silly not to have inoculated all the cows.

When Martin wants to follow the same procedure with human beings, and threatens to withhold the serum unless they "come to heel," the whites of St. Hubert's declare they will "die like men" instead. But a black doctor named Marchand (Clarence Brooks) offers the blacks on a small plague-stricken island: "It will be a privilege for my people to have served the world." Subsequently, we see Arrowsmith inoculating half the natives, sending away the other half with nothing, deciding to withhold the serum from a baby but giving it to the mother. The movie's morality seems slightly confused, for we seem expected to respond to the Negro doctor as a noble example of his race, whereas, if we hold that people are not cattle, he is instead a pitiable example of indoctrinated values and the mechanics of racism.* The latter interpretation is somewhat farfetched, given the film's am-

*In the novel, the black doctor did not make this offer, and Lewis's subsequent comment avoids the issue: "The negro doctor [in the film], I think, is the first one of his kind on the screen who has failed to come out as a quaint and obvious character. . . . I presented him honestly in my book . . . and the movie has miraculously [sic] presented him in the same honesty." (*The New York Times*, December 9, 1931, p. 23.)

bivalence on the issue of using humans as control groups (and its unwilling-ness ever to juxtapose starkly its implied antinomies), yet some credibility is given it by the unusually pyrotechnic camera movement with which Ford begins the St. Hubert's meeting: first we see a group of blacks; then the camera pulls back to show they are on a balcony loge with some whites seated in front; then the camera, on a crane, descends and pulls straight back across the hall's length and a long table where the meeting of whites is taking place. This indicates the power structure and the fate of the blacks, but the implications of moving camera linkage are too subtle, particularly coming at the very beginning of the sequence.

Other critics have not been bothered by the screenplay's inconsistencies. Lewis himself wrote to Colman, "I want to thank you for *Arrowsmith*; it completely carried out everything I tried to do in the novel."[11] And Richard Griffith, writing in 1956, saw the script as exemplifying "the 'Goldwyn touch': in its elusion of the incidental and highlighting of the genuinely the-matic elements of the plot." He declared it a "forerunner of 'message pic-tures.' . . . To make such a conflict of ideas and levels of knowledge the heart of a film drama was unheard of in 1931."[12]

Compared with the relative naturalism of Ford's four preceding Fox as-signments, *Arrowsmith* has elaborate demonstrations of depth of field and shows strongly Murnau's influence. But as the Black Death sequences begin, expressionistic stylization intensifies greatly, and elements of frenzy invade a hitherto sedate development. Leora's and Martin's aberrant motivations hereafter belong more properly to Ford's familiar "Duty Gone Astray" theme than to anything in Lewis. Five times Leora repeats, "I have no life without you," but Martin pays no attention as he sets out for Marchand's island: "I'm off to glory, Lee. If I pull this off I'll be a great man!" This key scene is shot from a low angle far back in the large room. Foreground chairs provide a proscenium arch, distancing and judging Leora and Martin, who appear iso-lated and small in the middle of the room. We may recall Leora's tremors of fear on the night of Martin's great discovery a year before. Outside her door now, overexposed in contrast to the dark menacing shadows inside, black na-tives pass carting their dead, chanting, "Lord help us!"

The picture's great accomplishment, and its definite advantage over the book is the mood it creates of paranoiac helplessness in confrontation with disease.* Set off against this central mood is the spectacle of the scientist who is at once the doctor-soldier and the dehumanized glory-hunter. On Martin's orders, native villages are burned, warehouses raided, a white-man's plantation commandeered, selective inoculations begun. Sondelius dies midst a gradual crescendo of the sound of rain and the incessant sobbing of a woman off-camera (expressionistic sound). Intercut with these scenes, Leora struggles alone in that dark-shadowed room, a bell tolling, blacks chanting, and dies, crawling on the floor calling for Martin. He later kneels

---

*Cf. the plague sequence in *The Prisoner of Shark Island* (1936).

beside her dead body in a mannerist-like composition; streams of racing natives express his craze as he screams, "To hell with science! To hell with Gottlieb!" and runs to stroke and kiss Leora's clothes.

Somewhat less comprehensible is Martin's similar exit from McGurk. Again, on paper, where conflicts are tidily stated, it is clear he desires to return to innocence. But in the movie's crescendo dynamics the ending is abrupt and crazed: Gottlieb found insane, Tubbs and Joyce quickly rejected, Martin racing madly down the hall, "Hey Terry, wait! Lee and I are coming too, we're both coming with you!" Close-up freeze-frame, fade out. Has Martin really found wisdom? Or has his galloping idealism merely shifted tracks? He still feels he betrayed Science by hysterically releasing serum to everyone after Leora's death.

What, furthermore, is the connection between the body of the film and its prologue—a line of covered wagons, in one of which a girl stares ahead determinedly, dissolving to the drunk town doctor telling young Arrowsmith (engrossed in Gray's *Anatomy*), "That was your grandmother, Martin, fine stock, pioneer stock, stubborn stock"—unless the conjunction of a drunk doctor and stubbornness intends to prefigure the fable's moral—whatever that moral is?

Considering, though, that Martin Arrowsmith is Ford's first real attempt at a profound character, and a confusedly complex one at that, it is not surprising that the personage is not entirely satisfying—especially given Colman's polished superficiality. What is surprising is that, a few scenes excepted, the picture has little period mood; Howard's telescoping has not been filled out with the normal, heavy dose of Fordian density. Perhaps there is too much plot, too much speed. Eight characters are developed to some degree, but some are left unfinished and others disappear, like John Qualen, as soon as their chapter concludes. And eight was a small number for Ford; even in 1931 his narrative technique was capable of developing far more tangential, cameo roles than this script's compression permits. Instead, opportunities walk on and off without even putting in their two cents. For example, when Sondelius and Martin get drunk in a Minneapolis beerhall, the eccentric Swedish Communist who (in the book) joins them is replaced (in the film) by a fellow who waltzes in with a chicken leg and a beer mug—and waltzes out again. One misses, too, Lewis's McGurk, the nefarious capitalist who has founded the Institute for his public image and entrusted its care to his wife Capitola.

Gustav Sondelius, on the other hand, is a triumph of Richard Bennett's burly flesh and gesture humanizing Lewis's sketch (which typically tries to grasp characters' essences in chronicling their deeds and words). No words could capture the grandiloquent and funny humanitarianism with which his thick accent and emphatic arm-raise announce, "And I will go wit' you! [to fight the plague]." Even, or especially, in this instance, however, it is apparent that the cinematic and the literary are rarely, if ever, synonymous in *Arrowsmith*.

Arrowsmith begins like a sad dream and concludes like a nightmare; moments of ebullience along the way seem in retrospect to have been so many alternatives that died prematurely. *Arrowsmith's* incredible modal intensity grows in richness and artifice, until its multiple thematic contradictions (personified in Dr. Arrowsmith) burst into crazed rejection. But this madcap rejection, resolving none of life's contradictions, seems more a continuation under new guise of Dr. Arrowsmith's galloping glory-quest than a correction of prior wrongness.

Air Mail (1932). In ensuing Ford pictures—*Air Mail, Flesh, Pilgrimage, Doctor Bull*—the very air is suffused with palpable weight of lonely, God-bereft existence. In *Air Mail*, the modal experiments of the past five years reach another culmination of sorts, and, with Murnau's frequent collaborator Karl Freund as photographer, no movie better illustrates Murnau's realist-expressionist influence on Ford. Pictorial subtleties abound: a brutalized young wife gazes desperately out rainy windows, whose gently dappling chiaroscuro midst contrasting stillness mirrors her mood with Antonioni-like expressivity; elsewhere, the psychic emptiness of "Desert Airport" is filled by glistening fog and darkness. But more important than lovely graytones is the neorealist intensity of space, the camera's meditative stare, the fact that every shot is already a world drenched by the personage inhabiting its space—whence the extraordinary dynamics of the contemplative two-shots: an intersection of "worlds." Surprisingly, such artiness occurs without strain in this supposedly tough male pic; in this we recognize, for the first time strongly, a most Fordian trait. And, indeed, *Air Mail*, both in 1932 and today, seems too much a depressed little commercial programmer to attract the critical attention it merits. But its characters, story, and milieu are handled with a complementary duplicity by Ford.

Air Mail's would-be mythic men ostensibly attract us as a movie's stars usually do; but, if we pay them closer attention, we may see that really they are unlikeable antiheroes, unwittingly subverting accepted values. It is easy to connect, in this respect, the screenwriter Frank "Spig" Wead biographied in *The Wings of Eagles* (1957, q.v.) with Frank W. Wead, scenarist of *Air Mail*. *Air Mail's* pilots are dominated by professionalism *in duty* (even as a wrecked flyer burns alive, we shift to saving his mail pouches); *in honor* (self-hate by a pilot who bailed out as his passengers crashed is heavier penance than the deafness of his ostracizing peers to his pleas for a chance to "save my soul"); *in machismo* (daredevil stunts by Duke [Pat O'Brien] are mere stage-setters to the articulate "Nuts!" he humphs when unanimous verdicts of "Impossible!" goad him into rescuing downed Mike [Ralph Bellamy] from a narrow canyon). But such dedication toward manly mannequinhood leaves gaping vacuities elsewhere in their lives. Woman may be the warrior's repose, but not for these misogynists. Husband Dizzy so tyrannizes Irene (Lillian Bond), and Mike is so righteous, it is difficult to disapprove her opportunism, as soon as Dizzy is killed, in running off with Duke. Duke, however, discards her to rescue Mike, thus redeeming himself while acknowledging her perfidy. Such conventional justice chimes ambiguously; we sense a story working on two levels of morality. Indeed, Ruth (Gloria Stuart), the "good" woman, provides a satisfying emotional focus for audiences unadventurous in their sympathies; but the true empathetic center (as often in this period) is the brash, alienated, victimized woman. But neither as victim nor as discarded refuse does Irene, the first such character in Ford, arouse our empathy without our conscious decision; ostensibly, she repulses us, symbolizing society's rot, and fixated solely on her own wants. Duke, moreover, will probably return to Irene; he has not rescued Mike out of humaneness but to prove he can do anything. Thus he survives a fatal crash not so much to provide a "happy ending" as because death would be inconsistent. "Say, how many of the stories you hear about that guy are true?" asks Slim. "All of 'em!" exclaims Mike, whereupon Duke zooms in out of nowhere. (One story: hired to bomb by revolutionaries, the princess fell in love with him, and so the government expelled him.) As in Murnau's *Last Laugh*, the impossible distances gloomy reality.

Isolation of professional caste binds the flyers together in a pseudo- and acerbic community and excludes the world. Gloom and desert serve not merely as props to express this isolation, as they would in pure expressionism, but extend and compound it in a realist dialectic. For, like the disgruntled, eccentric passengers stranded one foggy night in the terminal, the flyers are just passing through and refuse alliance with land or one another.

A subtext of racism, in form of local Indians lurking unobtrusively in backgrounds, contrasts this alienation; but they come stage center only once, to hold a *Donovan's-Reef*-like Christmas service (the children sing "Silent Night") and, as often in Ford, to point up the discordant impoverishment of white community. Slim Summerville plays the classic simpleman who, alone among the whites, does not war with life (anticipating later Francis Ford roles in this and in spitting across a room and making a can ring). Into this misanthropic murk intrudes Duke, scornful of propriety or danger, a figure of liberation, chaos, and nature, frolicking recklessly in his plane beneath a (for once) sunny sky—a typically Fordian disruption of which Tunga Khan in *7 Women* will be the ultimate representation.

Little of this "subversion" may be apparent to the casual viewer, who will like Duke and deplore Irene, and probably not bother to probe the discomfort of conventional moral attitudes. Similarly, special effects (by John P. Fulton, later of *Invisible Man* fame) so well integrate models and rear projection with actual stunts by flyer Paul Mantz (plus footage from *Pitz Palu*) that one never suspects the artifice. When Duke sees Mike from the air, he really sees a three-inch dummy with mechanical waving arm surrounded by six-foot mountains in a two-hundred-foot-long miniature canyon set.[13]

John Ford and Howard Hawks are frequently confused in the public mind. Ford himself often acknowledged plaudits for (Hawks's!) *Red River*. Yet, although *Air Mail* has some resemblances to Hawks's *Only Angels Have Wings* (1939), comparing Ford and Hawks is usually like comparing fruits and fishes: points of similitude are as few as points of difference. Hawks might be classed with Chaplin, Lubitsch, Wilder, and Cukor, all of whom appeal strongly to those who conceive cinema as an extension of theater, while Ford may be classed among the expressionists or even certain realists (Rossellini, Flaherty, Straub). The distinction is less that of "theater" versus "cinema" than of emphasis on body and dialogue versus emphasis on composition. Where expressionist Eisenstein will elaborate a point through a series of cuts, Chaplin will do a solo ballet, and Hawks will stage a long absurdist "duet," such as Jean Arthur's "Do you think I should?" dialogue with Dutch toward the end of *Only Angels*. Ford's dialogue normally is sparingly expressionist (as in *How Green Was My Valley*), but he too will use run-on talk-for-talk's-sake, particularly in his Irish pictures; the "Will you be wantin' the car, inspector?" exchange between Cyril Cusack and a gateguard at the start of *The Rising of the Moon* is typical. But such dialogues are rarely the rhythmic *pièces de résistance* they are for Hawks, and we tend to remember Ford's words within his total composition, while we remember Hawks's words with his actors and their (often frantic) gestures rather than with his compositions.

These facile distinctions correspond to deeper ones. Both Ford and Hawks movies can be described as series of skits by character actors. But whereas Ford's actors become fictional beings, Hawks's star personalities *are* his characters. Cary Grant, on paper, plays radically different people in *His Girl Friday, Only Angels,* and *Bringing Up Baby,* but in practice he seems a single identity, "Cary Grant," in three different moods. Artifice, in the best sense, is Hawks's aim; his art's realism is based on our delight at Cary Grant being "Cary Grant." In contrast, John Wayne in *Stagecoach, The Quiet Man, The Searchers, The Wings of Eagles,* and *Liberty Valance* is less "John Wayne" than five autonomous personages. True, no amount of auteur criticism will convince some people that *The Searchers* is not "a John Wayne movie." But Ford wants us to experience Ethan Edwards (John Wayne) and to believe as firmly in the "reality" of that character and that filmic world as we do in the characters and worlds of Balzac. He uses stars less for their personalities than for their presence, their ability to make a storybook character vivid.

Accordingly, Ford's characters have different cultural identities, Hawks's only have different jobs. Indeed, Hawks's people tend to be deracinated (no families in Hawks!) and their stories' locales—specific culture, atmosphere, and thereness—are relatively inconsequential. *Rio Bravo,* a western, and *The Big Sleep,* a gangster film, could exchange sets and costumes with little adjustment in scripting. Atmosphere in Hawks is mostly backdrop (the darkness in *Only Angels* has the unvarying constancy of a stage set), and his action typically involves the prolonged *development* of a few main characters (often just two or three) within a few situations and extremely long sequences. In contrast, Ford's intense pictorialness serves to create worlds both spatially and in cultural consciousness. Thus his atmosphere has variety, vim, and vigor, and is drenched with the sort of documentary details of daily life that Hawks reserves for feats of engineering, and his action, generally complex with many characters, involves constant cameo *exposition* of novel situations; a character is developed through constant insertion into short, contrasting sequences.

In sum, Ford movies are dialectics between world and sensibility; Hawks movies are between people. Hawks's people are bound together because they want to be: getting the mail through in *Only Angels* is a pretext for community. Ford's people are bound by ideology and purpose rather than affection: getting the mail through in *Air Mail is* the community's *raison d'être.* Accordingly, the mailbags play an infinitely greater part in *Air Mail* than in *Only Angels,* but often with heavy irony: tradition, almost nonexistent in Hawks, is always opprobrious in Ford. Correspondingly, while *Air Mail's* pilots shun the pilot who bailed out and deserted his *passengers,* Hawks's shun the pilot who abandoned his *mechanic.* For Ford, it is duty and pride that are at stake; for Hawks it is the team. Thus the Hawks man can be redeemed and accepted back onto the team, but the Ford man, having offended God, is held by his colleagues to be damned beyond human forgiveness.

Hawks characters are almost chameleons. But character is fate in Ford; people do not change; they undergo fortune and awake to destiny. His cinema is a tapestry of excommunications—in these years alone: blacks, half-castes, fallen women, illegitimate children, impolitic doctors, sons, and blacksmiths—and the ostracized can be saved only by the lonely hero (lacking in *Air Mail*). Hawks opposes Ford's notions of the lonely man who is great. His movies are about how people change each other and create community. The entire gargantuan structure of transcendental idealism that powers the Catholic Ford's worlds is reduced in Protestant Hawks's worlds to the immediate structures of personal loyalty, desire, and biology. It is not so much that Ford's people are undersexed or idealized (although his cameos *are* sometimes excessively iconic); indeed, Ford's people are scarcely less *physical* than the people of Renoir, Rossellini, Sirk, Walsh, Bresson, Hitchcock, Cukor, Minnelli, Ophuls, Sternberg, Capra, or Godard. It is that Hawks's people are hyperbolically physical, with sex as their motive force and animals or herds as their frequent metaphor (cattle, horses, leopards, minions who build pyramids). Personality, or physical emotion, stands atop Hawks's materialism, like a transcendent; in Ford, it is caught in the meshes of the cultural world ancestors have begotten, struggling to emerge, as in *Tabu*, from the masses that are nature.

Curiously, nature is more metaphorical in Hawks than in Ford, just as Hawks is verbal where Ford is visual. In treating a pilot's fatal attempt to land in fog, Hawks emphasizes dialogue between those on land and the (essentially) unseen pilot's voice; Ford alternates visual shots. The "moral" for Hawks, who dislikes dissension, lies in the attempted stoicism afterward by which death knits his community closer. But Ford emphasizes what Hawks elides: people's immediate anguish juxtaposed with the burning pilot, and his "moral" is a set of diffuse, multiple conflicts excited by the crash: the irony of the mailbags, the rapport between Mike and Ruth in contrast to the hatred between Irene and Dizzy (four cameos), and the pedantic, almost Brechtian observation to a teenager, "Still want to be a flyer, stupid?" Similarly, Ford's film is precisely about all the mundane realities Hawks's leaves out: what happens to Jean Arthurs and Cary Grants once they settle down.

Flesh (1932). Whereas *Arrowsmith* dealt with insanity and *Air Mail* with boredom, and gloom pervaded both, *Flesh* deals with a melodramatic conflict—alienation vs. simplicity—and offsets gloom with Fordian comedy. It thus marks an important step for Ford in the adaptation of his comic, vignette style to tragic material. But the step was probably made inadvertently. It is evident that Ford was not involved in *Flesh*'s initial planning and was subsequently prohibited from editing its script—dialogue is verbose, characters talk on and on without saying much—and it may be that he did not direct large chunks of it—scene after scene is filmed shallow focus in interminable three-quarter poses, with a dozen shots lasting almost ninety seconds and another dozen exceeding thirty (versus less than ten seconds for the average Ford shot). But most of *Flesh* feels like pure Fordian invention—sparse dialogue, lively action, articulate angles and cutting—

and with all its unevenness *Flesh* still is a serious study of America and creates in Lora Nash Ford's most profound character to date.*

Horrifying scenes begin *Flesh*: from high above a chimneyed rooftop, a circle of women tramping in a prison courtyard, then Lora, brash and alienated, in the self-righteous warden's office. Visually, these are Germanically expressionistic, but mood switches totally for the beergarden scenes. Polokai gaily takes his ritual postfight bath in a mammoth barrel, quaffs a gallon of beer, and submerges. Then the band plays, people sing, and he carries around a huge keg, filling mugs.

Another contrast sets off Germany, her officialdom grim but her people idyllic, from New York, a labyrinth of corruption. "You're not in Germany now; you're in America," says the wrestling-czar. And the meaning is ironic: the Germans were simple folk, all of a piece; they liked to sing, eat, and drink, but propriety was propriety. The Americans, consistent with Ford's depressing views in these years, are neurotic, conniving, and power hungry. Between the two there is no mutual language.

Contrast also sets off the three principal characters—Polokai: naive, oafish, good; Lora: alienated, pretty, amoral; Nicky: opportunistic, debonair, evil. Their qualities, and their isolation, are emphasized by Ford's vignette method through an abundance of portraitlike medium close-ups— Lora backed by translucent drapes or by dark water rippling in surreal serenity, like Monet's water lilies—that drench the character in her or his own mood. This technique reaches a high point when Nick reappears and discovers Lora has borne Polokai's child. After a three-shot and the baby's entry—Polokai hands him to Nicky—Ford cuts to portraitlike close shots of / Nicky, confused with the baby, glancing toward / Lora, implacable, then / Nicky turning toward / Polokai, beaming fraternally, then / Nicky, still confused with the baby.** The sequence needs no dialogue, and each little shot isolates each character in his own private world. Such cutting becomes typical of Ford—as in *Stagecoach*'s coach scenes.

But this isolation, this alienation, is, like our own initial impressions of the characters, something to be got beyond. Wallace Beery, although slightly more restrained than usual, with a bit more tenderness and hint of

---

*Just released from German prison (and awaiting Nicky's release), American Lora (Karen Morley) contemptuously accepts oafish Polokai's hospitality (Wallace Beery), and gets his money for her "brother" (boyfriend) Nicky (Ricardo Cortez). Nicky skips for America and Lora, bereft, marries Polokai, bearing a child the night he becomes Germany's champ wrestler. She makes him move to New York, where Nicky compels her to make him sign with Nicky's crooked syndicate. But learning German friends have all bet on a fight he is supposed to throw, Polokai gets drunk. Lora finds him in bed, Nicky enters, beats her, she tells Polokai the truth, he strangles Nicky, and, encouraged by Lora, breaks out of his stupor to win the match. In jail, he forgives Lora, who will await his release. Metro doubtless saw *Flesh* as a follow-up to Vidor's *The Champ* (1931), in which Beery played a boxer. (Compared to the post-1935 Metro of God, motherhood, and patria, Metro before 1935 was raw and earthy: compare Judy Garland chasing her dog around Oz in 1939 with Garbo playing phallus with her bedpost in 1934 in *Queen Christina*.)

** / = cut.

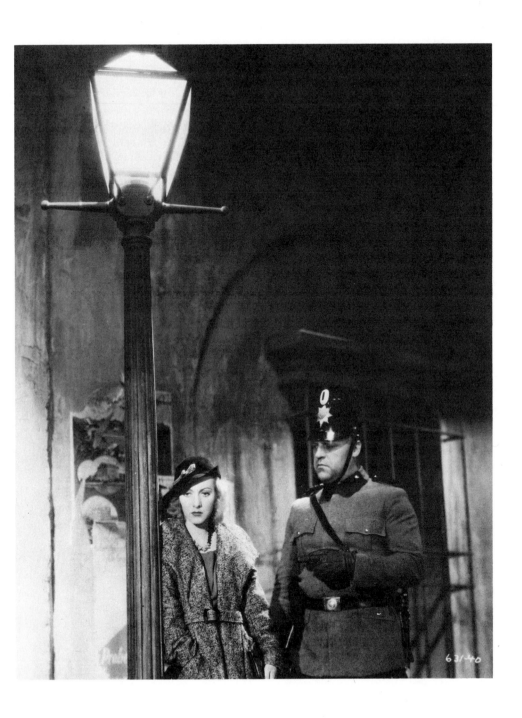

63-40

hidden depths, is typecast as a stupid but kind-hearted buffoon; we must come to accept the personage, forgetting the actor, and then must come to admire the man rather than the "big hunk of flesh." Ricardo Cortez's Nicky disengages our sympathies by his actions rather than by his body or manner; only from a benign distance can we summon compassion for him. Lora's heartless manipulation of Polokai all but destroys our nascent sympathy. She acts streetwise but she is a complete fool for Nicky (trembling sexually: "Love me . . . kiss me") and has none of the sweet appeal of, say, *Stagecoach*'s Claire Trevor. Yet her terrible realism, thrust into Polokai's compassion, in time enables us to feel her suffering, dread her isolation, and admire her guts; she seems to typify the Depression era.*

An easy ability to slip into deep feeling lifts these performances beyond the commonplace. The stock, stereotypical characters take on a certain independence as we, in line with the movie's moral, see beyond the flesh. Nicky himself never succeeds in this. Menacingly lit in close silhouette, he confronts Lora, hits her, and watches her fall back out of the frame as though she were just a thing he swats—and to him she *is* just a thing. A matching shot of Nick follows immediately, but now, as he gives his orders, his menace becomes frightening through blurred focus. Similarly, when Polokai kills Nick, it is Nick who, silhouetted with his back to the camera, dies like a thing. Thus do camera angles become moral statements. Lora's final rebellion against Nick is iterated by: /An empty frame: Lora jumps into frame, close-up, from *right*. /Medium shot of Lora: Nick jumps into frame, close-up, from *left*. The two shots with their two motions complement each other, convey kinetically the frenzy of the moment and the moral revolution in Lora's personality.

Lora is a development of the Irene character in *Air Mail*, but such an explored study of alienation is new to Ford. Early Ford characters embody their native culture without complexity or neuroses; even when an Irish family comes to America (*Shamrock Handicap*, 1926), no culture shocks prompt anyone to remeasure his existential awareness. Indeed, it probably is Murnau's chief contribution to Ford that he taught him that people live and breathe and feel within decor, and that consciousness is a continuously renewing dialectic between inner self and outer world. Hence in *Hangman's House* a Ford character finally falls into deep introspection over his life's failure to be what it yearns to be, and Ford sets the scene looking out to sea. In *The Black Watch*, the displacement is far more extreme: a Scotsman is transported to Pakistan and (to his guilt-ridden credit) begins to feel guilt and self-questioning. Similar displacements occur in *Arrowsmith* and *Air Mail*, and in *Flesh* Lora's dilemma is initially characterized by her being an

---

*Period evocations in films today have every prop accurate but ignore period atmosphere for "realism," and impose, as demythicization, revisionist mythologies upon bygone eras' feelings and beings.

American in Germany. But whereas such displacement was the *cause* of misery in earlier films, in *Flesh* it is merely the symbol. Lora's displacement extends to everywhere and everyone, even to her child, and the fact that in Nicky alone does she feel at home only emphasizes her displacement the more ironically. Her "dialectic" with reality is immeasurably more active and intense than that of any prior Ford character— precisely because her notions of reality are so blurred by alienation and delusion. Somewhat like Hannah (*Pilgrimage*), whom she anticipates, Lora's story is a passage toward consciousness of herself as an actor in life (rather than as a mere brunt of others' abuse or as an abuser of others herself), toward a realization not so much of her sinfulness as of her value.

The world Lora rises out of is suffused from its opening prison scenes with languid depression, loneliness, helplessness. The world that, through Polokai, beckons her is suffused by joviality. The pace is swift, the mood bubbles, *Flesh* becomes a comedy, and Ford adds amusing touches at every opportunity: the giant Polokai comes to the hospital to see his newborn with a three-foot elephant, and passes a little man walking proudly behind two nurses carrying three new babies. In a newspaper we read Polokai will fight "Zbyszko," and during the match, our attention on the fight, we may not notice some of Ford's "invisible humor," the hysterical gestures of Polokai's silhouetted trainer. Earlier, a shot of Ed Brophy in an office twiddling a toothpick in his mouth dissolves into a matching shot of Brophy still twiddling while bobbingly refereeing.

Lora confronts Polokai with an intensifying series of outrages: stealing his money, making him fight dishonestly, confessing Nicky is her boyfriend, causing him to murder Nicky; she drags him down into dishonor, drink, and finally prison, like herself. But at each confrontation Polokai replies with love and trust that, if at first they seem imbecilic, eventually seem redemptory. At times one half suspects that Polokai's simplicity may be a guise for guile—as when he breaks down a door that supposedly will not open (then does), or as when he breaks an egg after demonstrating that even the strongest man in the world could not break it. But it is the nature of the Fordian "fool"—a character developed in a number of directions in subsequent films—that he "sees true," or that (one is never sure) he refuses to see what he does not want to see, and therefore makes the world conform. At any rate, happiness in Ford will belong only to the determinedly simple. In *Flesh* it is the intertwining and eventual union of these two "stories" so mutually contradictory— the persistently simple man, the evolvingly alienated woman—that provides the catharsis.

Pilgrimage (1933). Yet Ford was searching in this period for a polyphony more sober than *Flesh's* boisterous melodramatics; two melancholic comedies—by far his finest films to date—marked his return to Fox. *Pilgrimage*, like *Four Sons*, is drawn from a simple, sentimental I. A. R.

Wylie story, and such it doubtless remains for the unexploring viewer. But *Pilgrimage*, like *Doctor Bull*, portrays the insipid mundanity of a culture; its dreary comedy stresses hard-souled individuals, intolerant communities, repressive ideologies, and idiosyncratic subcultures.

Three Cedars, Arkansas, 1918: Widow Hannah Jessop is a jealous, possessive mother; blind to her son Jim as an individual person, she mistakes her intolerance for love. "For his own good" she has Jim sent to war: "I'd rather see him dead than married to that girl!" And Jim dies, buried alive, but ten years later Hannah, unrepentant, shuns his posthumous son by Mary as proof that Jim was "no good." Hannah (Henrietta Crosman) is an old farmer woman, mean and nasty. Far from liking her despite herself (as we do Katharine Hepburn's obnoxious old ladies), our empathy for Hannah is unpleasant. Ford wants us to be empathetic, even sympathetic, but from the outside, where we can feel Hannah's "good reasons" without succumbing to them, and where we can understand her evilness as the eternally repeated tragedy of everyman. To show Hannah in such depth, Ford's direction becomes a distancing dialectic, rather like Murnau's in *Tabu*.

Through Ford's direction, objects become testimonials casting into perspective people enshrouded in private myopia and self-deception. Old Dad Saunders slumbers while Mary and Jim discuss him in the background, but a whiskey jug foreground tells the tale (frame 1). Gazing down a road, the pointed tops of a zig-zaggy fence tell us the sleigh is bringing Hannah news of Jim's death (2). Subtler roles for objects are prepared by the picture's initially deliberate pacing: we feel time heavily as we feel the dark, misty, palpable atmosphere of the farm. Mist, forest, pools, and barn doors enclose the lovers' *Sunrise*-like tryst (3); fiery blackness, a lamp, and a jutting bannister enclose a violent quarrel between mother and son (4). Thus, when mother and son debate while sawing a log and Ford watches through a proscenium-like gateway, the witnessing fence distances their drama into an "arena" or "court," encouraging a perspective of moral sympathy (5, 6). Similarly, a foreground table and lamp witness the long-shot scene when Hannah learns Jim is dead (7); their steadfast presence reminds us that time can neither be turned back nor halted: Hannah has to live every second. Comparable procedures distance many scenes in *Pilgrimage*—and throughout Ford's career. The tendency of distance to encourage reflection is additionally exploited during sharp altercations: frontal shots of Hannah's victims (Mary; later, Jimmy) are exceptionally close, projecting direct sensations of agonized appeal, but the answering frontal shots of Hannah are roomier head-to-chest, less projecting, less sensation-laden, and require us to "go in" toward Hannah, to reflect on her.

Sequencing, in linking one scene to another via ellipsis and thus implying cause-and-effect, also prompts the distance of reflection. A snowy window vista reinforces the ironic dimensioning of Ford's long single take as Hannah signs Jim into the army ("You are the first person to walk in here and offer up her own son. You have to love your country a lot to do that.") Whereupon a

1 2

3 4

5 6

7 8

9 10

 11 12

 13 14

 15 16

black locomotive hurtles toward us out of a black night—Hannah's love. (And we see the effect of the locomotive, which takes Jim away, during a remarkable sustained study of Mary, watching [8].) A similar instance, years later, pivots on a fencepost knob. The foreground, oversized knob "judges" a close-up of Hannah's piercing stare (9), then, in a matching long shot, with its fence stabbing diagonally into the frame (10), the knob "judges" tiny Jimmy fleeing Hannah's stare; after the ellipsis, Jimmy battles malicious gossip in a schoolyard fight, witnessed by a wide, prosceniumlike circle of children (11). A third ellipsis links Hannah's adamant refusal to join fifty Gold Star mothers on a pilgrimage to their sons' graves in France ("after spending ten years remembering to forget") to her standing on the station platform, going; and she is tiny, distanced a long perspective from the station entrance (12). The witnessing entranceway subsequently becomes personable when Mary and Jimmy enter frame bottom and stand in trepidation before petitioning Hannah to carry *their* flowers to Jim's grave (13).

This last ellipsis delicately demonstrates Hannah's inability to acknowledge her heart, which is confirmed when her hand, reaching down from the train window, accepts Mary and Jimmy's flowers without her face acknowledging their presence.

Pilgrimage, like many Fords, pleads for harmony between myth and human needs. Hannah's disharmony, however, reflects noxious distortions of reality by her culture. Her myopia is shared by the draftboard clerk who praises her love, by the farmhand who smokes on the haywagon, by the mayor (Francis Ford) who tries to stop the train with his cane, by the Wac who treats Hannah with amusement and undue respect, by the general's daughter who pompously declaims, "Think of how wonderful and reconciling it would be to really stand beside the graves of one's heroic dead!" The mayor of Three Cedars urges Hannah to take the pilgrimage because her "goin' will help put our town on the map," and his New York counterpart tells a reporter, as they watch the mothers board ship, that "that's the most eloquent speech this country ever made"; but Ford's foreground placement of the reporter (14) (who rushes off to quote the mayor) reinforces the irony between the motives of mothers visiting graves and the motives of a government that, having sent boys to die in a disastrously silly war, makes political capital ten years later by sending forth their mothers. (An ethnic cross-sample of mothers, too: Mrs. Goldstein, Mrs. Carluzzi, Mrs. MacGregor, Mrs. Quincannon, Mrs. Hammerschmidt.) The mothers do not question their culture's doctrines; patriotic sacrifice and maternal love coexist without protest. At the Arc de Triomphe they are told that "the altar of freedom is wet with your tears"; but it is hard not to wonder why Ford's French general strikes us as such an outrageous caricature during so sincere a ceremony (15). In fact, the ceremony precipitates an orgy of grief that evening in the mothers' commonroom. First (16), a foreground mother, all heart, dissolves into hysteric tears on hearing "Then You'll Remember Me" on the piano. Second, she is "comforted" by hillbilly Tally Hatfield,* who tells her, "I'd rather my [three] boys died as they did, than feuding with the McCallisters, 'cause they was all *good* boys"—which is not quite played for comic relief, making the Chekhovian absurdity all the more provocative. Are such memorial services worth their paroxysmal grief? Hannah's reaction, the third effect, is even worse: she publicly denounces her son as "no good," as an affront to "decent god-fearing people," and declares she will not join their pilgrimage to the graves. The all-heart mother in the foreground places Hannah's middle-ground hysteria into relief (17).

An altogether different sequence of events will indeed lead Hannah to Jim's grave. But then there is no talk of "heroic dead," and she does not "stand": she collapses. For Hannah herself was the war that killed her son, just as comparable intolerance in rival patriotic communities killed so many others.

Hannah's "bridge" scene is also the loveliest of George Schneiderman's varied photographic beauties. She walks across a Seine bridge at night, framed of course from afar, so as to include the arches below and the dark sky above (18). Street noise is blocked out by the soundtrack music. Fog mists drift thinly, and a few period automobiles and bicycles glide silently across. Now Hannah, just after having denounced her son, meets Gary, contemplating suicide. Her motherhood, in this dreamworld, responds to him, and morning shows life in a new context. Atmosphere in Three Cedars was glumly expressionist, the light always chrome-dark and the wheat fields studio-shot interiors. In the French country village Hannah visits with Gary and his friend Suzy, the atmosphere changes to heightened naturalism, light, freedom, real countryside. Hannah's intolerance of drink befitted Three Cedars as the plump, jolly curate with wine bottle befits France. Wealthy, bossy Mayor Elmer Briggs contrasts with the genial French mayor, whose wealth is his manure pile, and Hannah's tyrannical insistence on unending work (she even yells at her hens, "Come on! Lay some eggs! Earn your keep!") contrasts with French merrymaking. And in this new context Hannah responds differently to a doubled situation. From behind a distancing tree (19) she watches Gary tell Suzy he must leave her because of his mother's opposition, she watches Suzy's heart break, and abruptly Hannah slaps a palm to her forehead. This picture is frozen and over it is superimposed a series of flashbacks of Mary and Jim at the railroad station and the ominous black train roaring into the night taking Jim away. Three Cedars is imposed upon France, the old lovers upon the new, and Hannah recognizes the truth. She confesses to Gary's mother, stops her from hurting Gary as she did Jim (20), throws herself on Jim's grave and lays the flowers there, then goes home to embrace Mary and Jimmy (21).

---

*The outrageous hillbilly Tally Hatfield is played by Lucille La Verne, Griffith's Madame Frochard in *Orphans of the Storm* and the voice of the witch in Disney's *Snow White*.

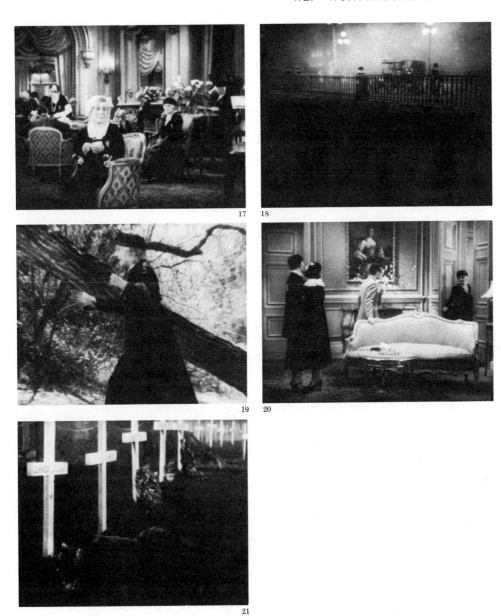

Almost alone among Ford characters, Hannah changes—from virulent, raging intolerance to the sowing of tolerance. If she can surpass her myopia, suggests Ford, there is an alternative to wars and to worlds like *Tabu*'s, where lovers are sacrificed to ideas (20). Hannah epitomizes her world, yet her hyperbolic qualities lead her to a wisdom from which her interference can save others from moralistic hypocrisies similar to those that led her to murder her own son. Hannah reunites a family, then walks away. Perhaps she is only a *deus ex machina* wrenched out of the necessities of Ford's fiction. Whatever, with this little old lady is born the first "Fordian hero," whom we will encounter in most subsequent Ford pictures in the guise of Will Rogers, Henry Fonda, and John Wayne, among others, and whose judging, priesting, Christ-like interventions will momentarily but repeatedly redeem mankind from its myopic intolerance. Flowers mark Hannah's passage. Ford's most constant symbol, they mark most heroes' loves—Lincoln, from and to Ann Rutledge; Nathan Brittles and Frank Skeffington, to their dead wives; Tom Doniphon, to and from Hallie; and so on. Hannah's flowers signify not only conscious intention (to honor the dead) and reversal (Hannah's initial refusal to honor her dead), but also their ultimate power: Hannah succumbs. Objects may do more than witness and judge. We so infuse the world with our feelings and thoughts, that eventually the world infuses us in return.

Doctor Bull **(1933).** As do dozens of Ford pictures, *Doctor Bull* begins and ends with a linking vehicle (a train here and in *Liberty Valance*, a steamboat in *The Sun Shines Bright*, a stagecoach in *Fort Apache*, etc.), which suggests the community's self-containment and isolation from the outer world. That Ford begins *Doctor Bull* with dead time—a long Bressonian stare at the New Winton station—before panning slowly toward the tracks and distant approaching train establishes both Ford's distancing consciousness and time's heavy presence. In contrast to the Odyssean *Pilgrimage*, the Iliadic *Doctor Bull* endures one Connecticut town through winter. Drama is placid and earthy, but the yearning desolation and labyrinthian prison of the social milieu impregnate light and air.

The train porter (a black man who shows no signs of racial oppression) hops off, calling "New Winton!" and greets the postmistress.

— "Why, good morning, Miss Helen. Did you have a good Christmas?"
— "Don't be silly! In this dull place, how could ya?"
— "Yes, it is dull, isn't it. All aboard! Next stop, New Haven!"

Inside the post-telephone office (where we frequently return for New Winton gossip), the mood for the rest of the picture is announced as May Tripping (Marian Nixon) reads to Helen from a book:

— "So he said: 'Death, where is thy victory?' So he passed over it, and all the trumpets blazed for him on the other side."

May was married only a week when her husband Joe became paralyzed from a fall. His legs, he later tells Doc Bull, are "like two slabs of stone."

Individual solitude is relieved (or, as often, exacerbated) by George Bull (Will Rogers), who, always tired, continues his rounds from one patient to the next. His aged aunt sits at home reading murder mysteries and ignoring the telephone. She persists in calling him "Kenneth," though her son Kenneth has been dead fifty years. Such oblivion is denied Bull. He is a sad man, yet cannot resist Abraham-Lincoln-like witticisms or inviting contempt by calling himself "a cow doctor." He passes a night without sleep, as usual, delivering an Italian family's seventh baby, then watches another patient die. "I've seen a hundred people die," he says, in a gauche attempt to console, "and none of them seemed to mind it. They was all too sick to care." Some women begin arguing whether the dead girl was seventeen or eighteen. "Hey, wait a minute!" he interrupts irascibly, "It doesn't make any difference, now does it?" (a sentiment echoed in *The Grapes of Wrath*'s funeral scene).

Bull has as clear an attitude toward death as toward life, in contrast to New Winton's myriad gossipy hypocrites and most especially to his counterpart, the hypochondriac Larry Ward (Andy Devine), a strident Fordian fool summing up a *doctor's* afflictions: Larry even wakes up Bull to recount his nightmares.

Bull is not a Capraesque hero. On the contrary, he is a strong man, authoritative and confident. The whole town has been his patient for twenty years and he has a weary sense of its lack of gratitude. He unloads himself during his visits with the widow Janet Cardmaker (Vera Allen, whose theatrical poise suits her role). Stretched out on her couch by the fire, dreaming of sleeping a month, he states the picture's theme when he tells her, "I kinda relax when I get up here on these wind-swept hills—with *thee*. . . . You know, some old early settler had the thing about right when he said that most of life is a storm and without a harbor a man is lost." "And a woman?" "Oh, a woman don't need refuge like a man." "I wonder . . . ."

When that I was and a little tiny boy,
With hey, ho, the wind and the rain,

sing George and Janet, in spontaneous reflection over approaching old age (both are nearing fifty). Janet keeps a jog of apple cider for Bull, and it too becomes a metaphor. "Guess I'm getting old," he muses, "or maybe your cider was younger in those days."

In the town below there is nothing but vicious gossip about the two friends. One old lady whispers into another's ear, "*I'll* tell you what they're doing up there . . . ." and Ford cuts to George lying on the couch while Janet reads from *Alice's Adventures in Wonderland* about the cat disappearing and leaving its smile behind. (Thirty years later, in *Donovan's Reef*, Lewis Carroll verses are again exchanged as code for understanding.)

"Another dividend check for Mr. Banning," says Helen in the post office, just as Ford cuts to the magnate and his wife making their ceremonious entrance (last) into the church and their front pew, where Herbert Banning (Berton Churchill, who plays obnoxious magnates also in *Judge Priest*, *Four Men and a Prayer*, and *Stagecoach*) magisterially removes his overcoat. As the choir starts "Hark the Herald Angels Sing," Doc Bull rushes in late and adds his bright, unmodest tenor. Outside, a beautifully desolate snowy scene, he joins them standing at a family grave and quips, "What're you all gathered here for? What's amatter? Somebody get out?" Ford often depicts the rich nastily (and New Englanders especially so), whereas Bull is as likeable as can be. But the resentment Bull builds against himself by a hundred insignificant things is, despite his compassion, charisma, and self-sacrifice, not unmerited. A common occurrence in real life, this sort of interpersonal friction is a rare topic in movies. Occasionally oblivious to the effects he produces, Bull takes delight in irritating the Bannings. Their nice daughter Virginia (Rochelle Hudson*) fights with her mother, gets drunk, then nearly kills herself in her spiffy sports car. Winning her confidence, Bull learns she is pregnant by a boy her parents will not accept and has her phone him for a rendezvous. The timid temerity with which she tells him, "Of course I like you . . . I mean . . . I love you," is among Ford's more sensitive moments. The Bannings read of Virginia's marriage in the paper; Mrs. Banning rises, addresses the maid, "Mary, will you leave the room, please," then announces the horror: "Virginia has married a German! O the disgrace of it!" Echo the others, as the scene fades, "O the disgrace of it!"

They soon find a weapon against Bull. Despite his warnings, their profitable power plant's pollution has caused a typhoid epidemic, and they manipulate a town meeting to hold Bull, as health officer, responsible. Mrs. Banning, sweet with amiable gentility, rises to call the vote and, with only five dissents, Bull is fired as town physician.

He tells them off (anticipating Judge Priest's more diplomatic acknowledgment of everyone's sinfulness in *The Sun Shines Bright*), then spends the night by Joe Tripping's bed. Despite an expected diagnosis of permanent paralysis and advice that Joe be consigned to a nursing home, Bull has injected Joe with "a little serum I brewed up at home." It worked on a cow and it works on Joe, and Bull and Janet ride honking and shouting through town.

Bull marries Janet and they leave New Winton. As before, the train pulls in and the porter calls out, "New Winton! . . . Why, good morning, Miss Helen. Did you have a good Easter?" "In this dull place!?" He shows her the New York paper headlining Bull's "Miracle Cure." "Why, medical circles are agog!" As Bull and Janet board, May and Joe (walking now) watch sadly (and step forward, as watching characters will do during the finales of *The Quiet Man, A Minute's Wait,* and *The Long Gray Line*). Larry Ward boards too, with his new shotgun wife, and her brother swats him with a big stick, breaking (a frequent Ford gag) his hip flask. Thus cadential slapstick concludes and brightens a typically depressed but varied series of vignettes, and the train pulls off.

Doctor Bull's 1933 New Winton seems at least as much a portrait of a bygone age as *Judge Priest*'s 1890s Kentucky. It exemplifies a depressed sub-

---

*An ingenue in *Laugh and Get Rich* (1930), *She Done Him Wrong* (1933), *Les Miserables* (1935), Natalie Wood's mother in *Rebel Without a Cause* (1955)—but never so interesting as here.

ject vivified by Ford's pacing (each scene leisurely, but fifty scenes in seventy-six minutes), constant whiffs of humor, and detailed characterization (everyone plays to the hilt, as in *Donovan's Reef*'s Boston scenes). "*Doctor Bull* was a downbeat story," said Ford, "but Bill [Will Rogers] managed to get a lot of humor into it—and it became a hell of a good picture. It was one of Bill's favorites."[14] Rogers must have reminded Ford of Harry Carey. Congenial, relaxed, conspiratial with characters and audience, Rogers gives Bull a pudgy weariness dissimilar to his other roles with Ford. His Bull can even tell his aunt that he wouldn't know anything without her reading the papers and not have the line remind us of Rogers's famous vaudeville line ("All I know is what I read in the papers"). His Bull is so dependent on Janet, like a small child that bares its every moan; this sort of lovers' relationship, though reminiscent of *Flesh*'s, is rarely encountered in films, where love is either just about to bloom or drifting into memory. And in many ways Bull as a Fordian hero contains contradictions that earlier heroes had either to resolve or burst. In *Pilgrimage*, a hero (Hannah Jessop) is born; in *Air Mail*, the hero (Duke) is a crass superman; in *Judge Priest*, he (Rogers again) is perhaps the compleat Fordian hero. But in *Doctor Bull*, the hero, both glorying in his alienation and accepting his priestly role, ultimately flees his community, escaping rather than just walking away. Yet as the picture's prologue states,

— Doctor Bull brings his neighbors into the world and postpones
   their departure as long as possible. He prescribes common sense
   and accepts his small rewards gratefully. His patients call
   him Doc.

The Lost Patrol (1934). Ford's next movie, about eleven British soldiers stranded midst sand dunes and being picked off one by one by unseen Arabs, has little relation to the themes and characters whose development we have been tracing. And it may seem unattractive today. But in 1934, while Ford's most personal work was passing unnoticed or being dismissed as commercial yuk, *The Lost Patrol*'s gutsy "realism" aroused critical raves. The National Board of Review placed it in the year's Top Ten, *The New York Times* sixth, and an Oscar went to Max Steiner for his (turgid) score. Had Ford correctly estimated contemporary tastes, or was success a fluke? Or did he make it just for the fun of "a character study—you got to know the life story of each of the men"?[15]

The critics were attracted partly by its claustrophobic, mechanical staginess, a quality usually attributed to scenarist Dudley Nichols's influence on Ford: a small group of isolated people, theatrically revealing their character under stress, within classical unities of space and time—as in *Men Without Women*, *The Informer*, *The Hurricane*, *Stagecoach*, and *The Long Voyage Home*. Yet, in the case of *The Lost Patrol*, the novel, already containing these features, had been purchased by Ford prior to RKO's or Nichols's involvement (and had already been filmed by Victor McLaglen's brother

Cyril). And while the "isolated group under stress" formula had been exploited in the first Nichols-Ford, *Men Without Women* (1930, also a prestigious critical success), it had equally been used in the Wead-Ford *Air Mail*
(1932). Probably Ford engaged Nichols because *The Lost Patrol*, like their
Men Without Women, Seas Beneath, and *Born Reckless*, was a drama about
men in war, and Nichols had served in the navy during the war. Frank Baker
was similarly employed as an expert in military ordnance.

Ford's practice of preparing each character's biography, with tastes,
opinions, and eccentricities, and then slipping in such tidbits mid the principal drama, is first noticeable here (albeit the situation left little alternative), and again in subsequent Nichols scripts. But strangely it is in the domain of character that the movie fails. The biographies are blatantly
present, but interest-arousing details invariably get announced just before
the character gets killed. A young soldier, for one example, talks about
home and mother and the future, and in the next scene he is dead. The
result, dramatically, is zero, repetitiously; and it is all the contrary to *Men
Without Women*, where a character's life conditions his actions and is not
merely a footnote to his death, and where Nichols's O'Neill-like drama of
reactions had been able to reap results. The distinction is one of plot leading
characters as opposed to characters producing plot. Nothing happens in *The
Lost Patrol* beyond the encroachment of aloneness and insanity (personified
by a variation on the Fordian fool, a Boris Karloff character who, like a
Nichols character in *Men Without Women*, goes berserk, tries to kill everyone, and shouts, "Vengeance is mine, saith the Lord!"), and no sooner is
Victor McLaglen alone, finally, than he kills the Arabs and is rescued by a
second patrol. Yet only at this penultimate moment does McLaglen com-
mence to engage us.

The movie might be called a study in the lack of leadership. The patrol is
lost because a young lieutenant dies without confiding anything in his sergeant. A man is killed when McLaglen lets him climb an exposed palm tree.
The Arabs are able to sneak up, kill two sentries, and steal horses. Most of
our men eventually die because they panic and run into the desert. In short,
McLaglen, an excellent top soldier, lacks the foresight and leadership an
officer is supposed to have. McLaglen is just "one of the men." The men are
not of lower class, or at least do not act or talk as though they were. Instead
they behave as a relatively educated next-door neighbor might have behaved in bourgeois America 1934, and not at all like British privates in 1916.
Their truncated roles increase their anonymity, and thus render them into
fashionable populist heroes—another Nichols trait. Ford repeated this idea
in *December 7th* (1943) when the same voice, speaking from the grave, together with scenes of various parents at home, describes itself in turn as the
voice of seven different dead GIs.

Max Steiner's style of scoring, in which each emotion is mimicked in the
music ("Mickey Mousing"), was less in fashion in 1934 than limited music

from on-set sources. And *The Lost Patrol*, according to Steiner, was at first "not intended to have any music, but after [it] was finished the producer decided that, because of the long silent scenes, it was necessary to underscore the entire production."[16] Steiner's subsequent Oscar brought "Mickey Mousing" back into vogue and led Ford to collaborate more intimately with him for *The Informer.*

The Lost Patrol was filmed with some hardship in the Yuma Desert. Tempers would flare and violent fights were not infrequent. Wallace Ford is reputed to have chased a cook over many a sand dune when the latter refused to serve a blackman. A more typical Ford-set incident occurred during a scene when McLaglen machine-guns an Arab. McLaglen was drunk to oblivion at the time, as Frank Baker, playing the Arab, knew. Thus Baker was vitally concerned when the bullets—Ford *always* used live ammunition—started grazing his feet. Charging furiously on the blubbering McLaglen, Baker might well have killed him, had he not noticed the second machine gun, manned by a sober marksman, which Ford had placed behind McLaglen, without, of course, mentioning the fact to Baker.

The World Moves On (1934). His next picture was even more incidental to Ford's career: "really a lousy picture—I fought like hell against doing it."[17] Yet these scenes of a family's hundred-year history are at least as entertaining and far more interesting than Winfield Sheehan's creaky *Cavalcade*, the smash-hit it mimics expensively. Ford went beyond himself for every other scene, but the invention never coheres. Midst talky nothings, magic moments occur: the way Mary drops back her head faintly when Richard goes to war; the way water mounts over struggling men inside a submarine, filling the screen till all is black and still; a vivaciously stylized dance, a glittering Prussian wedding, a romantic ship scene, the parade of life outside windows. The family's avarice and pernicious irresponsibility contribute to all woes, but its members too are mindlessly determined. To contrast them and mock the war, Ford inserts Stepin Fetchit within a mad five-minute battle montage (far surpassing *Cavalcade*'s): slightly wounded midst trench cacophony, he squawks, "You mean . . . ? I can *go*?!"

***Judge Priest* (1934).** One of 1934's top grossing movies, *Judge Priest* is also one of Ford's finest and most convivial works. Its 1890 Kentucky town is treated with a leisurely pacing and relaxed entrancement with the subtleties of diction, bearing, and facial expression that place it in another age entirely from the chic sophistication of other good movies of 1932–34. *Judge Priest* today has not aged; a storyland of myth and symbol, it looks just as fresh and old-fashioned as it did half a century ago (though, alas, extant prints are poor!). Based, like *The Sun Shines Bright* (1953), on Irvin S. Cobb stories, *Judge Priest*, in Cobb's words heading the picture, seeks to evoke "familiar ghosts of my own boyhood" and "the tolerance of the day and the wisdom of that almost vanished generation," as typified by "one man *down yonder*" in a "reasonably fair likeness" called Judge Priest.*

Will Rogers combines a laid-back Harry-Carey-like charisma with rich vocal characterization of each of his lines to make Bill Priest into possibly the most personable character in Ford, and a prototypical Fordian hero. "First thing I learned in politics," he tells Reverend Brand, "was when to say 'ain't'." The patrician Priest, cannier and less irascible than Dr. Bull, embodies the Southerner's political craftiness; but his ambitions are community centered. Ford often punctuates the tickling flow of Priest's high humor by cutting back from a close-up before a punchline's last word. A gag's effect is thus dispersed amid the community rather than employed to illuminate Priest's "star" quality. For, as with Rogers's other roles for Ford, the Priest character's tender humanity seems the fruit of secretive melancholy and loneliness. For this reason, his meetings with others—and most of the movie is a series of "duets"—seem engagements met with resourceful

*Kentucky, 1890. Judge Priest's court's folksy informalities irk prosecutor Maydew (who is running for Priest's seat), but Priest goes fishing with Jeff, a young black charged with loitering. Nephew Rome returns from law school and Priest encourages romance with Ellie May despite Rome's mother's disapproval of the girl's unknown parentage. When blacksmith Bob Gillis gets into a fight defending Ellie May's honor, Rome gets his first case, but when Gillis refuses to introduce Ellie May's name into the trial, Rev. Brand reveals Gillis's past life as a condemned prisoner pardoned for war heroism and as father and secret provider for Ellie May. All join in a Memorial Day parade.

This production still is possibly all that remains of a controversial lynch-mob sequence removed from *Judge Priest* before release. Paul McAllister, Will Rogers, Charley Grapewin, Hy Meyer, Tom Brown.

tact and delicacy. We know his encouraging remark to Rome, that no one ought live alone, refers to himself (see still). And we understand his reply, that he'd not gone to live with Rome's mother because he didn't care for her cooking, for we have just watched his desire to be charming overcome distaste for her haughty meanness. Later, his going to talk to his wife beside her and their children's tombstones is in itself almost less significant than his eagerness to get there; the words on the gravestone, "Margaret Beckenridge Priest, April 24, 1871," suggest how long he has been coming to visit her. Priest he is by celibacy and by a consciously transitory attitude toward his life; and by the moral superiority of those who, claiming knowledge of higher good and right of higher judgment, invade others' privacy: note that Billy Priest, judge and minister, refuses to return Gillis's accusing gaze as he proceeds to violate him. Priest's purpose is the Fordian hero's usual task—to reunite a family (Gillis's)—but does a good purpose justify moral arrogance? For good or ill, such types frequent Ford's worlds, constituting a major theme; but whether their arrogance stems from duty appointed or duty assumed, Ford is always critically concerned about their moral humility—or lack thereof.

The richness in Priest's characterization is complemented in Ford's cameo portraits of the other townspeople. During the trial, there is a se-

"No one ought live alone." Priest dominates the frame as he advises his nephew Rome. The enclosing porch rail suggests Priest's celibate aloneness. Then, across the backyard, Ellie May, Rome's love, comes out onto her porch. (Her frame-within-the-frame is illuminated, so that the composition anticipates *Citizen Kane*'s shot of boy Kane frolicking in the snow outside a window while, foreground, his parents decide his future.) Off-camera right, sounds of a rival suitor's arrival counterpoint Ellie May's entrance, causing Priest to gaze in the opposite direction.

quence that ought to astound us in its virtuosity: Francis Ford, a juror, does one of his famous spittoon-ringing spits. /Maydew (Berton Churchill) orates. /The first witness against Gillis testifies. /The second bad witness. / The judge speaks. /Ellie May (Anita Louise) reacts, concerned. These six shots of six characters are not edited in a fragmentary way. As with a similar sequence in *Flesh* (see page 84), each shot—each with formally articulated beginning, middle, and end—constitutes an autonomous scene in itself. Each character, in doing his "turn" (to borrow a vaudeville term apt here), expands on a basic archetype by a half-dozen inventive variations. Ford's ingeniously simple cutting places the six shots in linelike blocks, and the movie's real subject becomes not just our concern at diabolic developments in the trial, but rather the contrasts and interreactions of character.

As with most good Fords, our sense of experiencing a people's culture and values powerfully transports us into Ford's storybook world. Today's jargon on racism, for example, is not adequate to describe the intimate interactions of whites and blacks in *Judge Priest*. Just as the singing of "Anchors Aweigh" in *Salute* (1929) defines an era, a class, and an ideology, so too here does Priest's joining the blacks in "Old Kentucky Home." The blacks (roly-poly Hattie McDaniel and sloe-eyed Stepin Fetchit among them) relate readily to racial types, but so too do Ford's whites, and no values of existential individuality suffer on that account (indeed, the values become more complex in individuals derived from types). Priest, in his mediative role, bridges racial barriers not only in song, but in assuming—without condescension—comparable diction and crooked-neck pose when palling with Fetchit. No doubt that Ford captures the spirit of a racist community— Priest uses Jeff to fetch croquet balls, blacks sit in gutters, are called "boy," and treated like pets—but Ford also suggests that seeing, as Priest does, the attractive aspects in censorable individuals and societies is more promotive of true tolerance than seeing only the censorable. (Uglier sides of racism, however, were more apparent in Ford's original cut, which included a lynching scene and an antilynching plea by Priest ["one of the most scorching things you ever heard," said Ford]. These were excised by the studio, to Ford's chagrin, for lynchings were frequent during the thirties, but Ford used similar scenes in *The Sun Shines Bright*, 1953.)

For charisma, Rogers has his equal in Henry B. Walthall:* "a personality that just leaped from the screen," said Ford, "one of the greatest actors of all

---

*Walthall played a famous role as Griffith's "Little Colonel" in the Civil War sequence in *The Birth of a Nation* (1915).

time."[18] Walthall's Ashby Brand seems alone to appreciate the effort and intelligence behind Priest's personality. We can catch a gleam of playful recognition in his eye at Priest's trial ploy—giving Brand chance to correct reference to the "war of rebellion" to "The War for the Southern Confederacy" and thus attach the jury's sympathies, which the preacher in a long monologue immediately warms by recalling the shared deprivations of the war's last months. Grizzled veterans nod tearfully in empathetic recollection. "As many of you know, I am a Virginian," he begins, and relates how he recruited life-prisoners from a chain gang to fight "for what we thought was right." Ford superimposes scenes during Brand's chronicle, but keeps Brand's face in a corner of the screen.* As the camera tracks along prisoners' chains, Brand tells how they became known as "The Battalion from Hell" and Priest (who has directed this whole affair) signals out the window. Jeff, sitting on the curb in Priest's raccoon coat, starts "Dixie" on his banjo; other blacks join in. Meanwhile Brand, spiritualized by a halo, holds the courtroom entranced. He tells how one of those ex-convicts rescued a wounded Union officer, how he rode out ahead to recapture a flag, how he stood alone with a ramrod to face a cavalry charge (we see it all), and how

* Ford used similar tricks in *Lightnin'* (1925).

this man lives now in this town "watching over his daughter, providing for her education, through me, all unknown to Ellie May." Cut to Ellie May for her reaction at discovering her father; then back to Brand, who stands: "Gentlemen, you know him today as Robert Gillis."

The pandemonium of communal conviviality mustered by Brand is comically set off by Francis Ford shouting, "Hooray for Jeff Davis, the Southern Confederacy, and Bob Gillis!!!" And congeniality is orchestrated to "Dixie" in the parade coda: the blacks strut happily into the camera, Gillis is embraced into the veterans' ranks, Francis Ford spits into Maydew's tophat, and *Quiet-Man*-like curtain calls for the principals conclude, rather as in *The Black Watch*, with passing memorial wreaths and the sound of voices— one of Ford's finest finales.

Of course, the Reverend Brand's testimony is irrelevant: it is never brought out that Gillis was defending Ellie May. A comparable irrelevance occurred in the film's opening trial: the question of Jeff's guilt for stealing chickens got lost midst heated debate over what *kind* of chickens Priest's cronies stole during the war, and the next scene showed Jeff going fishing with Priest. These two anomalies explain a third: Priest's lachrymose lament at having to step down as judge for Gillis's trial, which, so clearly is he prejudiced in Gillis's behalf, seems absurd to modern sensibilities. But in all three instances the point is "higher knowledge"—the irrelevance of "facts" in face of the relevance of character. Priest *knows* Gillis, knows the man's craftsmanship, just as he *knows* barber Flem Tally (Gillis's accuser), and knows Tally's lousy shaves. Such knowledge would not be prejudice, even in a judge, but would serve justice—justice that would indeed have miscarried without Brand's last-minute revelations. Facts without character are almost always delusory. And Judge Priest's town concurs: Gillis, having shown his character during the war, would certainly have acted properly in his dealings with Flem Tally; further justification would be superfluous.

Does it strike us as odd, this notion that character does not change? R. G.

Collingwood, a philosopher of history, lambastes this notion in Tacitus enlighteningly:

> Furneaux pointed out long ago [*The Annals of Tacitus* (Oxford, 1896), vol. i, p. 158] that when Tacitus describes the way in which the character of a man like Tiberius broke down beneath the strain of empire, he represents the process not as a change in the structure or conformation of a personality but as the revelation of features in it which had hitherto been hypocritically concealed. Why does Tacitus so misrepresent facts? . . . It is because the idea of development in a character, an idea so familiar to ourselves, is to him a metaphysical impossibility. A "character" is an agent, not an action; actions come and go, but the "characters" (as we call them), the agents from whom they proceed, are substances, and therefore eternal and unchanging. Features in the character of a Tiberius or a Nero which only appeared comparatively late in life must have been there all the time. A good man cannot become bad. A man who shows himself bad when old must have been equally bad when young, and his vices concealed by hypocrisy. As the Greeks put it, *archē andra deixei.* Power does not alter a man's character; it only shows what kind of man he already was.[19]

If change in Ford, in most movies, in Dickens and Balzac and Greek tragedy, is essentially a stripping bare of character always there in the first place, perhaps it is because in all of them concern to express ideal "truths" surpasses the temptation to record the shifting surfaces of reality. Collingwood again quotes Furneaux:

> [Tacitus's] professed purpose in writing is to hold up signal examples of political vice and virtue for posterity to execrate or to admire, and to teach his readers, even through a narrative which he fears may weary them by its monotonous horrors, that good citizens may live under bad rulers; and that it is not mere destiny or the chapter of accidents, but personal character and discretion, dignified moderation and reserve, that best guard a senator of rank unharmed though time of peril.[20]

Ford's central characters—people like Priest, Lincoln, Ethan Edwards, Ransom Stoddard, Dr. Cartwright—are infinitely more complex morally than either the foils surrounding them (Maydew, Ellie May) or the normal protagonists of Manichaean melodrama. And destiny plays its own separate but important role in Ford, for like Augustine he feels history as a surging passage through time and as governed by God, rather than as the eternal and senseless cycle of repetition perceived by the Ancients. Still, there is something of Tacitus in Ford. It is not that his characters do not stare into Sartrian voids of freedom: Judge Priest does so constantly. It is that freedom is meaningless save as means to fulfillment of their nature—which is not a meaningless message for a film made in the middle of the Great Depression, or for a film (*Sergeant Rutledge*, 1960) made in the middle of the black struggle for freedom.

The notion that character is more trustworthy than logic or statistics is, of course, an axiom of popular wisdom as prevalent today as in 1890. Yet we are, if anything, more aware of a corollary danger: character is hard to distinguish from feeling; and where, as in the mass, demagogic politics of today, character can be manipulated to market consumer goods, presidents, and wars, we may place even *less* trust in our feelings than we do in logic or statistics. We can trust neither ourselves nor the information given us. And our virtuous leaders employ the same tactics of manipulation as history's arch villains. Judge Priest, like young Mr. Lincoln and like Lieutenant Cantrell (*Sergeant Rutledge*), recognizes that theatrics will reveal intuited truth better than mere facts or logic: he *stages* Brand's testimony, accompanies it with Jeff playing "Dixie," and has in Brand (as we have in Henry B. Walthall) one of the age's greatest orators. In real life, we seek, when we can, to know someone thoroughly before crediting the feelings his character projects. Still, all human knowledge is ultimately built upon feeling, and it is art's task in the scheme of things not only to heighten our sensibilities but also to educate them, so that our consciousness is no longer easily corruptible. Movies like Judge Priest do not simply move and manipulate us; they compel a subtle and critical analysis of the interplay of feeling, character, and the real world.

   The Whole Town's Talking (1935). As medicine for the Depression, or even as homily, Ford's messages may appear excessively traditional. But the identical message transposed from the stable 1890s of *Judge Priest* into the corrupt 1930s of *The Whole Town's Talking* becomes the lava of rebellion.* Critics, however, have tended to overlook one as much as the other, for both belong to despised genres—*Judge Priest* to sentimental, folksy melodrama, *The Whole Town's Talking* to low-budget comedy. Jean Mitry has described the latter in terms that might never occur to an American:

> Of all John Ford's films, *The Whole Town's Talking* is the most dynamic, brilliant and funny. . . . Not a work of genius, no, but dazzling and surpassingly virtuosic. . . . Edward Robinson's performance in the double role of Jones and Mannion is not just a brilliant tour de force. Along with memorable creations by Wallace Beery, Raimu, McLaglen, Spencer Tracy, Michel Simon or Fresnay, it is one of the summits of film acting. . . . The film's density is achieved by the greatest amount of action in

---

*After eight years' punctuality, Jones is late for work and discovers he looks like "Killer" Mannion. At lunch he is arrested, with his secret love, Miss Clark. After confusion, the D.A. gives him a passport and his boss asks him to write on Mannion for the papers. But at home he finds Mannion, who declares he will use Jones's passport at night and dictates his life story himself. To get Jones out of the way, the D.A. sends him to prison; but Mannion goes instead, to rub out an informer, then escapes. He sends Jones on an errand to the bank and informs police Mannion is coming, but Jones, having forgotten something, misses the ambush. When Mannion's mob suggest killing Jones, Jones lets them kill Mannion, then overpowers them with a tommy gun, rescues his kidnapped aunt, Clark, and Seaver, and wins an award and Miss Clark.

the least amount of time. . . . The situations jostle each other in a bewildering rhythm, in a species of chaos which mixes logic and illogic, truth and improbableness and, as Alexandre Arnoux said, "the peak of the natural at the very heart of artifice." Rapid, alert, wonderfully cut and mounted, supercharged, taut like a spring, it is a work of total perfection in its genre.

It is a minor genre, to be sure, merely a dexterous and witty game. And yet it is a game of a virtuoso who transforms drama into comedy and, juggling the resemblance of two characters, masterfully renews a stock situation treated hundreds of times on stage and screen. Is it not possible that genius, in a creator, *also* consists in gathering together all the commonplaces, all the clichés, all the things most used up and worn out everywhere else, in mixing them all together, and producing from them something absolutely new, original and personal?[21]

Swiftness and dynamism are accentuated in Ford's cutting of Robert Riskin's rapid-fire, newspaper-style script. The cuts break into action, not only just as dialogue lines begin, but often with the characters spinning around to speak. Amid the rapid crosscutting between rooms and characters, the same composition is rarely repeated. We return to Miss Clark being questioned by Boyle and Howe four or five times, and each time the camera setup is different. But cuts are never without logic. Boyle and Howe muse about collecting the $25,000 reward for Mannion while waiting outside Jones's apartment; a change of angle comes with a change of topic and tone, when they begin to wonder why Jones is taking so long.

We know that Ford's people are almost always conditioned by their society and beliefs and that, unless they are heroes, they are seldom able to see themselves outside of their situation. Still, we must time and again be struck by Jones's failure to complain—of the tyranny of the office, of the police, of Mannion. Yet some free will and self-determination remain. When Jones is able to have Mannion killed, it is true the occasion is handed him and he is desperately motivated by the plight of his great romantic love, Miss Clark (Jean Arthur); nonetheless he takes the initiative. Earlier, too, finding himself suddenly in a position of power, he can cry out to his office mates, "So long, slaves!"

As *Steamboat Round the Bend* will be, *The Whole Town's Talking* is structured around confusions of reality vs. appearance. The theme is suggested by the confusing resemblance of Jones and Mannion—at one point even *Jones* screams out, "My name's not Jones, it's Mannion, I mean, it's not Jannion, it's Mones . . . "—and is echoed by mirrors, by newspaper headlines that distort truth, by the bank doorman who thinks "Mannion" forgot his gun, by the verbal pun of "Boyle . . . and Howe!" But more important echoes center around the twin antinomies of (1) whether the real "killer" is Mannion or the system, and of (2) Jones's dreams vs. the real world, drab, oppressive, tyrannical. Jones's pets summarize the dilemma—his cat Abelard and his canary Heloïse. The monk Peter Abelard (1079–1142) is legendary for his tragic love affair with the nun Heloïse: Jones and Clark. The lovers' correspondence contained seditious conspiracies against the prevailing realism and wisdom of the age, and Abelard was condemned as a heretic. Abelard opposed the notion that freedom was simply unquestioning acceptance of God's plan and our nature. He suspected that each person is unique, that appearances may be deceiving, that individuals are not necessarily subsumable under universal concepts. He held we must also employ our intellect freely, not just our hearts, in order to discern the true nature of things. These are the movie's themes.

Ford's opening lateral track of Jones's office and its forty desks does not have the crushing, antlike feel of King Vidor's *The Crowd* (1928), with its progression from city, to skyscraper, to a particular outside floor and window, and into a particular desk; but the sense of oppression is at least as palpable, while Jones is more palpable an individual than Vidor's everyman John (James Murray). The monklike Jones typifies the Fordian character whose "virtue" consists in myopic reconciliation with poverty and hopelessness. He is fundamentally unrebellious, polite even to mobsters. But his dreams are of faraway places, of Egypt, Shanghai, and of Miss Clark. He sings myopically, "Oh, the world owes me a living . . . ," but four different clock faces contradict him: he is late for work; duty calls. Even in prison, where Seaver brings him "the McIntyre account" to work on, Jones is obsessed by his menial duties. There is a bookkeeperish compulsive quality to Jones, evident in the careful absorption he gives to putting on his glasses, that is comparable to Mannion's willfulness and that eventually breaks out in Jones's violence too. But for the moment Jones seems a symbol of the exploited working class and an illustration, along with the forces of crime, government, and business, of aberration in "duty and tradition." Duty has become meaningless role-playing. But perhaps habitual duty alone keeps the system functioning. And if this is the case, are we not serving a system, rather than being served by it, and ought we not to destroy this system?

Gangster films often give covert expression to such ideas as these, just as westerns often proffer escape to virgin land. But in treating gangster-film conventions parodically, Ford does not undermine the conventions' purposes; he satirizes arrogance of power simultaneously. Police always arrive in masses of forty or fifty, and shove everyone around brutally. After terrorizing poor Jones, when his true identity is discovered the D.A. sneers, "You're free to go. Get out!" And Jones, meekly holding his hat, replies typically: "Oh, thank you, sir. Oh! gentlemen, I'm sorry I caused you all this trouble!" "That's alright," snaps the D.A., brusquely. The prison warden is similarly rude a few scenes later. Even boss J. G. Carpenter complains of being "dragged down here without a word of explanation." And when the police take over the bank, they roughly grab employees' coats and herd everyone down to the basement.

One would expect this litany of misanthropes to climax in Killer Mannion. But though much is told of his dastardly deeds, nothing is shown. His disposals of Slugs Martin and the prison chauffeur both occur off-camera.

Although never sympathetic, Mannion embodies typical gangster symbolism: on one hand he is the rebellious little man, the populist hero who delights in making fools of bigshots and seeing his name in print; on the other hand, he personifies the unbridled aggrandizement of the reputable powers—government, police, wealth. Jones at first reacts to him as to established order: with fear and without antipathy. He does not inform on him, he does not shoot him when he gets the chance ("You don't shoot somebody who's asleep"), he goes to the bank for him, and even comes back when he thinks he has lost the money for Mannion's "mother." (Virtue then brings its own reward, for had Jones not returned, what would have happened to Miss Clark, Aunt Agatha, Seaver, and the $25,000?)

The Mannion story, until the fateful moment when his crimes touch at Jones's heart, is slightly comical. The real evil, as Joseph August's brooding photography reminds us continually, is the system. The cruelest scenes and actual climax of misanthropy are those of the columns of hundreds of prisoners marching in a claustrophobic prison yard, all dressed alike, all in conformity—just like "free" people. Naturally, a guard complains to the warden that Slugs Martin (hiding there from Mannion, and not a prisoner) is giving them a lot of trouble: he refuses to wear the prison uniform! Pointedly, the guard's attitude does not differ from that of the Seavers, Hoyts, and Carpenters.

Miss Clark (the "canary") is the antithesis of all this. She does not care when she is fired. She even thinks it might do Jones good to get fired. Imagine such insouciance in the heart of the Depression, with twelve million unemployed! She counsels courage and perseverance in one's dreams. And when Jones, the romantic dreamer, grabs the machine gun and starts it spurting, he acts not only for Miss Clark, but also in rebellion against all the tyranny of his life. Then, they all go to Shanghai, Abelard and Heloïse, too.

Seven of Ford's pre-1935 talkies are cynical portraits of somber oppression and tight-fisted misanthropy. The Depression itself is never mentioned directly; but the wealthy and powerful are the villains, while the populist classes abet their own exploitation. *The Whole Town's Talking*, despite its witty *allegretto* pacing, closes this series of pictures. Only once again, twenty-three years later, will Ford venture a portrayal of contemporary American city life, in *The Last Hurrah*.* Why? In part, perhaps, because the grimness of the urban present encouraged him to turn, like Jones, to the past and to faraway places to continue, allegorically, his themes of social

---

*The Grapes of Wrath and *Tobacco Road* (1940–41) are contemporary Americana, but depressing as they are, their *rural* settings are less suffocating, and offer wider possibilities, than the city films. *When Willie Comes Marching Home* (1950) is small-town America, and though the action misses being contemporary by only six years, the point of view (on World War II) is retrospective rather than modern, albeit cynical and deterministic. *The Long Gray Line* (1955) takes only a critical peek at contemporary life. *Gideon's Day* (1958), a police tragicomedy with London as its locale, offers a contrast with *The Whole Town's Talking*.

interaction. But, more practically, stricter enforcement of the Production Code (i.e., industry self-censorship) made topical subjects tabu. Hollywood retreated to adaptations of the classics, family pictures, or anything uncontroversial. Upon *The Whole Town's Talking*, the Code imposed deletion of the kidnapping scene (we see Jones's aunt captive, but not her capture) and an on-screen prison murder (now more interestingly rendered by shadows). But, ironically, Ford, by treating a crime movie as comedy, finessed the Code's effective prohibition of the crime genre, in force for about a year, and the picture's box-office success inspired a general resuscitation of crime movies from several years' doldrums.[22]

The Established Rebel

With *Araner* to retire to, John Ford found it easier to accommodate to life as an establishment figure. Perhaps he found it too easy. He played occasional, high-strung games of golf and abusive games of bridge (and cheated at both); he got drunk periodically at home, caught hell from Mary, and then escaped down the back alley to seek solace in the parish priest; and he passed his afternoons usually naked in the Hollywood Athletic Club's steamroom. His drinking buddies there formed an inner social club, the "Young Men's Purity, Total Abstinence, and Snooker Pool Association" (the latter part soon changed to "Yachting Association"), whose members included Emmett Flynn, Liam O'Flaherty, Dudley Nichols, Tay Garnett, Wingate Smith, Preston Foster, Harry Wurtzel, Gene Markey, Merian Cooper, Johnny Weismuller, Frank Morgan, John Wayne, and Ward Bond. To spoof establishment pomposity, the club renamed itself "The Emerald Bay Yacht Club" and chose "Jews But No Dues" as a motto.* The members all had elaborate uniforms and titles. But they continued to meet in steamroom or bar.

Ford was frequently considered cruel in these years, and he seems to have encouraged his reputation for masticating actors and getting drunk.

---

*Dan Ford (p. 114) quotes the slogan this way. Andrew Sinclair (p. 56) quotes it as "No Jews and No Dues"—Ford's riposte to his exclusion as a gentile from Jewish yacht clubs. Scenarist Henry Ephron has claimed Ford was prejudiced, but the claim seems based on miscomprehension of Ford's temperament and bitterness over Ford's cavalier rewriting of Ephron's script. Ephron's evidence is (1) that Ford pronounced his friend Daniel Fuchs's name as though ending in a K sound and (2) that when Phoebe Ephron remarked on an apparent overabundance of churches in the French village set of *What Price Glory* (a Ford regular would know such a remark was courting trouble), Ford replied, "Don't you think there are a lot of synagogues in a Jewish village?" The Ephrons stalked off, mortally offended. Sinclair, however, quotes Leon Selditz that Ford was not at all anti-Semitic (p. 56). Ford, of course, had a good many Jewish friends and even spoke some Yiddish; he once resigned from a club when it blackballed a Jewish army officer, and he donated a menorah to a Temple through his friend Jack Fier. His agent Harry Wurtzel was Jewish, and was something of a friend as well, having looked after Ford's family during the war. Nonetheless, Ford's nickname for Wurtzel was "Herschel," and in their correspondence he typically would advise him to hire a "smart hebe lawyer." (Ephron's allegations are in his *We Thought We Could Do Anything* [New York: Norton, 1977], pp. 117–20.)

The Emerald Bay Yacht Club, 1938, on board the *Araner*. Front row at right, John Ford and Preston Foster (?). Second row at left, John Wayne. Back row, center and right, Ward Bond and George Cleveland.

Philip Dunne contends that "Jack's courtesy to any individual was always in inverse proportion to his affection. I knew Jack liked me, because in all the years I knew him intimately he never said a polite word to me, not one."[23]

His relations with women, in contrast, could bring out a markedly different, kinder person in him. When he made *Mary of Scotland* his attraction toward Katharine Hepburn was immediate, and was reciprocated. On the first day of shooting, he found her seated in his chair mimicking him with a clay pipe and a hat pulled over her eyes—and, to her frustration, he typically ignored the gag. But her brassy ways eventually got to him. "You're a hell of a fine girl," he told her. "If you'd just learn to shut up and knuckle under you'd probably make somebody a nice wife."[24] She did not, of course, shut up. And when she found fault with Ford's lack of interest in her tower scene with Fredric March—its long expository speech for Queen Mary was the sort of thing Ford hated in scripts—he yelled for McNulty, told him to give Hepburn the megaphone and script, and walked out. She directed the

scene herself—for her first and only time—and it is perhaps the most moving scene in the film.[25] What fascinated her in Ford was his peculiar combination of qualities—"enormously rough, terribly arrogant, enormously tender . . . never smug, never phoney, and enormously, truly sensitive. . . . Spencer and Sean [Tracy and Ford] were very different, but they were similar in being able to be devastated by the world."[26] For his part, Ford found a kind of gumption in her he rarely met in women. Once, playing golf, she so irked him by insisting he shoot a three-foot putt that he actually missed it, and—his anger mounting—the follow-up, and the next shot as well! Enraged, he hurled his club fifty feet across the course. Katie was unintimidated. "I'd use an overlapping grip to get those distances,"[27] she teased.*
Weekends they sailed the *Araner*, and, when their picture was finished, Sean and Katie went east together to New York and to the Hepburn home in Connecticut, where they spent a month.[28]

Even before *Mary of Scotland*, John had felt dissatisfied in his marriage; now, during his six months with Katie, he probably felt happier with a woman than he ever had. Dan Ford has theorized that they were both "opinionated, pigheaded, and difficult to live with. John's masculine ego would never tolerate Kate's independence, and Kate instinctively knew that John Ford's house had to be a cold and lonely place for a woman. John was better off married to someone who had a stabilizing effect on him, a woman who could tolerate his energies and absences and could make him a home. Deep down, he knew he was better off with Mary."[29] But rather than such inordinate and unlikely pessimism, the real obstacles seem to have been John's children and, when all was said and done, his commitment to Mary, whatever the shortcomings of their marriage. In June 1936, Sean and Katie parted, and she, perhaps to distance herself, embarked on a very long national tour with the play *Jane Eyre*. In a letter the following April, she wrote, "Oh Sean, it will be heavenly to see you again—if I may—and if I may not I can drive by Odin St. in an open Ford and think a thousand things. In my mind and heart your place is everlasting."[30]

Their friendship endured until Ford's death. They avoided the closeness of filming together, although there was talk of her doing a picture with him in Ireland during the fifties and illness prevented her appearing in *7 Women*. It was she who persuaded Spencer Tracy to make *The Last Hurrah* with Ford; there had been some stubborn quarrel between the two men dating back to the early thirties.

Ford's father had died, quite unexpectedly and quickly, in June 1936, three years after his mother. He had been sending them $1,000 per month since the mid-1920s. Years later, he related an episode about his mother that had always interested him, as he said:

*Recollecting this incident in 1973, Ford commented to Hepburn, "I was mad at you for a week after that!" But she retorted, "I don't remember you ever being mad at me."

Ford and old woman who may be his mother (who died in 1933).

One of the members of one of our leading families went to Harvard and got a medical degree. He married a girl from Radcliffe. This girl was hooked on planned parenthood. She had a big tea at which she had all the leading doctors and expounded her plan. She said the population of Portland was too great and one of my closest friends—she wanted to know where she could go to, you know, with her theories—suggested that she go to 23 Sheridan Street, which was where we lived.

So she arrived and the ladies were there, Mrs. Mahoney, Mrs. Feeney, Mrs. Myers, etc., they were all there in bombazine in the parlor. They were very polite to this Yankee lady visiting from uptown, and she started talking and asked how many children they had and my mother said she had thirteen and this lady was horrified. "Much too many, Mrs. Feeney!" she said. "All the children can't be normal, they all can't get the proper upbringing!" My mother said, "All the children are normal," and she turned to my cousin and said in Irish, " ——." My cousin says, "Oh, yes, they are all normal except one—the youngest one, Johnny."

The lady says, "Well, you can't expect thirteen normal children. Where is Johnny now?" My mother says, "Oh, he's in a home." "Well, you see, that must be a terrific expense for you to support him in a home." "Oh," she said, "I don't support him." She says, "Well, where does he live? Where is the home?" My mother says, "Hollywood, California." "Hollywood? Why is it so far away?" "Well," she says, "I don't know, he's married, has children." "You say he has a home?" "Oh, yes he has a home—it's a very big, nice home." "Well," the lady says, "what is his work, what does he do for a living?" "Ah," my mother says, "he doesn't work at all. When he was growing up all he did was play football and read books. Johnny doesn't work at all." "He doesn't work?" "No, he just sits in a chair and yells at actors." "Oh! He's a movie director?" "Yes." "Oh."

"Now," my mother says, "tell me about yourself, darlin'. How many children do you have?" "I don't have any." "Well, that's too bad. How long have you been married?" "Fourteen months." "Ah, that's a shame. What's the matter? You better send your husband to see a doctor." She says, "My husband is a doctor." "What's the matter, can't he get his tallywhacker up?"

She arose in horror, and said, "I've never been so insulted in my life!" and she charged out of there. Mrs. Mahoney had nine, Mrs. Myers had eight, and my mother had thirteen—they were all past the age of child bearing.[31]

Meanwhile, Johnny was tolerating the new Hollywood, where it was becoming increasingly difficult for even a John Ford to do things his own way. He granted a rare interview, in order to publicize his dissatisfaction:

We're in a commercial *cul de sac*. We have time schedules, we are ordered to direct a certain story in a certain way because that's what the middle-west wants and after all the middle-west has the money. But the profession on the whole is progressing steadily. . . . Eventually motion pictures will all be in color, because it's a success and because it's a natural medium. And we'll go out to a Maine fishing port or to an Iowa hill and employ ordinary American citizens we find living and working there, and we'll plan a little story, and we'll photograph the scene and the people. That's all pictures should do anyway, and it'll be enough.[32]

It was fine to dream, but the movies Ford was actually making at the time were more studio-bound and artificial looking than ever. The era of the assembly line had come; directorial control was at a low point. Even Fox, Ford's bastion, had been invaded by a Napoleonic tycoon in boots and riding crop, Darryl F. Zanuck, whose new fangled Twentieth Century Productions had absorbed the venerable but ailing Fox Film Company in August 1935. And the producer system was becoming all-powerful; it was another means whereby studio bosses hoped to control directors who, until then, had enjoyed comparative freedom.

Some directors succumbed to the inevitable; others, like Maurice Tourneur, packed their bags and went home; a few, like Ford, connived to fight back. On *The Informer,* Ford introduced Cliff Reid to his troupe. Reid had collapsed from sunstroke during *The Lost Patrol,* his absence had pleased Ford, and he had asked for him again. "This," he said, gently turning Reid's head to a profile, "is an associate producer. Take a good look at him, because you will not see him again till the picture's finished." (Reid supposedly did show up again, on the last day of shooting, to congratulate Ford on the rushes as the latter sat contemplatively chewing a handkerchief. So Ford spent $25,000 reshooting the scenes Reid liked.[33])

Darryl Zanuck received a similar introduction on *Wee Willie Winkie,* except that this time Ford ordered the studio cop to keep Zanuck off the set. When, later, Zanuck complained Ford was behind schedule,[34] he tore out a bunch of pages from the script: "Now we're all caught up." And he never did shoot those pages. Sam Goldwyn once came on set to suggest, timidly, that Ford add some close-ups; Ford belted him thrice in demonstration of where he would crop close-ups when and if he, Ford, felt like taking them. "Oh, well," said Goldwyn, "at least I put the idea into his head." On another occasion when Goldwyn came on the set "just to watch you work," Ford called an immediate tea break, explaining that it would be very rude for him to go on working while his employer was there. Then, a few days later he sauntered casually into Goldwyn's office and sat down. "Can I help you, John?" asked Goldwyn. "Oh, I don't want anything," said Ford. Goldwyn continued going through his mail, time passed, and finally, knowing Ford was due on set, he asked him what he was doing there. "Oh, nothing, Sam. I just wanted to watch you work."[35]

Because Ford and Dudley Nichols had collaborated on two unusual, arty films at RKO — *The Lost Patrol* and *The Informer* — the theory grew that the RKO Ford was the *real* Ford, whereas the Fox Ford merely drew paychecks. But the follow-up Ford-Nichols RKO films — *The Plough and the Stars* and *Mary of Scotland* — were considered flops, and this was taken as evidence that Ford needed studio guidance. Actually, *Mary* did well commercially, but the quality of both pictures suffered from the most disastrous studio interference Ford ever endured. Contrariwise, his folksy Foxes (the Will Rogers movies among them) were smash hits, but critics never dreamed of taking them seriously. And even though Ford often did not initiate his Fox projects, they were more personal, had greater integrity, and suffered less supervisory meddling than the supposedly "independent" projects at RKO.

A legend grew, too: that Ford, to prevent others reediting his work, would only shoot the precise footage he needed. This was almost true. Many directors shot fifteen or twenty times more footage than ended up in the picture, whereas Ford's ratio was about 2½:1.[36] Yet RKO did reedit *Mary of Scotland,* and could and did take themselves the close-ups Ford avoided. Meanwhile at Fox, Darryl Zanuck outraged Ford by streamlining his movies' pace, but of all the big producers Zanuck was the most sensitive. Moreover, he was a superb editor, and did not interfere until after Ford had assembled his own first cut.

Yet Ford probably won more battles than most directors. "He was a man no one wanted to invoke the wrath of," said his researcher, Katherine Clifton.[37] "They were *very* scared of [him at RKO]," said Hepburn.[38] "John was a terrifying fellow," said Nunnally Johnson.[39] But it never occurred to Zanuck to be afraid of anyone working for him. When Ford failed to implement an order that Warner Baxter drop his phony Southern drawl during *The Prisoner of Shark Island* (actually, Ford was quite frustrated by Baxter), Zanuck stormed onto the set, and Ford immediately threatened to quit. Zanuck screamed: "Are you *threatening me*? Don't you threaten to quit. *I* throw people off sets!" Ford shut up. And a few days later, Nunnally Johnson, who had witnessed the scene, overheard someone ask Ford how he and Zanuck were getting along.

"'Oh,' said Ford, very casually, 'Darryl and I had a little talk, and after that there was no more trouble.'"

"A couple of seconds later Ford turned around and he noticed me sitting there, for the first time. 'That's right, isn't it, Nunnally?' he asked, finally."

"I just nodded," said Johnson.[40]

Another person Ford never could intimidate was John Carradine. The actor was terribly absent-minded and was forever messing things up. Few things made Ford more furious; over and over he would fly into a rage, and go on and on calling Carradine a god-damned stupid s.o.b. and every name he could think of. It did no good. Carradine would watch him with an indulgent smile and when Ford had finished would come over, pat him on the shoulder, and say, "You're o.k., John," and walk away. And Ford would be almost sputtering, because there was no way he could get under Carradine's skin.[41]

3 Second Period (1935–1947):
The Age of Idealism

"Who am I? What kind of a person am I to be?" These are questions posed constantly by Ford's people, as they search for, or grasp at, concepts of virtue and purpose in life. Cheyenne Harry, in *Straight Shooting,* found answers in love, and in himself. Later characters find their foundations in family, tradition, duty, occupation, or name.

Judge Priest recognizes virtue by the individual, and sees it manifested by how well a person performs his work: a good man is a good man. But in *The Prisoner of Shark Island,* Dr. Mudd defends himself by his occupation, not by his selfhood. A momentous change has occurred. *Judge Priest* is the last film in which it is enough for a person to do a good job at being himself. Henceforth, in an era of disintegration and chaotic flux, names or appearances are constantly confused with essence, as in *The Whole Town's Talking* and *Steamboat Round the Bend.* Accordingly, traditional values become uncertain and new ethical values must constantly be discovered. The Joads in *The Grapes of Wrath* search blindly for such new values—and Tom thinks finally he has found them in revolution, while his mother, like Huw in *How Green Was My Valley,* holds to the suicidal suppositions of old. For blind adherence to occupational duty, as in *The Hurricane,* breeds ruin. Young

Mr. Lincoln, like Priest, knows truth by knowing the person; and he attempts to redefine encrusted concepts like Law. But to convince the crowd he has to resort to tricks.

The idealism of the Depression decade found new certitude in the valorous struggles of World War II. Ideas seemed brighter and trustier—albeit distant—beacons in the postwar phase, as well. And by 1948, when Ford's third period begins, man has become the servant of myth, at first as a sort of partner, but soon as virtually a puppet.

EXOTICA (1935–1938)

The Informer	5.1.35	RKO Radio
Steamboat Round the Bend	9.6.35	Fox–20th Century–Fox
The Prisoner of Shark Island	2.12.36	20th Century–Fox
Mary of Scotland	7.24.36	RKO Radio
The Plough and the Stars	12.26.36	RKO Radio
Wee Willie Winkie	7.30.37	20th Century–Fox
The Hurricane	12.24.37	Goldwyn-United Artists
Four Men and a Prayer	4.29.38	20th Century–Fox
Submarine Patrol	11.25.38	20th Century–Fox

In mid-1934, as control of the motion picture industry became consolidated in the hands of outside financial interests, censorship, moral and political, was effectively imposed. And in August 1935, as Twentieth Century absorbed Fox Film, a politically more conservative administration took over that firm. Although the Depression had lost little of its vehemence, Hollywood films lost most of the acerbic social criticism. Seven of Ford's recent pictures had assumed antiestablishment views toward contemporary America, but the next twelve retreat into the past, into fantasy, introspection, and allegory, into historical romances set in Scotland, Ireland, India, and Samoa, or during our own Civil War or riverboat eras. This is a period of transition, of renewed, starker, single-mood expressionism, of an operatic, symbolic, and literary style.

Characters are introverted, egocentric, and obsessed with duty, because questions of identity become all-important when society drops out from an individual (Gypo, Duke, Mudd, Mary, DeLaage) and because people not only fail in duty, duty now begins to fail people. Duty and instinct are sometimes identical, sometimes in conflict. Duty is often wrapped up with ideologically governing myths, but these myths (midst the political and economic traumas of the thirties) are increasingly inadequate for human needs; they have become ossified, ripe for revolution, or else violent quarrels arise as to their meanings (totems in *Steamboat*, justice in *Shark Island*, priorities in *Plough*, queenhood in *Mary*, law in *Hurricane*). Whereas the fantasy-reality of social order tended to be stable (if sterile or noxious) in the previous period, fantasy now takes over, isolating individuals beyond hope of reintegration with real values. The hero no longer rises above the herd via alienation, but by primeval instinct stubbornly persisted in, without choice.

There is much stylistic diversity among these movies, but most of them are flawed and uneven, with only a single masterpiece, *Steamboat Round the Bend.*

The Informer (1935). Theodore Huff, writing some thirty-five years ago, summed up prevailing critical opinion on *The Informer*: "Nearly every list of 'ten best pictures of all time' includes it. Many consider it the greatest talking picture ever made in America. It is as much a landmark in the history of the sound film as *The Birth of a Nation* is in the silent era."[1] Indeed, *The Informer* had been inundated with awards,* Ford had been acclaimed the high priest of native cinema art, and still today he seems associated more with this than with any other of his films.

But in 1950, Ford told Lindsay Anderson, "I don't think [it's] one of my best. It's full of tricks. No, I think that comes a long way down the list."[2] He reiterated these feelings to students at UCLA in 1964[3] and again to Peter Bogdanovich, adding, "It lacks humor— which is my forte. . . . But I enjoyed making it."[4]

Ford had enjoyed the photography, Joseph August's radiant *Sunrise*-like tonalities; but he had subsequently come to realize that his real art lay in greater variety in mood and style. And today the very qualities that won *The Informer* its place as an official film classic seem even antithetical to Ford's virtues. Its single sustained mood, its heavy shadows and muffled sounds, its pedantic, heavy, slow tempo in acting and cutting, its "painstaking explicitness of a silent film grimly determined to tell its story without the aid of titles—an impression strengthened by Max Steiner's blatant, imitative music"[5] —all these qualities delighted thirties critics, most of whom failed to recall the waves of murky expressionism of the twenties or thirties. For them, *The Informer* stood out as new, different, and artistic, midst Hollywood's assembly-line product.

---

*Oscars: best direction, screenplay (Nichols); actor (McLaglen); score (Steiner); nomination for best picture, best editing. New York Film Critics awards: best picture, best direction. Belgian Crown: Chevalier Order of the Crown of Belgium (Ford); the Belgian Prix du Roi (Ford). L'Académie française: Officier de l'Académie française (Steiner). King of Belgium: bronze medal. International Artistic Motion Picture Exhibition (Venice): cup (Nichols). National Board of Review: best picture. Foreign Press Society of Holland: certificate of honor (Ford, McLaglen). Film Daily Poll: third best. Cinema Jumpo-sha (Japan): among eight best foreign films of the year. Daily Variety Poll rating (by 200 industry figures, 1950): fourth- best film of the first half-century of cinema. (List compiled by James L. Wilkinson), "An Introduction to the Career and Films of John Ford," unpublished M.A. thesis, University of California, Los Angeles, August, 1960.)

Dudley Nichols says he and Ford undertook the picture as "a deliberate and devoted stylistic experiment"[6]—though this explanation is too ingenuous to account for the motives of John Ford, to whom the "experiment" must have seemed pretty derivative, after eight years of conscious imitation of Germanic expressionism. He had met the Irish Marxist writer Liam O'Flaherty in Hollywood* and taken an option on his novel early in 1933, then had had the project rejected as uncommercial by almost every studio in town, until Merian Cooper at RKO decided, October 1934, that it might prove prestigious. Nearly every detail of production was dictated by Ford himself—including the script for which Nichols won an Oscar. Even more than usually, Ford used Nichols as a foil, critic, and sounding board in an exhausting process of countless rewrites during which maximum terseness was obtained. The browbeaten Nichols vowed never to work with Ford again.[7]

Perhaps Ford in 1935 wanted to do something flamingly extreme. Many of his pictures had been fast moving, rambling, variegated in mood and tempo, and quite popular. But it was only when he took on pretentious situation dramas, virtual theater pieces in their literary imagery, that he attracted critical attention for artistry: *Men Without Women, Arrowsmith, The Lost Patrol.* It seems incredible today that anyone could have enjoyed *The Informer* more than Ford's other 1935 films, *The Whole Town's Talking* and *Steamboat Round the Bend,* and, in fact, *The Informer* did earn much less, barely paying its $215,000 cost. (Yet Ford's personal dedication to it was certainly intense; Dan Ford tells us John was so distraught by its negative reception by its first preview audience that he vomited.)

And it was also precisely what tastemakers thought a film ought to be, and which they were evidently incapable of noticing unless bludgeoned. How else can we account for the fact that, seven years and more into the sound era, critics were raving over the use of the blind man's stick's "tap-tap"? Or that they were charmed by that reward poster for Frankie McPhillip,** which manages to blow against the foot of every Irishman in Dublin, and, as if that were not enough, keeps miraculously appearing every time Gypo looks at a

---

*The two became drinking buddies. Some years later they met in Paris and passed a night in a bar. O'Flaherty, taking no chances, had his own whiskey—Irish—with him in a suitcase, and it was not until 9 A.M. that John got back to his hotel. Alas, he then had to be carried from his bath to a hospital.

**The story: Dublin, one night during the Sinn Fein rebellion, 1922: Gypo Nolan (Victor McLaglen), cashiered from the IRA for failing to carry out an execution and thus left alone and destitute, betrays his friend Frankie McPhillip to the British for £20, for passage money to America for himself and a streetwalker. To shield himself, he accuses another, then nightmarishly carouses away the money. He breaks down before a rebel court, is sentenced to die, but escapes. The streetwalker unwittingly betrays him and, pursued and wounded, he dies in church begging Frankie's mother to forgive him.

We do not know if Ford was familiar with the 1929 English version of *The Informer,* less artily directed by Arthur Robison, and not distributed in the U. S. Ford's version was banned in Peru, because "it showed rebellion against authority."

brick wall. The same critics who raved over Ford's "innovative" use of subjectivity (i.e., the materializing poster; the "tap-tap" representing Gypo's conscience; Frankie's voice in Gypo's mind; the point-of-view camera techniques) failed and would fail to note subtler and more resonant subjectivity in *Pilgrimage*, *The Black Watch*, *Salute*, or *How Green Was My Valley*.[8]

Critical enthusiasm for Max Steiner's score is almost as bizarre. Steiner, going against fashion, which had favored on-screen music over background scoring, championed the through-composed movie in which music illustrated every action or object (e.g., Gypo's tinkling coins, or beer gurgling in a man's throat) and expanded a character's slightest emotion. Working from the completed, edited movie, Steiner would measure it and make up elaborate cue sheets detailing each action. From this he wrote his expanded musical commentary, or, as Oscar Levant termed it, his "Mickey Mousing." Perhaps Steiner's unwillingness to trust pictures to express themselves was (and is) justified by audience responses, yet he nullifies music's ability to counterpoint, and underlines *The Informer*'s pedantic heaviness.

Critics approved of Gypo Nolan, because in Victor McLaglen's performance he was a hulking stupid beast of a man, wandering in a friendless, depressed foggy night, and thus representative of the proletarian Everyman whom liberal critics felt Hollywood neglected. In fact, Ford all but eliminated O'Flaherty's protests against capitalist exploitation and British imperialism, reducing them to a generalized situation. And it seems strange that (considering only Ford and leaving aside hundreds of similar examples) the profounder and subtler social probings of the lower classes in pictures like *The Whole Town's Talking*, *Pilgrimage*, *Doctor Bull*, and *Flesh* were dismissed as "potboilers," while Gypo's simplistic and endlessly repetitious blusterings were hailed as evidence of a new social outlook.

Lindsay Anderson points out that McLaglen's performance seems "neo-realist in its suggestion of actual behaviors," and is thus at odds with the rigid formalism of the production. Of course, this is typical of Ford, whether with Will Rogers, Anne Bancroft, or Francis Ford. And his methods with McLaglen support appearances. He did everything possible to keep the actor confused: mocking him, lambasting him publicly, getting him plastered all night, then surprising him with dawn summonses to work, changing the script at the last moment, having people slip McLaglen Irish whiskey just before asking him to run through new lines. "I just want to get the timing, people have to leave; if you miss a line, just keep going," Ford would say, then shoot McLaglen's fumbling first take without the actor knowing it.[9] The sadism won McLaglen an Oscar, and Ford spent thirty-five years denying his tactics. But such is the public's conception of great acting that no one but Ford seems to have regarded the truth as insulting to McLaglen. And there is, perhaps, a connection between this and the Englishman John Baxter's remark that Ford's "most expressive symbol [of "Irishness"] is the character of Victor McLaglen, a personification of noisy, violent, drunken but loveable Ireland."[10] No one would cite Stepin Fetchit as the most expressive symbol of Negro culture or even Willis Bouchey of Wasp culture. Yet somehow out of all Ford's Irish stock company (Wayne, Bond, O'Hara, Shields, Fitzgerald, Francis Ford, MacDonald, Pennick, Malone . . .), it is the satiric buffoon character one finds identified as symbolic of the Irish. In fact, one wonders at the intelligentsia of the thirties, who could view Gypo as a model of the common man, rather than as an insult to humanity.

No character in *The Informer* is developed beyond the initial definition of his or her simplistic function within the gears and cogs of the mechanistic scenario. Instead, simple little ideas are pompously drawn out. In anguish, we watch an IRA man whimper in fright that he might draw the straw assigning the job of executing Gypo; of course he gets it, and three more chances to exhibit his sweaty whimper when Gypo escapes. This observation aside, neatly contrasted to the professional shooting by another IRA man, nothing whatsoever is told us regarding anything else in his life. This is typical. Commandant Dan Gallagher (Preston Foster) loves Mary and loves his IRA duty. This we learn, and nothing else, some fourteen times. And Mary loves Dan, loved her dead brother, and wants people to stop killing each other. That's Mary. (Ford repeats this winning formula with Foster and Stanwyck in *The Plough and the Stars*.) Ford does nothing to broaden his characters, or to humanize them with little snippets of spontaneity. Types they are born, and types they die.

The Informer takes extreme approaches to the themes and style Ford had been developing. Its society is devoid of heroes; Gypo indeed is the inverse of a Fordian hero. He fails in duty, destroys a family, is utterly determined by environment. Money is merely the proximate cause of his downfall; his true problem (like that of Depression America) is moral, not financial, poverty. Gypo, wholly externalized, lacks selfhood. Once ostracized by the community that defines him, he is prey to every attraction equally, whether vengeance, patriotism, drink, or comradeship. And, with guilt over murdering his friend, Gypo's existence becomes intolerable. He never makes choices. As instinctual as anything else is his dying plea for forgiveness; if this redeems Gypo socially, it scarcely redeems him morally. But social pardon suffices for Gypo. This mechanistic creature symbolizes the inadequateness of his society's sustaining myths—Ford frequently finds spinelessness characteristic of enslaved races, and simultaneously cause and effect of subjugation. But if Gypo is too vacuous to interest us in himself, lack of external reference similarly depletes his interest as mirror of his society: in contrast to the documentary-like detailing of social texture in previous movies, Dublin 1922 is a subjective fantasy, a mood far more than a place, an echo, like the sets of *Caligari*, of Gypo's gloom. Such interiorization marks all Ford movies, particularly those of the next three years, but, thankfully, never so limitingly again; nor are we again asked to participate in the subjectivity of such a troglodytic bore.

Steamboat Round the Bend (1935). In the premises of its plot, *Steamboat* resembles *The Informer.* Both Gypo and Dr. John (Will Rogers)* dwell in ideologically inadequate communities wherein reality and fantasy have merged, moral choices are few, and duty and instinct often conflict. And both Gypo and Dr. John seek solutions for initial failures, the one wandering around Dublin, the other wandering up and down the Mississippi River.

Beyond these premises, the two pictures diverge. That which in *The Informer* is definite becomes transmutable in *Steamboat*; surface denotes essence in one, but in the other, although densely layered, seems merely accidental to reality; one picture is pedantic and gloomy, the other poetic and mercurial.

A gentle morality fable, *Steamboat Round the Bend* reflects the American cinema at its most affable, the age of 1935 in its isolation, and, ever so delicately, the unspoken horrors of rural Southern life. The movie seems inspired by showboat melodrama: the folksy exoticism, the purposefully broad, "showboat" acting (more modulated than in Ford's "city" pictures), the easygoing romanticism, the less ostentatious (though equally inventive) visual technique. Is there anything lovelier or more careless than the way Fleety Belle, her first time at the wheel, yanks the whistle and joyfully calls, "Steamboat round the bend!!"?

Like *Pilgrimage, Dr. Bull,* and *The Whole Town's Talking, Steamboat* ravels itself around change in a static society populated by characters who are sometimes more and sometimes less than they appear to be. The opening screen legend suggests its anywhereness: "Time—The Early 90's, Place— The Mississippi River." Social contradictions are more pronounced than in *Judge Priest*: this is a regimented society where blacks are let out of their segregation cages for Fleety Belle's wedding, and where the train-station door says "Whites"; but it is also a fluid society (like *Straight Shooting*'s or like Vidor's all-black Southern society in *Hallelujah*) in which the principal characters change their occupations and social class every few minutes.

By today's standards, these characters are incredibly open; their simplicity—or rather, their insouciance in venting contradictions— is a major theme. In the very first episode, the New Moses (Berton Churchill, in

---

*Dr. John Pearly sells a cure-all, "Pocahontas Remedy," on his Mississippi steamboat, in the 1890s. Nephew Duke (John McGuire) accidentally kills a man to defend swampgirl Fleety Belle (Anne Shirley—twenties child-star under name Dawn O'Day, later in *Stella Dallas*, etc.), is sentenced to hang, and John starts a wax museum to finance an appeal, which fails. Fleety Belle and Duke marry in jail. She and John hunt the New Moses, who can clear Duke, but encounter a riverboat race, and Capt. Ely (Irvin S. Cobb—*Judge Priest* author, friend and rival of Will Rogers, with whom he ad-libs) taunts John not to renege on an old wager (both boats to winner). As they race, they lasso Moses aboard, burn wax figures and "medicine" for fuel, and win just in time to avert Duke's hanging. (In 1928 Ford was to have made *Captain Lash*, in which a Mississippi riverboat race climaxes when one boat explodes. Victor McLaglen was to star, but title and star were transferred to a wholly different subject ["Black Gang"] and directed by John Blystone.)

bedsheet, beard, and top hat), haranguing Demon Rum, shouts, "A sinner from hell!" and everyone stares at poor drunken Efe (a Francis Ford child-of-nature*), innocently holding his bottle. Efe looks round, shakes his head confessingly, offers his bottle in vain to all, and, as the New Moses utters the pledge, adds, "Me too!" and allows a ribbon to be pinned to his chest. But at the other end of the riverboat, another huckster, Dr. John, is hawking "Pocahontas Remedy," a medicine commercially popular, as it renders its patients unable to work while under treatment. Efe, to ensure his supply of the elixir, goes to work for John, quite happily, until the New Moses reappears to denounce Pocahontas as Demon Rum. Important here is the mania for superficial definitions—Demon Rum, Pocahontas, the New Moses, *Doctor* John, costumes, ribbons, rhetoric—that specify *function* rather than essence, or, rather, that assume function *is* essence. Efe recognizes this truth, which is why he need not recognize the identity of Demon Rum and Pocahontas. There is no paradox.

In this world, names, appearances, myths, symbols, and conventions *are* reality. In Professor Marvel's Wax Show sits "the very whale that swallowed Jonah"! But it is also a world of transmutation. Inside the whale, asleep, lies a Stepin Fetchit character who was baptized David Begat Solomon, changed his name to George Lincoln Washington, but whom Dr. John will call Jonah, of course. The wax figures' names are changed as well, to fit local occasion (Grant becomes Lee, two "old Moseses" becomes the James brothers, etc.). Not only do people mistake wax figures for real people (a mob is silenced when "the James Brothers" threaten), but real people are mistaken for wax figures, by some kids (who think Efe is wax) and even by us (who mistake Matt Abel, standing beside "Little Eva," for "Uncle Tom").

---

*The most developed of Ford's fool-characters, Francis Ford's Boudu-like coonskin wino appears notably in *Judge Priest, Young Mr. Lincoln, My Darling Clementine, Wagon Master, The Sun Shines Bright* and, less symbolically, *The Prisoner of Shark Island, Stagecoach, Fort Apache, 3 Godfathers, She Wore a Yellow Ribbon, The Quiet Man.*

And a farmer, whose sense of reality is as sophisticated as Efe's, accepts a lock of "George Washington"'s hair as an actual relic. Why not?

Simplicity seems gullible. People buy patent medicine, hail the New Moses or the New Elijah, trust that writing it in the Bible makes it so, even trust public institutions known to be corrupt, and declare with the astonishment of first discovery their greater insights: it *is* worth $500 to save Duke's life, decides Dr. John; "I ain't never had nothin' to love in my life, 'cept [Duke]," decides Fleety Belle. And simplicity and openness seem to be epitomized in her—her frank sexuality when Dr. John kisses her, her acute ingenuous passion during the prison-window love scene with Duke, the way her every emotion receives clear play, often physically, or even, as after the trial fiasco, when her blank stare outdoes the eloquence of Dr. John's verbalizing.

But the simple are not simply gullible. Jonah, for example, may seem a mere Uncle Tom stereotype, a fawning menial. In fact, his exaggerations satirize Uncle Tom: wanting to dress up as General Grant, offering a drink of water to the New Moses fished choking from the river, playing "Dixie" for gullible whites—such acts show he is not a witless underling, but (as Peter Rollins notes[11]) one of the country's many hucksters, all of whom (Dr. John, the New Moses, Elijah, Ely, Efe, Professor Marvel, the sheriff) wear several faces.

Such extensive skills at transmutation might seem to indicate a society's durability. But they may also signify moral hypocrisy and ossification. Merely changing names and appearances, while providing a "safety valve" for societal pressures, can prevent actual change, and embalm prejudice and the status quo. Indeed, in *Steamboat*'s world, people often *are* their functions: Jonah, for example, "belongs," as John observes, to the wax show. And Ford, in crosscutting between "General Lee" and farmers petrified waxlike in salute, demonstrates that people may become icons.

Moreover, taking things at face value is dangerous. Dr. John upbraids Duke for slumming with "swamp trash" (Fleety Belle), only to have the girl's family declare *her* irredeemably degraded for consorting with "river trash" (Duke). Similarly, because Duke has been labeled "guilty," officials who know him to be innocent and pure nonetheless enact with grandiloquent lethargy the government machinery culminating in his execution. Sheriff Rufe Jeffers (Eugene Pallette) is amiable, polite, and roly-poly (like his little daughter, who plays for the wedding, badly but appropriately, "Listen to the Mocking Bird"), but he sports a long buggy whip* and his quip, that it's "too bad" Duke must die, is maddeningly laissez-faire. Similarly matter-of-fact is the tone of the execution official, granting Duke's last request to see the race finish: "So if it's alright with you, Duke, we'll let it go when the *Pride of Paducah* comes around the bend." ("It won't be long," adds Rufe, consolingly.) But Duke accepts fate without murmur or protest; he finds no cause to object that the judge condemns him because of personal animosity toward Duke's lawyer, and he even refuses to escape. Duke is a dupe, a lamb fit for slaughter, trusting, as often in Ford (e.g., *Wagon Master*, *7 Women*), his fate to higher authority. Life is what he's got at the moment—which makes it all the more nostalgic.

*Villains have whips in *3 Bad Men*, *My Darling Clementine*, *Wagon Master*, and *Liberty Valance*. *Steamboat*'s officials resemble those in *The Whole Town's Talking*.

But Duke is wrong to be so trusting, for society's welfare depends on individual responsibility. And John's mistake is similar. Against Fleety Belle's outraged protests—"No! He ain't gonna do as you say! We've heard tell of that hangin' judge!"—John counsels Duke to surrender: "Trust me. They won't hang him." But she is right, of course, and John, a practiced huckster, *ought* not to have acted like a witless underling in trusting the corrupt judiciary. But in fact, he even awakens the law from bed, and complains at its lazy, reluctant attitude. "Guess I thought, 'cause I was older, I knew more about right and wrong than you," he apologizes later to Fleety Belle. And in effect, Dr. John is not quite the Fordian hero. He *is* a lonely bachelor, laboring to reunite a family threatened by society, but his wisdom is faulty and his efforts ineffectual. To finance an appeal (still trusting corrupt institutions) he takes on the wax show, revitalizing old myths, so to speak, by their transmutation (as the New Moses does). But John's archetypes, under any guise, are impotent: the appeal fails. And the New Moses (the archetype degenerated into a prohibitionist!) cannot be found.

Only collective iconoclasm will save Duke. For, as in *The Whole Town's Talking*, with its association of a liberated officeworker with the iconoclastic realism of Abelard, the old order has become so tyrannic that mere reform is hopeless. And, fittingly, it is Duke, the innocent lamb, who introduces the violent spark for the revolution, in his "forbidden" transmutation of Fleety Belle from swamp-girl to river-girl. Significantly, she wins John's respect by attacking him with a knife, and he will use this same knife, given him unawares by her, to save her from her swamp family; thus an alliance is formed. But it is Fleety Belle who knew better than to trust the establishment, and it is her goddesslike declaration that Duke shall not die—neither a command nor a prayer—that abruptly transforms defeat into victory and relaxation into raging violence. And many ideals perish as the *Claremore Queen* surges down river. The New Moses, kidnapped by John's lasso, protests, "I've got *souls* to save," but is corrected: he has a *life* to save. John, to keep going without fuel, cheats (making Ely tow him), hacks his boat into kindling wood, and burns the wax show figures. Finally, when only "the power of prayer" can save them, Pocahontas is revealed as Demon Rum, but finds its true function as fuel! As Efe, newly awaken, secretes away a jug, symbols and myths are fed "Into the fiery furnace! Hallelujah!! Glory Be!!!"

Does a new realism result? Yes and no. Duke's trust, after all, proves justified; and Ford's fetchingly brief concluding cameos suggest primeval values abide, even if today they can be achieved only with violence: Dr. John lounges fishing on his new riverboat, and Duke and Fleety Belle have gained Eden. As Duke said (and as all John Ford movies say), "There ain't nothin' nicer than goin' up and down the river."

"Steamboat Round the Bend should have been a great picture," grumbled Ford in 1965, "but at that time they had a change of studio and a new

manager came in who wanted to show off, so he recut the picture, and took all the comedy out."[12] Such acerbic sarcasm thirty years after the event—the new "manager" was Darryl F. Zanuck, the "change of studio" was Twentieth Century's absorption of Fox—suggests Zanuck's editing was significant. We shall never know. *Steamboat* has less comedy than other Fords, and little of his characteristic wackiness. Zanuck's defenders, Dan and Barbara Ford among them, suggest Zanuck quickened Ford's pacing and eliminated the inconsequential. Yet good Fords are often the sum of their inconsequentialities, and there *is* a peculiar episodic quality to *Steamboat*.

Will Rogers' death, shortly after completing *Steamboat*, ended what possibly was Ford's most fertile creative relationship. Naturally it was not without strains. There is an amusing story that Rogers—after characteristically giving Ford a continuous line of instructions on how to direct and then seeing Ford walk off the set, leaving him in charge—went sheepishly to tell Sheehan that Ford had just disappeared, for no apparent cause. But Rogers, like Carey, brought something more than folksy charisma into a Ford picture, namely an easing of tension and a rechanneling of directorial energy into gentler, more complex, yet less artificial representations of human relationships. The Rogers films are almost the only prewar Ford movies in which one does not sense Ford *making* things happen, but rather *letting* them happen. Not coincidentally, they, like the Carey silents, derive their magic primarily from the nuances with which characters relate in little things rather than from their larger dramas. Only in *Wagon Master* was Ford to recapture this magic, a movie about people first, and about events only inconsequentially.

Quite opposite such guileless art are Ford's next four films, brooding and ambition-heavy, in his *Informer* manner, each deeply flawed, and each dealing with deeply flawed worlds. Values and myths are inadequate for human needs; black expressionism befits conflicts of instinct and duty, in which duty's nature is ambiguous, and in which the combatants' commitment is so bound up with selfhood that, like Gypo, their moral choices seem predetermined, rather than free.

The Plough and the Stars (1936). The least imposing of the four, *The Plough and the Stars*, may well be Joseph August's photographic masterpiece—particularly in its dewy park scene. But like Hitchcock's *Juno and the Paycock*, this Sean O'Casey play, too, translates awkwardly into cinema. His Ireland—of quixotic revolutionaries, of oppressed barboors who loot, of balladeers and weeping women—is reduced to sixty-seven minutes of (often memorable) Easter Rebellion vignettes, unintegrated in their stylistic disparity and highlighted by Moroni Olsen and Arthur Shields. In face of RKO's interference, Ford lost interest. Denied a

The Plough and the Stars (1936). Note Ford crouched by camera at lower left corner of window.

The Plough and the Stars (1936).

cast of *only* Abbey Theatre Players* and forced to star Barbara Stanwyck (who wrought wonders for Capra), he transformed her into an incredibly blah stereotype. She whines repetitiously against her husband's fight for Ireland. But men will go on dying, and women will go on weeping, and neither, as she says, can help it.

The Prisoner of Shark Island (1936). Duty seems indistinguishable from instinct in *The Plough and the Stars*, and equally so in *The Prisoner of Shark Island.*** With the Civil War ending, Lincoln instinctually attempts to rechannel the duty with which the war was fought into a policy of *reconciliation:* upon announcing Lee's surrender, he asks the band to play "Dixie," claiming it for *all* Americans. But other factions instinctually feel that duty demands *revenge:* Lincoln is assassinated.

Dr. Mudd is a Southerner (as Ford's use of "Maryland, My Maryland" reminds us), but he shares Lincoln's positive sense of duty. And just as the accumulated kharma of years of war descends upon Lincoln, so too upon Mudd. A black filmworld evokes a grim epoch of repression, suspicion, cruelty, and hysteria. Beginning with bagged and ironed prisoners confronted, in ramming angulation, by their court, a dramatic nightmare progresses through executions, starkly lit horrors of geometric prisons, sharks, dank holes, and into the ultimate horror of plague.† But through it all, Mudd, a weary man, absorbed in duty to family and patients, obstinately defends himself *not* as unacquainted with Booth or Booth's deed, but as duty bound to aid the sick; and in prison, instinctually rejecting rancor, he will aid even his torturers, without hope of reward. In contrast, Secretary Erickson instructs the tribunal that duty demands they condemn Mudd and others accused, regardless of evidence; from duty, guards and the prison doctor instinctually hate Mudd. From duty, the commandant refuses to fire on the flag (to make the ship land medicine); but Mudd does so, because "I gotta look out for things."

This is the typical justification of a Fordian hero, and Mudd, no intellectual, has not reasoned his way to truer insights into society's welfare. He

---

*Among the Players Ford *did* import were Shields, his brother Barry Fitzgerald (né William Shields), Dennis O'Dea, Eileen Crowe, Una O'Conner, et al. (Backstage glimpses of O'Casey's plays at the Abbey occur in *The Rising of the Moon* and *Young Cassidy.*) Many players, like Shields, had actually been in the Dublin post office when it fell. And, years earlier, use of Irish and English veterans during *Hangman's House* resulted in brick-slinging battles.

**After setting a stranger's leg, Dr. Samuel A. Mudd is arrested, summarily tried, and given life at Dry Tortugas (Florida). Wife Peggy's escape plan fails; Mudd and black friend Buck are thrown into a dank pit; but yellow fever erupts and the commandant begs Mudd's aid. He squashes a black mutiny and fires on a federal ship, forcing its plague-fearing captain to land supplies and doctors. All petition Mudd's pardon. He and Buck return home. (The film follows Mrs. Mudd's biography, but elides the years in prison. Mudd [1833–83] was pardoned by Andrew Johnson on his last day in office [March 21, 1869], but appeals for his exoneration [recently, to President Carter] have not succeeded.)

†Cf. *Arrowsmith's* more harrowing plague. Here, Dr. McIntyre's slow, unwilling body-melt is juxtaposed to an onerous wheel.

merely persists in instinct, arriving at heroic actions simply because his stubbornness leaves no other choice. And, far from canonizing him, Ford omits appeals for our empathy, such as the information that Mudd freed his slaves years ago, and thus turns a scene such as Mudd's peremptory treatment of a carpetbagger into an instance of arrogance and politics. Nor does Ford palliate the refusal of Georgian Nunnally Johnson's script to cater to Northern tastes in racism. Black soldiers, though scarcely guileless, speak in musical, rhythmic patterns, with quasi-balletic gesture; and Ford changes Mudd's maid from a white to a black woman, and has her tremble not as a slave but as a servile woman, as she serves breakfast to Grandpa. Mudd defends, doctors, lives, and suffers with blacks; his friend Buck even enlists in the prison guard to help him escape. Still, Mudd can handle situations Northerners cannot, like quelling a black mutiny:

— They're gonna take you before the judge, gonna take ya out in the courtyard and build a scaffold, and yur gonna have to build it yurselves too, yur own scaffold. Now when ya get that done yur gonna do some diggin', yur gonna dig yur own graves, an' the law is gonna hang ya. They're gonna put a rope around yur necks, an' they're gonna choke ya, choke ya till yur eyeballs pop out an' yur tongue swells up.

Whereupon a mutineer comments:

— That ain't no Yankee talkin' just t' hear hisself talk. That's a Southern man, an' he mean it, yessir.

But Mudd ultimately emerges as a shallow, mechanistic character, more like Gypo Nolan than Judge Priest, and the fault lies in Ford's inability to direct Warner Baxter. Baxter's overprojected acting is mere representation; by wholly exteriorizing Mudd's innate arrogance, for example, he renders the character superficial; he substitutes nervousness for relating. In contrast, Harry Carey and Jack Pennick relax and swing their bodies nontheatrically, feeling out to each other, not "acting," but just "letting it happen."

Imagine Carey as Mudd, and note how the movie's emotions are clarified and deepened! In lieu of such humanity, Mudd's function is chiefly thematic, and Ford's overdependence on scenic values cannot compensate for this vapidity at the movie's core.

Also, despite its Ford-like themes and photography, *Shark Island* is a fairly cold, impersonal film. Even a nightmare needs atmospheric variety and more ironic relief (like Francis Ford comically slapping away flies while telling a twenty-yearer, "You'll never make it, Arnold, you're too old. The mosquitos'll get you!"). But Ford was not at ease under Zanuck's domination, had not at all (for the first time?) participated in writing the script, does not manage to interpolate his customary plethora of ritual, and seems rarely able to vivify personalities beyond Johnson's outline. Johnson wrote wonderful dialogue, but his emphasis on action results in fairly stratified characters, giving his work a mechanical, theatrical air. The "simple Fordian characters" of *Shark Island, The Grapes of Wrath,* and *Tobacco Road* are Johnson's, not Ford's, and far less complex and ambivalent. Lacking too is Ford's usual sense of a fabricated biography behind each character; Johnson's people have little past. Also, Ford's direction, in all three Johnson films, is deliberate. He parses Mudd's escape through moody corridors and archways, using barrack routine to heighten illusion and tension "with shrewd care for the pitch and speed of every move, every detail" (Otis Ferguson);[13] but such virtuoso executions seem on repeated viewings less interesting than Ford's visualization of what is not in the screenplay: moments of inconsequence, like Mudd sitting silently at his cell window with his legs curled up beneath him.*

Mary of Scotland (1936). Duty and instinct, synonymous in *Plough* and *Shark Island,* conflict in *Mary of Scotland* and *The Hurricane.* Mary Stuart, both as personage and character, is overwhelmed by the clatter of swords, thumping of armored men, deterministic compositions in monumental sets, ramming angles, and sweeping gestures, and by the cacophony of

---

*Other Ford additions include the freeze-frame of dead Lincoln, the reflection of Peggy's face in the window searching news of Mudd, the visual tour de force of the execution sequence, and the film's ending, when Buck's shadow swoops toward his thirteen kids like some homeward soaring eagle (Johnson had placed Buck's reunion inside, with Mudd's family). In Johnson, after Mudd has been recaptured in front of his wife, we return to Key West, where the child Martha's white nurse is reading to her: "And then the Prince leaned down and kissed Sleeping Beauty on both eyes—and she waked up." Cut to /Peggy coming in the door, then /to a shot of Peggy and her child, and she tells her that daddy and grandpa won't be coming home, daddy someday, but grandpa never. As Ford filmed it, the scene begins with the camera looking out the window toward the sea (= death; hope in afterlife; etc.), then, with the colored maid's voice *off*-camera, it pans slowly 90 degrees and we see Peggy wearily opening the door, while *off*-camera we hear: Maid: "And then the Prince leaned down and kissed the Sleeping Beauty on both eyes—and watcha s'pose?" Martha: "What?" Maid: "Sleeping Beauty waked up." Martha: "Mama!" *Now* Ford cuts to /a general shot of the room and we see Martha and the maid for the first time. One of Johnson's squarer scenes has been turned into something quite lovely.

complex events extended over years and beyond the temporal unity Ford-Nichols attempt to impose. History is a monstrous prop for Mary's collision with the world. She arrives (like so many Ford heroes) alone, in fog and night, and she kneels and prays to rule with "piety and wit"—virtues that will constantly elude her. Her dilemma, the conflict between her personality and office, is prefigured as she crouches helplessly beside a giant globe, and is articulated in Ford's presentation, alternately intimate and distanced—e.g., the familiarity we feel toward her as she greets James seems abruptly a trespass of manners when, in long shot, she mounts the stairs, the guards salute, and majesty is evoked. And Mary herself is girlish, even ingenuous, with only foolish dignity and sorry politics to oppose her ruthless barons and demonic cousin Elizabeth I. As often in Ford, virginity (Elizabeth) is associated with bitchiness, whereas uncontained sexuality (Mary) indicates purity.* And

*Flesh (Lora), Pilgrimage (widows vs. nubile daughters), Stagecoach (Dallas, Lucy), The Fugitive, What Price Glory, The Quiet Man, Mogambo, Donovan's Reef, 7 Women. Both petulant and prim, willful and self-destructive, the Ford heroines Mary most resembles are Shirley Temple, Grace Kelly, and (My Darling) Clementine.

Mary, in terror, will fling away her throne and her God for love of Bothwell ("Aye, and I'd do it again, a thousand times!").

Mary, though she tries, fails in her duty as queen even as she succeeds in her duty to herself. In Fordian terms, this ought to condemn her (albeit 1936 was the year a king of England resigned his throne for love) and, in the absence of any actual societal context, the contextualization of Mary's drama as a disembodied dynastic struggle occurring always in nightmarish castles, night, and fog, almost conceals the embarrassing truth: Mary really has no other cause as sovereign than herself. Having opted for "to thy own self be true," she expects her subjects to fight and die by tens of thousands, not that she might love as she chooses, but that she might rule as well.

Ford does not underline this hypocrisy. (Does he even acknowledge it?) On the contrary, he finds a moral victory in her defeat. She advocates tolerance and the right to marry whom she chooses. Her only alternative to being "a creature of love" is to become a machine like Elizabeth. Thus, in her penultimate scene, her lover dead, her throne gone, her execution hours away, she declares, "I win," meaning her progeny will inherit barren Elizabeth's throne: unlike Elizabeth, she has been a human, not just a queen. (But, alas for thematic sense, Mary's son was born of a marriage of state, not of love, and the victory she cites is political, not the moral one she and Ford accord her.)

Ford is intrigued by ideas, personages, and myths of history as background to Mary's moral odyssey, but almost none of it matches historical truth.* Indeed, *Mary of Scotland*, like Max Ophuls's *The Exile*, is irrelevant to history, retaining only the myths suitable for fairy-tale reflections on kingship and Manichaeanism, for which Charles II and Cromwell, or Mary and Elizabeth, provide the poetic subjects rather than the historical objects. Mary Stuart is a paradigmatic hero of this period: everything is given her—her duty, her glory, her downfall. Her native ingenuousness is under constant assault by a hostile world. Within a milieu determined by pageantry, the one element of freedom granted her is the possibility of rising above despair, through courage of purity.

Ford was unabashedly excited at the ideal casting of Katharine Hepburn as Mary, and he related to Howard Sharpe how he had carefully screened all her pictures, studying "every angle of her strange, sharp face—the chiseled nose, the mouth, the long neck."[14] It was a rare instance of Ford directing a major female star, while for her part Hepburn creates possibly her most multifaceted personage. Less rugged in the thirties and possessing greater range than in her Tracy years, the formality of her intonation and gesture,

---

*Ford's film echoes the Stuart-Catholic party line: villainous Bothwell is ever-pure, and Darnley's death is blamed on Mary's enemies; she herself never has a scheming thought. Also, Mary's long imprisonment is telescoped and she does not age; the real Mary died at forty-five, in 1587. And the meeting with Elizabeth (in Maxwell Anderson's verse drama from which Nichols adapted his scenario) never occurred.

her sense of her body in framed space, perfectly fit Ford's own manner. And she is well supported by an unusually subdued Fredric March (Bothwell), a morosely polychromatic John Carradine (Rizzio), and a bravura Moroni Olsen (Knox).* But the stiff prolixities of Nichols's script bog the movie's sweep, after its first half hour, midst detail and Korda-like dramaturgy. And RKO's reediting—ragged, jarring inserts, mismatched angles, and botched rhythms—produces a travesty of Fordian style.

The Hurricane (1937). In *The Hurricane,*** as in *Shark Island*, misguided duty underlies everything, exacerbated by the order / freedom dichotomy generic to South Sea movies. Governor DeLaage's refusal to allow his heart to influence his inhumane application of French law to an instinctual lifestyle makes him Ford's most irrational law-and-order extremist, and the character is infested with so much myopic arrogance that we may wonder what mitigating traits render him palatable to his wife and doctor, who vainly debate the meaning of DeLaage's ruling myth (order). Kersaint's prediction, that the hurricane will teach DeLaage there are things more important than the French penal code, suggests, along with shards of biblical allegory, that the storm represents God's wrath. Perhaps Depression America read a parable here (like *Steamboat Round the Bend*'s): establishment mythology, morally bankrupt, cannot suppress nature. But if this be true, the proletariat is in trouble, for the natives have no function other than as props for DeLaage's confusion, for it is they and their island (and the good priest and his church) who are destroyed and their oppressors who are spared. (Actually, the hurricane seems a manifestation of *DeLaage's* wrath sweeping, like Walter Pidgeon's destructive id in *Forbidden Planet,* over the world [and priest] that mock his personification of Law.) Afterward, confronted by ruination, DeLaage humbly concedes Terangi freedom.

*Knox's towering robed figure sweeps out of a crowd, bearing a striking resemblance in gesture and costume to Nicolai Cherkassov's Ivan the Terrible (1944), and Eisenstein's admiration for Ford was unbridled. The separate cuts of reluctant lords bowing woodenly to Mary, earlier, could have been copied by Eisenstein even in rhythm.

**Dr. Kersaint (Thomas Mitchell) reminisces about a sandbar, once an island paradise. *Flashback:* DeLaage (Raymond Massey), French governor of Manacura, denies mercy as Terangi's jailbreaks increase a six-month term for hitting back a Frenchman. After eight years, Terangi (Jon Hall) escapes across six hundred miles of ocean to his wife (Dorothy Lamour) and unseen daughter. DeLaage, deaf to pleas by his wife (Mary Astor), pursues—until a hurricane destroys everything.

Oscar to Thomas Moulton (sound recording); nominations to Thomas Mitchell and to Alfred Newman (music).

Before taking a trip, Ford had jotted down some possible names for the studio to look at, among them Charlie, who lived next door to him, was Tahitian and a good swimmer. One morning they were both driving out at the same moment. "Where are you going?" asked Ford. "U. A." "So am I. What are you going to do there?" "Well, I'm going to be in a picture." "What's it called?" "*Hurricane.*" While Ford was away, the studio had taken some tests of Charlie, liked them, and changed his name to Jon Hall. (The story is told by Ford in the John Ford Papers, Lilly Library, Indiana University.)

The Hurricane. Ford directing Dorothy Lamour.

All that, just to teach DeLaage a lesson? No wonder the sandbar set and its painted backdrop look so phoney: such obvious aestheticism recalls Kersaint's eyes' crazed gleam in the film's prologue. Nowhere else are we made conscious of studio re-creation. Yet, a few Samoan background shots aside, everything—village, church, buildings, palm trees—was constructed, for $150,000, on Goldwyn's back lot, even the lagoon (a 600-foot-long tank). Bert Glennon's expressionist photography even struggles to counteract the authentic look by melodramatizing land- and seascapes. And excess typifies this Goldwyn movie: full-blown, injudicious voluptuousness, repelling, compelling—but utterly unerotic. Ford could come no closer to *Tabu's* spirit than occasional touches and the casting of Murnau's heroine, Reri, in a bit part. The priest (C. Aubrey Smith) declaims like the Bible, usually with organ, as when he says, "This is between me—and Somebody Else," and a heavenly choir bursts through a glorious cloudscape. Massey and Astor are credible, if underdeveloped, as Frenchmen, and Dorothy Lamour is credible, if only physically, as a Polynesian—she is made to mouth colloquially poetic English supposedly representing native mentality. Severity toward

such generic wallowing would be thankless, but Jon Hall's bewildered, put-
on expressions deal poetic authenticity a fatal blow. (It was Hall's debut, and
Ford—trying to sabotage him?—had him beat with real whips and fired
upon with real bullets.)

The Hurricane was a box-office smash, due largely to the storm sequence
(by Jim Basevi with Stuart Heisler). Huge propellers simulated driving rain
"which," wrote Mary Astor, "kept us fighting for every step, with sand and
water whipping our faces, sometimes leaving little pinpricks of blood on our
cheeks from the stinging sand."[15] Wave machines churned the water. Then,
for $250,000, the set was destroyed by a tidal wave created by releasing
water from 2,000-gallon tanks mounted on sixty-five-foot towers (controlled by Ford with electric buttons). Detail shots, such as those of the stars
tied to the giant tree, were done indoors, with more wind machines, hoses,
and a papier-mâché tree suspended in a tank (so that it would turn as though
its roots were coming loose).

Ford seems to relish his repeated crosscuts from the horrified face of Mary
Astor to the horrifying face of the titanic onrushing wave. But what becomes
striking on repeated viewing is less the action of the storm than the serene and
lordly pacing of Ford's editing. Never has disaster been so majestic.

Wee Willie Winkie (1937). In contrast to the murky, darkly
subjective dreamworlds of the RKOs, *Hurricane* and *Shark Island*, Ford's
next three movies, all naive little matinee pieces, seem fresh, variegated,
and almost documentary-like. And one of them is, next to *Steamboat Round
the Bend*, the gem of the period. *Wee Willie Winkie** is so much a portrait of
a world, rather than merely a vehicle for the most profit-making star of the
thirties, that the viewer would do well to forget about Shirley Temple and
think instead of Priscilla Williams.

As she stares wide-eyed from her railroad car, Miss Priscilla Williams is
clearly thrilled to be in India. How India might feel about having her there
may be surmised from Ford's wry introduction of Priscilla emerging from a
smoky gorge. While his intentions might have been less than symbolic, people who *arrive* in Ford movies generally end up fulfilling rather awesome
purposes** and, as it happens, Priscilla will in her first few weeks in India

---

*1890s: Widowed American Joyce Williams (June Lang) with daughter Priscilla is obliged to
accept hospitality from her father-in-law (C. Aubrey Smith), a British colonel in India. There a
young officer (Coppy: Michael Whalen) courts Joyce, and Priscilla befriends a tough sergeant
(Victor McLaglen) and the notorious Khoda Khan (Cesar Romero). Thinking her abducted, the
regiment is about to storm an impregnable fortress when Priscilla shames the Indians into negoti-
ation. (There is almost no similarity to Kipling's poem.) Release prints were toned sepia for daytime, blue for night. Oscar nomination to Thomas Little (interior decoration).

**Mary Stuart arrives by boat, the Joads by truck, Sean Thornton by train, Wyatt Earp on
horse, and Clementine by stagecoach. Colonel Thursday also has a coach, Boats Gilhooley
rides a freighter, Amelia Dedham a ketch, Marty Maher has to walk, Ethan Edwards is alone
on a horse. Ransom Stoddard arrives once by train, once by stage and buckboard. The Fugitive
and Dr. Cartwright have mules. The Nordleys (*Mogambo*) arrive by steamer, Duke (*Air Mail*)
by plane. All arrive as loners into alien milieus.

sow flowers where'er she walks, humanize her grandfather, comfort the dying, win a boyfriend, marry off her widowed mother, and prevent a war. In effect, she is a true Fordian hero, celibate, mediating between repression and chaos (Britain and the Petans), and reuniting a family. Indeed, she is Ford's most affirmative hero, for her higher wisdom derives not from tragic experience or innate arrogance, but from an innocence reflecting humanity's innate virtue. Priscilla's innocent eye regards the world as her teddy bear, and therein lies her strength—for who dares disillusion such stubborn innocence? She does not know her mother's fragile naiveté, her grandfather's ruthless martial gravity, MacDuff's brute toughness, nor Khoda Khan's murderousness.

At times her mythology dominates the picture, as when a call grows louder passing from one mouth to another, until the camera jumps suddenly into a gaping close-up of MacDuff's huge orifice—a Homeric simile reflecting Priscilla's imagination. But if Priscilla does not always know how to interpret, she sees with a frankness denied unbiased observers. And Ford provides immense detail for her innocent eye, making *Wee Willie Winkie* as much a study of the British-India military as later films will be of the American.

This teddy-bear-documentary style is apparent in the reveille sequence: an Indian pulls energetically at a bell, the camera tracks along rows of barrack bunks, showing identically arranged kits and rifles chained to soldiers' feet; we follow the men through a raucous washroom scene. Priscilla awakes, sits up in bed and stares, entranced by pipes, drums, parades, cannon. She has a wide view from her window, out past the big tree, of the ferocious native hussars galloping by and the formations of tartaned infantry. (Ford and Shirley Temple repeat the sequence in *Fort Apache* [1948]. Later she visits MacDuff, not knowing he is dying. "Please God, honor the Queen, shoot straight, keep clean," says he, and she sings "Auld lang syne," which a piper takes up, after she leaves; and MacDuff is buried with pomp.

Elsewhere, too, in Ford happiness belongs to the perversely innocent, success to the blindly persistent. And Priscilla, who can mime the imperialist spirit Stepin-Fetchit-like, shares some of the qualities of the blessed Ford fool. But it is frightening that Priscilla is made the regiment's mascot, given a uniform, and trained in ordnance. For ordnance will regulate her spirit and merge her into that pleasant pageantry that is the arrogant, racist, and resented position of the British. We see that position in almost every scene, whether with English ladies shopping, English gentry in a tea shop, English officials supervising native police, English breaking through train-station crowds, or English balls interrupted by attacking Petans. Pax Britannica vs. native rule. Everywhere can be sensed the flag, the cross, and British music. "England's duty, my duty," huffs the colonel. English dominance is occasionally the butt of Ford's Irish amusement—e.g., a huge dour orderly gripping to his imperious chest a teensy-weensy teacup. But the tremendous barriers of rank (and race) seem constantly to terrify even the soldiers themselves.

The scene in which the colonel attempts to justify duty's point of view is set with stunning expressionism in a darkened room, he to the left engulfed in shadow, Priscilla and Joyce in the middle, their white dresses illuminated. The composition lends majesty to his words, but lends them subjectivity, too. He does not quite win his point. For to these Americans not so much India as the British are foreign, and the army even more so. But when Priscilla begs her mother to take her home, mother has to reply, "But this is home"— a line with considerable reverberation within an oeuvre in which the search for home is a constant theme. An old life, husband, and national identity are dead; new beginnings must be made. There is no choice.

One of Ford's finer ingenues, Joyce is hardly twenty-one and when she has to explain to Priscilla about "Indians," "India," and "Columbus," her sweet-serious parroting of history indicates her sheltered gentility. And her series of expressions while serving Coppy's parents tea— fright, bewilderment, anxiety lest she fail to please—are as entrancing as her shaded dance with him later—to a gentle "Comin' thro' the Rye," to camera movements *andante*.

Wee Willie Winkie is among Ford's most seminal prewar films not only because like virtually every postwar picture it studies militarist ethos, but also because it grasps the paradox that one must grow up, one must go on, one must belong, and that this is good, even though thereby one's conscience is arrogated and one is inculpated in collective evil. The future is to be entered into willingly.

Four Men and a Prayer, Submarine Patrol (1938). Neither movie explores any deep theme, yet both display *allegretto* virtuosity, deftly vignetting large casts and variegated modalities. Expressionism is moderated; and, as in *Winkie*, depth-of-field blocking and cutting, graceful camera movements, and animated reaction shots are employed more as in fifties than as in thirties Ford. The scripts, moreover, are trivial skeletons for the director's invention.

Four Men—with its subtle verbal gags, ridiculous costumes, butlers, and chewing gum, with Berton Churchill a hysterically sober tycoon, Loretta Young a Hawksian screwball, and George Sanders a pompous attorney, with Barry Fitzgerald drinking midst Ford's first friendly barroom brawl, every European in India carrying an umbrella, and Alexandrian bellboys wearing "Sphinx Hotel" sweaters—is an affair best appreciated by Ford cultists. Its uncharacteristically lampooning direction makes the story—of four sons globehopping to clear their father's name—almost meaningless.

In contrast, *Submarine Patrol*, which also stars Richard Greene, and studies a military society in miniature, is impressively self-effacing in technique and detail.* A brilliant bar sequence begins as Warren Hymer chains his taxi to a pole (an instance of "invisible humor"—easily missed, thus more delightful if noticed). Midst beery bedlam, "The monkeys have no tails in Zamboanga," and sailors' manic assault on a slot machine, a marine sergeant**, with cocky nonchalance, slips in a single coin, holds out his hat, and exits with his reward, as the sailors futilely resume. Meanwhile Perry absconds with Susan, having locked up morose John Carradine ("Dancing is a sinful pastime!") and discarded the key onto a passing tray. Later, when we find the sergeant dancing with Perry's society sweetheart, we recall a brief flirtation and a wry smile at Perry, and comprehend his cockiness of necessity toward the slot machine. But this subplot is executed with such deft innuendo that it may be all but overlooked.

Similarly subtle is the ingenious performance of the former Keystone comedian Slim Summerville, as Cookie. Cookie lives in a Tati-like world of his own with its private gestures, and the smile he gives the captain at a moment of potential crisis establishes his inviolable independence of even the navy. His gags typify Ford's invisible humor. While the crew pumps away at calisthenics, Cookie brings Quincannon (J. Farrell MacDonald) coffee and donuts, remarking, "That's great stuff! I do it myself every morning before I get out of bed"—a line thrown away and bringing no reaction from Quincannon. For all Cookie's gags occur in a separate universe—as when he steps forward to refuse, and finds himself included among the volunteers who have stepped forward too.

Sterner emotions counterpoint pleasantries: as in *Seas Beneath*, awkward individuality and mechanics dominate a depth-charge attack; fear dominates an *adagio* mine sequence, apoplexy a battle, orgiastic exhaustion its

---

*1918: Playboy Perry (Greene) and a motley crew shape up in convoy from Brooklyn to Brindisi on a wooden subchaser whose Capt. Drake needs to redeem himself for letting a destroyer run arock. Perry's attempt to wed Susan (Nancy Kelly) is thwarted by her freighter-captain father; Perry wins his respect on a mission, but orders to sail postpone marriage.

Ford once cited *Submarine Patrol* as a favorite, and *The New York Times* (Frank Nugent) gave it a rave review. Richard Greene's debut in *Four Men and a Prayer* won the British-stage import a Fox contract, but after a half-dozen movies he returned to England in 1940 to star there in adventure films and as TV's Robin Hood.

**Setting, song, machine, and character are repeated in *Donovan's Reef*.

aftermath. Schmaltz is juxtaposed to skillfully edited action, sailing past the Statue of Liberty (as in *The Growler Story*), or provides motivation, as when *Anchors Aweigh*, underlining an admiral's (Moroni Olsen's) soft sonorous delivery, conveys the officer-caste tradition behind Drake's determination. And while a lugubrious Italian waiter conducts a gooey "Santa Lucia," Perry and Susan stare straight ahead; he glances at her, then turns away; she does the same; the schmaltz throws their sincerity into relief.

PRE-WAR PRESTIGE (1939–1941)

Stagecoach	3.2.39	Argosy–Wanger–United Artists
Young Mr. Lincoln	6.9.39	Cosmopolitan–20th Century–Fox
Drums Along the Mohawk	11.3.39	20th Century–Fox
The Grapes of Wrath	3.15.40	20th Century–Fox
The Long Voyage Home	10.8.40	Argosy–United Artists
Tobacco Road	2.20.41	20th Century–Fox
How Green Was My Valley	12.?.41	20th Century–Fox

This is Ford's prestige period. These seven movies captured ten Oscars and thirty-four nominations, and in each of these three years the New York Film Critics chose Ford best director. Artistically, the period represents a renaissance after the dark ages of the preceding few years. But it is not without its impersonal tinges. Many of these movies were major studio productions, for which Ford had to contend with assigned scripts and Darryl Zanuck's supervision and editing. And to an extent, Ford played it safe and adapted himself to the tastes of the tastemakers and the instructions of his employers. He had striven for the lofty position he was now assuming—virtually unanimous recognition as Hollywood's foremost director—and he aimed to hold it.

On the other hand, Ford is far more profoundly and complexly engaged in these pictures than in any of the preceding period, which seems in retrospect to have been one of negativity, floundering, and indifference. Much that was contentious then is assured now. The Fordian hero reemerges; duty, no longer ambiguous, is synonymous with destiny; far from having identity problems, characters acquire fortification in class consciousness. Not only in *Stagecoach*, but in all these pictures, an individual represents his specific culture.

Themes of persistence, helplessness, and desperation pervaded preceding films. Themes of *survival* dominate now. This is very much a populist period. And characters are more instinctual, free will less in evidence, than ever before. In *Stagecoach*, *Young Mr. Lincoln*, and *Drums Along the Mohawk*, societies habitate premythic frontiers, where social structures are still defining themselves, rather than ossified, as earlier in the decade. And Ford's moody expressionism now seems almost a veneer barely containing a vigorous, variegated naturalness right below the surface. Yet matters take a sharp downturn with *The Grapes of Wrath*, *The Long Voyage Home*, *Tobacco Road*, and *How Green Was My Valley*. Now people are suffocated, entombed by social structures, and utterly destroyed; yet, even so, those who survive often emerge strengthened.

The period contains films such as *The Long Voyage Home* and *The Grapes of Wrath*, which brought Ford oceans of prestige in 1940, but which now seem fairly minor alongside the period's three great masterpieces: *Stagecoach* is more vigorously intense than any prior Ford movie. *Young Mr. Lincoln* has deepened characterizations and gives a more resonantly complex import to an individual's personality. *How Green Was My Valley* uses cinematic form as "spatial music," and to subvert the narrative's superficial meaning.*

---

*While Ford films and Fox films have a similar "look" (e.g., Henry King's 1939 *Stanley and Livingstone* looks more like fifties Ford than Ford does—except that scenery distracts from characters more than informing them), we ought not blithely to assume that Ford's three-dimensional lighting, fluid compositions, and expressive montage (if not his acting) derive from studio "tradition"—from the corporate talents of an oligarchy of photographers and editors. It is also possible that the Fox look owed much to Ford. Fox's fortunate vulnerability toward seeing a virtual "school" of a great artist had already been demonstrated under Murnau. But Ford was an even more valued and influential studio asset—after twenty-six years there he was still thought worth $600,000 a year. And by the mid-1950s, neither Zanuck nor King retained the Fox "look," but John Ford did.

Darryl F. Zanuck, looking back on these years, concluded that Ford was "the best director in the history of motion pictures" because "his placement of the camera almost had the effect of making even good dialogue unnecessary or secondary."[16]

Stagecoach **(1939).** Westerns, churned out in profusion by poverty-row firms for the lowest classes of audiences, had been shunned by big producers throughout the decade. But *Stagecoach* showed westerns could be intelligent, artful, great entertainment—and profitable. Budgeted at $392,000, it grossed over a million its first year, promoted John Wayne into big stardom, and gave Ford's reputation its first real boost since *The Informer*. Today still, *Stagecoach* is one of the freshest of official film classics.

"I found the story by reading it in *Collier's*," said Ford. "It wasn't too well developed, but the characters were good. 'This is a great story,' I thought, and I bought it for a small amount—I think it was $2,500. I tried to sell it to the studios, but nobody was buying. After the studio heads read it, they said to me, 'But this is a Western! People don't make Westerns anymore!' "[17] Ford shopped nearly a year for a producer, trying Joe Kennedy and David

Stagecoach. Ford with the coach and Benton Churchill.

Selznick before finding Walter Wanger, an independent producer releasing through United Artists. After urging Ford to cast Gary Cooper and Marlene Dietrich, Wanger agreed to Wayne and Trevor, relative nobodies, and subsequently had little influence on the production.

Ford's wisecrack to Bogdanovich that the story is really Maupassant's "Boule de suif" is farfetched. In Maupassant, when a coach carrying French refugees is halted during the Franco-Prussian War, the passengers intimidate a woman of reputedly easy virtue into sleeping with the German commandant. But, their release obtained, moral snobbery reasserts itself, and their savior is snubbed. Nor is there any more similarity to Maupassant in Ernest Haycox's *Collier's* story "Stage to Lordsburg" (but there is in *7 Women* and Sternberg's *Shanghai Express!*). Haycox's ending is like the film's, but Malpais Bill (i.e., the Ringo Kid) is not an escaped outlaw and boards the stage in Tonto. Dallas does not deliver a baby (nor do anything outstanding), the banker does not exist (but there is an English hunter), and the whiskey salesman succumbs to the heat rather than to Indians.*

When we think of *Stagecoach* we think of a coach traversing a giant vista of Monument Valley. Monument Valley, on the Navajo lands in northern Arizona, made its movie debut in *Stagecoach* and, always photographed with opulence, became a defining element in Ford's harsh, stony West through nine subsequent appearances. But even this first time, the valley is not simply a valley, but a valley melodramatized; and the coach is not simply a coach, but the historic mythos of "the West." Ford's previous evocations of history's magic moments (*Shark Island, Mary of Scotland* . . .) had usually originated from the diminishing confines of a soundstage; exteriors, curiously, had tended to represent a character's interior culture (the park in *The Plough and the Stars*, the riverbank in *Salute*, the river in *Steamboat*). But with *Stagecoach* a new magnitude of exteriority enters cinema, one touched

---

*Tonto, 1870s. Passengers board a stagecoach: Lucy Mallory (Louise Platt), a pregnant lady joining her officer husband; Dallas (Claire Trevor), a whore being evicted; Doc Boone (Thomas Mitchell), a drunk also ostracized; Peacock (Donald Meek), a meek whiskey salesman; Gatewood (Berton Churchill), a haughty banker. Cavalry ride guard, for Apache are loose. Hatfield (John Carradine), a gambler, goes along to "protect" Mrs. Mallory, and the sheriff (George Bancroft) to hunt the Ringo Kid (John Wayne), who escaped jail to avenge his brother, and who joins the coach outside town.

At Dry Ford Station, relief cavalry fail to rendezvous, but the passengers vote to go on without protection. At Apache Wells, Lucy learns her husband was wounded and Dallas and Boone deliver her baby. Ringo and Dallas fall in love, but smoke signals foil his escape. And, after fording a river, the coach is pursued by Apache across salt flats. Hatfield, about to kill Lucy to protect her, is killed himself, just as cavalry arrive.

In Lordsburg the travellers separate. Gatewood is arrested for robbing his bank. Ringo kills the three Plummer brothers and the sheriff lets him ride off with Dallas into the sunset.

Stagecoach won two Oscars (supporting actor: Thomas Mitchell; score: Richard Hageman et al.) and was nominated for five others (picture, direction, art direction, photography, editing—losing out generally to *Gone with the Wind*). The New York Film Critics chose Ford best director and the National Board of Review cited it as the year's third best. Current prints, however, give a totally false impression of the movie—grey, washed-out, soft, distant, old-fashioned looking, rather than sharp and vibrant.

on previously by *Tabu* and *Nanook*: a consciousness expanding forcibly; an alienated stare at the world's vastness, at an immensity embarrassing our trepidant love (rather like the mixture of passion and alienation with which nature is confronted in Rossellini's Bergman movies). *Stagecoach* in retrospect seems to be seeking heroic sensation and premythic purity, lost qualities needed in 1939, as the world turned toward global war. Scenery, then, is not simply a given, but a participant in drama.

On the other hand, there is a theatricality to *Stagecoach* that may seem to lie at the opposite extreme from this "realism." Story, Monument Valley, the Old West itself, all seem to have been transposed by Ford not into "re-creative realism" but into a dreamworld—to the extent that everything about *Stagecoach* works best when least plausible: the improbable collection of characters, the chase sequence, the 7th Cavalry, the Lordsburg shootout. *Stagecoach* seems to look *back* to Victorian theater's traditions and spectacle (whereas Griffith's movies, to which *Stagecoach* may appear to have stronger-than-usual relation, came *out* of Victorian theater). *Stagecoach*'s characters are as archetypal, generic, and basic as their adventures, and, here more than elsewhere, each character is given entrance and exit. Soon the fantasy takes on a dream's reality; the Old West is gone but *Stagecoach* will never die. It begins and ends with nostalgia—"I Dream of Jeannie"—and sadness is pointedly underlined in the first shot, when couriers emerge from distant vistas and gallop past a rising flag. Subsequent low-angle, deep-focus shots of the offices and streets of Tonto seem to stress that we are there, that this is it; but really the effect is like staring into a Matthew Brady photograph and imagining we are there. This is the *effort* that *Stagecoach* asks and obtains from its audiences, and this is why our belief in it and its impossible characters is as vivid as our belief in the reality of, say, Dickens's world, one now more real than the actual. So *Stagecoach* begins sadly, lamenting a dead world, and taking us back the way *The Lone Ranger* said it would. Lamenting what? Perhaps what Doc Boone says as Ringo and Dallas ride away: "Well, they're saved from the blessings of civilization!"—"I Dream of Jeannie."

Hence, if there is a tendency to think of *Stagecoach* as Ford's first large-sized masterpiece, the reason is less that it is a *better* movie than, say, *Judge Priest* (it is not), than that it is different. It sprawls; previous Fords seem tidy. And it sprawls in many ways: it seems to be three different movies stitched together; it has several climaxes; it has many stories, many cinematic styles, many locations, and many characters, who, for once, resist coherence into a community.

Stagecoach's structure is tripartite and unusually disparate: (1) the town of Tonto, where we meet the nine principals; (2) the journey to Lordsburg; (3) the town of Lordsburg, when the "story" really begins. Each section differs in script-method and cinematic style. The Lordsburg section, the third, is expressionistic melodrama, telling a normal story in parallel sequences (Ringo and Dallas, Luke Plummer in the bar) and then resolving the conflict. The second section, the journey, alternates between scenes en route and the way stations. On the road, Ford repeats the same pattern nearly a dozen times: (1) The coach in long shot rolling along the plain (to "Bury Me Not on the Lone Prairie"); (2) Curly and Buck in two-shot conversing on the driver's seat; (3) The passengers inside, always in isolated crosscuts. Three progressions occur simultaneously: space grows smaller, we pass from verité to comedy to chamber-drama, psychologies become more fragmented. At the way-stations, Ford composes model ensemble sequences. The first section, in Tonto, offers the most freedom for cutting around at will, and is probably scenarist Dudley Nichols's finest triumph:

the introductions are wittily and swiftly done, each vignette possessing a mood of its own and revealing personality and period.

Unfortunately this pace of revelation is not maintained in the second section, in which Ford and Nichols seem less interested in exploring individuals than in interactions. Each character, more than merely a dream-world archetype, represents a culture and class in microcosm (whereas other Fords contrast groups). If they are predictable, it is because they are vivid enough not to require demonstration. The surest route to ruining *Stagecoach* would have been to have cast these roles with vague, everyday-Joe faces, to have suppressed Ford's telltale, clichéd grimaces, gestures, clothing, and motives, and to have spent the movie in defining the characters' types. Ford, unpedantic, starts where another director would have concluded. True, such tight juxtaposing of so many archetypes in archetypal adventures seems an extreme application of Ford's vignette techniques of characterization (whereby a hypertypical cameo immediately defines a character); yet vignetting is blended with extended character development, and the result becomes a sort of archetypal fireworks show of increasing brilliance, as Ford freely plays each situation to an extreme degree of stylization and composes vignette "magic moments."

Interest in the characters stems from their interaction, from subtle details of gesture, intonation, and staging, and from tension between the type and the individual inhabiting it. Let us consider each of them.

Buck, the stage driver (Andy Devine), is a strident, stupid oaf, whose awkward voice makes anything he says sound not worth listening to—although it is, for the fascination of absurdity. But arriving in Lordsburg, he turns to Ringo and says, with a mature empathy that is "off-character," just "Lordsburg, Ringo" and one senses suddenly that Buck's public personality, his oafy side, is not the "real" one. Similarly, Yakima, the Apache woman, changes from a proud siren to a street urchin when she interrupts her song to tell three men (in Spanish), "OK, boys, get goin'!"

Similarly, Doc Boone: this Thomas Mitchell drunk is a variation on Mitchell's drunk doctor in *The Hurricane* and his drunk reporter in Capra's *Mr. Smith Goes to Washington;* and he is a variation on Ford's drunken doctors in *My Darling Clementine* and *The Colter Craven Story* and the drunk reporter in *Liberty Valance.* Yet nuances are brought to the role. When Boone weasels a parting drink from bartender Jack Pennick (Ford's perennial everybody's pal), the staging—he stands in a shaft of light in an empty bar—goes beyond mere cliché, seems *so* archetypal as to be pre-mythic. Rather than trying to be "original" (i.e., different), the character glories in being the "original" (i.e., archetype). But this personage too has distance within it, displayed in the film's last line, when Boone responds to Curly's offer of a drink with, "Just one," and sounds wholly himself for once.

Then there is Ringo, as basic and raw as a hero can be. Yet his magnificent admission, "I lied to you, Curly. I saved three bullets," not only glorifies the archetype (who needs only three bullets to kill three men); it also reflects a deeper side. Of all the passengers, Ringo seems the most community-minded, yet he gave vengeance priority over defense during the Indian chase. In fact, one wonders how Ringo got past the Hays office: for the movie certainly seems to excuse and even to laud Ringo's avenging his brother by calling out and shooting down three men in the streets, and we feel he deserves to ride off into the rising sun and happiness with Dallas. With Harry Carey, Wyatt Earp, or Ethan Edwards, Ford makes it clear that moral reckonings cannot be avoided; but Ringo's moral reckoning is his single-minded duty to vengeance. Untroubled by the complicated personality and social mission of the Fordian hero—he does not mediate, reunite families, or claim higher wisdom—Ringo's archetype (like Terangi's in *The Hurricane*) antedates civilization. Albeit, John Wayne, playing much younger than his thirty-two years, gives the character such laid-back personableness that his "realness," however simplistic, is instantly accepted by audiences.

Hatfield, we are told, has shot men in the back, but we meet him in a gallant hour trying to be again what he once was; his Satanic side nonetheless bursts out occasionally, as when he shouts, "Put out that cigar!" at Boone. Dallas, in contrast, is almost Shirley Temple dressed for a wicked Halloween. She may be an orphan and all but unemployable, yet her disgust at whoring is inconsistent with her persistence in it. Her underplayed bitterness does not flash to the surface as Hatfield's does, and thus at her moment of "transfiguration," when she presents the baby, she compares poorly with *7 Women*'s Dr. Cartwright in a similar moment. Cartwright's whore side is more explicit, her bitterness more matured, but when she gushes over a baby, the transfiguration is not only a greater contrast, it also occurs in a fleeting instant, not as a minor dramatic catharsis. Nonetheless, this catharsis is not as pronounced as in Nichols's script directions:

> The last trace of hardness has vanished from Dallas as she holds the infant in her arms, and there is a glow of wonder in her face. She stands a moment in the doorway, a smile in her eyes. . . . Her experience of the last few hours has deeply affected her, taken all the defiance out of her face, and softened it into beauty.[18]

Ford's realization is less grandiloquent. Dallas has all along been eager to be pleasant; she does not abruptly shift attitudes; she is merely relieved momentarily from self-shame, which soon returns. But Dallas's whole existence is a kind of dream: every moment, not just this one, has its glow or gloom, its warmth or chill; an accepting baby on one hand and a repelling propriety on the other dramatically define the boundaries of Dallas's affective consciousness, and thus exacerbate the vibrant oscillations twixt hope and despair with which Dallas experiences Ringo's presence, when every other moment threatens transfiguration. And it is this melodramatized representation of inner experience that Ford aims for and which reaches its height in the streaked blackness of the Lordsburg sequence, one of the finest achievements of Ford's career. Dallas is afraid to let Ringo know where she lives and what she is, and Ford's relentless tracking through the red-light district up to a ramp leading down into a nestle of dark shacks emphasizes how her whole life is at stake, and emphasizes the horror of the alternative awaiting her. She is an apt character for Ford's expressionism, for she is affective rather than philosophic; she does not contemplate her tragedy, she shares the naiveté of the youngsters we see in the Lordsburg bar, sheltered by their madam as though by a convent nun. We are not sure whether Ringo is noble or stupid, whether or not he knows Dallas is a whore, but his unflinching simplicity as he walks with her perfectly offsets her confusion. The honky-tonk piano that accompanies their walk contrasts with Richard Hageman's symphonic folk-tune score that elsewhere plays so major a role in making *Stagecoach* repeatedly enjoyable; a sort of apex of stylized populist melodrama is reached with the timpani roars accompanying the footsteps of Ringo and Plummer stalking each other. Dallas's tension climaxes just after the fight; typically Fordian is the way she first hears approaching footsteps and turns gradually around as the camera glides subjectively up to her, until Ringo emerges into the frame, and the storybook-spotted horses pull up with her wedding coach.

Lucy Mallory is typical of many Ford characters whose stereotype, patent at first glance, is ultimately elusive. As Hatfield says, she is "an angel in a jungle, a very wild jungle." A product of her gentle breeding and its unquestioning moralism, Lucy is also intelligent and impressionable. She seems the film's only person who really relates to the land. If her repugnance for Dallas is an indoctrinated intolerance, her repugnance for most of her other passengers comes more naturally. Her subtle pouts and attempts at formal politeness toward Gatewood are uproarious. When she first sees Hatfield she waits impatiently for the first opportunity, then excitedly gasps, "Who is that gentleman?" Her acts of courage are girlish, as when in bed she insists she will go on. Like Clementine Carter, she has come from the East alone, braving a wilderness to join her man. Passion and determination lie at the heart of many of Ford's misplaced gentle ladies, and always with a provocative thrill.

Thus in every character there are elements of contrast, some obvious, some hidden. Ringo, Boone, Dallas, Peacock, and (sometimes) Hatfield are "sympathetic"—no matter what they have done or will do; Lucy, Hatfield (generally), and Gatewood (always) are unsympathetic, their good sides left for discovery. The gentle Peacock, commonly mistaken for a clergyman, wants to "go back to the bosoms," but he is a businessman like Gatewood, with a business (whiskey) that wrought incalculable harm. But for Gatewood there is nary a saving grace. Dissolving from his snarling face to the Law and Order League suggests cause-and-effect, not only between establishment and intolerance, but between the banker's wife and *his* desire to flee town. Yet a forthright banker-villain had resonance in 1939 America.

Contrast and ambivalence create one of *Stagecoach*'s loveliest moments. At the first way station, Ringo has had the (inadvertent) audacity to seat the whore beside the lady. Everyone freezes and stares. Hatfield offers to "find" Mrs. Mallory a "cooler" seat by the window and Gatewood goes glaringly along. We hate them. Then Ford puts "I Dream of Jeannie" on the soundtrack and glides his camera dreamily into a poetic and intimate conversation between Lucy and Hatfield, into the nostalgia of the Old South and lost lives. We love them.

André Bazin initiated a lengthy debate when, after World War II, he lauded as "realistic" the long takes and composition in depth of *Citizen Kane* and *The Best Years of Our Lives* and disparaged in contrast the "classic" Hollywood editing styles of Ford and Capra, which he thought "manipulative."*

---

*Bazin, like other critics, grossly exaggerates *Citizen Kane*'s novelty and its importance as personal style as an end in itself. Said Welles: "John Ford was my teacher. My own style has nothing to do with his, but *Stagecoach* was my movie text-book. I ran it over forty times." (Quoted by Peter Cowie, *The Cinema of Orson Welles* [New York: A. S. Barnes, 1965], p. 27, from article by Dilys Powell in *The Sunday Times* [London, February 3, 1963].) Certainly Welles and Ford have diverse sensibilities, but Welles's visual style seems almost a hyperbolic parody of Ford's; where Ford is subtle, Welles is cramped, exaggerated, and ostentatious. For the record, both directors exploit depth of field, long takes, multiplane composition, avoidance of conventional intercutting, UFA-style expressionism, high-contrast lighting, low-level camera, sharp-focus objects near image surface between us and the main action, cameo cutting,

One might reply that Ford's cutting between and among characters in the coach—this isolating of one or two characters—is more psychologically realistic to one's experience within a carriage, whereas a single distanced long take of everyone would disperse the vividness of individual experience. Perhaps the coach cutting occasionally gets a bit ponderous, so that the laboring montage amplifies the sense of effort in the screenplay, and perhaps the repetitive contrasts are a commercial concession. Yet how enjoyable is this disjunctive editing! And such cutting and staging within ensemble scenes is, through movies such as *Mogambo* and *7 Women*, increasingly a Fordian forte.

Yet, even though *Stagecoach* is a rapidly cut movie (612 shots in ninety-seven minutes = 9½ seconds per shot, or 10½ without the chase), it is a mistake to overlook, as Bazin does, how much *Stagecoach* abounds in long, fluid camera takes and how much more integral to its style than to Welles's or Wyler's is composition in depth. The way-station episode illustrates how Ford synthesizes the two styles—montage and long take—that Bazin took for antitheses.

Dallas the whore has offended propriety by sitting next to Lucy the lady, who, by the morals of the day, must register shock. (To her credit, she hesitates before accepting Hatfield's offer.) Ford combines shots from his own narrating perspective (left column) with subjective shots (right column), which, although from Lucy's perspective, are not at first clearly defined as being from her gaze—even shot 5, of Lucy staring, may surprise some spectators who have missed the matching of her glance (3) with the forward dolly (4). The subjective shots from Lucy are not balanced with matching subjective shots from Dallas (there is no third column)—which emphasizes Dallas's passive victimhood and Lucy's active aggression, and also Dallas's

---

bringing actors into close shots by moving them rather than the camera; broad characterizations, particularly of bit players. Professor Robert Carringer argues Gregg Toland's credit for *Citizen Kane*'s visual style, citing as evidence Toland's similar work on Ford's *The Long Voyage Home* (1940, just before *Kane*). But Carringer's description of *Long Voyage* as "the first film . . . in which there is a consistent use of the deep-focus style" ("Orson Welles and Gregg Toland: Their Collaboration on *Citizen Kane*," *Critical Inquiry*, Summer 1982, pp. 658–70) suggests a profound unfamiliarity with Ford's (and others') visual style, in which we find abundant exploitation of all the skills of deep-focus style from 1929 onward. Carringer also repeats the false but generally accepted argument that it was not until *Kane*'s time that improved lighting, film stock, lenses, and the blimpless Mitchell camera enabled film to escape the "heavily diffused light, soft tonality [and] relatively shallow depth of field" that sound techniques had imposed on thirties Hollywood, and to "return to the sharper, crisper, still-photographic style characteristic of many silent films." But the soft, diffused style began in the late silent years (Charles Rosher, Karl Freund, Ben Reynolds, George Schneiderman, Karl Brown, Ernest Palmer, et al.), not with the first talkies, while, on the other hand, many early-thirties talkies are sharp and crisp (if one sees good prints), particularly Capra, Lubitsch, Vidor, and Ford (*Salute, Arrowsmith, Doctor Bull*)—but only when they wanted to be sharp and crisp. And the blimpless camera was (first?) used by Arthur Miller for *Wee Willie Winkie* in November 1936—four years before *Kane*. There were always ways to get around technical limitations (and a good artist capitalizes upon his limitations), although Bazin, in a fit of metaphysics, assumed things like faster film stock necessarily advanced cinema in that they help to perfect cinema's ability to be an "imprint" of reality—as if Bach's music would be better had he had modern instruments.

Figure 4. *Stagecoach:* Way-Station Episode

Objective point of view *(i.e., narrator's, Ford's)*	*Subjective point of view* *(i.e., Lucy's)*

1. **General shot:** room and table: Lucy at head.

2. Ringo offers to seat Dallas (from, approximately, Lucy's perspective).

3. **Closer** (from Dallas's side but not from her perspective): Gatewood (Boone and Hatfield background) and Lucy, who turns and stares toward:

Figure 4. (continued)

Objective point of view *(i.e., narrator's, Ford's)*	*Subjective point of view* *(i.e., Lucy's)*

4=2. **Dolly-in** on Dallas sitting
(Lucy's pov).

5. **Medium close-up:** Lucy staring
(frontal: i.e., not slanted from Dallas's
pov):

6=2. but closer. **Medium close-up:**
Dallas, who lowers her eyes under
Lucy's gaze.

Figure 4. *Stagecoach:* **Way-Station Episode (continued)**

Objective point of view *(i.e., narrator's, Ford's)*	*Subjective point of view* *(i.e., Lucy's)*

7=3. Four at table. Lucy turns away.

8=2. Dallas and Ringo react. (Same perspective as 2, but no longer under Lucy's gaze: i.e., Lucy is there, off-screen, but refuses to interact.)

9=3. Hatfield offers to find Lucy a cooler place by window.

Figure 4. (continued)

Objective point of view *(i.e., narrator's, Ford's)*	*Subjective point of view* *(i.e., Lucy's)*

10=2. Dallas and Ringo react.

11=3. Lucy rises and leaves.

12. **General shot** from head of
table, Ringo and Dallas seated left.
Lucy, Hatfield, Gatewood seat
themselves in rear.

Figure 4. *Stagecoach:* Way-Station Episode (continued)

Objective point of view *(i.e., narrator's, Ford's)*	*Subjective point of view* *(i.e., Lucy's)*

13

13. **Medium two-shot:** Dallas and Ringo (frontal: not former angle).

14a

14b

14. **Dolly in:** Lucy and Hatfield . . .

inferior position. The space-defining crosscutting thus not only underlines Lucy's brutality; geometric space itself graphically represents this brutality —the abrupt close-up (5), the piercing stare dollying-in on Dallas (4).

The shots exemplify what Bazin termed "expressionist montage" and clearly the drama's dialectics could not be so well represented in a single take. As it happens, however, Ford proceeds to reap a long take's advantages, for it seems to take an eternity for Lucy, Hatfield, and Gatewood to leave their seats, relocate, and settle anew; all the while we stare at their subtle interactions and refusals to interact with Dallas, their hypocrisies and confessions. And all this occurs within composition in depth, as they move up screen to the table's far end, leaving the outlaws isolated in the foreground. This distanced perspective (12) comes as a physical relief after the crosscuts. But, as a summary of the previously divided space, it also registers the result of the conflict. And, by its distance, the shot invokes our helpless inability to control the deeds of other people, despite our sense of their wrongness.

There follows, while *our* indignation is strongest, a cut to the sympathetic victims, and their togetherness is brought out in the interactions permitted by the long-take two-shot (such as Bazin likes: we do not know which of them to watch); but in order for their emotions to emerge, Ford had first to isolate them by cutting the others out of the frame. Similarly, he will isolate Hatfield and Lucy together (via a gentle dolly), but, subsequently, the privacy of crosscuts rather than a two-shot better suits their timidity.

Nick Browne, a theoretician, has published an ingenious study of the first portion of this sequence in which, however, he reaches conclusions diametrically opposed to central theses of my own study of Ford's cinema.[19] As Browne reads the shots, we, as spectators, *share* Lucy's gaze and are thus implicated with her; but our emotional identification with poor Dallas prompts us to repudiate Lucy's gaze, along with her moral authority. So strong is this process of identification and implication that, in effect, we experience the film as though we were part of it, and as though it were itself narrated by Lucy. Ford "masks" his activity as narrator, becomes "invisible," and employs Lucy as "a visible persona . . . to constitute and make legible and continuous the depicted space, by referring shots on the screen alternately to the authority of her eye or the place of her body, [so that] the story seem[s] to tell itself [and seems to deny] existence of a narrator different from character."[20] In other words, we experience the fiction directly, without the mediation of Ford's auteur presence. "Ford" does not exist; we are being manipulated; our own moral decisions are preempted.

The impracticality of Browne's propositions, from my view, is that Fordian cinema belongs to quite another syntactical system than those of the cinemas of star-system identification, *Star-Wars*-like sensation, or Hitchcockian subjectivity; rather than unquestioning involvement, Ford exacts empathetic distance, and his narrating presence is, even among auteur directors, exceptionally strong. Browne's tendency to approach Ford as though he were Hitchcock is analogous to approaching Vermeer as though he were Van Gogh. A sequence from Mizoguchi's *Sansho the Bailiff*, similar to the *Stagecoach* sequence, makes the distinction clearer:

Figure 5. *Sansho the Bailiff*

Objective point of view	*Subjective point of view*
1. The bailiff about to brand an old woman with a hot iron.	
	2. The woman (bailiff's point of view).
3. The bailiff's face as he brands off-camera.	

In neither film are we so implicated with the branders (Lucy; the bailiff) that we need to repudiate them. We see *that* they see and know that social custom decrees that their seeing is far less empathetic toward their victims than is ours! (We see suffering, angelic humans; they see institutions.) Ford makes this particularly clear, showing (shot 4) the victim from Lucy's perspective even before (5) Lucy herself gazes in the direction of that perspective, and having Lucy afterwards (7) turn away and pretend Dallas is not really there—although Lucy's perspective shot remains (8 and 10). (See Figs. 4 and 5 above.)

Importantly, neither Ford nor Mizoguchi shows the brander from the victim's perspective. There is no third column to the far left. The conflict and the terror such a perspective would convey would detract from the greater, philosophic question. Although we scream at one woman's pain and squirm at another's humiliation, these emotions lead our interest to the psychology of the branders (*How can they act that way?!*), not to the trauma of the victim, and for this reason we study the branders from impartial (unconflicting, un-terror-filled) perspectives. Thus neither Lucy nor the bailiff is a narrating persona; they are the *chief themes* of their scenes. Ford's and Mizoguchi's styles are both presentational, not subjective. The objectivity of Ford's shots of Lucy, particularly the frontal close-up (5), evinces his narrative presence. They are not merely "'objective,' or perhaps 'nobody's' shots" (Browne[21]), they are Ford's shots.

Ford's strategic intention, finally, is incompletely stated as "to ally us emotionally with the interests and fortune of the outsiders as against social customs" (Browne[22]), for it is also to solicit our understanding of the *insiders* who, because they cannot escape as easily as Dallas and Ringo, are far more the real victims of social custom. This is why Ford concentrates on Lucy. Lucy can no more socialize with a whore in a lunchroom than she can present her to society. The first impossibility stems from her own unacknowledged intolerance, the second from her newly discovered acknowledgment of the intolerance of her world. Thus the sheriff acts partly as her proxy in letting Ringo and Dallas quit civilization (social custom) after Ringo exhibits his wild-ness (a rival social code) by gunning down the Plummers. But in the 1880s, the only practical form for such tolerance was segregation. *Stagecoach*, then, is more concerned with studying social custom than with revolutionary alienation. And Ford is more concerned with the art of sensibility than with the pseudo art of excitation.

In fact, no other Ford western gives a more cynical verdict on the notion of the West as synthesis of nature and civilization. In *Liberty Valance* (1962), for contrast, Ransom Stoddard spends a lifetime to figure out what everyone in *Stagecoach* already knows: that civilization is corrupting. The idealism, progressivism, and enlightenment shared by virtually everyone in *Liberty Valance*'s Shinbone is absolutely absent in malodorous Lordsburg and Tonto — dirty, sleazy, full of mean, intolerant, aggressive people. Doc Boone's drinking and Dallas's prostitution symbolize their intolerable, "hippie" characteristics in a puritanical society. The fact that two do "escape the blessings of civilization" is no more a happy ending than are the conclusions of *The Grapes of Wrath* or *How Green Was My Valley*. Ringo, who ignores society rather than confronting it, who is less outlaw than oblivious, is a dumb god who snatches Dallas off to never-never land. Who of us resembles Ringo? What solution or reason for optimism does he offer *us*, who cannot escape? As always in Ford, happiness belongs only to fools and simpletons, and if we fantasize with Ringo it is only because hope is more primal than realism.

According to John Wayne, preview audiences found the chase sensational. They "yelled and screamed and stood up and cheered. I never saw anything like it."[23] Yet William S. Hart objected that the Indians could have shot one horse to stop the coach. And in other respects—the impossible accuracy of the passengers' six-guns and inaccuracy of the Indians, the trumpeting arrival of the cavalry — the chase, exciting as it still is, may seem a bit of a campy put-on. Such a reaction is not far from Ford's intentions, which, while not desiring suspension of belief, do intend release, release not only from melodramatic suspense, but also from suffocating Victorian repression. The chase climaxes a process (gratifyingly, even sadistically witnessed) during which these diverse types, thrown together and systematically stripped of civilization, pomposity, and inhibition, let loose their true selves. But the trumpet that climaxes the chase marks also civilization's reimposition. For Ringo and Dallas, fortunately, there is yet another frontier to escape to; for us, that is fairyland. The ultimate truth of the Fordian western is its own extinction.

Later Ford westerns repeat ideas from *Stagecoach*,* as *Stagecoach* presumably repeats ideas from Ford's silents. Like the Carey-Ford Universals, it envisions plots and characters in archetypal, mythic terms. Or rather, the

---

*For example: Buck's "legs, eh, limbs" to Lucy shows up in *Donovan's Reef;* both Buck and his coach are essentially the same in *The Man Who Shot Liberty Valance;* the dusty columns of soldiers show up again in *Fort Apache* and *Rio Grande;* the surprise discovery of the Indians via a pan is repeated in those films and in *Wagon Master* (and occurs via a cut in Francis Ford /

terms are *premythic*, in the sense that the characters are not, as in *Steamboat Round the Bend* (or any mature society), echoing myths, but seem to have relatively pure and secure self-identities—particularly when compared with the dependent, disintegrating beings inhabiting the threatening, repressive worlds of earlier thirties Ford films. On the other hand, *Stagecoach* is perhaps still too self-conscious to revive completely the earthy intimacy of those early silents, while its mixture of artfulness and commerciality set it apart from the Argosy westerns, too. Hence it is problematic how personal or typical of Ford *Stagecoach* really is. Coming out of the exotica period, it looks back to the *Men-Without-Women*, *Lost-Patrol*-type situation, and forward to the pretentiousness of *The Long Voyage Home* (all Dudley Nichols scripts), yet with less preciousness than any of the other 1939–41 movies. In some ways it resembles *The Hurricane*, yet with far more variety, speed, and vigor. Probably we shall never know what sort of movie and what sort of reception Ford expected from *Stagecoach*, but if a single quality makes it stand out from his previous work, it might be audacity.

> *Young Mr. Lincoln* (**1939**). A deeper, more multileveled work than *Stagecoach*, this film attracted little attention and no awards in 1939, and was not even successful financially. Yet it seems in retrospect one of the finest prewar pictures. It deals, in its prelude, with Lincoln's discovery of Law and his friendship with Ann Rutledge in New Salem, 1832, and in its second section depicts a trial in Springfield, 1837, a success that sets Lincoln on his road to glory.*

But as in *Liberty Valance* and *7 Women*, the movie's ultimate concern is the dubious dialectic between free will and a deterministic cosmos—

Ince's *Blazing the Trail* (2-reel 101 Bison, 1912); the Plummer brothers anticipate the Clantons of *My Darling Clementine* and the Cleggs of *Wagon Master*; the silent close crosscutting of the badmen recurs in those two films as well as in *Fort Apache*; the newspaper-office joke recurs in *Liberty Valance*; and the shot of Dallas and her lamp in the long narrow corridor is a big moment toward the end of *7 Women*. Ragtime piano recurs in *My Darling Clementine* and *The Sun Shines Bright*. The Dallas-Ringo relationship is probably more typical of prewar Ford (though, cf. Denver-Travis in *Wagon Master*), the Lucy-Hatfield one of postwar Ford. Most prophetic is the startling dolly-up introduction of John Wayne (against mountains), for *Stagecoach* introduced him to stardom. Ford had fought to get Wayne this role, a good-badman role, a Harry Carey role, and Ford, seeing Wayne as a Carey-type, had been urging him to copy Carey.

*The trial depicted occurred in 1857 in Cass [sic] County, Illinois; Lincoln used *The Old Farmer's Almanac* to break down a case against a certain Armstrong. The idea of two defendants derives from a trial covered by scenarist Lamar Trotti as a young reporter in Georgia: the mother of two young men was the sole witness, she refused to tell which one did the murder, and both were hanged.

The script is essentially Trotti's, but Trotti had worked with Ford on their Will Rogers Americana and much internal evidence confirms Ford's claimed collaboration (e.g., the Francis Ford character who is drunk and spits). Not since 1935 had Ford made a movie he cared deeply about at Fox, and to limit Zanuck's interference, he turned in scarcely a foot more film than he intended to use. Even so, Zanuck deleted shots, humor, and a scene when a young dandy, John Wilkes Booth, leaves a theater playing *Hamlet* and notices "this funny, incongruous man in a tall hat riding a mule" (Bogdanovich, p. 73) wishing he had money to go in.

between Lincoln as autonomous man and Lincoln as agent of history. Here, as in the later films, the case for free will is submerged within hints and glances, and all but overpowered by contexts rendered deterministic by various distancing devices—mood, myth, archetypes, genre, symbol, music, history, and time.

Time weighs heavy, Murnau-fashion, and the mood throughout is gloomy. Although the movie's thrust is passage (from immaturity to manhood, innocence to tainted wisdom, human to mythic stature), history, like God's omniscience, puts everything outside time, into the static determined; life is pilgrimage. And Lincoln seems haunted by this pilgrimage. Haunted, on one hand, by his *past*, by loss of Ann, and by general homelessness, which attract him to the family of Abigail Clay, whose two sons he defends against a murder charge; haunted, on the other hand, by his *future*—for Ford contextualizes the young Lincoln within a conditioning matrix of tenses. Time in various ways contributes a mystic determinism that pervades the film:

1. Cause-and-effect: Lincoln is seized in youth, on the threshold; thereafter all has been decided, with awesome finality, it seems, as Lincoln walks off screen at end.

2. Cause-and-effect bipartite structure: Events in 1837 seem determined by events in 1832. Ann inspires him from her grave.

3. Foreknowledge as cause: We know Lincoln's future, and premonitions of his tragic myth loom in anticipation.

4. Sense of destiny as cause: Lincoln combines ambition with mysticism, belief in free choice with conviction in ordained, appointed destiny; alternately, the character may be seen as a sort of Faust, a plaything of devilhistory. Does he pursue his future? Or does his future pursue him?

5. Finally, Rosemary Benét's poem prefaces a future-perfect from the outset:

> If Nancy Hanks
> Came back as a ghost
> Seeking news
> Of what she loved most,
> She'd ask first,
> "Where's my son?
> What's happened to Abe?
> What's he done?
> You wouldn't know
> About my son?
> Did he grow tall?
> Did he have fun?
> Did he learn to read?
> Did he get to town?
> Do you know his name?
> Did he get on?"

Of course *we* know the answers, we tell ourselves, but Ford tricks us, answering every question not in terms of 1865 but of 1837: the son is in Springfield, he became a lawyer, stood for right and mercy, did indeed grow tall, did not have much fun, certainly learned to read, and got to town too; a few of us know his name, and at movie's end he says he'll "walk *on* a bit farther." From our point of view, 1837 is in context of 1865, of what *shall* be; yet the film asks that we grasp 1837's happenings from the mother's point of view, implying that for her 1837 is a truer response to her questions than what happened later, because that future belonged to history, while this present belonged to Abe. It was now that his life defined its course.

In later pictures, John Ford would exploit a future-perfect perspective (vision of the past from a more recent viewpoint) through music in *Wagon Master*, or the flashback structures of *The Long Gray Line* or *Liberty Valance*. Here the poem provides perspective. Only the poem refers explicitly to Lincoln's mother. But it suggests Abe still under his absent mother's gaze, still conscious of that gaze, seeing himself serving a surrogate mother in Abigail Clay. His acceptance of payment from this impoverished mother-figure suggests umbilical severing: taking her money spares her humiliation and confirms their independence. He does not recall her as the woman who gave him the lawbooks in the movie's second scene, in 1832, nor does she remember him; but the circle has come round, and Lincoln enters into manhood, both released from his mother's gaze and launched by it.

> [When Ford discussed Lincoln] there was such an extraordinary sense of intimacy in his tone . . . that somehow it was no longer a director speaking of a great President, but a man talking about a friend.[24] [He didn't wish to film Mother Cabrini, objecting,] "I'm a Catholic and I'd treat such a subject with too much respect."[25] [But he cajoled Henry Fonda into being Lincoln:] "You think you'd be playing the goddamn great emancipator, huh? He's a goddamn fucking jake-legged lawyer in Springfield, for Christ's sake!"[26]

The myth of Lincoln also controls the character's freedom. The nineteenth-century theater had bequeathed an onerous tradition to Lincoln depictions, one that films had been thoroughly exploiting, too,* and Ford capitalizes on the tendency of any Lincoln movie to be an apotheosis of its own genre, with conventional mythic elements and shorthand narration. As with his later cavalry epics, Ford's starting point is less actual historic fact than inherited myth, which he reinterprets via history. Ford had Fonda's nose enlarged, played up his long, sinuous body and his big feet: Abe enters a scene a lank woodsman with slung ax and huge boots, and with scenery equally traditional. "Books?" exclaims the rustic youth; then, in typical Ford fashion, re-

---

*Francis Ford impersonated Lincoln frequently in the teens, but never for John. Frank McGlynn, Sr., held the role in *The Prisoner of Shark Island*. Both Fords read Lincolniana omnivorously.

peats, wondrously: "Books!" Or, the tall dark man stands alone silently, while a mob sweeps through streets. Or, from Lincoln's low-level point of view, Ann Rutledge suddenly appears, a mythic apotheosis of loveliness.

Like time, such magic moments, evocative of the mythic Lincoln, threaten, along with the suavity of Fonda, to submerge the real man. It requires the viewer's active participation to detect Lincoln's ignobility, silliness, awkwardness, arrogance, and fear. Comedic frontier roughness exonerates Lincoln for cheating at tug-of-war, or for ruthlessness toward two farmer plaintiffs or toward Jack Cass; and we admire his foxiness rather than his obnoxious guile in the way he dupes everyone during the trial. His silliness, too, is mitigated: as he rides into town, long legs draped over his mule, and tips his hat to the courthouse flag, the humor is a bit neutralized by Ford's characteristically unhurried and reflectively paced treatment, and by the scene's conclusion in a newspaper announcement of the opening of Lincoln's law office—thus bestowing upon the entire sequence an aura of "And so it happened . . . " Nor at Mary Todd's ball does he evince discomfort at finding himself in high society and admitting his humble origins ("No Lincoln I ever knew ever amounted to a hill of beans"). Perhaps he is caught off balance by Mary's offensive and by having to dance, but he does not seem to dance that badly. Ford even spares us the sight of Lincoln courting the venomous Miss Todd: few permutations of character are so extraordinary as their balcony scene when, as Lincoln abruptly tunes her out to stare at the river, bossy Mary docilely retreats to wait in a corner.* Even flirting with Douglas fails to arouse jealousy: Lincoln strums his Jew's harp nonchalantly. It is she who pursues, he whose timidity clothes power.

Yet this "angelic" Abe has a strong ego, can lord it over his fellows, is

---

*The way Mary flirts—leaving room and frame and forcing Abe to follow—anticipates Grace Kelly's similar tactics with Clark Gable in *Mogambo* (1954). Lincoln's ride into town on a mule (or ass?) has been compared by Jean Roy to Christ's entry into Jerusalem, but such an analogy strikes me as less intentional here than in *The Fugitive* or *7 Women*.

secretly, almost obnoxiously confident, and knows how to make the most of an opportunity. Whatever destiny's role, he chooses his road in life, even as he tips the stick on Ann's grave. "I'd feel such a fool," he mumbles then, "settin' myself up as knowin' so much." But scarcely a minute later (screen time) his head eclipses George Washington's portrait while quarreling farmers, behind a rockingchair* foreground, are coerced into peace by a sassily grinning Lincoln in the background. A little later, as he calms a lynch mob, he does not hide his cocky self-assurance, his enjoyment of what he is doing, or his exaltation after the event. In contrast, Judge Priest, in *The Sun Shines Bright* (1953), is nervous, calms a lynch mob with a weary sense of work, and, when all is over, wipes his brow with relief. Lincoln is proud, feels power, calms the mob with guile; the older man needs a gun and a drink.

Yet Lincoln seems dazed—surprised, almost scared—not at the danger he has faced, but by the power and destiny he is uncovering. The dazed expression comes again, more strongly, at Mary Todd's ball, as he stands transfigured on a balcony, suffused by the moonlit river's power, and, more strongly still, when he walks from the courthouse into the bright light and cheers of the masses. Destiny, as we know, is drawing him; but he himself only gradually becomes aware of it. The Lincoln who, at picture's end, strides resolutely up the hill (rather like Christ departing the Garden of Gethsemane) is a far cry from the whimpering, indecisive farmboy who, when he lets the fate of a falling twig decide his future, thinks he is only playing a game!

True, there is already a bit of a haunted look to Lincoln when we first see him lounging on a porch, awkward and unaware, and as he rises, the noisy chatter of a politician suddenly gives way to solemn calm: time will almost always slow down when Lincoln appears (he cannot dance to others' tempo). And Ford's camera watches him, passionately, repressively, yearningly, lovingly, but not innocently, recording every muscle movement all too intently, as young Abe puts down his board, lowers his legs, stands slowly, walks over, puts his hands in his pockets, begins to speak. Gloom, a mystic aura, seems to

*Cf. the rockingchair-as-stability in *The Searchers*.

impose itself, so that this Lincoln seems a dream creature, walking through a dream whose plot he cannot control but whose theme he begins to suspect.

> Fare thee well, my darling lass,
> Fare thee well and gone,
> With golden slippers on.

Ford does not tell us, but Nancy Hanks, like many pioneers, was a forest mystic (and Mary Todd took to spiritualism after Lincoln's death). Not surprisingly, then, Lincoln, in seeking what is in him, would expect to find guidance in Nature herself. Truth exists, within oneself and in the natural world consubstantially; the only "mystery" is the fog that blinds us to it. And Ford *does* tell us about Truth, for as Lincoln wonders, "Law!," gawking at the book, and then repeats, "Law!," the medium shot dissolves, nay, slowly explodes into an immense riverbent landscape, wherein Lincoln lies, against a big tree, reading the book. Thus we know that Law and Nature are one. "Why, gee," he says, "that's all there is to it, right and wrong!"—and thus we know that Law and innate intuitive knowledge are one with Nature, too. Whereupon, Ann Rutledge appears, cut to with a suddenness that marks her apparition as even more miraculous than the explosion of Law into Nature and that suggests she is Truth's angel. She alone, in fact, understands Abe Lincoln, revealing to him his own deepest thoughts:

— "Hello, Mr. Lincoln. Abe."
— "Hello, Ann. Give me a minute to try an' untangle myself."
— "Aren't you afraid you'll put your eyes out, reading like that upside down?"
— "Trouble is, Ann, when I'm standing up my mind's lying down. When I'm lying down my mind's standing up. Of course, allowin' I've got a mind."
— "You've a wonderful mind, Abe, and you know it."
— "River sure is pretty today, ain't it?"
— "You think a lot about things, don't you?"
— "Well, my brain gets to itchin' inside sometimes. I gotta scratch it."
— "Father says you've a real head on your shoulders, and a way with people too. He says it's not all just makin' me laugh. They remember what you say because it's got sense to it."
— "Mr. Rutledge is a mighty fine man, Ann, but if you ask me, I'm more like the old horse the fella's tryin' to sell. Sound of skin and skeleton and free from faults and faculties."
— "I know how smart you are, how ambitious you are too."
— "Ambitious?"
— "You are, deep down underneath. Even if you won't admit it."
— "Gotta have education these days to get anywhere. I never went to school as much as a year in my whole life."
— "O but you've educated yourself. You've read poetry and Shakespeare and . . . and now Law. I just had my heart set on your goin'

over to Jacksonville to college when I go to the seminary there
an' . . ."
— "You're mighty pretty, Ann."
— "Some folks I know don't like red hair."
— "I do."
— "Do ya, Abe?"
— "I love red hair."

The way Ford treats this dialogue—foolish Abe and sweet Ann strolling beside the river in an aura of intense enchantment— virtually overpowers the conflict that, reading the dialogue alone, is so obvious. Lincoln keeps trying to deflect their talk to romance, but Ann keeps turning it back to pushing Abe along, even to the point of using herself as bait. (This, of course, concurs with the puritan ethic. And Mary Todd would later assume a comparable role— pushing Abe on to the presidency.) After their parting, Lincoln's casting a stone into the river indicates a nonchalant surrender to her will (to fate, in effect: the ripples). But this surrender is sealed by winter's ice and Ann's death. Love and sexuality are transformed into duty—duty to the dead, duty to her plans for him, duty to discover "what's in" him. When Lincoln appears at her graveside to consecrate his surrender to her, he already seems a step closer to the legendary Lincoln figure (with his ax and huge boots), and Ford, as he does all his most significant moments between lovers, marks the occasion with a flower put by Abe on Ann's grave.* And the river, so often sacramental in Ford, will constantly recall him to this task. "You sure do love to look at that river," remarks a friend, "Think it's a pretty woman."

Ann points Lincoln's ambition, another woman (his mother) watches over

*Lincoln's consecration to duty foreshadows Wyatt Earp's in *My Darling Clementine*.

him, a third (Mrs. Clay) gives him lawbooks and opportunity, a fourth (Mary Todd) beckons him on. As memories, as ideals, as women, they guide the mystic Abraham, and they confirm his sense of divine appointment. "I may not know much of the law," he chides the prosecutor, "but I know what you're doing is wrong." What *does* he know of the law? "Not enough to hurt me." Indeed, even his knowledge that Jack Cass is lying during the trial is presented as though come from the moon, as it were, via an almanac, which he plucks from a top hat.

A set of melody-motifs (by Alfred Newman) reinforces the aura of divine guidance surrounding Lincoln:

1. "Lincoln's Destiny"
2. "Funny Lincoln"
3. "Mrs. Clay" = rightness (law, lawbooks)
4. "Ann Rutledge" = confirmation (duty, river).

Scene	Motif
Campaign speeches	"Destiny" / "Funny"
Mrs. Clay and books	"Clay" / "Destiny"
River: Tree	"Destiny"
Ann	"Funny" / "Rutledge"
Grave	"Rutledge"
Riding into town	"Funny"
Newspaper announcement	"Destiny"
Farmers' case	—no music—
Celebration: Pies	"Funny"
Carrie Sue and Adam	"Clay"
After killing:	
Sheriff and mother	"Clay"
Lincoln appears	"Destiny"
Lynchers and Lincoln	"Destiny"
Bye to Mrs. Clay	"Clay" / "Destiny" / "Clay"
Going to ball	"Funny"
Ball: river balcony	"Rutledge"
Ride out by river	"Rutledge"
Clay farm	"Destiny" / "Clay"

Curiously, no off-camera music at all appears in the film's entire second half (except for "The Battle Hymn of the Republic" at the very end). Even at points where one would expect music, there is silence, as when Lincoln walks out of the courthouse and is cheered. Are we to infer that here, as during the trial and the farmers' case, Lincoln is on his own?*

*The "Destiny" motif is used again by Ford to evoke the tragic Lincoln in the Civil War episode of *How the West Was Won* (1962) and in *Cheyenne Autumn* (1964) when Schurz looks at Lincoln's portrait; the association of Ransom Stoddard with Lincoln is reinforced in *The Man Who Shot Liberty Valance* by association of the "Rutledge" motif with the cactus rose plant and Hallie and youthful hopes and love, as in the Ann Rutledge scene here. The "Destiny" motif also appears in the Walter Lang–Shirley Temple–Fox *Blue Bird* (1940) when a pubescent Lin-

So possessed does Lincoln seem and so determining does Ford's treatment appear that the editors of *Cahiers du Cinéma*, in a much-paraphrased article in the August 1970 number of their magazine, stated that *Young Mr. Lincoln's* original intention—to be an edifying hagiography of Lincoln as an ideal representative of American (i.e., Republican) ideology—is routed by Ford's "excessive" treatment, which reveals instead the "truly repressive dimensions" of Lincoln and thus of America's ruling ideology. Although supposedly a man of the people and of peace, Lincoln receives Law from God, uses it with violence, and represses most human instincts in himself and others. When not outrightly ridiculous, Lincoln is a mediocrity, a mere agent of truth; rather than a human, he is an unchanging, glacial monster, a sort of Nosferatu.[27]

The tendency of Frenchmen to oversimplify America is an honorable tradition dating back at least to Rousseau and Stendahl; and Abraham Lincoln—sad, haunted, unafraid to look foolish—perhaps is hard to digest as a hero for those accustomed to heroes of the ilk of Louis XIV, Napoleon, or DeGaulle. But *Cahiers'* psycho-Marxist ideology particularly misses the dialectical complexities of the Lincoln myth—and of John Ford. True, tragedy piles on tragedy for Lincoln all his life, turning him into a figure of the night and ultimately killing him. True, it is the force of Lincoln's will, implemented by violence on the most massive scale, that counters the South's desire to secede. And true, Lincoln is ultimately not a man but a monument to will. But these themes, these contradictions, have always been essential attributes of the Lincoln myth.* Lincoln was not a man pulled up by "the banal game of universal suffrage," as *Cahiers* through the mouth of Engels claims, but a man whose ambition and conviction (self-righteous, undoubtedly) drove him on, so that each new tragedy became an impetus rather than a defeat; he accepted the course thrust upon him. There could be no relaxation for Mr. Lincoln: not for him the chance to play Father Abraham, the Great Emancipator, the Great Reconciler—except in legend. The

---

coln (looking Fonda-ish) is encountered in the Land of the Unborn Children; and in a World War II Signal Corps film, *It's Your America* (1944), when Arthur Kennedy muses on the meaning of democracy while studying a Lincoln-head penny as he dog-soldiers through the war; in Fox's *Belle Starr* (Irving Cummings, 1941) and *A Man Called Peter* (Henry Koster, 1955).

*The character of Ford's Lincoln is quite consistent with the Lincoln of the Robert Sherwood–John Cromwell *Abe Lincoln in Illinois* (Raymond Massey, 1939) and the Lincoln of D. W. Griffith's *Abraham Lincoln* (1930). But the latter does offer contrasts. Walter Huston's sprawling, declamatory, loutish Lincoln splits logs while Ann reads him law; Fonda's Lincoln, tidy, self-conscious, lies lazily on his back reading when Ann comes by. Both associate woman-law-nature, but Griffith concentrates on the ax: his Lincoln is the North's hammer, a man of perseverance in a dark psychodrama.

Both also have Mary Todd's ball. Ford's Mary is radiant, her gown freshly white, the ballroom spacious, floors waxed, walls high and clear; the men, all dressed nattily alike, swirl in circle to "Golden Slippers." Griffith's Mary is plain, her lace cream-colored, the room small, cluttered; the men, dressed variously in well-worn clothing, dance a languid waltz. Ford's past is glorious present, Griffith's antique; Ford exalts linearity and motion, Griffith the lovely in the commonplace. His Lincoln is awkward, straggly, vest too small, trousers short; but, unlike Fonda, he goes boldly to Mary and *he* asks *her* to dance.

mythic Lincoln is no monster, but a man ensnared by a potent conspiracy of his own character (formed by his life) and of historical forces (among them the ideological evolution of the "American dream"); both man and myth evolve, emerging out of gloom.

For while it is true that Ford's Lincoln often stands reflectively apart from everyone else—even, as J. A. Place observes, having himself draped like a proscenium arch over many of the trial scenes[28]—it is equally true that he is always being pulled into society. His proximity to tragedy, his duty to his dead, unite him with all who share a sense of loss. But in the world he inhabits there is little sense of "Fordian community"; only Lincoln's illusion of one, only isolation and hardship, and strife. When Lincoln visits the Clay farm and imagines himself a part of their family, he is actually speaking with three women related not by blood but—at the moment—by common tragedy: the threatened execution of the two Clay sons, one married, the other engaged to Carrie Sue. Mrs. Clay, when we first saw her, sparkled like Carrie Sue; a half-dozen years later, she is old, and widowed.* In the letter scene she speaks of those years: all the unremarkable, unquestioningly accepted horrors of pioneer life, the deaths, the unrewarded pain and toil. The letter concludes with a mawkish verse (a nice touch). Then, in a cell the family clings together singing, waiting (we see them in cameos); as Abigail leaves, the sheriff responds indifferently to her curtsy: she is nothing to him, nor does she expect attention from exalted personages. Midst all this, the real miracle is people's buoyancy—Carrie Sue's impetuosity: her unconscious eroticism, country accent, love for Sarah's baby, forwardness (like Mary Todd) in proposing marriage.**

Like Lincoln, the folk dwell in a mystic, forest dreamworld. The "blessings of civilization" have not yet come. People are instinctual, ingenuous; as in *Steamboat Round the Bend*, they are discovering things for the first time—books, law, their country's history as paraded on July 4th. But these "myths," without the hero's mediation, will not yet function properly. Without sufficient civilization, the law is a terrifying machine and the people are an unthinking mob. A Fordian fool (Francis Ford) exemplifies public volatility: a drunk (i.e., like most people, intoxicated by the moment), he will cheer lynchers or weep over a mother; yet Lincoln wants him on the jury.

*Alice Brady (1892–1939), Mrs. Clay, debuted on stage in 1911, somewhat against the will of her promoter father (William Brady: boxing and Broadway), then became his star at Brady Motion Pictures in 1914. She made fifty-two pictures (World, Select, Realart) before returning to the stage in 1923, where she was regarded as one of America's finest comediennes. She returned to films in 1933, made twenty-six more, and won an Oscar in *In Old Chicago* (Henry King, 1937). She was dying of cancer while making *Young Mr. Lincoln*, her seventy-eighth and last. Dewitt Bodeen cites her trial scene as "one of the profoundest manifestations of humanity's frightened bafflement before an inexplicable universe ever recorded by the camera." No wonder Lincoln understood her. ("Alice Brady," in *Films in Review*, November 1966, pp. 555–73.)

**The character's function anticipates Sue Lyon's in *7 Women*. Dorris Bowdon (Carrie Sue) receives no screen credit; she evidently replaced Judith Dickens, who is credited. She retired after marrying Nunnally Johnson in 1940 and playing Rosasharn in *The Grapes of Wrath*.

Lincoln appears nourished by the commonfolk; but he knows they are *common*folk. His introversion makes him so self-aware, so conscious of his apartness, of his "priesthood and judgeship," that (like Ransom Stoddard but unlike either Judge Priest) he cannot avoid condescension. He talks down to the lynchers and describes Mrs. Clay as, "Just a simple woman. I've seen [her] three times in my life, yet I know everything there is to know about her." Actually he has seen her four times, and does not know she gave him the lawbooks. For to him she stands for *all* mothers, just as Carrie Sue is like every young girl. (Indeed, the dramatic prominence of Lincoln's subjectivity may tend to blind even us to the individuality of the many "typed" supporting characters—and wrongly so, for it is they who save Lincoln from abstraction. As in *The Fugitive*, they root a hypertheoretical hero.)

Lincoln's sad, haunted, contradictory qualities are (unknown to *Cahiers*) shared by a remarkably large number of Fordian people, particularly from 1935 through 1947, all of whom feel chosen by destiny, secure in transcendental justification, and motivated by a sense of divinely appointed duty: Mary Stuart (*Mary of Scotland*), Dr. Mudd (*The Prisoner of Shark Island*), Casey and Tom Joad (*The Grapes of Wrath*), Wyatt Earp (*My Darling Clementine*), the Dubliners (*The Plough and the Stars*), the British (*Wee Willie Winkie*), the French (*The Hurricane*), the Americans (*Submarine Patrol, The Battle of Midway*). More generally, Lincoln is a paradigm of the Fordian hero of any date: solitary, celibate, almost impotent in grief, yet of the people; independent of logic, he arrogates authority to intervene, even violently, even by cheating, in order to mediate intolerance and to impress his personal convictions upon those whose thinking he faults (again: Judge and Priest); he reunites a family and walks away at the end.

The sense of tragic gloom haunting both film and Lincoln emanates from the shared knowledge (Ford, Lincoln, us) of the unity of life's passage from the necessary past into the necessary future. If Lincoln's belief during the twig episode is superstitious, later events in Springfield make him a more serious believer, until he realizes he no longer has the choice of going back: he must say goodbye to Ann, to Mrs. Clay, to his sidekick, to us and the screen, and "walk on a bit farther, up to that hill maybe": thunder, lightning, "Battle Hymn of the Republic," the Lincoln Memorial statue. But the man has become myth even before he dissolves into marble. That he is not entirely aware of this—nor entirely unaware, either—is evident from the manner in which the famous tall hat is made to dominate the forefront of the frame during the trial, while action occurs upframe from its perspective. We, but not cocky Lincoln, recognize the full irony of his putting this hat on, at his moment of triumph. The hero has been born.

***Drums Along the Mohawk* (1939).** Frontier life is depicted similarly in *Drums Along the Mohawk*, which sketches a gloomy series of events undergone by pioneer settlers in New York's Mohawk Valley, 1776–1781. The land is work; Indians attack periodically; farmhouses and crops are burnt; children are born, men march off to fight the British and die. But the land is virgin, the people young, the air suffused with freshness, the gloom something to be brushed aside. Even old widow McKlennan (Edna May Oliver—nominated for an Oscar here), momentarily overtaken by memory of her dead husband as she feeds twigs to a fire, quickly recovers her jaunty spirits. As in the early thirties, Ford shows the social structures that inspire people to endure, and even to die, in order to solidify those same structures. But such traditions—source of all evil elsewhere in Ford—here do not ossify under stress. Traditional male-female roles are constantly exchanged. Each helps the other persevere. Gil provides one home, Lana another. She searches for him after the first battle, and finds him dazed in the night. He, in a 100-second take, searches for her after the second battle—she dons a soldier coat and kills an Indian—and finds her dazed. And unlike *Stagecoach*'s or *Lincoln*'s frontiers, *Mohawk*'s is dense with embryonic institutions and myths. Rituals abound, often grim, occasionally of fairy-tale charm, but, whether the ritual be marriage, a doctor amputating a leg, or a U.S. flag being raised, people sense that what they do for their first time has been done since time immemorial.

But compared to *Young Mr. Lincoln*, *Drums* is artful naiveté, airy and bright in its use of Technicolor (Ford's first film in color and his least expressionistic since talkies began), and seeming a particularly commercial enterprise for Ford—why *did* Claudette Colbert insist on wearing full glamourpuss makeup even while raking hay? Still, it is dotted with magic moments, of which the finest, blending beauty, glory, and sadness, occurs as Lana stands gazing from a hilltop while, small in the distance, a column of troops, her husband among them, marches off to battle, piping "Yankee Doodle."

The battle in question, incidentally, was actually fought by Herkimer at Oriskany, August 16, 1777, against a corps of Burgoyne's army, one of a series of victories culminating at Saratoga October 17, which in turn brought about the French alliance by which the war was won. (Field forces were generally small; Cornwallis at Yorktown had 7,073 men.) The film's siege is fictitious.

Zanuck had been growing progressively more frantic as the date for the troupe's return from Utah drew near and Ford, already over budget and behind schedule, made no preparations for this huge battle—it had been scheduled for three weeks of shooting. He badgered Ford daily with telegrams. Then one day Ford replied: they were caught up, within budget, and the battle had been filmed that morning. What had happened was that Ford, out of a clear blue sky, had turned to Henry Fonda (Gil): "Henry, I have to shoot a battle scene that I don't want. I had a better idea today. You've studied the script and your role, you probably know more about the battle than I do. Sit down and lean against this wall." With the camera aimed at Fonda, Ford fired a series of questions: "So, Henry, how did the battle begin?" And Fonda replied, making up an account. "And Peter? What happened to Peter?" asked Ford; or, "What was it like to have killed that man, after seeing John die?" And Fonda went on improvising, giving a virtual psychoanalysis of the battle. "Cut," called Ford, and told the editors: "Cut out my questions and use it as it is." One long take.[29]

Weather conditions in Utah's Wasatch Mountains caused enormous delays and difficulties. When the light was not changing (making it impossible to match shots), it rained. Frank Baker recalls six days of rain beginning the day he arrived, and Ford's not speaking to him for weeks in retaliation.* To make matters worse, Fox had started production without a completed script. But Ford maintained strict discipline in camp. Beer was allowed only in the commissary and limited to two per man; violators were promptly sent home. Only Mae Marsh and Ruth Clifford were permitted to carry out beer—concealed in their aprons; in return, they knitted Ford socks. Every night Ford sent a bugler thirty feet into the woods to play "Taps"—distantly.

The Grapes of Wrath (1940). Following completion of the shooting of *Drums Along the Mohawk*, Ford's third picture without a break, he embarked, with scarcely a month's pause, upon the *Araner*, on *The Grapes of Wrath* (1940), the film, as Andrew Sarris has written, "that was

---

*Ford typically kept Baker ignorant of his role until Baker found himself leading a column of Continentals into the fort—with no instructions otherwise, so that all the way he tried desperately to divine where to stop and what to do. Such uncertainty was Ford's way of getting that little spark of spontaneity—and of keeping actors on their toes.

single-handedly to transform him from a storyteller of the screen to America's cinematic poet laureate."[30]

A variety of critical tendencies—literary, documentary, and social-conscious—contributed to placing this film on the "one small uncrowded shelf devoted to the cinema's masterworks," as Frank Nugent wrote in *The New York Times* at its release.[31] In 1940 its debt to British and American documentaries was evident, and the same qualities distinguished it from other commercial movies: not merely social concern, but the look of actuality, spare decor, location shooting (some of it), authentic-seeming actors, the understated tone of everything. Perhaps it did sweeten John Steinbeck's bitterness, and maybe its aura of outrage was belated, and some found it an amusing profanity—tinsel Hollywood mimicking the messianic underground. But it was difficult to recall any other movie from a major studio whose tone was anywhere near so "aware." Even today, after the radical-chic social-consciousness of the fifties, sixties, and seventies, few films appear quite so seditious, bitter, and damning.

It remains to be ascertained to what degree social criticism had been repressed in American films after the financial consolidation and stricter censorship codes wrought in the early thirties. True, protests were the norm in allegorical genres like the western and the gangster film, but such rabble-rousing was seldom taken or considered as serious social criticism. *The Grapes of Wrath*—its prestige guaranteed by the highly acclaimed novel from which it derived*—was to some degree unique. Had critics remembered the movies before 1935, they may have recalled the doleful, astringent, iconoclastic, and almost misanthropic terms in which Ford (to speak only of Ford) had depicted contemporary America in *Flesh, Pilgrimage, Doctor Bull,* and *The Whole Town's Talking,* and hence they might have thought *The Grapes of Wrath* less original, though preachier. Ford's wrath had been drenched in exotica since 1935, but he eagerly employed the license given by *Stagecoach* to vilify a banker over gamblers, whiskey-drummers, prostitutes, escaped convicts, street murderers, and marauding Apache.

> This here old man just lived a life,
> an' just died out of it.
> I don't know whether it was good or bad.
> An' it don't matter much.
> Heard a fella say a poem once.
> An' he says, "All that lives is holy."
> But I wouldn't pray just for an old man that's dead.

---

*It won two Oscars (direction; supporting actress: Darwell) and five nominations (best picture; actor: Fonda; script: Johnson; editing: Robert Simpson; sound: a group); New York Film Critics chose it best picture, and awarded Ford best director for it and *The Long Voyage Home*.

Many critics, some of them experts in literature, have compared this film to Steinbeck's novel (see Bibliography). My own tendency is to consider how a script or story serves a director, not how the director serves a script, and rather than duplicate the critical work of others, I have tried to limit my critique to locating Ford's personality in what is, after all, a studio collaboration and one of Ford's lesser movies—considered as art rather than as reputation.

'Cause he's alright.
If I was to pray, I'd pray for folks that's alive,
an' don't know which way to turn.
Granpa here, he ain't got no more trouble like that.
He's got his job all cut out for him.
So, cover him up an' let him get to it.
                    Casey's Funeral Oration

In *The Grapes of Wrath*, characters are less prototypical than in *Stage-coach*, and the anger they arouse is initially less totemic and, hence, more personally uncomfortable to us. The banker who throws Muley's family off its land seems initially a not-bad sort doing a job he hates. But doubts arise as we study his spiffy car, and as we watch him light a big cigar and drive off deaf to Muley's pathetic protests. Yet Ford mitigates the effect of these gestures by shifting the camera's gaze to the rear, so that the banker lights his cigar with his back to us and in far shot. So as we begin to hate him, we regard him less as a person. This process of alienation does not climax until the banker's second appearance, when he tells the Joads to be off by sunrise, and when we see him distanced and with a sheriff riding beside him. Now it's us against them.

This process of alienation is announced in the opening conversation between Tom Joad (Henry Fonda) and a truckdriver, and is repeated with the banker, the lunchroom people,* and the gas-station attendants, the New Deal camp director, and numberless policemen and contractors. We are led to identify with "Our People" (as Ma Joad puts it) and to regard the rest of the world as alien. Such a process of identification /alienation is essentially revolutionary. In many earlier Ford pictures, when society and its sustaining myths failed, individuals went into identity crises. Paradoxically, in *The Grapes of Wrath*, the opposite occurs: the individual is strengthened not only in self-identity, but in identity as a member of a class. Through this process Tom Joad comes to understand his mission in life, and goes off alone.

In later years Ford went out of his way to downplay this revolutionary side of the picture:

I was only interested in the Joad family as *characters*. I was sympathetic to people like the Joads, and contributed a lot of money to them, but I was not interested in *Grapes* as a social study. I admire John Steinbeck and enjoyed working on it. I bucked to do that picture, and put everything I had into it.[32]

And again:

Before all else, it is the story of a family, the way it reacts, how it is shaken by a serious problem which overwhelms it. It is not a social film on this problem, it's a study of a family.[33]

---

*Rather ironic: two truckdrivers reward with a large tip a waitress who grudgingly gave Pa Joad fifteen-cent bread for ten cents, and five-cent candy for one cent.

Such denials border suspiciously on affirmations. Ford "bucked," his politics are declared, he could hardly have been unaware of the project's uniqueness, and he rests his case on a distinction between a "family study" and a "social study." Furthermore, it had been typical of previous socially conscious documentaries (such as *Hallelujah, Our Daily Bread, Moana, Man of Aran*) to focus on exotic, alien subjects, on the lowest classes, and often on a family, and to employ "documentary" elements only as sorts of dramatic foils. This, of course, only the more hotly inflamed audience empathy.

But Ford is technically correct. *The Grapes of Wrath* is perhaps not a social study, because it concentrates on effects, not causes. The "system" is condemned, but remains unseen; impersonal tractors destroy homes; impersonal signs forbid rides. But oppression assaults the Joads without cessation (other than pointed reminders how much better they have it than others).

In later years Ford more typically concentrates on the causes, often neglecting the effects (e.g., *The Long Gray Line, The Man Who Shot Liberty Valance*), and his central characters are the soldiers or police or others within the power structure, while the oppressed are represented superficially. For example, in the cavalry films, it is the soldiers who are analyzed and the Indians who suffer iconically. But in *The Grapes of Wrath* the reverse is true. The focus is on the "Indians," the Oakies, while the oppressors and virtually everyone else are, if by no means dehumanized, the ones restricted to symbolic gestures. Even the federal camp director is presented as a prototypical New Deal knight.

A number of factors, however, alter the thrust of the film's "politics" of empathy and alienation. Primary is the unavoidable fact that "Our People"— these proud, folksy, hopelessly ignorant Oakies—are so exotic as to be almost unreal, while the classes and attitudes arousing our indignation are in reality our own. Thus audience indignation is inevitably intellectualized.

Secondly, the impact of revolutionary alienation is deflected in plot development. Empathy, as always in Ford, is aroused by situating narrative point of view at the level of the central characters. Usually these characters represent not only themselves but a society to which they belong. Often these societies are "enclosed": by profession—military bases; by geography—islands, towns; by vehicles—stagecoach; or, as in *The Grapes of Wrath*, by caste—the downtrodden. But generally they are less homogeneous than in *Wrath*, even though the society here is only a single family, and individuals achieve richer identities through elaborate patterns of contrast. "Our People," instead, are contrasted only with brutal simplicity, en masse, and as individuals they remain somewhat indistinct and distant (compared with other Ford films). Ford concentrates on one character, Tom Joad, while shoving far into the background most of the others in the family and their particular stories (e.g., Rosasharn). Perhaps it was at one time the intention to anchor the narrative in Tom Joad and his transmutation, through alienation, into revolutionary. A paroled convict, Tom's loyalty is contested between the immediate welfare of his family and the long-term survival of his class, i.e., between his mother and the preacher, Casey (John Carradine). By responding with violence to the martyrdom of the preacher, Tom becomes an outlaw, and must separate from his family, taking up Casey's torch. It is likely, however, that he would have accepted this torch in any case, even if he were not fleeing the law. For, in effect, we are witnessing the birth of a Fordian hero: Tom feels it his duty and destiny to become a mediator between order and the chaos it causes, in order to preserve families; and, like Casey, he accepts celibate aloneness as part of his mission.

It is interesting to reflect that this Christ-like Henry Fonda character carries with him reverberations of young Mr. Lincoln, whom he played for Ford the year before. Once again Fonda must isolate himself from family to a mission both times revolutionary, one to the Law, the other to the Out-law (though both above the Law), and both times he walks off at the end into his destiny. Lincoln's fate is to dissolve into granite mythhood, Tom's to ascend out of family-consciousness into richer (?) selfhood. In *My Darling Clementine* (1946), Fonda-warrior exits down a long road of aridity; in *The Fugitive* (1947), Fonda-priest ascends to martyrdom; in *Fort Apache* (1948), Fonda-Custer gallops to perdition with irony. His part is taken up by James Stewart in *Liberty Valance* and *Cheyenne Autumn*.

In point of fact, the film as Ford shot it did end with Tom Joad's linear separation from his mother, followed by the shot of him going up over the hill.* But, somewhere along the course of production, a counterplot began to mute this revolutionary trumpet: Ma Joad (Jane Darwell) and her feeble attempts to preserve her family midst patriarchal abdication (the preacher retires, Muley stays behind, Grampa dies, Pa goes senile, Rosasharn's husband flees, Tom flees).

Supposedly Ford agreed with producer Darryl F. Zanuck that the picture would benefit from an upbeat ending. A European might have introduced a chorus singing "The International," but Ford sailed off on his ketch, and a few days later Zanuck telephoned to say he had added a concluding sequence, in which Ma Joad delivers her now famous "We keep acomin'. We're the people that live. Can't nobody wipe us out. . . ." Ford liked it and asked Zanuck to direct it.

But even if Ford did like it, and even if, as he claimed, it was his idea to end with Ma, still it is difficult to reconcile Ford's hindsight with his eloquent departure from the set.** What is more, the capacious Jane Darwell

---

*Jean Mitry claims to have seen a print in Switzerland in 1945 that ended like Steinbeck: the Joads are living in a barn, picking cotton for a pitiful wage, and Rosasharn, having borne a dead baby, suckles an orphan. No one else has heard of this version; it is unlikely it ever existed. (*John Ford* [Paris: Editions Universitaires, 1954], p. 101.)

**Ford gives this account in an interview with Walter Wagner. Zanuck's biographer, Mel Gussow, assigns Zanuck credit for writing Ma's lines and using her scene to end the picture, but also quotes Ford as crediting Zanuck for limiting music to Dan Borzage's accordion —surely had been cast over his preference for the gaunt Beulah Bondi, whereas his preference for the strong Fonda won out over Zanuck's for the flabbier (but more box-office-popular) Don Ameche or Tyrone Power—partly because Zanuck saw the chance to bait Fonda into a seven-year contract. And even though Ma's speech sounds "Fordian," and even though those final shots echo the primal Fordian life-symbol, the parade, Ma's uncharacteristically prolix oration seems a tawdry resolution, in contrast to Ford's refusal to resolve. Nor is such sententiousness generally accorded Fordian characters without equal doses of irony. Of course, in this instance, it virtually destroys the film's trajectory toward inevitable *disintegration*/revolution, in favor of *perseverance*/abidance.

Ford pictures throughout the decade had been tackling social issues, characters determined to act, and instances of oppression, and we have seen how in many instances the natural response to repression and ossified convention (and inadequate myth) was a revolutionary upheaval—a burning of icons in *Steamboat*, a betrayal in *The Informer*, rebellion in *Plough*, revolt and disaster in *The Hurricane*. Persistence is the principal weapon of the oppressed. But persistence in itself is neither necessarily heroic (as Tom says, "It don't take no nerve to do something you can't do anything else *but* do") nor salutary (Hannah Jessop, Terangi, Mudd, Dr. John) *unless* directed toward erection of an alternative ideology (new myths). Ma offers no such alternatives; Tom does.

Grapes "was purposefully photographed black" by Gregg Toland, said Ford—although today most prints are gray—and seldom has a Ford picture been a world so unreal. Not even in *The Fugitive* is there so much abstraction from reality. Everything is submerged within a heavy shadowed mood, a dreamlike world mirroring Muley's insanity, like the desolation following nuclear war in a science-fiction film. Exteriors are carefully photographed to look like soundstages, the characters are lit like statues. People and objects are shorn of autonomy, emotions are *too* externalized (expressionistically). Elsewhere in Ford, subjectivity emanates from characters and it is they who create the spirit-world; here it is imposed a priori. It is unreason-

---

politely, as Borzage always played on Ford sets. Ford told Bogdanovich that the Fonda scene "was the *logical* end, but we wanted to see what was happening to the mother " (my italics)—which skirts the issue: we are even more curious about what happens to the central character. Tom Stempel, however, on scenarist Nunnally Johnson's authority, states that Johnson's original script ended with Ma's scene (whose words come from various places in the book, and which Steinbeck had enthusiastically approved as an ending, saying he had considered ending the book that way) but that Ford and Zanuck had not decided on the ending and left it out of the actual shooting script. Ford, in his reminiscences, claims Johnson wrote out the lines in front of Zanuck and him. (See: Wagner, *You Must Remember This* [New York: Putnam's, 1975], pp. 55–65; Gussow, *Don't Say Yes Until I Finish Talking* [New York: Pocket Books, 1972], p. 86; Peter Bogdanovich, *John Ford* [Berkeley and Los Angeles: University of California Press, 1978], p. 78; Stempel, *Screenwriter: The Life and Times of Nunnally Johnson* [New York: A. S. Barnes], pp. 78–87; Ford, in the John Ford Papers, Lilly Library, Indiana University.)

able, however, to lament *Grapes*'s expressionism: contemporary audiences
perceived the film as gritty actuality; it copies Thomas Hart Benton[34] and
photographic styles current in photo-journalism; and expressionism had
been prominently exploited in *Potemkin* and such hallowed "documentaries" as *Triumph of the Will, Night Mail,* and *Olympiad.* To suggest that a
blunt, natural style would be preferable to Ford's eerie lighting is to question the efficacy of art to comment on life.

The problems with *The Grapes of Wrath* resemble those of *The Informer:*
the mood is too restricted, too repetitive, too seldom varied. The story itself
seems to go on and on, episodically. And prolixity and monomania dominate
other aspects of Ford's style. What Orson Welles once said of him—that Ford
"does not move either his camera or his actors very much . . . there's little
movement in [his films]"[35]—is patently untrue in general of this most dynamic of all filmmakers, but is true in particular of *Grapes.* Takes are long,
cutting is slow, actors pose, and Ford will move them rather than the camera
when a closer shot is desired. The long conversation between Tom Joad and
Casey toward the beginning has a take two minutes forty seconds long, with
most movement occurring in the tree-leaves, and is followed by another that
is sixty seconds long. There is nothing "wrong" with this scene, one of the
better in the film, in fact—it does much to establish the picture's distinctive,
morose atmosphere—but, combined with a general fatigue in formal inventiveness, such techniques render *Grapes* a ponderous picture.

The Long Voyage Home (1940). Our poet laureate's second prestigious success of 1940* is even blacker and more single-minded than *Grapes*; stylistically, it seems a reversion to 1936.

Although the title could almost sum up Ford's work, the endless quest for a nonexistent home is seldom enunciated elsewhere than here, where most talk and all thought is of "home," and where again and again a death or departure is marked by John Qualen's commenting that someone has "gone home" (a line not to be found among the four Eugene O'Neill plays from which the movie derives). Even the contrast offered by the one seaman not seeking to escape the *Glencairn* is nihilistic; according to Donkeyman (Arthur Shields):

— The best thing to do with memories is—forget 'em. . . . When a man goes to sea he ought to give up thinking about things on shore. Land don't want him no more. I had me share of things going wrong, and it all came from the land. Now I'm through with the land, and the land's through with me.

Huw Morgan's attitude toward memory, in *How Green Was My Valley*, leads him into an isolation even more absolute than Donkeyman's, but that film's treatment of the memory motif is far subtler and variegated than *Voyage*'s, just as its brighter palette and recalcitrant optimism render it ultimately far more pessimistic than *Voyage*'s persistent repetition of the same few motifs of cosmic malevolence.

Yet this is a movie Ford was proud of—stills from it decorated his home. Those who delight chiefly in the spoken word relish it. And in 1940 it seemed a distinguished exception to Hollywood's "general worthlessness." Ford consulted with O'Neill and spent six weeks planning the adaptation with Dudley Nichols (a friend and fan of O'Neill, who in 1947 directed the film *Mourning Becomes Electra*); Nichols then locked himself away for twenty 16-hour days, haggled over his first draft with Ford for a week, then worked another month on the final script.[36] O'Neill loved the picture and screened it periodically.

O'Neill's stage words are frequently replaced by movie images. In *The Moon of the Caribbees*, restless men, native girls, a dance, and a fight translate the storyline with scarcely a single O'Neill line. Later, verbal poetry tends to be Nichols's, not O'Neill's. For instance, Donkeyman's "Memory" speech (quoted above) derives from a "land"-less O'Neill sentence ("Not that I ain't had my share o' things goin' wrong; but I puts 'em out o' me mind, like, an' forgets 'em"). Absent also from O'Neill is the grandiloquent cry by Driscoll (Thomas Mitchell), "Is there to be no more light in the world?" whose inspiration seems sprung from the long day's journey into night photographi-

*No Oscars, but seven nominations (best picture; screenplay: Nichols; music: Hageman; photography: Toland; editing: Sherman Todd; effects: Ray Binger and R. T. Layton; sound: Robert Parrish). New York Film Critics chose Ford best director for this and *Grapes*.

cally formalized by Gregg Toland's spots and shafts of brilliance midst total black, with the result that, far from the Ford-Toland pictures seeming to illustrate the text, it is rather the text that seems to be verbalizing the pictures— at least until the ineffable concluding sequence, when the sailors return downcast and scraps of refuse paper fly around in the patch of light dockside.

Thus, though fifty O'Neill words get telescoped into five or ten Nichols ones, the effect of Ford's expressionism is expansion, not contraction; each verbal idea becomes a fleshy personality, expressive gesture, or photographic space. Words are concretized even by words, as Donkeyman's "Memory" speech is tied to a "land/sea" theme. Elsewhere, Ole (John Wayne) is given a pet parrot by Ford, and Driscoll learns of Ole's fate by finding the parrot, whereas in O'Neill the news is merely verbal. Even changes seeming to debase O'Neill intentions actually strengthen emotional themes; for example, O'Neill's Smitty (whose letters the sailors steal and read) is just an alcoholic failure, but the film's Smitty (Ian Hunter) is an upper-class hero of the British Empire as well, so that, typically for Ford, he has sought escape not so much from physical weakness as, like Doc Holliday, from shamed social identity.

Characters may occasionally seem like too many Gypo Nolans— dunderheads wandering in the fog, almost too stupid to be pitied—and one might feel that here, as in *Tobacco Road* (Ford's next picture), the fascination with lower-class simpletons typical of this period of Ford's work is demeaning. It is all the more miraculous, then, that the casting of Hollywood "types" like John Wayne, Ward Bond, Thomas Mitchell, Barry Fitzgerald, or John Qualen never lessens credibility nor hints at that dreadful impression of actors "playing down."

***Tobacco Road* (1941).** Scenarist Nunnally Johnson thought *Tobacco Road* "a fiasco," for Ford relied on "old-fashioned bed-slat comedy . . . crude [and] clumsy."[37] Albeit there are magic moments: Arthur Miller's photographic prologue; Bible songs at City Hall and the car dealer's; walking to the poor farm; and Jeeter's final speech. But a condescending veneer of euphoric populism has replaced the uncomplicated gaze with which Ford previously viewed simple folk (e.g., *Steamboat Round the Bend*).

***How Green Was My Valley* (1941).** The film that beat out *Citizen Kane* for Oscars in production, direction, photography, and art direction. is often criticized as a "prestige" commercial picture, a tear-jerking bit of Hollywood gloss that improperly detracts from proletarian issues—as represented by such "realistic" (i.e., politically preachy) films as *Kameradshaft* or *The Stars Look Down*).* "A monstrous slurry of tears and coaldust,"

---

*Leaving his Welsh mining valley after fifty years, Huw Morgan recalls childhood as youngest in a large, working family. Flashback to c. 1900: Midst increasing economic recession, the valley quarrels over unions and liberal ideas of a new minister. Four brothers quit the valley

David Thomson calls it, and, echoing a common view of John Ford pictures as Pollyanna celebrations of tradition, charges, "Ford dumbly regrets the passing of a make-believe stability that has served as an obstacle to any necessary critical sensibility."[38]

As we shall see, only the most conventional and disingenuous readings of the film could support such conclusions.

Planning of the picture was dominated by 20th Century–Fox production chief Darryl F. Zanuck. Shot at Fox's San Fernando Valley ranch and costing $1,250,000, it was intended to win Academy Awards, which it did, six of them, and to gain wide popularity, which it did, grossing more than any film except *Sergeant York* during its year of release. But the project caused initial misgivings to the politically reactionary Zanuck. According to scenarist Philip Dunne: "Zanuck, Ford, and Nunnally Johnson had come under savage attack by right wingers for making *The Grapes of Wrath*. . . . Zanuck, who persisted in believing that I was much more of a radical fire-eater than I actually was . . . pretend[ed] to wring his hands over the great risk he was taking in turning me loose on a goddamn pro-labor picture."[39]

Zanuck had purchased the rights to Richard Llewellyn's novel, a best seller in 1939, and had at first assigned Liam O'Flaherty, then Ernest Pascal to script it. But in a memo in May 1940, he criticized Pascal's emphasis on the sociological over the human, and proposed taking a "*revolutionary viewpoint* of the screenplay of this story and [telling] it as the book does— through the eyes of Huw, the little boy. We should do the picture with him as an off-stage commentator with many of the scenes running silent and nothing but his voice over them."[40] (In effect, although it was about to become commonplace, voice-over narration by a character was virtually unknown in 1940.**) Pascal was replaced by Dunne, who worked with William Wyler, hired to direct, some three months on the script. In November 1940, Zanuck, having made the key decision for Huw as narrator, made two more critical decisions, writing Wyler that Huw "should never grow up" (Tyrone

---

to find work elsewhere, the eldest brother is killed in the mine, but Huw, who is the first in the valley to receive an education and could become a doctor, chooses to go down the colliery. Sister Angharad's divorce incites her excommunication, the minister (who loves her) quits in disgust, and Huw's father dies in Huw's arms in the mine. But in a second flashback, Huw recalls the good times.

The movie also won Oscars for supporting actor (Crisp), and was nominated in five other categories: supporting actress (Allgood), script, editing, music, sound. The art direction award was two separate Oscars, set direction and interior decoration. New York Film Critics chose Ford best director, and this was almost the only award he showed up personally to collect: he always shunned Oscar ceremonies.

**Kentucky Pride* (1925) excepted, this is the first voice-over narration in Ford. Aside from the documentaries and the special case of *Liberty Valance*, eight later films employ character narrators, but none to *Valley*'s extent: *When Willie Comes Marching Home, Rookie of the Year, The Quiet Man, The Long Gray Line, The Wings of Eagles, Gideon's Day, The Colter Craven Story, Sergeant Rutledge*. Noncharacter narrators occur in nine others: *Tobacco Road, The Fugitive, She Wore a Yellow Ribbon, Wagon Master* (the song), *What Price Glory, The Majesty of the Law, Flashing Spikes*, "The Civil War," *Cheyenne Autumn*.

Power was to have played the grown-up Huw) and that "now is the time for us to start talking in terms of drama and audience. I was bored to death by the repetition of the strike business and of starving babies, etc., etc. It all seems old hash to me."[41] By April, with script and casting completed, filming was put off until summer, by which time Ford was to be available.

Aside from its deemphasis of sociology, the script follows the book faithfully, and often word for word, allowing for tightening of time and telescoping of events. Most suppressions are expectable, such as the compromising sexual affairs of the Morgan sons and of Huw himself. Ford's most obvious addition to Dunne's script (which he otherwise followed closely) was the coda, in which idyllic memory triumphs over tragic actuality. Intended to finish the picture on an uplifting rather than depressing note, this "false happy ending" may fool a casual viewer (as it has fooled many a critic eager to accuse Ford of reactionariness and Hollywood of creampuffing social issues) into thinking that the movie is celebrating the very theme its double-leveled story is condemning. It is the movie's emphasis on memory, a motif only gradually enunciated in the book, that is the primary difference between it and the book. Huw's opening monologue

— I am leaving behind me fifty years of memory. Memory . . . Who shall say what is real and what is not? Can I believe my friends all gone when their voices are a glory in my ears? No. And I will stand to say no and no again, for they remain a living truth within my mind. There is no fence nor hedge around time that is gone. You can go back and have what you like of it . . . So I can close my eyes on my valley as it was . . .

is partly original, partly culled from scattered passages in the book, but its sense is quite different in the movie, because of the movie's more intense distinction between fact and fantasy. Huw's gaze looks out his window at the desolate slum his valley is today only to dissolve into his imagination's images of the lush valley of his childhood. The cameo scenes that immediately follow, in which quotidian events are spelled out as the essence of sacramental beauty, tell us what sort of person Huw is and prepare us: what we shall witness is a highly subjective, terribly colored depiction of reality, one in which a child's emotions of remembering take precedence over crass facts. The book's focus upon the change in the valley becomes in the movie the (non)change in Huw. In effect, the conventional stage fiction—that years may pass but Roddy McDowall (playing Huw) does not age—becomes a symbol of the character's and the culture's stasis. It is Huw who unites the myriad disparate persons, episodes, and styles of the movie's storyworld. To his progression from paradise to slag, from sunshine to mine, is juxtaposed his awakening to (and refusal of) consciousness. To experience the movie only as a celebration of Huw's dreamy myopia, denial of reality, and adhesion to tradition is to experience *only* Huw's point of view; it is not to experience *Ford's* point of view *of* Huw's point of view. And it is not even commonsensical. For it is quite clear in the movie that it is Huw's attitude, shared in different ways by his neighbors, that has destroyed the valley and mortified Huw. Huw is an antihero, and Ford, as in *The Man Who Shot Liberty Valance* (1962), calls into question the validity of Huw's point-of-view narrative. These ideas are not in the book.

Such a technique is commonplace in literature, but rare in film. True, almost every movie has shots reflecting a character's point of view or impressions; and dream sequences, too, are frequent. But mind's-eye narration sustained over an entire movie is virtually unknown.* It cannot work in ordinary films because audiences have no narrator to deal with. It is difficult to work in an auteur film—where audience should sense a narrating personality already—because the director must then interpose himself between the audience and the narrating character. What is easy in literature is nearly impossible in film (as the failure of literary-oriented critics to comprehend *How Green Was My Valley* demonstrates), for cinema, particularly auteur cinema, is less like literature than like painting made into music. The operative analogy is thus not with Joseph Conrad—who used narrating characters often—but with Vincent Van Gogh—who never did. Can we imagine a painting by Van Gogh showing the world as experienced by a well-adjusted Dutch businessman? in which both Van Gogh's *and* the businessman's sensibility are apparent? Even a single subjective shot, in cinema, can detract from a director's presence. Thus a Hitchcock always corrects, imposing his own point of view following a shot from a character's point of view. And thus *Citizen Kane* has not five narrators (unless they all see the world in identical echoing, black, deep-focus fashion), but only one, Welles, who is also Kane (and as vacuous as narrator as character).

In *How Green Was My Valley*, Ford's solution—and it is a successful solution for emotionally involved audiences—has been to sustain Huw's "I" both powerfully present and powerfully distanced. To the degree the viewer is conscious of Huw as narrator, he will be conscious of possible attitudes other than Huw's, and there he will find Ford. A large variety of devices, aural and visual, continually affirm Huw's narrating presence and distance the action:

- Most of the movie occurs in flashback.
- Huw's adult off-camera voice narrates (the voice is Irving Pichel's**).
- Scenes are shot from the visual point of view of boy Huw.
- Scenes frame Huw at their compositional focal point (e.g., when the family is presented to Bronwyn [Anna Lee] and Huw sits foreground while

---

*Only one other comes to mind: Max Ophuls's *Letter from an Unknown Woman* (1948). In *Liberty Valance* subjective distortion is more evident, since the narrator and many of the principals appear in expanded framing sequences.

**G. Dane Wilsonne, who knew Pichel, tells me that Rhys Williams had originally recorded the narration. But Ford, fearing on second thought lest audiences identify the voice with the boxer Dai Bando whom Williams plays in the film, substituted Irving Pichel. As the picture had already been completed, it was necessary for Pichel to match precisely Williams's rhythm and timing. Williams's (superior) version once circulated in Britain.

the others, spreading out before him, move as though in the dream of his persona memory)[frame 1].

• Scenes echo his mood in lighting (e.g., the shadowed corridor, his first day at school [frame 2]; expressionist shadowing emphasizes the interiority of Huw's image of community, his inner fantasy.

• Scenes echo his mood in cutting (e.g., when Huw opens the classroom door, Ford, crosscutting between Huw and the students at their desks, follows the pattern of Huw's timid attempt to take in the situation: in succeeding shots the large mass of students [frame 3] centers gradually on those few closest to him, while, correspondingly, the shots of Huw move closer to Huw; then Ford breaks this pattern and cuts startlingly to a medium close-up of the teacher, hitherto unnoticed, sitting high above and far away: the crosscuts now isolate Huw and teacher from the class, since Huw has now something more terrifying than the children with which to contend).

• Scenes echo his mood in sets (e.g., when Huw visits Angharad [Maureen O'Hara] at the Evans mansion, the gates and door are twice the size they actually would have been [frame 4]).

1   2

3   4

Huw's subjectivity, as we have seen, is established in his opening narration, as the adult Huw, gazing at the desolation his valley has become, is pulled back by memory. Harsh reality is swept away for a dream. And no doubt for Huw the same dream repeats itself eternally, has repeated itself these fifty years, and each time its "romance" will be subverted by its plot—the "slag" will come to the valley—until this plot is in turn subverted by renewed memory (the rosy-hued coda).

For Huw wishes to envision life as a succession of miracles; indeed, one such series is among the picture's most inspired stretches: after falling through the ice, Huw, in quick succession, is preached a wondrous sermon by Mr. Gruffydd, is introduced to the wonders of great books (are they the same books adult Huw is wrapping in his mother's scarf at the film's beginning?) while simultaneously Angharad discovers love, encounters the birds of spring, embraces again his mother, sees the whole village singing and his brothers returning home, and is taken by Mr. Gruffydd to a hilltop where, almost miraculously, he walks again [frame 5]. But, alas, Huw's enchanted outlook is the myopia of innocence; the movie is actually a succession of frightening tragedies, failures, oppressions. It is arguably Ford's most cynical and pessimistic film (and we recognize Ford in part by the staggering disparity between events and Huw's innocence). Even Huw's family is a failure, for it cannot tolerate discussion, and communication within it is severely circumscribed by patriarchal absolutism. (One gets the feeling, how-

5

ever, that the Morgan parents are closer and more liberal to Huw than to his much older siblings.)

Huw's view is remarkably distanced (even for Ford): he (and thus we) watch characters, particularly Angharad and Bronwyn, almost voyeuristically, from outside them, without penetrating (as we do matter-of-factly in most movies) into their motives and consciousnesses. This "apartness" in Huw largely accounts for *How Green Was My Valley's* seeming so "staged" an affair. In fact this "staginess"—the carefully noble manner in which the people talk, move, gesture—is one of Huw's chief contributions as "director" of his dream. He regiments his material into a mode of memory.

Consistent with the "stagey outsideness" of the characterizations is that Ford, here more ambitiously than with *Stagecoach*, is attempting (in his capacity as Huw's assistant director, so to speak) to adapt his vignette style of characterization, of comedy style, to the dark modalities of an introverted tragedy. Huw grasps his people in characterizing action: we shall, for example, always think of Bronwyn as Huw does, as she appears in the coda recapitulation of Huw's first encounter—coming round the corner with basket and bonnet, when he falls in love with her—and two or three more such simple vignettes complete her dramatic personality. In fact, we know nothing *about* her, except what seem to be vivid, tactile impressions of knowing *her*. In other words, in the script she is, as a dramatic personage, a nonentity, a simple foil for Huw, but in the picture she is, as a dramatic personage, among the most intimate and sure personalities in movies. Similarly, vignette narration is wondrously successful in the economic concreteness with which Angharad's marriage is sketched. We see her with her husband only as they leave the church, but so vivid later are her emotions in the tea scene with Huw that we in no way miss a scene between them.

But if such successes exemplify some advantages of Huw's distanced, awestruck vignette methods in a large-cast, quickly sequenced, ensemble movie, the obscurity of the Gruffydd personage (Walter Pidgeon) exemplifies its disadvantages in extended study of a *complicated* personality. Gruffydd's actions are rarely comprehensible to Huw (or to us?), yet *his* story, thrust into the background behind the stories of Huw, Huw's family, and the valley, is the film's "backbone." The long cameo exposition concludes in the marriage of Ivor and Bronwyn; here the "plot" begins, for now Mr. Gruffydd makes his entrance before his congregation and now—in a series of point-of-view crosscuts occurring almost without Huw's awareness, "underneath the thread of his narration"—Angharad falls instantly in love with the new minister (as Huw fell instantly in love with Bronwyn). It is by Ford's intervention that some of the lacunae in Gruffydd's tale are filled. For example, midst matters intimate to Huw (Bronwyn is reading to him in his window-bed), Ford's camera retreats discreetly to watch Angharad (out of Huw's sight) and Gruffydd, while keeping Huw and Bronwyn in the frame (6). (Such composition in depth seems infinitely more subtle than the scenes

6

praised by Bazin in *Kane* and *Little Foxes*.*) The presence of multiple narrators in the movie (Huw-adult; Huw-boy; Ford) allows such fascinating play
with point of view in which the fairly blunt ideas of *Stagecoach's* dinner
scene are developed with delicate, fugal complexity. But other sequences
dispense with Huw altogether: Gruffydd's rejection of Angharad; some labor scenes; the expressionistically caricatured women with teacups gossiping about Angharad's divorce. And Ford's additions allow us to see that Gruffydd's story parallels the valley's, a failure in relationship, a misconception of
the spiritual and the material. We realise Gruffydd is a Fordian hero manqué: celibate, solitary, claiming truth and authority, but a figure of impotence. He sermonizes about virtue and charity midst mountain daffodils,
but in the next scene allows his flock to excommunicate an unwed mother.
His congregation sit in their pews like soldiers in formation, and are shocked
by their minister's attempts at fellowship—singing and drinking and supporting a union. Gruffydd's self-appointed role is to mediate between revolution
and reaction, but he fails, as mediator, goodfellow, and leader, by virtue of an
idealism that, like Huw's, ignores the real world around him. Far from reuniting families, as the Fordian hero is supposed to do, Gruffydd watches
them be destroyed, and contributes to Angharad's own downfall. His inability to accept her love or realistically to acknowledge her, while yet courting
her like some chaste Parsifal, effectively condemns him—and the valley. An

---

*Bazin liked the long takes in *Little Foxes* during which Teresa Wright appears on a staircase behind and above her feuding in-laws. Ford had staged a similarly composed *coup de
théâtre* in *Mary of Scotland*, five years previously, when Mary appears on a staircase behind
and above the feuding Bothwell and Knox—and would repeat it in *The Searchers*, when Scar
appears on a dune behind and above the feuding Ethan and Marty. Such quarreling with Bazin
would be more gratuitous than it seems, did not Bazin specifically cite Wyler's compositional
style as superior to Ford's montage. (See: "The Evolution of the Language of Cinema," in Bazin's *What Is Cinema?*, translated by Hugh Gray [Berkeley and Los Angeles: University of
California Press, 1971], p. 35.)

inexorable chain of cinematic logic links this moment of denial (Gruffydd lights a lamp and notices Angharad in the dark; he flicks out his match as, in contrapuntal motion, Angharad rises to greet him; the rest of the scene is redundant, except as necessary ritual: we know their love is doomed) to Angharad's excommunication, the colliery explosion, the father's death, and the slag heap. As in *The Hurricane*, the cataclysm (storm or mine explosion) seems a sort of wrath of God: the shriveled minds of the valley people incite their just destruction; ironically it is the particularly innocent who are killed (Ivor, Gwilym—as in *The Hurricane*), while the "guilty" are preserved. Angharad will shiver, and Mr. Gruffydd, impotent rather than redemptive, will pose crucified, but it is Huw who will stare out blankly when the colliery lift rises.

The elusiveness of Gruffydd's personality and actions is partly connected to explanations elided by Zanuck. In Llewellyn's novel, unionism plays a more important role, the father is more sympathetic toward it, and less authoritative. The cause of the valley's desolation is analyzed as a combination of economic expediency and the workers' failure to unite behind the progressive socialism promoted by the Morgan sons. Also in the book, when Huw (not, as in the movie, Angharad) protests in chapel the excommunication of the unwed mother, Gruffydd explains that the valley has hitherto been self-governing; it has no police, no courts; the people have lived by the Bible; hopefully in time they will become more educated and kindlier, but until then it is only the sternness of their customs that has enabled them to function as a community without the evils of outside (English) intervention. The movie omits these explanations, instead implying that unionism, along with Gruffydd's new morality, is repugnant because it means change, and change is anathema to sinewy tradition: thus the valley cannot decide to unite in opposition to the diddle-brained mine owner and his dandy scion. Both valley and Huw ossify and decay because they prefer dream to reality.

In fact, the movie omits these explanations not *just* because of Zanuck, but because Huw omits them: the traditionalist attitudes are Huw's. When the dinner ritual is shattered toward the movie's beginning by dispute over the union, Huw protests that *he* has not deserted; and with each successive departure from the valley, Huw reaffirms that *he* shall not desert. (Actually, the father dismisses his sons for their *bad manners* at table, not because he disagrees with their position; but the sons walk out because they feel that being right is more important than manners. This "false" conflict confuses subsequent debate, and leads Huw irrationally to perceive all "new ideas" as threatening to home and tradition.) Conversely, the line "I'm leaving the valley" signals Gruffydd's capitulation. Indeed, Huw's one departure from the valley (going to school) was traumatic, and even at age fifty still there, his decision to leave conflicts with memory. For Huw sees *every* action as ritual, as part of sacramental tradition: coming home from work, washing, dinner, allowance, toffee shop, even just going around a corner becomes ritual—a consecrated, instantly legendary, special magic moment.* Change is mirrored in disrupted ritual: that Bronwyn continues to put out fresh clothes for Ivor a year after Ivor's death evinces her refusal to admit change. And Huw, confronting his heart with reality, tries like Bronwyn to force reality to bend to his heart's needs: tiny details become heart-rending nuances, bigger than life and set in scenes hyperdramatic; a plethora of incidents spin the spectator far out of the duration of normal time (i.e., the movie seems longer than its 118 minutes). It would, for instance, require a page to relate the miniature drama enacted in a few seconds by Angharad as she waits excitedly inside her door for Mr. Gruffydd coming to call; this is a tiny moment, almost a period of punctuation, yet so typical of the picture as a whole.

When the sons leave the table and Huw stays, he pities but admires his father. And the idealism with which Huw views him is inseparable from the aura of defeat he equally surrounds him with. As in the famous "Lord is my shepherd" sequence when father Morgan grieves the breakup of his family, Huw's father is always seen from his son's spiritual and often physical perspective (and Donald Crisp conveys Gwilym Morgan's bilevel presence—as real man and as Huw's fantasy), and this reflects Huw's obligation and (scarcely acknowledged) guilt toward this defeated nobility. Initially Huw is torn between his reactionary father and the progressive Gruffydd; but the choice is not so simple. The father is not so much reactionary as a believer in first principles—that people ought and will perform the duties of their stations and that legislation and institutional strife cannot remedy failure in individual duty. Gruffydd, on the other hand, backs institutions over individuals, fails toward individuals, and sees all institutions—mine, union, church, and family—break down. But Huw *will* not fail; he *will* tend his station. To follow tradition for Huw means not to leave the valley, means to be a miner, as was his father; to leave the valley, to become a doctor or lawyer, this would be to deny his father, to put down his father's life. Or, at least, this is how his *mother* feels. (She and Bronwyn, with baby, stand in a background doorway, in ceilinged depth of field, framed foreground by Huw announcing to his father his decision, which they apparently cause, to affirm tradition; appropriately, the scene is a static tableau.) His father's ardent hope, to the contrary, is that Huw *will* contradict him, will leave the valley, will leave the old ways, will surpass the father, and yet take with him the good in family tradition.

Alas, in this world, the best-laid hopes run aground on the reefs of human instinct. Nothing was ever so necessary as that Huw leave the valley. But Huw misjudges the force of tradition, apprehends only its inward spiral, its negative, closing-out-the-world face, and, intending his life to be an act of consummate purity in devotion to a supreme beauty, he rejects the path of

---

*Lisa, in Ophuls's *Letter from an Unknown Woman*, suffers similarly; and she is also a point-of-view persona narrator, tempting us to believe her suicide is merely romantic, rather than also unconsciously sado-masochistic.

growth, chooses that of decay, and thus is ultimately responsible for the end of his tradition's evolution.

In Huw's linkage with his mother in defiance of his father, is there implication that Huw wishes, oedipally, not merely to follow father's footsteps, but to replace father?—as, in fact, he does, just as he replaces Ivor in Bronwyn's house (he moves his bed there). Curiously, the mother-Huw alliance not only shares aversion to change and leaving the valley-womb, but also, like Bronwyn, even to acknowledgment: the mother also denies the father's death, just as she denies the map showing her sons' diaspora ("They are here. In the house!"). And Huw, as he looks, age fifty or more, out his window and glimpses slag and desolation, speaks of leaving this valley at last, wrapping his belongings in his mother's shawl (tradition), but boasting proudly that it doesn't matter, that he can cancel out Now, can close his eyes and remember how it was. And there it is: the whole movie running by in flashback, but the story one of destruction, of dismemberment of the family, of its destruction, and of Huw's guilt—all unacknowledged. Tradition itself has become, unrecognized, the malignant slag, has itself become change; and once again in Ford it is a question of duty and tradition gone astray. Huw's innocence undergoes successive shocks culminating in Angharad's excommunication, Gruffydd's desertion, and his father, in pitted darkness, in earth womb, dying in his arms. Oedipal guilt mingles with utter futility; only suffering has meaning. Huw's blank stare into nothingness, when the colliery lift reaches light, is (I think) the movie's key shot. The eyes fix inward, not outward, into a desolate soul without a thing to look at, for life has meaning because seeing is a moral act. Evil change has triumphed (as it always shall in Ford), the Morgan family has been slaughtered, as Ivor predicted, the valley turns arid and Huw bereft, which necessitates that he in the mine of his own identity subsist all the more strongly within the fantasy purity Gruffydd (so cruelly?) bequeathed him.

Hence, as the colliery lifts, Huw's heart flees into memory, and is wholly absorbed by it. Reality *becomes* memory, and ignites a rerun of Huw's dream (i.e., the coda in which the valley blooms in youth and Huw walks with the father he has betrayed), and Huw, Gruffydd's appointed successor, *rejects* reality, as do, in various ways, his mentor, mother, sisters, and valley (in contrast to the brothers, who fight and emigrate, and to the father, who bends to events). Huw's act (the coda) is both tragic and courageous. Memory subdues reality, isolates the mind, but at what a cost!

Although scenarist Philip Dunne feels Ford filmed his script virtually without change,* *How Green Was My Valley* is far more John Ford's picture

*Nonetheless, as Dunne has acknowledged, Ford's contributions were many. Among them: changing Dunne's two fighters into a comic team, with Barry Fitzgerald as the slapstick part-

than Philip Dunne's script. Ford's cinematization does not merely "realize" Dunne's intentions, it transmutes and even subverts them, and creates an expressionist fantasy of ritual whose subjectivity Ford faults.

The music helps convey Huw's cloying saccharinity, counterpointing here, reinforcing there; yet the music is usually more sentimental than the image, where Ford's rigorous purposefulness, in staging and framing and gesturing eyes, combats the maudlin Huw by clear and simple strength. As usual (although here it is probably Dunne's doing), he makes everything concrete: a dispute between mistress and servant is represented by a tea pitcher. The scenes of valley life opening the film and orienting us have the principal effect of causing sensations of depth, memory, and déjà-vu, of vertical structure during the movie's course, so that as these scenes recur (e.g., the paymaster's window) they take on more intimate significance. But most notably, everything has been choreographed, the better to reflect Huw's notion of life as ritual: everywhere, whether in church or at Bronwyn's presentation, ritual is expressed as flowing geometric motions. The choreography, moreover, constantly opposes motion and stillness, echoing the movie's antinomy of changing reality vs. (Huw's) static idealism. Not only is all motion choreographed within each shot, but (what is rarer) between shots as well, so that shots join into movements of a suite.

An exemplary sequence occurs when the mother (Sara Allgood) comes downstairs after a long recuperation and is reunited with Huw, still restricted to his window-bed: MS: Mother, at bottom of stairs, moves out of frame right, FS (low level): and hobbles across room diagonally down frame toward Huw; /CU: Huw sits up in bed, puts hand to breast. X MCU: Mother opens arms and bends toward Huw: /2MS: they embrace. /GS: The room, with them in far corner.*

Nothing could be more classic than Ford's treatment, the tight opposition of matching close shots exploding into a two-shot, and then the long shot for relief and distance. But the sequence is exceptional in that the cutting seems demanded not so much by dialectic of ideas as by internal motions and gestures within each shot. This is a peculiarity of Ford and of this movie in particular.

Ford's "rule" (though frequently violated) can be seen in the school fight. The two boys move left to a knockdown, /then right / and so on, until Huw, beaten, sinks in a spiraling combination of boy and camera. Here each shot contains a single line of motion; a cut occurs when this single motion is

---

ner; lines like " 'Tis a coward I am but I will hold your coat"; the women calling to each other in song; Crisp slapping Huw's wrist with a spoon when Huw grabs some bread, or putting on his bowler hat and announcing "I'm going to get drunk"—both in imitation of Ford's own father; putting Crisp's feet in a bowl of water when Evans comes to ask for Angharad's hand; having Sara Allgood behave somewhat like Ford's own mother. In addition, Ford participated in most of the picture's casting. (See interviews with Dunne, and with Josephine Feeney, in the John Ford Papers, Lilly Library, Indiana University.)

* / = cut; X = crosscut (matching angle); FS = full shot; MS = medium shot; GS = general shot (bigger); CU = close-up; MCU = medium close-up.

caesuraed. The same rule is employed in the Huw and mother sequence quoted above: one take, one motion.

When a number of characters occupy a single take, their motions may be utilized in contrapuntal vectors. For example, the camera stands inside Mrs. Tossle's toffee shop, looking out onto the street. Huw, outside, moves from window to door; but as he does so two women pass in the background in the opposite direction, so that the two motions (Huw/women) cross in the doorway; the women move on as Huw enters the shop. Such an instant may seem trivial, but the "collision" does not happen by chance. Such devices, frequent and important in Ford's film language, reinforce a principal motion.*

Contrasting employment of stasis is also frequent. Outside their door, suddenly realizing two sons are leaving, the mother shivers and the father is stunned, a portrait of repressed trembling, and the camera prolongs the shot. Similarly treated are the dinner scene, Huw seeing Bronwyn, presentations of the sons to her, Huw's decision to become a miner, the colliery-life group—all tableaux immortalizing tradition.

In the most elaborate scene (not contained in Llewellyn), Ford capitalizes on his one-motion, one-take rule: Ivor (Patrick Knowles) has been killed in a mine explosion and his body is being carried down the road from the colliery, past the cottages on the right, to his wife Bronwyn. On the left, hundreds of miners stream down the hill-road, their passing an obligato of motion through the frame. Above, in the background, the colliery whistle screams and fiery black smoke belches from the hills, sprinkling the valley

*Jean Renoir discusses such devices in his *My Life and My Films* (New York: Atheneum, 1974), p. 156–57.

with cinders. Townswomen swarm distraughtly in black veils. Bronwyn is pushed forward (i.e., down-frame) toward her house by the mass of Ivor's friends carrying his body. She trips on a small stone wall, reacts slowly, then rushes suddenly to Ivor. But it does not matter where she goes, for the parade (and the retreating camera) bearing Ivor dead will not stop till it reaches her door and enters her home. She is led back by Mr. Gruffydd and father Morgan, separates herself, and alone in a halo of space retreats sobbing toward her yard, and then to her door, her path a crazy pattern of zigs and zags. A low picket fence frames screen-bottom. She reaches her door on extreme right, screams "Ivor!" and collapses. Gruffydd and Morgan rush across-frame to her; then Gruffydd rushes back to the left, as the camera pans with him. All this while the stream of miners continues. Reality, motion, change cannot be resisted by idealism, but only by participating in life's flow: next scene, Bronwyn's baby is born.*

Ford never took a second take, recalls Anna Lee (Bronwyn), and the above sequence, like most, was unrehearsed: the men were told merely to keep pushing her back. Instead, Ford fussed over wardrobes. "He would take one of his old handkerchiefs and tie it around your neck, which was a real mark that he liked you, and he'd come up and either adjust something or pick up your apron and tell you to put it in your hand and almost use it as a prop. He'd do all kinds of little things with wardrobe, and he must have had some idea why he was doing it. I never quite got the idea."[42] But it would change her mood. Like Ford's other bizarre tactics—his refusal to explain or rehearse—the wardrobe fetish channeled the actor into attentiveness to milieu, and thus to natural spontaneity.** "I was twelve years old," said Roddy McDowall. "I had already made about twenty films in England, and I wasn't naive. I knew what was going on. What stands out in my mind is that I never remember being directed. It all just happened. Ford played me like a harp. I remember him as very dear and very gentle. . . . He forged a unique sense of family with all of us."[43]

Along with *The Grapes of Wrath* and *Tobacco Road, How Green Was My Valley* may seem to constitute a social-consciousness trilogy. The pictures share a common theme: disintegration of a family, a culture, and part of the earth, due to economic oppression by the larger world outside. In fact, this is not really a Fordian theme and occurs in none other of his films (wherein there are more elements of growth and more multiclass viewpoints) but

---

*Death/birth juxtapositions occur in *Pilgrimage, Doctor Bull, Fort Apache,* and *7 Women;* cf. *The Long Gray Line.*

**Wyler had hoped to cast Greer Garson as Bronwyn; Ford cast Anna Lee. She feels the role compensated for the brighter career she would probably have had, had she not left her native England. She actually was pregnant during filming of this scene—unknown to Ford—and suffered the loss of a twin in miscarriage. This devastated Ford who, ever after, when casting her, would inquire, using his pet name for her, "Boniface, I want to know one thing: Are you pregnant?" (Anna Lee's real name is Joan Boniface.) (From author's interview with Anna Lee, March 1979.) Maureen O'Hara named her daughter Bronwyn.

doubtless owes its genesis to Zanuck, Dunne, and Nunnally Johnson. None-theless, Ford has been criticized, in each case, for neglecting "documen-tary" for "Hollywood" entertainment, and for emphasizing political *effects*, rather than causes and solutions. One might dismiss these arrant com-plaints, arguing that, even if they were true, people do not themselves al-ways comprehend the forces moving them and that, therefore, it is not nec-essary for us to understand, either, within the movie; in fact, it is more realistic (at least subjectively) if we do not. But, in fact, we do understand. For what *is* specifically Fordian in these pictures (we have seen it before, notably in *Judge Priest*) is the notion that people behave not from logic but from feeling. Facts have no value without character and character is feeling (indeed, a film character is essentially a locus of emotional forms). Social and economic analysis cannot precede merely from concepts and statistics: it requires emotional sensitivity as well; and this is why we have art, despite the efforts of those who would subvert it to political action.

In any case, more sociology would scarcely make *How Green Was My Valley* better, for it is not at all trying to be a movie about labor or even about coal, but rather about psychosis and the dialectics of individuality within family and social change. Moreover, the picture does explicitly pose the question. Why did the green valley turn to slag? And it does provide thorough answers: blind adherence to tradition, resistance to change. What is ironic is that these same complainers cite these movies as instances of *Ford*'s reactionism, as though, in light of his analysis of the valley's decay and Huw's wasted, psychotic life, he were inviting his audience to follow such example, and to "take [their] intelligence down a mine shaft"!

At the time he was making *How Green Was My Valley*, Ford, sensing America's entry into World War II, had already begun training his Field Photo Unit. As the youngest in a big family and as one who had also discov-ered books as a bedridden child, perhaps he identified with Huw, and with Huw's "fifty years of memories." Ford was forty-seven, and he too found it always difficult to let go of the past; but he could not countenance a fantasy isolationism that would lead to slaughter; it was time to quit the valley for-ever. In Ford's next movie, *The Battle of Midway*, the "drama" would lie in the hope to maintain Huw-like purity in face of war reality. But hope is dim in *How Green Was My Valley*; the holocaust looms. By the time of its re-lease, war had come to America.

WAR (1941–1945)

Sex Hygiene	1941	Audio Productions–U.S. Army
The Battle of Midway	Sept. 1942	U.S. Navy–20th Century–Fox
December 7th	1943	U.S. Navy

Numerous training, coverage, and reportage projects (see Filmography).

John Ford in Navy uniform.

Nearly a hundred films are credited John Ford before his war service resulted in his first documentary in 1941. Many of his subsequent documentaries are curious, collective, or anonymous projects, but, especially in the cases of *The Battle of Midway* and *This Is Korea!* (two personal masterpieces), they represent unique aspects of Ford, explore alternate styles of cinema, exploit various dialectical relationships with the audience, and anticipate many of the "modernist" techniques of Rossellini, or even Godard and Straub.

Briefly, Ford's stance is more didactic than in his story films, visual and aural elements are more disjunctively combined, and montage becomes linear and simple, designed, in Vertov's phrase, to describe "fragments of actuality," and from their accumulation to evoke actuality. But greater objectivity is not an aim. Quite the contrary: Ford's documentaries are all propaganda movies (with the qualified exception of *This Is Korea!*), and their attitude is unequivocal compared to the story pictures, wherein military duty gone astray is a constant theme.

Unlike some modernists, Ford did not throw away Hollywood notions of the reality of the cinematic image; but Ford did wish to exploit tensions between apparent actuality and obvious fabrication. Curiously, it is at those points that tension is most taut, at which both oppositions are being most fully exploited, that both cinematic and actual reality are most potently thrown at us.

> I am really a coward. I know I am, so that's why I did foolish things. I was decorated eight or nine times, trying to prove that I was not a coward, but after it was all over I still knew, know, that I was a coward. Courage is something . . . I don't know . . . it's pretty hard to define. All I know is *I'm* not courageous. Oh, we'd go ahead and do a thing but after it was over, your knees would start shaking. I was not gallant or anything else. It just happened that way.[44]

War was another test for Ford. He plunged into it typically, with consuming commitment and total detachment. That was always his tragedy and genius: he was never exhausted by his passions; part of him remained outside, lonely and unsatisfied. Photos of him during the war are often breathtakingly romantic: his eyes hide beneath dark glasses, he wears leather jackets, sports a pipe mythically, his poses are larger than life. But if Ford adored military panoply, he abhorred its stupid slaughter. Perhaps he acted out boyhood fantasies, but he went off to war carrying not a gun but a camera, trading shots of film for shots of bullets.

He had been rejected by the navy during World War I for his poor eyesight, and an appointment as a photographer in the Navy Flying Corps, politically wrangled by his father, did not come through—if it ever did—until after the armistice; but somehow he got a Victory Medal.[45] Through his wife he had many friends in the Pacific fleet; he was given a reserve commission as a lieutenant commander in September 1934. He regularly filed intelligence reports on Japanese activity off the Mexican coast—on land he would stroll from bar to bar, accompanied by Wayne and Bond and followed by a hired mariachi band—and it has been claimed that he was acting as an undercover spy during his two trips to the Philippines. (If so, he fooled George O'Brien.)

Now, to record the history of the coming war, he began in 1939 to plan the most ambitious documentary film project ever undertaken. To this purpose, he recruited and trained his own film corps, consisting of Hollywood technicians each of whom became able to do everything. And they were drilled weekly by ex-marine Jack Pennick. Most were "over age and rich," as Mary Ford said, "people who could never have been drafted, but when Jack said, 'Let's go,' they obeyed him."[46] At first, the navy declined to take them as a reserve unit, but finally Colonel "Wild Bill" Donovan accepted them into the foreign intelligence agency Roosevelt had secretly ordered him to set up. Ford became chief of the Field Photographic Branch of the Office of Strategic Services (OSS, later the CIA); his only superior was Donovan, whose only superior was Roosevelt. "Our job," explained Ford, "was to photograph both for the Records and for our intelligence assessment, the work of guerrillas, saboteurs, Resistance outfits. . . . Besides this, there were special assignments."[47] Ford's unit made a great many films, some of which were only projected once, and in the greatest secret, before a few government leaders.

Sex Hygiene (1941). The first project, apparently undertaken prior to the unit's acceptance, was a curious instructional epic produced by Zanuck for the army and titled *Sex Hygiene*—VD ignorance had caused more harm than all World War I's battle casualties. Ford's first documentary shows tendencies that reappear in the others: the enclosure of the documentary material within an outer narrative or theatrical framework, and repetition. GIs are marched into a theater, where they view a film in which a doctor shows films (films within a film within a film) of pus-oozing penises, raving maniacs, and, as an example of how not to get help, a boy getting a bottle from an evil-looking pharmacist. We learn disease may spread by hand contact while watching Pete buckle his belt beside a statue of Venus before passing his cigarette to another guy. Over the doctor's final warning come fourteen close reaction shots of soldiers, a tiny track inward with each. A musical comedy was being filmed on a stage next to the one Ford was using at Fox, and he caused quite a stir when he sent his syphilitics over in wheelchairs to watch the half-naked dancing girls.

Field Photo was ordered to Washington in September 1941; it consisted of fifteen crews (ultimately, 175 men and 35 officers), a lab, and offices in the South Agriculture Building. Ford's home for two years was "a tiny broom closet of a room" (number 501) in the Carlton Hotel, until he finally found an apartment on the third floor of 1636 Connecticut Avenue. In December he accompanied his crews to Iceland to film a report on the Atlantic fleet and to Panama to report on canal defense. Since documentaries by regular army or navy photo crews would have tended to be whitewashed within service bureaucracy, Ford's OSS unit proved its worth to Roosevelt immediately.

The afternoon of December 7th, Ford, Mary, and Barbara were dining at the Alexandria home of Admiral William Pickens, chief of navigation. "The phone rang," Mary recalled, "and the maid brought the telephone to the admiral, and she called him 'animal,' and she said, 'It's for you, animal.' He said, 'I've told you not to disturb me while I'm at dinner.' 'It's the war department.'

We all bristled up. And he said, 'Yes, yes, yes,' and he hung up. And he said, 'Gentlemen, Pearl Harbor has just been attacked by the Japanese. We are now at war.' Everyone at that table, their lives changed that minute. We all walked out of the dining room. Then Mrs. Pickens said, 'It's no use getting excited. This is the seventh war that's been announced in this dining room.' "[48]

Mary came from "a war-fighting family. Most of my brothers were lost in wars." She was to see almost nothing of Jack or Pat (in the navy) during the next three and a half years. In World War I, she had been a psychiatric nurse, and active in charity between the wars. Now she took over the kitchens at the famous Hollywood Canteen, a free club where celebrities entertained 6,000 servicemen a night; it kept her busy—and stable. *Araner* was leased to the navy for the duration for one dollar. The Fords joked later that they never got the dollar (but the navy did assume large upkeep and repair expenses).

The regular military resented OSS people snooping around. MacArthur never did allow them into his theater, and Ford had tried and failed to countervail FDR's order restricting OSS operations to outside the United States.[49] Ford himself was strongly disapproved of in many circles. He acted as unmilitary as he possibly could, and most of the men in his unit probably did not know how to execute a right-face.[50] He would skip important meetings, was seldom in uniform or even reasonably tidy, ran his branch with his customary disrespect for bureaucratic niceties, generally failed to show proper awe toward chiefs of staff, and outraged navy regulars by dining publicly with enlistees. To win friends, he would invite various officers and chiefs to screenings of his movies, when he would deliver a stock speech: "I've been wanting to see this picture myself. I never saw it after it was all put together." This was in line with his legend—the brash, instinctual Irish hard-nose who could knock off a *How Green Was My Valley* and not bother to look at it. Then after the screenings, Ford would pull out his big white handkerchief, wipe away a tear, and croak, "I'm glad I waited until I could see it with you. I didn't realize it was so moving."[51] His personal filming of the battle of Midway also won him esteem (plus a Purple Heart) for boosting the nation's fortitude as it sent forth its sons to die.

The Battle of Midway (1942). This type of film was virtually lacking formal precedent, one for which Ford had to invent something "new." And it was an occasion when critical reception mattered little but when the reaction of the *masses* to Ford's deeply personal essay on "war, and peace, and all-of-us" mattered terribly. Rarely is an artist given so vast a subject for his canvas, and rarely does his thought receive the interested attention of so vast an audience.

To this aim *The Battle of Midway* is directly manipulative: it seeks a deeper level of consciousness through a fuller exploitation of multimedia art. To be sure, Ford did not abandon staginess altogether, but he did not again stand so far off from his material after *The Battle of Midway* as he did before it. This is the deepening of feeling to which critics referred, after the war. It is the difference, perhaps, between a man who films his ideas and a man who films his experience. His vision expanded, to darken considerably, but also to discover a greater beauty in a cactus rose than was seen in *Stagecoach*. Compared to the moody thirties pictures, *The Battle of Midway* has a broader, more open style—mood contrasts are freewheelingly juxtaposed, hokum mixes with sublimity, man is viewed less transcendentally and more ambiguously.

Whatever else war might be, Ford tells us, it is regardless an ultimate sort of experience of one's life. What is life, or love, or death compared to it?

War at the Battle of Midway (June 4–6, 1942) took place over a three-hundred-mile battle area, the film informs us. It would be impossible to report such an event in cinema, if by "report" we intend a record not simply of events but rather of deeds and thoughts and emotions. War is an experience, but also it is an attitude: whoever experiences war or thinks deeply about it is altered in his thought.

> Ford shot it himself, standing on an exposed water tower and, according to onlookers, yelling at the attacking Zeroes to swing left or right—and cursing them out when they disobeyed directions.[52]

> I was not ready and when the attack arrived I had only an Eyemo, a 16mm camera. I shot film and continued to change the film magazines and to stuff them in my pockets. The image jumps a lot because the grenades were exploding right next to me. Since then, they do that on purpose, shaking the camera when filming war scenes. For me it was authentic because the shells were exploding at my feet.[53]

We frequently see the walls of Ford's shelter.

> I was on this tower to report to the officers who were 50 feet under the ground, to report exactly the position of the Japanese planes and the numbers and so on. I had one boy[54] with me, but I said, "You're too young to get killed," and I hid him away, I thought in a safe place. I just kept reporting. I'd say, "There's a plane up there, one of our planes shot down, man in a parachute, Japs have shot the parachute, the man landed and the PT boat went out . . ." I just reported those things and took the picture. I was getting paid for it. That's what I was in the Navy for.

> I was doing alright till I had a blast of shrapnel that knocked me out. I was wounded pretty badly there, however I managed to come to long enough to finish the job.[55]

Ford's tower was on top of the power house—the first objective in a raid. A wound in his left arm plagued him the rest of his life. And at his funeral in 1973 the flag from his Midway headquarters was draped on his coffin.

It was not a coincidence that Ford was there photographing it himself.

Ford at Midway Island, 1942.

He had asked to be there, to photograph the battle. And the thought is staggering, particularly if one regards Ford as the great poetic chronicler of American history. For this was the biggest naval battle of history, the turning point of the greatest sea war ever fought and, is it too much to say?—the moment when the United States became the dominant global power.

The most significant fact of *The Battle of Midway* is that it is authentic, and Ford at every moment wishes to remind us of this. The film goes as far as possible toward being an exception to Godard's dictum of the similarity of documentary and fictional cinema (i.e., that, once images reach the screen, there is no essential difference between a "real" Nanook building an igloo ["documentary"] and a staged Hitchcockian murderer lurking in the shadows ["fiction"]). There is all the difference in the world between the historical films of Ford and Rossellini and this actuality; and all the difference in the world, too, between filming the actuality of Forty-Second Street and filming the actuality of the Battle of Midway. The twin facts of its historic importance and of the ultimate nature of war draw us more deeply into its documentary than would otherwise happen. There is a unique sort of "reality" here; there is a closer proximity to life than exists in Ford's fiction films. The confrontation is starker, more vivid, more deeply encountered.

And it is personal. Since Ford was there, he reports the deeds, the thoughts, the emotions of this ultimate experience, reports them as he felt and experienced and performed them. It is even a sort of autobiography, for war is an extension of one's cognition, down toward hell, up toward heaven, and broadly across a horizon no longer two-dimensional.

Ford is filming philosophy along with experience. One thinks constantly of what it is to kill, to be killed, to be in deadly peril, to be a mechanic fueling death. Is it heroism? How scared are they? Do not misinterpret Ford's sentimentality: it is a sign of his breadth, not of his simpleness. These are our people, our friends, or they could be. The voices of the narrators throw us into the terrifying mundane reality of it, of war unthinkable. They speak directly to us—"You!" Like it or not, we are forced to respond.

There is a dialectic to this film that is posed to us constantly, one that turns itself into an argument for the justness of this war by one who hates war with profound feeling. Yet Ford argues not so much with logic as with sentiment. There are streams of emotion that run the gamut of nearly every emotion. The succession of emotional forms—from peace to war to victory, from heroism to fear to courage, from individuality to paranoia to community, from innocence to sin to redemption, from dawn to night to dawn— constitute a reflective philosophy written into cinema and as such untranslatable into words. The film's title symbolizes a struggle of conscience.

The Battle of Midway is a symphony in its succession of tones of light, of tones of emotion, of tones of movement. The wonderful score is inextricably woven together with the images involved at a given moment, the cutting, the words spoken by the narrators. The two battle sequences are not long, but for me real time slows, and each shot seems to last a hellish eternity. There are no dead bodies, and no blood; no more than Sophocles does Ford need to resort to such devices.* Here, as in battle scenes in all his other pictures, he relies on an intense, often surreal, "impressionism." *The Battle of Midway* is a picture that demands deep concentration and total involvement to yield its riches. It is not a movie for a small screen, or for soft speakers. The music and battle sounds stand in relation to the pictures somewhat as a rich musical accompaniment stands to a vocal line; the two are equally important and reciprocally supportive. If a formal precedent be sought, it can be found in the battle compositions so popular in nineteenthcentury music. Only Beethoven's *Battle of Vittorio* (*Wellington's Victory*) is widely known today, but there were many such pieces, often for piano solo, and their tripartite structure (presentation, battle, aftermath—each of fairly equal length) is the same as that of Ford's picture. In cinema, there was

---

*Compared with most U.S. war-propaganda film, *The Battle of Midway* emphasizes death, danger, and vulnerability. *Fighting Lady* (de Rochemont–Steichen, 1945), for example, borrows much from *Midway* but is calculated to make parents think their sons are in capable hands against an inept enemy—with little sense of danger.

Eisenstein's *Alexander Nevsky* (1938), which, unlike Ford's film, places the Jubilation *after* the Lamentation, leading one to observe that all battle pieces may, by that choice, be divided into those who leave one celebrating or lamenting war. In any case, Ford's musical movie exemplifies the operatic Ford, an aspect of his style occurring at the high point of most of his movies, particularly—on a through-composed basis—in *The Black Watch, Mary of Scotland, Wagon Master,* and *The Sun Shines Bright.*

Nothing happens by chance in this film. And Ford's calculation in getting it released exactly as he wanted, and to the widest possible audience, belies the image of a man who would "just go out and shoot it" and then take off on a yacht trip leaving everything in the hands of the studio. After stopping in Hollywood to have the film processed, he flew straight to D.C. "His left arm was still bandaged, he needed a shave, and he looked as though he hadn't slept for a week," recalls editor Robert Parrish.[56] There was need for secrecy and haste. Word had gotten out of Ford's exploit and there was danger the film would be seized for interservice news pools. To prevent this, Ford dispatched Parrish and the film to Los Angeles—without orders—telling him to hide out at his mother's.

Ford assembled a rough cut, gave Parrish further instructions (one wonders how much initiative was Parrish's), brought in Phil Scott to dub sound effects and Al Newman to provide a score (Ford supplying the tunes). Dudley Nichols stayed up all night writing a florid commentary, which Ford had James Kevin McGuinness (a Metro production head) rewrite more folksily. Henry Fonda, Jane Darwell, Donald Crisp, and Irving Pichel came upon instant summons; Ford, reading from notes, told them what to say, and they said it into a microphone, imitating him—a twenty-minute session. During the editing, Parrish omitted McGuinness's lines, spoken by Darwell, about getting the boys to the hospital, which he found maudlin, and a furious debate ensued. "It's for the mothers of America," Ford explained. "It's to let them know that we're in a war and that we've been getting the shit kicked out of us for five months, and now we're starting to hit back. Do you think we can make a movie that the mothers of America will be interested in?"[57]

Because of interservice rivalry, it was important to give army, navy, and marines equal footage. When Parrish told Ford they were five feet short on the marines, Ford pulled from his pocket a five-foot close-up in 35mm color of the president's son, marine major James Roosevelt. That night, they took the print to the White House, FDR's support being necessary to get it released. He chatted all through the movie, then suddenly froze into silence when his son appeared. At the end Eleanor was crying, and the president proclaimed: "I want every mother in America to see this picture!"

Most of them did.* Ford, to prove a point, ordered Parrish to attend the

---

*Not without further difficulties: Eastman-Kodak, according to Wilkinson, at first claimed 16mm Kodachrome could not be successfully blown up to 35mm. Ford suspected the company feared cheaper production methods; after a month dragged by, veiled threats of government seizure helped loose the film from the lab. Then Technicolor made five hundred prints.

Radio City Music Hall premiere. "*The Battle of Midway* was the first film of its kind," said Parrish. "It was a stunning, amazing thing to see. Women screamed, people cried, and the ushers had to take them out. And it was all over the material that we had fought about. . . . The people, they just went crazy." And the film went on to win an Academy Award.[58]

Never was Ford to make a film more cinematically and formally perfect than *The Battle of Midway*. The concision of its seventeen minutes never demands concession to amplitude.

Titles. A legend emphasizes: report, actual, authentic. A map situates Midway Island midway in the Pacific.

I. Exposition. (1) *Midway Island.* Bright blue Kodachrome sky and lively music induct one into the movie. Crisp's voice addresses *us:* "Our outpost. Your front yard." (2) *The Marines.* But cutting abruptly closer to a marching marine column, just as a male chorus enters the instrumental hymn ("*First* to fight . . . "), Ford produces an operatic effect: the future heroes present themselves. This is a necessary device in an epic; but we know some of them will actually die, soon. (3) *The Birds.* Crisp: "These are the natives of Midway. Tojo has sworn to liberate them." But our flag dissolving into blue sky and birds (whose voices abruptly follow the "Hymn"'s cadence) suggests they are *American* birds, free as the sky. (4) *Sunset Before Battle.* "The birds seem nervous." A sailor plays "Red River Valley" (dubbed by Dan Borzage) as others gaze into a sunset whose red flames suggest the Japanese battle flag: muffled explosions.

(5) *The Air Force.* As B-29s are prepared, Jane Darwell exclaims: "That fellow's walk looks familiar. My neighbor's boy used to amble along just like that. Say, is that one of them Flying Fortresses?" Henry Fonda: "Yes, ma'am. It sure is!" Darwell: "Why it's that young lieutenant! He's from my home town, Springfield, Ohio. He's not gonna fly that great big bomber?!" Fonda: "Yes, ma'am! That's his job! He's the skipper!"

Darwell's and Fonda's voices play a different role than Crisp's and Pichel's. The latter are informed commentators; the former seem to speak from the audience, speaking *to* the film. They engage us in actuality, in a dialectic with it, and help us admit these soldiers as representative of our friends and neighbors. (Also, Darwell and Fonda were readily identifiable as folks from *The Grapes of Wrath*, while Crisp carried patriarchal authority from *How Green Was My Valley*.)

But Darwell's role is more complex: she questions the film and it replies to her. When she says, "Will's dad is an engineer. Thirty-eight years on the old Ironton Railroad," the film obediently dissolves, with homey music, to Dad oiling a locomotive, then turning in a closer shot to look into the camera. (Gregg Toland shot the "Ohio" scenes.) Darwell, not so much narrating as

Figure 6. *The Battle of Midway*

Timing	Divisions	Music /(Sound)
0:30	**Titles**	"My Country 'Tis of Thee"
4:56	I. **Exposition**	
1:00	1. Midway Island	"Anchors Aweigh"; "Yankee Doodle"
0:22	2. The Marines	"Marine Hymn"
0:35	3. The Birds	(Bird sounds); bird motif
0:35	4. Sunset Before Battle	"Red River Valley"; (bombs)
2:22	5. The Air Force	
0:50	a. Council	"Columbia, Gem of the Ocean"; "Off We Go"
0:40	b. Crew and flash home	Homey folk tune
0:52	c. B-29s take off	(Engine sounds)
5:35	II. **The Battle**	
3:35	1. U.S. Defense	
1:25	a. Japs attack, bomb	(Gunfire, plane drones, bombs falling)
0:35	b. Flag-raising	"Star Spangled Banner" (explosions)
1:35	c. Jap planes shot down	(Battle sounds)
2:00	2. U.S. Counteroffensive	(Battle sounds) "Anchors Aweigh"
4:50	III. **Aftermath**	
1:00	1. Flyers return	"Anchors Aweigh"
0:35	2. Birds still free	"Marine Hymn"—slow
0:20	3. Search for survivors	"Anchors Aweigh"
0:55	4. Survivors return; hospital destroyed.	"Anchors Aweigh"; "Onward Christian Soldiers"
2:00	5. Funeral on land; on sea; recapitulation.	"My Country 'Tis of Thee"
0:50	**Coda**	"Off We Go"; "Anchors Aweigh"; "Marine Hymn"; "Over There"

16:51

talking privately to someone else, continues: "And his mother. Huh, well, she's just like the rest of us mothers in Springfield, or any other American town." Mother sits knitting, red flowers beside her, a service star on the wall; then we see a girl talking on the phone, a red ribbon in her hair: "And his sister Patricia! Eh! She's about as pretty as they come!" Fonda: "I'll say so!"

As the B-29s take off, Darwell calls, "Good luck! God bless you, son!" Again Ford wants to engage us, but even if we do not support Darwell's sentiment, we must relate to its ramifications. Eight consecutive pans of B-29s taking off set a tone of mechanical strength thrusting forth. The constant birds increase their association with America: like the airmen, they amble and fly.

       II. The Battle. (1) *The U.S. Defense* (3:35). 1/Sky, five Jap planes. Crisp, hurried: "Suddenly, from behind the clouds: The Japs Attack!" (Din of battle noises.) 2/Soldier with field glasses looks from foxhole. 3/Sky. 4/AA gun-barrel fires from foxhole. 5/Japanese plane flies through shrapnel. 6/AA gun again. 7/Plane through shrapnel. 8/Two boy soldiers at AA gun in foxhole.

    9/Two USMC planes take off, pan right. Unidentifiable male voices call, "There go the Marines!" 10/Pan right with two more USMC planes. 11/Again, several more. 12/=2: soldier with field glasses looking up. 13/Planes directly overhead. 14/Two boys in foxhole, from above. 15/Their AA gun firing. 16/From Ford's hut: plane flies along beach, suddenly there's an immense EXPLOSION; film slips sprockets, rights, camera shakes. 17/In long-focal lens and perhaps slow motion: debris floats through air (cf. Antonioni's *Zabriskie Point*). 18/Plane swoops overhead in CU. 19/AA gun firing. 20/Sea and sky full of shrapnel. 21/Two boys. 22/Their gun again. 23/Planes above; EXPLOSION loosens film; explosion on beach and its smoke. 24/Overlooking base, fires and beach. 25/Similar. 26/Island ground: fire and wreckage. 27/Hangar, burning, pan right into smoke. 28/Plane above: EXPLOSION, loosening film; looking out from hut, debris falling. (Instrumental strains of "The Star Spangled Banner" begin just after this explosion.)

    29/Men running rapidly through fiery debris. 30/*A flag detail is attaching U.S. flag, while others race by seeking shelter. Behind them a marine with field glasses kneels on one knee looking up at sky. Choir enters with,* "And the rockets' red glare . . ." *The flag is raised, slowly, the camera panning up in steady steps: a lengthy shot midst rapidly cut ones. As the flag is raised Irving Pichel's voice says,* "Yes, this really happened." 31/White sky

The Battle of Midway (1942).

with bursting shrapnel—". . . bombs bursting in air . . ." 32/Fiery smoke-cloud—". . . gave . . ." 33/The flag, frame filled with black smoke—". . . proof through the night . . ." 34/Long shot, slightly tilted up, the brilliantly sunlit *flag*, its pole; the *blue* sky filling upper left diagonal, the *black smoke* churning through right diagonal. A few *birds* fly through smoke—". . . that our flag was still . . ." 35/Quick shot of plane flying through fiery smoke—". . . there!"

36/Beach, abrupt EXPLOSION. (End of music.) 37/Fiery smoke-clouds. 38/Black smoke. 39/Billowing fire and black smoke. 40/Two boys in foxhole shooting. 41/Shrapnel-filled sky. (Plane drone, distinct.) 42/AA gun-barrel firing. (Drone continues.) 43/Droning plane in air is hit and ex-plodes. 44/Jeep careens through fiery debris. 45/Tremendous EXPLO-SION on ground rocks film; camera jerks around to left, then pans right to medic attending man. 46/Plane flying in air. Camera pans around base; sound of bomb falling, then EXPLOSION. Film jumps and when it steadies, camera looks out from hut toward base. 47/Again, from the hut.

48/The base, with huge black smoke-cloud, pan up along it. One bird flies through. (During this shot begins distinct drone of plane, which will occupy the soundtrack through shot 55.) 49/Long shot: hangar, billowing cloud of fire pours from it, and out of the fire pours the huge black smoke-cloud. (Drone continues.) 50/Closer shot of fire-cloud. (Drone . . .) 51/Two boys in foxhole firing AA gun. (Drone . . .) 52/Air filled with shrapnel. A metallic CLANK. Camera rocks. The clank stops the droning sound: now the plane is heard to cough a few times and then starts falling earthward. This sound continues in ever-rising crescendo for almost fifteen seconds. 53/During this crescendo, the camera looks over burning installations, smoke rising, then pans slowly leftward. 54/The two boys—crescendo nearly deafening. 55/Look-ing up to sky from sandbag ridge in foxhole: plane careens diagonally across sky, crescendo increasing; it hits earth, rocking camera, which jerks. 56/Plane wing: fire burns in circular Japanese emblem. (Fire sound.)

It goes without saying that, while the footage is actual, the soundtrack was added later.

(2) *U.S. Counteroffensive.* In terms of the film, the flag-raising inspires courage, the plane-downings signal the turn of battle, which now switches to the sea. Planes swirl dizzily above, but Ford keeps cutting to the carrier men fueling ammunition, their guns flaring the film red; he is fascinated by men and their might, by mechanical discipline in crisis, by the job of war, by the impersonal, unseen enemy. On our men's faces we glimpse intense ex-citement, happiness beyond intoxication. Strains of "Anchors Aweigh" suc-ceed an immense explosion. We dissolve to Ford's hut window: the shot says "I was there. I am safe." (Lt. Kenneth M. Pier shot most air/sea footage.)

III. Aftermath. (1) *Flyers Return.* As pilots gaze joyously at the camera, Pichel says: "Men and women of America, here come your neighbors' sons. . . . You ought to meet them." But his phrase "home from a day's work" is disturbing. War may be a job, but killing and winning are not so intoxicating for us as for those living it. The faces alienate while attracting. Ford is fascinated: they are heroes, but theirs are deeds difficult to comprehend. (4) *Survivors Return.* As Crisp speaks of pilots "eight days . . . nine days . . . ten days without food or water," the film flares red between his words, as an exposure-shocked survivor emerges, expressing painful endurance. Others arrive, Pichel's stern naming becomes epithetical, mythic. The melody "Onward Christian Soldiers" enters, cutting and panning take on lofty, jubilant rhythms. "Logan Ramsey." Pans with a stretcher, cut to another . . . ; the hymn swells. "Frank Sessler." As two enter an ambulance and it pulls off, the hymn begins a glorious canon; Darwell: "Get those boys to the hospital! Please do! Quickly. Get them to clean cots and cool sheets. Get them doctors and medicine and nurses' soft hands. Get them to the hospital! Hurry. Please." A choir enters the hymn on "clean": "*Onward Christian soldiers, marching as to war! With the cross of Jesus marching on before!*" Meanwhile we pan a destroyed building; as the choir sings, "*war,*" the pan switches direction, ending on the red cross that was to have safeguarded the bombed hospital. Poignantly, the movie has tried to respond to Darwell with images. The hymn is a prayer; it says: "*Be* Christian." It is a hope. Ford seeks reassurance, justification, for war. Darwell's plea is part of this dialectic; these soldiers are "ours": how would *our* mother react were we in the ambulance?

With tolling bell, the red cross fades into (5) *The Funeral.* Deep-hued light of late afternoon, the camera tilted up toward faces shadowed by dusk and history. PT-boats churn through sea deeply blue, as a choir sings the second chorus of "My Country 'Tis of Thee"—"*Author of liberty*"—directly over a coffin draped in gleaming red flag. Even the white-topped waves rise and fall with the hymn, as we pan up to billowy clouds ("*Freedom's holy light*"), then down to the island ("*Protect*"), dissolve into a pan in opposite direction, following three planes to center on a shot recapitulating four themes: a soldier kneeling with field glasses (*watchfulness*), birds flying (*freedom*), both oblivious to the huge black smoke-cloud (*danger*); the planes (*strength*) ("*and Guide Thy might*"). Cut to a scene overlooking the base ("*Great God our King*"), then to the flag, its colors strongly etched against black smoke, but this time the camera is not tilted upward: the difference between courage and faith, hope and security ("*Amen*").

A coda, added at FDR's request, swishes paint across three successive signs tabulating the Japanese vessels destroyed.

Meanwhile, after accompanying Doolittle toward Tokyo and participating in raids on Marcus Island and Wotje, Ford in August 1942 flew to London, and checked comfortably into Claridge's. (His flight had laid over in Ireland, where John had joked, "There are only two neutral countries in all of Europe: the peace-loving Irish and those cowardly Swedes."[59]) His job in England was to prepare Field Photo crews for the invasion of North Africa—at Oran, Algiers, and Casablanca, November 8—and for this purpose his men were sent to commando schools in Scotland. Ford himself reached Algiers November 14 and a few days later encountered Darryl Zanuck at Bone. Zanuck, now a colonel in the Signal Corps, was going through the war in such luxury and with such intense self-promotion that he was later singled out as an example of a "Hollywood Colonel" and forced into inactive service—one reason Ford took care to document his own contributions. At Bone Zanuck snapped a satiric photo—from behind—of Ford astride a donkey, then had it published in all the newspapers, to Ford's disgust. They had a sole cigar between them when a bomb nearly blew them to kingdom come; "Did it hurt the cigar?" Ford asked.[60] After Zanuck departed, Ford followed the American advance to Tebourba, where Field Photo filmed a gargantuan tank battle. On the way, near Souk El Arba, while photographing a dogfight directly over his head, Ford captured a downed German fighter, turned him over to Free French forces, then repossessed him when the French began torture. By late January Ford was back in Washington. He was responsible now for nearly six hundred people. Jack Pennick moved in with him, which made life a bit less lonely.

Around this time, Ford saw *The Ox-Bow Incident* and sent a note to director William Wellman congratulating him. And he added: "The only thing in the picture that didn't strike me as being real, Billie, was my brother Frank refusing a drink and making such a fuss about getting hung. After all, most of his ancestors have been hung and I just can't see Frank refusing a drink."[61] That June, Frank, aged sixty-one, dyed his hair and enlisted in the army, noting he had been too old for World War I. All went well during basic training at Fort Ord, until Frank tried to cash a Social Security check—and got discharged.[62]

Son Pat had gotten married in Maine and received a commission in the navy; but his eyesight was wretched and to his disgust he found himself stationed in Los Angeles as a public information officer. Only toward the end of the war was Ford able to pull enough strings to get Pat headed toward intelligence work. Mary was up to her neck in the Hollywood canteen and also was worrying over Ward Bond and John Wayne. Neither was in the service; they were both over the draft age, Bond was epileptic, while "Duke" (the nickname came from a dog he had had as a boy), with four children, had waited until too late to apply for a commission and was unwilling to enlist as a private. Ford got Wayne onto a USO tour in MacArthur's theater in the South Pacific—where the OSS was banned—and then had Wayne write up a report for the OSS.[63] But much of the time Duke and Ward were hanging around Ford's house engaged in antics. Duke set Ward's bedclothes on fire to wake him up once, and another time, after Ward bet him he could not knock him off a newspaper and then closed a door between them, Duke punched Ward by driving his fist right through the door.[64] There were more serious problems, too. "Can't you write and try and beat something into Duke's head," wrote Mary to Jack. "I've practically been sitting on Josie [Wayne's wife] to prevent a divorce but now guess she will have to get up for decency's sake and try and save a little for the kids before it's too late. He has gone completely berserk over that Esperanza Bauer and cares for no one. Thinks he is the hottest set in pictures and says he is madly in love and nothing else matters. It's a damn shame that with a war going on he has to think about his lousy stinking tail. I only think of those gorgeous kids. It's really tragic. Bond is drunk three-fourths of the time and as Pat says, 'When the cat's away how the mice will play.' Guess without you they're bound for destruction. . . . [One of Duke's leading ladies] was talking about him the other day and said (this is funny), 'I tried to help him. I knew he couldn't act without being coached. He said Ford took him home at eight and helped him with his next day's scenes. I tried that too but it didn't work.'"[65]

Meanwhile in Washington, Ford was under considerable opprobrium. Soon after Pearl Harbor, Donovan had ordered Field Photo to film a secret report on the attack—what happened and who was to blame. The perilous situation of OSS units poking into that sensitive affair had been further exacerbated at Pearl by the somewhat undiplomatic manner of Gregg Toland, famed cinematographer of *Little Foxes, Grapes of Wrath, Citizen Kane*, etc., whom Ford had assigned to direct. (Ford went out to Pearl in May 1942 and is listed as co-director.) The finished film, *December 7th*, a bitter exposé of how administrative oversight had left Hawaii vulnerable, was judged outrageous and politically disruptive. It was confiscated, never released, and Roosevelt issued a directive subjecting all future Field Photo material to censorship, lest it injure national morale. Disgusted, Toland had gone to Rio to film a report on Brazil (Ford visited him there during a month-long trip in May 1943). And Donovan, to avoid having Ford officially reprimanded, got him out of the way by putting him on an unescorted munitions freighter that left New York October 4 and reached Calcutta November 25. While Ford's men were puzzled why they had not flown, Ford himself was glad for the rest and, as usual, loved a fifty-five-day sea voyage.[66]

December 7th (1943). The eighty-five minute, unreleased version of *December 7th* survives in the National Archives. On December 6, 1941, a character called "U.S."—a traditionally garbed Uncle Sam (Walter Huston)—is musing about "Hawaii, Territory of Heaven," but white-suited Mr. C (for Conscience: Harry Davenport) suggests U.S. is complacent. U.S. narrates the cultivation of Hawaii, comparing it to the winning of the West. Sugar cane, pineapples, big business. From grass huts to modern Honolulu, its university libraries, schools, arts academy, streets, homes, trees, churches, hotels, beaches, ports (typically repetitive: e.g., not *one* exemplary church, but eight different churches), businesses. "The Big Five" companies: "Castle & Cook, Alexander & Baldwin," etc., "the nerve center . . . of the territory. Grandsons, aunts, held together by blood ties and interlocking directorates. Scratch one and the other bleeds."

But, says C, the laborers are mostly Japanese, 37 percent of the population, at work in fields, restaurants, flowermarts, their streets, slums, Japanese telephone book, magazines, banks, their own "Big Five." Thirty-two(!) Japanese shop signs, with superimpressions of street life. Japanese boy scouts salute the flag. But the Japanese language is taught, too, "along with their morality and their culture" and their Shinto churches. Declares a monk:

— In Shintoism we worship the first Japanese emperor, whose creation started the world of mankind. . . . [Emperor Hirohito] is the mortal image of our immortal deity. . . . Shintoism preaches honor of the ancestor, thereby keeping alive the fires of nationalism and preserving a racial and social bond with the unbroken and divinely descended Imperial dynasty. To be a Shinto is to be a Japanese. This is not, nor can it be, a matter of choice. It is a duty.

Seventeen thousand Hawaiian children are registered for Japanese citizenship; the consulate carries on extensive espionage. We see various eavesdropping Japanese: a gardener outside a men's room, girls in a barbershop, a chauffeur, a girl on a date. A Nazi tells the consul how overheard club talk helped him sink a destroyer (a frequent "plot" in propaganda films).

But U.S. remains optimistic. Nine lovely girls represent minority groups; children perform ethnic customs; six girls say "Aloha." But U.S. dreams of the war in Europe. And, Sunday morning, the squadrons appear, "swooping down like flights of tiny locusts," as Japanese envoys confer in Washington. Ten minutes of battle footage.* Fifty of two hundred planes are downed,

*All this footage (accepted as actual for years) was staged by Toland and Ray Kellogg, mostly at Fox, using rearscreen. Similarly, actors and studio sets were employed for much of the background material. According to William T. Murphy ("John Ford and the Wartime Doc-

but 2,343 Americans die. The camera frames a grave. "Who are you boys? Come on, speak up some of you!"

A voice identifies itself as Robert L. Kelly, USMC. We see his picture on the wall at home. He comes from Ohio, he tells us, and introduces his parents. The *same* voice continues through six more dead soldiers, each representing different services, different regions, different racial origins. Iowa parents pose American-Gothic-like before their silo; a black mother hangs laundry. "But, how does it happen that all of you sound and talk alike?" "Because we *are* all alike. We are *all* Americans." Notably Fordian is the funeral held on a shore midst white sand and flags (terribly beautiful photography). A tenor sings "My Country 'Tis of Thee"; an elderly officer and wife stand in attendance, she struck with such fragile sorrow that, though it looks actual, one suspects Ford posed her in his patented way; tracking shot looking up at palm trees.

From a map of Japan a radio tower arises, a Godzilla-like monster sprouting waves: our narrator corrects Tojo's victory claims. Before-and-after shots chronicle salvage operations. "Who is that saucy little girl . . . ? [A small ship sailing past.] By George, it looks like . . . Yes! It is! The mine-layer *Oglala* . . . !" *Now* Hawaii prepares for attack. Barbed wire, tunnels, drills, children in gas masks. Some Japanese buy war bonds; others are forced out of business, others arrested. But not a single act of sabotage. All traces of Japanese language are removed, all those signs changed, temples closed.

In Arlington Cemetery a Pearl victim talks to a Marine casualty, who points out where everyone's buried. "I saw the General the other day," he says, meaning Washington. The World War I vet is cynical but the sailor says, "I'm putting my bets on the Roosevelts, the Churchills, the Stalins, the Chiang Kai-sheks!" Twenty-four UN flags pass in review.

In 1943, Ford eliminated *December 7th*'s finger-pointing, changing it from an investigation to a paean of the navy's ability to bounce back. This thirty-four-minute version omits U.S., Mr. C, and the analysis. And it won Ford his fourth Oscar in a row.

After some time in New Delhi, Ford, always accompanied by Jack Pennick, flew to Rangoon where Field Photo was making a propaganda film in support of Mountbatten (*Victory in Burma*, directed by Irving Asner). In Rangoon he met Donovan and together they flew to Assam. Donovan insisted on parachuting into Nazira, and Ford of course was obliged to parachute too, with some fright. The next day he saw planes landing at the airstrip and realized Donovan and he could have as well. Colonel Carl Eifler

umentary," *Film and History*, February, 1976, pp. 1–8) there was no actual U.S. film of the attack, only Japanese, C. Daughtery, however, shot two hundred feet in 16mm and Lt. Comd. Edward Young shot one hundred feet of 8mm Kodachrome, and this footage was lent to Field Photo as reference, according to documents in the John Ford Papers (Lilly Library, Indiana University).

was in command of OSS operations in the Far East, and Donovan wanted to prove to Congress that the OSS's daredevil guerrilla activities behind Japanese lines deserved support. Here in the jungle a priest, James Stuart, was training Kachin tribesmen as guerrillas, and Ford, deciding to incorporate the Kachins into the Mountbatten film, left Guy Bolte, Bob Rhea, and Butch Meehan with Father Stuart; a few months later, Meehan was killed in action. Ford and Donovan went on over the Himalayas to Chungking and Kunming in order to establish OSS operations in China. Field Photo began an extensive program of aerial mapping, and Ford spent a month there training his men.[67] He also visited Tibet. After one camera crew was killed parachuting, Ford had to send in a second. In mid-January, he and Pennick flew back to New Delhi, and then, in a nine-day series of hops (Karachi, Masira, Aden, Khartoum, El Fasher, Maiduguri, Kano, Accra, Ascension Island, Natal [Brazil], Belem, Georgetown, Trinidad, Boringuin, Miami), they reached Washington on January 23, 1944.

In March, Ford took two weeks' leave at home—his only leave thus far, except for two days after Midway—and then in April was off for London, for D Day. Ford was in charge of U.S. Navy, U.S. Coast Guard, British, Dutch, Polish, and French camera installations—all seaborne photography for the United Nations.

When Ford had left Mark Armistead in charge of Field Photo in London, his only orders (for two years) were, "Do a good job for the OSS and the navy." Armistead's group made a few documentaries, but their chief labor was in the invention of reconnaissance methods, such as photographing through submarine periscopes. Armistead's biggest task was to develop aerial mapping techniques, for the Allies possessed no detailed maps of the Normandy beaches. (Later, after D-Day, with five planes known [but not to Ford] as "John Ford's air force," Armistead mapped most of Western Europe and had started on Russian-held portions, when Allied governments, realizing at last what valuable military information the U.S. was gaining, put a stop to it. Ford had to save him from a court martial, but Eisenhower told Donovan that Armistead's work alone justified the whole OSS.)[68]

The day before the invasion, Ford sent cameramen Brick Marquard and Junius Stout (Archie Stout's son; he was killed some months later) onto Omaha Beach with the Rangers, to prepare camera positions; others were sent in on the first wave. Armistead had mounted springwound cameras on five hundred landing craft. Ford rode a destroyer in the first attack. (There is a story, perhaps apocryphal, that he was commanding an observation vessel and, receiving a signal to turn starboard, he turned to port instead. A message came: "You turned the wrong way, you idiot." Ford read it and handed it to an aide. "Take this down to decoding," he ordered, "and have it translated immediately."[69]) Later on D-Day, Ford joined Armistead in a PT boat commanded by Johnny Bulkeley (the hero of *They Were Expendable*), where he spent the next five days. Bulkeley piloted Ford into some excursions with the French underground—experiences Ford recreated comically in *When Willie Comes Marching Home*—and Ford, keeping a promise, brought back some wine for director George Stevens, whom he had placed in command of British photography. Then he returned to London and got uncontrollably drunk.

Ford participated with Bulkeley in a PT boat operation in support of Yugoslav partisans, on the side of Tito's anti-Communist rival, Mikhailovitch. Ford groused that the business was "too full of lousy Oxford dons and aristocracy, princes and dukes and God knows what kind of White Russians."[70] Then he was detached by order of the secretary of the navy to make a propaganda movie about Bulkeley and the PT boats, *They Were Expendable*. When Ford got back to the real war, in July 1945, it was almost over. He went to Budapest to assist in the repatriation of Jewish refugees, filmed French forces entering St. Nazaire and Bordeaux, and sent a detail from Field Photo to cover the Nuremberg trials (see Filmography). On August 11 he was promoted to captain and on September 29 was detached from service.

As a condition of making *They Were Expendable*, Ford had asked MGM's Louis B. Mayer for the highest price ever paid a director, all of which he would contribute to the "Field Photo Farm." Sam Briskin, a Columbia Pictures executive, owned a twenty-acre estate in the San Fernando valley with a five-bedroom house, swimming pool, stables, and tennis court. Ford wanted to turn it into a clubhouse for his unit. He told Mayer that Mayer had been making money and movies while others had been fighting Nazis; now was the time to pay his bill. "Just pay me two hundred fifty thousand dollars. That will be my contribution. Then you throw in another two hundred fifty thousand to show that you are grateful to the lads for suppressing Nazism, and I'll direct *They Were Expendable* and get John Wayne to star in it. We'll get Cliff Reid as associate producer. . . . He's the best goddam associate producer in the business. Did a hell of a job on *The Informer*."[71]

Ford's motives were mixed. The war had made him no less egotistical than he had been before it, but, in almost everyone's opinion, it had made him a much *kinder* person. He wanted to perpetuate his leadership, and his unit's *esprit de corps*, into civilian life, but he also wanted to provide for his men. Any of them could live at the Farm free of charge, and this was initially a boon to those whose marriages and lives had been disrupted by the war. The Farm also served as a recuperation center for paraplegic veterans condemned to nearby Birmingham Hospital. Mary Ford organized regular entertainments for them. Christmas Eve and St. Patrick's Day were big, family occasions, with stars like Wayne, Fonda, or Andy Devine as Santa Claus. A small barn was converted into a chapel, a replica of Washington's at Mount Vernon, with stained glass windows from the church set of *How Green Was My Valley*. Here the central service of Ford's life was enacted each Memorial Day. Everyone from the unit (and most of the Ford stock company) was expected to be there. Bagpipers would march, a black choir sang "The Battle Hymn of the Republic," and the honor role of the dead was read. Ford knew every member of his unit, their wives and families, and supported many of the paraplegics, in addition to subsidizing the Farm by about $10,000 a year. Ford, said Mark Armistead, "was the only one of the Hollywood directors that fought who did not forget his men."[72]

Thirteen of them died in action; more than half were decorated.

POSTWAR: TRANSITIONAL PHASE (1945–1947)

They Were Expendable	12.20.45	Metro-Goldwyn-Mayer
My Darling Clementine	11.?.46	20th Century–Fox
The Fugitive	11.3.47	Argosy Pictures–RKO Radio

While all of the second period, 1939–41 in particular, is marked by themes of survival and persistence, Ford's three postwar films meditate on ruination, rather than on the victory culminating World War II and the preceding decade of social strife. *They Were Expendable* stares at destruction and regards survival as an onerous duty; *My Darling Clementine* allegorizes the war and loss of innocence; *The Fugitive* ruminates on destruction caused by attempts to impose justice (postwar foreign policy) and sees hope only in God. Thus, these movies are blacker than ever. Consciousness seems expanded, bolder, less facile, with a greater sense of evil and a searching quality. Also, expressionistic style seems fiercer, montage more articulating, and the operatic side of Ford in the ascendant. But these are sad films, there is a sense of waiting; this is a transitional period.

A dialogue with destiny begins. In contrast to the transcendental assurance with which duty was previously regarded, its source now seems more imminent. The hero may be mistaken about his duty, feel incapable of it, or wonder what it is. Free will returns, slightly.

In March 1946, Ford, seeking independence as numerous filmmakers were doing, incorporated his own production company, Argosy Pictures. In addition to eight brilliant Ford movies, the company also made *Mighty Joe Young*, with Ernest Schoedsack as director. The principal investors, besides Ford (chairman) and Merian Coldwell Cooper (president), were all OSS veterans: William Donovan, Ole Doering (a member of Donovan's Wall Street law firm), David Bruce (married to a Mellon and variously ambassador to England, France, Germany, and China), and William Vanderbilt.* So eager was Ford for this independence that he turned down a Fox offer guarantee-

---

*Argosy Pictures Corporation was capitalized at $500,000. Ten thousand shares were issued. Upon dissolution in 1956, Ford and his wife held 2,475 shares, Cooper and his wife 1,130, with another 1,095 in trust for relatives, Bruce and his (?) wife 1,992, Doering 2,000, Donovan's law firm 250. Sixteen other shareholders held small blocks of stock.

ing $600,000 per year. (His first attempt at independence—a cooperative group called Renowned Artists formed in June 1937 with Tay Garnett and Ronald Colman—had failed to get off the ground.) Argosy had actually produced *The Long Voyage Home* in 1940 and, very unofficially, *Stagecoach*, both through Walter Wanger. Its initial distribution agreement with RKO specified backing for *The Quiet Man* if its first picture were successful, but *The Fugitive* failed, and then Howard Hughes took over RKO. A new agreement with Republic was similarly formulated, but this time Ford made a western first. To hold down costs, and to bail out from *The Fugitive* disaster, Ford was especially sparing with film, perhaps exposing no more than one and a half times the finished length of *Fort Apache* and completing it and *She Wore a Yellow Ribbon* for about a million dollars *under* budget. Long disputes with Republic over *The Quiet Man*'s earnings—it appeared Republic was underreporting them—eventually resulted in a large settlement in Argosy's favor ($546,360.25 as I read the papers, twice that according to Dan Ford[73]), but the company ceased production in 1953 after Republic butchered *The Sun Shines Bright*. The new era of the superproduction made companies like Argosy less viable, even aside from the problems that were encountered with Republic. It had, however, realized a 600 percent capital gain for its major-risk investors, 30 percent for its minor-risk investors. Ford, in addition, had been paid approximately $1.5 million in salary, Cooper about $500,000. Cooper again worked with Ford on *The Searchers*, this time with C. V. Whitney money. Cooper's immense importance as Ford's producer, in handling myriad administrative details, became painfully evident in later years when Ford had to perform these tasks himself.*

*Cooper (1894–1973) was born in Jacksonville to a Scotch-Irish plantation family; his lawyer father became chairman of the Federal Reserve Board in Florida. After Lawrenceville and Annapolis (whence he resigned in his last year because of excessive exuberance), Cooper was a merchant seaman, a midwest reporter, a national guardsman fighting Pancho Villa, and an army flyer in France, where the Germans shot him down in 1918. He got shot down again, fighting Bolsheviks with Poland's Kosciusko Squadron, but escaped Russian prison after ten months, making it to Latvia with two others in twenty-six days. He worked for *The New York Times* and did a quasi-autobiography, *Things Men Die For* (Putnam, 1927) under the pseudonym "C." He then enlisted with cameraman Ernest Schoedsack in Edward Salisbury's round-the-world exploration; their movies of Ethiopia were burnt up in Italy, they wrote a book, *The Sea Gypsy* (1924), then with Marguerite Harrison filmed the 350-mile migration of Iran's Bakhtiaria tribe. This became the famous documentary *Grass* (1925), whose success inspired Paramount to finance Cooper and Schoedsack in *Chang*, in Thailand, and *Four Feathers* (1929). Well advised, Cooper had invested in aviation stock and soon found himself on the boards of Pan Am and several other airways. In September 1931 he became production assistant at RKO, taking over Selznick's job as production chief in February 1933. Along with the Whitney brothers, he invested heavily in the new Technicolor process, teamed Fred Astaire and Ginger Rogers, brought John Ford from Fox to make *The Lost Patrol*, and, with Schoedsack, made *King Kong*, in which transparencies were first used. In May 1933 he married Dorothy Jordan (Lucy Lee's mother in *The Sun Shines Bright*, Martha in *The Searchers*), resigned as production head, but continued to produce specials, such as *The Last Days of Pompeii*. In 1936 he became vice-president of Selznick-International but, failing to interest Selznick in a Technicolor *Stagecoach*, quit to form Argosy, bringing along some Whitney money. During the war, he was Chennault's chief of staff in China, assisted Whitehead's airborne invasion of New Guinea,

***They Were Expendable* (1945).** The story is drawn from a short best-seller by W. L. White, an account of America's disastrous defeat in the Philippines from the viewpoint of a torpedo squadron and its commander, Lieutenant John D. Bulkeley (= Brickley here), edited from interviews with the second in command, Lieutenant Robert Balling Kelly (= Rusty Ryan).* Ford:

> What I had in mind was doing it exactly as it had happened. It was strange to do this picture about Johnny Bulkeley—I knew him so well. He was the fellow in Guantanamo who, when Castro cut the lines off, quickly installed the water system. During the [world] war, my district was around Bayeux, practically on the Coast, and it was pretty well populated with the SS and Gestapo. So instead of dropping an agent in, we took a PT boat, which Johnny always skippered himself—he refused to let me go in unless he skippered the ship. We used to go back and forth— we could always slip in there, if the signals were right—because the Resistance had told us the Germans never thought of guarding this one creek. We'd go in there on one engine, drop an agent off or pick up information, and disappear.[74]

Among the film's most ardent champions was the English critic (now director) Lindsay Anderson, who discussed it with Ford in 1950:

> Ford's attitude toward [*They Were Expendable*] so dumbfounded me that a whole tract of conversation was wiped from my memory. As a matter of fact, we were both dumbfounded. He was looking at me in extreme surprise. "You really think that's a good picture?" He was amazed. "I just can't believe that film's any good." I was amazed. "But—didn't you want to make it?" Ford snorted. "I was ordered to do it. I wouldn't have done it at all if they hadn't agreed to make over my salary to the men in my unit." He added: "I have never *actually* seen a goddamn foot of that film." I told him that horrified me. "I'll use the same word," he said, "I was horrified to have to make it. . . ." "Didn't you feel at least that you were getting something into it, even though you hadn't wanted to take it on?" He scorned the idea. "Not a goddamned thing," he said, "I didn't put a goddamned thing into that picture." He had been pulled out of the front line to make it, had just lost thirteen men from his unit, and had to go back to

---

then became deputy chief of staff for all air force units under MacArthur. He produced the first Cinerama spectaculars with Lowell Thomas, but left, with the Whitneys, when Warner Brothers took over. In 1952 he was awarded a special Academy Award "for his many innovations and contributions to the art of the motion picture." (See Rudy Behlmer, "Merian C. Cooper," *Films in Review*, January 1966, pp. 17–35.)

*A lawsuit followed the film's release: Commander Kelly was awarded $3,000 for John Wayne's "libelous" portrayal of him, while Lt. Beulah Greenwalt won $290,000 for Donna Reed's portrayal of her.

Robert Montgomery (Brickley), a navy officer, had actually commanded a PT-boat squadron in the Solomon Islands. He also directed the last few days of the movie (some back-projection plates) when Ford broke his left leg falling twenty feet from a scaffold and spent two weeks in traction.

Hollywood to direct a lot of actors who wouldn't even cut their hair to look like sailors. I said I found this particularly extraordinary because the film contains so much that needn't have been there if it had been made just as a chore. "What, for instance?" I made example of the old boat-builder (played by Russell Simpson), who appears only in a few shots, yet emerges as a fully, and affectionately conceived person. Ford relented slightly: "Yes, I liked that. . . ." He shifted his ground: "The trouble was, they cut the only bits I liked. . . . Is that scene in the shell-hole still there, between the priest and the boy who says he's an atheist?" "What priest?" I asked. "Played by Wallace Ford." "There's no priest in the film at all." This surprised him. I said I found it extraordinary that one could cut a whole (presumably integral) character from a story without leaving any trace. "M-G-M could," said Ford. I said: "But *Expendable* runs two and a quarter hours as it is. . . ." Ford said: "I shot that picture to run an hour and forty minutes—it should have been cut down to that." I said that this could not be done without ruining the film." "I think I know more about making pictures than you do," said Ford.

He asked me what the music was like; he had had fierce arguments over it. "But surely—it's full of just the tunes you always like to use in your pictures." But Ford had found it too thickly orchestrated, too symphonic. "I wanted almost no music in it at all—just in a very few places, like 'Red River Valley' over Russell Simpson's last scene. We played and recorded that as we shot it. Otherwise I didn't want any music; the picture was shot as a documentary, you know. No reflectors were used at any time, and we kept the interiors dark and realistic." He asked if that last shot was still in, with the aeroplane flying out, and the Spanish tower silhouetted against the sky; and what music was over it. He seemed satisfied when I told him it was "The Battle Hymn of the Republic."

But chiefly Ford was amazed at the thought that anyone could find *They Were Expendable* an even tolerable picture. "John Wayne had it run for him just recently—before he went back to the States. And afterwards he said to me: 'You know, that's still a great picture.' I thought he was just trying to say something nice about it; but perhaps he really meant it."[75]

Three years later, Anderson persisted in another article:

But made with reluctance or not, it is evident from the result that the subject and theme stirred [Ford]. . . . The film he made . . . had from the beginning to end the vividness and force of profound personal experience. Although (presumably) a recruiting picture in intention, it transcended its origins completely: fundamentally, the values and human responses of the film were those of *The Grapes of Wrath*—love and comradeship, devotion to a faith, the spirit of endurance that can make victory out of defeat. In its sustained intensity of expression, it was perhaps even superior as a poetic achievement.[76]

A month after their chat, Ford sent Anderson a telegram: HAVE SEEN EXPENDABLE. YOU WERE RIGHT. FORD. But thirteen years later, at UCLA, he again claimed he disliked it.[77] His ambivalence is understandable. He had been pressured into doing it, by Frank Wead and Jim McGuinness for over two years, then by Secretary of the Navy Forrestal. Meanwhile, he had met and come to admire Bulkeley and had tried to distill into the picture his own war reflections and experience. "Jack was awfully intense on that picture," recalls John Wayne, "and working with more concentration than I had ever seen. I think he was really out to achieve something."[78] Then MGM hacked away.

It is easier to imagine what MGM hoped to achieve: support for reconquest of the Philippines, with MacArthur beginning that task. But the war ended sooner than expected and what had been urgent present became historic past, a memory of sacrifice. The film now ends in 1941, with a lighthouse invoking the hopes of those left behind, and a preface by MacArthur recalls us to times gone. It is difficult not to believe that this was what Ford intended all along, for nothing in this plaintive, meditative movie seems calculated to arouse war fervor. And although almost every writer on Ford states that *They Were Expendable* was a critical and popular failure due to its release some months after the war had ended, when no one was in the mood for war pictures—Dan Ford writes it lost money and was soon withdrawn, Andrew Sarris claims it marked Ford's estrangement from the cultural establishment—in actuality *They Were Expendable* ranked among the year's top moneymakers. Like *The Grapes of Wrath*, it is a tale of disintegration and employs a protracted documentary-like approach, mingled with touches of expressionism. But, judging by the box office, Americans were overwhelmingly more stirred by Ford's lamentation for the war than by his lamentation for the Depression.

They Were Expendable resembles other Spig Wead scripts—*Air Mail, The Wings of Eagles*—an all-male world, almost self-sufficient, to which women contribute awkwardly. Men stand watching as comrades sail off to battle, then feign nonchalance at medals and tales of derring-do. For it's a job to be done— in this case, a sacrifice "bunt" to be laid down—and it's the team that counts. Which makes it all the more affecting that the team disintegrates through no will of its own: bases are deserted, men reassigned, boats junked, till only a few men remain, on foot yet. Along with materiel, life's normal rituals, too, are disrupted: dances, romances, phone calls, funerals. Only the professional, sporty traditions of duty and team remain. "Take care of him," says Brickley to a soldier, in parting, because—the final ignominy—the commanders, the coaches, are ordered to desert their own team.

All this Ford dedramatizes as much as possible. Rather than a charging plot, *They Were Expendable* is a series of quotidian episodes moving unemphatically but inexorably toward nullity. For these are the little men who see only the war in front of them, and rarely see even that. No Japanese are seen; the struggle is interiorized. Only the evacuation of MacArthur—not even the battles—takes on dimensions of an "event," and this for the man's symbolic value, rather than for the trip itself, which Ford elides. And so much is the emphasis on the group, not on the individual, that characterizations are extraordinarily recessive for Ford. Even in Robert Montgomery's Brickley it requires our aggressive attention to discern tics of personality, to discern an unprepossessing hero and a study in the art of command, as that command slowly evaporates.

Yet the picture's worth depends precisely upon our insights into those privileged instants when the individual does emerge in the group-member (and through his individuality reconsecrates the sanctity of the whole). Performances are gentle, laid back (but with some jaunty one-liners). As in *Wagon Master*, Ford enjoys extended two-shots of people chatting, but most dialogue here gets exchanged during "moments between," as though passing in a corridor or while awaiting a bus. Thus character seems all the more fugitive and precious a quality.

The victories Ford perceived in this defeat—proof of the PT boat and proof of moral fiber—are, however, exceeded by mortification that it happened as it did. Much of his outrage was deleted,* as with the censoring of *December 7th*, but much of it remains still: words of puzzlement that we were so unprepared, that the Japanese attacked so easily, that the navy ran away and the air force was gone, that so many men were expended to no purpose, in obedience to orders from an invisible and seemingly uncaring command on high.

Perhaps the reason Ford felt *They Were Expendable* a failure is that it is too protracted. No more than Lindsay Anderson can I suggest where Ford would prune thirty-five minutes, but even the dedramatized, episodic quality of the film would gain from concentration. As it stands, *They Were Expendable* lacks two qualities typical of Ford's best work: it is too seldom rich in invention (notably excepting its last fifteen minutes) and, partly because of MGM's ubiquitous jaunty march tune, there seems to be little sense of progression in its modal textures. Documentary style for Ford, after all, always meant not the unvarying flatness of Grierson but the structured variety of the "cinephonic" suites of Murnau or Jennings. Some moments of intense expressionism—the mysteriously lit face of the admiral issuing orders as retreating troops pour by in the background, or the fire-bordered road near the end—suggest Ford may have intended a film wierder, more psychotic, more like *Arrowsmith*, than what we have. At present, the battle scenes are so unintegrated into the atmosphere we experience that some critics have questioned whether Ford even wished them in the movie at all. He surely did, but as in all his other war pictures, as interludes of exhausting, preternatural catharsis, not, as now, as mere kiddie-matinee-like action.

---

*Sinclair (pp. 118–22) writes that the script had called for "voices" to ask questions about American unpreparedness, that Ford shot a bitter farewell address by Brickley to his men, and that "Ford's private message about valiant self-sacrifice for inscrutable commands" is perverted by the studio's having added "The Battle Hymn of the Republic" at the end.

My Darling Clementine (1946). With *They Were Expendable* and *The Fugitive*, *My Darling Clementine* forms a dark trilogy of sadness, hope, endurance, and yearning, of Manichaean drama pitting light against darkness. While all three react to the experiences of World War II, *My Darling Clementine* approaches allegory. Wyatt Earp (the U.S.) gives up marshalling in Dodge City (World War I), but takes up arms again to combat the Clantons (World War II) to make the world safe. Victory is horrible, and Wyatt must return to the wilderness, to his father (confession; reconstruction), leaving innocence, hope, and civilization (Clementine) behind, "lost and gone forever," a distant memory (the long road) in Tombstone (the world of 1946).

So familiar is the mythic iconography of the hero within generic conventions of the western, that one may take Ford's mythicizing of Wyatt Earp a bit too much for granted, even though *My Darling Clementine*'s black, expressionist, music-drama style, closely resembling *The Fugitive*, is remarkably self-conscious and exaggerated, even for Ford. Earp (like most Henry Fonda roles for Ford) is a hero pure who knows his mind, talks seldom, lopes calmly, gazes steadily, gets the job done; his very name inspires gapes of awe. Initially, in the wilderness, he is framed with upward-gazing angles, sky-backed poses, and Monument Valley monuments. Indoors, counterpointed by mournful honky folk tunes, he inhabits a blackness streaked by clouds of cigarette smoke and spotted by gaseous lamps, and is sighted along distant lines of

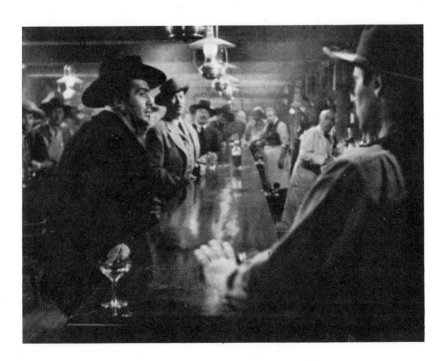

perspective. Wyatt combines the godhood of Lincoln, the passion of Tom Joad, the directness of the Ringo Kid. Like many another Fordian hero, he comes out of the wilderness, rights wrongs, and goes on his way.

But Ford's topic is less the hero as archetype than the archetype's moody sensibility within a world of contradictions. Outwardly, Wyatt is perennially in passage—from black wilderness to white civilization—and in this he resembles Tombstone, which Ford typically seizes upon at a moment of transition in the making of America. "Wide-awake, wide-open town, Tombstone! You can get anything you want there," says Pa Clanton. But the nightly atmosphere of sinful roisterousness, in which nomads throw each other out of town and Jane Darwell's madam represents distinguished stability, is quickly giving way by day to a community of schools, churches, and Clementine Carters.

Inwardly, as Wyatt passes from one world to the next, his sensibility (like the community's) comes more and more into scarcely acknowledged conflict with itself, conflict between the Wyatt dutiful to the "high moral codes" of the wilderness actually existing and the Wyatt yearning for the values of civilization. Just sitting is a sensual, soulful pleasure, as for Judge Priest on his porch, Ole Mose in his rocker, Lincoln anywhere. But Wyatt's loafing, like his shave, poker, and (three!) meals, is repeatedly interrupted by violence and by duty (always paired). Duty disrupts his journey home to stop in Tombstone, and duty calls him back into the wilderness when that job is done. Wyatt embodies the Fordian hero's traditional urge to squat with his traditional obligation to wander. He likes to think of himself as an "*Ex-marshall*," but he becomes one again to find his brother's murderer. The weary gloom with which he accepts this duty, the self-consciousness with which he casts himself as an angel of vengeance and order, are not unfamiliar qualities for the hero, but the contradictions they imply are dwelt upon with unaccustomed emphasis (no doubt reflecting Ford's reaction to the war). Wyatt consecrates himself at James's graveside to the loftiest goals of civilized utopia ("When we leave this country, kids like you will be able to grow up and live free"), but he equally consecrates his personal vengeance, his honor of family, as lawful authority. Nobility in Ford seems often a virtue blooming in hypocritical soil: Huw's loyalty, Lincoln's bossy assumption of truth, the Fugitive's of martyrdom. We do not object to Wyatt killing the Clantons, nor even to his assumption of right to do so; what is worrisome is his alliance of implacable vengeance with legal and moral justification. Although he is in the community, even defines it, and helps establish civilization, he is actually a wilderness figure just passing through; he cloaks his wilderness moral code with the laws of civilization, and leaves a bloodbath behind him. He stays in Tombstone only four days, with motives initially opportunistic and only belatedly communal: i.e., he quiets the drunken Indian to get a shave, takes the marshall's job for family honor. True, he finds himself drawn to communal involvement: reversing earlier priorities, he ignores Brother Morg's plea to finish dinner, because he has "got" to get Doc to bed, and, characteristically, he allows himself to be seduced into attending the camp meeting, while his brothers exclude themselves from the community to pursue their private visit to James's grave. But when it comes to Wyatt's chief purpose, to get the Clantons, he seeks to exclude the community (the mayor and the deacon)—"*strictly* a family affair."

If Wyatt is aware of his contradictions, he is not perplexed by them. His simplicity encloses his philosophy. "*What kind of* town is this?" he exclaims. "*What sort of* town is this where a man can't even get a peaceful shave?" "*What kind of* town is this that sells liquor to Indians?"* Such lines are jokes, because Wyatt utters them with the sincere amazement with which Louis XIV once remarked, "I almost had to wait!" But Wyatt's lines also typify the questioning, Tom-Joad-like mixture of emotion and morality with which he confronts life. "Have you taken it into your head to deliver us from all evil?" someone asks; and Wyatt replies, "Not a bad idea. That's what I'm being paid for." Hamlet's soliloquy is not out of place midst this muddle of duty, vengeance, right, and doubt. Just what sort of world *do* we live in? And how do we define our answers? Does new awareness entail political consequences? Must we take up arms? As for Hamlet, the cost for Wyatt of "quietus" is bloody: a second brother's life is sacrificed to family honor. But we get the feeling Old Man Earp would agree with Old Man Clanton, that family duty precedes everything. This is the West, and moral codes rise monumentally out of the wilderness. Wyatt is enslaved to them. But can a land where people "live free" be built on such codes? Can civilization be founded on wilderness law?

This heart-of-darkness inquiry particularly permeates Ford's postwar films, notably, of course, *Liberty Valance*. Its irony is underscored in *My*

---

*"What kind of . . ." phrases occur often in Ford, often as dramatic-rhetorical devices— e.g., "What kind of man am I that . . . ?"

Darling Clementine with graphic expressionism. In frame 1 (p. 227), the need to arrest his friend Doc Holliday and the onus of avenging his murdered brother weigh heavily on Wyatt: the bar ramming massively against his guts symbolizes his duty, conscience, and heavy recognition of his own moral world determining what he shall do; he seems all the more heroic for being so humanly puny. So strong is the dynamic force of the bar-line across the screen, that when the Clantons lumber in from off-frame, their motion across the screen seems uncomfortably contrapuntal—the two compositional ideas seem more dissonant than complementary. And in fact, with the Clantons lined up along the bar (upper left) like feathers on an arrow, the bar no longer symbolizes Wyatt's superego, but an external hostility independent of his awareness. From being a crushed human enduring self-inflicted martyrdom, Wyatt becomes a portrait of comic myopia. Obsessed idealistically, he is oblivious to actual, threatening evil.

The same point is made earlier, when Ford sets an encounter between Wyatt and the Clantons, just after Wyatt takes the marshall job, in an eerie series of confrontational close-ups:* the Clantons' knowledge (they seem to be waiting for him) and Wyatt's intent obliviousness enclose them and him in worlds absolutely disparate, albeit momentarily tangential. People, in this movie, do not live in an objective reality, but in subjective ones enclosed by the limits of their knowledge, moral philosophy, and, above all, their sensibility. Subjectivity may be communal—e.g., the Clantons, the Earps, Tombstone, individual relationships. But by and large solipsism and loneliness suffuse this precommunal, precivilized world ("Ten thousand cattle gone astray," sings Chihuahua); people live separate lives and relate to divergent experiences. Ford "creates" these disparate emotional worlds cinematically, through composition, cutting, music, and acting styles, and by modalities mirroring subjectivity as they shift from *film noir* nightmare to poetic realism. The movie is virtually a series of skits, or turns, illustrating mostly abortive attempts at community: the Clantons vs. Earp; the Clantons and the Shakespearian actor; the deliberate grouping in one theater box of a bizarre collection of stereotypes; the actor's wacky embrace of the town drunk ("Great souls by instinct to each other turn, demand allegiance and in friendship burn. Good night, sweet prince"); the silhouetted argument between Holliday and Clementine; the crosscuts between Holliday operating and Chihuahua being operated on; the interrupted dinners; Clementine's pretending not to notice Wyatt when she gets off the stage; his farewell kiss to her; and, perhaps most spectacularly, this remarkable series of vignettes:

---

*180-degree crosscut CUs recur in *Wagon Master* between the goodies and the even more evil Cleggs who, like the Clantons, are given as degenerate, are motherless families with four perverted sons, whose father dies last trying to sneak a shot. Cf. *Two Rode Together, Liberty Valance* —more degenerate motherless families.

1. Pa Clanton leaves his empty, crypt-shadowed room. (His son Billy lies dead abed; Pa has just murdered Virgil Earp in revenge.)

2. Chihuahua: long-held close-up; melancholy after being operated on without sedation.

3. Doc Holliday, happily victorious after managing to perform the operation, is toasted by Wyatt. (The jovial town madam, who never has any trouble relating, points up the awkwardness of everyone else.)

4. But Clementine, at the saloon door, is snubbed trying to congratulate him.

5. Wyatt and bartender Mac (framed foreground, the Clementine-Holliday doorway scene occurring way downscreen between them) discuss romance.

In each case, the frame is the character's world, its atmosphere an extension of his personality; his or her viewpoint becomes the "only truth." Hence we pass from Clanton's black dementia, to Chihuahua's mortal despair, to Holliday's elation, to Clementine's depression, and now to Wyatt's jubilation— for Clem's failure with Holliday leaves her available for Wyatt. "Mac, have you ever been in love?" he asks, happily. "No," replies the bartender, concluding this series of solipsistic vignettes, "I've been a bartender all my life."

Diversity of sensibility, one setting another in relief, is consistent with Ford's penchant for juxtaposing scenes of contrasting moods. Pa Clanton brutally whipping his sons sets into relief the magical scene next morning, when Wyatt balances his feet on the porch post, then awkwardly rises and takes off his hat as Clementine Carter (Cathy Downs) steps out of the stage-coach. From his reluctance to speak and from his lithe body's measured movements lofting her trunk, you know he has rarely felt so self-conscious—though his back is turned. Two Indians glide by on ponies, so quietly is the scene drenched in the air of vivid awareness. The gruff joke of Brother Morg (Ward Bond) ordering a gargantuan breakfast counterpoints this mood, but then everyone stares: a lady, civilization, has come to Tombstone. Being from Boston, she will start a school, and it is she, or perhaps what she repre-sents, that entices Wyatt into their enchanted Sunday walk toward the toll-ing bell of the church-to-be and singing choir ("Shall we gather at the river," aptly). Their walk is prefigured earlier, as Wyatt escorts her down a hotel corridor toward Doc's room: its churchy shadows, like the walk to church, predict an alliance between Clementine and Wyatt, which will, however, probably never be, and predict the hallowed fulfillment of her lengthy quest for John Holliday, which will, however, be futile. The way she fondles John's things, in a room describing his personality, recalls the fondling of loved ones' objects in *Straight Shooting* and *The Grapes of Wrath*, except that there is a hint of repressed sexuality in Clementine's immersion of self into John's room. It is she who is evoked by the film's title, because it is darling Clementine who personifies the hopes and dreams of both men, one decay-ing, the other rising: their yearning for what is lost irretrievably—whether as Wyatt gallops down an endless road, destined to wander forever toward some mountainous fate as Clementine waits forever within the town fence

("I'll be loving you forever, O my darling Clementine!"), or whether as Holliday spurns her attempts to reach out to him:

— "You *are* pleased that I came . . . ? My coming has made you unhappy."
— "It was ill advised."
— "Was it ill advised the way you left Boston?"
— "How'd you know I was here?"
— "I didn't. Finding you hasn't been easy. Cow town to cow town. One mining town to another.* I would think that if nothing more, you'd be at least flattered to have a girl chase you!"
— "Look, Clem, you've got to get out of here . . . "
— "But I won't!"
— "This is no place for your kind of person."
— "What kind of a person am I, John?"
— "Please go back home, Clem, back where you belong. Forget that you ever . . . [coughing fit]. The man you once knew is no more, there's not a vestige of him left. Nothing!"
— "You can't send me away like this. Now I know why you don't care whether you live or die, why you're trying to get yourself killed. You're wrong, so wrong. You have a world of friends back home who love you as I love you."

"What kind of a person am I?" If John Holliday does not understand Clementine, she understands him even less. Now, destroying himself, dying from consumption and alcoholism, his lost ideals undimmed in memory, his stuffed bookcases and diplomas belying the stereotype he has become, he is the opposite of the Boston physician she recalls. "In fact," observes Wyatt, "a man could almost follow [Doc's] trail from graveyard to graveyard."

*The eliptical dialogue is typical of Ford.

Clementine has been pursuing a fantasy and, rebuffed, decides to go home.

"If you ask me, you're giving up too easy," says Wyatt. "If you ask me," she retorts, "you don't know much about a woman's pride." Her gentle control of her voice and refinement of gesture always contradict the passion of her words. Ford has made her manner opposite to her character. Clementine is from *Boston* (we know what that means, in Ford): she is willful, pushy, has crossed a continent all alone in search of her man, will found a school. It is she who asks Wyatt to church, and she who hints he ask her to dance.*

The situations of Wyatt, Holliday, and (the absent) Clementine are focused in the "To be or not to be" sequence. The pretentiousness of inserting Shakespeare into a western mirrors the advent of culture in the wilderness, and is both undercut and underscored by staging the soliloquy on a saloon table with a drunken actor (Alan Mowbray) and an uncomprehending savage audience (the Clanton boys). For once, Shakespeare is directed for maximum expressivity and intelligibility, as Ford has Mowbray speak slowly and with long pauses (indicated by □), and uses music, from an on-screen pianist, to accompany exactly, balance the verse into musical quatrains, and expand the actor's voice-pitch into melody of sorts.

> To be, or not to be: □ that is the question: □
> Whether 'tis nobler in the mind to suffer
> The slings and arrows of outrageous fortune, □
> Or to take arms against a sea of troubles, □
> And by opposing □ end them?

Wyatt, of course, opposes troubles (ought he to?), and Clementine and the Clantons also decide to take action. But Holliday prefers

> To die: □ to sleep; □
> No more; □ and, by a sleep to say we end
> The heart-ache □ and the thousand natural shocks
> That flesh is heir to, □ 'tis a consummation □
> Devoutly to be wish'd. □

Is not Wyatt in a kind of "sleep"? Holliday in a nightmare? Clementine in a kind of dream?

---

*Commentators are wont to contrast Clementine and Chihuahua as Ford's opposite female stereotypes. Clementine does resemble Grace Kelly (*Mogambo*) and many early ingenues, while good-whore Chihuahua resembles freely friendly Charmaine (*What Price Glory*). But to reduce Ford's women to two stereotypes is as superficial a criticism as it would be to reduce Ford's men to goodies and baddies. As always, the stereotype only begins to define a character. It is curious, though, how both women, with ambivalent mixtures of fickleness and survival-instinct, switch their gazes quickly from their hearts' desire to new lovers (Chihuahua to Billy Clanton, Clementine to Earp). In contrast to Hawks's western women—who are treated essentially as erotic fantasies and whose eroticism is always updated to the era of the film's release (e.g., the women in *Rio Lobo* are 1970-like Californians)—Ford's Clementine has her feet firmly planted on the earth. She pursues Holliday not simply from desire but to help him; rejected, she is independent enough to stake out her own future in Tombstone.

> To die, to sleep; □
> To sleep: □ perchance to dream: □ ay, there's the rub; □
> For in that sleep of death □ what dreams may come
> When we have shuffled off this mortal coil, □

These are thoughts that haunt Holliday specifically. Thus he silences the mocking Clantons—at whom the actor spits:

> Must give us pause: □ There's the respect □
> That makes calamity of so long life; □
> For who would bear the whips and scorns of time, □ . . .
> . . . the law's delay, □
> The insolence of office, □ and the spurns
> That patient merit of the unworthy take[s], □
> When he himself □ might his quietus make □
> With a bare bodkin? □ Who would fardels bear, □
> To grunt and sweat [under] a weary life, □
> . . . life . . . , life . . . *Please help me!*

And Holliday takes it up:

> But that the dread of something after death,

Although he has forgotten how to be a doctor, he remembers his Shakespeare and, as Wyatt watches with wondering concern, Holliday gives soulsearching resonance, with clouds of tobacco smoke swirling around him, to the next three words:

> The undiscover'd country □ from whose bourn □
> No traveller returns, □ puzzles the will, □
> And makes us rather bear those ills we have, □
> Than fly to others that we know not of? □
> Thus conscience does make cowards of us all . . .

Whereupon he breaks into a coughing fit.

Thus, *My Darling Clementine* concerns a search for a dream of justice, oblivion, or love, and breathes the langorous airs of loss. As if looking for answers, the camera stares at the sky after the battle and down the long road at the finish, at the moment that picture's title—and theme—become clear.

For a sad movie, *My Darling Clementine* is invigorated by much humor, invention, and sudden shifts of mood. Although Ford is at his best at moments of digression, Dan and Barbara Ford claim that Darryl Zanuck markedly improved the movie by reediting Ford's original cut frame by frame, deleting some humor and "sentimentality" (thirty minutes in all), and thus strengthened the storyline and pace. At this point the picture was previewed to an audience of two thousand that was immensely appreciative up until the final minute. Then, however, they laughed at Ford's original ending, wherein Wyatt shakes hands with Clementine rather than kissing her. Accordingly, but to Ford's chagrin, a kiss was inserted.

The real Wyatt Earp used to visit friends working at Universal during Ford's apprentice years, and Ford claimed to have recreated the Battle of the OK Corral according to Earp's account. Today, however, historians consider the movie's once respected sourcebook, Stuart N. Lake's *Wyatt Earp, Frontier Marshall*, to be a tissue of untruths designed by an Earp relative to create a legend around an unsavory character. Actually, Earp, Holliday, and the Clantons were leagued in a holdup racket; disagreements led to the OK Corral incident, which was a massacre, not a battle; afterward, Wyatt and Holliday quit town and the Clantons' bodies were left hanging in the butcher's shop. It was brother Virgil, not Wyatt, who was the sheriff in Tombstone; his wife's account is in Frank Waters's revisionist history, *The Earp Brothers of Tombstone* (New York, 1960). Ford's truer, and utterly different, portrait of Wyatt in *Cheyenne Autumn* (1964) probably reflects his reading since *My Darling Clementine*.

The Fugitive (1946). For his first independent production, Ford chose Graham Greene's *The Labyrinthine Ways* (or *The Power and the Glory*) which he had been planning to make before the war at Fox, but with C. V. Whitney financing it and with Thomas Mitchell as the priest. Most of what made Greene's novel famous—a fornicating, alcoholic priest drifting into ambivalent martyrdom—could not be filmed because of the Production Code,*and in a letter to Zanuck in 1946 Ford confessed, "It is really not a sound commercial gamble but my heart and my faith compel me to do it."[79] So, Henry Fonda was cast as the priest, and, with Dudley Nichols, Ford wrote a sort of Passion Play allegory as a screenplay. But once in Mexico, Ford jettisoned most of the script and, giving leave to his fancy, made a highly abstract art film. *The Fugitive* lost considerable money, caused a rift between Nichols and Ford, and has posed problems even for Ford's most devoted followers. Only the director himself consistently defended it. "I just enjoy looking at it."[80] "To me, it was perfect."[81]

And in terms of composition, lighting, and editing, *The Fugitive* may be among the most enjoyable pictures. For example, the opposing internal angles of frames 1 and 2 interlock with an interesting dynamism and, in bringing the peasant forward while placing the interrogating police lieutenant behind the peasants, the compositions reverse each man's actual power and

---

*The film: Pursued by a tormented police lieutenant (Pedro Armendariz), a priest (Henry Fonda) holds furtive baptisms, is nearly betrayed, almost escapes but returns for a dying man, is arrested trying to buy Mass wine, watches a hostage die in his place, is aided by the lieutenant's ex-mistress (Dolores Del Rio), and an outlaw (Ward Bond). Free at last, he is tricked into returning for the dying outlaw, and executed.

Two curious ironies of our prejudices toward film vs. literature: what was prohibited on the screen was widely assigned reading in Catholic schools; and rights to the picture have now reverted (as provided), not to Ford, but to its literary forebear, Greene, who, however, wrote me: "I have never been able to bring myself to see the film as it was a total travesty of my book, perhaps due to Ford's Irish type of Catholicism. The illegitimate child was given to the police officer instead of to the priest!" (March 7, 1979.) There is little reason to approach Ford's picture as though it intended to be a staging of Greene's novel rather than as a work in itself.

1 2

illuminate their psychologies: the threatened lieutenant, the secure peasant. And some of the more brilliant technical feats in film may be found in
The Fugitive, such as the police attack on the peasant market, or the moment when a gramophone horn is swung away and a dancer, in one close *brio*
pan, gets chased into a saloon, into a soldier's arms, and is lifted up onto a
bar, where her legs begin to dance.

But Lindsay Anderson, among many, attacks "the over-luscious images [as]
frequently vulgar in their sentimental appeal; a lame child in a church doorway, holding a lighted candle."[82] Could not Ford have been less obvious with
such holycard images, however typical they may be of naive Catholicism? Yet
Ford's artfulness is intimate rather than synthetic; he celebrates openly cultural aspects that repel Anglo-Saxon sternness. Just as the movie's marvelous
score, which might initially seem overly expressionistic, is an emanation from
the characters rather than a "Hollywood" touch, so too the pathos of the images emerges from their content rather than from Ford's direction. His camerawork during crowd scenes resembles the realism of Rossellini or Buñuel
during the next few years, rather than the contrivance of a Goldwyn; and
music in Rossellini and Buñuel is certainly no less emotional.

An attack from opposite grounds comes from Jean Mitry: "A theoretical
drama in theoretical reality . . . depersonalized . . . cold." Perhaps Ford is
excessively iconic (even the credits underline such intentions: "*a* fugitive, *an*
Indian woman, *a* lieutenant of police . . .") but his abstraction of his characters from their milieu is deliberate. They are persons depersonalized in a cold
world. A terribly fractured world, in the cutting, a terribly shadowed world, a
terribly formalized world. Yet it is their world, the most subjective of any Ford
movie — and, I suppose, in that sense, theoretical. The priest's dilemma, we
might say, lies in trying to reconcile substance and appearance, or in trying to
control his monstrous imagination, which so often runs away with him — as in
the (much imitated) temporal ellipses as he debates whether to board the
boat or go with the boy, or as he flees the city. In an ultimate prolongation of
Ford's vignette techniques, the priest's subjectivity swamps objective reality:
he cannot palliate the excruciating torture (unbearable equally to us!) of the

3

hotel-room scene. Or, try as he will, to the priest, Diego (J. Carroll Naish) appears snakelike, Judas-like, repulsive; Maria Dolores seems a sort of Mary Magdalen seeking out iconic poses as refuge; and the inner agony which El Gringo's bluff refuses to acknowledge is patent to the priest in the way the outlaw keeps his chin thrust in throughout. Beauty midst this agony—little children singing with big happy faces, a refugee doctor (John Qualen) uttering placidities—only serves to remind the priest (and us) of the *constraint* of the film's world, of its theoreticalness, its subjectivity—and thus naturalness seems prodigiously unnatural. Where is truth? The question sounds pompous. But the priest's dilemma revolves far less around the ultimate ramifications of God's presence in the world than around the priest's inability to separate the subjective colorings of his perceptions from "actual" reality. Do the peasants he is baptizing really smile up at him so humbly—or is that partly the way he conceives the event? (In 1960 I heard an American priest sermonize of a visit to Mexico in terms every bit as "over-luscious" as Ford's—and I wondered then at the accuracy of his impressions.) How isolated this priest is! Five years in such a country, traveling from village to village, the only priest in the land, adored on one side and hunted on the other, the adoration more isolating than the pursuit. The discomfort that Mitry and Anderson and Fonda have remarked in Fonda's performance is—why should it be necessary to point this out?—precisely what Ford wanted. It is just this discomfort that renders the character palpable. Frame 4 is held for over a minute and requires

4

Fonda, against accepted portrait technique, to hold his hand outstretched, thus distorting his torso proportions (more in the movie than here). Spatially, we know he is sick, indrawn, involuted, feels awkward, tiny, helpless. His head is too big; he is even "outside" his body (the hand). His hand represents an annoyance, something bigger than himself. His speech is self-flagellating:

> It wasn't courage, Doctor, it was only pride. . . . I began to lose grace. . . . I began to think I was a *brave* man, who knows? a martyr. I suddenly realized I was the only priest left in the country. . . .

The Doctor pooh-poohs: "Oh, don't be so hard on yourself, Father. A man is entitled to a little pride." The priest's agitation mounts:

> Not in my profession. I was building a fine lie, wearing it like a proud cloak. . . . [But] when the first real test came I couldn't measure up. I let men die for me. . . .

Indeed, the priest flees throughout the movie, first in one direction, then in another. His cowardice stems from the quality that Ford's pictures (*The Quiet Man, 7 Women*) identify as the clergy's essential problem: pride, moral arrogance, separation from the world. In short, a hypocrisy—but a hypocrisy perhaps necessary to the profession—and it is with this *abstract* flaw that Ford has replaced the *concrete* flaws (alcoholism, simony, fornication) of Greene's novel. The priest's flight is from his own impurity, and from that there is no "sanctuary" in the doctor's hospital; there is sanctuary only in martyrdom. He flees safety to do what saints are supposed to do, knowingly. He is not discouraged when he learns El Gringo did not write the note asking him to come and does not want the sacraments. Is he mad? Like Ingrid Bergman in Rossellini's *Europe '51*, he is obsessed in isolation, is posed with solipsistic dilemmas, is marching to the step of a different drummer. As in the Bresson-Bernanos *Diary of a Country Priest*, flight leads to a sort of gnosticism ("All is grace"): a thunderclap and a rainstorm give courage and recall him not only to God by the experience of power, but also to the cosmos by the experience of having an eternal, if tiny, spot within Being. "I want to live my death," he says.

Don Rafael, the lieutenant, is the priest's Doppelgänger. He too engages the peasants in rituals (but sermonizes them, whereas the priest is tongue-tied), is depicted riding (but a horse rather than a donkey), is obsessed with cowardice and his abstraction from everyone else's reality, and like the priest is constantly associated with geometric backgrounds, divine shafts of light, and doorways (leading through labyrinthine ways to God). More marked in his hypocrisy, he believes in the revolution, believes he is "making a better world," but leaves trails of blood in his wake; his release is violence. He is frustrated by officials who profit from blackmarket liquor, and by his own people: "I'm an Indian like you are," he harangues, riding back and forth, "Stand up straight! I want to give you—Everything!" Yet he is unable to acknowledge his child by Maria Dolores. Frame 5 shows her defying him by genuflecting; her action relates to the foreground font, in which the child has been baptized, to the lieutenant's chagrin; the zigzagging angles through four layers of depth, and the contrapuntal angles of light and wall, create multitudinous relationships between the characters and their situations. The lieutenant's men become beasts when he is not present, and in battle bloody madness possesses him as well, as sometimes seems to happen to Third-world revolutionaries today. But, given that Ford tells us little of anticlericalism's good reasons in Mexico, the lieutenant does not come off badly. The priest tells him, "I'm the sort of man you lock up every day, and give money to."

The outlaw, El Gringo (Ward Bond), may have started out in Nichols's treatment as a sort of Good Thief. In the movie, he shows no sign of faith or repentance, but represents the ostensibly accidental but actually providential figure that brings priest and lieutenant together and to God (cf. the Cleggs in *Wagon Master*). As in St. Augustine's theory of history, God's ways are mysteries. Almost all *The Fugitive*'s characters are outcasts, yet they are ruled by formalized codes. Warmth and integrity exist in their Sternbergian world, but any real communication between them can occur only in stolen instants, in subtleties of expression and glances within codes. Yet Sternberg does not erect such formidable barriers of obviousness, abstraction, and Latin Catholicism. What are we to think of the scene when the priest, after riding up to the hillside on his mule, returns to his ruined church and stands

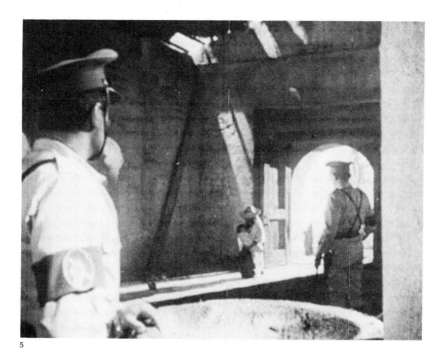

5

gazing at a high round window streaking light into the darkness? Later, Don Rafael confronts this same window and laughs hysterically. The priest in prison will find comfort through a similar window. God is the light of the world, and shadow, which seems at first His antithesis, is perhaps really another, labyrinthine, way. The grace that flows into rooms flows also into souls who confront it, and it illuminates these souls dramatically. Were the priest, or Don Rafael, not the sort of persons who react the way they do, the symbolic light would be merely pompous. But Ford is trying to capture the level of their existence: a Latin priest who thinks he is a saint, a Latin revolutionary who thinks he is destroying God. The priest can no more escape the light than he can escape the myriad arches that, as signs of formalized culture (i.e., of his belief in a rational, God-inhabited cosmos), follow him everywhere—the arched aqueduct on the plain (frames 6, 7), the arched sidewalks in the city (8), the arched tree-shadows at the river (9), even the arched walls in prison (10*). The horrible question, of course, is whether these are signs *from* God or only signs *for* God. No matter; for the priest the world's architecture is a sermon: myriad angles jutting inward hound him

*This frame forms part of a remarkable montage: /Full shot (as here): the priest sees: /LS: hostage and cops crossing courtyard. /Medium CU: the priest gawks: /Full shot (frame shown), drops buckets and runs /into a long shot chasing the cops. The varying of space (between CU, FS, and LS) and the dropping buckets create a crescendo of motion, while the stasis of the principal figure is relieved when the priest drops the buckets, then runs.

6   7

8   9

10   11

12

toward his duty, angles spreading outward conduct him heavenward—as in frame 11, when he ascends to execution. Nor is the lieutenant spared similarly continual assaults by the physical world, which violently attacks him at the moment the priest is killed (12)—at which point he crosses himself, testifying to superstition, to belief, to proof of God, to who knows? For the priest, the dilemma between appearance and substance is solved only in surrender, when truth becomes legible.

Simple definitions, simple people with simple paradoxes, yet paradigmatic of every culture's inherited dilemmas; these are simplicities that become almost unmanageably complex because of the intensity and profundity of people's belief in them, simplicities that drive people mad, and whose intense profundity must be felt also by us: a difficult task, since it all seems so alien and so simple.

Don Rafael bursts into the cantina, screams at the dancer, "What kind of woman are you?!" (like Wyatt Earp asking what sort of town this is). Then he sees who it is. Maria Dolores drops her fan, he bends to pick it up. "I don't know, Don Rafael. What sort of woman am I?" An instant of gallantry, when each stands helpless in love and defiance, and when, as throughout the film, everything is washed with the melancholic dreams of a past world. *The Fugitive* is already *The Man Who Shot Liberty Valance*. With great passion it looks back, as did *How Green Was My Valley*, to a more innocent world (specifically to the world before World War II—for *The Fugitive* is an allegory for Reconstruction). The fugitives are outcast by time and history, and they are searching, half in the old world, half in the new, for ways of coping.

It is such resonances as these, along with the way characters' souls emerge together with their public poses, that give pungency to *The Fugitive*'s flat, stark dialogue. The conversation between the priest and Maria Dolores is composed of an ingeniously inventive series of reverse-angles and two-shots:

— "Will there be churches again, Father?"
— "We must hope so."
— "In the village they have no hope. They say . . . the Church is dead."

And the priest climbs to the rooftop and rings a bell.

From *Tabu* to *The Passenger*, films like *The Fugitive* have sought out privileged and private landscapes and have dressed themselves in the most formalized expression in order to evoke the most unformalized realities of life.

Although *The Fugitive* presents unique difficulties, its stylistic invention is typically Fordian, only concentrated. If in its allegoric, operatic ways, it resembles *The Battle of Midway*, in its unanswered questions it is closer to *7 Women;* or, it can be seen as a journey to God such as *3 Godfathers* and *Wagon Master*, or even *Mogambo*—a mixture of the quotidian and the mysterious. But basically *The Fugitive* is a western: land, Indians, army, robber barons, outlaws. Otherwise it resembles *My Darling Clementine* (*film noir;* do-gooders moved by divinely appointed duty), *Stagecoach* (the Gringo's theme is "Bury Me Not on the Lone Prairie"), *Fort Apache* (arrogance), and *When Willie Comes Marching Home* (mindless patriotism).

Funerals

When Will Rogers had died in an air crash in 1935, Ford had gone to pieces; and for the next couple of decades he wore a hat with a funny hole in it Rogers had given him. When Tom Mix died in a car crash in 1940, Ford had rushed to the wake, placed a Stetson on Mix's head and interceded with the War Department for burial in the flag. (Technically, Mix had been AWOL since the Spanish-American War.) Ford always came on strong at death—whatever life's disputes.

Harry Carey's last years had seen memorable roles in *The Last Outlaw, Mr. Smith Goes to Washington, Duel in the Sun,* and *Red River.* But he had worked with Ford only once since 1921, in *The Prisoner of Shark Island.* They had drifted apart partly due to rival tale-carrying by two old bachelors, Joe Harris and J. Farrell MacDonald. When the Careys and Fords would get together, about twice a year, Dobe used to wonder why his mild-mannered father would get so excited. "Now, Jack, that's a lot of crap!" Harry would exclaim, slamming down his fist, "For Chrissake! *I* wrote that story, the story was *my* idea!" "No, it was *my* story," Ford would rebut. And on they would go. Dobe took Harry to see *Stagecoach* in 1939, and all through it Harry hardly ever stopped talking: "We did *that*! We did *that*!"[83]

But Ford was at Harry's bedside, September 24, 1947, the day he died. Afterward, Ollie Carey went and stood on the porch. "And I remember Jack came out and he took hold of me and put his head on my breast and cried, and the whole front of my sweater was sopping wet. For at least fifteen or twenty minutes he cried, just solid sobbing, solid sobbing, and the more he cried, the stronger I'd get. It was very good for me, it was wonderful. Oh, God, he shook and cried. I thought, it's chilly here and here I am sopping wet all the way down."[84]

Harry's death gave Ford a chance to fulfill his dreams of having a wedding or funeral at the Farm, and an Irish wake, too. Four uniformed sailors stood guard all night outside the Field Photo chapel, with Carey's horse, Sonny, tied to the hitching post. Ford, Wayne, Bond, and Spencer Tracy were pall-bearers. Dan Borzage played "Red River Valley," and John Wayne read Tennyson's "Crossing the Bar." *3 Godfathers* was in production at the time, a remake of Ford's favorite of his movies with Carey, *Marked Men* (1919), and Ford prefaced it with a dedication. A lone rider appears, half-silhouetted in the dusk, and removes his hat: "To the memory of Harry Carey—Bright Star of the early Western Sky," reads the legend, while "Good Bye Ole Paint" (" . . . I'm a-leavin' Cheyenne"—a reference to Carey's Cheyenne Harry character) is quoted musically. And Ford used *3 Godfathers* to promote Dobe's stardom as Harry Carey, Jr. (Henry George "Dobe" Carey yielded reluctantly to billing as Harry Carey, Jr., on pressure from Ford and Wayne; he had appeared briefly in three earlier films—notably *Red River*, but without meeting his father on screen. The rider on the horse, however, is Cliff Lyons, and Wayne rather than Dobe assumes Harry Carey's former role.) "I think he felt duty-bound by his higher power to launch me on a film career," said Dobe. Was this in compensation? "Yes. And I think that's why he caused me so much hell. When we got back to town he was marvelous, but in Death Valley he was really tough. I used to think, 'Gee, if you were mad at my dad, don't take it out on me.' "[85]

Ford's next funeral of atonement came with Francis Ford, who died, painfully, of cancer, September 6, 1953. Shortly before, Dan Ford, then a boy, recalls stopping beside one of Hollywood's giant studios. "John and Francis exchanged a look. Then Francis turned to me and said. 'I used to own that studio.' For a moment he smiled and the old twinkle was there in his eyes. Then it faded away. 'You know,' he said, 'I've really had a very wonderful life.' "[86] But jobs had been scarce for the aging actor. His wife had written John a year earlier, "I am terribly worried about Frank. He hasn't worked for over one year . . . He walks the floors constantly."[87] Some years before John had lent Frank money to open a saloon, but business went poorly, Frank got discouraged, and so one night he locked the doors and drank all the booze. John was scarcely uncaring, but his pathological attitude toward Frank, which so infuriated Harry Carey and other old-timers, continued to the end. Once John was sitting back acting nonchalant as a procession of people admired a camera setup he had arranged. Then Billy Ford, Frank's son, took a look. "Whadya think?" asked John. "Well, it's great but it looks just like something my father once . . . " John threw him off the set right then and there.[88]

The funeral was a grand affair. Frank Baker had never attended funerals, not even his wife's, but he went to this one. Afterward, he did not speak to John, but sat across the street in a car. Ford, while chatting with various groups of people for five or ten minutes, kept staring silently over toward Baker. Some weeks later they met. "Were you at Frank's funeral?" Ford asked, immediately. "You know very well I was there. You saw me." "We gave him a good send-off, didn't we?"

Baker made no reply. Yet for the next few years, every time Ford saw him, he would ask, "We gave Frank a good send-off, didn't we?" He knew Baker as among those most critical of his treatment of Frank and hoped for approval of the funeral. He never got it.

John Ford probably felt guilt toward any friend who died. His ability in life to bestow affection was impaired by his self-protectiveness. He hid. Toward women he could be utterly tender, but men he loved combatively—and how much more so Frank, who was probably the person in his life he held most in awe.

4 Third Period (1948–1961): The Age of Myth

"From *Fort Apache* on," writes Andrew Sarris, "Ford's films seemed to have abandoned the Tradition of Quality for a Cult of Personality."[1] As the critical mainstream veered increasingly toward astringent social relevance, the ex–poet laureate looked increasingly irrelevant, holed up in Monument Valley churning out matinee westerns. In fact, the bitterness of social comment in Ford's movies was more acerbic than before. The thirties revolutionary had not embraced the establishment. But what Ford had to say, America did not wish to hear. To his credit, he no longer sought prestige by couching his thought within trendy styles. His pictures instead became intensely private, formulated within well-worn commercial genres, fraught with myth, irony, and double-leveled narratives. Still today, many a casual critic, underestimating Ford, misses not only the subtlety, but misconstrues denunciations as celebrations.

BRILLIANCE (1948–1956)

Fort Apache	3.9.48	Argosy Pictures–RKO Radio
3 Godfathers	12.1.48	Argosy Pictures–MGM

She Wore a Yellow Ribbon	10.22.49	Argosy Pictures–RKO Radio
When Willie Comes Marching Home	2.50	20th Century–Fox
Wagon Master	4.19.50	Argosy Pictures–RKO Radio
Rio Grande	11.15.50	Argosy Pictures–Republic
This Is Korea!	8.10.51	U.S. Navy–Republic
The Quiet Man	9.14.52	Argosy Pictures–Republic
What Price Glory	8.52	20th Century–Fox
The Sun Shines Bright	5.2.53	Argosy Pictures–Republic
Mogambo	10.9.53	Metro-Goldwyn-Mayer
The Long Gray Line	2.9.55	Rota Productions– Columbia
Rookie of the Year (TV short)	12.?.55	*Screen Directors Playhouse*
The Bamboo Cross (TV short)	12.6.55	*Fireside Theatre*
The Searchers	5.26.56	C. V. Whitney Pictures –Warner Bros.

This period is distinguished by the vitality of its invention, at every level of cinema, but with particular intensity in montage, motion, and music. Ford at his most energetic intellectually is also Ford at his most optimistic. The defeatism of the preceding period has been largely rejected—or, at least, recontextualized. Although virtually all the pictures take place in the past (or in Africa or Korea) it is evident that Ford felt some hope in America. This is the period of *3 Godfathers, Wagon Master,* and *The Sun Shines Bright.* But it is also the period of *Mogambo* —is man different than the ape?—and it is evident Ford finds more to criticize than to praise in American society: *Fort Apache, When Willie Comes Marching Home, The Long Gray Line.*

In this period the community theme in Ford is in ascendance, a period of social analysis, akin to the early thirties pictures. Military or military-like societies are chosen because they provide clear sets of the customs, ideologies, and structures relevant to America. Although ten prior pictures dealt with such groups, only *Wee Willie Winkie* and *Salute* had attempted quasi-documentary approaches to such communities. But of the thirty-three films made after 1948, eighteen are directly concerned with studying the problems of military communities, while nine others treat, in much the same terms, quasi-military communities (wagon trains, missionaries, political parties, police), while two others have military life as a background (*The Searchers, Donovan's Reef*). In all thirty-three films the specific question is, What makes people tick? Why do they do what they do? or, twenty-nine times, What makes people fight?

There is less determinism and more free will than elsewhere in Ford in this period. Duty, previously regarded by the hero as divinely appointed, henceforth resides in the group and is socially assigned.

Previously people lived in idealistic commitment; individuals might die but the Idea would endure (e.g., Ma Joad). This theme continues, but the static concept is replaced by a dynamic antinomy and given concrete representation: *subsistence* and *change* —and an uncertain change—become the matrices through which all other themes must operate. And henceforth the films of John Ford essentially constitute a cinema of passage, whose central symbolic antinomies are the parade and the house.

Expressionism virtually disappears in its purer forms, and though Ford exploits operatic cinema more than ever, most of his mannerist tendencies are subsumed into brighter palettes and cleaner compositions.

But the films grow progressively darker. A few old men sustain the viability of society, only faith can find an ontological distinction between man and ape, the parade is a substitute for the insufficiency of reason. The films dwell on the coercive tendencies of society, of instruments becoming malevolent institutions. The period concludes with *The Searchers*, a farewell to youth and the entry into Ford's work of acute ambivalence, of a dialectic equivalent to pessimism and uncertainty about Good and Evil. Yet even so, these eight years constitute a period of glory, of stability and sureness, more blessed with masterpieces than any other period.

Five Westerns

"I made four or five westerns . . . , potboilers, but they served a purpose," said Ford.[2] "I had to do something to put my company back on its feet after what we lost [with *The Fugitive. Fort Apache*] was a very concocted story. But very good box-office."[3] "[It] is a variation inspired by Custer's last battle. We changed the tribe and the topography."[4]

Ford's prewar reputation had been based on "quality" adaptations of literature conceived to tastemakers' appeal. Now, needing to appeal to new, wider audiences, his style became more forceful, his palette more colorful; his better instincts were refreshingly liberated. *Fort Apache*'s style owes more to *The Battle of Midway* than to *The Grapes of Wrath*, or even to *Wee Willie Winkie*—although it was the notion of making a movie about the intimate life of an isolated cavalry post that had led Ford to purchase James Warner Bellah's Kiplingesque story, "Massacre." Army-post pictures had been common enough in Hollywood. But when the troops ride in and out of their garrison in Curtiz's 1936 *Charge of the Light Brigade*, music and countryside are dramatically banal in contrast to the dynamic significance of Ford's folk tunes and Monument Valley. What Ford brought new to the genre—and what now enters more intensely into his work—is a conscious vivification of his material as mythic actuality. The land, its indigenous inhabitants, quotidian ritual, and documentary detail assume awesome symbolic roles. The complex social forces that formerly determined Fordian people are henceforth concentrated into myth. Myth rules man.

Fort Apache (1948). Here began a long association with Frank S. Nugent, who had been hired as an in-house critic by Darryl Zanuck back in 1940 (in order, some gossiped, to stop Nugent's pans of Zanuck films in

The New York Times), but who, like another newspaperman, Dudley Nichols, had not written a script until hired by Ford.

> [Ford] gave me a list of about fifty books to read—memoirs, novels, anything about the period. Later he sent me down into the old Apache country to nose around. . . . He made me do something that had never occurred to me before—but something I've practised ever since: write out complete biographies of every character in the picture. Where born, educated, politics, drinking habits (if any), quirks. You take your character from his childhood and write all the salient events in his life leading up to the moment the picture finds him—or her. The advantages are tremendous, because having thought a character out this way, his actions, his speech are thereafter compulsory; you know how he'll react to any given situation. . . . Bellah's short story, *Massacre*, touched the character and provided the ending. But the first 80 percent had to be worked back from the ending—and the key to it was in the character development.[5]

Indeed, *Fort Apache* is dense with character interrelationships and prior biography, ethnicity, religion, manners, and mores. Innumerable happenings—riding lessons, dances, drills, drinking bouts, romances, visits, punishments, home-makings, serenades, dinners—have been "concocted" to detail documentary, along with a multitude of richly individuated personalities—five sergeants, two corporals, four officers, four women (plus Francis Ford doing his famous spit). There is a Grand March* (to "St. Patrick's Day") and some magical dancing (to, as so often, "Golden Slippers"). And there is Shirley Temple, absolutely right and beautifully subtle as Philadelphia Thursday, an ingenuous, rascally sixteen, fresh from school in Europe, devoted to her father and unafraid to express frank thrills for a dashing young lieutenant ("Wonderful!").** Indian-killers though they be, the soldiers engage our warmest sympathies. As we watch Sergeant O'Rourke (Ward Bond) deliberately finishing his Bible-reading before raising his head to greet his son returned home, every detail of the home—its textiles, plates, religious statue, fireplace, and lighters—articulates the man's identity and aids our affection. We know the moment fulfills a lifelong dream: an immigrant's son has become an officer.[†]

Despite this achievement, Colonel Thursday justifiably discourages courting of his daughter by O'Rourke's officer-son, because the latter, as an enlisted man's son, will never advance. And all life at Fort Apache is domi-

---

*Similar to but not so fine as in *The Sun Shines Bright*; Ford's first Grand March occurred in *The Prince of Avenue A* (1920).

**John Agar (Lt. O'Rourke) had actually married Shirley Temple shortly before the film. Alas, the fascination of *her* eroticism was not of the stuff that created adult stars in 1948. But Ford recreates an episode from their 1937 *Wee Willie Winkie*, when she wakes up her first morning, goes to her window, and sees the flag being raised, the cannon shot, horse, wagons, dust. She was paid the same salary as Wayne and Fonda—$100,000. McLaglen got $35,000; Bond $25,000; O'Brien $15,000; Kibbes $12,000; Withers $7,500; Lee $7,000; Rich and Agar $5,000.

[†]A similar scene occurs in Francis Ford's *The Burning Brand* (1912).

nated by the military's caste system. Alcohol, for instance, is always be-
stowed from a higher rank to a lower (Thursday buys drinks for the men at
the way station; officers spike the noncoms' ball punch; Thursday orders
Meachum's whiskey "destroyed"; Thursday offers Collingwood a drink;
York gives Sergeant Beaufort a drink at the canyon). A higher-ranking soldier is always in authority, in military thinking, and reality must conform to
theory. Thus, when a recruit is thrown from his horse and chases after it, his

sergeants shout, "Hey! Where are you going with that horse! Come back
here with that horse!" Here, as generally, Ford's slapstick is making a point.
In fact, another gag virtually explains the whole film: Sergeant Mulcahy
(Victor McLaglen), cautioned to behave at the ball, pledges: "We'll be the
morals of decorum!" For, in actuality, decorum dictates the only morality
they have.

For the people of Fort Apache serve a system, in which group, duty, and
order are more important than individual, morality, or life itself. They are
warrior-priests. But they will be destroyed by the system, by duty gone
astray; willingly, they will charge into a canyon of slaughter, led by a man
particularly dedicated to ritual glory. Even though Colonel Owen Thursday
(Henry Fonda) has been told the Apache wait in ambush, the soldiers obey
his orders, knowing him wrong, and they die.

The Indians are outside the system; they are the Other, the enemy (by
definition rather than cause); they are like the land, something to be controlled. And dust is their constant ally: dust thrown by Cochise as sign he
will engage the cavalry (conveying sorrow at having to fight, in contrast to
Thursday's elation, and telling us also that the soldiers are already dead);
dust clouds warning York the Apache are near; dust clouds squaws create to
fool Thursday; dust engulfing the trapped regiment; dust into which the
Apache disappear after planting the destroyed regiment's banner in front of
York and which then rolls over York's men. Cochise tells Thursday the
Apache had surrendered, but then came the Indian agent:

— He is worse than war. He not only killed the men, but the women,
   and the children, and the old ones. We looked to the Great White
   Father for protection: he gave us slow death. . . . Send him [the
   agent] away and we will speak of peace.

Thursday has previously indicated his disgust for the agent, but, insulted
by Cochise's threat of war, he calls him a "recalcitrant swine . . . without
honor"—though it was Thursday who was just now about to attack treacher-

ously under a flag of truce. A martinet, stiff-backed, hungry for glory, shamed to fight "breech-clad savages," affected with his cigars, Thursday's arrogance is motivated by the blind prejudice of his racism—which Ford instances in Thursday's attitude toward the Irish (forgetting O'Rourke's name twice and calling him O'Brien or Murphy); need it be said, Thursday comes from Boston, like most screwballs in Ford.

Ford sees the cause of army barbarity in disgruntled officers trying to make a name for themselves so they can return east. But glory is an acceptable goal in the system, as Mrs. Collingwood (Anna Lee) proves by refusing to call her husband back from the fatal campaign when a long-awaited promotion to West Point comes through, even though she has a premonition of his death ("All I can see is the flags"). And glory is the response the system makes to Thursday's mass suicide.

In the picture's last scene, the camera dollies back from the B Troop banner, an oil portrait of Thursday, and his saber. Captain York (John Wayne), whose oath to Cochise Thursday betrayed, whose advice of the ambush Thursday scorned, talks with two reporters:

Rep. 1: [Looking reverently at the portrait:] He must have been a great
       man. And a great soldier.

York:	[In an official but convincing tone:] No man died more gallantly. Nor won more honor for his regiment.
Rep. 1:	Of course you are familiar with the famous painting of Thursday's Charge.
York:	Yes, I saw it the last time I was in Washington.
Rep. 2:	That was a magnificent work. There were these massed columns of Apache in their warpaint and feather bonnets, and here was Thursday leading his men in that heroic charge.
York:	Correct in every detail. [In fact, the description *is* exact.]
Rep. 2:	He's become almost a legend already. He's the hero of every schoolboy in America. But what of the men who died with him. What of Collingworth . . .
York:	Colling*wood.*
Rep. 2:	Oh, of course. Collingwood.
Rep. 1:	That's the ironic part of it. We always remember the Thursdays, but the other men are forgotten.
York:	You're wrong there. They aren't forgotten, because they haven't died. They're living, right out there. [York has moved to the window; ghosts of the cavalrymen appear superimposed on the pane—"Battle Hymn of the Republic."] Collingwood and the rest. And they'll keep on living, as long as the regiment lives. The pay is thirteen dollars a month, their diet beans and

hay—they'll eat horsemeat before this campaign is over—fight over cards or rotgut whisky, but share the last drop in their canteens. The faces may change, and the names, but they're there, they're the regiment, the regular army, now and fifty years from now. They're better men than they used to be. Thursday did that. He made it a command to be proud of.

Thus the archdemon becomes a hero, and the individuals are proud, undisturbed by the murder committed upon them; in fact, O'Rourke, whose father Thursday sacrificed, has named his son after Thursday. How can this be? The answer is that their lives *are* the system; life is not questioned; no additional act of the will is required to honor Thursday.

And the epilogue of *She Wore a Yellow Ribbon* consists of a similar epitaph, narrated over a color brigade in Monument Valley:

— So here they are, the dog-faced soldiers, the regulars, the fifty-cents-a-day professionals, riding the outposts of a nation. From Fort Reno to Fort Apache, from Sheridan to Stark, they were all the same: men in dirty-shirt blue and only a cold page in the history books to mark their passing. But wherever they rode, and whatever they fought for, that place became the United States.

We may not like these conclusions, but Ford's intentions are to give accurate depictions of the system, not to give us "happy endings." What sounds like a paean to American imperialism happens to be simple truth. These *are* our heroes, our forefathers who have given us what we have today; in a way, they are ourselves. A Kubrick applies placeboes to our consciences, showing us that evil, warped men cause evil; but Ford makes us uncomfortable, showing us that fine, noble people cause evil—and reminding us that, however much we decry what they did, we are not about to undo their work. Thus, Ford shows us facts, but also an "inside" perspective on those facts.

Bogdanovich: The end of *Fort Apache* anticipates the newspaper editor's line in *Liberty Valance,* "When the legend becomes a fact, print the legend." Do you agree with that?

Ford: Yes—because I think it's good for the country.[6]

Really? How come, then, that in both movies Ford "prints" the facts, while exploding (and explaining) the legends?* His portrait of the cavalry is a scathing indictment of arrogance, idiocy, racism, and caste-ridden inefficiency. It is puzzling that so flagrant an irony as *Fort Apache*'s is commonly mistaken for chauvinism by so many of Ford's critics.

---

*Peter Watkin's *Culloden* had a similar conclusion: despite the ruination Bonnie Prince Charlie's arrogance visits upon them, the Highlanders continue to venerate him as a rallying symbol of national identity.

And the movie is also one of the few in which Indians emerge both honorable and victorious. That they remain alien testifies to Ford's honesty.* He certainly does them no injustice. But here and in *She Wore a Yellow Ribbon* he sights them across the gap of culture and history, and lavishes upon them some of the finest epic photography of his career. John Ford:

> My sympathy was always with the Indians. Do you consider the invasion of the Black and Tan into Ireland a blot on English history? It's the same thing, all countries do the same thing. There's British doing it, Hitler doing it, there's Stalin. Genocide seems to be a commonplace in our lives. But it was not a systematic destruction of the Indians. All I know is the cavalry got the hell kicked out of them, and the Indians practically destroyed themselves. It was the loss of the buffalo that wiped them out.[7]

Fort Apache is the first (and maybe the best) of the so-called trilogy of 7th Cavalry films—all based on James Warner Bellah stories. Stretches of it meander and there is some careless mismatching of shots due to haste, but much of it is first-rate Ford, with powerful photography (frequently on infrared stock). More impressive even than the credit sequence's sweeps across Monument Valley are the vast, epic compositions of Thursday leading his columns, backed by thunderous skies, with Archie Stout's camera scarcely a foot off the ground.

Fort Apache's action, at the time of Custer's 1876 Battle of the Little Big Horn, chronicles a fresher, more meaningful cavalry era than the later, mopping-up operations of *Yellow Ribbon* or *Rio Grande*. It is, relatively speaking, a picture of actuality, whereas *She Wore a Yellow Ribbon*, the second of the "trilogy," celebrates the generic ritual established by the first.

Here, in *She Wore a Yellow Ribbon* (1949), the nostalgic dreamworld, the old man's reverie of *Rio Grande*, the third of the series, is confronted in the bright sunshine of Technicolor. We can thus trace, in the span of three years and three pictures, a retreat into mythic re-creation. Gone already are the documentary reenactments of nineteenth-century life. The palpable feel of grit and guts is transposed into the purely iconic, icons stunningly recreating the colors and movement of Remington (other icons, other myths),** visually actual and executed with bold romantic panache, but already given within the context of a leading character grown old, to whom the present (1876) is a pale remnant of the Old West, and whose living memories find their most natural companionship beside the grave of his wife and children—like Will Rogers's Judge Priest.†

---

*An accurate Indian movie, in which everything is viewed through an Indian consciousness, would, language aside, pose insurmountable problems for our comprehension—not to mention commercial disaster. Nicholas Ray made a (heavily compromised) attempt to do this, with Eskimos, in *The Savage Innocents* (1959). Ford attempted honest pictures from *our* viewpoint.

**Ford and Carey's *Hell Bent* (1918) opened with an author contemplating a Remington canvas ("The Misdeal") that comes to life to start the story.

†Just after Custer's massacre, Fort Stark is threatened, and Capt. Brittles, due to retire,

The window of Captain Nathan Brittles's quarters at Fort Stark looks "out" onto the close-set wooden posts of the stockade—two feet away. On a printed calendar (curiously lacking a month name), each day is crossed out as retirement approaches, but really Brittles's life is marking time until death reunites him with a happier reality, with that family whose portraits he falls asleep with on his lap. Meanwhile the man is indistinguishable from the jargon and protocol of military duty. His motto is, "Never apologize. It's a sign of weakness," and, just like George Washington, he stays mounted and in clear view during battle. The mentality of a professional soldier has become his second nature. And because of this, we understand the depths of his mortification at the manifold failures of his last patrol, even though such a mentality is, like that of many Fordian heroes, not the sort many of us would be comfortable with in everyday life. Brittles, however, comes

---

leads his last patrol. But, escorting two ladies, he cannot intervene when he sights Arapaho, arrives late for one rendezvous to find men dead, late for another to find the stage burnt and more dead, and cannot stop a white trading rifles to Indians. Leaving a rear guard, he returns dejected. Since he retires at midnight, he is denied permission to lead the relief. His men give him a silver watch and he sees them ride off. But he takes command on personal authority and, when a parley fails, stealthily drives away the Indian horses, thus ending the war-threat. At 12:02 he retires, officially. And he starts west alone, but Tyree is sent after him, with news of appointment as chief of scouts. A dance is held in his honor, but he prefers to visit alone the small cemetery where his wife and children are buried.

through as a more palpable, "brittle" human being than did Wyatt Earp or Colonel Thursday, and, unlike them, his interventions save lives and bring peace, rather than wreaking havoc and death. Ford:

> Some years ago Douglas MacArthur asked me to stop by to see him in Tokyo. "We're showing one of your films tonight, *She Wore a Yellow Ribbon.*" He added that he had it shown at least once a month and that he still wasn't tired of it.[8]

"I'll be back, men, I'll be back," calls Captain Brittles as he leaves his troop to guard a ford, and, later, "Old soldiers," he says, "how they hate to grow old!"

At the time of the action, the redmen, spurred on by the destruction of Custer and the miraculous reappearance of the buffalo, are enjoying the illusion that history can be reversed, and, for moments during his last patrol, Brittles intersects this Indian summer, and the days of his youth are reborn under the bright sun. Coincidentally at such moments the picture, dropping its mask of theatricality, rises to a high level of present-anterior actuality: in the distance an entire tribe of Arapaho moves nomadically across the plains; later a herd of buffalo grazes with much the same naturalness. Sergeant Tyree gallops across the prairie pursued by Indians, and jumps a ravine to escape, one man alone in the wilderness. At Sudrow's Wells, Private John Smith dies and is buried with a general's honors: he was Rome Clay, CSA. Like Tyree ("I ain't gittin paid fer thinkin"), many of the cavalry's common soldiers are former Confederate officers who, like Brittles, seem to regard the army as a kind of monastic retreat from a bitter world. Even Pony That Walks* finds himself ignored by his younger tribesmen, and, when Nathan says, "Old men should stop wars," the chief replies, "Too late," and suggests they go away together to hunt buffalo and get drunk. And when the troop sights the herd, a soldier exclaims, "Sure hanker for a piece of buffalo meat!" "Me too!" adds a second soldier, "'Hain't never had none." But before this reference to the passing wilderness rings too sententiously, a third soldier interjects, "Beans is safer!" Couples may float deathlessly into a sweet slow waltz midst the dark, glowing colors of the final reception, but a new age is at hand. No wonder Brittles retreats to his graveyard.

John Wayne carries the drama single-handed, virtually, with more dialogue than ever before or since. His roles in *Stagecoach, The Long Voyage Home,* and *Fort Apache* had been small, taciturn, and distinctive, but his performance in Hawks's *Red River* had convinced Ford he could act, and in *3 Godfathers* Wayne recited the longest monologue in any Ford movie. In *Yellow Ribbon,* he has the added novelty of playing in makeup a man a

---

*Played by Chief John Big Tree (1875–?), 100 percent Seneca, who in 1912 posed for the Indian-head nickel and from 1915 appeared in innumerable pictures, including *Drums Along the Mohawk.*

generation older than himself. At times, like the movie alternating between storybook theatricality and realism, he gets a bit hammy, but that is the character.

Ford westerns tend to be epitomes of the genre, rather than variations upon it. Brittles exemplifies this tendency, as does the photography—the expressionistic black-and-red skies with bright low-drifting night-clouds; or the day-for-night stampede, sepia, black-and-white, traced with blue*— and as do the gags. Speed makes Victor McLaglen's hammy barroom brawl one of Ford's best friendly fights (what else would army types do for recreation?). For Quincannon, who retires himself in two weeks, this is the final "battle" and his blows seem inspired by Dumas's description of Porthos's Herculean death. But this tendency toward epitome seems to handicap *She Wore a Yellow Ribbon*'s attempts toward being a Fordian comedy. The rugged, crass, even vulgar professionals of Ford's cavalry movies are all-of-a-piece types; they lack the ability of *Submarine Patrol*'s citizen sailors or of *When Willie Comes Marching Home*'s pixilated Punxatawnians to explode readily into chimeric manifestations of individuality.

Magic moments aside, however, the fact remains that *She Wore a Yellow Ribbon*, and *Rio Grande* even more, were made to make money from kiddie-matinee audiences. They were shot hurriedly, and their scripts are concocted banalities played at the broadest levels. Never was Ford more careless with his players. Joanne Dru, fascinating in *Wagon Master*, has the least personality of any Ford female, and John Agar and Harry Carey, Jr., are correspondingly simple. Takes are long, with little of the inventive montage or composition of Ford's more personal movies.

***Rio Grande* (1950),** Ford's seventh western in eight pictures, was undertaken because Republic would not back *The Quiet Man* without a successful first project. But if Ford began with indifference, warming up O'Hara, Wayne, and McLaglen for the Irish movie, he seems to have grown enchanted eventually. And, after all, the Argosy westerns' magic is inseparable from their rawness and careless production—one notes even more mismatching of infrared than in *Fort Apache*.

Rio Grande is so obvious technically, yet so successful, that many may find here an initiation to Ford. It is a storybook movie, accessible and privileged, cozy and strong, almost a chapter of reveille in an old man's fireside reverie, a mixture of epic and corn. It is a textbook in the rendering and exploiting of empathy.**

Victor Young's melodies yearn over vast strong valleys; the wide swift river inculcates rhapsodic beatitudes. A color brigade bursts dustily

---

*Winton C. Hoch's Technicolor won an Oscar—despite his formal, written protest against shooting the famous thunderstorm sequence, which Hoch was certain would not come out.

**Texas, 1878: Midst rescuing children captured by Apache, Lt. Col. Kirby Yorke is reunited with his family after fifteen years, when wife Kathleen comes pursuing their son Jeff who has enlisted.

through a gate, and the camera pushes forward to stare commandingly at an approaching horseman. Such dynamics evoke Remington or Delacroix, but mostly Matthew Brady: actuality mingling with theater (i.e., those Civil War soldiers could not have been as mysterious as Brady portrays them). Cut closer: he is dirty, unshaved, weary, but a small gesture he makes—straightening, trying to look proud—affords us immediate entry into the human being within the professional. Partly because of the moustache, it takes effort to remember this is John Wayne.

Knee-level camera angles both distance and personalize; but empathy is secured chiefly by extensive use (most atypical for Ford) of point-of-view camera. Kathleen (Maureen O'Hara) stands in close shot while soldiers ride off behind her; /she pops into an empty frame after her son rides out of it; /the reverse-angle shows a desert vista with a speck of a rider, before we cut back to /Kathleen gazing.

Jeff (Claude Jarman, Jr.*) combines sensitivity, cuteness, and lanky toughness, almost erotically, and Ford promotes identity with him. He sits singing in a tent with three buddies, but only his face faces the camera and only he is spotlit and not shadowed: our experience is his. When, of all people, his mother walks in—she was supposed to be back in Virginia—his embarrassment almost overpowers the humor, because we are still meant to identify with him (he is spotlit, his mother is in the crosscut). His wake-up is entirely in reaction shots:** Jeff wakes, looks, /Heinze smiles, /Jeff reacts, /Tyree and Boone smile, /doctor offers spoon, /Yorke looks in window, /Doc gives spoon, Jeffs says "ough," /Yorke smiles—all over a bugle blowing reveille. Later: Yorke leads sorties down the Apache street: /Indian takes aim /Yorke /Indian shoots /Yorke falls off horse /close shot: and onto ground, writhing QUICK DISSOLVES high-angle long shot: horsemen form circle around wounded leader. /High-angle CU: Yorke. X low-angle CU: Jeff. X Yorke: "Pull it out, Jeff." X Jeff hesitates. /Low-angle two-shot: Tyree and Boone: "Get it done, Reb." "Yo," adds Boone. /Jeff yanks; X Yorke cringes. X Jeff wipes nose. /Long shot: Yorke is helped to horse, bugle sounds recall. This is textbook crosscutting; the matching high- /low-angles mirror growing intimacy between father and son; the cut-aways to friends supply moral support; "Yo" and Jeff-wiping-nose are devices milked throughout the movie.

Ford crosscuts between Kathleen and Yorke when they first see each other, and even puts "I'll Take You Home Again, Kathleen" on the soundtrack, but the moment is more perfunctory than Earp seeing Clementine or Marty Maher meeting Mary O'Donnell. Kathleen is so vague, her life a void except for quadruple repetition of the he-burnt-her-plantation story;† she seems summed up by her gazes into off-space. She is affecting when most wifely, when she finally joins the plain-faced young wives and overalled boys waiting on the road for their men, and when she spins her parasol while the band plays "Dixie." There's nothing vague about Jeff, though, and his scenes with Yorke have the chemistry lacking between husband and wife. Low-angles add seriousness to their first conversation, and crosscuts ascending to close-ups add intensity. *Rio Grande* is a succession of intimacies with pungent dialogue: "What kind of man is he, mother?" "He's a lonely man."

---

*Jarman (1934–) starred in *The Yearling* (1946), *Intruder in the Dust*, *The Great Locomotive Chase*; recently directed the San Francisco Film Festival.

** / = cut. X = crosscut, or reverse-angle.

†"Silent as death she was, with her babes in her arms," says McLaglen. Ford's wife's Carolina ancestors had their house burnt by Sheridan.

"They say he's a great soldier." "What makes soldiers great is hateful to me." Sacrifice of self to duty is explicit in the uniform.

Sheridan (J. Carroll Naish) is depicted almost as mythically as MacArthur in *They Were Expendable*. His spiffy horse belies his personal dirt, and, after being serenaded ("We may have more great men but we'll never have better . . . Glory-O!"), queries, "I wonder what History will say about Shenandoah?" "I can tell you what my wife said about it," quips Yorke, but the magical moment of history and humanity has had its effect, and when the scene concludes with Sheridan pouring himself coffee, we are programmed to wonder at the Great Man's simplicity.

Tyree (Ben Johnson) echoes myths more archetypal. Silent and capable, he gallops free and sovereign across the horizons of Monument Valley, summing up, like the cactus rose later, Ford's West. At one special moment, as Tyree's charger careens into an unsuspecting Apache happily pursuing a soldier, the epic mythologies of Ford join those of Buster Keaton.

Archetypal, too, is the status, largely symbolic, of women, who exist for the warriors' repose. Yorke wanders along a riverbank: Wayne, as instructed, keeps his face blank, thinks nothing; the moonlit water and haggard twilight tell us he is thinking of Kathleen. Later he stands in the dust watching his wife's wagon depart; presently we discover the music is coming not from the soundtrack, but from a sentimental tribute by the men of the fort. In such a world, poor Kathleen will find no peace until she accepts her prescribed role within the army. But then, no existential choices exist for men, either. All is duty.

Rio Grande is Ford at his best and worst. Its images rest in the mind—a little girl yanking a church bell, Jeff holding his swooned mother, wives tramping beside stretchers—and at worst it has at least the virtues of intimacy. Ford must have felt some pride: the mounted bugler on the horizon under the words "Directed by John Ford" is scarcely modest.

3 Godfathers (1948), and *Wagon Master* (1950) both stand in marked contrast to "the cavalry trilogy," being freely structured around historical and biblical myths, rather than demonstrative of institutional dynamics. Particularly dear to Ford was *3 Godfathers*'s story, of three bad men who, after robbing a bank and escaping into the desert, rescue a newborn baby and, guided by the Bible, take it to New Jerusalem, two of them dying on the way. The good badman, as we know, was a frequent Ford character, as was also a trio of badmen, whom he would usually liken to the three magi. Besides *Marked Men* (1919), his first filming of Peter B. Kyne's story and his favorite of his films with Harry Carey, *The Secret Man* (1917) and *Action* (1921) have similar stories, and there is a 1915 Francis Ford two-reeler, *Three Bad Men and a Girl*, in which Jack and Francis play two of the badmen. Three good badmen show up in *3 Bad Men* (1926) and there are similar triplets in *The Iron Horse* (1924) and the cavalry trilogy sergeants, not to mention the three magi in *Donovan's Reef* (1963).

As in *Donovan's Reef,* everything in *3 Godfathers* looks forward to Christmas, as to a moment of universal renewal. The badmen are ingenuous and respectful, and far too inept for the wilderness (one gets shot, they drink all their water, lose their horses, have to consult books for advice, and fumble into suicide). And civilization has provided a train by which the posse outflanks them. Yet it was clear at the outset, when B. Sweet (Ward Bond) emerged from behind his flowers and picket fence, that badmen have become anachronistic less by triumph of history than by triumph of virtue. This is the Mormons' promised land. The town "Tarantula" has changed its name to "Welcome" ("Welcome to Welcome") and, as in Mrs. Sweet's coffee, "egg shells . . . settle the grounds." As in *Liberty Valance,* the desert had bloomed—and in glorious Technicolor. But *3 Godfathers* tends to be a minor movie, its long stretches of desert monotony redeemed by magic moments, of which by far the best is the finale, when sparkling cutting and framing rhyme spunky, swingy girls singing "Bringing in the Sheaves."

That **Wagon Master (1950),** one of Ford's major masterpieces, grossed about a third of any of the cavalry pictures surely came as no surprise. It was a personal project, with no stars, little story, deflated drama, almost nothing to attract box office or trendy critics. The story, resembling the Carey-Fords of the teens more than a fifties western, was written by Ford himself, the only such instance after 1930, and he was ruthless with the script. Said Frank Nugent: "We did not work at all closely. . . . His script cutting—especially of dialogue—was rather harsh."[9] Of all his pictures, said Ford, "*Wagon Master* came closest to what I had hoped to achieve."[10] It is "the purest and simplest western I have made."[11]

The magic that places *Wagon Master* among Ford's most enduringly rewarding movies tends, alas, to elude many viewers, particularly upon first viewing and particularly because purity and simplicity define that magic, for such qualities are far from those usually associated in the public mind with Great Motion Pictures. But *Wagon Master* is more poetry than drama, weaving together the West's purest myths with the simplest, most natural characters.

The opening (credit) sequences pose the themes:

1. The *Cleggs:* over their own "Wanted" poster rob Crystal City express office and kill clerk in spite.

2. The *Mormons:* wagons ford sparkling river. (Evil vs. good; association of Mormons with river image.)

3. The *Cleggs:* ride on twilit horizon.

4. The *Mormons:* camera pans thrice as Mormon wagons pass. (Evil vs. good again; accent on family [women and children in wagons] of Mormons, as opposed to femaleless Cleggs.)

5. Sister Ledeyard (Jane Darwell): blows her *bullhorn:* dissolve:

6. Longshot: *Horsetraders* Travis Blue (Ben Johnson) and Sandy Owens (Harry Carey, Jr.) driving with horses *toward* Crystal City.

7. The *Cleggs:* riding *away* from Crystal City.

8. Crystal City: horsetraders sell horse to marshall and meet Mormons: Elder Wiggs (Ward Bond), Elder Adam Perkins (Russell Simpson), his daughter Prudence (Kathleen O'Malley).

Note the mediating role of the *bullhorn* between the *Mormons* and the *horsetraders*, framed by the *Cleggs* on either side. This prefigures a later sequence: the Mormons, as Wiggs puts it, are heading for "the San Juan— to a valley that . . . that's been reserved for us by the Lord, been reserved for His people, so we can plough it and seed it and make it fruitful in His eyes." They need a guide, however, and Wiggs suggests that Travis and Sandy are the answer to this prayer. But the boys decline, and the Mormons set off alone, yet Wiggs, scratching his head, gives it another try (note the blend of corn [scratching] and apotheosis [words]): "Kinda wishing those young horse traders had given the Lord a hand! Sister Ledeyard! Supposin' you blow that horn again!" She does, and, as though answering her prayer, we dissolve to Travis and Sandy riding up to a fence, on which they sit to watch the wagons pass; suddenly, in *song*, they decide to take the job.

Note how the reprise of the prefigured image of the bullhorn as linkage between Mormons and horsetraders (and Cleggs) suggests not only that the Mormon-horsetrader alliance is divinely preordained, but also apotheosizes into poetic themes the various social groups. These groups correspond to the basic mythic elements of the West, and throughout the movie will be interwoven in similarly forthright fashions:

A. The Cleggs, outlaws

B. The Mormons, the ordained

C. Travis and Sandy, horsetraders (cowboys), drifters, and agents of the Lord

D. Marshall and posse, the establishment, who persecute A, B, and E

E. The showfolk

F. The Indians

Wagon Master meditates on the *difference* of these thematic groups. A and B are presented almost as two polarities of sonata form, with C as a bridge or catalyst. In the second movement, B, C, and E climax in the communal harmony of the dance scene. Thirdly, the Cleggs intrude and oppose everyone, and then the posse intrudes, also opposing everyone. In the fourth movement, B, C, and E combine to climb the last mountain, then in a swift sudden gunfight C annihilates A. A coda reprises in free combinations of B, D, and E — a sort of *stretto.*

The showfolk (a patent-medicine salesman, two loose women, and Francis Ford as a drummer) are, like other groups, outcasts, expelled from Crystal City. Ford's West, just like America itself, was colonized by urban refuse — outlaws, religious pilgrims, whores, swindlers, and free-spirited youngsters; not surprisingly, the wilderness knows its own: the Indians are friendly.

Two "obbligatos" add dimension to the allegorical mythos of the social groups. One, of course, is the land. Details of geography and time are vague, the better to be mythic, but the journey appears to take about a week and cover a hundred miles.* And the westward parade is persistent. Over and over again the off-screen chorus repeats, "rollin', rollin', rollin' . . . Goin' West, goin' West, goin' West . . ." In one key, minute-long sequence, the pilgrims trudge wearily through the dust toward the end of a forty-mile waterless trek, and here as elsewhere Ford strikingly sharpens the elements of mineral (desert — Monument Valley) and vegetable (brush) to contrast animal and man. The Mormons with children, horses, and dogs (ever-present on the soundtrack) are a herd in migration, a people pushed on by social and elemental forces, and by their will to find paradise. "We're just a small group of families," says Wiggs. And they *walked* West, step by step. Small in number, humble with faith rather than heroic, nothing could better explain the invincibility and inevitability of the conquest of the West than these images of walking people. Their columns form a parade, glorious, tawdry, and religious, but primarily their phenomenon seems lustily biological. The wilderness, in contrast to the civilization of Crystal City, seems to cradle man and to welcome him as a means to its fulfillment.

Music adds additional dimension: legend. "A hundred years have come and gone since 1849," sing the Sons of the Pioneers, and their unmistakably 1949 sound disturbingly distances the movie's pictorial action. That Ford's oxymoron is intentional is evident from the juxtaposition of the chorus's references to "the mighty wagon train" whose "thunder echoes in the sky" and the actual group of eleven or twelve wagons and sixty people. The blatant

---

*The San Juan River is some hundred miles northwest of Crystal (= Crystal City?), New Mexico. After fording a river, the Mormons encounter the showfolk (stranded without water, but evidently too far from Crystal to walk back). The next water is now forty miles, or two or three days as the wagon master says. After reaching the river, they entertain the Cleggs for about three days before entering their valley. The action is anterior to *3 Godfathers'*, in which the Mormons and Ward Bond are settled and growing flowers.

artificiality of this Stan Jones music apotheosizes the you-are-there authenticity of the images, underlines the stuff of legend (cf. *Fort Apache* and *Liberty Valance*), and serves a narrative function. Alas, it also seems to alienate many audiences completely, who, in trying to ignore the music, miss both the historic dialectic and *Wagon Master*'s essence as a *music* drama (or horse opera?). Music supports its tendency to epiphanize everything into primal symbology: the colt mounting the riverbank, the Cleggs' arrival, a gallop over the prairie, a lovingly prolonged shot of Travis taking his horse for a bath, even a bed or a rockinghorse. (Still, it seems a shame that at the dance, the participants' folksy instruments are faded out for a studio band and the Sons of the Pioneers.)

It almost seems as though Ford tried to promote Ward Bond, Ben Johnson, Harry Carey, Jr., and Joanne Dru; he listed their parts next to their names in the opening credits—the only time he was ever to do so. And each of them gets plenty of evocative cameo shots, with the three men frequently lined up in front of the camera to trade remarks and gesticulate. But normal Hollywood star-creation employs quite different techniques: high-energy performances rather than laid-back ones, and subjective rather than distancing camera techniques. For example, in an Errol Flynn film, in contrast to Ford, we see everything from Flynn's point of view; we are encouraged toward empathetic "identification" with *him*. But in *Wagon Master* folks just "be." And we watch. For as always in Ford, symbols, apotheoses, and poetry are counterbalanced by the relaxed "realism" of individuals, although nowhere else to this degree of simplicity, purity, and naturalness. Here above all is where *Wagon Master*'s magic resides. Watching Ward Bond whittle becomes wonderful, and the moment on the fence when Travis and Sandy sing to each other becomes one of the miracles in Ford. As in *Steamboat Round the Bend* and *How Green Was My Valley*, it is *Wagon Master*'s thesis that each little happening is grace.

Singing, for example, in John Ford pictures, besides its importance in ordinary community rituals such as marriages and funerals, is often symbolic of the most intimate act of social commitment a person can be capable of. Sons serenade their parents in *How Green Was My Valley* to mark restoration of family togetherness, peasants come serenade their priest in *The Fugitive* and their queen in *Mary of Scotland*; singing signifies Sean Thornton's acceptance into the community in *The Quiet Man*, becomes the sign of fellowship in *Up the River*, and even in *Straight Shooting* (1917), the act of listening to a recording together becomes quasi-mystical. (Contrarily, attacks on phonographs reflect broken unions in *Air Mail*, *The Wings of Eagles*, and *Donovan's Reef*.) Yet more intimate by far are the few occasions in which characters actually sing to each other: Helen Chandler's teaching William Janney "Anchors Aweigh" in *Salute* sums up deep traditions of romance and social duty intermingled; Will Rogers's joining the blacks in "Old Kentucky Home" in *Judge Priest* momentarily transcends all barriers of racism; Colleen Townsend and Dan Dailey express fellowship that redeems their utter conventionality in their song and dance in *When Willie Comes Marching Home*.

In *Wagon Master*, Travis and Sandy's resort to song to express a decision to guide the Mormons has at least three significations. By its formality, it suggests a commitment to the Mormons and an acquiescence in "the Lord's will"; by its connection to music's role throughout the film, it suggests mythic adventurousness; but more importantly, it suggests their friendship. This male-male partnership, lacking combativeness, macho manners, or sexual overtones, is a rare thing in American movies. Showing such a relaxed and natural friendship is what Ford had in mind by "pure and simple."

Meanwhile, the two romances proceed with tender economy. The mystery of a Fordian character is not the mystery of what he will do next; it is the mystery of his life such as it is at a given moment. It is not so much what happens to him that matters, as what he is; not so much what he does, as what he is in doing it. Thus Ford's peculiar power to evoke the atmosphere of a frontier era, with characters and culture father to our own, yet alien to us. Sandy ("carrot-topped") begins gazing at Prudence ("red-headed") at their first meeting, in Crystal City, and she quietly avoids and seeks his eyes; the relationship throughout is developed subtly to the side of whatever other action is occurring, so their courtship is the sort of event one might not wholly notice on first viewing the picture.

The Travis-Denver (Joanne Dru) romance, though given more prominence, is also articulated in undertones. Ford had taken the Ringo-Dallas love affair from *Stagecoach* (1939) and sublimated it. Travis is a steadier, quieter, and more intelligent sort than Ringo*; Denver seems attracted partially by her inability to fluster him.** Without overtly displaying it, they enjoy each other—which is what makes watching them interesting. Sexual innuendoes are especially covert: for example, the way Travis mounts his horse to bathe in the river, after telling Denver he will "join her." When Travis, like Ringo before him, offers marriage and a lonely life on a cattle ranch to a prostitute, Denver for an instant gazes joyously, then rushes wildly away, as the camera tracks with her in a tear-wrenching motion (eight seconds); she trips and falls, but the camera never stops its relentless motion—one of Ford's most extraordinary scenes. Then, instead of explicating her reasons as he did with Dallas, Ford dissolves to a twenty-five-second study of Denver slouched in the back of her wagon, puffing once on a cigarette then throwing it away (like Ava Gardner, *Mogambo*, or Anne Bancroft, *7 Women*, both of whom she resembles in style).

The Cleggs, though fleeing like the Mormons and showfolk, are not in search of peace; their goal resembles the biblical snake's. Long, secure shots give way to eight frightened and frightening rhythmic close-ups and eerie, hymnal music, to mark their intrusion into the Mormon dance. The close-ups recall Ford's similar parsing of a confrontation in *My Darling Clementine* between Wyatt Earp and the Clanton family. Both Clanton and Clegg

---

*Ben Johnson (Travis) (1919?– , Oklahoma) is more properly in the line of Ford's relaxed naturals stemming from Harry Carey and Will Rogers than is Wayne. Curiously, he used to be impossibly nervous, but "once Ford relaxed him, he stayed relaxed," recalls Dobe Carey while demonstrating how Ford aped relaxation by standing in a grotesque droop. Johnson entered films as a stuntrider, catching Ford's eye when, doubling Wayne in *Fort Apache*, his quick thinking saved some lives. Alas, his type of hero was as out-of-date in his day as Harry Carey would have been, and he did not get the recognition he deserved until his grossly inferior role in Bogdanovich's *Last Picture Show* (1971).

**Joanne Dru (1923–), a friend of Ford's daughter, starred in Hawks's *Red River* (1947). In contrast to her cocky slinkiness there, she was rather nondescript in *She Wore a Yellow Ribbon*, but achieved her most real-to-life presence in *Wagon Master*.

families are womanless, number four sons (Fred Libby and Mickey Simpson appear in both), and are ruled by despotic patriarchs hostile to all the world, who whimper their dead sons' names at the end, then try to draw and are themselves shot dead. Of the two fathers, Shiloh [sic] Clegg is the more deranged, and his family has an insular criminality closer to that in such seventies films as *Bloody Mama* or *Dirty Harry* than to 1951's *White Heat*. But Shiloh is well rounded with sardonic wit: "The Lord will bless you for [taking us in], brother," he tells Wiggs; "He marks the sparrow's fall." Shiloh, of course, was to be one of history's bloodiest battles.

As the wagons climb the final mountain at the end, instead of the expected apotheosis, Ford runs through another series of close-ups of the Cleggs, preceded by one of Wiggs, thus anticipating for us the Clegg decision to kill Wiggs and destroy the seed grain. "Grain is more valuable to us than gold itself," Wiggs had said (reviving an antithesis Ford exploited in *3 Bad Men* in 1926), inadvertently giving Clegg means to avenge the whipping administered Reese Clegg. To the Clegg sense of things, it mattered not that Reese had outraged an Indian girl in an Indian camp, that Wiggs's quick punishment prevented general massacre, nor that the beating was not so severe that Reese rode his horse less well next day, nor that the Mormons have saved the Cleggs from the posse and given them freedom. The whipper is shot dead, for family honor, as the express-office clerk was shot dead for *disrespect*; rudeness is sacrilegious. When Shiloh assumes control, his haughtiness has the majesty of an ancient autocrat. There is no need for Charles Kemper to play the part satirically or in an overblown Rod Steiger fashion, for Shiloh is self-righteous beyond display, able to slap Wiggs with his hat in the same calm, sane, unpretentious manner one would govern a horse. (In contrast, when Wiggs realizes he has unjustly yelled at his horse for tripping in quicksand and throwing him, he says, "Sorry, horse.")

The Cleggs represent the absolute evil of myth. They ooze dementia, foreboding fatality for whomever they meet. We have not yet discovered their purpose (nor that of the "snakes" in *The Fugitive*). Perhaps they have none, are only a "mistake." Yet they rekindle the age-old theological mystery of evil and divine omniscience. For their encounter with the Mormons seems preordained—in the film's first shots. "Providential," Cleggs terms this encounter, and his blasphemy proves true: innocence obliterates him. Yet the Mormons are lambs, not willing to protect themselves. Without Travis they would have maintained their pacifism, Wiggs would have died, the grain would have been lost and the colony destroyed. Yet—and this compromise of ideology for practicality fascinates Ford—the Mormons will accept protection from a shepherd, thus (a trifle hypocritically?) maintaining their innocence.* "No toil nor labor fear," sing the people; "The Lord will provide," affirms Wiggs.

---

*The same notion appears in *7 Women* (1965), but then the myth is less pure (or perhaps more pure), for the sheep are saved, but their innocence, where intact, is turned into psychosis.

Travis is an odd sort of Fordian hero to mediate between order and chaos, for, reluctant to draw on a man ("only on snakes!") and seeing violence as violence whatever its rationale, he intervenes more from instinct than from higher knowledge. He is, reluctantly, the instrument of the Lord, the gun is appropriately supplied by a small child (an angel), Travis uses it only to prevent a second murder, and even then Sandy forces his hand by throwing the gun at him. The violence—scarcely the film's only "action"—is so swift and sudden that it is over almost before we realize it has begun. And Travis throws away his gun, disgusted at having the snake-killing job thrust upon him.

In contrast to the depressed quality of his prewar work, Ford's optimism reaches a beatific apex in *Wagon Master*. Here, surely, is paradise gained. The debt to constant struggle is acknowledged, and man becomes in some sense the creator, the molder of destiny, while equally the shriven pilgrim gathered at new rivers. The deserts seem constantly in bloom, and the valley entered with innocence and purity intact is the Lord's own and needs only man for its completion. It is not Eden; it is better than Eden, for the "snakes" have been killed by Travis, the Lord's agent, "the answer to a prayer."

As Travis throws away his gun, Ford fades into a clutching moonlit shot of a lush virgin valley and glimmering river (one of the finer moments in constantly fascinating photography by Bert Glennon and Archie Stout). A Mormon hymn (off-camera) accompanies:

Come, come ye saints, no toil nor labor fear,
But with joy wend your way.

Though hard to you this journey may appear,
Grace shall be as your day.
'Tis better far for us to strive
Our useless cares from us to drive;
Do this and joy your hearts will swell—
All is well! All is well!

Dissolve: a vast high-shot of the wagons and of the people walking in a mass away from them. Dissolve: an intentionally theatrical, black-drop night shot: they mount onto a small platform of stones and gaze forward joyfully at / unbridled horses drinking tranquilly from the valley river. / Mormon men and women drink the vision rapturously; / among the children, Elder Wiggs stands in foreground and, along with the final lines of the hymn, he (Ward Bond) takes off his hat and says twice with boyish gusto, "I'll be dog-gone!"—what filmmaker today would venture such accurate simplicity? Quick fade into the recapitulation shots of the finale, with rollicking chorus.

More, perhaps, than any other film, *Wagon Master* is less interested in where it is going (plot), than in where it is (the moment). Still, obviously, it is a movie about *passage*—a "parade" West. Only briefly is "home," the antinomy of passage, suggested. And immediately upon its suggestion, it is abruptly refused by the film, which obstinately cuts back into flashbacks, back to passage rather than fulfillment, back to the past, to distance. And the movie fades out during a pan as a young colt steps up onto firm ground after fording a river—an image of eager progeny that sums up *Wagon Master* in the forward motion of life.

Three War Films

Three war films pass, like the westerns, from social study to mythic evocation. The three employ widely disparate styles of, respectively, comedy, surreal farce, and documentary. But in each case Ford's purpose is identical: a critical portrayal of the virtually unacknowledged ideologies that—in, respectively, hometown America, the frontline army, or national consciousness—establish war's possibility. (The theme is taken up again in *The Long Gray Line*.)

When Willie Comes Marching Home (1950). Ford called *Willie* "one of the funniest films ever made," and in later years would often lament, "I feel I'm essentially a comedy director, but they won't give me a comedy to do."[12] (Of Ford's postwar films, only *The Quiet Man, Donovan's Reef*, an episode of *The Rising of the Moon*, and a TV show, *Flashing Spikes*, could also be classified as comedies.) *Willie* resembles Ford's silent and prewar comedies—economical production, a huge cast of nearly fifty speaking parts, wacky gags, abundant detail, and invention. It would almost be comprehensible as a silent picture. Signs often substitute for spoken words: four newspapers with headlines, successive officers introduced by name plaques (lieutenant, captain, major, colonel), besides seventeen actual signs. More series dot the movie: drinks (wine, rum, whiskey, cognac, bourbon, sherry, compared to milk and ice cream at home), vehicles (trains, planes, fighters, parachutes, boats, motorcycles, bicycles, jeeps, taxis, hay wagon). The hero progresses through all enlisted ranks, while progressively encountering all officer ranks. And there are series of maps (2), radios (3), chasing dogs (2), a "Who's that?" gag (2), parades (2), and parties (3).

Yet *Willie* is chiefly a document on hometown American war fever. * Its obvious serious point is that war pictures never celebrate the guys who do not get into battle. "I'd rather fly dawn patrol in an F-6," declares an ace pilot, "than fool around with a bunch of rookies—that's rough stuff!" But everyone in town ignores poor Kluggs. Near-fatal training accidents are ignored, people ridicule him, small dogs attack him.

Willie's less obvious serious point is yet another Fordian essay in social dynamics, on his "Why They Fight" theme. But satire is more obvious. Punxatawney is a platitude, as are its citizens, institutions, buildings, rites, lifestyle, and attitudes (like Sternberg's masterful short, *The Town*, and Preston Sturges's *Hail the Conquering Hero* and *Miracle of Morgan's Creek*). Our hero loves the girl next door and runs across their yards like True Heart Susie. Their two houses are identical, differing only slightly in tasteful but unadmirable lower-middle-class decor. The two mothers (Evelyn Varden and Mae Marsh) are hilarious models of pixilated lubby-dub. Kluggs's father's every gesture affirms his stereotype—like grabbing a cigar out of his mouth when the radio broadcasts news of Pearl Harbor, or carrying the bass drum in the American Legion Band. Rituals, too, are repeatedly lampooned—church collections, parties, and tearful train-station goodbyes. And when Ford builds up to one of his typical finale-revues, the obvious irony is that Kluggs is leaving: both times Willie came marching home he was greeted with suspicion. And Ford's TV-style pans and dollies mimic the platitudinous material, as do his patterns of master shot followed by crosscuts. The latter, typical of Hollywood cheapies but not of Ford, is capitalized on for the opportunities for variation afforded by its formal clarity. Performances, too, broad and satiric but subtle and economic in gesture, mimic the platitude. In marked contrast to other Fords, characters do not

---

*Punxatawney, West Virginia, 1941: Bill Kluggs (Dan Dailey), first to enlist, gets a hero's send-off and a welcome-home party after training, only to spend a miserable war as a gunnery instructor at home watching others leave. Finally, opportunity comes, but his B-17 has to be abandoned. Kluggs, asleep, bails out later, is captured by French partisans photographing a V-2, gotten drunk, quizzed in London, quizzed in Washington, exhausted by forced drinks, and finally hops a freight to escape a psychiatric ward, only to be clubbed by his father who mistakes him for a spy when he climbs in his kitchen window—four days after leaving. But MPs will escort him to Washington for a presidential decoration, and Kluggs leaves a hero.

Sy Gomberg was nominated for an Oscar for original story. Lt. Gomberg had actually left an air base Friday noon on a B-17, been strafed by a Japanese plane that he then shot down, and found himself home and haggard Monday.

surpass stereotypical expectations, except in exaggeration, and society is homogeneous rather than stratified. Even national differences are incidental: the war mentality is the same whether French, English, German, or American.

The French village is an equivalent of Punxatawney. It has the requisite picturesque square, the inn, and cross-section of indigenous types, all exactly as they ought to be—even the Germans. The partisan Yvonne (Corinne Calvet) is young, beautiful, sexy, pert, and mysterious; she wears lipstick, low-necked blouse, and gunbelt; she puts Kluggs's bracelet down her bosom and stores her notebook there too. Ford pokes fun over the French word *impossible* (meaning: I-don't-want-to) and Dan Dailey's double-takes over a question about the "Yonkees" imitates Ford's own tomfoolery with British interviewers. But Kluggs himself cannot speak standard English: quizzed who Dick Tracy is, he replies, "A flatfoot, a cop, a *gendarme.*" What is comic in Punxatawney, however, here has the depressed earnestness of a neorealist war drama, with the intimate proximity of war. All the same, hidden amidst the melancholia occur the same gags, the same pompous seriousness so absurd in the context of Punxatawney. The Frenchman looks silly when he kneels with his gun to cover friends fleeing into a crypt. A German officer kicks down a farmhouse door, then carefully hides behind as his men barge in shooting. The gray-suited *madame le professeur* blinks her eye comically when cautioned. But nothing is funny, least of all the farewell to Yvonne, her hair wafting in the wind, the flat grassy hills and low-lying clouds. Even photographic style has changed: subdued Renoiresque light, white skies, restricted depth of field, giving poetry to bare tree branches. And music, rare elsewhere, has melodramatic functions in France.

From the dark silhouettes of the French coast, we progress to seacoast dusk, then to London and the Thames, somewhat brighter but with blimps hanging in the sky and sirens sounding, while over Washington, the Pentagon and Potomac, the sun shines bright and strong. Clothing, too, progresses toward lighter colors. Those back home can only make believe, and so paranoia steadily increases. The elder Kluggs (William Demarest) assumes the Germans would go to the trouble of spying on his kitchen. And the gruff MPs who show up clubbing and pounding their way into his home resemble the Nazis seen earlier. That scary suggestion culminates Ford's satire. MPs act like MPs, soldiers like soldiers, good patriotic civilians like good patriotic civilians. Such was the structure of society during World War II and everything follows from that. Sang Kluggs, "I say hello to the people I know in a vague sort of way. Baffled and blue I go stumbling through the day." And the band plays, "We're poor little lambs who have gone astray, baa, baa, baa."

Ford presents the platitude that today we name "Middle America," how those who live within this platitude are uncritically conditioned by it, how innocent they are, and how dangerous. Despite humor, the portrait is distinctly melancholic and would be overtly cynical, were the characters less affectionately drawn. As it is, we may remember best how Kluggs mimics Fred Astaire's pointing hand and top hat, doing a period song and dance, how he and Marge (Colleen Townsend) swing with delighted rapport, graceful and marionettelike, how Ford treats this—the sole classic-musical sequence in all his films—with élan and fun, panning and cutting with rhythmic symmetry from his proscenium-framing camera.

What Price Glory (1952). The original idea had been to remake Raoul Walsh's celebrated silent as a musical, but Fox executives from Darryl Zanuck down were surprised when they saw what Ford had wrought. "If you want music, *you* put it in," said Ford, as he walked out.

There *are* musical numbers, mostly at the beginning, though fewer of them than were shot. But, neither fish nor fowl, the movie was received coldly and dismissed as a weird miscalculation by the maker of *The Quiet Man* (which had debuted the day before in New York). Among a surfeit of war movies, this one seemed neither sufficiently pro- nor antiwar to a public fatigued by Korean "police actions." For, like *This Is Korea!*, the support-the-boys documentary Ford had made the year before, *What Price Glory* is a eulogy for the dog soldier, and not a defense of the politics of war.

Of the 1926 version, Walsh has written that his message was

that war is not only futile but a dirty, bungled mess. There was no glory for the men on the rifle pits and the trenches. They had to launch or repel an attack against the enemy because their generals and congress said it was their duty.[13]

Ford, whose war experience was intimate, intensifies this message. But instead of belittling the soldiers for their helplessness, he stands back in awe at their persistence. Whether, as Flagg wonders, there is a kind of religion to the profession of arms that a soldier can't shake loose from, or whether it is merely that the drums, the bugles, and the marching columns offer a more rational order than the farcical hysteria of life behind the lines, Ford finds a kind of nobility in these men. Their "glory," their "truth" that "goes marching on"—cited in the opening tableaux—is more universal than the heroism of military duty.

Flagg's type of soldier is not a normal human. He and Quirt bitch incessantly, go nearly insane with paranoia at the front, but they have no other life. "I almost got married . . . 25 times . . . but I was saving myself. From what? From what?" For war. War, Flagg wails, "was alright when you had 30 or 40 men in the hills who knew their jobs, but now there are so many little boys, little boys who have no business being here at all." Yet war's infection is contagious. The wounded boy who shrieks, "What price glory now, Captain Flagg?" hobbles out the door with his gun a few minutes later.

Actually, what he walks into is a theatrical mist lit bright red, with a hymn on the soundtrack, a more intense version of the artificiality of the gold wheat field and its bright white clouds against pink skies, or the blue-tinted night scenes. And this artificiality continues into the hysteria of the acting. In the midst of this surreal hell, there is a moment of happiness when Flagg and Quirt capture a German colonel. Now they can go home. The comedy Ford introduces here (Keaton's salute joke) aims to mirror their mood. But like much of the picture's comedy—and like the love song (substituting for Walsh's chewing-gum scene) that Marisa Pavan sings to Robert Wagner—it may strike us as a bit excessive and misplaced. (When Ford fails, at least he does not fail timidly.) In *What Price Glory* both comedy and melodrama are contrasting species of the same hysteria, and serve to equate Ford's odd style with his theme: that war is an extension of reality into farce, and also into lunacy, and yet seems, deceptively, more purposeful and rational than the ambiguous games of peacetime. This is portrayed in the poker game, when Flagg's hysteria bursts even *his* ample bounds. These soldiers grasp, without option, for the only *raison d'être* their lives possess: marching on. "We don't know where we're going—nobody knows."

The parade as a substitute for reason is, like duty earlier, an important metaphor in most of Ford's postwar pictures (the journey of the Mormons in *Wagon Master*, the dragging home of Maureen O'Hara in *The Quiet Man*, the parades in *The Long Gray Line*, the search in *The Searchers*). Life is a constant passage without a map, and with only immediate purposes; the seduction of the moment gives life its vitality. Since the opposition between the precariousness of freedom and self-responsibility and the surety of order and prescribed duty is strongest in the military, it is hardly surprising that Ford almost always chooses disciplined social organisms for his subjects. But the sense of duty that sustains his individuals also commonly leads them astray into aberrations or death. Racism becomes a function of society, like war. If the army exists for war, Ford's pictures also show us that war exists for the army.

Although all Ford's movies of the early fifties are eccentric, *What Price Glory* is the weirdest of the lot. Perhaps it is too much of a good—or horrific—thing. The concentration on the frightening process by which individuals coalesce into a fighting organism deprives the picture of deep peaks and valleys of contour. Despite the contrasts between love and war (prefiguring in their extremity the films of Ford's transitional period), the modal variation is insufficient to relieve a certain erosion in interest. And unlike most Fords, the last act is the weakest of the three.

Both Flagg and Quirt are hollow heroes for Ford. Since neither of them has any life beyond the histrionic, Ford is forced to develop Lewisohn, a weak minor character, in compensation. But it does not work. Curiously, Ford never spends time mourning the dead; he focuses intensely on the living, and the scene between Flagg and Nicole, about Lewisohn's death, is strangely flat.

What Price Glory is the *volte face* of *When Willie Comes Marching Home*, and it works best when closest to comedy. Act I has a gag nearly every ten seconds, some broad, most subtle sleight of hand. James Cagney and Dan Dailey slouch throughout the picture and deliver their intensity from the neck up. This reinforces the spring-wound tautness of Ford's farce, and of course adds to the impression that *What Price Glory* relaxes too seldom.

Ford had wanted John Wayne in the part of Flagg (Wayne had played the role in Ford's 1949 stage production of the play—see Filmography) and his mood was not improved when Henry and Phoebe Ephron, the scenarists, took one of his off-handed barbs to heart and walked off the set in a huff, mistakenly convinced he was anti-Jewish. Unable to work with any of his usual scriptwrights, Ford largely ignored the Ephron text.

This Is Korea! **(1951).** No genre of film arouses such controversy as poetic documentary. Distortion of fact, fabrication, omission and commission, prejudicing viewpoint, blatant chauvinism, all supposedly anathema to documentary, are in fact the modus operandi of *Potemkin, Listen to Britain, Triumph of the Will* (and, perhaps less consciously, TV news). Distance (aesthetic and geopolitical) may, for some viewers, excuse Eisenstein, Jennings, or Riefenstahl (and myopia disguises the news). But with America's own John Ford, so much do his films seem personal statements and so prevalent is the tendency to confuse Ford's intentions with his characters' (as in misreadings of *Fort Apache*), that distance contracts to confrontation, when his mythicizing treatment of history (through aestheticized images and idiomatic dialogue) deals not with storybook past but with newsreel now, as in *This Is Korea!*

That picture's failure in the fifties to earn its cost (financed by Republic, not the republic) was surely due less to politics than to awkward length and thoroughly depressing mood. But it suffers irrelevantly when those determined to see it as propaganda point out (correctly) its scarce success explaining an unpopular war or engaging homefront solidarity with the boys over there. For closer inspection reveals, superficial evidence to the contrary, that anything so practical as propaganda was merely Ford's excuse, not his purpose, for a project initiated wholly by himself: to document a moment, an attitude, that even today seems shrouded in poetry.

Thus he is not concerned with detailing strategy, movements, dates, or statistics; merely the soldiers' worm's-eye view. Nor for Ford the journalist's heady assumption to report truth, or both sides, of a war; more relevant to capture the spirit of his own side (distinct, at least). For Ford the consequential mythology of the Korean War lay not in judicious debate over its wisdom, but in our dominant ideology, as represented in the attitudes of those defending the Pax Americana.

It was "Christmas in the year of grace, 1950," and marines were giving bubble gum to kids and dying for them thinking of home; they were retreating in desolate cold and tending myriad war machines and killing people, and all this was for God, mother, and orphaned children, for Christmas and the flag and things that make life worthwhile. Still, they wondered why they were there; something seemed wrong. It was a job to be done, duty, and there were the kids, but, god, it was awful. There are glimpses of heroes: MacArthur in silhouette, Chesty Puller growling ("Put some more fire down on those people! Thank ya!"); but mostly there is marching, drudgery, and, above all, machines: again and again Ford cuts away to name weapons. The enemy in person is almost never encountered; but others keep returning dead or maimed. * We go on, leaving cemeteries behind, one hill after another, endlessly, until space and time merge into dreary sameness and it no longer matters whether we are "advancing" north or south or whether it is now or then.

This is the attitude Ford shows, and the movie is more distanced, less folksy, and not at all optimistic, compared with *The Battle of Midway*, and the soldiers never come disarmingly alive as they did there. That was Ford's war, not this. But this was Korea, this was the cold war. Ford arrived January 1, 1951, two months after a million Chinese hurtled across the border pushing UN forces into desperate retreat midst snow and ice; a month or so later our counterattack began. Characteristically, Ford had found the moment of defeat. No past film of his, not *The Informer* and not *The Long Voyage Home*, has such long-sustained sensuousness: somber, sober, empty. But bleakness is not conveyed through sacrificing aesthetic brilliance; instead of desaturating color, he found a yellow-green-blue option to create mood. Pale greenish fields fade into yellowish hills blending into bluish skies; wintry landscapes, otherwise pretty, are framed behind gnarled trees. Only when orphans jump for bubble gum do bright reds and other gay colors appear. But there is a cut-away to a deep-hued hospital ship, and deep tones paint a scene in Tokyo as command officers reenact historic moments with stiff superconsciousness (recalling the independence proclamation in *The Plough and the Stars*). Meanwhile, retreat and weather worsen, and white skies haze everything; marines, unlike the 7th Cavalry, are not etched against the sky but blended in *sfumato* to the earth. Carrier planes take off into stark skies, with motor and water sounds replacing music. Through the night the *Missouri*'s cannon** flash and thunder (as in *The Wings of Eagles*).

* Ford once lamented not being able to show the Chinese attacking at night; but the enemy's absence has Sophoclean eloquence. (The Chinese are never mentioned in the film.)

** The scene of the battleship firing all its sixteen-footers simultaneously—referred to by several biographers—is not in the movie.

Quickening montage and crackling fire-wind climax long seasons in hell as marines plunge into maelstroms of flame and acrid smoke ("For this is Korea, chums. This is Korea. And we go in"). The camera watches from doorways, anticipating Ethan's descent into hell in *The Searchers;* no wonder Ford's next movie, *The Quiet Man,* is so Edenesque.

Outside any context but this, the effect of a small boy's wry grin as Korean nuns accept him into an orphanage might be bathetic ("You'll be alright now!" tenderly). Elsewhere we see an endless road of refugees ("Now look at this, and look at it, and look at it!"). Korean faces stare frequently at the camera (at us), blankly or inquisitively, whilst GI faces tend to ignore us. It is the familiar Fordian theme of privacy invaded—usually by the hero, now by us.

The movie concludes quietly, in perhaps the most refulgently haunting montage of Ford's career. There is no glorification here; but in this infinite purgatory, what magnificence! what weary, Iliadic persistence and sacrifice to undergo, so that somewhere way around the world in some semi-stone-age nation, little kids can have bubble gum. Such an effort is inseparable from the preppy cold-war jargon of the narration, which makes us wince, yes, but which Ford was so right to use. For this is a definitive memento of the uncertain hope that America could make things all right in the world.

The Quiet Man (1952). Like so many other Ford heroes, Sean Thornton enters this movie by arriving on a vehicle (a train), a touch personal to Ford that confirms the intimacy suggested by the credit sequence's warm tones, dark waters, and cello motifs. Sean arrives in Innisfree from Pittsburgh and has his buggy stop on a little stone bridge near a small cottage, and he hears in his mind his dead mother's voice:

— Don't you remember it, Seannie, and how it was?
The road led up past the chapel and it wind and it wound.
And there is the field where Dan Tobin's bullock chased you.
It was a lovely little house, Seanin,
and the roses,
well, your father used to tease me about them,
but he was that fond of them too.

Quips the coachman, "Ah, that's nothin' but a wee humble cottage." But comes the reply, "I'm Sean Thornton and I was born in that little cottage. I'm home and home I'm going to stay." *The Quiet Man* will be the reverse of *How Green Was My Valley.*

Ford liked to say he was born *Sean;** his parents came from this part of Ireland and he had made trips there as a boy. "I shot it on my native heath," he said; "the actors were old family friends."[14] Indeed, they were more than

---

*He had Irish cousins named Thornton, and dubbed Jack McGowan's runty character "Feeney."

that: *The Quiet Man* so abounds in family ties that its communal "feel" arises naturally. Besides Ford's brother Francis and son-in-law Ken Curtis in the cast, daughter Barbara and son Patrick participated in the production. Barry Fitzgerald and Arthur Shields were brothers in real life (and old friends of many of the picture's Abbey Theatre players), Bond and Wayne had gone to school together, and four of Wayne's children (Ford's godchildren) sit at the race with Maureen O'Hara, whose brother is Charles Fitzsimmons. Other old acquaintances included Merian C. Cooper, Archie Stout, Mae Marsh, Harry Tenbrook, and Victor McLaglen, whose son Andrew was assistant director.

Ford had wanted to make *The Quiet Man* for many years and had almost done so back in 1937 in association with a co-op called Renowned Artists Company. And then had come the financial problems of Argosy Pictures. "Remember," Ford told Lindsay Anderson, "that with all these pictures [the Argosy westerns] I wasn't just working to pay off on *The Fugitive*, but to make enough for *The Quiet Man* as well. Of course, it'll probably lose the lot; but that's the way it always goes."[15]

But when Ford got to Ireland in 1951 things did not go well. Lindsay Anderson, who interviewed him just after location shooting in Cong, reports Ford's remarks:

> Injuries inherited from the war gave him, intermittently, a good deal of pain; they had put him out of action for a few days on *The Quiet Man* [when Wayne and Patrick Ford shot the race sequence], and generally made studio shooting—in the glare and oppressive atmosphere of a sound stage—a penance. "I was out in Korea before coming to Ireland—I made a documentary there called *This Is Korea*—and oddly enough I never had a twinge. But out at Cong it really got me down."[16]

No doubt the weather was the cause; it "was photographed in the rain—or Irish mist, as they call it in Ireland. That helped the picture a lot."[17] But, Ford continued,

> "The unit seemed to go soft too; they started standing about looking at the scenery. I had to start watching for points of continuity—people looking out of windows, that sort of thing, which no one else noticed. Then, of course, our technicians work a lot faster than yours. It was really too big a job for one man to tackle on his own."[18]

"I'm just going back to making Westerns," Ford concluded, and even mused about quitting films entirely: "I want to be a tugboat captain."[19]

Perhaps no Ford picture has been so popular as *The Quiet Man.** But when François Truffaut wrote of his dislike for Ford's "slap-on-the-rump"

---

*The Quiet Man was Ford's top-grossing picture to date. It won Oscars for direction and photography, and was nominated in six other categories: best picture, supporting actor

style of comedy, he summed up both a prevalent critical antagonism and a popular enthusiasm. Yet both attitudes miss the forest for the trees. According to Ford,

> The customs shown in *The Quiet Man* are true and prevail in Connemara, which is the poorest county in Ireland and the only one Cromwell never conquered.[20]

Indeed, the picture's commercialism and intoxicating Technicolor tend to obscure its documentary and Brechtian aspects. Ford moves rapidly through an analysis of Innisfree society. We go from train station to countryside to town to church to pub, meeting trainmen, coachmen, priests, aristocrats, squires, the IRA, drinkers, field hands, Anglican clergy. But again, the many characters provide such atmospheric vignettes (and their theatrics and comedy are so engaging and funny) that the community's sociologic complexity—despite the picture's obsession with public custom—is not readily apparent. Yet Connemara is a Third-world culture, fundamentally Gaelic-Irish, but with the Roman Church and England superimposed upon the palimpsest.*

Well may Widow Tillane maintain that "Innisfree is very far from being heaven." She will never be believed. Thick though it be with stultifying formalities, to Sean (and to us, after World War II), this land of simplicity and community, where horses and bicycles are the means of transport and life is close to the soil, seems Shangri-La, without Shangri-La's asexual intellectualism. Yet Ford's story should be evident enough: a peaceful American returns to his native village, but can only find peace there after bullying his wife and brawling with her brother; until then he will feel himself an outsider, confused in his manhood, a gentleman surrounded by peasants and clergy.

The Reverend Peter Lonergan is among the more interesting characters. "What I detest more than anything are the Irish priests," Ford told Tavernier, adding, "The parish priest [of Innisfree] has more money than the Lord Mayor of Dublin."[21] And in opposition to the amiable tones of Father Lonergan's narrating voice, Ford in pictures, without doing anything overt enough to offend the Legion of Decency, depicts Lonergan in his first meeting with Thornton as repressed, twisted, and sanctimonious. I cannot reproduce the grotesque shadow his hat casts over his face, nor the lurid sound of his voice:

(McLaglen), screenplay (Nugent), art direction (Frank Hotaling), set decoration (John McCarthy, Jr., and Charles Thompson), sound recording. The Screen Directors Guild gave its crown to Ford, and the Screen Writers Guild its to Nugent, the National Board of Review and Look Magazine chose it best film, and it was one of three runners-up at Venice.

*Ford said: "This is a very sexy story, you know. I like good lusty sex but I object to dirty innuendoes. . . . I was born in Cape Elizabeth, Maine, but I went to school in Ireland for a while and was brought up to speak both English and Gaelic. Every Irishman is an actor. The Irish and the colored people are the most natural actors in the world."

> Lonergan: Ah yes. I knew your people, Sean. Your grandfather. He died in Australia. In a penal colony. And your father. He was a good man too. Bad accident that. And your mother.
> Sean: She's dead. America when I was twelve.
> Lonergan: [Piously:] I'll remember her in the mass tomorrow, Sean. [Sternly:] You'll be there. Seven o'clock.
> Sean: [With Yankee ingenuousness:] Sure I will.

And come next morning Sean is there in church. And Ford's floor-level shot down the nave is the strongest image in the film, and indicates the curious power of an institution that has integrated itself with local custom: Mary Kate will use Gaelic to confess her marital difficulties, and Lonergan, with an appetite for violence beyond his calling, hypocritically performs penance by upbraiding his effeminate curate. (A similarly practical morality consists in forbidding sale of intoxicating liquors at horse races—but just during the race itself.)

Ford called *The Quiet Man* "a love story, a mature love story"[22] and "a very sexy story."[23] And as one might expect, he exploits a love story's traditional archetypal situations—skipping through fields, embracing in a cemetery during a storm—with artful novelty, but not with such novelty as to make us forget them as symbolic reminders of the repression within which the romance is enacted. The first glances occur within painterly formality (green foliage and sheep, then the scarlet-skirted redhead), ecclesiastical formality (the holy-water font), or atavistic longing (Thornton's balletic sexual clash with Mary Kate's blue blouse and red skirt at night in his cottage). When Sean comes to call he is greeted with formulaic phrases and Mary Kate (as often) is framed by a window.* Formal courtship is initiated with the whole village gazing in witness; the wedding itself is given Victorian distance as they pose for their portrait (Lonergan narrates, "So they were married—in the same little chapel I gave them their Baptism") and flash powder explodes. But the dispute over the dowry disrupts the love "process"—as indeed Sean's Yankee ways so often disrupt Gaelic custom.

In one of the few scenes in which he and Mary Kate talk reasonably, Sean is working in the yard. "Roses?!" she gasps, "Are you plantin' roses?! Fine farmer you are—not a turnip or a cabbage or a potato on the place. . . ." "Or children," says Sean. She changes the subject to getting a horse for the ploughing; Sean suggests a tractor. "A tractor!" she responds, "Nasty, smelly things, an' besides, they're an awful price. With a horse you get other advantages. . . ." "For the roses," says Sean, handing her a buttercup.

The scene, though one of the least overt in a declamatory movie, is one of Ford's finest. The flower symbol is particularly dear to his work and conveys major ideas in more than twenty pictures: Hannah Jessop is given flowers to carry to France in *Pilgrimage;* families hold pieces of heather in *The Black Watch* as they bid farewell to sons off to war; Lana throws her bouquet in *Drums Along the Mohawk;* Lincoln puts a flower on Ann Rutledge's grave; Dr. Mudd returns home to flowers in *The Prisoner of Shark Island;* Joanne Dru brings John Wayne a plant for his wife's grave in *She Wore a Yellow Ribbon;* cadets bring flowers for old Marty Maher in *The Long Gray Line;* Minne's flowers get Spig Wead to move his toe in *The Wings of Eagles;* a single flower is carried in the slum church in *Gideon's Day;* the Irish mistake the British couple for newlyweds because of their flowers in *A Minute's Wait;* Frank Skeffington puts a fresh flower daily beneath his wife's portrait;

---

*The scene recalls Mr. Gruffydd outside Angharad's window in *How Green Was My Valley.*

Tom Doniphon gives Hallie a cactus rose in *The Man Who Shot Liberty Valance*, and half a century later she gives one to him; in *Donovan's Reef*, in one of many floral metaphors, Dr. Dedham's outcast children lay flowers on his lawn Christmas morning; in *7 Women*, Woody Strode picks flowers for Dr. Cartwright.

Sean's mother's voice spoke of the roses she used to grow in this very same yard. But Sean not only wishes to renew a tradition; in the form of the buttercup he expresses his wish to give roses to Mary Kate, roses that now express all he wishes to be and all he hopes for. Indeed, this sequence began inside the house, with a lengthy, formalized shot of their empty dining room, a large bowl of red roses (the same red as Mary Kate's skirt) prominent on the center-set table. Now she fastens Sean's buttercup to her lapel.

Earlier, red roses were thrown away by Sean when Danaher rejected his courtship. Later at the wedding, Mary Kate's bouquet is a prominent motif; then, when he brutally carries her to the bedroom and she momentarily submits to him, she embraces him with this bouquet; then, thrown upon the bed alone, she cries with it.

It is significant that Ford externalizes their conflict. The statuesque crowds that gather for each step of the battle remind us that in this society no relationship is private. And when Thornton and Danaher at last confront each other by the field oven, the village women standing veiled and separate from their men remind us that the stick both Mary Kate (by the fireside) and an older woman (coming from the train) offer Sean is no mere prop of Fordian-concocted comedy. The parade back from the station (with the "kick-on-the-rump") is not only a form of the Fordian parade, as in *What Price Glory* a substitute for reason, it is also a graphic illustration that marriage is a community function. Mary Kate wants her things about her because it is the *inside* of the house that is the woman's power base. Sean fails to grasp this, because he fails to grasp that, *external* appearances to the contrary, in Ireland the man merely reigns: it is the woman, controlling bed and board, who rules ("They'll be no dinner tonight," saith Mary Kate). Thus for today's audiences, *The Quiet Man*, like many Fords, poses the worrisome proposition that primitive sexism might not be without advantages; for liberation is often another form of compulsory conformity, one all too often deracinating the individual. In Innisfree, Sean *must* conform; and when he does, Ford hits high gear for his wonderful finale-revue of cameo portraits. There is irony, to be sure, but more profound than bitter. For is it ever possible to watch those smiling, cheering faces, shot out at you with the brazenness of Eisenstein peasants, and the moment when Mary Kate throws away Sean Thornton's stick and they join hands and run at last into their cottage and the bagpipes come in to climax, is it really possible to resist Ford's poetry?

Ford is still an expressionist, and in *The Quiet Man* emotions are not merely represented, but articulated. One notes the lovers' balletic clashes, or (an almost more typical instance) the way Mary Kate interrupts a lengthy, sedate conversation with the marriage broker (Barry Fitzgerald) to jump to her feet and race to the forescreen (the camera cuts rapidly backward to expand the frame), both camera and actress giving kinetic and spatial articulation of her reaction to Sean's words (that she come "with the clothes on her back—or without them"). Equally expressionistic is Ford's use of color in his artful, closed-formed, painterly compositions. One might argue that in *The Rising of the Moon* (1956), Ford's second made-in-Ireland film, the subtle black-and-white photos have a more "realist" air and better serve to document Ireland's countryside; but we should beware falling sophomorically into the illusion that "realist" is innately superior to (or more truthful than) "expressionist." Three-strip dye-transfer Technicolor was (like Rimsky-Korsakov's orchestration) generally used not for naturalism but for glorious artifice. The deep scarlet of the roses is one such example, the greenness of the fields another—Ford was actually accused of having painted the fields. But similar logic is a mite less successfully applicable to the scores of the two pictures. *The Rising of the Moon*'s discreet use of tenor and recorder weighs less heavily upon its (admittedly less fortified) images than does Victor Young's richly symphonic one upon *The Quiet Man*'s; a few snatches of accordion and spinet are all we get of on-screen music, alas.

In the original story, by Maurice Walsh, Sean Thornton is a featherweight whose size belies his ferocity, and no one can imagine his skill. In Ford's version no one doubts John Wayne's strength, they only think him a quaint American, perhaps a coward. Obviously Ford's "quiet" man is different from Walsh's, and it is difficult to say whether the decision to alter the character's size was for the best, although there is something to be said for Ford's eliminating a facile gimmick in favor of a subtler structure of *moral* tensions. Wayne, in any case, tended to be vulnerable rather than domineering in Ford pictures—perhaps reflecting their original relationship as a polite college boy working for a famous, patriarchal director. Wayne's Sean Thornton is closer to the shy, sensitive brother in *Salute* (1929) than to the cocky, bossy older brother who lectures him to grab what he wants and fight to keep it. This, of course, is what Sean Thornton is reluctant to do. Thus, while on one hand, it is he who upholds the tenets of liberalism against his wife's traditional sexism, on the other hand, Wayne's low-energy, suppressed, dead-rhythmed performance, especially juxtaposed with Maureen O'Hara's passion and the flamboyance of all the Irish, marks Sean Thornton as a dead man emotionally. "That was a goddam hard script," said Wayne. "For nine weeks I was just playing a straight man to those wonderful characters, and that's really hard."[24] Indeed, in his emotional repression, Sean resembles the Fonda heroes in Ford (Lincoln, Tom Joad, Wyatt Earp, the Fugitive) and is in fact a typical Ford hero trying to moderate intolerance. But this time the hero's inability to join the community derives not from his priesthood or even from the moral principles Sean espouses, but from his inabilities to accept reality (the reality of himself as one who killed and one who likes to fight, the reality of Innisfree and of Red Danaher and their traditions); the true hero does not shrink from violence, whose salutary place in life he concedes. Sean Thornton, like so many Ford characters (and particularly after World War II), has learned to forget the horrid, violent past, and to return home (thus the deep significance of the scene behind the film's title credits); but he is one of the few who actually make it home and find rebirth there, albeit ironically, as a macho male.

Francis Ford plays the next-to-last of his twenty-nine appearances in brother John's pictures: Dan Tobin, an old man with long white beard who jumps from his deathbed to see the fight. Francis's parts had progressively less dialogue as the years rolled by—he was a marvellous mime—and his last spoken word here comes toward the middle, during the wedding sequence when, echoing Danaher, he says, "Without further eloquence." It would make a better story to say he never spoke again on screen, but in fact in his large role in *The Sun Shines Bright* he does say a single word, "refreshments!" The cameo of brother Francis, incidentally, is *The Quiet Man*'s penultimate: he's jumping for joy.

The Sun Shines Bright (1953). John Ford:

> Maybe there's one that I love to look at again and again. That's *The Sun Shines Bright*. That's really my favorite. At Republic, old man [studio head Herbert] Yates didn't know what to do with it. The picture had comedy, drama, pathos, but he didn't understand it. His kind of picture had to have plenty of sex or violence. This one had neither, it was just a good picture. But Yates fooled around with it after I left the studio and almost ruined it.[25]

The Sun Shines Bright is one of two or three John Ford pictures one would like to call his finest. Yet it never had a New York first run, was dismissed by the *Times* as so many sentimental clichés, and was quickly cut from ninety to sixty-five minutes. Its failure contributed to the demise of Ford's Argosy Pictures, and even today its depictions of blacks may, wrongfully, incite indignation. Any treatment of this obscure film must try to evoke its artistic magnitude and to clarify its attitudes toward race.

It might well have been titled *Intolerance*, not alone for its theme, but for its formal complexity as well. Unlike Griffith's film, however, its structuring antinomies are simultaneously thematic and formal. And its complex subtleties are hidden beneath an air of effortless ingenuousness. For, despite four intricate story lines and twenty or so distinct characters, the movie's narrative, composed in tidy sequences with a Mozartian concision and nakedness of technique, unfolds most of the time midst dancing and parading through suites of beautiful and intriguing compositions. Rarely has a movie been so inventive—and playful—with montage.* Yet each separate shot seems a

---

*Minus titles, the film runs 88 minutes 33 seconds and has 640 shots (8.3" average). But, leaving out a 60-second shot and the slowly cut funeral (7'15", 16 shots), there are 623 shots in 80

Figure 7. *The Sun Shines Bright*

A small western Kentucky town c. 1905

ACT I. The First "Day"—Morning
1. Levy. Ashby Corwin comes home, and romances Lucy Lee Lake.
2. Courtroom. Judge Priest prevents his opponent Maydew from persecuting banjoist U. S. Grant Woodford (whose rendition of "Dixie" causes patriotic bedlam) and town madam Mallie Cramp.

ACT II. The First "Day"—Night
1. a. As he has for eighteen years—ever since Dr. Lake brought home his granddaughter Lucy Lee, whom he does not recognize—General Fairfield refuses to attend the CSA veterans meeting.
   b. Priest tells the eleven vets he will take home their portrait of the general and his wife, lest Lucy Lee see it and realize who she is (for she looks exactly like her grandmother).
   c. And Priest returns to the USA vets their "captured" flag.
2. Outside. Drunk, Ashby sees Lucy Lee, then whips Buck for gossiping about her, but Priest explains General Fairfield's son was killed in a riverboat fight over her mother.
3. The mother arrives in town, collapses on her way to Mallie's and is taken to Dr. Lake's, where, glimpsing Lucy Lee, she fulfills her dying wish.
4. Lucy Lee runs to Priest's home, spies the portrait, and realizes who she is. Then the sheriff arrives: Mendy Ramser has been raped and the bloodhounds treed U. S.

ACT III. The Second "Day"—Morning.
Jeff fetches Priest, who confronts a lynch mob outside U. S.'s cell.

ACT IV. The Second "Day"—Night
1. Mallie comes to see Priest, who promises "the Lord will provide" the dead woman a proper funeral.
2. Ashby takes Lucy Lee to the festival dance, but discreet stares chase her out, just as
3. The sheriff arrives: Mendy has identified Buck, who her father shoots, Buck flees in Lucy Lee's carriage, is shot by Brother Finney, while Ashby rescues Lucy Lee.

ACT V. The Third "Day"
1. Maydew's election-day oration is interrupted by
2. A white hearse, a carriage of whores, and Priest. Eventually, a hundred townsmen join him.
3. At the blacks' church, General Fairfield joins Lucy Lee, and Priest recites the parable of the woman taken in adultery.
4. Maydew is confident, but the lynch mob tie the vote for Priest, and he votes for himself.
5. That night: the whites parade past Priest's door, then the blacks come serenade him.

---

minutes, for a 7.7" average. Republic's prerelease excisions—including a scene in which Priest chats to portraits of the dead—are presumably lost for all time (?).

complete little movie in itself—like Lumière's one-shot films. And each shot *tells*: we are not merely *shown* a storyland, but are led, *by means of* Ford's narrative and cinematic textures, into an analysis of the class structures of Fairfield, Kentucky, 1905, its people, their manners and civilization, and, finally, into their collective consciousness.

The small world of Fairfield is fraught with divisions: the Southern faction, holding firmly to the Old South's traditions and the CSA's glories; the Northern faction, sometimes miming progress in carpetbagger terms and maintaining GAR traditions; the Negro population, not far enlightened out of slavery's traditions and rigidly segregated; the ignorant, tough farmers from the Tornado District; the prostitutes, the military-school cadets, the temperance women. There are the aristocrats, the businessmen, the politicians, the townsfolk, the farmers and the subproletariat, the blacks. Within each of these groups, ingenuous adherence to tradition sets the stage for intolerant persecution not only between factions but even within families. Various aspects of intolerance are illustrated in the four story lines (in two of which it is the appearance of the steamboat—Fairfield's link with the outer world—that precipitates crisis): (1) Priest's reelection campaign against Republican Maydew—who employs labels to stigmatize people and discredit tolerant attitudes; (2) Ashby Corwin's return to Fairfield and romance with Lucy Lee—the bitter profligate humanized by the outcast orphan; (3) U. S. Woodford's near lynching for rape—the true culprit incites racist hatred but is thwarted by Priest and exposed; (4) The mystery of Lucy Lee's parentage, revealed when her mother, a whore, returns to Fairfield to die—moral intolerance dividing families and persecuting an innocent child. *

Fairfield's whites are depicted as militarist and rambunctious—by means of uniforms and deportment, but chiefly by music: when they dance they also march; in the funeral procession they march; even standing in place they march. Only thrice do they produce their own music: march

---

*The picture claims to derive from three of Irvin S. Cobb's many Judge Priest stories. In Cobb's "The Sun Shines Bright," Dr. Lake tells how young lawyer Priest faced down with a gun some whites wanting to "coon" young Pleasant Woolfolk. Later, Priest is about to lose his first election, when Pleasant brings all his people to vote. The only element used in the movie is that after the election the blacks began to sing "Old Kentucky Home" and 1,500 whites joined in around Priest in the street.

"The Mob from Massac" is the movie's Tornado gang, but the Jim they try to lynch is unrelated and unknown to anyone. Priest faces down the mob as in the movie, but with fewer words. The true culprit, another black, dies confessing and the eighty-four Massac men vote for Priest—who does not need his own vote.

In "The Lord Provides," Mallie Cramp visits a half dozen churches by streetcar before coming to Priest. The dead woman has no connection to anyone. The funeral procession resembles the movie's except that Lake and the equivalent of Amora have been carefully alerted. The Lord provides the other mourners. In Priest's short sermon, he decides *not* to tell the adultery parable and instead quotes the verse, "Suffer little children. . . . " Ashby Corwin, "a nobody, financial or otherwise," says a prayer. No election is at stake. Neither Lucy Lee nor the general is referred to in these stories, nor Buck or U. S. Woodford.

tunes, at the GAR meeting ("Marching Through Georgia"), Maydew's brassy parade ("Hail, Hail . . ."), Priest's brassy victory parade ("Dixie"). And their funeral procession has only mechanical sounds—until it reaches the blacks.

For it is given to the blacks to supply music for the whites. Jeff plays harmonica on Priest's porch (steps!) and at the CSA meeting; U.S. plays "Dixie" in court; the blacks sing black hymns at the funeral, play for the steamboat's arrival, play for the whitefolk's dance, and sing "Old Kentucky Home" at the end.

The abiding peacefulness of the blacks contrasts to white militancy, politics, lynch mobs, class strife, haughty mien, and endless parading. None of the four black principals is discontent. Uncle Zach has a coach business. Uncle Pleas carried his master's body back from Chickamauga and now looks after drunken Ashby. His nephew hangs around the levee strumming banjo. And then there is Jeff Poindexter, played by an aged Stepin Fetchit with the squeaky voice, bent head, and bumbling gestures of the comic darkie. But unlike earlier Fetchit characters, this one is not *quite* the traditional Fordian fool who, in *The Black Watch*, *Salute*, or *The Searchers*, satirically reflects establishment values. Even in Fairfield, Jeff, like Priest, seems a type who has survived beyond his era, only to find his fashion obsolete. None of the other blacks share his "comic" traits. Yet Jeff is not funny in what he says or does, and he continually earns our respect. Nor do the whites find him silly, although by habit they condescend toward all blacks. Even Judge Priest addresses the noble, gray-haired Uncle Pleas as "boy." And the mark of oppression exists in every black action, in the ununderlined contrast between their part of town and the whites' part, in the attitude (or nonattitude) of whites toward them, in their own acquiescence to their state. In the peaceful coexistence of a segregated society the mechanics of racism are most apparent. But they are less apparent when an audience, due to its own racism, sees Stepin Fetchit's character as merely a comic darkie and misses the man.

As always, it is the Fordian hero who mediates community tensions, searching for a middle way between chaos and repression—a way of tolerance. He is celibate, lonely, willing to resort to violence; he reunites a family, then walks away at the end. And Judge Priest, possessed by long experience of higher wisdom, always acts judiciously, if paternalistically. Unlike impractical reformers, like Governor DeLaage, Mr. Gruffydd, or Mary Stuart, whose immoderate idealism leads to failure, Priest knows when to accept reality. We see him often recoil smilingly from a shock: e.g., Pleas's war recollections, Lucy Lee's discovery of the portrait, the vote tally showing him behind by sixty-two and particularly after Brother Finney shoots Buck when the camera tracks rapidly up to a close-up of stunned Priest (a rare technique for Ford), who then decides, melancholically: "Good shootin'! Saves the expense of a trial."

Fairfield needs Priest's paternalism. It is no lovely, peaceful haven, but a town torn by class feuds, racism, violence, lust, and hypocritical social standards. Political opposition, the GAR, is led less by the noble banker, Colonel Jody Habersham, than by the Nixon-like prosecutor, Horace K. Maydew. Forever orating, or shouting for "Order!", Maydew proclaims:

> It is a great and glorious day for Kentucky, when no longer, no longer, can an empty sleeve or a gimpy knee serve as a blanket to smother the progress of the twentieth century . . . [Cheers]

To gain political capital, Maydew persecutes people—Mallie Cramp, Brother Finney, U.S.—as though they personified vice, moonshine, and indolence. His haughty Northern racial intolerance contrasts with Priest's tolerant racism. But Priest labors quietly, tolerating some disorder, and respecting individuals. Now, when he walks into the town hall to vote for himself and win the election, he walks toward a picture of George Washington. But there are strong intimations that the Republicans, younger and more numerous, will win next time. Thus it seems the last victory for the Confederacy, the Last Hurrah for an old order (and for America?), the twilight before the Maydews take over. The picture ends at night.

Sound and Sight. Sound's role is prominent. More than half the movie has music, all but five minutes from on-screen sources (far more than most musicals). Effects include things as minor and foxy as crickets outside Priest's house or something like the footsteps we suddenly *hear* over reaction shots of Priest and friends *before* we *see* Mallie Cramp at the gate. Ford repeats this scheme often: ten reaction shots of terrified blacks and a grinding turbulent score with added barks, guns, and female screams, before we see the lynch mob; hearse sounds and Maydew's reaction before the procession; in the "Dixie" number, Bagby in his smithy reacts to the bugle before we see Priest blowing it—and Ford builds to the climax of this joke by having Lake, Bagby, and Felsburg burst consecutively into the courtroom and stare, before reverse-cutting to the scene of mayhem. In 1935 in *The Informer* we knew what was going on when we heard tapping, because we had previously been introduced to the blind man and his cane; but in 1953 we do not know to what the sounds refer. Reaction shots before the fact are used elsewhere in postwar Ford (and in *How Green Was My Valley*); he generally gives temporal precedence to emotional form over facts, to effects over causes, for his cinema is largely one of reactions. This allows audience thought to flow from reflection rather than articulation. For example, by the time we finally *see* the lynch mob and come to know the cause of commotion, some of the rawer emotion has been drained, and the "thought" of the scene clarifies: i.e., the horror of violence.

Sound is used impressionistically while Ashby walks Lucy Lee to school (see Figure 7:I.1), and this emphasis on the subtle and close-at-hand sounds of a rural lane enhances by contrast the sudden cut from the close tracking to the open-space long shot of the schoolhouse, and the effect is further under-lined by the flock of small black children who run gaily diagonally down-frame toward Lucy Lee like a fan unfolding. Elsewhere, during the funeral procession, we hear almost nothing for six long minutes but hearse wheels, hooves, and the remarkable, steadily augmenting volume of human feet as the procession grows. Elsewhere, some marvelous rag piano accompanies the mother's walk to the whorehouse (as in *Stagecoach*). Her arrival in town is presaged by an off-camera steamboat whistle during the preceding scene between Ashby and Priest, just after the latter says, "You can't suppress truth" (II.2), and thus the whistle seems a sort of divine intervention.

Providence seems also represented through the tune "Genevieve," which (like the strum tune in *Donovan's Reef* and the jungle sounds in *Mogambo*) seems also to conspire that truth come to light. "Genevieve" occurs six times:

1. Soundtrack, Lucy Lee in buggy outside Ashby's (II.2).
2. Soundtrack, her mother cries for her (II.3).
3. Jeff's harmonica, Dr. Lake tells Priest "somebody" has come back to town (i.e., the mother) (II.4).
4. Soundtrack, Priest goes to look at portrait of Lucy Lee's grandmother (II.4).
5. Soundtrack, same sequence, just after Lucy Lee recognizes grand-mother.
6. Banjo band, when she dances with Ashby (IV.2).

"Genevieve," then, seems associated with mothering, or, perhaps more pre-cisely, with the prodigious consequence of a child wrongfully separated from its parents—one of Ford's major themes, for nothing more acutely manifests intolerance. It is fitting that when in the last instance Lucy Lee rushes out of the ballroom, "Genevieve" seems to be chasing her. Her at-tendance at the dance (so wrongfully counseled by Priest and his cronies) is an attempt to overcome shame, to brave public gossip, in short, to refuse to recognize that the whore who has just died was her mother. Dancing the day her mother dies! Lucy Lee forfeits her innocence, applauds heinous hypocrisy, and will have much to expiate; fortunately for her, her guilt will have the consolation of communal contrition.

Angles. Judge Priest may be the "star" of the picture, but he never quite dominates his scenes. An exemplary sequence occurs in his courtroom dialogue with Uncle Pleas:

Priest: Uncle Pleas Woodford . . . ! Are *you* the boy that brought Bainbridge Corwin's body back from Chickamauga?
Pleas: Yessir, judge. You remember. I brought him all the way back in these two arms. [*Wistfully*:] Don't you remember?
Priest: [*Grave nostalgia, nodding*:] Yes. I do.

Pleas: [*Extreme melancholy:*] O what a time that was.
Priest: [*Suddenly cheerful:*] Yeah! Ha ha!

As Ford crosscuts between them, one is left free to view each character both within and without the other's prejudicial view. We are not permitted to "identify" with Priest; his subjectivity does not dominate the scene: Ford remains narrator.

But at certain brutal confrontations, Ford employs a character's point of view. The recognition scene (II.4) warrants extended analysis:

Lucy Lee rushes into Priest's hallway. The camera stares down-hall; a doorway left leads into the room with the portrait of General Fairfield and his wife. (If Lucy Lee, who resembles her grandmother, sees it, she will know who she is.) Priest comes out this door, into the shot of the hall. A lamp inside the room and off-camera lights the *left* side of the frame (Priest) but puts most of the right (Lucy Lee) in shadow:

Lucy Lee: Uncle Billy! Uncle Billy . . .! I had to see you, Judge. I must know what's going on. Who am I? I know Dr. Lake loved me like a daughter, but tell me, Judge, who am I?
Priest: Why, you're his adopted daughter, honey.
Lucy Lee: That's not enough anymore, Uncle Billy.
Priest: You're mine, too. You belong to every one of us, every man jack that ever rode for Gen . . .

The camera position cuts to one *inside* the room, in fact, from the point of view of the portrait! It now looks out into the hall doorway, and Lucy Lee has changed position in the frame. Now she is on the *left* and he is on the *right*! Priest, startled, stops talking when he sees her see the portrait. The cut across the axis* exemplifies the drama of the event, and simultaneously Lucy Lee moves her face forward out of the shadow and into the light. Ford crosscuts to the portrait briefly from her perspective, then comes back to the previous shot. She now goes into the room, up to the portrait, and Victor Young's music illustrates her "awakening":

1. /MS, side: Lucy Lee approaches portrait on left.

2. /MCU: Priest steps forward in concern; his face enters light and moves into CU.

---

*For sake of smoothness, characters ordinarily maintain identical relative position during shifts of camera position between shots. If their positions are exchanged (e.g., Lucy to Priest's right in one shot, to his left in the next), the transition is rough and confuses space—and is termed "cutting across the axis." Another example: showing a motion (a car moving) first from its left, then from its right, so that on screens it appears to reverse direction.

3. /CU, 180°: Lucy Lee, staring.

4. XCU, matching, 180°: her grandmother's identical face in portrait.

5. X(= 3)CU: Lucy Lee.

6. /(= 2)CU: Priest wipes perspiring brow.

7. /(= 1)MS, side: Lucy Lee moves a step closer to portrait, and lifts drape, thus revealing General Fairfield.

8. /(= 6)CU: Priest, smiles now (an instance of his coming to terms with reality).

9. /(= 7)MS, side: Lucy Lee leaves portrait, and

10. /(= 2)MCU: kisses Priest: "Thank you, Uncle Billy. Now I know who I am."

The music follows the melodrama step by step, building up to a Straussian *Verklärung* during the 180-degree crosscut close-ups, then a cello moves gently into "Genevieve," consolingly. This is Ford's unabashed operatic manner. The crosscuts, however, are severe, both in closeness and angle, and are previously used by Ford only during the menacing confrontations in *My Darling Clementine* and *Wagon Master*. Here Lucy Lee confronts truth, herself: significantly, and this is the point of the 180-degrees, *she* not only looks at the portrait, the portrait looks at her. The portrait, like that of Manulani in *Donovan's Reef*, thus plays a providential role, along with "Genevieve" and the mother's return. The portrait's sudden appearance is particularly unexplained, but this only emphasizes its *deus ex machina*, or providential, intervention.

The clarity of this sequence—each shot *tells*, and is perfectly composed and lit, so that each shot is a miniature drama in itself—the clarity is deceptive. Ford so subordinates plot explanation to the individual moment, and the nature of Lucy Lee's mystery unfolds in such slow stages, a line here, another there, and with such lack of emphasis, that many have found the plot line baffling on first viewing. This is rather typical of Ford, who hated plot exposition; *The Sun Shines Bright* demands highly active attention. But Ford seems to be mocking himself at the CSA meeting, when, as the veterans deliberate mysteriously about what to do with the portrait, Ford cut to a little moment between Brother Finney and Mink in the back. Mink looks quizzically at Finney, who shrugs a pantomime equivalent of, "I haven't the faintest idea, either, of what they're talking about."

Depth of Field. Ford regularly divides his compositions into three distinct planes of depth. Action commonly occurs in mid-field. Both lighting and placement of objects and people contribute to the impression of depth. Ford's compositional style becomes a play upon internal angles. The screen, the camera's focal plane, may be regarded as the stable side of a box, whose rear wall, almost never parallel to the screen-wall, forms an oblique angle to the screen, thus accentuating depth of field and interior angles. Characters are placed within this box in lines or in a bent line forming an angle of its own; such angles, in relation to the screen-plane, form triangles and pyramids. Ford's pictures make us look *in*—into these angles and pyramids—but because they do so, they also make us continuously jump out, to view the screen as a whole.

At the CSA meeting (II.1), frame-top and frame-bottom are darkened; the gray-bright middle draws us into the depth of field. As Priest enters the room, the camera, distantly gazing over rows of empty wooden chairs, pans 40 degrees with him across the hall, then reverse-pans left, then right again, as flags are fetched. The deep-focus panning accentuates the empty chairs. At this long take's end, the camera stares down a striking alley (formed by wall, chairs, and men in gray, and punctuated by objects, such as a cannon, in the darkened foreground); then, at the moment of salute, Ford cuts deep into this alley, into a tenser alley of men and flags. Silver-gray textures reflect the poetry's image: "Dashed with honorable scars, lo in glory's lap they lie. Though they fell, they fell like stars, streaming splendor through the sky." Space informs emotion.

Nowhere is Ford's montaged choreography of motion in deep space better achieved than at the Grand Lemonade and Strawberry Festival, the finest of his dance sequences and an exemplary definition of Fordian cinema. Tonal values again play counterpoint to kinetic and musical ones: the Negro banjo band alternate black suit, white suit; the twenty cadets wear gray coats and white trousers, their partners light-shaded long dresses. Spectators line all four walls; march and dance take place *within* this square of townspeople, within the community. Additional "boxiness" (the camera, with floor and ceiling, views five box-sides and itself forms the sixth) amplifies kinesis within each shot composition and across seams of montage. A dazzling suite of shots during the Grand March ends with a frontal shot overlooking five rows, eight abreast, stiff at attention. With a banjo tattoo, Ford cuts snappily closer, accentuating militarist qualities and reinforcing the music change (to "Golden Slippers").* With the downbeat, the dancers clack their heels and in a rapid flowing wave from rear rank to front, jump into the dance with leaping gusto—O how the girls love it!

Similarly: when Ashby and Lucy Lee make their entrance in a beautifully conceived pan and track from the rear of the auditorium up to Amora Ratchitt (who tells her, as she has told every girl tonight, "Why Lucy Lee! You're the prettiest girl at the party!" and Mae Marsh adds a long shrieking, "Yeeessss!"), Ford doesn't wait for laughter. The banjo band has just started "Genevieve," sprightly. Lucy Lee, in the midst of her curtsy, rises in the same movement and joins with Ashby to swirl into the melee. Space and motion inform emotion.

The Gift to be Simple. A Ford character may be a simpleton, or a person who never amounted to much, or someone we don't like; but he claims our attention by sensitivity and activity. Emotions are implanted into his every gesture and posture. When Lucy Lee and her father come out of their house (I.1.ii), it is one instance among hundreds of a stylized portrait Ford wishes to eternalize. It is not simply the occurrence that may attract us, it is Ford's narrative presence, as though he were telling us, "Lucy Lee and Dr. Lake walked out into the street . . ." and we were feeling in his voice the meanings and memories of the event. As with dramatic situations, so with the characters themselves: elemental generic structures provide palpable qualities that are then vivified by invention. Each "point" is made separately, but in retrospect the number of points is vast. Several personages illustrate this.

Ford's brother Francis appears in the role of Brother Finney (the name is close enough to their family name, Feeney). It was his twenty-ninth appearance for John, his last on film (he died September 6, 1953), and the final development of his latter-day screen persona, a tattered coonskin remnant of former glory. He could spit across a room and make the spittoon ring. He was usually drunk, he was always good-natured and as cooperative as a leaf in a breeze, and more and more he came to be a character of silent pantomime (as befits a silent screen star). Jeff, at the CSA meeting, recognizes Finney's sidekick Mink and asks Priest if he remembers the little boy at Shiloh: Finney nods his head and shakes, and beats his hands as though holding drumsticks while imitating a drum roll, "*Bssss-bzzzz.*" Otherwise

---

*Ford uses similar techniques to punctuate voice entry into "The Marine Hymn" over the color brigade in *The Battle of Midway.*

he speaks only a single word, the last of his career: "Refreshments!" He personified a variety of raw instinct, the Fordian idyllic human being, irresponsible and innocent in a nature supremely simple. It is he who shoots Buck Ramsey in the back, and the exchange of shots afterward between a horrified Priest and a gleefully proud Finney says much about the differing natures of the two. Apparently only "Brother Feeney" can kill and retain his innocence, and Priest's decision to accept it for the best adds to the suggestion that Finney acts for God and Brother John. Indeed, Finney and Mink are the only whites who, like the blacks, resist Fairfield's white society. Finney even brings a jug to the temperance ladies' dance, and later we see him drinking happily beneath a campaign sign, "Maydew will drive out the Moonshiners"!

Two others contain Finney's simplicity but contrast markedly. Ashby Corwin's (John Russell*) woodenness is the soul of his character and reflects his discomfort when obliged to step out of the narrow confines of his cliché nature. He (*Ash*-be) has the aristocratic gesture-and-do of the dead Confederacy without its depth of personality; glory is denied him because his proper epoch died before his birth. General Fairfield, on the other hand, is a magnificent relic, a recluse who writes his memoirs in full-length smoking jacket in a study crowded with mementos half a century old. When "Trumpeter" Priest

*Russell (1921–) played Tytyl in *The Blue Bird* (1940), *Rio Bravo* (1959), etc.

comes to call, he enters like a soldier, marches to the desk, and becomes a boy. It is the most stylized sequence of an extremely stylized movie, and James Kirkwood's * posture and voicing yield not an inch to legend, myth, or humanity. When last we see him he stands watching Priest's "Dixie" parade like a tin soldier, straight and proud, his drawn sabre held arm's length at his side. In a single shot Ford evokes the flower, grace, and lustrous glory of vanished aristocracy. And the parade is passing by.

Procession. The funeral procession is a tour de force of angles. Itself a line, it traverses Ford's box in nearly every possible direction. Twice Ford cuts across the axis and the procession, without disequilibrium, changes direction across the screen: first, at shot 22, when GAR Habersham takes his place beside Priest— the *first* person to join the tiny procession of Priest, the white hearse, and the prostitutes. By the second cut across axis, shot 48, the procession has become a vector (a line in motion, a force) to which a good part of the town has fastened, like an arrow gathering feathers. Now, as Lucy Lee, acknowledging her mother and sin, joins the procession, its direction again changes across the screen.

Equally, the procession is a culmination of Ford's vignette methods. The whole of *The Sun Shines Bright* resembles a riverboat melodrama, in which each scene is a skit, every shot a turn, and every character a cameo. And the procession is a procession of cameos—Priest, the prostitutes, Bagby, Felsburg, Habersham, Amora Ratchett, Mae Marsh, the jeering women with parasols, ** a farmer, Lake, Redcliffe, Finney, Mink, and dozens more—a congregating of cameos into a community. En masses they announce their guilt.

This climax is formalized in a panorama. As the procession snakes downframe into a large open space between white and black quarters of Fairfield, Ashby runs in from the right; the camera begins panning leftward with him, then shot at 60 cuts to a matching pan as he joins Lucy Lee. For twenty-five seconds the slow pan moves leftward, only 90 degrees, but seeming greater, for its arc is tangent to the procession's curve. And gradually the tight shot of the carriage opens into a long vista, down whose right side the procession files toward the colored church and a small Negro choir.

*Kirkwood (1883–1963), a flamboyant, hard-drinking, legendary show-business figure, went from stage to pictures as actor and later director under Griffith. He appears in the latter's *A Corner in Wheat* (1909). Before marrying actress Gertrude Robinson, he briefly romanced Mary Pickford and later directed her in nine pictures at Majestic (1911) and Paramount (1914–15); he directed a number of Mary Miles Minter vehicles at Metro (1916) but did not direct again in film after 1919. He was wiped out in 1929 and after the mid-thirties he found it impossible to get work. "He lived out a precarious alcoholic existence until his death at eighty," writes Jack Spears (*Hollywood: The Golden Era* [New York: Castle, 1971], p. 167), and quotes actor John Griggs: "'I recall Jim Kirkwood not so much for his illustriousness as for the fact that never in a lifetime have I seen an actor so gallant in adversity.'" His son authored *A Chorus Line* and many other plays.

**Ford was fond of parasols' visual effect: women on the boat deck at the beginning; a yellow one in *Mogambo*, red in *Donovan's Reef*.

The white sound of marching feet joins the black sound of song. The choir sways earthily to "Swing Lo," but the procession marches even in place. This contrast is reiterated: "Detail, halt!" cries Priest; "The first three ranks will fall out, act as pallbearers." But Uncle Pleas comes forward to sing "Deep River." His action is a typically Fordian device: it combines music and movement, underlines sentiment, and changes—by his stepping forward from his place in the line—the simple diagonal line of the choir into an angle, thus realizing a static composition's dynamic potential.

As the camera shifts position, it seems that casket and mourners funnel away from us and upward into the chapel. This, and the fact that inside the chapel is stony and cavelike, is appropriate for the goal of a symbolic journey. The blacks stand outside, not by custom of segregation, but because this is a ceremony of *white* penance. Priest's sermon will transform public confession through absolution into redemption. Whatever his motive for choosing it, the black chapel is the perfect site for humble confession of intolerance. The whites enter into this black womb, so to speak, and thus acknowledge that the basis, heart, and conscience of their community is black.

"'Whosoever receives a child into his arms receiveth me,'" quotes Priest from Saint Mark, referring to Lucy Lee's mother; then, after General Fairfield enters like a repentant child, he continues the parable of the woman taken in adultery.

— You remember, Jesus raised himself up, and he looked those accusers in the eye. And this is what he said: "He that is without sin among you let him first cast a stone at her." . . . And by and by . . . every last one of them common scoundrels were gone! And only the woman herself stood there! And he said to her . . .

Here we cut from Priest (and coffin) to /the front row of the chapel, where sits the strange combination of General Fairfield, Lucy Lee, and Mallie Cramp, with Ashby standing protectively (but displaced) behind Lucy Lee. It is with these four framed, and the casket significantly unseen, that Priest, looking them in the eye, says:

— . . . "Woman, where are those, thine accusers? . . .

Cut back to /Priest:

— . . . "Hath no man condemned thee?" And she said, "No man, Lord." And he said unto her, "Then neither do *I* condemn thee!"!!!

Shouting ecstatically, Priest slams shut the Bible in triumph.

Thus would he anneal his community and bring it into the innocence and light of God. Yet innocence is at the root of the community's endemic intolerance: duty gone astray (as always in Ford). It is simplicity that is pernicious, whether in the indignant righteousness of General Fairfield, Ashby, or Maydew, or in the pagan Finney, who, flowing with chance and fate, carries a gun, is drunk, kills without pang, yet remains pure. Well might Ashby

pray God to "pity . . . simplicity," for this funeral is a ceremony not of purification but of guilt. All share place with the whores; no man lives immune
to this contagion, blameless for his innocence of (i.e., unconscious responsibility for) almost infinite guilt—not even Judge Priest, who most of all in
this community confronts moral choices consciously, is capable of real sin,
and embodies Ford's notion that principled good intentions lurk behind
most human tragedy. Such knowledge breeds caution: Priest always carries
an umbrella. Warily, defending U.S. with a gun, he, unlike cocky Young Mr.
Lincoln, does not feign cuteness or reason with a lynch mob, nor glory in
forcing them back: he wipes his brow and begs for a drink. He has the practical sense to acknowledge, in acquiescing in Buck's murder, violence he
cannot control, and takes concrete steps to atone for his silence's share in the
wrong done Lucy Lee's mother. And, judge, soldier, and priest, he is also, as
friend Felsburg says, "a cunning, unscrupulous politician," and wisely ships
off the prostitutes right after the funeral. * Yet even Priest is innocent (unaware) of his own racism.

Parade and House. Priest wins reelection by one vote (his
own). The band plays "Dixie," Brother Finney grabs the stick to beat the
drum himself,** properly, and music and picture dissolve into the victory
parade past Priest's house that night.

It is a movie of parades: funeral parades and victory parades. The Tornado boys parade to a lynching and, later, to vote. Maydew's band parades
twice (so that "Hail, Hail, the Gang's All Here" frames the funeral sequence!). There is a Grand March at the dance. Lucy Lee and Ashby have
several little parades all to themselves, while her mother's solitary trail is
marked by Uncle Zach as she limps toward Mallie Cramp's. Now, finally, the
whites parade past Priest in groups: the CSA, the GAR, the band, the Tornado boys ("He saved US from ourselves"), the cadets, two-score women
with fans. Cinematically a parade is an angle, a vector, an image that is
simultaneously the dramatic core, formal figure, and primary symbol of
Ford's film. The people parade, the compositions play with vectors, and life
is dynamic subsisting, form its manifestation, providence its rule.

This is an Augustinian viewpoint. Ford's people are pilgrims, and in *The
Sun Shines Bright* (curious name for a movie that could be titled *Intolerance!*) he relates to his material while suggesting a more perfect City of
God. Although Priest's victory parade resolves complex plots and relationships into a single gesture of communal unity, it also gives formal expression
to a yet existent disunity. For the blacks who come at the end sing a different
tune—"The sun shines bright on my Old Kentucky Home," not "Dixie."

---

*In *The Soul Herder* (1917—Ford liked to think it his first picture), Cheyenne Harry cleans
up *his* town by giving whores money to go away and "start a new life." Harry too was a fighting
clergyman, like Capt. Rev. Clayton in *The Searchers* and many another of Ford's characters.

**"The first [movie] part handed to me was that of a fresh drummer"—in 1907!—wrote
Francis Ford in 1914 (in *Universal Weekly*, December 20, 1913, p. 4).

And they do not march; they stroll, softly—in the opposite direction. Nor does the sun shine bright; it is night. And while crosscuts twixt Priest and whites are nearly level, when he looks at /the blacks, the camera gazes up at him gazing down.

But this is a 1952 picture about 1905, and, unless we favor Maydew, we realize that the world's problems are not to be solved in a few days, and that, meanwhile, such men as Judge Priest, albeit racist, are to be treasured. Hence as Priest retreats through one door of his home, then another, carrying his lamp deeper into successive rooms and then disappearing at last, Jeff, the black man, sits outside on the porch steps, serenading and guarding this white "motherless child," just as blacks have guarded and serenaded whites throughout Fairfield's history, and as Judge Priest has guarded them.

As silhouettes of Lucy Lee and Ashby pass off the frame (she having prevented his intruding), the camera, having panned slowly to the left as though taking a deep, slow breath, releases itself quickly rightward and into an expansive embrace —the most benedictory camera movement in Ford's oeuvre. Except for Jeff's fingers on the harmonica, all motion has ceased. The parade has passed. The town glistens in white and black like some jewel, the bushes seem suddenly green, the bricks red, and the white frame house of Judge Priest glows abidingly.

> My most beautiful pictures are not westerns; they're little stories without big stars about communities of very simple people.[26]

Judge Priest vs. *The Sun Shines Bright:*
How Does Ford Change?

Rather than occurring randomly throughout his career, Ford's best pictures (those most inventive and emotionally balanced) tend to date from four narrow points:

1933	*Pilgrimage, Judge Priest* ('34)
1939	*Stagecoach, Young Mr. Lincoln, How Green Was My Valley* ('41)
1952	*Wagon Master* ('50), *The Quiet Man, The Sun Shines Bright, Mogambo*
1962–65	*The Man Who Shot Liberty Valance, How the West Was Won:* "The Civil War," *Donovan's Reef, 7 Women*

There are, naturally, fine pictures in between these points (especially *The Black Watch, Steamboat Round the Bend, The Battle of Midway, My Darling Clementine, The Fugitive, The Searchers, The Majesty of the Law, Gideon's Day,* et al.), but each of the four points epitomizes the spirit of one of the four periods of Ford's career.

Comparisons between the four points are tempting, but fraught with danger. Received wisdom has it that Ford's work "evolved" into deeper expression, deeper self-consciousness, deeper style, deeper criticism of his material. Indeed, it seems a virtual truism among genre critics that sometime around 1960 happy Hollywood became neurotic New Wave and that John Ford repented of his Pollyanna simplicities. Closer inspection, however, reveals 1952 as a rare burst of optimism midst the general depression of Ford's output. Nineteen thirty-three offers scant evidence of simplicity, Pollyanna spirit, or dearth of self-reflexivity, and no western, not *Liberty Valance* and certainly not the parodies of Peckinpah or Altman, proffer estimates of the West *more* critical or cynical than does *Stagecoach.* Perhaps there are other ways, equally facile perhaps, of characterizing the four periods:

1933	dark; humane characters (organic)
1939	black; ideal characters
1952	light; iconic characters
1962+	fiery; humane characters (metallic)

From 1948 on, Ford's compositions are generally more classical, less mannerist, while the pictures of the final period are striking demonstrations of the range and variety classical styles may assume. Compared with *Judge Priest* and *Stagecoach, The Sun Shines Bright* and *Liberty Valance* have more straight lines, more flat surfaces, more rectangles, flatter lighting, and compositions less filled, whether by props or by modeling light. Thirties Ford is more Murnauian. Everything is more curved, pliable, rotund,

fleshy. Not only is there more scenic clutter, the clutter itself is more clut-
tered: contrast the randomly scattered candy-pull lanterns in 1934 (*Judge
Priest*) with the neatly patterned strawberry-festival lanterns in 1952 (*The
Sun Shines Bright*) with the geometric fishnet Lelani peers through in 1964
(*Donovan's Reef*). Light in the 1930s is a thing of great interest; rather as in
Caravaggio, it has mannerist depth and seems three-dimensional. Blurred
chiaroscuro plays upon walls or forms pools through which characters move,
or encloses them in haloes; space is less distance than an illuminated mist.
The vast quantities of stylization in thirties Ford evince intense self-
consciousness: style itself is clearly a distancing device, requiring us to
come to terms with an interpretation rather than with simple reality.

In one aspect, at least, "improvement" can be sensed. The cutting of
1933, though insightful, conceptual, and playful with contrasting moods and
worlds, is nonetheless off-hand, abrupt, and even crude in comparison to
the cultivated, musiclike cutting of 1939 and after, so that here one may
make analogies to the "evolution" of Mozart or Beethoven and suggest that
"improvement" is a matter of each "note" coming to seem more expressive
in more ways.

But in another aspect, as his characters become less anatomical and more
iconic, Ford perhaps loses something. There is a fleshy sprawl to the people
of 1933 and a patience in their voices and gestures that in later years seems
sacrificed to greater purposefulness: even Jeff Poindexter (Stepin Fetchit)
seems leaner and more "edited" in 1952 than in 1934. It is true, perhaps,
that later Fords have vaster visions, place buglers on horizons and fire in the
night, and sense the flow of historical destiny in ways that 1934 does not yet
even dream of, but sometimes their characters seem distanced to Cimabue
proportions and reliant, Godard-like, on specific signifying gestures, alongside the more naked, mercurial, and sensual presence of 1933's characters.
As the later Ford sometimes seems unwilling or unable to build his art as
much on Henry Fonda and John Wayne as he formerly did on Harry Carey
and Will Rogers, so too he grows progressively more contemplative toward
landscapes, so that a Rossellini-like dialectic with "raw" reality almost
seems to compel Ford, as it does Bresson, to treat his actors iconically.

If Ford becomes less mannered, less intrigued by his actors, more puzzled by land, it is partly because he becomes more distanced, and not only
in style but personally as well: simply put, he grows older. The dreams of
youth are more valuable but less immediate. Decreased physical participation with his characters is the price Ford sometimes (but not always!) pays
for more understanding —and for a heightened sense of *in*comprehension,
too. It is perhaps true to suggest that awareness of complexity and contradiction and dialectical struggle is more clearly and completely written into
the scripts of late Ford, whereas it is more sensuously contained in the actors of earlier Ford. *The Sun Shines Bright* is easier to talk about than *Judge
Priest*. But there are prewar and postwar pictures that belie this facile dis-

tinction: *Stagecoach, Young Mr. Lincoln, How Green Was My Valley, Wagon Master, Liberty Valance, 7 Women.*

Mogambo (1953). Shortly after the release of *Mogambo*, Jean Mitry questioned Ford about his penchant for introducing a group of people into a difficult situation, and Ford replied:

> For me, it's a way of confronting individuals, of bringing them face to face. This situation, the tragic moment, permits them to define themselves, to become conscious of what they are, to rise above their indifference, their inertia, their conventionality, the "mediocrity" they'd be without that situation. To find the exceptional in the ordinary, heroism in everyday life, to exalt man "in depth," this is the dramatic device I like. And also, to find humor in tragedy, because tragedy is never totally tragic. Sometimes it's absurd. I'd love to do a tragedy which would turn ridiculous, very seriously . . . What interests me are the consequences of a tragic moment upon diverse individuals, to see how they behave, respectively, in confrontation with a crucial fact, or in an exceptional adventure.[27]

We shall see that this applies to *Mogambo*.

Deep in Africa, c. 1953:

Day 1: Vic (Clark Gable) traps animals for zoos. He has an affair with Kelly, a stranded playgirl (Ava Gardner).

Day 2: Vic summarily kicks her out a week later when safari clients arrive: anthropologist Donald Nordley (Donald Sinden) and his wife Linda (Grace Kelly), who's fatally attracted to Vic. Kelly returns when the boat busts.

Day 3: Linda spars with Kelly, takes a walk, is rescued by Vic, flirts with him; complicated repartee at dinner.

Day 4: Safari in jeep: more repartee. Flirting in camp.

Day 5: Mission station: Vic undergoes "Ceremony of Courage" (natives throw spears); Kelly confesses to priest.

Day 6: Linda rebuffs Kelly's friendship; on river; Samburu tribe hostile at Kenya Station; Kelly confides in Brownie; Linda kisses Vic at waterfall; bitter tent scene with Don.

Day 7: Mountains of the Moon. Gorillas: Linda, frightened, grabs Vic; later they plot to tell Don.

Day 8: But instead Vic saves Don from gorilla attack. Later he gets drunk with Kelly, Linda sees and shoots him in arm, and Kelly tells Don Vic was making passes.

Day 9: The Nordleys leave. Vic and Kelly will marry.

Mogambo is a comedy of manners, blarney, and sophistication, set in the jungle. It is an essay on ethics, uncertain that "ethics" is not merely a synonym for "cultural instinct." It observes four orders—land, animals, primitive tribes, cultured whites—wondering whether the same law (a Hobbesian law of the jungle) governs each, or whether man possesses power to impose a higher law of his own.

Donald Nordley is an anthropologist. "He studies man, man's development . . . he examines heads." He wants to study the giant gorillas because he has a "theory of derivative evolution." He says, "I can't wait to see them in their natural habitat: the truest exemplary link between modern man and his primitive derivation." "Yes," opposes a priest, "I think you and I could have a lusty debate on the origin of man."

In the key sequence the question is only partly resolved: Waiting for the gorillas, Vic, instead of telling Don he is taking Linda away from him, saves his life. At the first sound of gorillas, Ford cuts back to a proscenium shot of the jungle clearing, announcing a "stage." And after Vic shoots a gorilla, dead silence reigns for the first time; he walks up and stands behind the fallen beast, the camera tracking in to a three-quarter shot of him, then / crosscutting to a high-angle shot, from Vic's perspective, of the dead gorilla's face. Then /back to the shot of Vic. He brushes off Don, "Do you think I planned this?! The last thing I wanted to do was to knock him over [i.e., metaphorically: Don]. Let's stop the chatter." And Brownie says, "Sorry, Vic, the little one got away [i.e., the baby ape; metaphorically: Linda]."

In Ford's syntax, the track-in on Vic is a momentous figure of style reserved for key moments of confrontation, a moment when interior and exterior realism join. (Such a track occurs, for example, in *The Sun Shines Bright* when Judge Priest sees Buck Ramsey shot dead—Figure 7: IV.3.) Vic has been constantly associated with beasts, pictorially and verbally; the ambivalence inherent in crosscutting* allows him to be read either as equivalent or opposite to a beast. But in shooting the gorilla has he denied the beast in himself? Has he acted sensibly, persuaded by Don's words of Linda's unsuitability? Did he act nobly, or only by a cultural conditioning that made him instinctively save a life that by jungle law he ought to have let the gorilla take?** Kelly says, twice, "You went noble." Vic says, "I went yellow." Did he fail in courage, or did he act like a man? (And what is man?)

Mogambo is somewhat vague. The land and animals, which play so constant a role in the movie, act, of course, without moral qualm or responsibility. Nor are the tribes *seen* as much better; rather they are primitive, corporate, alien, and with (to the whites) arational ethical systems; they offer no ethical contrast to the land and animals—with the single exception that they will not follow Vic into "that strange territory . . . the Mountains of the Moon" until he passes the "Ceremony of Courage." That is, the gorilla country represents truth (anthropologically, for Don; ethically for the film; confrontation with reality, for the characters); "Africa" is the test.

---

*When a shot of one person is paired with, for example, a gorilla, we will sense either comparison or contrast (or both). Similarly, crosscuts between people can indicate either comparison or contradiction.

**Vic's dramatic itinerary closely resembles Tom Doniphon's in *Liberty Valance*.

But the question of the possible uniqueness of man is confused in that each of them is a "split" personality. Vic is not a hunter, he is a trapper who loves animals; he is passive rather than active; he loves the wilderness but encages it for zoos and circuses; he cannot confront Don; he cannot confront reality. And he is split between two women. His two assistants, kindly Brownie and bestial Boltchak, reflect also his split.

But the film, Africa, will bring each of the four principals into a forced confrontation with reality, and in each case passion (*mogambo*) rather than rational decision will prompt the confrontation and acceptance. Each character's "moral itinerary" is prefigured in a short sequence before repeating itself at greater length (the characters have their own cyclicism). In Vic's case, the film's prelude serves as an allegory: the prey is trapped but escapes because the net is too weak. His prefiguration sequence is also Linda's.

Linda is twenty-seven, looks younger (and in fact is: Grace Kelly was twenty-four), has been married seven years to a boy she has known since they were five. She is sheltered, wealthy, pampered, ingenuous; in manner she is either too correct, bitchy, or disarmingly girlish. Of all the characters, she is psychologically the most complex. It is Linda, ostensibly the most civilized, whose repressed savagery, once released by Africa, wills Vic's involvement with her; by coming to Africa she falls into a situation, actually a trap, which at first (and then again) seems idyllic but which also will bring her (twice) into the savage's jaws.

Linda and Vic share a prefiguring sequence that is parsed in classic montage. She walks into the jungle and at first is enchanted, an innocent in paradise, crosscut with monkeys and birds (frames 1–3) and happily leaving the frame (3A). Then Vic rushes after her (4), and the idyll is interrupted; Linda, turning, is crosscut with fighting animals and becomes frightened (5–15). In panic she falls into a pit-trap (18)(one of *Vic's* traps). A black panther on a tree limb snarls downward, as Linda, looking upward in crosscut, cringes and shrieks (19–20). But this pair of shots is crosscut with Vic, in a low-angle shot (matching that of the panther, thus suggesting their mutual interest in Linda); he takes aim and kills the panther (24–25). Then he comes to the pit and pulls /Linda out. Ford breaks this action into *two* shots (26–27), typically, because the experience of being pulled out of a pit is different from that of standing beside Vic (27A, the continuation of shot 27).

Rescued, Linda seems to want to be taken. She stands emotionally naked (27A), then strolls off swinging her sweater and obliging Vic to follow (28). Then (29), simultaneously thrusting out her bosom while retreating her body, glimpsing up with her blushing, downcast eyes, she plays at seduction, coy, teasing, girlish. "Donald's one husband who's believed everything I've told him since I was five years old." She taunts Vic with remarks like, "That could be the remark of a cynical man . . . of a lonely man." Again walking off (30), she almost skips, and forces Vic to follow her. She poses (31) weakly and birdlike against a fallen trunk, and her feelings seem reflected in

15

16

17

18

18A

19

20

21

22

23

24

25

26

27

27A

Ford's composition, wherein Vic appears twice her size, and in the subsequent crosscuts (32–33), sexually menacing—with a low-angle for him and a high-angle for her. A fierce storm begins, she falls, so that Vic lifts her, whereupon she throws her arms around his neck—intercut with images of wind, river, rain-swept trees. At her door he closes in on her, trembling and wet (35). Vic has become the hunter again, and he pulls her scarf off, leaving her (35A) naked emotionally, her head birdishly tilted; she quickly retreats inside after an all-revealing glance. (The same figure of birdlike neck and scarf recurs in *The Horse Soldiers;* Ford found necks attractive.)

As in this sequence, *Mogambo* often creates dialogue between its "stage-play" artifice and its jungle "documentary." But the two are distinct, even though at times comparable or equivalent. The big ensemble scenes occur in rooms or tents, around tables, beds, or piano; and this melodrama is marked off from Africa by studio lighting (or, in closer exterior shots, by lamps and reflectors). The women come with full wardrobes and change for virtually every scene. The script is Ford's talkiest; lines snap with sardonic wit, weaving intricate networks of double entendre. But purposefully and metaphorically, much of the dialogue is *chatter*, the whiteman's sound, just as land, animals, and tribes possess their sounds. In terms of the film, stageplay vs. Africa is the question of external and internal realism. Africa not only brings out the unconscious of the characters; its juxtaposition also gives the stageplay whatever aesthetic-ethical meaning and realism it possesses, by placing its artifice within a context of actuality. Africa, on the other hand, may possess actuality, but it gains meaning only in juxtaposition (through the montage analysis) with the stageplay. *Mogambo* is full of magic, deeply intimate, and emotional exchanges between its characters. Time and again they gaze into the off-space, into Africa, seeking meaning, and then turn back to the surer comforts of human society. Such moments in *Mogambo* are fleeting instants, scarcely accentuated, when time seems suspended. Quickly and impassionately these moments are absorbed into the chitter-chatter of the stageplay and into the vastness of Africa. No one in *Mogambo* sings "Shall We Gather at the River," but rivers punctuate repeatedly with the varied metaphors their presence bestows.

What seems contemptible, sinful, in Linda is her lack of courage, her deceit. After her second love scene with Vic, by the waterfall, she returns to Don in the tent and repulses his advances. The camera looks through the tent from the rear, past Linda and Don and their cots, left and right; beyond the tent-flap doorway, the campfire sends smouldering white smoke into the night sky. Crickets, instead of the waterfall, are the background sound. As Donald talks to Linda he shines a flashlight into her face (twice), blinding her and making her cry. Across the rear of the tent is mosquito netting; the camera looks through this netting to Linda, whilst it sees Don through an open flap of the netting. The netting serves as a theatrical scrim: the backlight from the fire throws the shadow of Linda's head onto the scrim above her actual head, thus giving her two heads. He asks her calmly, "Lin, darling, are you still my girl?" "Don't be childish!" she retorts, moving hurriedly toward the door. "That's good enough for me," he says, stretching out on his cot.

Comparable to Donald's flashlight is the flash of his Leica. Twice, before and after this scene, he surprises Linda with his flash, each time freezing her in deception; the second occasion she stands in wide ensemble scene, holds her pose with an indescribable expression of naked truth for three or four lengthy seconds. (At picture's end, marriage reaffirmed, he snaps her picture without a flash.)

How much does Don suspect? This is an intrigue the movie poses. He is a scientist who does not leap to conclusions, and a proper British gentleman who presumes others are honorable until contrary evidence becomes overwhelming. Donald too has a "split." He observes reality, records it via film, tape, and notebook, but another side of him prefers the myth. (He and Linda are alike: each feels sophisticated and thinks the other innocent and innocuous.) *Mogambo* permits three interpretations of him: he is naively trusting; he is suspicious but afraid to discover the truth; he is all-knowing. In the third interpretation (which I lean to), Donald is seen as coldly setting up a "test" for Linda when he sends her back to camp with Vic after the first encounter with the gorillas; and he is seen as deliberately manipulating Vic's emotions during their talk before the second encounter with the gorillas. This interpretation suggests the moral deficiencies of the scientific method when applied to human relations. In the subsequent scene with Boltchak (when he gets mad at Boltchak for saying what he already suspects or knows), the natives in the background are dissecting the dead gorilla, and the scene is staged with images of decadence. In any case Donald's conduct is frighteningly efficient. He puts just the right amount of pressure on Linda. He preserves the trust-bonds of their wedlock through his deceitful trust (thus the significance of taking her picture without the flash). He clearly makes the right (i.e., human as opposed to jungle) choice when he "accepts" her innocence and the Vic-Kelly lie (cf. *Fort Apache, Liberty Valance*: preference for myth over fact when the former is more utilitarian). And he effectively disarms Vic. His motives, however, are rooted in passion.

A second question is whether Donald's "survival" abilities bring him closer to the beast or to man. He suggests that certain compromises must, and ought, to be made in life. Hypocrisy is sometimes laudable (as in Renoir). Everyone unites in the lie that will preserve Linda and her marriage, and yet she is the least responsible and the most culpable. She throws onto Vic her own obligation of confessing to her husband. When she feels she has been tricked, she reaches instinctively for a gun and fires at Vic. Is her reversion to jungle law duplicated by her civilized husband? "If she hadn't [shot you] I'd have done it myself!" But Linda is restored to Donald's comforting arms, to "home and Devonshire" and "raising that family." She will never learn the "truth" about Vic, but she has learnt the dangers of "Africa" and thus a "truth" about herself. *Mogambo* itself happily mocks the clichés of its fantasy drama. When Linda catches Kelly in his arms, she pulls back the tent flap (= stage curtain) and Vic says:

> Listen Mrs. N, you're not gonna tell me that you've been taking all this [love affair] seriously, are you?! You know how it is on safari — it's in all the books — the woman *always* falls for the White Hunter, and we guys make the most of it. Can you blame us? When you come along with that look in your eye there's no one who . . . [at this point Linda shoots him.]

The gorillas are described as unpredictable and dangerous. In their fascination they prompt us to question ourselves (man / beast) and to wonder what is real. In *Mogambo* the apes were photographed by a second unit equipped with 16mm equipment using the same methods Donald does.

(There are a couple of 16mm shots of natives beating bush in costumes different from those beating bush in 35mm.) What is curious, however, is that these 16mm shots (recognizable by their paler color) are *almost* (the operative word in discussing *Mogambo*) always crosscut with Donald's Bolex 16mm movie camera, so that the cinematic result *suggests* we are seeing the film he is taking. I say "suggest" because obviously we are not: Donald's film is still in the camera and Ford does not provide the usual masking that would indicate it. *Mogambo* is essentially a story of a bunch of people who make a long arduous trek (pilgrimage, parade) into strange territory in search of gorillas (truth, home). Linda finds fear and excitement—she cringes but keeps looking. Vic, crosscut with a (35mm) dead gorilla, finds himself. Don finds only a paler (i.e., 16mm) image. Cinema, like life, turns in upon itself. Artifice and document, man and ape, theater and life, myth and reality, white and black, are equated, divided, subtracted, and multiplied.

Kelly alone does not go to see the apes. She has come to Africa by mistake in the first place. Besides, she was unwillingly stuck at Vic's a week, she was again prevented from leaving by the Kenya Station tribal revolt, and even in the last scene as she climbs into the canoe, Brownie asks her, "Are you sure you're ready to go?"

Kelly is a bit like Father Josef (even including his sanctimonious side); she is Catholic, learns to avoid dangerous animals (devils?), and is close to knowing the beast within herself. As Brownie says, she has "scars" (cf. the Indian named Scar in *The Searchers*). She is the legitimately tragic figure in *Mogambo*, Linda is the playgirl.

Kelly is initially presented as a brainless toy; Vic says:

> That's playgirl stuff, Brownie. I've seen 'em in London, Paris, Rome. They start life in a New York nightclub and end up covering the world like a paint advertisement. Not an honest feeling from her kneecap to her neck.

She jokes about her "split": hearing Brownie describe an anthropologist as someone who examines heads, she quickly parries, "He could have examined both of mine!"

In Kelly's "prefiguration," she takes a shower, approaches dangerous animals that look cute, refuses to discuss her scars, goes after Vic, falls for him, and is jilted. Then, after her confession, she gathers water from the river, tells about her scars, ignores the gorillas, and finally, at first refuses to fall for Vic a second time, then pushed by passion gives in, plunges into the river, and wades to him.

What motivates her confession and change? One presumes she confesses fornication and was moved by the shock of her encounter with Vic, her battles with Linda, the initial encounter with a primitive tribe threatening to kill her, the availability of a priest, the need to confide. But there is another element, one subtly presented, that brings her moral adventures into parallel with Vic's: they both would like to see their rivals dead.

Kelly allows Linda to take her walk without warning her about the dangers of the jungle. Since Kelly has been there a week, she must be aware of these dangers. And as Linda leaves, Ford inserts a shot of Kelly's watching; not only does the camera look at Kelly from behind a bamboo curtain (staging used frequently throughout *Mogambo* to indicate hidden motives), but also the camera tracks up to Kelly (we have already discussed this figure of style in reference to Vic). When, however, Vic brings Linda back, Kelly, standing with rain pouring down in back of her, realizes her scheme has backfired. ("Scheme" is much too strong a word: after all, she herself tells Vic about Linda's walk.) Ford follows this shot with a strange tracking shot of Kelly walking in the rain in a black raincoat and black rainhat—strange colors for Kelly but ones which in the psychochromatic terms of *Mogambo* suggest a state of sin. The subsequent juxtaposition of the confession scenes and her attempted apology to Linda suggests action motivated by advice given by Father Josef.

Kelly is the one courageous member of the quartet. Her second confession, to Brownie, indicates her "great strength of character" after her husband's death; in the jeep scene we see her fighting back tears. She says constantly what no one else will say, cutting through the polite innuendos with which Vic and Linda masquerade their hypocrisy. She has one of her finest moments after the famous dinner scene. Standing beside the piano in her white gown, with Don and Brownie gathered 'round, she uses her white handkerchief as a prop while singing "Comin' thro' the Rye." The song's words accurately taunt Vic and Linda, who flee into the shadows, and the words also capture Kelly's dilemma, placing it in context of Vic's polygamy:

When a body meets a body comin' thro' the rye,
If a body kiss a body, need a body cry?
Every lassie has a laddie; none they say have I.
But all the boys they smile at me, comin' thro' the rye.

Kelly represents Western culture at its best. She has the savoir faire to lie at the proper time. Least prepared for Africa (as Etula says, she "can't even cook an egg"), her toughness and openness make her the least incompatible with it (she joins in the native chant and dance). She best suggests the sort of harmony into which the various ethical dilemmas merge at the end. A rainbow is in the sky and as at the end of *The Sun Shines Bright* order reigns as best it might in a beautiful, wild, and changing world.

It is difficult to ignore Ford's use of color in the female costuming. Vic refers to Kelly as a "paint advertisement." Offset against white, black, and tan (jungle colors) are patches of red, pink, and yellow. There is virtually no blue in *Mogambo*, except the sky. These colors operate psychochromatically, though again not with total consistency: they reinforce what is already there, rather than themselves producing something. Red may be equated with attack, yellow with cowardice, green with harmony. That is, Linda and

Kelly wear red or yellow depending on how they are faring toward Vic. Kelly assumes a green blouse after her conversion, white for her scar talk with Brownie, and green when she accepts Vic at the end. Colors are used to great effect in the crosscut dinner scenes. One might cite the declaration of blood implied by Kelly in her white gown pouring a glass of red wine. (True-blue Brownie wears a blue kerchief.)

Although *Mogambo* possesses not a note of an off-camera musical score, it is through-composed: on-camera native chants, Kelly's song, the sounds of the jungle and the land. This "score" is of considerable importance.

Ford was not considered a woman's director. With the exception of *Mogambo*, he worked with major female stars on only five occasions in the sound era: *Arrowsmith* (Helen Hayes), 1931; *Drums Along the Mohawk* (Claudette Colbert), 1939; *Mary of Scotland* (Katharine Hepburn), 1936; *Tobacco Road* (Gene Tierney), 1941; and *7 Women* (Anne Bancroft), 1965. Hardly an imposing collection of "sex goddesses." In *Mogambo* Ava Gardner is cast quite differently from her customary siren and vamp roles: more tenderness, health, and layers of depth. Her character closely resembles Bancroft's in *7 Women*, and they both perform during dinner scenes. Grace Kelly had stellar roles after *Mogambo*—*Dial M for Murder, Rear Window, The Country Girl*—but had not yet earned star billing at the time of *Mogambo*, the picture that *made* her a star: both she and Ava Gardner received Academy Award nominations for it; Grace also got a Metro contract. Ford had insisted on Grace Kelly over the Metro hierarchy's opposition; *they* thought her "ordinary, drab and uninteresting" in her minor role in *High Noon* and a Fox screen test. "As far as this test," argued Ford, "Darryl [Zanuck] miscast her. But this dame has breeding, quality, class. I want to make a test of her— in color—I'll bet she'll knock us on our ass."[28] Hitchcock came upon Kelly after *Mogambo* and used her mechanically, subordinating her personality to fairly iconic conceptions; under Ford she is looser, with more humor, relaxation, and complexity, more physically projecting and improvisatory, and she appears to greater erotic effect than with any of her other directors. Her feigned English accent—although quite good— adds another dimension to the artifice of Linda. It is a pity Ford did not direct "sex goddesses" more often.

Mogambo was also a major picture for Clark Gable. His career on the wane, Metro had not planned to renew his contract, but *Mogambo* put "the King" on top again.

The role of the packboat skipper, Captain John, played by Laurence Naismith, was probably intended for Francis Ford, who had died a few months before.

The production safari, one of the largest safaris of modern times, left Nairobi November 1, 1952, and in eight days traveled a thousand miles to the Kagera River in Tanganyika, near the Ugandan border, a hundred miles from the west shore of Lake Victoria. Footage was also shot in Kenya, Uganda, and French Equatorial Africa. Interiors were filmed in London.

Not atypically for Ford, he molded the screen personages partly upon characteristics in the actors themselves, in this case managing to find more sensitivity and sweetness in Kelly, Gardner, and Gable than they displayed elsewhere. Many of the episodes in the movie reflect actual events of the production. A leopard did walk into Ava's tent one night, and she cooked for everyone once, too. The absurd luxury of Vic's safari (tons of vanity luggage, two or three chairs in each tent, etc.) was mirrored in Metro's, except that some of the stars stayed in hotels in Kenya and flew back and forth each day to location (then bragged how they "roughed" it). Various rumors (never substantiated) had it that Kelly and Gable were having an affair; other rumors (even vaguer) had it that she was allowing *two* men to seek her favors—consequently fostering considerable tension on a production already potentially troubled by Frank Sinatra hanging around trying to patch up his marriage with Ava.

Mogambo holds the record for first-year grosses of all Ford's pictures. Artistically it is a worthy companion to *The Sun Shines Bright* and *The Long Gray Line*. It is a remake of an earlier Metro, *Red Dust* (Victor Fleming, 1932), in which Gable plays his same role; Jean Harlow, Gardner's; Mary Astor, Kelly's. The two movies have little in common.

The Long Gray Line (1955).

> We're always afraid of what we do not know. I'm
> curious why people love military marches. Why do
> people follow them automatically, marching quite
> naturally in step? Simply because each time we hear a
> march we know, we know what's coming next, and this
> gives us an absolute confidence in the next minute,
> while in obscurity we're all afraid. We need to have
> confidence in the second, the minute, the hour which
> is coming. And with a march we know that second,
> that minute.   JACQUES TOURNEUR

The questionable sense, or worth, of life, a frequent Ford theme, receives increasingly pessimistic treatment in his later years. *The Long Gray Line* suggests a philosophy that, while seeking to transcend the bewildering contradictions of life's ordeal, is yet rooted in the immediate existential moment. Tidily summed up in Old Martin's parting blessing, "Subsist, subsist," this notion of *balance* is central to Ford's oeuvre. All creation is in passage, man is a pilgrim ever in motion; at times we may feel a moment that is "out of time," but really we are caught up in powerful and mysterious currents, can never stop, rest, and take our bearings, arational chaos can erupt at any instant, but the wise man subsists.

Marty Maher is a bit of a simpleton; his life is basically an experience of sentiment. He is thus an apt character to illustrate desire for order midst life's dazzling confusion. A parade catches him up, he follows its step, and in this engagement of self into the pace set for him by the parade—an engagement requiring repeated renewals of persistence—he finds subsistence. But has he chosen the right parade? At the parade's heart, how can he know?

Subsistence. Affection, too, dazzles, but provides its own satisfaction. Unpalatable truths lie frequently within bonhomie, particularly in Ford. Old Martin is a typical "wolf in sheep's clothing": Donald Crisp makes him so engaging, one happily agrees to disregard how obnoxious, rude, intolerant, egocentric, chauvinistic, and domineering he is. "When I was a lad," he tells Kitty seconds after meeting her, "a girl that cluttered up her head with education was sure to turn out flat-chested and with a squint" (whereupon she removes her glasses). Milburn Stone's John J. Pershing is so mythic that we overlook how terribly *nasty* a sonovabitch *he* is. Marty and Mary have an abiding love; nonetheless, she is something of a nag. And so on. Things are not obvious in *The Long Gray Line;* they merely seem so.

Now, John Ford failed Annapolis's entrance exam but ended up an admiral anyway. He appreciated a cadet's decision to enter West Point and as a "professional soldier" himself subscribed to duty; yet such moral subordination did not conflict with his clarity and honesty as a moviemaker. Hence, *The Long Gray Line* pleases, on one level, militarist viewers, while yet, on another level, it is objectively a critical, damning portrait of the "heart" of the military. In this picture the wisdom of hindsight can see not only explanation for the Vietnam War, but also—in showing what "made" (Marty's phrase) Eisenhower—the picture enlightens us about certain qualities of fifties America.

Figure 8. *The Long Gray Line*

A	Parades (Titles), *P1*[a]	1954
B	Marty and Eisenhower.	

	C	(1) Arrives at Point, *P2*. (2) Breakfast hazing, plates. (3) No pay; plates.	1896

Part I

	D	(1) Enlists. (2) Paints ball. (3) Dance sentry *P3*. (4) Punishment *P4*; fights Rudy; guardhouse. (5) Boxes Koehler, cadets; Mary. (6) Asks Koehler for (7) kitchen work. (8) *P5*, picnic. (9) proposes.	1900?

	E	(1) Mary welcomes home; flag 1. (2) Father and Dinny, prayer. (3) Swimming; Red. (4) Dinner for Red and Kitty; Old Martin and superintendent. (5) Notre Dame game, *P6*; locker room, and Church. (6) Dinny's new car; Mary pregnant. (7) Hospital birth. (8) Walk home with Old Martin; party; death. (9) Bar and cadets. (10) Punishment 2, *P7*. Mary in hospital, *P8*.	1913 1914 1915

INTERLUDE	(1) Parade Review, *P9* (2) Graduation 1915 (3) Parade Review, *P10*	1915

Part II

	E	(1) Red and Kitty married, *P11*. (2) Station—off to war, *P12*. (3) Marty refused combat; Old Martin tries to enlist. (4) Posting of casualties. (5) Black ribbons; Kitty and Mary. (6) Armistice; Red dead; quits army. (7) Farewell to Old Martin. (8) Visits Kitty and baby; decides to reenlist.	1917 1918

	D	(1) Red, Jr., sworn in. (2) Marty and ball; hazing. (3) Red, Jr., off to "hop." (4) Pearl Harbor announcement. (5) Marty and Mary at son's grave; Red, Jr. (6) Red confesses honor violation to Marty; Mary and flag 2. (7) Night argument between Marty and Mary over Red; Red and Kitty: Red off to war as sergeant. (8) Marty tells off governor about tradition. (9) Mary's death, *P13*.	1938 1941

	C	(1) Marty in church; crèche. (2) Walks home in snow. (3) Alone; cadets; Kitty and Red, Jr. (now captain) give him party.	1944

B	Marty and Eisenhower.	1954
A	Parade Review, *P14*	(Actually: May 23, 1946)

[a]*P* = Parade

"What a fine ruin it would make!" exclaims Marty, and his original observation remains as true as the attacks by "the youngest governor in the
United States" on tradition vs. reality. Life may go on outside, but at the
Point everything stays the same (almost): the cadets (with a couple of exceptions) are wooden, uninteresting, and impersonally similar (or so they would
seem to Irish Marty); a man here has a good chance to end up a monument
(like Major Koehler). West Point's justification is that it *works*.

Marty Maher is an immigrant; like his wife, he arrives in America wearing his ticket (for entrance, for life's journey). "Things are cruel hard in
Ireland . . . but not for a man that owns a pub in a hard-drinking community." But West Point, the only America either of them knows, "is a fine
proud place." A place of absolute order: "A prison, an insane asylum!"
Marty calls it. "What!" he says of his father, "Himself? Him that's always
lived free—bring him here among the regulations . . . ?!" In truth, Marty
longs to return to Ireland; he does not like the army. What keeps him?

1. He joins to avoid losing his earnings by paying for the dishes he
breaks as a waiter (Fig. 8: I. D. 1).

2. Koehler tricks him into reenlisting by his desire to win Mary O'Donnell (I. D. 8, 9).

3. He reenlists when Mary is pregnant; then, the baby dead, he is
trapped midst reminders of dead hopes (I. E. 10).

4. During World War I Marty is needed at the Point (II. E. 3).

5. Pershing calls West Point the "heart" of the army (I. D. 1.); but at war's
end Marty sees it as a death factory and quits. But like a good Irishman he
sees in another what he cannot in himself. Kitty's baby is a link to the future
(as Ford demonstrates by dissolving from Old Martin ["Subsist!"] waiting to

die to the little naked baby), and the child's duty ("to follow in his father's glorious footsteps") also provides Marty with a sense to his own life, past and future. So he reenlists.

6. Finally (I.B.), Marty tells Eisenhower, "It took me thirty or forty years just to get the hang of it [army life], you know." Now, says Marty, sitting posed with a vase of *flowers* left rear and a large *urn* right rear, "Everything that I treasure in my heart, *living* or *dead*, is at West Point. I wouldn't know where else to go."

The Point's holding power is clarified in the hospital sequence that concludes part I (and complements the Christmas party concluding part II). There is a crescendo of motion: cadets march in to bring Marty home from the bar; his shadowing father walks behind in the dark; next morning cadets walk punishment duty for having gone off-limits for Marty—a sort of formal symbol of a funeral procession; Marty comes with flowers, whose symbolism is dual (and which the nurse bars from Mary's room). Then, after momentary stillness in the hospital room, comes the gargantuan parade outside.

Multiple dramas unfold, in that stillness, between husband and wife: sorrow for dead Martin Maher III; Marty's fury that he will never have a child (cf. Old Martin's "I'm on my way to becoming an ancestor!" and the continuity expressed in the joke that the babe will be named not after Marty Jr. but after the older man); Mary's sense of empathy, but also of guilt at her barrenness; the mutual need for comfort, which they seem unable to give. In the silence, a faint drum beat, slow and ominous, then, eventually, some fifes, and finally the marching tune loud and clear (the same tune cadets sang going to breakfast the day Marty arrived, and even then it suggested permanent motion). Down below, from afar down the long straight campus road, come four-abreast columns of cadets. The loudness of the drum beats is exaggerated. And the portentousness of the confrontation is marked by Ford with (1) no less than three exchanged crosscuts, plus (2) a dolly-in on Marty (which we know as a Fordian figure marking coming-to-terms with reality), and with (3) virtually the only "impossible" camera angle in postwar Ford (i.e., the window is on an upper story), an unnaturalness accentuating the rational act portrayed. Says Mary, in the crosscut from outside the window, "It's a cruel thing, but try to find it in your heart, Martin, to accept the will of God . . . or would [these cadets] only be putting you in mind of the son we had for such a little while . . . so that you'll wish you could go away from here and never have to look at them again?" Marty's face, in fact, is shadowed, but Mary's is lighted, for of course the parade means not only doom but also that life marches on; her heart flies to it for succor. But this grim, implacable parade, though Marty does not know it, is really what seals his fate and defeats his desire to leave the army and to live "free";* it indicates the inexorable power of the tradition of military discipline—and tells us why men will kill and die.

*Sgt. Rutledge, another racial underling, also rejects "freedom" for the army.

More than an institution, West Point is a giant family, and the friends who half a dozen times come to console mark the links of love that bind. When Kitty, expressionistically shadowed with Red's Medal of Honor, bitterly complains of her widowhood, "Professional soldiers are trained to die, is that it?" Marty replies, "They're trained to do a job, Kitty. Some die young and some don't, but they all give their lives for their country, they're ready when they're needed. They set the example—and their wives, Kitty!" "Alright," she says, with flat desperation, "I'll set the example too." The baby cries: dissolve to his enlistment as a plebe. Did this Red, Jr., whom at movie's end Kitty will proudly present on crutches as a "professional soldier," ever have a choice? "The *Corps*!!" proclaims the title music—a hymn, solemn and implacable.

Marty shares many of the characteristics of the Fordian hero: celibate, even impotent, able to "balance," able to keep atop the maelstrom; but he lacks the authority and critical consciousness of the true Fordian soldier-priest. Having made the initial move, by casually walking into West Point, he spends the rest of his life watching as others walk (or parade) into it. He is oft separate in the movie, often spatially, because he is an observer, a feeler, but not quite an outsider. He is an Irishman among Yankees. He is West Point's oldest living tradition, but he can never graduate. The real Point, the cadets, pass in review through half a century, always changing; Marty grows old, people die, and he will soon; the institution is permanent. West Point, one might say, becomes a woman, a womb. To leave the Point is like leaving the womb: some die, some are injured, some become great men. But Marty cannot leave. He prepares others to leave and die, but remains on the sidelines. Even midst celebration of his son's birth, Marty sits typically to the side, contemplating a dress sabre given him by the cadets to mark the occasion. Little does he imagine the sword symbolism (death; phallus), for the doctor has not yet come announcing death, and Marty has probably forgotten how, years earlier, he was ordered to report to "the Master of the Sword" (i.e., Major Koehler).

The cannon at West Point are harmless. Marty tells Pershing the balls don't fit (and is told to mind his duty). The cannon suggest aggression, but they cannot fire. The biological image of Marty sitting abreast the barrel and dropping a ball between his legs suggests the barrenness of his issue, intimates the coming scandal of Red, Jr., reminds us of futility: of the questionable worth of our life when we turn ashen gray, of the cruelness of renewing seasons and of brass cannon, which, dumb as they are, have a permanence denied to us. One would not read too much into these cannon, but they appear in two other important scenes: dominating, from above, the parents, suddenly grown old, as they watch Red's oath-taking; leaned on by Marty and Red, side by side, as Red confesses. Implacable, almost sinister cannon.

In a film full of dinners and luscious inviting food, it is strange that Marty never eats: he never tastes that cake with the light green icing (Fig. 8: I.D.7); Mary's picnic basket goes to Rudy Heinz (I.D.8); when Old Martin and Dinny arrive, Marty's dinner is forgotten and they all go to the living room and pray; he takes not a mouthful during the dinner for Red and Kitty. In the flashback's last sequence (II.C.3), he burns an egg (!) that he tries to cook; Kitty asks him when he last ate and orders the cadets to work: they place Marty in an armchair, holding a fork and an elaborate pipe he has just been given, they put a pillow behind him and Mary's old shawl on his lap, they place a tray and eggs in front of him, and around his neck, as a bib, they tie a red-checkered napkin exactly like the one Mary had in Rudy's picnic basket, they give him Red, Jr., a hero, set up a Christmas tree, decorate it, and sing him a serenade.

Still Marty does not eat. What he does do, throughout the movie, is smoke his pipe. He does not fully join with life, but he subsists, smolderingly, an image of West Point tradition. The barrenness of Marty's life seems particularly strong in this last act, in that house so amazingly changed with Mary's departure, in colors turned brown and blue-gray, a brown barrenness even a Christmas tree cannot redeem. Yet how important *things* have become, things like the cannon, the house, the uniform. As Mary died, Marty placed her glass on a shelf and dropped her shawl on the floor. How important they seemed, being there as Marty clung to Mary's dead body, dead traditions pointing like the Point itself to death. Far brighter is the gold statue of Mary Queen of Heaven holding the infant Jesus, with the Christmas crèche below it, to which Ford dissolves across the years after Mary's death scene: an image of spiritual rebirth corresponding to the renewal of the seasons on earth, another tradition, a "response" or "answer" to the question posed by Mary's death.

Cyclicity. Figure 8 illustrates *The Long Gray Line*'s structure, which may be conceived of in various ways:

1. It is circular: the structure mounts, then regresses toward its beginning. The keystone of the structural arch is the 1915 graduation ceremony, flanked by two parade reviews. Parades begin (I. A) and end (II. A) the film; the scene in Eisenhower's office is both the second (I. B) and penultimate (II. B) sequence. These (A and B) "frame" the flashback; but within the flashback itself, the archlike structure is continued.

2. It is additive: a flashback (*b*) not only occurs within bracketing present-time sequences, *aba'*; a flashback is also an equation, *a = b*, because such a structure suggests causal (and other) relations between past and present. In fact, Marty tells his story to prove he ought to be allowed to stay at West Point: here has revolved his life's struggle, the "thirty or forty"-year process of changing a "free" Irish immigrant into a unit of that alien society of "regulations . . . sobriety . . . duty."*

3. The second section repeats the first. The first son died, the celebration party was interrupted; the second son enlists, has Marty pin on his officer's bars (as Overton, in 1917, requested his first salute), and the second party concludes successfully, with the same song sung at the first:

> Come fill your glasses, fellows,
> And stand up in a row,
> We're singing sentimentally,
> We're going for to go.
>
> In the Army there's sobriety,
> Promotion's very slow . . .

As events occur and recur, repetition appears predestined.

For example: Red, Jr., is not only the son of two close friends (one dead) and a substitute for Marty's own dead son, he is also intended to fulfill hopes that, like Ward Bond's in *Fort Apache*, are really Marty's own desire to relive his life as a cadet rather than just a coach. We dissolve from Marty's reenlistment decision to Red, Jr., and his class taking the enlistment oath, which corresponds to: the 1915 graduation, Marty's 1896 enlistment, the fulfillment denied Marty's baby. The next scene finds Marty astride a cannon dropping a ball as in 1900, and Red, Jr., is hazed with identical recitations of 1896 by sons and grandsons of cadets Marty knew back then. And as Marty places flowers on his son's grave, Red, Jr., confesses he has broken his oath (by marrying before graduation) but plans to conceal his violation (the marriage was quickly annulled). But those cannon and the Hudson's granite cliffs and, of course, Marty himself are implacably hostile to Red's dishonor; Marty watches the flag lowered to half mast (as he watched decades earlier) and in Rembrandtesque darkness tells Mary he wants to quit: failure.

---

*The Man Who Shot Liberty Valance's similar (*aba* ; *a = b*) structure also explains the present by the past, and shows the present to be a result, or product, of the past.

Thus events occur and recur over fifty years. But as Marty ages, their pace quickens. Autumns pass into winters, springs turn barren. More and more, each scene contrasts starkly with its neighbor, happiness thrust against tragedy.

Parade. Such dialectical clashes are the structuring motifs of postwar Ford. Change and subsistence; parade and house; chaos and order; theater and reality. In *The Long Gray Line* parades frame the story; a parade celebrates Marty's courtship of Mary; another mourns his son's death and another provides courage to go on living; the parade suggests madness, as troop-trains depart for World War I and crowds surge in wild confusion behind Marty; the parade bridges the gaps of years; and, manifested by only its distant sounds, the parade signals the coming of death to Mary O'Donnell. (Parades are indicated on Figure 8, the plot diagram, by *P.*) Antinomally, the image of the house has been almost as frequent, along with a dying father's parting blessing to "subsist," advice that Marty, searching frantically for something to say as Red, Jr., hurries off to World War II, suddenly and intuitively finds to repeat to this *his* "son"* —while Mary gazes bereftly.

The four-and-a-half-minute parade review for Marty (with Irish tunes) with which the picture concludes bursts almost like a miracle the dialectical tensions of *The Long Gray Line.* As in the finale of Renoir's *French Cancan,* we enter rare realms of evocative spectacle, poetry, and symbolism. At any rate, this is clearly another world: we are struck by the sudden proliferation of automobiles and buses onto these hallowed grounds, and by the new bleachers overflowing with tourists. The grass is green, the military is benign, innocuous, overflowing with good fellowship. The squads of cadets now seem like toy soldiers; the music provides the glory, the pictures are of cute, sprightly, but faceless, mechanical toy soldiers. And Marty's dead appear: Mary, Old Martin, Koehler, Red, Sr., Overton! The only disturbing,

---

*Red, Jr., scarcely notices these words, and Marty himself utters them almost without thought. The disorder of the scene contrasts markedly with the original, careful ritual when Marty walked to his father, saying, "I ask for your blessing, daddo," and there came the formal, but magically prophetic response, "You'll always have that, my boy. Subsist, subsist."

*un*theatrical element in the spectacle is Marty himself, forever dropping out of attention, shaking hands, reaching out for his ghosts, crying. He alone seem "real." When Kitty answers her son's "It's been a great day for Marty" with "It's been a great *life* for Marty," her delivery is deliberately shorn of dramatic nuance; the essential question of the film (Does life make sense?) is answered affirmatively in negation of its patent tragedy, and for the simple reason that experience itself is precious. The contradictions of life at a death factory, of course, are not resolved; they are lifted instead into a higher order. The parade substitutes itself for reason, an arational, atemporal framing of Marty's flashback narrative of his life. He knows now, reaching for his ghosts, that the past *is* present ($b = a$), tradition is now, human experience is essentially permanent within memory, whose reality, in this "Viking's Funeral," transcends that of death—as in *How Green Was My Valley*. The sequence dazzles, then, not by apprehension of a preternatural miracle, but of a natural one: consciousness of the import of one's own existence as a permanent particle of time. The final shot is not of the parade but of Marty breathing heavily beside two generals. Like us, he has become a spectator of his life.

The Long Gray Line has fared badly with critics, and although it certainly is not a movie without faults,* it *is* one of Ford's most ambitious works, and complaints of its supposed chauvinism, sentimentality, and manipulative facility misconstrue the movie's nature, which is allegorical (rather than realist) and subjective (rather than objective).

The appearance of Marty's dead during the parade finale ought not to surprise us. We should recall the montage earlier, during another parade, as

---

*A couple of marginal scenes threaten to blight one's appreciation of the whole: absurdities like someone soaping the kitchen ramp—when Marty slides and falls—while waiters serve breakfast, or that half a dozen cadets disappear during swimming class. We could dispense with the swimming scenes and with Old Martin trying to enlist (albeit modeled on Ford's sexagenerian brother Francis). It is a shame Ford's determination to remain within Marty's point of view deprives us of a wonderful dance sequence just because Marty is outside on sentry duty: true, he is always outside, but he could have peeked. At least we do see the lovely young girls throw their boys bouquets, framed fittingly in an archway.

Marty, from behind a tree, watched Mary O'Donnell and her picnic basket (Fig. 8: I.D.8): two-shot: Marty and Mary at bench /LS: parade /two-shot again /MS: three cadets, in parade, salute /two-shot again. Ford's remarkable interjection of utter nonrealism here, the saluting cadets midst a love tryst, allegorizes the tryst much as Renoir allegorizes a tryst in *The River* by using *Invitation to the Dance* as background music. The whole of *The Long Gray Line* unfurls within this allegorical dialectic between life (the parade) and Marty's subjectivity.

But characters here do not so much develop as watch themselves exist through time and other people. With Marty as central persona, we learn that life is not so much ours to live, as for others to live for us. No doubt Marty's narration reflects his Irishness, lowerclassness, and "redneck" immigrant mentality; no doubt he distorts some portraits (e.g., his animated wife, in Maureen O'Hara's marvelously full-bodied stylization, contrasting with Tyrone Power's woodenness—Marty's passivity). No doubt Ford romanticizes events, and chooses to relate the precious moments, and those only, the moments of utmost feeling. But far from passing facilely through many intoxicated incidents, Ford typically fills out each episode with density of decor (e.g., the love and detail of the Maher living room) and disciplined performances that often vivify (Ford's typically) taciturn scripting: e.g., Mary steps down a step, turns her neck in that Irish birdlike way of hers: "Is it sorry you are already, Martin Maher?" "It's sorry I'll never be, Mary O'Donnell" (I.D.9).

Ford's virtues are often his most attacked features: his up-front showmanship, degrees of unabashed stylization of actors and emotions never attained even in Metro musicals, bold clarity in gesture, frightening precision in effects. Each shot has beginning, middle, and end. Even the simplest reaction shot receives inventive treatment (e.g., Rudy Heinz, watching Koehler box with Marty, leaps on an exercise bar). Marty, first entering West Point, is struck by the cadets marching in the quadrangle (I.D.1); in the parade finale, Koehler and two cadets strut into a low-angle proscenium shot and tip their hats like Pall Mall boys. Such effects evince confidence in emotions. Perhaps Koehler's swimming instructions ("There are four things to remember: confidence, timing, relaxation, and breathing") apply also to cinematic technique. (But when Marty falls into the pool, his friends save him from drowning.)

Ford's subtle structuring of moods and emotions appears in sequence II.E.5: During World War I, Marty puts a black ribbon next to Overton's yearbook picture; as he mentions Rudy Heinz was also a casualty, the camera shows Mary reacting to the news. The doorbell rings, she stands still a moment, then walks straight back to open the door. Ford cuts on the door movement to Marty's reaction, hearing Kitty's voice. When we cut to a general scene of the living room and see Kitty, Marty is already coming into the room. Now, a lesser director would have shown us Kitty's entry; by sticking in the reaction shot, Ford preserves Marty as the central character: had he shown Kitty bubbling into this sullen scene he would have turned our attention to her. Now Kitty and Mary sit gossiping, and Marty, to his chagrin, must set table for tea, and, outraged at a tea ceremony while his boys are dying and he's stuck at the Point, he stalks off in fury. By having the two women chatter at a frenetic pace, Ford: 1) contrasts stylized, satiric comedy to the sullen mood; 2) preserves a juxtaposition to set off Marty's weightier mood while preserving his primacy; 3) provides a telling moment in a throw-away reaction: Kitty gleefully reports news of "Cherub Overton" in Paris— "Imagine! In Paris!!" But Mary O'Donnell lets fall not a hint that Overton is dead.

The Long Gray Line was Ford's first picture in Cinemascope, a format he disliked at the time. He felt compelled to use extremely long takes and to shoot entire scenes in single shots with characters framed full length. Five hundred and fifty-seven shots in 213 minutes results in about 15 seconds per shot, deceptively low because of some quick sequences; versus a deceptively high average of 8.4 seconds per shot for *The Sun Shines Bright*. There are less than forty camera movements, most tiny, and early Cinemascope's shallow focus constrains Ford's usual depth of field (but clever staging partly compensates). Pictorial style otherwise resembles *The Sun Shines Bright*, but however creative Ford's long shots (and most are indeed wonderful), Ford without cutting is Ford sorely lacking.*

Though ostensibly based on Marty's autobiography, *Bringing Up the Brass: My 55 Years at West Point* (1951), and proclaiming itself "The *True* Story of an Enlisted Man Who Was There for 50 . . . Years," virtually all of the movie is pure invention. Marty Maher enlisted in 1896 and retired in 1946, when the parade review was held in his honor and when, by order of the commander-in-chief (Truman), he was allowed to stay at West Point. He was still alive at the time the picture was released, but I have not found accounts of his reactions. In actual fact, the Mahers had no children, but adopted a niece; the Red Sundstrom characters are not in the book, nor are most of the other incidents. Instead the chronicle is a fairly unreadable collection of locker-room stories and talk of old Ireland—with a foreword by Eisenhower.

***The Searchers* (1956).** Texas, 1868, a solitary cabin: Ethan Edwards returns from the Civil War and Mexico still a Reb; affection for brother Aaron's wife makes him an outsider. Indians massacre Aaron's family, but Ethan vows to find little niece Debbie, who may be captive, and is joined by Martin Pawley, an orphan Aaron adopted whom Laurie Jorgensen hopes to marry. For seven years the living suffer while the (probably) dead are

---

*Cheyenne Autumn (1964) is also in long takes, appropriately; but *7 Women*, Ford's third anamorphic feature, shows complete adaptation to scope format and is among his most rapidly edited pictures.

Figure 9. *The Searchers*

The division below is somewhat arbitrary. But within each "act" there is considerable unity of time. By merging together the three middle acts, a tripartite structure is revealed: exposition, development, resolution.

1. Exposition	**ACT I**			
	1.	Edwardses'	Ethan arrives / living room / dinner / fireplace and gold / bedtime	Day 1: evening
	2.	Edwardses'	Breakfast and rangers / departure	Day 2: morning
	3.	Desert	Indian grave: posse splits	Day 2: afternoon
	4.	Edwardses'	Indians heard; Debbie at tomb	Day 2: evening
	5.	Edwardses'	Ethan and co. / Edwardses' ruins	Day 3: morning
	6.	Edwardses'	Funeral	Day 4
	7.	Desert	Swamp / chase and battle / posse splits off	Day c. 5
	8.	Desert	At cliffs	Day c.6?
	9.	Desert	Brad's death	Night 6?
	10.	Desert	Snow	Much later
	ACT II			
	1.	Jorgensens'	Arrival / home scenes / Texacans	2 years later
	2.	Jorgensens'	Home scenes, leave	Day "2"
	3.	Futterman's	Bar	Later
	4.	Desert	Rock ambush	Evening
2. Development	**ACT III**			
	1.a.	Jorgensens'	Letter arrives . . .	2 years later
	FB-1	Desert	(Trade with Indians / Look)	(Day 1 . . .)
	1.b.	Jorgensens'	. . . Letter continued . . .	---
	FB-2	Desert	(Bed, Look / morning)	(. . . night 1 . . .)
	1.c.	Jorgensens'	. . . Letter continued . . .	---
	FB-3	Desert	(Killing buffalo / slaughtered Indians / 7th Cavalry / lunatic captives)	(. . . much later)
	1.d.	Jorgensens'	. . . Letter concluded	---
	2.	Desert	Wilderness sunset ride	Every day
	ACT IV			
	1.	Cantina		3 years later
	2.	Scar's camp		(7 years from start)
	3.	Debbie, Scar's attack		
	4.	Cliffs and wounds		
3. Resolution	**ACT V**			
	1.	Jorgensens'	Dance and wedding / Ethan and Marty arrive / fight / Mose and lieutenant	Some months later: Night 1
	2.	Desert	Night camp debate / rope / night march / Scar killed / attack: Ethan and Debbie / slapstick	Morning 2 / Morning 2
	3.	Return home		

searched. Then Debbie is found, married to her mother's assassin, Comanche chief Scar, and only Marty's intervention and Scar's attack prevent Ethan killing her. Their return, after five years unseen, stops Laurie marrying another. They join rangers to destroy Scar's band and Ethan is about to kill Debbie when, lifting her as he did seven years ago, he hugs her instead and takes her "home."*

In order to distance Ethan (John Wayne), and to define him within his culture, Ford and scenarist Frank Nugent have placed a "letter scene" in the middle of *The Searchers*.

III.1.a. Jorgensens': The only letter Laurie (Vera Miles) gets from Marty (Jeffrey Hunter) in five years is delivered by Charlie McCorry (Ken Curtis). In a comic sequence, she is forced to read it aloud in front of Charlie (an oaf courting her) and her parents. Marty writes how he acquired an Indian wife . . .

Flashback 1: (Laurie reads, voice-off.) Ethan and Marty trade with Indians, then find a chubby girl following them, a wife Marty has unwittingly purchased. "Come on, Mrs. Pawley!" jokes Ethan. They call her "Look."

1.b. Jorgensens': Charlie is overjoyed ("Hawh! Hawh! So he got himself an Indian wife!"); Laurie throws the letter into the fire. Her father retrieves it, scolds her, pitilessly orders she read on. "'She wasn't nearly as old as you'!" she reads, fuming . . .

Flashback 2: That night, Look tries to lie with Marty, who kicks her down a hill. At mention of Scar she shows terror. Next morning (Marty narrates) they follow her trail marks.

1.c. Jorgensens': Laurie, eyes filled with tears.

Two points deserve note thus far. First is the intricate structure of narrative points of view. *We* are watching *the movie* (Ford) wherein *Laurie* reads *Marty's words* about *Ethan's attitude* toward *Look*. Secondly, each character offers a contrasting sensibility. We are at once aware of the disparity between Laurie's comprehension of Marty's letter and what actually happened. Within her home, we see her distress contrasted by Charlie's oafish opportunism, her father's obliviousness, her mother's wish that Laurie forget Marty. In the flashback, we may feel inclined to participate in Ethan's humor at Marty's plight. If so, we do so because we perceive Look through the filters of others' sensibilities (all of them racist: Ethan, Marty, Laurie). Our lack of regard for Look's feelings parallels the general lack of regard for Laurie's feelings. Empathy is rare in the world of *The Searchers*, as in our own. Ford hopes, by means of the intricate contrasts of this letter scene, to make us aware of how each person's attitudes color reality. To do so, he must "distance" us from the

---

The Searchers was shot in 1955 in fifty days, all over the West from Gunnison, Colorado for snow, to Edmonton, Alberta, for buffalo. Its producer and backer, C. V. Whitney, had, with John Hay Whitney, been a Selznick backer and was frequently involved in projects with Merian C. Cooper.

sympathy we automatically feel for the John Wayne character and must turn our participation in Ethan's callous racism against us:

Flashback 3: (Marty, voice-off:) They lose Look's trail in snow. Later, Ethan slaughters buffalo, to deprive the Indians. Then they come upon an Indian camp raided by cavalry, with corpses everywhere: men, women, children, and Look. (See Fig. 9)

Ethan kills buffalo to kill Indians; soldiers kill Look. Do we now feel sorry for laughing at her? But this sequence's chief effect is to distance Ethan. As we dissolve from Laurie into a long shot of Ethan about to slaughter buffalo, Marty's voice tells us we are about to see something that he still has not been able to figure out: the way Ethan goes wild killing the buffalo. This episode, then, and in fact this entire third act, is a sort of "medical report" on Ethan. Elsewhere, Ethan tends to be the dramatic focal point of *The Searchers* and an empathy-identity figure for the audience; but in this act we see him through others' eyes, others comment on him, his deeds are complexly contextualized, his sanity is dissected, he becomes a phenomenon to be studied, and is least able to guard from view the tenderness and terror inside him. As a result, not only is our compassion for him enriched, but his actions are objectified against the tapestry of his culture.

Flashback 3 (continued): Later, they sight the renowned 7th Cavalry, with flags, beautiful horses, and a bright Irish jig. At the fort entrance three peaceful Indians, each in different-colored blanket, enter the frame as silent onlookers. The music dies into tough-faced soldiers whipping captives, herding them like cattle into the stockade.

Ford *shows* the 7th Cavalry in its mythic glory, because its myth is an essential portion of its historical actuality. And he shows the Searchers responding to that glory, because that is how they felt about the cavalry. But Ford does not thereby glorify the cavalry. On the contrary, he "frames" the evocation of their glory between scenes of massacred Indians and whipped captives. Without its glory, properly contextualized, the 7th Cavalry cannot be understood. Thus Ford treats it as he treats Ethan. And Ford shows reasons for their brutality:

Flashback 3 (continued): In the fort Ethan and Marty inspect whites rescued from Comanche. All are half-crazy; perhaps one is Debbie. In a sustained close-up, Ethan's eyes react to the broken humans he sees and the lunatic howls he hears.

Everyone inhabits a private world: Laurie, her father, her mother, Charlie; the 7th Cavalry, the captive Indians, the peaceful Indians, the indifferent sergeant (Jack Pennick) who shows Ethan the rescued whites. The privacy of the lunatics may differ in dimension from this universal solipsism, but does it differ in kind? Where is truth midst such myriad solitudes? In all probability Debbie is a lunatic, too: why does Ethan persist in his search? Perhaps because he recognizes something of himself in others' lunacy: his stare outward at the terrified lunatics is really the stare inward we noted in

Huw at the end of *How Green Was My Valley*. And Ethan had a similar moment earlier (resting his horse and gazing anxiously across the desert toward his brother's house [Fig. 9: I.3]) when his sensitivity broke through his armor. His vision of a comfy home is impaired by his vision of "wilderness" (in his threatened family, in the lunatics, in Debbie, in himself), but his kindnesses—his concern for Martha and Mrs. Jorgensen, his stopping Marty and Brad from seeing their dead—explain Ethan's unbridled hate as a form of terror, a terror he can only control by exteriorizing it into the search for Debbie.

III.1.d. Jorgensens': Marty's letter offers not a word of love; Laurie is disconsolate. Her father takes the letter, folds it into his pocket, and exits nonchalantly smoking his pipe. Laurie stares bereftly out the window (a stare mirroring Ethan's), but Charlie, strumming guitar, saunters coyly to her side, singing, "Gone again, skip to my Lou, my darling."

2. Laurie's thoughts are visualized by a long dissolve into a sunset vista of Ethan and Marty riding the wilderness. (See Fig. 9)

The worst fears come true: cruel waiting, endless searching, lack of empathy, hostility, deaths of whites and reds, brutality, torture, all ending perhaps in lunacy. Ford shows the cause and effect of these phenomena in each personage. Through comic techniques the viewer is indicted as a participant in the mechanics of racism. The glory of the 7th Cavalry is a paradox—like any man's justification. Empathy is almost nonexistent: whites have no feeling for reds, nor has Marty much concern for Laurie, Laurie for Marty's cause, Jorgensen for his daughter, or Charlie for anything but his opportunism. Ford shows each autonomous point of view and contrasts them, thus throwing them into relief. The juxtaposition of wilderness horrors against home's comfy fireside makes us both question the quest and comprehend its necessity. Laurie's authentic tragedy is not diminished by a comic presentation necessary to contrast it with the starker horrors of the hostile world outside. All this is Ethan's context.

There is need to insist upon this context, and to present it as a sort of conglomerate of tunnel-vision points of view. For in 1868 Texas homesteads are dispersed, people gather (seldom) for weddings and Indian hunts, survival discourages empathy. In place of a dramatic world constructed upon ever-present multitudes of interlocking relationships, it is mostly an arid wilderness that Ethan wanders, with social bonds more theoretic than concrete. Few westerns inhabit grimmer worlds. *The Searchers* is an atypical Ford movie in its concentration on a solitary hero rather than a social group and in its emphasis on the bright open spaces of the desert rather than the angulated chiaroscuro of rooms. It could be classed among Ford's allegorical pieces—*The Fugitive, Wagon Master, 3 Godfathers*—but even more than they it is a morality play, in which all hostilities of wilderness and man flow from a consummate sin.

Intolerance was always a major Ford theme, and racism became a dominant motif (generally misunderstood by critics and thus increasingly strident)
in *The Sun Shines Bright, The Searchers, The Last Hurrah, Sergeant Rutledge, Two Rode Together* (1952–61). In *The Searchers*, racism first destroys
Debbie's family, then nearly destroys her; not until Ethan overcomes his racism will he regain Debbie. Meanwhile, the community leader, Captain-
Reverend Samuel Clayton (Ward Bond), totes both Bible and gun* (the tools
of American expansion according to Ford), and few greater pleasures exist
than killing Indians. Even fleeing women and tiny children, we see, are exterminated joyously. "O Lord, for what we are about to receive we thank you!"
prays Mose Harper (Hank Worden) just before a slaughter. Of course Ole
Mose is a "fool," and accepted as such, but like his alter ego Ethan his actions
represent the actual morality, if not the decorum, of the whites.

For attitudes in *The Searchers* are externalized and theatricalized. The
movie itself, with each bright Technicolor frame organized into painterly,
definitive portraiture, expressionistically composed and lighted, and with
the yearning tune "Laurina," is not realistic but symbol of reality; everything
is saturated in myth, everything is a commentary upon myth.** "I used
a Charles Russell motif," said Ford,[29] as if to remind us that his own myths
are based on the myths devised by others. Perhaps *The Searchers'* "Texas
1868" looks nothing like the *real* Texas; but it does look the way "Texas"
ought to look. And who has made a more mythic entrance into a movie than
Ethan's slow ride out of the distance? Ethan, in a repressed but incessant
ascent toward fury, dominates *The Searchers* through strength and stature
(in his back and walk), through fragility (in his voice and eyes), and through
humanness (supporting performances are more stylized comically, expressionistically, even statuesquely); but most of all Ethan dominates as the focal point of mythic tensions. All these qualities of style combine in some of
Ford's finest moments, fully choreographed to affecting music, such as the
way the Edwards family walk to their porch positions to see Ethan arrive, or
Ethan's background farewell to his sister-in-law Martha while gruff Sam
Clayton stands foreground sipping coffee with feigned unmindfulness; in
both instances, characters frozen on the porch or at the table stop time,

---

*One of many Fordian soldier-priests.
**Technicolor is itself a medium better suited to mythicization than to realism. In addi-
tion, Ford organizes his 1:1.65 VistaVision compositions far more expansively than the narrower ones of *The Sun Shines Bright* or *Mogambo.* Frame space favors the horizontal: tops and
bottoms tend to be darker, the center swath brighter; characters are posed horizontally, horizon lines and scenery and props also emphasize the horizontal. All this frame-space-to-be-
traversed fits the notion of a search. But the effect is mitigated in 16mm (and of course on
television), where side-space present in 35mm is cropped and aspect-ratio consequently reduced to 1:1.33. VistaVision was originally a "high fidelity" process by which a larger image
was obtained on the film by printing frames sideways rather than vertically, resulting in a much
sharper image.

emphasizing the import of Ethan's arrival or departure. And well they might. Insofar as myths are conflicts safely sublimated for the reasonableness of daily life, nothing is less comfortable than a myth incarnate.

During Ethan's first evening home with Aaron's family, the rockingchair, its back to us and its face to the fire, dominates the scene with Ford's usual subtle obviousness (cf. young Lincoln's hat). Ethan jumps out of it, never to return to it, in fury over Aaron's remark that Ethan, before the war, seemed anxious to leave the farm. Ethan, curiously, takes this in exactly the opposite sense, and replies that he is perfectly willing to pay for his stay now. Then next morning, Mose arrives, grabs the rocker, departs saying to Martha, "Grateful to [sic] the hospitality of your rockingchair," and then grabs the chair again, during the scene outside the smouldering ruins of dead Martha's home [Fig. 9, I.5], whilst Ethan goes stalking off. To have his own rockingchair becomes the nomadic Mose's dream. And repeatedly throughout the movie, the rockingchair-by-the-fire is contrasted (by camera, script, and character) to Ethan's never-ending motion across arid open space. Even the peaceful, trading Comanche possess a rockingchair, in contrast to Scar's nomadic band. As always in Ford, happiness is for fools and society is for the simple, not for the idealists, the romantics, the hyperconscious, like the widowed Judge Priests or the haunted Lincoln.

"What makes a man leave house and home and wander off alone?" asks the title music, announcing once again the familiar Fordian antinomy of passage / subsistence, parade / home—and, as in *What Price Glory* and *The Long Gray Line*, the parade (the searching) seems a sort of *substitute* for reason as well as a *search* for reason. For Ethan, who like Tom Joad keeps trying to return home, paradoxically leaves home to search for home, deserts humanity to discover what humanity is, gives up meaningful existence to seek out meaning. As in *Mogambo*, a long trek is a search for "man," and the hero has a "split" within himself as a social and interior being; Ethan's confrontation with Scar thus parallels Vic's (Clark Gable's) confrontation with the dead gorilla, in that the hero really confronts the ambivalence in himself (civilized or savage?). This paradox too is proclaimed in *The Searchers'* title song: "A man will search his heart and soul, go searchin' way out there." Only metaphorically can Ethan's soul be "way out there." His inner search—for home, for resolution of fury, for peace—manifests itself in the outward search for Debbie.*

The wilderness Ethan wanders is metaphorical as well, not, as in Hawks's *El Dorado* or as in the familiar "wilderness / civilization" antinomy some

---

*These lyrics *were* specifically chosen by Ford.

critics ascribe to Ford, a territory in which anything is permitted and to which civilization has yet to come. In Ford, wherever man is, he brings with him his culture, laws, and codes. The Comanche are not linked to absolute wilderness but to their own, rival culture—as our first, hypericonic glimpse of an Indian emphasizes; indeed, with feathers, horn, and warpaint, Scar sports all the totemic paraphernalia we expect in a Fordian vignette. Reiterated crosscuts between Scar and little Debbie contrast cultural icons while presaging their future importance in each others' lives; he picks her up from a cemetery and takes her into another world—but not exactly into a "wilderness." The Indians of *The Searchers* are constantly paralleled with the whites—riding abreast of them, in battle, or parleying. As with Look, our tendency to look upon Indians as totem poles is reversed against us when we finally meet Scar intimately (Fig. 9, IV. 2), discover that he is human and that his racial hatred is equated with Ethan's. (Scar's raid on the Edwards was in revenge for sons killed by whitemen; now he lives surrounded by the trophies of his hate: his scalps, the medallion, and Debbie.) The struggle between reds and whites is thus an all-or-nothing war between two civilizations, with the land as both prize and battlefield. For now, the Indians and their tepees blend into the landscape like integral parts of its rocks, towers, and pinnacles. The whiteman is the invader, the stranger in this land: witness the peculiarity of the Edwards house, perched in nowhere. But the whites will conquer this land and transform it, so that no longer will they seem strange here, transforming the land as now the Comanche transform white captives. "Whoo whoo whoo," sings the crazed woman to her doll, as Ethan gazes numbed by the frightful fragility of the human mind: how utterly we are like weeds. It is fear, a psychological wasteland, that is the wilderness Ethan wanders. He emerges from and returns into this wilderness not because he, like Shane or like Vidor's Man Without a Star, is a wild thing, but because he embodies quintessentially human longings for which society offers no fulfillment. His longings all symbolize an *excess* of civilized values rather than wilderness ones. Society deserts Ethan as much as Ethan deserts society. Others give up; he persists. "That'll be the day!"—his favorite retort—virtually defines him: Ethan is someone who does not change, does not give up, does not miss a shot, does not get parties thrown for him, cannot be seriously threatened by the likes of Marty or Brad. He appears to be a loner, yet his absence from home is motivated by desire to preserve a family that his love for Martha might threaten, just as, subsequently, desire to preserve that family's remnants keeps him apart for the course of the film. He appears, like the dead Indian whose eyes he shoots out, doomed "to wander forever between the winds." His love of family, his need to restore it by rescuing Debbie, his racism and intolerance, all assume a purity and persistence that set him uncomfortably apart. If character is fate, feelings are character: his persistence through seven years of obsessive love/hate causes a crisis, a "split," in Ethan. Unable to reconcile his love of family with his outrage that this white child has given herself to her mother's red despoiler, he is impelled to destroy her.

Ethan's conflict mirrors ideally the racism of society. Brad Jorgensen gave up his own life, unable to deal with the thought that his beloved died less than pure. And Ethan's desire to see Debbie dead is endorsed by almost everyone, particularly by Laurie, who tells Marty that Debbie's mother (Martha) would *want* Ethan to put a bullet through the girl's brain. The captain-reverend endorses this attitude *but* also endorses Marty's effort to preserve Debbie's life; he is a captain-reverend, after all (and similarly, earlier [Fig. 9, I.7], he shoots attacking Indians and, as opposed to Ethan, spares retreating ones). Mose Harper also combines both attitudes, but in a more exuberantly theatrical manner (just as he mirrors Ethan's rocking-chair-vs.-wandering duality). The captain-reverend and Ole Mose can tolerate the essential paradoxes of racial violence, however, and so can society as a whole —the Edwards family fondly watches their boy's central placement of Ethan's sword over the hearth. But in Ethan, who is extraordinary in being a student of his hate—an expert on the Comanche and even speaking their language—the desire to kill that which is most essential to him produces acute conflict, obliging him finally, as he hurls Debbie above his head to kill her, to confront a racism that society accepts unthinkingly.

Ford aptly described *The Searchers* as "a kind of psychological epic,"[30] and it is worth noting that the Comanche—who have the mythic qualities of being constantly discussed, feared, and pursued, of marking their passage as violently as possible with ravaged and stricken victims, but of being themselves virtually never *seen*—appear almost magically when they *are* seen. A dead Comanche is found beneath a stone; Scar is suddenly *there* in the cemetery; the Comanche who battle the rangers are suddenly *there* on the horizon; Scar is suddenly *there* to save Debbie by shooting Ethan (IV.3).

The Comanche, then, appear as shocks of terror, as an element Ethan cannot control. And they become associated with even deeper terrors within him. And with another chain of images:

When, in *The Searchers'* first shot, Martha opens her door from blackness to the bright world outside, the equation of home with blackness suggests (as is subsequently confirmed) that within the doorway dwells our innerness, heart and womb, our vulnerability, even our unconscious. On this occasion Martha is opening herself to Ethan—the imagery accounts for the sequence's extraordinary emotional power—but the necessity to protect, to seal off our interiority from the world outside, from other people, produces psychic isolation, the consummate sin from which stems all the lack of empathy we noted in the letter scene, and all the intolerance, racism, opportunism, obsessive hate, and insanity of *The Searchers'* world.

Martha and her home seem the prime desires of Ethan's interiority. But they are also the prime frustrations: Ethan is left outside alone at night as Aaron takes Martha indoors to bed. The languorous timidity with which Ethan rode up to the house is contrasted with the robustness with which Marty charges up and bolts through the door, and with the way the children suddenly burst open a door to tease Lucy and Brad kissing, and, later, with the way Laurie teasingly and uninhibitedly bursts into Marty's bath.

Doorways, then, are linked to sex, and usually with a degree of shock, for sex is another feeling Ethan cannot control.

The doorway image in all its connotations recurs, now associated with the Comanche, as the worst conceivable nightmare, as a screeching searing of consciousness: Ethan, midst swirling smoke, stands framed by Martha's burnt doorway, within which lies her body, dead and dead after unthinkable torture. All Ethan's terrors unite; from this moment, unable to face them, he goes insane. The seven-year search he now undertakes is thus a search for peace of mind; but in the meantime Ethan's mind is anything but peaceful. Two goals torment him. He pursues Scar to avenge the murderous rape of the woman he himself could not possess. And he pursues Debbie not only because she is Martha's child but also as a sublimation of his inability to have Martha, of his impotence in *anything* that matters to him.

The searches for years are for unseen ideals—ideal evil and ideal good. Then Ethan finds Scar and enters his tepee. His eyes follow the camera's pan along the rod of Scar's collection of white women's scalps, and Debbie is suddenly there, holding it, appearing magically, with a shock, out of nowhere, like a Comanche. That she has become a Comanche she herself confirms after she appears a second time, again like a miracle, on the horizon of a sand dune. Beautiful, nubile, but unharmed, she has evidently given herself freely to Scar. No wonder Ethan wants to kill her. *

*At the base of the sand dunes, just before Ethan tries to kill her (but is himself shot by Scar [IV. 3]), Debbie, at first speaking in Comanche, tells Marty she had hoped for years they would come, then gave up, is now Indian, they should go away. Does Debbie, then, *want* to go home?

And so, later, he hurls her above his head. But the setting is a doorway—
a cave entrance—and the sand is swirling in duplication of the smoke that
engulfed Ethan outside dead Martha's ruins. Does he recall lifting Debbie
the night before that massacre (I:1)? Regardless, he finally *touches* Debbie,
grasps the *person* rather than ideas, and all his hate, fury, and insanity is
transmuted into love.*

The moment and the image are justly among the most celebrated in
American cinema. Ethan, in an iconic gesture that is strikingly original yet
rooted in tradition and myth, personifies a new moral awareness of self and
humanity. In rising above the universal racism and solipsism, he acts as
surrogate for his society—and for us, too.

Fordian heroes tend to act as surrogates. They have seen themselves as
agents of the Lord (Travis and Sandy), the law (Lincoln), justice (Rogers),
medicine (Mudd), high ideals (Huw Morgan). They must purify the world:
right a wrong, restore honor, purge disease, avenge crime, purify law, up-
hold ideals. But Fordian heroes are lonely; isolation and self-exclusion are
the prices they pay. Tom Joad cannot rest while society's outcasts tread the
road; Mr. Gruffydd must leave the valley. All are obsessed by duty, all be-

---

Can she be a white woman? Are not the whites about to destroy her second family much as the
reds destroyed her first family? Given what we see of other captured whites (here and in *Two
Rode Together*), Debbie's physical and mental health can be accounted for only by a miracle—
or by extraordinary gentleness on Scar's part. We do not know the answers to these questions,
nor can we say to what degree she has found peace with the man who perhaps displays her
mother's scalp (as he displays the scalp of Marty's mother). But Debbie has come not to chat but
to warn of Scar's attack. Does a fourteen-year-old have clear ideas of what she wants, after
seven years of rigorous conditioning to be an Indian, when she suddenly finds infant fantasies
close to fulfillment? She does begin to hope again, for later (V.2) she embraces Marty joyfully
when he tells her he is taking her home. (In Paul Schrader's 1979 *Hardcore*, *The Searchers* is
remade as a modern Methodist [George C. Scott] trying to rescue his daughter from slavery to
a porno producer; she too instinctively refuses at first to return home.)

*Lifting up Debbie = pulling down the branch in Mizoguchi's *Sansho the Bailiff* (1954). In
both cases a gesture repeated years later restores a hero to sanity, family, and first principles.

come "priests," take vows equivalent to chastity, give up everything for their task. And over the years Ford's concept of his hero evolves toward ever more pronounced obsession and introversion. The heroes played by Fonda illustrate this evolution—Lincoln, Tom Joad, Wyatt Earp, the Fugitive priest—and the process continues through the Wayne heroes, climaxing in the suicides of Tom Doniphon (*Liberty Valance*) and Dr. Cartwright (Anne Bancroft, *7 Women*). The hero's ability to moderate intolerance becomes progressively more questionable, and the cost to him more ruinous.

Among these heroes Ethan is distinctive not so much by his neuroses (he may even seem fairly normal alongside DeLaage, Terangi, Rankin, Arrowsmith, Mary Stuart, John Knox, Muley, Gruffydd and Huw, Lincoln, the Cleggs, and the Clantons) as by the resonant complexities of his contradictions. It is true that he so thoroughly perverts the hero's traditional tasks—to moderate intolerance and reunite families— that Marty has to stay by his side to hold him in check. Although in many respects Ethan's alter ego ("He-Who-Follows," Scar names him), and with even his own set of doorway images, Marty, part Indian himself, does not share the common horror at racial pollution, and is the only person to recognize the absurdity of granting ideology dominion over human life—only begrudgingly do the rangers permit him to slip in ahead of their raid to try to save Debbie. But Marty is not a Fordian hero. He has no affect on Ethan; his attempts to save Debbie fail (Scar saves her the first time, Ethan abducts her the second); Ethan, not Marty, saves the family; and Marty's devotion to duty does not cost him Laurie. We ought not, then, discount Ethan for his neuroses. His hate is cogent, his loyalty to a dead woman noble. No one finds him absurd. A man with very human qualities, he is forced to deal with his surroundings in a superhuman way. The arguments that he should care for the living, that Debbie is dead or "the leavings of a Comanche buck" (Laurie) are refuted and Ethan vindicated when Debbie is found. Even Ethan's hate appears ultimately as the other face of his compassion. Thus when he rides up to the Jorgensens holding Debbie, her arms childishly around his neck, we must, I think, feel awe and admiration for him. He did what no one else would bother to do. His loneliness and sin humanize his heroic stature and heroize his humanity.

The Searchers, initially so grimly antiromantic, comes, with the improbable recovery of a healthy Debbie and the nullification of Ethan's hate, to reassert hope with expressionistic vehemence. The miracle recalls *Wagon Master*'s apotheosis. Even the wandering old Moses has gained the promised land—the rockingchair. But, unlike in *Pilgrimage*, the resolution of inner conflict culminating a journey does not mark reconciliation with society. Ethan, the new Moses, modern man, stands outside, grasps his left elbow with his right hand, and turns and walks away, as Mrs. Jorgensen's door closes to end the picture in the same darkness out of which Martha Edwards opened her door to begin it. Why did Ethan not enter?

Many explanations are plausible, from ones traditional to the western (distant horizons beckon; new duties call; the task is done; the hero belongs to the wilderness), to ones particular to *The Searchers* (Ethan is doomed to wander; happiness is for the simple; his new moral awareness excludes him from the older order). And there is the special explanation (as noted earlier, pages 22–23) that the arm gesture Ethan makes was the signal gesture of Harry Carey, who often walked away at the end of pictures, and who greatly influenced Ford and Wayne—and, in fact, the house Wayne walks away from here is Carey's widow's (Olive Carey, playing Mrs. Jorgensen). Wayne's homage acknowledges debts and links Ethan to past Fordian heroes.

But, on the other hand, why—beyond the requirements of a happy ending—should Ethan *not* be left alone? Is he to live with fourteen-year-old Debbie? Surely she is better off with the Jorgensens. Is he to live with the Jorgensens? They are relative strangers. No, as in our own world, people live separately, not in utopian communes: Ethan walks away for the most commonplace of reasons. That his walking away *seems* extraordinarily meaningful, that his arm gesture seems an admission of impotence, is perhaps because, in a moment, the hero disappears and only a lonely, aging man is left.

Ford and Politics

Once at Goulding's Lodge in Monument Valley, Ford hired a gorgeous woman to wait on Ward Bond's table, act enamored of him, and give him devoted service. One evening she told Ward her husband would be back next day; this would be her last night alone; he should bring a six-pack and a watermelon. So that night, with six-pack and watermelon, Ward set out for her bungalow. Little did he suspect that Ford, Wayne, and four others were waiting with blank-loaded pistols. When he opened the door, they started firing. Ward dropped the six-pack and raced away for his life, still carrying the watermelon.[31]

Ford and Wayne were constantly thinking up tricks to play on Bond. Because Bond *strove* to be pretentious and was always griping about his role, his room, or whatever, he was Ford's pet patsy, with Wayne as the audience. No insult could dent Bond's thick hide. And, consciously or not, he was a superlative actor, perhaps the most underappreciated in films. He was also among the Ford family's most intimate friends, godfather to Jack's children and grandchildren. He even got married on the *Araner.*

But Ward Bond was president of the Motion Picture Alliance for the Preservation of American Ideals, an organization determined to root out Communists and "fellow travelers" and to aid the House Un-American Activities Committee in its witch hunts. This caused problems for liberal thinkers. "I didn't know if I should like Ward," said Dobe Carey. "I didn't like that outfit. But I did like Ward. Ford said Ward would do anything that made him feel important, even at the expense of stomping on people, 'cause he was just too thickheaded to really analyze it and see what a phoney thing it was. It was terrifying. But I don't think Ward knew what he was doing. As Ford used to say, 'Let's face it. Ward Bond is a shit, but he's our favorite shit.' "[32] Indeed, Bond was infamous for putting his foot in his mouth. Once while Ford was shooting a scene for *The Searchers,* the power suddenly went off. People scrambled hither and yon to find out what had gone wrong. It turned out Bond had innocently unplugged the camera so he could take a shave.[33] Ward, said Ford, "was a great, big, ugly, wonderful guy. But he was . . . the greatest snob I have ever known."[34]

John Wayne, an equally close friend, was reputedly an authentic Jew-baiter and Red-baiter in the early fifties. Ford, who seems to have regarded him as something of an intellectual lummox only fools could take seriously, used to rib him endlessly.[35]

Ford, as a child of immigrants and a member of a (then) persecuted racial and religious minority, tended to ally himself with blacks or Indians or anyone victimized by discrimination. He came from a time when loyalty to family, friends, country, and principles counted more than life itself. Thus he did not turn his back on cronies who descended into bigotry. But he did not support them in it either.

While Ford was principled, he was basically apolitical and would rarely voice an opinion. But if someone's integrity or job were at stake, he was the first to speak up. The speech he made in 1933 to the Screen Directors Guild (an organization he had helped organize) was such a case:

In the past few weeks, despite the most profitable year that the motion picture industry has ever known, there have been more studio people fired than at any other time. Hundreds have been let go at all the studios. Directors and assistants, writers and stock players, craftsmen and office

workers of every classification. Now, after this eminently successful financial year, just why is this going on? Why are so many people being let out?
The usual answer is, of course, business depression. Stock market is going down. Business is bad. I don't believe it. Your Board of Directors
doesn't believe it. President of the United States doesn't believe it. The
Attorney-General's Office in Washington doesn't believe it. Their inves-
tigator, Mr. Jackson, doesn't believe it. In fact, he boldly states that the
banking industry is going on a sit-down strike. Why? To bring about a
financial crisis. So that wages and wage-earners can be pushed back to
where they were in 1910. . . . How does it affect this Guild? Look, Gentlemen, I don't think that we are stupid enough to deny that the picture
racket is controlled from Wall Street. All right, last year, again I repeat,
the most profitable year of all, this Guild was unrecognized. Big finance
won the first round. Now they are going to try to win the second round.
They are going to keep us unrecognized in bad times. . . .[36]

At the same time, intolerant of endless committees and infighting, he
avoided the 1930s wars between the studios and the incipient trade guilds.
Behind the scenes he helped; and Mary Ford aided the unemployed
through the Assistance League.

The blacklisting of the McCarthy era disgusted him. * "Send the commie
bastard to me, I'll hire him," he'd say.[37] He had the Military Order of the
Purple Heart condemn the 1947 HUAC hearings as "defamatory and slan-
derous . . . witchhunts."[38] When in 1951 the Department of Defense charged
Frank Capra (of all people!) with Communist involvement, Ford retorted, "I
never heard him [object] to the Congressional Investigation of Hollywood
Communists. I don't believe he did. Frankly, I objected to it loudly and
vociferously. I'll now go on record as saying I think it was a publicity stunt
and taxpayers would have saved a lot of money in railfares if the investigation
had stayed in Washington."[39] In 1950, he refused to back Cecil B. DeMille's
loyalty oath for the Guild; DeMille proposed that names of those declining to
sign be sent to the studios. Then, to confound opposition, DeMille rumored
that Guild president Joseph Mankiewicz was "pinko" (then a serious charge)
and attempted a quick coup by sending recall ballots—only to his allies! But
the liberals forced a general meeting, at which Ford's intervention, concluding four hours of debate, was decisive. He identified himself for the stenogra-
pher, "My name's John Ford. I am a director of Westerns," and declared
himself "ashamed" at "what looks to me like a blacklist. I don't think we
should . . . put ourselves in a position of putting out derogatory information
about a director, whether he is a Communist, beats his mother-in-law, or
beats dogs. . . . I don't agree with C. B. DeMille. I admire him. I don't like

---

*Ford discovered Anna Lee had been blacklisted for a year, due to confusion with another
woman of similar name. For subsequent jobs, producers obliged her to sign a disclaimer that
she was not "Ann Lee." (Author's interview with Anna Lee, March 1979.)

him, but I admire him." The assembly passed Ford's motion for DeMille's
resignation and endorsement of Mankiewicz.[40]

Cultural identity, to Ford's generation, was something to be profited
from, preserved, and celebrated. But in popular jargon after the mid-fifties,
it was confused with racism, and "integration" seemed often to imply cultural uniformity. Strangely, what began as an effort to assure individual
rights threatened to turn into ideological fascism. The depiction in movies,
even in historical setting, of communities whose attitudes the new ideology
deemed racist, jingoist, or antifeminist was declared "offensive." Since
Ford's pictures deal obsessively with themes of race, ideology, and class, it
was easy for well-meaning observers to mistake the man himself for a racist
and a reactionary. Such damnation was infuriatingly ironic, for no other film
artist had sought so persistently to uncloak society's noxious patterns and to
sift out existential freedom. For Ford it was always a question of inquiring
into the tensions and adhesions between an individual, his origins, and his
present situation. Whether Irish, Negro, Indian, British, Wasp, or whore,
the individual was always played against his stereotype. Ford's detractors
saw only that stereotype. It is a pitiable reflection on American criticism
that Ford, virtually the *only* filmmaker to concern himself with racism before it became commercially fashionable to do so, is virtually the only filmmaker whom critics attack as racist.

One reason he filmed so often in Monument Valley was that his Navajo
friends needed the money his projects brought them. He paid them union
wages at a time when Indians were not commanding even fifty cents a day.
He studied their language, played their sports, was adopted into their tribe,
and named Natani Nez—"Tall Soldier." A blizzard covered the Valley in the
fifties, and Ford got army planes to drop food in. "To the Navajos," said
Harry Goulding, who operated a lodge there, "Mr. Ford is holy, sorta."[41]
Indians, in Ford's movies, are both noble and savage, just like the whites.
"They say I took pleasure in killing Indians in the movies," said Ford, late in
life. "But while today film people shed tears over the fate of the Indians,
write humanitarian pamphlets and make declarations of intention without
ever, *ever* putting their hands in their pockets, more humbly I gave them
work. . . . More than having received Oscars, what counts for me is having
been made a blood brother of various Indian nations. Perhaps it's my Irish
atavism, my sense of reality, of the beauty of clans, in contrast to the modern world, the masses, the collective irresponsibility. Who better than an
Irishman could understand the Indians, while still being stirred by the tales
of the U.S. Cavalry? We were on both sides of the epic."[42]

The complexity of Ford's treatments of blacks and the military—core
themes best considered in context of the pictures themselves—was obscured
by his public career as a naval officer. An Air Medal gained making *This Is*

Korea! had earned him retirement promotion to rear admiral in 1951, and he would periodically train navy film crews at sea or make a documentary, not so much in support of a war, as of the men fighting it. For him the muddled ambiguities of Vietnam were overshadowed by his immersion in those of the past. Ironically, his defense of the notion, in all its simplicity, that this was a struggle for freedom against tyranny embarrassed official hypocrisy, for the government withdrew his movie enunciating this simplicity.

In 1937 Ford had contributed $1000 for an ambulance for the Loyalists in Spain, and had written his nephew Bob Ford, "Politically, I am a definite socialist democrat—always left. Communism to my mind is not the remedy this sick world is seeking. I have watched the Russian experiment with great interest. Like the French commune I am afraid it might lead to another Buonaparte [sic]. Mussolini was in early manhood an anarchist, Hitler almost."[43] His name appeared on the masthead of liberal antifascist organizations such as the Motion Picture Democratic Committee. If he later seemed to drift to the right, it was because its ideological purity occasionally seemed preferable to the general carpetbaggery. More than ever, he was basically uninvolved with politics. He was unusually candid during a visit to Paris in 1967, as Bertrand Tavernier reported: "I'm a liberal Democrat. Mostly, I'm a rebel." His favorite presidents? "Lincoln, Roosevelt and John Kennedy. I adored Kennedy . . . but Johnson is a detestable person, a murderer." Bob Kennedy he thought "an ambitious opportunist." "In the last elections, I didn't vote. Goldwater had no serious program and I hated Johnson." He opposed organizations like the American Legion mixing in politics. "I hate people who try to dictate your conduct." Asked about the McCarthy purges, Ford replied, "I was the first to protest." Tavernier continues:

> Several times he spoke vehemently about communists, like a middle American. Nonetheless, when we introduced Samuel Lachize, from *l'Humanité,* as a communist critic, Ford didn't blink. "Let him come in . . . I'd love to talk with a communist . . . I'm a liberal."
>
> And then, to our great astonishment, the conversation unrolled beautifully. The two were instantly sympathetic and Ford didn't play games with Lachize's questions. He responded at length, a very rare thing, and only became angry when Lachize told him some people thought (wrongly, added Lachize) there were racist aspects in his work:
>
> "The people who say that are mad, insane. I'm a Northerner. I detest segregation and I've employed hundreds of blacks at the same wages as whites. I got the production companies to pay a tribe of Indians, who were starving, at the same rate as the highest paid Hollywood extras and I saved them. Racist, me? My best friends are blacks: Woody Strode and my servant who's lived with me for thirty years. I've even made a picture which exalted the blacks. . . . No, I'm not a racist. I consider the blacks as completely American."
>
> He came back to the subject a number of times, and we had immense difficulty trying to calm him down. He even mentioned how Jews were

treated in the USSR, the only time he made a critical reference to his questioner's ideology. The tone remained very cordial, but the reference had struck him. All at once, he called me in a stentorian voice and asked me to bring him his rosary. [Ford was receiving in bed, with his dirty night shirt, cigar butts and chocolate bars.] When he had it in his hand, he gave it to Lachize, saying, "Take it, it's a gift. Join our group."

Lachize was stupefied. Ford took back the rosary. "I'll pray to Our Lady for you."[44]

DECOMPOSITION (1956–1961)

In 1952 *The Quiet Man* had been released to universal acclaim, and Ford had won his final Oscar. All six of his Oscars were displayed in his office or home, although publicly he feigned disinterest and had always skirted attending award ceremonies.* But Ford had ceased since the war, as Andrew Sarris has observed, to exercise fashionable leadership. One did not look to Ford for films like *Key Largo, On the Waterfront, The Country Girl, Rebel Without a Cause, Man with a Golden Arm,* or *Psycho.* His ideas no longer resounded within the new ideology, but seemed instead to be backward-looking. True, Ford movies continued to be popular, almost all popular movies seemed far more backward-looking than Ford's, and Hollywood as a whole was even less concerned than Ford with the latest fancies of New York critics, who themselves scarcely reflected the mainstream. But Ford was a special case. The rites of his cult obscured the newness and evolution of his work. Fashionable progressives did not want careful analyses of functioning racism and mythmaking; they wanted to see suffering minorities screaming for justice and myths rejected. Conservatives, meanwhile, were blind to Ford's ridicule and revisionism, and saw only celebrations of tradition; their interpretations reinforced progressive rejection of Ford. For example, *Fort Apache:* here is a picture glorifying the Indians and debunking myths of the 7th Cavalry; yet it is incessantly cited as a typical example of exactly the opposite and of everything wrong with John Ford. Such failure to communicate seems due neither to directorial or audience incompetence but to the role ballyhoo plays in shaping not only how we see movies but our ideologies and national politics as well. Ford's image was linked to the establishment and his pictures were too strongly within the classic mainstream for his wisdom's subtle complexities to be perceived.

The Ford aura of these years was linked to the image of John Wayne kicking Maureen O'Hara, to Victor McLaglen's drunken bluster, and to the director's endless cigarsmoke-laden games of "pitch" with piles of silver dol-

---

*But he had accepted an honorary doctorate from the University of Maine, Orono, in 1947, and an honorary master's from Bowdoin College the same year. Williams College offered him an honorary master's provided he show up to accept it; he went to Brazil instead—May 1943. Maine schools only, apparently, although he may have received LL. D. from Brandeis.

lars and such macho stalwarts as Wayne and Ward Bond. (Humphrey Bogart joined the gang occasionally. Once, having been slipped the Queen of Spades during a game of Hearts, he flew into a towering rage, swore never again to set foot in the house, and stormed out. He returned, sheepishly, after fifteen minutes: it was his own house.) Ford's hard-nosed, man's-man image and his wild eccentricities hid the real person. It was more fun to contemplate his slow, theatricalized antics chewing handkerchiefs and lighting his pipe, the long silences prefacing explosions of sarcasm. But as Anna Lee, to whom he gave candy on Valentine's Day, has said, people neglect what a kind and wonderful man he was—if he liked you; if he did not, he could be very unkind. Lindsay Anderson wrote these impressions in 1951:

> It is natural that anecdotists should concentrate on his wild Irish temper, his fondness for horseplay, the violence of his conflicts with producers and high-stepping actresses; and there is no reason to suppose these stories exaggerated. (Ford has only to protest "I'm a quiet, gentle person" for one to be quite sure they are not.) But besides the stampedes, the war parties, the knockabout fights, there are those quiet moments in his films, equally characteristic, of tenderness and insight; and these too his presence reflects. This was the Ford I found in Dublin—a man of fascinating contradictions; of authority in no way diminished by a complete rejection of apparatus; of instinctive personal warmth as likely to evidence itself in violence as in gentleness; confident of his powers, yet unpretentious about their achievement. A patriarchal figure, sitting among friends; it was easy to understand the devotion he inspires in those who work for him.[45]

We must, then, accept Ford anecdotes within context of his immense charisma. No one could have gotten away for decades with being so abusive and such a prima donna in the petty-petty ego-glorious worlds of Hollywood and the navy had he not possessed a fascination that more than compensated. Kindness and humor were his chief traits. Even midst aggravation, the madder he got, the wittier he became.

People so often approached him expecting the worst and emerged charmed. Robert Parrish's journalist aunt had been meeting popes, statesmen, plutocrats, and celebrities for thirty years; after chatting in Gaelic with Ford, she remarked he was among the most delightful people she had ever met—but it was a pity he had not continued his studies for the priesthood (!).[46]

Allan Dwan, after some four hundred films beginning in 1911, had adopted a rather casual approach to direction by 1949. Then one day Ford, who had worked for Dwan as a prop boy back at Universal, came into his office. Dwan, sixty-four, was about to start *The Sands of Iwo Jima*, and Ford, Dwan relates, said, "'Will you throw yourself into this one? Will you really *do* this one? For me, will you do it?' Like a coach talking to a guy who was going to play halfback for him. He pepped me up so much I said, 'All right, for your sake I'll make a good picture.'" Ford then talked John Wayne into starring in it, and *The Sands of Iwo Jima* is today the picture that Allan Dwan is best remembered for, out of all those four hundred.[47]

Yet even in 1954, surrounded by friends, wealth, medals, and unparalleled prestige, Ford's self-esteem was prey to the same anxieties that had made him ill during previews of *The Informer*. Filming of *Mister Roberts* had begun in a party spirit as the Ford regulars, and *Araner*, too, gathered in Hawaii for Ward Bond's marriage to his friend of many years, Mary Lou May. Henry Fonda, who had been out of films since *Fort Apache* in 1948, was there as well. He was to play the title role in *Mister Roberts*, as he had in the play's Broadway production. Unknown to Fonda, Warners had thought William Holden or Marlon Brando would be better box office and had consented to Fonda only when Ford threatened not to make the movie unless they did so. But Fonda had spent seven years playing *Mister Roberts* and now quickly became disgruntled with Ford's approach: "I didn't like the kind of roughhouse humor that Pappy was bringing to it. . . . Pappy shot it all wrong. He didn't know the timing. He didn't know where the laughs were and how long to wait for them to die down. He had them all talking at once, throwing one line in on top of another. When I said something he just handed me the script and said, 'Here, you wanna direct?'"[48] The producer, Leland Haywood, sided with the actor, and during a meeting of the three of

Mr. Roberts (1955). Cast and crew relaxing.

them, Ford socked Fonda in the jaw, knocking him across the room. He apologized an hour later, but the rift never healed.

Of course, what is best for the stage is seldom best for a film, and an actor who thought he knew more than the director was scarcely a novelty. One would expect that "hard-nosed" Ford would have surmounted discord this time as he had so often in the past. But instead Ford started drinking and, as the weeks passed, he became more and more morose; he took to retreating to the *Araner,* and finally hid there, refusing to eat or see anyone. Production was shut down for five days. Ford sobered up and got back to work, but shortly afterward his gallbladder ruptured and he was hospitalized for an operation. Mervyn LeRoy was brought in to replace him. *

The "betrayal" of a friend is not enough to account for Ford's behavior; fear of failure is a likelier explanation. His ability with comedy, which *he* thought his strong point, had always been questioned. He was taking a large risk in transmogrifying a fashionable Broadway play into the quite different thing that is a Fordian comedy. He lost confidence in himself. His need to achieve was undiminished.

There were many reversals in the fifties. Besides Francis Ford's death, the fights with Republic, and the dissolution of Argosy, home and health came under attack. After thirty-four years in their unfashionable Odin Street home (to which they had occasionally added extra rooms), the Fords were summarily given sixty days to vacate: the City of Los Angeles wanted the hill for a Hollywood Bowl parking lot. Protest was useless; so was a two-week binge on the *Araner.* They moved in May 1953 to a Mexican-style Bel Air house, 125 Copo de Oro Road, formerly owned by the William Wylers, and by the Frank Lloyds before that. Very Hollywood, it did not seem like home.

Both *Araner* and Ford were deteriorating physically. The $100,000 he spent repairing the boat's dry rot was only the beginning of a constant financial drain. Ford's attack of "shingles" in 1949 was probably just a means of getting out of doing *Pinky,* a film he disliked. But there was nothing phony about the gallbladder attack that forced him off *Mister Roberts* in 1954; his stomach blew up like a balloon. He suffered also from periodic pain in his

---

*Ford shot most of the exteriors, but there are few of these, and many of them are integrated with studio work, so that there are virtually no significant sequences of Fordian cinema, with the editing Ford intended. His segments are recognizable by their faster tempo, spiffier style, greater physicality, and more inventive employment of space. The LeRoy segments—long, sparsely edited, talky, and static—lack visual interest and resemble a filmed play, as Fonda wished. Ford can be distinguished during the nurses' visit; in the altercation (in crosscuts) between Fonda and James Cagney over shirtless sailors; and in individual shots of the Liberty Port sequence. Ford evidently intended a speedier, many-charactered portrait of a crew, and more ambivalence about duty and obedience. His Roberts, in contrast to the fairly simple one of LeRoy and Fonda, would have enriched contradictions: his druggy pomposity and thirst for glory that make him prefer to be the crew's hero rather than an effective intermediary. Ford had wished to eliminate the scotch-making and the laundry scenes—which Joshua Logan directed after *LeRoy* left. Some of the slapstick comedy Ford inserted—such as the drunk sailor riding a motorcycle off a pier—was cut out by Fonda and Haywood and then restored by Warners.

left arm (where he had been wounded at Midway) and, more seriously, from his eyes.

His eyesight had always been terrible. He had begun sporting his famous black eyepatch in the early thirties, partly for its rakishness, partly to protect his light-sensitive left eye; but he wore it only now and then and would lift it up in order to read. Dark glasses and the eyepatch also kept others from seeing the tenderness that all who knew him well found in his eyes. And naturally he profited from no one being quite sure how much he could see. Sometimes he would not see something six feet in front of him; but if he were filming and an actor readjusted his hat a hundred yards away, he would stop the shot. In Africa, however, blurred vision and amoebic dysentery had led him to shorten *Mogambo*'s location shooting schedule; planned exteriors were moved into tents and filmed later in London. Mary then accompanied John on a holiday drive down to Naples, from where, on April 2, 1953, they sailed home on the *Andrea Doria*; but Ford's vision had grown worse, and he spent the voyage in his darkened cabin. On June 30 he entered the hospital for a critical operation; he was afflicted with conical myopia and with external cataracts on both eyes. The operation gave him the experience of total blindness for a number of weeks and only slightly improved his sight.

The effect on Ford of these multiple afflictions is apparent in the pictures of the next five years.

Decomposition: The Films

	Filmed / released	
The Rising of the Moon	Spring '56 / May '57	Four Province Prodns. – Warner Bros.
The Wings of Eagles	Aug. '56 / Feb. '57	Metro-Goldwyn-Mayer
The Growler Story (documentary)	Nov. '56 /	U.S. Navy
Gideon's Day	Spring '57 / Mar. '58 (G.B.)	Columbia British Prodns.
The Last Hurrah	/ Nov. '58	Columbia
Korea: Battleground for Liberty (documentary)	Fall '58 /	U.S. Dept. of Defense
The Horse Soldiers	Fall '58 / June '59	Mirisch–United Artists
Sergeant Rutledge	May '59 / May '60	Ford Prodns.–Warner Bros.
The Colter Craven Story (TV)	/ May '60	*Wagon Train* series
Two Rode Together	Nov. '60 / July '61	Ford–Sheptner Prodns.–Columbia

The films comprising this period are distinguished by disequilibrium, stark modal contrasts, cynical pessimism, and experimentation. These are pictures with myriad magic moments, but (except for *Gideon's Day*) without overall coherence. Often one feels Ford is uninspired and merely doing his job.

It is an era of confusion in the movie industry, of the disappearance of the studios, of independent superproductions. Without much difficulty we can discern the itinerary of Ford's private life, his struggles with the decay of age, his search to reconcile his religion and the world's evil, his faltering faith in America.

In contrast to other divisions in Ford's oeuvre, the boundaries of this transitional period are somewhat vague. *The Long Gray Line* and *The Searchers* contain incipient traits of "decomposition." And similarly, at the other end, *The Man Who Liberty Valance* is flawed by traces of misanthropy.

All of these movies, from *The Searchers* on, concern themselves with persistent heroes in increasingly malevolent worlds. There is, as a result, a growing polarization between the sweet and the horrible, which Ford, attempting to expand the dimensions of his realism, tries to embrace with altered expressionistic techniques—and fails, fails because his style is inordinately strained. The solution, aesthetically and philosophically, will be found in the final period, in a transcendent approach capable of containing otherwise incommensurate contradictions.

The Wings of Eagles (1957).

The title was lousy [recalled Ford]—I screamed at that. I just wanted to call it "The Spig Wead Story." . . . I didn't want to do the picture because Spig was a great pal of mine. But I didn't want anyone *else* to make it. I knew him first when he was deck officer, black shoe, with the old *Mississippi*—before he went flying. . . . We did quite a few pictures together. He died in my arms. I tried to tell the story as truthfully as possible, and everything in the picture was true. The fight in the club—throwing the cake . . . , the plane landing in the swimming pool—right in the middle of the Admiral's tea—[all] that really happened.[49]

The Long Gray Line dealt with West Point and an immigrant outsider's subsumption into its culture. *The Wings of Eagles*, Ford's only other extended biography, deals with the navy (like *Salute*) and with Spig Wead's efforts to fit into life—navy, marriage, writing.

Ford concentrates on Wead's inner itinerary. His public life, in contrast, is narrated so obliquely*—via newspapers (three), film clips (three), off-screen narrators (two, three times), meetings, a marquee, a chartroom, and battle (like *When Willie Comes Marching Home*)—that one may well finish the movie wondering who Wead was to have a movie made about him.** But then

---

*For example: attention is called to insignia whenever promotions occur, but ranks are never identified. This is probably an inside joke, since fewer people recognize navy than army insignia. Similarly, names are carelessly given. Clark Gable is never identified in the *Hell Divers* clip. Admiral John Dale Price, an actual Wead friend who (played by Ken Curtis) narrates the movie and is credited as "technical advisor," is referred to in the movie only as "Johnny Dale."

**Besides naval aviation and devising World War II's "jeep" carriers (to replace disabled planes), Frank Wead, Jr., after recovering from total paralysis, received credit for some thirty-

The Wings of Eagles (1957). Ford talks to Ward Bond (imitating Ford) and
John Wayne.

it is typical of "transitional" films that they provoke questions and leave one
with incoherence. This picture, and Spig, gravitate around four motifs whose
correspondence is, annoyingly, suggested but ultimately unclear (to me, at
least): illusion/reality and friendship/separation. The key would appear to
be that Spig is destructive to himself and to others; this is the reality, which he
attempts to avoid through situations of irreality and isolation.

Military life, and Ford's least attractive portrait of it, is part of irreality—
poke-in-the-ribs rivalry among rah-rah locker-room jocks unimaginable
outside their own weird world. Wead, like his peers, fights, as though playing football, for money and power for his service, and Ford, whatever the
merits of Wead's crusade for air-power, displays the mechanics of self-
perpetuating military institutions run by brotherhoods of jingoistic myo-
pics. Even the classic defense is given to the particularly unsympathetic
Willis Bouchey, a perennial Ford heavy here playing a senator:

two Hollywood screenplays, from *Flying Fleet* (G. Hill, 1929) to *Blaze of Noon* (Farrow, 1947).
For Ford: *Air Mail, They Were Expendable.* Also: *Ceiling Zero* (Hawks), *Test Pilot* (Fleming),
The Citadel (Vidor), and many service pictures. Wead died in 1947.

— We've got a country yelling pacifism at us, disarmament, the world is going to live together like one big happy family, there'll be no more wars, the Army and the Navy are going out of business. Now, you fight maybe one war every generation, but we have to fight those voters every blame two years.

There is, in addition, a strange self-consciousness about military things. One finds oneself wondering what it would be like, every time one entered a room, to have somebody run ahead, shout "'Tention!" and have everyone stand stiff. Perhaps because Ford participated in many of these events (he ducked the cake), perhaps because this bland, broad, tough lifestyle was one side (of many contradictory sides) of Ford, his choice of dramatic tone is often uncertain and distanced. The free-for-all fight, for example, prompts less laughter than puzzlement—especially after two rival noncoms call a truce and drink beer instead. Why these strange pleasures? Does their energetic and artificial existence breed an unfulfillment that finds release in a good fight? Ford's friendly fights are blatant sadism. Those in *The Long Voyage Home* and *Mister Roberts* gain eroticism from repression, but elsewhere (*She Wore a Yellow Ribbon, What Price Glory, The Quiet Man, Donovan's Reef*) heterosexual needs seem secondary to male comradery. The first lines of Johnny Dale's voice-off narration—"Spig knew he wanted to fly and I knew I wanted whatever Spig wanted"—set the tone for this portrait of a friend: Spig is always viewed from slightly uncomprehending third-person distance, but he is viewed always with devotion.

Partially because Spig prefers the world of men, partially because Minne is the only Ford service wife unwilling to accept her subservient role, Spig is never able to integrate career and marriage. This dimension of impotence becomes more palpable with paralysis and his final ride down the cable. In one sense Spig's dilemma is the familiar Ford theme of outside forces determining an individual (as Ford said of Wead, "Life disappointed him"), but here it is also a quasi-sexual theme, and military life, if not labeled deviant, is at least viewed as destructive. Wead is compared to Frank Merriwell, a foolish hero who leaves confusion in his wake (as is Mr. Peter in 7 *Women*). Wead proceeds from slapstick* through melodrama to tragedy, but his era is portrayed as sad and subdued (consistent with Ford's contemporary movies) and so is he: "Half man, half worm, half wit," he describes himself. "Damn the martinis, full speed ahead . . . star-spangled Spig," his wife calls him. For an obstinate persistence replaces *The Long Gray Line*'s theme of subsistence. Spig persists, but fate (?) has a will of its own.

Reality, illusion, and friendship. Unfortunate in not having a more compatible mate, Spig suffers as deeply as Minne but never gives up hope—nor surrenders his independence. Ford does not simplify (or clarify); at least three motives might explain why, paralyzed, Wead sends her away: the heroic gesture of sacrifice, the despair and neuroses induced by sudden helplessness, the unbearable pain of being an object of pity.

Spig endures hell (reality). Ford's matured expressionism, the sun and rain, the shadows, the bright white streak across the mattress, the burning-yellow coloration, Wead's horizontal pose, all convey a state of soul. He is forced to accept help, because Carson, unlike Minne, is not the sort to be sent away. "I'm gonna help you through this little trouble," declares this paragon of friendship. The principles of military training are adaptable to every situation: for days, and even with music, Spig chants, "I'm gonna move that toe!" From this lugubriousness springs an oddly heroic distance, bringing into relief a polyphony of strong emotional motifs, emphasized in Ford's unusual Mizoguchian tracking shot back from the window, over Spig, and across the room, a gesture of classic distancing wedded to Murnau expressionism—awed withdrawal.

To this point, newspapers and newsreels have hinted at the film's play between irreality (e.g., seeing Daddy on a moviescreen—a movie within a movie) and brute evidence (being paralyzed). Now the simile accelerates. Always the myopic, always living the immediate moment, Spig looks into the mirror that Carson places under him and, at first—it's a gag—sees not his toes, but the names written on the mirror's surface; Carson obliges him

---

*The airplane stunts repeat gags in the Ford-Wead *Air Mail* (1931).

to look deeper into the reflection. And Wead, persisting in his chant, eventually turns deeper into himself: the second time we see the mirror he is looking at his own face in it. But this is not all. Wead must learn he *needs* others. The third time we see the mirror he sees in it the roses that Minne (he knows) has sent anonymously: now he moves his toe. Once again flowers play an important role in Ford. Earlier, when Spig comes home to a messy living room, he throws a bouquet into the wastebasket. Minne, wandering home tipsy, discovers it there and realizes Spig is back. The bouquet continues to counterpoint their reconciliation as Minne throws it beside Spig, washing dishes in the kitchen, and he typically puts it in a vase and plops it down in front of her.

Spig inspires devotion, but he is afraid to admit his need for friends and is never seen giving back as much as he receives. Typically, we never hear him tell Minne he loves or wants her. Typically, he replies, "That was yesterday, what do we do now?" when Carson complains Spig has not written in years. Typically, he forgets all about Johnny Dale when Dale provides the key word, "jeep," to solve a tactical dilemma.

This last incident is bathed in irreality: a darkened chartroom in which Wead, sleeping there in search of solution, flashes his flashlight on and off around the room; whenever the door is opened, alarms ring and glaring lights pop on. But there does not appear to be an exact correspondence in the movie between Wead's treatment of friends and the motif of reality / irreality. Yet reality is generally hostile. The Victrola (representing reality) that spits records at Minne* when Pearl Harbor thwarts her reunion with Spig is the same sort of symbolic idea as recurs, benignly, with the slot machine in *Donovan's Reef.* War has provided another intrusion of reality, and, like paralysis, comes clothed in its own artifice.

Midst the potent expressionism of the authentic battle scenes (Kwaja-lein, January 1944), the 1956 scenes of Wead (Wayne) during the battle con-trast obviously; thus it is not surprising that Spig emerges unscathed, but that Carson is wounded protecting Wead.

Spig gets Carson wounded, but Carson rejects from Wead (again coming too late) assistance similar to that which Carson gave Wead earlier. Again the motivation is complex: pride, anger, a hint that Wead should retire. Spig has a heart attack, and now comes the climax: a rapid montage of seventeen shots of sea battle at night, cannons thunder, balls of fire streak gold-red through the pitch-black sky. Reality replies to Spig with persistent repeti-tion of its own, with a dreadful might that achieves the most implacable figure of hostile determinism in Ford, and which, while dwarfing even the indomitable Spig** and proclaiming the folly of any individual's indepen-dence, simultaneously reverses itself and becomes the formalized expres-sion, again, of Spig's state of soul.

He decides to retire; death is approaching and he has caused enough damage. "Let 'em think I'm licked." But clearing out his desk, photographs (i.e., illusions) of Minne start him dreaming of happier times. The black-and-white photo dissolves, with the fantasy sparkle of thirties Hollywood, into hazy color flashbacks of life with Minne. As in *How Green Was My*

*Perhaps in vengeance for a record broken in *Air Mail.*
**Spig's strength is apparent when he holds a telephone—the old, heavy metal type—aloft and steady with one hand, keeping the arm above its cradle, while dialing with the other hand.

Valley, some we have not seen before (but we did see Spig taking one he is now fantasizing over), and all memories are glorified. Yet the memories and parade concluding Spig's life lack the affirmation of those concluding Marty Maher's in *The Long Gray Line*. In place of that optimism, it now seems (as it will again in *The Last Hurrah*) that at the end all you have, and the best any man can hope for, is friends. Lined up on deck to see Spig off, these admirals and generals set a seal of moral redemption to Wead's life; but they also attest to its failure. The old buddies have grown into their uniforms to the point that they look almost alike, all of the same mold, while Spig, at last reduced to tears of friendship and public avowal of incapacity, melts into an outsider: a human being first, a soldier not at all.

Another thing Spig persisted in was writing: through thirty-nine(?) rejections. Writing, says Carson, "is just a bunch of lies wrapped up in paper," so Spig ought to be able to do it well (i.e., irreality again). The Hollywood director he goes to work for is called John Dodge in the film; in real life it was George Hill; in actuality it is Ward Bond imitating John Ford. Ford claims this was Bond's idea, but Ford was more than cooperative. We see the Old Man's Oscars, his hat, pipe, whiskey-holding cane, prize Mexican saddle, pictures, and who knows what else. Bond imitates Ford's boots, his white handkerchief that he played with, and walk, and numerous small tics. The way Bond-Dodge-Ford gives Wead instructions—just write about "people, Navy people"—recalls Frank Nugent's account of his first *Fort Apache* story conference with Ford. Earlier, when Wead asks John Dale, "How does he know I can write?" Dale (i.e., Ken Curtis, Ford's son-in-law) replies, "Well, he knows *he* can't!"—a line whose truth is confirmed by Nunnally Johnson's account of Ford's frustration at not being able to write. Dodge's secretary of twenty-two years has her counterpart in Ford's. And on the office wall are pictures of Harry Carey and Tom Mix. The little skit with the matchbook during *Hell Divers* has the look of another Ford imitation, used in *Rookie of the Year*.

At one point, trying to warn Wead away from the theater, Dodge cites his own experience, throwing a copy of *The Odyssey* onto the table:

Dodge: I even played in this thing once.
Wead: *Ulysses?* You played in *Ulysses?*
Dodge: Yep, Bowling Green, Kentucky. I played Robert E. Lee.

Does this joke have any meaning? Apparently not. Does Wead's life have any meaning? Apparently not. *Meanings*, perhaps, to those who knew him and to himself. But for us . . . ? We are struck more by its incoherence, its defeats and failures. It remains a mystery marked by persistence, endurance, and more than a hint of futility. Wead may remind us of Sisyphus, but we do not think of him as happy.

Such a vision of life may be realistic. But is such irresolution consistent with the needs of art, in which we expect aesthetic completion? Can the film have meaning, when its subject does not? The question nags at Ford's film in this period. He had always sought to *equate* form and meaning. But now meaning begins to disintegrate, and so form decomposes, too. Peter Bogdanovich found a message in these movies: "glory in defeat." Of course, in Wead's case, glory may have been in his life, but certainly was not in his defeat. Nonetheless, the theme, scarcely hinted at in previous pictures, lurks throughout these years. Initially, when defeated heroes survive, as in the opening story of *The Rising of the Moon*, glory appears redemptive. But by *The Last Hurrah* and *The Horse Soldiers*, when defeated heroes die, glory resounds emptily as mere rationalization of waste.

The Rising of the Moon (1957). The relative optimism of *The Rising of the Moon* and *Gideon's Day*, scarred though it may be, derives also from their being made in the British Isles, where Ford, taking no salary, was able to escape professional and personal problems in America and to make movies his own way. *

---

*Producer of both (and actual, though uncredited, producer of *The Quiet Man*) was the Lord Killanin (Michael Morris), hereditary peer, Shell Oil director, one of the world's leading aspirin distributors, and, recently, head of the World Olympic Committee. His barony adjoined Ford's father's birthplace, and there were blood ties between the families. With Ford, Killanin formed Four Province Productions, including Roger Greene, Brian Desmond Hurst, and Michael Scott, and struggled tirelessly to promote filmmaking in Eire. There were ambitious plans (see the list of unrealized projects at the end of the Filmography), but none of them materialized. *The Rising of the Moon*'s negative cost $256,016.53, and with distribution costs it netted a loss of around $250,000. World grosses scarcely exceeded $100,000. Before deciding on "A Minute's Wait," Ford had thought of doing "Ghost Story," with Katharine Hepburn. *The Rising of the Moon* was controversial in Ireland: it was banned by the city of Belfast and caused protests among IRA sympathizers in the South.

Uncommercial, ethnic in character, with an almost overwhelming sense of place, and employing Abbey Theatre Players, *The Rising of the Moon* was originally called "Three Leaves of a Shamrock." The shamrock was once the symbol of Irish resistance, and the movie's three stories have revolution as their—covert—theme. In "The Majesty of the Law," Inspector Dillon follows narrow lanes into the country, along a stream where sunlight and tree-shadows ripple gently.

> Come back, Paddy Reilly!
> . . . The Garden of Eden has vanished, they say,
> But I know the lie of it still . . .

sings a background tenor, with recorder. We glimpse an old man walking stiffly, and a moonshiner, indicating a ruined tower, quips, "From there to a wee thatched cottage." " 'Tisn't the cottage that makes the king," replies Dillon, and Mickey J. echoes, as if savoring poetic wisdom.

The old man, in rhymed motion, throws himself backward into the air while slamming his hat to the ground; just then, the inspector bursts into and across the frame. All this equals "Welcome." The extravagant warmth and sincerity of Dan O'Flaherty (authentically overplayed by Noel Purcell) suit the granite will his arthritic movements reflect. A certain Feeney called him a liar, accordingly Dan bashed his skull; Feeney sued, Dan will not pay the £5 fine. So Dillon has been sent to arrest him. This is revealed midst vehement fireside prolixities on every subject under the sun: mostly traditions lost, songs, secrets, cures. * Much of the movie's charm lies in the lilt of its dialogue. But, as Mickey J. demonstrated, running round the tower enclosing his still while the inspector waited for him to complete his circle instead of chasing him, the inevitable cannot be evaded.

Friday evening Dan sets out for prison, kissing his stone as neighbors stand silent witness. Suddenly Feeney appears, hobbling in bathrobe and bandages, begging to pay the fine himself. O'Flaherty's cane implacably bars the frame:

> I will punish you, you weak snivering man. I will lie on bare boards for you. I will suffer for you, so that neither you nor your children nor their children after them will be able to raise their heads for the shame of it! Who walks with me to the top of the hill?

Farmwomen bow; poor as he may be, he is their king.

"The Majesty of the Law" bids hail-and-farewell to heroism for lost principles. The reactionary old man today is revolutionary, as the moonshiner represents sedition, and the inspector a reluctant instrument of alien codes superimposed on native order. **

*The notion of youth's loss of traditional knowledge recurs in *The Long Gray Line* when cadets forget Maj. Keough, and in *The Searchers* when young Pat Wayne cannot locate places not mentioned on maps, and in *Liberty Valance* when newspapermen have never heard of Tom Doniphon.

**Dialogue was added to Frank O'Connor's story, wherein "Dan Bride" was a simple farmer, without the royal ancestors Ford adds; the rebuke to Feeney is announced to the in-

The other two stories seem less significant. Yet "A Minute's Wait," a delightful train-station vignette comedy, demonstrates deft virtuosity with some twenty characters. And the residual oppression of modern Eire depicted in the first two stories becomes overt in the stark contrasts and vertiginous angles of "1921." A patriot escapes prison disguised as a nun, then Ireland disguised as a balladeer.* A policeman, distracted by his wife, allows the escape, and comes in the process to a consciousness of self and oppression—the first step toward revolution.

Gideon's Day (**1958**). "The freest, most direct, least fabricated film ever to sprout from one of Her Majesty's studios," was the verdict of the prestigious *Cahiers du Cinéma*.[50] But when the picture got released in America, its title had been changed (to *Gideon of Scotland Yard*) and it was relegated to the "art house" circuits of the day (then specializing in Margaret Rutherford and coffee), and rather than go to the expense of Technicolor prints, Columbia distributed it in black-and-white.

Yet *Gideon*, following a Scotland Yard inspector through a single day, with thirty episodes and fifty speaking parts tidily compressed into ninety

---

spector, not in confrontation, and the fight resulted from an argument: there was no question of being accused of lying!

*Francis Ford's 1916 *The Cry of Erin* concerns an Irish peasant escaping execution by changing clothes with a priest, then sailing from Cork.

minutes, is among Ford's most personal and ambitious movies, although costing only $543,600. One senses how delighted he was with his cast of English actors, especially Jack Hawkins (Gideon), whom Ford, extravagant with praise, called "the finest dramatic actor with whom I have worked."[51]

This particular Gideon's day gets a high score: a rapist, two mobsters, a female con artist, a murderer, a corrupt policeman, three bank robbers. But Gideon gets the wrong fish—an old haddock instead of the fresh salmon his wife requested. And his personal life is ill-fated: he loses his morning bath to his daughter, gets hit with a ball coming downstairs, gets a traffic ticket, forgets his concert ticket (and the fish), can't find a parking space, rips his coat, has a drink thrown in his face, is interrupted at breakfast, at morning tea, lunch at home, porkpie in pub, sandwich in office, and midnight dinner at home. Customarily frantic—he literally spends the whole movie going in and out of doors—often driven to fury by crime, he nonetheless has that strange English ability to relax totally when his job calls for him to interview someone. Yet as the opening shots tell us—beautiful Technicolor of sunny happy London, followed by a beshadowed Gideon burning the night oil in his bare drab office—Gideon is a hero because he deals all day with things everyone else can afford to ignore, and because when he gets home he has no stories to tell. Not that he is untainted: he is overly alarmed when Kate tells him "some young man" took Sally home from her concert; his job deprives his family of his presence, and its problems make him difficult. As Sally says, "Just because something's gone wrong—we all have to suffer!"

Kate is like one of Ford's cavalry wives at some remote outpost and, thanks to Anna Lee's beautifully poised and assuredly modest performance, she does her job with hardly an unangelic whimper. The world's "wrongness," however, afflicts women with much suffering. "Promise me one thing. Never marry a policeman," says Kate. But love and compassion for Gideon shine in her eyes, and Sally, answering "Yes mother," gazes dreamily after Constable Farnaby-Green, thus proving Gideon's daughter's love for her very human father. The charm of these home scenes (the happy light-greens, yellows, and red-checked tablecloths of Kate's kitchen, balanced by her blue dress) makes them the picture's nicest parts. Indeed, George Gideon is one of those rarest of Fordian people—a man with a wife, family, and real home at film's end. But, as in *The Searchers*, this cheer exists to contrast the hostility beyond.

Ford's sole tragicomedy, *Gideon's Day* is about London, the British, and 1957, about the claustrophobia, craziness, and complacent despair of modern life ("London Bridge is falling down . . ." mocks the theme tune—and it is surely not unintentional when we glimpse a headline about the H-bomb). Yet if *Gideon's Day*, of all the 1956–61 films, comes closest to solving the aesthetic problem of molding such wildly disparate material into modal forms with overall coherence, this is because its tone is generally light and its characters deep and clear.

The humor is often Ford's traditional, understated wackiness: the squeak of Farnaby-Green's shoes and his slightly Chaplinesque walk; the chief's obsession with his moose head; the way the vicar's daughter enters the church carrying one large flower; Sergeant Gully snapping to attention when Gideon enters, and the latter's bemused reproof that the war has been over for years. One relishes the way Farnaby-Green, giving Gideon his ticket, remarks to his daughter with polite snottiness, "The law, Miss Gideon, allows no distinction between high-ranking police officers and other members of the public," and the way Gideon repeats the same words to Farnaby-Green in the last scene. Eighteen-year-old Sally Gideon is delightfully puckish, particularly mimicking Farnaby-Green to his face.*

The characters, as an interview with producer Killanin clarifies, owe more to Ford than to their conventional scripting**:

> *Killanin:* You more often than not suggest types quite different to that indicated in the script.
>
> *Ford:* But don't you see, I am interested in *people.* That is why [in] a picture like *Gideon's Day* and, indeed, *The Rising of the*

---

*In the last scene, the way Gideon pushes back his hat and throws away his match, when it turns out Farnaby-Green has forgotten his license, is an imitation of Ford by Hawkins.

**By T. E. B. Clarke, whose credits include Ealing comedies, *Hue and Cry, Passport to Pimlico, The Lavender Hill Mob.*

Moon where we had some 50 speaking characters, all the parts "sing." I certainly don't like type casting. I like casting for individuals, for I photograph people.

Killanin: Both the eventual pictures have gone a long way from the shooting script.

Ford: Because as the basic story develops one must develop each character in the actor, besides the mood and the tempo, so that the drama is correctly mixed with humor.[52]

Ford's point is paraphrased by Louis Marcorelles, in *Cahiers*:

For anyone who takes the trouble to open his eyes, to follow the progression of each shot and each detail in the shot, nothing happens in Ford except that which is rigorously desired, willed not by some higher decree of the scenario, but because each personage possesses his own internal logic, and is inscribed according to very precise limits onto space and time.[53]

Each portrait receives detailed care, in Ford's vignette method. For example, a decorous middle-aged secretary Duke interviews among three reports we see of an investigation into Joanna Delafield's past—surely a minor character if ever there were one!—grabs our interest: she tells nothing of

Gideon's Day. In the Gideons' kitchen: Jack Hawkins, Ford, Anna Lee, Anna Massey, and visitor John Wayne (without toupee).

Joanna we have not observed ourselves, but she chooses to complain of the same faults of character apparent in herself.

The quiet matter-of-factness of Ford's staging captures events as they are to their participants, thereby intensifying the horror of our passive witnessing. And comedy's *allegretto* tempo has an advantage over tragedy's *adagio*, in the effects to be gained through agogic emphases to serve as contemplative points of relaxation or tension. To cite a few instances: The second or two the camera rests on Mason's dead body; Mrs. Kirby's closed door after Gideon's terrible visit; Sayer climbing the stairs (deprived of all suspense because we know he will kill Dolly); the moments stolen to watch Sergeant Gully crease Gideon's hat; the half-startled glance Mrs. Kirby gives Gully when he brings her tea and announces, "Milk and sugar" (a bit like the fleeting instants of sweetness in *7 Women*; in fact, Mrs. Kirby resembles Agatha Andrews). Similarly, when Gideon hears the rape-murderer of a fourteen-year-old is on his way to London, his remark is trite, "Well, let's hope he gets here." But Ford has him walking slowly across the room as he says it, has him pause to fiddle with his pipe as he says it, and then has him walk out of the frame (then cutting back to him immediately!), and has Hawkins recite the line with a manly matter-of-factness that barely masks inner fury, so that what resonates is psychological insight into a character whose sense of purpose is even more potent and terrifying than *The Searchers'* Ethan Edwards's. And as with Edwards, a forward dolly to Gideon's eyes shows crusty professionalism has not inured him from caring deeply.

As Gideon's day darkens with nightfall, Ford becomes giddy, the craziness facile, color combinations jangly, discordant. And just violence in green contrasts with unjust violence in red. A slum church bathed in green light (exotic expressionism) with painted backdrop, neon lights of downtown London, jangly red, gold, white, and black of the Delafield apartment: color and artifice climax when the affectatious Fitzhubert complacently fires three bullets into Mason, a sympathetic vault guard, whose red blood Ford links with Fitzhubert's red carnation. This is one of few studied death scenes in Ford: he wants to impress evil's actuality, to make us hate it as Gideon does nearly slamming his fist into Fitzhubert, but above all to convey banality. Both the clichéd mad painter and Fitzhubert *bore* Gideon: he has seen such triteness-posing-as-genius hundreds of times. (Accordingly, Ford throws away his only action scene in one long dark take.) "You're due for a promotion—in ten or twenty years," Gideon cracks to one of his men, quoting from some John Ford western he must have seen.

Because one aspect of *Gideon's Day* is that it is a "crime prevention" film, Ford is able to elaborate his belief in justice "when it is virile." For justice, the police must be respected, as honest as effective. Unlike most police in pictures, Ford's bobbies never stumble. Nor are they ever particularly intelligent or heroic. Instead it is all routine performed with the placidity of a short-order cook.

The Last Hurrah (1958). Gideon & Co. are nonetheless fighting a rear-guard action. The relative absolutes that previously secured society are crumbling, to be replaced by brief moments of love midst general carnage. Still, in London *Gideon's Day* manages to find *some* hope within a psychotic world's ordered chaos, whereas in the chaotic order of Boston, *The Last Hurrah* finds only cynicism, misanthropy, and despair. (It becomes clear, at least, why Ford had avoided subjects dealing with contemporary America or with cities since *The Whole Town's Talking* in 1935.)

The personages surrounding Mayor Frank Skeffington—the potent cast surrounding Spencer Tracy—are mere satellites of an aging Irish king, whose unscrupulous ambition has for decades promoted the welfare, security, and future of his people. His ethnic patriarchal system has survived past its time, however, and Skeffington's defeat for reelection marks the emergence of a new—but unsecured—order. Skeffington is a Fordian hero in the Judge Priest mold; but this time the Maydews take over.

As in "The Majesty of the Law," tradition and ethnicity are heavily emphasized in the Ford-Nugent screenplay, but not in the literary source. "You wouldn't have me break with tradition, would you?" asks Skeffington. "Remember the day we took office. Frank Skeffington is available to every man and woman in this state." But only the last sentence is in Edwin O'Connor's novel, not the evocation of tradition. And far more than O'Connor, Ford sees this Dan-O'Flaherty-like majesty leading a bitter, dirty, racial struggle. All opposition, as far as Ford's Skeffington is concerned, is motivated by "the fact that the city is no longer yours [the Wasps']—it's ours." Skeffington is often contemptible (and Ford tastelessly misanthropic), as when blackmailing a slum-clearance loan by making the chief banker's mentally deficient son fire commissioner. But a Fordian hero always employs violence, and more often Skeffington is lovable, as when meeting his nephew's wife:

— Do you know? Your mother was the most beautiful woman I ever saw. Except for one. Your grandmother Ellen. And, you know? You look exactly like her.

Tradition for Skeffington is a living force, spearheaded by himself. He takes his nephew on a pilgrimage to his childhood tenement (another scene not in O'Connor):

— I was born here, Adam. Your father-in-law, the eminent Sir Roger, was born down there—oh, that of course is before it became a Chinese laundry. See that window: Martin Burke. ["You mean the Cardinal?!" interjects Adam, as the soundtrack quotes a tune associated with Donald Crisp in *The Long Gray Line*.] Yes. This is it. We were all born down here together, then drifted our different ways. [He strikes a match to peer at initials carved in a heart on a post:] Still there. I guess I was about six years old when I met your Aunt Kate. I've loved her ever since.

But tradition has not ennobled the younger generation. Cocky, foolish and superficial as Ford's young men are wont to be (in the postwar pictures), they never fare worse than in *The Last Hurrah.* Adam (Jeffrey Hunter), slightly urbane, slightly arrogant, slightly vapid, is the best of the lot; beyond loyalty (to his uncle) and contempt (for politics and numerous people) he almost never commits himself to a point of view. The pampered obliviousness of Skeffington's wishy-washy playboy son and the enemy banker's idiot son illustrate the dangers of patriarchy. It weighs too squarely on the shoulders of old men and enfeebles everyone else. Skeffington's victories have been obtained at too great a moral cost: there is ironic justice that his generation's corruption gives birth to the class-traitor who defeats him — the marshmallowy Kevin McCluskey (whose TV appearance seems a Fordian lampoon of Nixon's Checkers speech).

In *Drums Along the Mohawk*, a pastor warns a girl against an unfit suitor, praying, "He's a Massachusetts man, O Lord, and Thou knowest no good can come from Massachusetts!" *The Last Hurrah*'s host of misanthropic characters would not alter the pastor's mind: McCluskey's wife, Amos Force, Roger Sugrue, undertaker Johnny Degnan, among others. "I certainly do know Boston* and those people," said Ford. "Half of them are half-witted and half of them are bright, but there's always a couple of kooks among them."[54] Indeed, most of the kooks in Ford—Colonel Thursday, Doc Holliday, Amelia Dedham—come from Boston. And Ford's bitterness extends even into the unsympathetic satire of the Irish wake.

Skeffington, glorious in defeat, announces his candidacy for governor as he concedes the mayoralty. Yet he walks home alone, as McCluskey's victory parade passes behind him on a direction of its own: passage and continuity. He feels his heart give at home and (another interpolation) looks beseechingly toward his wife's portrait before collapsing down the stairs.

An ethnically authentic ritual has been established around this portrait of the dead Kate Skeffington. A lonely and isolated man, despite his active life, Skeffington places a fresh flower in front of it each morning. Now the parade of his supporters troops slowly into the house bringing him flowers. Adam, after Skeffington's death, puts a new flower beneath the portrait. But the action does not promise survival of tradition. Instead, the parade returns finally to Skeffington in the last shot when, from outside the door, we watch his old sidekicks and their shadows parade mournfully up the staircase to view their dead leader. As in *The Wings of Eagles*, life's ultimate achievement is having friends at the end.

---

*Though the picture says only "A New England City," one senses Boston, and O'Connor's novel was supposedly based on the career of Congressman, Mayor, Governor James Curley, who sued Columbia and settled for $25,000 in damages, then $15,000 when the first check went mysteriously astray. But Ford's picture never accuses Skeffington of personal corruption — beyond his blackmailing through a loan. (For Curley, see Francis Russell, "The Last of the Bosses," in *American Heritage,* June 1959.)

The Last Hurrah, in its major moments, develops Fordian symbology into a dark despair of dissolved traditions and social orders. Life and ideology seem futile—except for flowers.

But the picture as a whole is weak. "Something went out of it in the cutting," said Anna Lee, adding that Ford was disappointed with the picture and had not been permitted by Columbia to supervise its editing.[55] Perhaps it is not the editing's fault that the Adam character is a useless bystander, not even a narrator. But it is the editing's fault that *The Last Hurrah* is lethargic and long (121 minutes), with the lengthiest sequences and shots of Ford's career. No wonder his interest seems often merely casual, and cynicism rather than inspiration spikes banality. It should be a beautiful moment when Skeffington, inviting nephew Adam to watch the last old-style campaign, leans against the window and says, "The last hu-rrah." But it is tepid. The long monologue is essentially expository. Ford always avoided exposition and kept things stationary when words were important. Here, however, Skeffington wanders awkwardly from spot to spot, within a continual long shot, and energy and character are dissipated. Ford-Tracy's Skeffington is more symbolic than O'Connor's, but he is far more shallow. Tracy conveys worlds of emotion through restrained visceral force, but, with Columbia's editing, he seems an actor without a director.

The Horse Soldiers (1959). Similar problems—and greater ones—haunt *The Horse Soldiers.* "No! I don't want to make great sprawling

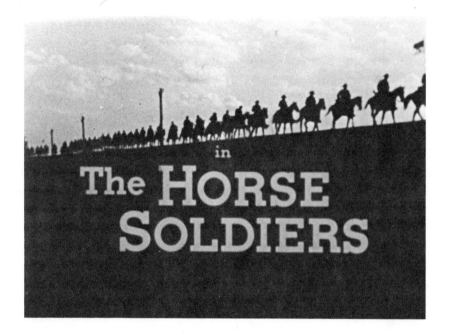

pictures. I want to make films in a kitchen. . . . The old enthusiasm has gone, maybe. But don't quote that—oh, hell, you can quote it."⁵⁶ Ford's usual postfilm depression was justified. *The Horse Soldiers* sprawled all over the South, its 250-page six-corporation contract had taken dozens of lawyers half a year to iron out,* Ford was deteriorating physically, had never felt enthusiasm for the script or hit it off with his producer-scenarist Martin Rackin, and stuntman Fred Kennedy had broken his neck during shooting.

Yet, as Louis Marcorelles concluded, after a highly unfavorable review in *Cahiers du Cinéma*, magic moments mitigate *The Horse Soldiers'* failure:

> Ford in cinema has attained summits difficult to equal, not so much by totally perfect works as by instants of unbearable beauty, where man calmly turns back into himself, harmonizes himself with the world, and goes off to continue the struggle. . . . Judged by the standard of elegant defeatism in nearly all contemporary cinema, *The Horse Soldiers* is still passionate. Both as filmmaker and man, Ford always releases that same Herculean force, tempered with tenderness. But the contours are increasingly blurry. Ford is very close to imitating himself. But, for the unhappy souls, it should be made clear that, at its best moments, *The*

---

*Wayne and Holden each got $750,000, Ford $375,000 plus 10 percent of the producers share after it reached twice negative cost. The six corporations belonged to Wayne, Holden, Ford, Mahin-Rackin, Mirisch, and United Artists. Moviemaking was becoming a craft for dealers, not moviemakers. Similar problems drove Frank Capra into retirement.

Horse Soldiers struck us as quite superior to both *Stagecoach* and *How Green Was My Valley.*[57]

The picture's faults begin with its story, a free adaptation of Harold Sinclair's account of Colonel Benjamin Grierson's 600-mile, sixteen-day raid from La Grange, Tennessee, to Baton Rouge during the Vicksburg campaign, April 1863. A story of incidents, the film never passes beyond the incidental. Lacking a fixed locale, it lacks depth in character and culture. Unlike other "travelogues," such as *Stagecoach* or *Mogambo*, the principal characters are vapid, they lack biography, their subdramas are tawdry. Cameo vignettes are shallow, for Ford, and there is little evocation of the past. Thematic ambiguities are incoherent, symbols often are without referent, interrelations are obscure.

Particularly noisome is the heavy reiteration of doctor-hatred by Colonel Marlowe (John Wayne) and his consequent running feud with Dr. Kendall (William Holden). Marlow's explanation—how he held down his young wife while doctors cut her open for a nonexistent tumor and killed her—is undercut by juxtaposition to the slaughter of Confederates and Kendall's efforts to save the wounded. The subplot becomes macabre: Kendall treats a soldier's leg with tree moss, Marlowe scoffs, soldier removes moss, gets gangrene, dies after amputation.* Marlowe mocks Kendall, and Ford ridicules their fight by intercutting it with boy cadets parading to battle. It is difficult to care about this talky subplot, but it and some tangential concoctions between Marlowe and Hannah Hunter (Constance Towers**) constitute the movie's internal drama.

The Horse Soldiers could be transposed to Monument Valley, with the Southerners becoming Indians combating manifest destiny, except that mythic stylization of the blue-coats is tempered and key types made repugnant. Major Gray (Walter Reed) is a less empathetic version of the glory-hungry lieutenant, Colonel Secord (Willis Bouchey) an obnoxious Colonel Thursday, Sergeant Kirby (Judson Pratt) a disgusting version of Victor McLaglen's amiable sadist, Marlowe a repressed Nathan Brittles without Brittles's compelling humanism. Ken Curtis, Hank Worden, Jack Pennick, O. Z. Whitehead, and Hoot Gibson[†] bestow moments of personality, but briefly.

---

*Similar images of physical helplessness recur frequently in late Ford. Cf. *The Wings of Eagles, The Last Hurrah, 7 Women.*

**The real Hannah was in her sixties. Towers in her twenties brings beauty and amusement to the role, but Ford repeats many Maureen O'Hara gags.

[†] Ford and Gibson were ex-roommates and Ford directed his first feature, *Action*, in 1921. The great B-western star was fondly remembered in Tennessee. The day Wayne and Holden arrived, the *Natchez Times* banner-headlined: "Filming Stars. Hoot Gibson, Others Arrive"; and next day, still snubbing the superstars, a four-column picture was headlined, "White Haired Hoot Star Attraction." Hoot got $5,000 for his tiny part. (*The New York Times Magazine*, September 20, 1959, p. 62.)

In contrast, the South is bathed in myth. The long rebel column passing on the distant far riverbank (singing "For Southern Rights Hurrah") recalls the migrating Arapaho in *She Wore a Yellow Ribbon* (and Wayne hides his men both times). Southern cameos are strong and empathetic: magnificent one-armed Jonathan Miles (Carleton Young) carrying the Stars and Bars alone at the end of the Battle of Newton Station; the headmaster (Basil Ruysdael: another reverend-colonel) carrying a Bible to battle; the proud sheriff (Russell Simpson) nearly hung by dastardly deserters.

When we think of the industrial North, its politicians and carpetbaggers, its dirty cities and sober citizenry, it is easy to forget that the Confederate constitution sought not only a slave-based economy but also hegemony over the vast majority of whites by a landed plutocracy. Yet the racial theme is minimized* and the populist one neglected entirely. Though the blacks look threadbare and famished, the Southerners are virtually never depicted as slavers or racists; they fight for "Southern rights, hurrah!" As for the Union forces, Hannah mocks their pious talk of "preserving the Union," calls them "plundering pirates," while they themselves only say they're doing a job.

*After the battle, Union troops pass a Negro congregation outside its church. "Jubilo," an emancipation song (used also in *Sergeant Rutledge*) is on the soundtrack, but the blacks only remove their hats, expressionless. Then two CSA snipers accidentally kill Hannah's black maid (Althea Gibson). Why? Cut to next scene: no explanation. This is an instance of the referentless symbolism referred to earlier.

One might, therefore, conclude with J. A. Place that "Ford's sympathies are with the South throughout,"[58] but this, like Place's claim that Ford is saying that war is senseless, simplifies too much.

The episodic narrative has two unifying elements: both appear in the last shot—a cabin and a passing column of horsemen. In most scenes, horsemen move, foreground or background, usually Northern, but here they are Southern. Their carriage suggests triumphal heroes, whereas they are actually vanquished minor players. In any case, they pass by and are gone, and their oddly inconclusive image is confirmed as the familiar Fordian parade, transitory life. What remains on the screen is the cabin.

"A house divided against itself cannot stand." The cabin represents subsistence, the effort to save the Union. It looks just like the cabin a few scenes back that is blown up by Confederate cannon, while the boy cadets attack the Yankees. Now, the cadets are able to attack because Marlowe has paused in his flight to destroy some salt deposits ("as valuable as ammunition"). Midst the conference deciding this, Deacon (Hank Worden) stands in the background, the exact image of ole Abe Lincoln. For it is the divine Lincoln who is directing this war, and Ford subtly invokes him to justify more destruction. Deacon, in fact, saves the Yanks. After Newton Station, they are three-hundred miles within Southern territory with a large CSA force on their tail. Their fate seems sealed. But Deacon used to live hereabouts and smuggle runaway slaves through the underground railway, the swamp: "The Garden of Eden had its sufferin' too. Follow me, Brother Colonel, through the swamps, all the way to the River Amite. 'Lead kindly Lord!'" Thus, as in *Wagon Master*, the voyagers are saved by an angel of the Lord. (And an underground railway is provided for the railway engineer who destroys railways.)

True, the Yanks are the invaders; housewives throw dust at them. Some Yanks enjoy their orgies of murder, whereas the South is always depicted in desperate struggle (e.g., the many Southern hands vainly trying to ignite a cannon during the final battle). Marlowe himself, tough as nails but refusing to carry a gun, is horrified at bloodshed, and, as a railroad engineer, shamed to be destroying railroads. But Grant has told him that failure to destroy the Confederate supply station to Vicksburg "might cost us 100,000 men, might cost us the war."

A word more about those gallant boys, whose heart-catching action is the movie's highpoint:* Their uniforms and presentation recall *The Long Gray Line*, but now they not only look like toy soldiers, they effectively are toy soldiers. Why are they sent against Marlowe's men? In order to sacrifice themselves by delaying Marlowe, so that the grown-up rebels can catch him. Which side, then, engages in senseless killing? Or at Newton Station?

---

*Such incidents did happen, except that the boys usually got killed, whereas here Marlowe prevents sadist Kirby killing the minister, orders retreat, and gives the cadets a gallant charge. The incident of the drummer boy sneaking out of his mother's window occurred as early as 1913 in Ince's famous *Drummer of the 8th* (1-reel Broncho, May 28, 1913).

Aren't those heroic rebels engaging in one of the stupidest suicidal exploits in cinematic war?

The South's glorious gestures are repeated by the Yankees, but with subdued treatment. We see the Rebels massacred charging Union guns, we see their flagbearers killed again and again but the flag is always raised again. And we see their children march off to war. But it's the Union soldiers we see die in close-up (the boy in the hospital; the man with gangrene). The Southern struggle is invoked verbally, but it's the Union men we watch enduring a six-hundred-mile campaign. They too charge into the mouth of a cannon, their flag is lifted again and again too, and they have an equivalent to the one-armed Southern colonel in Major Grey, who toasts quoting *Richard III*, replies "Thank you for the opportunity" when ordered to charge, cries "Blow, trumpet, blow" when fallen wounded, and will now, like other Northern casualties, be sent to dreaded Andersonville prison.

Ford's Civil War references generally "side" with the Yankees: no portraits of Lee, but many icons of Lincoln; Grant, Sherman, and Sheridan are the great men who fascinated him.

In the final sequence, Marlowe has neither time nor words to tell Hannah he loves her. But he pulls off her bandanna, revealing her neck (like Sean Thornton in *The Quiet Man* with Maureen O'Hara, or Clark Gable in *Mogambo* with Grace Kelly). She watches him gallop across as the bridge explodes behind him. "Laurina" (the *Searchers* theme) peals forth in sound and picture as she puts her hand to her eyes, looking after him. "Laurina" appeared earlier, at another river, just before encountering Hannah, intimating Marlowe's quest to heal wounds left by his wife's death.

The Confederates cannot catch the Yankees now, but they will try. Their general salutes Kendall gallantly: "Can our regimental surgeon be of any assistance to you, Doctor?" and then races off. These twin treaties of war-transcending humanity are combined, midst the theme music, with the twin images of moving horsemen and stationary cabin, until we are left with only the cabin. An ending as mysterious and beautiful as Ford ever achieved.

***Sergeant Rutledge* (1960).** In contrast to *The Horse Soldiers*, *Sergeant Rutledge* never opens up to the natural world. It is shut up in tortured subjectivity, which nature merely mirrors, and Bert Glennon's photography makes it Ford's most expressionistic color film (and possibly his most brilliant—characters set against black, light-streamed fog, trains roaring through the night). Even out-of-doors, emotions are intense, angry, pent-up; even in Monument Valley emphasis is not on the sky but on grim red clay; even lovers are furious. The movie is molded of space between people, space enclosing them, constricting space, constraining light, a world of terror and loneliness. It is not a movie of dialogue between man and environment (like *Wagon Master*): Mary runs to the tracks, looking out into space as people did in *The Searchers;* but this time there is nothing there.

Sergeant Rutledge sets an episode of a black cavalryman's life within a trial, ostensibly a trial for rape and murder, actually a farce for white passion to release itself upon a Negro whippingboy. High-angle shots, numerous close-ups, foreground figures glaring wrathfully downscreen toward background figures, all add portentous tones quickly undercut by their own exaggeration, as well as by the court's idiotic dickerings, by prosecutor Shattuck's racist demagogy and caricatured mannerisms, and by Cordelia Fosgate (Billie Burke) befuddling his name—Shattuck, haddock—and calling him Captain Fish.

Sergeant Rutledge takes up the theme, broached by *The Sun Shines Bright*, *The Long Gray Line*, and *The Searchers*, among others, of a militarist society's hostility toward anything not held in sway by its moral tyranny. Few pictures depict "order" so distastefully or the military so repugnantly. The violence in themselves that the whites disguise as order and do not acknowledge, they project into the land they strive to dominate—the inimicably inhospitable landscape of arid stone, red like the Indians who strike back like the furies of white subconsciousness—and they project into the blacks they do dominate—the blacks who the whites in their repressed sexuality think want to rape them. When the real rapist, a white man, confesses, his personality collapses completely, he pounds the chair on his knees—"I had to, I had to"—and chaos erupts. Is civilization, then, merely a cloak for savagery? or does it encourage savagery? Denial of reality produces violence, and propriety cloaks the prurient. Ford's exaggeration and humor exemplify these hypocrisies: the rhetoric disguising racism, the clock the colonel snitched during the burning of Atlanta, Cordelia's ladies fanning as they contemplate rape, the judge's whiskey that everyone calls "water." As in *Steamboat Round the Bend*, discombobulation between names and things signifies social rot. Thus when Mary Beecher (or another) testifies facing Shattuck across the frame, with the five judges along the rear, and the court is given a proscenium frame with lights dimmed theatrically, leaving the witness spotlit and her voice echoing, it seems the court rather than Rutledge that is on trial.

As in *The Sun Shines Bright* the blackman is the surrogate for white self-flagellation and conscience. Ironically, while the Indians and their land wish to keep the whites out, the blacks wish to join white society more fully. "Someday," we'll be free, says Rutledge (Woody Strode). "Someday" your little girl will be awfully proud of you, he tells a dying black. "Someday" this will be a *good* land, Cantrell (Jeffrey Hunter) tells Mary. But not yet, not now.

Freedom, indeed, is hauntingly evoked midst strains of "Jubilo" (a song of the black emancipation), but Rutledge rejects it (a chance to escape) and returns to constriction. Why? "Because the 9th Cavalry was my home, my real freedom, and my self-respect, and the way I was deserting it, I wasn't nothin' but a swamprunnin' nigger. [Sobbing loudly, always in close-up, he leaps to his feet, the camera arching up toward him.] And I ain't that! Do you hear me?! I'm a man!"*

Rutledge's decision resembles Captain York's at the end of *Fort Apache*. There is no "someday" outside of society. And even though public hypocrisy has thoroughly corrupted established order, truth will still be found in the emotions of the pure of heart. Rutledge, like Lincoln and Judge Priest,

---

*As with McLaglen in *The Informer*, Ford tricked Strode into getting drunk the night before, then called him at 6 A.M. for his big trial scene.

knows facts cannot be argued against prejudice. And like Sternberg's Shanghai Lily (*Shanghai Express*) the only response he makes to a friend's accusations is his own character. Of what value, ask Ford films repeatedly, are mere facts compared to character? The little gold cross at the crux of *Sergeant Rutledge*'s murder mystery symbolizes burden, salvation, and the inner truth that someday will bring someday.

"Taller than a redwood tree," sing his comrades of Rutledge, a sort of underground Fordian hero. "I've never gotten over *Sergeant Rutledge*," said Woody Strode (Rutledge) years later. "It had dignity. John Ford put classic words in my mouth. . . . You never seen a Negro come off a mountain like John Wayne before. I had the greatest Glory Hallelujah ride across the Pecos River that any blackman ever had on the screen. And I did it myself. I carried the whole black race across that river."[59]

But *Sergeant Rutledge* was not a commercial success. It was half-heartedly marketed as a suspense picture, with no one allowed to enter during its last five minutes — a tactic that must have highlighted the movie's most annoying flaws. Theoretically, suspense is served by the eerie lighting, stark angles, and dozen flashbacks, which dribble "facts" piecemeal and backwards. (Not until the sixth flashback do we learn Rutledge's crime, not until the twelfth do we learn his side of the story, and all the while false suspicions are shoddily implied by interruptions at crucial points.) But suspense is not Ford's forte, and, anyway, *Sergeant Rutledge* is too much a discombobulation of genres — suspense film, western, racial melodrama, theoretical expressionism. We know almost immediately that Rutledge is 100 percent good, our interest in the murder mystery quickly evaporates, and the last-minute histrionic confession by an all-but-new character seems contrived. Granted, all this is Ford's intention: to reveal the farce and exalt character. But it destroys the suspense film, so that, in practice even more than in concept, *Sergeant Rutledge* shares the problems of other Fords of the period — weird, uneven, strident, dispersed in effects, ultimately incoherent. And, unhappily, the script's structural premises are unfulfilled: the twelve flashbacks do not reflect their six narrators' personal knowledge (i.e., events occur outside their sight and contrary to their description), while the only instance of real tension between narrator and event occurs with Cordelia's reminiscence of her attitude toward Lucy. Given that subjectivity is at the heart both of prejudice and nobility, it is curious Ford did not exploit the possibilities inherent in multiple subjective narration. Finally, Ford never seems at his best when, as with *The Informer*, he forces a single mood of constriction to dominate a film without large doses of off-setting humor. The few instants of hope, far from trying to balance grimness, possess a crazed disequilibrium — the scenes heroizing Rutledge at campfire, the awkward, unrehearsed spontaneity of the love scenes. This lack of balance is a consistent problem throughout this period, a problem solved in the years ahead.

Two Rode Together (**1961**). According to Ford, he undertook
Two Rode Together as a favor to Columbia's Harry Cohn, hated it, and "just
tried to make James Stewart's character as humorous as possible."[60] According to Dan Ford, Ford did it for the money ($225,000 plus 25 percent net
profits) and lost enthusiasm while working on the script with Frank Nugent.
Whatever, once again, despite magnificent passages, themes (including that
of "moral ambiguity") do not cohere. It is not clear even to whom the title's
"Two" refers.* The bitterness, revisionism, disjunctiveness and experimentation of this transitional period climax in this film.

It is a grim, claustrophobic movie, set mostly at night against solid black,
occasionally in overcast daytime. The Comanche are ignoble rabble (compared to *The Searchers*' Comanche), willing to sell a white boy who has
become a warrior in their own tribe, subjecting their women to dreadful
slavery. Midst blackness and fire, Stone Calf orgiastically invokes his war
gods, while Quanah Parker sneers, "He still thinks buffalo shields can turn
away bullets!"

The redman's myth-ridden paranoia is matched by the whiteman's obsessive fantasies. Families dwell in guilty pasts, outside present reality, their
lives and relationships suspended, their search for missing members kidnapped by Comanche also a search for personal redemption. Grief-crazed
Anna McCandless is martyring her husband. Marty Purcell (Shirley Jones)
blames herself for her brother's capture, though she was a little girl at the
time; she is a tomboy, doesn't go to dances, confesses, "I used to pray to be
changed into a boy. At times I still do"—to compensate her father. The
motherless Clegg boys have grown into uncouth effeminate roughnecks.**

It is strange the army does not convince these people of their futility, of
what happens to youngsters reared as Indians. In *The Searchers* Debbie
came back safe and sane, but in the more realistic *Two Rode Together* Hannah Clegg refuses to go back; Freda Knudsen is too daft to return; Running
Wolf is savage and hates whites (due to difficulties growing up Indian) and
has to be locked up; Elena (Linda Cristal), having accepted slavery proudly
as Stone Calf's woman, allows herself to be taken back as though changing
masters, but is greeted as a degraded freak. The last dance scene in Ford
masks poisonous inhumanity: Elena prefers to return to the Comanche,
McCabe (James Stewart) denounces the assembly. Simultaneously, Running Wolf, having quite naturally killed the psychotic Anna, is "tried" and
hanged. Instinct replies to instinct. The whites release pent-up rage against
not only Comanche but also their own fantasies. But on his way to be
hanged, in one of Ford's finest sequences, the boy hears Marty's music box

---

*The Gary–McCabe dominant storyline is intimate but a nonrelation: they do not in-
fluence each other, cooperate only once, and McCabe, manically asserting independence,
once threatens to kill Gary. At the end, McCabe rides off with Elena, together, while the
"ride" with Gary remains a fleeting incident.
**Like *My Darling Clementine*'s Clantons and *Wagon Master*'s Cleggs.

(already established as a fantasy object from the past), rushes to it shouting "Mine," and is dragged away just as Marty realizes he is her brother. (Ford's counterpointing of stasis and propulsion to convey Marty's terrible multifaceted realization creates the picture's catharsis.)

If *Mogambo* shows men as different from beasts, *Two Rode Together* shows them as weeds. Reality is subjective, morality too, and they and personal identity depend upon the conditioning milieu. Instinct and necessity determine everything. No other Ford picture is played so constantly at a level of gut response. Elena, reluctant to leave the Indian camp when there, accepts McCabe as her savior once out of it; but when McCabe kills Stone Calf she hurls herself onto his body wailing a Comanche dirge and streaming sandy soil through her upraised hands—until McCabe shouts her back to consciousness. Similarly, Running Wolf reveals himself slave to conditioned reflex when he jumps for the music box and speaks his first English word, but in him split nature is total and inimical. Hannah Clegg (Mae Marsh) alone in the movie seems to have a transcendent awareness of her situation—"I am dead," she says.

As Running Wolf is hanged, Ford cuts back to Marty and Jim Gary (Richard Widmark) separated across the space of the frame. She rises to her feet, sculpturally, and comes to embrace him. This and the following shot to which Ford will dissolve—an altar boy ringing a bell—resolve the catharsis. And since the movie began with boy-and-bell, the Fordian notion that life is an ongoing journey (people ride together in *Two Rode Together* but they do not parade) is expressed in consolation.

The love scenes between McCabe and Elena (particularly the lovely one when he plays with her hair and encourages her to go to the dance) and even more so, the Gary and Marty scenes, are played on a high level of spontaneous ingenuousness typical of Ford's experimental representationalism, in order to contrast the general grimness and rabid constriction.* They come off like cute innocent teenagers. Naturally this comedic style seems more artificial than the grim, sculptural *verismo*. Long single takes are used, too, such as the three-minute fifty-one-second riverbank chat between McCabe and Gary, improvised by the actors when they thought they were rehearsing. All this marks Ford's return to his roots; he said in 1964:

> Since actors used to play natural roles simply, people always assumed they were lousy actors. But, in those silent westerns, look how much more natural and "modern" their acting is, compared to the romantic stars of the time. Critics, however, seem to think acting is better when it's self-conscious.[61]

McCabe—who lounges on a porch, feet balanced on a railing, and sees gamblers tremble at learning his name—seems a cynical parody of *My Dar-*

---

*Less defensible, to my tastes, are the comedy of Widmark's fight with the Cleggs and Andy Devine's stomach buffoonery.

ling Clementine's Wyatt Earp, for McCabe is a mercantile marshall who gets 10 percent of everything. And it would appear that James Stewart (McCabe)* has taken over the intellectual-hero roles Henry Fonda used to play. But McCabe is really a corruption of the traditional Fordian hero, and of *The Searcher's* Ethan Edwards in particular. He rides off in the end, but uncelibate and rejecting—rather than barred from—society. Also, unlike the Fordian hero, McCabe refuses to play God: he *does* reunite families, even brings people "back from the dead," but does so for the sake of money rather than principle. And it is because McCabe, with unacknowledged hypocrisy, disclaims godlike arrogance that he dislikes Wringle (Willis Bouchey). Wringle is willing to pay $1,000 for "*any*" boy, in order to appease his wife and get himself out of the wilderness and back to business. And yet, is this not an instance of Ford tricking us, his audience, by using our facile willingness to define characters at face value?

The *obnoxious* Wringle is apparently contrasted with, but actually mirrored by, the *nobly sympathetic* McCandless, who is willing to dupe *his* wife out of pity for her. But we ought not to judge methods by motives alone. And, in fact, McCandless's action of adopting a boy (sixteen years old?) he knows is not his own amounts to racist enslavement (so, explicitly, Ford depicts it— the boy must be encaged), whilst *only* Wringle has the moral sense to do the right thing: "Send the boy back where he belongs," he shouts, obnoxiously, "Let the past bury the past." Again, good intentions are the true evil.

By means of these hypocrisies, and through Elena, McCabe discovers his own mercantile morality is not so bad after all. The major, a figure of supposed righteousness, breaks the bargain he made when he hired McCabe to ransom the captives: he refuses to honor McCabe's deal with Wringle, refuses to repay McCabe for the goods traded the Indians, and when McCabe protests, has him thrown into jail! When Gary protests, the major utters, profoundly, what (save for our auteurist insight into the Fordian hero) may be the most incomprehensible non sequitur in Ford: "I thought McCabe might be able to teach you what I was never able to—that only God can play God!"** Has Ford rejected the Fordian hero—which Gary wanted to become? Or has this transitional period, like the 1935–38 one, been merely one of reassessment and of heroes manqué?

---

*"Wayne, Cooper, and Gable are what you call natural actors," said Ford. "They are the same off the screen as they are playing a part. Stewart isn't like that. He isn't a thing like he is on the screen. Stewart did a whale of a job manufacturing a character the public went for. He studied acting." (Quoted by George Capozzi, Jr., *The John Wayne Story* [New Rochelle, N.Y.: Arlington, 1972.])

**Gary is called "Natani Nez" by Quanah Parker—Ford's own Navajo name, meaning "Tall Soldier."

fisted, hard-drinking Irish sonovabitch, and so he used people like O'Brien, Wayne, and McLaglen in his films and as poker companions. But, as Dobe Carey says, "there was that incredible tenderness, poetry, and pathos underneath all that muscle. Dad would get sarcastic, 'Gee, he loves to take guys' shirts off with the muscle!'"[5] There were rumors of this sort—a stuntboy once quit after Ford slapped him on the rump[6]—but they were simply inevitable consequences of Ford's secretive ways. "He wouldn't let you see those eyes: so soft and tender." As he hid his feminine sensitivity, so too he hid his erudition and intellectual subtlety, for nothing could be more damning in Hollywood. He once confessed being able to speak German to Hedda Hopper, then added, "You know, I don't want this to get out—I pose as an illiterate."[7] To be an artist, he had to hide artistic intention. At other times, of course, he hid because it was fun, manipulative, or just easier. "I take exception to your remark, 'he doesn't give a hang,' etc., etc.," wrote Bea Benjamin, Ford's business manager, to Henry Yeager, his captain of the *Araner.* "Mr. Ford keeps in touch with all of his financial business but likes to create an impression of indifference to deliberately confuse or befuddle the listener or to pass the buck."[8]

Some who knew Ford thought him a basically happy person, indeed a blessèd one. Others saw darker sides as well. "He was never relaxed, never mellow, never allowed you to relax either," said Frank Baker. "He was always unhappy. He never had a day's happiness. Will he find peace? Lonely spirit! What was he looking for?"[9]

Religion he approached with minglings of piety, casualness, and Celtic superstition. He felt debts to the dead. He carried a sort of necklace on which were his navy dogtag, a St. Christopher medal, a rabbit's foot, a Star of David, an elk's tooth, a small black ring of rhinoceros hair, and others; if he were talking to a Catholic or Jew or whatever, he would shamelessly pull out the appropriate charm. Scripts had to be worked over on the *Araner,* in his "lucky spot." He distrusted clergy and his movies focus on their hypocrisy, but he depended on them, too. The parish priest—a Jesuit—was frequently called into family affairs. And when on location, Ford would arrange for services and sometimes serve the Mass himself. But he was not above putting a five-dollar bill in the collection and telling the priest afterward he had not been able to find change for the twenty he had contributed. Once in Honolulu Jack stopped to call on Cardinal Spellman; Mary, who had never met him, waited in the car, because she was wearing jeans. "This little man walked over to the car," she recalls, "and he said, 'Are you Mary? Why don't you come in.' 'I can't go in there. Look how I look.' 'If it's the Cardinal you're afraid of, don't give it a thought, because I'm the Cardinal.' And he had some strawberry shortcake he'd saved for me. That would convert anyone!"[10] It did convert Mary.

Some Universal executives, all dressed like undertakers, came onto Ford's set. "I'm an associate producer," said one. "Gosh!" said Ford, "Are you really? God! For years I've been wanting to meet an associate producer! Tell me all about what it is you do!" Ford was reminded not to give extras dialogue, for by union rules a full week's actor's wage would have to be paid. Well, *Flashing Spikes* had a baseball game in it, and Ford found a couple of words for every player and nearly every spectator.

Once, as usual, Frank Baker found himself about to play a scene he knew nothing about. "Ford would never tell you anything!" "Okay," called Ford from atop a boom, "Ready?" Baker gasped: "But what do I say?" "You say, 'Father Sister Father.' Okay? Okay. Ready!" Only halfway through the scene, as he watched things happen, did Baker unfathom the cryptic line. Ford snarled afterward: "So! You figured it out, did you?!"

This was on *The Bamboo Cross*, but was typical of Ford's methods. Sometimes, though, he would casually walk through a scene himself, but without announcing he was doing it. Old-timers knew to watch, and knew if they did not copy exactly, he would not say what was wrong, but would just make them try again. When Ford went through a scene in *Liberty Valance*, he ended with his hand *drooped* over a railing. Edmond O'Brien noticed, but deliberately placed his *on* the railing. Forty-two times. Ford would not give in and tell him.

Photographer William Clothier said:

> Ford used to wear the same clothes day after day. Christ, he wore the same hat for 20 years. He also had things he'd say all the time, commonplace things like, "I guess I'll have to pull a rabbit out of my hat," whenever a scene wasn't going well. One day we were doing a tough scene in *Cheyenne Autumn* and the Old Man must have taken 30 minutes moving Carroll Baker and Richard Widmark around, trying to get the scene to work. Nothing. So he turned to me and said, "This isn't going to work, is it?" I said, "No." So then he said, "Well, I guess I'll have to pull a rabbit out of my hat." So he took his hat off and pulled a [toy] rabbit out of it! He must have had it hidden there all morning."[11]

"Nuttier than a fruitcake and a genius," Widmark called him.[12] But he was growing old. He had always kept everything in his head making a film; unlike other directors, he had never depended on his assistants or script girl. But as he aged, he became forgetful and it would have been contrary to habit to turn to others for help, even had there been people to turn to. And Hollywood had changed. In an era of independent production, he was obliged to make "great, sprawling films" to get backing. Months spent setting up deals would exhaust him and myriad tedious details previously handled by line producers fell now upon him. Then the financiers would intervene and spoil his best efforts. It was not simply due to old age that he would get bored and throw away pages of script.

But "directing's like dope addiction," he moaned to Hedda Hopper in 1962, "something you can't leave. The only thing is now that the present cycle has rolled around, I have no choice but to make westerns. Talk about moral bankruptcy! In the past 18 months I've had three good stories okayed at the studios—warm, human stories. It's not the studio that turned them down, but the Madison Avenue and Wall Street people who do the financing. They sent them back saying there wasn't enough sex and violence!" He offered to ghostwrite a sports column for Hedda.[13]

In the late years of old age and accumulated tradition, filming with Ford became an even more intense celebration of community. Partying had been inherent in his methods, even in the teens. Players made it a point to be on set every day, for they never knew when Ford might invent some marvelous business for them unforeseen in the script. *Donovan's Reef*, in Hawaii, climaxed this tendency, with old friends and children gathered together. Yet every night Ford would have Frank Baker accompany him on a drive up to a cliff, where he would pass several hours in utter silence, staring out to sea.*

TRANSCENDENCE

The Man Who Shot Liberty Valance	April '62	Ford Prodns.–Paramount
Flashing Spikes (TV)	October '62	Alcoa Premiere TV series
"The Civil War" (in *How the West Was Won*)	November '62	Cinerama-MGM
Donovan's Reef	July '63	Ford Prodns.–Paramount
Cheyenne Autumn	October '64	Ford-Smith Prodns.–Warner Bros.
7 Women	November '65	Ford-Smith Prodns.–MGM

If, as Ford's films have shown, so much of human response is determined by societal environment, is there any hope of finding a firm basis to support claims that life is worthwhile, struggle for virtue justified, and free will not an illusion? For many Ford characters, service to ideas offers hope, whether in duty to regiment or job, or in the commingling of loyalty to a loved one and vision of a better world expressed by a cactus rose upon a coffin. Man is often propelled upon his "unceasing search for something he will never find"[14] by such goals, substitutes for lost home and childhood. But if all vestiges of home and, indeed, of civilization disappear (all those things that it is usually the Fordian hero's duty to preserve and purify), then what? Implicit in all Ford, these problems are increasingly explicit in this and the preceding period, and in *7 Women* most particularly.

*Baker in 1962 had been suddenly summoned to *How the West Was Won*'s location battle scene, where Ford told him to climb a tree and go to sleep. When he awoke, everyone had gone home. Next day he received $1,000 for two weeks' work. It was a typical Ford stunt for a friend in need. Often though, Baker would deliberately goad Ford out of his "guru" implacability, Ford was forever firing him in the middle of scenes, whereupon Baker would refuse to return without a personal apology. And Ford, stuck with half a scene, would have no choice.

In contrast to the transitional years, Ford now reconciles classical, balanced style with thematic ambiguity. He finds a moral vision able to contemplate anguish and uncertainty without destroying itself. It sees the individual within an intricate nexus of determinants, but sees him both intimately and transcendently, both empathetically and dispassionately. A person's inner self is often at odds with his actions and social manifestations; similarly, the chaotic, determining manifestations of the world beyond the individual (society, the cosmos) are often at odds with the ordering principles whose existence one posits. Thus the "transcendent" is both beyond and within, both God and the inner ego. And Ford's vision may be interpreted either as Catholic or materialist or both.

Just as this final creative effort is one of conscious revision and summation thematically, so too it strives for summation formally. Of such formal summation no description, in the instance of Fordian cinema, seems more apposite than "kinetic sublimity." *The Man Who Shot Liberty Valance, Donovan's Reef,* and *7 Women* represent John Ford at his apex.

The Man Who Shot Liberty Valance (1962). The picture opens with a small steam train churning its way across a plain, blowing its whistle: coming.* The movie will close with the same train on a larger plain, again blowing its whistle: going. It is the train that is the film's principal protagonist, the train that changed the West. We might also think of the train as relating to the Fordian symbol of the parade in the more general sense, a formalized progression, a *passage*. Life keeps going; the motion is constant and to a certain extent unfocusable: good and evil, happiness and sorrow, gain and loss, all blend into one another.

This is the first of three masterpieces of Ford's last period, in which earlier ambiguities—intensified yet viewed from a heightened perspective—are subsumed into a higher level of consciousness, one in which struggle seems only another phenomenon—perhaps. *Liberty Valance* and *Donovan's Reef* (twin in many respects) do seem an old man's pictures; but less vigorous inventiveness is compensated, as in many great artists' last works, by deftness and vision.**

The Fordian hero is now more than ever restricted by his inability to act freely. There seems something above man, call it fate, motion, society, or history, but there is a dynamism in human society that moves society without its ken or will. Ford's Augustinian notion of man as pilgrim has been retained, strong as ever for the individual, but with an ironic touch, for the pilgrim has become a spectator of his own life, an actor in a play whose ending he cannot anticipate.

---

*Most 16mm prints have an aspect ratio of 1:1.33, which crops off the sides from images intended to be 1.65, with the result that the entire movie loses much of its subtle distancing.

**Frank Baker stated to author that the scenarios of both pictures were substantially improvised by Ford from day to day during production—*Liberty Valance* more so.

Familiar themes have grown in ambiguity. Evil is still associated with chaos, and good with order. But without chaos there is no freedom. And order may inhibit freedom, ossify hope, and destroy the wild and heroic beauty of man. Duty has become entirely immanent and personal. Memory is no less vital than present experience, as in earlier Fords, but now it tells far too many lies, and each lie, like each action, reverberates endlessly through history. The hero has gone into exile and been forgotten; the Maydews have inherited the earth.

Ford has a reputation for spacious landscapes, somewhat undeserved since his art has been to use vistas effectively rather than frequently; but *Liberty Valance* lacks exteriors almost entirely. Its manner is theatrical— long scenes of talk—and it focuses on the town, as opposed to the range; statehood as opposed to territory, civilization as opposed to wilderness; words (law and education) as opposed to the gun. The application of all of this to the USA, 1962, or today, is implicit, and a major intention of the film: the past as prelude.

If there is little in the way of landscape, there is not much more in the way of "action." Yet much happens with intensity in speechless scenes, on the level of gazes between characters, on such levels as the slow unwinding dances enacted by Vera Miles and Woody Strode when they recognize each other in the coffin room. This, it seems to me, is properly the world of a great movie, one in which the bodies of the actors, their eyes, and the spaces between them become the chief forms of expression.

As the train moves across the plain at the beginning, the soundtrack music is martial, almost like gladiator music (it resembles *7 Women's* score). From this low-angled long shot Ford cuts to old Link Appleyard (Andy Devine) waiting at the depot, then crosscuts to the depot itself, the tracks stretching diagonally up screen, and the train pulls in, nearly filling the screen. Link moves into range, and we cut briefly to him, age and expectancy written on his face.

Hallie Stoddard (Vera Miles) and Senator Ransom Stoddard (James Stewart) descend slowly from the train, pause to take in their bearings, and then Hallie, carrying a hatbox, walks slowly down a descending diagonal up to the camera, where Link is standing. Just as she reaches him we cut to a medium close-up as they embrace.

The beauty here is subtle. We are given an opposition between Link in close shots and two people in distant ones. We are given a town quiet and still, except for the train's sounds, its smoke, the low incessant tolling of its bell and, occasionally, almost inaudible muffled timpani thumps on the soundtrack. Everything speaks of age, not the characters' makeup so much as the calculation with which they move, the intensity and selectivity with which they give their attention, their presence, to something or someone. The Fordian absence of extraneous movement has been pushed to an extreme of simplicity. One thing happens at a time and the result is clarity.

This abstract richness in motion and cutting becomes as soulful as Mozart's music for Sarastro. When Ford shows Hallie descending, almost falling, down the screen, and then cuts around to the medium shot of his two characters together in one filled space, the effect is at once a resolution and explosion of everything the preceding compositions had been working to achieve.

In *The Man Who Shot Liberty Valance* one concentrates on the eyes of the characters, thence their souls, and thence their world. It is a world so methodical, so simple in its cinematic manifestation that as our characters walk slowly along the street, their every step a calculation, their participation in where they are so total, the town so quiet (save for the tolling bell*) that everything reveals a shattering intensity of repression somewhere between awareness of life and awareness of death. It seems, here, that a sudden movement, a jerk in the camera's slow ponderous motion, might burst self-control into chaotic convulsions.

There is something terribly unsettling about this scene. Just as the actors appear to be looking inward while at the same time trying to take in the external world, so we are faced with an image whose motion reveals each new detail, unmasks each new "framing." The intensity is quiet but no less borders upon the shattering; it is a combination of a viewpoint that attempts to *grip* objects while at the same time leaving them behind: passage.

As always Ford detests exposition. Not for nearly two hours will we learn precisely why these people have come to Shinbone. Now, though, a newspaper editor (Carleton Young) questions Stoddard. We learn Stoddard is a fa-

---

*The bell was tolling too, but differently, during a similar walk through town in *My Darling Clementine*.

mous senator, once from this town, here now for the funeral of Tom Doniphon, an old friend no one has heard of. This fails to satisfy the editor, so Stoddard reluctantly goes off to talk, while Hallie goes to a buckboard with Link Appleyard.

The same deep silence reigns as they sit together on the buckboard, Link's eyes toward the floor, Hallie's on the hatbox on her lap. As they begin stilted conversation the camera moves us closer into their dispositions:

> *Hallie:* Th' place has sure changed. Churches, highschool, shops.
> *Link:* Well, the railroad done that. Desert's still the same.
> *Hallie:* The cactus rose is in blossom.
> *Link:* Maybe, maybe you'd like to take a ride out desert way an maybe look around.
> *Hallie:* Maybe.

During this strange, terse dialogue, they do not move or look at one another. As Link starts off, we cut to gaze down the street: the overhead electric wires, the buildings, the town they were discussing.

Somewhere outside of town, gazing at burnt ruins Hallie and Link sit silently, her hat's black veil softly waving in the breeze. Crosscut to some cactus plants, then back to them:

> *Hallie:* You knew where I wanted to go, didn't you?
> *Link:* Well, you said you wanted to see the cactus blossoms. There's his house down there, what's left of it, blossoms all around it.
> *Hallie:* He never did finish that room he started to build on, did he?
> *Link:* No. Oh well, you know all about that.
> *Hallie:* There's a lovely one there.

Link labors down from the buckboard, moving as always with weary exertion; Hallie puts her hand round the hatbox.

On the soundtrack appears a nostalgic melody, the same nameless tune Ford used in 1939 in *Young Mr. Lincoln*, associated with Ann Rutledge, as Lincoln talks to her grave. Its connotation is the same now, although it is a woman rather than a man that lives. But just as we do not know these cactus plants have any importance, so too we do not know that the melody has: it is Ford's general principle that he makes you *feel* first and understand afterward.

At the paper, Stoddard sees the buckboard return. The reporters follow him and his wife down narrow streets, past wood houses, down an alley and into a stable, through it and into a backroom doorway. Crosscut: a coffin; then back to them. An aged Negro (Pompey: Woody Strode) sits alone looking up at them. Pan in as he rises–the same "gladiator music" as at the film's start—and Hallie starts toward him. Through this series of crosscuts repressed stony faces melt laboriously into recognitions of old friendship. Stoddard opens the coffin, asks the undertaker angrily what has happened to the corpse's boots, and orders they be put back on, his gunbelt and spurs, too. Then he sits; but there is no room on the bench with Link, Hallie, and Pompey, and he sits alone, perpendicular, not parallel, to the coffin.

The editor intrudes, demanding an explanation. Stoddard looks at his wife. She nods and so, with evident feeling of painful necessity, he gets up and goes out with the editor. Hallie, with great care, takes the hatbox from Link and starts to open it. Cut to the outer room, to Stoddard and the newspapermen.

As before with the hatbox, we do not yet know even that it is important. We do not think about it. We are more interested in Stoddard and the re-porters. They gather round a stove. Behind them is an old stagecoach. Stod-dard wipes dust off its name, "Overland Stage Lines," and discovers it is the same vehicle that carried him West years before. (It also looks like the vehi-cle used in *Stagecoach* in 1939.) He tells how as a young lawyer he came west, following the *words* of Horace Greeley, "Go West, young man, go West! And seek fame, fortune, adventure!" Dissolve into a flashback: the stagecoach hurtles through the night, into a clearing.

This flashback continues for all but the last few minutes, giving *Liberty Valance* a form similar to *The Long Gray Line*'s, almost entirely flashback. And as in that picture, *Liberty Valance* is essentially a montage of its two sections, the one resulting from the other. But there is an eeriness to the style of this flashback (and not until much later shall we understand why). It is composed of long, loping sequences, and of takes uncommonly long for Ford, shot for the most part in general shots. People move somewhat as in a dream. The artificiality is subtle, as is the contrast with the acting style in the "modern" sequences. The playing is freer, almost haphazard. While Stoddard is presumably in his early twenties in the flashback and Hallie perhaps still a teenager, only a token effort has been made to make them look young (Miles was thirty-three, Stewart fifty-three) and this is purpose-ful. There is precious little decor in the sets. Nearly all the scenes occur in town, indoors and often at night. William Clothier's black-and-white pho-tography is mostly medium gray tones, unlike Ford's usual richness (as in the "modern" sequences—although Clothier's style is always less opulent than Glennon's, August's, Stout's, or Schneiderman's).

The stagecoach is halted by robbers headed by Liberty Valance (Lee Marvin). Valance rips apart Stoddard's lawbook (chaos /order). Their brutality is emphasized, rather than mitigated, in Ford's direction (which generally avoids dwelling on violence), and as Valance begins to whip Stoddard* orgiastically, the camera quickly dollies to a close-up of Valance's face making horrible gestures. It would be easy to dismiss this as simply a device to hide the fact that Lee Marvin is not actually whipping James Stewart but, just as in Mizoguchi's *Sansho Dayu* when the bailiff brands an old woman and the camera moves in to gaze steadily at the bailiff's face, Ford is intent on the psychological truth of violence. In addition, he departs from his usual practice, and shows the event from *Stoddard*'s viewpoint; we shall see why.

Next night, in town. "Genevieve, Sweet Genevieve" comes from a bar nearby; a rider (John Wayne) comes from the darkness down the street, leading a buckboard with Stoddard lying in it, some horses behind. As he rides slowly across the screen, the camera, on the porch, pans along porch-posts and around a corner. This is one of Ford's moments that gain so much from seeming like awestruck religious contemplations. Here it specifically anticipates Dr. Cartwright's entrance into the mission in *7 Women*, the point being that in both instances emphasis is put upon a normal unselfconscious action that in retrospect has great meaning for those involved, although Ford's art is here again creating an *aura* of significance without our yet knowing the significance. In the present scene there is first of all the nostalgic re-creation

*Stoddard is leaning against a wagon wheel, a Ford symbol of suffering.

of passed time, the Old West, into which the sentimental music invites us. Second, the moment will have far-reaching consequences for the John Wayne character. Third, Valance will later be driven *out* of town lying dead on a similar cart. Fourth, there is the contrast between Wayne's entrance and the two entrances (now and years later on the train) by Stoddard. In any case, entrances always have great import for Ford.

Wayne stops beneath a window and calls Hallie, who looks out and calls his name, Tom Doniphon. Now we learn who the man in the coffin is (will be) and the iconographic significance is great, for Wayne has assumed in the public eye (and to some extent in Ford's) a position as the archetypal hero of the West and as representative of certain aspects of the American character. Now he lies dead in a coffin without his boots and nobody knows his name. We shall learn he was a Fordian hero.

"Wayne actually played the lead," said Ford; "Jimmy Stewart had most of the scenes, but Wayne was the central character, the motivation for the whole thing."[15] (One can also understand the film profitably by placing Hallie at its center.)

Doniphon takes Stoddard into the kitchen of a restaurant owned by Hallie's parents, Peter and Nora Ericson (John Qualen, Jeanette Nolan), Scandinavian immigrants with accents.* Of the six sequences composing the hundred-minute flashback, the first two center around the kitchen, the others a schoolroom, a bar used as assembly room, a convention hall, all gather-

---

*In *The Searchers* Miles was also Qualen's daughter and then, too, they were Scandinavian.

ing places of a settled society, of which the kitchen is perhaps the symbolic heart. In contrast to these town scenes, those few of the "outside" suggest, like the stagecoach holdup, a wilderness of insecurity. The townspeople gather in their town, an artificial world, for protection from a menacing and chaotic outer space, from which they isolate themselves.

Ford had dealt frequently with closed worlds: *The Lost Patrol, Stagecoach, The Long Voyage Home,* most notably, but equally it is implied in pictures like *Doctor Bull, The Hurricane, Drums Along the Mohawk, The Informer, My Darling Clementine, The Sun Shines Bright, The Long Gray Line, Donovan's Reef,* and *7 Women.* More than simply a treatment of confined characters it is a treatment of confined space, of a virtually closed society both sufficient and insufficient unto itself. In a sense, the world beyond does not exist. We deal with the interaction between this closed space and society, between individuals and society and how they mutually determine one another, and how the social island is determined by forces from without. But these forces are seldom seen. They are spoken of and their effects are manifest. The railroad is yet to come to Shinbone, and we do not see the cattlemen and their ranges (any more than we saw battlefields in *The Long Gray Line*).

Lying in the kitchen, his wounds being swathed by (first Hallie, then) Doniphon, Stoddard reveals he is a lawyer, with even a shingle: "Ransom Stoddard: Attorney at Law." Doniphon mocks him: Liberty Valance respects only the gun. "I don't want a gun," moans Stoddard sententiously; "I don't want to kill him. I want to put him in jail." "Out here a man solves his own problems," humphs Doniphon. "You know what you're saying to me?!" cries Stoddard. "You're as bad as he is! What kind of a community have I come to here?" he wonders, echoing Wyatt Earp in *My Darling Clementine*, and echoing himself asking Valance, at the holdup, "What kind of man are you?" "Now what kind of man are you, Dude?" Valance replied.

Here an essential conflict is enunciated: the battle between orders imposed by words (law) and by force (guns). Already the name "Liberty Valance" is a word-play: the "valence" of liberty depends on force (which is why order and liberty are not identical). In line with this, and moreover typically, Ford has gone to the trouble of providing a representation of Stoddard by his own device—his shingle, *words*—both his trade and his weapon represented by *actual written* words. Words play a significant part in this allegory of the establishment of law and order. Recall that it was Horace Greeley's *words* that sent Stoddard west. (Two years hence, in *Cheyenne Autumn*, words will be seen as the whiteman's chief and treacherous weapon in genocide of the Indian.)

The Man Who Shot Liberty Valance abounds with words in the form of signs: the funeral parlor has its sign, the newspaper, the stagecoach, Doniphon's ranch, the restaurant ("Peter's Place—Home Cooking"), all have their signs. And each person has his prop, as Valance has his whip, and his product. As always in postwar Ford, each abstract idea has a physical correlative. No character in Ford ever acts in simple space; it is always in direct relation to another person or object. Everything receives physical representation.

Doniphon seems engaged to Hallie, and is building an extra room onto his ranch. But their relationship strikes us as less than entirely comfortable. Doniphon seems to regard her from a distance with equal proportions of presumption and fear. When Stoddard is given whiskey as medicine, Doniphon takes the bottle and jokes about not letting Stoddard drink alone; Hallie impersonally pulls it away and goes about her business, but Doniphon smiles coyly, happy to get attention.

Link Appleyard, the town marshall, comes into the kitchen. Although in the "modern" sequence the character is entirely serious, in the flashback he is the drama's buffoon, whose bits of slapstick are slipped into the general austerity to engage the audience. But at times this slapstick seems tasteless, as with O. Z. Whitehead as a man-child always licking lollipops. Alas, "good jokes" get encored, for example when Link's hat, which he has neglected to remove, is snatched off by Doniphon onto the floor. Joke number one. Then as he reaches down for it Hallie walks by and kicks it across the room. Joke number two. And the marshall is forever eating on the cuff, and each time Nora checks another X on the blackboard already crowded with twenty-some X's following the name "Marshall"; and this joke is encored later with a much bigger X. This ilk of comedy does, however, provide contrast.

Of course the implication is that the Law is a buffoon in Shinbone. (Equally: the Law is a "Link" to bring "Appleyards" to Shinbone; but for now Law has many X's against it.) And hence Ransom Stoddard will ransom the Law, while "Stoddard" suggests his stubbornness. In fact, when Link enters Doniphon quips, "Here comes Mr. Law and Order himself!"

Stoddard wants Link to arrest Valance, but the marshall babbles, ". . . Put Liberty Valance in jail . . .?!"

"Somebody better listen to somebody about Liberty Valance!" shouts Nora.

"I'm only the town marshall," whines Link, "and what Liberty [sic] does out on the road ain't no business of mine."

Doniphon takes his leave, but before he does there is a rare moment between him and Hallie. Shot close up, he tells her she's pretty when she's mad; crosscutting to her we see from her reaction that she does love him.

The next sequence, again at night, begins on the street, and things are hopping inside the bar. To a honky-tonk "Golden Slippers" a drunk is bounced out of the saloon and rushes in again. Through his office window we find Dutton Peabody (Edmond O'Brien), editor of "The Shinbone Star." He frightens the marshall on the way to the restaurant, where he lectures Hallie on silverware placement, only to be mocked as superstitious. (The scene relates to the limitations and artifice of the order coming to the West.)

In the kitchen Stoddard is washing dishes. Behind him we can see Hallie through the doorway taking orders. He wants to show her in his lawbook (now *taped* together after Valance's manhandling) that the marshall does have jurisdiction. Her mother pushes them together, and they sit with a lamp between them (a common Fordian suggestion of hope). Hallie with hot embarrassment has admitted she cannot read.

The scene is one of those extraordinarily ingenuous ones that occur occasionally between Ford's men and women (e.g., in *Steamboat Round the*

Bend or *Two Rode Together*). Hallie is simple and modest; reading to her means the Bible. What occurs between them is personal more than physical and in such moments Ford encourages broad playing (though, as we shall see, there is additional reason for their wide-eyed manner). "Do you think I *could*? Do you think I *could* learn to read . . .?" "Why *sure* you can, Hallie!" Ranse's face lights up in a patented James Stewart glow; and the Ann Rutledge melody appears.

And here begins (if it has not begun sooner) a second conflict; Hallie becomes torn between Stoddard and Doniphon, and not simply between them as individuals but between what they seem to represent. While Doniphon might conquer by competence, charm, and simple dominance, Stoddard does so ingenuously by his idealism (and by his *words*): she admires his learning and feels accordingly inferior to him, just as she reacts toward Doniphon's granite strength. Yet at the same time she can mother Stoddard whereas Doniphon poses a sexual threat. The picture's two themes will develop in parallel; as legal order changes, so too will the order between the sexes.

The scene is broken up when Link yells for a second steak and when Doniphon enters with his devoted lackey Pompey. He has brought Hallie a cactus rose plant, which Pompey (in this action symbolizing the blackman's role in American history?) takes out back, plants, and waters. She calls Ranse to admire it.

"Hallie, did you ever see a real rose?" he asks, again unintentionally shaming her.

"No," she replies at last, and then gaining confidence, "but maybe some-day, if they ever dam the river we'll have lots of water, and all kinds of flow-ers!" This motif of making the wilderness bloom recurs at various moments in *Liberty Valance*. And recall the climactic sequence in *Wagon Master* when the Mormons enter their promised land in religious glory, or in *The Grapes of Wrath* when the Okies gaze at California to "Red River Valley," or Mrs. Jorgensen's impassioned speech in *The Searchers*. For Ford the land is a great neutrality waiting for man to come and establish there his order, to give it form. And words play a role in this.

Tom Doniphon has taken a seat with Peabody. The editor is anxious to publicize his engagement to Hallie, but Doniphon holds him back—proba-bly he noticed the vase of flowers on the kitchen shelf where Stoddard keeps his shingle. Liberty Valance and his two dirty henchmen come into the res-taurant, typically bringing violence and chaos; they throw out some diners and arrogate their places.

Ford cuts unabashedly to a reaction shot of Hallie: she turns around and looks scared, and as she does so the camera describes a quick dolly around her and up to a medium close-up of her surprise and alarm. Ford could scarcely have been more obvious in the tricks of his trade, and there are hundreds of similar reaction shots in his pictures. But it fulfills its main purpose here, which is to depict *fear* and to influence the viewer to experi-ence the body of the sequence within an aura of fear. Just a bit later, in the same scene, there is another reaction shot, in which Link suddenly jumps up and scrambles out the door when he learns Valance is present. Here the slapstick contrast produces a laugh (and whether the laugh is with or at the joke makes no difference).

Stoddard backs in with Doniphon's dinner on a tray, and spots Valance's leather whip, the one with which Valance beat him. Ford frames it close-up on the white table. Valance sticks out his foot, tripping Stoddard, who sprawls lengthwise on the floor on top of the food. Valance stands over him, hand on gun, malevolently commanding, "Pick it up, Dude!" Stoddard stares back from the floor, his face masked with fury.

We'll never know what might have happened, for Doniphon, seated at the far end of Stoddard's body, rises: "That was *my* steak, Valance. *You* pick it up!" Valance starts for his gun, but Doniphon indicates Pompey covering him from the kitchen door. Cut to Pompey who cocks his rifle with a menac-ing motion of chin and mouth—typical of Ford, this simple, precise, and deliberate narration.

Stoddard and Valance think Doniphon intervenes from friendship for Stoddard or desire to impress Hallie, but Doniphon seems eager to find any excuse to kill Valance. He says he intervened because of "my steak, pil-grim," but Stoddard probably misses the (probably) unintentional pun: Doniphon has a "stake" in this town, Hallie, and Stoddard doesn't yet.

(Oddly enough, the point is made that *everyone* at the restaurant eats steak, big ones too, but on Ranse's plate, as he tells Hallie about reading, there is no steak: just two slices of bread and some beans.) In any case, as Tom and Liberty stand in tense silence—Ford crosscutting between them— Doniphon with his polished black suit, his white hat and vest, his tie, and his gently mocking smile, is the shining knight, indomitably strong, inviting Valance to die, but always within the etiquette of chivalry. He will not take Valance on principle, only when actually threatened.

But Stoddard, alas, prevents the skirmish. *He* picks up the steak, announcing he does so in the name of common sense and reason (lawyer, order, words); but later, when Doniphon quips, "Thanks for saving my life, pilgrim!" Stoddard's real motives come clear: "That isn't why I did it: *Nobody fights my battles!*"

Valance sneers, knocks over some chairs and people, sweeps a few tables and, thrashing his lackeys, leaves. Outside they throw a bottle through the window, fire some random shots (all duck but Stoddard), and ride violently out of town.

Liberty Valance is rather unique in Ford: a singular example of an absolutely one-dimensional character: pure unadulterated violence and chaos without hint of redeeming feature. But it is not shameful, dramatically, that all his gestures and words are clichés, that he himself is a cliché. This is the point: Liberty Valance types do exist, are clichés, and do respect only force. But evil though he be, within the film's symbolic drama he manifests his violence within society and as such his actions are sacerdotal. For he, as much if not more than anyone else, will be an architect of the future order.

Stoddard has retreated disheartened to the kitchen; Hallie runs to comfort. Doniphon enters, sees he is interrupting, and announces he will be away a few days. Just after he exits Hallie runs to the door, feeling a bit lost, perhaps sensing that their relationship is changing and she is losing something irretrievably. In a beautiful contemplative scene we see her standing outside the back door, lit white midst surrounding blackness, watching, staring out into the distance alone. It is a reprise of a typical Fordian moment. How often before have we seen him evoke this magical nostalgia of someone watching another departing—and always the emphasis is on the person gazing. This haunting blank stare is itself practically a John Ford signature. It is the only exception to the rule that his personages always relate to an object or person; thus the shock when they confront nothingness. His characters stare when someone leaves, when someone dies, when a reality is becoming suddenly memory. But it is usually the stare of a lost soul who can find nothing to look at. Life has meaning because seeing is a moral action.

But Hallie's future is presaged via the dissolve into the next sequence, daytime weeks later: Hallie's image, framed in her doorway saying goodbye to Tom, is momentarily superimposed within *another* doorway: Stoddard's law office.

Her image vanishes as Stoddard pulls a carriage up outside the Shinbone Star. His shingle now hangs beside the door. He is nattily dressed and his self-esteem noticeably higher, and when he praises Peabody's statehood editorial, the editor laps up every word. Hallie tells him class is waiting; she rings the bell for the students.

Stoddard takes the newspaper into a connecting room, where a class of various ages awaits. He rings the bell, calls to order, says hello to a ranch hand (who stutters that he is there because they cut cards and he lost), and stops someone smoking ("None of us smokes here!"). He nods at Hallie and she leads the children through the alphabet song. (There are classes of children in some earlier Fords [e.g., *How Green Was My Valley, Air Mail, Rio Grande*] but the class as an important *theme*—the young being educated— only becomes obsessive in his last movies: here, *Cheyenne Autumn, 7 Women*, and, humorously, *Donovan's Reef.* In each case, education is seen as indoctrination and as a method of imposing repressive order.)

Stoddard sits in front of a blackboard (an Overland Stage Company timetable board) on which are written the words, "Education is the basis of law and order." There is a flag and a picture of George Washington. He reads Peabody's editorial, commenting how statehood will mean safety and schools and development. He asks Pompey, standing beside a picture of Lincoln, to recite the preamble to the Constitution. Pompey starts, "We hold these truths . . ." but stumbles, forgetting "all men are created equal."

— "I knew that, Mr. Ranse, but I just plumb forgot it."
— "That's alright, Pompey. A *lot* of people [*sneer*] forget that part of it."

So here we have more of the words theme, words as a means of indoctrination, as a *force* of order, education as the peculiar American method of fulfilling the dream of an age of idealism.

Words are also Stoddard's means to power, his authority within the society of the town and the weapon he hopes to use against Valance. Note how he rules the classroom by force of ego, how in praising the editor he wins respect for himself and is considered qualified to judge and in some manner superior. There is something slightly pompous in his posture as a teacher, the self-righteousness with which he corrects the smoker, passes over a little girl who always knows the right answer, his condescension toward Pompey. All men may indeed be created equal, but it is rather late for Pompey: he never loses his master/slave attitude; education prejudices everything and gives power into the hands of those who possess it.

The class is broken up when Doniphon comes by to order Pompey back to chores; he brings news of atrocities committed by Valance, whom the anti-statehood cattlemen have hired to terrorize the townsfolk. Peabody hurries to print the news. "Print that and Valance'll kill you," says Doniphon. He advises Hallie to avoid the school for her safety, which infuriates her; he tells her again she's pretty when mad, then exits. And she sees Stoddard *erasing* the words on the blackboard; he repeats in disgust Doniphon's parting words: "When force threatens, talk's no good anymore."

Stoddard leaves Hallie alone in the classroom. She fondles the bell on his desk, sadly, and then walks around the rows of benches fingering the books lovingly. The Ann Rutledge melody again appears, recalling the linkage between hope and learning (in *Young Mr. Lincoln*, too) and manifesting her love for Ransom. (There were, to this effect, some telling scenes of her earlier, as she gazed up at him during class.)

Then from the window she sees Stoddard riding out of town and learns in horror he has been practicing shooting in case of another encounter with Valance. She runs to the porch, the camera subjectively pans right with her as she looks out and off (into outer space, it seems) and calls desperately, "Tom, Tom Doniphon . . . !!!" As she calls, the camera juts up a fraction.

The shots, almost the words, it seems, are suspended through a long dissolve into the next scene, of Stoddard's buckboard speeding along in the country being overtaken by Doniphon on horseback. It is a typical Ford ellipsis, the dissolve suggesting cause and effect, or, "And so it came to pass that Tom Doniphon went galloping after Ransom. . . ." You never see her asking Tom, just the result.

They go to Doniphon's ranch, where Stoddard denies he is after Hallie and fails to hit a tin can. Confronted with Doniphon's authority and out of his own element (the town) he seems as incompetent as Pompey in class. Every time he steps out of shelter he gets into trouble. Now Doniphon, demonstrating as warning how well a gun can be handled, shoots three paint cans, splattering Stoddard. Pompey laughs: Doniphon's honor is his. But Stoddard charges diagonally across the distance up to Doniphon and swings a colossal rounded punch, following through. The follow-through gives a slight pause to the shot before the cut to Doniphon falling back: a well-timed cutting effect. As Stoddard, furious still, climbs onto his buckboard, good-natured Doniphon pitches him his gun; usually he calls him "Pilgrim," now it's "Gunslinger."

The townspeople gather in the saloon to choose two representatives for the Capital City statehood convention. Outside, two officials check off those who enter. Pompey leans against a porch-pole, rifle across his lap, hat on his knee, eyes half closed.

Pompey recalls Stepin Fetchit's character in *The Sun Shines Bright*. During production, when Ford asked Stewart what he thought of Woody Strode's costume, Stewart replied it seemed a bit like Uncle Remus. "And what's wrong with Uncle Remus? I put that costume together—that's just what I *intended!*" Ford called some people over, continuing, "One of the players seems to have some objection! One of the players here doesn't seem to *like* Uncle Remus! As a matter of fact, I'm not at all sure he even likes Negroes!"[16]

Peter Ericson and his wife arrive and he proudly exhibits his citizenship papers. Such naiveté was considered dated in 1962, but here, as in a comparable instance in *Donovan's Reef,* Ford employs Ericson's ingenuous pride as part of the film's nostalgia, part not only of the lost idealism of the age but also of the knowledge that there is some reason for lessened pride in American citizenship today.

A wino in coonskin, Kentuck (Shug Fisher), comes along and the judges make him leave his jug outside. The character is a homage to the dead Francis Ford's coonskin type. But Francis, unlike Kentuck, never had to leave his jug outside; he even had it in the jurybox in *Young Mr. Lincoln.* How times have changed!

Inside it is Tom Doniphon who grabs the mallet, pushes people to seats, enforces the bar's closing ("This is a democracy, isn't it?"—again the ambiguity of liberty and law) and pushes Stoddard into chairing the meeting. "We want statehood," proclaims Ranse, "because statehood means the protection of our farms and our fences, and it means schools for our children and it means progress for the future."

The nominations follow. Stoddard puts up Tom's name. Ford cuts to a general shot placing Stoddard in posture as chairman, the theatrical distancing (Stoddard seems upon a stage) suggesting historical nostalgia and underlining the import of Doniphon's refusal: "'Cause I got other plans, personal plans." This is Doniphon's curious nature; he provides the muscle to get things done and yet stubbornly declines responsibility. While this suggests democracy's tragedy, that those who are strong and good are often reluctant to assume duty, it is Doniphon's adhesion to his concept of personal freedom that makes him act as he does. His world and Stoddard's are mutually exclusive and belong to different ages. Stoddard is from the East, Doniphon probably from Texas. The triumph of one will entail the eclipse of the other, just as only one of them will get Hallie. Doniphon's glory, and that of his order, is that he will continually bring about destruction of himself and his order by remaining true to his notions of chivalry: for he must defend those who are against force, those who are loved by those he loves.

So he seconds nomination of Stoddard ("Not only because he knows the law, but because he throws a good punch") and of course Stoddard accepts. Dutton Peabody also accepts, after a drunken oration about how the press (like the knight?) should stand apart from politics.

Meanwhile Valance and henchmen enter, strewing chaos, and he tries to force his own election as delegate. (Pompey again appears to contain Valance; when he clicks his gun the marshall jumps.) Note the symbolic evocation of Valance spotlit (like Jack Palance in Godard's *Contempt*) against the wall brandishing his whip high over the heads of the voting assembly. He loses, Doniphon laughs, and Valance challenges Stoddard either to get out of town by nightfall or else to meet him on the street with a gun. Then he stalks out, throwing a chair.

The meeting adjourned, everyone rushes madly to the bar. The band plays "Ring, Ring the Banjo." Again Ford punctuates with humor. Stoddard hears

Doniphon's advice (to leave), then walks out, through the swinging doors. This shot is held some time and is carefully composed. Doniphon in the foreground gazes after Stoddard down the screen's diagonal, toward the swinging door (through which we can see Valance ride by). The scene is held long because it will be paralleled later when Doniphon stands outside swinging doors watching Stoddard walk back into the convention for the nomination (and Hallie). For us the second scene underlines the import of the first, not simply as intimation of fate, but as a decisive moment in Doniphon's tragedy.

That night Peabody is in his office, drunk as usual. (It is curious that this word man is always intoxicated. We are intended to infer that words are untrustworthy: Peabody is as intoxicated by words as by liquor and it may justly be asked who is the master, Peabody or liquor, Peabody or words. And we shall see that words do eventually dominate those who use them. As order dominates liberty.)

Peabody notices he has misspelled a headline ("Liberty Valance Defeeted")—surely an omen of coming disaster, this breakdown of words! (Significantly the paper has no date or place name: had Rossellini made this picture he might have titled it *America Year Zero*.) Discovering his jug is dry (that too!), he quips, "What's this? No courage left? Well, courage can be purchased at yonder tavern!" Music (*My Darling Clementine*'s sombrero song) comes from a Mexican bar next door and as Peabody extinguishes his lamp to the accompaniment of this yearning music, he says—and the words are suspended meaningfully—"Go West, old man, and grow *young* with the country!" Peabody is rather old for that pilgrimage.

Meanwhile in the kitchen Pompey and Peter urge Ranse to leave, and he quarrels with Hallie about meeting Valance, in the midst of which he corrects her grammar (surely his character!) and she retorts in fury, "'Isn't,' 'ain't'—what difference does it make?" So again, words are questioned.

Peabody wobbles back to his office, quoting *Henry V*'s Crispin's Day speech, and, illuminating his lamp, he finds Liberty Valance in the shadows with the offending headline. "What have we here," Peabody jokes, "Liberty Valance and his Myrmidons? Liberty Valance taking liberties with the liberty of the press?" Rather than fearful, Peabody derives joy from his pun, as though he were a martyr and the puns a cherished crucifix. Valance beats hell out of him and tears up the printshop, spilling typeblocks all over the floor (the enemy of words). His henchman, giggling fiendishly, vividly experiences something resembling a sadistic orgasm; once again Ford concentrates on the one who *does* violence. Peabody is left with his paper planted on his face; the lamp is thrown through the window (the symbol of hope crashing through the *word* "STAR") and Stoddard's shingle is half shot down: the sign is split, the words "Attorney at Law" drop, the name "Ransom Stoddard" remains hanging.

Hallie sends Pompey for Doniphon. Stoddard, finding Peabody, sends Link to tell Valance (winning at poker in the bar—but with a "dead man's hand") he is waiting outside with a gun. "You all heard it," says Liberty, "A clear-cut case of self-defense!" He quaffs whiskey and crashes his glass on the bar; the scene cuts from *clash* to the *click* of Stoddard's gun, as he cocks it in medium shot. (This familiar technique, often used obviously, is here nearly "invisible," since our attention is concentrated on the characters.)

Stoddard, who earlier said he did not want a gun but just wanted to put Valance in jail, is confronted by his half-destroyed shingle. The shingle is first shown close up at an epic angle, and is then crosscut with Stoddard looking at it. Shall he be true to his concepts of law or shall he take the law into his own hands? Note that Ford *shows* this. Stoddard tears down his sign, his name, throws it to the ground, and walks off, leaving us looking briefly at the broken sign.

The camera tracks in front of him, as he roves around and encounters two farmers, one of whom stutters, comically. This bit of humor is subtly conveyed midst mounting intensity; the further breakdown in words is not underlined and the pun that the valence of liberty is coming right now is scarcely perceptible.

(Though I have been at pains to indicate symbolic progressions, Ford never permits his symbology to intrude, and an analysis such as this one risks obscuring that a movie is meaningful chiefly because of the humanness of the gestures and speeches of the actors. That an audience may be oblivious to deeper ambiguities or to this picture's real subject, that some would even dismiss it as a "yeoman-like western" [Judith Crist] is a tribute to Ford's skill as an entertainer. An audience will feel these many subtleties even if failing to understand them consciously. It is, I think, only the cavalier fashion in which Americans view westerns and segregate art and entertainment that hinders deeper appreciation, except when, in cases like *High Noon*, the pretense is inescapable.)

So at last Stoddard and Valance confront each other. Valance, drunk, plays with Stoddard, calls him "Professor," "Dude," and shoots a wine jug hanging on the wall, splattering Ranse as Doniphon did earlier. Finally, in long shot, they fire at the same time. Valance drops and sprawls into a spot-

light on the street (the livery stable light). Ford cuts back and, in a beautifully evocative use of contrapuntal motion, has Stoddard, holding his
wounded arm, stumble off toward the left as people rush in (in the opposite
direction) in the background, and horses rush by, all converging round Valance's body spotlit at rear: "It's Liberty! Liberty's dead!"—a scene of historical transition, fraught with motion (i.e., passage, the parade).

The camera crosscuts to Stoddard walking up the step to the restaurant
and Hallie. Back where Valance lies dead: Ford goes immediately to comedy. Doc Willoughby shouts, "Whiskey! Quick!" A bottle is handed him, he
takes a snort, kicks over Valance, exclaims, "Dead," and walks off.

In the kitchen Hallie once again kneels before Ranse binding his
wounds. Again the Ann Rutledge melody recurs. "I feel so guilty," Hallie
sobs. "I didn't want you to run away, I wanted you to stay." At the sound of
the door opening they both look up, worried. Doniphon enters on the side,
the gladiator music melancholic now; he apologizes to Hallie that he came
too late to help, then, seeing he is an intruder, he leaves.

Outside the camera pans 45 degrees to the right in extreme long shot,
following Doniphon and Pompey. Meanwhile a cart carrying Valance's body,
his legs dangling from the rear, is driven in from the right, moving opposite
Doniphon's direction. When it reaches screen-center the camera, having
finished its pan to the right, moves back leftward with the cart, following it
off and down the street. Gay music comes from the saloon, some Mexicans
pass singing and strumming guitars, and someone throws Valance's hat onto
the wagon. Again Ford matches music and contrapuntal motion evocatively.
And note, of course, that Valance and Doniphon exit simultaneously.

But first Tom stomps into the bar, in a terrible state of mind. "Come on
home, Mars' Tom," begs Pompey, but Doniphon gulps whiskey. One of Valance's men shouts for a lynch mob to hang Stoddard, and Doniphon throws
him out of the saloon, the camera swaying to echo his fury. The second bad
man faces up to him, inches apart. Cut to a close-up of the bad man's face,
then an abrupt swift drop down to his gunbelt as he grabs his gun from its
holster, then a rapid cut to a medium shot, as Doniphon *kicks* the gun out of
his hand. He hands the vermin over to Link (who now, ridiculously, brags of
his prowess) and, shouting at the band to continue and throwing them coins
and pushing Link out of his way and into a window (which breaks), he dis-
gustedly stalks out.

Reaching his ranch, he stumbles into the room for Hallie, splatters whiskey around, throws a lantern into it, and crumples into a corner as flames
erupt everywhere. Pompey drags him into a buckboard (like Valance).

Cut to a "WELCOME" banner on the woodframe convention hall in
Capital City.* Bands play, parades pass. (Cutting from day to night, to here

---

*Ford has been quoted to the effect that *Liberty Valance*, like *Fort Apache*, is based on "an
historic fact" (*Positif* 82, March 1967, p. 17). Just which historic fact is unrevealed. A letter in
the *Village Voice* (quoted by Sarris, *The John Ford Movie Mystery* [Bloomington: Indiana Uni-

from Doniphon's burning house, amounts to a moral-historical statement: destruction of the old order gives birth to the new.) Ranse and Peabody (bandaged) walk to the door, Stoddard loitering to gaze like a kid at the parade, until an official extends a hand in enthusiasm: "Well, now, I sure do want to shake the hand of the man who shot Liberty Valance!" which instantly destroys Ranse's poise. He is clearly feeling qualms of conscience.

The convention scenes seem to drag on forever, perhaps because Ford dislikes politicians; certainly these satiric festivities are the picture's weakest minutes. After the cattlemen's tempest Peabody nominates Stoddard as a champion of law and order. When the rival orator (John Carradine) replies that Stoddard's sole qualification is that he killed a man, a tumult breaks out and Stoddard ducks away.

Meanwhile Tom Doniphon has slunk into the hall, dirty, unshaven, disheveled. As Stoddard goes out the door Tom throws away his cigarette, John Wayne fashion, and follows him into a coatroom.

— "Pilgrim, where're you going?"
— "I'm going home, Tom. I'm going back East where I belong."
— "What is it now, Pilgrim? Your conscience?
— "Isn't it enough to kill a man, without trying to build a life on it?"

But Doniphon tells him he didn't kill Valance, and as Stoddard gawks, he lights a cigarette and, blowing smoke into the camera, says, "Think back . . ." and the smoke accompanies a dissolve into a flashback: Stoddard and Valance on the street, but this time from an alley perpendicular to the street where they stand. Pompey throws Doniphon his rifle and he fires as they do, dropping Valance. The geometric setup concentrates two vectors of order on Valance as the valence between them. Neither Stoddard nor Doniphon can any longer tolerate Liberty; but Valance's vector is aimed only at Stoddard, for he could exist with Doniphon. The flashback not only corrects Stoddard's notion of who killed Valance; it corrects a geometry that was incorrect in terms of the allegory. Of course both Ranse and Tom compromise their principles: Stoddard by resorting to gun-force and taking the law into his own hands (Valance was technically correct calling his part self-defense), Doniphon by violating chivalry. "Cold-blooded murder. But I can live with it. Hallie's happy. She wanted you alive . . . Hallie's your girl now. Go on back in there and take that nomination. You taught her to read and write, now give her something to read and write about."

It is at this point that themes and symbols reach their penultimate collision. The players have all along acted not from choice but from dictates of their philosophies. Ultimately they are controlled by these philosophies. As representatives of two different orders of society they could be said to repre-

---

versity Press, 1976, p. 179]) from James D. Vizzini states that the "picket wire" referred to in the film is a cowboy bastardization of the Purgatoire River in southeast Colorado.

sent a Fordian philosophy of history. But it is not so simple. Fate, or the unperceived forces of society, plays the game it will, but plays it with human agents, persons who to some extent (what?) exercise free will. It is this free will that will alter the nature of fate somewhat, even if it cannot change its course.

Had fate had its way (if one may use such a phrase), Stoddard might eventually have prosecuted Valance or Doniphon killed him fairly. Instead Stoddard tries to kill Valance because of abhorrence of Valance's deeds (i.e., devotion to order even above the law) and, the major reason, because Valance has challenged Stoddard at his most sensitive point, his vanity. So here we might say that the "valence" lies in the imperfection of mankind. It is Stoddard's pride that causes him to break the law to establish order, his tragic flaw that will corrupt liberty so that the triumph of order will also be a loss of idealism. Thus Stoddard is the man who shot Liberty Valance.

Doniphon's case is a more legitimate double bind. He could have allowed Stoddard to die and thus obtained Hallie. But his knight-and-lady attitude forces him to follow her wishes and to protect Ranse without showing Ranse up (as he did earlier in the restaurant). To do so entails dishonoring himself. No matter what he does he loses Hallie. See how strangely fate closes in on him, how the forces of history converge upon him and erase him. Heroically he chooses the "love-death" alternative. With him one order of liberty dies and another is born, one less free in the absolute sense. For liberty entails disorder. Thus the ironic truth to the shout, "Liberty's dead!" Valance, as long as he lived, represented a potential for either order to succeed. His perpetuation in the world represented an alternative between liberty and order. Thus Doniphon is the man who destroyed (shot) the valence.

One might equally say freedom destroys itself through its abuse. Valance brought about his own destruction, as did Doniphon. Order is a necessity, not just from the viewpoint of those humans who wish it but from the nature of this philosophy of history: all elements move toward cohesion. Thus free will was, perhaps, irrelevant.

Must a government that seeks order through law (words) employ guns? In fact, just before the critical shooting, words, threatened by force, had been failing all over the place. And this occurred not by fate but by human agency, by free will. If order entails a loss of liberty it is because of the imperfection, the sin, of man. Liberals may be more coercive than those who simply use guns. Education is the basis of law and order, and also a tool of totalitarianism.

Words are a higher form of social order than force, for they can only exist where force is not present: they require civilization. The triumph of words appears inevitable, fate will take care of that. But the opportunity still exists for man to corrupt their meaning.

Stoddard's triumph, however, is ironic. He will go on to a glorious political career on the strength of words, the publicity that his vanity has won him, that he is "the man who shot Liberty Valance," words that in the sense intended, are in fact *not true*. But no matter. Stoddard has made himself the tool of words; and in place of his apron gets a spiffy suit.

Doniphon, through the "letter" of the law, has absolved Stoddard of conscience pangs just enough for his ambition to trample his scruples. Here Stoddard exercises free will: he lies. He scoots back into the convention hall and goes on to fame and power on the strength of a lie; goes on too to get Hallie, thus robbing Tom.

She, it appears, is true to her hero-worshipping and inferior-feeling nature, and chooses the "braver warrior" and the higher star. She can in addition relate ideally to Stoddard, while to Doniphon her relationship would have been more primitive. She is always mothering Ranse, tending his wounds; she is sexually awed by Doniphon, and dependent on his strength. She may not have had a choice, however, for Doniphon, his pride lost, has given her up. And so again the nature of society changes and something is lost. The woman chooses security over passion, law over nobility.

Had Stoddard not chosen to go after Valance, had he not broken his own codes, he would not have forced Doniphon to intervene, he could not have forced Doniphon to compromise himself, and he would not have gotten Hallie by default.

And so, when Stoddard returns in old age to Shinbone, he must in some sense come as the murderer of Tom Doniphon, but he does not yet appear to realize this. Hallie, on the other hand, does recognize responsibility for the destruction of a man who loved her. We do not know when Ranse told her Doniphon shot Valance (for she seems to know). But she did not rush to

Doniphon in his moment of need as she did to Stoddard, and it is implied she has not seen him since. Ironically, it was Doniphon who had the more basic need for her; it is hardly imaginable that Stoddard's ambition would have been affected had he not gotten Hallie.

Thus when they arrive in Shinbone at the beginning of the picture, it is Hallie who wears the Fordian stare, looking inward, silent and grave. Stoddard in contrast is his garrulous political self, goes off to talk politics with the reporters, and seems disturbed by his life (that is, seems anxious to prove he did *not* kill a man, even though, by establishing his innocence of possible murder, he establishes his guilt of fraud), rather than conscious of the relationship between Hallie and Tom.

"Shinbone" is so called because it is where liberty stumbled (and even suggests a biblical "rib bone," Adam's sin for Eve). And it stumbled through Ransom's egomania—his "stoddard," his persistence ("a persistent cuss" is what Tom calls him). His stubbornness ransoms order (himself) in exchange for liberty (Tom). Similarly, he has ransomed Tom's love for Hallie. But in contrast to whatever one may read into Stoddard's name, Tom Doniphon is just plain Tom Doniphon. Yet, true to his myth, the Fordian hero, attempting to mediate between order and chaos, has intervened for higher good; and now, having united the lovers and sealed his own celibacy, he goes off alone.

When Stoddard goes back into the convention hall the saloon-type doors continue to swing open and shut for a long time afterward as Doniphon, throwing off a cigarette again, watches Stoddard and then exits, plainly, without fanfare. But standing there he is ironically juxtaposed with big campaign posters, "Vote territory and the open range." It is obvious some preternatural Fordian hand keeps these doors swinging long after they ought to have stopped, but it does not matter: the device underlines the actual significance of the scene: like a stop-motion film, the continual interruption of our seeing what is happening inside the room beyond the doors (just people jumping up and down and making noise) with Doniphon's quiet departure outside increases our feeling that time is passing, that something is happening. And this, after all, is the point.

At long last the scene dissolves back into the "present." Senator Stoddard finishes his story, sitting guiltily outside the room where Doniphon lies bootless and gunless and spurless in his coffin, sitting beside the stagecoach that started it all.

It is immediately obvious that things are, literally, much brighter in the present: we're back into the brighter and more contrasty style of photography and decor, back into a style of acting in which the players seem more vital and stylized. Or rather, into a style of behavior more "educated": the characters in the flashback seemed more physical, their movements more rounded, their consciousnesses more vegetable. Now people act as though they are not limited to the town, they project their personalities more forcibly, they think more intellectually, they move more angularly, more self-consciously.

It is noteworthy too that in all the flashback little occurs that Stoddard himself has not witnessed. Some of the few exceptions are events he could well have imagined: Hallie alone in the schoolroom; Valance in the bar and what Doniphon did after the shooting. Only one shot, that of Hallie outside the kitchen watching Doniphon ride away, strikes one as being beyond Stoddard's narration. It is not, in any case, necessary that Ford have followed slavishly the point of view of Stoddard as narrator; it is sufficient that his point of view be constantly suggested, that the "surface" reflect his limits while the "underneath" express (Ford's) deeper reality.

And, in fact, the flashback is pretty consistently distorted by Stoddard's subjective memory. Hallie, interestingly, is never seen alone with Tom. To the contrary, we have noted a definite ellipsis of such a moment before the shooting lesson. Doniphon's appearances are always handled matter-of-factly. In the key scene in which Doniphon presents a cactus rose plant to Hallie (the importance of which will be clear momentarily) no dramatic or rhetorical emphasis whatsoever is placed upon Doniphon's role: it is just something that happened in between things more important to Stoddard. In fact one has to look hard and deeply at the scenes in which Hallie and Tom are both present to detect a rapport between them. On the other hand, the moments in the flashback that are most alive and intense and on which the greatest amounts of poetry and music are expended are those involving Ranse and Hallie.

Each of the characters of the various personages is colored toward Stoddard's bias: Valance is irredeemably despicable, utterly outside the protection of the law, totally evil incarnate—Stoddard seems less troubled that he killed a man than that he broke the letter of the law; Peabody is lovable but a lesser and foolish rival in the game of words; Pompey despite his heroic side has a slave mentality; Link is a buffoon; everyone looks up to Ranse. Tom Doniphon is relatively incomprehensible, almost a blank mask (superficially), and in his scenes with Hallie wooden, cavalier, seemingly uncaring, even awkward; he is overbearing toward Pompey and ambivalent toward

Stoddard. Hallie is always radiant, soft, and kind, always looking up at Ranse (recall the high-angle shots down at her in the classroom), always looking up to him to form her, but not particularly erotic. The camera generally takes a position proximate to Stoddard's point of view. Recall, for example, the concentration of the face of Valance whipping him.

In the modern sequences, however, we immediately see that Hallie is more independent and more Stoddard's equal. Link is not a buffoon. Pompey is meeker and more subservient, older; and Stoddard is more condescending toward him: when he leaves Pompey in the coffin room, he will squeeze money into his hand, and when Pompey tries to decline it, Stoddard will mumble, "Porkchop money, Pompey"—patting his hand professionally. And, in fact, the sun does shine occasionally in Shinbone.

Ransom Stoddard himself now seems even more pompous and even more a caricature of a politician than he was during the flashback, where, as painstakingly shown, these qualities in him were always hinted at: his was a passage from "Pilgrim" (as Tom saw him) to "Dude" (Valance's truer estimate!). To his credit Stoddard recognizes his failing, if not its full dimension. But his tragic realization and comeuppance are approaching.

Meanwhile, the editor concludes Stoddard's history: "Three terms as governor, two terms in the Senate, Ambassador to the Court of St. James, back again to the Senate, and a man who with a snap of his fingers could be the next vice-president of the United States!"

—   "Well, you're not going to use the story, Mr. Scott?"
—   "No sir! This is the West, sir. When the legend becomes fact, print the legend."

So it is too late. Stoddard cannot change his lie now. The consequences of his action cannot be undone, nor the falsity of his fame. Words and time have conquered. And thus, more basically, the newspaperman is correct (though we are free to disagree): the real truth is that which has become fact and the legend has indeed become fact. The historical truth is merely a footnote, and, need it be said, this is the problem. Every student of history (and Ford was one) must continually marvel at the disparity between historical fact and tradition. People prefer fantasy and, often, they need it.

A similar point was made by Ford in *Fort Apache* (q.v.), yet in both pictures, though he says he agrees with the notion of printing the legend, he himself "prints" both the facts and the legend. He would maintain that the ideals that form society are more important than the functionaries of society.

Ranse now turns and goes toward the door to the room with the coffin. As he opens the door the camera shoots from the point of view of Hallie, sitting still on the bench against the wall, opposite the door. The camera gazes at a low level across the length of the casket (whose side is in the bottom foreground of the shot: thus definitely Hallie's seated point of view) and up at a gentle angle to show Stoddard at the door. Prominently sitting on the closed casket is a cactus rose plant (like the one Doniphon gave to Hallie years before: it is this that she carried back in a hatbox from the charred, wilderness-overrun ruins of Doniphon's ranch). It dominates the scene, but subtly (like all Ford's symbols) because it is naturally Stoddard who draws our attention and because the prior references to the plant have all been *sotto voce*.* Stoddard notices the rose plant but acts as though he does not see it. The crosscut now shows the room with Hallie sitting on the bench, the camera gazing down at her from Stoddard's point of view, with him in the foreground. She rises and walks toward the camera and out of the room with Stoddard, the camera following her around so that it now looks over the casket toward the door. She exits first, followed by Stoddard, but he looks back again, frowning, at the cactus rose, then closes the door. But the camera stays, moves up closer to the cactus rose and holds that frame. (One recalls this as the stylistic reply to a matching dolly-up to Stoddard when he entered the coffin room at the beginning of the movie.)

This peculiar gesture has several facets. The camera dollies in not simply to draw our attention to the plant, but rather as a (typically deliberative) narrative device. By means of this emphasis Ford tells us something about the plant. Naturally we sense its importance, but without fully divining its meaning. Secondly, the sustained image suggests that, as is the case, both Hallie's and Stoddard's thoughts remain on this rose plant after they leave the room.

The close-up of the cactus rose dissolves into the final sequence, a medium shot of Hallie and Ranse seated alone in a railroad car, the countryside passing by in the window to the right, Hallie beside it, Stoddard on the left. Their eyes and expressions are clearly displayed. Now Stoddard too wears the Fordian stare, along with his wife, but with *The Man Who Shot Liberty Valance* the stare has changed from a stare outward to a stare inward.**

*If proof be needed of subtleness: when the picture was nationally telecast some years ago on NBC only one cut was made: the scene in which Doniphon gives Hallie the cactus rose plant! This of course makes nonsense of its role.

**A similar transition from outward to inward stare occurs in *The Wings of Eagles* (1957) with Spig Wead and his mirror. Cf. Huw in *How Green Was My Valley*.

Something appears changed in his manner, he is more sober and austere. They are both deep in meditation, a great silence reigns, broken only by the clatter of the train wheels. When they speak, their words are soft, heavy, and careful, the rhythms flat, the expression repressed.

> — "Hallie, Hallie, would you be too sorry if once I get the new irrigation bill through, would you be too sorry if we just up and left Washington? 'Cause I, I sort of have a hankering to come back here to live, maybe open up a law office."

(Note the terseness of the following dialogue:)

> — "Ranse, if you knew how often I dreamed of it. [*Pause*] My roots are here. [*Short pause*] I guess my heart is here. [*Long pause: her eyes, but not her head, turn slightly toward the window*] Yes let's come back. Look at it. [*Short pause*] It was once a wilderness, now it's a garden. Aren't you proud?"

There is a long pause. Stoddard does not reply and Hallie does not change her gaze. He just sits there without moving a muscle and you know that he is not feeling proud now. Finally he replies,

> — "Hallie, who put the cactus roses on Tom's coffin?"
> — "I did."

The camera holds the shot a few moments, holding her voice suspended over the scene.

The camera cuts back to a higher fuller shot, as the conductor comes by, interrupting and getting an ashtray for Stoddard. He tells the senator that "these tracks lead straight to Washington" (once again Stoddard is going contrary to his intentions) and that he has wired ahead to clear the road, so that they may go as quickly as possible.

Stoddard, a big cigar in one hand and a match in the other, bows his head pompously, back in his politician character now, and says, "Thank you, Jason, thank you, and I'm going to write a letter to the officials of this railroad and thank them for their kindness and for going to all this trouble."

"You think nothing of it! Nothing's too good for the man who shot Liberty Valance!" replies the conductor as Stoddard strikes his match and brings it toward the cigar in his mouth while the conductor is walking off. The camera dollies in closer to Stoddard.

Hallie has reacted just a bit to this remark, but she returns to her poise immediately and sits motionless. But Stoddard stops his match in midflight to his cigar, holds the cigar just out of his mouth, his mouth slightly open, frozen for a moment by the conductor's words, then weakly blows out the match and lowers the cigar. There is no escape. The camera holds the scene for a long time.

It is clear, then, that while the long caesura of the flashback was necessary for Stoddard, the talker, to exercise his duty toward Doniphon, it was not necessary for Hallie. For her the cactus rose represents Tom Doniphon and represents as well hope for the future, hope perhaps that held a dream finer than the one fulfilled. Of course it is age looking back upon the dreams of its youth, but one might suggest too that perhaps Ranse has not lived up to her expectations.

And for Stoddard the cactus rose seems to have awakened him to an aspect of Hallie—her love for Doniphon—that he had not before recognized (judging by his narrative), and perhaps, too, to an aspect of himself.

For them both it is an acknowledgment that something beautiful and natural to those rugged days of youth, that something and someone have died, that a better dream existed. We see death written all over the modern sequences, though nowhere more deeply than on the faces of Ransom and Hallie at this moment. We see not only their age (contrasted to the "garden" that has bloomed), but we see that the world is passing them by—but not only going by outside their window, and not only in the transformation of the wilderness (their world) into a garden. Their true death is that, despite the garden, they have ultimately failed, each of them, in deep personal ways. It was a failure they shared, and like some Adam and Eve they have sacrificed their innocence and idealism for something less than their idealism.

The close-up of the cactus rose was sustained in order that it might balance, might hang suspended, over the conversation between Hallie and Ranse on the train—thus the dissolve between the shots. The result of the combination of the two shots suggests that, beyond being a tribute to an old love, the plant sums up thematic threads: the duality of order and liberty, the better dream, the loss of innocence, youth, perfection, beauty, the loss of a wilderness for a garden, of the physical for the verbal, the loss of what Tom would have given Hallie and which Stoddard has not. And then it is Tom who deserves the symbol of fruition.

The shot of Stoddard and Hallie cuts to the last composition of the film. It is a sort of crosscut, an answer, to the shot on the train, and comes just after the train whistle begins to blow. At a low angle, but on a rise, the camera gazes over stalks of wheat and takes in an immense plain. The train is heading upscreen, the tracks wending across the screen, near the bottom, from left to right and then vertically up the right side. The train, the railroad that has changed the West, is billowing smoke and blowing its whistle. On the soundtrack is the Ann Rutledge theme.

It is the final triumph of fate: things go on: passage. Whatever may happen to Ranse or Hallie or Tom, whatever happens in life or history, the parade goes on. Our sadness remains with us.

Donovan's Reef (1963). The South Pacific island Haleakaloha is, like many Fordian societies, cut off from the world but equally a nexus (and uniquely a resolution) of everything the outside world offers. It is a polyglot society, with strata, an apparent paradise, like Innisfree, but overflowing with flaws ("busted things"), a portrait of imperialism, racism, and hypocrisy. But *Donovan's Reef* never ceases being a comedy; its characters are unfashionably middle-aged and banal, and Haleakaloha's dark side is whimsically reduced to symbol.

Its theology is pantheistic: everything is god. The universe is alive. Animation and moral force belong not only to people, their institutions and communities, but also to weather, to land and sea, to flowers and music, to machines, to pictures, to colors. Every prop has its personality, its influence—particularly the portrait of the island's dead princess, Manulani. As in *Liberty Valance*, there seems a certain ordering principle at work in the world—especially in Manulani's Haleakaloha—which ultimately exerts control over our lives. Slight events partake of epiphany; accord is inevitable; meanwhile, *Donovan's Reef* unravels like necessary ritual. Mythicizing lighting transforms all—emphasizing depth, extending shadows, endowing persons (and occasionally a prop) with consecrating illumination while darkening surroundings, so that actions assume sacerdotal significance. *Donovan's Reef* is close to a cinematic experience of pure form (particularly its last third), moving stubbornly twixt chaos and (repressive) order toward harmony, inexhaustibly gifted with visual beauty (dynamic form). Idealistic and artificial, *Donovan's Reef* is a love affair with a best of all possible worlds. When a flaw is created in "paradise," by the introduction of racism into the family core, these gods become reproving: broken music, slot ma-

chines, leaky roofs, thunder and lightning, pratfalls. But the gods are benign, and everyone is equipped with an umbrella—quite a contrast to the
way things turned out in *The Hurricane*. The gods are righteous, but tolerant, and their order transcends the optimism of *Wagon Master*, the pessimistic optimism of *The Sun Shines Bright*. The bestial in man, so worrisome in
Mogambo, is now a variant no more condemnable than a lightning storm as a
variant of weather. Even Liberty Valance (i.e., Lee Marvin) ends up happily
married, settled, and playing with a toy train, whose intrusion he formerly
opposed. The off-duty law, the anarchy and violence that in *The Man Who
Shot Liberty Valance* were intolerable are in *Donovan's Reef* not only tolerable, but condoned and rewarded. Implacable, historical fatalism has
changed to cozy, animistic predestination.

   Donovan's Reef is of the suitelike, operatic Ford. But what was once expressionism has evolved into a purer sort of classicism (the shot, for example, of the native blowing into a seashell—a homage to Murnau's *Tabu*). The
structure is generally tripartite, not only in sequencing, and in the fluid
fashion many sequences divide themselves into three scenes, but within
each scene, montage and gesture describe a rhythm that, balancing two
alternatives, moves toward a third state of accord (i.e., a "pax"—a peace).

   Much as *The Sun Shines Bright* began with a riverboat and *Liberty Valance* with a train, *Donovan's Reef* begins with a merchant ship at sea—a
closed society's link with the world. Gilhooley (Lee Marvin), shanghaied,

Figure 10. *Donovan's Reef*

ACT I. 1.i.   At sea: Gilhooley jumps ship.
        ii.   Island riverbank: Dr. Dedham's goodbye to kids and Donovan in canoe; DeLage dictates transfer request; DeLage greets kids and Donovan, sees Gilhooley coming; Donovan leaves.
        iii.   Gilhooley greeted on shore; converses; DeLage.
        2.i.   Donovan leaves kids at their home.
        ii.   Gilhooley enters saloon; Donovan coming.
        iii.   Gilhooley and Donovan (fight); Dedham.
        3.i.   Boston: conference.
        ii.   Donovan et al. confer in saloon about Amelia coming.
        iii.   They interrupt piano lesson; tell Lelani of deception play; she runs to her bed.
        (Interlude) Moving parade.

ACT II. 1.i. Amelia greeted; she and boat captain; Donovan helps her into canoe; on shore she meets Gilhooley.
        ii.   She has her picture taken outside saloon.
        iii.   At her father's house, she sees Manulani's portrait.
        iv.   Rain that night; priest in chapel.
        v.   Amelia awakened by storm and open doors, finds Luki and Donovan.
        2.i.   Next morning: DeLage lends Amelia his car and Eu.
        ii.   Saloon: Cluzeot and Gilhooley and jukebox; Amelia asks Donovan for boat, makes pax; jukebox; she visits terrace; and meets kids and Cluzeot.
        iii.   General store: she meets Lafleur and buys swimsuit.
        iv.   Water skiing with Donovan; pax.
        3.i.   Later: cutting Christmas tree in mountains; Manulani.
        ii.   On return, Donovan leaves kids at saloon; Manulani.
        iii.   That night: Eu sees Donovan and Amelia canoeing;
        iv.   and, during Lafleur song at saloon, plots with DeLage.
        v.   After love scene with Amelia, Donovan throws Lafleur out of his bed.
        4.i.   Later: Donovan and Gilhooley signal Dedham from lighthouse about Amelia.
        ii.   Dedham lands and meets Amelia.
        iii.   At home, she displays Christmas tree and its lights.
        iv.   Long talk over tea is interrupted by hospital call.
        5.   Christmas Eve service.

ACT III. 1.i. Sunrise and Cluzeot; Amelia sees servants honoring Manulani; bicycles to hospital; questions Cluzeot at cemetery: Manulani.
        ii.   Luncheon with DeLage.
        iii.   Christmas saloon fight; Cluzeot and jukebox miracle.
        iv.   Pageant honoring Queen Lelani: Amelia discovers all.
        v.   She brings presents to saloon, fights with Donovan.
        2.i.   Later: Cluzeot fixing chapel roof.
        ii.   Amelia escorted to pier for departure.
        iii.   But she returns to fight and pax with Donovan.
        (Coda) Moving parade.

clubs the bo's'n to escape, and the latter's slapstick reaction announces the movie's acting style: comic, theatrical, (chaotic?), broadly forward, in contrast to *Liberty Valance*'s measured tragedy. The first hints of symbolism are subtle: it is December 7 and Gilhooley wonders what people at Pearl will say; *later*, we learn Gilhooley and Donovan (John Wayne) were both born this day and have been celebrating the event for twenty-two years with annual birthday brawls. (No one tells us, but twenty-two years before 1963 is December 7, 1941: the Pearl Harbor attack.) Gilhooley is a figure of instinctual anarchy—like Liberty Valance, or resembling a development of the Francis Ford character. An eternal cigar-in-mouth marks his oral personality; when not kissing or drinking from bottles, "Boats" Gilhooley enjoys playing soldier with "Guns" Donovan. The two fought the war on Haleakaloha. Donovan now owns a bar there ("Donovan's Reef") and Dedham, a third buddy, is a doctor with three young children.

But as with December 7th, the narration is extremely oblique. Everything in the picture's first sequences anticipates the Donovan-Gilhooley meeting, but the telltale lines of dialogue are not marked off. Individual events overshadow suspense, and it requires a bit of work to figure out what has happened and why. Typically, for example, it is left for us to reflect that Gilhooley has come halfway round the world to keep his birthday ritual.

In any case, as the lines and angles of character placement in the prefight portion of the saloon scene (see Fig. 10: I.2.iii) illustrate, *Donovan's Reef* is basically a movie of motion and beauty. Its seminal articulation comes as the native girls swarm shoreward to welcome Gilhooley (I.1.iii): 90-degree pan right to left; at midpoint we gaze out to sea, down the pier, centering on two Polynesian totem posts. As the pan began girls ran right-to-left down toward the pier; when the pan reaches the far side, a second stream of girls runs left-to-right down toward the pier, to join the others. They start to sing as the camera reverses its motions, panning back toward the right to center on the posts.

This tripartite structure (left/right—back to center) is imitated in the montage frequently in the picture's course (shot/countershot—two-shot), wherein it is stated also thematically (fight/fight—pax; male/female—couple; chaos/order—harmony). *And* it is imitated as well in sequencing: In I.1: Gilhooley/the island and people—their combination. In I.2: Donovan/Gilhooley—their combination, with Dedham added from part one. In I.3: Boston/island reaction—*subtraction!* The remainder of the picture labors toward resolution of the formal deficiency of this opening triptych (I: 1, 2, 3), suspending until film's end this dissonance (the subtraction of the Dedham children). The movement is toward accord.

In I.3, we cut to Boston. The board meeting of the Dedham Shipping Company is one of Ford's finest comic sequences: mythically lit, highly stylized and pungent, and his penultimate satire of the New England dotard.

Four paintings* summarize four aspects of the Dedhams: /portrait of a nineteenth-century businessman; /of a sea captain; /of a nineteenth-century minister; /tilt down from a portrait of a pirate, past a wooden ship model, to Amelia Dedham, very proper in blue suit, glasses, and hat.** The decision is made that she will visit her father, whom she has never met, in hope of discovering moral turpitude sufficient to disqualify his inheritance of a controlling interest of Dedham stock.

Meanwhile in Haleakaloha the decision is made, in Dedham's absence, to pretend his half-caste children are Guns's, from fear of a Bostonian rather than from suspicion of her mission. To this end, the children's piano lesson is interrupted (a bad sign in itself) and Lelani summoned to the living room. Dissolve: The camera frames Lelani at a high angle, then tracks back across the room as Donovan concludes, "So you and the kids must move in with me and pretend you're mine." "But Uncle Guns, I don't understand. First you tell me I have a sister coming from America, and then you say we're to leave home . . . Wouldn't it be proper for me and my brother and sister to welcome her here, in the absence of my father?" The scene exhibits Ford's "postexpressionism": the slow track-out from Lelani, the high angle (un-

---

*These pictures, as well as the Manulani portrait, as well as all other portraits in Ford (e.g., the one in *The Sun Shines Bright*), seem painted by the same hand. Whose?
** / = cut.

usual for Ford), the obtrusively theatrical lighting, all accentuate her position in the center of an arena, surrounded; stark shadows are outlined on the
floor; a few touches of primary color are offset, in the brilliant color coordination of costumes, by white and black: one of Ford's loveliest color scenes.
Cluzeot protests, "Monstrous," but is ignored (like *The Hurricane*'s priest)
and Lelani understands: "It's because I'm not white!" (As in *Stagecoach*'s
dinner scene, when Ford turns our hatred of characters to empathy,
Donovan's pain as he tries to comfort Lelani turns our alienation at his
"cruelty" to empathy: the eternal Ford portrait of a person suffering
through his own misplaced value systems.) In a sad parade, with a strum
tune (a recurrent musical motif), the children move out of the Dedham
house, each character carrying an attribute: Cluzeot (music books), Luki
(baseball stuff), Sally (dolls), Lelani (ceremonial gown: cf. III.1.iv),
Donovan (their luggage), four servants (the piano), Gilhooley (cigar and piano stool). With this "sin" of subtraction, in which racism and family separation, two favorite Ford themes, are combined, *Donovan's Reef*'s first "Act"
concludes.

Amelia's arrival (on Ford's ketch, *Araner*, captained by Frank Baker) du-
plicates the singing-girls business previously staged for Gilhooley. But this
time, more solemn angles and Mizoguchian pans (which seem mystic revelations of reality) underline this ritual—an indication it contains meanings of

a permanence transcending its human agents. This solemnity is extended in the formalized fashion in which, on the shore, the children, Cluzeot, and two nuns *walk* (always this motion into and out of frames!) *into* a shot screened by a net, or André de Lage* unfolds a bright red umbrella, or Lelani, in a perfect instance of Ford's "postexpressionism," wipes away a tear, framed behind the fishing net. In contrast, Amelia, now and throughout, wears red, white, and blue. Her first hint of the mystic comes when finally she finds herself alone in her father's house; a Polynesian hymn accompanies a camera track as she enters the mythically lit living room and stares at the portrait of a native woman (Manulani): crosscuts between Amelia and portrait work as does similar montage in *The Sun Shines Bright* when Lucy Lee sees her grandmother's picture: Amelia starts wondering. In point of fact, Amelia meets nearly everyone in crosscuts, exchanges that stand out both as rare moments of relating and as rare quasi-point-of-view shots. But the Manulani portrait is key: there is no "mother" on the island, only this *idea* (and ideal), which will always be related to native music and forces of nature. Now Manulani's disapproval is suggested in a dissolve to Cluzeot praying in church beneath an umbrella, in protection from the same storm that wakes up Amelia. And prayers and storm lead to the bringing together of Luki and Amelia, and thus to resolution of conflict.

A strum tune and crosscuts accompany a gently satiric cigarette tryst between stuffed-shirt Amelia and redneck Donovan; romance, of course, becomes possible the instant she learns he is a man of means. Rising, they switch sides in the frame, and, in the shot/countershot/two-shot pattern, make "pax," extending their hands across the distance. The delicate agogics in play and montage both here and in the following patio scene (accompanied by the *Don Giovanni* minuet—from Lelani's off-screen piano) make these some of the most entrancing scenes in late Ford. On the minuet's final

*This French governor's name is sufficiently close to DeLaage, the French governor in Ford's other South Sea movie, *The Hurricane*. Among his titles, the Marquis de Lage lists Baron de Fienne, a reference to Ford's birth name.

note, they enter the children's room (all white and black) and Amelia meets Lelani, then Sally, in crosscuts: "Well," she exclaims with effusion, "You're a little *doll!* What's your name?" "Sarah, but they call me Sally." "*Sarah!* Well, my name's Amelia, Sarah. Nobody ever called me Sally!" "No?" This is typical Frank Nugent dialogue. Like the line "Raincheck?" in the saloon and like many other lines it invites figuring out meanings not immediately clear. Nugent has characters express themselves in codes of their own class. Amelia, coldly raised, believes in proper names (she calls Guns "Michael") but her baby talk is typical of her condescension toward everyone.

Instances of her attitude came just before the patio scene, as she ignored Gilhooley and questioned the Chinese pumping the slot machine despite the three signs—one of them in Chinese: "'*Dérange*,' 'Out of Order,' and so forth. Explanation?"

Donovan:	Slot machine. Was shipped in here six years ago, busted. It is still busted.
Amelia:	Well . . . why . . .?
Donovan:	I do not attempt to explore the depths of the Oriental mind, Miss Dedham. [*Turning toward Mr. Eu standing stiffly beside them*] Perhaps your Ivy League chaperon here could explain to my clients again that it's busted.
Amelia:	That's reasonable. Mr. Eu!
Eu:	I will try to explain it to them, in their *barbarian* tongue!

Evident here is Donovan's caustic racism, Amelia's formidable impersonableness toward Eu, and Eu's own, colonialized (satire of) racism. For like the children whom Cluzeot calls "Monsters" when they twist to "Frère Jacques" the moment his back is turned, there is a monster side to everything on the island: chaos veneered with order. Lelani and Sally wear sailor suits, which could also be Catholic-school uniforms; these "half-castes" are being raised as proper Europeans, which marks, as in *Cheyenne Autumn*, a stage in white imperialism. The whites live in palaces and control: government, religion, commerce, medicine, gambling, liquor. The priest is a private priest, apparently instructing only the children of aristocrats (the children are, in fact, native royalty). Notable by its absence from Ford's little community here is a school for the natives. Instead, the Polynesians operate like a sort of chorus, in the background; church and medicine excepted (for imperialism has its good sides), they are ignored by the upper-class whites,* and judging by the few references (Cluzeot to starvation, Fig. 10: I.1.iii; Dedham to sickness, II.4.iv) their condition is precarious. Note that the shopkeepers and saloon-folk, the petit bourgeois, are Chinese rather than Polynesian. They have, however, a mystic service within Ford's pantheist allegory, for although there is little

---

*But note the native who suddenly races by with a towel when Amelia swims to shore, confirming the suspicions aroused by the singing-greeting girls that the island caters to the tourist trade.

(alas!) of the sounds of ocean and wind (which one got in *Mogambo*), there is much symbolically present music (as in *the Sun Shines Bright*), the "voice-off" presence of the Polynesians who, like the land and the flowers, survey everything and conduct it to accord. Cluzeot's function in this scheme is not quite clear to me. He has a passion for music (a moral good) and is encouraged to regard the slot machine as a lamentably broken jukebox; but he is also the puritanic suppressor of violence, chastizing the kids for cheering at the Donovan-Gilhooley battle, and he believes beauty must be taught through discipline. He is, then, the Ransom Stoddard of the movie, and he *always* carries an umbrella: one never knows . . .

Mysticism returns (after a boring too-absurd water-ski sequence, climaxed by a pax) when, as Guns chops a Christmas tree atop gargantuan vistas of mountains, valleys, waterfalls, Lelani *sings* a Polynesian prayer, "thanking the goddess of the canyon for our tree," as she explains to Amelia. "*Goddess?!*" chortles Amelia, "You believe in gods and goddesses?!" "Well, I believe in the one god as we all do. But I respect the beliefs and customs of my people." This with snotty sententiousness, as Lelani struts away from Amelia, who stares puzzled. What may sound like bad acting by little Jacqueline Malouf is actually appropriate: whether or not we have figured it out yet, the serious, lofty Lelani is Haleakaloha's reigning queen.

Mystic and melancholic, the strum tune accompanies Amelia's marveling at the valleys' power, echoing the pantheism of Rossellini's *Stromboli*, and summoning her toward a war memorial, which, as it threatens to reveal the Manulani secret, Donovan hastens to block from view. His voice grows vicious, his face hard, and Ford has them posed against the sky, as he talks of the war here. The Japanese are gone now, but Americans, French, and Chinese remain, and so, somewhere below, do the Polynesians midst the silent vistas toward which Lelani chants. Somehow the Americans are repeatedly associated with war and destruction—the anachronistic World War II jeep doubly so, since it tears ugly ruts in the sod. Donovan and Gilhooley fight for pleasure, and celebrate a war day as their birthday. Amelia was marked as a pirate imperialist, and associated with the degenerate French governor in constant red, white, and blue.

But perhaps because Dedham is "one of their own," the natives do not perform their ritual for his return—the picture's third arrival and of them all the most lovingly composed. The camera pans down from the beach's rise, following nurses and natives, slowly to the surf, the strum tune melancholic on the soundtrack. Each of the thirteen shots uses motion, within the frame; this is Ford's "kinetic sublimity." Amelia *enters* (theatrically), from the rear, a medium-high-angle shot. At the surf, a patient is carried from a longboat, laid on a stretcher; others start up the beach and exit the frame, for the camera pans only with Dedham, small in the shot, who walks behind the others. The effect is languorous and the beach is all but deserted by the time the pan moves far enough to include Amelia at far right. Crosscuts, next, of

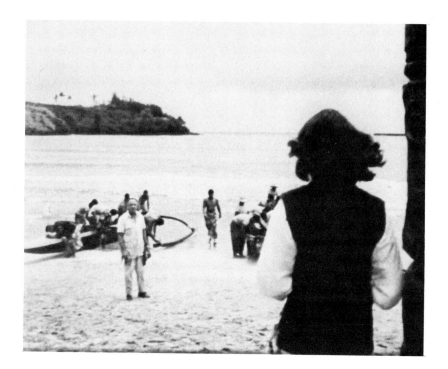

her moving gradually toward him, but from head-on, not from the side, and of Dedham staring at her, before they embrace, between the pax posts (the totem poles on the beach). The choir comments approval, with one word twice: "Haleakaloha."

Ford cuts marvelously to a bright, lively interior. The Christmas tree has been decorated and gifts lie wrapped beneath it. "Look," cries Amelia, flashing on and off the tree lights, "generator's working!" And darkish soundtrack music alters to a slow, premonitory "Jingle Bells," presaging the film's formal resolution and the end of "monstrous" segregation. The list of broken things, among other deficiencies, is awesomely long: besides the generator, a busted photo, busted record, busted bottles, busted slot machine with upside-down sign, leaky chapel roof, starvation, poverty, war, fights, monstrous children, distorted looking glass, backfiring jeep, rain, the United States of America, off-duty law, Donovan's racial fear, Eu's racism, nets, de Lage wishing transfer to Miami Beach or Hollywood, broken mirrors and sixty-three years' bad luck, misspelled words, legion/legend, the bump on the road, Amelia's six pratfalls, elitism, Maydays, Limeys, mispronounced Irish names, wrong words (dove, legs), rose and thorn, the "reef," and a broken piano. But now, finally, something is working. The flashing lights and the "Jingle Bells" look forward to flashing lights and bells and whistles to come, all of which will celebrate the arrival of . . . Christmas!

This and the following sequence are among Ford's finest. The latter consists of three "scenes," the first of which is an interesting étude on the formulaic treatment of a conversation in crosscuts. Dedham is struggling to explain to Amelia that the "little half-castes" are his and why he never told her dead mother's family he married Manulani. The exchange of shot / countershot, pivoting (upon some flowers) across a table, occurs twelve times, but then, as Dedham speaks of war-time dangers, the flat countershot of him is replaced by a deeper, low-angle one, whose depth and rhythm (it is repeated twice fairly rapidly) suggest torpedoing and darkness. But the shot is deeper also because Dedham is *approaching* the "truth," of course, *is* Manulani, whose portrait is, for the first time, present in the depth of this low-angle shot of Dedham. Manulani's portrait forms both (1) the end point of a perspectival, truth-searching line running from Amelia's back, through the flowers, through Dedham, and thence to the portrait, and also (2) the reverse line: Manulani, in back of Dedham, reaching out toward Amelia through Dedham and the flowers. Manulani and the flowers are, recall, both sorts of gods: they represent passions and transcendent forces. The flowers operate somewhat as light does in *The Fugitive* or as the lamp does in *Liberty Valance*. Amelia is altered by contact with Haleakaloha, by its beauty (the flowers), and thus becomes receptive to Donovan, to her father, and eventually to Manulani and her half-caste siblings. Thus the flowers properly act as the axis upon which the crosscuts turn.

The rhythms of the montage are quadruple: the actual time of each shot, the placements of the low-angle shots, and the psychological times: the quantity of words and gesture, and their (agogic) quality. Alternation of patches of color propose rhythms too, of course, for here as often elsewhere in *Donovan's Reef* color is a kinetic gesture.

Dedham's attempt to confess is interrupted when the kids lay flower wreaths on the lawn; Amelia watches through a slatted screen (as her siblings watched her through a net). Intending to fetch them, she leaves the frame; pan right with Dedham, who swallows some rum and, with Manulani's portrait behind him, says, "Amelia," in the picture's most intimate moment; "Yes?" she responds from off-camera; "Well," he continues, " 'The time has come, the Walrus said, to speak of many things' "; " 'Of sailing ships and sealing wax,' " she adds, reentering the frame; and Dedham concludes melancholically, " 'And cabbages and kings.'* I'd been here about . . ." but is again interrupted: the hospital bell; and he leaves the frame, the camera resting on Amelia, then panning with her, alone, as she goes to the door. From the window until now, a single take has marked passage from Amelia at the drama's center, to Dedham, and then, through her just-aroused curiosity, back again to Amelia. The shot's "discourse" is contained in this entering and exiting; it is not a crosscut conversation, nor a two-shot, but rather an attempt at accord. The sensitive agogics of Jack Warden's delivery and gesture take on an almost decorative import; it suffices that they trade lines of poetry, for the words themselves have no use except poetically. One is tempted to call the shot Ford's finest "magic moment."

The Christmas service recalls *The Fugitive's* baptism (community in song, expressionism) and *The Sun Shines Bright's* funeral, but in *Donovan's Reef* all the community's groups are present (cf. the funeral's excluded blacks): Americans, French, Chinese, Polynesians, businessmen, religious, government, medical, military, children, rich and poor, aristocrat and commoner.** As for Lafleur's song sequence earlier, hurricane lamps suggest a theater. The children dressed as angels parade to "Silent Night" in Polynesian, and André reads, "And from the East came three wise men, three kings,† bearing gifts." Each country is represented by its attribute. "The King of Polynesia"— Sergeant Munk (Mike Mazurki)—comes barechested and wreath-crowned with a basket of fruits, to /kneel before the crèche. "The Emperor of China"—Mr. Eu—comes in oriental robes with tea service and rice, to / kneel. And "The King of the United States of America"—Gilhooley—in white sheet and gold paper crown with the antique phonograph, to /kneel. Gilhooley's entrance is underlined by its position (last), a new and heroic

---

*Perhaps the sailing ships are the navy, the sealing wax the marriage to Manulani, the cabbage the kids, the kings Dedham and Manulani. Ford quotes Lewis Carroll also in *Doctor Bull*.

**Dedham, however, is called to hospital just before the pageant; i.e., the Dedham family is yet to come together.

†Once again Ford invokes his favorite myth of the three (*3 Bad Men, 3 Godfathers,* etc.).

angle, flaming torches behind him, stark shadows, and the stately loving manner in which de Lage draws out the U.S.'s full name; all this, combined with Gilhooley, his cigar, and the benign, musical symbol of the phonograph, suggest a deliberate nostalgia for the *idea* of America. Gilhooley is spotlit upon the sanctuary stage, evoking the symbolic dimension across time and space of America's role and man's genuflection before God. Similarly expressionistic shadows fall across the congregation, and they have occurred earlier in the movie whenever Amelia or the house-servants approached the Manulani portrait, and when Lelani is told she must hide from Amelia.

But the cozy warm community's offerings are not accepted. "All is calm," Lafleur sings, followed by thunder, lightning, and rain; "All is bright," and the chapel goes dark and the umbrellas come out. A heavy stream of water cascades onto Gilhooley's head, toppling America's crown. "Steady on, men! Steady! Sing out!" commands Pat Wayne, and all obey.

It is uncertain how much Amelia knows by Christmas dawn. Maids Yoshi and Koshi place wreaths before Manulani's portrait and, theatrically shadowed, bow ritualistically three times, but flee when Amelia spots them. She places flowers there herself and exchanges quizzical crosscut stares with the painting. A series of paintinglike images, unusually beautiful even for this movie, narrate Amelia's bicycle search for information; at the cemetery she demands "the truth" from Cluzeot, while the camera, independently, tracks into a close-up of the cross on Manulani's grave. Earlier, it panned from Cluzeot, to Amelia watching him, and then back again to Cluzeot; this double-motion is exceedingly rare for Ford (who generally limits pronounced movements to one per shot), and suggests a linkage comparable to the attempted accord in the "Cabbages and Kings" scene. Everything leads to Manulani; she is the *contrechamp* of the pan, the chief god, the cactus rose. Everyone tries to keep Amelia away from her, but at every turn she finds her.

Meanwhile at the Reef a miracle occurs. After a song ("Waltzing Mathilda," which music Ford translates into motion),* and a grand Christmas brawl, Cluzeot refuses a coin, given out foretellingly by the clobbered slot machine during the fight, insisting that it belongs to the "juke box." "Music! Comme ça, musique!" he says, throwing the lever; Donovan and Gilhooley, on the floor, watch in awe as a mighty fountain of coins gushes forth. "Whoop, whoop, whoop!" sings the slot machine, jingle-jangling and flashing red and white. Expressionistic shadows mark what is, in many ways, the climactic moment of the film. The machine is a sort of god; the persistence of the Chinese (and Gilhooley), despite the signs, indicates hope and stubbornness (traditional Fordian virtues). Oddly, Donovan has neither put the machine out of reach nor emptied its treasures; instead, he respects the laws of chance. The machine discharges because it is Christmas. All man's most destructive and sadistic temptations may today be joyfully indulged as

---

*Sung by Dick Foran, a singing cowboy star of the forties.

tolerable exercise of "liberty"; even the Lee Marvin character (whom Cluzeot calls a "devil" and whose haircut is indeed satanic) is tolerable; even the
piano's destruction can be condoned today. The black-caped priest, leading
the police, a puritanic enforcer of harmony, musical and otherwise, appears
a benign agent of order (in contradistinction to Sergeant Munk who, like
Link Appleyard, is always off-duty). As in many other Fords, it is the innocent who reaps the fruits of others' labors. Cluzeot asks nothing from the
machine but music; he says the money *belongs* to it, and renders unto god.

And all of this happens because it is Haleakaloha's national day; Lelani
sits enthroned; a choreograph of motion, music, color, and flowers pay her
homage.* *Donovan's Reef*'s natives exercise a redemptive power; Amelia
finds her family; all is brought to accord (indeed, formally: Amelia curtsies
to Lelani in syncopation with a curtsying double line of natives). And, as in a
commedia dell'arte, there comes the curtain-call procession: The *Araner* is
in harbor, Captain Martin is loading Amelia's luggage. The camera gazes
from the surf up at the pier and its two posts, as though a spectator up at a
stage, and most of the players—Amelia, the kids, Dedham, Cluzeot, nuns,
nurses, natives—walk slowly forward to stand in line; the strum tune,
happy, accompanies. But, challenged by her father, Amelia goes back to say
goodbye to Guns (whom she clobbered with her umbrella in the last scene).

---

*A subtle but important instant: Dedham and Amelia, instead of mounting the dais to pay
homage, stand conversing; but the Polynesian master of ceremonies raps his staff commandingly.
Would so authoritative an interruption, of a white by a native, be conceivable any other day?

As she starts back, Dedham calls her, and, "pax-ly," their arms stretch across the screen as she surrenders her umbrella.

Passing Donovan, she falls off the jeep and onto her ass once again. Midst fights and paxes they agree to wed. Her reference, "If what you said is true," refers to his "I made a human being out of you"—by treating her like a woman. In fact, this is true. She is lordly and condescending with everyone, maintaining a genteel decorum also with her father. But with Guns she has no control: her voice, particularly, betrays her, becoming with Donovan squeaky and mousey, enraged, or low and vampish. Their hit-and-kiss skit* endorses neither Donovan's chauvinism nor Amelia's, any more than the barfight comedy endorsed macho sadism. Donovan's and Amelia's lifestyles were established at the beginning, and their affair has progressed with stated satire. The irony, akin to *Liberty Valance*'s, is that the Bostonian has succumbed to the call of the wild. Does Donovan, as he spanks her, say, "I wear the *pants* in this family" or "I wear the *pax* . . ."? Surely the latter. And "pax" is truer. Those who decry such sexist behavior in this film might ponder that the essence of comedy rules that this "happy ending" need only be acceptable to the characters involved, not to us. Why does this ultimate succession of fights and paxes accelerate in this long, balletic tracking shot, only to conclude at a weed-infested, dry fountain?

*The skit was used, a bit differently, in *A Minute's Wait.*

The conclusion, as happy as could be wished, is ironic. Money solves everything. Amelia (= USA) will become the new mother-figure, the new Manulani—as the crosscuts between her and the portrait suggest. A long parade, as earlier, wends down the path to the Dedham house, returning the kids' possessions. Once again Ford concludes with his primal antinomies: parade / house. The camera's pan does not come to a halt; it still moves slowly across the screen as the picture fades and the movie ends: a long "Alōhaaa."

No sooner had Ford arrived in Hawaii to begin production of *Donovan's Reef* than he learned that Paramount had pulled out of their financing arrangement with him. Rather than abandon the picture, he became his own producer. But, strange to say, here even more than with *Liberty Valance* there was no real script and Ford more or less improvised from day to day. Perhaps his nightly trips up to the cliff for twelve weeks with Frank Baker, when he would brood silently, were meditations for the next day's work.

To some, *Donovan's Reef* showed signs of dotage. Ford once got set up to shoot a scene only to be reminded, when he called for action, that the dialogue had not been written yet. Back stateside, crews readied studio retakes, only to have Ford walk in, yell, "Finished. Pau!" and walk out. On the islands, so many old friends and children were present, that the affairs took on airs of a last reunion rather than of a film production. Indeed, *Donovan's Reef* is a picture whose claims to greatness seem recognizable only to the initiate, and by no means even to many of them. The comedy seems often terribly broad, the children overly indulged in, and, as may happen while watching a movie, the presence of two or three weak and relatively inane sequences tends to elongate and devalue the entire movie. Lastly, there are those who find the scene of Wayne spanking Elizabeth Allen to be inexcusably offensive.

Yet flawed as it is, and perhaps *too* deceptively shallow, *Donovan's Reef* ranks with Ford's sublimest work for at least 89 of its 109 minutes. It combines and advances upon thematic and articulative figures from *The Hurricane* (nature as mysterious transcendent), *The Fugitive* (theocratic labyrinth, expressionism), *Wagon Master* (moral grace, use of music), *The Sun Shines Bright* (social analysis, racism), and *Mogambo* (man and nature). *Donovan's Reef* is the reverse of *The Man Who Shot Liberty Valance*: tragedy / comedy; black-and-white / color; man comes west to establish order and kills liberty / woman comes east to steal and discovers liberty; continent / island; repression / anarchy; pessimism / optimism; long shots and scenes / fast paced; verbal / pictorial; looking / acting; death / birth. . . .

Perhaps, as Jean-Marie Straub and Danièle Huillet once observed, the operative comparison is with Jean Renoir's *The Golden Coach*.[17] Both have somewhat similar pictorial styles, ethereal musical movements and gestures, and a commedia-dell'arte-like stylization of stereotypes and situations. Both are symbolic in anthropology and politics; both are materialist, Brechtian-like critiques of reality and society.

Cheyenne Autumn (1964). As Ford sank into old age his public persona became more quarrelsome and obliviously irresponsible. Yet it is hard to see how he could otherwise have gotten away with making such determinedly philosophic and abstract films as those of his last five years. It would be stretching the point to suggest that the old man's spells of drunken depression were merely theater cleverly plotted to get his way in the end, but it is true that such spells were scarcely new and that his Hollywood career had been theater from early on. Ford liked sports and poker, but his basic idea of a good time was to retire to his boat and read undisturbed. In the 1960s, Ford's act, his pose as a hard-nosed antiintellectual who magically turned out good pictures, grew progressively more outrageous, while his pictures became less than ever similar to his public character. With *Cheyenne Autumn*, Ford's act backfired.*

Critical essays rarely deal with the film itself. They deal instead with obstacles Ford encountered. Supposedly, his producers vetoed his plans to treat the Cheyenne as a kind of alien Greek chorus unable to communicate to whites, and insisted on casting the middle-aged Quaker schoolteacher with nubile Carroll Baker and the principal Indians with Caucasians. Supposedly, Ford did not work happily with Ricardo Montalban or Sal Mineo, was forced to retain Karl Malden footage he did not want and to jettison Sal Mineo footage he did want, and had a "bad score" foisted upon him. Supposedly, location shooting was arduous on the sixty-nine-year old Ford, who started shooting before the script was solved and who lost interest before he had finished.[18]

Some of these stories may be true. It is certainly true that Spencer Tracy, as Schurz, fell ill and was replaced with Edward G. Robinson, and that, it being impossible to go back onto location with hundreds of extras to restage the

---

*1878. The Cheyenne nation, reduced by disease and starvation from 1,000 to 286, all its appeals ignored, escapes its Oklahoma reservation and begins an 1,800-mile trek home to Dakota. A young Quaker teacher, Deborah Wright, goes along. Capt. Thomas Archer's troop reluctantly pursues, but when Maj. Braden attacks with artillery the major is killed and their horses lost. Dull Knife, appointed war chief by his dying father, swears celibacy for the duration and watches Red Shirt, son of his elder brother Little Wolf, woo his young wife. Back East, the press hyperbolizes facts and Interior Secretary Schurz is under fire. Archer catches up to the Cheyenne, but Lt. Scott's impetuous charge loses a battle. The starving Cheyenne beg food en route—and are murdered for sport by trailhands—and they find the buffalo herds slaughtered.

Interlude. Archer's troop enters winter camp but renew pursuit when the Cheyenne trail is discovered. But the Cheyenne, dying in the snow from hunger, split in two. Most of the women and children surrender but, brutalized by Capt. Wessels and the War Department's demand they immediately march back to the reservation, they escape again, many dying in the attempt, and rendezvous at Victory Cave. There, only the presence of Schurz, summoned by Archer, prevents their massacre by an army battalion. Afterward, Dull Knife kills Red Shirt in a duel and rides into exile; Wright and Archer send a little girl home to her tribe.

treaty scene, Robinson's body was collaged awkwardly onto existent footage. But problems plague most productions, and few movies adhere to their first script concepts. To cite such problems as excuses—as Hitchcock does in complaining to Truffaut of miscastings spoiling his original concepts[19]—is to ignore art's need to capitalize on limitation (Hitchcock should have altered his concepts). Some of what *Cheyenne Autumn* bystanders took for problems may not have been problems at all—Ford never explained—and others, like nubile Carroll Baker, now seem inspired choices.

The pseudocriticism lavished on *Cheyenne Autumn*'s production "problems" of course had a purpose. The film lost money, even critics were bored, and rather than accept the fact that, having gone expecting another *She Wore a Yellow Ribbon*, they had got another *Fugitive* instead, they clung to the meta-film they had wanted. The $4.2 million movie had been ballyhooed as the master's farewell to Monument Valley, only *this* time from the Indian side, and even Andrew Sarris assumed it was "a failure simply because Ford cannot get inside the Indians he is trying to ennoble."[20] Perhaps suspecting Ford had not been trying to "get inside," Sarris later retrenched, noted that no filmmaker has ever seen the West through the eyes of an Indian, and that Ford "had always scrupulously respected the dignity and honour of the Other in the remorselessly racist dialectic of the [Western] genre."[21]

Ford himself had contributed to the confusion, telling Bogdanovich, "I've killed more Indians than Custer, Beecher and Chivington put together,"[22] and even his apologists have blithely assumed Ford needed to expiate injustices done Indians in his earlier pictures. True, those who like *Soldier Blue* (Ralph Nelson, 1970), in which every white atrocity is parsed, will never be content with John Ford. But *Soldier Blue*'s Indians are stupid, misguided, and semisavage, while its whites are troglodytes from whom we can comfortably dissociate ourselves. *Fort Apache*'s Indians, in contrast, were clever and victorious, and the soldiers—unavoidably empathetic and like ourselves—were unwitting instruments of their ideological conditioning. Finally, Ford kept insisting that *Cheyenne Autumn* told "a true story, authentic, the reality as it was,"[23] whereas in fact the movie bears only slight resemblance to the historical facts in Mari Sandoz's well-researched book of the same name. *Her* story is far grimmer, the characters quite different, most events quite otherwise; even in the last scene Ford has changed matters: Dull Knife actually killed "Thin Elk" (not "Red Shirt") in a trading post, not a tribal ceremony; Lone Wolf was drunk, not a noble warrior, and the girl in question was his daughter, not his wife. Afterwards, he went up into the hills, the Elk family destroyed his lodge, and he was no longer chief. And Carl Schurz was basically uninvolved in the Cheyenne affair, and did not come West to parley with them.

Let us, then, put aside worries about the movie John Ford did not make and deal instead with the one he did. What is the *Cheyenne Autumn* we have?

The actual *Cheyenne Autumn,* not surprisingly, corresponds to what our study of Ford would lead us to suspect from him at this date. Its action is not so much genocide as the sway of absurdity, with the Cheyenne as its victims. Almost nothing occurs *with* reason. The Cheyenne parade homeward seeking reason, the cavalry pursue without reason, the parade more than ever substitutes instinct for reason. A major shoots cannon at children, a lieutenant charges for glory, the eastern press goes berserk, the telegram spouts instructions for genocide, sportsmen slaughter buffalo, the army worships orders— all act instinctually. When finally Schurz asks, "Just one question, General. Do you enjoy killing Indians, women, children?" he misses the point. It is comforting to imagine that genocide is the product of evil, sadistic people and so to shift the blame for a holocaust away from ourselves. Alas, Ford indicts every white person: the brutely mechanical army is merely the visible agent of policies engendered by government, press, and average citizen. But they are not sadists. Even Wessels, the archcaricature, is humane and compassionate, a student of Indian culture, while the trailhands who shoot Indians for fun are no more sadistic than rabbit hunters. No reason explains genocide—except that the Cheyenne want to live and that everyone is myopic.

Those who know Ford will not be surprised by the Dodge City episode strangely inserted into the middle of the picture. Comic absurdity offsets absurd tragedy frequently in Ford's work, the novelty in *Cheyenne Autumn* being that the snappy, immediate farce is concentrated together rather than interspersed throughout, the better to throw into relief *Cheyenne Autumn's* ponderous distanced dirge. The episode repeats gags from *My Darling Clementine* as Wyatt Earp tries to have a quiet game of poker. But there is an air of moral decadence, Wyatt's character is a bored selfish cynic rather than a stimulated idealist, and familiar pictorial motives, like the long shot along the bar, are exaggerated into parody. The Ionesco-like dialogue and pantomime—a marvelously intense, volatile vaudeville of pouts between James Stewart, Arthur Kennedy, and John Carradine, triply offset by skits by Elizabeth Allen's whore, the gassy trailhands, and the panic-struck mayor—requires no further justification.* But its point is surely our solipsism, our inability to think or even to see beyond the clichés of our specific cultural determination. The theme goes back beyond *Tabu.* Intolerance is not cruel, it is a limitation of sensibility whereby we protect, define, and assert ourselves. Horribly, genocide of the Indian was not a policy or even a conscious act but the natural voraciousness of a youthful culture's expansiveness, just as the Cheyenne pil-

---

*There are those who judge this episode one of Ford's greater miracles and regard Warner Brothers' extermination of its second half as a loss greater than the complete *Greed.* In the missing portion Earp and Holliday lead Dodge City's citizens out to battle the Cheyenne but, sighting a lonely Indian scout, they rush back home and hide in their cellars. (Ford corrects some facts: in *My Darling Clementine* Earp is young in 1882, having left Dodge City for Tombstone, where he meets Holliday. Now Earp is older, it is 1878, and he and Holliday play poker in Dodge City.)

grimage is the primal urge of a dying nation. A tiny herd collides with a gigantic one; is anyone responsible?

This is the familiar Fordian scheme, the same ravaged world we knew in *Pilgrimage*, but with contradictions vaster, action less immediate, and beauty deepened. But, as in other late Fords, the Hero is problematic—the tasks are greater, their significance overwhelming, the hero's means almost nonexistent.

Is Deborah Wright the hero? She alone possesses higher knowledge of right and wrong (and puts out flowers, but no one comes), and she rejects convention and family to go off alone with the Cheyenne to strive to preserve their children. But she is not terribly successful. Miss Wright is right to teach the Cheyenne to write; without history reason has even less hope. And she teaches spelling while drawing pictures: a buffalo, later a train, thus conceptualizing why Indian life is doomed. (The train brought sportsmen who exterminated the herds on which Indian civilization depended.) Yet also, Miss Wright assures white domination by teaching its language. Education as indoctrination is an obsessive theme in late Ford (Ransom Stoddard, Father Cluzeot, and Mr. Pether labor in classrooms to impose *their* values), and words are never to be trusted. Dull Knife claims he learned words "when white men still spoke truth" (when was that?), but treaties lie, newspapers lie, telegrams are absurd, and all Wessels's book knowledge fails to raise his consciousness. "Confidentially—I want to know the truth," whispers Schurz, but the truth is words, words that, as in *Liberty Valance*, control men and are distorted by men. Words, the conduit of civilization, are the amoral instrument by which intolerance imposes itself. (It is worth noting that Ford's concern with the relativities of point of view and the validity of language anticipates by almost a decade the "modernist" attitudes of Jean-Luc Godard.)

Is Archer (Richard Widmark) the hero? He seems particularly impotent, cast reluctantly as the Cheyenne's most immediate enemy, forgetting the names of his men, shirking moral responsibility, trying to shift it onto the doctor; and when Archer does at last accept higher knowledge, he must run to Schurz to do anything. Back in 1948, *Fort Apache*'s Captain York expressed outrage less verbosely than does Sergeant Wichowsky (Mike Mazurki) in his vaudevillian tent dialogue with Archer (likening the army to Cossacks), but York rode into battle under protests and threats of arrest, whereas Wichowsky, after his binge, reenlists because he cannot resist "Boots and Saddles."

Then is Schurz the hero? Yes, but despite his looking for guidance to Lincoln (midst Lincoln's melody from *Young Mr. Lincoln*), Schurz is a magnificent *deus ex machina*, appearing from nowhere to mediate between a few dozen Cheyenne and an artillery-equipped army battalion bent on their destruction. The cigars he hands out when the Cheyenne admit they have no tobacco for their peace pipes seem ironic proof of white victory. If the land that needs a hero is unhappy, what may be said of the land that needs a *deus ex machina?* Fordian heroes, while never plentiful, formerly sprang up organically.

The world without heroes lacks glory as well. No bands play or voices sing as E Troop parades across Monument Valley. Ben Johnson's "Yoh" and horsemanship have lost their youthful zest. And none of the soldiers nor any of the whites outside Dodge City (save Schurz, the god) possess the cameo individuality we associate with Ford. Toned down, recessive, their actions seem progressively more dehumanized enactments of ritual patterns.

Yet the "truth," the Cheyenne story, is still more distanced. Their gilded statue during the titles, the opening legend, and a history-book narrator frame them in their mythic past. Viewed almost always from immense physical distance, in meditative stares, with a presentational style such as Noel Burch would ascribe to prewar Japanese cinema,[24] the individual Cheyenne are purely iconic, recalling *The Fugitive*'s most abstract moments. Their story, particularly the love story, appears virtually in subtext. Again, the heroes are clay footed. Red Shirt, whose shirt is almost the only bright color in the main film, has the ridiculous glory of a truly lost cause—he recalls Ashby Corwin in *The Sun Shines Bright*—but he also epitomizes the moral decay of the reservation years, arrogating rights to fire first shots and to steal his chief's wife. Dull Knife struggles too for heroism. But his leadership as his people trek homeward has witnessed repeated disasters and when, upholding right, he kills Red Shirt, his violence exiles him from his community. More than any hero, Dull Knife must ride away at the end, barred from the promised land.

Like *This Is Korea!* or *The Fugitive*, *Cheyenne Autumn* works not so much in terms of theme or character as by the presence of its physical beauty. (Needless to say, it must be seen in full Cinemascope; anything else completely alters Ford's magisterial distance and pace.) When, as it did in *Rio Grande*, the troop rides into winter quarters and the women stand sunstreaked watching in the dust and autumn foliage, Victorian tenderness beats in the frame; but there is a similar awe at beauty in even Ford's most implacable scenes, as when he stares Antonioni-like at the pastel tints of desert bush and sky while the slimy trailhands shoot Cheyenne for sport. We are not so far from the expressionism of *Pilgrimage* when Ford blackens the sky over the bone-laden plain of dead buffalo, or, mournfully, as the hospital's bluish grays chill into the muted reddish grays of prison and then into the ocherous grays of "Victory Cave." Ford never evades his obligation to aestheticize human tragedy. When Little Wolf raises his knife in threat of suicide and pale light refracts softly off the statuesque faces of the Cheyenne chorus surrounding him, it is not merely the picture that is iconic; the moment is as well. Similarly, from outside their prison we see Cheyenne faces peering out through frost-framed windows; the scene is almost totally dark, save for a lamp, which then too is extinguished.

This is the nadir. But blackness in late Ford also means torches blazing in the night—in *Two Rode Together*, *7 Women*, *Vietnam! Vietnam!*, and here, along with cannon in the night in *The Wings of Eagles* and "The Civil War," and candles in the night in *Donovan's Reef*. These images—out of Blake?— tell us that however elusive truth or useless reason, however dependent we ultimately are in miracles that do not come, the obligation to strive remains. The young—Deborah and Red Shirt—do not question this. And as the Cheyenne wend their way toward extinction, they gradually doff their Western clothes and don Indian ones, achieving victory of sorts in their finale, which Ford sets on a meadow against a Renaissance-like perspective of background wilderness, and in which rejuvenation, violent purification, and funeral are combined.

The Dodge City sequence aside, *Cheyenne Autumn* maintains a style of stern formality: figures engulfed by landscape alternate with iconic figures posed against landscape. As in *The Fugitive*, soft breaths of humanity occasionally break through this grimness—generally as confessions of helplessness: the old Quaker sitting uncomprehendingly in the sunstream, Schurz gazing woefully at Lincoln's portrait, O'Carberry wishing he were a better doctor, Little Wolf staring at his brother who has just killed his son, the little girl running home.

"The Civil War" (1962). Cinerama was a three-camera process (now generally seen in anamorphic editions that crop its frame's top and bottom) which, as it suffered from elongated depth perspective, befitted travelogue epics and roller-coaster rides. Merian Cooper was one of its backers, however, and Ford contributed a twenty-five-minute episode, "The Civil War," to Cinerama's 162-minute *How the West Was Won* (1962):

> The Civil War erupts, Zeb's pa was off at the first shot to join the Union army, and now the eager youngster leaves his Ohio farm, Ma, brother, dog. / Shiloh, night: heaps of dead, mass graves, hospital gore. A friend in the dark warns Zeb not to drink from the pink stream and suggests they "jus' leave this war to the folks that want it." Outside the church-hospital, mid cherry blossoms, Sherman urges Grant not to give up, and Zeb knifes his (Rebel) friend before the latter can kill Grant. Bombs and battle scenes. Zeb comes home by riverboat, finds Ma buried beside Pa. He leaves brother on the farm, and heads west.

It is as epitomizing and anthological as anything in Ford: how a youth came off a farm, discovered the world; how this experience killed the past and thrust the will toward expansion. Vast tides of history are concentrated at their point of transition into the immediate emotions of a single individual. Everything is said; and with such formidable elegance and concision that the neighboring episodes of "The Civil War" (behemoths by Henry Hathaway and George Marshall) seem like so much bad disco momentarily ceasing for the *St. Matthew Passion*'s final funereal chorus.

A somewhat similar approach to history was taken in *Liberty Valance*, and would have been taken in a picture Ford desperately wanted to make, but never could, *April Morning*—about the battle of Lexington and the American Revolution.

> I'd devote most of my work to describing the daily life of the future Americans of that time, the life of those farmers just starting to get attached to this new world, taking root here, the existence of those farmers who then begin to revolt against the English soldiers. This aspect of the birth of the United States, rustic, rural, interests me much more than the battle, which is only its crystallization. It's this approach to history that stirs me. I like to make my pictures about the little people, who begin to feel the thirst for self-respect growing within themselves, who become aware of their belonging to a community.[25]

U.S. Grant makes a brief appearance in "The Civil War." Ford thought Grant's life "one of the great American stories—but you can't do it. You can't show him as a drunkard, getting kicked out of the Army."[26] But Ford, in a poignantly elegant and, at nine minutes, even *more* concise episode in *The Colter Craven Story,* had shown Sam Grant coming home in disgrace to Wilmette and being denounced by his father in front of his wife, then suddenly taking charge of some raw volunteers who march off to war piping "Johnny Comes Marching Home," while Sam goes off to a clerical job "sharpening lead pencils." Later, his friends from Wilmette meet him at

The Rookie of the Year. Wayne protects son Pat Wayne. James Gleason watches.

Shiloh in deep despair, and realize what became of Sam Grant. The episode, made for Ward Bond's long-running TV series, *Wagon Train* (a spin-off of *Wagon Master*), was Bond's twenty-second appearance in a Ford picture—and his last in any film. He died November 5, 1960. John Wayne plays Sherman in both these sketches of Shiloh, and he also turns up umpiring a baseball game—with outrageously hammy calls—in *Flashing Spikes*, a hilarious TV episode starring James Stewart. Wayne had played a reporter in an earlier, also inventive, Ford TV baseball film, *Rookie of the Year.*

   7 Women (1965). "Ford represents pure classicism of expression in which an economy of means yields a profusion of effects," wrote Andrew Sarris,[27] and nowhere is this truer than in *7 Women,* in this culmination of Ford's vignette methods, where every gesture, every word, every object resonates into the indefinably symbolic. Each of its characters contains worlds, each of their actions permits multiple interpretations, each of them relates to each of the others on so many diverse levels as to invite virtually endless dissection. And, given the quality of Ford's work during the ten years preceding *7 Women*—the noticeable slowing down, the weariness, the pessimism, and even the misanthropy—*7 Women* is astonishing for its vitality. It may be the most quickly cut of all Ford's movies; it is certainly the most inventive, as rich in detail and revelation as any picture ever made. It constitutes not only a summation of all Ford's prior career; it is also, as so often before, a new beginning, as far above and beyond *The Man Who Shot Liberty Valance* as that picture was in relation to *Two Rode Together.* Each moment confronts us with unequaled virtuosity and unsurpassed depths of humanism.

   But, before continuing in this vein, it should be noted that my view is, alas, in the minority. More typical was *The Morning Telegraph*'s comment in 1966: "A maudlin, mawkish, gooey, dripping hunk of simpering slush"; or Arthur Knight's enlightened chuckle in the *Saturday Review:* "I suspect that his admirers among the *auteur* critics will be hard put to it to explain away this work of The Master."[28]

   Its commercial* and critical failure, and Ford's plaintive remark in *Cahiers du Cinéma,* "I think it's one of my best, but the public didn't like it. It wasn't that they wanted,"[29] moved me to write him how much I liked it. And he responded with the letter reproduced here.

   7 Women scored critical successes in England and France, as an art film, but in the U.S. Metro abandoned it long before release. Its New York debut came after four or five months showcasing around the country as a cheap thriller, and then at a Forty-Second Street theater on the bottom half of a double bill with Burt Kennedy's *The Money Trap.* Its subject, typical for the thirties, alienated 1965's pseudosophisticates and camp followers in com-

---

*7 *Women*'s negative cost $2,308,190. Ford was paid $262,258. With distribution costs it had lost $2,300,000 by 1970. Grosses *worldwide* came to only $937,432 by then.

My dear Thomas Gallagher =

Thank you for your very Kind
letter. Perhaps its only us
Irish that can appreiate good
cinema fare (2 was born Sean
Aloysius O'Feeney).

    Hollywood now is run by
Wall St. + Madison Ave who
demand "Sex + Violence". This
is against my conscience + religion.
again my heartfelt thanks

     John Ford.

P.S. Just now 2 received a most
imposing diploma from the London
film festival notifying me that
"Seven women" has been chosen as
the out standing American film !!!
Is This ironic? Or is it just fate?

     J. F.

mand of trends in taste. Audience psychology is a fragile affair; a few detached cynics can easily condition everyone, so that people laugh instead of cry. Yet an all-black audience in Philadelphia's colored ghetto was perfectly in tune with 7 Women, even applauding at the end, and I have never known it not to make a profound impression upon anyone to whom I have introduced it.

Superficially, adverse reactions are comprehensible. 7 Women is pitched continually on the brink of bathos; its dialogue is a string of terse clichés, its emotions embarrassingly naked. Though distinctly a film of interior realism and dark tragedy, it is on the surface an essay in pure fantasy with a constant obbligato of humor and satire. What at first glance might excusably be mistaken for an overly broad, obvious, and emphatic work is in reality an affair of infinitely subtle distancing.

7 Women derives from Norah Lofts's short story, "Chinese Finale" (1936). Miss Argent narrates; all the women are English, and the Pi Lung mission is forewarned that Dr. Cartwright is a woman. She wears a skirt, not pants; her hair is short, but she has no interest in fashion; her motives for wanting a faraway job are not specified. Miss Andrews (without the Agatha) is a typical unremarkable mission chief, without Margaret Leighton's extraordinary characteristics; thus Cartwright's abrasive manners are not balanced by excesses in Andrews and must stand on their own merits. There are no refugees; an influenza epidemic lasts three weeks; Andrews retains her authority throughout. But Cartwright spends two days drinking alone in her room, drives Andrews to tears, and decides to leave.

That night she and Argent see the town afire. She goes to town with Arthur Pether, is wounded in the arm, and returns with news of his death; but Florrie's never told. Next morning the women awake to find themselves prisoners

Figure 11. *7 Women*

Numbers following each entry indicate duration in minutes (e.g., 7:32 or just in seconds (e.g., 95″). Numbers in parentheses indicate number of shots.

ACT I	30:00(246)	Shot average = 7.3 seconds.
	1:35(7)	Titles: Mongol cavalry.
Day One	7:32(65)	
1. Morning	2:45(25)	Courtyard 87″ (19). Dining room and letter 78″ (6).
2. Afternoon	4:47(40)	Classroom 48″ (12). Andrews and Emma 100″ (13). Porch and tree 139″ (15).
Day "Two"[a]	21:53(174)	
1. Evening	2:00(17)	Children sing; Cartwright arrives; meets Florrie.
2. Dinner	4:15(48)	
3. Clinic	3:37(31)	Cartwright, Florrie, Pether.
4. Office	3:14(21)	Andrews cautions Emma against Cartwright.
5. Courtyard	3:51(29)	Kum-cha refugees arrive.

Figure 11. (continued)

6. Diningroom	1:37(13)	Andrews and British.
7. Office	2:25(15)	Cartwright lectures Andrews on Florrie.
ACT II	17:30(107)	Shot average = 9.5 seconds
Day Three	11:22(75)	
1. Morning & c	4:11(29)	Clinic: cholera! courtyard 166″ (18). Vaccinations and clothes firing 85″ (11).
2. Night	6:51(46)	Binns relieves Cartwright 60″ (5). Pether digs grave 34″ (2). Pether leaves Florrie's tray 72″ (11). Andrews and Cartwright: Emma sick 88″ (8). Andrews and Cartwright under tree 157″ (20).
Day "Four"[a]	6:08(32)	
1. Road	0:08(1)	Plague sign removed.
2. Dinner	3:50(25)	Cartwright drunk!
3. Night	2:30(6)	Cartwright and Pether see village burning.
ACT III	38:30(232)	Shot average = 9.95 seconds.
Day Five [b]	12:30(77)	
1. Courtyard	2:07(14)	Army retreats. Pether and Kim to village.
2. Courtyard	5:07(36)	Packing 67″ (7); bandits arrive 230″ (29).
3. Night	5:13(27)	Massacre 162″ (7); bandits arrive 230″ (29).
3. Night	5:13(27)	Massacre 162″ (18). "Ransom" demand and Florrie's labor 151″ (9).
Day Six [b]	15:01(124)	
1. Morning	4:05(32)	Hut: Cartwright calls 64″ (7); dining room bargain for medical bag 85″ (15); meditates 46″ (6); returns to hut 50″ (4).
2. Afternoon	5:25(29)	Tunga hears of birth 24″ (3); goes to hut 138″ (13). Cartwright to Tunga 77″ (6). Woman in hut 86″ (7).
3. Night	7:27(63)	Hut: Cartwright and food 167″ (15). Woman in dining room 111″ (12). Wrestling 169″ (36).
Day Seven	9:02(42)	
1. Morning	2:53(15)	Women, Cartwright and Emma.
2. Evening	0:46(7)	Riding in gate. Women.
3. Night	5:22(30)	Cartwright in corridor; releases women 137″ (5). She watches them leave in cart 71″ (18). She in corridor 20″ (1). Gives poison 94″ (6).
	0:30	End titles.
Total:	86:00(485)	Shot average = 10.63 seconds.

[a]Time is elided for dramatic unity.

[b]Nonanamorphic television editions of 7 Women run 100 minutes. Editor Leon Selditz says Ford did not intend to use this additional footage. And some of these scenes, added to make the film optimum television length, are redundant or even not by Ford (such as the Mongol attack on the town surreally suggested by birds, sun-streaked branches, wasp sounds, horse hooves, and shadows). Nonetheless, the Ford-Selditz edition may have been shortened by MGM for theatrical release. For example, while it is clear that Ford shot the riding sequence, it is problematic whether he intended to retain it: it is lovely but redundant, and it destroys the formal unity of never leaving the mission. (Cartwright, Tunga Khan, Lean Warrior, and two Mongols ride out gate. /Extreme LS: Lean plucks flower. /Tunga reacts. /MS: Lean gives Cartwright flowers. /LS: Tunga grabs flowers, swats Lean. /Lean reacts. /LS: They gallop off.)

of Tonga, but there are no executions. They're taken away in a wagon, and the second night, in some town, in a fetid room and without any water, Florrie gives birth. After repeated attempts, Cartwright obtains an interview with Tonga, rides with him, and the women are moved to clean rooms. Andrews, become somewhat vague with Tonga's arrival, objects sternly (but not vociferously) to Cartwright's conduct, and after three days goes crazy and mumbles incoherent verses. Miss Clark, otherwise unmentioned, joins Andrews in turning her face to the wall when Cartwright enters.

Cartwright wakes up the four women to tell them they are going. She has gotten Tonga drunk, and has found a man, who was to have his head chopped off the next day, to drive them away in a wagon; by the time Tonga awakes, they will have escaped. Cartwright's wound has infected her and she expects to be dead within a day. Argent concludes:

— She nodded to the driver, who picked up his whip. I saw through the tears that were pouring down my face the lonely figure at the gate, the Chinese coat—evidently Tonga's present—gleaming in the lantern-light. I thought of the poison being carried with every beat of her pulses. . . . I knew that I should never speak to Miss Andrews again.

Tyger! Tyger! burning bright
In the forests of the night,
What immortal hand or eye
Could frame thy fearful symmetry?

Religion and the search for God is a major theme in only one other Ford, *The Fugitive*, and there too were the problems of evil, of God's silence, and the labyrinthine ways. In both instances the subjects are missionaries, religious who regard themselves as privileged, while being tormented over their conscious inadequacies.

Agatha Andrews (Margaret Leighton) is a bit like Colonel Thursday in *Fort Apache*; she takes things too seriously. She refers to herself often as "the head" of the mission, and indeed it is her head, forever twitching nervously on her spindly neck, that attracts our attention when we first see her, from the back, driving into her mission. Superficially, on the broadest level, Andrews is offered as a dislikeable character.

As in Ford's military pictures, Andrews's colleagues are a motley crew. But, she says, "They have all enlisted in a war. They are soldiers in the army of the Lord." Miss Binns (Flora Robson), the head of another mission, is equally severe when she reminds Mrs. Russell, "When you joined the mission at Kum-cha, you shut the door on your life with Colonel Russell. Leave it shut!"

Juxtaposed to Andrews's army of professionals and amateurs is, as in *The Horse Soldiers*, a doctor, and the clash between ideologies is immediate and fiery. Expected to be a man, Cartwright (Anne Bancroft) turns out to be a woman and unreligious; worse, she appears riding a mule, in britches, carrying a riding stick, with short hair and coarse words. Within two days, with cholera raging, Andrews finds herself deposed and obliged to place her hopes in science rather than in God. Cartwright's common sense appears in refreshing contrast to the kookie pietism of the religious,* and she is offered as a sympathetic character.

As the picture proceeds, still reading it on its broadest level, the contrast between Andrews and Cartwright is intensified. Andrews becomes psychotic and isolated within her own repression, while one by one the other missionaries turn against her. Meanwhile, Cartwright becomes increasingly heroic and beloved.

But neither matters nor morality are so simple. The question of empathy and likeableness is only relevant because the characters, their deeds and dispositions, are placed constantly in question. Starting with the simply definable, Ford quickly passes into the ineffable, to the beyond-good-and-evil within each character. And so perhaps because there is so much that is repellent in Agatha Andrews, she emerges as the most empathetic of all, at least for me. Margaret Leighton does lovable things when she gives tangerines to the children, or sits under her tree. (The tree scene recalls *Stagecoach*'s lunch-table scene: in both pictures Ford alternately arouses our antipathy and sympathy for a given character.)

Ford, as we have seen elsewhere, has a fondness for turning the tables on his audience, and Emma Clark is a fascinating instance. A girl of about eighteen, pretty, healthy, enthusiastic and outgoing, she always stands out from her shriveled, embattled colleagues. She seems the most nearly "normal," "the only one who still has a chance in life." Emma's supreme innocence is due to her sheltered life; both her father and two brothers were ministers. She is mentally young for her age; she has evidently been subjected to a rigorous upbringing, has been trained to be agreeable, has been trained to mime approved sentiments.

Now, Sue Lyon rose to stardom playing Lolita, and there is something still of Lolita in her Emma Clark. The traces of lesbianism, which we may read in Andrews's crushed and complex affections for Emma (daughter-figure, disciple, herself young again) and which make Emma nervous, can also be found in Emma's cautious transference of her affections to Cartwright (as superwoman, glamor, the real world, and manliness). Emma, however, loves babies best.

There seems a certain shallowness in Emma, one suggesting insincerity and detachment from reality. She bursts out of the hut when the children are shot, but it seems odd that, a few seconds later, she looks up from her noisy sobbing and says, "Dr. Cartwright! Now I know what evil really is!"

---

*The sign on the mission says that World Headquarters are in "Boston, Mass., U.S.A." which should tip us off about what to expect to find inside.

What has been criticized as horribly bad acting from Sue Lyon (who could hardly be expected to shine alongside Dunnock, Leighton, Bancroft, Robson, Lee, and Field) is perhaps the reality of the character herself (Ford capitalizing on Sue Lyon). Looking back as she rides off in the oxcart, Emma announces, loudly: "Dr. Cartwright! I'll never forget her as long as I live!" It is difficult to believe that Emma's love, either for the children or for Cartwright, is terribly deep.

Does Emma really have no idea at all of what is happening? How ingenuously she watches Cartwright go off to Tunga Khan, and how excitedly she asks, "What's going on? Where's she going? Isn't she coming back?"! But, by the time Binns has finished her delicate explanation ("Dr. Cartwright has taken an oath to preserve human life"), Emma has turned her attentions back to the baby and seems to have forgotten her question. "Whatever doctor's doing," she lectures Andrews, "is for our good, and you should be thankful!" "*Whatever*"?! Are we to conclude that of all these missionaries Emma has the *least* contact with reality? When Cartwright comes to liberate them, Emma spurts out again: "What are you . . . why are you staying here? Why aren't you coming with us?" (Emma always speaks ten times faster than anyone else; each character has her particular tempo.) "Beat it," answers Cartwright; and even when Emma is riding in the cart, she does not seem to have thought out what has happened. Emma's character wears like a prayer shawl, and her concentration on babies to the avoidance of any other reality has a sort of instinctual quality to it, a survival instinct that contrasts markedly with Andrews's physical psychosis.

Some justification for Andrews acting like "a small-time dictator" is the lamblike nature of her flock. "Though He slay me," quoth Charles Pether, "yet will I trust Him!" (Which is just what happens to Pether.) "Yes, Jesus loves me, We are weak but He is strong," sing the children. "Give us what Thou wilt, when Thou wilt, as much as Thou willest; Thou alone knowest what is good for us," prays Andrews at grace. The missionaries, sitting in the room, wait to be slaughtered, sing hymns, and dream of Christmas, Thanksgiving Day, and home. Their danger is actual. But, at the same time, they have hope in Cartwright, and the situation is quite similar to the Mormons in *Wagon Master* who, unwilling to soil their own hands, leave the immoral task of killing to the "Lord's angel," Travis. Andrews, uncharitable to a fault, at least has the virtue of consistency, in refusing to touch the "contaminated" food and in refusing to condone prostitution.

Often in Ford it is the empathetic fool who delivers the gut punch. Emma runs up to Cartwright and says, uncharacteristically purposefully, "Dr. Cartwright, you got us out of the hut. Maybe you could get the baby away from here altogether?" Cartwright stares at Emma, then looks away, surprised and perhaps even angry, then (deciding Emma has no inkling of what she is suggesting?) she pats Emma on the arm, calls her a "good kid," and leaves to carry out the suggestion. What comes next is obscure to me. Emma leans against the door and breathes deeply, almost as if to say, "Well, that's done!" and then walks slowly across the room and back to the baby. Ford is making a point with this scene, but what? Is Emma less naive than she puts on? Do the glances that the other women make at her indicate their willingness to accept, and hope for, Cartwright's sacrifice?

In any case, we make allowances for Emma, just as we do for Tunga Khan, and also because Emma is young, has never had a choice; but the same is true of everyone. Florrie and Charles Pether (Betty Field, Eddie Albert), both graying in their forties, are still mental teenagers. Their normal lives were suspended, waiting for Pether's invalid mother to die; now they are married, now Charles may fulfill his dream of being a missionary (every bit as much a "Frank Merriwell" gesture as his foray into the village: Charles is lovably awkward in everything), and now Florrie can have a baby. She is both frightening and compassionate when she exclaims: "All my chums at school had babies! Betsy Chapman had twins! Now it's my turn!" As we saw as early as 1933, in *Pilgrimage*, Ford realizes that people never grow up inside. And *7 Women* is a film made by a man struggling against the decay of his own body, struggling against the despair fomented in him by the world, and yet also possessed of a faith, inexplicable even to himself, and therefore of a value that he doubts but cannot avoid affirming, which allows him to acknowledge death confronting him and the evil in the world.

When Agatha Andrews recites that grace—"Give us what Thou wilt . . ." —she does not suspect that a cholera epidemic and Tunga Khan are about to be given, nor does she realize that the positive gift, Dr. Cartwright, has already arrived. Dr. Cartwright will furnish the cart in which the seven women will leave their mission (and only of Miss Binns could it be said that she acted as a Christian). It is for this reason, and because we know what it signifies, having seen the film, that the arrival shot of Dr. Cartwright riding her mule into the mission courtyard is one of the loveliest images in Ford. The children are singing "Yes, Jesus loves me," and here is the proof, as it were, arriving in an unexpected form (female) and at an unexpected time, though no one knows this yet, and though Cartwright does not know that she has found her mission (though she does know it, but not in the more real and symbolic sense—her destiny). But fate blows the leaves this way and that, and the threads of life are as variegated as the row of multicolored bobbins set so beautifully on the dining room windowsill, and which serve as a background to Cartwright's meditation before submitting to Tunga Khan, and after she has bid the seven women goodbye. Cartwright is the eighth woman, first because she seems like a man, secondly because as soon as she trades her riding britches for a gold robe, as soon as her female sex betrays her to Tunga Khan (as it made it impossible to get a decent job as a doctor, and as a tragic love affair had set her on the run), Miss Ling is thrown

Dr. Cartwright (Anne Bancroft) announces she will give herself to Tunga Khan
(Mike Mazurki).

back among the women to raise their number to seven again.* Now she has
become "The Scarlet Woman, the Whore of Babylon"; now also she carries
the lamp in the darkness. The corollary to her arrival shot is that of her
standing golden, with her lamp, at the gate, watching the women leave her
alone, while the camera tracks hopelessly away from her; and then she turns

---

*The baby is another instance of substitution: for the baby dead from cholera, the old man
dead from cholera, the children shot by the Mongols, and his father, Charles Pether.

to go through the gate, and into a mission that is now, ironically, exclusively her own.

When Cartwright takes the vial of poison, Argent protests, "Don't, please don't, it's a sin, it's a sin against God, it's a sin." "Then pray for me," replies Cartwright. But if she cares little for this concept of sin, she cares mightily for her oath to preserve life, for the profession to which she has sacrificed her life as completely as Agatha has sacrificed hers. The two hero-ines are frequently parallel. Not for nothing does Agatha mean "good." *Blessed are the clean of heart, for they shall see God.* But this is torture, Agatha's eyes almost always have tears in them. She must fill her life, and God is not enough. Nor is medicine. And neither lady has a vocation to celibacy. Both are imperious, both do everything "too much," both drive frail bodies by sheer will, slouching wearily (Cartwright with dangling ciga-rettes), neither has free choices. Agatha, by being consistent to the letter of the law, violates the spirit of Christianity; even so, her barren psychosis attains an Old Testament grandeur. Cartwright, by being consistent to her oath, finds herself confronted with two choices: either to stay on as Tunga Khan's mistress, until he tires of her, or else to kill them both, as she does; Cartwright's murder and suicide are violations of her oath, acts of ultimate despair, defeat, and negation, but there is a pagan glory to her, and a Chris-tian one too. Her moral abnegation of self to save her "family" mark her as

Dr. Cartwright about to poison Tunga Khan and herself.

the Fordian hero in the tradition of Carey, Rogers, Fonda, and Wayne. But the hero's traditional celibacy now has an ironic twist, and the decision to intervene entails, even more forcibly than for Tom Doniphon, exclusion from life itself. Yet this was her "case," so she stayed. So simple. And her manner at death . . . do we not all see our death this way—as a thing we violently detest yet wish we could assent to? She assents, and her suicide seems heroic, an ultimate act of defiance and submission.

Andrews ought to have been proud. "I founded this mission, and I made it a part of the life of the entire province." Education appears to be the prime task; as usual in Ford, the white man conquers with the alphabet. It is easy to judge the missionaries racist, for they seem so displaced in this "last place on earth," "this Chinese hole-in-the-wall"; they are all homeless searchers. As Miss Argent puts it, "We're not like those poor creatures in the village." One may see a questioning of the role of American imperialism here, though there is no denying the sacrifice, poverty, and humane intentions of these missionaries. And the truth is, as in *Cheyenne Autumn* and as in much of the world today, Western civilization's triumph (and often its welcome) is infinitely greater than any attempt at assessing the balance of gain or loss or good or evil.

Yet these missionaries fail, as the French failed in *The Hurricane* (the bandits are like a hurricane), and the implications of many traditional Fordian devices have turned funereal in *7 Women*. The children, as they flee the plague, sing "Shall We Gather at the River" as though it were a desperate "*Dies Irae*" rather than a celebration of community. The favorite image of the parade has dwindled to a procession of refugees, to a doctor and her coolies, to an oxcart of expelled missionaries—and yet, also, has exploded to a hoard of savages roaring across the screen in slashing diagonals. The antinomal image of stable subsistence is almost absent; only a restless serenity is found beneath the large tree in the yard. Life has become more consuming than ever; Marty Maher's pipe is replaced by Cartwright's innumerable cigarettes. But then comes the baby.

All is paradox, like the problems of evil and God, and Ford has no private revelation to communicate. Regardless of right or wrong, historical necessity, as in *Liberty Valance*, is not to be denied. As Tunga Khan gawks quizzically at the rockingchair on the mission porch, the white head of the nomad's horse juts into the frame, reminding us that, as in *The Searchers*, wilderness and civilization confront each other across an abyss. The Mongols are not insensitive to beauty: of the scenes missing from the theatrical edition of *7 Women* the least expendable is the moment, all in long shot, when Lean Warrior jumps from his horse to pluck a bunch of flowers for Cartwright. Yet the Mongols are savages, they kill little children and laugh. The women will all die in a ditch, predicts Florrie Pether, "like animals," and they nearly do, and Charles was "shot down like a dog," and Andrews calls the baby an "animal" and calls Cartwright the "mother of hogs." As in *Mogambo*, the humanity of man is placed in question. For it seems that neither the whites nor the Asians have much more than a shred of free will within the determining forces of culture, history, biology, libido, and profession.

Nothing is revealed, all is mystery. What remains is the image of gold midst black, of a flaming torch passing by, of bright threads, of flashes of vibrant, all-feeling persons who shine in the intimately awesome beauty of human interior life, and who then pass on. This is the immanent transcendent into which Ford has merged his terrible, Blakean ambiguities. Gone is the misanthropy of *Liberty Valance;* the only palpable truth is individual consciousness.

Much of 7 *Women's* artistic interest is difficult to discuss on paper. One small example: we cannot reproduce here the manner in which Mildred Dunnock delivers a line such as "Everybody has turkey [*pause*] on Thanksgiving Day," and it is surprising how difficult, if not impossible, it is to imitate her, even if one tapes that line and listens to it a dozen times. Virtuosity is often greatest in the simplest of things, and complexity is properly the clear combination of a multitude of simple articulations.

The complexity of 7 *Women,* a movie that, like its individual characters and their actions, utterly evades description, is due largely to the integrity of character presentation. As in playing a melody, or delivering a verse, the highest art in direction occurs when, through total stylization (clarification), the subject emerges with a separate life peculiarly its own. Ford and Renoir are similar, in that they both start with simple particles of elements, and then produce ingenious combinations; but generally they are also dissimilar, in that Renoir's particles often have an indefinable nondimensionality to them, while Ford's often have a certain definiteness and squareness. But 7 *Women* is a film in which Ford comes closest to Renoir's manner. Or to Murnau's cinema of presence: for character in 7 *Women* is no longer a conception, but a manifestation, a phenomenon, in which distance no longer disunites actor and role. Thus the fascination of the dining room scenes, in which we can watch the chameleonlike comportment of ten individuals whom we know fairly well, yet who are surprising us constantly. Ford's art is to have each nuance of articulation reveal something novel and interesting (and yet consistent); a character's initial typing becomes the basis for the diversity his personality later manifests.

To the paradox of style/realism correspond other paradoxes: God/evil, opinion/fact, the mission/the world, faith/science, free will/determinism, woman/man, Christian-medical mores/Mongol savagery, and, most especially, interior life/social life. Irish Catholicism has within it a deep streak of Manichaeanism, which Ford manages to pose here at every second, while yet subsuming the polarities of "soul" and "matter" within a mysterious, labyrinthine unity into which they dissolve. To this effect, the feminist angle on 7 *Women* is interesting, because it points out that the life of an individual is a constant struggle against definitions imposed not only by immediate society, but also by history and even by one's own body. Age shall wither, regardless of the youth of the mind.

When Agatha Andrews enters Emma's room, Ford rests his camera for a long time upon Agatha looking, before cutting to what she is looking at (Emma washing). The pause is meditative, rather than suspenseful; it establishes Agatha, rather than Emma, as the scene's emotional center. For Emma will arouse our empathy far more easily than Andrews, and the pause on Agatha intends to correct an imbalance before it occurs. She enters slowly and uncertainly, because Emma is in her bra. The pause at the door engenders conflicts of desire and guilt; she wants to touch Emma's hair, but pulls back her hand.

Crosscutting often indicates conflict. When Andrews and Cartwright argue in the office, angles, subtly oblique at the outset, grow parallel as their mutual fury reaches its height. But, more frequently, the cutting's alternation of isolation and combination suggests the struggle, so continuous in each of these people, to liberate the self from its impediments. Formally, the struggle resembles a concerto grosso—alternations of *soli* (cameo vignettes) and *tutti* (intricate ensembles)—while the vertical (i.e., simultaneous) juxtapositions of disparate emotions attains a quasi-fugal complexity. Tempo slows and shots become longer in the movie's course, simply because the women are forced together by Tunga Khan. In this context, a camera movement may be more precise than a cut, as in expressing Agatha's dual dilemma of mental isolation and inability to escape from forced community.

Since, most of the time, these people are awkward, since they usually communicate something different than what they would like to, the brief moments of nakedness are all the more telling. Such moments may make us wince, as Cartwright winces, when Florrie tells the story of her life in one cliché ("What's a woman without a child?") or when Pether juts his chin out into the frame and declares, "For the first time in my life I'm not scared." Or the moments may be voyeuristic, catching a character unawares, like the placid figure Miss Argent makes eating her rice and trying to hide from the battle of wills raging around her. Or they may be tiny things that later become important, like Mrs. Russell staring at Pether, but avoiding his helping hand, when she climbs out of the oxcart on her arrival at the mission. Or they may come with sudden unexpectancy, as experiences revealed as devoutly wished, like the combination of silver (Argent) and gold when Miss Argent, remembering to love, returns to embrace Cartwright, and Cartwright kisses passionately in return, grateful for a little friendship, the need for which she, in her bereft loneliness, has kept concealed.

Cutting often establishes connections that we would otherwise not make: the surprising image of water being poured over Tunga Khan is followed by the sound of the baby's cry; both image and sound stand out as life symbols. Or, Cartwright surrenders herself to Tunga Khan, then we see the baby being oiled: biological cause and effect. In the first act of the picture, Cartwright says, "It'll be a miracle if that baby lives." Then, in the third act, that baby is born, and Cartwright is on her way out the door to fulfill her deal with Tunga Khan, but finds her way barred by Miss Binns. But, in her role as ingenuous agent, Emma carries the baby between the Cartwright-Binns confrontation, and says, "Isn't it a miracle! He's alive and he's breathing!" And Binns lets Cartwright go, for it is both a miracle and not a miracle.

Seldom has Ford been so exciting in his organization of ensemble movement within a scene; the careful choreography of past films is often replaced by brief, spontaneous contrapuntal gestures: Emma leading the children to the fields, while Cartwright races around in the background; Binns jutting her head into the left-bottom foreground of a scene to offer assistance during the plague, causing Cartwright in the center to pivot away from Andrews at upper-right, thus marking Andrews's fall from authority; the commotion in the hut, when Florrie begins her labor pains, and Ford pans with Argent away from cringing Andrews, over the group on the floor, then follows the excited Emma searching for a stick for Florrie to bite; Cartwright stalking into Tunga Khan's room, simultaneously surrendering her body and asserting her authority "simply by striding toward the camera and forcing three people to react to her movement within the same frame. This movement triggers a series of abrupt actions with explosive force. When Ford finally does cut back and forth between [Cartwright and Tunga Khan], the

Eisensteinian collision is supplemented by a more supple sensibility capable of transmitting a touch of tenderness between two deadly antagonists" (Sarris);[30] or, the conclusion of the wrestling match when, in four quick shots: /Tunga Khan reaches down to the ground, seizes Lean Warrior's head, lifts it up to the camera and twists it and throws him down dead; / abruptly Ford cuts to a flute and drum playing cheery folk music; /a wide shot of the fight-circle, Tunga Khan striding toward Cartwright searchingly, as Lean Warrior's body, lifted high, is carried out Viking-fashion; /Cartwright on the porch, throwing away her cigarette and strolling off.

Seldom have Ford's images been so beautiful. The colors pass from orange-brown, to the Vermeer-like blues, purples, and slanting white light of the women locked in the dining room, to the gold and black of Cartwright in the corridor. And the vitally inventive, quickly cut exploitation of anamorphic wide screen's possibilities contrasts glaringly with the comparatively stilted long takes of *The Long Gray Line*.

Seldom has Ford's music been so apt. Elmer Bernstein's score makes *7 Women* into a virtual tone poem. The Mongol theme (recalling *Liberty Valance*'s "gladiator" theme), the intimations of derangement, the excited signals of warning as Cartwright examines the sick refugees, the ominous cantus firmus beneath "Shall We Gather at the River," and, most of all, those lovely fragile passages of quasi-serenity bring to fulfillment this spiritual odyssey of John Ford. For visually, too, *7 Women* is music: organization of time and space to purify, isolate, and interrelate gesture. As lines of motion parade across the frame and characters traverse from one blocking toward another, agogic pauses mark their solitary pilgrimages through life as quests—no sooner attained than denied—for understanding, fulfillment, and closeness to another soul.

★

7 Women was Ford's final picture. "I think he was ready for it," says Anna Lee (Miss Russell), "because he was absolutely charming to everybody. We'd break for tea as we always did at 4:30 and have the table brought out and the teapot and the cakes. He was particularly gracious on this one, never raised his voice." (The only explosion came when Flora Robson protested her dressing-room door lacked "Dame" before her name; and she would argue with Ford. "I saw her being absolutely shredded, because she did not realize you could not argue with or question Mr. Ford. It was always like that when someone was new.")

The picture was shot in continuity, in order to get good performances; for the same reason, Ford exposed three and a half to four times as much negative as he eventually used. *7 Women*'s scenarists were in France and would telephone portions of the script daily during shooting. Producer Bernard Smith, recalls Anna Lee, "would come over to the long table [where

Ford introducing *The Rookie of the Year* (1955).

the cast gathered] with new pages hot off the wire. Ford would lift his patch and look at them, study them for a few moments, and then deliberately, right in front of Bernie Smith, he would tear them up, throw them on the floor, and say, 'Now, what are we going to say?' From then on he would give us ideas and we'd start improvising the dialogue, and that's why I don't think probably more than a dozen pages in the original script were ever used.* He would say, 'Well, I think you should say this,' and we'd make notes. He'd give us a line and Anne [Bancroft] would say, 'Well, I think I'll say it this way. . . . '"31

Shot on a sound stage, sparing Ford the fatigue of location, *7 Women* came out just as he wanted. But, even though directing was like "dope addiction," he was not to have another chance at it. The gossips said he was senile, *7 Women* could be cited to prove their point, and production insurance was hard to obtain for sickly old directors. For whatever reason, Ford's

---

*Actually, comparison between the film and preliminary scripts shows Ford followed the screenplay quite exactly. The points of departure are in the precise ways things are staged (e.g., the script calls for Cartwright to stand up in shock when Tunga Khan breaks Lean Warrior's neck, whereas Ford merely has her indicate bored disgust) and in that every third line is rewritten to make it less literary, slangier, and more clipped. The line "So long, you bastard" is not in the script.

Patricia Neal began the picture as Cartwright but was paralyzed by a stroke after a couple of days' shooting.

Ford being interviewed by Philip Jenkinson.

next picture, *The Miracle of Merriford*, was scrapped by Metro in October 1965, scarcely a week before shooting was to have begun. A few years afterwards, his marginal involvement in two minor documentaries, on Vietnam and on Marine General Chesty Puller, were taken as evidence of his isolation. Many feature projects came tantalizingly close to fulfillment, only to have backing dissolve at the last moment. John Wayne was reluctant to involve himself in a film with Ford. As late as May 1973, Ford was quoted as having always dreamed of filming Conan Doyle's *White Company,* which he claimed to have read each year since he was eight.[32] In his hands, it would have resembled his Civil War episode: the bright hopes of youth go off to war only to find disillusionment and unsought-for wisdom.

Personally, he was as messy as ever. Clothes and piles of books would be strewn everywhere. He consumed chocolate bars and tobacco like a glutton. He liked watching movies, but if he did so critically, he never let on.* Natu-

*A "ten-favorite" list Ford compiled for *Cinema* in 1964 is whimsical: (1) *The Birth of a Nation;* (2) *The Honor System* (Walsh, 1916—a thief is let out of prison on his word, and returns); (3) *3 Godfathers* (Ford); (4) *Ninotchka* (Lubitsch); (5) *The High and the Mighty* (Wellman), (6) *Tol'able David* (King, 1921); (7) *The Song of Bernadette* (King); (8) *Lady for a Day* (Capra); (9) *Going My Way* (McCarey); (10) *The Alamo* (Wayne). (Always extravagant with public praise, Ford once said: "*The Alamo* is the greatest picture I've ever seen. It will last forever, rally he enjoyed pictures friends had made, and complained he never could be objective about his own work. Asked his favorite, his choice would vary: *The Sun Shines Bright, Wagon Master, Young Mr. Lincoln, The Fugitive.* He told Tavernier he liked "Leo McCarey—I love *Make Way for Tomorrow*—Frank Capra, and then people like Raoul Walsh, who's a bit like me, but more seductive and pleasing to women, Tay Garnett, Henry King. I also like Sammy Fuller a lot, a fine fellow with great integrity. I don't like John Huston, who's a faker."[33]

In 1966 he made a tour of duty in the navy, sailing from the Mediterranean to the Philippines and then to Vietnam. One grandson, Timothy, was in the merchant marine; the other, Dan, had received a battlefield promotion in Vietnam. In 1968 the *Araner* was sold. It was in ill repair, too old, and costing a fortune to maintain. Ford considered himself lucky to get $25,000 and some Hawaiian resort shares for her. In 1970, he and Mary celebrated their fiftieth anniversary by being married again, in the Field Photo chapel, and she pronounced her advice to young couples: "Believe nothing you hear, and only half of what you see."[34]

The Farm itself had been sold in 1965. Its purpose had become less compelling as the veterans grew into lives of their own. Funerals, such as Ward Bond's in 1960, had become its chief events. Although half the land had been sold in 1961, the financial burden on Ford became immense, and there were tax problems, as well. The $300,000 it fetched, together with the chapel, intact, were given to the Motion Picture Country Home, a lavish industry-endowed retirement community in Woodland Hills. The sweeping portrait of Ford that once dominated the Farm's tavern room now hangs in the lodge.

Ford's acknowledged debtors, among directors, included Elia Kazan, Sergei Eisenstein, Samuel Fuller, Jean-Marie Straub, Peter Bogdanovich, Budd Boetticher, Mark Donskoi, John Milius, Lindsay Anderson, Orson Welles, Bertrand Tavernier, Ingmar Bergman, Frank Capra, Douglas Sirk, and Howard Hawks. In Japan, Akira Kurosawa wore dark glasses while directing, not to protect his eyes, but in order to look like John Ford. In Paris in 1967, and at Venice in 1971, Ford was fêted royally.

But in America he no longer counted for anything. His last years were lonely, and he suffered from forced retirement. And he was aging rapidly. A broken hip put him into a wheelchair in 1970 and compelled him to move from the Bel Air house to a single-level one Katharine Hepburn located in Palm Desert, near Eisenhower Hospital, where he was receiving radiation treatment for cancer.

---

run forever, for all peoples, all families, everywhere." Anything for a buddy.) On another occasion he cited Laurel and Hardy's *The Battle of the Century* (McCarey, 1927) as his favorite. And he was so taken by Renoir's *Grand Illusions* (1938) that he wanted to remake it in English, with English prisoners.

There was not much time left. In October 1972 the Screen Directors Guild staged a salute to him—Ford chose *How Green Was My Valley* for the occasion. Katharine Hepburn came for a week's visit. And finally, on March 31, 1973, the American Film Institute honored him with its first Life Achievement Award. It was his last hurrah, and was telecast nationwide. President Richard Nixon appeared to wheel Ford around, present him with the Medal of Freedom, and promote him to full admiral. Ford talked, cried really, about the prisoners of war returning home from Vietnam and, for this, prayed "God bless Richard Nixon!" The remark disconcerted those who had forgotten the stinging satires of Nixon in *The Last Hurrah* and *The Sun Shines Bright;* but Nixon was president, and needed blessing.

John Ford died in his sleep, attended by priests, August 31, 1973, at 6:05 P.M., in the house on Old Prospect Trail in the desert. Cancer was the cause. He was alert until the end, using painkillers only during the last two weeks. He was survived by Mary, who had Parkinson's disease, their children, and a sister, Josephine.

His will, signed March 31, 1973, left an estate of $500,000, excluding real estate, to be divided, after his wife's death, half in trust to daughter Barbara and half to son Patrick's two children. Patrick himself was excluded, without explanation, but $10,000 was bequeathed to Pat's daughter by his second marriage. (A few years later, Mary Ford brought suit for $4,100,000 against the executors, charging they had sold the Rolls Royce and the Copa de Oro house for less than true value and had made the will in a tax-costly fashion; the suit is still pending.)

Ford, out of pure cussedness, would fight the IRS even when his lawyers said not to. But money, as his business manager, Bea Benjamin, said, was something "he never cared about."[35] The *Araner* was his sole extravagance—he spent $75,000 prettying her up for *Donovan's Reef*, in return for a $5,000 leasing fee—and aside from her, his lifestyle was modest indeed by Hollywood standards. Not only did he turn a deaf ear to most tax and investment advice—such as real estate—but he never exploited his name for gain. Compared with Hitchcock, for example, who did pursue wealth, Ford earned barely 5 *percent* as much money during the fifties and sixties. What Ford pursued was the freedom to make his kind of movies. He not only turned down an offer from Zanuck guaranteeing him $600,000 per year, he went ahead and made, independently, *The Fugitive, 3 Godfathers, Wagon Master,* and *The Sun Shines Bright*—projects which, from their conception, he knew would be lucky even to earn back their cost. Subsequently, when he was commanding $250,000-plus per picture, he chose instead to do *The Rising of the Moon* and *Gideon's Day* for no salary at all, and then *Young Cassidy* for only $50,000. His personal charities were considerable, even apart from the $300,000 donated to found the Field Photo Farm and the annual subsidies he gave to maintain it. His war service, too, cost him heavily: from averaging around $175,000 before the war, his yearly earnings dropped to $27,000, $14,000, and $23,000 in 1942, '43, and '44. He griped constantly, of course, about the sums Mary spent—and they appear to have been fairly lavish—but he never restrained her, at least not for long.

The funeral was held September 5, at Hollywood's Church of the Blessed Sacrament. Richard Koszarski reports that, before the service, the church was empty except for the coffin and a single mourner, Woody Strode—a scene out of *Liberty Valance*.[36] On the coffin lay the flag from Ford's headquarters during the battle of Midway. He was buried in Holy Cross Cemetery, Culver City.

His last public appearance had been for the Memorial Day services at the Motion Picture Country Home. Frank Baker:

"When he said goodbye to me, it was a very touching thing. He had enormous respect for my wife, Helen Broneau, whose picture is here, and who'd worked with him around 1916. I didn't approach him up there at the chapel. I was sitting here [in my room at the Home], and I heard a car draw up out there, and a knock came on the door, and there was a warrant officer who was taking him around. And he said, "Admiral Ford is in the car outside, and he would like to see you." I said, "Sure, bring him in." So he came in in his wheelchair, and he was sitting where you are. And I didn't have any liquor in the place—I don't drink myself. And he was dying; he didn't have many days to live. He said, "Have you got a drink, Frank?" And I suddenly realized I didn't have one. Now some months before a girl from Australia, a girl named Joan Long, had been out here, and was going to do a picture on my family. And she'd brought me a bottle of Scotch, so I suddenly thought of that—and she was a great admirer of John Ford's work. So I took it out, and to excuse my mess-up, I told him the story of this girl's film, and that he had been her favorite director or some damn thing. And Ford went back into the past. He was dragging up figures that I'd forgotten, speaking with a terribly deep sentimental feeling about them. And bringing up Frank again, and Frank in an entirely different light. And I was hoping he'd just get out and not say goodbye. And he kept staring at this picture, and he was looking at her. I'd poured him the drink, and he had it in his hand. And he wanted to say, "So long, I won't be seeing you again," and he didn't know what to say. He always brought my wife into everything. My wife, he'd get her advice. Certain stories he wouldn't do till she had read them. Suddenly he said, "Well," and he's staring right at her. And he wants to include me, but he can't bring himself to. And he suddenly raises that glass, and he's staring right at this picture, "To . . ." and he's going to say Helen, my wife, and he knew that would shock me I guess, for he says, "To Joan Long." And we downed the drink. And then he looked around for someplace to throw the glass, you know, so it wouldn't be used again. I told him I'd take care of it. He said, "Well, I guess all good things must end. Quartermaster!" and he went out, never shook hands with me or anything. He went out and got in the car, and I stood down there. He's just staring right ahead, and the car starts to move, and he didn't turn towards me, but he raised his hand in salute as he went by. And he did a funny thing, as he started going out, the petty officer left us for a moment to go and open the door and he turned around and he started to put his hand out. And he said a very strange thing which I today value very much, knowing Ford. He said, "Well, I guess this is it. I'd like you to know that you're one of the very few people I ever respected. You never crawled on your belly to me."[37]

Mary Ford, 1977:

To me, he was the greatest man that ever lived in every way. I just thought he was great because he had a wonderful sense of humor; he made me laugh. I'd seen a lot of misery, a lot of unhappiness. I don't know, there was something about him. It certainly wasn't his looks. I just fell in love with him . . . Oh such a life. It was like a dream . . . I wouldn't change a day in my life. Each one has been so perfect. Up in my room, I have a large picture of Jack, and people say to me, "Why do you sit and look at that?" Because every minute of it was a laugh, something worth having.[38]

6 Conclusion

*People are incorrect to compare a director
to an author. If he's a creator, he's more
like an architect. And an architect
conceives his plans according to precise
circumstances.* JOHN FORD

      The notion of a Hollywood director as auteur, author, archi-
tect, or central creative force of a movie is complex. For a Hollywood director rarely wrote his own story or screenplay, chose his actors, designed his
sets, or edited his shots. Even in telling actors where to stand, the director
had often to bow to the wishes of a producer or star. Yet only when a director
does succeed in imposing his will over the various contributions to a picture
is he considered an auteur.

    Broadly speaking, we can discern three types of such auteurs: the collab-
orator, who keeps a low profile (e.g., Cukor); the author, who dominates
completely (Welles, Sternberg); the architect, who reigns (Ford, Renoir).

    Ford had the advantage of entering his profession in the teens, when
directorial authority was greatest. Four years' apprenticeship to brother
Francis had already earned him a reservoir of friends within the industry
and a thorough technical acumen. His liberty, during five years and thirty-
nine pictures at Universal, was secured by the facts that his stars (Harry
Carey, Hoot Gibson) were coincidentally close friends and the studio's biggest moneymakers and that front-office interference with low-budget westerns was minimal. He continued to avoid day-to-day supervision by trans-
ferring to a "director's studio," Fox, and by establishing himself as their

"fair-haired boy." In the thirties, when filmmaking became less personal, Ford lost considerable independence, but his box-office record and personal authority still allowed him uncommon control. Even in 1936, at the height of the assembly-line studio system, Howard Sharpe could write in *Photoplay* that Ford "works directly with each department during [preparation]. His hand draws the design for a set fireplace.* His own suggestions are the inspiration for certain gowns and coiffures and uniforms—and most important of all, much of the dialogue (especially in his Irish portraits) comes from the Ford typewriter."[1]

In all but five or so of his films, Ford worked intimately with his scenarist from the movie's inception. He tended to work with the same people through many decades—writers, cameramen, technicians, actors, editors—and they knew what he wanted. Far from squashing these individual talents, Ford had eccentric ways of putting them on their own and goading them to surpass themselves. Yet at the same time Ford fashioned these collective efforts into a movie-world as detailed a product of his imagination as the Paris of Balzac or the London of Dickens.

How did he manage to do this?

Ford's Working Methods

Actors. Ford sets had a special air to them. For most people it was a reunion, for newcomers it was often trial under fire. "You had to be able to do everything," said Frank Baker. "He didn't care for the rules of the Screen Actors Guild. He'd have you playing a major part, and suddenly say, 'You're doing nothing, I want somebody to sit on that seat there, and when the coach goes by, get up and walk across.' And you'd better do it too, otherwise he'd ride you. He picked on people. He always picked somebody at the beginning of a picture, and he'd let them have it. You couldn't do anything right. You could *not* do anything right! I've seen big Victor McLaglen stand there and cry like a child, and I've seen Duke Wayne do exactly the same thing. Blubber like a child, and Ford just sitting there, humiliating the hell out of his star player. He was doing it for a purpose all the while. He's getting the best discipline out of that company than any company that ever went before a camera. He just had to open his mouth, and 'Yes sir, yes sir.'"[2]

Yet his sets were not tense. An atmosphere of seriousness, of reverence, even, would often prevail, enhanced by Danny Borzage's accordion music, and punctuated by the ritual traditions of afternoon tea and the director's humorous eccentricities—the scapegoat, the chewed handkerchiefs, the long pauses leading up to sarcasms. However disconcerting to the uninitiate, these were among life's stranger joys to the cultists. And Ford's sadisms were the exception. More often he was the soul of kindness. His troupe

---

*This was *Mary of Scotland*'s fireplace, which reappeared in Xanadu in *Citizen Kane*.

became affectionate families and years later many would still speak of the time they were making a Ford picture as one of the most enjoyable experiences of their lives.

"After photographing several John Ford pictures, I didn't notice any pattern or method. . . . He could not be compared even to himself from one day to the next," said Arthur C. Miller.[3] "This man directs less than any man in the business. As a matter of fact, he doesn't direct—he doesn't want any actor to give an imitation of him playing the part. He wants the actor to create the part—that's why he hired him, because he saw him in the part. You'd sit at a big coffee table in the morning—everybody was there, whether you worked that day or not. You'd drink coffee until you couldn't swig it down any more."[4] They would discuss anything, from football to aviation, and occasionally Ford would interject something concerning the picture. "He'd start telling *you* about some scenes, and suddenly a guy over *there* would realize that he was talking about the character *he* was playing—but he'd be talking to you. Now the actor would start using his imagination—I caught wise to this after a year or so—and you could see it, he wasn't listening to the conversation any more, he'd be thinking. This was the way Ford got performances out of people."[5] According to Miller, "There were never any long rehearsals, especially in the dialogue, nor did I ever see him act a piece of business for an actor, or tell when to look at someone, or read a line. There were no marks on the floor for the actors to position themselves [—they might look down for the marks]; he simply gave them a general idea of where to be. I heard Ford tell a writer that if he gave detailed instructions, all he would get would be a well-rehearsed line of chatter. I am sure that this is the reason he never had drilled rehearsals and was displeased when he had to make a second take of a scene, which he seldom did."[6]

Miller photographed *How Green Was My Valley*, among others, and it seems a miracle that Ford obtained the control he did with these methods— every scene and gesture so meaningfully choreographed. But others confirm Miller. "[Ford] doesn't like to talk about it," says Henry Fonda, "there's practically no communication."[7] "He never talked the part you were playing," said Pat O'Brien; "he'd tell you what he wanted . . . , 'I hope you can get it,' he'd say, with that patch over his eye and chewing that handkerchief. When you failed, he'd say, 'that wasn't what I wanted. Try to get what I wanted.' When it was finally good, he'd go over and hug you. 'Why the hell didn't you get it in the first place?' "[8] " 'Laconic' is a good word for John Ford and his technique of direction," wrote Mary Astor; "no big deal about communication with John. Terse, pithy, to the point. Very Irish, a dark personality, a sensitivity which he did everything to conceal, but once he said to me . . . , 'Make it *scan*, Mary.' And I said to myself, 'Aha! I know you now!' "[9] "I know I never worked with another movie director who knew as much about acting as he did or cared so much about performance," wrote Raymond Massey; "to me he rarely made a direct comment or suggestion. It was mostly brief innuendo, laced with Irish wit and always constructive, frequently confidential."[10]

Ford centered attention on himself, as actors hoped (sometimes desperately) for a hint of guidance. "You become so tuned to him," said Maureen O'Hara, "one word of his becomes a volume. You become aware that he understands the story and knows how to get it out of you. It's a frame of mind he creates. He puts you at ease and sets you free to think, and you can move easily."[11] "He wouldn't tell you what to do," said Anna Lee, "but you'd find yourself doing things that obviously had come from somewhere. It was some kind of thought transference that he did. And I think that's why he liked people who worked with him to be totally absorbed in him as a director, in other words, not to have too many ideas yourself. You were the vessel in which he injected what he wanted, and then it sort of flowed out of you." Occasionally Ford would walk through a scene, without telling you he was doing it. Nonetheless, you were expected to imitate his tiniest gesture. "People who worked with Ford a lot, like Duke Wayne or James Stewart, have so adapted themselves to his mannerisms," says Anna Lee, "that now, if I see Jimmy Stewart on a talk show, I'm looking at Jack Ford. I mean the way he moves his mouth. And I found this with my sons, when they were little; they'd copy the way Jack Ford would mutter."[12]

Ford's direction was sometimes mechanical, as when during *Rio Grande* he instructed John Wayne to keep his face blank and allow the scenery to provide the thought, or as during *The Battle of Midway* when Ford took notes from his pocket and told his four "voices": "When I point to you, say what I tell you to say," and in twenty minutes they were done.[13] But he could go to the opposite extreme and have Henry Fonda improvise a long, long monologue during *Drums Along the Mohawk* while shooting questions to him from off-camera. And Ford, at other times, might employ the intimate associations that are part of "Method" acting. Ruth Clifford was playing a Comanche captive in *The Searchers* who goes berserk when she sees a doll, and Ford confided to her almost off-handedly, "You know, I'd almost whisper it. She's . . . just . . . lost her . . . No English." Ford sensed Ruth was thinking of her own lost child; he put a piece of wood in her arms, and told her to let go her emotion midway through the scene. It played searingly. "I'm proud of you," he whispered afterward. But such praise was rare.[14]

Ford "rehearsed, rehearsed and rehearsed till you could practically do it blindfolded," says Dobe Carey.[15] "I never remember being directed. It all just happened," says Roddy McDowall.[16] Anne Bancroft:

> We realized why he is considered to be one of the greatest directors in Hollywood. He arrives each morning knowing exactly what he intends to film and with every scene visually worked out in his mind. He is never in a hurry, yet doesn't waste a minute. His rehearsals are so thorough that more often than not he will film the most difficult scene in one 'take,' rarely more than two. . . . If there were any differences of opinion as to how a scene

should be played, the actor invariably ended up agreeing with Mr. Ford. He is infinitely patient in explaining his reasons for what he wants. At the same time, he is in command and can be firm when necessary.[17]

Often he would rewrite lines, Dobe Carey recalls. He would say, "Come on, kids, let's get chairs and gather round here. Has anybody got a script?" They would run through the dialogue, and this would give him ideas. Then they would start again, and he would point to you and say a line. "And if you didn't catch on, if you didn't know how he'd work, it would infuriate him. The minute he would point to you and say, '*I ain't taking that from you*,' you were supposed to say it right back at him." Then, they would block the scene for the cameraman, relax while the set was lit, and rehearse five or six more times. Ford would never use typical director-talk like, "Jump on your cues! Pick it up! Pick it up! Let's have a lot of energy, kids!" He had *body language*, says Carey. "He'd get very grotesque looking (people would snicker, which would infuriate him); he'd act things out for you in an extremely exaggerated version of what he wanted."[18]

Thus Ford's methods varied radically. But one does note, grossly simplifying, three main "modes" of play: tragic, or epic (in which every superfluous movement was repressed); comedic, or natural (more spontaneous); and slapstick (broad, exaggerated, often used for perverse actions). While the individual actor was usually given liberty to discover himself, "in sequences with a large number of people he [paid] attention to every movement and gesture, almost as though he was directing a ballet," said Flora Robson.[19] Indeed, Ford's direction is most discernible in the choreographed fashion five or more people will move about a room.

Actors were never permitted to view rushes, and though the scenarist might have traced a complete biography for his character, the actor might not even know which part he was playing till just before shooting. Ford delighted in throwing disconcerted actors in otherwise carefully prepared scenes.

In 1936, he used a silent camera 40 percent of the time. "I can talk while a scene is shooting," explained Ford, "and give suggestions about expression or movement; as a result I don't have to make so many takes. I've discovered that if you rehearse a scene too much it looks artificial and— well, *rehearsed*."[20]

Ford was obsessed with adjusting actors' clothing, particularly hats. He would stamp on hats, crumple them, then put them back on the actor—and grab his hand if he started to readjust it. "The lines of the costume react on the lines of the face just as in music a note has its overtones," writes art historian Frederick T. Weber; "this is why artists are always glad to use scarfs, furs or anything they can themselves arrange on their subjects."[21] No actor dared suggest it, if he wanted a particular hat. But, according to Wayne, if you gave your hat to wardrobe and let it get mixed up with all the other hats, nine times out of ten Ford would pick that one for you.

According to Katherine Hepburn, it was Ford's sensitivity that made him a great director of actors. He could always sense what people were feeling—even across a room (and if he sensed hostility he would get up, go over, and find out why). With this sensitivity—which amounted to an ability to read minds, almost—Ford could prompt an actor to do what Ford wanted him to do, but in the actor's own way. Similar ability, to some degree, has been possessed by many great directors—especially by those who do not treat their actors as marionettes.

Photography. "I think first as a cameraman," said Ford.[22] "He knew more about photography than any other man who ever worked in the movies," declared cinematographer William Clothier.[23]

It may come as a surprise, then, to understand that Ford, like many other good directors, almost never looked through the camera. Gabriel Figueroa, who shot *The Fugitive,* explains how this worked. He met with Ford and they discussed the film's general ambience and looked over the sets. The first sequence was to be shot the following day. Ford gave him some instructions, and said, "Gaby, find the best set-up for a long shot."

Next day the basic lighting was ready when Ford arrived.

I asked him if he would like to check the set-up through the camera. He looked at me, and after a puff on his pipe, simply answered:

"I am just the director, you are the photographer. But tell me: which lens are we using?"

"28mm." I said.

"Okay. So you are cutting here and there," and he began to indicate the imaginary limits of the space covered by the camera lens. It took Ford years of experience to be able to do this, and it made my staff and me aware of the kind of person we were going to work with.[24]

Ford's favorite cameramen—Joseph August, Arthur Miller, Gregg Toland, George Schneiderman, Bert Glennon, Archie Stout—each had recognizable styles of their own, yet their work for Ford *also* looks Fordian. A Ford movie, it cannot be overstressed, is first of all an aesthetic pleasure visually; it demanded beautiful images. Often it is the painterly style of Ford's pictures that first distinguishes him to audiences. At times this painterly manner has fallen into fashionable disrepute, and people have claimed preference for, say, the newsreel-like straightforwardness of De Sica or the extremely desaturated color of the early seventies. Yet Ford believed that "pictures, not words, should tell the story,"[25] and the conscious aestheticism of his compositions is not separable from his narration.

He preferred black-and-white. "You can get a guy off the street and he can shoot a picture in color. But it takes a real artist to do a black-and-white picture."[26] And he liked a rich array of gray tones, from a velvet black to an ermine white. He liked to brag about his lighting, which tended toward a rich chiaroscuro, with pools of light and dark. No other director so consistently exploited the sides, corners, and depth of the frame. Action was staged, usually, triplanarly, with the principal subject in midground.

Ford's reputation for getting "all outdoors" onto film was a matter of effectiveness rather than quantity. Indeed, his interiors are far more creative, simply because he had more angles, shadows, and objects to play with.

He had a reputation for being cheap with film. The typical practice in Hollywood in the thirties was to film a "master shot" of a scene, five or ten times, then move in and cover all the parts of the scene in profuse variety of medium shots and close-ups. All of this footage would then be delivered to an editor who would play around with it until he came up with a way of putting it together that met the approval of various committees of producers. To get this ultimate two minutes of screen time, the director may have exposed two hours or more of negative.

Not Ford. "I don't give 'em a lot of film to play with. In fact, Eastman used to complain that I exposed so little film. I *do* cut in the camera. Otherwise, if you give them a lot of film 'the committee' takes over. They start juggling scenes around and taking out this and putting in that. They can't do it with my pictures. I cut in the camera and that's it. There's not a lot of film left on the floor when I'm finished."[27]

Not only did Ford expose just a little film (say, two and a half times his final footage), but he only shot the precise pictures he knew he would use, and he tended to stage scenes in (short) "sequence shots," moving actors in to close shots, rather than adding inserts later. In Hollywood of the twenties and thirties, Ford's methods were revolutionary and deeply influenced masters as diverse as Vidor and Capra.

Robert Parrish explains what it was like to edit a Ford film:

> I was once given a sequence of *Drums Along the Mohawk* to edit. It was the first time I had done that kind of work and I really worked hard at it. I sweat blood and water. Suddenly Ford came into the cutting room and asked me how it was going. I told him it wasn't going well. He stared at me and said simply, "If, with the stuff I've given you, you can't manage, go learn some other job." Since I was gawking at him, surprised, he added, "All you have to do is cut at the frames where I say [on the film], "Start!" and at the frames where I say, "Cut!" and to splice one shot onto the next. That's all." And he left. It was true. Ford didn't need an editor.[28]

Ford, said Lefty Hough, his assistant over many decades, "was such a different character than any of these other fellows—the Capras, the Wellmans. Much smarter director. Very brilliant man. Only director I ever remember walking on a set and never see this guy open up a script. . . . He knew exactly what he was going to do. . . . He had every cut in his head [even] on *The Iron Horse* [back in 1924]—he didn't have it [written] on a dialogue [page of the script]." Ford could not understand why his assistants would not remember shots when he would recite what they were going to do.[29]

Ford did his own editing in the teens, parts of the thirties, and frequently after World War II. At Fox, Darryl F. Zanuck occasionally reedited his films, at times to Ford's grudging approval. ("My father was the second greatest editor who ever lived," said Barbara Ford, who worked many years as a Fox editor; "Zanuck was the greatest."[30])

What is amazing about Ford is not simply that he did not have to compose his pictures in the cutting room (as many directors did—and do), but that he never went to the opposite extreme and storyboarded. Storyboarding—a fairly standard technique today—is best exemplified by Hitchcock's films: the entire movie is first drawn, like a comic strip, with the composition of each shot (or camera movement) precisely indicated. Subsequently, the technicians on the set need only duplicate the drawn illustrations; and, later, the film is cut according to the storyboard. "No wonder Hitchcock's films look like that!" was Barbara Ford's comment. Ford pictures look nothing like Hitchcock's because they never have Hitchcock's mechanicalness. Ford composed the picture entirely in his head, without even a written outline of the shots he would use.

Scriptwrights. "I think John Ford almost dies because he can't write. It just runs him nuts, that he has thoughts and ideas and has never trained himself to put them down on paper."[31] Thus Nunnally Johnson, who did not collaborate with Ford on their three pictures together. Frank Nugent, who did collaborate, remarked on Ford's "astonishing flair for dialogue." Ford—who admittedly could not sit down and fill a sheet of paper—used a writer as a sounding board, and as someone to perform the drudgery of producing successive drafts of material to be worked on. Anywhere but Hollywood he would automatically have received script credit.

Writing conferences were lengthy, often extending through weeks on Ford's boat. Ford behaved like "a real tyrant, needling and picking away at you," said James Warner Bellah.[32] "Sometimes," noted Nugent, "he is groping, like a musician who has a theme but doesn't quite know how to develop it. I've had the feeling often—in story conferences—that he's like a kid whistling a bar of music, and faltering; then if I come up with the next notes and they're what he wanted, he beams and says that's right, that's what he was trying to get over. . . . Usually a script is written scene by scene, gone over, discussed, rewritten maybe, then okayed—and you don't go back over it again—which, again, is good for a writer."[33] "I'm not sure, but I suspect that when he starts thinking about a story, he calmly devotes himself to personal research, gets hold of the music of the period and, generally, comes to his office well provided with a mixture of facts and fancy, so that he can tussle, if the occasion arises, with the scenarist, costume designer or anyone else who comes within range of his Celtic eye."[34]

Ford hated expository scenes, and would cut dialogue so brutally that talk in his movies usually resembles some elliptical pidgin English. "He loves to tear pages out of scripts," said James Stewart, "cut scenes down to phrases and phrases to words."[35] The finished film, notes Nugent, is "always

Ford's, never the scriptwriter's." After shooting *Wagon Master*, Ford told him, "I liked your script. In fact, I actually shot a few pages of it."[36]

The remark was not a joke. To understand the script's role in Ford's methods, we must reexamine Johnson's notion that it frustrated Ford that he could not write. In America, with our literary biases, we tend to conceive of movies as fundamentally illustrations of stories and words; in fact, our copyright laws allow ownership of the pictures to the person who wrote the original plot (even after the plot is mangled)! For Johnson, for most critics of the old school as for most academicians, the script elements *are* the film. Ford's cinema, on the other hand, is almost unique in rarely giving the impression of having been born via translation from prose. His movies seem rather to have been conceived directly in visual terms (and not so much antiliterary, as aliterary, in origin). Ford never outlined what he was going to do on paper, and he treated his finished script almost as a preliminary outline. Once on set, huge quantities of pages would be discarded, much dialogue would be improvised, all the staging and cutting (rarely indicated in the script) would be "invented." Thus the question of whether or not Ford was capable of writing his scripts alone should be weighed against the more important question of whether it would have been desirable. In fact, Ford believed a director profits more than he loses by not having had to restrict his creative vision first of all to a page of words, and by being able to bring a degree of critical detachment into his utilization of a scenario not entirely his own. For example, Ford thought Sam Fuller's work suffered because Fuller wrote his own scripts.[37]

In point of fact, Ford "grew up" within a collaborative process. Francis Ford collaborated with Grace Cunard, and Ford wrote his films at Universal in collaboration with Harry Carey. This was his preferred method, which he was able to practice in all but four or five instances (Johnson's *The Prisoner of Shark Island*, *The Grapes of Wrath*, *Tobacco Road*, and Philip Dunne's *How Green Was My Valley*).

Some of the Dudley Nichols scripts of the prewar years were followed rather slavishly, but these were products of intense collaboration. Ford himself appears to have written most of *The Informer*, and Nichols's influence generally seems to have been more theoretical than conceptual. Paul Jensen, for example, notes Nichols was impressed by a line from O'Neill's *Strange Interlude*, "The present is a strange interlude in which we call upon the past and future to bear witness that we are still living."[38] But Ford liked O'Neill, too, and the line's notion is evident in the pre-Nichols *Black Watch*, *Hangman's House*, *Salute*, even *The Iron Horse*, and especially in the non-Nichols *Young Mr. Lincoln*, wherein Lincoln is pulled by his future and pushed by his past. And Joseph McBride has observed that in Ford, "Moments occur in the eye of eternity to be re-enacted in the mind forever."[39]

The Ford-Nichols movies were characterized by literary pretense, theatrical values, and heavy Germanic stylization. Nichols provided Ford, in some instances, with script-architecture, character interaction, and more complex dramatic structures than possessed by Ford's simple, storybook pictures of the twenties. In contrast, the postwar collaboration with Frank Nugent was less schematic in verbal revelation of character, but Nugent's ability to capture a character in a single nugget of unliterary dialogue better suited Ford's vignette techniques.

"Two of the most beautiful things in the world," Ford was fond of reminding his scenarists, "are a horse running and a couple waltzing."[40] His late movies are richly but sparsely scripted, almost epigrammatic in their economy, and their "action" is subtle but direct. "With Ford," said Flora Robson, one of the 7 Women, "the actor is continually conscious of the fact that he is making a motion picture and that it must move, move, move. His scenes are never static or dominated by the dialogue."[41] "When movies are best," said Ford, "the action's long and the talk's short. When a film tells its story and reveals its characters to us in a suite of simple, beautiful and animated shots, that's a movie."[42]

Characterization. A typical Ford drama centers on a group rather than on one or two characters, and is enclosed within a greater drama, that of a society, as represented by a dozen or more well-defined characters. For this reason, Ford's characters are designed for easy recognition, for memorableness. As Jean Mitry put it, they are "almost always strongly typed, indeed, stereotyped. [But then Ford] gives them life and realism by stuffing them with a thousand details, a thousand original or singular nuances, nuances which burst the seams of the ready-made clothing the characters wore at first, when it was necessary to define them and situate them dramatically."[43]

"What makes someone a type," wrote Stanley Cavell, "is not his similarity with other members of that type but his striking separateness from other people."[44] The alternative to using such types is to present characters who are amorphous and undifferentiated and then allow them, during the film's course, gradually to reveal their individuality, so that, at film's end, they emerge as stereotypes. This sort of characterization has been modish in recent years; in a sense, it ends where Ford begins. Sometimes, by initially presenting a character as belonging to an *archetype* (a symbolic personage evocative of universal myths), Ford can not only construct dramas of primordial resonance, but can play that character against his generic type.

Ford *was* highly dependent most of his career upon cameo, or vignette approaches to characterization. The term *vignette* is used here not in the sense of a *masked* photograph but in the emphasis put in such photographs on posing the subject in ways strikingly characteristic. Thus, a single medium shot may instantly convey volumes of information about its character—somewhat akin to a Norman Rockwell portrait. Hence Ford's description of himself as fundamentally a comedian is profoundly true, for his native capabilities were early and consistently displayed in *comedy* skills: in vignetting, accent, deftness, in quicksilver shifts of moods. He had to struggle to master techniques of the tragedian, groping to find a suitable manner, whereas his comic technique required comparatively slight development from *The Shamrock Handicap* in 1925 through *Donovan's Reef* in 1964. Not surprisingly, his finer tragedies, e.g., *7 Women*, are constructed like his comedies, not like such (for him) misdirected approaches as *The Informer*, whose single-minded efforts are antithetical to those of the comedic Ford. Indeed, ability to create an extended study of a complex character (one embodying contradictions, or conscious of existential ones) long eluded Ford. Correspondingly, his cameo technique not only aided him in developing his unique sort of "all-star" ensemble drama, but in fact made this type of movie the *only* fertile direction for his talents. He thus capitalized upon his major limitation, while continuing to experiment in search of extended characterization.

The validity of cameo characterization, so richly a part not only of Ford but of Walsh, Capra, Renoir, Ophuls, and Vidor as well, is often missed midst the craze for mistaken notions of "truth" in art inherited from the nineteenth century. Even George Bernard Shaw saw the critical trend inherited from Wagner and Ibsen as "all along . . . a pious dialectical fraud, because it applies the test of realism and revelation to the arts of illusion and transfiguration."[45] And Jacques Barzun observes that "the truth of a character does not depend on any particular substance or mode of presentation, but on his fitting the purpose and environment provided by his creator. If you take an interest, *any* interest, in Lysistrata or Gulliver, they are real to that extent and for that purpose. Panurge is real in Rabelais and would be false in Meredith, and the converse is true about a Meredithian figure. As for 'real life,' it is impossible to say whether it furnishes Meredithian or Rabelaisian or Shavian characters in the raw. Fictional life is so much harder to live than actual life that most people would wither away in the rich atmosphere of Hamlet or Mr. Pickwick."[46]

"He made me write out complete biographies of every character," said Frank Nugent,[47] for story considerations were secondary to those of character, and it was necessary to give a sense of "life lived" to these cameolike apparitions. "You've got to tell your story through the people who portray it," insisted Ford. "As the basic story develops one must develop each character in the actor, besides the mood and the tempo, so that the drama is correctly mixed with humor."[48] "You can have a weak, utterly bad script — and a good cast will turn it into a good picture. . . . With the exception of the stars who [were in the thirties] signed for parts by the studio in advance, I insist on choosing names for myself. And I spend more time on that task than on any other."[49]

Thus much of Ford's work was done before actual rehearsals began, which explains how his laconic, indeed uncommunicative methods nonetheless achieved results. Often he constructed a screen character by build-

ing on foibles or eccentricities already there in the actor.* Thus, for example, Harry Carey became more Harry Carey than he actually was, i.e., more
charismatic and relaxed, while in Harry Carey, Jr., the notable characteristic was stumbling over things or walking into walls.[50] Thus Ford was usually
less concerned that an actor speak the exact words written for him than that
he be comfortable saying them; dialogue, too, tended to be "cameo-
typical."

The same care was expended casting minor parts, and it was in this way
that the "Ford Stock Company" originated, for he had a penchant for casting ex-celebrities such as Mae Marsh, Russell Simpson, or Francis Ford in
small roles. Though columnists played up this stock company as early as
1931, community filmmaking had been a general practice in the teens,
when a director had "his company," consisting of stars, bit players, cameramen, and grip. But by 1936 Ford had to explain the practice: "Ex-stars will,
after all, give a better performance even in the smallest part than any casual
extra would; and it's my contention that the bits in any picture are just as
important as the starring role, since they round out the story—complete the
atmosphere—make the whole plausible. . . . The other, and just as important reason, is that when I was starting out in this town those people were
kind to me. I want to repay a little of that if it's in my power."[51]

Ford's subordinate parts tend to be quite broadly played—"in the English theater style," as Anna Lee describes it[52]—and this is a quality disconcerting to those who mistake "realism" for the apparent absence of stylization. Equally puzzling to modern audiences can be his fondness for
mixing actors of theatrical sophistication with untrained ones (e.g., Sue
Lyon in 7 *Women*).

Framing and Cutting. Ford had a reputation, fueled by personages such as Orson Welles, François Truffaut, André Bazin, and Andrew
Sarris, for long takes, slight camera movement, and "invisible" editing.** In
fact, Ford's typical shot lasts about ten seconds, often less, which is brief
indeed by any but *Potemkin* standards, and probably one out of four Ford
shots involves camera movement. True, Ford avoids like poison the showiness
of a Lelouch or a Welles, but such quantitative comparisons have little mean-

---

*Concentration on Ford as director may obscure his role in creating stars or launching
careers. To name a few: Harry Carey, Harry Carey, Jr., Hoot Gibson, John Wayne, Ward Bond,
Spencer Tracy, George O'Brien, Grace Kelly, Jon Hall, Dorothy Lamour, Richard Greene,
Barry Fitzgerald, Arthur Shields, Vera Miles, John Carradine, Ben Johnson.

**Ford early on attracted attention for avoiding close-ups and maintaining long shots
where others would cut to a close-up, and for moving actors in relation to the camera, sometimes into close-up, rather than cutting to them. He was also reputed one of the first to use long
takes in ensemble scenes. Long takes were normal during the early sound era (1928–31), when
Ford avoided using them statically, but by 1939 montage style was the rule, 1931 seemed a
thousand years ago, and anyone departing from current fashion was regarded as a pioneer.

ing in judging aesthetic articulations; Mozart's music contains fewer dissonant chords than Stravinsky's, but Mozart's dissonance is more stinging. Ford's cuts, rather like Mozart's progressions, match smoothly enough that people determined not to perceive cutting will seldom be bothered by them. But to watch a Ford movie without *feeling*—physically, emotionally, intellectually—his cutting is like listening to music while being oblivious to rhythm and harmony, or like looking at Renaissance painting while being oblivious to composition. Cutting and framing are Ford's most basic aesthetic articulations; until perception of them becomes a vital part of one's movie watching, the cinema of John Ford will remain essentially unexperienced.

Before discussing Ford's montage, however, we must single out three "heresies" that have worked their way into montage theory. The first of these is the axiom that the individual shot has no value in itself, that all of its meaning and emotive force derive from its linkage with other shots. While the axiom *is* sufficiently true to justify such an overstatement (for people seldom recognize montage's power), still, at the same time, it *is* an overstatement. The dialectic between shots that conditions each of them can, obviously, only be as rich as the richness of each shot. To concentrate solely on the *relation* between shots in discussing montage is to put the cart before the horse. Secondly, montage has fallen into ill repute through its ability to govern our ideology and manipulate our emotions. Such suspicion of montage is valid enough and, in essence, goes back to Plato's distrust of art. But the remedy lies neither in expulsion of art from the republic nor in expulsion of cuts from films; it lies in the moral responsibility of the artist and the intelligence of the perceiver. Despite Bazin, "invisible" editing only exists in the decision of one who will not see. Thirdly, the need for literary-minded critics and semioticians to reduce films to "narratives" has resulted in approaches to movies that are excessively conceptual, whereas the more vital aesthetic functions have been overlooked: montage's ability to isolate moods and emotions. We all know the trick of cutting to express emotional change—from calm to surprise; more important is the cut that accords each emotion its due—from surprise to calm, for example. The example is simplistic, but by this route cinema may effect an *aesthetic* dialectic between shots. Why is this important? Because despite much effort, human beings do not confront the world or each other in terms of logic or even in clear conceptual terms. If we think back in our lives to an event that was personally vital to us, our visual memory of what happened and our aural memory of what was said are likely to be considerably more vague than our aesthetic memory of what was felt. And for this reason those who truly want to understand life do not limit themselves to the social sciences or the semioticians but consult art as well.

Returning to Ford, we have seen how the major influence in his evolving utilization of the semiautonomous shot as a modal element of montage was the work of F. W. Murnau. Although Ford did not adopt Murnau's florid camera (for reasons we shall examine presently), he did adopt Murnau's intense exploitation of characterizing body posture, poeticization of spatial relationships within the frame, and moody, chiaroscuro lighting—all techniques whereby compositional form is aestheticized. And Ford further intensified Murnau's tension and movements—dynamics that in Murnau favor the *curve*—by placing them within a geometry of *straight* lines: most signally within the triplanar space generated by Ford's depth of field, planar lighting, and arrangement of props (with actors generally in middle ground).

Ford's cutting, next, extends and develops the emotional/compositional ideas begun in the individual frame. Let us take a terribly simplistic example to demonstrate how this works. The pattern of three shots—John × Mary/John and Mary—is among the most formulaic in cinematic syntax, and Ford uses it often.* What distinguishes his use of it is first of all the degree to which he relates motion, gesture, and graphics so that the reverse-angles rhyme; when the paired crosscuts conclude in a two-shot, the opposition of their contrasting angles is neutralized. Also, the spatial relationships supposed by the crosscutting are confirmed (i.e., we assumed that John was looking at Mary, then that Mary was looking at John, and that thus the two were in spatial proximity; but this is not confirmed until the two-shot). The sequence is the cinematic equivalent of a musical cadence that progresses through alternative dissonances to resolution.

But spatial and kinetic relationships are not separable in Ford from content and emotion. As Frank Nugent said, "he works from the character more than anything else"; and the key to Ford's style is the dialectic between his cutting and his vignette characterization. In our simple example, the discursive content (boy alone, girl alone, the couple united) may, in its formal presentation (each alone, then two together), arouse in an audience emotions rooted first in existential loneliness, then in societal fulfillment. The point here is that this formal presentation is not simply "content": John could have met Mary in a single shot, but the director has chosen to emphasize their solitary stares into space. And what distinguishes Ford's use of this formula is the fervency with which, thanks to Ford's vignette characterization and Murnau-like intensity of mood, each character inhabits his or her separate world and saturates it with the vibrations of his or her soul. In such a case, their eventual union in a two-shot may be eventful indeed.

Since Ford wishes to maintain his strong presence as narrator, his camera's physical point of view is generally *objective*. Only terribly rarely is it *subjective* (i.e., when the camera gazes from the physical position of one of the characters). "Over-the-shoulder" shots—which may be called *conversational* point of view—are, however, common; unlike a shot from a charac-

---

* /=cut. × = crosscut.

ter's subjective perspective, the over-the-shoulder shot retains an objective narrative presence (Ford's) exterior to the action: rather than seeing *Mary* (as seen by John), we see *John looking at Mary.*

The result of Ford's objective camera style is that we do not "identify" with the characters. Instead, we stare *at* them and relate *to* them. There is an instance of a character's (i.e., subjective) point of view during *Stage-coach's* dinner scene, when Mrs. Mallory's piercing dolly-in on Dallas comes *before* the near-180° crosscut identifying the dolly as having been from Mrs. Mallory's point of view. Typically, Ford shows a "reaction" shot before showing what prompts the reaction, thus discouraging identification and securing his own narrative posture. But, subsequently, by varying the intensity of his narrative presence (through camera placement, but also through lighting and all other techniques), Ford intriguingly exploits the tensions between various gradations of identity and distancing.

There is, of course, a difference between "distance" and "distancing." It is an artist's entire aesthetic sensibility rather than simply the long shot that accounts for distancing. Hitchcock's movies contrast violently with Ford's, so intensely subjective and manipulative, literally *plucking* emotion out of the audience, that we may be said to be *participants,* whereas with Ford, no matter how intensely emotional, we are also critical, judging *witnesses.* Ford's cinema, in other words, is presentational; his painterly style suits "comedies of manners" in which a culture's mores are displayed. Style itself becomes a distancing device, because his thorough aestheticism, the Mozart-like importance he accords to beauty for its own sake, strikes up a dialectic with his documentary-like subjects. It is style, rather than an artist's real-life personality, that we refer to in speaking of his personality or presence. The example of Stendhal and Balzac make it clear, as Arnold Hauser has written, "that the service an artist renders to progress depends not so much on his personal convictions and sympathies as on the power with which he portrays the problems and contradictions of social reality."[53] And what is "power," if not style?

Although Ford's presentational style means he avoids setting up identification mechanisms (as Hitchcock does), he does "set up" personality. That is, after getting accustomed to Ford, it is curious how often so many other filmmakers, particularly shop directors like Lloyd, Fleming, or Whale (who rarely controlled their own cutting), seem constantly to be cutting *away* from characters. With Ford, on the other hand, characters are cut *to,* and then they are there for (apparently) leisurely absorption, to be empathized with, but not identified with. (Few dead spots occur midst the kinetic happenings of a Ford film, but each little event occurs with such clarity and proportion that haste never intrudes.)

Antonioni too does everything possible to create forms expressive of mood; but rather than exploiting montage, he prefers to roam with his camera through spaces that, although thus unstructured themselves, are littered with (often cubist) structures. Ford's space, in contrast, is almost always structured; he is obsessed with lines, planes, interior angles, depth-of-field alleys, which take on force in relation to defined space (the frame), and even this he empha- sizes, by angling his stage slightly to his focal plane. Ford's highly active mon- tage creates dynamic poetry out of elements that have no existence in Anto- nioni's movies, and whose exclusion there signifies man's ideological rootlessness and uncertainty. A moving camera tends to deemphasize real space and time; a still camera tends to emphasize them. The moving camera distracts from movement within the frame, whereas the still reinforces it. The moving camera (even gentle follow-pans) tends to separate a character from his milieu, the still to emphasize the milieu.

A pan of 45 degrees, or perhaps much less, is a grandiloquent gesture in Ford. He rejects florid movement not because it threatens the illusion of reality, but because he does not wish to sacrifice the advantages of the au- tonomous shot, and because (given the quasi-determinist role milieu plays) he does wish to emphasize the rapport between character and milieu. Ex- tended camera movement, as in Ophuls, tends to leave characters adrift in (structured) time but divorced from structured space, and Ford once in a while will employ camera movement for disorienting effect. In contempo- rary subjects, too, like *When Willie Comes Marching Home* or *Gideon's Day,* he may adopt a fairly mobile "TV style," though even here the hint of disorientation is deliberate. Elaborate trackings are reserved for occasions when the movement is capable of defining space; the track of the priest in *The Fugitive* riding against twilighted arches is a good instance. And even here, as in the track of Denver in *Wagon Master* running away from Travis's marriage proposal, the Godard-like abstractness distances and indicates disorientation.

Sound and Music. Ford welcomed the talking picture with elation, and thirty-five years later declared, "It's still a silent medium. . . . Pictures, not words, should tell the story."[54] Nevertheless, it was only in the talking movie that Ford mastered silent cinema. His silents have so many titles that they are virtually illustrated storybooks. Given spoken dialogue, Ford could become more complex visually; given control over music and sound effects, he could create the powerful, modal cinema Murnau has suggested. In 1928 he called for development of "auditory images," for "the use of sound as well as sight images."[55]

He conceived his pictures while listening to period music; thus his films are modal music-dramas from the moment of their conception. Composer Richard Hageman says Ford directed "with one ear on the music. . . . We didn't have to rescore a scene [of 3 *Godfathers*], because he knows in ad- vance what the music is and paces the action to it."[56] Although Ford complained once of "too much music," he generally used a symphony orchestra during wilderness scenes when he was in charge (and, generally, he *was* responsible for his movies' music). Often, as in *Stagecoach*, music is densely expressionistic, shunning realism, like other aspects of his cinema, for the sake of atmosphere. While he never made a "musical," many of his movies have more music than some musicals. Rare indeed is the Ford movie not essentially a choreography to music through most of its duration.

Often, too, music derives from on-camera sources. But the patently anachronistic score of *Wagon Master* interrupts on-camera music in order to serve a narrative and distancing function. Music in *Donovan's Reef* impersonates an unseen character and chorus, as do background sounds in *Mogambo*. Folk songs, folk tunes, and patriotic hymns function, as surely as do manners, costumes, and decor, as symbols of the ethos of an age and culture. Other "auditory images" include sounds for mood and psychology. The latter reached a nadir (but gained an Oscar) in Max Steiner's "Mickey Mousing" scores for *The Informer* and *Mary of Scotland*, where every word or feeling was imitated musically. Far more subtle are Elmer Bernstein's contrapuntal signals in *7 Women*, or Alfred Newman's leitmotifs, which begin by designating characters, in *Young Mr. Lincoln*, and finish by evoking worlds of specific emotions associated with them, and even appear in much later pictures, setting up complex cross-relations.

Ford customarily used only a single microphone. Whenever possible, he showed rather than told: thus the abundance of signs, newspapers, and words themselves.

Preliminaries and Structures. Ford contended that the short story was the perfect form for a motion picture. It provided him with just enough of a trend, a frame, for the character delineation in which he was far more interested than the plot itself. Then, according to Ford, "Usually I take the story, and get every line of printed material I can find on the subject. And then I take the boat and simply cruise until I've read it all. I eat, sleep, and drink whatever picture I'm working on—read nothing else, think of nothing else; which is probably the reason the continuity and mood of my products stay at an exact level."[57]

"Ford," said Frank Nugent, "thinks in terms of a complete story line, a general conception of what he wants to do, and he thinks in the forms of individual scenes, bits, and characters. He works something like a painter, selecting his colors and doing a palette—blues, greens, yellows, he lays them all out in his mind. Then, putting his thumb in here with a broad splash of color, then a little touch on the other side. He goes home at night after a day's talk and reads books, or listens to records. And, listening to the music, pictures, colors, or moods come into his mind. He has a great feeling for characters, some from his own imagination. These series of impressions, images, moods—music moods, character moods, atmosphere—become in effect his raw material."⁵⁸ One could go so far as to define Ford's cinema as the "musicalization" of painting.

This attention to shifting moods, reminiscent of Mozart and Chekhov, is a principal hallmark of Ford's style. To structure these moods he preferred fairly definite sequences, optimally about two minutes long. Thus when Dudley Nichols worried that he could write a play but not a script, Ford told him to write a play in fifty or sixty scenes.⁵⁹ Such a large number of discrete sequences results in incredible density of mood, detail, and character.

If a movie is to be fundamentally formal, cinematically, its screenplay will outline the structure of its formal movements. As a result of clear structure—each sequence autonomous in mood, tempo, action, theme, setting—one gets a definite feeling of suitelike *progression:* developing movement, in plot, form, and theme. Ford: "I very seldom play a sequence to its full effect, and so my stuff is usually confusing to both cast and producers in its uncut form. Before I make a single set-call I outline the story, as it will appear on the screen, in my mind, and separate details are subordinated to the final complete effect."⁶⁰

Contrast. "Realism," said Brecht, "doesn't consist in reproducing reality, but in showing how things really are." Thus realism is a function of style (and thus differing greatly from one artist to another); but too often the term is used in ways both meaningless and confusing. What critics praised in 1935 as the ultimate word in realism seems today ultimate contrivance. To many casual movie-goers, any film made before 1970 looks artificial and anything made today looks realistic. This state of affairs exists because people are reluctant to engage a movie on a stylistic level.

Among movie artists Ford should be classed with Murnau, Sternberg, Vidor, Renoir, Ophuls, Mizoguchi, and Rossellini, as denoting a cinema of felt expression through aesthetic form. Ford's sort of movie implies complete stylization of every element. All content becomes formalized; every quality of sight or sound is thoroughly aestheticized. This process of stylization was, it seems, prompted by Murnau's demonstration of the artistic potential of cinema: how cinema could formalize feelings, and be "modal." Such stylization, far from being antipathetic to "realism," treats our sense of reality as a feeling to be formalized and intensified.

On the other hand, there was a second vein of theatricality in Ford, already well developed, of vignette characterization ("turns") and intense changefulness. The distinction between the two veins is that this simpler theatricality was concerned mostly with the subject before the camera only, whereas the Murnau process of modification formalized the cinematic medium itself.

The mature Ford was a fusion of these two tendencies. He began to "compose" his movies in terms of mood, dramatic style, and cinematic form (angles, lines, light, gesture, movement, montage). The aspects of contrast resulting from this fusion fall into three modes:

1. Mixture of contrasting styles. Within a single scene Ford will juxtapose elements of naturalness, expressionism, slapstick, impressionism, neorealism, or whatever; e. g., the combination of "theatricality" and "documentary realism" in *She Wore a Yellow Ribbon*.

2. Mixture of contrasting moods. A tragic moment is typically contrasted with a happy one. Comedy is injected whenever possible. In Ford's view of human drama, as McBride put it, "what is most noble, poignant and terrifying is frequently a hair's-breadth away from howling absurdity."[61] Most better Fords switch rapidly through a wide gamut of emotional moods.

3. Mixture of contrasting modes. Cinema by its nature is a combining medium. Ford treats shapes, motions, light and dark, colors, sound, music, cutting, and camera movement, each of them expressively and autonomously, and juxtaposes them polyphonically rather than simply combining them toward a single effect.

Thus it may be said Ford exploits every aspect of multimedia cinema. At its ideal, his cinema is "operatic": everything is choreographed. Diverse aspects of cinema are interrelated, sometimes harmonically, sometimes polyphonically. There is a baroque sense of contrast.* Sequence contrasts with sequence, motion with motion. Multiple stories are told simultaneously with multiple classes of society, multiple dramas unfold within the same scene, often reflecting multiple sensitivities. Ford's disposition toward the vignette combined with the Murnau influence to result in swift changes of mood, large casts (ensemble pictures rather than one- or two-character ones), multiple plot lines, coordination of technique and theme into suitelike sequences that build schematically. The style implied its evolution toward increasingly ambiguous characters and structures.

---

*Vsevolod Pudovkin during a conference on Ford held in Moscow in 1946 was also struck by these aspects in Ford's work: "Even in superficial analysis you will find in his pictures a collision of most divergent methods, up to and including the method defining the genre of the work itself. Side by side with sharp grotesque you will find painstaking and minutely detailed realistic elaboration of scenes, at times bordering on naturalism. And suddenly arises a sentimental tale, filled with abstract symbolism, like an illustration to a Sunday bible sermon. Recall the scene showing the pastor in *How Green Was My Valley*, where Christ in a jacket teaches a child to walk on the blossoming and blessed earth as in a valley of paradise. And a second later the factory chimneys are belching smoke, water pours from the dirty roofs, dark crowds are moving through the gloomy, dirty streets, and the tale acquires the epic austerity of an unconcerned and thoughtful onlooker."

Pudovkin also praised Ford because, despite having grown up in the American environment and thus not yet being "able to envisage man of the masses as the historical master of life, still . . . he tries to envisage man not isolated but included within the diversified world." Pudovkin found a "sub-text" or "spirit" in Ford that "in its most general aspect says: 'Everything in our life is not as it should be. There can be dreams of a beautiful world, but how to find the path to this beautiful world I know not.'" (Pudovkin's text along with those of others was sent to Ford and is among the Ford Papers, Lilly Library, Indiana University. Parts of it are also in Philippe Haudiquet, *John Ford* [Paris: Seghers, 1966], pp. 141–142.)

Form and Theme

Chaos (incoherence)	*Order* (stasis, repression)
motion	rest
freedom	determinism
liberty	law
reality (documentary re-creation)	theater (re-created documentary)
parade	house
change	subsistence

Ford's master antinomy is probably chaos/order. Art (and men) labor to exist (and balance) between such extremes, and motion and rest are so much the formal bases of Ford's cinema that they would alone suffice to render *How Green Was My Valley* personal. But Ford liked, also, to philosophize over History (History, he once said, was his "real profession"); and his better movies chronicle change and speculate on man's dubious authority over his own fate. Often, in later years, the *parade* proved a splendid image by which to suggest change, continuity, and man's doubtful ability to control his own fate.

The parade represents life's pilgrimage, in the Augustinian sense, but Ford never lost sight of the void that is faith's *volte face*. The parade—"man's unceasing search for something he can never find"[62]—is often a substitute for reason. And in daily life the parade, without even its elusive goal, may become form without meaning. Thus life is a constant passage without a map, with only immediate purposes, but with the seduction of the moment giving life its validity. For most people, perfect freedom is too precarious and its attendant self-responsibility is too onerous; the surety of order and prescribed duty is more comfortable. Nowhere better than in the military is this opposition between freedom and order exemplified, and for this reason Ford in later years increasingly chose such disciplined social organisms for his subjects. With such societal contexts, commonplace actions become rituals, partake of myth, and are contemplated with awe. But myths may breed myopia.

There is evil of the common sort in Ford—characters who wallow in the intrigues, deceptions, and callow practicalities that distinguish the real world—but, for Ford, lack of commitment, honor, or friendship damn beyond the pale. The evil, the true evil, that haunts his films is the evil of good intentions.

Any effort persisted in becomes corrupt. The sense of duty that sustains Ford's individuals (and also their sense of faith) commonly leads them astray into aberrations or death. Duty-bound, they invade others' privacy, and arrogate knowledge of higher good, right, and judgment: judges, ministers, soldiers, outlaws, priests. Thus racism, war, or any form of intolerance, becomes a function of society.

In tracing Ford's pictures (particularly *Judge Priest, How Green Was My Valley, This Is Korea!, The Man Who Shot Liberty Valance*) we have seen how people (and governments) act from feeling, not from logic. Man is made of dreams as much as of reality. And we have seen how Ford, in awakening around 1927 to cinema's ability to be art through total stylization, awakened simultaneously to his art's high task: to help us free ourselves from determining ideologies. Art, after all, has the capability of making us understand things through emotion that we would be absolutely incapable of understanding through the intellect. Within a determining milieu, particularly when that milieu is challenged, free will, human nature, life's worth, a benign divinity's existence, all must necessarily be posed in question. And so Ford pictures ideally construct in minute detail a social set of apparent homogeneity (thus often military-like) in order to analyze that society within its historic moment, and in order to demonstrate how the garments of society, together with history itself, operate on the individual. It is for these reasons that Jean-Marie Straub has called Ford the most "Brechtian" of all filmmakers.[63] (Footnote 63 elucidates the comparison further.)

Civilization always attempts to impose order in Ford, and repression and chaos always result. Augustine, Hegel, and Marx also envisioned history as a process of dialectical clashes. But where they all saw this dialectic leading toward an ideal state, Ford was always bothered by the possibility that the apparent movement of history may only be the chance by-product of chaos, or merely the cosmos's eternally violent quest for equilibrium. One senses the contest between order and freedom in Ford as early as the 1927–1935 period, although only in his final period is it full and dynamic. In between, after 1935, repression reigns. Feeble heroes occasionally challenge, and suppressed violence once in a while erupts; but, like hurricanes, these interruptions pass. In such an atmosphere, ideological clashes occur on mundane levels—conflicts with Indians and outlaws and gangsters—and otherwise are sublimated into myths.

Pilgrimages and long voyages end where hope does, midst disintegration and defeat, yet they fail to dim the gentle confidences exchanged en route. Bleak indeed are the ways of the world in Ford, save for a congeniality forever contradicting life's essential sadness.

Community and Family

Fordian communities are islands apart, and stress is usually laid, at beginning and end of movie, on the need to traverse the outer world in order to arrive (by train, boat, stagecoach . . .) *here*. Thus a community has a sense of "us and them." "Us" includes, of course, a set of groups, each defined by class, culture, and race, perpetually divisive, and each thinking "us and them." Finally comes the family; the family, almost always depicted as an isolated pocket of existential security, as a refuge from loneliness (but, like "home," it is an ideal rarely attained, and generally imperfect, fragmented, lacking one parent*). The individual's self-identity is, contrary to some current assumptions, constituted far less by his individuality than by his sense of identity within the family unity, thence within his specific class, culture, race, religion, etc.

A Fordian character is always distinctly characterized as representative of a specific culture. There is no confusing a Boston Wasp with an Irish-American or Swede. And people do not rebel consciously against socioethical-religious prescriptions of childhood. For Ford's pioneers, virgin land represents opportunity not for innovation but for continuity; even for Ford's blacks, true freedom can be envisioned only within existent structures.

Twin problems arise from this situation. The first of these is that the family is always being threatened from without: members are kidnapped, persecuted, or separated by prejudice. But whatever the variation, the specific threat to the family is always a form of intolerance. Intolerance, whether racial or "moral" (e.g., illegitimate birth), means denial that another shares fully our humanity; in other words, intolerance springs not only from self-identity, from recognition of membership in a unity, but also from basic *misunderstanding* of identity and unity, from well-meaning attempts to pursue virtue. In fact, these threaten the things they seek to preserve.

The second problem occurs when a family member, say, a child grown up, seeks to extend himself into the world outside. As, axiomatically, he cannot leave his family, he must extend it, into marriage, into new lands, into alien cultures. Such fusion will encounter difficulty: intolerance.

When a community falls into intolerance, to restore itself, to mediate between the twin evils of chaos and order, it requires a hero. The hero's specific task is always to restore a missing family member, one fallen victim to intolerance.

The Fordian Hero

$$\frac{\text{Myths}}{\text{Reality}} : \frac{\text{apparent harmony}}{\text{actual disharmony}} : \left. \frac{\text{visions of good}}{\text{fact of evil}} \right\} \text{Subsist}$$

Ford's tendencies toward stylization match his inclination to treat people as archetypes and quotidian events as sacred ritual. In his art, style so encodes reality that cinema necessarily becomes myth.

---

*Of Ford's fifty-five sound pictures, thirty-seven feature families, of which seven are complete families and thirty either fragmented or (ten times) about to become so. Family structures disintegrate in twenty-one instances, and are threatened but preserved in eighteen others (mostly earlier). Only in one instance, *Rio Grande*, is a family refabricated. In fact, families fare badly under most better American directors. There are none in Chaplin, Lang, Lubitsch, Aldrich, Mankiewicz, DeMille, Edwards, Losey, Mann, Wilder, Huston, Allen, Zimmermann, or Hawks; and only a couple in Ophuls, Sternberg, Wyler, Walsh, Penn, Sturges, or

That myth hides (and preserves) truths about life, often by rendering palatable the unpalatable, suits the Hollywood moviemaker's dual task, to entertain and enlighten, and invites "double-level" narratives. An inevitable, unhappy ending can be hidden (and preserved) under a "false" happy ending or a *deus ex machina;* * a disgusting character can be rendered comic; actions wrong, pernicious, suicidal can be justified subjectively and greeted with approbation. Thus is revealed discordancy between myth and reality, which breeds misdirected attempts to act rightly, which is the intolerance from which most human suffering flows. Some would remedy this situation by destroying the myths; others would destroy reality. The Fordian hero, perceiving that myths (even defective) are necessary to sustain us, seeks to mediate between myth (repressive order) and reality (chaos), in order, by purifying myth, to revitalize society.

To this end, he may not be passive, a "sheep" crying for a "shepherd" (like the Mormons in *Wagon Master*), or a passive drifter (like Marty Maher in *The Long Gray Line*). He must, perceiving that life can be hell, strive to keep atop the maelstrom; like Tom Joad, he must climb to critical consciousness of life's contradictions. And then, he must be willing to act, to intervene, to assume authority over others. Such intervention, often entailing immense moral arrogance, even violence (e.g., Mudd, Lincoln, Priest, Doniphon, Cartwright), he justifies by claimed knowledge of transcendent truth: he cites duty, justice, rightness.

Occasionally, a false hero forgets his role as mediator, fixates on myopic truths, and sows chaos in the guise of order (Hannah Jessop, DeLaage, Wyatt Earp, Ransom Stoddard, Colonel Thursday, et al.). The true hero mediates, "balances," encourages subsistence and peace—often symbolized by reunification of a family: Harry Carey, Will Rogers, Lincoln, Priest, Ethan Edwards (oddly), Doniphon, Cartwright.

Emotional vulnerability rather than physical prowess characterizes the Fordian hero, and he acts from the pressure of outer events or inner conscience rather than from free will. (The false hero, indeed, often seems arbitrary.) Sometimes the Fordian hero resembles a Hegelian one: his native prescience leads mankind closer toward the ideal but he himself is placed outside normal, biological history—he is almost always celibate, almost never "gets the girl," seldom reaps life's humble pleasures. He is often a combination of soldier, judge, and priest, symbolizing his intervention, authority, and self-sacrifice. And although he may be a fixture of society, he is yet an outsider, because he is purer than the average man in service of

---

Mulligan. Others see more to lament than to praise in the family: Ray, McCarey, Welles, Coppola, Sirk, Minnelli, Capra, Hitchcock. Vidor and Ford emphasize families. (See my "Looking Homeward—in Vain: The Family in American Film," *Mosaic* [Winnipeg] 16, no. 1–2 [Winter / Spring 1983], pp. 71–82.)

*E.g., *Air Mail, How Green Was My Valley, Fort Apache;* also many Capras, such as *Mr. Smith Goes to Washington, American Madness, It's a Wonderful Life.*

such accepted values as tolerance, justice, medical duty, preservation of family, and love (whereas the false hero serves racism, vengeance, law, "duty," intolerance, and glory). As shepherd, the hero cannot be sheep; others subsist within contradictions, he must get outside them. He, like Moses, is denied the promised land; he walks away after uniting couples, families, or communities. Interiorly compelled to acquiesce in appointed duty, he is fully conscious that his redemptive acts will, like Christ's, efface, condemn, even destroy him.* Yet always he upholds for humanity, for his community, or merely for a friend, a lantern, a flower, pointing toward a better vision.

Individual Consciousness

I remarked, and have often remarked since, how most people do not care for things which are authentic. They prefer mixtures and make-up. JEAN RENOIR,
Les Cahiers du
Capitaine Georges

When all is said and done, in life as in art what counts is the discovery of soul. Yet nothing is more difficult in the dramatic arts than the creation of a true-to-life character. Dramatization by its nature tends to schematize and concentrate, to make things neat and tidy, to present ideas and conflicts in clear patterns. A dramatic character tends also to be schematized: he is very definitely one way and not another; he professes and exhibits one mind and not another; he is consistent with himself from one moment to the next. But generally, as we know, this is not at all the way matters stand in real life with real people. Real people sprawl, they contradict themselves, they behave in ways contrary to their intentions, and their personalities are subject to innumerable momentary distractions.

Audiences contribute to the dramatist's dilemma, for they often prefer conflicts of ideas to conflicts of persons, and, in any case, they tend to try to force characters into molds. A character (like Ethan Edwards, in *The Searchers*) may fascinate by spilling out of his mold, but if he sprawls too much, the audience will reject him as incoherent. The writer too contributes to the dilemma, for his very task is to make solid the things that the director wishes to be ephemeral. Thus most directors devise methods to encourage accidental nuances, and thus Ford rigorously refused to verbalize in preproduction (by script or storyboard) what he would do on set. The problem is to get "life" into a character.

*Conventional wisdom is viewed cynically from early on. Arrowsmith, Duke Talbot (*Air Mail*), and Doctor Bull flee their communities loathingly. In later years, heroes grow increasingly desperate and isolated. John Wayne kills for vengeance unquestioningly in *Stagecoach*, but fights only after soul-searching in *The Quiet Man*; his struggle is existential and private in *The Searchers*, is waged against his own body in *The Wings of Eagles*, and, in *Liberty Valance*, he is compelled to heroic action entailing self-destruction.

But there are limits to what a director can do. For all Ford's technical acumen, formal inventiveness, and dialectical philosophy, at a certain level he was dependent upon the actor. Cinema, almost all the time, is a method of manipulating an actor, of using him as a piece of décor, and of injecting life and spontaneity into him. And virtually all respected actors support this effort.

But the quality in an actor Ford most valued was "naturalness." Naturalness cannot be treated like décor, it cannot be created by a director if it is not already latent in the actor (although it may be encouraged), and it is the rarest quality. It is difficult to appreciate, impossible to analyze, and very few stars ever possessed it. One who did was Will Rogers. Rogers, at least in his Ford pictures, did not *play* his roles.

To explain this, contrast him with Katherine Hepburn or John Wayne, both of whom *play* their parts. Hepburn does so at an intellectual level. Both she and Ford made thorough *studies* of Mary Stuart (in this instance), by reading books and researching costumes, and the character as a result is a synthetic product of their studies: the emotions portrayed result from cogitations by actor and director. The intrigue or fascination of any Hepburn character lies in our attempt to get past the "construct" of her character to the person we sense present before us. But such intellectualization can be limiting: it tends to schematization, since it results from analysis, and real people are usually not schematic. Wayne, in comparison, tends to relate emotionally to his character, rather than seeking to understand him intellectually; this method of feeling (rather than thinking) his way into a character allows the possibility of distractions at the intellectual level—of nuances which do not entirely cohere to an intellectual concept of the character—and which thus give an appealing autonomy to fleeting instants of emotion. Nonetheless, in Wayne too one is slightly (and pleasantly) conscious of a distance between player and character.

Other sorts of distance may be found in, say, Cary Grant, under either Hawks or Hitchcock. To a certain extent, both these directors encourage actors not only to *perform*—to exaggerate, to stylize, often to have a good time *playing*—but also, within this performance, to be themselves. Thus, in speaking of characters in many Hawks or Hitchcock movies, we can often talk interchangeably of, say, "Cary Grant" or the specific name of his personage. And, again, we are conscious of acting.

But we are not conscious of acting with Will Rogers, nor with Harry Carey, Ben Johnson, Francis Ford, J. Farrell MacDonald, Wayne (in *Stagecoach* and occasionally elsewhere), Slim Summerville (in *Submarine Patrol*), Jack Pennick, Helen Chandler (*Salute*), Anna Massey (*Gideon's Day*), Mae Marsh, Ruth Clifford, nor perhaps with Ward Bond, or Grace Kelly (in *Mogambo*). Naturalness, in these and other cases, means the absence of an apparent distance between character and player. Thus, in discussing John

Ford pictures, it seems more appropriate to designate a character *solely* by the name of his personage, and almost never by the name of the actor. Of course, naturalness is an immeasurable quality, and evaluations of it may differ. But one thing is certain: the sort of performances that generally win plaudits from critics and admiration from audiences are not of this sort at all, but precisely those in which distance is most evident (i.e., in which one senses the actor acting). Ford, for all his exploitation of distancing devices, tried to avoid distance between player and role (with the special-case exception of *The Man Who Shot Liberty Valance*). He resembles, in this respect, Ophuls and Rossellini, and together they might be contrasted to Sternberg, Hawks, Hitchcock, Lang, Griffith, even Murnau, among whom characters are externalizations or representations, at any rate something other than the essences incorporating them.

Many, but not all, of Ford's nonsynthetic, natural performances are of simple-souled characters, yet they invariably emerge as far more complex than such heady types as Arrowsmith or Mary Stuart. They are all not-of-a-piece types; they are individuals but their glances and gestures do not cohere, do not uniformly contribute to a single impression; they always leave us feeling that we are seeing only bits and pieces of who they really are. They do not "satisfy," they just "be," tantalizingly, hidden, but free, self-willed, naturally theatrical, and alive.

"I learned a great deal from Harry Carey," said Ford. "He was a slow moving actor when he was afoot. You could read his mind, peer into his eyes and see him think."[64] "The secret," said Ford of moviemaking, "is people's faces, their eye expression, their movements."[65]

It is because John Ford's movies center contemplatively on the most real qualities of actors that a corrective balance is attained with his synthetic qualities of expressionism, just as emotional instinct balances intellectual analysis.

Notes

Abbreviations

Anderson   Lindsay Anderson, *About John Ford* (London: Plexus, 1981).

Bogdanovich   Peter Bogdanovich, *John Ford*, 2d ed. (Berkeley: University of California Press, 1978).

Dan Ford   *Pappy: The Life of John Ford* (Englewood Cliffs, N. J.: Prentice-Hall, 1979).

JFP   The John Ford Papers, Lilly Library, Indiana University. Includes reminiscences undated, but presumably c. 1973.

Parrish   Robert Parrish, *Growing Up in Hollywood* (New York: Harcourt Brace Jovanovich, 1976).

Sinclair   Andrew Sinclair, *John Ford: A Biography* (New York: Dial, 1979).

Wilkinson   James L. Wilkinson, *An Introduction to the Career and Films of John Ford*, unpublished M.A. thesis, UCLA, August 1960 (microfilm copy in Library and Museum of the Performing Arts, Lincoln Center, New York).

1 Prologue: Youth and Apprenticeship

1. Biographical information throughout the book derives chiefly from Dan Ford, Sinclair, Wilkinson (whose family tree I have revised), the John Ford Papers, and interviews with Cecil McLean de Prida, Harry Carey, Jr., and George O'Brien.

Ford's birth certificate is reproduced in Wilkinson and in the Film Study Center at the Museum of Modern Art, New York. Baptismal information was obtained by Grafton Nunes.

2. Philip Jenkinson, unreleased filmed interview with Ford, 1969.

3. Quoted in Wilkinson, p. 17, from his interview with Francis Ford, January 21, 1951.

4. Ford's reminiscences, JFP.

5. Quoted in Walter Wagner, *You Must Remember This* (New York: Putnam's, 1975), p. 57.

6. Quoted in Sinclair, p. 11, from taped interview by Bogdanovich, JFP.

7. Ford's reminiscences, JFP.

8. Bogdanovich, p. 108.

9. Wilkinson, p. 23, from letter from boyhood friend Joseph D. McDonnell.

10. Josephine Feeney's reminiscences, JFP.

11. Ford's reminiscences, JFP.

12. Quoted in Wagner, *You Must Remember This*, p. 57.

13. Quoted in Eric Leguèbe, *Le Cinéma Americain par ses auteurs* (Paris: Guy Authier, 1977), p. 75. My translation.

14. For Francis Ford, see my "Brother Feeney," *Film Comment*, November 1976, pp. 12–18. For the Melies Company, see runs of *Film Index* and *Moving Picture World*; Madeleine Malthête-Méliès, *Méliès l'enchanteur* (Paris: Hachette, 1973); Patrick McInroy, "Hollywood Ruined S. A. Filming," *San Antonio Light*, May 30, 1976, "Today" section, p. 1. For Ince, see Ince, "The Early Days at Kay Bee," *Photoplay*, March 1919, pp. 42–46; George Pratt, "See Mr. Ince . . . ," *Image*, 1956, pp. 100–111; George Mitchell, "Thomas Ince," *Films in Review*, October 1960, pp. 464–84; Paul O'Dell, *Griffith and the Rise of Hollywood* (New York: Castle, 1970); David Robinson, *Hollywood in the Twenties* (New York: A. S. Barnes, 1968); Jean Mitry, *Histoire du cinéma*, vol. 1. (Paris: Editions Universitaires, 1968), pp. 332, 342, 437–43, a great improvement over his earlier articles but still a bit fanciful. Jon Tuska, *The Filming of the West* (New York: Doubleday, 1976), pp. 25–30, perhaps overstates somewhat the case for Francis Ford. See also Fred C. Balshofer and Arthur Miller, *One Reel a Week* (Berkeley: University of California Press, 1967), as well as the records of the New York Motion Picture Company from 1913 onward, at the Wisconsin Center for Film Research, Madison, which, however, provide only scant information.

15. *Motion Picture Directory*, 1921, p. 263.

16. "Francis Ford Expresses His Ideas on Serials," *Moving Picture World*, August 16, 1919, p. 998.

17. Bogdanovich, p. 40.

18. Universal's *Moving Picture Weekly*, October 16, 1915, p. 41.

19. Richard Willis, "Francis Ford, of the Gold Seal Company," *Motion Picture Magazine*, June 1915, p. 104.

20. Ibid., pp. 101–2.

21. Ibid., p. 104.

22. Ince, "Early Days," p. 44.

23. Anthony Slide and Robert Gitt, "Frank Baker," unpublished interview, July 30, 1977, unpaginated.

24. Theodore Huff Memorial Film Society, handout, March 23, 1970.

25. "Francis Ford Expresses His Ideas on Serials."

26. *Moving Picture World*, August 27, 1927, p. 588.

27. Slide and Gitt, "Frank Baker."

28. Willis, "Francis Ford," p. 101.

29. Quoted in Frank S. Nugent, "Hollywood's Favorite Rebel," *The Saturday Evening Post*, September 23, 1949, p. 97.

30. Ibid.

31. Quoted in Cecilia Ager, "Then and Now," *The New York Times Magazine*, September 20, 1959, p. 62.

32. Ford's reminiscences, JFP.

33. Quoted in Richard Schickel, "Good Days, Good Years," *Harpers*, October 1970, p. 46.

34. Author's interview with Cecil McLean de Prida, March 1979.

35. April 28, 1917.

36. *Moving Picture Weekly*, May 19, 1917, p. 18.

37. Ibid., June 2, 1917, p. 19.

38. Quoted in Wilkinson, p. 186.

39. Ibid.

40. Quoted in *Moving Picture Weekly*, July 28, 1917, p. 11.

41. *Los Angeles Evening Herald Examiner*, February 28, 1944, p. B4.

42. Bogdanovich, p. 39.

43. *Moving Picture Weekly*, August 18, 1917; also, *Moving Picture World*, September 1, 1917, p. 1433. But the present "happy" ending is given in *Moving Picture Weekly*, January ?, 1925.

44. Bogdanovich, p. 108.

45. Wagner, *You Must Remember This*, p. 59.

46. Author's interview with Olive Carey, March 1979.

47. Author's interview with Harry Carey, Jr., March 1979.

48. Olive Carey's reminiscences, JFP.

49. Author's interview with Olive Carey.

50. *Los Angeles Evening Herald Examiner*, February 28, 1944, p. B4.

51. Arthur H. Lewis, *It Was Fun While It Lasted* (New York: Trident Press, 1973), p. 313.

52. Author's interview with Harry Carey, Jr.

53. *Moving Picture World*, March 29, 1919, p. 1768.

54. Anthony Slide and June Banker, unpublished interview with Mary Ford, 1970, unpaginated.

55. Ibid.

56. Letter begun November 19, 1921, from John to Mary Ford, JFP.

57. Letter, January (?), 1922, from John to Mary Ford, JFP.

58. Dan Ford, p. 24.

59. List from George N. Fenin and William K. Everson, *The Western* (New York: Grossman, 1973), p. 139.

60. Quoted in Bertrand Tavernier, "John Ford à Paris," *Positif* 82 (March 1967), p. 20. My translation.

61. Anderson, p. 20.

62. Quoted in Kevin Brownlow, *The War, the West, and the Wilderness* (New York: Knopf, 1978), p. 392.

63. Author's interview with Frank Baker, March 1979.

64. Author's interview with Cecil McLean de Prida.

65. Bogdanovich, p. 47.

66. Dan Ford, p. 33

67. Many mysteries would clarify, were less early Ford lost.

68. Author's interview with George O'Brien, May 1979.

69. Quoted in notes of Maurice Zolotow, Zolotow Manuscripts, Library of the University of Texas, Austin.

70. Quoted by Dan Ford, JFP.

71. Author's interview with Frank Baker.

72. Ibid.

73. Ibid.

74. Ibid.

75. Ibid.

76. Ibid.

77. Ibid.

78. Quoted by Dan Ford, JFP.

79. Slide and Banker, interview with Mary Ford.

80. Mary Ford's reminiscences, JFP.

81. John Ford's reminiscences, JFP.

82. Author's interview with George O'Brien.

83. Letter from John to Mary Ford, January 1931, JFP.

84. Author's interview with George O'Brien.

85. Ibid.

86. Jon Tuska, interview with H. Bruce Humberstone, in *Close Up: The Contract Director* (Metuchen, N.J.: Scarecrow Press, 1976).

87. Dan Ford, p. 67.

88. Ibid., p. 68.

89. Sinclair, p. 38, and author's interview with Cecil McLean de Prida.

90. Author's interview with Frank Baker.

2 First Period (1927–1935): The Age of Introspection

1. *Moving Picture World*, March 26, 1927, p. 342. Most sources estimate audiences were roughly equally male and female, but no definite information exists.

2. Ibid., March 3, 1927, p. 35.

3. Erich Rohmer, *L'organisation de l'espace dans le "Faust" de Murnau* (Paris: Editions 10/18, 1977), pp. 112, 118. My translation.

4. *Moving Picture World*, April 2, 1927, p. 490.

5. Rohmer, "Faust," p. 32.

6. John Ford, "Veteran Producer Muses," *The New York Times*, June 10, 1928, sec. 8, p. 4.

7. *Moving Picture World*, April 21, 1928, p. 342.

8. *Film Spectator*, May 12, 1928, pp. 5–7.

9. Ibid., November 3, 1928, p. 10, and November 10, 1928, pp. 6–7.

10. *The New York Times*, October 11, 1930, p. 21.

11. Quoted in Juliet Benita Colman, *Ronald Colman: A Very Private Person* (New York: Morrow, 1975), p. 113.

12. Richard Griffith, *Samuel Goldwyn: The Producer and His Film* (New York: Simon & Schuster, 1956), p. 21.

13. John Brosnan, *Movie Magic* (New York: St. Martin's Press, 1974), pp. 68–71.

14. Bogdanovich, p. 57.

15. Ibid.

16. Max Steiner, "Scoring the Film," in Nancy Naumburg, ed., *We Make the Movies* (New York: Norton, 1937), p. 221.

17. Bogdanovich, p. 59.

18. Ibid., p. 47.

19. R. G. Collingwood, *The Idea of History* (New York: Oxford University Press, 1946), p. 44.

20. Ibid., p. 39, quoting Furneaux, ed., *Cornelii Taciti Annalium*, Libri I–IV (Oxford, 1886), pp. 3–4.

21. Jean Mitry, *John Ford* (Paris: Editions Universitaires, 1954), pp. 23, 28–29. My translation.

22. See Carlos Clarens, *Crime Movies* (New York: Norton, 1980), p. 141.

23. Philip Dunne, *Take Two: A Life in Movies and Politics* (New York: McGraw-Hill, 1980), p. 92.

24. Dan Ford, p. 98.

25. Author's interview with Frank Baker.

26. Reminiscences of Katharine Hepburn (with John Ford), c. 1972, JFP.

27. Ibid.

28. Dan Ford, p. 99.

29. Ibid.

30. Letter from Katharine Hepburn to John Ford, April 10, 1937, JFP.

31. Reminiscences of John Ford, JFP. The assertion that his mother had thirteen children is most likely blarney; that he was the last certainly is.

32. Quoted in Howard Sharpe, "The Star Creators of Hollywood," *Photoplay*, October 1936, p. 100. Reprint: see Biliography.

33. Parrish, p. 131.

34. Author's interview with Frank Baker. The story has been told many times, but Baker claims to have witnessed it.

35. Recounted by Dan Ford, JFP.

36. Author's interview with Leon Selditz, April 1979.

37. Reminiscences of Katherine Clifton, JFP.

38. Reminiscences of Katharine Hepburn, JFP.

39. Reminiscences of Nunnally Johnson, JFP.

40. Quoted in Max Wilk, *The Wit and Wisdom of Hollywood* (New York: Atheneum, 1971), pp. 278–79.

41. Reminiscences of Nunnally Johnson, JFP.

3   Second Period (1935–1947): The Age of Idealism

1. Quoted in Anderson, p. 63.

2. Anderson, p. 22.

3. George J. Mitchell, "Ford on Ford," *Films in Review*, June 1964, pp. 324–25.

4. Bogdanovich, p. 59.

5. Anderson, p. 88.

6. Quoted in Anderson, p. 86.

7. Dan Ford, p. 84. Nichols, in Anderson (p. 240), gives a quite different account, claiming the script was essentially his own—and suggesting that Ford may

imagine after a film that his (Ford's) contributions were greater than they were.

8. See, for example, in Lewis Jacobs, *The Rise of the American Film* (New York: Teachers College Press, 1967), pp. 479–84.

9. Author's interview with Frank Baker.

10. John Baxter, *The Cinema of John Ford* (New York: A. S. Barnes, 1971), p. 49.

11. Peter C. Rollins, "Will Rogers and the Relevance of Nostalgia: *Steamboat Round the Bend*," in John E. O'Connor and Martin A. Jackson, eds., *American History /American Film* (New York: Ungar, 1979), pp. 78–79.

12. Bogdanovich, p. 57.

13. Robert Wilson, ed., *The Film Criticism of Otis Ferguson* (Philadelphia: Temple University Press, 1971), p. 121.

14. Sharpe, "Star Creators," p. 98.

15. Mary Astor, *A Life on Film* (New York: Dell, 1972), p. 134.

16. Mel Gussow, *Don't Say Yes Until I Finish Talking* (New York: Pocket Books, 1972), p. 150.

17. Quoted in Bob Thomas, ed., *Directors in Action* (New York: Bobbs Merrill, 1973), pp. 143–44.

18. Quoted in Paul Jensen, "Dudley Nichols," in Richard Corliss, ed., *The Hollywood Screenwriters* (New York: Avon, 1972), p. 118.

19. Nick Browne, "The Spectator-in-the-Text: The Rhetoric of *Stagecoach*," *Film Quarterly*, Winter 1975, pp. 26–38.

20. Ibid., pp. 35–37.

21. Ibid., p. 31.

22. Ibid., p. 38.

23. Quoted in Thomas, *Directors in Action*, p. 160.

24. Bogdanovich, p. 20.

25. Quoted in Axel Madsen, interview with Ford, *Cahiers du Cinéma* 183 (October 1966), p. 48. My translation.

26. Quoted by Fonda in Mike Steen, "Henry Fonda," in *Hollywood Speaks! An Oral History* (New York: Putnam's, 1974), p. 40.

27. Editors of *Cahiers du Cinéma*, "John Ford's *Young Mr. Lincoln*," *Cahiers du Cinéma* 223 (August 1970), pp. 29–47. Translation by Helene Lackner and Diana Matias, in *Screen*, Autumn 1972, pp. 5–28. Reprinted in Gerald Mast and Marshall Cohen, eds., *Film Theory and Criticism*, 2d ed. (New York: Oxford University Press, 1979), pp. 778–831. The *Cahiers* article, although thoroughly meretricious, has spawned a host of admiring commentaries—for which reason I have felt obliged to consider it here. Some of the commentaries are listed in the Bibliography.

28. J. A. Place, *The Non-Western Films of John Ford* (New York: Citadel, 1979), pp. 56–67.

29. Robert Parrish, "Témoignage sur John Ford," *Présence du Cinéma* 21 (March 1965), pp. 18–20. My translation.

30. Andrew Sarris, *The John Ford Movie Mystery* (Bloomington: Indiana University Press, 1976), p. 50.

31. *The New York Times*, January 25, 1940, p. 17; January 28, 1940, sec. 9, p. 5.

32. Mitchell, "Ford on Ford," p. 331.

33. Quoted in Tavernier, "John Ford à Paris," p. 18. My translation.

34. Dan Ford, p. 143.

35. *Cahiers du Cinéma* 165 (April 1965), p. 11.

36. *Friday,* August 9, 1940.

37. Quoted in Anderson, p. 247.

38. David Thomson, "John Ford," in *A Biographical Dictionary of Film* (New York: Morrow, 1979), pp. 185–86. Anderson (p. 71) writes in similar terms, alas.

39. Dunne, *Take Two,* p. 94.

40. Quoted in Gussow, *Don't Say Yes,* p. 87.

41. Ibid., p. 88.

42. Author's interview with Anna Lee, March 1979.

43. Quoted by Dan Ford, p. 158.

44. Jenkinson, interview with Ford.

45. Author's interview with Cecil McLean de Prida. Information about Ford's activities during the war derives from Mrs. de Prida, Dan Ford, Sinclair, Parrish, author's interview with George O'Brien, and materials in JFP.

46. Slide and Banker, interview with Mary Ford.

47. Quoted in *Los Angeles Evening Herald Examiner,* February 28, 1944, p. B4.

48. Slide and Banker, interview with Mary Ford.

49. Parrish (pp. 137–42) describes in detail how Ford sent him and another man to take spy photos of the White House; Parrish was arrested, but Ford presided over his court of inquiry.

50. Author's interview with Harry Carey, Jr.

51. Parrish, p. 142.

52. Nugent, "Hollywood's Favorite Rebel," p. 25.

53. Madsen, interview with Ford, October 1966, pp. 48–51.

54. Photographer Second Class Jack MacKenzie, Jr., tells a slightly different story regarding his activity. See *American Cinematographer,* February 1944.

55. Jenkinson, interview with Ford.

56. Parrish (pp. 144–51) describes Ford's machinations in great detail.

57. Ibid., p. 145.

58. Ibid., p. 151.

59. Dan Ford, p. 176.

60. Sinclair, p. 114.

61. Letter, dated 1942, from Ford to Wellman, JFP.

62. Dan Ford, p. 183.

63. Ibid., p. 182.

64. Ibid.

65. Letter, dated June 1, 1943, from Mary to John Ford, JFP.

66. Parrish (p. 152), Sinclair (p. 115), and numerous references in JFP contradict Dan Ford's statement (p. 185) that Ford flew.

67. Dan Ford, p. 188.

68. Sinclair, p. 124.

69. Author's interview with John Stafford.

70. Sinclair, p. 118.

71. Parrish, p. 159.

72. Sinclair, p. 126.

73. Dan Ford, p. 274.

74. Bogdanovich, p. 82.

75. Anderson, pp. 20–21.

76. Ibid., p. 73.

77. Mitchell, "Ford on Ford," p. 331.

78. Dan Ford, p. 199.

79. Letter, October 17, 1946, from Ford to Zanuck, JFP.

80. Anderson, p. 22.

81. Bogdanovich, p. 85.

82. Anderson, p. 90.

83. Author's interview with Harry Carey, Jr.

84. Reminiscences of Olive Carey, JFP.

85. Author's interview with Harry Carey, Jr.

86. Dan Ford, p. 259.

87. Letter, dated 1952, from Mary Ford (Frank's wife) to Mary Ford (John's wife).

88. Author's interview with Frank Baker.

4   Third Period (1948–1961): The Age of Myth

1. Sarris, *John Ford Movie Mystery*, p. 124.

2. "Burt Kennedy Interviews John Ford," *Action*, August 1968. Reprinted in Thomas, *Directors in Action*, p. 134.

3. Anderson, p. 22.

4. Tavernier, "John Ford à Paris," p. 17. My translation.

5. Quoted in Anderson, p. 244.

6. Bogdanovich, p. 86.

7. Jenkinson, interview with Ford.

8. Madsen, interview with Ford, October 1966, p. 51.

9. Quoted in Anderson, p. 244.

10. Bogdanovich, p. 88.

11. Tavernier, "John Ford à Paris," p. 20. My translation.

12. Mitchell, "Ford on Ford," p. 33.

13. Raoul Walsh, *Each Man in His Time* (New York: Farrar Straus Giroux, 1974), p. 186.

14. Jean Mitry, interview with Ford, *Cahiers du Cinéma* 45 (March 1955), p. 5. My translation.

15. Anderson, p. 22.

16. Ibid.

17. Mitchell, "Ford on Ford," p. 332.

18. Anderson, p. 19.

19. Ibid.

20. Mitchell, "Ford on Ford," p. 332.

21. Bogdanovich, p. 19.

22. Anderson, p. 22.

23. Mitchell, "Ford on Ford," p. 332.

24. Joe McInerney, "John Wayne Talks Tough," *Film Comment*, September 1972, p. 53.

25. "Kennedy Interviews Ford," p. 134.

26. Tavernier, "John Ford à Paris," p. 17. My translation.

27. Mitry, interview with Ford, p. 6. My translation.

28. Quoted by Dore Schary, *Heyday* (New York: Berkeley Books, 1979), p. 256.

29. Quoted in Bill Libby, "The Old Wrangler Rides Again," *Cosmopolitan*, March 1964.

30. Quoted in Joseph McBride, "*The Searchers*," *Sight and Sound*, Spring 1972, p. 212.

31. Ford recounts this story in Mark Haggard, "Ford in Person," *Focus on Film* 6 (Spring 1971), p. 33.

32. Author's interview with Harry Carey, Jr.

33. Author's interview with John Stafford.

34. Haggard, "Ford in Person," p. 32.

35. Author's interview with Harry Carey, Jr.

36. Draft of speech, dated 1933, JFP.

37. Remark to author by Maurice Rapf, 1976.

38. Resolution, dated 1947, JFP.

39. Draft of letter, dated January 1952, from Ford to Department of Defense, JFP.

40. Kenneth L. Geist, *Pictures Will Talk* (New York: Scribner's, 1978), pp. 202–4.

41. Bogdanovich, p. 14.

42. Leguèbe, "John Ford," p. 77. My translation.

43. Letter, dated September 1937, from Ford to Bob Ford, JFP.

44. Tavernier, "John Ford à Paris," pp. 13–14. My translation. On other occasions, Ford made vague allusions to having voted for Goldwater and, later, for Nixon, his reason being that he *knew* them both, rather than for political motives.

45. Anderson, p. 25.

46. Parrish, p. 154.

47. Allan Dwan's reminiscences (with Dan Ford), JFP.

48. Dan Ford, p. 268.

49. Bogdanovich, p. 96.

50. Louis Marcorelles, *Cahiers du Cinéma* 85 (July 1958), p. 54. My translation.

51. Michael Killanin, "Poet in an Iron Mask," *Films and Filming*, February 1958, p. 9.

52. Ibid.

53. Marcorelles, *Cahiers* 85, p. 54. My translation.

54. Bogdanovich, p. 102.

55. Author's interview with Anna Lee.

56. Colin Young, "The Old Dependables," *Film Quarterly*, Fall 1969, pp. 8–9.

57. Louis Marcorelles, *Cahiers du Cinéma* 101 (November 1959), pp. 48–49. My translation.

58. J. A. Place, *The Western Films of John Ford* (New York: Citadel, 1975), p. 179.

59. Quoted in Joseph McBride and Michael Wilmington, *John Ford* (New York: Da Capo, 1975), p. 169.

60. Bogdanovich, p. 97.

61. Madsen, interview with Ford, *Cahiers du Cinéma* 168 (July 1965), p. 79. My translation.

5 **Final Period (1962–1965): The Age of Mortality**

1. Letter, dated June 20, 1951, from Barbara to John Ford, JFP.

2. Author's interview with Frank Baker.

3. If, however, I read allusions in the correspondence in JFP of this period cor-

rectly, Pat ended up living on a lot in which John had invested money—his sole real estate investment.

4. Bob Thomas, *Selznick* (New York: Pocket Books, 1970), p. 259.

5. Author's interview with Harry Carey, Jr.

6. Author's interview with Frank Baker.

7. Hedda Hopper, unpublished conversation with Ford, April 13, 1962, Library of Motion Picture Arts and Sciences, Beverly Hills.

8. Letter, dated May 19, 1959, from Bea Benjamin to Captain Henry Yeager, JFP.

9. Author's interview with Frank Baker.

10. Slide and Banker, interview with Mary Ford.

11. Scott Eyman, interview with William Clothier, *Take One* 4, no. 8 (November–December 1973 [published March 1975], p. 13. That it was a *toy:* reminiscences of Clothier (with Dan Ford), JFP.

12. Quoted in author's interview with Harry Carey, Jr.

13. Hedda Hopper, conversation with Ford.

14. John Ford, "Veteran Producer Muses," p. 4.

15. Bogdanovich, p. 99.

16. Ibid., p. 16.

17. Remark to author, 1975.

18. See Jean-Louis Comolli, "Signes de piste," *Cahiers du Cinéma* 164 (March 1965), p. 75; Dan Ford, pp. 296–305; Sinclair, pp. 198–200; remarks by scenarist James R. Webb, in Philippe Haudiquet, *John Ford* (Paris: Seghers, 1966), pp. 128–30.

19. François Truffaut, *Hitchcock* (New York: Simon and Schuster, 1966); e.g., on *Paradine Case*, p. 127; on *Strangers on a Train*, p. 146; on *I Confess*, p. 149; et al.

20. Andrew Sarris, "John Ford," in *The American Cinema* (New York: Dutton, 1968), p. 48.

21. Sarris, *John Ford Movie Mystery*, p. 160.

22. Bogdanovich, p. 104.

23. Madsen, interview with Ford, October 1966, p. 42. My translation.

24. Noel Burch, *To the Distant Observer* (Berkeley: University of California Press, 1979). One of Burch's principal theses lies in his attempt to contrast Japan's prewar *presentational* modes of cinema with Hollywood's *representational* (i.e., illusion of realism) modes, but his argument seems to me to reveal prejudices that blind him to the essential features of Western cinema—certainly to auteurist cinema.

25. Leguèbe, "John Ford," pp. 78–79. My translation.

26. Bogdanovich, p. 141.

27. Sarris, *John Ford Movie Mystery*, p. 185.

28. Arthur Knight, a review of *7 Women*, *Saturday Review*, January 8, 1966, p. 97.

29. Madsen, interview with Ford, October 1966, p. 51. My translation.

30. Sarris, *John Ford Movie Mystery*, p. 185.

31. Author's interview with Anna Lee.

32. Joyce Haber, "If I Could Film a Dream . . ." *Philadelphia Inquirer*, May 13, 1972.

33. Tavernier, "John Ford à Paris," p. 18.

34. Slide and Banker, interview with Mary Ford.

35. Reminiscences of Bea Benjamin, in JFP.

36. Remark to author, 1974.

37. Author's interview with Frank Baker.

38. Slide and Banker, interview with Mary Ford.

6 Conclusion

1. Sharpe, "Star Creators," p. 98.
2. Slide and Gitt, "Frank Baker."
3. Balshofer and Miller, *One Reel a Week*, p. 186.
4. Quoted in Leonard Maltin, *The Art of the Cinematographer* (New York: Dover, 1978), p. 70.
5. Ibid.
6. Balshofer and Miller, *One Reel a Week*, p. 187.
7. Quoted in Steen, "Henry Fonda," p. 27.
8. Karyn Kay and Gerald Peary, "Talking to Pat O'Brien," *Velvet Light Trap* 15 (Fall 1975), p. 32.
9. Astor, *A Life on Film*, p. 134.
10. Raymond Massey, *A Hundred Different Lives* (Boston: Little Brown, 1979), pp. 212, 215.
11. Quoted in Sinclair, p. 168.
12. Author's interview with Anna Lee.
13. Parrish, p. 149.
14. Author's interview with Ruth Clifford, March 1979.
15. Author's interview with Harry Carey, Jr.
16. Dan Ford, p. 158.
17. *7 Women* pressbook, Free Library of Philadelphia Theater Collection.
18. Author's interview with Harry Carey, Jr.
19. *7 Women* pressbook.
20. Sharpe, "Star Creators," p. 100.
21. Frederick T. Weber, "Portrait Painting," *Encyclopaedia Britannica* (1957).
22. Mitchell, "Ford on Ford," p. 33.
23. Eyman, interview with William Clothier, p. 32.
24. Gabriel Figueroa, letter to author, May 1979.
25. Mitchell, "Ford on Ford," p. 26.
26. "Kennedy Interviews Ford," p. 135.
27. Ibid., p. 136.
28. Robert Parrish, "De Chaplin à Fuller," *Cahiers du Cinéma* 142 (April 1963), p. 11. My translation.
29. Lefty Hough's reminiscences, JFP.
30. Author's interview with Barbara Ford, March 1979.
31. Quoted in William Frough, *The Screenwriter Looks at the Screenwriter* (New York: Macmillan, 1972), p. 240.
32. Dan Ford, p. 284.
33. Anderson, p. 244.
34. Quoted in Wilkinson.
35. Quoted in Sinclair (p. 194), from *Films and Filming*, April 1966.
36. Frank Nugent, "In Remembrance of Hot-Foots Past," *The New York Times*, March 3, 1949, p. 33.
37. Tavernier, "John Ford à Paris," p. 18.
38. Jensen, "Dudley Nichols," p. 111.
39. McBride and Wilmington, *John Ford*, p. 24.
40. Hal Humphrey, "Veteran John Ford Looks Back," *Philadelphia Bulletin*, April 11, 1965.
41. *7 Women* pressbook.

42. Madsen, interview with Ford, July 1965, p. 79. My translation.

43. Mitry, *John Ford*, p. 26. My translation.

44. Stanley Cavell, *The World Viewed* (Cambridge: Harvard University Press, 1979), p. 33.

45. Quoted in Jacques Barzun, *The Energies of Art* (New York: Harper Bros., 1956), p. 257.

46. Ibid., p. 262.

47. Anderson, p. 242.

48. Killanin, "Poet in an Iron Mask," p. 9.

49. Sharpe, "Star Creators," p. 98.

50. Author's interview with Harry Carey, Jr.

51. Sharpe, "Star Creators," p. 99.

52. Author's interview with Anna Lee.

53. Arnold Hauser, *The Social History of Art,* vol. 4 (New York: Random House), p. 30.

54. Mitchell, "Ford on Ford," p. 330.

55. Ford, "Veteran Producer Muses," p. 4.

56. Grady Johnson, "A Paean of Economy," *The New York Times*, June 27, 1944, sec. 2, p. 4.

57. Sharpe, "Star Creators," p. 98.

58. Wilkinson.

59. Anderson, p. 237.

60. Sharpe, "Star Creators," p. 100.

61. McBride and Wilmington, *John Ford*, p. 32.

62. Ford, "Veteran Producer Muses," p. 4.

63. When Straub made this remark to the author in 1975 (after seeing *Pilgrimage* and *Donovan's Reef*) he was referring not so much to Ford's *acting style*—in that sense *no* films are truly Brechtian—as to Ford's manner of stripping naked social ideologies that are elsewhere unacknowledged. To Joseph McBride, Straub said Ford is the most Brechtian of filmmakers, "because he shows things that make people think . . . by [making] the audience collaborate on the film" (McBride and Wilmington, *John Ford*, p. 108). McBride analyzes *Fort Apache* in this light, pointing out how Captain York donning Colonel Thursday's hat at the end is a Brechtian device [like the cardinal donning the pope's robes in Brecht's *Galileo*], and that we see clearly that an insane system needs the dedication of noble men to perpetuate itself.) Less simply, one might call Ford Brechtian because every element in his cinema is engaged dialectically with every other element (whether one speaks of elements of—or between—style, content, myth, ideology, or whatever), with the result that Ford's films are self-reflexive and transparent in their workings.

This notion—essentially the thesis of this book—flies violently in the face of a recent critical tendency to regard the "classical" cinema of Hollywood as a monolithic system that sought to mask its "codes" (e.g., its *montage*) in order to create an apparently unmediated representation of the real world; it sought to entertain passively and left unacknowledged its own governing ideology. (Cf., *Stagecoach*: my argument with Browne ("Spectator-in-the-Text"); also Burch, *Distant Observer;* Robert Phillip Kolker, *The Altering Eye* [New York: Oxford, 1983]; Thomas Schatz, *Hollywood Genres* [New York: Random House, 1981]). "Modernist" (i.e., some post-1960) cinema, on the other hand, subverts our absorption in emotion, story, or character, and exposes its "codes" (e.g., by showing the camera, discordant editing, having an actor speak directly to us), in order to force us to relate intellectually rather than through emotional identification.

In these circles, Straub is admired as epitomizing "modernist" cinema, while Ford is often derided (although not by most of the above-named critics) as a sentimental reactionary. Thus Straub's comparison of Brecht and Ford caused considerable head-shaking. It is, of course, generally agreed that many films cater exclusively to an audience's desire for passive spectacle (e.g., *Star Wars*, some of Hitchcock); and all research shows that audiences generally watch movies in order *not* to think. Nonetheless, the fallacies of "modernist" critics are multitudinous (even including their arrogation of the label "modern"). Firstly, their premise of a monolithic classical system is a pure fantasy that reveals little sensibility for the complexity of pre-1960 cinema and almost no acquaintance with the actual films themselves. Secondly, they naively assume that audiences can be *forced* to think, whereas "modernist" techniques soon lose their initial shock and audiences happily re-immerse themselves into the fictional worlds of even the most determinedly antipathetic movies. Thirdly, because their basis is exclusively materialist, they, like Grierson and Aristarco before them, distrust emotions and aestheticism and would destroy the art of cinema in favor of a cinema of political propaganda.

An examination of Brecht's 1930 table, in which he gave cursory comparison between the (bad) "dramatic" and the (good, Brechtian) "epic" theaters, will, in the light of Straub and this book, show Ford very much on the "epic" side—the "modernist":

Dramatic Theater	Epic Theater
plot	narrative
implicates spectator into drama	makes spectator an observer
wears down his capacity for action	arouses his capacity for action
provides him with sensations	forces him to make decisions
provides experience	provides a picture of the world
involves the spectator	confronts the spectator
suggestion	argument
feelings are preserved	feelings are propelled into perceptions
man is assumed known	man is the object of inquiry
man unalterable	man alterable and altering
suspense about the outcome	suspense about the progress
each scene exists for another	each scene for itself
linear development	in curves
evolutionary determinism	evolutionary leaps
the world, as it is	the world, as it becomes
what man ought to do	what man is forced to do
man as a fixed point	man as a process
his instincts	his motivations
thought determines being	social being determines thought

(Brecht did not intend, obviously, that epic theater be absolutely one way and not at all the other way; it is a question more of tendency.)

64. Ford, unpublished, untitled article, supposed to be on "The Man's Story," for a projected book by Bill Hawkes, 1946, JFP. Ford, of course, went out of his way to show that he was not to be categorized as a "man's director."

65. Reminiscences of Barbara Ford, with John Ford, JFP.

Appendix:

Grosses and Earnings

Ford's yearly earnings are taken from working copies of his federal or (when asterisked) state tax forms, supplemented by figures given on film contracts or as noted by Dan Ford. Salary figures for specific films are given when known and are included in the yearly earnings totals (but not necessarily during the year of the film's release). When a salary includes a percentage (e.g., +10%), such additional payment was due only after twice the cost of the negative had been earned, and, usually, after distribution costs were deducted as well. The latter were not inconsiderable. 7 *Women*, for example, cost $2,308,000 to make ("negative cost") and by 1970 had grossed $937,432 worldwide, but distribution costs amounted to $930,000, bringing 7 *Women*'s net loss to $2,300,000.

Grosses generally are listed for the first year of release domestically; foreign first year earnings often equalled domestic ones. The figure after a film title is the cost of the negative. Business is rated *Excellent, Good, Fair,* or *Poor,* and for this information I am indebted to Lee Beaupré, who, however, cautions that prewar figures may be extremely untrustworthy. E = Estimate. A = Actual rental figure.

Year	Ford's Earnings Year (total) Film fees	Title—Negative Cost (when known)	Domestic Gross (first year)
1917	$75 to $100 weekly		
1918	$150 weekly		
1919	$300 weekly		

Year	Ford's Earnings Year (total)	Film fees	Title—Negative Cost (when known)	Domestic Gross (first year)
1920	$300 to $600 weekly			
1921	$13,618			
1922	$27,891			
1923	$44,910			
1924	$30,118		The Iron Horse— $280,000	E: $2 million plus (worldwide)
1925	$73,954			
1926	$82,272		3 Bad Men—$650,000	
1927	$83,114			
1928	$47,112			
1929	$133,977		Strong Boy	Fair to Poor
			The Black Watch— $400,000	Good: E: $800,000
			Salute	Fox's best in 1929
1930	$145,094 minus stock loss	$14,000	Men Without Women	Fair to poor
			Born Reckless	Fair to poor
			Up the River	Fair. E: $650,000
1931	$41,952 minus stock loss	$12,000	Seas Beneath	Fair to poor
			The Brat	Poor
			Arrowsmith	Excellent, among year's top 20. A: $1,250,000
1932	$81,130 minus $50,000 stock loss	$36,000	Air Mail—$305,000	Fair
			Flesh	Good. E: $850,000
1933	$72,903		Pilgrimage	Fair to good. E: $650,000
			Doctor Bull	Fair
1934	$141,355		The Lost Patrol— $254,000	Good. E: $750,000
			The World Moves On	Fair. E: $450,000
			Judge Priest	Very good. E: $900,000
1935	$121,290	$50,000	The Whole Town's Talking	Fair. A: $300,000
			The Informer—$215,000	Fair to poor
			Steamboat Round the Bend	Very good. E: $1,000,000
1936	$192,586		The Prisoner of Shark Island	Fair to good. E: $750,000
			Mary of Scotland	Very good. E: $1,000,000
			The Plough and the Stars	Poor
1937	$159,066		Wee Willie Winkie	Very good. E: $1,250,000
		$100,000 + 12%	The Hurricane	Excellent, among year's top 20. E: $1,400,000

Year	Ford's Earnings Year (total)	Film fees	Title—Negative Cost (when known)	Domestic Gross (first year)
1938	$220,068	$75,000	*Four Men and a Prayer*	Fair. E: $600,000
		$75,000	*Submarine Patrol*	Fair to good. E: $750,000
1939	No information	$50,000	*Stagecoach*	Good. E: $1,000,000
		$75,000	*Young Mr. Lincoln*	Fair to good. E: $750,000
		$75,000	*Drums Along the Mohawk*	Very good. E: $1,250,000
1940	$178,000	$75,000	*The Grapes of Wrath*	Good to very good. E: $1,100,000
			The Long Voyage Home	Fair. E: $600,000
1941	$168,000		*Tobacco Road*	Fair to good. E: $900,000
			How Green Was My Valley—$1,300,000	2nd biggest of year, after *Sergeant York*. A: $2,800,000
1942	$27,000			
1943	$14,300			
1944	$22,650			
1945	$115,000	$300,000 (donated)	*They Were Expendable*	Among year's top 20. A: $3,250,000
1946	$141,000		*My Darling Clementine*	Very good. A: $2,750,000 domestic $1,750,000 foreign
1947	$199,000		*The Fugitive*	Poor. E: $750,000
1948	$176,000		*Fort Apache*—$1,200,000	Among year's top 20. A: $3,000,000 domestic $1,900,000 foreign
			3 Godfathers	Fair to good. A: $2,700,000
1949	No information		*She Wore a Yellow Ribbon*—$1,600,000	Very good. A: $2,700,000 domestic $2,500,000 foreign
1950	$188,000		*When Willie Comes Marching Home*	Fair to good. A: $1,700,000
			Wagon Master	Fair to poor. E: $1,000,000
			Rio Grande—$1,238,000	Very good. A: $2,250,000
1951	$133,000			
1952	$258,000		*The Quiet Man*—$1,750,000	In top 10. A: $3,800,000
			What Price Glory	Good. A: $2,000,000
1953	No information		*The Sun Shines Bright*	Poor
1954	$84,000		*Mogambo*	In top 10. A: $5,200,000
1955	$317,000		*The Long Gray Line*—$1,748,000	Very good. A: $3,450,000 domestic $2,150,000 foreign

Year	Ford's Earnings Year (total)	Film fees	Title—Negative Cost (when known)	Domestic Gross (first year)
1956	No information	$175,000 + 10%	*The Searchers*	In top 20. A: $4,450,000
1957	$144,000	No Salary	*The Rising of the Moon—* $256,016	Very poor. A: $950,000 worldwide
			The Wings of Eagles	Good. A: $2,250,000
1958	No information	No salary	*Gideon of Scotland Yard* (U.S.) $453,600	Poor. E: $400,000
		$125,000 + 25%	*The Last Hurrah*	Poor to fair. A: $950,000
1959	No information	$375,000 + 10%	*The Horse Soldiers*	In top 20. A: $3,600,000
1960	$180,000*		*Sergeant Rutledge*	Poor
		$3,500	*The Colter Craven Story*	(Television)
1961	$267,000*	$225,000 + 25% (includes Pat Ford salary)	*Two Rode Together*	Fair. A: $1,600,000
1962	$189,000*	$150,000 + 25% ownership	*The Man Who Shot Liberty Valance—* $3,200,000	Very good. A: $3,200,000
		$50,000	"The Civil War," *How the West Was Won*	
1963	$184,000*		*Donovan's Reef—* $2,686,585	Very good. A: $3,300,000
1964	$137,000	$200,000 + %	*Cheyenne Autumn—* $4,200,000	Good. A: $3,150,000
1965	No information	*$262,00 + %*	*7 Women—*$2,308,190	Very poor. A: (by 1966): $204,000 domestic $51,00 foreign $433,000 domestic $504,000 foreign
1966	$102,000			

No information for years after 1966.
Net worth (1965): E: $1,700,000

Filmography

The present filmography is based upon previously published ones but contains many corrections and additions. Plot summaries for the silent period have been drawn from contemporary periodicals and differ from those in Peter Bogdanovich's filmography, where they appear to have been drawn from Universal's records.

Information on John Ford's work prior to *The Tornado* in 1917 is sketchy. His niece speaks of a film co-directed with Edward Laemmle, for example, of which nothing is known. Ford liked to say he got his start as a director with some action sequences for Carl Laemmle's guests in 1916; these were incorporated into a western directed by someone else (not one by Francis Ford), but nothing else is known. Although John participated in some fashion in thirty or more Francis Ford pictures (possibly beginning with *Lucille Love,* a fifteen-chapter serial issued weekly from April 14, 1914) and worked also for other filmmakers (such as Allan Dwan), only those pictures in which he has been definitely identified have been listed. John Stewart's *Filmarama* (Metuchen, N.J.: Scarecrow Press, 1975) lists, without further detail, two *stage* appearances for Ford: in 1901 (!) in *King's Carnival* and in 1919 in *Tumble In.*

*denotes a presumably lost film.

†denotes films in which Ford participated but which he did not direct.

All films prior to 1928 are silent; all those after 1929 are all-talking. Films in the transition years are identified accordingly.

All films are in black and white, unless otherwise described. For silents, quoted reviews are from trade journals from the weekly number closest to the film's issue date.

*†1914 *The Mysterious Rose* (Gold Seal–Universal). 2 reels. November 24. Director: Francis Ford. Writer: Grace Cunard. Filmed August 7–15. With Francis Ford (Phil Kelly), Grace Cunard (Raffles), Jack Ford (Dopey), Harry Schumm (D.A.'s son), Wilbur Higby (ward boss), Eddie Boland (Yeen Kee).

Political wars between ward bosses and D. A. Detective Kelly solves assassination with two roses as clue, and lets Raffles escape. Sixth in the "My Lady Raffles" series.

*†1915 *Smuggler's Island* (Gold Seal–Universal). 2 reels. January 19. Director: Francis Ford. Writer: Grace Cunard. With Ford, Cunard, Jack Ford (smuggler).

Ford saves Grace from smugglers who capture her when she discovers their lair.

†1915 *The Birth of a Nation* (Epoch Producing Corp.). 12 reels. February 8. Director: D. W. Griffith.

Jack Ford supposedly played a Ku Klux Klansman.

*†1915 *Three Bad Men and a Girl* (101 Bison–Universal). 2 reels. February 20. Director: Francis Ford. Writer: Grace Cunard. Filmed December 23–29. With Francis Ford (Joe), Jack Ford (Jim), Major Paleolagus (Shorty), Grace Cunard (girl), Lewis Short (sheriff), F. J. Denecke (his assistant).

Mistaken for badmen, three good men capture real badmen and free girl from Mexican settlement. Satire on fanciful westerns, murders every fifty feet; Ford leaps seventy-nine feet; Grace crosses chasm on laundryline.

*†1915 *The Hidden City* (101 Bison–Universal). 2 reels. March 27. Director: Francis Ford. Writer: Grace Cunard. With Francis Ford (Lt. Johns), Grace Cunard (princess), Jack Ford (Johns's brother), Eddie Polo (Minister Poleau).

Captured after losing a battle, Johns refuses love of a princess of desert city in India, but she helps Jim escape and substitutes herself as sacrifice to fire god.

*†1915 *The Doorway of Destruction* (101 Bison–Universal). 2 reels. April 17. Director: Francis Ford. Writer: Grace Cunard. Assistant: Jack Ford. Filmed February 26–March 4. With Francis Ford (Col. Patrick Feeney), Jack Ford (Edward Feeney), Mina Cunard (Cecille McLain), Harry Schumm (Gen. McLain), Howard Daniels (Frank).

Sent by British on a suicide mission, an Irish regiment assaults a Sepoy citadel waving an Irish flag made by Feeney's mother.

*†1915 *The Broken Coin* (Special Features–Universal). 44-reel serial: 22 two-reelers released weekly from June 21. Director: Francis Ford. Writer: Grace Cunard, novelized by Emerson Hough. Cameramen: R. E. Irish, Harry Maguire. Assistant: Jack Ford. Exteriors: Bisbee, Calif. With Grace Cunard (Kitty Gray), Francis Ford (Count Frederick), Eddie Polo (Roleau), Harry Schumm (King Michael II), Ernest Schields (Count Sacchio), Jack Ford (Sacchio's accomplice), W. C. Canfield (Gorgas the outlaw), Reese Gardiner (the Apache), Doc Crane (pawnbroker), Harry Mann (servant), Vic Goss (servant), Lewis Short (prime minister), Mr. Uttal (henchman), Bert Wilson (confidante), Mina Cunard (king's sweetheart [also doubled for Grace]), Carl Laemmle (editor).

Girl reporter finds half a coin hinting at vast treasure and sets off to Balkan kingdom of Gretzhoffen, where she becomes involved in palace intrigues and daredevil adventures.

*†1915 *The Campbells Are Coming* (Broadway Feature–Universal). 4 reels. October 16. Director: Francis Ford. Writer: Grace Cunard. With portions filmed in late 1914. With Francis Ford (Nana Sahib), Duke Worne (Azimooah), Grace Cunard (Scotch lassie), F. J. Denecke (Campbell), Harry Schumm (lassie's sweetheart), Lewis Short (her father), Jack Ford, 7,000 extras. Working titles: "The Lumber Yard Gang," "The Yellow Streak."

Sepoy, 1857: Nana Sahib ascends throne, sends Azimooah to Queen Victoria to learn father's pension discontinued because Nan is only an adopted son. Returning, Azimooah falls in love with Scotch lassie, whom Nan seizes for harem but who escapes during rebellion. The Campbells attack Lucknow in mammoth battle, and Nan is left prey to jungle beasts without food or water.

*†1916 *The Strong Arm Squad* (Rex-Universal). 1 reel. February 15. Director: Francis Ford. Writer: Grace Cunard. Filmed in Maine, November 26–29, 1915. With Francis Ford (Phil Kelly), Elsie Maison, Cecil McLean, Jack Ford (crook), William White (detective), Dandy Bowen (police chief), John, Abbie, Pat, Eddie, Mary, and Jo Feeney.

Kelly allows sweetheart's brother to escape when proved head of the Lumber Yard Gang.

*†1916 *Chicken-Hearted Jim* (Rex-Universal). 1 reel. April 23. Director-writer: Francis Ford. Filmed in Maine, November 10–17, 1915. With Francis Ford (Jimmie Endicott), John A. Feeney (his father), Abbie Feeney (his mother), Cecil McLean (Jib), Phil Kelly (her father, captain), Pat Feeney (mate), Jack Ford, Eddie Feeney (crew), Mary Feeney, Jo Feeney (Jim's sisters).

Jim worries his parents by his nightly debauches; fleeing the cops, he joins a schooner, single-handedly thwarts a mutiny, and marries the captain's daughter. (Almost exactly the same plot as Ford-Cunard's *Captain Billie's Mate* (2 reels, September 27, 1913).

*†1916 *Peg O' the Ring*. (Universal). 31-reel serial: 15 2-reelers (except chapter 1: 3 reels) released weekly from May 1. Director: Francis Ford. Writers: Grace Cunard, with Joe Brandy (Universal general manager), Walter Hill (circus publicity man). Photographers: Harry Grant, Abel Vallet. With Grace Cunard (Peg; Peg's mother), Francis Ford (Dr. Lund, Jr.), Mark Fenton (Dr. Lund), Jack Ford (his accomplice), Pete Gerald (Flip), Jean Hathaway (Mrs. Lund), Irving Lippner (Marcus, the Hindoo), Eddie Boland (his pal), Ruth Stonehouse, Charles Munn, G. Raymond Nye, Eddie Polo.

Circus girl is subject to spells because mother clawed by lion.

*†1916 *The Bandit's Wager* (Big U-Universal). 1 reel. November 15. Director: Francis Ford. Writer: Grace Cunard. With Grace Cunard (Nan Jefferson), Francis Ford (her brother), Jack Ford.

Nan comes west to keep house for brother. Her car breaks down one day, and she meets bandits, but it's her brother testing her courage.

*†1916 *The Purple Mask* (Universal). 33-reel serial: 16 2-reelers (except chapter 1: 3 reels) released weekly from December 25. Director: Francis Ford. Writer: Grace Cunard. With Francis Ford (Phil Kelly, "The Sphinx"), Grace Cunard (Patricia Montez), Jean Hathaway, Peter Gerald, Jerry Ash, Mario Bianchi, John Featherstone, John Duffy, Jack Ford.

Parisian society tomboy steals aunt's jewels to baffle detective who snubbed her; but jewels are stolen again and she joins Apache to trace them.

*1917 *The Tornado* (101 Bison–Universal). 2 reels. March 3. Director-writer: Jack Ford. With Ford (Jack Dayton, the No-Gun Man), Jean Hathaway (his Irish mother), John Duffy (Slick, his partner), Peter Gerald (Pendleton, banker of Rock River), Elsie Thornton (his daughter Bess), Duke Worne (Lesparre, chief of the Coyote Gang).

Jack Dayton, the No-Gun Man, son of Old Ireland, wants to send money to his mother in Ireland to pay for her cottage. In Rock River, Lesparre, chief of the Coyote Gang, covets the mayor's daughter; his gang robs the bank and kidnaps Bess. $5,000 reward. Jack joins gang to save Bess, jumps a passing train from his horse to fight Lesparre, whom he throws off the train. He gets the girl and the money.

*1917 *The Trail of Hate* (101 Bison –Universal). 2 reels. April 28. Director-writer: Jack Ford. With Ford (Lt. Jack Brewer), Duke Worne (Capt. Dana Holden), Louise Granville (Madge), Jack Lawton.

Lt. Brewer, risen from the ranks in the 67th, is adored by his men but hated by West Pointer Holden. When Madge's father is killed in a stage holdup, Jack marries her after an awkward courtship, but Madge leaves him for Holden. Years later, in the Philippines, Jack is leading troops against the Moros. Holden, trapped in the interior, abandons his men, his post, and Madge (now his wife) to save himself. When Jack saves Madge, she begs his forgiveness but is rejected in disgust.

Bogdanovich, citing a notice in *Motion Picture News* (April 28, 1917), credits direction to Francis Ford. But *Universal Weekly* (April 21, 1917) makes a big fuss about it being directed by Jack.

*1917 *The Scrapper* (101 Bison–Universal). 2 reels. June 9. Director-writer: Jack Ford. Photographer: Ben Reynolds. With Ford (Buck Logan, the scrapper), Louise Granville (Helen Dawson), Duke Worne (Jerry Martin, a parasite), Jean Hathaway (Martha Hayes).

All the guys on the ranch like the teacher, Helen, and the pugnacious Buck saves her life when her team runs away. But she decides to return to the city. Buck proposes for the twentieth time, but she won't promise anything. Meanwhile the town madam (Martha) and pimp (Martin) plan to use her to snare Col. Stanton and fake an attack so that Martin can rescue her and gain her confidence. She is given a new gown and taken to a party to meet the colonel, but Buck and the boys arrive and wreck the brothel, saving Helen. All escort Buck and Helen to board the train west.

*1917 *The Soul Herder* (101 Bison–Universal). 3 reels. August 7. Director: Jack Ford. Writer: George Hively. Photographer: Ben Reynolds. With Harry Carey (Cheyenne Harry), Jean Hersholt (the parson), Elizabeth Jones (his daughter, Mary Ann), Fritzi Ridgeway (June Brown), Vester Pegg (Topeka Jack), Hoot Gibson (Chuck Rafferty), Bill Gettinger (Bill Young), Duke Lee, Molly Malone. Working titles: "Buckhorn Hits the Trail," "The Sky Pilot." Reissued as 2-reeler in 1922.

A badman becomes a minister. For plot, see text, page 17.

*1917 *Cheyenne's Pal* (Universal Star Featurette). 2 reels. August 13. Director: Jack Ford. Scenarist: Charles J. Wilson, Jr., from story by Ford. Photographer: Friend F. Baker. Filmed May 20–23. With Harry Carey (Cheyenne Harry), Jim Corey (Noisy Jim), Gertrude Aster (dancehall girl), Vester Pegg, Steve Pimento, Hoot Gibson, Bill Gettinger, Ed Jones (cowboys), Pete Carey (Cactus, the horse). Working titles: "Cactus My Pal," "A Dumb Friend." Made to promote sales of war bonds.

Cheyenne Harry sells horses to the British Army, but not Cactus My Pal. But he blows his money and, drunk, sells Cactus for $350, which he loses gambling. So Harry gets a horse-tending job on the boat, but at midnight jumps off (with horse) and swims to shore. Jim Corey lets them go.

1917 *Straight Shooting* (Universal Butterfly). 5 reels (music timing: 67 minutes, 55 seconds). August 27. Director: Jack Ford. Writer: George Hively. Photographer: George Scott. With Harry Carey (Cheyenne Harry), Molly Malone (Joan Sims), Duke Lee (Thunder Flint), Vester Pegg (Placer Fremont), Hoot Gibson (Sam Turner), George Berrell (Sweetwater Sims), Ted Brooks (Ted Sims), Milt Brown (Black-Eyed Pete). Working titles: "The Cattle War," "Joan of the Cattle Country." Reissued as 2-reeler, *Straight Shootin'*, January 1925.

Cattlemen vs. homesteaders. For plot, see text, page 19.

*1917 *The Secret Man* (Universal Butterfly). 5 reels. October 1. Director: Jack Ford. Writer: George Hively. Photographer: Ben Reynolds. With Harry Carey (Cheyenne Harry), Morris Foster (Harry Beaufort), Elizabeth Jones (his child), Steve Clemente (Pedro, foreman), Vester Pegg (Bill), Elizabeth Sterling (Molly, his sister), Hoot Gibson (Chuck Fadden), Bill Gettinger. Working titles: "The Round Up," "Up Against It."

Molly gets a note about a sick child and runs away from her brother Bill and lover Chuck. Meanwhile, Cheyenne Harry escapes from prison in a garbage truck and is aided on a train by Harry Beaufort, who gives him a job on his ranch. But when the sheriff starts poking around, Cheyenne leaves, and Beaufort has Pedro take his little girl to another town. When Molly hears Pedro has had an accident and the child is dead, she loses her mind, because she is secretly married to Beaufort. Meanwhile, Cheyenne finds the child and spends the night with her. The posse shoots his horse, and the girl is hurt when they fall down a cliff. They find no water, only bones, so Cheyenne signals for the posse. Back in town, the girl is to be raffled at a church bazaar, but Cheyenne reunites the family and stops Bill from killing Beaufort, who explains that his uncle from whom they had concealed their marriage is now dead. Molly forgives him; Cheyenne and Chuck look at each other, and one after the other they go out into the night.

*1917 *A Marked Man* (Universal Butterfly). 5 reels. October 29. Director: Jack Ford. Scenarist: George Hively, from story by Ford. Photographer: John W. Brown. With Harry Carey (Cheyenne Harry), Molly Malone (Molly Young), Harry Rattenbury (Young, her father, a rancher), Vester Pegg (Kent), Mrs. Townsend (Harry's mother), Bill Gettinger (sheriff), Hoot Gibson.

Hiding in rain in rocks from posse, Harry reads letter from his mother, who thinks he has a ranch and wife. He stumbles into a house, helped by Molly and her father (Harry had held up Molly's train and allowed her to keep her dead mother's brooch), who then lend Harry money to enter the rodeo—to get money to visit his mother back East. But Ben Kent cuts Harry's cinch, so that Harry, losing the rodeo, will help Ben hold up a stage, which they do, in a river, and Harry protests when Ben shoots the driver. They are caught and sentenced to hang, but when news arrives that his mother is coming, Harry is given two weeks' grace and the use of Young's ranch and Molly. After a wonderful visit, Harry gives himself up, but a stagecoach passenger testifies he is innocent.

Remade as *Under Sentence* (1920) by Ford's brother Edward.

*1917 *Bucking Broadway* (Universal Butterfly). 5 reels. December 24. Director: Jack Ford. Producer: Harry Carey. Writer: George Hively. Photographer: John W. Brown. With Harry Carey (Cheyenne Harry), Molly Malone (Helen Clayton), L. M. Wells (Ben Clayton, her father), Vester Pegg (Capt. Thornton, a cattle buyer).

Harry's fiancée, Helen, is seduced away to New York by horse-buyer Thornton. Harry, distraught, follows in pursuit. Sharpshooters try to take his money, but a lady crook befriends him and helps him locate Helen. Thornton, still putting off marriage, holds a party, and Helen sends Harry a little redwood heart he once gave her. The V-Plus Ranch boys show up to help, riding down Broadway, and brawl along the rooftops.

*1918 *The Phantom Riders* (Universal Special). 5 reels. January 28. Director: Jack Ford. Producer: Harry Carey. Scenarist: George Hively, from a story by Henry McRae. Photographer: John W. Brown. Filmed September 8–27, 1917. With Harry Carey (Cheyenne Harry), Molly Malone (Molly), Buck Connor (Pebble, her father), Bill Gettinger (Dave Bland), Vester Pegg (leader of the Phantom Riders), Jim Corey (foreman).

Bland dominates Paradise Creek Valley, open government grazing land, through masked, white-coated riders led by Unknown, and he wants Molly too. Harry brings a small herd into the valley, is warned to leave, replies he will fight Bland single-handed, slaps him for insulting Molly, and is sentenced to hang by Bland. Molly's father goes to his aid, Harry finds him hanging dead from a tree, then is captured again after routing six phantoms in a bar celebrating Bland's marriage to unwilling Molly, who rides for help and rescues Harry with U.S. Rangers.

*1918 *Wild Women* (Universal Special). 5 reels. February 25. Director: Jack Ford. Producer: Harry Carey. Writer: George Hively. Photographer: John W. Brown. With Harry Carey (Cheyenne Harry), Molly Malone (the princess), Martha Maddox (the queen), Vester Pegg, Ed Jones, E. Van Beaver, W. Taylor.

Harry gets drunk celebrating a rodeo victory in San Francisco and passes out. He and his pals are shanghaied, mutiny, and cast onto a desert island with native girls; the possessive queen pursues him as he pursues the princess—till he wakes up with a hangover.

*1918 *Thieves' Gold* (Universal Special Feature). 5 reels. March 18. Director: Jack Ford. Scenarist: George Hively, from story "Back to the Right Train," by Frederick R. Bechdolt. Photographer: John W. Brown. With Harry Carey (Cheyenne Harry), Molly Malone (Alice Norris), L. M. Wells (Savage), Vester Pegg (Simmons, or Padden, an outlaw), Harry Tenbrook, M. K. Wilson, Martha Maddox.

Harry leaves the herds for Mexico with Padden, who, drunk, shoots someone. Next day Harry holds up an auto, is arrested, but will not rat on Padden. When fiancée Alice deserts him, Harry goes to Mexico, beats Padden at cards, Padden wounds Harry and dies, and Alice finds Harry unconscious and forgives him.

Received poor reviews.

*1918 *The Scarlet Drop* (Universal Special). 5 reels. April 22. Director: Jack Ford. Scenarist: George Hively, from story by Ford. Photographer: Ben Reynolds. With Harry Carey (Kaintuck Cass), Molly Malone (Molly Calvert), Vester Pegg (Capt. Marley Calvert), M. K. Wilson (Graham Lyons), Betty Schade, Martha Maddox, Steve Clemente. Working title: "Hill Billy."

Kaintuck Cass hates the Calverts, aristocrats, and they consider Casses trash, unworthy to fight with the Confederacy in the Civil War. So Cass becomes a bandit, holds up a stage, and takes Molly Calvert prisoner, but falls in love with her and sends her home. Later she falls in love with him when he saves her from rape by gentleman Lyons (blackmailing her because her mother was Negro). Calvert hides Cass from cops in attic, while Molly offers them tea, but a falling drop of blood betrays Cass. He eventually escapes back to Molly.

The plot resembles Francis Ford's *War Time Reformation* (1914). Reviewers found it "old hat."

*1918 *Hell Bent* (Universal Special Attraction). 5,700 feet. June 29. Director: Jack Ford. Writers: Ford, Harry Carey. Photographer: Ben Reynolds. With Harry Carey (Cheyenne Harry), Neva Gerber (Bess Thurston, his girl), Duke Lee (Cimarron Bill, his pal), Vester Pegg (Jack Thurston), Joseph Harris (Beau, an outlaw), M. K. Wilson, Steve Clemente.

Escaping to Rawhide after a shooting spree and finding dancehall and hotel full, Harry forces Cimarron to share a room; friendship. Harry meets Bess, whose brother Jack has been fired from Wells Fargo and whose mother is ill, and who has to earn money in dancehall, so Harry gets himself hired as bouncer to protect her. Beau covets Bess, hates Harry, and persuades Jack to join his holdup gang, who kidnap Bess. Harry pursues, corners Beau, but to avoid Bess thinking him cowardly, challenges Beau to race on foot fifty miles across desert to Yaqui waterhole; but the hole is dry, Beau dies, and Cimarron rescues Harry, who marries Bess.

The film begins with author of story rejected for lack of punch admiring Remington picture called "The Misdeal," which comes to life to start the story — which pokes fun at itself.

Exhibitors' Trade Review: "Typical Harry Carey picture, which means that thrills and excitement are plentifully distributed about, and that speed and more speed is the keynote . . . A tickling tone of merriment."

*1918 *A Woman's Fool* (Universal Special Attraction). 60 minutes. August 12. Director: Jack Ford. Scenarist: George Hively, from novel *Lin McLean*, by Owen Wister. Photographer: Ben Reynolds. With Harry Carey (Lin McLean), Betty Schade (Katy), Roy Clark (Tommy Lusk), Molly Malone (Jessamine).

Lin loves Katy, a biscuit shooter in a Denver railroad restaurant, and offers her a home in the West. Then there is a drought and Katy's husband shows up offering to make it rain for six hours for $1,000, and does so, and Katy returns to him. Broken-hearted Lin goes to another town, where he meets a young pal, Tommy, who turns out to be Katy's abandoned child.

Lin adopts him, and falls in love with Jessamine, a station agent; Katy reappears and, after failing to wreck their marriage, kills herself, and Tommy reunites the couple.

*1918 *Three Mounted Men* (Universal Special Attraction). 6 reels. October 7. Director: Jack Ford. Writer: Eugene B. Lewis. Photographer: John W. Brown. With Harry Carey (Cheyenne Harry), Joe Harris (Buck Masters), Neva Gerber (Lola Masters), Harry Carter (the warden's son), Ella Hall.

Harry is put in solitary for fighting with Buck. Buck is a friend of warden's son, a forger, and pardoned. But Buck bribes son for hush money, so Harry, on hard labor, is released to get Buck. Harry arranges a holdup with Buck and Buck is arrested. But then Harry discovers Buck is Lola's brother, and so he rescues him from cops and marries Lola.

Exhibitors' Trade Review (November 21, 1918) complained of too much realism, too much filth and rats in prison. "Carey consistently portrays a rough character throughout the picture. The only wonder of it is that anyone should attempt to heroize such a type. There may be such men in the west, but it is best on the screen to show them up as horrible examples of what a man may be."

*†1919 *The Craving* (Universal-Bluebird). 5 reels. January 6. Directors: Francis and Jack Ford. Story and scenario: Francis Ford. With Francis Ford (Carroll Wayles), Mae Gaston (Beaulah Grey), Peter Gerald (Ala Kasarib), Duke Worne (Dick Wayles), Jean Hathaway (Mrs. Wayles). Working title: "Delirium."

Carroll Wayles, scientist with powerful explosive, has a rival, Ala Kasarib, an East Indian come to America for the formula with Beaulah Grey, under Kasarib's hypnotic control, to seduce Wayles. Wayles refuses to drink, recounting his past deliria (special effects recreate girls poured from bottles into wineglasses, battlefields in Europe, etc. "Everywhere he looked he saw nude women"). In a mental battle in his lab, Kasarib gets the formula, and Wayles takes to drink. Later, he fights Kasarib in the latter's lab, an explosion leaves Kasarib dead, and Wayles and Beaulah fall in love.

Bogdanovich removes *The Craving* from Ford's credit, and even quotes Ford's disclaimer. Yet *Universal Weekly* (January 14, 1919) insists Jack participated. Curiously, *Moving Picture World* (October 12, 1918!) reviews it unfavorably and credits distribution to M. H. Hoffman, a states' rights agent, rather than to Universal. Everything about the picture smells of Francis; if Jack helped, it was just help.

* 1919 *Roped* (Universal Special). 6 reels. January 13. Director: Jack Ford. Writer: Eugene B. Lewis. Photographer: John W. Brown. With Harry Carey (Cheyenne Harry), Neva Gerber (Aileen Judson Brown), Molly McConnell (Mrs. Judson Brown), J. Farrell MacDonald (butler), Arthur Shirley (Ferdie Van Duzen).

Harry is a millionaire cattleraiser in Arizona in need of a housekeeper, so his hands put a marry ad in the newspaper and a note arrives from a poor but beautiful girl living at the Ritz in New York City. Harry goes east and marries Aileen, ensnared by her bankrupt society mother who, when a baby is born, will not let him see it and tells him it is dead (preferring alimony and a lounge lizard to marriage). Harry returns from a business trip to find them gone, but the butler tips him off, and Harry and his cowboys find them, knock out the lounge-lizard, and the couple takes a honeymoon to Grand Canyon.

* 1919 *Harry Carey Tour Promotional Film* (Universal). ½ reel (500 feet). February. Directors: Harry Carey, and Jack Ford. With Harry Carey.

A compilation of sensational stunts to illustrate Carey's tour talk.

* 1919 *The Fighting Brothers* (Universal). 2 reels. March 10. Director: Jack Ford. Scenarist: George Hively, from story by George C. Hull. Photographer: John W. Brown. Filmed February 8–15. With Pete Morrison (Sheriff Pete Larkin), Hoot Gibson (Lonnie Larkin), Yvette Mitchell (Conchita), Jack Woods (Ben Crawley), Duke Lee (Slim). Working title: "His Buddy."

Sheriff Larkin does his duty, arresting for murder his brother, whom he knows to be innocent. Then he takes off his badge and helps him escape.

* 1919 *A Fight for Love* (Universal Special Attraction). 6 reels. March 24. Director: Jack Ford. Writer: Eugene B. Lewis. Photographer: John W. Brown. Exteriors

filmed in California's Big Bear region. With Harry Carey (Cheyenne Harry), Joe Harris (Black Michael), Neva Gerber (Kate McDougall), Mark Fenton (Angus McDougall, her father), J. Farrell MacDonald (the priest), Princess Neola Mae (Little Fawn), Chief Big Tree (Swift Deer). Working title: "Hell's Neck."

Harry crosses to Canada and rolls a cigarette gazing at the posse pursuing him. But the Americans call the Mounties and Harry hides with Indians and fights with whiskey-runner Black Michael over an Indian girl. Michael is also Harry's rival for Kate, whom he abducts, killing an Indian boy and confessing to a priest; then, pursued by Harry and falling from a cliff, he confesses again to the law and dies.

Exhibitors' Trade Review commented on its many fights for love, exciting chases, Indians, and spellbinding locations.

* 1919 *By Indian Post* (Universal). 2 reels. April 12. Director: Jack Ford. Scenarist: H. Tipton Steck, from story "The Trail of the Billy-Doo," by William Wallace Cook. Filming began February 18. With Pete Morrison (Jode McWilliams), Duke Lee (Pa Owens), Madga Lane (Peg Owens), Ed Jones (Stumpy, the cook), Jack Woods (Dutch), Harley Chambers (Fritz), Hoot Gibson (Chub), Jack Walters (Andy), Otto Myers (Swede), Jim Moore (Two-Horns, an Indian). Working title: "The Love Letter."

Stumpy writes a love letter to Peg for Jode, copying it from "Lothario's Compendium," but other cowboys find the letter and tack it to a door, where Two-Horns, admiring the "paper talk," finds it and shows it to everyone he meets. Before Jode can catch him, Two-Horns shows it to Peg, with happy effect. Working title: "The Love Letter."

* 1919 *The Rustlers* (Universal). 2 reels. April 26. Director: Jack Ford. Writer: George Hively. Photographer: John W. Brown. Filmed February 22–March 8. With Pete Morrison (Ben Clayburn), Helen Gibson (Postmistress Nell Wyndham), Jack Woods (Sheriff Buck Farley), Hoot Gibson (his deputy). Working title: "Even Money."

A government ranger infiltrates a rustler gang so effectively that Nell has to save him from a lynch mob.

* 1919 *Bare Fists* (Universal Special). 5,500 feet. May 5. Director: Jack Ford. Scenarist: Eugene B. Lewis, from story by

Bernard McConville. Photographer: John W. Brown. Filming began July 20, 1918. With Harry Carey (Cheyenne Harry), Molly McConnell (his mother), Joseph Girard (his father), Howard Ensteadt (his brother, Bud), Betty Schade (Conchita), Vester Pegg (Lopez), Joe Harris (Boone Travis), Anna Mae Walthall (Ruby, a dancehall girl). Working title: "The Man Who Wouldn't Shoot."

Harry's father is marshall of Hays City, a lawless bordertown. His mother begs them not to intervene in a saloon fight, but they do and Pa is killed, Harry killing two of the slayers. So mother makes him swear on the Bible not to carry a gun again. But Harry is framed for Boone's murder of Conchita and sentenced to die, and when his mother makes her last visit, he learns brother Bud has been branded a cattle thief. So Harry escapes and gets the real thieves.

*1919 *Gun Law* (Universal). 2 reels. May 10. Director: Jack Ford. Writer: H. Tipton Steck. Photographer: John W. Brown. Filmed March 11–21. With Peter Morrison (Dick Allen), Hoot Gibson (Bart Stevens, alias Smoke Gublen), Helen Gibson (Letty), Jack Woods (Cayuse Yates), Otto Myers, Ed Jones, H. Chambers (Yates's gang). Working title: "The Posse's Prey."

A government agent infiltrates a mine to prove its owner is a mail robber, but in the process he falls in love with the guy's sister and the guy saves his life, causing a dilemma alleviated by recovery of the intact mailbags.

*1919 *The Gun Packer* (Universal). 2 reels. May 24. Director: Jack Ford. Scenarist: Karl R. Coolidge, from a story by Ford and Harry Carey. Photographer: John W. Brown. Filming began March 25. With Ed Jones (Sandy McLoughlin), Pete Morrison ("Pearl Handle" Wiley), Magda Lane (Rose McLoughlin), Jack Woods (Pecos Smith), Hoot Gibson (outlaw leader), Jack Walters (Brown), Duke Lee (Buck Landers), Howard Ensteadt (Bobby McLoughlin). Working title: "Out Wyoming Way." Reissued August 1924.

A reformed gunman, sheepmen, and a gang of outlaws unite to win water rights from cattle barons.

*1919 *Riders of Vengeance* (Universal Special). 6 reels. June 9. Director: Jack Ford. Producer: P. A. Powers. Writers: Ford, Harry Carey. Photographer: John W.

Brown. With Harry Carey (Cheyenne Harry), Seena Owen (the Girl), Joe Harris (Sherriff Gale Thurman), J. Farrell MacDonald (Buell), Jennie Lee (Harry's mother), Glita Lee (Virginia), Alfred Allen, Betty Schade, Vester Pegg, M. K. Wilson.

As Harry and his bride emerge from the church, she and his parents are murdered. Harry reappears a year later to post the names of those he will kill in revenge, which he does, one by one, till Gale Thurman. But Harry rescues Thurman's girl from stage holdup, cares for her in his cave / home after considering harming her, and falls in love. Then, trapped with Thurman in the desert and fighting off Apache, he discovers the man's innocence and tries to save him for the girl's sake, but Thurman dies.

According to W. P. Wooten, Ford, taking over when the original director took ill, only directed portions. *Exhibitors' Trade Review* used phrases like: "sympathetic," "strenuous," "action," "color," "lots of suspense." *Moving Picture World* (May 24, 1919): "scenic," "lots of killings."

*1919 *The Last Outlaw* (Universal). 2 reels. June 14. Director: Jack Ford. Scenarist: H. Tipton Steck, from story by Evelyne Murray Campbell. Photographer: John W. Brown. Filmed April 8–12. With Ed "King Fisher" Jones (Bud Coburn), Richard Cumming (Sheriff Brownlo), Lucille Hutton (Idaleen Coburn), Jack Walters (Chad Allen), Billie Hutton. Working title: "A Man of Peace." Reissued December 1923; remade as feature, 1936.

Bud returns home from ten years in jail to find his town gone "civilized and dry" and his daughter in the clutches of a bootlegger. So the old outlaw kidnaps his daughter and is wounded saving her.

*1919 *The Outcasts of Poker Flat* (Universal Special). 6 reels. July 6. Director: Jack Ford. Producer: P. A. Powers. Scenarist: H. Tipton Steck, from stories "The Outcasts of Poker Flat" and "The Luck of Roaring Camp," by Bret Harte. Photographer: John W. Brown. With Harry Carey (Square Shootin' Lanyon; John Oakhurst), Cullen Landis (Billy Lanyon; Tommy Oakhurst), Gloria Hope (Ruth Watson; Sophy), J. Farrell MacDonald, Charles H. Mailes, Victor Postel, Joe Harris, Duke R. Lee, Vester Pegg.

Square Shootin' Harry Lanyon, owner of Arizona gambling hall, loves ward Ruth but thinks she loves his adopted son Billy and will not interfere. Then he reads Harte's "Outcasts of Poker Flat" and sees in it similarities to his own situation. (John Oakhurst befriends Sophy as she is about to kill herself on a steamboat, deserted by gambler fiancé Stratton. Oakhurst brings Sophy to Poker Flat and encourages her to marry his son Tommy. Then Stratton reappears, coveting Sophy; but vigilantes drive everyone out of the town, where they are caught in a storm and only Sophy and Tommy survive.) Impressed, Lanyon vows not to make similar mistakes and discovers Ruth loves him, not Billy. Remakes by Christy Cabanne, 1937, and Joseph Newman, 1952.

Moving Picture World (June 28, 1919): "Catches admirably the spirit of the early days in California." *Photoplay:* "Two remarkable things are Harry Carey's rise to real acting power, and director Ford's marvelous river locations and absolutely incomparable photography. This photoplay is an optic symphony."

*1919 *The Age of the Saddle* (Universal Special). 6 reels. August 18. Director: Jack Ford. Producer: P. A. Powers. Scenarist: George Hively, from story by B. J. Jackson. Photographer: John W. Brown. Exteriors filmed in the Rio Grande Valley. With Harry Carey (Cheyenne Harry Henderson), Joe Harris (Sheriff "Two Gun" Hildebrand of Yucca County), Duke R. Lee (Sheriff Faulkner of Pinkerton County), Peggy Pearce (Madeline Faulkner, his daughter), Jack Walters (Inky O'Day), Vester Pegg (gambler), Zoe Ray, Howard Ensteadt (the children), Ed "King Fisher" Jones (Home Sweet Holmes), William Cartwright (Humpy Anderson), Andy Devine. Working title: "A Man of Peace."

Yucca's sheriff is in cahoots with rustlers of Harry's steers, and it is outside of Pinkerton sheriff's jurisdiction; but Harry falls in love with latter's daughter, who makes him give up guns. When his water is poisoned, Harry drags his cabin into Pinkerton County with six horses. Rustlers kidnap Madeline, Harry rescues her, and posse captures leaders, who, however, are saved by a raid at their trial, only to be lured by Harry to his cabin, knocked out with the poisoned water, and recaptured.

*1919 *The Rider of the Law* (Universal Special). 5 reels. November 3. Director: Jack Ford. Producer: P. A. Powers. Scenarist: H. Tipton Steck, from story

"Jim of the Rangers" by G. P. Lancaster. Photographer: John W. Brown. With Harry Carey (Jim Kyneton), Gloria Hope (Betty, his girl), Vester Pegg (Nick Kyneton), Theodore Brooks (the Kid), Joe Harris (Buck Souter), Jack Woods (Jack West), Duke R. Lee (Capt. Graham Saltire), Claire Anderson (Roseen), Jennie Lee (mother).

Jim loves mother's ward Betty, but thinks she loves brother Nick. Betty loves Jim, thinks he loves pretty, treacherous Roseen. Saloonman Buck loves Roseen, but vows vengeance on Jim, thinking Roseen loves Jim. Jim is a Texas Ranger after Midas Mine thieves; duty is his middle name and he arrests his own brother Nick and locks all in cabin; but Roseen, repulsed by Jim, lets them out. Jim, accused a traitor, captures them again, but Nick rides off cliff rather than be captured. Jim marries Roseen.

Exhibitors' Trade Review (October 18, 1919): "Typical Harry Carey . . . wild chases, commingling of bathos and humor, realistic."

*1919 *A Gun Fightin' Gentleman* (Universal Special). 5 reels. November 30. Director: Jack Ford. Producer: P. A. Powers. Scenarist: Hal Hoadley, from story by Ford and Harry Carey. Photographer: John W. Brown. With Harry Carey (Cheyenne Harry), J. Barney Sherry (John Merritt), Kathleen O'Conner (Helen Merritt), Lydia Yeamans Titus (her aunt), Harry von Meter (Earl of Jollywell), Duke R. Lee (Buck Regan), Joe Harris (Seymour), Johnny Cooke (the old sheriff), Ted Brooks (the Youngster).

Harry refuses to surrender land to Merritt Packing Co., eludes their hired men, but is dispossessed when a lawyer finds a title flaw. Harry goes to Chicago, but at dinner Merritt mocks his clothes and manners. So Harry becomes an outlaw, robs Merritt's payrolls, finally abducts his daughter Helen, and falls in love. When Merritt comes to save her, she makes him right wrong.

*1919 *Marked Men* (Universal Special). 5 reels. December 21. Director: Jack Ford. Producer: P. A. Powers. Scenarist: H. Tipton Steck, from story "The Three Godfathers," by Peter B. Kyne. Photographer: John W. Brown. Editors: Frank Lawrence, Frank Atkinson. With Harry Carey (Cheyenne Harry), J. Farrell

MacDonald (Tom "Placer" McGraw), Joe Harris (Tom Gibbons), Winifred Westover (Ruby Merrill), Ted Brooks (Tony Garcia), Charles Lemoyne (Sheriff Pete Cushing), David Kirby (Warden "Bruiser" Kelly). Working title: "The Trail of Shadows."

Harry, Bill, and Tom, in state pen for train robbery, escape. Later Harry leaves Ruby to rob bank with Bill and Tom. but they are chased into Mojave Desert, encounter a dying mother and vow to save her baby; only Harry survives, staggering into a dancehall Christmas Eve. Ruby and sheriff learn the baby is his nephew and obtain pardon from governor. Numerous remakes, including Ford's 3 *Godfathers*, 1948.

*1920 *The Prince of Avenue A* (Universal Special). 5 reels. February 23. Director: Jack Ford. Scenarist: Charles J. Wilson, Jr., from story by Charles and Frank Dazey. Photographer: John W. Brown. With James J. "Gentleman Jim" Corbett (Barry O'Conner), Mary Warren (Mary Tompkins), Harry Northrup (Edgard Jones), Cora Drew (Mary O'Conner), Richard Cummings (Patrick O'Conner), Frederik Vroom (William Tompkins), Mark Fenton (Father O'Toole), George Vanderlip (Reggie Vanderlip), Johnny Cooke (butler), Lydia Yeamans Titus (housekeeper), George Fisher.

The prince is Barry O'Conner, whose father, Patrick, is district ward boss and supports Tompkins for mayor, whose daughter Mary is pleasant to Barry for political reasons, but Barry falls in love. At her dance, all refuse to dance with him, so he invites a maid to "trip the light fantastic" and Mary, humiliated, orders him out. Patrick, insulted, demands apology, and Tompkins and Mary come to call and Mary consents to be Barry's partner at Grand Ball. There, O'Conner's rival insults Mary, and Barry defends her in a gigantic brawl, winning Mary.

Exhibitors' Trade Review (January 17, 1920): "Wealth of human interest, good comedy, a bit of pathos . . . atmosphere . . . one can always be sure of clever details when Ford has taken a hand at things." *Moving Picture World* (January 17, 1920): "A triumph among unique character stories . . . a story of genuine life . . . an undercurrent of humor." Ford's first non-western.

*1920 *The Girl in No. 29* (Universal Special). 4,775 feet. April 3. Director: Jack Ford. Scenarist: Philip J. Hurn, from story

"The Girl in the Mirror," by Elizabeth Jordan. Photographer: John W. Brown. With Frank Mayo (Laurie Devon), Harry Hilliard (Rodney Bangs), Claire Anderson (Doris Williams), Elinor Fair (Barbara Devon), Bull Montana (Abdullah, the strangler), Ray Ripley (Ransome Shaw), Robert Bolder (Jacob Epstein).

Laurie Devon wrote a successful play and will not work again. Friends deplore his rut. One day he sees a girl across the way holding a revolver to her head, breaks in to prevent her suicide, begs to be her protector, discovers Shaw is bothering her, follows Shaw, gets dumped into cellar, escapes, learns girl abducted, rescues her from thugs, thinks he has killed Shaw, then learns the whole thing is a joke by his friends, and marries the girl. (Lots of rain and night.)

*†1920 *Under Sentence* (Universal). 2 reels. June 12. Director: Edward Feeney. Scenarist: George Hively, from story by Jack Ford. Shooting started April 12. With Bob Anderson, Ethel Ritchie, Jennie Lee, J. Farrell MacDonald, Cap Anderson, Jack Woods.

Remake of Ford's *A Marked Man*, 1917, by younger brother Edward, who later changed his name to O'Fearna and served as assistant director on many of John's pictures.

*1920 *Hitchin' Posts* (Universal Special). 5 reels. August 29. Director: Jack Ford. Scenarist: George C. Hull, from story by Harold M. Schumate. Photographer: Benjamin Kline. With Frank Mayo (Jefferson Todd), Beatrice Burnham (Ophelia Bereton), Joe Harris (Raoul Castiga), J. Farrell MacDonald (Joe Alabam), Mark Fenton (Col. Carl Bereton), Dagmar Godowsky (octoroon), Duke R. Lee (Col. Lancy), C. E. Anderson (steamboat captain), M. Biddulph (Maj. Gray).

Todd, a Southern gentleman whose lands are confiscated by Yankees, takes to gambling for livelihood and on a Mississippi riverboat wins last possessions of Col. Bereton—four race horses. Bereton commits suicide that night, and the captain asks Todd to inform Bereton's daughter Barbara; but Bereton had already asked Castiga to do this. Todd and Castiga meet on plantation, and Todd dislikes Castiga for his treatment of his wife, Todd's sister. They duel: Castiga fires before allowed, but Todd reserves his shot in accord with promise to Todd's sister. Barbara, penniless, goes West to homestead, Todd and Castiga, too, separately, and unknown to Barbara. Todd and Castiga race for oil claim on Bereton's horses, fight, and Castiga drowns. Todd's sister has died and he marries Barbara.

1920 *Just Pals* (William Fox–20th Century Brand). 5 reels. November 14. Director: Jack Ford. Scenarist: Paul Schofield, from story by John McDermott. Photographer: George Schneiderman. With Buck Jones (Bim), Helen Ferguson (Mary Bruce, schoolteacher), George E. Stone (Bill), Duke R. Lee (sheriff), William Buckley (Harvey Cahill), Edwin Booth Tilton (Dr. Stone), Eunice Murdock Moore (Mrs. Stone), Burt Apling (brakeman), Slim Padgett, Pedro Leone, (outlaws), Ida Tenbrook (maid), John J. Cooke (elder).

Norwalk, a village on the border between Wyoming and Nebraska: Bim, the town bum, befriends a ten-year-old hobo, and together they thwart an express office robbery and win the schoolteacher's heart.

*1921 *The Big Punch* (William Fox–20th Century Brand). 5 reels. January 30. Director: Jack Ford. Scenarists: Ford, Jules Furthman, from story "Fighting Back," by Furthman. Photographer: Frank Good. With Buck Jones (Buck), Barbard Bedford (Hope Standish), George Siegmann (Flash McGraw), Jack Curtis (Jef, Buck's brother), Jennie Lee (Buck's mother), Jack McDonald, Al Fremont (Jed's friends), Edgar Jones (sheriff), Irene Hunt (dancehall girl), Eleanor Gilmore (Salvation Army girl).

Buck is planning to go to theological seminary, his mother a widow alone on ranch. Buck finds brother Jed drunk with pals in saloon listening to McGraw plan new crime. Hope Standish, Salvation Army girl, comes selling *War Crys*, and McGraw will throw her out if she does not kiss him, so she does, coldly, and crowd buys all her papers. Buck forces Jed to come home, McGraw's gang attacks him, but Jed and pals support Buck, and McGraw swears revenge. He has crony sheriff arrest them for sheep rustling and Buck, trying to warn them, is arrested too, getting two years, the others ten. In prison, Buck loves Hope, who visits, and studies for ministry. Ordained after release, he takes over the

old circuit rider's route, lives down his "reputation," learns to love work and Hope, and converts Jed when Jed escapes from prison.

Exhibitors' Trade Review: "Action," "full of human touches," "heart tugs."

*1921 *The Freeze Out* (Universal Special). 4,400 feet. April 9. Director: Jack Ford. Writer: George C. Hull. Photographer: Harry C. Fowler. With Harry Carey (Ohio, the Stranger), Helen Ferguson (Zoe Whipple), Joe Harris (Headling Whipple), Charles Lemoyne (Denver Red), J. Farrell MacDonald (Bobtail McGuire), Lydia Yeamans Titus (Mrs. McGuire).

A stranger rides into Broken Buckle to open a gamblinghouse to rival Red and Whipple's. Teacher Zoe, who disapproves of brother Whipple's house, tries to interest the Stranger in reform but is ignored. But the new house turns out to be a school and library.

*1921 *The Wallop* (Universal Special). 4,539 feet. May 7. Director: Jack Ford. Scenarist: George C. Hull, from story "The Girl He Left Behind Him," by Eugene Manlove Rhodes. Photographer: Harry C. Fowler. With Harry Carey (John Wesley Pringle), Joe Harris (Barela), Charles Lemoyne (Matt Lisner), J. Farrell MacDonald (Neuces River), Mignonne Golden (Stella Vorhis), Bill Gettinger (Christopher Foy), Noble Johnson (Espinol), C. E. Anderson (Applegate), Mark Fenton (Major Vorhis). Working title: "The Homeward Trail."

Adventurer Harry Pringle makes his strike and returns home and recognizes his lost love, Stella, in a movie theater. Alas, she loves another, Chris, who is running for sheriff against incumbent Lisner. Foiled by Harry in an attempt to kill Chris, Lisner frames Chris for murder. A posse pursues Chris and Stella, who hide in a cave; Harry finds them, ties up Chris, claims the reward, then frees him, reveals Lisner's corruption and, having reunited Chris and Stella, goes back alone to his mine.

Exhibitors' Trade Review: "Pleasing to all . . . interesting story . . . big outdoors . . . night and rain, with only a campfire for light."

*1921 *Desperate Trails* (Universal Special). 4,577 feet. July 9. Director: Jack

Ford. Scenarist: Elliot J. Clawson, from story "Christmas Eve at Pilot Butte," by Courtney Riley Cooper. Photographers: Harry C. Fowler, Robert DeGrasse. Filmed March 14–April 11. With Harry Carey (Bert Carson), Irene Rich (Mrs. Walker), George E. Stone (Danny Boy), Helen Field (Carrie), Barbara La Marr (Lady Lou), George Siegmann (Sheriff Price), Charles Insley (Dr. Higgins), Ed Coxen (Walter A. Walker). Working title: "Christmas Eve at Pilot Butte."

Loved by Widow Walker, Harry loves Lady Lou, and goes to prison to protect Lou's brother, where, discovering the "brother" is her lover, he escapes and kills him. To give Widow Walker the reward for his capture, he turns himself in to her boy on Christmas eve; but Lou has confessed the frame-up.

Exhibitors' Trade Review: "No padding," "good night scenes." *Motion Picture News:* "The closing reels show the slow change of seasons in the trackless forest."

*1921 *Action* (Universal Special). 4,590 feet. September 12. Director: Jack Ford. Scenarist: Harvey Gates, from "The Mascotte of the Three Star," by J. Allen Dunn. Photographer: John W. Brown. With Hoot Gibson (Sandy Brooke), Francis Ford (Soda Water Manning), J. Farrell MacDonald (Mormon Peters), Buck Conners (Pat Casey), Byron Munson (Henry Meekin), Clara Horton (Molly Casey), William R. Daley (J. Plimsoll), Charles Newton (Sheriff Dipple), Jim Corey (Sam Waters), Ed "King Fisher" Jones (Art Smith), Dorothea Wolburt (Mirandy Meekin). Working title: "Let's Go."

Molly is an orphan, heir to ranch and mine, alone, threatened. Sandy, Soda Water, and Mormon wander in from range and take interest. Sandy falls in love, works mine, fends off conspirators and sends Molly east to school. But conspirators conspire and Molly returns to find all in jail, but she straighten things out.

Hoot Gibson's first feature starring role, and Francis Ford's first appearance under Jack's direction. "*Exhibitors' Trade Review:* 'Unusually good," "artistic," "box office," "original."

*1921 *Sure Fire* (Universal Special). 4,481 feet. November 5. Director: Jack Ford. Scenarist: George C. Hull, from story "Bransford of Rainbow Ridge," by Eugene Manlove Rhodes. Photographer: Virgil G. Miller. With Hoot Gibson (Jeff Bransford), Molly Malone (Marian Hoffman), Reeves "Breezy" Eason, Jr. (Sonny), Harry Carter (Rufus Coulter), Murdock MacQuarrie (Major Parker), Fritzi Brunette (Elinor Parker), George Fisher (Burt Rawlings), Charles Newton (Leo Ballinger), Jack Woods (Brazos Bart), Jack Walters (Overland Kid), Joe Harris (Romero), Steve Clemente (Gomez), Mary Philbin.

Jeff's girl, Marian, is down on him for lack of ambition, and *her* married sister, Elinor, is about to elope with an Eastern lover (who, her child tells Jeff, has just stolen $5,000 mortgage money for Elinor's house). Mr. Parker discovers Jeff there, and Elinor Parker puts the blame on Jeff, who escapes to a cabin. Meanwhile, bandits kill the Easterner, take the money, abduct Marian, and escape to the same cabin, where Jeff saves Marian. Posse arrives, finds loot on a baddy. Elinor's secret is safe, her husband (still complaisantly ignorant) gives Jeff the $5,000 for his marriage to Marian.

*1921 *Jackie* (William Fox). 4,943 feet. November 27. Director: Jack Ford. Scenarist: Dorothy Yost, from story by Countess Helena Barcynska (pseudonym for Marguerite Florence Helene Jervis Evans). Photographer: George Schneiderman. With Shirley Mason (Jackie), William Scott (Mervyn Carter), Harry Carter (Bill Bowman), George E. Stone (Benny), John Cooke (Winter), Elsie Bambrick (Millie).

Jackie, a Russian waif, is apprenticed to a cheap roadshow. But her lustful manager assaults her, and she flees with Benny, a crippled boy, to London, where she dances on the street. Carter, a wealthy American, picks her up, pays for an operation for Benny and lessons for her. Then, after her successful debut, he has to dispose of her former master before marrying her.

Exhibitors' Trade Review: "Wealth of pathos," "colorful." "The production is remarkable for the insistent adherence to accurate and artistic detail which have distinguished director Jack Ford's contributions to the screen in the past."

*1922 *Little Miss Smiles* (William Fox). 4,884 feet. January 15. Director: Jack Ford. Scenarist: Dorothy Yost, from "Little Aliens," by Myra Kelly, adapted by Yost and Jack Strumwasser. Photographer: David Abel. With Shirley Mason (Esther Aaronson), Gaston Glass

(Dr. Jack Washton), George Williams
(Papa Aaronson), Martha Franklin
(Mama Aaronson), Arthur Rankin
(Dave Aaronson), Baby Blumfield
(Baby Aaronson), Richard Lapan (Leon
Aaronson), Alfred Testa (Louis Aaronson),
Sidney D'Albrook (the Spider).

Ups and downs of a Jewish family in New
York ghetto tenement. The mother is losing
her eyesight, daughter Esther loves young
Dr. Jack, and brother Dave's ambitions to
become a prizefighter worry his parents.
Complications arise when Dave, in bad
company, shoots a gangster for insulting
Esther. But Dr. Jack restores mother's
eyesight and marries Esther.

Exhibitors' Trade Review: "Ghetto stories usually popular, this one is unoriginal,
but very good: pathos and comedy, realistic people and places."

*†1922 *Silver Wings* (William Fox). 8,271
feet. August 26. Directors: Jack Ford (the
Prologue), Edwin Carewe (the Play).
Writer: Paul H. Stone. Photographers:
Joseph Ruttenberg, Robert Kurle. With
(in the Prologue): Mary Carr (Anna Webb),
Lynn Hammond (John Webb), Knox
Kincaid (John, their child), Joseph
Monahan (Harry, another son), Maybeth
Carr (Ruth, their daughter), Claude Brook
(Uncle Andrews), Robert Hazelton (the
priest), Florence Short (widow), May
Kaiser (baby); and (in the Play): Mary Carr
(Anna Webb), Percy Halton (John), Joseph
Striker (Harry), Jane Thomas (Ruth), Roy
Gordon (George), Florence Haas (Little
Anna), Claude Brook (Uncle Andrews),
Roger Lytton (banker), Ernest
Hilliard (Jerry).

The Prologue: John Webb invents an improved sewing machine, enriching his family, then dies. The Play: Eldest son Harry,
however, mismanages affairs, John skips
town, accused of stealing the money Harry
embezzled, Ruth elopes. Mother Abba
sells the business to cover Harry's debts
and, impoverished, takes a menial factory
job. Later, a magazine story of her life
helps reunite the family.

The Ford sequence contained an affecting scene of a baby's death.

*†1922 *Nero* (William Fox). c. 11,500
feet. September 17. Director: J. Gordon
Edwards. With Jacques Gretillat, Alexander Salvini. Filmed mostly in Italy.

Ford wrote and directed scenes to
heighten Edwards's climax. As Edwards's

Christians are being torn apart by lions,
Ford, in parallel montage, added scenes of
horsemen gathering, like Griffith's klans,
while enormous drums beat. These horsemen, spearheading the rebellious army of
Galba, assault the city, but are opposed by
Nero's soldiers at a bridge over the Tiber;
some of them fall into the Tiber spectacularly before they gain the bridge. At this
point the film returned to Edwards's shot
of the horsemen entering the arena just in
time to save the star Christians.

*1922 *The Village Blacksmith* (William
Fox). 7,540 feet. November 2. Director:
Jack Ford. Scenarist: Paul H. Sloane, from
poem by Henry Wadsworth Longfellow.
Photographer: George Schneiderman.
With William Walling (John Hammond,
blacksmith), Virginia True Boardman (his
wife), Virginia Valli (Alice Hammond),
David Butler (Bill Hammond), Gordon
Griffith (Bill, as child), Ida Nan McKenzie
(Alice, as child), George Hackthorne
(Johnnie), Pat Moore (Johnnie, as child),
Tully Marshall (Squire Ezra Brigham),
Caroline Rankin (Mrs. Brigham), Ralph
Yeardsley (Anson Brigham), Henri de la
Garrique (Anson, as child), Francis Ford
(Asa Martin), Bessie Love (Rosemary
Martin), Helen Field (Rosemary, as child),
Mark Fenton (Dr. Brewster), Lon Poff
(Gideon Crane, schoolteacher), Cordelia
Callahan (Aunt Hattie), Eddie Gribbon
(village gossip), Lucille Hutton (flapper).

In a prologue, Johnnie Hammond, one
of the blacksmith's two sons, falls crippling
himself from a tree young Anson Brigham
has dared him to climb. Anson is the son of
the squire, who hates the blacksmith for
marrying the woman the squire loved. She
dies. Years later (around 1923), son Bill
Hammond goes off to medical school (for
Johnnie), and Anson, back from college,
ensnares Hammond's daughter, Alice,
arousing gossip. Bill is injured in a train
accident, and Alice, accused of stealing
church money (actually stolen by Anson),
tries suicide in storm; crippled Johnnie
pursues Anson. The blacksmith arrives to
save Alice and forces Anson and the squire
to confess. Bill recovers and operates
successfully on Johnnie.

*1923 *The Face on the Barroom Floor*
(William Fox). 5,787 feet. January 1.
Director: Jack Ford. Scenarists: Eugene
B. Lewis, G. Marion Burton, from poem
by Hugh Antoine D'Arcy. Photographer:

George Schneiderman. With Henry B.
Walthall (Robert Stevens, an artist), Ruth
Clifford (Marion Von Vleck), Walter
Emerson (Richard Von Vleck), Alma
Bennett (Lottie), Norval McGregor (gover-
nor), Michael Dark (Henry Drew), Gus
Saville (fisherman).

As a derelict paints a girl's face on a barroom floor, flashbacks tell his story: Robert
Stevens is a famous artist engaged to social-
ite Marion. In Maine he paints a charming
fisherman's daughter, but Marion's brother
dishonors her and she kills herself. Stevens,
shielding Marion's brother, is blamed and
Marion drops him. He drifts from bad to
worse; when thieves plant a stolen wallet
on him, he is sent to prison. During a riot
he escapes, saves the governor's life, swims
to a lighthouse, and when the keeper is too
ill to work, signals for him and saves ships.
Returning to prison, he is pardoned and
eventually reunited with Marion.

*1923 *Three Jumps Ahead* (William Fox).
4,854 feet. March 25. Director-writer:
Jack Ford. Photographer: Daniel B. Clark.
With Tom Mix (Steve Clancy), Alma
Bennett (Annie Darrell), Virginia True
Boardman (Mrs. Darrell), Edward Piel
(Taggit), Joe E. Girard (Annie's father),
Francis Ford (Virgil Clancy), Margaret
Joslin (Juliet), Henry Todd (Cicero), Buster
Gardner (Brutus).

Steve Clancy and his uncle Virgil are captured by outlaws and imprisoned in their
mountain hideout cave, where another prisoner, Darrell, imprisoned there two years, is
forced to flog them. Darrell escapes, and the
baddies promise Steve they will release his
uncle if he recaptures Darrell but will kill
him if he fails. Steve, outside, meets Ann,
traps Darrell, returns him, discovers he is
Ann's father, rescues him.

1923 *Cameo Kirby* (William Fox). 5,910
feet. October 21. Director: John Ford. Sce-
narist: Robert N. Lee, from play by Harry
Leon Wilson and Booth Tarkington.
Photographer: George Schneiderman.
Released with tinted sequences. With
John Gilbert (Cameo Kirby), Gertrude
Olmstead (Adele Randall), Alan Hale
(Col. Moreau), William E. Lawrence (Col.
Randall), Jean Arthur (Ann Playdell),
Richard Tucker (Cousin Aaron), Phillips
Smalley (Judge Playdell), Jack McDonald
(Larkin Bruce), Eugenie Ford (Mme.
Dauezac), Frank Baker.

Riverboat gambler Kirby wins Colonel
Randall's estate solely to save him from
crooked Moreau. But Randall kills himself
and Moreau, blaming Kirby, shoots him in
the back. Kirby kills Moreau in a second
duel, but a Randall brother, deceived by
Moreau, pursues Kirby, who, hiding in the
Randall house, discovers his secret love
Adele is Randall's daughter and proves
his innocence. Remade, 1929, by Irving
Cummings.

Ford's first billing as "John Ford." *Exhibitors' Trade Review* (October 27, 1923): "As
though the men and women of that pre–
Civil War period had come to life again
in the full vigor and beauty of their joy of
living. Ranks with the best of the year."
Despite some pretty pictures, it seems
overtitled tedium today.

*1923 *North of Hudson Bay* (William
Fox). 4,973 feet. November 19. Direc-
tor: John Ford. Writer: Jules Furthman.
Photographer: Daniel B. Clark. Released
with tinted sequences. With Tom Mix
(Michael Dane, a rancher), Kathleen Kay
(Estelle MacDonald), Jennie Lee (Dane's
mother), Frank Campeau (Cameron
MacDonald), Eugene Pallette (Peter
Dane), Will Walling (Angus MacKenzie),
Frank Leigh (Jeffrey Clough), Fred Kohler
(Armand LeMoir). Working title: "Journey
to Death."

Rancher Michael Dane falls in love with
Estelle while en route to northern Canada,
where his brother Peter has struck gold.
But there he finds his brother dead and his
partner MacKenzie sentenced to walk the
"death trail" until dead. Dane tries to help
MacKenzie, earns the same sentence, but
both escape, battling wolves, and meet
Estelle, pursued by her uncle, the real
murderer, who dies after a canoe chase
over a waterfall.

Only portions of the film survive—with
Czech titles.

*1923 *Hoodman Blind* (William Fox). 5,434
feet. December 20. Director: John Ford.
Scenarist: Charles Kenyon, from play
by Henry Arthur Jones and Wilson Barrett.
Photographer: George Schneiderman.
With David Butler (Jack Yeulette), Gladys
Hulette (Nance Yeulette; Jessie Walton),
Regina Connelly (Jessie Walton, the first),
Frank Campeau (Mark Lezzard), Marc
MacDermott (John Linden), Trilby Clark
(Mrs. John Linden), Eddie Gribbon

(Battling Brown), Jack Walters (Bull Yeaman).

John Linden, a victim of wanderlust, deserts wife and daughter and goes West with a village girl, with whom he has a second daughter, then leaves them as well. In South Africa he finds wealth. Meanwhile, both mothers die. Nancy, the legitimate daughter, marries a fisherman; look-alike Jessie, the illegitimate daughter, becomes a whore. Through their resemblance, crooked lawyer Mark Lezzard arouses the jealousy of Nancy's husband, hoping to gain Nancy for himself and thus the money that Linden sends her through Lezzard. Linden returns and is reunited with his daughters, after Nancy's husband heroically rescues Jessie from a sinking boat.

Exhibitors' Trade Review: Atmospheric, crooked streets, character studies, almost all outside and at night, "with that eerie and striking contrast of flickering light and sharp shadows." "Heavy melodrama that seems to depress instead of entertain," wrote an exhibitor to *Moving Picture World* (August 29, 1925).

1924 *The Iron Horse* (William Fox). 11,335 feet. August 28. Director: John Ford. Scenarist: Charles Kenyon, from story by Kenyon and John Russell. Photographers: George Schneiderman, Burnett Guffey. Titles: Charles Darnton. Music score: Erno Rapee. Assistant director: Edward O'Fearna. Released with tinted sequences. Filmed January–March. With George O'Brien (Davy Brandon), Madge Bellamy (Miriam Marsh), Judge Charles Edward Bull (Abraham Lincoln), William Walling (Thomas Marsh), Fred Kohler (Deroux), Cyril Chadwick (Peter Jesson), Gladys Hulette (Rudy), James Marcus (Judge Haller), Francis Powers (Sgt. Slattery), J. Farrell MacDonald (Cpl. Casey), James Welch (Pvt. Schultz), Colin Chase (Tony), Walter Rogers (Gen. Dodge), Jack O'Brien (Dinny), George Waggner (Col. Buffalo Bill Cody), John Padjan (Wild Bill Hickok), Charles O'Malley (Maj. North), Charles Newton (Collis P. Huntington), Delbert Mann (Charles Crocker), Chief Big Tree (Cheyenne chief), Chief White Spear (Sioux chief), Edward Piel (old Chinaman), James Gordon (David Brandon, Sr.), Winston Miller (Davy, as child), Peggy Cartwright (Miriam, as child), Thomas Durant (Jack Ganzhorn), Stanhope Wheatcroft (John Hay), Frances Teague

(Polka Dot), Dan Borzage, Frank Baker. Working titles: "The TransContinental Railroad," "The Iron Trail."

Building the transcontinental railroad.

Most prints derive from a poorly edited British negative.

*1924 *Hearts of Oak* (William Fox). 5,336 feet. October 5. Director: John Ford. Scenarist: Charles Kenyon, from play by James A. Herne. Photographer: George Schneiderman. With Hobart Bosworth (Terry Dunnivan, a sea captain), Pauline Starke (Chrystal), Theodore von Eltz (Ned Fairweather), James Gordon (John Owen), Francis Powers (Grandpa Dunnivan), Jennie Lee (Grandma Dunnivan), Francis Ford, Frank Baker.

Terry Dunnivan, an elderly sea captain, adopts orphan Chrystal, who grows up and loves Ned. But Ned voyages and is reported missing. Two years pass, the old captain is about to wed his ward, but a steamer is wrecked and Ned is a survivor. The captain marries Nancy, but learns of her love for Ned, follows him, takes him on an Arctic trip, and, dying midst frozen wastes, hears the voice of his wife and baby ("Goodby Daddy"). Ned and Chrystal wed.

Exhibitors' Trade Review: "Great Bosworth." "Photos of sea, Arctic, New England" —"a veritable triumph of realism." "Good box-office."

1925 *Lightnin'* (William Fox). 8,050 feet. August 23. Director: John Ford. Scenarist: Frances Marion, from play by Winchell Smith and Frank Bacon. Photographer: Joseph A. August. Assistant director: Edward O'Fearna. With Jay Hunt (Lightnin' Bill Jones), Madge Bellamy (Millie), Edythe Chapman (Mother Jones), Wallace McDonald (John Marvin), J. Farrell MacDonald (Judge Lemuel Townsend), Ethel Clayton (Margaret Davis), Richard Travers (Raymond Thomas), James Marcus (Sheriff Blodgett), Otis Harlan (Zeb), Brandon Hurst (Everett Hammond), Peter Mazutis (Oscar).

Lightnin' Bill Jones is thin, lazy old codger, named in jest, who, with his wife, owns the Calivada Hotel on the California-Nevada border. "Mother" Jones wants to sell the hotel, but a young lawyer, John Marvin convinces Lightnin' that the offer is fraudulent. When Mother persists, Lightnin' exiles himself to the veterans' home, but everything is cleared up in court, and Marvin wins the Joneses' adopted daughter.

A downbeat comedy from a record-running stageplay, the prestige production received excellent distribution and played around for almost two years—unusual for the 1920s. Exhibitors invariably praised it, but said its box-office appeal was mediocre. Today, Madge Bellamy aside, the humor seems ponderous and mostly in the titles. Remade, 1930, by Henry King, with Will Rogers.

1925 *Kentucky Pride* (William Fox). 6,597 feet. September 6. Director: John Ford. Writer: Dorothy Yost. Photographers: George Schneiderman, Edmund Reek. Assistant director: Edward O'Fearna. Filmed in Kentucky. With Henry B. Walthall (Roger Beaumont), J. Farrell MacDonald (Mike Donovan), Gertrude Astor (Mrs. Beaumont), Malcolm Waite (Greve Carter), Belle Stoddard (Mrs. Donovan), Winston Miller (Danny Donovan), George Read (butler), Peaches Jackson (Virginia Beaumont), and the horses Man O'War, Fair Play, The Finn, Confederacy, and Virginia's Future (herself), Negofol (her sire), Morvich (her husband).

A horse story.

*1925 *The Fighting Heart* (William Fox). 6,978 feet. October 18. Director: John Ford. Scenarist: Lillie Hayward, from "Once to Every Man," by Larry Evans. Photographer: Joseph H. August. Released with tinted sequences. With George O'Brien (Danny Bolton), Billie Dove (Doris Anderson), J. Farrell MacDonald (Jerry), Diana Miller (Helen Van Allen), Victor McLaglen (Soapy Williams), Bert Woodruff (Grandfather Bolton), James Marcus (Judge Maynard), Lynn Cowan (Chub Morehouse), Harvey Clark (Dennison), Hank Mann (his assistant), Francis Ford (the town fool), Francis Powers (John Anderson), Hazel Howell (Oklahoma Kate), Edward Piel (Flash Fogarty), Frank Baker (manager).

The townspeople look down on the Boltons, the male members having all succumbed to drink except young Denny, who feels the situation keenly. He gives Soapy Williams a sound thrashing when he discovers him selling bootleg hootch to his grandfather. When grandfather dies and sweetheart Doris turns against him (suspecting he is drinking), Denny follows a reporter's advice to go to New York and become a prizefighter. He gets a tryout at Flash Fogarty's gym and earns a match against Williams (now heavyweight champ), but Williams's fan Helen vamps Denny into breaking training, so he loses the fight. Later Denny meets Williams and Helen outside a nightclub and, taunted, licks him on the street and returns home to Doris.

Moving Picture World (September 26, 1925): George O'Brien a he-man, not a "dude like Mix." Just a good programmer. Too much character and atmosphere, slow pace.

*1925 *Thank You* (William Fox). 6,900 feet. November 1. Director: John Ford. Producer: John Golden. Scenarist: Frances Marion, from play by Winchell Smith and Tom Cushing. Photographer: George Schneiderman. Released with tinted sequences. With George O'Brien (Kenneth Jamieson), Jacqueline Logan (Diana Lee, the mother), Alec Francis (David Lee), J. Farrell MacDonald (Andy), Cyril Chadwick (Mr. Jones), Edith Bostwick (Mrs. Jones), Vivian Ogden (Miss Glodgett), James Neill (Dr. Cobb), Billy Rinaldi (Sweet, Jr.), Maurice Murphy (Willie Jones), Robert Milasch (Sweet, Sr.), George Fawcett (Jamieson, Sr.), Marion Harlan (Millie Jones), Ida Moore, Frankie Bailey (gossips).

After a series of escapades, Kenneth Jamieson's millionaire father banishes him to a chicken farm in the slow village of Dedham, where, on the same day, Diane, niece of Rev. David Lee, arrives from Paris with French clothes and delights David. A few days later Kenneth gets drunk and offends Diane, but David talks to him and he reforms. David, underpaid and always having to beg, is refused an increase in pay unless he sends Diane away; busybody Jones notifies Jamieson, Sr., who goes after Diane roughshod, expecting to find a gold-digger. But Diane wins him over, particularly after she nurses Kenneth back from an illness, and Jamieson, Sr. gives the townspeople a sound verbal thrashing, calling them hypocrites and pharisees at their treatment of David. Not long after, David and Jamieson, Sr., who were old cronies, are overjoyed at engagement of Diane and Kenneth.

Moving Picture World (October 3, 1925): "sympathetic, but too much characterization slows story."

1926 *The Shamrock Handicap* (William Fox). 5,685 feet. May 2. Director: John Ford. Scenarist: John Stone, from story by Peter B. Kyne. Photographer: George Schneiderman. Titles: Elizabeth Pickett. Assistant director: Edward O'Fearna. Released with tinted sequences. With Leslie Fenton (Neil Ross), J. Farrell MacDonald (Con O'Shea), Janet Gaynor (Sheila O'Hara), Louis Payne (Sir Michael O'Hara), Claire McDowell (Molly O'Shea), Willard Louis (Orville Finch), Andy Clark (Chesty Morgan), George Harris (Benny Ginsburg), Ely Reynolds (Virus Cakes), Thomas Delmar (Michael), Brandon Hurst (the procurer).

Horse racing, Ireland and America.

Some filmographies give different character names; those above correspond to the existing print.

1926 *3 Bad Men* (William Fox). 8,710 feet. August 28. Director: John Ford. Scenarists: Ford, John Stone, from the novel *Over the Border*, by Herman Whitaker. Photographer: George Schneiderman. Filmed at Jackson Hole, Wyoming, and in the Mojave Desert, March–May. Released with tinted sequences. With George O'Brien (Dan O'Malley), Olive Borden (Lee Carlton), J. Farrell MacDonald (Mike Costigan), Tom Santschi (Bull Stanley), Frank Campeau (Spade Allen), Louis Tellegen (Sheriff Layne Hunter), George Harris (Joe Minsk), Jay Hunt (old prospector), Priscilla Bonner (Millie Stanley), Otis Harlan (Zack Leslie), Walter Perry (Pat Monahan), Grace Gordon (Millie's friend), Alec B. Francis (Rev. Calvin Benson), George Irving (Gen. Neville), Phyllis Haver (prairie beauty), Vester Pegg, Bud Osbone.

Dakota land rush, 1876.

1926 *The Blue Eagle* (William Fox). 6,200 feet. September 12. Director: John Ford. Scenarist: L. G. Rigby, from story "The Lord's Referee," by Gerald Beaumont. Photographer: George Schneiderman. Assistant director: Edward O'Fearna. Released with tinted sequences. With George O'Brien (George Darcy), Janet Gaynor (Rose Cooper), William Russell (Big Tim Ryan), Robert Edeson (Father Joe), David Butler (Nick Galvani), Phillip Ford (Limpy Darcy), Ralph Sipperly (Slats Mulligan), Margaret Livingston (Mary Rohan), Jerry Madden (Baby Tom), Harry Tenbrook (Bascom), Lew Short (Capt. McCarthy), Frank Baker.

On shipboard, a submarine attack interrupts a grudge fight between Darcy and Ryan, who both love Rose Cooper. After the war, their skipper (and pastor of a dock-front parish) unites them momentarily to blow up a submarine used by dope smugglers; then he referees their fight. Darcy wins and gets Rose. But Father Joe finds a widow for Ryan and it all ends with an American Legion parade.

The soldier-priest prefigures Ward Bond's pugnacious roles, and inventive humor redeems a pedestrian film. Janet Gaynor has only a couple of scenes, alas. Rated good entertainment in 1926. The surviving print is missing a number of sequences.

†1926 *What Price Glory?* (William Fox). 12 reels. November 23. Director: Raoul Walsh. With Victor McLaglen, Edmund Lowe, et al.

Ford is said to have directed shots in the going-off-to-the-front sequence.

*1927 *Upstream* (William Fox). 5,510 feet. January 30. Director: John Ford. Scenarist: Randall H. Faye, from story "The Snake's Wife," by Wallace Smith. Photographer: Charles G. Clarke. Assistant director: Edward O'Fearna. With Nancy Nash (Gertie King), Earle Foxe (Eric Brasingham), Grant Withers (Jack LeVelle), Raymond Hitchcock (the star boarder), Lydia Yeamans Titus (Miss Breckenbridge), Emile Chautard (Campbell Mandare), Ted McNamara, Sammy Cohen (a dance team), Francis Ford (juggler), Judy King, Lillian Worth (sister team), Jane Winton (soubrette), Harry Bailey (Gus Hoffman), Ely Reynolds (Deerfoot), Frank Baker.

In a vaudeville boardinghouse, conceited Brasingham is chosen (for his wealthy name) for a West End revival of Hamlet and makes good. But he fails to credit his coach and coming home to a wedding (his sweetheart marrying her knife-throwing partner) assumes it's a part for him, and gets kicked out; but he smiles for photographers.

Derived from Francis Ford's unreleased *Matinee* (1925).

†1927 *7th Heaven* (William Fox). 12 reels. May 6. Director: Frank Borzage. With

Janet Gaynor, Charles Farrell, etc.
Ford directed portions of the taxis-to-the-Marne sequence.

*1928 *Mother Machree* (William Fox). 75 minutes. January 22. Director: John Ford. Scenarist: Gertrude Orr, from lyric and song by Rida Johnson Young. Photographer: Chester Lyons. Editors and title-writers: Katherine Hilliker, H. H. Caldwell. Assistant director: Edward O'Fearna. Released with sequences tinted light amber, lavender, green, and blue. General release: March 5. Synchronized music and sound effects, with the title song sung with voice synch. With Belle Bennett (Ellen McHugh, Mother Machree), Neil Hamilton (Brian McHugh), Philippe de Lacy (Brian, as child), Pat Somerset (Bobby De Puyster), Victor McLaglen (Terence O'Dowd, Giant of Kilkenny), Ted McNamara (Harper of Wexford), William Platt (Pips, Dwarf of Munster), John MacSweeney (Irish priest), Eulalie Jensen (Rachel van Studdiford), Constance Howard (Edith Cutting), Ethel Clayton (Mrs. Cutting), Jacques Rollens (Signor Bellini), Rodney Hildebrand (Brian McHugh, Sr.), Joyce Wirard (Edith Cutting, as child), Robert Parrish (child).

A family is divided in 1899 Ireland, reunited years later in America.

The Story of Mother Machree was announced in Fox publicity in June 1926 and went into production that September. In November its premiere was announced for December 12, 1926, tied in to marketing of music and discs of the title song. But no film appeared. In February, just after completion of *Sunrise*, Ford voyaged to Germany, returning in April. In May 1927, at Fox sales convention in Atlantic City, *Sunrise*, *7th Heaven*, and *Mother Machree* were privately screened (with Movietone scores?), and in April the first Movietone Sound newsreels were shown at the Roxy. In September *Sunrise* opened, with Movietone track, and *Four Sons* was nearing completion. In January 1928 *Mother Machree* was said to have cost $750,000 and its "delay" to have been worthwhile. (It was, however, shown in prerelease at the Astoria Theater, London, in September 1927—presumably a silent version.) Only three reels (one of them mostly entry music) survive.

1928 *Four Sons* (William Fox). 100 minutes. February 13. Director: John Ford.

Scenarist: Philip Klein, from story "Grandma Bernle Learns Her Letters," by I. A. R. Wylie, and from a treatment thereof by Herman Bing (uncredited). Photographers: George Schneiderman, Charles G. Clarke. Music arranger: S. L. Rothafel. Original score: Carli Elinor. Theme song: "Little Mother," by Erno Rapee, Lee Pollack; sung by Harold van Duzee and the Roxy Male Quartette. Editor: Margaret V. Clancey. Title writers: Katherine Hilliker, H. H. Caldwell. Assistant director: Edward O'Fearna. Released with music and synchronized sound effects. With Margaret Mann (Frau Bernle), James Hall (Joseph Bernle), Charles Morton (Johann Bernle), George Meeker (Andres Bernle), Francis X. Bushman, Jr. (Franz Bernle), June Collyer (Annabelle Bernle), Albert Gran (postman), Earle Foxe (Major Von Stomm), Frank Reicher (headmaster), Jack Pennick (Joseph's American friend), Archduke Leopold of Austria (German captain), Hughie Mack (innkeeper), Wendell Franklin (James Henry), Auguste Tollaire (Major), Ruth Mix (Johann's girl), Robert Parrish (child), Michael Mark (Von Stomm's orderly), L. J. O'Conner (aubergiste), Ferdinand Schumann-Heink, Capt. John Porters, Carl Boheme, Constant Franke, Hans Furberg, Tibor von Janny, Stanley Blystone, Lt. George Blagoi (officers), Frank Baker (soldier).

A Bavarian mother loses three sons in World War I and goes to America to join the fourth.

1928 *Hangman's House* (William Fox). 6,518 feet. May 13. Silent. Director: John Ford. Scenarists: Marion Orth, Willard Mack, from novel by Brian Oswald Donn-Byrne, adapted by Philip Klein. Photographer: George Schneiderman. Editor: Margaret V. Clancey. Title-writer: Malcolm Stuart Boylan. Assistant director: Phil Ford. With Victor McLaglen (Citizen Hogan), Hobart Bosworth (James O'Brien, Lord Chief Justice), June Collyer (Connaught O'Brien), Larry Kent (Dermott McDermott), Earle Foxe (John D'Arcy), Eric Mayne (legionnaire colonel), Joseph Burke (Neddy Joe), Belle Stoddard (Anne McDermott), John Wayne (spectator at horse race; hanging man), Frank Baker (English officer).

An exile returns to Ireland to rid it of a scoundrel.

*1928 *Napoleon's Barber* (William Fox–Movietone). 2,980 feet. November 24. All-talking. Director: John Ford. Scenarist: Arthur Caesar, from his own play. Photographer: George Schneiderman. Title-writer: Malcolm Stuart Boylan. Released with talking sound. With Otto Matiesen (Napoleon), Frank Reicher (the barber), Natalie Golitzin (Josephine), Helen Ware (barber's wife), Philippe De Lacy (barber's son), Russell Powell (blacksmith), Buddy Roosevelt, Ervin Renard, Joe Waddell, Youcca-Troubetzkoy (French officers), Henry Herbert (soldier), D'Arcy Corrigan (tailor), Michael Mark (peasant).

A barber brags what he would do to Napoleon, not knowing his customer *is* Napoleon.

Ford recorded Josephine's coach crossing a bridge, against the advice of the sound man, and achieved perfect results. His claim that it was "the first time anyone ever went outside with a sound system" is correct only in dramatic films. Fox Movietone News had frequently recorded outdoors, notably the West Point cadets (shown April 30, 1927 at the Roxy) and the Lindbergh takeoff, May 20, 1927.

Moving Picture World (February 26, 1927), noting a Georges Renavant production of *Napoleon's Barber* at the Grove Street Theater, called it a gem of a "screen laugh-maker that would be almost certain to go big with a star like Buster Keaton or Harry Langdon." Ford began filming September 29, 1928.

1928 *Riley the Cop* (William Fox). 67 minutes. November 25. Director: John Ford. Writers: James Gruen, Fred Stanley. Photographer: Charles G. Clarke. Editor: Alex Troffey. Assistant director: Phil Ford. Released with music and synchronized sound effects. With J. Farrell MacDonald (Aloysius Riley), Louise Fazenda (Lena Krausmeyer), Nancy Drexel (Mary), David Rollins (Davy Collins), Harry Schultz (Hans Krausmeyer), Billy Bevan (Paris cab driver), Mildred Boyd (Caroline), Ferdinand Schumann-Heink (Julius), Del Henderson (judge), Russell Powell (Kuchendorf), Mike Donlin (crook), Robert Parrish.

A kindly New York cop travels to Germany.

?*?1929 *Strong Boy* (William Fox). 63 minutes. March 3. Director: John Ford. Scenarists: James Kevin McGuinness, Andrew Bennison, John McLain, from story by Frederick Hazlett Brennan. Photographer: Joseph H. August. Title-writer: Malcolm Stuart Boyland. Released with music and synchronized sound effects. With Victor McLaglen (William "Strong Boy" Bloss), Leatrice Joy (Mary McGregor), Clyde Cook (Pete), Slim Summerville (Slim), Kent Sanderson (Wilbur Watkins), Tom Wilson (baggage master), Jack Pennick (baggageman), Eulalie Jensen (the queen), David Torrence (railroad president), J. Farrell MacDonald (Angus McGregor), Dolores Johnson (usherette), Douglas Scott (Wobby), Robert Ryan (porter), Frank Baker. Working title: "The Baggage Smasher."

A railroad porter becomes a hero and marries the boss's daughter.

The only print of this film—a 35mm nitrate—was reportedly in a private collection in Australia. Does it still exist?

1929 *The Black Watch* (William Fox). 93 minutes. May 8. All-talking. Director: John Ford. "Staged by": Lumsden Hare. Scenarists: James Kevin McGuinness, John Stone, Frank Barber, from novel *King of the Khyber Rifles*, by Talbot Mundy. Photographer: Joseph H. August. Art director: William Darling. Song: "Flowers of Delight," by William Kernell. Editor: Alex Troffey. Assistant director: Edward O'Fearna. Filmed: January–February. With Victor McLaglen (Capt. Donald King), Myrna Loy (Yasmani), Roy D'Arcy (Rewa Ghunga), Pat Somerset (Highlanders' officer), David Rollins (Lt. Malcolm King), Mitchell Lewis (Mohammed Khan), Walter Long (Harem Bey), Frank Baker, David Percy (Highlanders' officers), Lumsden Hare (colonel), Cyril Chadwick (Maj. Twynes), David Torrence (Marechal), Francis Ford (Maj. MacGregor), Claude King (general in India), Frederick Sullivan (general's aide), Joseph Diskay (muezzin), Richard Travers (adjutant), Joyzelle.

Remade 1954, by Henry King, as *King of the Khyber Rifles*.

1929 *Salute* (William Fox). 86 minutes. September 1. All-talking. Director: John Ford. Scenarist: James K. McGuinness, from story by Tristram Tupper, John Stone. Photographer: Joseph H. August. Editor: Alex Troffey. Title-writer: Wilbur Morse, Jr. Assistant directors: Edward

O'Fearna, R. L. Hough. Filmed at Annapolis, May–July. With William Janney (Midshipman Paul Randall), Helen Chandler (Nancy Wayne), Stepin Fetchit (Smoke Screen), Frank Albertson (Midshipman Albert Edward Price), George O'Brien (Cadet John Randall), Joyce Compton (Marion Wilson), Cliff Dempsey (Maj. Gen. Somers), Lumsden Hare (Rear Adm. Randall), David Butler (navy coach), Rex Bell (cadet), John Breeden, Ward Bond, John Wayne (midshipmen).

A young man enters Annapolis.

*†1929 *Big Time* (William Fox). 83 or 87 minutes. September 7. All-talking. Director: Kenneth Hawks. With Lee Tracy, Mae Clark, Stepin Fetchit, John Ford (as himself).

A melodrama about a vaudeville family drifting to Hollywood.

*1930 *Men Without Women* (William Fox). 77 minutes. January 31. Director: John Ford. "Staged by": Andrew Bennison. Scenarist: Dudley Nichols, from story "Submarine," by Ford, James K. McGuinness. Photographer: Joseph H. August. Art director: William S. Darling. Music: Peter Brunelli, Glen Knight. Editor: Paul Weatherwax. Assistant director: Edward O'Fearna. Technical advisor: Schuyler E. Gray. Filmed at Catalina, fall 1929. With Kenneth MacKenna (Burke), Frank Albertson (Price), Paul Page (Handsome), Pat Somerset (Lt. Digby, R. N.), Walter McGrail (Cobb), Stuart Erwin (Jenkins, radio operator), Warren Hymer (Kaufman), J. Farrell MacDonald (Costello), Roy Stewart (Capt. Carson), Warner Richmond (Lt. Commander Bridewell), Harry Tenbrook (Winkler), Ben Hendricks, Jr. (Murphy), George LeGuere (Pollosk), Charles Gerrard (Weymouth), John Wayne, Robert Parrish, Frank Baker.

A Shanghai nightclub: Weymouth thinks "Burke" is Quartermain, sole survivor of a destroyer torpedoed carrying "England's greated Field Marshall"; there had been scandal about a Lady Patricia, whom Quartermain had visited, but "I voted to clear the woman and damned the memory of my best friend." Later, one man must stay behind in a trapped submarine. Burke tells Price about Quartermain, "a man whose name are dead but who didn't die himself." When Price surfaces he tells

Weymouth, "His name was Burke, he's from my home town."

The only known surviving prints are of a silent edition with intertitles. The talking version seems lost.

1930 *Born Reckless* (William Fox). 82 minutes. May 11. Director: John Ford. "Staged by": Andrew Bennison. Scenarist: Dudley Nichols, from novel *Louis Beretti*, by Donald Henderson Clarke. Photographer: George Schneiderman. Art director: Jack Schulze. Associate producer: James K. McGuinness. Editor: Frank E. Hull. Assistant director: Edward O'Fearna. With Edmond Lowe (Louis Beretti), Catherine Dale Owen (Joan Sheldon), Lee Tracy (Bill O'Brien), Marguerite Churchill (Rosa Beretti), Warren Hymer (Big Shot), Pat Somerset (Duke), William Harrigan (Good News Brophy), Frank Albertson (Frank Sheldon), Ferike Boros (Ma Beretti), J. Farrell MacDonald (district attorney), Paul Porcasi (Pa Beretti), Eddie Gribbon (Bugs), Mike Donlin (Fingy Moscovitz), Ben Bard (Joe Bergman), Paul Page (Ritzy Reilly), Joe Brown (Needle Beer Grogan), Jack Pennick, Ward Bond (soldiers), Roy Stewart (District Attorney Cardigan), Yola D'Avril (French girl).

New York, 1917: For publicity, a D.A. sends three burglars to war instead of "up the river." After France, one, Louie Beretti, swears vengeance on a mobster who shot his sister's husband, but we hear no more of that storyline. He goes to propose to Joan, but meets her fiancé; so much for love. 1920: prospering with a speakeasy, he alibis for Big Shot, who shot a stoolie. 1922: Big Shot kidnaps Joan's child; Louie rescues her and kills Big Shot.

1930 *Up the River* (William Fox). 92 minutes. October 12. Director: John Ford. "Staged by": William Collier, Jr. Writers: Maurine Watkins with Ford, William Collier, Sr. Photographer: Joseph H. August. Set designer: Duncan Cramer. Music and lyrics: Joseph McCarthy, James F. Hanley. Wardrobe: Sophia Wachner. Editor: Frank E. Hull. Assistant directors: Edward O'Fearna, Wingate Smith. Filmed: summer. With Spencer Tracy (St. Louis), Warren Hymer (Dannemora Dan), Humphrey Bogart (Steve), Claire Luce (Judy), Joan Lawes (Jean), Sharon Lynn (Edith La Verne), George McFarlane

(Jessup), Gaylord Pendleton (Morris), Morgan Wallace (Frosby), William Collier, Sr. (Pop), Robert E. O'Connor (warden), Louise MacIntosh (Mrs. Massey), Edythe Chapman (Mrs. Jordan), Johnny Walker (Happy), Noel Francis (Sophie), Mildred Vincent (Annie), Wilbur Mack (Whitelay), Goodee Montgomery (Kit), Althea Henley (Cynthia), Carol Wines (Daisy Elmore), Adele Windsor (Minnie), Richard Keene (Dick), Elizabeth and Helen Keating (May and June), Robert Burns (Slim), John Swor (Clem), Pat Somerset (Beauchamp), Joe Brown (Deputy Warden), Harvey Clark (Nash), Black and Blue (Slim and Klem), Morgan Wallace (Fosby), Robert Parrish.

A comedy set in a prison.

The surviving print is missing numerous shots.

1931 *Seas Beneath* (William Fox). 99 minutes. January 30. Director: John Ford. Scenarist: Dudley Nichols, from story by James Parker, Jr. Photographer: Joseph H. August. Editor: Frank E. Hull. Filmed at Catalina, November. With George O'Brien (Comdr. Bob Kingsley, USN), Marion Lessing (Anna Marie Von Steuben), Warren Hymer (Lug Kaufman), William Collier, Sr. (Mugs O'Flaherty), John Loder (Franz Schilling), Walter C. "Judge" Kelly (Chief Mike "Guns" Costello), Walter McGrail (Joe Cobb), Henry Victor (Ernst Von Steuben, commandant, U-boat 172), Mona Maris (Lolita), Larry Kent (Lt. MacGregor), Gaylord Pendleton (Ens. Richard Cabot), Nat Pendleton (Butch Wagner), Harry Tenbrook (Winkler), Terry Ray (Reilly), Hans Furberg (Fritz Kampf, 2nd officer, U-172), Ferdinand Schumann-Heink (Adolph Brucker, engineer, U-172), Francis Ford (trawler captain), Kurt Furberg (Hoffman), Ben Hall (Harrigan), Harry Weil (Jevinsky), Maurice Murphy (Merkel), Frank Baker.

World War I: A U.S. freighter, disguised, decoys German subs.

1931 *The Brat* (Fox Film). 81 minutes. August 23. Director: John Ford. Scenarists: Sonya Levien, S. N. Behrman, Maud Fulton, from play by Fulton. Photographer: Joseph H. August. Editor: Alex Troffey. With Sally O'Neil (the brat), Alan Dinehart (MacMillan Forester), Frank Albertson (Stephen Forester), Virginia Cherrill (Angela), June Collyer (Jane), J. Farrell MacDonald (Timson, the butler), William Collier, Sr. (judge), Margaret Mann (housekeeper), Albert Gran (bishop), Mary Forbes (Mrs. Forester), Louise MacIntosh (Lena), Ward Bond (policeman).

In court for not paying for spaghetti, a waif is discharged for book research to writer MacMillan and taken to his mother's Long Island estates, where she encounters mother, two courting ladies, a jovial bishop, and a proper butler. MacMillan coldly has his way with her until she chooses drunk brother Steve and goes to his Wyoming ranch (which mother had wished to sell for a two-story yacht for MacMillan).

1931 *Arrowsmith* (Samuel Goldwyn–United Artists). 108 minutes. December 1. Director: John Ford. Producer: Samuel Goldwyn. Scenarist: Sidney Howard, from the novel by Sinclair Lewis. Photographer: Ray June. Art director: Richard Day. Music: Alfred Newman. Editor: Hugh Bennett. With Ronald Colman (Dr. Martin Arrowsmith), Helen Hayes (Leora), A. E. Anson (Prof. Gottlieb), Richard Bennett (Sondelius), Claude King (Dr. Tubbs), Beulah Bondi (Mrs. Tozer), Myrna Loy (Joyce Lanyon), Russell Hopton (Terry Wickett), De Witt Jennings (Mr. Tozer), John Qualen (Henry Novak), Adele Watson (Mrs. Novak), Lumsden Hare (Sir Robert Fairland), Bert Roach (Bert Tozer), Charlotte Henry (a young girl), Clarence Brooks (Oliver Marchand), Walter Downing (city clerk), David Landau, James Marcus, Alec B. Francis, Sidney Grey, Florence Britton, Bobby Watson, Ward Bond (policeman), Frank Baker (ship captain).

Glory, medicine, and his wife compete for a doctor's loyalties. Four Oscar nominations: best picture, best adaptation (Sidney Howard); art direction (Richard Day); photography (Ray June).

†1932 *Hot Pepper* (Fox Film). 76 minutes. Director: John G. Blystone. With Victor McLaglen, Edmund Lowe, Lupe Velez.

A sequel to *What Price Glory?*

Ford directed some second unit scenes.

1932 *Air Mail* (Universal). 83 minutes. November 3. Director: John Ford. Producer: Carl Laemmle, Jr. Scenarists: Dale Van Every, Lt. Comdr. Frank W. Wead, from story by Wead. Photographer: Karl Freund. Special effects: John P. Fulton.

Aerial stunts: Paul Mantz. With Pat
O'Brien (Duke Talbot), Ralph Bellamy
(Mike Miller), Gloria Stuart (Ruth Barnes),
Lillian Bond (Irene Wilkins), Russell
Hopton ("Dizzy" Wilkins), Slim
Summerville (Slim McCune), Frank
Albertson (Tommy Bogan), Leslie Fenton
(Tony Dressel), David Landau (Pop), Tom
Corrigan (Sleepy Collins), William Daly
(Tex Lane), Hans Furberg (Heinie
Kramer), Lew Kelly (drunkard), Frank
Beal, Francis Ford, James Donlan, Louise
MacIntosh, Katherine Perry (passengers),
Beth Milton (place attendant), Edmund
Burns (radio announcer), Charles de la
Montte, Lt. Pat Davis (passenger plane
pilots), Jim Thorpe (Indian), Enrico
Caruso, Jr., Billy Thorpe, Alene Carroll,
Jack Pennick.
　Conflicts and daredevilry punctuate
pilots' dreary days.

1932 *Flesh* (Metro-Goldwyn-Mayer). 95
minutes. December 9. Director: John
Ford. Scenarists: Leonard Praskins, Edgar
Allen Woolf, and (uncredited) William
Faulkner, from story by Edmund
Goulding. Dialogue: Moss Hart. Photogra-
pher: Arthur Edeson. Editor: William S.
Gray. With Wallace Beery (Polokai), Karen
Morley (Lora Nash), Ricardo Cortez
(Nicky), Jean Hersholt (Mr. Herman), John
Miljan (Joe Willard), Vince Barnett
(waiter), Herman Bing (Pepi), Greta Meyer
(Mrs. Herman), Ed Brophy (Dolan), Ward
Bond (wrestler), Nat Pendleton.
　A female ex-con marries a German wres-
tler, but sells him out for her boyfriend.

1933 *Pilgrimage* (Fox Film). 90 minutes.
July 12. Director: John Ford. Scenarists:
Philip Klein, Barry Connors, from story
"Gold Star Mother," by I. A. R. Wylie. Dia-
logue: Dudley Nichols. Photographer:
George Schneiderman. Art director:
William Darling. Music: R. H. Bassett.
Musical direction: Samuel Kaylin. Ward-
robe: A. R. Luick. Editor: Louis R.
Loeffler. Assistant director: Edward
O'Fearna. Dialogue director: William
Collier, Sr. Filmed in February. With
Henrietta Crosman (Hannah Jessop),
Heather Angel (Suzanne), Norman Foster
(Jim Jessop), Marian Nixon (Mary
Saunders), Maurice Murphy (Gary Worth),
Lucille La Verne (Mrs. Tally Hatfield),
Charles Grapewin (Dad Saunders), Hedda
Hopper (Mrs. Worth), Robert Warwick
(Maj. Albertson), Betty Blythe (Janet

Prescot), Francis Ford (Mayor Elmer
Briggs), Louise Carter (Mrs. Rogers), Jay
Ward (Jim Saunders), Francis Rich (nurse),
Adele Watson (Mrs. Simms), Jack Pennick
(sergeant).
　An Arkansas mother realizes her guilt
during a journey to France.

1933 *Doctor Bull* (Fox Film). 76 minutes.
September 22. Director: John Ford. Sce-
narist: Paul Green, from novel *The Last
Adam*, by James Gould Cozzens. Dia-
logue: Jane Storm. Photographer: George
Schneiderman. Music: Samuel Kaylin.
Filmed in June. With Will Rogers (Dr.
Bull), Marian Nixon (May Tripping),
Berton Churchill (Herbert Banning),
Louise Dresser (Mrs. Banning), Howard
Lally (Joe Tripping), Rochelle Hudson
(Virginia Banning), Vera Allen (Janet
Cardmaker), Tempe Pigotte (Grandma),
Elizabeth Patterson (Aunt Patricia), Ralph
Morgan (Dr. Verney), Andy Devine (Larry
Ward), Nora Cecil (Aunt Emily), Patsy
O'Byrne (Susan), Effie Ellsler (Aunt Myra),
Veda Buckland (Mary), Helen Freeman
(Helen Upjohn), Robert Parrish, Francis
Ford (mayor). Working title: "Life's
Worth Living."
　A folksy doctor tries to help an intolerant
community.

1934 *The Lost Patrol* (RKO Radio). 74
minutes. February 16. Director: John
Ford. Executive producer: Merian C.
Cooper. Associate producer: Cliff Reid.
Scenarists: Dudley Nichols, Garrett Fort,
and (uncredited) Frank Baker from story
"Patrol," by Philip MacDonald. Photogra-
pher: Harold Wenstrom. Art directors: Van
Nest Polglase, Sidney Ullman. Music: Max
Steiner. Editor: Paul Weatherwax. Techni-
cal advisor: Frank Baker. Filmed in the
Yuma desert. With Victor McLaglen (ser-
geant), Boris Karloff (Sanders), Wallace
Ford (Morelli), Reginald Denny (George
Brown), J. M. Kerrigan (Quincannon), Billy
Bevan (Herbert Hale), Alan Hale (cook),
Brandon Hurst (Bell), Douglas Walton
(Pearson), Sammy Stein (Abelson), Howard
Wilson (flyer), Neville Clark (Lt. Hawkins),
Paul Hanson (Jock Mackay), Francis Ford,
Frank Baker (relieving colonel; Arab).
　A British patrol is picked off one by one
by unseen desert Arabs.
　Remake, 1943: *Bataan*, by Tay Garnett.

1934 *The World Moves On* (Fox Film). 90
minutes. June 27. Director: John Ford.

Producer: Winfield Sheehan. Writer: Reginald C. Berkeley. Photographer: George Schneiderman. Art director: William Darling. Set decorator: Thomas Little. Costumes: Rita Kaufman. Music: Max Steiner, Louis De Francesco, R. H. Bassett, David Buttolph, Hugo Friedhofer, George Gershwin. Songs: "Should She Desire Me Not," by De Francesco; "Ave Maria," by Charles Gounod. With Madeleine Carroll (Mrs. Warburton, 1824; Mary Warburton, 1914), Franchot Tone (Richard Girard, 1824 and 1914), Lumsden Hare (Gabriel Warburton, 1824; Sir John Warburton, 1914), Raul Roulien (Carlos Girard, 1824; Henri Gerard, 1914), Reginald Denny (Erik von Gerhardt), Siegfried Rumann (Baron von Gerhardt), Louise Dresser (Baroness von Gerhardt), Stepin Fetchit (Dixie), Dudley Diggs (Mr. Manning), Frank Melton (John Girard, 1824), Brenda Fowler (Mrs. Girard, 1824), Russell Simpson (notary public, 1824), Walter McGrail (French duelist, 1824), Marcelle Corday (Miss Girard, 1824), Charles Bastin (Jacques Girard, 1914), Barry Norton (Jacques Girard, 1929), George Irving (Charles Girard, 1914), Ferdinand Schumann-Heink (Fritz von Gerhardt), Georgette Rhodes (Jeanne Girard, 1914), Claude King (Braithwaite), Ivan Simpson (Clumber), Frank Moran (Culbert), Jack Pennick, Francis Ford (legionnaires), Torbin Mayer (German chamberlain, 1914).

1825, New Orleans: Cotton King Sebastian Girard's will directs his sons to set up branches in France, Prussia, America, and, with Warburton, Manchester; all vow unity. Richard kills Mary's offender in a duel, but, the vow barring love, she sails for England with her husband. 1914: New generations renew the vow. Richard and Mary think they recognize each other. Germany: Jeanne marries Fritz. World War I: Richard and Henri enlist for France, Fritz and Erik for Germany, Fritz's sub sinks a liner carrying Girards, then is sunk itself. Mary runs English firm, marries Richard. Henri is killed, Erik maimed, Richard, wounded in Germany, is cared for by Erik's parents. 1924: Manic Richard tries to corner cotton. 1929: Bankruptcy returns him to Mary.

1934 *Judge Priest* (Fox Film). 81 minutes. October 5. Director: John Ford. Producer: Sol Wurtzel. Scenarists: Dudley Nichols, Lamar Trotti, from stories by Irvin S.

Cobb. Photographer: George Schneiderman. Music: Samuel Kaylin. With Will Rogers (Judge William Priest), Henry B. Walthall (Rev. Ashby Brand), Tom Brown (Jerome Priest), Anita Louise (Ellie May Gillespie), Rochelle Hudson (Virginia Maydew), Berton Churchill (Senator Horace K. Maydew), David Landau (Bob Gillis), Brenda Fowler (Mrs. Caroline Priest), Hattie McDaniel (Aunt Dilsey), Stepin Fetchit (Jeff Poindexter), Frank Melton (Flem Tally), Roger Imhof (Billy Gaynor), Charley Grapewin (Sgt. Jimmy Bagby), Francis Ford (juror no. 12), Paul McAllister (Doc Lake), Matt McHugh (Gabby Rives), Hy Meyer (Herman Feldsburg), Louis Mason (Sheriff Birdsong), Robert Parrish.

1890 Kentucky.

1935 *The Whole Town's Talking* (Columbia). 95 minutes. February 22. Director: John Ford. Producer: Lester Cowan. Scenarist: Jo Swerling, from novel by W. R. Burnett. Dialogue: Robert Riskin. Photographer: Joseph H. August. Editor: Viola Lawrence. Assistant director: Wilbur McGaugh. With Edward G. Robinson (Arthur Ferguson Jones; Killer Mannion), Jean Arthur (Miss "Bill" Clark), Wallace Ford (Mr. Healy), Arthur Byron (Mr. Spencer), Arthur Hohl (Det. Sgt. Michael Boyle), Donald Meek (Mr. Hoyt), Paul Harvey (J. G. Carpenter), Edward Brophy (Slugs Martin), J. Farrell MacDonald (warden), Etienne Girardot (Mr. Seaver), James Donlan (Howe), John Wray (henchman), Effie Ellsler (Aunt Agatha), Robert Emmett O'Connor (police lieutenant), Joseph Sawyer, Francis Ford, Robert Parrish. Working title: "Passport to Fame."

A timid clerk resembles Public Enemy No. 1.

Prison footage from Hawks's *The Criminal Code* (1931).

1935 *The Informer* (RKO Radio). 91 minutes. May 1. Director: John Ford. Associate producer: Cliff Reid. Scenarist: Dudley Nichols, from novel by Liam O'Flaherty. Photographer: Joseph H. August. Art directors: Van Nest Polglase, Charles Kirk. Set decorator: Julia Heron. Costumes: Walter Plunkett. Music: Max Steiner. Editor: George Hively. Assistant directors: Eddie Donahue, Edward O'Fearna. Filmed: February. With Victor McLaglen (Gypo Nolan), Heather Angel (Mary McPhillip), Preston Foster (Dan

Gallagher), Margo Grahame (Katie Madden), Wallace Ford (Frankie McPhillip), Una O'Connor (Mrs. McPhillip), J. M. Kerrigan (Terry), Joseph Sawyer (Bartley Muiholland), Neil Fitzgerald (Tommy Conner), Donald Meek (Pat Mulligan), D'Arcy Corrigan (the blindman), Leo McCabe (Donahue), Gaylord Pendleton (Daley), Francis Ford (Judge Flynn), May Boley (Mrs. Betty), Grizelda Harvey (an obedient girl), Dennis O'Dea (street singer), Jack Mulhall (lookout), Robert Parrish (soldier), Clyde Cook, Barlowe Borland, Frank Moran, Arthur McLaglen, Frank Baker.

1922 Dublin: Gypo Nolan informs on a buddy.

Awards: See main text, page 121.

1935 *Steamboat Round the Bend* (Fox Film—20th Century–Fox). 80 minutes. September 6. Director: John Ford. Producer: Sol M. Wurtzel. Scenarists: Dudley Nichols, Lamar Trotti, from story by Ben Lucian Burman. Photographer: George Schneiderman. Art director: William Darling. Set decorator: Albert Hogsett. Music director: Samuel Kaylin. Title song: Oscar Levant (uncredited). Editor: Alfred De Gaetano. Assistant director: Edward O'Fearna. Casting: Al Smith. Script clerk: Stanley Scheuer. Camera: James Gordon, Paul Lockwood. Location photography on Sacramento River. With Will Rogers (Dr. John Pearly), Anne Shirley (Fleety Belle), Eugene Pallette (Sheriff Rufe Jeffers), John McGuire (Duke), Berton Churchill ("The New Moses"), Stepin Fetchit (George Lincoln Washington), Francis Ford (Efe), Irvin S. Cobb (Capt. Eli), Roger Imhof (Pappy), Raymond Hatton (Matt Abel), Hobart Bosworth (Chaplin), Louis Mason (boat race organizer), Charles B. Middleton (Fleety's father), Si Jenks (a drunk), Jack Pennick (ringleader of boat attack).

Patent medicine and waxworks fuel a riverboat race to save a life.

1936 *The Prisoner of Shark Island* (20th Century–Fox). 95 minutes. February 12. Director: John Ford. Producer: Darryl F. Zanuck. Associate producer–scenarist: Nunnally Johnson, from life of Dr. Samuel A. Mudd. Photographer: Bert Glennon. Art director: William Darling. Set decorator: Thomas Little. Costumes: Gwen Wakeling. Music director: Louis

Silvers. Editor: Jack Murray. Assistant director: Edward O'Fearna. With Warner Baxter (Dr. Samuel A. Mudd), Gloria Stuart (Mrs. Peggy Mudd), Claude Gillingwater (Col. Jeremiah Milford Dyer), Arthur Byron (Mr. Erickson), O. P. Heggie (Dr. McIntyre), Harry Carey (Comdt. of Fort Jefferson, "Shark Island"), Francis Ford (Cpl. O'Toole), John Carradine (Sgt. Rankin), Frank McGlynne, Sr. (Abraham Lincoln), Douglas Wood (Gen. Ewing), Joyce Kay (Martha Mudd), Fred Kohler, Jr. (Sgt. Cooper), Francis McDonald (John Wilkes Booth), John McGuire (Lt. Lovell), Ernest Whitman (Buckingham Montmorency Milford), Paul Fix (David Herold), Frank Shannon (Holt), Leila McIntyre (Mrs. Lincoln), Etta McDaniel (Rosabelle Milford), Arthur Loft (carpetbagger), Paul McVey (Gen. Hunter), Maurice Murphy (orderly), Jack Pennick (soldier who sends flag messages), J.M. Kerrigan (Judge Maiben), Whitney Bourne, Robert Parrish, Frank Baker.

True story of doctor who innocently helped John Wilkes Booth and got condemned to life imprisonment.

†1936 *The Last Outlaw* (RKO Radio). 62 minutes. June 19. Director: Christy Cabane. Associate producer: Robert Sisk. Screenplay: John Twist, Jack Townley, from story by John Ford and Evelyne Murray Campbell. Photographer: Jack MacKenzie. Art director: Van Nest Polglase. Associate: Jack Gray. Musical direction: Alberto Colombo. Song: "My Heart's on the Trail," music by Nathaniel Shilkret, lyrics by Frank Luther. Sound: Denzil A. Cutler. Editor: George Hively. With Harry Carey (Dean Payton), Hoot Gibson (Chuck Wilson), Margaret Callahan (Sally Mason), Tom Tyler (Al Goss), Henry B. Walthall (Bill Yates), Ray Meyer (Joe), Harry Hans (Jess), Frank M. Thomas (Dr. Mason), Russell Hopton (Sheriff Billings), Frank Jenks (Tom), Maxine Jennings (receptionist), Fred Scott (Larry Dixon).

A remake of Ford's 1919 two-reeler.

1936 *Mary of Scotland* (RKO Radio). 123 minutes. July 24. Director: John Ford. Producer: Pandro S. Berman. Scenarist: Dudley Nichols, from play by Maxwell Anderson. Photography: Joseph H. August. Art directors: Van Nest Polglase, Carroll Clark. Set decorator: Darrell Silvera. Costumes: Walter Plunkett. Music: Max Steiner. Editor: Jane Loring.

Assistant editor: Robert Parrish. Special effects: Vernon L. Walker. Filmed in January–March. With Katharine Hepburn (Mary Stuart), Fredric March (Bothwell), Florence Eldridge (Elizabeth), Douglas Walton (Darnley), John Carradine (David Rizzio), Monte Blue (Messager), Jean Fenwick (Mary Seton), Robert Barrat (Morton), Gavin Muir (Leicester), Ian Keith (James Stuart Moray), Moroni Olsen (John Knox), Donald Crisp (Huntley), William Stack (Ruthven), Molly Lamont (Mary Livingston), Walter Byron (Sir Francis Walsingham), Ralph Forbes (Randolph), Alan Mowbray (Trockmorton), Frieda Inescort (Mary Beaton), David Torrence (Lindsay), Anita Colby (Mary Fleming), Lionel Belmore (English fisherman), Doris Lloyd (his wife), Bobby Watson (his son), Lionel Pape (Burghley), Ivan Simpson, Murray Kinnell, Lawrence Grant, Nigel DeBrulier, Barlowe Borland (judges), Alec Craig (Donal), Mary Gordon (nurse), Wilfred Lucas (Lexington), Leonard Mudie (Maitland), Brandon Hurst (Arian), D'Arcy Corrigan (Kirkcaldy), Frank Baker (Douglas), Cyril McLaglen (Faudoncide), Robert Warwick (Sir Francis Knellys), Earle Foxe (Duke of Kent), Wyndham Standing (sergeant), Gaston Glass (Chatelard), Neil Fitzgerald (nobleman), Paul McAllister (Du Croche).

1936 *The Plough and the Stars* (RKO Radio). 67 minutes. December 26. Director: John Ford. Associate producers: Cliff Reid, Robert Sisk. Scenarist: Dudley Nichols, from play by Sean O'Casey. Photography: Joseph H. August. Art director: Van Nest Polglase. Music: Nathaniel Shilkret, Roy Webb. Editor: George Hively. With Barbara Stanwyck (Mora Clitheroe), Preston Foster (Jack Clitheroe), Barry Fitzgerald (Fluther Good), Dennis O'Day (the Young Covey), Eileen Crowe (Bessie Burgess), Arthur Shields (Padraic Pearse), Erin O'Brien Moore (Rosie Redmond), Brandon Hurst (Sgt. Tinley), F. J. McCormick (Capt. Brennon), Una O'Conner (Maggie Corgan), Moroni Olsen (Gen. Connolly), J. M. Kerrigan (Peter Flynn), Neil Fitzgerald (Lt. Kangon), Bonita Granville (Mollser Gogan), Cyril McLaglen (Cpl. Stoddart), Robert Homans (barman), Mary Gordon (first woman), Mary Quinn (second woman), Lionel Pape (Englishman), Michael Fitzmaurice (ICA), Gaylord Pendleton (ICA), Doris Lloyd, D'Arcy

Corrigan, Wesley Barry, Frank Baker (English officer).

Dublin, Easter Rebellion.

1937 *Wee Willie Winkie.* (20th Century–Fox). 99 minutes. July 30. Director: John Ford. Producer: Darryl F. Zanuck. Associate producer: Gene Markey. Scenarists: Ernest Pascal, Julian Josephson, from story by Rudyard Kipling. Photography: Arthur Miller. Art director: William Darling. Set decorator: Thomas Little. Music: Louis Silvers. Editor: Walter Thompson. Released with tinted sequences (sepia for day, blue for night). With Shirley Temple (Priscilla Williams), Victor McLaglen (Sgt. MacDuff), C. Aubrey Smith (Col. Williams), June Lang (Joyce Williams), Michael Whalen (Lt. "Coppy" Brandes), Cesar Romero (Khoda Khan), Constance Collier (Mrs. Allardyce), Douglas Scott (Mott), Gavin Muir (Capt. Bibberbeigh), Willie Fung (Mohammed Dihn), Brandon Hurst (Bagby), Lionel Pape (Major Allardyce), Clyde Cook (Pipe Maj. Sneath), Lauri Beatty (Elsi Allardyce), Lionel Braham (Maj. Gen. Hammond), Mary Forbes (Mrs. MacMonachie), Cyril McLaglen (Cpl. Tummel), Pat Somerset (officer), Hector Sarno (conductor).

A little girl stops a war in 1890s India.

Many prints in circulation have been abridged to about 80 minutes. Oscar nomination: interior decoration (Thomas Little).

1937 *The Hurricane* (Samuel Goldwyn–United Artists). 102 minutes. December 24. Director: John Ford. Producer: Samuel Goldwyn. Associate producer: Merritt Hulburd. Scenarists: Dudley Nichols, Ben Hecht (uncredited), from novel by Charles Nordhoff, James Horman Hall, adapted by Oliver H. P. Garrett. Associate director: Stuart Heisler. Hurricane sequence: James Basevi. Photographer: Bert Glennon, Archie Stout (second unit). Art directors: Richard Day, Alex Golitzen. Set decorator: Julie Heron. Costumes: Omar Kiam. Music: Alfred Newman. Editor: Lloyd Nosler. Sound recording: Thomas Moulton. Assistant director: Wingate Smith. Exterior locations at Samoa, Catalina. Filmed in summer. With Dorothy Lamour (Marama), Jon Hall (Terangi), Mary Astor (Mrs. DeLaage), C. Aubrey Smith (Father Paul), Thomas Mitchell (Dr. Kersaint), Raymond

Massey (Gov. Eugene DeLaage), John
Carradine (guard), Jerome Cowan (Capt.
Nagle), Al Kikume (Chief Meheir), Kuulei
DeClercq (Tita), Layne Tom, Jr. (Mako),
Mamo Clark (Hitia), Movita Castenada
(Arai), Reri (Reri), Francis Kaai (Tavi),
Pauline Steele (Mata), Flora Hayes (Mama
Rua), Mary Shaw (Marunga), Spencer
Charters (judge), Roger Drake (captain of
the guards), Inez Courtney (girl on boat),
Paul Strader, *Araner.*

After completion of rough cut, some
interiors were reshot with new dialogue by
Ben Hecht.

South Sea Island.

Awards: See text, page 137.

†1938 *The Adventures of Marco Polo*
(Samuel Goldwyn–United Artists). 100
minutes. April 15. Director: Archie Mayo.
Producer: Samuel Goldwyn. Scenarist:
Robert E. Sherwood, from story by N. A.
Pogson. Photography: Rudolph Maté. Art
director: Richard Day. Music: Alfred
Newman. Special effects: James Basevi.
With Gary Cooper, Sigrid Gurie, Basil
Rathbone.

Ford shot scenes for a brief montage in
which, in seconds, Polo is shipwrecked by a
storm, caught in a desert sandstorm, and
crosses a mountain.

1938 *Four Men and a Prayer* (20th
Century–Fox). 85 minutes. April 29.
Director: John Ford. Producer: Darryl F.
Zanuck. Associate producer: Kenneth
MacGowan. Scenarists: Richard Sherman,
Sonya Levien, Walter Ferris, and (un-
credited) William Faulkner, from novel
by David Garth. Photographer: Ernest
Palmer. Art directors: Bernard Herzbrun,
Rudolph Sternad. Set decorator: Thomas
Little. Music: Louis Silvers, Ernst Toch.
Editor: Louis R. Loeffler. Costumes:
Royer. With Loretta Young (Lynn
Cherrington), Richard Greene (Geoffrey
Leigh), George Sanders (Wyatt Leigh),
David Niven (Christopher Leigh), William
Henry (Rodney Leigh), C. Aubrey Smith
(Col. Loring Leigh), J. Edward Bromberg
(Gen. Torres), Alan Hale (Farnoy), John
Carradine (Gen. Adolfo Arturo Sebastian),
Reginald Denny (Douglas Loveland),
Berton Churchill (Martin Cherrington),
Claude King (Gen. Bryce), John Sutton
(Capt. Drake), Barry Fitzgerald (Mulcahy),
Cecil Cunningham (Pyer), Frank Baker
(defense attorney), Frank Dawson, Lina
Basquette (Ah-nee), Winter Hall (judge),
Will Stanton (Cockney), John Spacey, C.
Montague Shaw (lawyers), Lionel Pape
(coroner), Brandon Hurst (jury foreman).

Four sons roam the world to establish
the innocence of their disgraced (and
murdered) father.

1938 *Submarine Patrol* (20th
Century–Fox). 95 minutes. November 25.
Director: John Ford. Producer: Darryl
F. Zanuck. Associate producer: Gene
Markey. Scenarists: Rian James, Darrell
Ware, Jack Yellen and (uncredited)
William Faulkner, from novel *The Splinter
Fleet,* by John Milholland. Photography:
Arthur Miller. Art directors: William
Darling, Hans Peters. Costumes: Gwen
Wakeling. Set decorator: Thomas Little.
Music director: Arthur Lange. Editor:
Robert Simpson. With Richard Greene
(Perry Townsend III), Nancy Kelly (Susan
Leeds), Preston Foster (Lt. John C.
Drake), George Bancroft (Capt. Leeds),
Slim Summerville (Ellsworth "Spuggs"
Ficketts—"Cookie"), Joan Valerie (Anne),
John Carradine (Matt McAllison), Warren
Hymer (Rocky Haggerty), Henry Armetta
(Luigi), Douglas Fowley (Brett), J. Farrell
MacDonald (Quincannon), Dick Hogan
(Johnny), Maxie Rosenbloom (Sgt. Joe
Duffy), Ward Bond (Olaf Swanson), Robert
Lowery (Sparks), Charles Tannen (Kelly),
George E. Stone (Irving Goldfarb), Moroni
Olsen (Capt. Wilson), Jack Pennick (Guns
McPeck), Elisha Cook, Jr. ("Professor"
Pratt), Harry Strang (Grainger), Charles
Trowbridge (Adm. Joseph Maitland),
Victor Varconi (chaplain), Murray Alper
(sailor), E. E. Clive.

World War I: Citizen sailors on a
wooden sub chaser.

1939 *Stagecoach.* (Walter Wanger–United
Artists). 97 minutes. March 2. Director:
John Ford. Executive producer: Walter
Wanger. Scenarist: Dudley Nichols, from
story "Stage to Lordsburg," by Ernest
Haycox. Photography: Bert Glennon. Art
director: Alexander Toluboff (credited;
actually, set decorator: Wiard B. Ihnen).
Costumes: Walter Plunkett. Music
(adapted from seventeen American folk
tunes of early 1880s): Richard Hageman,
W. Franke Harling, John Leipold, Leo
Shuken, Louis Gruenberg. Editorial
supervision: Otho Lovering. Editors:
Dorothy Spencer, Walter Reynolds.
Assistant director: Wingate Smith. Filmed
in Monument Valley and other locations in

Arizona, Utah, and California, October–December. With John Wayne (the Ringo Kid), Claire Trevor (Dallas), John Carradine (Hatfield), Thomas Mitchell (Dr. Josiah Boone), Andy Devine (Buck), Donald Meek (Samuel Peacock), Louise Platt (Lucy Mallory), Tim Holt (Lt. Blanchard), George Bancroft (Sheriff Curly Willcox), Berton Churchill (Henry Gatewood), Tom Tyler (Hank Plummer), Chris Pin Martin (Chris), Elvira Rios (Yakima, his wife), Francis Ford (Billy Pickett), Marga Daighton (Mrs. Pickett), Kent Odell (Billy Pickett, Jr.), Yakima Canutt, Chief Big Tree (stuntman), Henry Tenbrook (telegraph operator), Jack Pennick (Jerry, barman), Paul McVey (Express agent), Cornelius Keefe (Capt. Whitney), Florence Lake (Mrs. Nancy Whitney), Louis Mason (sheriff), Brenda Fowler (Mrs. Gatewood), Walter McGrail (Capt. Sickel), Joseph Rickson (Luke Plummer), Vester Pegg (Ike Plummer), William Hoffer (sergeant), Bryant Washburn (Capt. Simmons), Nora Cecil (Dr. Boone's housekeeper), Helen Gibson, Dorothy Annleby (dancing girls), Buddy Roosevelt, Bill Cody (ranchers), Chief White Horse (Indian chief), Duke Lee (sheriff of Lordsburg), Mary Kathleen Walker (Lucy's baby), Many Mules (Geronimo), Ed Brady, Steve Clemente, Theodore Larch, Fritzi Brunette, Leonard Trainor, Chris Phillips, Tex Driscoll, Teddy Billings, John Eckert, Al Lee, Jack Mohr, Patsy Doyle, Wiggie Blowne, Margaret Smith, Frank Baker (scalped corpse).

1884, a stagecoach journey in New Mexico.

Awards: See text, page 146.

1939 *Young Mr. Lincoln* (Cosmopolitan–20th Century–Fox). 101 minutes. June 9. Director: John Ford. Executive producer: Darryl F. Zanuck. Producer: Kenneth Macgowan. Scenarist: Lamar Trotti, based on life of Abraham Lincoln. Photography: Bert Glennon, Arthur Miller (uncredited, river locations). Art directors: Richard Day, Mark Lee Kirk. Set decorator: Thomas Little. Music: Alfred Newman. Editor: Walter Thompson. Costumes: Royer. Sound effects editor: Robert Parrish. Filmed in February. With Henry Fonda (Abraham Lincoln), Alice Brady (Abigail Clay), Marjorie Weaver (Mary Todd), Dorris Bowdon (uncredited) (Carrie Sue Clay),

Eddie Collins (Efe Turner), Pauline Moore (Ann Rutledge), Arleen Whelan (Sarah Clay), Richard Cromwell (Matt Clay), Ward Bond (John Palmer Cass), Donald Meek (John Felder), Spencer Charters (Judge Herbert A. Bell), Eddie Quillan (Adam Clay), Milburn Stone (Stephen Douglas), Cliff Clark (Sheriff Billings), Robert Lowery (juror), Charles Tannen (Ninian Edwards), Francis Ford (Sam Boone), Fred Kohler, Jr. (Scrub White), Kay Linaker (Mrs. Edwards), Russell Simpson (Woolridge), Charles Halton (Hawthorne), Edwin Maxwell (John T. Stuart), Robert Homans (Mr. Clay), Jack Kelly (Matt Clay, as child), Dicky Jones (Adam Clay, as child), Harry Tyler (hairdresser), Louis Mason (court clerk), Jack Pennick (Big Buck), Steven Randall (juror), Clarence Wilson, Elizabeth Jones. Credited as Carrie Sue, but not appearing: Judith Dickens.

Lincoln's discovery of the Law, his love for Ann Rutledge, and his first public victory—in a murder trial.

1939 *Drums Along the Mohawk* (20th Century–Fox). Technicolor. 103 minutes. November 3. Director: John Ford. Executive producer: Darryl F. Zanuck. Producer: Raymond Griffith. Scenarists: Lamar Trotti, Sonya Levien, and (uncredited) William Faulkner, from novel by Walter D. Edmonds. Photography: Bert Glennon, Ray Rennahan. Art directors: Richard Day, Mark Lee Kirk. Color consultant: Natalie Kalmus, Henri Jaffa. Costumes: Gwen Wakeling. Set decorator: Thomas Little. Music: Alfred Newman. Editor: Robert Simpson. Sound effects editor: Robert Parrish. Filmed in Utah's Wasatch Mountains, summer. With Claudette Colbert (Lana Borst Martin), Henry Fonda (Gilbert Martin), Edna May Oliver (Mrs. McKlennan), Eddie Collins (Christian Reall), John Carradine (Caldwell), Dorris Bowdon (Mary Reall), Jessie Ralph (Mrs. Weaver), Arthur Shields (Fr. Rosenkranz), Robert Lowery (John Weaver), Roger Imhof (Gen. Nicholas Herkimer), Francis Ford (Joe Boleo), Ward Bond (Adam Hartmann), Kay Linaker (Mrs. Demooth), Russell Simpson (Dr. Petry), Chief Big Tree (Blue Back), Spencer Charters (Fisk, innkeeper), Arthur Aylesworth (George), Si Jenks (Jacobs), Jack Pennick (Amos), Charles Tannen (Robert Johnson), Paul McVey (Capt. Mark Demooth), Elizabeth Jones

(Mrs. Reall), Lionel Pape (general), Clarence Wilson (paymaster), Edwin Maxwell (pastor), Clara Blandick (Mrs. Borst), Beulah Hall Jones (Daisy), Robert Greig (Mr. Borst), Mae Marsh, Ruth Clifford, Frank Baker (commander of colonial troops).

Mohawk Valley pioneers during Revolutionary War.

Oscar nominations: Best supporting actress (Edna May Oliver).

1940 *The Grapes of Wrath* (20th Century–Fox). 129 minutes. March 15. Director: John Ford. Producer: Darryl F. Zanuck. Associate producer–scenarist: Nunnally Johnson, from novel by John Steinbeck. Photography: Gregg Toland. Art directors: Richard Day, Mark Lee Kirk. Set decorator: Thomas Little. Music: Alfred Newman. Song "Red River Valley" played on accordion by Dan Borzage. Technical consultant: Tom Collins. Costumes: Gwen Wakeling. Second-unit director: Otto Brower. Editor: Robert Simpson. Sound: George Leverett, Roger Heman. Sound effects editor: Robert Parrish. Assistant editor: Edward O'Fearna. Filmed: September–November. With Henry Fonda (Tom Joad), Jane Darwell (Ma Joad), John Carradine (Casey), Charley Grapewin (Grampa Joad), Dorris Bowdon (Rosasharn), Russell Simpson (Pa Joad), O. Z. Whitehead (Al), John Qualen (Muley), Eddie Quillan (Connie), Zeffie Tilbury (Grandma Joad), Frank Sully (Noah), Frank Darien (Uncle John), Darryl Hickman (Winfield), Shirley Mills (Ruth Joad), Grant Mitchell (guardian), Ward Bond (policeman), Frank Faylen (Tim), Joe Sawyer (accountant), Harry Tyler (Bert), Charles B. Middleton (conductor), John Arledge (Davis), Hollis Jewell (Muley's son), Paul Guilfoyle (Floyd), Charles D. Brown (Wilkie), Roger Imhof (Thomas), William Pawley (Bill), Arthur Aylesworth (father), Charles Tannen (Joe), Selmar Jackson (inspector), Eddie C. Waller (proprietor), David Hughes (Frank), Cliff Clark (townsman), Adrian Morris (agent), Robert Homans (Spencer), Irving Bacon (conductor), Kitty McHugh (Mae), Mae Marsh, Francis Ford, Jack Pennick.

An evicted Oakie family seeks a new home during the 1930s.

Awards: See text, page 176.

1940 *The Long Voyage Home* (Argosy Pictures–Wanger–United Artists). 105 minutes. October 8. Director: John Ford. Producer: Walter Wanger. Scenarist: Dudley Nichols, from one-act plays "The Moon of the Caribbees," "In the Zone," "Bound East for Cardiff," "The Long Voyage Home," by Eugene O'Neill. Photography: Gregg Toland. Art director: James Basevi. Set decorator: Julia Heron. Music: Richard Hageman. Editor: Sherman Todd. Sound editor: Robert Parrish. Special effects: Ray Binger, R. T. Layton. Filmed in summer. With Thomas Mitchell (Aloysius Driscoll), John Wayne (Ole Olsen), Ian Hunter (Thomas Fenwick, "Smitty"), Barry Fitzgerald (Cocky), Wilfred Lawson (captain), Mildred Natwick (Freda), John Qualen (Axel Swanson), Ward Bond (Yank), Joe Sawyer (Davis), Arthur Shields (Donkeyman), J.M. Kerrigan (Crimp), David Hughes (Scotty), Billy Bevan (Joe), Cyril McLaglen (mate), Robert E. Perry (Paddy), Jack Pennick, (Johnny Bergman), Constantin Frenke (Narvey), Constantin Romanoff (Big Frank), Dan Borzage (Tim), Harry Tenbrook (Max), Douglas Walton (second lieutenant), Raphaela Ottiano (Daughter of the Tropics), Carmen Morales, Carmen d'Antonio (girls in canoe), Harry Woods (the admiral's sailor), Edgar "Blue" Washington, Lionel Pape, Jane Crowley, Maureen Roden-Ryan.

The Glencairn's crew dream of land, but always return to the sea.

Awards: See text, page 182.

1941 *Tobacco Road* (20th Century Fox). 84 minutes. February 20. Director: John Ford. Producer: Darryl F. Zanuck. Associate producers: Jack Kirkland, Harry H. Oshrin. Scenarist: Nunnally Johnson, from play by Kirkland and novel by Erskine Caldwell. Photography: Arthur C. Miller. Art directors: Richard Day, James Basevi. Set decorator: Thomas Little. Music: David Buttolph. Editor: Barbara McLean. Sound effects editor: Robert Parrish. With Charley Grapewin (Jeeter Lester), Marjorie Rambeau (Sister Bessie), Gene Tierney (Ellie May Lester), William Tracy (Dude Lester), Elizabeth Patterson (Ada Lester), Dana Andrews (Dr. Tim), Slim Summerville (Henry Peabody), Ward Bond (Lov Bensey), Grant Mitchell (George Payne), Zeffie Tilbury (Grandma Lester), Russell Simpson (sherriff), Spencer Charters (employee), Irving Bacon (teller), Harry Tyler (auto salesman), George Chandler (employee), Charles Halton (mayor), Jack Pennick (deputy sheriff), Dorothy Adams (Payne's secretary), Francis Ford (vagabond).

Life among decadent rural whites in Georgia.

1941 *Sex Hygiene* (Audio Productions– U.S. Army). 30 minutes. Director: John Ford. Producer: Darryl F. Zanuck. Photographer: George Barnes. Editor: Gene Fowler, Jr. With Charles Trowbridge, Robert Lowery, George Reeves.

An army training film on venereal disease.

1941 *How Green Was My Valley* (20th Century–Fox). 118 minutes. December. Director: John Ford. Producer: Darryl F. Zanuck. Scenarist: Philip Dunne, from novel by Richard Llewellyn. Photography: Arthur Miller. Art directors: Richard Day, Nathan Juran. Set decorator: Thomas Little. Costumes: Gwen Wakeling. Music: Alfred Newman. Choral effects: Eisteddfod Singers of Wales. Editor: James B. Clark. Narrator: Irving Pichel. U.K. version narrator: Rhys Williams. Filmed in June–August. With Walter Pidgeon (Mr. Gruffydd), Maureen O'Hara (Angharad Morgan), Donald Crisp (Gwilym Morgan), Sara Allgood (Mrs. Beth Morgan), Anna Lee (Bronwyn Morgan), Roddy McDowall (Huw Morgan), John Loder (Ianto Morgan), Patrick Knowles (Ivor Morgan), Richard Fraser (Davy Morgan), James Monks (Owen Morgan), Barry Fitzgerald (Cyfartha), The Welsh Singers (singers), Morton Lowery (Mr. Jonas), Arthur Shields (Mr. Parry), Ann Todd (Ceiwen), Frederick Worlock (Dr. Richards), Evan E. Evans (Gwinlyn), Rhys Williams (Dai Bando), Lionel Pape (Old Evans), Ethel Griffies (Mrs. Nicholas), Marten Lamont (Jestyn Evans), Mae Marsh (miner's wife), Louis Jean Heydt (miner), Denis Hoey (Motschell), Tudor Williams (singer), Clifford Severn, Eva March, Frank Baker.

A Welsh mining family in the 1890s. Awards: See Text, Page 184.

†1941–46 Field Photo films for OSS: Many training films and documentaries for restricted use made by Ford's crews under his general supervision (amounting to zero or greater?), including: *How to Operate Behind Enemy Lines* (with Dana Andrews?); *How to Interrogate Enemy Prisoners; Living Off the Land; Nazi Industrial Manpower; Dunkirk in Reverse; Inside Tibet* (Kodachrome, in National Archives), etc.

Report, November 1941: Condition of Atlantic Fleet (by Ford, Ray Kellogg). *Canal Report:* on Panama defenses, December–January 1942 (Ford directed, photographed, edited, wrote, and spoke narration; also by Al Jolkes, Al Ziegler, Robert Parrish). Report: Doolittle raid on Tokyo, April 1942 (Ford, et al.). Coverage: Allied landings at Oran, Algiers, Casablanca, November 1942.

1942 *The Battle of Midway* (U.S. Navy–20th Century–Fox). Kodachrome /Technicolor. 17 minutes. September. Director: Lt. Comdr. John Ford, USNR. Narration: Ford, Dudley Nichols, James Kevin McGuinness. Photography: Ford, Jack McKenzie, Lt. Kenneth M. Pier, Gregg Toland. Music: Alfred Newman. Editors: Ford, Robert Parrish. Sound effects editor: Phil Scott. With voices of Henry Fonda, Jane Darwell, Donald Crisp, Irving Pichel.

A report on the actual battle. Oscar: Best documentary.

1942 *Torpedo Squadron* (U.S. Navy). Kodachrome. 8 minutes (8mm). Director: Lt. Comdr. John Ford, USNR.

According to Bogdanovich, Ford's unit took some footage of life on a PT-boat (Torpedo Squadron 8) in 16mm color shortly before the Battle of Midway. All but one of the squadron were killed, and the edited footage was delivered by personal envoys (such as Joe August) to the dead sailors' families.

1943 *December 7th* (U.S. Navy). 85 and 34 minutes. Directors: Lt. Gregg Toland, USNR, Lt. Comdr. John Ford, USNR. Photography: Toland. Second-unit directors: Ray Kellogg, James C. Havens, USMC. Music: Alfred Newman. Editor: Robert Parrish. Additional narration: James K. McGuinness. With Harry Davenport, Walter Huston.

A study of life in Hawaii, before and after Pearl Harbor. Mostly Toland's work.

Originally made 85 minutes long, but unreleased; nontheatrically distributed in a 34-minute version.

Oscar: Best documentary.

1943 *Victory in Burma:* On Mountbatten and Father Stuart; (directed by Irving Asner, assisted by Jack Swain, Bob Rhea, Arthur Meehan).

etc. (Mark Armistead, supervisor; Ford shot some China portions).
Coverage: Allied landings at Normandy, June 1944.
Research: documentary footage for use at Nuremberg trials (by Ray Kellogg, Budd and Stewart Schulberg, Joe Ziegler, Bob Webb), later released as *Nuremberg* (War Dept.: 1946, 76 minutes); compiled by Pare Lorentz and Stuart Schulberg. Prints available from National Archives).

†1943 *We Sail at Midnight* (Crown Film Unity–U.S. Navy), 20 minutes. July. Director: Ford (?). Narration written by Clifford Odets. Music: Richard Addinsell.
Hazards of merchant shipping in combat zones.
An extant fragment shows cargo handling in New York City and trucks on Broadway. Attribution to Ford is *very* dubious.

1945 *They Were Expendable* (Metro-Goldwyn-Mayer). 136 minutes. December 20. Director-producer: John Ford. Associate producer: Cliff Reid. Scenarist: Frank W. Wead, from book by William L. White. Photography: Joseph H. August. Art directors: Cedric Gibbons, Malcolm F. Brown. Set decorators: Edwin B. Willis, Ralph S. Hurst. Music: Herbert Stothert. Editors: Frank E. Hull, Douglas Biggs. Second-unit director: James C. Havens (rear projection plates by Robert Montgomery). Assistant director: Edward O'Fearna. Filmed in Florida, February–April. With Robert Montgomery (Lt. John Brickley), John Wayne (Lt. Rusty Ryan), Donna Reed (Lt. Sandy Davis), Jack Holt (Gen. Martin), Ward Bond (Boots Mulcahey), Louis Jean Heydt (Ohio, flyer in hospital), Marshall Thompson (Snake Gardner), Russell Simpson (Dad, chief of shipyard), Leon Ames (Maj. Morton), Paul Langton (Andy Andrews), Arthur Walsh (Jones), Donald Curtis (Shorty Long), Cameron Mitchell (George Cross), Jeff York (Tony Aiken), Murray Alper (Slug Mahan), Harry Tenbrook (Larsen), Jack Pennick (Doc Charlie), Charles Trowbridge (Adm. Blackwell), Robert Barrat (Gen. Douglas MacArthur), Bruce Kellogg (Tomkins), Tim Murdock (Ens. Brown), Vernon Steele (doctor), Trina Lowe (Gardner's girlfriend), Alex Havier (Benny), Eva March (nurse), Pedro de Cordoba (priest), Pacita Tod-Tod (nightclub singer), William B. Davidson

(hotel manager), Robert Emmett O'Conner (Silver Dollar bartender), Max Ong (mayor of Cebu), Bill Wilkerson (Sgt. Smith), John Carlyre (Lt. James), Philip Ahn (orderly), Betty Blythe (officer's wife), Kermit Maynard (airport officer), Stubby Kruger, Sammu Steon, Michael Kirby, Blake Edwards (boat crew), Wallace Ford, Tom Tyler, Frank Baker.
Brickley and Ryan pioneer PT-boats in combat during America's defeat in the Philippines.

1946? *In Memoriam Manuel Quezon.* c. 20 minutes. A print of this film, 16 mm Kodachrome, is among the John Ford Papers, Lilly Library, Indiana University, but it was not permitted that it be examined. Dan Ford thinks John Ford is responsible for it. Manuel Quezon was the first president of the Philippines, in 1935.

1946 *My Darling Clementine* (20th Century–Fox). 97 minutes. November. Director: John Ford. Producer: Samuel G. Engel. Scenarists: Engel, Winston Miller, from story by Sam Hellman, based on book *Wyatt Earp, Frontier Marshall*, by Stuart N. Lake. Photography: Joseph P. McDonald. Art directors: James Basevi, Lyle R. Wheeler. Set decorators: Thomas Little, Fred J. Rode. Costumes: René Hubert. Music: Cyril J. Mockridge. Editors: Dorothy Spencer, (uncredited) Darryl F. Zanuck. Special effects: Fred Sersen. Assistant director: William Eckhardt. Exteriors filmed in Monument Valley, May–June. With Henry Fonda (Wyatt Earp), Linda Darnell (Chihuahua), Victor Mature (Doc John Holliday), Walter Brennan (Old Man Clanton), Tim Holt (Virgil Earp), Ward Bond (Morgan Earp), Cathy Downs (Clementine Carter), Alan Mowbray (Granville Thorndyke), John Ireland (Billy Clanton), Grant Withers (Ike Clanton), Roy Roberts (Mayor), Jane Darwell (Kate Nelson), Russell Simpson (John Simpson), Francis Ford (Dad, old soldier), J. Farrell MacDonald (Mac, barman), Don Garner (James Earp), Ben Hall (barber), Arthur Walsh (hotel clerk), Jack Pennick, Robert Adler (stagecoach drivers), Louis Mercier (François), Mickey Simpson (Sam Clanton), Fred Libby (Phin Clanton), Harry Woods (Luke), Charles Stevens (Indian troublemaker), William B. Davidson (Oriental saloon owner), Earle Foxe (gambler), Aleth "Speed" Hansen (guitarist), Danny Borzage (accordionist),

Frank Conlan (pianist), Don Barclay (opera house owner), Mae Marsh (old lady going to church).

Based on myths of Wyatt Earp, Doc Holliday, and the Battle of the O. K. Corral. A remake of *Frontier Marshall* (Allan Dwan, 1939): remade as *Wichita* (Jacques Tourneur, 1955), *Gunfight at the O. K. Corral* (John Sturges, 1957), and others.

1947 *The Fugitive* (Argosy Pictures– RKO Radio). 104 minutes. November 3. Director: John Ford. Producers: Ford, Merian C. Cooper. Associate producer: Emilio Fernandez. Scenarist: Dudley Nichols, from novel *The Labyrinthine Ways* (or *The Power and the Glory*), by Graham Greene. Photography: Gabriel Figueroa. Art director: Alfred Ybarra. Set decorator: Manuel Parra. Music: Richard Hageman. Orchestration: Lucien. Editor: Jack Murray. Executive assistant: Jack Pennick. Directorial assistant: Melchor Ferrer. Assistant director: Jesse Hibbs. Filmed in forty-seven days on locations in Mexico and at Churubusco Studios, Mexico City. With Henry Fonda (A Fugitive), Dolores Del Rio (An Indian Woman), Pedro Armendariz (A Lieutenant of Police), Ward Bond (El Gringo), Leo Carrillo (A Chief of Police), John Qualen (A Refugee Doctor), Fortunio Bonanova (The Governor's Cousin), Chris-Pin Martin (An Organ Player), Miguel Inclan (A Hostage), Fernando Fernandez (A Singer), Jose I. Torvay (A Mexican), Melchor Ferrer.

A hunted priest struggles with his conscience.

1948 *Fort Apache* (Argosy Pictures–RKO Radio). 127 minutes. March 9. Director: John Ford. Producers: Ford, Merian C. Cooper. Scenarist: Frank S. Nugent, from story "Massacre," by James Warner Bellah. Photography: Archie Stout, William Clothier (second unit). Art director: James Basevi. Set decorator: Joe Kish. Music: Richard Hageman. Editor: Jack Murray. Special effects: Dave Koehler. Costumes: Michael Meyers, Ann Peck. Camera: Eddie Fitzgerald. Script supervisor: Meta Sterne. Choreography: Kenny Williams. Technical consultants: Maj. Philip Kieffer, Katharine Spaatz. Research editor: Katharine Clifton. Costume research: D. R. O. Hatswell. Second-unit director: Cliff Lyons. Production manager: Bernard McEveety. Assistant directors: Lowell

Farrell, Jack Pennick. Filmed in forty-five days on locations in Utah and Monument Valley, June 1947. With John Wayne (Capt. Kirby York), Henry Fonda (Lt. Col. Owen Thursday), Shirley Temple (Philadelphia Thursday), John Agar (Lt. Michael O'Rourke), Ward Bond (Sgt. Maj. O'Rourke), George O'Brien (Capt. Sam Collingwood), Victor McLaglen (Sgt. Mulcahy), Pedro Armendariz (Sgt. Beaufort), Anna Lee (Mrs. Collingwood), Irene Rich (Mrs. O'Rourke), Guy Kibbee (Dr. Wilkens), Grant Withers (Silas Meachum), Miguel Inclan (Cochise), Jack Pennick (Sgt. Shattuck), Mae Marsh (Mrs. Gates), Dick Foran (Sgt. Quincannon), Frank Ferguson (newspaperman), Francis Ford (bartender), Ray Hyke (Gates), Movita Castenada (Guadalupe), Hank Worden (Southern recruit), Harry Tenbrook (courier), Mary Gordon (woman in stagecoach), Frank Baker, Ben Johnson (stunt riders).

Life on a calvary post, 1876.

†1948 *Red River* (Monterey Productions–United Artists). Director: Howard Hawks. With John Wayne, Montgomery Clift, Joanne Dru.

Hawks was having great difficulties getting the footage he had shot worked into a coherent film. Ford made numerous editing suggestions, including the use of a narrator.

1948 *3 Godfathers* (Argosy Pictures–Metro-Goldwyn-Mayer). Technicolor. 106 minutes. December 1. Director: John Ford. Producers: Ford, Merian C. Cooper. Scenarists: Laurence Stallings, Frank S. Nugent, from story by Peter B. Kyne. Photography: Winton C. Hoch, Charles P. Boyle (second unit). Art director: James Basevi. Set decorator: Joe Kish. Music: Richard Hageman. Editor: Jack Murray. Color consultants: Natalie Kalmus, Morgan Padelford. Camera: Harvey Gould, Edward Fitzgerald (second unit). Production manager: Lowell Farrell. Assistant directors: Wingate Smith, Edward O'Fearna. Filmed in thirty-two days on locations in the Mojave Desert. With John Wayne (Robert Marmaduke Sangster Hightower), Pedro Armendariz (Pedro Roca Fuerte), Harry Carey, Jr. (William Kearney, "the Abilene Kid"), Ward Bond (Perley "Buck" Sweet), Mildred Natwick (mother), Charles Halton (Mr. Latham), Jane Darwell (Miss Florie),

Mae Marsh (Mrs. Perley Sweet), Guy Kibbee (judge), Dorothy Ford (Ruby Latham), Ben Johnson, Michael Dugan, Don Summers (patrolman), Fred Libby (deputy sheriff), Hank Worden (deputy sheriff), Jack Pennick (Luke, train conductor), Francis Ford (drunk), Ruth Clifford (woman in bar).

Three bandits fleeing across a desert adopt a baby.

Remake of Ford's *Marked Men* (1919), G. M. Anderson's *Bronco Billy and the Baby* (1915), Wyler's *Hell's Heroes* (1929), and Boleslawski's *Three Godfathers* (1936).

†1949 *What Price Glory* Stage production. Supervisor: John Ford. Assistant supervisor: George O'Brien. Directed by: Ralph Murphy. Produced by the Masquers Club of Hollywood for the Military Order of the Purple Heart. Producer: Harry Joe Brown. Assistant: Eddie Oxford. Management: Jacques Pierre. Stage manager: G. Pat Collins. Performed: February 22, 1949, Long Beach; February 24, 1949, San Jose; February 25, 1949, Oakland; February 27, 1949, San Francisco; March 1, 1949, Pasadena; March 2, 1949, Los Angeles. With Ward Bond (Flagg), Pat O'Brien (Quirt), George O'Brien, Alan Hale, Sr., Robert Armstrong, Wallace Ford, Oliver (Babe) Hardy, Charles Kemper, Henry O'Neill, Jimmy Lydon, Herbert Rawlinson, Louis Alberni, Harry Carey, Jr., Forrest Tucker, Fred Graham, Larry Blake, Michael J. Dugan, Don Summers, G. Pat Collins, Gregory Peck, John Wayne, Maureen O'Hara.

Pat O'Brien: "It was always Ford's wish to do a stage play because he loved actors for the theater. . . . It was all for charity. None of us got a quarter." (Karyn Kay and Gerald Peary, "Talking to Pat O'Brien," *Velvet Light Trap,* Fall 1975.) The proceeds, $30,000, went to build a clubhouse for paraplegic veterans. Ford was then president of the Purple Heart organization.

†1949 *Mighty Joe Young* (Argosy Pictures–RKO Radio). 94 minutes. Director: Ernest B. Schoedsack. Producers: John Ford, Merian C. Cooper. Scenarist: Ruth Rose, from story by Cooper. Photography: J. Roy Hunt. Art director: James Basevi. With Terry Moore, Ben Johnson, Robert Armstrong, Frank McHugh, Regis Toomey.

"I had nothing to do with it," said Ford to Bogdanovich.

1949 *She Wore a Yellow Ribbon* (Argosy Pictures–RKO Radio). Technicolor. 103 minutes. October 22. Director: John Ford. Producers: Ford, Merian C. Cooper. Associate producer: Lowell Farrell. Scenarists: Frank S. Nugent, Laurence Stallings, from story "War Party," by James Warner Bellah. Photography: Winton C. Hoch, Charles P. Boyle (second unit). Art director: James Basevi. Set decorator: Joe Kish. Music: Richard Hageman. Conductor: Constantin Bakaleinikoff. Editor: Jack Murray. Assistant editor: Barbara Ford. Second-unit director: Cliff Lyons. Assistant directors: Wingate Smith, Edward O'Fearna. Technical consultants: Cliff Lyons, Maj. Philip Kieffer. Color consultants: Natalie Kalmus, Morgan Padelford. Special effects: Jack Caffee. Costumes: Michael Meyers, Ann Peck. Camera: Harvey Gould. Historical technical advisor: D. R. O. Hatswell. Filmed in thirty-two days on locations in Monument Valley, October 1948. With John Wayne (Capt. Nathan Brittles), Joanne Dru (Olivia), John Agar (Lt. Flint Cohill), Ben Johnson (Sgt. Tyree), Harry Carey, Jr. (Lt. Pennell), Victor McLaglen (Sgt. Quincannon), Mildred Natwick (Mrs. Abbey Allshard), George O'Brien (Maj. Mack Allshard), Arthur Shields (Dr. O'Laughlin), Francis Ford (barman, Irish), Harry Woods (Karl Rynders), Chief Big Tree (Pony That Walks), Noble Johnson (Red Shirt), Cliff Lyons (Trooper Cliff), Tom Tyler (Quayne), Michael Dugan (Hochbauer), Mickey Simpson (Wagner), Fred Graham (Hench), Frank McGrath (trumpeter), Don Summers (Jenkins), Fred Libby (Cpl. Krumrein), Jack Pennick (Sgt. Major), Billy Jones (courier), Bill Gettinger (officer), Fred Kennedy (Badger), Rudy Bowman (Pvt. Smith), Post Park (officer), Ray Hyke (McCarthy), Lee Bradley (interpreter), Chief Sky Eagle, Dan White, Frank Baker.

An aging captain leads a final cavalry patrol, 1876.

Oscar: Photography—Winton C. Hoch.

†1949 *Pinky* (20th Century–Fox). 102 minutes. November. Director: Elia Kazan. Producer: Darryl F. Zanuck. Scenarists: Philip Dunne, Dudley Nichols, from novel *Quality*, by Cid Ricketts Summer.

Photography: Joseph MacDonald. Music: Alfred Newman. Assistant director: Wingate Smith. With Jeanne Crain, Ethel Barrymore, Ethel Waters, William Lundigan, Basil Ruysdael.

A Negro girl passes for white.

Ford prepared the production and worked a day on it before taking ill, although illness was apparently a pretext for his withdrawal, desired both by himself and Zanuck. Nothing in the finished film seems Fordian.

1950 *When Willie Comes Marching Home* (20th Century–Fox). 82 minutes. February. Director: John Ford. Producer: Fred Kohlmar. Scenarists: Mary Loos, Richard Sale, from story "When Leo Comes Marching Home," by Sy Gomberg. Photography: Leo Tover. Art directors: Lyle R. Wheeler, Chester Gore. Set decorators: Thomas Little, Bruce MacDonald. Music: Alfred Newman. Editor: James B. Clark. Assistant director: Wingate Smith. Production manager: Joe Behm. Special effects: James B. Clarke. Choreography: Kenny Williams. Camera: Till Gabbani. Costumes: Charles LeMaire, Travilla. Script supervisor: Meta Sterne. With Dan Dailey (Bill Kluggs), Corinne Calvet (Yvonne), Colleen Townsend (Marge Fettles), Lloyd Corrigan (Major Adams), William Demarest (Herman Kluggs), James Lydon (Charles Fettles), Evelyn Varden (Gertrude Kluggs), Kenny Williams (musician), Lee Clark (musician), Charles Halton (Mr. Fettles), Mae Marsh (Mrs. Fettles), Jack Pennick (sergeant), Mickey Simpson (MP Kerrigan), Frank Pershing (Maj. Bickford), Don Summers (MP Sherve), Gil Herman (Lt. Comdr. Crown), Peter Ortiz (Pierre), Luis Alberni (barman), John Shulick (pilot), Clarke Gordon, Robin Hughes (marine officers), Cecil Weston (Mrs. Barnes), Harry Tenbrook (Joe, taxi driver), Russ Clark (Sgt. Wilson), George Spaulding (Judge Tate), James Eagle (reporter), Harry Strang (sergeant), George Magrill (chief petty officer), Hank Worden (choir leader), John McKee (pilot), Larry Keating (Gen. G. Reeding), Dan Riss (Gen. Adams), Robert Einer (Lt. Bagley), Russ Conway (Maj. J. A. White), Whit Bissell (Lt. Handley), Ann Codee (French instructor), Ray Hyke (Maj. Crawford), Gene Collins (Andy), James Flavin (Gen. Brevort), David McMahon (Col. Ainsley), Charles Trowbridge (Gen.

Merrill), Kenneth Tobey (Lt. K. Geiger), Maj. Sam Harris (hospital patient), Alberto Morin, Louis Mercier (resistance fighters), Paul Harvey (officer), James Waters, Ken Lynch, Frank Baker, J. Farrell MacDonald, Vera Miles.

Comedy about small-town war fever.

1950 *Wagon Master* (Argosy Pictures– RKO Radio). 86 minutes. April 19. Director: John Ford. Producers: Ford, Merian C. Cooper. Associate producer: Lowell Farrell. Writers: Frank S. Nugent, Patrick Ford. Photography: Bert Glennon, Archie Stout (second unit). Art director: James Basevi. Set decorator: Joe Kish. Music: Richard Hageman. Songs: "Wagons West," "Rollin' Shadows in the Dust," "Song of the Wagon Master," "Chuck A-Walla-Swing," by Stan Jones, sung by the Sons of the Pioneers. Editor: Jack Murray. Assistant editor: Barbara Ford. Second-unit director: Cliff Lyons. Assistant director: Wingate Smith. Costumes: Wes Jeffries, Adele Parmenter. Special effects: Jack Caffee. Technical consultant: D. R. O. Hatswell. Filmed in Monument Valley and in Professor Valley, Utah. With Ben Johnson (Travis Blue), Harry Carey, Jr. (Sandy Owens), Joanne Dru (Denver), Ward Bond (Elder Wiggs), Charles Kemper (Uncle Shiloh Clegg), Alan Mowbray (Dr. A. Locksley Hall), Jane Darwell (Sister Ledeyard), Ruth Clifford (Fleuretty Phyffe), Russell Simpson (Adam Perkins), Kathleen O'Malley (Prudence Perkins), James Arness (Floyd Clegg), Fred Libby (Reese Clegg), Hank Worden (Luke Clegg), Mickey Simpson (Jesse Clegg), Francis Ford (Mr. Peachtree), Cliff Lyons (sheriff of Crystal City), Don Summers (Sam Jenkins), Movita Castenada (young Navajo girl), Jim Thorpe (Navajo), Chuck Haywood (Jackson).

A Mormon wagon train, 1849.

1950 *Rio Grande* (Argosy Pictures– Republic). 105 minutes. November 15. Director: John Ford. Producers: Ford, Merian C. Cooper. Scenarist: James Kevin McGuinness, from story "Mission with No Record," by James Warner Bellah. Photography: Bert Glennon, Archie Stout (second unit). Art director: Frank Hotaling. Set decorators: John McCarthy, Jr., Charles Thompson. Music: Victor Young. Songs, sung by the Sons of the

Pioneers: "My Gal Is Purple," "Footsore Cavalry," "Yellow Stripes," by Stan Jones; "Aha, San Antone," by Dale Evans; "Cattle Call," by Tex Owens; and "Down by the Glen Side," "You're in the Army Now." Editor: Jack Murray. Assistant editor: Barbara Ford. Second-unit director: Cliff Lyons. Costumes: Adele Palmer. Special effects: Howard and Theodore Lydecker. Filmed in Monument Valley, June–July. With John Wayne (Lt. Col. Kirby Yorke), Maureen O'Hara (Mrs. Yorke), Ben Johnson (Trooper Tyree), Claude Jarman, Jr. (Trooper Jeff Yorke), Harry Carey, Jr. (Trooper Daniel Boone), Chill Wills (Dr. Wilkins), J. Carroll Naish (Gen. Philip Sheridan), Victor McLaglen (Sgt. Quincannon), Grant Withers (deputy marshall), Peter Ortiz (Capt. St. Jacques), Steve Pendleton (Capt. Prescott), Karolyn Grimes (Margaret Mary), Alberto Morin (lieutenant), Stan Jones (sergeant), Fred Kennedy (Heinze), Jack Pennick, Pat Wayne, Chuck Roberson, The Sons of the Pioneers (regimental singers): Ken Curtis, Hugh Farr, Karl Farr, Lloyd Perryman, Shug Fisher, Tom Doss.

A family reunites on a cavalry post.

†1950 *The Bullfighter and the Lady* (Republic). 87 minutes. Director: Budd Boetticher. With Robert Stack.

Ford assisted Boetticher in editing the picture.

1951 *This Is Korea!* (U.S. Navy–Republic). 3-Strip Trucolor. 50 minutes. August 10. Director: Rear Adm. John Ford, USNR. Narration: James Warner Bellah, Frank Nugent, Ford. Photography: Charles Bohuy, Bob Rhea, Mark Armistead. With the voices of John Ireland, Irving Pichel, George O'Brien.

An on-the-spot documentary of the marines in Korea.

1952 *The Quiet Man* (Argosy Pictures–Republic). Technicolor. 129 minutes. September 14. Director: John Ford. Producers: Ford, Merian C. Cooper, and (uncredited, Michael Killanin). Scenarists: Frank S. Nugent, from story by Maurice Walsh (*The Saturday Evening Post*, February 11, 1933), adapted by Richard Llewellyn (uncredited). Photography: Winton C. Hoch, Archie Stout (second unit). Art director: Frank Hotaling. Set decorators: John McCarthy, Jr., Charles Tompson. Music: Victor

Young. Songs: "The Isle of Innisfree," by Richard Farrelly; "Galway Bay," by Dr. Arthur Colahan, Michael Donovan; "The Humour Is on Me Now," by Richard Haywood; "The Young May Moon," by Thomas Moore; and "The Wild Colonial Boy," "Mush-Mush-Mush." Editor: Jack Murray. Assistant editor: Barbara Ford. Second-unit directors (uncredited): John Wayne, Patrick Ford. Assistant director: Andrew McLaglen. Color consultant: Francis Cugat. Costumes: Adele Palmer. Exteriors filmed in Ireland, June–July. With John Wayne (Sean Thornton), Maureen O'Hara (Mary Kate Danaher), Barry Fitzgerald (Michaeleen Og Flynn), Ward Bond (Fr. Peter Lonergan), Victor McLaglen (Red Will Danaher), Mildred Natwick (Mrs. Sarah Tillane), Francis Ford (Dan Tobin), Eileen Crowe (Mrs. Elizabeth Playfair), May Craig (woman at railroad station), Arthur Shields (Rev. Cyril Playfair), Charles FitzSimmons (Forbes), Sean McClory (Owen Glynn), James Lilburn (Fr. Paul), Jack McGowran (Feeney), Ken Curtis (Dermot Fahy), Mae Marsh (Fr. Paul's mother), Harry Tenbrook (policeman), Maj. Sam Harris (general), Joseph O'Dea (guard), Eric Gorman (railroad conductor), Kevin Lawless (fireman), Paddy O'Donnell (porter), Webb Overlander (railroad station chief), Hank Worden (trainer in flashback), Harry Tyler (Pat Cohen), Don Hatswell (Guppy), David H. Hughes (constable), Douglas Evans (physician), Jack Roper (boxer), Al Murphy (referee), Patrick Wayne, Antonia Wayne, Melinda Wayne, Michael Wayne (children at race), Pat O'Malley, Bob Perry, Frank Baker.

A Yank returns to his birthland in Ireland.

Awards: See text, page 278–279.

1952 *What Price Glory* (20th Century–Fox). Technicolor. 111 minutes. August. Director: John Ford. Producer: Sol C. Siegel. Scenarists: Phoebe and Henry Ephron, from play by Maxwell Anderson, Laurence Stallings. Photography: Joseph MacDonald. Art directors: Lyle R. Wheeler, George W. Davis. Set decorators: Thomas Little, Stuart A. Reiss. Music: Alfred Newman. Song: "My Love, My Life," by Jay Livingston, Roy Evans. Editor: Dorothy Spencer. Color consultant: Leonard Doss. Costumes: Charles LeMaire, Edward Stevenson. Special effects: Ray Kellogg. Choreography: Billy

Daniel. With James Cagney (Capt. Flagg), Corinne Calvet (Charmaine), Dan Dailey (Sgt. Quirt), William Demarest (Cpl. Kiper), Craig Hill (Lt. Aldrich), Robert Wagner (Lewisohn), Marisa Pavan (Nichole Bouchard), Casey Adams (Lt. Moore), James Gleason (Gen. Cokely), Wally Vernon (Lipinsky), Henry Letondal (Cognac Pete), Fred Libby (Lt. Schmidt), Ray Hyke (Mulcahy), Paul Fix (Gowdy), James Lilburn (young soldier), Henry Morgan (Morgan), Dan Borzage (Gilbert), Bill Henry (Holsen), Henry "Bomber" Kulkovich (company cook), Jack Pennick (Ferguson), Ann Codee (nun), Stanley Johnson (Lt. Cunningham), Tom Tyler (Capt. Davis), Olga André (Sister Clotilde), Barry Norton (priest), Luis Alberni (the great uncle), Torben Meyer (mayor), Alfred Zeisler (English colonel), George Bruggeman (English lieutenant), Scott Forbes (Lt. Bennett), Sean McClory (Lt. Austin), Charles FitzSimmons (Capt. Wickham), Louis Mercier (Bouchard), Mickey Simpson (MP), Peter Ortiz, Paul Guilfoyle.

World War I in France.

1953 *The Sun Shines Bright* (Argosy Pictures–Republic). 90 minutes. May 2. Director: John Ford. Producers: Ford, Merian C. Cooper. Scenarist: Laurence Stallings, from stories "The Sun Shines Bright," "The Mob from Massac," "The Lord Provides," by Irvin S. Cobb. Photography: Archie Stout. Art director: Frank Hotaling. Set decorators: John McCarthy, Jr., George Milo. Costumes: Adele Palmer. Music: Victor Young. Editor: Jack Murray. Assistant editor: Barbara Ford. Assistant director: Wingate Smith. Filmed in 1952. With Charles Winninger (Judge William Pittman Priest), Arleen Whelan (Lucy Lee Lake), John Russell (Ashby Corwin), Stepin Fetchit (Jeff Poindexter), Russell Simpson (Dr. Lewt Lake), Ludwig Stossel (Herman Felsburg), Francis Ford (Brother Finney), Paul Hurst (Sgt. Jimmy Bagby), Mitchell Lewis (Andy Radcliffe), Grant Withers (Buck), Milburn Stone (Horace K. Maydew), Dorothy Jordan (Lucy's mother), Elzie Emanuel (U. S. Grant Woodford), Henry O'Neill (Jody Habersham), Slim Pickens (Sterling), James Kirkwood (Gen. Fairfield), Mae Marsh (Amora's companion), Jane Darwell (Amora Ratchitt), Ernest Whitman (Uncle Pleasant Woodford), Trevor Bardette (Rufe, leader of lynch

mob), Hal Baylor (his son), Eva March (Mallie Cramp), Clarence Muse (Uncle Zack), Jack Pennick (Beaker), Ken Williams, Patrick Wayne (cadet).

Portrait of a 1905 Kentucky town.

1953 *Mogambo* (Metro-Goldwyn-Mayer). Technicolor. 116 minutes. October 9. Director: John Ford. Producer: Sam Zimbalist. Scenarist: John Lee Mahin, from play "Red Dust," by Wilson Collison. Photography: Robert Surtees, Fredrick A. Young. Art director: Alfred Junge. Costumes: Helen Rose. Editor: Frank Clarke. Second-unit directors: Richard Rossen, Yakima Canutt, James C. Havens. Assistant directors: Wingate Smith, Cecil Ford. Color consultant: Joan Bridge. Special effects: Tom Howard. Safari director: Carr Hartley, superintendent of Mount Kenya reserve. Interiors filmed in London. Exteriors filmed in Tanganyika, Kenya, Uganda, French Equatorial Africa, October–February. With Clark Gable (Victor Marswell), Ava Gardner (Eloise Y. Kelly), Grace Kelly (Linda Nordley), Donald Sinden (Donald Nordley), Philip Stainton (John Brown Pryce), Erick Pohlmann (Leon Boltchak), Laurence Naismith (Skipper John), Dennis O'Dea (Fr. Joseph), Asa Etula (native male), Wagenia Tribe of Belgian Congo, Smuru Tribe of Kenya Colony, Bahaya Tribe of Tanganyika, M'Beti Tribe of French Equatorial Africa.

A game hunter, a playgirl, and a sheltered English couple on safari in Africa.

Remake of Victor Fleming's *Red Dust* (1932). In Vincente Minnelli's *The Courtship of Eddie's Father* (1963), Glenn Ford sees a scene from *Mogambo* on TV (Gable and Kelly by a waterfall.)

†1954 *Hondo* (Wayne-Fellows–Warner Brothers). Warnercolor / 3-D. 83 minutes. December. Director: John Farrow. Producer: Robert Fellows. Scenarist: James Edward Grant, from story by Louis L'Amour. Photography: Robert Burks, Archie Stout. With John Wayne, Geraldine Page, Ward Bond.

Two shots, only, were directed by Ford—of a troop of cavalry that Wayne sees when he visits an army post—but they stand out in this film like Delacroixes in a gallery of *TV Guide* covers.

1955 *The Long Gray Line* (Rota Productions–Columbia). Technicolor /

Cinemascope. 138 minutes. February 9.
Director: John Ford. Producer: Robert
Arthur. Scenarist: Edward Hope, from
autobiography *Bringing up the Brass,* by
Marty Maher with Nardi Reeder
Champion. Photography: Charles Lawton,
Jr. Art director: Robert Peterson. Set
decorator: Frank Tuttle. Music adaptation:
George Duning. Music conductor: Morris
Stoloff. Editor: William Lyon. Assistant
directors: Wingate Smith, Jack Corrick.
Costumes: Jean Louis. Color consultant:
Francis Cugat. Filmed at West Point,
March–May 1954. With Tyrone Power
(Martin Maher), Maureen O'Hara (Mary
O'Donnell), Robert Francis (James
Sunstrom, Jr.), Donald Crisp (Old Martin),
Ward Bond (Capt. Herman J. Koehler),
Betsy Palmer (Kitty Carter), Phil Carey
(Charles Dotson), William Leslie (Red
Sundstrom), Harry Carey, Jr. (Dwight
Eisenhower), Patrick Wayne (Cherub
Overton), Sean McClory (Dinny Maher),
Peter Graves (Sgt. Rudolph Heinz),
Milburn Stone (Capt. John Pershing), Erin
O'Brien-Moore (Mrs. Koehler), Walter
D. Ehlers (Mike Shannon), Don Barclay
(Maj. Thomas), Martin Milner (Jom
O'Carberry), Chuck Courtney (Whitey
Larson), Willis Bouchey (doctor), Jack
Pennick (Tommy, sergeant).

Fifty years of an Irish immigrant at
West Point.

1955 *The Red, White and Blue Line* (U.S.
Treasury Dept.–Columbia). Technicolor /
Cinemascope. 10 minutes. Director: John
Ford (?). Writer: Edward Hope. Photog-
raphy: Charles Lawton, Jr. Narrator:
Ward Bond.

A savings bond promotional made on
set of *The Long Gray Line* and featuring,
according to Joseph McBride, about seven
minutes from that picture, plus scenes
on set of cast at supper table, discussing
bonds, during which Donald Crisp
serves stew.

†1955 *Mister Roberts* (Orange Productions–
Warner Brothers). Warnercolor / Cinema-
scope. 123 minutes. July 30. Directors:
John Ford, Mervyn LeRoy, and
(uncredited) Joshua Logan. Producer:
Leland Hayward. Scenarists: Frank
Nugent, Joshua Logan, from play
by Logan, Thomas Heggen, and novel by
Heggen. Photography: Winton C. Hoch.
Art director: Art Loel. Set decorator:
William L. Kuehl. Music: Franz Waxman.

Editor: Jack Murray. Assistant director:
Wingate Smith. Costumes: Moss Mabry.
Production manager: Norman Cook.
Technical consultants: Adm. John Dale
Price, USN, Ret., Comdr. Merle MacBain,
USN. Exteriors filmed in the Pacific,
Midway Island, September 1954. With
Henry Fonda (Lt. (jg) Roberts), James
Cagney (captain), Jack Lemmon (Ens.
Frank Thurlowe Pulver), William Powell
(Doc), Ward Bond (CPO Dowdy), Betsey
Palmer (Lt. Ann Girard), Phil Carey
(Mannion), Nick Adams (Reber), Harry
Carey, Jr. (Stefanowski), Ken Curtis
(Dolan), Frank Aletter (Gerhart), Fritz
Ford (Lidstrom), Buck Kartalian (Mason),
William Henry (Lt. Billings), William
Hudson (Olson), Studdy Kruger
(Schlemmer), Harry Tenbrook (Cookie),
Perry Lopez (Rodriguez), Robert Roark
(Insigna), Pat Wayne (Bookser), Tige
Andrews (Wiley), Jim Maloney (Kennedy),
Denny Niles (Gilbert), Francis Conner
(Johnson), Shug Fisher (Cochran), Danny
Borzage (Jonesey), Jim Murphy (Taylor),
Kathleen O'Malley, Maura Murphy, Mimi
Doyle, Jeanne Murray-Vanderbilt, Lonnie
Pierce (nurses), Martin Milner (shore
patrol officer), Gregory Walcott (shore
patrolman), James Flavin (MP), Jack
Pennick (marine sergeant), Duke
Kahanamoko (native chief).

Life on a backwater cargo boat,
World War II.

1955 *Rookie of the Year* (Hal Roach
Studios, episode for the *Screen Directors
Playhouse* TV series). 29 minutes.
December. Director: John Ford. Scenarist:
Frank S. Nugent. Photography: Hal Mohr.
Filmed in summer 1955. With John Wayne
(Mike Cronin), Vera Miles (Ruth Delbert),
Pat Wayne (Lyn Goodhue), Ward Bond
(Larry Goodhue, alias Buck Garrison),
James Gleason (Ed Shaeffer), Willis
Bouchey (Mr. Cully, newspaper editor),
Henry Tyler (Wright), William Forrest
(Walker), Robert Leyden (Willie). John
Ford appears in the introduction, spotlit
on a director's chair, with baseball gear.

A cynical newsman thinks he has
discovered a great story, one that will
liberate him from ten years with the
"Emeryville Post-Gazette": the Rookie of
the Year is the son of Buck Garrison, a great
player who took a bribe. But he withholds
the story, out of decency to Buck, and lands
a tour of the Orient.

Rapidly paced, loaded with invention, fantastic dialogue, and great caricatures.

1955 *The Bamboo Cross* (Lewman Ltd.–Revue; episode for the *Fireside Theatre* TV series). 27 minutes. December 6. Director: John Ford. Producer: William Asher. Scenarist: Laurence Stallings, from play by Theophane Lee. Photographer: John MacBurnie. Art director: Martin Obzina. Set decorator: James S. Redd. Music supervisor: Stanley Wilson. Supervising editor: Richard G. Wray. Assistant director: Wingate Smith. Filmed November 7–11. With Jane Wyman (Sister Regina), Betty Lynn (Sister Anne), Soo Yong (Sichi Sao), Jim Hong (Mark Chu), Judy Wong (Tanya), Don Summers (Ho Kwong), Kurt Katch (King Fat), Pat O'Malley (priest), Frank Baker.

Maryknoll nuns are captured by Chinese Communists eager to prove the "unmarried ladies" kill babies with "poisoned cakes" (i.e., Communion wafers). Sister Regina oozes pietism, the commissar is rarely less than apoplectic—until a servant, who had joined the Communists to learn "the truth of the poverty and ignorance of my people," leaps into the frame brandishing a long knife. The commissar dies gurgling percussively off-camera, and the nuns are saved.

The low point of Ford's career.

1956 *The Searchers* (C. V. Whitney Pictures–Warner Brothers). Technicolor / Vista Vision. 119 minutes. May 26. Director: John Ford. Producers: Merian C. Cooper, C. V. Whitney. Scenarist: Frank S. Nugent, from novel by Alan LeMay. Associate producer: Patrick Ford. Photography: Winton C. Hoch, Alfred Gilks (second unit). Art directors: Frank Hotaling, James Basevi. Set decorator: Victor Gangelin. Music: Max Steiner. Title song: Stan Jones. Editor: Jack Murray. Production supervisor: Lowell Farrell. Assistant director: Wingate Smith. Color consultant: James Gooch. Costumes: Frank Beetson (M), Ann Peck (F). Special effects: George Brown. Script supervisor: Robert Gary. Filmed in Colorado and Monument Valley, summer and fall 1955. With John Wayne (Ethan Edwards), Jeffrey Hunter (Martin Pawley), Vera Miles (Laurie Jorgensen), Ward Bond (Capt. Rev. Samuel Clayton), Natalie Wood (Debbie Edwards), John Qualen (Lars Jorgensen),

Olive Carey (Mrs. Jorgensen), Henry Brandon (Chief Scar), Ken Curtis (Charlie McCorry), Harry Carey, Jr. (Brad Jorgensen), Antonio Moreno (Emilio Figueroa), Hank Worden (Mose Harper), Lana Wood (Debbie as child), Walter Coy (Aaron Edwards), Dorothy Jordan (Martha Edwards), Pippa Scott (Lucy Edwards), Pat Wayne (Lt. Greenhill), Beulah Archuletta (Look), Jack Pennick (private), Peter Mamokos (Futterman), Bill Steele (Nesby), Cliff Lyons (Col. Greenhill), Chuck Roberson (man at wedding), Ruth Clifford (deranged woman at fort), Mae Marsh (woman at fort), Dan Borzage (accordionist at funeral), Billy Cartledge, Chuck Hayward, Slim Hightower, Fred Kennedy, Frank McGrath, Dale van Sickle, Henry Wills, Terry Wilson (stuntman), Away Luna, Billy Yellow, Bob Many Mules, Exactly Sonnie Betsuie, Feather Hat, Jr., Harry Black Horse, Jack Tin Horn, Many Mules Son, Percy Shooting Star, Pete Grey Eyes, Pipe Line Begishe, Smile White Sheep (Comanche).

Seven years roaming the West in search of a girl kidnapped by Comanche.

1957 *The Rising of the Moon* (Four Province Productions–Warner Brothers). 81 minutes. May 16 (Dublin); June (G.B.); August 10 (U.S.). Director: John Ford. Producer: Michael Killanin. Scenarist: Frank S. Nugent, from stories. Photography: Robert Krasker. Art director: Ray Simm. Costumes: Jimmy Bourke. Music: Eamonn O'Gallagher. Editor: Michael Gordon. Assistant editor: Dennies Bertera. Continuity: Angela Martell. Production manager: Teddy Joseph. Camera: Dennys Coop. Technical consultants: Earnon O'Malley, Lennox Robinson, Patrick Scott. Filmed in Ireland, spring 1956. Introduced by Tyrone Power.

"The Majesty of the Law," from story by Frank O'Connor. 23 minutes, 24 seconds. Noel Purcell (Dan O'Flaherty), Cyril Cusack (Inspector Michael Dillon), Jack McGowran (the poteen maker: Mickey J.), Eric Gorman, Paul Farrell (neighbors), John Cowley (the Gombeen Man).

An old farmer goes to jail to defend his honor.

"A Minute's Wait," from play by Michael J. McHugh. 23 minutes, 43 seconds. Jimmy O'Dea (porter), Tony Quinn (railroad station chief), Paul Farrell (chauffeur), J. G. Devlin (guard), Michael Trubshawe (Col. Frobisher), Anita Sharp

Bolster (Mrs. Frobisher), Maureen Porter (barmaid), Maureen O'Connell (May Ann McMahon), May Craig (May's aunt), Michael O'Duffy (singer), Ann Dalton (fisherman's wife), Kevin Casey (Mr. McTigue).

A train stops at a station.

"1921," from play "The Rising of the Moon," by Lady Gregory. 27 minutes, 53 seconds. Dennis O'Dea (police sergeant), Eileen Crowe (his wife), Maurice Good (P. C. O'Grady), Frank Lawton (major), Edward Lexy (ROMS), Donal Donnelly (Sean Curran), Joseph O'Dea (chief of guards), Dennis Bennan, David Marlowe, Dennis Franks (English officers), Doreen Madden, Maureen Cusack (false nuns), Maureen Delaney (old woman), Martin Thornton (sergeant), John Horan (bill poster), Joe Hone, John Comeford, Mafra McDonagh (IRA men), and members of the Abbey Theatre Company.

A patriot escapes during 1921 rebellion. (This episode resembles Francis Ford's 1916 *The Cry of Erin*.)

Ford did not personally direct the framing scenes with Tyrone Power.

1957 *The Wings of Eagles* (Metro-Goldwyn-Mayer). Metrocolor. 110 minutes. February 22. Director: John Ford. Producer: Charles Schnee. Associate producer: James E. Newcom. Scenarists: Frank Fenton, William Wister Haines, based on life and writings of Comdr. Frank W. Wead, USN. Photography: Paul C. Vogel. Art directors: William A. Horning, Malcolm Brown. Set decorators: Edwin B. Willis, Keogh Gleason. Maureen O'Hara's wardrobe: Walter Plunkett. Music: Jeff Alexander. Editor: Gene Ruggiero. Aerial stunts: Paul Mantz. Recording supervisor: Dr. Wesley G. Miller. Makeup: William Tuttle. Assistant director: Wingate Smith. Color consultant: Charles K. Hagedon. Technical advisors: Adm. John Dale Price, USN, Ret., Dr. John Keye. Special effects: A. Arnold Gillespie, Warren Newcombe. Filmed in August 1956. With John Wayne (Frank W. "Spig" Wead), Maureen O'Hara (Minne Wead), Dan Dailey (Carson), Ward Bond (John Dodge), Ken Curtis (John Dale Price), Edmund Lowe (Adm. Moffett), Kenneth Tobey (Herbert Allen Hazard), James Todd (Jack Travis), Barry Kelley (Capt. Jock Clark), Sig Ruman (manager), Henry O'Neill (Capt. Spear), Willis Bouchey (Barton), Dorothy Jordan (Rose

Brentmann), Peter Ortiz (Lt. Charles Dexter), Louis Jean Heydt (Dr. John Keye), Tige Andrews (Arizona Pincus), Dan Borzage (Pete), William Tracy (air force officer), Harlan Warde (executive officer), Jack Pennick (Joe), Bill Henry (naval aide), Alberto Morin (second manager), Mimi Gibson (Lila Wead), Evelyn Rudie (Doris Wead), Charles Trowbridge (Adm. Crown), Mae Marsh (Nurse Crumley), Janet Lake (nurse), Fred Graham (officer in brawl), Stuart Holmes (producer), Olive Carey (Bridy O'Faolain), Maj. Sam Harris (patient), May McEvoy (nurse), William Paul Lowery (Wead's baby, Commodore), Chuck Roberson (officer), Cliff Lyons, Veda Ann Borg, Christopher James.

Story of a navy man between the wars who became a screenwriter after being paralyzed.

1957 *The Growler Story* (U.S. Navy). Eastmancolor. 22 minutes. Director: John Ford. Producer: Mark Armistead. Photography: Pacific Fleet Combat Camera Group. Editor: Jack Murray. Assistant editor: Barbara Ford. Narrator: Dan Dailey. Filmed in the Pacific, November 1956 (Navy Film No. MN 8679). With Ward Bond (Quincannon), Ken Curtis (Capt. Howard W. Gilmore), and navy personnel, wives, and children.

Made for navy personnel. An actual World War II incident. Capt. Gilmore bids farewell to his tearful wife and two children; Quincannon leaves his wife and eight children. A dockside band plays "Far Away Places," wives wave anxiously, flower wreaths are thrown into the water as the submarine sails out of Pearl Harbor. At sea the log records the sinking of a freighter, the rescue of downed flyers, until one day an enemy vessel emerges from the fog: Gilmore is wounded but gives the order to submerge, saving the ship at the cost of his life. Back at Pearl his wife receives his Medal of Honor and a wreath floats from *The Growler*'s prow. Gilmore is a background character, as Ford lavishes cornball sentimentality on Ward Bond's Quincannon, whose eight kids stand in line from tallest to shortest to salute goodbye, who hears of a ninth child coming while giving blood, and who grins broadly when *The Growler* gets her first kill. Such (inhumane?) exuberance is typical of Ford's documentaries, in contrast to his usual moral responsiveness. The picture employs open forms and a zoom lens, and spends half its length poeticizing the farewell.

1958 *Gideon's Day* (Columbia British Productions). Technicolor. 91 minutes. March 1958 (G. B.); February 1959 (U. S.). U.S. title: *Gideon of Scotland Yard.* Director: John Ford. Producer: Michael Killanin. Associate producer: Wingate Smith. Scenarist: T. E. B. Clarke, from novel by J. J. Marric (pseudonym for John Creasey). Photography: Frederick A. Young. Art director: Ken Adam. Music: Douglas Gamley. Editor: Raymond Poulton. Assistant director: Tom Pevsner. Costumes: Jack Dalmayne. Production manager: Bill Kuly. Filmed in London, September 1957. With Jack Hawkins (Inspector George Gideon), Dianne Foster (Joanna Delafield), Anna Massey (Sally Gideon), Anna Lee (Mrs. Kate Gideon), Cyril Cusack (Herbert "Birdie" Sparrow), Andrew Ray (P. C. Simon Farnaby-Green), James Hayter (Robert Mason), Ronald Howard (Paul Delafield), Howard Marion-Crawford (chief of Scotland Yard), Laurence Naismith (Arthur Sayer), Derek Bond (Det. Sgt. Eric Kirby), Griselda Harvey (Mrs. Kirby), Frank Lawton (Det. Sgt. Liggott), John Loder (Ponsford, the Duke), Doreen Madden (Miss Courtney), Miles Malleson (judge at Old Bailey), Marjorie Rhodes (Mrs. Rosie Saparelli), Michael Shepley (Sir Rupert Bellamy), Michael Trubshawe (Sgt. Golightly), Jack Watling (Rev. Julian Small), Hermione Bell (Dolly Saparelli), Donal Donnelly (Feeney), Billie Whitelaw (Christine), Malcolm Ranson (Ronnie Gideon), Mavis Ranson (Jane Gideon), Francis Crowdy (Fitzhubert), David Aylmer and Brian Smith (Manners and White-Douglas, Fitzhubert's acolytes), Barry Keegan (Riley, chauffeur), Maureen Potter (Ethel Sparrow), Henry Longhurst (Rev. Mr. Courtney), Charles Maunsell (Walker), Stuart Saunders (Chancery Lane policeman), Dervis Ward (Simmo), Joan Ingram (Lady Bellamy), Nigel Fitzgerald (Insp. Cameron), Robert Raglan (Dawson), John Warwick (Insp. Gillick), John LeMesurier (prosecuting attorney), Peter Godsell (Jimmy), Robert Bruce (defending attorney), Alan Rolfe (CID man at hospital), Derek Prentice (first employer), Alastair Hunter (second employer), Helen Goss (woman employer), Susan Richmond (Aunt May), Raymond Rollett (Uncle Dick), Lucy Griffiths (cashier), Mary Donevan (usherette), O'Donovan Shiell, Bart Allison, Michael O'Duffy (policemen), Diana Chesney (barmaid), David Storm (court clerk), Gordon Harris (CID man).

A day in the life of a Scotland Yard detective.

1958 *The Last Hurrah* (Columbia). 121 minutes. November. Director-producer: John Ford. Scenarist: Frank Nugent, from novel by Edwin O'Connor. Photographer: Charles Lawton, Jr. Art Director: Robert Peterson. Set decorator: William Kiernan. Editor: Jack Murray. Assistant directors: Wingate Smith, Sam Nelson. With Spencer Tracy (Frank Skeffington), Jeffrey Hunter (Adam Caulfield), Dianne Foster (Maeve Caulfield), Pat O'Brien (John Gorman), Basil Rathbone (Norman Cass, Sr.), Donald Crisp (the cardinal), James Gleason (Cuke Gillen), Edward Brophy (Ditto Boland), John Carradine (Amos Force), Willis Bouchey (Roger Sugrue), Basil Ruysdael (Bishop Gardner), Ricardo Cortez (Sam Weinberg), Wallace Force (Charles J. Hennessey), Frank McHugh (Festus Garvey), Anna Lee (Gert Minihan), Jane Darwell (Delia Boylan), Frank Albertson (Jack Mangan), Charles FitzSimmons (Kevin McCluskey), Carleton Young (Mr. Winslow), Bob Sweeney (Johnny Degnan), Edmund Lowe (Johnny Byrne), William Leslie (Dan Herlihy), Ken Curtis (Monseigneur Killian), O. Z. Whitehead (Norman Cass, Jr.), Arthur Walsh (Frank Skeffington, Jr.), Helen Westcott (Mrs. McCluskey), Ruth Warren (Ellen Davin), Mimi Doyle (Mamie Burns), Dan Borzage (Pete), James Flavin (police captain), William Forrest (doctor), Frank Sully (fire chief), Charlie Sullivan (chauffeur), Ruth Clifford (nurse), Jack Pennick (policeman), Richard Deacon (Plymouth Club director), Harry Tenbrook, Eve March, Bill Henry, James Waters, Frank Baker.

An old-style politician's last campaign.

1959 *Korea: Battleground for Liberty* (U. S. Dept. of Defense). Eastmancolor. c. 40 minutes. Director: Rear Adm. John Ford, USNR. Producers: Ford, Capt. George O'Brien, USN, Ret. Filmed in and around Seoul, fall 1958. With O'Brien, Kim-Chi Mi, Choi My Ryonk.

An orientation film for American

soldiers being stationed in Korea. Cameos trace life and culture as Sgt. Cliff Walker, at first terrified, befriends a Korean family, serves on a community council, and combats prostitution with a 4H club. Speeches by Eisenhower and Rhee conclude, dissolving into bathers at a rock pool; pop musicians; Walker and Korean picnicking; DMZ lookout post. The film encourages fraternization between U.S. soldiers and Korean civilians. Ford had planned to direct additional such films on Taiwan and Vietnam, and may have consulted on their scripts.

1959 *The Horse Soldiers* (Mirisch Company–United Artists). Deluxe Color. 119 minutes. June. Director: John Ford. Producers-scenarists: John Lee Mahin, Martin Rackin, from novel by Harold Sinclair. Photography: William H. Clothier. Art director: Frank Hotaling. Set decorator: Victor Gangelin. Music: David Buttolph. Song: "I Left My Love," by Stan Jones. Editor: Jack Murray. Special effects: Augie Lohman. Costumes: Frank Beetson (M), Ann Peck (F). Assistant directors: Wingate Smith, Ray Gosnell, Jr. Filmed in Louisiana and Mississippi, October–December 1958. With John Wayne (Col. John Marlowe), William Holden (Maj. Hank Kendall), Constance Towers (Hannah Hunter), Althea Gibson (Lukey), Hoot Gibson (Brown), Anna Lee (Mrs. Buford), Russell Simpson (Sheriff Capt. Henry Goodboy), Stan Jones (Gen. U.S. Grant), Carleton Young (Col. Jonathan Miles), Basil Ruysdael (commandant, Jefferson Military Academy), Willis Bouchey (Col. Phil Secord), Ken Curtis (Wiklie), O. Z. Whitehead (Hoppy Hopkins), Judson Pratt (Sgt. Major Kirby), Denver Pyle (Jagger Jo), Strother Martin (Virgil), Hank Worden (Deacon), Walter Reed (Union officer), Jack Pennick (Sgt. Maj. Mitchell), Fred Graham (Union soldier), Chuck Hayward (Union captain), Charles Seel (Newton Station bartender), Stuart Holmes, Maj. Sam Harris (passengers to Newton Station), Richard Cutting (Gen. Sherman), Bing Russell, William Forrest, William Leslie, Bill Henry, Ron Hagherty, Dan Borzage, Fred Kennedy.
    Civil War: Union cavalry raids deep within Confederate lines.

1960 *Sergeant Rutledge* (Ford Productions–Warner Brothers). Technicolor. 111 minutes.

May. Director: John Ford. Producers: Patrick Ford, Willis Goldbeck. Writers: Goldbeck, James Warner Bellah. Photography: Bert Glennon. Art director: Edie Imazu. Set decorator: Frank M. Miller. Music: Howard Jackson. Song: "Captain Buffalo," by Mark David, Jerry Livingston. Editor: Jack Murray. Assistant directors: Russ Saunders, Wingate Smith. Costumes: Marjorie Best. Filmed in Monument Valley, May–June 1959. With Jeffrey Hunter (Lt. Tom Cantrell), Constance Towers (Mary Beecher), Woody Strode (Sgt. Braxton Rutledge), Billie Burke (Mrs. Cordelia Fosgate), Juano Hernandez (Sgt. Matthew Luke Skidmore), Willis Bouchey (Col. Otis Fosgate), Carleton Young (Capt. Shattuck), Judson Pratt (Lt. Mulqueen), Bill Henry (Capt. Dwyer), Walter Reed (Capt. MacAfee), Chuck Hayward (Capt. Dickinson), Mae Marsh (Nellie), Fred Libby (Chandler Hubble), Toby Richards (Lucy Dabney), Jan Styne (Chris Hubble), Cliff Lyons (Sam Beecher), Charles Seel (Dr. Eckner), Jack Pennick (sergeant), Hank Worden (Laredo), Chuck Roberson (juror), Eva Novak, Estelle Winwood (spectators), Shug Fisher (Mr. Owens).
    1880s: The trial of a Negro cavalry sergeant for rape and murder of a white girl.

1960 *The Colter Craven Story* (Revue Productions–MCA; episode for the *Wagon Train* series.) 53 minutes. May. Director: John Ford. Producer: Howard Christie. Writer: Tony Paulson. Photographer: Benjamin N. Kline. Art director: Martin Obzina. Music: Stanley Wilson. Theme tune: Jerome Morros. Set decorator: Ralph Sylos. Editors: Marston Fay, David O'Connell. Costumes: Vincent Dee. Assistant director: James H. Brown. With Ward Bond (Maj. Seth Adams), Carleton Young (Colter Craven), Frank McGrath (Chuck Wooster), Terry Wilson (Bill Hawks), John Carradine (Park), Chuck Hayward (Quentin), Ken Curtis (Kyle), Anna Lee (Alarice Craven), Cliff Lyons (Weatherby), Paul Birch (Sam Grant), Annelle Hayes (Mrs. Grant), Willis Bouchey (Jesse Grant), Mae March (Mrs. Jesse Grant), Jack Pennick (drill sergeant), Hank Worden (Shelley), Charles Seel (Mort), Bill Henry (Krindle), Chuck Roberson (Junior), Dennis Rush (Jamie), Harry Tenbrook (Shelley's friend), Beulah Blaze, Lon Chaney, Jr., John Wayne (billed as Michael Morris) (Gen. Sherman).
    The wagon train picks up Craven and

his wife. Craven is a doctor who worked through med school in a slaughter house, then graduated to Shiloh, where 500 of his patients died. Now, taken to drink, he is afraid to perform a caesarian. But Adams tells him the story of his friend Sam, who was a failure back in Wilmette, but whom he met again at Shiloh, after losing all but 19 of his 223 townsmen. But Sam (Grant) had 30,000 casualties and still overcame "defeat." Craven delivers the baby.

The episode uses footage from Ford's *Wagon Master* (on which the series was based). Only the wonderful nine-minute Wilmette flashback looks strongly Fordian, within an otherwise shoddy film.

† 1960 *The Alamo* (Batjac–United Artists). Technicolor/Todd-A.O. 190 minutes. October. Director-producer: John Wayne. Writer: James Edward Grant. Photography: William H. Clothier. With John Wayne, Richard Widmark.

Ford directed various shots—Mexican artillery fording a river; a wide sweep of Santa Anna's army approaching the mission; a dance; a Mexican shot just before Travis closes the gate; Ken Curtis swimming a river—and one entire sequence (by far the best thing in the film) of Frankie Avalon delivering a message to Richard Boone by a riverside.

1961 *Two Rode Together* (Ford-Sheptner Productions—Columbia). Pathecolor. 109 minutes. July. Director: John Ford. Producer: Stan Sheptner. Scenarist: Frank Nugent, from novel *Comanche Captives*, by Will Cook. Photography: Charles Lawton, Jr. Art director: Robert Peterson. Set decorator: James M. Crowe. Music: George Duning. Editor: Jack Murray. Assistant director: Wingate Smith. Costumes: Frank Beetsson. Filmed in southwest Texas, November 1960. With James Stewart (Guthrie McCabe), Richard Widmark (Lt. Jim Gary), Shirley Jones (Marty Purcell), Linda Cristal (Elena de la Madriaga), Andy Devine (Sgt. Darius P. Posey), John McIntire (Maj. Frazer), Paul Birch (Edward Purcell), Willis Bouchey (Harry J. Wringle), Henry Brandon (Quanah Parker), Harry Carey, Jr. (Ortho Clegg), Ken Curtis (Greely Clegg), Olive Carey (Abby Frazer), Chet Douglas (Ward Corbey), Annelle Hayes (Belle Aragon), David Kent (Running Wolf), Anna Lee (Mrs. Malaprop), Jeanette Nolan (Mrs. McCandless), John Qualen (Ole Knudsen), Ford Rainey (Henry Clegg),

Woody Strode (Stone Calf), O. Z. Whitehead (Lt. Chase), Cliff Lyons (William McCandless), Mae Marsh (Hannah Clegg), Frank Baker (Capt. Malaprop), Ruth Clifford (woman), Ted Knight (Lt. Upton), Maj. Sam Harris (post doctor), Jack Pennick (sergeant), Chuck Roberson (Comanche), Dan Borzage, Bill Henry, Chuck Hayward, Edward Brophy.

A cynical sheriff and a cavalry officer ride into Comanche territory to ransom white captives.

1962 *The Man Who Shot Liberty Valance* (Ford Productions– Paramount). 122 minutes. April. Director: John Ford. Producer: Willis Goldbeck. Scenarists: Goldbeck, James Warner Bellah, from story by Dorothy M. Johnson. Photography: William H. Clothier. Art directors: Hal Pereira, Eddie Imazu. Set decorators: Sam Comer, Darrell Silvera. Costumes: Edith Head. Music: Cyril J. Mockridge; theme from *Young Mr. Lincoln*, by Alfred Newman. Editor: Otho Lovering. Assistant director: Wingate Smith. Filmed in September 1961. With James Stewart (Ransom Stoddard), John Wayne (Tom Doniphon), Vera Miles (Hallie Stoddard), Lee Marvin (Liberty Valance), Edmond O'Brien (Dutton Peabody), Andy Devine (Link Appleyard), Ken Murray (Doc Willoughby), John Carradine (Starbuckle), Jeanette Nolan (Nora Ericson), John Qualen (Peter Ericson), Willis Bouchey (Jason Tully), Carleton Young (Maxwell Scott), Woody Strode (Pompey), Denver Pyle (Amos Carruthers), Strother Martin (Floyd), Lee Van Cleef (Reese), Robert F. Simon (Handy Strong), O. Z. Whitehead (Ben Carruthers), Paul Birch (Mayor Winder), Joseph Hoover (Hasbrouck), Jack Pennick (barman), Anna Lee (passenger), Charles Seel (president, election council), Shug Fisher (drunk), Earle Hodgins, Stuart Holmes, Dorothy Phillips, Buddy Roosevelt, Gertrude Astor, Eva Novak, Slim Talbot, Monty Montana, Bill Henry (credited, but not appearing, as a poker player), Frank Baker (uncredited, replacing Henry), John B. Whiteford, Helen Gibson, Maj. Sam Harris.

A senator returns to Shinbone for a pauper's funeral and tells the true story of his youth.

1962 *Flashing Spikes* (Avista Productions– Revue–MCA; episode for the *Alcoa Premiere* TV series). 53 minutes. October 4. Director: John Ford. Associate producer: Frank Baur. Scenarist: Jameson Brewer, from novel by Frank O'Rourke. Photographer: William H. Clothier. Art director: Martin Obzina. Set decorators: John McCarthy, Martin C. Bradfield. Music: Johnny Williams, Stanley Wilson. Costumes: Vincent Dee. Editors: Richard Belding, Tony Martinelli. Titles: Saul Bass. Sound editor: David J. O'Connell. Technical consultant: Cy Malis. Series host: Fred Astaire. With James Stewart (Slim Conway), Jack Warden (commissioner), Pat Wayne (Bill Riley), Edgar Buchanan (Crab Holcomb), Tige Andrews (Gaby Lasalle), Carleton Young (Rex Short), Willis Bouchey (mayor), Don Drysdale (Gomer), Stephanie Hill (Mary Riley), Charles Seel (judge), Bing Russell (Hogan), Harry Carey, Jr. (man in dugout), Vin Scully (announcer), Walter Reed (second reporter), Sally Hughes (nurse), Larry Blake (first reporter), Charles Morton (umpire), Cy Malis (the bit man), Bill Henry (commissioner's assistant), John Wayne (umpire in Korea), Art Passarella (umpire), Vern Stephens, Ralph Volkie, Earl Gilpin, Bud Harden, Whitey Campbell (baseball players).

At a hearing, columnist Short charges rookie sensation Riley took a bribe from blacklisted Slim Conway to throw a series game. In flashback, Conway recounts a semipro game in which, midst myriad wondrous cameos, a riot nearly breaks out over Conway, and Conway is spiked by Riley—who, however, apologizes. So Conway gets old pal Lasalle to give Riley a tryout; but Riley is drafted and has to go to Korea first. Then, at spring training, Conway intervenes to prevent a fight when Short insults Riley's wife. Barred from the Series stadium, he listens in the parking lot, where Short sees him hand Riley an envelope, presumably a bribe. Actually, it was a brochure of Conway's fishing place. Riley is cleared, and it turns out Conway was framed, years ago.

First rate Ford.

1962 *How the West Was Won* (Cinerama–Metro-Goldwyn-Mayer). Technicolor / Cinerama / Ultra Panavision. 162 minutes. November. Directors: John Ford ("The Civil War"), George Marshall ("The Railroad"), Henry Hathaway ("The Rivers," "The Plains," "The Outlaws"). Producer: Bernard Smith. Scenarist: James R. Webb, suggested by series in *Life*. Art directors: George W. Davis, William Ferrari, Addison Hehr. Set decorators: Henry Grace, Don Greenwood, Jr., Jack Mills. Music: Alfred Newman, Ken Darby. Editor: Harold F. Kress. Costumes: Walter Plunkett. Cinerama supervisors: Thomas Conroy, Walter Gibbons-Fly. Historical consultant: David Miller. Special effects: A. Arnold Gillespie, Robert R. Hoag. Color consultant: Charles K. Hagedon. Narrator: Spencer Tracy.

Ford sequence ("The Civil War"): 25 minutes, 13 seconds. Photography: Joseph La Shelle. Assistant director: Wingate Smith. With George Peppard (Zeb Rawlings), Carroll Baker (Eve Prescott Rawlings), Russ Tamblyn (Confederate deserter), Claude Johnson (Jeremiah Rawlings), Andy Devine (Cpl. Peterson), Willis Bouchey (surgeon), Henry (Harry) Morgan (Gen. U. S. Grant), John Wayne (Gen. Sherman), Raymond Massey (Abraham Lincoln).

A farm boy leaves home to go to war.

1963 *Donovan's Reef* (Ford Productions–Paramount). Technicolor. 109 minutes. July. Director-producer: John Ford. Scenarists: Frank Nugent, James Edward Grant, from story by Edmond Beloin, adapted by James Michener. Photography: William Clothier. Art directors: Hal Pereira, Eddie Imazu. Set decorators: Sam Comer, Darrell Silvera. Costumes: Edith Head. Music: Cyril J. Mockridge. Editor: Otho Lovering. Assistant director: Wingate Smith. Special effects: Paul K. Lerpae, Farciot Edouart. Color consultant: Richard Mueller. Filmed on the island of Kauai (Hawaii) in the South Pacific. With John Wayne (Michael Patrick "Guns" Donovan), Lee Marvin (Thomas Aloysius "Boats" Gilhooley), Elizabeth Allen (Amelia Sarah Dedham), Jack Warden (Dr. William Dedham), Cesar Romero (Marquis André de Lage), Dorothy Lamour (Miss Lafleur), Jacqueline Malouf (Lelani Dedham), Mike Mazurki (Sgt. Menkowicz), Marcel Dalio (Fr. Cluzeot), Jon Fong (Mister Eu), Cheryline Lee (Sally Dedham), Tim Stafford (Luki Dedham), Carmen Estrabeau (Sister Gabrielle), Yvonne Peattie (Sister Matthew), Frank Baker (Captain Martin), Edgar Buchanan (Boston notary), Pat Wayne (navy lieutenant), Dan Ford, John Stafford (children), Charles Seel (Grand Uncle

Sedley Atterbury), Chuck Roberson (Festus), Mae Marsh, Maj. Sam Harris (members of family council), Dick Foran, Cliff Lyons (officers), and Ford's ketch, *Araner*.

A comedy of manners—and racism—on a South Pacific isle.

1964 *Cheyenne Autumn* (Ford-Smith Productions–Warner Brothers). Technicolor / Panavision 70. 159 minutes. October. Director: John Ford. Producer: Bernard Smith. Scenarists: James R. Webb and (uncredited) Patrick Ford, from book by Mari Sandoz. Photography: William Clothier. Art director: Richard Day. Set decorator: Darrell Silvera. Associate director: Ray Kellogg. Music: Alex North. Editor: Otho Lovering. Sound editor: Francis E. Stahl. Assistant directors: Wingate Smith, Russ Saunders. Technical consultant: David H. Miller. Filmed in Monument Valley; Moab, Utah; Gunnison, Colorado, October–December 1963. With Richard Widmark (Capt. Thomas Archer), Carroll Baker (Deborah Wright), James Stewart (Wyatt Earp), Edward G. Robinson (Secretary of the Interior Carl Schurz), Karl Malden (Capt. Wessels), Sal Mineo (Red Shirt), Dolores Del Rio (Spanish woman), Ricardo Montalban (Little Wolf), Gilbert Roland (Dull Knife), Arthur Kennedy (Doc Holliday), Patrick Wayne (2nd Lt. Scott), Elizabeth Allen (Guinevere Plantagenet), John Carradine (Maj. Jeff Blair), Victor Jory (Tall Tree), Mike Mazurki (Top Sgt. Stanislaw Wichowsky), George O'Brien (Maj. Braden), Sean McClory (Dr. O'Carberry), Judson Pratt (Maj. "Dog" Kelly), Carmen D'Antonio (Pawnee woman), Ken Curtis (Joe), Walter Baldwin (Jeremy Wright), Shug Fisher (Skinny), Nancy Hsueh (Little Bird), Chuck Roberson (platoon sergeant), Harry Carey, Jr. (Trooper Smith), Ben Johnson (Trooper Plumtree), Jimmy O'Hara (trooper), Chuck Hayward (trooper), Lee Bradley (Cheyenne), Walter Reed (Lt. Peterson), Willis Bouchey (colonel), Carleton Young (aide to Carl Schurz), Denver Pyle (Senator Henry), John Qualen (Svenson), Nanomba "Moonbeam" Morton (Running Deer), Dan Borzage, Dean Smith, David H. Miller, Bing Russell (troopers). Narrators: Spencer Tracy, Richard Widmark. Working title: "The Long Flight."

Two-hundred-eighty-five Cheyenne flee a reservation to go back home.

†1965 *Young Cassidy* (Sextant Films–Metro-Goldwyn-Mayer). Technicolor. 110 minutes. March. Directors: Jack Cardiff, John Ford. "A John Ford Film." Producers: Robert D. Graff, Robert Emmett Ginna. Associate producer: Michael Killanin. Scenarist: John Whiting, from autobiography *Mirror in My House*, by Sean O'Casey. Photography: Ted Scaife. Art director: Michael Stringer. Costumes: Margaret Furse. Music: Sean O'Riada. Editor: Anne V. Coates. Production manager: Teddy Joseph. Assistant director: John Quested. Titles: Maurice Binder. Casting: Miriam Brickman. Technical consultant (for teaching Rod Taylor a Dublin accent): Jack McGowan. Camera: Jack Atchelor. Filmed in Ireland in July. With Rod Taylor (Sean Cassidy), Maggie Smith (Nora), Julie Christie (Daisy Battles), Flora Robson (Mrs. Cassidy), Sian Phillips (Ella), Michael Redgrave (William Butler Yeats), Dame Edith Evans (Lady Gregory), Jack McGowan (Archie), T. P. McKenna (Tom), Julie Ross (Sara), Robin Sumner (Michael), Philip O'Flynn (Mick Mullen), Pauline Delaney (Bessie Ballynoy), Arthur O'Sullivan (foreman), Tom Irwin (constable), John Cowley (barman), William Foley (publisher's clerk), John Franklyn (bank teller), Harry Brogan (Murphy), James Fitzgerlad (Charlie Ballynoy), Donald Donnelly (undertaker's man), Harold Goldblatt (director of Abbey Theatre), Ronald Ibbs (theatre employee), May Craig, May Cluskey (women in the hall), Tom Irwin, Shivaun O'Casey, and members of the Abbey Theatre.

Young Sean O'Casey in Dublin: his romances, his mother's death, his first production.

Ford prepared script, cast, and locations, but fell sick after two weeks' shooting, which included the scene with Daisy Battles (but the close-ups were added later by Cardiff); the opening scene when Cassidy becomes a laborer; the inn scene with the three sons and football players; some scenes with Mrs. Cassidy; a scene with Rod Taylor and the tree in bloom after his mother's death—about ten minutes in total. The script seems poor, but Ford scripts rely for sense on his direction. The key Nora-Cassidy relationship lacks motivation, and boring monotonality has replaced Ford's intense changefulness. Only the inn scene has spontaneity and economy.

1965 *7 Women* (Ford-Smith Productions–
Metro-Goldwyn-Mayer). Metrocolor /
anamorphic Panavision. 86 minutes.
November. Director: John Ford. Producer:
Bernard Smith. Scenarists: Janet Green,
John McCormick, from story "Chinese
Finale," by Norah Lofts. Photography:
Joseph LaShelle. Art directors: George W.
Davis, Eddie Imazu. Set directors: Henry
Grace, Jack Mills. Costumes: Walter
Plunkett. Music: Elmer Bernstein. Editor:
Otho S. Lovering. Assistant director:
Wingate Smith. Production manager: Rex
Bailey. Special effects: J. McMillan
Johnson. Filmed in February–April. With
Anne Bancroft (Dr. D. R. Cartwright),
Margaret Leighton (Agatha Andrews),
Flora Robson (Miss Binns), Sue Lyon
(Emma Clark), Mildred Dunnock (Jane
Argent), Betty Field (Florrie Pether), Anna
Lee (Mrs. Russell), Eddie Albert (Charles
Pether), Mike Mazurki (Tunga Khan),
Woody Strode (Lean Warrior), Jane Chang
(Miss Ling), Hans William Lee (Kim),
H. W. Gim (coolie), Irene Tsu (Chinese
girl).

1935 China: women missionaries
encounter plague and bandits.

Anne Bancroft replaced Patricia Neal
when the latter became ill after three days'
shooting. Prints released for television
include additional scenes.

†1972 *Vietnam! Vietnam!* (Ford
Production–USIA). Eastmancolor. 58
minutes. September 1971. Director:
Sherman Beck. Executive producer: John
Ford. Producer: Bruce Herschensohn.
Scenario: Thomas Duggan, Ford. Editor:
Leon Selditz. Location photography:
Vietnam, October–December 1968.
Narrator: Charlton Heston.

Although Ford went to Vietnam, he did
not participate in production, nor does the
zoom work, rack-focusing, or light texture
suggest Ford. But subsequently Ford
supervised the editing and rewrote the
scenario. Although longer and costlier
($252,751) than any other USIA production,
its interpretation of the war had become

embarrassing by the time of its release,
and, after a few overseas showings in U.S.
Information Agency libraries and cultural
offices, it was withdrawn from circulation.

Its prologue is a montage of stills of
some fifty 1960s headliners (Koufax, the
Beatles, the pill, etc.), ending with
Vietnam. Part 1 explores the country's
background, culture, and the war. Shots of
refugees, mutilated children, burnt bodies
of babies, sobbing women, mass graves.
"To those in command of North Vietnam
and the Vietcong the pursuit was a united
Vietnam under Hanoi with a Communist
government. To those in South Vietnam
the pursuit was to be left alone." POW
wives describe their efforts for information; the USSR's involvement is shown;
American "End the War" demonstrators
parade with North Vietnamese flags. In
Part 2, cameos of a couple of dozen people
debate the war: Rush, Reagan, Johnson,
McCarthy, U.S. soldiers, Fulbright, Sam
Brown, hippies, a Hungarian freedom
fighter. Vietnamese parade at night with
7-Up–can torches, people singing hymns.
"The flames were still bright on December
31, 1969, but if that fire would be a permanent light of freedom or would be
extinguished was not to be known within
the decade."

1976 *Chesty* (James Ellsworth Productions).
28 minutes. April 4. Director: John Ford.
Producer: James Ellsworth. Writer: Jay
Simms. Photography: Brick Marquard.
Music: Jack Marshall. Editor–associate
producer: Leon Selditz. Assistant to
producer: Charles C. Townsend. Filmed
August 1968–April 1970. First public
showing at Filmex, Los Angeles.
Unreleased. Host: John Wayne.

A documentary about Lt. Gen. Lewis
"Chesty" Puller, USMC. Made for TV,
but never sold or released. Originally
sixty minutes, but shortened to encourage
sale. Ford is said to have preferred the
shorter version.

Unrealized Projects (among many)

1926 *Corncob Kelly's Romance,* story by
Peter B. Kyne.

1928 *Blockade,* story by Berthold Viertel.

1928 *Captain Lash.* A Mississippi
riverboat story to star Victor McLaglen.

1928 *Frozen Justice,* an Alaskan saga
which Murnau lost to Ford and neither
made.

1940 *Four Sons.* A remake.

1941 *The African Queen.*

1943 *The Last Outlaw.* A remake of Ford's 1919 two-reeler and Cabanne's 1936 feature, to star Harry Carey, for Republic Pictures.

1947 *The Family.* A White Russian family exiled to China after the revolution, from Nina Federova's 1940 novel, with John Wayne and Ethel Barrymore, for Argosy.

1947 *Janitzio.* To be made in Mexico, after *The Fugitive*, by Argosy.

1952 *Famine,* story by Liam O'Flaherty, for Four Provinces in Ireland.

1952 *Demi-Gods,* story by James Stephen, for Four Provinces in Ireland.

1952 *Seven Pillars of Wisdom,* by T. E. Lawrence.

1952 *Two-Headed Spy,* to be filmed in Germany with Kirk Douglas; at Douglas's initiation. Filmed in 1958 in England by André de Toth with Jack Hawkins.

1952 "Ghost Story," an episode for *The Rising of the Moon*, with Katharine Hepburn.

1956 *The Judge and the Hangman,* a mystery, to be filmed in Munich and ski country in the Alps, with Spencer Tracy or John Wayne.

1956 *Drama of Inish,* aka *Is Life Worth Living*, story by Lennox Robinson, for Four Provinces, in Ireland, with Katharine Hepburn.

1956 *The Valiant Virginians,* by James Warner Bellah, to be made for C. V. Whitney, at first as a trilogy of three features, then as a single film; with John Wayne.

1960 *The White Company,* by Sir Arthur Conan Doyle. A youth goes to fight in France during the Hundred Years War. John Wayne, Laurence Olivier, Alec Guinness, Susan Hampshire. Negotiations were carried on for nearly ten years and filming almost took place in Spain, for Samuel Bronston Productions, but Doyle's estate demanded colossally unreasonable sums for the literary rights: $100,000 plus 25 percent of producer's net at one point; $200,000 flat at another. Ford was still talking about doing it in the 1970s.

1962 *A Scout for Custer,* by Willis Goldbeck and John Ford. The story, both comic and tragic, of General Custer's younger brother Tom's stubborn and repeated attempts to bring common sense into the general's reckless campaigning. A story of gallant failure of a man who was brave without conviction in what he was attempting.

1964 *Rupert of Hentzau,* a project promoted by David Selznick for Jennifer Jones.

1965 *The Miracle of Merriford,* aka *Trumpets over Merriford.* A small English town's church is damaged during World War II by Americans, who then try to raise money for repairs. A comedy in the vein of *The Quiet Man*, from a novel by Reginald Arkell. Ford had signed with Metro, Dan Dailey had been cast, and the script by Willis Goldbeck and James Warner Bellah was completed, when Metro shelved the project barely a week before filming was to begin in Utah.

1967 *April Morning.* A boy's family during the battles of Lexington and Concord. From novel by Howard Fast. Scripted by Michael Wilson, to have been produced by Samuel Goldwyn, Jr.

1967 *OSS.* The story of Maj. Gen. William J. "Wild Bill" Donovan and the intelligence agency during World War II. With John Wayne.

1969 *Valley Forge.* To have been co-produced with Frank Capra.

1970? *Comanche Stallion.* A stallion, stolen from Apache and believed by them to be a god who will restore their greatness, tramples to death the son of a drunk cavalry officer, who vows to capture and torture it, but fails.

1973 *The Josh Clayton Story.* About the first black to graduate from West Point. With Fred Williamson. Alternate title: "Appointment with Precedence."

Radio and Television Appearances

1957 *This Is Your Life.* Appeared on Ralph Edwards's television show devoted to Maureen O'Hara.

1958 *Wide Wide World.* Appeared on television June 8, to promote *Horse Soldiers.*

1962 *The Unreal West.* CBC Radio (Toronto). Producer: Jack Vance. Scenarist-narrator: Tony Thomas. Broadcast: July 25. 60 minutes. Interviews with Richard Boone, John Wayne, Olive Stokes Mix (a Cherokee, and Tom Mix's widow), Randolph Scott, Tom McCoy, Johnny Mack Brown, Yakima Canutt, John Ford.

1966 *John Ford,* in the ORTF (Paris) *Cinéastes de notre temps* series. A lengthy interview broadcast June 16.

1973 *American Film Institute First Annual Life Achievement Award* (CBS). Producer: George Stevens, Jr. Taped March 31, broadcast April 2. President Richard Nixon presented Ford with the Civilian Medal of Honor and promoted him to admiral. John Wayne, Maureen O'Hara, Danny Kae, Jack Lemmon, and others.

Films about Ford

1971 *Directed by John Ford* (California Arts Commission–AFI). Color. Director-writer-interviewer: Peter Bogdanovich. Producers: George Stevens, Jr., James R. Silke. Interview photography: Laszlo Kovacs, Gregory Sandor, Brick Marquard, Eric Sherman. Editor: Richard Patterson. Assistant: Mae Woods. Associate producer: David Shepard. Narrator: Orson Welles. First shown: Thirty-second Venice Film Festival, September 15, Ford present to receive festival award. With Ford, John Wayne, Henry Fonda, James Stewart.

Interviews with actors and brief glimpses of Ford; most of the picture consumes excerpts from twenty-seven Ford films.

1971 *The American West of John Ford* (Group One–Timex–CBX). Director: Denis Sanders. Executive producer: Bob Banner. Producers: Tom Egan, Britt Lomond, Dan Ford. Writer: David H. Vowell. Photographer: Bob Collins.

Editor: Keith Olson. Broadcast December 5. With Ford, John Wayne, James Stewart, Henry Fonda.

According to Bogdanovich, this documentary includes clips from Ford westerns, interviews with Stewart and Fonda at Ford's home, with Wayne in Monument Valley directing a stunt, and material with Fonda overlooking the old Fox lot in Century City.

1974 *John Ford: Memorial Day 1970.* Director-writer-editor: Mark Haggard. Producers: Haggard, Paul Magwood, Lowell Peterson. Photographer: Douglas Knapp. Narrator: Linda Strawn. 12 minutes. First shown: April. With John Ford, Walter Pidgeon, Anna Lee, Harry Carey, Jr., Olive Carey, Dan Borzage, Dick Amador, Meta Sterne, George Bagnall, Ray Kellogg, Mary Ford, Wingate Smith.

Members of Ford's field unit at twenty-fourth Annual Memorial Day Service at the Motion Picture Country Home in Woodland Hills, California.

Selected Bibliography

Titles preceded by an asterisk have been found particularly valuable.

BOOKS AND ARTICLES

Ager, Cecilia. "Then and Now." *The New York Times Magazine*, September 20, 1959, p. 62. An interview with Ford and Hoot Gibson.
*Anderson, Lindsay. *About John Ford*. London: Plexus, 1981. Contains reprints of interviews, letters, and articles previously published in *Sequence* and *Cinema*, plus new material.
Astor, Mary. *A Life on Film*. New York: Dell, 1972.
Baby, Yvonne. "John Ford à Paris." *Le Monde*, September 16, 1966.
*Balshofer, Fred C., and Arthur Miller. *One Reel a Week*. Berkeley: University of California Press, 1967.
Baroncelli, Jean de. "Avec Alfred Hitchcock et John Ford." *Le Monde*, January 7, 1955.
Baxter, John. *The Cinema of John Ford*. New York: A. S. Barnes, 1971.
Behlmer, Rudy. "Merian C. Cooper." *Films in Review*, January 1966, pp. 17–35.
Berggen, Noel. "Arsenic and Old Directors." *Esquire*, April 1972, p. 135.

Bogdanovich, Peter. "The Autumn of John Ford." *Esquire*, April 1964, pp. 102–7, 144–45. Expanded version in Bogdanovich, *Pieces of Time*. New York: Arbor House, 1973, pp. 172–93.

*———. *John Ford*. 2d ed. Berkeley: University of California Press, 1978.

Browne, Nick. "The Spectator-in-the-Text: The Rhetoric of Stagecoach." *Film Quarterly*, Winter 1975, pp. 26–38.

Calum, Per, ed. *John Ford: En Dokumentation*. Copenhagen: Dankse Filmmuseum, 1968.

Capozzi, George, Jr. *The John Wayne Story*. New Rochelle, N. Y.: Arlington, 1972.

Comolli, Jean-Louis. "Ford et forme." *Cahiers du Cinéma* 183 (October 1966), p. 54.

Corliss, Richard. "Dudley Nichols" and "Frank Nugent." In *Talking Pictures*. Woodstock, Conn.: Overlook, 1974, pp. 225–35, 330–35.

Delahaye, Michel. "De John Ford à Sean O'Feeney, jalons et repères." *Cahiers du Cinéma* 183 (October 1966), pp. 55–59.

Dempsey, Michael. "John Ford: A Reassessment." *Film Quarterly*, Summer 1975, pp. 2–15. An anti-Ford diatribe.

Dunne, Philip. *Take Two: A Life in Movies and Politics*. New York: McGraw-Hill, 1980.

Eisenburg, Emanuel. Interview with Ford. *New Theater*, April 1936, p. 18.

Ericson, Peter. "Recent Works of John Ford." *Sequence* 2 (Winter 1947), pp. 18–25.

Everett, Eldon K. "The Great Grace Cunard—Francis Ford Mystery." *Classic Film Collector*, Summer 1973, pp. 22–25.

Everson, William K. "Forgotten Ford." *Focus on Film*, Spring 1971, pp. 13–19.

Eyman, Scott. Interview with William Clothier. *Take One* 4, no. 8, (November–December 1973 [published March 1975]), pp. 8–14.

Ferrini, Franco. *John Ford*. Florence: La Nuova Italia, 1974.

*Ford, Dan. *Pappy: The Life of John Ford*. Englewood Cliffs, N. J.: Prentice-Hall, 1979.

*Ford, John. "Veteran Producer Muses." *The New York Times*, June 10, 1928, sec. 8, p. 4. Reprinted in *Hollywood Directors 1914–1940*, by Richard Koszarski, New York: Oxford University Press, 1976, p. 198–201.

———. "Forward." In *The Name Above the Title*, by Frank Capra, New York: Macmillan, 1971. Actually ghost-written, but with Ford's collaboration, by Katherine Clifton.

———. John Ford Presents: *Cowboy Kings of Western Fame: John Ford Series of Famous Western Stars*. Western Series, 1973. $120 collection of 11 × 16 reproductions of templates by artist Will Williams.

———. "Il mio amico John Wayne," *Bis* 4, no. 33, August 18, 1951, p. 15. (No English language source is known for this 1500 word Italian article, lacking detail, in praise of John Wayne.)

"Francis Ford." *Universal Weekly*, December 20, 1913, p. 4.

"Francis Ford Expresses His Ideas on Serials." *Moving Picture World*, August 16, 1919, p. 998.

Gallagher, Tag. "Brother Feeney." *Film Comment*, November 1976, pp. 12–18. Reprinted with changes and a Francis Ford filmography, in *Griffithiana*, edited by Paolo Cherchi Usai and Livio Iacob, "Thomas Ince: Il Profeta del Western," special edition (Genoa, Italy), year 7, nos. 18–21, October 1984, pp. 59–72 and (filmography) 205–20.

Gussow, Mel. *Don't Say Yes Until I Finish Talking.* New York: Pocket Books, 1972.

Haber, Joyce. "If I Could Film a Dream . . . ." *Philadelphia Inquirer*, May 13, 1972. Ford muses about the White Company.

Haggard, Mark. "Ford in Person." *Focus on Film* 6 (Spring 1971), pp. 31–37. Ford at the University of Southern California, March 1969 and February 1970.

Haudiquet, Philippe. "En bavardant avec John Ford." *Les lettres françaises*, July 21, 1966.

———. *John Ford.* Paris: Seghers, 1966.

Hopper, Hedda. Unpublished conversation with Ford, April 13, 1962. Library of Academy of Motion Picture Arts and Sciences, Beverly Hills.

Humphrey, Hal. "Veteran John Ford Looks Back." *Philadelphia Bulletin*, April 11, 1965.

"An Interview with John Ford." *Focus!*, October 1969, pp. 3–4. Ford at the University of Chicago.

*Jenkinson, Philip. Unreleased filmed interview with Ford, 1969.

———. "John Ford Talks to Philip Jenkinson About Not Being Interested in Movies." *The Listener*, February 12, 1970, pp. 217–18. Excerpts from the filmed interview.

Jensen, Paul. "Dudley Nichols." In *The Hollywood Screenwriters*, edited by Richard Corliss. New York: Avon, 1972, pp. 107–24.

Johnson, Grady. "A Paean of Economy." *The New York Times*, June 27, 1948, sec. 2, p. 4.

Kay, Karyn, and Gerald Peary. "Talking to Pat O'Brien." *Velvet Light Trap* 15 (Fall 1975), pp. 29–32.

Kennedy, Burt. "Burt Kennedy Interviews John Ford." *Action*, August 1968. Reprinted in *Directors in Action*, edited by Bob Thomas. New York: Bobbs Merrill, 1973, pp. 133–37.

Kezich, Tullio. *John Ford.* Parma: Guanda, 1958.

Killanin, Michael. "Poet in an Iron Mask." *Films and Filming*, February 1958, pp. 9–10. A conversation with Ford.

Lachize, Samuel. "Brève rencontre avec John Ford." *Cinéma 61* (February 1961).

Lahue, Kalton C. *Continued Next Week: A History of the Moving Picture Serial.* Oklahoma City: University of Oklahoma, 1964.

———. "Grace Cunard," In *Ladies in Distress.* New York: A. S. Barnes, 1973, pp. 52–61.

Leguèbe, Eric, "John Ford." In *Le Cinéma Americain par ses auteurs.* Paris: Guy Authier, 1977, pp. 71–81.

Libby, Bill. "The Old Wrangler Rides Again." *Cosmopolitan*, March 1964, pp. 12–21. Ford on the western.

McBride, Joseph. "County Mayo Go Bragh." *Sight and Sound*, Winter 1970–71, pp. 43–44, 52. Interview with Ford.

———. "Bringing in the Sheaves." *Sight and Sound*, Winter 1973–74, pp. 9–11. Ford's funeral.

McBride, Joseph, and Gerald Peary. Interview with Howard Hawks. *Film Comment*, May 1974, pp. 44–53.

McBride, Joseph, and Michael Wilmington. *John Ford.* New York: Da Capo, 1975.

McHenry, William. "Her Grace and Francis I: The Royal Pair of Photo-Melodrama." *Motion Picture Photoplay*, January 1916.

McInerney, Joe. "John Wayne Talks Tough." *Film Comment*, September 1972, pp. 52–55.

McInroy, Patrick. "Hollywood Ruined S. A. Filming." *San Antonio Light*, May 30, 1976, Today section, pp. 1–2.

Madsen, Axel. Interview with Ford. *Cahiers du Cinéma* 168 (July 1965), p. 79.

*———. Interview with Ford. *Cahiers du Cinéma* 183 (October 1966), pp. 38–53.

Malthête-Méliès, Madeleine. *Méliès l'enchanteur*. Paris: Hachette, 1973.

Maltin, Leonard. *The Art of the Cinematographer*. New York: Dover, 1978.

*Mitchell, George J. "Ford on Ford." *Films in Review*, June 1964, pp. 321–32. Ford at a University of California, Los Angeles, tribute.

Mitry, Jean. *John Ford*. Paris: Editions Universitaires, 1954.

———. Interview with Ford. *Cahiers du Cinéma* 45 (March 1955), pp. 3–9. Abridged translation in *Interviews with Film Directors*, edited by Andrew Sarris. New York: Avon, 1969, pp. 193–201.

———. *Histoire du cinéma*. vols. 1–3. Paris: Editions Universitaires, n.d. (c. 1968).

Motte, Michele. "Le Vieux John Ford parle du western." *Paris-Presse*, July 12, 1966.

Murphy, William T. "John Ford and the Wartime Documentary." *Film and History*, February 1976, pp. 1–8.

Nichols, Dudley. "The Writer and the Film." In *Film: A Montage of Theories*, edited by Richard Dyer McCann. New York: Dutton, 1966, pp. 73–87.

Nugent, Frank S. "In Remembrance of Hot-Foots Past." *The New York Times*, March 3, 1949, p. 33.

*———. "Hollywood's Favorite Rebel." *The Saturday Evening Post*, September 23, 1949, pp. 26, 96–98.

———. "Eire Happily Revisited." *The New York Times*, July 14, 1957, sec. 2, p. 5.

Parrish, Robert. "De Chaplin à Fuller." *Cahiers du Cinéma* 142 (April 1963), pp. 1–16.

———. "Témoignage sur John Ford." *Présence du Cinéma* 21 (March 1965), pp. 18–20.

*———. *Growing Up in Hollywood*. New York: Harcourt Brace Jovanovich, 1976.

Philippe, Claude-Jean. "John Ford en chair et en os." *Télérama*, July 31, 1966.

Place, J. A. *The Western Films of John Ford*. New York: Citadel, 1975.

———. *The Non-Western Films of John Ford*. New York: Citadel, 1979.

Reed, Joseph W. *Three American Originals: John Ford, William Faulkner, and Charles Ives*. Middletown, Conn.: Wesleyan University Press, 1984. Excellent critical treatment of Ford's later films.

Rieupeyront, Jean-Louis. "Rencontre avec John Ford." *Cinéma 61* (February 1961).

Roy, Jean. *Pour John Ford*. Paris: Editions du Cerf, 1977.

Sarris, Andrew. "John Ford." In *The American Cinema*. New York: Dutton, 1968, pp. 43–49.

———. *The John Ford Movie Mystery*. Bloomington: Indiana University Press, 1976.

Schickel, Richard. "Good Days, Good Years." *Harper's*, October 1970, p. 46.

*Sharpe, Howard. "The Star Creators of Hollywood." *Photoplay*, October 1936, pp. 15, 98–100. Reprinted in *The Talkies*, edited by Richard Griffith. New York: Dover, 1971; pp. 116, 167, 333–37.

*Sinclair, Andrew. *John Ford: A Biography*. New York: Dial, 1979.

"Six Pioneers." *Action*, November 1972; pp. 17–18. John Ford at Directors Guild theater.

*Slide, Anthony, and June Banker. Unpublished interview with Mary Ford, 1970.

*Slide, Anthony, and Robert Gitt. "Frank Baker." Unpublished interview, July 30, 1977. Sponsored by the Archival Acquisitions Program of the Los Angeles Film and Television Study Group.

Tavernier, Bertrand. "La Chevauchée de Sganarelle." *Présence du Cinéma* 21 (March 1965), pp. 1–6.

*———. "John Ford à Paris." *Positif* 82 (March 1967), pp. 7–22. An interview.

Tavernier, Claudine. "Le 4ème dimension de la vieillesse." *Cinéma 69.* (June 1969).

Wagner, Walter. "John Ford." In *You Must Remember This.* New York: Putnam's, 1975, pp. 55–65.

*Wilkinson, James L. *An Introduction to the Career and Films of John Ford.* Unpublished M.A. thesis, University of California, Los Angeles, August 1960. Microfilm copy, Library and Museum of the Performing Arts, Lincoln Center, New York.

Willis, Richard. "Francis Ford: A Director with a Heart." *Motion Picture Magazine*, February 1915, p. 112.

———. "Francis Ford of the Gold Seal Company." *Motion Picture Magazine*, June 1915, pp. 101–4.

Young, Colin. "The Old Dependables." *Film Quarterly*, Fall 1969, pp. 2–17.

Zolotow, Maurice. *Shooting Star: A Biography of John Wayne.* New York: Simon & Schuster, 1974.

REVIEWS AND ARTICLES ON PARTICULAR PICTURES

In order of film chronology.

Hangman's House (1928)
Beaton, Cecil. *Film Spectator*, May 12, 1928, pp. 5–7.

Riley the Cop (1928)
Beaton, Cecil. *Film Spectator*, November 3, 1928, p. 10; November 10, 1928, pp. 6–7.

Doctor Bull (1933), *Judge Priest* (1934), and *Steamboat Round the Bend* (1935)
Rollins, Peter C. "Will Rogers and the Relevance of Nostalgia: *Steamboat Round the Bend.*" In John E. O'Connor and Martin Jackson, eds., *American History / American Film.* New York: Ungar, 1979, pp. 77–96.
Rubin, Martin. *Film Comment*, January 1974, pp. 54–57.

Submarine Patrol (1938)
Nugent, Frank S. *The New York Times*, November 19, 1938, p. 9.

Stagecoach (1939)
Anobile, Richard, ed. *Stagecoach.* New York: Avon, 1974. A shot-by-shot series of frame blow-ups.
Interviews with Ford, Wayne, Trevor, Canutt, Smith, Reynolds, Spencer, Devine, Plunkett, Carradine. Articles by A. Sarris and A. Knight. In *Directors in Action*, edited by Bob Thomas. New York: Bobbs Merrill, 1973, pp. 140–73.

Young Mr. Lincoln (1939)

Brewster, Ben. "Notes on the Text 'John Ford's *Young Mr. Lincoln.*'" *Screen*, Autumn 1972, pp. 29–41. A critique of the *Cahiers* article below.

Editors of *Cahiers du Cinéma*. "John Ford's *Young Mr. Lincoln.*" *Cahiers du Cinéma* 223 (August 1970), pp. 29–47. Translation by Helene Lackner and Diana Matias in *Screen*, Autumn 1972, pp. 5–28. Reprinted in *Film Theory and Criticism*, edited by Gerald Mast and Marshall Cohen. 2d ed. New York: Oxford University Press, 1979, pp. 778–831.

Eisenstein, Sergei. "Mister Lincoln par Mister Ford." *Positif* 74 (March 1966), pp. 74–83. French translation of article written in 1945.

Fluck, von Winfried, ed. *Young Mr. Lincoln —der Text der Cahiers du Cinéma und der Film von John Ford: Ergebnisse und Materialien eines Seminars*. Berlin: J. F. Kennedy-Institut für Nordamerikastudien, Freie Universität Berlin, 1978.

The Grapes of Wrath (1940)

Bluestone, George. *Novels into Film*. Baltimore: Johns Hopkins Press, 1957.

French, Warren. *Filmguide to "The Grapes of Wrath."* Bloomington: Indiana University Press, 1973.

Semple, Tom. *Screenwriter: The Life and Times of Nunnally Johnson*. New York: A. S. Barnes, 1980.

The Long Voyage Home (1940)

Friday, August 9, 1940. Ford on the film.

My Darling Clementine (1946)

Lyons, Robert, ed. *My Darling Clementine* [script]. New Brunswick, NJ: Rutgers University Press, 1984.

The Searchers (1956)

Arizona Highways, April 1956. Feature story on production.

Cahiers du Cinéma 63 (November 1956), p. 61. Anonymous unfavorable three-line review.

The Searchers: Materials and Approaches," special number of *Screen Educator*, 17 (Winter 1975–76). (Contents: John Caughie, "Teaching through Authorship," pp. 3–13; David Lusted, "*The Searchers* and the Study of the Image," pp. 14–26; Tom Ryall, "Teaching Through Genre," pp. 27–33; Douglas Pye, "*The Searchers* and Teaching the Industry," pp. 34–48; Edward Buscombe, "Critics and *The Searchers*," pp. 49–51; Alan Lovell, "*The Searchers* and the Pleasure Principle," pp. 52–57.)

Gideon's Day (1958)

Marcorelles, Louis. *Cahiers du Cinéma* 85 (September 1958), p. 54.

The Horse Soldiers (1959)

Marcorelles, Louis. *Cahiers du Cinéma* 101 (November 1959), pp. 46–49.

Robinson, David. *Sight and Sound*, Winter 1959–60, p. 36.

Sergeant Rutledge (1960)

Givray, Claude de. *Cahiers du Cinéma* 114 (December 1960), pp. 63–64.

How the West Was Won (1962)

Fieschi, Jean-André. *Cahiers du Cinéma* 148 (October 1963), pp. 58–60.

Cheyenne Autumn (**1964**)

Comolli, Jean-Louis, *Cahiers du Cinéma* 164 (March 1965), p. 75.

7 Women (**1965**)

Aprà, Adriano. *Cinema e Film* (Rome) 1 (Winter 1966–67), pp. 139–43.
Clipping from *New York Morning Telegraph*, 1966. *7 Women* file, Library and
    Museum of the Performing Arts, Lincoln Center, New York.
Comolli, Jean-Louis. *Cahiers du Cinéma* 182 (September 1966), pp. 14–20.
Knight, Arthur. *Saturday Review*, January 8, 1966, p. 97.
Narboni, Jean. *Cahiers du Cinéma* 182 (September 1966), pp. 20–24.
Pressbook. Theater collection, Free Library of Philadelphia.

Vietnam! Vietnam! (**1972**)

McBride, Joseph. "Drums Along the Mekong." *Sight and Sound*, Autumn 1972,
    pp. 213–16.
Morgenstern, Joseph. *Newsweek*, May 15, 1972, p. 38.

Chesty (**1976**)

McBride, Joseph. *Variety*, December 26, 1974, p. 13.

FILMOGRAPHIES

Bogdanovich, Peter. In *John Ford*. 2d ed. Berkeley: University of California Press,
    1976, pp. 113–49.
Brion, Patrick. In *Cahiers du Cinéma* 183 (October 1966), pp. 60–70.
Mitchell, George J. In *Films in Review*, March 1963, pp. 129–45.

COLLECTIONS

John Ford issues

Cahiers du Cinéma 183 (October 1966). John Ford issue.
Cinema & Cinema (Florence) 31 (April–June, 1982). John Ford issue.
Cult Movie (Florence) 9/10 (April–July 1982). John Ford issue.
Filmkritik 181 (January 1972). John Ford issue.
Focus on Film 6 (Spring 1971). John Ford issue.
Presénce du Cinéma 21 (March 1965). John Ford issue.
Velvet Light Trap 2 (August 1971). John Ford issue.
Wide Angle 2, no. 4 (1978). John Ford issue.

Journal runs

Exhibitors' Trade Review (*Motion Picture Daily*), 1916– .
Film Index, 1907–11.
Motion Picture (*Story*) *Magazine*, 1911– .
Motion Picture News, 1909– .
Motography, 1909– .
Moving Picture World (Herald), 1907– .
Photoplay, 1913– .
Universal Weekly (*Moving Picture Weekly*), 1913– .

Library collections

Clipping collections. Free Library of Philadelphia Theater Collection.
Clipping collections. Library of the Academy of Motion Picture Arts and Sciences, Beverly Hills.
Clipping collections. Library and Museum of the Performing Arts, Lincoln Center, New York.
John Ford Papers. Lilly Library, Indiana University.

Author's interviews

Interviews with Frank Baker, Olive Carey, Harry Carey, Jr., Ruth Clifford, Cecil McLean de Prida, Barbara Ford, Anna Lee, George O'Brien, Leon Selditz, John Stafford. March–May, 1979.

Index

An asterisk after a subject entry indicates a character from a film.
Boldface type used for a subject entry indicates a theme or motif in Ford's pictures.
Boldface type used for a page reference indicates the principal discussion.